CONTRACT AND RELATED OBLIGATION

THEORY, DOCTRINE, AND PRACTICE

Eighth Edition

■ ■ ■

Robert S. Summers
Late McRoberts Research Professor of Law, Emeritus
Cornell Law School

Robert A. Hillman
Edwin H. Woodruff Professor of Law, Emeritus
Cornell Law School

David A. Hoffman
Professor of Law,
University of Pennsylvania Law School

AMERICAN CASEBOOK SERIES®

WEST ACADEMIC PUBLISHING

444 Cedar Street, Suite 700
St. Paul, MN 55101
1-877-888-1330

Printed in the United States of America

ISBN: 978-1-68467-015-4

IN MEMORY OF ROBERT S. SUMMERS

1933–2019

PREFACE TO THE EIGHTH EDITION

This Eighth Edition updates and freshens the materials with new cases, excerpts and notes on important developments in contract law. The new materials focus on how contract law is adapting to the digital age, including with respect to formation, enforcement, defenses, and remedies. Unfortunately, we prepared most of this edition during the pandemic of 2020, but it made us mindful to include materials on contract law's response to the many thousands of contracts that have not been performed under these circumstances. We have also omitted cases and materials that have grown stale, and streamlined our coverage of the lawyer's role in the agreement process and the remedies after a rightful cessation of a contract. But the book's structure and much of the materials remain as in the earlier editions. We have included in this front matter the Preface to the First Edition, which explains the goals and organization of the book.

Robert Summers passed away in 2019 and we dedicate this edition to him. Nevertheless, Bob's insights and learned contributions remain the heart of this book.

We hope (and believe) that students will find that these materials introduce theory, doctrine, and practice in an accessible interesting, and enjoyable manner. Of course, we cannot promise that all cases will equal the stakes or flair of one of our squibs, Alfred v. Walt Disney, wherein the plaintiff relied on the

> epic of Gilgamesh, Woody Guthrie, the Declaration of Independence, Noah and The Great Flood, *Game of Thrones, Star Wars Episode V: The Empire Strikes Back, Star Trek*, President Obama, and Euclid's proof of the Infinity of Primes, among other references. * * * If the Plaintiff needed to sum up this entire case in one sentence, it is this: "Two executives of the Disney Company are stalling the next evolution of human transportation on this planet."

Those scoundrels. Did the plaintiff win? Read on and find out.

ROBERT A. HILLMAN
MYRON TAYLOR HALL
ITHACA, N.Y.

DAVID A. HOFFMAN
SILVERMAN HALL
PHILADELPHIA, P.A.

September 2020

PREFACE TO THE FIRST EDITION

Goals. Five primary goals have guided the design and content of this book. We have sought to provide materials that will enable students to:

—understand the leading rules and principles governing contract and related obligation, including the substantive reasons behind these rules and principles;

—develop substantially the basic lawyer skills required to plan, draft, interpret, counsel, litigate, and negotiate in this field;

—understand and deploy general theories of the nature, functions, and limits of contract and related law;

—develop the general analytical and critical abilities and attitudes (including a keen regard for facts) that typify the good lawyer;

—learn not only the deficiencies of, but also some of what is best about, American contract law, including its intellectual richness and what it teaches us about ourselves and our society.

Our Philosophy of Instruction. We believe in the case method, and in extensive dialectical exchange between teacher and student, and between student and student. Accordingly, this is predominantly a case book. The book also provides a framework, and numerous opportunities, for concentrated dialogue on the justificatory reasoning, authoritative and substantive, to be found in the opinions. (See Appendix A: "Judicial Reasons".)

We have generally chosen not to impose our own personal pedagogical grid on the cases and other materials, so that, except in the first chapter, we pose very few questions of our own. In each chapter, we have inserted several problems devoted to planning, drafting, and other roles of lawyers.

Criteria Affecting Selection of Materials. We have selected cases with an eye to the usual factors: the richness of the facts (including their potential for hypothetical variation), the quality of the opinion, the doctrinal, transactional, or relational significance, the depiction of lawyer performances, historical or social import, and more. Occasionally, we have included a case partly for cultural reasons. Various statutes appear here, including many sections from Article Two of the Uniform Commercial Code. The book includes additional materials on the sale of goods, for the teacher who chooses (or is required) to cover this subject.

We also include extracts from the two Restatements of Contracts. For students who acquire too much of a taste for the ready-made formulas of a restatement, and thus tend to think of the common law case merely as something to be "boiled down" into a sentence or phrase, we also offer Appendix C: "The Restatement Idea—Some Skepticism".

The book includes some sample documents drawn from the world of practice. These consist of actual contracts, opinion and other letters, portions of briefs, and some comments from lawyers who litigated a few of the cases in the book.

Role of Text. We have seldom relied on text to convey knowledge of law. More often, we have used text to introduce the subject of each chapter, to treat lawyer' roles, to convey a sense of structure within an area, and to provide background material to facilitate discussion.

Organization. The organization of our book furthers our primary goals. In Part One, called "Foundations of Contract and Related Obligation," we include three chapters. The first opens with an actual agreement and stresses the function of contracts as social exchange devices frequently planned and drafted by lawyers, but which the parties normally perform without any involvement of lawyers, let alone courts. The second chapter systematically presents the major general theories of obligation operative in contract and related areas. (Of course, remedies inevitably enter here, too.) The emergence and development of one general theory of obligation—promissory estoppel—is treated historically. Some of the major forms of interplay between contract and tort are also considered. The third chapter treats the general law of remedies as it applies to each theory of obligation.

Together, Chapters One, Two, and Three introduce most of the basic themes of the book. Although we follow many of the ideas of the late Professor Fuller, we emphasize that the reality of contract obligations resides more in their voluntary observance and in the force of the normative reasoning the obligations generate, than in the predicted efficacy of remedies for their breach.

Parts Two through Four are organized to reflect the main chronological stages of contractual activity: agreement, performance, and cessation. In Part Two, "The Agreement Process," we stress contract planning, the law governing the formation of agreements, the private administration of agreements (with and without the aid of lawyers), and the theories on which agreements are policed. Part Three, "The Performance Process," deals mainly with the parol evidence rule, the interpretation of agreements, the general obligation of good faith, the law of conditions, and breach and the permissible responses thereto. Part Four, "The Cessation Process," presents the grounds of rightful cessation and any remedies available thereafter. Here we offer systematic treatment of the complex interplay between such grounds of cessation as mistake, impracticability, and frustration on the one hand, and general theories of obligation and remedies on the other. (See especially Chapter Nine.)

Part Five is devoted to the rights and duties of third parties.

Hours. The book is designed for a six semester hour course, but the book can, of course, readily suit other hour allocations.

Some Words of Justification. There are already some outstanding teaching books in this field. Why add to them? Here we undertake briefly to explain ourselves, and perhaps we may be forgiven if we sometimes overstate a bit.

(1) We include much material designed to acquaint students with the entire range of lawyer roles in contractual matters, and to foster the development of sophistication and skill required in most of these roles. We stress the lawyer's planning role. Our effort here is reflected in a variety of forms, including various planning problems and some materials gathered from practitioners who handled recent cases included in the book.

(2) We focus on privately-made law in the form of agreements and customary norms. For example, as already noted, we begin with detailed consideration of an actual agreement. We emphasize that lawyers not only create and apply state-made law but create and apply the terms of private agreements as well. We stress, too, that judges frequently invoke the terms of privately created law as authoritative reasons for judicial decisions.

(3) We draw on the writings of Atiyah, Corbin, Dawson, Eisenberg, Farnsworth, Fried, Fuller, Gilmore, Llewellyn, Macneil, Posner, and others, all of whom have contributed significantly to the enrichment of contract theory. In addition, we add some theorizing of our own. For example, we introduce the concept of a multi-dimensional general theory of obligation in Chapter One, explore and compare a variety of such theories in Chapter Two, and regularly return to these theories in later chapters.

(4) We believe that today there is far less dialectical teaching in the first year of law school than was true only twenty years ago. In our view, the students are the main losers in this development. Gradual and cumulative changes in the nature of published teaching materials help explain this decline. The smaller proportion of principal cases, the heavy editing of those cases, the inclusion of numerous summaries and notes after each principal case, the extensive use of general textual notes on the law aimed at covering ground, the frequent resort to extracts from black-letter Restatements, the use of numerous lengthy excerpts from articles, and the infrequent sequences of principal cases on a single topic, all illustrate what we perceive to be an unfortunate trend. We have tried to prepare a book that will maximize analysis, criticism, and dialogue, both in and out of the classroom.

(5) In our view, contract teaching materials should not present all valid law as something essentially laid down or acted upon by officials, nor present formal legal reasoning and substantive moral reasoning as sharply distinct. Contrary to these positivist views, contract and related law

comprise a complex intermixture of private agreement (tacit as well as express), custom, case law, statute, regulatory law, *and* substantive reasoning—moral, political, economic, and other. We show from the beginning that substantive reasoning is far from "extra-legal" in nature. It is intrinsic to law, and no sharp line can be drawn here between the legal and the non-legal.

(6) This is not just a book about contract and related law. We also seek to develop a number of other more general perspectives and insights, including the power of general theory; the strengths and limits of a common law system; the recent rise of statutory and regulatory law, and the problems that this poses for lawyers and private parties; the differences between formalistic and instrumentalist legal method; the interactions of substantive right and judicial remedy in private law fields; the inevitable overlap among fields of private law; the subtlety and pervasiveness of the obligation of good faith; the interactions of law and fact; the social uses and limits of private ordering; the multi-faceted character of contract as a social institution; and the decline of freedom of contract.

Conventions. Bracketed material in cases and excerpts are ours, as are lettered footnotes. Other footnotes by judges in opinions or by authors in excerpts have been renumbered. We omitted some footnotes from these materials without indication.

R.A.H.
R.S.S.

February 1987

GENERAL ACKNOWLEDGMENTS TO THE EIGHTH EDITION

We gratefully acknowledge our indebtedness to the following authors and publishers who gave us permission to reprint excerpts from copyrighted articles in this or previous editions: Albany Law Review, for excerpts from Note, Risk of Loss and Distribution of Insurance Proceeds Under Real Estate Contracts in New York, 28 Albany L.Rev. 253 (1964); American Bar Association Journal, for excerpts from Williston, Restatement of Contracts is Published by the American Law Institute, 18 A.B.A.J. 775 (1932)—Reprinted with permission from the *ABA Journal,* The Lawyer's Magazine; The American Law Institute, for excerpts from 1970 Proceedings of the American Law Institute, 47 A.L.I.Proc. 489–91 (1970)—Copyright © 1970 by The American Law Institute, reprinted with the permission of The American Law Institute; The American Law Institute and Professor Stewart Macaulay, for excerpts from Macaulay, The Use and Non-Use of Contract in the Manufacturing Industry, 9 Practical Lawyer, Nov. 1963—Copyright © 1963 by The American Law Institute, reprinted with the permission of *The Practical Lawyer.* Subscription rates $25 a year; $5.00 a single issue (this article appeared in 9 *The Practical Lawyer*; Annual Survey of American Law and Professor Charles L. Knapp, for excerpts from Knapp, Judgment Call: Theoretical Approaches to Contract Decisionmaking, 1988 Ann.Surv.Am.L. 307, 333, 336; Boston University Law Review and the Trustee of the Literary Estate of John P. Dawson, for excerpts from Dawson, Judicial Revision of Frustrated Contracts: Germany, 63 B.U.L.Rev. 1039 (1983); Boston University Law Review and the Trustee of the Literary Estate of John P. Dawson, for excerpts from Dawson, Judicial Revision of Frustrated Contracts: The United States, 64 B.U.L.Rev. 1 (1984); Boston University Law Review and the Trustee of the Literary Estate of John P. Dawson, for excerpts from Dawson, Restitution Without Enrichment, 61 B.U.L.Rev. 563 (1981); Boston University Law Review and Professor Mark Pettit, Jr., for excerpts from Pettit, Modern Unilateral Contracts, 63 B.U.L.Rev. 551 (1983); California Law Review and Professor Andrew Kull, for excerpts from Kull, Rationalizing Restitution, © 1995 by California Law Review Inc., reprinted from California Law Review, Vol. 83 No. 5; California Law Review, for excerpts from Whittier, The Restatement of Contracts and Mutual Assent, 17 Cal.L.Rev. 441 (1929)—1929 by 17 California Law Review, reprinted by permission; Columbia Law Review and Professor E. Allan Farnsworth, for excerpts from Farnsworth, Disputes Over Omission in Contracts, 68 Colum.L.Rev. 860 (1968)—Copyright © 1968 by the Directors of the Columbia Law Review Association, Inc. All rights reserved (this article originally appeared at 68 Colum.L.Rev. 860 (1968)), reprinted by permission; Columbia Law Review, for excerpts from Fuller, Consideration and Form, 41 Colum.L.Rev. 799 (1941); Columbia Law Review and Professor James Gordley, for excerpts from Gordley, European Codes and American Restatements: Some Difficulties, 81 Colum.L.Rev. 140 (1981)—Copyright © 1981 by the Directors of the Columbia Law Review Association, Inc. All rights reserved. Reprinted by permission; Columbia Law Review, for excerpts from Kessler, Contracts of Adhesion—Some Thoughts About Freedom of Contract, 43 Colum.L.Rev. 629 (1943); Columbia Law Review, for excerpts from Patterson, Constructive Conditions in Contracts, 42 Colum.L.Rev. 903 (1942); Columbia Law Review and Professor Joseph M. Perillo, for excerpts from Perillo, Restitution in a Contractual Context, 73 Colum. L.Rev. 1208 (1973)—Copyright © 1973 by the Directors of the Columbia Law Review Association, Inc. All rights reserved (this article originally appeared at 73 Colum.L.Rev. 1208 (1973)), reprinted by permission; Columbia Law Review and Professor Joseph M. Perillo, for excerpts from Perillo, Restitution in the Second Restatement of Contracts, 81 Colum.L.Rev. 37 (1981)—Copyright © 1981 by the Directors of the Columbia Law Review Association, Inc. All rights reserved (this article originally appeared at 81 Colum.L.Rev. 37 (1981)), reprinted by permission; Columbia Law Review and Professor William F. Young, for excerpts from Young, Half Measures, 81 Colum.L.Rev. 19 (1981)—Copyright © 1981 by the Directors of the Columbia Law Review Association, Inc. All rights reserved (this article originally appeared at 81 Colum.L.Rev. 19 (1981)), reprinted by permission; Cornell Law Review, Fred B. Rothman & Co., for excerpts from Hillman, An Analysis of the Cessation of Contractual Relations, 68 Cornell L.Rev. 617 (1983); Cornell Law Review, Fred B. Rothman & Co., for excerpts from Hillman, Contract Modification Under the Restatement (Second) of Contracts, 67 Cornell L.Rev. 680 (1982); Cornell Law Review, Fred B. Rothman & Co., for excerpts from Hillman, Debunking Some Myths About Unconscionability: A New Framework for U.C.C. Section 2–302, 67 Cornell L.Rev. 1 (1982); Cornell Law Review, Fred B. Rothman & Co. and Professor Robert Hudec, for excerpts from Hudec, Restating the "Reliance Interest," 67 Cornell L.Rev. 704 (1982); Cornell Law Review, Fred B. Rothman & Co., for excerpts from Summers, The General Duty of Good Faith—Its Recognition and Conceptualization, 67 Cornell L.Rev. 810 (1982); Cornell Law Review, Fred B. Rothman & Co. and Professor James J. White, for excerpts from White, Eight Cases and Section 251, 67 Cornell L.Rev. 841 (1982); Barak Richman and Dennis Schmelzer, Barak Richman and Dennis Schmelzer, *When Money Grows on Trees: Lucy v. Zehmer and Contracting in a Boom Market*, 61 Duke L.J. 1511, 1552–55 (2012). Duke Law Journal and Professor John Weistart, for excerpts from Weistart, Requirements and Output Contracts: Quantity Variations Under the UCC, 1973 Duke L.J. 599; Fordham Law Review and Professor John D.

Calamari, for excerpts from Calamari, Duty to Read—A Changing Concept, 43 Fordham L.Rev. 341 (1974); Fordham Law Review and Alexander Radus, for Hoffman and Radus, Instructing Juries on Noneconomic Contract Damages, 81 Fordham L. Rev. 1221 (2013); Professor Patricia B. Fry for excerpts from Fry, X Marks the Spot: New Technologies Compel New Concepts for Commercial Law, 26 Loy.L.A.L.Rev. 607 (1993); Harvard Law Review Association and Professor Patrick Atiyah, for excerpts from Atiyah, Book Review: C. Fried, Contract as Promise, 95 Harv.L.Rev. 509 (1981); Harvard Law Review Association and Professor Melvin Eisenberg, for excerpts from Eisenberg, The Bargain Principle and Its Limits, 95 Harv.L.Rev. 741 (1982); Harvard Law Review Association, for excerpts from Holmes, The Path of the Law, 10 Harv. L.Rev. 457 (1897); Harvard Law Review Association, for excerpts from Kessler & Fine, *ulpa in Contrahendo,* Bargaining in Good Faith, and Freedom of Contract: A Comparative Study, 77 Harv.L.Rev. 401 (1964); Harvard Law Review Association and Professor W. David Slawson, for excerpts from Slawson, Standard Form Contracts and Democratic Control of Lawmaking Power, 84 Harv.L.Rev. 529 (1971); Harvard Law Review Association and Professor Anthony J. Waters, for excerpts from Waters, The Property in the Promise: A Study of the Third Party Beneficiary Rule, 98 Harv.L.Rev. 1109 (1985); Hastings Law Journal and Professors William Whitford and Stewart Macaulay, for excerpts from Whitford and Macaulay, Hoffman v. Red Owl Stores: The Rest of the Story, 61 Hastings L.J. 801 (2010); Indiana Law Journal and Fred B. Rothman & Co., for excerpts from Calamari & Perillo, A Plea for a Uniform Parol Evidence Rule and Principles of Contract Interpretation, 42 Indiana Law Journal 333 (1967); Journal of Law & Commerce and Professor Richard Speidel, for excerpts from Speidel, The New Spirit of Contract, 2 J.L. & Com. 193 (1982)—Copyright © *The Journal of Law & Commerce,* University of Pittsburgh, 1982, reprinted with permission from 2 J.L. & Com. 193 (1982); Journal of Legal Education and Professor Walter E. Oberer, for excerpts from Oberer, On Law, Lawyering and Law Professing: The Golden Sand, 39 J.Leg.Educ. 203 (1989); Journal of Legal Studies and Professor Anthony Kronman, for excerpts from Kronman, Mistake, Disclosure, Information and the Law of Contracts, 7 J. of Legal Stud. 1 (1978); Journal of Legal Studies, The University of Chicago Press and Judge Richard Posner, for excerpts from Posner & Rosenfield, Impossibility and Related Doctrines in Contract Law: An Economic Analysis, 6 Journal of Legal Studies 83 (1977); Michigan Law Review, for excerpts from Hillman, Online Boilerplate: Would Mandatory Website Disclosure of E-Standard Terms Backfire?, 104 Mich.L. Rev. 837 (2006); North Carolina Law Review Association, for excerpts from Dalzell, Duress by Economic Pressure I, 20 N.C.L.Rev. 237 (1942)—Reprinted with permission from 20 N.C.L.Rev. (1942), Copyright © 1942 by the North Carolina Law Review Association; Northern Kentucky Law Review and Professor Richard Speidel, for excerpts from Speidel, The Borderland of

Contract, 10 N.Ky.L.Rev. 164 (1983); Northwestern University Law Review, for excerpts from Childres & Garamella, The Law of Restitution and the Reliance Interest in Contract, 64 Nw.U.L.Rev. 433 (1969)—Reprinted by special permission of Northwestern University, School of Law, 64 Nw.U.L.Rev. 433 (1969); Northwestern University Law Review, for excerpts from Havighurst, The Restatement of the Law of Contracts, 27 Ill.L.Rev. 910 (1933)—Reprinted by special permission of Northwestern University, School of Law, 27 Ill.L.Rev. 910 (1933); Ohio State Law Journal, for excerpts from Dunbar, Drafting the Liquidated Damages Clause—When and How, 20 Ohio State L.J. 221 (1959); Pennsylvania Bar Association and David W. Maxey, for excerpts from Maxey, Fundamentals of Draftsmanship—A Guide for the Apprentice in Preparing Agreements, 51 Pa.Bar Ass'n Quarterly 47 (1980); Saint Louis Law Journal and Professor Donald King, for excerpts from King, The Tort of Unconscionability: A New Tort for New Times, 23 St. Louis L.J. 97 (1979); Southern California Law Review and Professor Ian Macneil, for excerpts from Macneil, A Primer of Contract Planning, 48 S.Cal.L. Rev. 627 (1975); Stanford Law Review and Tess Wilkinson-Ryan, for excerpts from Wilkinson-Ryan and Hoffman, The Common Sense of Contract Formation, Stan.L.Rev. 1269 (2015); Stanford Law Review and Professor Melvin Eisenberg, for excerpts from Eisenberg, The Responsive Model of Contract Law, 36 Stan.L.Rev. 1107 (1984); Stanford Law Review and Professor Lawrence Friedman, for excerpts from Friedman, Legal Rules and the Process of Social Change, 19 Stan.L.Rev. 786 (1967); Tulane Law Review, for excerpts from Dawson, Economic Duress and the Fair Exchange in French and German Law, 11 Tulane L.Rev. 345 (1937); UCLA Law Review, Fred B. Rothman & Co., and Professor Arthur Rosett, for excerpts from Rosett, Contract Performance: Promises, Conditions and the Obligation to Communicate, 22 U.C.L.A.L.Rev. 1083 (1975); University of Chicago Law Review and Professor Melvin Eisenberg, for excerpts from Eisenberg, Donative Promises, 47 U.Chicago L.Rev. 1 (1979); University of Chicago Law Review, for excerpts from Lieberman & Henry, Lessons from Alternative Dispute Resolution, 53 U.Chi.L.Rev. 424 (1996); University of Chicago Law Review, for excerpts from Schultz, The Firm Offer Puzzle: A Study of Business Practice in the Construction Industry, 19 U.Chi. L.Rev. 237 (1952); Virginia Law Review Association, for excerpts from Cavers, Legal Education and Lawyer-Made Law, 54 Va.L.Rev. 177 (1952); Virginia Law Review Association, Fred B. Rothman & Co. and Professor Stanley Henderson, for excerpts from Henderson, Promises Grounded in the Past: The Idea of Unjust Enrichment and the Law of Contracts, 57 Va.L.Rev. 1115 (1971); Virginia Law Review Association & Fred B. Rothman & Co., for excerpts from Summers, "Good Faith" in General Contract Law and the Sales Provisions of the Uniform Commercial Code, 54 Va.L.Rev. 195 (1968); Wisconsin Law Review and Professor Russell J. Weintraub, for excerpts from Weintraub, A Survey of Contract Practice and Policy, 1992 Wis.L.Rev.

1, reprinted by permission of the Wisconsin Law Review; Wisconsin Law Review and Professor William Whitford, for excerpts from Whitford, Ian Macneil's Contribution to Contracts Scholarship, 1985 Wis.L.Rev. 545; The Yale Law Journal Company and William S. Hein Company, for excerpts from Ben-Shahar & Bernstein, The Secrecy Interest in Contract Law, 109 Yale L.J. 1885 (2000)—Reprinted by permission of the Yale Journal Company and William S. Hein Company from the Yale Law Journal, Vol. 109, pages 1885–1925; The Yale Law Journal Co. and Fred B. Rothman & Co., for excerpts from Clark, The Restatement of the Law of Contracts, 42 Yale L.J. 643 (1933)—Reprinted by permission of The Yale Law Journal Company and Fred B. Rothman & Co. from *The Yale Law Journal,* Vol. 42, p. 643; The Yale Law Journal Co. and Fred B. Rothman & Co., for excerpts from Comment, Apportioning Loss After Discharge of a Burdensome Contract: A Statutory Solution, 69 Yale L.J. 1054 (1960)—Reprinted by permission of The Yale Law Journal Company and Fred B. Rothman & Co. from *The Yale Law Journal,* Vol. 69, pp. 1054, 1056–1057; The Yale Law Journal Co. and Fred B. Rothman & Co., for excerpts from Corbin, Conditions in the Law of Contract, 28 Yale L.J. 739 (1919)—Reprinted by permission of The Yale Law Journal Company and Fred B. Rothman & Co. from *The Yale Law Journal,* Vol. 28, pp. 739, 743, 745–746; The Yale Law journal Co. and Fred B. Rothman & Co., for excerpts from Corbin, Offer and Acceptance, and Some of the Resulting Legal Relations, 26 Yale L.J. 169 (1917)—Reprinted by permission of The Yale Law Journal Company and Fred B. Rothman & Co. from *The Yale Law Journal,* Vol. 26, pp. 169, 199–200; The Yale Law Journal Co., Fred B. Rothman & Co., and Marjorie Fuller, for excerpts from Fuller & Perdue, The Reliance Interest in Contract Damages, 46 Yale L.J. 52 (1963)—Reprinted by permission of The Yale Law Journal Company and Fred B. Rothman & Co. from *The Yale Law Journal,* Vol. 46, pp. 52, 53–57, 60–62, 75–80; The Yale Law Journal Co., Fred B. Rothman & Co. and Professor Paul Gewirtz, for excerpts from Gewirtz, Commentary on Karl N. Llewellyn, What Price Contract?—An Essay in Perspective, 100 Yale L.J. 1508 (1991)—Reprinted by permission of The Yale Law journal Company and Fred B. Rothman & Co. from *The Yale Law journal,* Vol. 100, pp. 1508, 1508–10; The Yale Law Journal Co., Fred B. Rothman & Co., and Professor Stanley Henderson, for excerpts from Henderson, Promissory Estoppel and Traditional Contract Doctrine, 78 Yale L.J. 343 (1969)—Reprinted by permission of The Yale Law Journal Company and Fred B. Rothman & Co. from *The Yale Law Journal,* Vol. 78, pp. 343, 358–360; The Yale Law Journal Co. and Fred B. Rothman & Co., for excerpts from Llewellyn, Our Case-Law of Contract: Offer and Acceptance II, 48 Yale L.J. 779 (1939)—Reprinted by permission of The Yale Law Journal Company and Fred B. Rothman & Co. from *The Yale Law Journal,* Vol. 48, pp. 779, 803–04; and The Yale Law Journal Co. and Fred B. Rothman & Co., for excerpts from Wormser, The True Conception of Unilateral Contracts, 26 Yale L.J. 136 (1916).

We also gratefully acknowledge our indebtedness to the following authors and publishers who gave us permission to reprint excerpts from copyrighted books in this or previous editions: The American Law Institute, for excerpts from Restatement (First) of Contracts, copyright © 1932 by The American Law Institute, reprinted with the permission of The American Law Institute; The American Law Institute, for excerpts from Restatement (Second) of Contracts, copyright © 1981 by The American Law Institute, reprinted with the permission of The American Law Institute; The American Law Institute, for excerpts from Restatement (Second) of Torts, copyright © 1965 by The American Law Institute, reprinted with the permission of The American Law Institute; The American Law Institute and the National Conference of Commissioners on Uniform State Laws, for excerpts from Uniform Commercial Code, copyright © 1990 by The American Law Institute and the National Conference of Commissioners on Uniform State Laws. Reprinted with the permission of the Permanent Editorial Board for the Uniform Commercial Code; Aspen Law & Business, for excerpts from Farnsworth, Contracts (4th ed. 2004); Harvard University Press and Professor Charles Fried, for excerpts from Fried, Contract as Promise (1981); The Lawyers Cooperative Publishing Co., for excerpts from Williston & Jaeger, A Treatise on the Law of Contracts (3d ed. 1957); Little Brown & Co. and Judge Richard Posner, for excerpts from Posner, Economic Analysis of Law (2d ed. 1977); J.C.B. Mohr (Paul Siebeck), for excerpts from Arthur von Mehren, Contracts in General, International Encyclopedia of Comparative Law VII; Northwestern University Press, for excerpts from Fuller, The Law in Quest of Itself (1940); Oceana Publications, Inc. and Professor Rudolf Schlesinger, for excerpts from Schlesinger, Formation of Contracts (R. Schlesinger ed., 1968); Ohio State University, for excerpts from Gilmore, The Death of Contract—Excerpts from THE DEATH OF CONTRACT, by Grant Gilmore, copyright © 1974 by the Ohio State University Press, reprinted by permission; Professor George Palmer, for excerpts from Palmer, Mistake and Unjust Enrichment (1962); University of Chicago Law School and Professor William Twining, for excerpts from Twining, The Karl Llewellyn Papers (1968); West Publishing Company and Professor Dan B. Dobbs, for excerpts from Dobbs, Remedies (1973); West Publishing Company, for excerpts from 19 Leopold, Beyer, Park, West's Legal Forms (2d ed. 1986); West Publishing Company, for excerpts from Prosser & Keeton on Torts (5th ed. 1984); West Group and Professors James J. White and Robert S. Summers for excerpts from Uniform Commercial Code (6th ed. 2010); Yale University Law School, for excerpts from 1 Corbin on Contracts (1963), 3 Corbin on Contracts (1960), and 3A Corbin on Contracts (1960); and Yale University Press and the Trustee of the Literary Estate of John P. Dawson, for excerpts from Dawson, Gifts and Promises (1980).

The authors also wish to thank the following practitioners for permitting us to use materials from their files: Mr. John A. Coppeler of

Flynn, Py & Krause, Sandusky, Ohio; Mr. David B. Cotner of Datsopoulos, MacDonald & Lind, Missoula, Montana; Mr. Michael S. Danian, Attorney at Law, Waukegan, Illinois; Mr. James E. Dixon, Attorney at Law, Dixon, Illinois; Mr. Lawrence C. Force of Force & Baldwin, Adrian, Michigan; Mr. Stephen J. Hajduch, Attorney at Law, Milwaukee, Wisconsin; Mr. Edward A. Monsky of Fine & Wyatt, Scranton, Pennsylvania; Mr. Donald L. Steerman of the Shinn law firm, Lamar, Colorado; Mr. Charles T. Rubin of Kroll & Tract, New York, New York; Mr. John B. Waldron of Courey, Schwinn, Kodadek & McRoberts, P.A., Minneapolis, Minnesota; and Mr. Timothy W. Woods of Jones, Obenchain, Ford, Pankow, Lewis & Woods, South Bend, Indiana.

PERSONAL ACKNOWLEDGMENTS TO THE EIGHTH EDITION

Professors Hillman and Hoffman thank Cornell Law School students Conor Cathey and Yan Li, and Penn Law students Alana Bevan, Blanche Helbling and Michael White. We also thank Bill Draper, of the Biddle Law Library, for excellent assistance.

We also thank Dean Eduardo Peñalver and Dean Ted Ruger for their support.

As always, Betsy Hillman and Sue Back provided the necessary encouragement.

SUMMARY OF CONTENTS

PART TWO. THE AGREEMENT PROCESS

PART THREE. THE PERFORMANCE PROCESS

TABLE OF CONTENTS

PART FOUR. THE CESSATION PROCESS

PART FIVE. RIGHTS AND DUTIES OF THIRD PARTIES

TABLE OF CASES

The principal cases are in bold type.

TABLE OF UNIFORM COMMERCIAL CODE SECTIONS

TABLE OF RESTATEMENTS

CONTRACT AND RELATED OBLIGATION

THEORY, DOCTRINE, AND PRACTICE

Eighth Edition

PART ONE

FOUNDATIONS OF CONTRACT AND RELATED OBLIGATION

■ ■ ■

CHAPTER ONE

INTRODUCTION

■ ■ ■

Suppose contracts freely made and effectively sanctioned and the most elaborate social organization becomes possible.

SIDGWICK

This book is about the theory, doctrine, and practice of contract and related law. We will study several general theories of legal obligation and several types of law. We define a theory of obligation as a recognized general basis for imposing legal duties. The predominant theory of obligation we will study is that legal duties arise from a contract, which consists of an agreement supported by *consideration*. Nevertheless, legal duties arise pursuant to other theories of obligation as well. For example, we will study the theory called "promissory estoppel" in which duties arise from a party's justified reliance on a promise. Thus, although we concentrate on contract in the sense of "agreement with consideration," our subject is much broader.

Among the types of law to be studied here are judge-made common law, statutes adopted by legislatures, and regulations made by administrators. Government officials make all of these types of law. But most of the law in this field is not made by the government. It is made by private parties (with or without the aid of lawyers), and consists of the terms of their agreements, express and implied. Moreover, officials have relatively little to do with the administration of most such agreements. Instead, the parties themselves administer them in countless situations that never come before courts at all. For example, when you agree to mow your neighbor's lawn for $20, perform the services, and receive payment, you and your neighbor have made and administered private contract law. People enter contracts almost daily. Only a small number of these contracts end up in court.

Of these rare, litigated, contracts, even fewer end up reported as written opinions. This book consists largely of such "reported" cases—the heavily disputed, sometimes strange, remnant of what once was a promising set of out-of-court promises and agreements. You might ask:

Why study such odd arcana, when most contracts you will create as a lawyer, or encounter as a citizen, will never lead to an appellate opinion?

Within the American law school, the basic course on contract law is a wonderful vehicle for developing the analytical and critical faculties that mark the good lawyer. Without these skills, a lawyer cannot effectively find facts, plan, draft, interpret, counsel, negotiate, or litigate. Knowledge of the relevant principles of the common law and of common law method is likewise an essential prerequisite to effective practice in this field. The intensive study of appellate cases is indispensable to the acquisition of these faculties and forms of knowledge. In addition, cases are vital sources of authentic knowledge about the social institution of contract as it actually functions in our society. By studying opinions, you learn how to be a lawyer, learn what lawyers do, and learn how to make arguments that will persuade judges.

Generally, judges in contract cases follow or create what is called "common law." The common law is a set of principles drawn from precedent and policy that helps judges to decide disputes. In most of the opinions you will read, the express or implied terms of the parties' agreement generate strong reasons for deciding in favor of one party, reasons that judges often adopt either as the sole or as a partial basis for their decisions. Even when judges do not decide on the basis of such reasons, they frequently invoke principles and policies that facilitate and implement private agreements.

Moreover, when a private agreement conflicts with the common law, the private agreement generally prevails. Private parties generally have the right to adopt terms that displace or override common law rules that would otherwise govern. Most of the opinions you will read in this course therefore create *default* rules—rules that govern if the parties are silent in their contract on the matter in question. This flexible characteristic of contract law distinguishes it from many of the rules you will learn in other first-year courses. However, we will also study some important rules of the common law that judges may invoke to invalidate or police the terms of private agreements.

In addition to the terms of agreements and the common law, we will study some statutory law. We will focus on various sections of Article 2 of the Uniform Commercial Code governing the sale of goods.[a] Parties can

---

[a] The National Conference of Commissioners on Uniform State Laws (NCCUSL) and the American Law Institute (ALI) combined forces to draft the Code. Pennsylvania, in 1953, became the first state to enact it. After some editorial revision, many other states adopted it in the 1960s and 1970s. Today the Code is law in all states except Louisiana (where parts of it are in force). The Code is divided into eleven articles. Insofar as we study the Code in this course, we will focus almost entirely on Article 2, which deals with the sale of goods. On the history of the Code project, see J. White and R. Summers, *Handbook of the Law Under the Uniform Commercial Code 1–7* (5th ed. 2000). NCCUSL and the ALI produced amendments to Article 2, but no states have enacted them. We therefore cite the pre-amendment version of Article 2 throughout this book. (We cite the 2001 revision to Article 1, however, because a majority of states have adopted this version.)

also displace or override almost all of the rules of Article 2 by agreement. Article 2 is designed primarily to facilitate and implement the terms of private sales agreements. Article 2 also includes some exceptional sections that displace or override contrary terms in private agreements. In addition, in various specialized fields of contract, studied in upper level law courses, such as consumer protection, insurance, employee collective bargaining, automobile dealer franchising, storage, and transportation, numerous regulatory statutes apply. Many of the provisions of such regulatory statutes cannot be superseded by private agreement.

What roles do lawyers perform when they practice in this field? Their practice consists mainly of activities outside of the courtroom such as fact-finding, planning, drafting, interpreting, counseling, and negotiating. Accordingly, a major focus of this book is on the lawyer's work outside of court.

HILLMAN AND SUMMERS, THE BEST LAW SCHOOL SUBJECT

21 Seattle L. Rev. 735, 735 (1981).

As far as we are concerned, there is no mystery to the title of this essay. For lots of reasons, contract law is by far the best law school subject to teach and to learn. What other subject contains such a wealth of theory, doctrine, and substantive reasoning? What other subject focuses so clearly on essential components of economic and other organization in our society, namely private agreements and exchange transactions? What subject better exemplifies the power of general theory, the functions and limits of the common law, the rise of statutory law, the interaction of right and remedy, and the role of various legal actors in our system (including transactors, lawyers in their various roles, judges, and lawmakers)?

SECTION ONE: CONTRACT AND RELATED OBLIGATION

An important professor of our subject, Karl N. Llewellyn, once stressed that "[i]n the normal modern case the first measure of the parties' rights is the contract."[b]

A. THE NONCOMMERCIAL SPECIALLY DRAFTED AGREEMENT

Many thousands of noncommercial specially drafted agreements are made every day in the United States. The episode set forth below is based on actual facts.

---

[b] K. Llewellyn, *Cases And Materials On Sales* xiv (1930).

FACTS

In the fall of 1962, Virgil White (a police officer) and his wife, Gwynneth, wished to buy a residence in Oak Creek, Wisconsin, located next to a home owned by Paul and Ruth Benkowski, Jr. The water supply for the residence the Whites wished to purchase came through pipes from a well on the Benkowskis' property, and the control valves for that water system were located inside the Benkowskis' residence. Mr. White concluded it would be too costly to drill a well on the residence he wished to buy. He talked with the Benkowskis and they agreed to supply water to the Whites through the pipes from their well. Accordingly, the Whites went ahead with their purchase. Afterwards, the Whites proposed that the Benkowskis enter a formal agreement for the supply of water to the Whites' residence. Mr. Benkowski agreed but, instead of consulting a lawyer, he had a friend, Joe Artz, a real estate agent, draft an agreement. As part of the overall arrangement, the Whites paid $400 to the Benkowskis to enable them to buy the new pump and larger tank required to serve both premises. The actual agreement drafted by the real estate agent is set forth below:

AGREEMENT AS TO SUPPLY OF WATER

This agreement, made this 28 day of November, 1962, between Paul Benkowski Jr., and Ruth Benkowski, his wife (first parties), and Virgil A. White and Gwynneth A. White, his wife (second parties),

WITNESSETH

WHEREAS, first parties are the owners of the following described real estate situated in the City of Oak Creek, Milwaukee County, Wisconsin, to-wit:

[legal description of real estate omitted]

AND, WHEREAS, second parties are the owners of the following described real estate situated in the City of Oak Creek, Milwaukee County, Wisconsin, to-wit:

[legal description of real estate omitted]

> *This agreement shall become null and void whenever water is supplied by any municipal system or if the existing well should go dry or become inadequate to supply said 2 homes or if second parties would drill their own well.

AND, WHEREAS, there is now situated on the above real estate of first parties, one certain water well operated by an electric submersible system motor,

AND, WHEREAS, the parties hereto desire that the source of water from the well upon parties of the first part's property be supplied unto the parties of the second part's home through the system of piping now there existing, it is hereby mutually agreed:

1. That first parties will furnish water for the use of the occupants of the house located on the lands of the second parties for a period of ten (10) years from November, _____ 1962.

2. That the second parties will pay for said water supply service the sum of Three ($3.00) Dollars per month, commencing with 1 December, 1962, payable on the first day of each and every month, in advance, and that in addition, second parties shall contribute to first parties, one-half (½) of the cost of any repairs or maintenance expense to said water system; also including replacements of motor, tank or accessories; (* above)

3. It is further hereby agreed between the parties hereto that at the end of the ten year period referred to in Paragraph One above, parties of the second part shall have the option to renew this agreement.

This agreement shall be binding upon and shall extend unto the respective grantees, successors, heirs, executors, administrators and assigns of each of the respective parties hereto.

IN WITNESS WHEREOF, the parties hereto have hereunto set their hands and seals of the day and year first above written.

WITNESSES TO FOUR SIGNATURES:

Ron Allen ——— Paul Benkowski Jr. (SEAL)
Paul Benkowski Jr.

James J. White ——— Ruth Benkowski (SEAL)
Ruth Benkowski

Virgil A. White (SEAL)
Virgil A. White

Gwynneth A. White (SEAL)
Gwynneth A. White

COMMENTS AND QUESTIONS

1. Assuming the above agreement meets all the requirements of a valid contract, is it law? Theorists of jurisprudence have sought to define "law." According to the "positivist" tradition in jurisprudence, law is defined essentially as something laid down by officials in power. For example, John Austin (1790–1859), a leading English positivist whose influence is still widespread, defined positive law as the "general commands of a sovereign legislature backed by sanctions." J. Austin, *I Lectures on Jurisprudence* 180–185, 225–26 (4th ed. Campbell 1873). If this definition is applied strictly, did the Whites and Benkowskis make law here? Nevertheless, if their agreement gave rise to "legal obligations," and if a court would provide a remedy for breach of their agreement, is it not appropriate to call their agreement law?

2. Consider the importance for the Whites and Benkowskis of legal recognition of their agreement. For one thing, the agreement provided for an exchange. What are the basic elements of the White-Benkowski exchange? Why does exchange occur? Consider this view: "[I]t is precisely the disparity in the value attached to the objects exchanged that results in their being exchanged. People buy and sell only because they appraise the things they give up less than those received." L. Von Mises, *Human Action: A Treatise on Economics* 204 (3d ed. 1963). Apply this analysis to both sides of the White-Benkowski exchange.

Another value of a legally valid agreement is that it allocates risks. What risks are allocated to the Whites? To the Benkowskis?

3. Consider the special importance to society of legal recognition of agreements. Such recognition is one way a society expresses its regard for freedom. Through agreements, individuals such as the Whites and the Benkowskis can, within the limits of their own resources, organize important elements of their own lives, and thereby experience self-determination. This is a value to the parties themselves, as well. Of course, freedom of contract and self-governance are less meaningful to persons who have relatively little bargaining power. In addition, people have used contracts for nefarious purposes too, such as slavery contracts and sales of organs. Contracts can be used for good or evil.

Society can also benefit from the legal recognition of private agreements because private exchange usually provides a more efficient allocation and distribution of resources than a system of governmental allocation and distribution. The French economist, Frederic Bastiat, once cited this example:

> On entering Paris, which I had come to visit, I said to myself—Here are a million of human beings who would all die in a short time if provisions of every kind ceased to flow towards this great metropolis. Imagination is baffled when it tries to appreciate the vast multiplicity of commodities which must enter to-morrow through the barriers in order to preserve the inhabitants from falling a prey to the convulsions of famine, rebellion and pillage. And yet all sleep at this moment, and their peaceful slumbers are not disturbed for a single instant by the prospect of such a frightful catastrophe. On the other hand, eighty departments have been labouring to-day, without concern, without any mutual understanding, for the provisioning of Paris. How does each succeeding day bring what is wanted, nothing more, nothing less, to so gigantic a market? What, then, is the ingenious and secret power which governs the astonishing regularity of movements so complicated, a regularity in which everybody has implicit faith, although happiness and life itself are at stake? That power is an *absolute principle,* the principle of freedom in transactions.

F. Bastiat, *Economic Sophisms* 104–05 (1922).

4. Why did the Whites and Benkowskis rely on Joe Artz, a real estate broker, to draft their agreement? Some lawyers have complained that such activity by real estate agents is a source of unnecessary litigation. Of course, not everyone can afford a lawyer. And even if a person can afford a lawyer, there may be additional reasons why he or she might not wish to retain one. For example, Rollie Massimino, formerly head coach of Villanova's basketball team, is reported to have said in response to why he turned down a coaching job with the New Jersey Nets: "The Nets were very professional in all their dealings. We had some 20 telephone conversations and about five face-to-face meetings. Everything was agreed on verbally and then the lawyers took over with their legalese and there were snags. * * * " Ithaca Journal, June 26, 1985, § 2, at 16 Col. 3 & 4.

If the Whites and the Benkowskis had retained lawyers, their roles would likely have included: ascertaining the facts, determining the parties' goals, evaluating alternative possible means to achieve those goals, anticipating possible problems and conflicts of interests between the parties, identifying any legal issues, researching and applying applicable law, planning and drafting a proposed agreement, negotiating with the other side concerning problems and conflicts, revising the proposed agreement accordingly, and securing a final signed agreement. Before preparing a draft of the agreement, the lawyers would have had conferences with their clients. Let us assume that the Whites and their lawyer had such a conference pursuant to a letter such as the one set out below:

> Virgil & Gwynneth White
> 3837 East Garden Place
> Oak Creek, Wisconsin
>
> Dear Mr. & Mrs. White:
>
> You have asked me to draft an agreement with Paul and Ruth Benkowski to supply you with water from their well through existing pipes connected to your new home. You have told me that you have already agreed to a monthly service charge of $3.00 to be paid in advance on the first day of each month, that you have agreed to pay $400 for a new pump and an additional tank, and that you have agreed to pay one-half of the cost of additional repairs, maintenance or replacement expenses. The agreement is to last for ten years with an option to renew, but will terminate when water is supplied by a municipal system, or the Benkowskis' well goes dry or is inadequate to supply the two homes, or if you drill your own well.
>
> Before I draft the agreement there are certain additional issues that we should clear up with the Benkowskis. Concerning

the duration of the agreement, if you exercise the renewal option is the renewal period for ten years? May you renew the agreement more than once? You certainly should have that right since you do not want to be without a water supply after one renewal period. Are you *required* to be connected to the municipal system if it becomes available or may you continue to receive water from the Benkowskis' well (it may be cheaper from the Benkowskis)? When does the Benkowskis' well "become inadequate" to supply both homes? For example, will merely one or a few periods of low water pressure be sufficient? We need to discuss this further with the Benkowskis and see if we can nail down some agreement on precisely when the well "becomes inadequate."

Concerning the price to you of the water service, does the $3.00 per month charge continue under all circumstances during the period of the agreement? For example, suppose the value of water in this general area increases dramatically because of a drought or pollution or the like? We need to include a provision specifically indicating that such events do not trigger a right of the Benkowskis to raise the price (or to get out of the agreement). In addition, you agree to pay one-half of repairs, maintenance and replacement costs to the system. We should make it clear that only such repairs, maintenance and replacement costs that are necessary to continue the supply of water to both homes are included, not repairs, etc. that are solely beneficial to the Benkowskis.

You have not reached an agreement concerning water quality. We should seek to include a provision in which the Benkowskis warrant the quality of the water they will supply to you. Quality should be tied to Milwaukee County Health Department regulations.

Are there to be any limits on your usage of water? I assume that the Benkowskis' attorney (if they retain one) will raise this issue. If the issue is not raised, we need to decide whether to raise it ourselves by seeking a provision specifically ensuring that you can use all of the water you desire. Offering such a provision may prod the Benkowskis into seeking a price scheme based on the amount of water usage. I assume that we can agree on a mutually agreeable scale. If we remain silent on this issue, I can foresee disagreements about water usage later on, so perhaps we should consider the issue now.

Finally, while I know you people are on good terms now, unfortunately we lawyers have seen too many deals go sour. So it is appropriate to think of remedies that you desire if the

Benkowskis break their agreement, for example, by turning off the water on you. We should try to get an agreement as to how much the Benkowskis will have to pay you for each hour that the water is purposefully turned off to discourage such behavior, should your relationship with the Benkowskis not remain cordial. Such an amount must necessarily reflect the damages to you or it will not be legally enforceable.

We need to have a meeting first on these matters, and then later with the Benkowskis. Of course we will need to compromise on many of them, but the important thing is to have your agreement clearly deal with these issues so as to avoid trouble in the future.

SINCERELY YOURS,
JEAN L. SMITH

COMMENTS AND QUESTIONS

1. Does it appear that Joe Artz, the real estate broker who drafted the White-Benkowski agreement, satisfactorily ascertained the facts, determined the parties' goals, and anticipated problems prior to planning and drafting the agreement? Identify what you consider to be the biggest deficiency in the agreement from the Whites' point of view. In thinking about this, consider Jean Smith's letter.

2. Assume that after Jean Smith wrote the foregoing letter, she had conferences with the Whites and, after further fact finding, planned and drafted a proposed agreement. Assume the agreement included the following clause:

> The Benkowskis promise that the water they are to supply under this agreement shall be potable according to the standard of water potability incorporated in the regulations of the Milwaukee County Health Department applicable to residential use. The Benkowskis warrant that the water in their well, as presently chlorinated by them, now complies with the foregoing standard. If the water falls below the foregoing standard, the Whites shall have no duty to pay for water affected and shall have all other legal remedies.

Does the agreement drafted by Joe Artz deal with this problem? In light of the clause above and Jean Smith's letter, in what ways does it appear that Jean Smith could have done a better overall job for the Whites than Joe Artz? How might this be explained? An obvious factor is that Jean Smith has had formal education and training. But is there rather more to it than this? What are the attributes of a lawyer?

3. It is one thing to plan and draft a proposed agreement for a client and quite another to secure the assent of the other party. Thus the lawyer may be called upon to negotiate. What is the most opportune time to negotiate for a

clause such as that in question 2 above—at the stage of initial agreement or later, after a breakdown? Why?

4. It appears that Joe Artz purported here to act for both sides. Would it have been appropriate for Jean Smith to have done this? Consider the following provision.

MODEL RULES OF PROFESSIONAL CONDUCT

Rule 1.7 (2002).

Client-Lawyer Relationship
Rule 1.7 Conflict Of Interest: Current Clients

(a) Except as provided in paragraph (b), a lawyer shall not represent a client if the representation involves a concurrent conflict of interest. A concurrent conflict of interest exists if:

(1) the representation of one client will be directly adverse to another client; or

(2) there is a significant risk that the representation of one or more clients will be materially limited by the lawyer's responsibilities to another client, a former client or a third person or by a personal interest of the lawyer.

(b) Notwithstanding the existence of a concurrent conflict of interest under paragraph (a), a lawyer may represent a client if:

(1) the lawyer reasonably believes that the lawyer will be able to provide competent and diligent representation to each affected client;

(2) the representation is not prohibited by law;

(3) the representation does not involve the assertion of a claim by one client against another client represented by the lawyer in the same litigation or other proceeding before a tribunal; and

(4) each affected client gives informed consent, confirmed in writing

THE RELATIONSHIP BREAKS DOWN

As we know, Joe Artz, the real-estate broker, wrote no such letter as Jean Smith's, and conducted no fact-finding conferences or negotiations. Instead, he simply drafted the agreement set forth earlier (copying partly from a standard form), and the parties signed it on November 28, 1962. The Benkowskis eventually claimed that the Whites were using "too much" water! Beginning on March 5, 1964, on several occasions the Benkowskis turned off the Whites' water supply. The Whites were very distressed. Let us now assume that Jean Smith contacted the Benkowskis by means of the following letter:

July 7, 1964

Mr. & Mrs. Paul Benkowski, Jr.
3835 East Garden Place
Oak Creek, Wisconsin

Dear Mr. & Mrs. Benkowski:

My clients, Mr. and Mrs. Virgil White, have informed me of difficulties they are having with you over their water supply. They have shown me their agreement with you which assures them an adequate supply of water for the life of the agreement. Would you or your lawyer get in touch with me at your earliest convenience?

SINCERELY YOURS,
JEAN L. SMITH
ATTORNEY-AT-LAW

Assume that the Benkowskis also saw a lawyer, Mr. Joel Westin, and that Mr. Westin began to negotiate with Jean Smith over the foregoing matters.

COMMENTS AND QUESTIONS

1. Private agreements are usually performed without dispute. Why? What are the possible explanations for the breakdown here? Would a breakdown have been as likely if lawyers had planned and drafted the agreement?

2. How strong is the Whites' negotiating position? In particular, do you agree with Jean Smith's interpretation of the agreement as set forth in her letter, namely that the language of the agreement "assures" the Whites of an "adequate supply of water for the life of the agreement"? What arguments might be made, pro and con, as to the proper interpretation of the agreement in this regard? Interpretation is itself a complex and significant lawyer skill. (We study it systematically in Chapter Six.)

3. What do you think would be the usual result of efforts between lawyers to negotiate the settlement of such a dispute? A voluntary settlement with, perhaps, the Whites agreeing to pay $1.00 a month more for water and agreeing not to use more than a given number of gallons per day? A lawsuit in which the dispute is ultimately resolved by a judge or jury in a court of law? Actually, we need not speculate at all. Only a tiny fraction of disputes arising under written agreements is ultimately resolved by court decision. How might this be explained? Here are some possibilities. Try to think of others.

(a) Parties prefer (or are compelled by circumstances) to order their own affairs.

(b) Many written agreements are carefully planned and drafted. As a result, they ultimately serve as effective bases for private settlement without resort to courts.

(c) Lawyers expert in the conduct of negotiations are readily available, and they regularly achieve settlements.

THE LAWSUIT

In the actual episode, possibly in part because the parties had not asked lawyers to prepare their agreement, the unusual happened. The relationship between the Whites and the Benkowskis not only broke down, but the parties were unable to resolve their differences through negotiation. As a result, the Whites sued the Benkowskis, seeking through a pleading called a complaint: (1) a sum of money as compensatory damages for the losses they sustained, and (2) a sum of money as "punitive" damages.[c]

The principal "legal papers" filed in this case prior to trial are set forth below:

STATE OF WISCONSIN: CIRCUIT COURT: MILWAUKEE COUNTY CIVIL DIVISION

VIRGIL A. WHITE and	)	
GWYNNETH A. WHITE, his wife,	)	
Plaintiffs,	)	COMPLAINT
vs.	)	Case No. 324–264
PAUL BENKOWSKI, JR. and	)	
RUTH BENKOWSKI, his wife,	)	
Defendants.	)	

NOW come the above named plaintiffs, VIRGIL A. WHITE and GWYNNETH A. WHITE, his wife, by their attorney, JEAN L. SMITH, and as for a cause of action against the above named defendants, PAUL BENKOWSKI, JR. and RUTH BENKOWSKI, his wife, and allege * * * as follows: to-wit:

1. That the plaintiffs, VIRGIL A. WHITE and GWYNNETH A. WHITE, his wife * * * reside at 3837 East Garden Place.

2. That the defendants, PAUL BENKOWSKI, JR. and RUTH BENKOWSKI, his wife * * * reside at 3835 East Garden Place.

---

[c] The Whites also initially sought a court order (a temporary restraining order) directing the Benkowskis to perform their contract to supply water without interruption, a preliminary form of the remedy called "specific performance," to be studied in Chapter Three. The Whites sought this remedy through a document called an "order to show cause," but abandoned their request when they decided to change residences.

3. That on or about the 28th day of November, 1962, the plaintiffs and defendants entered into an agreement entitled "AGREEMENT AS TO SUPPLY OF WATER", said agreement constituting a valid contract. * * *

4. That said agreement provided, among other things, that the defendants would furnish water for use of the plaintiffs, their respective grantees, successors, heirs, executors, administrators and assignees for a period of ten (10) years commencing on the 28th day of November 1962, providing further that the plaintiffs have an option to renew said agreement at the end of the ten year period; said agreement being further conditioned on the payment of the sum of Three ($3.00) Dollars per month to the defendants, said sum to be payable on the first day of each and every month, and further to pay one-half (½) of the cost of repairs and maintenance expenses to said water system.

5. That the plaintiffs duly performed all the conditions and covenants of the said agreement on their part to be performed * * * and that the defendants have failed to live up to the conditions and covenants of said agreement and still refuse to do so.

6. That the defendants have, on many occasions violated the conditions and covenants of said agreement by turning off the water supply to the home of the plaintiffs and as instances of such violations when the water was completely shut off, cite the following:

March 5,	1964—	From	7:10 P.M.	to	7:25 P.M.
March 9,	1964—	"	3:40 P.M.	to	4:00 P.M.
March 11,	1964—	"	6:00 P.M.	to	6:15 P.M.
April 14,	1964—	"	9:30 P.M.	to	10:55 P.M.
June 10,	1964—	"	6:20 P.M.	to	7:03 P.M.
July 1,	1964—	"	5:30 P.M.	to	9:40 P.M.
July 6,	1964—	"	2:00 P.M.	to	4:00 P.M.
July 6,	1964—	"	4:05 P.M.	to	5:15 P.M.
July 6,	1964—	"	8:50 P.M.	to	9:20 P.M.

7. That further the defendants on several occasions turned the water off partially, allowing only a trickle of water to be obtained by the plaintiffs on their premises. * * *

8. That such action on the part of the defendants has caused great inconvenience to the plaintiffs, creating an unhealthy and unsanitary condition on the plaintiffs' premises; such condition being damaging to the health and safety of the plaintiffs and their family and causing them great

mental anguish and consequently suffered compensatory and punitive damages in the sum of Five thousand ($5,000.00) Dollars.

WHEREFORE, plaintiffs demand judgment against the defendants for compensatory and punitive damages in the sum of Five thousand ($5,000.00) Dollars, plus the costs and disbursements of this action and for such other and further relief as the Court may deem just and equitable.

JEAN L. SMITH
ATTORNEY FOR THE PLAINTIFFS
SEPTEMBER 4, 1964

COMMENTS AND QUESTIONS

1. Does the foregoing pleading cite legal authorities? Set forth evidence in proof of facts? Allege facts which, if proved or admitted, constitute a valid claim in law?

2. Assume that the foregoing pleading alleges facts which, if proved, would constitute a valid claim for breach of contract. Reread the complaint and see if you can isolate and formulate the various elements of such a claim.

3. What preparation was necessary before Jean Smith drafted this complaint?

STATE OF WISCONSIN: CIRCUIT COURT:
MILWAUKEE COUNTY CIVIL DIVISION

VIRGIL A. WHITE and	)	
GWYNNETH A. WHITE, his wife,	)	MOTION TO DISMISS FOR
Plaintiffs,	)	FAILURE TO STATE A CLAIM
vs.	)	Case No. 324–264
PAUL BENKOWSKI, JR. and	)	
RUTH BENKOWSKI, his wife,	)	
Defendants.	)	

Defendants, by Joel Westin, their attorney, move the Court for an order dismissing that portion of Plaintiffs' complaint in the above entitled action demanding punitive damages, on the ground that such relief cannot be awarded in a contract action.

JOEL WESTIN
ATTORNEY FOR DEFENDANTS
SEPTEMBER 20, 1964

Assume the trial judge set October 9, 1964 as the date for a hearing on the above motion to dismiss (also sometimes called a demurrer). Consider whether this motion raises a question of fact or only a question of law. On October 9, after hearing argument from both lawyers, the judge denied the defendants' motion. (We see later that the judge was in error.) The Benkowskis then served their answer.

STATE OF WISCONSIN: CIRCUIT COURT:
MILWAUKEE COUNTY CIVIL DIVISION

VIRGIL A. WHITE and	)	
GWYNNETH A. WHITE, his wife,	)	
Plaintiffs,	)	ANSWER
vs.	)	Case No. 324–264
PAUL BENKOWSKI, JR. and	)	
RUTH BENKOWSKI, his wife,	)	
Defendants.	)	

Now come the above named defendants by Joel Westin, their attorney, and as for an answer to the plaintiffs' complaint, admit, deny, allege and show to the court as follows:

[In paragraphs 1–3 of this answer, the defendants admitted the allegations of paragraphs 1–4 of the plaintiffs' complaint.]

4. Answering Paragraph 5 of the plaintiffs' complaint, the defendants admit that the plaintiffs have paid the monthly service charge of $3.00 provided for in said agreement although some of these payments have been made late; the defendants deny that the plaintiffs have paid any sums towards the cost of repair and maintenance of the water system because there have been no such costs; * * * the defendants' [sic] admit that the plaintiffs have performed one of the express conditions and covenants of said agreement on their part to be performed, namely, the payment of the monthly charge of $3.00 but deny that the plaintiffs have performed any other express conditions and covenants of said agreement. * * *

5. Answering Paragraph 6 of the plaintiffs' complaint, the defendants deny that they have * * * turned off the water supply to the home of the plaintiffs and in particular the defendants deny that they turned off the water supply to the home of the plaintiffs on the occasions cited in Paragraph 6 of the plaintiffs' complaint.

6. Answering Paragraph 7 of the plaintiffs' complaint, the defendants deny that on any occasion they turned off the water supply to the plaintiffs' home partially. * * *

7. Answering Paragraph 8 of the plaintiffs' complaint, the defendants deny that any action on their part has caused any inconvenience to the plaintiffs and has created an unhealthy and unsanitary condition on the plaintiffs' premises, that they have damaged the health and safety of the plaintiffs and their family in any way, that they have caused them any mental anguish and that the plaintiffs have, consequently, suffered compensatory and punitive damages to the sum of $5000.00 or in any other amount. * * *

And as and for an affirmative defense, the defendants allege:

1. that said agreement provides that it shall become null and void whenever the existing well shall go dry or become inadequate to supply said homes, and

2. that the existing well has become inadequate. * * *

WHEREFORE, the defendants demand judgment as follows:

1. Dismissing the plaintiffs' complaint upon its merits.

2. Terminating the said agreement between the parties hereto.

3. For the costs and disbursements of this action.

JOEL WESTIN
ATTORNEY FOR DEFENDANTS
OCTOBER 28, 1964

NOTE: RESPONSES TO A COMPLAINT

Upon examining the preceding motion and pleadings filed by counsel for the Benkowskis, you can see that a defendant may make various responses to a complaint. A defendant may assume the facts alleged and assert that the plaintiff still has no valid claim in light of applicable law. (See the motion to dismiss, above.) Or a defendant may simply admit the facts alleged, or deny them, or state that the defendant does not have information sufficient to form a belief as to the truth of the facts. A defendant may also set forth "new matter"—make new allegations that would, if proved, afford a defense. This response is called an "affirmative defense." For example, the Benkowskis' affirmative defense was that the well had become inadequate. A defendant may also assert a counterclaim. For example, the Benkowskis might have claimed that the Whites failed to pay their water bills on time and owed the Benkowskis money damages. Knowledge of the foregoing possible responses to a complaint will help you grasp the procedural posture of many of the cases to be studied in the rest of this book.

THE TRIAL

After the foregoing papers were filed, the Whites moved to another residence. Further attempts at a negotiated settlement were made, but without success. Thus a trial of the factual issues in dispute became necessary. Make a list of these issues by rereading the above complaint and answer. A jury trial was held on September 26–27, 1966.

At trial, Virgil White testified that Paul Benkowski told him that the water was shut off to remind the Whites that they were using too much water and that the Benkowskis wished to terminate the water agreement because the well was not adequate for the two families. Virgil White also testified that he asked his wife to keep a record of the times the water was turned off. The Whites both testified about an odor on one occasion and inconveniences caused by the water interruptions, including the necessity of taking their children to a neighbor's home to be bathed.

Virgil and Gwynneth White also testified about the relationship of the families just prior to and during the period of water interruptions. Gwynneth testified that the relationship of the families was good until about September of 1963, when the Whites' daughter picked an apple in the Benkowskis' yard. Ruth Benkowski then called the daughter an "S.O.B." Gwynneth told Ruth that "she didn't like this." Later Ruth called Gwynneth "a redheaded bitch." Virgil White stated that Paul Benkowski lodged a complaint with Virgil's superior that Virgil had tried to run over Paul's child. The district attorney's investigation absolved Virgil. Paul Benkowski also complained to the police chief that Virgil took too long for lunch at home from time to time, and had wild parties at home. Virgil was again absolved of any wrongdoing.

Paul Benkowski, in his testimony, denied that there were "hard feelings" between the families. He testified that "most of the difficulty" with the water supply was because of a blown fuse or because sand got into the pump and nozzle, thereby "reducing the water to a trickle." Ruth Benkowski testified that she concluded that the Whites used an excessive amount of water "because dirty water was drawn into the system and the pump was going on and off and we were drawing sand and dirty water." The Benkowskis therefore felt the system was inadequate to supply the two families. Ruth stated that the Benkowskis never had an expert come out to test the amount of water that was in the well.

At the close of the trial on September 27, 1966, the trial judge requested counsel for both parties to submit proposed instructions to the jury. Thereafter, he instructed the jury on the law applicable to the facts of this case as follows:

EXCERPTS FROM JUDGE HOLR'S INSTRUCTIONS TO THE JURY, SEPTEMBER 27, 1966

Now, as counsel have indicated, there are two questions. The first one reads: "Did the defendants maliciously, vindictively or wantonly shut off the water supply of the plaintiffs for the purpose of harassing the plaintiffs?"[d]

If you answer the first question "Yes", then answer this second set of questions: "(a) What compensatory damages did the plaintiffs suffer? (b) What punitive damages should be assessed?"

Now, in an action for a breach of contract the plaintiff is entitled to such damages as shall have been sustained by him which resulted naturally and directly from the breach if you find that the defendants did in fact breach the contract. Such damages include pecuniary loss and inconvenience suffered as a natural result of the breach and are called compensatory damages. In this case the plaintiffs have proved no pecuniary damages which you or the Court could compute. In a situation where there has been a breach of contract which you find to have damaged the plaintiff but for which the plaintiffs have proven no actual damages, the plaintiffs may recover nominal damages.

By nominal damages is meant trivial—a trivial sum of money.

Now, the second part of the second question refers to punitive damages. Punitive damages cannot be awarded for a mere breach of a contract alone. The mere fact that the breach has distressed the parties against whom the contract was breached is not sufficient to award punitive damages. However, if you find from the evidence that the defendants acted maliciously, vindictively or wantonly for the purpose of harassing the plaintiffs by shutting off the water, you may, if you see fit, but you're not obliged to do so, award, in addition to the nominal damages, such sum as you think proper under the circumstances as punitive damages by way of an example or punishment in order to deter the defendants and others from offending in a like manner in the future. You may also consider the seriousness of the wrong committed in reaching your answer.

Punitive damages are never a matter of right, but when allowable may be awarded or withheld in the discretion of the jury. Punitive damages may not be awarded unless the acts of the defendants in question were done maliciously, vindictively or wantonly as I will define those terms to you. Even if you find malice, vindictiveness or wantonness, you may award or withhold punitive damages as you see fit.

---

[d] The parties had agreed that for purposes of the trial, the Whites' theory of recovery was that the Benkowskis maliciously, vindictively, and wantonly broke the contract by turning off the water.

Now, by malice is meant ill will, bad intent or malevolence towards the plaintiff.

Vindictively means revengeful or desire to see another person suffer.

By wanton we mean a reckless or intentional disregard of the consequences to others.

If you award punitive damages you may consider the defendants' wealth so far as it appears from the evidence because such damages, to accomplish their purpose, may be proportionate in some general way to the defendants' ability to respond.

Assume that after giving the above instructions, Judge Holr requested the jury to remain seated while he retired to his chambers to hear possible objections from counsel to the instructions given. The Whites' attorney, Jean Smith, objected to the judge's instruction that no compensatory damages could be recovered. The judge overruled this objection and Smith took exception. The Benkowskis' attorney, Joel Westin, objected to the judge's instruction that punitive damages could be awarded and moved to strike the question pertaining to punitive damages on the "special verdict"[e] form to be submitted by the judge to the jury. The judge reserved his ruling on this objection and motion. Thereafter, he returned to the courtroom and asked the jury to retire and deliberate on the evidence in light of his instructions on the law, and to return its answers on the special verdict form. The form, and the answers the jury returned, appear below:

STATE OF WISCONSIN: CIRCUIT COURT:
MILWAUKEE COUNTY CIVIL DIVISION

VIRGIL A. WHITE and)
GWYNNETH A. WHITE, his wife,)
Plaintiffs,)
vs.) Case No. 324–264
PAUL BENKOWSKI, JR. and)
RUTH BENKOWSKI, his wife,)
Defendants.)

---

[e] In a special verdict, the jury reports to the judge specific factual findings, while in a general verdict the jury finds generally in favor of one of the parties.

SPECIAL VERDICT

QUESTION 1: Did the defendants maliciously, vindictively or wantonly shut off the water supply of the plaintiffs for the purpose of harassing the plaintiffs?

ANSWER: Yes

DISSENTING
JURORS: ________________
____

QUESTION 2: If you answered Question 1 "Yes", then answer this question:

(a) What compensatory damages, if any, did the plaintiffs suffer?[f]

ANSWER: Ten Dollars

DISSENTING
JURORS: ________________
____

(b) What punitive damages should be assessed?

ANSWER: $2,000.00

Dissenting
Jurors: ________________
____

Edwin West
Foreman or Forelady

Dated at Milwaukee, Wisconsin, this 28 day of September, 1966.

Some weeks after the verdict was returned, a post-trial proceeding was held in which counsel for the parties were given an opportunity to make motions requesting the trial judge to correct claimed errors that might have occurred during the proceedings. On December 17, 1966, the trial judge rendered his decision on these motions:

---

[f] The judge submitted this special verdict form allowing for compensatory damages, but apparently expected the jury to award only nominal damages pursuant to his instructions.

STATE OF WISCONSIN: CIRCUIT COURT:
MILWAUKEE COUNTY CIVIL DIVISION

VIRGIL A. WHITE and	)	
GWYNNETH A. WHITE, his wife,	)	
Plaintiffs,	)	
vs.	)	Case No. 324–264
PAUL BENKOWSKI, JR. and	)	
RUTH BENKOWSKI, his wife,	)	
Defendants.	)	

DECISION—MOTIONS AFTER VERDICT

* * * The defendants now move for a new trial for the reason that the Court erred in submitting the issue of punitive damages to the jury, that the verdict is contrary to the evidence and the law, that the damages awarded are excessive, and not in the interest of justice. In the alternative the defendants move to strike the answer as to punitive damages. The plaintiffs move the judgment upon the verdict. [The Court discussed the facts]

* * *

Upon this record counsel were advised that the Court would and did instruct the jury that no pecuniary loss had been proven, but that if the jury found that there was a breach of contract which damaged the plaintiff the plaintiff could recover nominal damages which was defined as a trivial sum.

* * *

This Court's research and analysis of the Wisconsin decision leads it to the conclusion that a claim for punitive damages must be supported by a showing of actual injury which justifies an award of something more than nominal compensatory damages.

* * *

The Court concludes that the rule in Wisconsin is to the effect that punitive damages are not allowable where there can be a finding of only nominal damages from the evidence. Thus the court should not have instructed the jury that it could find punitive damages.

Because the jury's findings of a deliberate breach is supported by the evidence and the plaintiffs conceded that they had proven only nominal damages there is no need for a new trial. The Court grants the defendants' motion to strike from the verdict the question and answer concerning punitive damages.

The defendants also challenge the jury's answer of $10.00 for compensatory damages. This finding was contrary to the Court's instruction and cannot be sustained upon the evidence. The Court considers this situation to be one within the authority of Campbell v. Sutliff (1927), 193 Wis. 370 which authorizes the Court to reduce damages without a new trial. Therefore it is ordered that the answer to that part of the verdict be reduced to nominal damages in the amount of $1.00.

Plaintiff is entitled to judgment for $1.00 together with costs and disbursements.

Marvin C. Holr, Circuit Judge

After the trial court entered judgment for $1.00 in damages against the Benkowskis, the Whites appealed to the Wisconsin Supreme Court. Their lawyer filed a formal notice of appeal and thereafter prepared and filed several copies of a brief and a transcript of the trial record with the Wisconsin Supreme Court. In preparing the brief, Jean Smith reviewed a copy of the trial transcript and studied applicable law to identify rulings made by the trial judge that might be legally erroneous and prejudicial. The major function of the appellant's brief is to demonstrate that, in light of applicable law, the trial judge did prejudicially err and that a new trial or some other appropriate relief is required. Once the parties have completed their briefs, a time is set for oral argument. Following the oral argument, the judges deliberate, decide the case, and hand down a written opinion (in most cases).

Bear in mind this general observation while studying the Wisconsin Supreme Court's opinion:

> Now a case never reaches a court of review until it has first been through a tribunal of trial—else there would be nothing to review. But the cases, so called, in your casebooks are almost exclusively chosen from courts of review. To understand them, therefore, you must get at what has gone on before they got there. * * * [A] court of review has as its business of review to listen to complaints that a lower court has done some job improperly, i.e. as the phrase goes, has been in error, has made some ruling not in accord with the rules of law, correctly understood. (K. Llewellyn, The Bramble Bush 26 (1930).)

WHITE V. BENKOWSKI

Supreme Court of Wisconsin, 1967.
37 Wis.2d 285, 155 N.W.2d 74.

This case involves a neighborhood squabble between two adjacent property owners.

Prior to November 28, 1962, Virgil and Gwynneth White, the plaintiffs, were desirous of purchasing a home in Oak Creek. Unfortunately, the particular home that the Whites were interested in was without a water supply. Despite this fact, the Whites purchased the home.

The adjacent home was owned and occupied by Paul and Ruth Benkowski, the defendants. The Benkowskis had a well in their yard which had piping that connected with the Whites' home.

On November 28, 1962, the Whites and Benkowskis entered into a written agreement wherein the Benkowskis promised to supply water to the White home for ten years or until an earlier date when either water was supplied by the municipality, the well became inadequate, or the Whites drilled their own well. The Whites promised to pay $3 a month for the water and one-half the cost of any future repairs or maintenance that the Benkowski well might require. As part of the transaction, but not included in the written agreement, the Whites gave the Benkowskis $400 which was used to purchase and install a new pump and an additional tank that would increase the capacity of the well.

Initially, the relationship between the new neighbors was friendly. With the passing of time, however, their relationship deteriorated and the neighbors actually became hostile. In 1964, the water supply, which was controlled by the Benkowskis, was intermittently shut off. Mrs. White kept a record of the dates and durations that her water supply was not operative. Her record showed that the water was shut off on the following occasions:

(1) March 5, 1964, from 7:10 p.m. to 7:25 p.m.

(2) March 9, 1964, from 3:40 p.m. to 4:00 p.m.

(3) March 11, 1964, from 6:00 p.m. to 6:15 p.m.

(4) June 10, 1964, from 6:20 p.m. to 7:03 p.m.

The record also discloses that the water was shut off completely or partially for varying lengths of time on July 1, 6, 7, and 17, 1964.

Mr. Benkowski claimed that the water was shut off either to allow accumulated sand in the pipes to settle or to remind the Whites that their use of the water was excessive. Mr. White claimed that the Benkowskis breached their contract by shutting off the water.

Following the date which the water was last shut off * * * the Whites commenced an action to recover compensatory and punitive damages for an alleged violation of the agreement to supply water. A jury trial was held. Apparently it was agreed by counsel that for purposes of the trial "plaintiffs' case was based upon an alleged deliberate violation of the contract consisting of turning off the water at the times specified in the plaintiffs' complaint." * * *

[The court then set forth the special verdict submitted to the jury.]

Before the case was submitted to the jury, the defendants moved to strike the verdict's punitive-damage question. The court reserved its ruling on the motion. The jury returned a verdict which found the Benkowskis maliciously shut off the Whites' water supply for harassment purposes. Compensatory damages were set at $10 and punitive damages at $2,000. On motions after verdict, the court reduced the compensatory award to $1 and granted defendants' motion to strike the punitive-damage question and answer.

Judgment for plaintiffs of $1 was entered and they appeal. * * *

WILKIE, J. Two issues are raised on this appeal.

1. Was the trial court correct in reducing the award of compensatory damages from $10 to $1?

2. Are punitive damages available in actions for breach of contract?

Reduction of Jury Award

The evidence of damage adduced during the trial here was that the water supply had been shut off during several short periods. Three incidents of inconvenience resulting from these shut-offs were detailed by the plaintiffs. Mrs. White testified that the lack of water in the bathroom on one occasion caused an odor and that on two other occasions she was forced to take her children to a neighbor's home to bathe them. Based on this evidence, the court instructed the jury that: [The court set forth the portion of the jury charge indicating that the Whites could recover only nominal damages for their harm suffered from the breach.]

* * * In the trial court's decisions on motions after verdict it states that the court so instructed the jury because, based on the fact that the plaintiffs paid for services they did not receive, their loss in proportion to the contract rate was approximately 25 cents. This rationale indicates that the court disregarded or overlooked Mrs. White's testimony of inconvenience. In viewing the evidence most favorable to the plaintiffs, there was some injury. The plaintiffs are not required to ascertain their damages with mathematical precision, but rather the trier of fact must set damages at a reasonable amount. Notwithstanding this instruction, the jury set the

plaintiffs' damages at $10. The court was in error in reducing that amount to $1.

The jury finding of $10 in actual damages, though small, takes it out of the mere nominal status. The award is predicated on an actual injury. This was not the situation present in Sunderman v. Warnken.[1] Sunderman was a wrongful-entry action by a tenant against his landlord. No actual injury could be shown by the mere fact that the landlord entered the tenant's apartment, therefore damages were nominal and no punitory award could be made. Here there was credible evidence which showed inconvenience and thus actual injury, and the jury's finding as to compensatory damages should be reinstated.

Punitive Damages

> "If a man shall steal an ox, or a sheep, and kill it, or sell it; he shall restore five oxen for an ox, and four sheep for a sheep."[2]

Over one hundred years ago this court held that, under proper circumstances, a plaintiff was entitled to recover exemplary or punitive damages.[3]

Kink v. Coombs[4] is the most recent case in this state which deals with the practice of permitting punitive damages. In *Kink* the court relied on Fuchs v. Kupper[5] and reaffirmed its adherence to the rule of punitive damages.

In Wisconsin compensatory damages are given to make whole the damage or injury suffered by the injured party. On the other hand, punitive damages are given

> " * * * on the basis of punishment to the injured party not because he has been injured, which injury has been compensated with compensatory damages, but to punish the wrongdoer for this malice and to deter others from like conduct."[6]

Thus we reach the question of whether the plaintiffs are entitled to punitive damages for a breach of the water agreement.

The overwhelming weight of the authority supports the proposition that punitive damages are not recoverable in actions for breach of contract. In Chitty on Contracts, the author states that the right to receive punitive damages for breach of contract is now confined to the single case of damages for breach of a promise to marry.

---

1 1 Wis. 471, 29 N.W.2d 496 (1947).

2 Exodus 22:1.

3 *McWilliams v. Bragg*, 3 Wis. 377, 424 (1854).

4 28 Wis.2d 65, 135 N.W.2d 789 (1965).

5 22 Wis.2d 107, 125 N.W.2d 360 (1963).

6 *Malco, Inc. v. Midwest Aluminum Sales*, 14 Wis.2d 57, 66, 109 N.W.2d 516, 521 (1961).

Simpson states:

> "Although damages in excess of compensation for loss are in some instances permitted in tort actions by way of punishment * * * in contract actions the damages recoverable are limited to compensation for pecuniary loss sustained by the breach."[7]

Corbin states that as a general rule punitive damages are not recoverable for breach of contract.[8]

* * *

Persuasive authority from other jurisdictions supports the proposition (without exception) that punitive damages are not available in breach of contract actions. This is true even if the breach, as in the instant case, is wilful.

Although it is well recognized that breach of a contractual duty may be a tort, in such situations the contract creates the relation out of which grows the duty to use care in the performance of a responsibility prescribed by the contract. Not so here. No tort was pleaded or proved.

Reversed in part by reinstating the jury verdict [$10] relating to compensatory damages and otherwise affirmed. Costs to appellants.

COMMENTS AND QUESTIONS

1. You should consider at least the following questions about each appellate opinion you study in this book (and some instructors will want you to prepare written "briefs" dealing with all such matters).

    a. What were the essential facts of the case (as set forth in the appellate opinion)?

    b. What was the procedural posture of the case on appeal? For example, was the appeal from a ruling on demurrer? From a ruling on the admissibility of evidence? From an instruction to the jury? From a post-trial ruling? And so on.

    c. What substantive legal issue (or issues) did the case present?

    d. How did the court rule on the issue (or issues)?

    e. What were the court's reasons for the decision? Did the court rely on previous cases or other legal authority? Did the court offer substantive reasons (moral, economic, social, institutional etc.)?[g] Other reasons?

---

7 Simpson, *Contracts*, § 195, 394 (2d ed. Hornbook series).

8 5 Corbin, *Contracts*, § 1077, 438.

g See Appendix A.

f. Is the decision sound? The reasoning?

2. An influential professor of law, John Henry Wigmore, once wrote that "[w]e must be students of reasons as well as of rules." The point is important. For example: (1) a court's reasons frequently clarify the decision; (2) a court decision, as an exercise of state power, must be justified, which depends on the availability of supporting reasons; (3) stated reasons commonly influence future cases.

3. As a matter of policy, should the Benkowskis have been liable for punitive damages? As we saw in *White v. Benkowski*, Wisconsin generally does not permit their recovery for breach of contract. This is a very common rule in the United States and has many explanations that you will study later.

Notwithstanding the general rule, punitive damages may be available for an "independent tort" associated with a breach of contract, such as a deliberate misrepresentation at the time of contracting. The Benkowskis did not engage in any such misrepresentation. Another *possible* independent tort, however, is malicious breach of contract, recognized in some jurisdictions. Note that the jury found that the Benkowskis acted "maliciously, vindictively or wantonly * * * for purposes of harassing the plaintiffs." Moreover, compensatory damages here were so low ($10) that they could not effectively deter a breach. Given these factors, should the court have held that there was an "independent tort"? What principles and policies favor denial of punitive damages even for malicious breach of contract?

Even if Wisconsin recognized the independent tort cause of action for punitive damages, the Whites would have had to give the Benkowskis appropriate advance notice of this claim. Would it be sufficient that the Whites asked for punitive damages in their formal complaint and that the parties at trial stipulated that the case was being tried on the theory of "deliberate violation"?

4. Could the Whites' attorney, Jean Smith, have done a better job of conducting the litigation? What seems to have been her most serious mistake?

5. Was the Whites' decision to pursue legal remedies a sound decision? What else could they have done? Should Jean Smith have advised the Whites not to sue because of the probability of a small recovery?

6. We return now to our opening theme: Could this litigation have been avoided by better planning and drafting? Suppose the agreement had provided a careful definition of when the Benkowskis were entitled to cease supplying water? Would this have helped to avoid litigation? Suppose the Whites had consulted Jean Smith before they purchased their home and she had prepared a well-drawn agreement (from the Whites' point of view), but the Benkowskis had refused to sign it. Would Jean Smith necessarily have failed to serve her clients? What if, as a result of Jean Smith's advice, the Whites did not enter a contract with the Benkowskis at all?

NOTE: *THE GENERAL THEORY OF OBLIGATION IN WHITE V. BENKOWSKI*

According to the Supreme Court of Wisconsin, the Benkowskis owed a legal duty to the Whites to provide water. We saw that the primary source of this duty was the agreement between the parties. Without the agreement, the Benkowskis' duty would not have arisen. (Nor would the lawsuit.) The agreement was not the sole source of the Benkowskis' legal duty, however. The legal system determines which agreements give rise to legal duties. Most of the law giving legal effect to agreements is common law made by courts. The common law recognizes several *general theories of obligation.* As we have said, a theory of obligation is a recognized general basis for imposing legal duties. The predominant theory in contract and related law, invoked by the Whites against the Benkowskis, is that legal duties arise from a valid agreement with consideration (a contract). We study the concept of valid agreement in Chapters Four and Five. We study consideration in Chapter Two, along with other general theories of obligation.

For now, we will offer *preliminary* definitions of "agreement" and "consideration." Professor Arthur L. Corbin, an important scholar of our subject,[h] once defined an agreement as follows: "To say that there is an agreement generally means that two or more persons have expressed themselves in harmony." *1 Corbin on Contracts*, § 1.9 (2019). Professor Corbin refused, however, to define consideration, and denied that our law recognizes a unitary concept of consideration. Other authorities, however, have been willing to define consideration as a "bargained for exchange." We will later see that this definition, and the above definition of agreement, are useful points of departure, but require much elaboration and some modification.

B. OTHER BASIC TYPES OF AGREEMENTS

In addition to noncommercial specially drafted agreements of the type studied in *White v. Benkowski*, there are other basic types of agreements. Of course, commercial parties also enter specially drafted agreements. In addition, both commercial and non-commercial parties also enter standard form agreements, oral agreements, and informal agreements. Examples of the latter include ordering a meal at a restaurant for a price or buying a coat off the rack. We will see throughout this book that the lawyer's planning and drafting role, if any, varies with the type of agreement involved. For now, consider these introductory materials on standard form agreements:

---

[h] Arthur L. Corbin (1874–1967) taught contract law at Yale Law School from 1903 to 1943. His treatise, *Corbin on Contracts*, is perhaps the most respected of all legal treatises.

SLAWSON, STANDARD FORM CONTRACTS AND DEMOCRATIC CONTROL OF LAW MAKING POWER

84 Harv. L. Rev. 529, 530, 532 (1971).

Standard form contracts probably account for more than ninety-nine percent of all the contracts now made. Most persons have difficulty remembering the last time they contracted other than by standard form; except for casual oral agreements, they probably never have. But if they are active, they contract by standard form several times a day. Parking lot and theater tickets, package receipts, department store charge slips, and gas station credit card purchase slips are all standard form contracts.

Moreover, standard forms have come to dominate more than just routine transactions. For individuals, if not quite yet for corporations, form contracts are in common use for even such important matters as insurance, leases, deeds, mortgages, automobile purchases, and all of the various forms of consumer credit. The contracting still imagined by courts and law teachers as typical, in which both parties participate in choosing the language of their entire agreement, is no longer of much more than historical importance.

* * *

The predominance of standard forms is the best evidence of their necessity. They are characteristic of a mass production society and an integral part of it. They provide information and enforce order. A typical automobile insurance policy, for example, informs the policyholder how to conduct himself should he become involved in an accident or other kind of occurrence from which liability of the kind covered may arise. It enforces all or a part of such conduct by the sanction of denying insurance protection unless it is performed. These services are essential, and if they are to be provided at reasonable cost, they must be standardized and mass-produced like other goods and services in an industrial economy. The need for order could, in theory, be fully satisfied by officially drafted rules—by laws in the traditional sense. One of the beliefs by which our society is organized, however, is that at least some lawmaking is better accomplished in a decentralized manner. We therefore prefer that the economy be controlled privately to a large extent, and private control today means control largely by standard form.

In some settings in which lawyers use form agreements, one of the parties is virtually certain not to consult a lawyer and not to bargain with the other party over terms. Can you imagine bringing a lawyer along with you to a local Apple Store when you buy a new computer? In today's world, Apple has the power to dictate the terms of its sale to you. You must accept its terms or not buy from Apple. (Of course, the power of buyers in the aggregate will affect some of Apple's decisions.) In Chapter Five, we will see that the law may intercede on behalf of consumers in such "contracts of adhesion," but lawyers have no role when the consumer purchases an item. Of course, on the other hand, lawyers for Apple draft its forms.

Form agreements are also common in commercial transactions. Examples are purchase orders and sales confirmations. In addition to drafting such forms, lawyers may be asked to review them to help clients decide whether to sign. Even a consumer may ask a lawyer for such advice if the transaction is important enough.

When a lawyer chooses to use a standard form, he or she may still alter it in some way. This is often done in real estate transactions, for example. Consider these general thoughts on when a lawyer should utilize a standard form in a particular transaction:

MACNEIL, A PRIMER OF CONTRACT PLANNING

48 S. Cal. L. Rev. 627, 653–56 (1975).

Advantages of forms in legal framework planning itself are obvious: they are convenient and efficient. There is, however, vast variation in the quality of forms. Moreover, using any form can be dangerous. First, the legal framework contained in the form simply may not fit the relationship being planned. In addition, however good the form may be as far as it goes, it may not constitute complete legal framework planning. Finally, a form may have become outdated because of changes in the law.

Every lawyer has to decide for himself on numerous occasions the extent to which he will utilize a form. Few will or should always rise to Dickerson's suggestion that:

> the danger that the form will lull him into a false sense of accomplishment is so great that in other than the most routine situations he is wise to use it mainly as a cross check.[i]

But the lawyer failing to follow Dickerson's next dictum is no lawyer, simply a hack: "He must not forget that he has been engaged to exercise his professional judgment, not to serve as a mere retrieval system."

C. A BRIEF INTRODUCTION TO RELATIONAL EXCHANGE

Planning the White-Benkowski agreement entailed special challenges. Unlike buying a coat off the rack (sometimes called a discrete exchange largely because there is relatively little interaction between the parties), the White-Benkowski exchange was relational in nature in that it occurred through time in a process of continuous interaction between the parties.

---

[i] Dickerson, *Fundamentals of Legal Drafting*, § 19, 53 (1965).

The differences between discrete and relational exchanges are important for the lawyer planning an agreement. The more "relational" an exchange, that is, the more it is projected into the future and requires ongoing party interraction, the more likely the parties and their lawyers cannot precisely define performance obligations or allocate risks optimally. One result is that the parties and their lawyers may rely on norms to govern their relationship other than those arising from the original agreement. These norms may call for cooperation and compromise, if the parties are to achieve the fruits of their agreement.[j]

SECTION TWO: MAJOR SOCIAL RESOURCES THAT FACILITATE AGREEMENTS AND THEIR PERFORMANCE

The making and performance of agreements flourish in our society. Consider how many agreements you are a party to at this moment. Presumably you have one with your law school and one with your landlord. What others?

The reasons why agreements are so widespread in our society are complex. One explanation is that specialization of labor, which results because of its efficiency, creates the need for exchange behavior. As individuals specialize, they become less self-sufficient and more dependent on others' goods and services, which they then must secure through agreements.

K. LLEWELLYN, CONTRACT: INSTITUTIONAL ASPECTS

Encyclopedia of Soc. Sci. 330–31 (1931).

Bargain is * * * the social and legal machinery appropriate to arranging affairs in any specialized economy which relies on exchange rather than tradition (the manor) or authority (the army) for apportionment of productive energy and of product. Contract in the strict sense is the specifically legal machinery appropriate when such an economy moves into the phase of credit dealings, i.e. of future dealings in general—in which aspect the mutual reliance of two dealers on their respective promises comes of course into major importance. This machinery of contract applies in general to the market for land, goods, services, credit or any combination of these. * * *

---

[j] The pioneering scholarship on relational exchange is by Professor Ian R. Macneil of Northwestern University Law School (formerly of Cornell and Virginia). See, e.g., Macneil, *The New Social Contract* (1980); Macneil, *Contracts: Adjustment of Long-Term Economic Relations Under Classical, Neoclassical, and Relational Contract Law*, 72 Nw. U. L. Rev. 854 (1978).

We now introduce in subsections A and B below a number of major resources of society deployed directly and indirectly to facilitate agreements and to secure the benefits that may come from them.

A. RESOURCES NOT PRIMARY OBJECTS OF STUDY IN THIS BOOK, BUT OF IMPORTANCE TO ITS THEMES

Our society invests enormous resources in ways that directly or indirectly facilitate the making and performance of agreements. Some of these, while very important, are not the focus of this book. For example, we expend vast legal resources every day to keep order and social peace. The criminal law, for example, is deployed in part to this end. If our society were not tolerably well-ordered, the making and performance of agreements could not flourish.

At least of equal importance, our society provides a system of public education. As a result, people have much greater capacity to plan and manage their lives. Among other things, they are better able to realize personal goals through agreements. Our educational system also fosters technological and other advances that vastly expand the range of human choice and thus the fruits of agreements.

Our society also deploys resources to help people obtain jobs and to help business entities succeed. As a result, more people have the means to enter agreements. Examples range from the use of a central banking system to provide credit and stimulate investment to a social security system that helps people meet the basic needs of life.

Through governmental activity, society also facilitates the daily functioning of communications networks and transportation systems. These networks and systems today extend the reach of markets far beyond what they once were.

Our legal system also invests resources to prevent private parties and governmental bodies from erecting unjustified barriers to the making and performance of agreements. For example, we have constitutional and other laws forbidding one state from imposing tariffs against goods from another state. In this and other ways our legal system nurtures and protects national markets in which private parties from different states may contract freely. Our system has also adopted antitrust and other regulatory laws prohibiting various forms of anti-competitive behavior that reduce the range and variety of choice. (Of course, not all such laws work well toward these ends.)

The legal system also provides for the creation and operation of various kinds of business organizations and other entities capable of entering and performing agreements. These include: unions, corporations, trade associations, partnerships, and so on.

A great many additional laws facilitate exchange through agreements. These laws include rules providing for a uniform monetary system, establishing a uniform system of weights and measures, imposing regulatory obligations of disclosure, setting standards of product quality, protecting against third party interference with contractual rights, and recognizing property interests in the fruits of exchange—in goods bought, in houses purchased, in wages and salaries earned, and so on.

B. RESOURCES TO BE STUDIED IN THIS BOOK

We now turn to the main types of resources to be studied closely in this course. All these resources are deployed directly or indirectly to facilitate agreements and the realization of benefits from them.

A Legal Profession with Generalists and Specialists in Contract and Related Law. As indicated in the case of *White v. Benkowski*, our system recognizes and facilitates the availability of specially trained personnel—lawyers—who can, in various ways, help parties realize their goals through agreements. We have now identified most of the diverse roles of the lawyer in the practice of contract and related law. Throughout this book we will study these roles, and will develop standards for evaluating the performance of the lawyer.

Valid Agreements Between Individuals and Various Entities. This book opened with the White-Benkowski agreement, and we will encounter a number of other more or less complete agreements in the course of our study. Such agreements are the main source of legal duties that parties incur in this field. When such agreements are drafted by third parties, they are usually drafted by lawyers. The requirements of a valid legal agreement are studied in Chapters Four and Five.

Law Recognizing and Structuring General Theories of Legal Obligation. As we have noted, the predominant theory of legal obligation studied in this book is agreement with consideration. The Whites invoked this theory as the basis for their legal claim against the Benkowskis for compensatory damages. We will study this and other theories of obligation in Chapter Two.

Law Defining the Boundaries of Freedom to Enter Agreements. Various forms of law define limitations on the freedom of parties to enter agreements. In *White v. Benkowski*, the parties did not include any language in their agreement that ran afoul of legal limitations on their freedom. But there are several such limitations. Suppose, for example, that the Whites and the Benkowskis had agreed that if the Benkowskis turned off the Whites' water, the Whites would be entitled to exact a private "fine" of $100 for each such occasion? This would not have been upheld in court. We will study this particular limitation in Section Six of Chapter Three, and others in later chapters. Upper-level law courses consider numerous other limitations.

Law Policing the Consummation and Content of Agreements. A major function of our law is to police the consummation and content of agreements. We will study several policing doctrines, mainly in Chapter Five. One such doctrine is that a contract or a clause of a contract may be unenforceable because "unconscionable." One authoritative version of this doctrine appears in § 2–302(1) of the Uniform Commercial Code:

> If the court as a matter of law finds the contract or any clause of the contract to have been unconscionable at the time it was made the court may refuse to enforce the contract, or it may enforce the remainder of the contract without the unconscionable clause, or it may so limit the application of any unconscionable clause as to avoid any unconscionable result.

Can you think of a clause the Whites and Benkowskis might have included that would have been unconscionable? We will see that this general body of law overlaps with the law defining the freedom to enter agreements.

Law Determining the Content of Duties to Perform Agreements. As we saw in *White v. Benkowski*, agreements are often incomplete or unclear. For example, what is the meaning of "become inadequate" in the clause providing for termination of the agreement if the well "should * * * become inadequate to supply said 2 homes"? In such situations, various forms of general law—law not explicitly embodied in the agreement—may be applied to determine the duties imposed by the agreement. This general law includes rules of interpretation, rules governing the sequence of performance, rules filling gaps in agreements, rules governing the admissibility of evidence of terms not included in written agreements, rules structuring the effect of custom, rules of good faith, and more. These are the subject of Chapters Six and Seven.

Rules and techniques of interpretation facilitate drafting, counseling, and negotiating, and guide the courts in the event of a lawsuit. For example, suppose water agreements such as the Whites' and Benkowskis' were common in Oak Creek, Wisconsin, and that in Oak Creek, the phrase "inadequate water supply" had taken on special meaning (e.g., muddy water more than once a week). Courts often rely on such evidence under the rubric of "custom and usage." When this is so, the parties' lawyers can use such language in the agreement and can tell their clients with some confidence how the language will be interpreted in court. If a dispute arises as to the meaning of the language, the parties can be expected to settle their differences without litigation.

Law Governing Breach, Repudiation, and Permissible Responses. Whether action or inaction constitutes a breach or repudiation depends largely on the content of the parties' agreement. For example, the agreement between the Whites and the Benkowskis might have provided that the Whites would be in breach for failing to pay $400 for a new pump by a particular date. The agreement might also have set forth the Benkowskis' appropriate responses to any such breach. On the other hand, the agreement might fail to define breach or to set forth responses or both. Here, legal rules fill the gaps. See Chapter Seven.

Law Governing the Maturation and Excuse of Contract Duties. For various reasons, a party's duty to perform may not mature under the language of the agreement. Assume, for example, that the Benkowskis agreed to deliver water only after the Whites performed their promise to provide $400 for a new pump. Must the Benkowskis deliver any water if the Whites breach by failing to pay the $400? This breach would constitute a failure of an express condition and would excuse the Benkowskis from delivering any water. A change in circumstances following the consummation of an agreement also may excuse a party from performance. For example, an unanticipated drought might greatly reduce the water supply from the Benkowskis' well, and thereby excuse the Benkowskis from performance. These matters are studied in Chapters Seven and Eight.

Law Governing the Rights and Duties of Third Parties. Contract and related law governs not only the rights and duties of immediate parties, but also the rights and duties of more remote parties, such as those who "buy" a contract right from an immediate party and those non-parties who benefit from a contract performance. For example, this area of the law determines whether a purchaser of the Whites' home could enforce the Benkowskis' obligation to supply water to the home. We study third-party rights and duties in Chapters Nine and Ten.

Law Defining and Providing Remedies. Much general law in this field deals with the availability of judicial remedies. We caught a glimpse of some of this law "in action" in the case of *White v. Benkowski*, including law on both compensatory and punitive damages. We will now introduce two basic questions which we will study intensively in Chapters Two and Three: (1) What judicial remedies are available in this field? (2) What is the relationship between these remedies and the general theories of obligation operative here?

SECTION THREE: GENERAL THEORIES OF OBLIGATION AND REMEDIES—AN INTRODUCTION

A. THEORIES OF OBLIGATION

In general, judges and lawyers do not recognize legal duties merely in an *ad hoc* fashion from case to case. Rather, they decide on the existence of such duties largely in accord with the requirements of a general theory of obligation. We introduced this concept earlier and defined it as a recognized general basis for imposing legal duties. Recall that the applicable general theory of obligation in *White v. Benkowski* is an agreement with consideration—an enforceable contract.

Although the rights and duties of the Whites and Benkowskis arose from an agreement with consideration and although this is the predominant theory of obligation in this field, we study other important theories of obligation as well. We study in detail the following general theories of obligation in Chapter Two:

1. Obligation arising from an agreement with *consideration* (and any required writing)

2. Obligation arising from *justified reliance on a promise*—"promissory estoppel"

3. Obligation arising from *unjust enrichment*

4. Obligation arising from promises for *benefit received*

5. Obligation arising from *tort*

6. Obligation arising solely from "*form*"

7. Obligation arising from a *statutory warranty*

In light of these various theories of obligation, you can see that the law may enforce an obligation even in the absence of an enforceable contract. To put it differently, your goal in this course is not simply to ask "is there a contract," but rather, is there a "theory of obligation" that justifies relief, and, if so, which one?

We now briefly introduce the reliance and unjust enrichment theories merely to demonstrate the range and variety of potentially operative theories in this field. The facts of *White v. Benkowski* illustrate these theories. Suppose the water-supply agreement required the Whites to buy a pump for $400 to be installed on the Benkowskis' premises and, after purchase but prior to installation, the Benkowskis repudiated the agreement. Suppose further that the Whites resold the pump for $350. In this example, the Whites reasonably relied on the Benkowskis' promise to supply water and sustained a loss. If the agreement was not enforceable (let us assume, for example, that the agreement left too many gaps), the Whites could not recover the $50 loss on the theory that the Benkowskis breached an enforceable agreement with consideration. Nevertheless, they likely could recover on the independent theory of justified reliance—"promissory estoppel."

Another theory affords relief for unjust enrichment in contract and related contexts. Suppose the Benkowskis actually installed on their premises the pump that the Whites purchased for $400 and put it to use, but thereafter the Benkowskis repudiated their deal with the Whites.

Assume again that the agreement was too incomplete. The Benkowskis would nevertheless be enriched at the Whites' expense. Pursuant to a widely accepted general theory of obligation, the Whites would be entitled to the value of the benefit conferred, which would prevent unjust enrichment of the Benkowskis.

Sometimes more than one theory of obligation will be applicable to the same set of facts. Even so, each theory may have independent significance.

B. REMEDIES

Successful theories of obligation lead to various possible remedies. Monetary remedies include: (1) lost expectancy damages designed to put the plaintiff in the same monetary position as if there had been no breach; (2) reliance damages designed to restore the plaintiff to the same monetary position as before the defendant made the promise; and (3) a sum equivalent to the value of any benefit the plaintiff conferred on the defendant. Beyond these monetary remedies are other possibilities, as we will see in Chapter Three.

We explore basic remedial possibilities and their relationships to theories of obligation in the problem and case that follow.

PROBLEM 1-1

Sam Grainseller was a grain dealer in Omaha where there is a well-organized grain market. Grainbuyer Inc. was a milling company in a town 20 miles away. On January 10, Sam agreed in writing to sell 1000 bushels of Orfed bearded white wheat to Grainbuyer for $3.55 per bushel, delivery September 1 at Sam's grain elevator in Omaha. On September 1, Grainbuyer sent trucks to Sam's elevator at a cost of $500, but when they arrived the drivers were told that Sam would not deliver, having "sold out." On September 2, after a careful survey of possibilities, Grainbuyer bought 1000 bushels of the same type of wheat from another seller near Sam at $5.55 a bushel, and again incurred $500 shipping costs. Grainbuyer Inc. wants to know its rights and remedies against Sam.

This deal is governed by the Uniform Commercial Code.[k] Article 2 of the Code, entitled "Sales," by its terms applies to "transactions in goods." U.C.C. § 2–102. "Goods" include "all things * * * which are movable at the time of identification to the contract for sale * * *." U.C.C. § 2–105(1). Although the "transactions in goods" language is broader than mere sales and presumably includes transactions such as bailments of goods, many sections of Article 2

[k] Most of Articles 1 and 2 of the Code (the latter dealing with the sale of goods) were drafted by Professor Karl N. Llewellyn (1893–1962). He was a professor of law at Columbia University, Yale University and the University of Chicago, and was one of this country's leading legal scholars and a major theorist of jurisprudence. He was chief draftsman of the Uniform Commercial Code and author of many articles and books, including *The Bramble Bush* (1930) (a set of lectures for beginning law students), and *The Common Law Tradition—Deciding Appeals* (1960). A fine biography is *W. Twining, Karl Llewellyn and The Realist Movement* (1972).

refer specifically to sales. For example, note the definition of goods in § 2–105(1), above. This curious approach to the scope of Article 2 produces some confusion. In this problem, however, is there any question as to whether Article 2 applies? Article 1 of the Code, entitled "General Provisions," also is relevant whenever another Article applies to a problem. Among the various Code sections applicable here is § 1–305(a), set forth below. Under § 1–305(a), what damages would Grainbuyer receive for Sam's breach? Is this appropriate? On what theory of obligation would this remedy be based?

UNIFORM COMMERCIAL CODE § 1–305(a).

Remedies to be Liberally Administered

The remedies provided by [the Uniform Commercial Code] must be liberally administered to the end that the aggrieved party may be put in as good a position as if the other party had fully performed but neither consequential or special damages nor penal damages may be had except as specifically provided in [the Uniform Commercial Code] or by other rule of law.

SULLIVAN V. O'CONNOR

Supreme Judicial Court of Massachusetts, 1973.
363 Mass. 579, 296 N.E.2d 183.

KAPLAN, JUSTICE.

The plaintiff patient secured a jury verdict of $13,500 against the defendant surgeon for breach of contract in respect to an operation upon the plaintiff's nose. The substituted consolidated bill of exceptions presents questions about the correctness of the judge's instructions on the issue of damages.

The declaration was in two counts. In the first count, the plaintiff alleged that she, as patient, entered into a contract with the defendant, a surgeon, wherein the defendant promised to perform plastic surgery on her nose and thereby to enhance her beauty and improve her appearance; that he performed the surgery but failed to achieve the promised result; rather the result of the surgery was to disfigure and deform her nose, to cause her pain in body and mind, and to subject her to other damage and expense. The second count, based on the same transaction, was in the conventional form for malpractice, charging that the defendant had been guilty of negligence in performing the surgery. Answering, the defendant entered a general denial.

On the plaintiff's demand, the case was tried by jury. At the close of the evidence, the judge put to the jury, as special questions, the issues of liability under the two counts, and instructed them accordingly. The jury returned a verdict for the plaintiff on the contract count, and for the defendant on the negligence count. The judge then instructed the jury on the issue of damages.

As background to the instructions and the parties' exceptions, we mention certain facts as the jury could find them. The plaintiff was a professional entertainer, and this was known to the defendant. The agreement was as alleged in the declaration. More particularly, judging from exhibits, the plaintiff's nose had been straight, but long and prominent; the defendant undertook by two operations to reduce its prominence and somewhat to shorten it, thus making it more pleasing in relation to the plaintiff's other features. Actually the plaintiff was obliged to undergo three operations, and her appearance was worsened. Her nose now had a concave line to about the midpoint, at which it became bulbous; viewed frontally, the nose from bridge to midpoint was flattened and broadened, and the two sides of the tip had lost symmetry. This configuration evidently could not be improved by further surgery. The plaintiff did not demonstrate, however, that her change of appearance had resulted in loss of employment. Payments by the plaintiff covering the defendant's fee and hospital expenses were stipulated at $622.65.

The judge instructed the jury, first, that the plaintiff was entitled to recover her out-of-pocket expenses incident to the operations. Second, she could recover the damages flowing directly, naturally, proximately, and foreseeably from the defendant's breach of promise. These would comprehend damages for any disfigurement of the plaintiff's nose—that is, any change of appearance for the worse—including the effects of the consciousness of such disfigurement on the plaintiff's mind, and in this connection the jury should consider the nature of the plaintiff's profession. Also consequent upon the defendant's breach, and compensable, were the pain and suffering involved in the third operation, but not in the first two. As there was no proof that any loss of earnings by the plaintiff resulted from the breach, that element should not enter into the calculation of damages.

By his exceptions the defendant contends that the judge erred in allowing the jury to take into account anything but the plaintiff's out-of-pocket expenses (presumably at the stipulated amount). The defendant excepted to the judge's refusal of his request for a general charge to that effect, and, more specifically, to the judge's refusal of a charge that the plaintiff could not recover for pain and suffering connected with the third operation or for impairment of the plaintiff's appearance and associated mental distress.

The plaintiff on her part excepted to the judge's refusal of a request to charge that the plaintiff could recover the difference in value between the nose as promised and the nose as it appeared after the operations. However, the plaintiff in her brief expressly waives this exception and others made by her in case this court overrules the defendant's exceptions; thus she would be content to hold the jury's verdict in her favor.

We conclude that the defendant's exceptions should be overruled.

It has been suggested on occasion that agreements between patients and physicians by which the physician undertakes to effect a cure or to bring about a given result should be declared unenforceable on grounds of public policy. See Guilmet v. Campbell, 385 Mich. 57, 76, 188 N.W.2d 601 (dissenting opinion). But there are many decisions recognizing and enforcing such contracts, see annotation, 43 A.L.R.3d 1221, 1225, 1229–1233, and the law of Massachusetts has treated them as valid, although we have had no decision meeting head on the contention that they should be denied legal sanction. Small v. Howard, 128 Mass. 131; Gabrunas v. Miniter, 289 Mass. 20, 193 N.E. 551; Forman v. Wolfson, 327 Mass. 341, 98 N.E.2d 615. These causes of action are, however, considered a little suspect, and thus we find courts straining sometimes to read the pleadings as sounding only in tort for negligence, and not in contract for breach of promise, despite sedulous efforts by the pleaders to pursue the latter theory. See Gault v. Sideman, 42 Ill.App.2d 96, 191 N.E.2d 436 * * *.

It is not hard to see why the courts should be unenthusiastic or skeptical about the contract theory. Considering the uncertainties of medical science and the variations in the physical and psychological conditions of individual patients, doctors can seldom in good faith promise specific results. Therefore it is unlikely that physicians of even average integrity will in fact make such promises. Statements of opinion by the physician with some optimistic coloring are a different thing, and may indeed have therapeutic value. But patients may transform such statements into firm promises in their own minds, especially when they have been disappointed in the event, and testify in that sense to sympathetic juries.[1] If actions for breach of promise can be readily maintained, doctors, so it is said, will be frightened into practising "defensive medicine." On the other hand, if these actions were outlawed, leaving only the possibility of suits for malpractice, there is fear that the public might be exposed to the enticements of charlatans, and confidence in the profession might ultimately be shaken. See Miller, The Contractual Liability of Physicians and Surgeons, 1953 Wash.L.Q. 413, 416–423. The law has taken the middle of the road position of allowing actions based on alleged contract, but insisting on clear proof. Instructions to the jury may well stress this requirement and point to tests of truth, such as the

1 Judicial skepticism about whether a promise was in fact made derives also from the possibility that the truth has been tortured to give the plaintiff the advantage of the longer period of limitations sometimes available for actions on contract as distinguished from those in tort or for malpractice. See Lillich, The Malpractice Statute of Limitations in New York and Other Jurisdictions, 47 Cornell L.Q. 339; annotation, 80 A.L.R.2d 368.

complexity or difficulty of an operation as bearing on the probability that a given result was promised. See annotation, 43 A.L.R.3d 1225, 1225–1227.

If an action on the basis of contract is allowed, we have next the question of the measure of damages to be applied where liability is found. Some cases have taken the simple view that the promise by the physician is to be treated like an ordinary commercial promise, and accordingly that the successful plaintiff is entitled to a standard measure of recovery for breach of contract—"compensatory" ("expectancy") damages, an amount intended to put the plaintiff in the position he would be in if the contract had been performed, or, presumably, at the plaintiff's election, "restitution" damages, an amount corresponding to any benefit conferred by the plaintiff upon the defendant in the performance of the contract disrupted by the defendant's breach. See Restatement: Contracts § 329 and comment a, §§ 347, 384(1). Thus in Hawkins v. McGee, 84 N.H. 114, 146 A. 641, the defendant doctor was taken to have promised the plaintiff to convert his damaged hand by means of an operation into a good or perfect hand, but the doctor so operated as to damage the hand still further. The court, following the usual expectancy formula, would have asked the jury to estimate and award to the plaintiff the difference between the value of a good or perfect hand, as promised, and the value of the hand after the operation. (The same formula would apply, although the dollar result would be less, if the operation had neither worsened nor improved the condition of the hand.) If the plaintiff had not yet paid the doctor his fee, that amount would be deducted from the recovery. There could be no recovery for the pain and suffering of the operation, since that detriment would have been incurred even if the operation had been successful; one can say that this detriment was not "caused" by the breach. But where the plaintiff by reason of the operation was put to more pain than he would have had to endure, had the doctor performed as promised, he should be compensated for that difference as a proper part of his expectancy recovery. It may be noted that on an alternative count for malpractice the plaintiff in the *Hawkins* case had been nonsuited; but on ordinary principles this could not affect the contract claim, for it is hardly a defence to a breach of contract that the promisor acted innocently and without negligence. The New Hampshire court further refined the *Hawkins* analysis in McQuaid v. Michou, 85 N.H. 299, 157 A. 881, all in the direction of treating the patient-physician cases on the ordinary footing of expectancy. * * *

Other cases, including a number in New York, without distinctly repudiating the *Hawkins* type of analysis, have indicated that a different and generally more lenient measure of damages is to be applied in patient-physician actions based on breach of alleged special agreements to effect a cure, attain a stated result, or employ a given medical method. This measure is expressed in somewhat variant ways, but the substance is that the plaintiff is to recover any expenditures made by him and for other detriment (usually not specifically described in the opinions) following proximately and foreseeably upon the defendant's failure to carry out his promise. Robins v. Finestone, 308 N.Y. 543, 546, 127 N.E.2d 330. * * * This, be it noted, is not a "restitution" measure, for it is not limited to restoration of the benefit conferred on the defendant (the fee paid) but includes other expenditures, for example, amounts paid for medicine and nurses; so also it would seem according to its logic to take in damages for any worsening of the plaintiff's condition due to the breach. Nor is it an "expectancy" measure, for it does not appear to contemplate recovery of the whole difference in value between the condition as promised and the condition actually resulting from the treatment. Rather the tendency of the formulation is to put the plaintiff back in the position he occupied just before the parties entered upon the agreement, to compensate him for the detriments he suffered in reliance upon the agreement. This kind of intermediate pattern of recovery for breach of contract is discussed in the suggestive article by Fuller and Perdue, The Reliance Interest in Contract Damages, 46 Yale L.J. 52, 373, where the authors show that, although not attaining the currency of the standard measures, a "reliance" measure has for special reasons been applied by the courts in a variety of settings, including noncommercial settings. See 46 Yale L.J. at 396–401.[2]

For breach of the patient-physician agreements under consideration, a recovery limited to restitution seems plainly too meager, if the agreements are to be enforced at all. On the other hand, an expectancy recovery may well be excessive. The factors, already mentioned, which have made the cause of action somewhat suspect, also suggest moderation as to the breadth of the recovery that should be permitted. Where, as in the case at bar and in a number of the reported cases, the doctor has been absolved of negligence by the trier, an expectancy measure may be thought harsh. We should recall here that the fee paid by the patient to the doctor for the alleged promise would usually be quite disproportionate to the putative expectancy recovery. To attempt, moreover, to put a value on the condition that would or might have resulted, had the treatment succeeded as promised, may sometimes put an exceptional strain on the imagination of the fact finder. As a general consideration, Fuller and Perdue argue that the reasons for granting damages for broken promises to the extent of the expectancy are at their strongest when the promises are made in a business context, when they have to do with the production or distribution of goods or the allocation of functions in the market place; they become weaker as the context shifts from a commercial to a noncommercial field. 46 Yale L.J. at 60–63.

---

[2] Some of the exceptional situations mentioned where reliance may be preferred to expectancy are those in which the latter measure would be hard to apply or would impose too great a burden; performance was interfered with by external circumstances; the contract was indefinite. See 46 Yale L.J. at 373–386; 394–396.

There is much to be said, then, for applying a reliance measure to the present facts, and we have only to add that our cases are not unreceptive to the use of that formula in special situations. We have, however, had no previous occasion to apply it to patient-physician cases.[3]

The question of recovery on a reliance basis for pain and suffering or mental distress requires further attention. We find expressions in the decisions that pain and suffering (or the like) are simply not compensable in actions for breach of contract. The defendant seemingly espouses this proposition in the present case. True, if the buyer under a contract for the purchase of a lot of merchandise, in suing for the seller's breach, should claim damages for mental anguish caused by his disappointment in the transaction, he would not succeed; he would be told, perhaps, that the asserted psychological injury was not fairly foreseeable by the defendant as a probable consequence of the breach of such a business contract. See Restatement: Contracts, § 341, and comment a. But there is no general rule barring such items of damage in actions for breach of contract. It is all a question of the subject matter and background of the contract, and when the contract calls for an operation on the person of the plaintiff, psychological as well as physical injury may be expected to figure somewhere in the recovery, depending on the particular circumstances. The point is explained in Stewart v. Rudner, 349 Mich. 459, 469, 84 N.W.2d 816. Cf. Frewen v. Page, 238 Mass. 499, 131 N.E. 475; McClean v. University Club, 327 Mass. 68, 97 N.E.2d 174. Again, it is said in a few of the New York cases, concerned with the classification of actions for statute of limitations purposes, that the absence of allegations demanding recovery for pain and suffering is characteristic of a contract claim by a patient against a physician, that such allegations rather belong in a claim for malpractice. See Robins v. Finestone, 308 N.Y. 543, 547, 127 N.E.2d 330; Budoff v. Kessler, 2 A.D.2d 760, 153 N.Y.S.2d 654. These remarks seem

[3] In Mt. Pleasant Stable Co. v. Steinberg, 238 Mass. 567, 131 N.E. 295, the plaintiff company agreed to supply teams of horses at agreed rates as required from day to day by the defendant for his business. To prepare itself to fulfill the contract and in reliance on it, the plaintiff bought two "Cliest" horses at a certain price. When the defendant repudiated the contract, the plaintiff sold the horses at a loss and in its action for breach claimed the loss as an element of damages. The court properly held that the plaintiff was not entitled to this item as it was also claiming (and recovering) its lost profits (expectancy) on the contract as a whole. Cf. Noble v. Ames Mfg. Co., 112 Mass. 492. (The loss on sale of the horses is analogous to the pain and suffering for which the patient would be disallowed a recovery in Hawkins v. McGee, 84 N.H. 114, 146 A. 641, because he was claiming and recovering expectancy damages.) The court in the *Mt. Pleasant* case referred, however, to Pond v. Harris, 113 Mass. 114, as a contrasting situation where the expectancy could not be fairly determined. There the defendant had wrongfully revoked an agreement to arbitrate a dispute with the plaintiff (this was before such agreements were made specifically enforceable). In an action for the breach, the plaintiff was held entitled to recover for his preparations for the arbitration which had been rendered useless and a waste, including the plaintiff's time and trouble and his expenditures for counsel and witnesses. The context apparently was commercial but reliance elements were held compensable when there was no fair way of estimating an expectancy. See, generally, annotation, 17 A.L.R.2d 1300. A noncommercial example is Smith v. Sherman, 4 Cush. 408, 413–414, suggesting that a conventional recovery for breach of promise of marriage included a recompense for various efforts and expenditures by the plaintiff preparatory to the promised wedding. * * *

unduly sweeping. Suffering or distress resulting from the breach going beyond that which was envisaged by the treatment as agreed, should be compensable on the same ground as the worsening of the patient's condition because of the breach. Indeed it can be argued that the very suffering or distress "contracted for"—that which would have been incurred if the treatment achieved the promised result—should also be compensable on the theory underlying the New York cases. For that suffering is "wasted" if the treatment fails. Otherwise stated, compensation for this waste is arguably required in order to complete the restoration of the status quo ante.[4]

In the light of the foregoing discussion, all the defendant's exceptions fail: the plaintiff was not confined to the recovery of her out-of-pocket expenditures; she was entitled to recover also for the worsening of her condition,[5] and for the pain and suffering and mental distress involved in the third operation. These items were compensable on either an expectancy or a reliance view. We might have been required to elect between the two views if the pain and suffering connected with the first two operations contemplated by the agreement, or the whole difference in value between the present and the promised conditions, were being claimed as elements of damage. But the plaintiff waives her possible claim to the former element, and to so much of the latter as represents the difference in value between the promised condition and the condition before the operations.

Plaintiff's exceptions waived.[1]

Defendant's exceptions overruled.

---

[4] Recovery on a reliance basis for breach of the physician's promise tends to equate with the usual recovery for malpractice, since the latter also looks in general to restoration of the condition before the injury. But this is not paradoxical, especially when it is noted that the origins of contract lie in tort. See Farnsworth, The Past of Promise: An Historical Introduction to Contract, 69 Col.L.Rev. 576, 594–596. * * *

It would, however, be a mistake to think in terms of strict "formulas." For example, a jurisdiction which would apply a reliance measure to the present facts might impose a more severe damage sanction for the wilful use by the physician of a method of operation that he undertook not to employ.

[5] That condition involves a mental element and appraisal of it properly called for consideration of the fact that the plaintiff was an entertainer. Cf. McQuaid v. Michou, 85 N.H. 299, 303–304, 157 A. 881 (discussion of continuing condition resulting from physician's breach).

[1] For a discussion of the different types of reasons set forth by Justice Kaplan, see Appendix A of this book.

Dec. 8, 1938

Professor Karl N. Llewellyn
School of Law
Columbia University
New York City

Dear Karl:

* * * To me it seems clear that no analysis of contract law can be realistic or adequate which does not recognize that there exists a hierarchy of contract interests, which may be sloganized by saying that they extend from restitution through the reliance interest to the expectation interest, with a number of little midstations, disturbing to elegantia juris, along the way. * * * I feel, incidentally, that your failure to employ this approach is attributable in part to your preoccupation with businessmen's business agreements, especially sales. * * * I consider the contribution made in my article on the reliance interest to lie, not in calling attention to the reliance interest itself, but in an analysis which breaks down the contract-no contract dichotomy, and substitutes an ascending scale of enforceability. * * *

SINCERELY YOURS,
LON L. FULLER[m]

FULLER,[n] PROFESSIONAL RESPONSIBILITY

44 A.B.A. J. 1159, 1161–62 (1958).

In our society the great bulk of human relations are set, not by government decree, but by the voluntary action of the affected parties. * * * Successful voluntary collaboration usually requires for its guidance something equivalent to a formal charter, defining the terms of collaboration, anticipating and forfending against possible disputes, and generally providing a framework for the parties' future dealings. In our society the natural architect of this framework is the lawyer. * * * [Here] the lawyer functions, not as an expert in the rules of an existing government, but as one who brings into existence a government for the regulation of the parties' own relation. * * * The fruits of [the lawyer's] skill enter in large measure into the drafting of ordinary legal documents, though this fact is obscured by the mistaken notion that the lawyer's only concern in such cases is with possible future litigation, it being forgotten

[m] Harvard Law School Library, Lon L. Fuller Papers.

[n] Lon L. Fuller (1902–1978) was probably the leading American contract theorist of the twentieth century. He was also a major figure in the fields of jurisprudence and legal philosophy. He taught at Oregon, Illinois, Duke, and Harvard. His article, *The Reliance Interest in Contract Damages*, 46 Yale L.J. 52 (1936), is one of the two or three most influential articles in the history of the subject. Another important article is Fuller, *Consideration and Form*, 41 Colum. L. Rev. 799 (1941). For a systematic introductory treatment of Fuller's work, see R. Summers, *Lon L. Fuller* (1984).

that an important part of his task is to design a framework of collaboration that will function in such a way that litigation will not arise.

CHAPTER TWO

GENERAL THEORIES OF OBLIGATION

■ ■ ■

The most important general feature of law is that certain kinds of human conduct are no longer optional, but in some sense obligatory.

H.L.A. HART

SECTION ONE: THEORIES OF OBLIGATION AND THEIR RELEVANCE TO THE LAWYER'S ROLE

In this chapter, we study in depth various theories of obligation operative in contractual and related affairs that were introduced in Chapter One, including agreement with consideration, promissory estoppel, and unjust enrichment. The number of such theories is not fixed and occasionally new theories emerge. Moreover, the dimensions of existing theories may change. Further, even the most developed theory of obligation may not alone resolve all the legal issues that arise in a case. Thus, a court may decide a case soundly even though the outcome cannot be justified solely on the basis of an existing theory of obligation. For example, in Sullivan v. O'Connor in Chapter One, the court decided the issues partly on the basis of a general theory and partly on the basis of attention to the particular circumstances.

Nevertheless, general theories of obligation predominate in this field. The lawyer must understand these theories and deploy them effectively as a planner, drafter, counselor, negotiator, and litigator. The primacy of basic theory is hardly exceptional. As Justice Oliver Wendell Holmes, Jr. once remarked, "[t]heory is the most important part * * * of the law, as the architect is the most important man who takes part in the building of a house."[a]

---

[a] Holmes, *The Path of the Law*, 10 Harv. L. Rev. 457, 477 (1897). Oliver Wendell Holmes, Jr. (1841–1935) practiced law, taught law briefly at Harvard, served as a justice of the Supreme Judicial Court of Massachusetts for twenty years, and served for thirty years as a Justice of the Supreme Court of the United States. His writings have had great influence. All students of the law should read something by and about him. Perhaps the most readable biography is C. Bowen, Yankee from Olympus (1943). Holmes's book, The Common Law (1881), is a landmark that includes three important chapters on contract. The late Justice Felix Frankfurter said of this book that it "is a classic in the sense that its stock of ideas has been absorbed and become part of common juristic thought. * * * " *F. Frankfurter, Of Law and Men* 167 (1956).

When the requirements of a general theory of obligation are satisfied, the parties incur both rights and duties. For example, when the Benkowskis and the Whites entered into a valid agreement with consideration, the Benkowskis incurred a duty to provide household water to the Whites and the Whites acquired a right to that water.

Upon breach of their duty, the Benkowski owed damages. Does that mean that the only significance of an obligation is the legal remedy that it generates? Holmes (again) thought so:

> [T]he duty to keep a contract at common law means a prediction that you must pay damages if you do not keep it,—and nothing else. If you commit a tort, you are liable to pay a compensatory sum. If you commit a contract, you are liable to pay a compensatory sum unless the promised event comes to pass, and that is all the difference.[b]

Of course, the "cash value" of the breach of a primary duty *is* important to business people and others. It must also be conceded that remedial considerations may distinctively influence judges when they decide whether and how far a theory of obligation applies to a particular case. (Again, see Sullivan v. O'Connor.) It follows that the lawyer practicing in this field must be remedies-minded.

But the *why* of contract law doesn't just matter in how it cashes out in the end. Real people also want their agreements to have legal force because of what happens *out of court*—the "normative significance"[c] of an agreement. When parties believe in the legal weight of their agreements, disputes in contractual and related affairs arise less frequently, and may be settled more simply and cheaply. Indeed, as empiricists have shown, parties see breaches of "legal" contracts as moral wrongs to be punished rather than taxed as Holmes would have done.[d]

In the materials that follow in this chapter, we concentrate mainly on two basic dimensions of general theories of obligation of major interest to the lawyer. The first consists of the substantive requirements, defined by law, for the prima facie applicability of each theory. For example: what are the requirements of a valid agreement with consideration? The second dimension consists of the general justifying rationale (or rationales)

---

[b] Holmes, *The Path of the Law*, 10 Harv. L. Rev. 457, 462 (1897).

[c] See H.L.A. Hart, THE CONCEPT OF LAW, chs. IV and V (1961). Professor Hart is the first Anglo-American legal theorist to clarify and stress the normative character of private law duties. He is one of the two or three most influential English speaking legal theorists of the twentieth century. After study at Oxford and preparation for the bar, he practiced for nine years at the Chancery bar (1931–1939). He was at the British War Office during World War II and then returned to Oxford, where he became professor of jurisprudence in 1952. Hart is an innovative adherent of the positivist tradition. For a fine general treatment and a bibliography, see D. Neil MacCormick, H.L.A. Hart (Stanford, 1981).

[d] See Tess Wilkinson-Ryan and Jonathan Baron, Moral Judgment and Moral Heuristics in Breach of Contract, 6 J. Emp. Leg. Stud. 405 (2009).

supporting each theory. We will see that theories vary not only in their basic requirements for applicability, but also in their justifying rationales. We stress these rationales here because they often influence judicial decisions on whether a theory applies.

In later chapters, we will see that theories of obligation have still other dimensions. For example, although the basic requirements of an agreement with consideration may be satisfied so that a prima facie duty arises, the party obligated may assert a defense such as the "unconscionability" of a term, or a "material breach" by the other party.

SECTION TWO: OBLIGATION ARISING FROM AN AGREEMENT WITH CONSIDERATION—THE LEADING THEORY

In this section, we concentrate on the "bargain" concept of consideration. Consideration is one of the basic requirements of the leading theory of obligation in contractual and related affairs. We also touch on aspects of the second basic requirement of this theory, a valid "agreement," but we postpone systematic study of this requirement until Chapter Four.

We open with cases on the concept of consideration as bargained-for exchange. This concept has deep historical roots, including roots in ancient common-law pleading and procedure. We explore these early roots in Appendix B.

HARDESTY V. SMITH

Supreme Court of Indiana, 1851.
3 Ind. 39.

[One Isham sold the rights to an invention, allegedly improving a lamp, to the defendant, Smith. Smith paid for the rights by signing some promissory notes. Isham assigned the notes to the plaintiff, Hardesty, who sought to collect on them. Smith alleged an affirmative defense that the supposed improvement in the lamp was worthless.]

PERKINS, J.

[T]he plaintiff demurred generally. The Court * * * overruled [the demurrer] * * * and the defendant had final judgment in his favor.

* * *

* * * [T]he Court erred in not sustaining the demurrer. * * * The simple fact that the improvement in the lamp was of no utility, is not sufficient to bar a suit on these notes. Parties of sufficient mental capacity for the management of their own business, have a right to make their own bargains. The owner of a thing has the right to fix the price at which he will part with it, and a buyer's own judgment ought to be his best guide as

to what he should give to obtain it. The consideration agreed upon may indefinitely exceed the value of the thing for which it is promised, and still the bargain stand. The doing of an act by one at the request of another, which may be a detriment or inconvenience, however slight, to the party doing it, or may be a benefit, however slight, to the party at whose request it is performed, is a legal consideration for a promise by such requesting party. So the parting with a right, which one possesses, to another, at his request, may constitute a good consideration. And where one person examines an invention to the use of which another has the exclusive right, and, upon his own judgment, uninfluenced by fraud, or warranty, or mistake of facts, agrees to give a certain sum for the conveyance of that right to him, such conveyance forms a valid consideration for such agreement. The judgment of the purchaser is the best arbiter of whether the thing is of any value, and how great, to him. The chance he may acquire of gain, the power he may obtain of preventing any other person from attempting to introduce the use of the invention in competition with some rival one such purchaser may, at the time, own the right to, or some other motive, may induce him willingly to pay a sum of money, in such case, for that which, in the end, may prove valueless in itself. On the other hand, as we have already said, loss, or trouble, or inconvenience, or expense, on the part of the grantor, or seller, without any profit to the buyer, is a good consideration. So the simple parting with a right which is one's own, and which he has a right to fix a price upon, must be a good consideration for a promise to pay that price. In such cases, the purchaser *gets a something* * * *.

* * * When a party gets all the consideration he honestly contracted for, he cannot say he gets no consideration, or that it has failed. If this doctrine be not correct, then it is not true that parties are at liberty to make their own contracts. And if, where an article is fairly sold and purchased, for a stipulated consideration, a Court or jury may annul the bargain if they come to the conclusion the article sold was of no value, then they should be permitted, in every case, where they may conclude the article is worth something, to determine whether it is worth as much as has been promised for it, and, if it is not, to reduce the amount to be paid to that point; thus doing away with all special contracts. * * *

PER CURIAM.—The judgment is reversed with costs. Cause remanded.

DEAN WITTER REYNOLDS, INC. v. VARIABLE ANNUITY LIFE INS. CO., 373 F.3d 1100, 1110–11 (10th Cir. 2004). The common law has long maintained that an assignee stands in the shoes of the assignor. Thus, when Dean Witter brings a claim as an assignee of Mrs. Bass, the law conceptualizes the matter as if Mrs. Bass, not Dean Witter, stands before the court.

DOUGHERTY V. SALT

New York Court of Appeals, 1919.
227 N.Y. 200, 125 N.E. 94.

Appeal from Supreme Court, Appellate Division, Second Department.

Action by Charles Napoleon Dougherty, an infant, by Susan M. Teves, his guardian, against Emma L. Salt, as executrix of the last will and testament of Helena M. Dougherty, deceased. From a judgment of the second department of the Appellate Division of the Supreme Court (184 App.Div. 910, 170 N.Y.Supp. 1076), reversing a judgment of the Trial Term, which set aside a verdict of the jury in favor of plaintiff and dismissed the complaint, and reinstating the verdict and directing judgment thereon, the defendant appeals. Judgment of Appellate Division reversed, and judgment of Trial Term modified by granting a new trial. Affirmed.

CARDOZO, J.[e] The plaintiff, a boy of eight years, received from his aunt, the defendant's testatrix, a promissory note for $3,000, payable at her death or before. Use was made of a printed form, which contains the words "value received." How the note came to be given was explained by the boy's guardian, who was a witness for his ward. The aunt was visiting her nephew.

> "When she saw Charley coming in, she said, 'Isn't he a nice boy?' I answered her, Yes; that he is getting along very nice, and getting along nice in school; and I showed where he had progressed in school, having good reports, and so forth, and she told me that she was going to take care of that child; that she loved him very much. I said, 'I know you do, Tillie, but your taking care of the child will be done probably like your brother and sister done, take it out in talk.' She said, 'I don't intend to take it out in talk; I would like to take care of him now.' I said, 'Well, that is up to you.' She said, 'Why can't I make out a note to him?' I said, 'You can, if you wish to.' She said, 'Would that be right?' And I said, 'I do not know, but I guess it would; I do not know why it would not.' And she said, 'Well, will you make out a note for me?' I said, 'Yes, if you wish me to,' and she said, 'Well, I wish you would.' "

A blank was then produced, filled out, and signed. The aunt handed the note to her nephew, with these words:

> "You have always done for me, and I have signed this note for you. Now, do not lose it. Some day it will be valuable."

[e] Benjamin N. Cardozo (1870–1938) was a judge of the New York Court of Appeals from 1914 until 1932 (Chief Judge the last six years). In 1932, President Hoover appointed Cardozo to the United States Supreme Court to replace the retiring Oliver Wendell Holmes, Jr. A highly literate judge, Cardozo also wrote a number of books. The best known is The Nature of the Judicial Process (1921).

The trial judge submitted to the jury the question whether there was any consideration for the promised payment. Afterwards, he set aside the verdict in favor of the plaintiff, and dismissed the complaint. The Appellate Division, by a divided court, reversed the judgment of dismissal, and reinstated the verdict on the ground that the note was sufficient evidence of consideration.

We reach a different conclusion. The inference of consideration to be drawn from the form of the note has been so overcome and rebutted as to leave no question for a jury. This is not a case where witnesses, summoned by the defendant and friendly to the defendant's cause, supply the testimony in disproof of value. Strickland v. Henry, 175 N.Y. 372, 67 N.E. 611. This is a case where the testimony in disproof of value comes from the plaintiff's own witness, speaking at the plaintiff's instance. The transaction thus revealed admits of one interpretation, and one only. The note was the voluntary and unenforcible promise of an executory gift. Harris v. Clark, 3 N.Y. 93, 51 Am.Dec. 352; Holmes v. Roper, 141 N.Y. 64, 66, 36 N.E. 180. This child of eight was not a creditor, nor dealt with as one. The aunt was not paying a debt. She was conferring a bounty. Fink v. Cox, 18 Johns. 145, 9 Am.Dec. 191. The promise was neither offered nor accepted with any other purpose. "Nothing is consideration that is not regarded as such by both parties." (Philpot v. Gruninger, 14 Wall. 570, 577 * * *).

A note so given is not made for "value received," however its maker may have labeled it. The formula of the printed blank becomes, in the light of the conceded facts, a mere erroneous conclusion, which cannot overcome the inconsistent conclusion of the law. * * * The plaintiff through his own witness, has explained the genesis of the promise, and consideration has been disproved. Neg.Instr.Law, § 54 (Consol. Laws, c. 38).

We hold, therefore, that the verdict of the jury was contrary to law, and that the trial judge was right in setting it aside.

[The court then ordered a new trial based on a New York procedural rule.]

* * *

The judgment of the Appellate Division should be reversed, and the judgment of the Trial Term modified by granting a new trial, and, as modified, affirmed, with costs in all courts to abide the event.

Judgment accordingly.

STONESTREET v. SOUTHERN OIL CO., 226 N.C. 261, 263, 37 S.E.2d 676, 677 (1946). [W]hen one receives a naked promise and such promise is not kept, he is no worse off than he was before the promise was made. He gave nothing for it, loses nothing by it, and upon its breach he suffers no recoverable damage.

PROBLEM 2-1

Suppose you had been counsel to the guardian of Charles Napoleon Dougherty and had been asked to draft an agreement with consideration obligating Helena M. Dougherty to pay the sum promised. Draft the agreement.

RESTATEMENT (FIRST) OF CONTRACTS § 75.

Definition of Consideration.

(1) Consideration for a promise is

(a) an act other than a promise, or

(b) a forbearance, or

(c) the creation, modification or destruction of a legal relation, or

(d) a return promise,

bargained for and given in exchange for the promise.

(2) Consideration may be given to the promisor or to some other person. It may be given by the promisee or by some other person.

WILLISTON,[f] RESTATEMENT OF CONTRACTS IS PUBLISHED BY THE AMERICAN LAW INSTITUTE

18 A.B.A. J. 775, 776–77 (1932).

The rules to be derived from a multitude of decisions are sometimes clear and sometimes open to dispute; but in any event the sources from which the rules are to be sought become more and more bulky as time passes. Inconsistencies, uncertainties and complexities are the sure accompaniments of bulk, as well as increased expenditure of time in seeking applicable rules. The difficulty has not become overwhelming as yet, but surely must become so. One need only multiply the annual production of law reports by a number of years, say fifty to one hundred, small in the history of a country, to realize what search in an accumulated mass of decisions may mean.

[f] Samuel Williston (1861–1963) was a Professor of Law at Harvard Law School. He was one of the two foremost scholars of American contract law in the last century, and was Reporter of the Restatement (First) of Contracts. He authored an influential multi-volume treatise, WILLISTON ON CONTRACTS, and drafted a number of influential statutes, including the Uniform Sales Act. He also wrote an autobiography, LIFE AND LAW (1940).

* * * The situation is sufficiently serious now to make it evident that the prodigious material from which our law must be sought should be summarized as effectively and as soon as possible.

* * *

* * * Statutes, however, are not likely at present, or in the immediate future, to afford an adequate solution to the problem presented by the bulk and diversity of decisions. And so far as a solution is ultimately approximated in that way the solution will be aided and more satisfactorily carried out if a preliminary attempt is made, as it is in the Restatement, to frame rules in statutory form, the correctness of which can be tested by the courts when there is not the rigidity that statutes necessarily have.

* * *

It was the essence of the plan that it should be a cooperative effort in which each statement should receive the careful thought of the body of experts, and later receive the approval of the Council and of the whole body of the Institute. Every sentence of the Restatement of Contracts has been prepared and considered in this way. * * * It seemed that the Restatement would be more likely to achieve an authority of its own that would to some extent, at least, free courts from part of the troublesome weighing of cases and arguments if exact rules were clearly stated without argument. Those who have prepared the Restatement have had arguments among themselves—hundreds of them. They believe it better to give the net results of their arguments than to present the arguments themselves with supporting authorities.

K. LLEWELLYN, THE BRAMBLE BUSH

157–58 (1951 ed.).

[T]he rule follows where its reason leads; where the reason stops, there stops the rule.

NOTE: CONSIDERATION AND FORM

One of the more famous pieces of contract law scholarship is *Consideration and Form*, by Lon Fuller.[g] In it, Fuller attempted to explain the nature and function of legal formalities. He argued that such devices play three important roles:

> § 2. *The Evidentiary Function.*—The most obvious function of a legal formality is, to use Austin's words, that of providing "evidence of the existence and purport of the contract, in case of controversy." The need for evidentiary security may be satisfied in a variety of ways: by

[g] 41 Colum. L. Rev. 799 (1941).

> requiring a writing, or attestation, or the certification of a notary. * * *
>
> § 3. *The Cautionary Function.*—A formality may also perform a cautionary or deterrent function by acting as a check against inconsiderate action. The seal in its original form fulfilled this purpose remarkably well. The affixing and impressing of a wax wafer—symbol in the popular mind of legalism and weightiness—was an excellent device for inducing the circumspective frame of mind appropriate in one pledging his future. To a less extent any requirement of a writing, of course, serves the same purpose, as do requirements of attestation, notarization, etc.
>
> § 4. *The Channeling Function.*—Though most discussions of the purposes served by formalities go no further than the analysis just presented, this analysis stops short of recognizing one of the most important functions of form. * * * In seeking to understand [the] channeling function of form, perhaps the most useful analogy is that of language * * *. One who wishes to communicate his thoughts to others must force the raw materials of meaning into defined and recognizable channels; he must reduce the fleeting entities of wordless thought to the patterns of conventional speech. One planning to enter a legal transaction faces a similar problem. His mind first conceives an economic or sentimental objective, or * * * set of overlapping objectives. He must then, with or without the aid of a lawyer, cast about for the legal transaction (written memorandum, sealed contract, lease, conveyance of the fee, etc.) which will most nearly accomplish these objectives.
>
> * * *

After setting forth these functions, Fuller argued that courts' treatment of formalities, i.e., whether they applied the consideration requirement strictly or laxly, depended not just on their superficial nature but also on the characteristics of the underlying agreement that they marked. The law enforces bargains to vindicate interests of *private autonomy*, to remedy injuries done to those who have *relied on promises*, and to make sure that promisors are not *unjustly enriched.* As Fuller put it:

> Form has an obvious relationship to the principle of private autonomy. Where men make laws for themselves it is desirable that they should do so under conditions guaranteeing the desiderata described in our analysis of the functions of form. Furthermore, the greater the assurance that these desiderata are satisfied, the larger the scope we may be willing to ascribe to private autonomy. * * *

For example, when a promisor has not changed her position in reliance on a promise, nor laid out money for its fulfillment, nor promised to perform herself, enforcement is denied because, courts say, there is no consideration. But the underlying *reason* for the denial is that there is no substantive bases of contractual liability . . . If on 'substantive' grounds the balance already inclines away from judicial intervention, the case against enforcement becomes stronger when we draw into account the desiderata underlying the use of formalities.

That there is in the instant case a lack of evidentiary and cautionary safeguards is obvious. As to the channeling function of form, we may observe that the promise is made in a field where intention is not naturally canalized. There is nothing here to effect a neat division between tentative and exploratory expressions of intention, on the one hand, and legally effective transactions, on the other. In contrast to the situation of the immediate gift of a chattel (where title will pass by the manual tradition), there is here no 'natural formality' on which the courts might seize as a test of enforceability.

PROBLEM 2-2

Fuller offered what he calls "substantive reasons" and "reasons of form" that may provide supporting justifications for the *content* of Restatement (First) of Contracts section 75. He thus fleshes out the bare bones of the section, drafted by Professor Williston, who thought such "exact rules" should be "clearly stated" *without* supporting reasons. Fuller also undertakes to fill gaps in many judicial opinions. According to him, "the policies underlying the doctrine [of consideration] are generally left unexamined in the decisions." Were these policies in fact left unexamined in the first two decisions in this chapter? In light of Fuller's reasons of substance and reasons of form, were these two cases correctly decided? What of the cases that immediately follow?

MAUGHS V. PORTER

Virginia Supreme Court of Appeals, 1931.
157 Va. 415, 161 S.E. 242.

PRENTIS, C.J.

The record discloses that to the plaintiff's notice of motion for $461 the defendant filed a general demurrer, which was sustained. To that judgment plaintiff has been allowed a writ of error.

The motion is based upon these facts: The defendant inserted this advertisement in the "Daily Progress," a newspaper published in Charlottesville, Va.:

"New Model Ford Free

"At the auction fifty (50) beautiful residence lots Fry's Spring, Thursday, October 13, 1:30 on time. Every white person over sixteen (16) years of age has an equal chance at the New Ford regardless of buying or bidding. Come to the auction of Oak Lawns."

Responding to that advertisement, the plaintiff, a white person over sixteen years of age, attended the sale, and received from the defendant a slip of paper upon which, by direction of the auctioneer, she placed her name, and deposited it in a box held by the auctioneer. Upon the drawing of the slip from the box, she was adjudged the winner of the automobile. In response to the auctioneer's demand, she paid him $3 for his services in drawing the lucky number.

The defendant placed an order for the car with the Albemarle Motor Company, but refused to pay for it when it was ready for delivery, and has also refused the demand of the plaintiff that he pay her the value of the car, alleged to be $461.

The defendant demurred to the notice of motion, alleging two grounds, thus stated: (1) That the matters alleged in the plaintiff's notice of motion fail to show a sufficient consideration for defendant's promise, and that defendant's promise is nudum pactum, and hence unenforceable; (2) that, in so far as there was any consideration for defendant's promise, the scheme alleged in the notice of motion is a lottery or raffle, and any contract which might otherwise arise therefrom is illegal and unenforceable.

The questions then are: (1) Whether the alleged offer to make the gift can be enforced as supported by a sufficient consideration; and, if it should be determined that there was such a consideration as would otherwise support the gift, then (2) whether the transaction constitutes a lottery, which is prohibited by Constitution, § 60, and by statute, Code, §§ 4693, 4694.

First. In Spooner v. Hilbish, 92 Va. 333, 23 S.E. 751, 753, we find this clear statement by RIELY, J.: "A gift is a contract without a consideration, and, to be valid, must be executed. A valid gift is therefore a contract executed. It is to be executed by the actual delivery by the donor to the donee, or to some one for him, of the thing given, or by the delivery of the means of obtaining the subject of the gift, without further act of the donor to enable the donee to reduce it to his own possession. 'The intention to give must be accompanied by a delivery, and the delivery must be made with an intention to give.' Otherwise there is only an intention or promise to give, which, being gratuitous, would be a mere nullity. Delivery of possession of the thing given, or of the means of obtaining it so as to make the disposal of it irrevocable, is indispensable to a valid gift." * * *

* * *

Clearly then the plaintiff, under the facts shown here, cannot recover, unless defendant is bound by a promise which is supported by a consideration sufficient to support the action.

It is often quite difficult to determine in such cases whether or not there is such a consideration.

1 Williston on Contracts, § 112, p. 232, thus illustrates the difficulty: "If a benevolent man says to a tramp: 'If you go around the corner to the clothing shop there, you may purchase an overcoat on my credit,' no reasonable person would understand that the short walk was requested as the consideration for the promise, but that in the event of the tramp going to the shop the promisor would make him a gift. Yet the walk to the shop is in its nature capable of being consideration. It is a legal detriment to the tramp to make the walk, and the only reason why the walk is not consideration is because on a reasonable construction it must be held that the walk was not requested as the price of the promise, but was merely a condition of a gratuitous promise. It is often difficult to determine whether words of condition in a promise indicate a request for consideration or state a mere condition in a gratuitous promise. An aid, though not a conclusive test in determining which construction of the promise is more reasonable is an inquiry whether the happening of the condition will be a benefit to the promisor. If so, it is a fair inference that the happening was requested as a consideration. On the other hand, if, as in the case of the tramp stated above, the happening of the condition will be not only of no benefit to the promisor but is obviously merely for the purpose of enabling the promisee to receive a gift, the happening of the event on which the promise is conditional, though brought about by the promisee in reliance on the promise, will not properly be construed as consideration. In case of doubt where the promisee has incurred a detriment on the faith of the promise, courts will naturally be loath to regard the promise as a mere gratuity and the detriment incurred as merely a condition. But in some cases it is so clear that a conditional gift was intended that even though the promisee has incurred detriment, the promise has been held unenforceable."

Under the first ground of demurrer in this case it is contended for the defendant that this was not a promise for a consideration, but on the contrary, was a mere condition of the proposed gift.

We conclude, however, that there was sufficient consideration to support the gift and but for the other question involved this would determine the case. The object of the defendant unquestionably was to attract persons to the auction sale with the hope of deriving benefit from the crowd so augmented. Even though persons attracted by the advertisement of the free automobile might attend only because hoping to draw the automobile, and with the determination not to bid for any of the lots, some of these even might nevertheless be induced to bid after reaching the place of sale. So we conclude that the attendance of the plaintiff at the sale was a sufficient consideration for the promise to give an automobile, which could be enforced if otherwise legal.

[The court went on to hold that defendant's promise was unenforceable as a lottery.]

Affirmed.

BARFIELD V. COMMERCE BANK, N.A.

United States Court of Appeals, Tenth Circuit, 2007.
484 F.3d 1276.

Chris Barfield, an African-American man, entered a Commerce Bank branch in Wichita, Kansas, and requested change for a $50 bill. He was refused change on the ground that he was not an account-holder. The next day, Chris Barfield's father, James Barfield, asked a white friend, John Polson, to make the same request from the bank. Mr. Polson was given change, and the teller never asked whether he held an account with the bank. A few minutes later, James Barfield entered the bank, asked for change for a $100 bill, and was told that he would not be given change unless he was an account-holder.

James Barfield then enlisted the help of a white news reporter and his African-American colleague. The two men, separately, visited the bank to request change. The African-American man was asked whether he was an account holder, and the white man was not.

The Barfields filed suit under 42 U.S.C. § 1981, alleging racial discrimination in the impairment of the ability to contract. The Bank moved to dismiss for failure to state a claim. While that motion was pending, the two sides engaged in extended mediation and negotiation, which ultimately failed. During that period, the Barfields moved for class certification and to amend their complaint to include a claim under Title VI of the Civil Rights Act of 1964. The judge denied both plaintiffs' motions and granted the defendant's motion to dismiss. The Barfields timely appealed.

I.

Originally enacted in the wake of the Civil War, Section 1981(a) states:

> All persons within the jurisdiction of the United States shall have the same right in every State and Territory to *make and enforce contracts,* to sue, be parties, give evidence, and to the full and equal benefit of all laws and proceedings for the security of persons and property as is enjoyed by white citizens, and shall be subject to like punishment, pains, penalties, taxes, licenses, and exactions of every kind, and no other.

42 U.S.C. § 1981(a) (emphasis added). As part of the Civil Rights Act of 1991, Congress added part b to the statute: "For purposes of this section, the term 'make and enforce contracts' includes the making, performance, modification, and termination of contracts, and the enjoyment of all benefits, privileges, terms, and conditions of the contractual relationship." *Id.* § 1981(b). The purpose of part b was to expand the statute to encompass

"all phases and incidents of the contractual relationship." *Rivers v. Roadway Express, Inc.,* 511 U.S. 298, 302, 308, 114 S.Ct. 1510, 128 L.Ed.2d 274 (1994).

Section 1981 claims are subject to a three-part test. The claimant must demonstrate: "(1) that the plaintiff is a member of a protected class; (2) that the defendant had the intent to discriminate on the basis of race; and (3) that the discrimination interfered with a protected activity as defined in § 1981." *Hampton v. Dillard Dep't Stores, Inc.,* 247 F.3d 1091, 1102 (10th Cir.2001). Only the third prong is at issue here.

All courts to have addressed the issue have held that a customer's offer to do business in a retail setting qualifies as a "phase[ ] and incident[ ] of the contractual relationship" under § 1981. In *Christian v. Wal-Mart Stores, Inc.,* 252 F.3d 862 (6th Cir.2001), the Sixth Circuit upheld a § 1981 claim where an African-American customer, ready to make a purchase, was accused of shoplifting and removed from the store:

> we have no trouble concluding that [the appellant] made herself available to enter into a contractual relationship for services ordinarily provided by Wal-Mart: the record reflects that she had selected merchandise to purchase, had the means to complete the transaction, and would, in fact, have completed her purchase had she not been asked to leave the store.

Id. at 874. The Fifth Circuit has written that "when a merchant denies service or outright refuses to engage in business with a consumer attempting to contract with the merchant, that is a violation of § 1981." *Causey v. Sewell Cadillac-Chevrolet, Inc.,* 394 F.3d 285, 290 (5th Cir.2004). * * *

The question, then, is whether the Barfields' proposal to exchange money at a bank is a contract offer in the same way as an offer to purchase doughnuts or apple juice. The claim made by the appellees, and accepted by the district court, is that the Barfields' proposed exchange was not a contract because it involved no consideration: "The bank would not have received any benefit or incurred a detriment if it had agreed to change the Barfields' bills." App. at 56. That reasoning, however, departs in several significant ways from our understanding of contract law.

To determine the contours of a contract, we look to state common law. *Hampton,* 247 F.3d at 1104; 42 U.S.C. § 1988(a). Under Kansas law:

> A contract must be supported by consideration in order to be enforceable. *State ex rel. Ludwick v. Bryant,* 237 Kan. 47, 697 P.2d 858 (1985); *Mitchell v. Miller,* 27 Kan.App.2d 666, 8 P.3d 26 (2000). 'Consideration is defined as some right, interest, profit, or benefit accruing to one party, or some forbearance, detriment, loss, or responsibility, given, suffered, or undertaken by the other.'

> 17A Am.Jur.2d, Contracts § 113, p. 129. A promise is without consideration when the promise is given by one party to another without anything being bargained for and given in exchange for it. 2 Corbin on Contracts § 5.20 (rev.ed.1995).

Varney Bus. Servs., Inc. v. Pottroff, 275 Kan. 20, 59 P.3d 1003, 1014 (2002). * * *

In the most straightforward sense, the transaction proposed by the Barfields was a contract of exchange: they would give up something of value (a large-denomination bill) in exchange for something they valued more (smaller-denomination bills). It is hard to see why this is not a contract. If two boys exchange marbles, their transaction is a contract, even if it is hard for outsiders to fathom why either preferred the one or the other. Consideration does not need to have a quantifiable financial value:

> [T]he legal sufficiency of a consideration for a promise [does not] depend upon the comparative economic value of the consideration and of what is promised in return, for the parties are deemed to be the best judges of the bargains entered into. . . . Where a party contracts for the performance of an act which will afford him pleasure, gratify his ambition, please his fancy, or express his appreciation of a service another has rendered him, his estimate of value must be left undisturbed. . . .

In re Shirk's Estate, 186 Kan. 311, 350 P.2d 1, 10 (1960).

The Bank, however, argues that the proposed exchange was not a contract because it received no remuneration for performing the service of bill exchange. In other words, rather than view the transaction as an exchange of one thing for another, the Bank urges us to treat the transaction as a gratuitous service provided by the Bank, for no consideration. We cannot regard the Bank's provision of bill exchange services as "gratuitous" in any legal sense. Profit-making establishments often offer to engage in transactions with no immediate gain, or even at a loss, as a means of inducing customers to engage in other transactions that are more lucrative; such offers may nonetheless be contractual, and they do not lack consideration. *See Idbeis v. Wichita Surgical Specialists, P.A.,* 279 Kan. 755, 112 P.3d 81, 90 (2005) (holding that unquantifiable consideration, such as an employee's goodwill and professional contacts, is adequate to sustain a contract). If, as is alleged in the complaint, the Bank effectively extends bill exchange services to persons of one race and not the other, that is sufficient to come within the ambit of § 1981.

Appellee relies heavily on a part of this Court's holding in *Hampton v. Dillard Department Stores, Inc.,* 247 F.3d 1091 (10th Cir.2001). That case involved two individuals—an aunt and a niece—shopping together at a department store. *Id.* at 1099. After the aunt, Ms. Hampton, made a purchase, a store clerk offered each of the two women a coupon for a free fragrance sample. *Id.* at 1100. The women went to the fragrance counter and were in the process of redeeming their coupons when they were stopped by a security guard, who suspected them of shoplifting. *Id.* The guard searched Ms. Hampton's bag and found no stolen merchandise; the women, after verbally expressing their displeasure, left the store without renewing their attempts to obtain fragrance samples. *Id.*

They brought suit in federal court alleging interference with contractual rights under § 1981. Although the district court allowed Ms. Hampton's § 1981 claim to proceed to the jury and this Court upheld the jury verdict in her favor, the district court dismissed the claim of her niece, Ms. Cooper, on summary judgment, and this Court affirmed. Appellee suggests that our affirmance of summary judgment against Ms. Cooper stands for the broad proposition that gratuitous offers do not constitute contracts within the meaning of Section 1981, and argues that because the Bank's service of providing change was gratuitous, any racial discrimination with respect to that service would fall outside the ambit of the statute.

Appellee reads *Hampton* too broadly. *Hampton* did not establish any sweeping limitations on the coverage of Section 1981. Rather, *Hampton* was based on a specific finding that the coupon in question in that case was a contract benefit valid only upon purchase of merchandise. *Id.* at 1104–05. Because Ms. Cooper's aunt made a purchase, "she completed the invited performance in accordance with the terms of the offer" and thus had a valid contractual right to the coupon and its attendant benefits. *Id.* at 1104. In contrast, Ms. Cooper never "ma[de] or attempt[ed] to make a purchase at Dillard's," *id.* at 1118, and thus she had no right to the contractual benefit. *Hampton* thus stands for the sensible proposition that a customer who fails to comply with a store's contractual terms cannot then claim that subsequent conduct by the store's employees interfered with her contractual right.

Instead of holding, as the Bank asserts, that offers of free merchandise can never constitute contracts under § 1981, *Hampton* reserves that question for another day. *Id.* at 1105. However, its consideration of the issue in dicta supports the conclusion we come to today. In describing the coupon, the *Hampton* Court noted that a retail establishment's offer of a free service or sample in fact could constitute a contract within the meaning of Section 1981. The establishment receives a benefit from such offers because "to sample those products, the customer would traverse the store, perhaps eyeing other merchandise for purchase." *Id.* at 1105.

We therefore reverse the district court's dismissal of the Barfield's Section 1981 claim.

[The court affirmed the trial court's denial of the Barfields' move to amend their complaint to add class action certification and a claim unter Title VI because the new allegations consisted of generalized conclusions, not specific facts.]

CARLISLE v. T & R EXCAVATING, INC., 704 N.E.2d 39, 123 Ohio App. 3d 277 (1997). Without consideration, there can be no contract. * * * [C]onsideration consists of either a benefit to the promisor or a detriment to the promisee. To constitute consideration, the benefit or detriment must be "bargained for". Something is bargained for if it is sought by the promisor in exchange for his promise and is given by the promisee in exchange for that promise. The benefit or detriment does not need to be great. In fact, a benefit need not even be actual, as in the nature of a profit, or be as economically valuable as whatever the promisor promises in exchange for the benefit; it need only be something regarded by the promisor as beneficial enough to induce his promise. Generally, therefore, a court will not inquire into the adequacy of consideration once it is found to exist.

Whether there is consideration at all, however, is a proper question for a court. Gratuitous promises are not enforceable as contracts, because there is no consideration. A written gratuitous promise, even if it evidences an intent by the promisor to be bound, is not a contract. Likewise, conditional gratuitous promises, which require the promisee to do something before the promised act or omission will take place, are not enforceable as contracts. While it is true, therefore, that courts generally do not inquire into the adequacy of consideration once it is found to exist, it must be determined in a contract case whether any "consideration" was really bargained for. If it was not bargained for, it could not support a contract.

HAMER V. SIDWAY

Court of Appeals of New York, 1891.
124 N.Y. 538, 27 N.E. 256.

Appeal from an order of the general term of the supreme court in the fourth judicial department, reversing a judgment entered on the decision of the court at special term in the county clerk's office of Chemung county on the 1st day of October, 1889. The plaintiff presented a claim to the executor of William E. Story, Sr., for $5,000 and interest from the 6th day of February, 1875. She acquired it through several mesne assignments from William E. Story, 2d. The claim being rejected by the executor, this action was brought. It appears that William E. Story, Sr., was the uncle of William E. Story, 2d; that at the celebration of the golden wedding of Samuel Story and wife, father and mother of William E. Story, Sr., on the

20th day of March, 1869, in the presence of the family and invited guests, he promised his nephew that if he would refrain from drinking, using tobacco, swearing, and playing cards or billiards for money until he became 21 years of age, he would pay him the sum of $5,000. The nephew assented thereto, and fully performed the conditions inducing the promise. When the nephew arrived at the age of 21 years, and on the 31st day of January, 1875, he wrote to his uncle, informing him that he had performed his part of the agreement, and had thereby become entitled to the sum of $5,000. The uncle received the letter, and a few days later, and on the 6th day of February, he wrote and mailed to his nephew the following letter: "Buffalo, Feb. 6, 1875. W.E. Story, Jr.—Dear Nephew: Your letter of the 31st ult. came to hand all right, saying that you had lived up to the promise made to me several years ago. I have no doubt but you have, for which you shall have five thousand dollars, as I promised you. I had the money in the bank the day you was twenty-one years old that I intend for you, and you shall have the money certain. Now, Willie, I do not intend to interfere with this money in any way till I think you are capable of taking care of it, and the sooner that time comes the better it will please me. I would hate very much to have you start out in some adventure that you thought all right and lose this money in one year. The first five thousand dollars that I got together cost me a heap of hard work. You would hardly believe me when I tell you that to obtain this I shoved a jack-plane many a day, butchered three or four years, then came to this city, and, after three months' perseverance, I obtained a situation in a grocery store. I opened this store early, closed late, slept in the fourth story of the building in a room 30 by 40 feet, and not a human being in the building but myself. All this I done to live as cheap as I could to save something. I don't want you to take up with this kind of fare. * * * Willie, you are twenty-one, and you have many a thing to learn yet. This money you have earned much easier than I did, besides acquiring good habits at the same time, and you are quite welcome to the money. Hope you will make good use of it. I was ten long years getting this together after I was your age. * * * Truly yours, W.E. STORY. P.S. You can consider this money on interest." The nephew received the letter, and thereafter consented that the money should remain with his uncle in accordance with the terms and conditions of the letter. The uncle died on the 29th day of January, 1887, without having paid over to his nephew any portion of the said $5,000 and interest. * * *

PARKER, J. * * * The defendant contends that the contract was without consideration to support it, and therefore invalid. He asserts that the promisee, by refraining from the use of liquor and tobacco, was not harmed, but benefited; that that which he did was best for him to do, independently of his uncle's promise,—and insists that it follows that, unless the promisor was benefited, the contract was without consideration,—a contention which, if well founded, would seem to leave open for controversy in many cases whether that which the promisee did or omitted to do was in fact of such benefit to him as to leave no consideration to support the enforcement of the promisor's agreement. Such a rule could not be tolerated, and is without foundation in the law. The exchequer chamber in 1875 defined "consideration" as follows: "A valuable consideration, in the sense of the law, may consist either in some right, interest, profit, or benefit accruing to the one party, or some forbearance, detriment, loss, or responsibility given, suffered, or undertaken by the other." Courts "will not ask whether the thing which forms the consideration does in fact benefit the promisee or a third party, or is of any substantial value to any one. It is enough that something is promised, done, forborne, or suffered by the party to whom the promise is made as consideration for the promise made to him." Anson, Cont. 63. "In general a waiver of any legal right at the request of another party is a sufficient consideration for a promise." Pars.Cont. *444. "Any damage, or suspension, or forbearance of a right will be sufficient to sustain a promise." 2 Kent, Comm. (12th Ed.) *465. Pollock in his work on Contracts, (page 166,) after citing the definition given by the exchequer chamber, already quoted, says: "The second branch of this judicial description is really the most important one. 'Consideration' means not so much that one party is profiting as that the other abandons some legal right in the present, or limits his legal freedom of action in the future, as an inducement for the promise of the first." Now, applying this rule to the facts before us, the promisee used tobacco, occasionally drank liquor, and he had a legal right to do so. That right he abandoned for a period of years upon the strength of the promise of the testator that for such forbearance he would give him $5,000. We need not speculate on the effort which may have been required to give up the use of those stimulants. It is sufficient that he restricted his lawful freedom of action within certain prescribed limits upon the faith of his uncle's agreement, and now, having fully performed the conditions imposed, it is of no moment whether such performance actually proved a benefit to the promisor, and the court will not inquire into it; but, were it a proper subject of inquiry, we see nothing in this record that would permit a determination that the uncle was not benefited in a legal sense. Few cases have been found which may be said to be precisely in point, but such as have been, support the position we have taken. * * *

The order appealed from should be reversed, and the judgment of the special term affirmed, with costs payable out of the estate. All concur.

RESTATEMENT (SECOND) OF CONTRACTS § 71.

Requirement of Exchange: Types of Exchange

(1) To constitute consideration, a performance or a return promise must be bargained for.

(2) A performance or return promise is bargained for if it is sought by the promisor in exchange for his promise and is given by the promisee in exchange for that promise.

(3) The performance may consist of

(a) an act other than a promise, or

(b) a forbearance, or

(c) the creation, modification, or destruction of a legal relation.

(4) The performance or return promise may be given to the promisor or to some other person. It may be given by the promisee or by some other person.

RESTATEMENT (SECOND) OF CONTRACTS § 81.

Consideration as Motive or Inducing Cause

(1) The fact that what is bargained for does not of itself induce the making of a promise does not prevent it from being consideration for the promise.

(2) The fact that a promise does not of itself induce a performance or return promise does not prevent the performance or return promise from being consideration for the promise.[h]

Comment:

a. *"Bargained for."* Consideration requires that a performance or return promise be "bargained for" in exchange for a promise; this means that the promisor must manifest an intention to induce the performance or return promise and to be induced by it, and that the promisee must manifest an intention to induce the making of the promise and to be induced by it. * * * In most commercial bargains the consideration is the object of the promisor's desire and that desire is a material motive or cause inducing the making of the promise, and the reciprocal desire of the promisee for the making of the promise similarly induces the furnishing of the consideration.

b. *Immateriality of motive or cause.* This Section makes explicit a limitation on the requirement that consideration be bargained for. Even in the typical commercial bargain, the promisor may have more than one motive, and the person furnishing the consideration need not inquire into the promisor's motives. Unless both parties know that the purported consideration is mere pretense, it is immaterial that the promisor's desire for the consideration is incidental to other objectives and even that the

[h] Does this section of the second Restatement also consist solely of bare bones in need of Fullerian flesh? Do Comments a and b provide some flesh?

other party knows this to be so. * * * Subsection (2) states a similar rule with respect to the motives of the promisee.

ALLEGHENY COLLEGE v. NATIONAL CHAUTAUQUA COUNTY BANK OF JAMESTOWN, 246 N.Y. 369, 373, 159 N.E. 173, 174 (1927).

CARDOZO, C.J.

A classic form of statement identifies consideration with detriment to the promisee sustained by virtue of the promise. (Hamer v. Sidway * * *.) So compendious a formula is little more than a half truth. There is need of many a supplementary gloss before the outline can be so filled in as to depict the classic doctrine. 'The promise and the consideration must purport to be the motive each for the other, in whole or at least in part. It is not enough that the promise induces the detriment or that the detriment induces the promise if the other half is wanting.' * * * If A promises B to make him a gift, consideration may be lacking, though B has renounced other opportunities for betterment in the faith that the promise will be kept.

G. GILMORE, THE DEATH OF CONTRACT

111 n. 34 (1974).

Hamer v. Sidway * * * illustrates * * * that the New York Court of Appeals (unlike most American courts) * * * rejected the so-called bargain theory of consideration.

PROBLEM 2-3

According to the Website the Grio, the following transpired between Rapper Lil Uzi Vert and a student at Temple University, Raheel Ahmad:

> "Yo Uzi, can you pay for my college tuition?" Ahmad asked politely as the group walked by. "Ninety grand—I go to Temple, bro," Ahmad continued, causing [Uzi] to suddenly stop and turn around. "Ninety grand? I could pay for that," [Uzi] replied, before quickly running off what he would require in exchange for the gift. * * * "Make sure you show me all of your transcripts, everything," he explained. "Show me all your papers and everything, and you can get $90,000 from me." Ahmad later admitted to local station WPVI that he actually "wasn't expecting anything" but thought "why not" ask for the favor. The 20-year-old political science student also confirmed that he kept up his part of the deal and sent all of the documents requested. "I'll just say shout-out to Uzi, and thank you if you actually do come through with this, greatly appreciate it, and one love," he said.

Suppose Ahmad comes to your law office and asks whether he has any legal rights against Lil Uzi Vert if he doesn't pay. Please respond.

BAEHR V. PENN-O-TEX OIL CORP.

Supreme Court of Minnesota, 1960.
258 Minn. 533, 104 N.W.2d 661.

LOEVINGER, JUSTICE.

This is an action for rents which defendant is claimed to owe plaintiff because of possession and contract.

Plaintiff leased certain gasoline filling stations to one Kemp, doing business as Webb Oil Company, under written leases. Kemp was purchasing the business known as Webb Oil Company and certain related property from defendant. On account of these transactions and purchases of petroleum products, Kemp was heavily indebted to defendant. Kemp became unable to meet payments due to defendant and on December 10, 1955, gave defendant an assignment of accounts receivable and to become receivable, including those involving the plaintiff's filling stations. Thereafter, during the period involved here, defendant collected rents paid by the operators of the filling stations, received other payments made to Webb Oil Company, paid some of its debts at Kemp's direction out of these sums, and installed its agent in the office to run the business.

Plaintiff was in Florida when he received a letter dated December 28, 1955, from Kemp, stating that defendant had all of Kemp's assets tied up. A short time after this, plaintiff called defendant's agent to ask about payment of the filling station rents. Plaintiff was told "that Mr. Kemp's affairs were in a very mixed up form but that he would get them straightened out and mail me [plaintiff] my checks for the rent." Hearing nothing further, plaintiff wrote a letter to defendant asking what he had to do to get his rent checks and adding: "Or will I have to give it to an attorney to sue."

Defendant replied by letter stating it was attempting to assist Kemp in keeping the business going, "but in no way are operating or taken possession." The letter denied knowledge of or responsibility for any rent due plaintiff. A week or 10 days after receiving this letter, plaintiff again called defendant and asked for his rent. Defendant's agent then said to plaintiff, "they [the company] were interested and that they would see that I [plaintiff] got my rent, and would take care of it, and they would work it out with the head office. * * * He said he would take it up with them and they would assure me my rent."

The rent was not paid, and in April or May 1956 plaintiff returned to Minneapolis from Florida. Soon after this plaintiff consulted a lawyer, and "shortly thereafter, as rapidly as the lawyer could get moving, a suit was started." On June 2, 1956, plaintiff sent defendant a letter advising that he was reentering and taking possession under the leases of the filling stations and because of failure to receive rent. On July 10, 1956, this suit was started for rents due on the filling stations for the period December 1, 1955, through June 2, 1956, upon the grounds that defendant was in possession of the stations and had contracted to pay the rent during this period.

The case was fully tried on all issues in the district court. At the conclusion of plaintiff's evidence, the court ruled that the evidence was conclusive that defendant neither took possession of the filling stations nor an assignment of Kemp's leases. Defendant then presented evidence on the issue of a contract to pay the rents, and this issue was submitted to the jury under proper instructions. The amount that would be due under such a contract was agreed upon; and the jury returned a verdict for plaintiff in that amount. Thereafter, the district court granted defendant's motion for judgment notwithstanding the verdict; and ordered a new trial in the event of reversal. Plaintiff appealed.

[The court first affirmed the trial court's ruling that defendant did not take possession of the stations or an assignment of the leases.]

The issue whether there was a contract by defendant to pay plaintiff is more doubtful. Unfortunately, contract, like most of the basic terms constituting the intellectual tools of law, is conventionally defined in a circular fashion. By the most common definition, a contract is a promise or set of promises for the breach of which the law gives a remedy or the performance of which the law recognizes as a duty. This amounts to saying that a contract is a legally enforceable promise. But a promise is legally enforceable only if it is a contract. Thus nothing less than the whole body of applicable precedents suffices to define the term "contract."

Although the definition of contract does not help much in determining what expressions shall be held to impose legal obligations, it does direct attention to a promise as the starting point of inquiry. Both in popular and legal usage, a promise is an assurance, in whatever form of expression given, that a thing will or will not be done. While we must take care to distinguish between statements meant to express merely present intention and those meant to give an assurance as to a future event, this involves no more than the common difficulty of seeking precise meaning in the usually imprecise, and often careless, expressions of ordinary colloquy.

If we accept plaintiff's version of the statements made by defendant's agent, as we are required to do by the verdict, there was an unequivocal assurance given that the rents would be paid. This cannot be anything but a promise.

However, the fact that a promise was given does not necessarily mean that a contract was made. It is clear that not every promise is legally enforceable. Much of the vast body of law in the field of contracts is concerned with determining which promises should be legally enforced. On the one hand, in a civilized community men must be able to assume that those with whom they deal will carry out their undertakings according to reasonable expectations. On the other hand, it is neither practical nor reasonable to expect full performance of every assurance given, whether it be thoughtless, casual and gratuitous, or deliberately and seriously made.

The test that has been developed by the common law for determining the enforceability of promises is the doctrine of consideration. This is a crude and not altogether successful attempt to generalize the conditions under which promises will be legally enforced. Consideration requires that a contractual promise be the product of a bargain. However, in this usage, "bargain" does not mean an exchange of things of equivalent, or any, value. It means a negotiation resulting in the voluntary assumption of an obligation by one party upon condition of an act or forbearance by the other. Consideration thus insures that the promise enforced as a contract is not accidental, casual, or gratuitous, but has been uttered intentionally as the result of some deliberation, manifested by reciprocal bargaining or negotiation. In this view, the requirement of consideration is no mere technicality, historical anachronism, or arbitrary formality. It is an attempt to be as reasonable as we can in deciding which promises constitute contracts. Although the doctrine has been criticized, no satisfactory substitute has been suggested. It is noteworthy that the civil law has a corresponding doctrine of "causa" which, to the eye of a common-law lawyer, is not much different than consideration.

Consideration, as essential evidence of the parties' intent to create a legal obligation, must be something adopted and regarded by the parties as such. Thus, the same thing may be consideration or not, as it is dealt with by the parties. In substance, a contractual promise must be of the logical form: "If * * * (consideration is given) * * * then I promise that * * *." Of course, the substance may be expressed in any form of words, but essentially this is the logical structure of those promises enforced by the law as contracts.

Applying these principles to the present case, it appears that although defendant's agent made a promise to plaintiff, it was not in such circumstances that a contract was created. Plaintiff correctly states that an agreement of forbearance to sue may be sufficient consideration for a contract. Plaintiff further contends that his failure to institute suit immediately upon learning of Kemp's assignment to defendant permits an inference of an agreement to forbear from suit in consideration for defendant's assurance of payment of rents to plaintiff. This court has held that circumstantial evidence may support the inference of such an agreement to forbear. However, such an inference must rest upon something more than the mere failure to institute immediate suit. The difficulty with plaintiff's case is that there is no more than this.

Plaintiff's conversation with defendant's agent was about the middle of February 1956 while plaintiff was in Florida. Plaintiff returned to Minneapolis, which was his residence as well as the jurisdiction where defendant was found, about the latter part of April or the first of May 1956. Soon after this he consulted a lawyer, and suit was started "as rapidly as the lawyer could get moving." There is nothing in the evidence to suggest that plaintiff deferred initiating legal action any longer than suited his own personal convenience. There is nothing in the evidence to suggest that defendant sought any forbearance by plaintiff or thought that it was securing such action; nor is there any evidence that plaintiff's delay from the middle of February until April or May in undertaking legal action was related to defendant's promises. There is no evidence that either of the parties took defendant's assurances seriously or acted upon them in any way. There was, therefore, no consideration, and the promises did not amount to a contract. Since the district court was correct in ordering judgment entered for the defendant, notwithstanding the verdict, on this ground, it is unnecessary to consider other points relating to enforceability of the alleged contract.

Affirmed.

NEUHOFF V. MARVIN LUMBER AND CEDAR CO.

United States Court of Appeals, First Circuit, 2004.
370 F.3d 197.

TORRUELLA, CIRCUIT JUDGE.

The Neuhoffs allege that Marvin breached an oral contract to provide replacement windows for free. The oral contract was allegedly made in March 1998 when [Marvin's agent] informed the Neuhoffs that their decaying [Marvin] windows would be replaced once Marvin's production problems were fixed and the windows reached a more advanced stage of decay. * * *

[T]he Neuhoffs' breach of contract claim fails because Marvin's alleged promise to repair lacked consideration. * * *

The Neuhoffs allege three types of consideration: (1) forbearance of their legal claims, (2) the time and labor expended assisting Marvin in connection with Marvin's promise to replace the defective windows, and (3) the benefit Marvin received to their reputation by agreeing to replace the windows.

It is well-settled that "abandonment of a claim believed to be well founded * * * is the surrender of a thing of value and is a sufficient consideration for a contract." * * * The claim need not be "of such character in law or fact or both as finally to commend itself to the judgment of the tribunal of last resort," rather it need only be "well founded and made in good faith and not frivolous, vexatious or unlawful." *Id.* (internal quotations and citations omitted). But, "[m]ere forbearance to sue [on] a claim, without any promise either in express terms or by fair implication from all of the circumstances, does not form sufficient consideration. * * * " *Merrimac Chem. Co. v. Moore,* 279 Mass. 147, 181 N.E. 219, 222 (1932). It is undisputed that the Neuhoffs never expressed their willingness to forbear suit before or after the promise to replace the defective windows was made. Nonetheless, the Neuhoffs argue that their willingness to forbear suit could be implied. An "agreement to forbear to sue may be implied when the circumstances are such as to lead to the reasonable conclusion that the * * * thing of value was given to induce the [other party] to forbear." *Id.* The record shows that the alleged promise to replace all of the windows was not given to induce the Neuhoffs to relinquish a claim against Marvin. Thus, the Neuhoffs' claims of forbearance is not sufficient for consideration since such forbearance was neither express nor could be found by fair implication from all the circumstances.

[The court went on to hold that the record did not support Neuhoffs' claims that they assisted Marvin or that Marvin wanted to improve its reputation. Further, as to the latter, the court held that "not every benefit is consideration. * * * We cannot conclude, based on the record, that a hypothetical and tangential benefit to Marvin's reputation is sufficient consideration to make Marvin's statement a binding contract."]

SPRINGSTEAD V. NEES

Supreme Court of New York, Appellate Division, 1908.
125 App. Div. 230, 109 N.Y.S. 148.

Action by Anna Springstead and others against George Nees and another. Judgment for defendants, and plaintiffs appeal. Affirmed.

JENKS, J. This action was tried by stipulation as a common-law action before the court without a jury. The parties are all of the surviving children of Nees, deceased, who died intestate, leaving them his sole heirs at law. Nees died, the owner and seised of realty called the "Sackett Street Property" and the owner of realty, called the "Atlantic Avenue Property," which he held by deed to him as trustee for his children, Sophia and George. Shortly after Nees' death all of the parties, an attorney at law, and friends met in Nees' house. Nees' strong box was opened, and when the deed to the Atlantic avenue property was found therein the attorney handed it to Sophia, saying: "This is yours." The evidence for the plaintiffs is that they, or some of them, were surprised to learn that this deed was to their father in trust for two of the children; for theretofore they had believed that he was the owner and seised in fee. They expressed their surprise, and there were murmurings. Thereupon Sophia spoke up, saying, "We will give you our share in the Sackett street property if you don't bother us about the Atlantic avenue property," and George assented. The Sackett street property was sold thereafter. This action is brought by the other three children against Sophia and George, upon that alleged promise of Sophia and George, to recover their proportionate share of the proceeds of that sale. Sophia and George testified that no such promise ever was made. The learned court gave judgment for the defendants, dismissing the complaint, with costs.

After finding the preliminary facts, which were not disputed, the court found that the defendants, after the death of their father, were seised in fee simple of the Atlantic avenue property and held indefeasible title thereto; that the plaintiffs had no color of right in the Atlantic avenue property, and did not at any time threaten or attempt to assert any claim of right hostile to the defendants in that property; that there was no compromise, either wholly or partly executed, between the parties, affecting rights which the plaintiffs might have in that property; that the plaintiffs had given up no rights in that property, nor had they changed their position therein; and that a promise (referring to which I have heretofore described as shown by the testimony for the plaintiffs) made by the defendants to the plaintiffs that, if the plaintiffs "would not 'molest,' or 'bother,' or 'make a fuss' about, the defendants' rights on the Atlantic avenue property, the defendants would give the plaintiffs their share in the Sackett street property, if made, would have been without consideration." The plaintiffs appeal.

The record sustains the facts found. Assuming that such promise was made, I am of opinion that there was no consideration shown. * * *

The consideration for the promise cannot be found in the fact that there was a compromise of a disputed claim, for there is no evidence thereof. It must rest, then, upon the forbearance to exercise a legal right. Forbearance to assert either a legal or an equitable claim is sufficient consideration, as we have seen. * * * It seems unnecessary to consider the conflict over the question whether forbearance as to a claim without foundation can constitute good consideration. See 1 Parsons on Contracts (8th Ed.) p. 441, note, discussing the various authorities. It seems to be the rule with us that it is not essential that the claim should be valid; but it is enough if it could be regarded as doubtful or colorable. But if the claim be not even doubtful, or colorable, or plausible, in that there is no reason for an honest belief that it has some foundation in law or in equity, then forbearance applied to it is not good consideration. * * *

* * *

In the case at bar the court, as I have said, found properly that the plaintiffs had no color of right in the Atlantic avenue property; nor did they at any time threaten or attempt to assert any claim. The evidence of the plaintiffs is that, when they were surprised to find that the deed to the Atlantic avenue property was in trust for but two of their number, thereupon and without any further reason, save that they expressed surprise and were dissatisfied, the defendants made the promise in question. The promise was not even in response to any suggestion of any possible claim then or thereafter against the deed, or despite it, or of any action adverse to it. There was no suggestion, then or at any time thereafter, made that the deed was invalid for any reason, or of any ground upon which it was open to attack. Indeed, I can discover no reason upon the evidence how any of the parties could seriously suppose that even a doubtful or a colorable claim could be asserted then or thereafter. It does not appear that anything was ever done, then or thereafter, in consequence of the alleged promise, or that the rights of the parties were in any way thereby changed or affected.

I think that the judgment must be affirmed, with costs. All concur, except HOOKER, J., who dissents.

HOOKER, J. (dissenting). The circumstances surrounding the opening of the strong box after decedent's death and the finding there of a deed running to the defendants, and the conversation then between the children, seem to me such as to present a situation where there was at least color of a valid claim by the plaintiffs, by reason of their heirship, to the Atlantic avenue property. One of these circumstances is that the strong box where the deed was found belonged to the decedent, and it might well be doubted whether there had ever been a delivery of the deed before the grantor's death, which was necessary to pass title. If such claim was open to be urged, there was consideration for the promise.

The judgment should be reversed.

2 CORBIN ON CONTRACTS

§ 7.17 (2019).

Forbearance to bring a suit, or to proceed with one already brought, or to press a claim in any other way, is not consideration if the forbearance is made with knowledge that the claim is invalid. This is on grounds of public policy, not because the forbearance is not beneficial to the promisor or detrimental to the promisee. * * * [The reason for this is that, if such forbearance] * * * were recognized as consideration, invalid claims would be infinitely increased in number and blackmail would become a profitable racket.

* * *

In a good many court opinions, it is stated that forbearance to press a claim (or a promise to forbear) is not consideration unless the claim is doubtful, that is, unless the claimant had some reasonable ground for belief in the justice of the claim. * * * Many courts are satisfied if the claimant had an honest belief in the claim, without regard for whether the claimant had a reasonable basis for it. * * * As a practical matter, the difference between the last two stated doctrines may not be great. * * * The claimant must be asserting the claim "in good faith." This does not mean that the claimant must believe that the suit can be won. It means that the claimant must not be threatening suit for purposes of vexation, or in order to realize on its "nuisance value." It should be emphasized that under the good faith standard, the reasonableness of the asserted claim is not irrelevant. The absence of any reasonable ground for belief in its validity is strong evidence, though not conclusive evidence, that the claim was not asserted in good faith.

NOTE:
PROMISE FOR PROMISE AS CONSIDERATION

In Baehr v. Penn-O-Tex Oil Corp., Justice Loevinger points out that a bargained-for *promise* is a sufficient consideration for a promise. See also Restatement (Second) of Contracts § 71(1); Restatement (First) of Contracts § 75(1)(d). Thus, one of Baehr's approaches to recovery was based on his alleged promise to forbear from suing in exchange for defendant's promise to pay the rents. See also Neuhoff v. Marvin Lumber and Cedar Co. Similarly, in Springstead v. Nees, a bargained for *promise* by the other children not to "bother" George and Sophie about the Atlantic Avenue property would have been sufficient consideration for the promise of George and Sophie to give up their share of the Sackett Street property (assuming the other children had a colorable claim in the Atlantic Avenue property).

Because a bargained-for promise may constitute consideration, a party may become obligated to perform even though the other has not relied on the agreement. Thus, if Arnold promises to sell his car to Kate for $400, delivery next Saturday, and Kate promises to pay the $400, Arnold is legally bound to perform even if he attempts to recant five minutes after the deal is made and before any change of position by Kate. The same applies, of course, to a promissory exchange involving millions of dollars between corporate titans. Why such a rule? Would the following rule be superior? A party is always free, upon giving appropriate advanced notice, to back out of a wholly executory exchange except when the other party has reasonably relied in some way. Consider the material below.

FULLER, CONSIDERATION AND FORM

41 Colum. L. Rev. 799, 816–17 (1941).

The Wholly Executory Exchange.—B promises to build a house for A, and A, in return, promises to pay B $5,000 on the completion of the house. B defaults on his promise, and A, without having had occasion to pay anything on the contract, sues B for damages. Judicial intervention in this kind of case apparently began in England toward the end of the sixteenth century . . .

Where a bilateral contract remains wholly executory the arguments for judicial intervention have been considerably diminished in comparison with the situation of the half-completed exchange. There is here no unjust enrichment. Reliance may or may not exist, but in any event will not be so tangible and direct as where it consists in the rendition of the price of the defendant's performance. On the side of form, we have lost the natural formality involved in the turning over of property or the rendition and acceptance of services. There remains simply the fact that the transaction is an exchange and not a gift. This fact alone does offer some guaranty so far as the cautionary and channeling functions of form are concerned, though, except as the Statute of Frauds interposes to supply the deficiency, evidentiary safeguards are largely lacking. This lessening of the factors arguing for enforcement not only helps to explain why liability in this situation was late in developing, but also explains why even today the executory bilateral contract cannot be put on complete parity with the situation of the half-completed exchange.

In the situation of the half-completed exchange, the element of exchange is only one factor tending toward enforcement. Since that element is there reinforced by reliance, unjust enrichment, and the natural formality involved in the surrender and acceptance of a tangible benefit, it is unnecessary to analyze the concept of exchange closely, and it may properly be left vague. In the executory bilateral contract, on the other hand, the element of exchange stands largely alone as a basis of liability and its definition becomes crucial. Various definitions are possible. We may define exchange vaguely as a transaction from which each participant derives a benefit, or, more restrictively, as a transaction in which the motives of the parties are primarily economic rather than sentimental. Following Adam Smith, we may say that it is a transaction which, directly or indirectly, conduces to the division of labor. Or we may take Demogue's notion that the most important characteristic of exchange is that it is a situation in which the interests of the transacting parties are opposed, so that the social utility of the contract is guaranteed in some degree by the fact that it emerges as a compromise of those conflicting interests. The problem of choosing among these varying conceptions may seem remote and unimportant, yet it underlies some of the most familiar problems of contract law. For example, suppose a nephew promises his uncle that he will not smoke until he is twenty-one, and the uncle promises him $5,000 as a reward if he will keep his promise. Where the nephew sues after having earned the reward by following the prescribed line of conduct recovery has been permitted. But would such an agreement be enforced as an executory bilateral contract? Could the uncle, for example, sue the nephew for smoking a cigarette? In answering this question it is at once apparent that we are faced with the necessity of defining the particular kind of exchange which is essential to the enforcement of a bilateral contract.

VON MEHREN, CONTRACTS IN GENERAL

7 Int'l Ency. of Comp. L. 20 (ch. 1) (1982).

But if contracts are not enforceable, in nonsimultaneous exchanges one party runs the risk that the other will not render his performance in due course. Hence, the enforceability of contract can also be viewed as a response to the sequential character of much economic activity. Indeed,

> "the absence of legally enforceable rights would, among other consequences, bias investment toward economic activities where the interval in which the contemplated economic activity could be completed was short, and this would reduce the efficiency of resource use."[i]

In the absence of enforceable contract rights, many sequential transactions would presumably still be carried on. But the party who performed first would seek to protect himself against the possibility of nonperformance by the other party; the resulting

> "system would not be very efficient. Apart from the costs involved in maintaining credit bureaus and administering security deposits (especially in a world where the return of the deposit could not be legally compelled), self-protection would not always work."[j]

There are thus strong economic arguments to support the enforceability of contracts.

FULLER & PERDUE, THE RELIANCE INTEREST IN CONTRACT DAMAGES

46 Yale L.J. 52, 61–62 (1936).

It may be said that there is not only a policy in favor of preventing and undoing the harms resulting from reliance, but also a policy in favor of promoting and facilitating reliance on business agreements. * * * Agreements can accomplish little, either for their makers or for society, unless they are made the basis for action. When business agreements are not only made but are also acted on, the division of labor is facilitated, goods find their way to the places where they are most needed, and economic activity is generally stimulated. These advantages would be threatened by any rule which limited legal protection to the reliance

---

[i] R. Posner, *Economic Analysis of Law* § 4.1 at 66 (1977).

[j] *Id.* at 67.

interest. Such a rule would in practice tend to discourage reliance. The difficulties in proving reliance and subjecting it to pecuniary measurement are such that the business man knowing, or sensing, that these obstacles stood in the way of judicial relief would hesitate to rely on a promise in any case where the legal sanction was of significance to him. To encourage reliance we must therefore dispense with its proof. For this reason it has been found wise to make recovery on a promise independent of reliance, both in the sense that in some cases the promise is enforced though not relied on (as in the bilateral business agreement) and in the sense that recovery is not limited to the detriment incurred in reliance.

DE LOS SANTOS V. GREAT WESTERN SUGAR COMPANY

Supreme Court of Nebraska, 1984.
217 Neb. 282, 348 N.W.2d 842.

CAMBRIDGE, DISTRICT JUDGE.

This is an appeal by the plaintiff of a summary judgment entered by the trial court in favor of the defendant in an action for breach of contract.

* * *

This appeal centers around the following provision contained in the "Hauling Contract" executed by the plaintiff and the defendant in October 1980:

> The Contractor [i.e., plaintiff] shall transport in the Contractor's trucks *such tonnage of beets as may be loaded by the Company* [i.e., defendant] from piles at the beet receiving stations of the Company, and unload said beets at such factory or factories as may be designated by the Company. The term of this contract shall be from October 1, 1980, until February 15, 1981.

(Emphasis supplied.) The plaintiff, as an independent contractor, was obligated under the "Hauling Contract" to furnish certain insurance, suitable trucks and equipment, and all necessary labor, maintenance, fuel, and licenses required for his operations thereunder, and the compensation which he was to receive for his services was based solely upon the amount of beets which he transported, the rate per ton varying with the length of the haul.

It is undisputed that upon executing the hauling contract the plaintiff knew that the defendant had executed identical such contracts with other independent truckers who would also be hauling the defendant's beets and that the plaintiff would therefore transport on his trucks only "such tonnage of beets as may be loaded by" the defendant upon the plaintiff's trucks, not all of the beets "as may be loaded by" the defendant from piles at the defendant's beet receiving stations. The plaintiff had been transporting beets under the contract for approximately 2 months when, in early December 1980, the defendant informed the plaintiff that his services would no longer be needed. The plaintiff does not claim that he was entitled to transport all of the beets, but he does contend that he was entitled to continue to haul until all of the beets had been transported to the factory, that the defendant did not allow him to do so, and that the defendant thereby wrongfully terminated the hauling contract, causing the plaintiff loss of profits, forced sale of his trucks at a loss, and other damages to be proved on trial. In his petition the plaintiff predicated his action against the defendant upon the hauling contract. The defendant in its amended answer thereto alleged, among other defenses not relevant to the disposition of this appeal, that the defendant was not obligated under the contract to allow the plaintiff to haul any particular amount of tonnage and that its determination that it would no longer require the plaintiff's services was a determination which was within the defendant's discretion under the terms of the contract. * * * The plaintiff was paid in full for all beets which were in fact hauled by him, and there is no issue in this case in that regard.

Considering the words contained therein together with the aforesaid undisputed facts known to both the plaintiff and the defendant when they executed the hauling contract, it is clear that neither the plaintiff nor the defendant intended to or did, either in fact or law, promise to transport a specific quantity of beets or promise to transport beets during a specific period of time. The term of the contract set forth therein, i.e., October 1, 1980, until February 15, 1981, did not constitute a promise, but merely established the period of time during which the promises which were contained in the contract would be in effect. Although the plaintiff made a number of promises in the hauling contract, all centered around the plaintiff's promise to transport beets as loaded by the defendant on the plaintiff's trucks during the period of October 1, 1980, through February 15, 1981, the defendant made no promises at all other than the promise to pay for the transportation of those beets which were in fact loaded by the defendant onto the trucks of the plaintiff during that period. An agreement which depends upon the wish, will, or pleasure of one of the parties is unenforceable. See 56 C.J.S. *Master and Servant* § 6 (1948). In *Garsick v. Dehner,* 145 Neb. 73, 79, 15 N.W.2d 235, 238 (1944), this court stated:

> Speaking generally, mutuality of obligation is an essential element of every enforceable agreement. However, "Mutuality of contract consists in the obligation on each party to do, or to permit something to be done, in consideration of the act or promise of the other. * * * Mutuality is absent when one only of the contracting parties is bound to perform, and the rights of the parties exist at the option of one only."

Where a promisor agrees to purchase services from the promisee on a per unit basis, but the agreement specifies no quantity and the parties did not intend that the promisor should take all of his needs from the promisee, there is no enforceable agreement, and the promisor is not obligated to accept any services from the promisee and may terminate the relationship at any time without liability other than to pay for the services accepted. The fact that the promisor has accepted services from the promisee in the past under such an agreement does not furnish the consideration necessary to require the promisor to accept such services in the future under the agreement. Nor does the specification in such an agreement of the period of time during which it will be operative impose an obligation that is not already present under the agreement. *Waco Fire & C. Ins. Co. v. Plant,* 150 Ga.App. 888, 259 S.E.2d 95 (1979). * * * Applying the foregoing to this case, it is apparent that the right of the defendant to control the amount of beets loaded onto the plaintiff's trucks was in effect a right to terminate the contract at any time, and this rendered the contract as to its unexecuted portions void for want of mutuality. In the absence of a specification of quantity, the defendant had no obligation to use any of the plaintiff's services, and the defendant's decision to cease using those services after a certain point is not actionable.

* * *

AFFIRMED.

WOOD V. LUCY, LADY DUFF-GORDON

Court of Appeals of New York, 1917.
222 N.Y. 88, 118 N.E. 214.

CARDOZO, J. The defendant styles herself "a creator of fashions." Her favor helps a sale. Manufacturers of dresses, millinery, and like articles are glad to pay for a certificate of her approval. The things which she designs, fabrics, parasols, and what not, have a new value in the public mind when issued in her name. She employed the plaintiff to help her to turn this vogue into money. He was to have the exclusive right, subject always to her approval, to place her indorsements on the designs of others. He was also to have the exclusive right to place her own designs on sale, or to license others to market them. In return she was to have one-half of "all profits and revenues" derived from any contracts he might make. The exclusive right was to last at least one year from April 1, 1915, and thereafter from year to year unless terminated by notice of 90 days. The plaintiff says that he kept the contract on his part, and that the defendant broke it. She placed her indorsement on fabrics, dresses, and millinery without his knowledge, and withheld the profits. He sues her for the damages, and the case comes here on demurrer.

The agreement of employment is signed by both parties. It has a wealth of recitals. The defendant insists, however, that it lacks the elements of a contract. She says that the plaintiff does not bind himself to anything. It is true that he does not promise in so many words that he will use reasonable efforts to place the defendant's indorsements and market her designs. We think, however, that such a promise is fairly to be implied. The law has outgrown its primitive stage of formalism when the precise word was the sovereign talisman, and every slip was fatal. It takes a broader view today. A promise may be lacking, and yet the whole writing may be "instinct with an obligation," imperfectly expressed (Scott, J., in McCall Co. v. Wright, 133 App.Div. 62, 117 N.Y.Supp. 775; Moran v. Standard Oil Co., 211 N.Y. 187, 198, 105 N.E. 217). If that is so, there is a contract.

The implication of a promise here finds support in many circumstances. The defendant gave an exclusive privilege. She was to have no right for at least a year to place her own indorsements or market her own designs except through the agency of the plaintiff. The acceptance of the exclusive agency was an assumption of its duties. * * * We are not to suppose that one party was to be placed at the mercy of the other. * * *

Many other terms of the agreement point the same way. We are told at the outset by way of recital that:

> "The said Otis F. Wood possesses a business organization adapted to the placing of such indorsements as the said Lucy, Lady Duff-Gordon, has approved."

The implication is that the plaintiff's business organization will be used for the purpose for which it is adapted. But the terms of the defendant's compensation are even more significant. Her sole compensation for the grant of an exclusive agency is to be one-half of all the profits resulting from the plaintiff's efforts. Unless he gave his efforts, she could never get anything. Without an implied promise, the transaction cannot have such business "efficacy, as both parties must have intended that at all events it should have." Bowen, L.J., in the Moorcock, 14 P.D. 64, 68. But the contract does not stop there. The plaintiff goes on to promise that he will account monthly for all moneys received by him, and that he will take out all such patents and copyrights and trade-marks as may in his judgment be necessary to protect the rights and articles affected by the agreement. It is true, of course, as the Appellate Division has said, that if he was under no duty to try to market designs or to place certificates of indorsement, his promise to account for profits or take out copyrights would be valueless. But in determining the intention of the parties the promise has a value. It helps to enforce the conclusion that the plaintiff had some duties. His promise to pay the defendant one-half of the profits and revenues resulting from the exclusive agency and to render accounts monthly was a promise to use reasonable efforts to bring profits and revenues into existence. For this conclusion the authorities are ample. * * *

The judgment of the Appellate Division should be reversed, and the order of the Special Term affirmed, with costs in the Appellate Division and in this court.

CUDDEBACK, MCLAUGHLIN, and ANDREWS, JJ., concur. HISCOCK, C.J., and CHASE and CRANE, JJ., dissent.

UNIFORM COMMERCIAL CODE § 1–304.

Obligation of Good Faith

Every contract or duty within [the Uniform Commercial Code] imposes an obligation of good faith in its performance and enforcement.

UNIFORM COMMERCIAL CODE § 2–306(2).

A lawful agreement by either the seller or the buyer for exclusive dealing in the kind of goods concerned imposes unless otherwise agreed an obligation by the seller to use best efforts to supply the goods and by the buyer to use best efforts to promote their sale.

PROBLEM 2-4

1. Assume that U.C.C. § 1–304 and § 2–306(2) applied to the Wood and De Los Santos cases. Would they change the results? On the meaning of good faith, see Chapter Six.

2. Assume you were counsel for Wood in Wood v. Lucy, Lady Duff-Gordon, and he had asked you at the outset to set up the arrangement so it would "without doubt be legal without having to go to court." What wording would you have included? What approach in De Los Santos to ensure the enforceability of the "hauling contract"?

H.G. WOOD, A TREATISE ON THE LAW OF MASTER AND SERVANT

§ 134 (1877).

With us the rule is inflexible that a general or indefinite hiring is *prima facie* a hiring at will, and if the servant seeks to make it out a yearly hiring, the burden is upon him to establish it by proof. A hiring at so much a day, week, month, or year, or no time being specified, is an indefinite hiring, and no presumption attaches that it was for a day even, but only at the rate fixed for whatever time the party may serve.

WEINER v. MCGRAW-HILL, INC.

Court of Appeals of New York, 1982.
57 N.Y.2d 458, 443 N.E.2d 441.

FUCHSBERG, JUDGE.

In a matter raising an issue of wide concern to employers and employees, we must decide whether, in the circumstances of this case, the plaintiff, though not engaged for a fixed term of employment, pleaded a good cause of action for breach of contract against his employer * * *.

The operative facts deserve emphasis. Taken most favorably to the plaintiff, as they must in the context of an appeal [from an order dismissing the complaint] they show that, in 1969, the plaintiff, Walton Lewis Weiner, a young man who four years earlier had entered upon a career in book publishing with another employer, Prentice-Hall, was invited to engage in discussions looking towards his joining the staff of the defendant, McGraw-Hill, Inc. In the course of these talks, McGraw's representative, aware of Weiner's position with Prentice-Hall, assured his prospect that, since his company's firm policy was not to terminate employees without "just cause", employment by it would, among other things, bring him the advantage of job security. Concomitantly, the application Weiner thereafter signed and submitted, on a printed McGraw form, specified that his employment would be subject to the provisions of McGraw's "handbook on personnel policies and procedures". This reference as relevant here, represented that "[t]he company will resort to dismissal for just and sufficient cause only, and only after all practical steps toward rehabilitation or salvage of the employee have been taken and failed. However, if the welfare of the company indicates that dismissal is necessary, then that decision is arrived at and is carried out forthrightly" (Handbook, § 8.20, par. [8]).

These undertakings were important to Weiner, who alleges not only that he placed "good faith reliance" on them in leaving his existing employer, but in the process forfeited all his accrued fringe benefits and a salary increase proffered by Prentice-Hall to induce him to remain in its employ.

Following written approval, affixed at the foot of the application form by two members of the defendant's staff, one the interviewer and the other a supervisor, McGraw engaged Weiner's services. For the next eight years, so far as escalation in rank (to director of promotion services) and periodic raises in his level of compensation would seem to indicate, Weiner had every reason to believe he had, if anything, more than met the reasonable requirements of his new post. Other offers of employment he routinely rejected. Nevertheless, in February, 1977, he suddenly found himself discharged for "lack of application".

There ensued this litigation, by which, in a complaint speaking broadly in the language of breach of contract, the plaintiff seeks damages for his wrongful termination. To support its * * * motion to dismiss, defendant's argument was, and is, that there existed no contract of employment under which McGraw-Hill's evaluation of Weiner's job performance could be challenged in a court of law. In its view, the form signed by the parties was just an application for employment and nothing more. Defendant further contends that its oral promise of job security was in no way binding on it.

* * *

[The trial court upheld the complaint, but the Appellate Division reversed and granted the motion to dismiss on the basis that Weiner's employment was at will.]

For the reasons which follow, we believe the plaintiff stated a cause of action.

* * *

Turning now to substance, it is * * * clear that the fact that plaintiff was free to quit his employment at will, standing by itself, was not entitled to conclusory effect. Such a position proceeds on the oversimplified premise that, since the plaintiff was not bound to stay on, the agreement for his employment lacked "mutuality", thus leaving the defendant free to terminate at its pleasure. But this would lead to the not uncommon analytical error of engaging in a search for "mutuality", which is not always essential to a binding contract, rather than of seeking to determine the presence of consideration, which is a fundamental requisite. For, while coextensive promises may constitute consideration for each other, "mutuality", in the sense of requiring such reciprocity, is not necessary when a promisor receives other valid consideration * * *.

* * *

Apt * * * in the circumstances before us now is the following comment by Corbin: "[I]f the employer made a promise, either express or implied, not only to pay for the service but also that the employment should continue for a period of time that is either definite or capable of being determined, that employment is not terminable by him 'at will' after the employee has begun or rendered some of the requested service or has given any other consideration * * * This is true even though the employee has made no return promise and has retained the power and legal privilege of terminating the employment 'at will'. The employer's promise is supported by the service that has been begun or rendered or by the other executed consideration" (1A Corbin, Contracts, § 152, p. 14). So understood, an agreement on the part of an employer not to dismiss an employee except for "good and sufficient cause only" and, if such cause was given, until the prescribed procedures to rehabilitate had failed, does not create an ineluctable employment at will.

These propositions in mind, we find * * * sufficient evidence of a contract and a breach to sustain a cause of action. First, plaintiff was induced to leave Prentice-Hall with the assurance that McGraw-Hill would not discharge him without cause. Second, this assurance was incorporated into the employment application. Third, plaintiff rejected other offers of employment in reliance on the assurance. Fourth, appellant alleged that, on several occasions when he had recommended that certain of his subordinates be dismissed, he was instructed by his supervisors to proceed in strict compliance with the handbook and policy manuals because employees could be discharged only for just cause. He also claims that he was told that, if he did not proceed in accordance with the strict procedures set forth in the handbook, McGraw-Hill would be liable for legal action. In our view, these factors combine to present a question for trial: Was defendant bound to a promise not to discharge plaintiff without just and sufficient cause and an opportunity for rehabilitation? * * *

* * *

Consequently, the order of the Appellate Division should be reversed and the order of Special Term reinstated.

[JUDGE WACHTLER'S dissent is omitted.]

KAMBOJ v. ELI LILLY & CO., 2007 WL 178434 at *24 (N.D. Ill. 2007). Absent special circumstances, the mere relinquishment of a prior job to take a new job is insufficient consideration. But if the employee's forbearance is a "specially bargained for detriment" * * * it can be said that the employee has surrendered something of value in exchange for the promise of employment and therefore that adequate consideration exists.

BLADES, EMPLOYMENT AT WILL VS. INDIVIDUAL FREEDOM: ON LIMITING THE ABUSIVE EXERCISE OF EMPLOYER POWER

67 Colum. L. Rev. 1404, 1419 (1967).

[T]here is a multitude of cases in which even contracts for permanent employment, that is, for indefinite terms, have been held unenforceable on the ground that they lack mutuality of obligation. But these cases demonstrate that mutuality is a high-sounding phrase of little use as an analytical tool. If the employee in addition to his services has given other "good" consideration, such as foregoing a claim against the employer or giving up a business to accept the employment, the agreement will be enforced on behalf of the employee even though he is free to quit at any time. Thus it seems clear that mutuality of obligation is not an inexorable requirement and that lack of mutuality is simply, as many courts have come to recognize, an imperfect way of referring to the real obstacle to enforcing any kind of contractual limitation on the employer's right of discharge—lack of consideration.

BRC RUBBER & PLASTICS, INC. V. CONTINENTAL CARBON CO.

United States Court of Appeals, Seventh Circuit, 2018.
900 F.3d 529.

RIPPLE, CIRCUIT JUDGE.

This case involves a contract dispute over the sale and purchase of carbon black, an important ingredient in rubber products. BRC Rubber & Plastics, Inc. ("BRC") seeks to recover from Continental Carbon Co. ("Continental") costs that it incurred in purchasing carbon black from another supplier following Continental's alleged repudiation of the parties' supply agreement.

Initially, BRC claimed that the agreement was a requirements contract, *i.e.*, a supply agreement in which Continental promised to provide all of the carbon black that BRC required. Because Continental failed to do so, the district court awarded summary judgment to BRC.

In a prior appeal, we rejected the characterization of the agreement as a requirements contract and, therefore, vacated the judgment. In remanded proceedings, BRC, without amending its complaint, pursued the alternative theory that the agreement is for the supply of a fixed amount of carbon black. The district court granted summary judgment to Continental for two reasons: BRC's complaint failed to state a claim for relief under any theory of the agreement other than as a requirements contract; in the alternative, the agreement is unenforceable for a lack of mutuality and consideration.

BRC now appeals. For the reasons set forth in this opinion, we conclude that the parties' agreement is enforceable and that BRC can proceed on its alternative characterization of the contract as an agreement for a fixed amount of carbon black. We, therefore, reverse and remand the case for proceedings consistent with this opinion.

Background

BRC produces rubber-based products for the automotive industry. Continental is a supplier of carbon black, a raw material that is a key ingredient in rubber products. On January 1, 2010, BRC and Continental entered into a five-year agreement (the "Agreement"). Under its terms, Continental "agree[d] to sell to [BRC] approximately 1.8 million pounds of prime [carbon] black annually . . . to be taken in approximately equal monthly quantities." The Agreement set out baseline prices for three different grades of carbon black (N339, N550, and N762) and stated that those prices were "to remain firm throughout the term." In return,

Continental obtained the right to review and meet any better offers that BRC received during the term.

In 2010, Continental shipped 2.6 million pounds of carbon black to BRC. Shipments continued regularly into mid-2011, with Continental providing more than one million pounds by the spring of 2011. However, in March 2011, demand for carbon black began to exceed Continental's ability to produce it. In April 2011, Continental notified all of its buyers that the N762 grade of carbon black would be unavailable in May due to plant outages and lack of inventory. BRC nonetheless placed an order for 360,000 pounds of carbon black, including N762, for delivery in the coming weeks.

The parties dispute the nature of their communications during this period. In mid-April 2011, a Continental sales representative emailed BRC's Vice President of Purchasing seeking to increase the baseline prices of carbon black by $.02 per pound. BRC rejected this request, citing the "firm" prices set out in the Agreement. In late April, the same Continental representative informed BRC that Continental might withhold shipments from BRC. Continental does not deny that this communication occurred but maintains that the representative, who was about to be terminated from the company, delivered a false message.

Given Continental's limited inventory and obligations to other customers, it neither confirmed BRC's last order nor shipped the requested carbon black. BRC's counsel then sent a letter to Continental, dated May 16, 2011, demanding immediate shipment of the unfulfilled order and immediate assurance that Continental would uphold its end of the bargain in the future. Continental responded that it did "not have N762 available at the moment." As a result, on May 18, 2011, BRC purchased one railcar's worth of N762 from another supplier at a higher price than set forth in the Agreement.

Two days later, Continental offered to ship BRC multiple railcars of carbon black at price increases up to $.06 per pound. Continental claims that this offer mistakenly quoted higher prices than the Agreement. When BRC refused to pay higher prices, a Continental Director suggested that BRC "call another supplier." Continental maintains that this response was based on a misunderstanding. Indeed, within hours, counsel for both parties conferred and Continental's attorney sent an email to BRC stating that Continental would "continue producing and shipping timely at the contract prices, and would not cut off supply to BRC.

Later that same day, BRC sought further confirmation as to when Continental would fulfill BRC's outstanding order. Continental responded, "we will ship one car next week and do the best we can re future orders based on our intent to supply 1.8 million lbs." BRC requested a status update three days later, and Continental gave a similar response.

On the next business day, BRC again inquired about the status of its order, and Continental said that it would ship one railcar of carbon black the following day. At this point, Continental emphasized that the Agreement required it to supply only 1.8 million pounds per year—or approximately 150,000 pounds per month—and that it already had shipped 1.2 million pounds that year—or approximately 300,000 pounds per month. Continental shipped one railcar of carbon black to BRC the next day. Within a week, Continental emailed BRC seeking to increase the baseline prices again and to accelerate the payment terms in the Agreement. On June 2, 2011, BRC filed this lawsuit.

* * *

Discussion

We review the district court's decision on summary judgment de novo. *E.T. Prods., LLC v. D.E. Miller Holdings, Inc.*, 872 F.3d 464, 467 (7th Cir. 2017). Summary judgment is proper when the moving party shows that there is no genuine dispute as to any material fact and that it is entitled to judgment as a matter of law. Fed. R. Civ. P. 56(a). When ruling on a motion for summary judgment, we, like the district court, view the record in the light most favorable to the nonmoving party; if a reasonable factfinder could return a verdict in favor of that party, the motion must be denied. *Payne v. Pauley*, 337 F.3d 767, 770 (7th Cir. 2003).

We begin with the district court's holding that the Agreement is unenforceable for lack of mutuality and consideration. The court reasoned that "[b]ecause the Supply Agreement is not a requirements contract, and because even the 'Meet or Release' provision in the Supply Agreement does not require BRC to purchase carbon black exclusively from Continental, there is no mutuality of obligation in the Supply Agreement. [It] is therefore unenforceable for lack of consideration." The court went on to adopt Continental's characterization of the Agreement as an unenforceable "buyer's option," or "open offer to sell.

We review the district court's interpretation of the Agreement de novo.

* * * For the reasons explained in the following paragraphs, we hold that the Agreement is supported by mutuality and consideration and is, thus, enforceable.

Under Indiana law, a contract must impose mutual obligations on the parties in order to be enforceable. *Terre Haute Reg'l Hosp., Inc. v. El-Issa*, 470 N.E.2d 1371, 1377 (Ind. Ct. App. 1984). "If both parties to the [Agreement] are not bound, neither is bound," *id.*, and consideration is lacking. Obligations that give rise to consideration can take the form of legal benefits or legal detriments. *Kelly v. Levandoski*, 825 N.E.2d 850, 860 (Ind. Ct. App. 2005) ("A benefit is a legal right given to the promisor to which the promisor would not otherwise be entitled. A detriment, on the other hand, is a legal right the promisee has forborne." (citation omitted) (quoting *DiMizio v. Romo*, 756 N.E.2d 1018, 1023 (Ind. Ct. App. 2001))). Furthermore, the obligations on both parties must be "reasonably definite and certain," *Zeyher v. S.S. & S. Mfg. Co.*, 319 F.2d 606, 607 (7th Cir. 1963) (applying Indiana law); they cannot be illusory promises that, by their terms, make performance entirely optional, *Pardieck v. Pardieck*, 676 N.E.2d 359, 364 n.3 (Ind. Ct. App. 1997). That said, so long as a contract imposes definite obligations on both parties, courts do not question whether the value of consideration is adequate. *Tanton v. Grochow*, 707 N.E.2d 1010, 1013 (Ind. Ct. App. 1999).

Here, the Agreement imposes sufficiently definite obligations on both parties. Continental is obligated to make available "approximately 1.8 million pounds of prime [carbon] black annually . . . to be taken in approximately equal monthly quantities," at the baseline prices set out "firm[ly]" in the Agreement. In return, BRC has accepted a legal detriment under the "Meet or Release" provision, which is "naturally read as a 'right of first refusal,' meaning *if* BRC sought to buy carbon black from another seller at a lower price, Continental had to be given the chance to meet that price." *BRC Rubber & Plastics, Inc.*, 804 F.3d at 1232. As we noted in the previous appeal, BRC is not obligated to purchase any carbon black from Continental; BRC can purchase it at higher prices from other suppliers or it can produce its own. However, BRC is prohibited from purchasing carbon black from other suppliers on better terms than the Agreement unless Continental reviews the offer and decides not to match it.

Under Indiana law, a right of first refusal to sell can support mutuality of obligation. * * * The Indiana Court of Appeals has described a right of first refusal as "a 'valuable contractual right' in which the right-holder may 'preempt' a third-party offer for a protected interest." *B&R Oil Co. v. Stoler*, 77 N.E.3d 823, 828 (Ind. Ct. App. 2017). Furthermore, the value of a right of first refusal is not undermined by its conditional nature. *See Saviano v. Comm'r of Internal Revenue*, 765 F.2d 643, 653 (7th Cir. 1985) (recognizing conditional right of first refusal). Therefore, the right that Continental acquired through the "Meet or Release" provision is not legally diminished as a result of its limited application to only those offers that are "better" than the terms of the Agreement. It is not our place to question the value of this consideration. *See Tanton*, 707 N.E.2d at 1013.

On the other side of the bargain, Continental has promised to make available to BRC approximately 1.8 million pounds of carbon black per year at the stated prices. Contrary to Continental's argument, mutuality of obligation does not require that "the seller . . . be required to sell and the buyer . . . be required to buy." It is clear under Indiana law that "the doctrine of mutuality of obligation does not require that every duty within an agreement be based upon a corresponding obligation." *Terre Haute Reg'l Hosp.*, 470 N.E.2d at 1377. Therefore, BRC's obligation under the

Agreement need not mirror that of Continental; it is not the case that the seller be required to sell and the buyer be required to buy. *See id.* ("Certainly a contract does not become unenforceable merely because the obligations of the parties differ in quality or quantity."). Because the Agreement imposes a definite obligation on both parties, there is mutuality and consideration.

* * *

Conclusion

In sum, we conclude that the Agreement is supported by mutuality of obligation and, thus, consideration. * * *

REVERSED and REMANDED

FAGERSTROM v. AMAZON.COM, INC., 141 F.Supp.3d 1051 (S.D.Cal. 2016). [Fagerstrom and others purchased products from Amazon, but claimed that Amazon engaged in false advertising by setting forth discounted prices that actually were the retail price offered by other retailers. Amazon sought to enforce an arbitration agreement in which Amazon reserved the right to make changes "at any time." The court held that the agreement was not illusory in part because Amazon was bound by the duty of good faith and fair dealing. The court explained:]

The restriction on Amazon's discretion imposed by the duty of good faith and fair dealing saves the Agreement from being illusory. * * * Here, Amazon made a promise to Plaintiffs that 'any dispute or claim . . . will be resolved by binding arbitration.' Plaintiffs are justified in expecting Amazon to carry out this core obligation should a dispute or claim arise, just as Amazon is attempting to do here. * * * As the party who retains discretion to make changes to the Arbitration Agreement, Amazon must exercise this discretion in a manner consistent with 'the spirit of the bargain' and Plaintiffs' justified expectations under the contract. * * * Thus, Plaintiffs' concern that Amazon could modify the Agreement to avoid pending arbitration if Amazon determined that arbitration was no longer in its interest is unfounded. Amazon could not, in fact, interpret the Agreement to allow Amazon to arbitrate or not arbitrate particular disputes as it saw fit, and Washington courts will not give effect to an interpretation that would produce such a result.

PROBLEM 2-5

On January 10, Seller agrees to deliver 12 jet engines to Buyer on February 1. Payment is due on delivery of the engines. The agreement also provides that "Seller may terminate this agreement on 24 hours-notice." Valid contract? Suppose on January 11, Seller notifies Buyer that Seller "will not perform"? Suppose on February 1, Seller failed to deliver without having given notice?

Professors Ben-Shahar and White report that automaker Ford's contract with its suppliers states that "[t]he buyer may terminate the Purchase Order, in whole or in part, at any time and for any or no reason, upon Written Notice to the Supplier." They observe that this provision "come[s] close to rendering the contract[ ] illusory. Still, the requirement of a written notice in Ford's contract * * * may constitute the necessary restriction to render these contracts enforceable." Omri Ben-Shahar & James J. White, Boilerplate and Economic Power In Auto Manufacturing Contracts, 104 Mich. L. Rev. 953, 958 n. 20 (2006).

NOTE:
THE PREEXISTING DUTY DOCTRINE

The "preexisting duty" doctrine is the subject of much discussion among contract scholars. In his treatise, Professor Corbin stated:

> Most acts and forbearances, or promises of future performance, are a sufficient consideration for a promise if they are bargained for by the maker of that promise and are given in exchange for it. One of the most important exceptions consists of those performances that are required of the performer, exactly as rendered by him, by a pre-existing legal duty. The same is true of a promise to render such a performance. The very frequently stated rule is that neither the performance of duty nor the promise to render a performance already required by duty is a sufficient consideration for a return promise.
>
> There has been a growing doubt as to the soundness of this doctrine.[k]

Suppose Ajax Construction Company agrees to construct a drive-in theatre for Brown's Cinema for $60,000. The contract provides that Ajax will clear the site and provide all of the fill necessary for the job. After Ajax begins performance, it discovers that the amount of fill needed will be greater than it contemplated. The cost of additional fill will be over $5,000. Ajax therefore seeks and receives Brown's promise to pay an additional $5,000 for the completed work. According to standard doctrine, Ajax gave no consideration for Brown's promise to pay the additional $5000 because Ajax had a preexisting duty to provide all of the fill necessary for $60,000. Thus, under the preexisting duty rule, Brown's promise to pay the extra $5000 would be unenforceable.

Assume, however, that the parties had freely and fairly agreed to their contract modification. For example, suppose Brown's believed rightly that it had received too good a deal, but Brown's later refuses to pay the $5,000. Predictably, many courts decline to apply the preexisting duty rule to such a case. Conversely, assume that Brown's was the victim of unfair pressure. For

[k] 1A CORBIN ON CONTRACTS § 171 at 105 (1963).

example, knowing that Brown's could not find another contractor, Ajax refuses to perform without a price increase even though it would not suffer higher costs in providing the fill. Here, courts usually "apply" the preexisting duty rule. Because the rule is thus principally a policing doctrine, we consider it more fully in Chapter 5.

HAIGH v. BROOKS, 113 Eng. Rep. 119 (Q.B. 1839), *aff'd,* 113 Eng. Rep. 124 (Ex. 1840). [Brooks allegedly gave Haigh an objectively valuable guarantee. In return Haigh surrendered a piece of paper Brooks had earlier given Haigh, which Brooks apparently assumed rendered him legally liable to Haigh, but which may have had no objective legal effect. The court held that giving up this piece of paper (however objectively worthless it may have been) would be consideration.]

2 CORBIN ON CONTRACTS

§ 5.14 (2019).

Parting with a document, the contents of which can in fact render no service, has been held to be a consideration for a promise to pay a large sum of money. Services or property are consideration for a promise to pay much more money than anyone else would pay for them. * * *

* * *

The rule that market equivalence of consideration is * * * to be left solely to the free bargaining process of the parties, leads in extreme cases to seeming absurdities. When the consideration is only a "peppercorn" or a "tomtit" or a worthless piece of paper, the requirement of a consideration appeared to Holmes to be as much of a mere formality as is a seal. In such extreme cases, a tendency may be observed to refuse to apply the rule, but it is a tendency that has not been carried very far. Such cases can sometimes be explained on the ground that the court feels that there was no bargain in fact and that the stated consideration was a mere pretense.

PROBLEM 2-6

Compare the following two provisions of the Restatement (Second) of Contracts:

> § 79. Adequacy of Consideration * * *
>
> If the requirement of consideration is met, there is no additional requirement of * * * equivalence in the values exchanged. * * *
>
> § 208. Unconscionable Contract or Term
>
> If a contract or term thereof is unconscionable at the time the contract is made a court may refuse to enforce the contract, or may

> enforce the remainder of the contract without the unconscionable term, or may so limit the application of any unconscionable term as to avoid any unconscionable result.

How might such provisions be reconciled? If the owner of a car worth $10,000, offers to trade it for a worthless wrist watch, will the law uphold the deal? Does the imbalance in such an exchange suggest that something else is wrong with the deal?

HILLMAN AND O'ROURKE, RETHINKING CONSIDERATION IN THE ELECTRONIC AGE

61 Hastings L. J. 311, 321–322 (2009).

The bargain theory is neither descriptively nor normatively very coherent. As Professor Charles Fried pointed out * * *, the theory leaves ample room for courts to dodge issues and for theorists to ponder. Courts sometimes police the adequacy of consideration despite contract law's freedom-of-contract norm to leave that issue to the parties. Courts enforce gift promises that induce reliance or for a benefit already received despite the absence of a bargain. Courts enforce without consideration contract modifications, option contracts, waivers, and promises made to charitable institutions. Courts enforce promises even if the return consideration is only an ephemeral reason for making the promise. Courts manipulate or dispense with consideration if they believe a gift promise is important enough to enforce. Consideration to support a promise can come from a party other than the promisee. Theorists offer conflicting moral, economic, and libertarian theories, among others, to "explain" promise enforcement. No wonder Professor Grant Gilmore was moved to announce the wholesale demise of the bargain theory of consideration.

Notwithstanding Gilmore, we believe that the bargain theory survives as the best the law can do at line drawing between those promises that should be legally enforceable and those that should be left to the promisor's "foro conscientiae." Despite its malleability, consideration serves a minimal gatekeeper role, corralling the large category of gift promises in which the cost of enforcement outweighs the benefit. Nevertheless, the bargain theory's relative indeterminacy means that courts can enlarge the category of promises within its ranks if they believe a promise is important and enforcement is administratively feasible. Two examples of the latter should suffice. To preserve the flexibility of contracting parties in the face of changed circumstances, contract law recognized the importance of enforcing contract modifications that are not supported by consideration. Courts therefore devised mutual rescission, waiver, and other theories within the framework of the consideration doctrine to allow for enforcement of such modifications. Similarly, contract law began to enforce promises not to revoke offers (option contracts) in the absence of consideration because of the importance of options to our economy: "The fact that the option is an appropriate preliminary step in the conclusion of a socially useful transaction provides a sufficient substantive basis for enforcement." * * *

In short, under the rubric of "consideration," twentieth-century courts enforced promises that increased society's welfare, interpreted broadly, and that were capable of judicial administration. Lines were drawn, but courts could adjust them if necessary.

NOTE: RELATING CONSIDERATION TO AGREEMENT LAW AND THE STATUTE OF FRAUDS

The parties must make a valid agreement before a prima facie duty arises under an agreement with consideration. Although this chapter includes materials on agreement law, the subject is studied systematically in Chapters Four and Five. Some types of agreements with consideration also require a writing. We encounter cases involving the writing requirement in the next several sections, and return to it again in Section Nine of this Chapter.

SECTION THREE: OBLIGATION ARISING FROM JUSTIFIED RELIANCE—PROMISSORY ESTOPPEL

S. PUFENDORF, DE JURE NATURAE ET GENTIUM

Book III, ch. v., sec. 11 (1688).

[I]f a man has suffered any damage from the non-fulfilment of a promise (suppose a man has trusted another's word, and has in some way or other neglected to look to his own necessities), the promisor is bound by natural law to make good the matter; and from this it is right to conclude that a promise can be exacted, and a person must perform it, lest another suffer loss thereby.

ATIYAH, CONTRACTS, PROMISES AND THE LAW OF OBLIGATIONS

94 L.Q. Rev. 193, 202–03 (1978).

Is it not manifest that a person who has actually worsened his position by reliance on a promise has a more powerful case for redress than one who has not acted in reliance on the promise at all? A person who has not relied on a promise (nor paid for it) may suffer a disappointment of his expectations, but he does not actually suffer a pecuniary loss. The disappointment of an expectation may of course be treated as a species of loss by definition, as indeed, the law generally does treat it, if the expectation derives from Contract. But no definitional jugglery can actually equate the position of the party who suffers a diminution of his assets in reliance on a promise, and a person who suffers no such diminution.

KIRKSEY V. KIRKSEY

Supreme Court of Alabama, 1845.
8 Ala. 131.

Assumpsit by the defendant, against the plaintiff in error. The question is presented in this Court, upon a case agreed, which shows the following facts:

The plaintiff was the wife of defendant's brother, but had for some time been a widow, and had several children. In 1840, the plaintiff resided on public land, under a contract of lease, she had held over, and was comfortably settled, and would have attempted to secure the land she lived on. The defendant resided in Talladega County, some sixty or seventy miles off. On the 10th October, 1840, he wrote to her the following letter:

> "Dear Sister Antillico,—Much to my mortification, I heard that brother Henry was dead, and one of his children. I know that your situation is one of grief and difficulty. You had a bad chance before, but a great deal worse now. I should like to come and see you, but cannot with convenience at present. * * * I do not know whether you have a preference on the place you live on or not. If you had, I would advise you to obtain your preference, and sell the land and quit the country, as I understand it is very unhealthy, and I know society is very bad. If you will come down and see me, I will let you have a place to raise your family, and I have more open land than I can tend; and on account of your situation, and that of your family, I feel like I want you and the children to do well."

Within a month or two after the receipt of this letter, the plaintiff abandoned her possession, without disposing of it, and removed with her family, to the residence of the defendant, who put her in comfortable houses, and gave her land to cultivate for two years, at the end of which time he notified her to remove, and put her in a house, not comfortable, in the woods, which he afterwards required her to leave.

A verdict being found for the plaintiff, for $200, the above facts were agreed, and if they will sustain the action, the judgment is to be affirmed, otherwise it is to be reversed.

* * *

ORMOND, J. The inclination of my mind is that the loss and inconvenience which the plaintiff sustained in breaking up and moving to the defendant's, a distance of sixty miles, is a sufficient consideration to support the promise to furnish her with a house, and land to cultivate, until she could raise her family. My brothers, however, think that the promise on the part of the defendant was a mere gratuity, and that an action will not lie for its breach. The judgment of the court below must therefore be reversed, pursuant to the agreement of the parties.

NOTE: FROM EQUITABLE ESTOPPEL TO PROMISSORY ESTOPPEL

Cases like Kirksey posed a pickle for humane jurists: couldn't a way be found to protect promisees who relied on promises that were gratuitously made? One approach—adopted in the late 19th and early 20th century—used principles of *equity* to bar promisors from asserting the absence of consideration. For example, in Ryerss v. Trustees of Presbyterian Congregation of Blossburg, 33 Pa. 114 (Pa. 1859), Ryerss promised to (but didn't) give $100 if a congregation built a church in a particular place. The court found consideration in "the labour, trouble, and expense to which he subjected the party promised, as well as in the benefit he expected * * * would accrue from the enterprise, to property wherein he was interested, in the neighbourhood." Given that "good and valuable consideration", the court concluded that there were "no grounds of defence against a promise so well proved." Or, consider Seavey v. Drake, 62 N.H. 393 (N.H. 1882). In Seavey, a father orally promised his son to deed him a tract of land, which the son then improved and lived on. The court concluded that the "expenditure in money or labor in the improvement of the land induced by the donor's promise to give the land to the party making the expenditure, constitutes, in *equity*, a consideration for the promise and the promise will be enforced."

But what is *equity*? During the Middle Ages in England, a legal system emerged in which there were courts of law and a court of equity. Judges sitting in courts of law applied what was called the common law, which consisted primarily of judge-made law. The court of equity evolved partly because of the rigidity and inflexibility of substantive common law rules. Although the court of equity usually followed the common law, that court also evolved some distinctively equitable doctrines that modified the common law. These doctrines included such equitable defenses as fraud, mistake, estoppel, unclean hands, laches, and unconscionability.

The English court of equity also arose because it met distinct remedial needs. For example, courts of law in contract actions would ordinarily grant only money damages for breach of contract. The court of equity, on the other hand, would grant "specific relief"—a decree directing the defendant to do or refrain from specific action. For example, the court of equity might order the defendant to perform a contract (a remedy called specific performance), or not to commit a tort (a remedy called an injunction). Ordinarily, the court of equity would require the party seeking relief to show that the remedy available in a court of law (usually a claim for money damages) would be inadequate. Only then would the court of equity grant specific relief. For example, a plaintiff in a contract action would have to show that money damages would be difficult to measure or that the goods promised were unique.

Most of the distinctions between law and equity were transported to America in colonial times. Today in England and in nearly all states in this country, courts of law and courts of equity have merged into one court—a trial court of general jurisdiction with power to grant all remedies formerly granted by the two separate courts, and with power to apply all applicable substantive law, whether it originated as common law or as equitable doctrine.

American equity courts (and courts of general jurisdiction applying equitable principles) developed a robust and complex set of rules that shaped (and limited) *equitable estoppel* in contract cases. According to a learned 1886 treatise,[1] the doctrine required that:

> (1) There must be conduct—acts, language, or silence—amounting to a representation or concealment of material facts. (2) These facts must be known to the party estopped at the time of his said conduct, or at least, the circumstances must be such that knowledge of them is necessarily imputed to him. (3) The truth concerning these facts must be unknown to the other party claiming the benefit of the estoppel, at the time when such conduct was done, and at the time when it was acted upon by him. (4) The conduct must be done with the intention, or at least with the expectation, that it will be acted upon by the other party; or under such circumstances that it is both natural and probable that it will be so acted upon. * * * (5) The conduct must be relied upon by the other party, and thus relying he must be led to act upon it. (6) He must in fact act upon it in such a manner as to change his position for the worse; in other words, he must so act that he would suffer a loss if he were compelled to surrender or forego or alter what he has done by reason of the first party being permitted to repudiate his conduct and to assert rights inconsistent with it. * * * The conduct creating the estoppel must be something which amounts either to a representation or a concealment of the existence of facts. * * * The facts represented or concealed must, in general, be either existing or past, or at least represented to be so. A statement concerning future facts would either be a mere expression of opinion, or would constitute a contract and be governed by rules applicable to contracts.

Some plaintiffs were able to navigate this unwieldy doctrine to win their case notwithstanding the absence of consideration. For example, in Ricketts v. Scothorn, 57 Neb. 51 (1898), a grandfather told his bookkeeper granddaughter, "I have fixed out something that you have not got to work any more. None of my grandchildren work and you don't have to." He then gave her a promissory note for $2,000 and she immediately quit her job. More than a year later she took another job. Her grandfather died without paying the note. The court, ruling for the granddaughter, reasoned that the grandfather's executor was

[1] J. Pomeroy's EQUITY JURISPRUDENCE 264, 272–73.

estopped from denying that there was consideration for the promissory note: "Having intentionally influenced the plaintiff to alter her position for the worse on the faith of the note being paid when due, it would be grossly inequitable to permit the maker, or his executor, to resist payment on the ground that the promise was given without consideration."

However, courts and commentators were dissatisfied with the *ad hoc* nature of these equitable results. Sometimes courts would frankly state that equity was the source of the rule, other times they would find consideration by feats of imaginative legerdemain. Consider again the reasoning of the courts in Ryerss and Seavey. When the American Law Institute adopted section 90 of the Restatement (First) of Contracts in 1931, it tried to start afresh by recognizing a new theory of obligation called "promissory estoppel." It stated:

> A promise which the promisor should reasonably expect to induce action or forebearance of a definite and substantial character on the part of the promisee and which does induce such action or forebearance is binding if injustice can be avoided only by enforcement of the promise.

The Restatement (Second) of Contracts, published in 1981, includes a new version of section 90. It provides:

> (1) A promise which the promisor should reasonably expect to induce action or forbearance on the part of the promisee or a third person and which does induce such action or forbearance is binding if injustice can be avoided only by enforcement of the promise. The remedy granted for breach may be limited as justice requires.
>
> (2) A charitable subscription or a marriage settlement is binding under Subsection (1) without proof that the promise induced action or forbearance.

In the Restatement (Second), one finds at least four changes in the wording of old § 90. Can you identify them? Do they all expand or do some of them restrict the scope of the theory?[m]

Consider the foregoing history when reading the next set of cases. Would Cochran have been able to make out the elements of equitable estoppel? Why or why not?

COCHRAN V. ROBINHOOD LANE BAPTIST CHURCH

Court of Appeals of Tennessee, 2005.
2005 WL 3527627.

ALAN E. HIGHERS, J. On September 18, 1981, Reverend Eugene Cochran ("Reverend Cochran") began his tenure as Pastor of Robinhood Lane Baptist Church (the "Church"). Thereafter, Reverend Cochran maintained the position of head pastor at the Church until his death on

[m] Among other sections of the new restatement that apply § 90 are § 87 (on option contracts) and § 139 (on the statute of frauds). We study both later.

August 20, 1995. In return for his services, the Church paid Reverend Cochran a salary as well as providing him with certain additional benefits such as cell phone services, beeper services, lawn services, and gas and vehicle maintenance services. At Reverend Cochran's request, the Church also accorded the majority of these benefits directly to Reverend Cochran's wife, Mrs. Annie Cochran ("Wife" or "Appellant").

Before his death, Reverend Cochran spoke to several deacons of the Church requesting that the Church provide for Wife if the Church was able. On September 3, 1995, the Church entered into an agreement (the "Agreement") with Wife wherein the Church agreed to provide Wife with $ 783.56 on the first and third Sunday every month until September 5, 2010 and would provide lawn services for Wife's residence. Pursuant to the agreement, Wife would receive these benefits until one of two terminating events occurred: (1) her death; or (2) she remarried. However, if she remarried within five years of the inception of the contract, Wife would continue to receive these benefits for five years total. If Wife remarried after five years, she would no longer receive any benefits. Moreover, the agreement terminated all benefits that Wife previously received from the Church under the Church's oral agreement with Reverend Cochran for his services as pastor.

In March 1996, the Church discontinued making payments to Wife. On August 9, 1996, Wife filed suit against the Church * * * for breach of contract and declaratory judgment. On October 9, 1996, Wife amended her complaint to include the theory of promissory estoppel as a justification for upholding the contract. * * * The chancery court granted the motion for summary judgment as to the Church.

On appeal, Appellant contends that (1) Appellant's presence at the Church as first lady of the Church; (2) Appellant's loss of benefits previously received from the Church; and/or (3) Appellant's restraint of marriage pursuant to the Agreement constituted legally adequate consideration for the Agreement. We disagree.

A. Consideration

First, Appellant contends that the benefit of her presence at the Church as first lady of the Church was adequate consideration to support a contract. However, nowhere in the limited record on appeal demonstrates that Appellees benefitted from her presence at the Church. Appellant did not take on any additional responsibilities with the Church or promise to continue her activities with the Church. If Appellant chose to no longer attend the Church as a member, she would still be eligible for the benefits conferred to her pursuant to the terms of the Agreement. Accordingly, her mere presence at the Church does not constitute consideration.

Second, Appellant asserts that her loss of benefits previously received from the Church constituted legally adequate consideration. In order for this loss to constitute consideration, Appellant must have had a vested right to these benefits at the time of execution of the Agreement.

[The Court concluded that she had no such contractual right.]

Finally, Appellant asserts that the provision in the Agreement restraining her from marrying constituted consideration for the Agreement. * * * [T]his provision is void as a matter of public policy and cannot constitute consideration.

B. Promissory Estoppel

Appellant contends on appeal, as she did at trial, that even if the Agreement did not have legally adequate consideration, the Agreement should be upheld on a theory of promissory estoppel. We disagree.

Previously our supreme court has defined promissory estoppel as follows:

> "A promise which the promisor should reasonably expect to induce action or forbearance of a definite and substantial character on the part of the promisee and which does induce such action or forbearance is binding if injustice can be avoided only by enforcement of the promise."

Alden v. Presley, 637 S.W.2d 862, 864 (Tenn. 1982) (quoting Restatement of Contracts § 90). While broad in its definition, the theory of promissory estoppel does have its limits. As our supreme court has previously noted,

> "detrimental action or forbearance by the promisee in reliance on a gratuitous promise, within limits constitutes a substitute for consideration, or a sufficient reason for enforcement of the promise without consideration. This doctrine is known as promissory estoppel. A promisor who induces substantial change of position by the promisee in reliance on the promise is estopped to deny its enforceability as lacking consideration. The reason for the doctrine is to avoid an unjust result, and its reason defines its limits. No injustice results in refusal to enforce a gratuitous promise where the loss suffered in reliance is negligible, nor where the promisee's action in reliance was unreasonable or unjustified by the promise. The limits of promissory estoppel are: (1) the detriment suffered in reliance must be substantial in an economic sense; (2) the substantial loss to the promisee in acting in reliance must have been foreseeable by the promisor; (3) the promisee must have acted reasonable in justifiable reliance on the promise as made."

Id. * * * [W]e conclude that Appellant has not demonstrated that she detrimentally relied on the promises of Appellees.

Appellant argues on appeal that she conducted her life in reliance on the benefit she received from the Church. However, in order for the theory of promissory estoppel to apply, Appellant must show that the promises made in the Agreement induced an action or forbearance by Appellant to her detriment in reliance on those promises after Appellees made those promises. Appellant has failed to demonstrate such detrimental reliance. The only act of forbearance or action taken since the execution of the Agreement on the part of Appellant in reliance on the promises made by Appellees in the Agreement was that Appellant declined a proposal of marriage in order to adhere to the conditions of the Agreement.[1] As we have stated earlier, this restraint of marriage is void as a matter of public policy. Since this restraint cannot be adequate consideration for the Agreement, it is counterintuitive to allow this restraint to serve as a basis for upholding the Agreement on a theory of promissory estoppel. Accordingly, the theory of promissory estoppel is inapplicable in this case.

Conclusion

For the reasons set forth herein, we affirm the decision of the chancery court granting summary judgment to Appellee. Costs of this appeal are taxed to Appellant, Mrs. Annie B. Cochran, and her surety, for which execution may issue if necessary.

CONTRACTS, PROMISSORY ESTOPPEL

20 Va. L. Rev. 214, 218–219 (1933).

The prime objection to the recognition of promissory estoppel lies in the upheaval which would be caused in the law of contract, especially with regard to the rules of consideration, consequent upon its application. The fear that general adoption of the doctrine would tend to abolish consideration in contract cases is almost universal. * * * The doctrine definitely lies outside of contract law; * * * the question of what limits would be applied to it, once adopted, seems potent; the certainty which seems requisite in a great basic branch of law like that of contract, would seem doomed to demolition * * *. On the other hand, we must consider the plight into which the courts have forced themselves by their general refusal to acknowledge the applicability of promissory estoppel. In the main they have resorted to contract law, and by indulging in fictions and unfortunate analogies have jammed, stretched, and distorted "rules" of consideration * * * where consideration has no real application according to its established conception. * * *

---

[1] Appellant also claims that she took out a loan in reliance on the Agreement. However, Appellant took this loan out after the Church stopped making payments pursuant to the agreement * * *. A promisee does not act reasonably when he or she acts in reliance on a promise that has already been breached.

WHEELER V. WHITE

Supreme Court of Texas, 1965.
398 S.W.2d 93.

SMITH, JUSTICE.

This is a suit for damages brought by petitioner, Ellis D. Wheeler, against respondent, S.E. White. Wheeler alleged that White had breached a contract[1] to secure a loan or furnish the money to finance the construction of improvements upon land owned by Wheeler. Wheeler further pleaded, in the alternative, that if the contract itself was not sufficiently definite,

---

[1] Contract between Ellis D. Wheeler, Party of the First Part, and S.E. White, Party of the Second Part:

"That said Party of the First Part is the owner of Lots Nine (9), Ten (10), and Eleven (11) (excepting the South one hundred ten (110) feet of Lot Nine (9), all of Block Number Seven (7), of BRINKMAN ADDITION to the City of Port Arthur, Jefferson County, Texas. Said Party of the First Part hereby employs Party of the Second Part for the purpose of securing a loan to finance the construction of improvements upon said property; said improvements to face on the Port Arthur-Orange Highway one hundred forty feet (140) and extend back a depth of eighty feet (80); said building to be constructed according to plans and specifications heretofore agreed on by the parties hereto. The loan to be made by, or obtained by, Party of the Second Part for the Party of the First Part, and to be in the sum of SEVENTY THOUSAND AND 00/100 ($70,000.00) DOLLARS and to be payable in monthly installments over a term of fifteen (15) years and bear interest at a rate of not more than six (6%) per cent per annum.

"Said loan is to be obtained on or before six (6) months from date of this contract, either from funds provided by Party of the Second Part or from third persons whom Party of the Second Part may negotiate with to provide such funds. In either event Party of the First Part agrees to sign all necessary papers required of Lendor to create proper liens.

"Party of the First Part agrees to pay to Party of the Second Part the sum of FIVE THOUSAND AND 00/100 ($5,000.00) DOLLARS for his services in making or securing said loan for Party of the First Part. Said FIVE THOUSAND AND 00/100 ($5,000.00) DOLLARS shall be due and payable to Party of the Second Part as soon as the SEVENTY THOUSAND AND 00/100 ($70,000.00) DOLLARS loan is made available for construction of said premises; and should party of the First Part fail and refuse to pay said FIVE THOUSAND DOLLARS ($5,000.00) when due, Party of the Second Part shall have the right to enforce payment by filing suit in a Court of competent jurisdiction, and Party of the First Part hereby specifically agrees to pay ten (10%) per cent additional on said sum as Attorney Fees and all costs of Court in connection with said suit.

"This agreement voids and takes precedence over previous agreements by and between Ellis D. Wheeler and S.E. White, concerning the hereinabove described property.

"Party of the First Part agrees that when said loan has been obtained that he will proceed with all reasonable haste and diligence in having the improvements for which said loan is obtained constructed, and to execute all necessary agreements, liens, etc., that may be required in the process of, and consummating said loan. In the event that Party of the Second Part obtains said loan but Party of the First Part does not use the financing thus obtained by Party of the Second Part for any reason, then Party of the First Part will pay to Party of the Second Part the sum of FIVE THOUSAND AND 00/100 ($5,000.00) DOLLARS for his services in obtaining said loan.

"In addition to the above, Party of the First Part agrees to allow Party of the Second Part six (6) months exclusive right to secure reliable tenants to occupy seventy (70′) feet frontage in the Commercial Building which he contemplates building, said seventy (70′) feet fronting on the Port Arthur-Orange Highway; said rentals to be not less than ONE AND 60/100 ($1.60) DOLLARS per square foot per year. Should Party of the Second Part secure tenants to the remaining seventy (70) feet frontage before tenants are secured by Party of the First Part, or others, then Party of the Second Part may secure tenants for the remaining portion of said building. Party of the First Part agrees to pay Party of the Second Part, in addition to the payment of said FIVE THOUSAND AND 00/100 ($5,000.00) DOLLARS as above specified, a five (5%) per cent commission on all rentals paid by tenants obtained by Party of the Second Part; said five (5%) per cent commission to be paid for the life of the lease granted to said tenants."

then nevertheless White was estopped from asserting such insufficiency. White filed special exceptions to all of Wheeler's Third Amended Original Petition. The special exceptions asserted that the pleaded contract did not contain essential elements to its enforceability in that it failed to provide the amount of monthly installments, the amount of interest due upon the obligation, how such interest would be computed, when such interest would be paid, and that the alternative plea of estoppel was, as a matter of law, insufficient to establish any ground of recovery. All special exceptions were sustained, and upon Wheeler's declination to amend his pleadings, the trial court entered its judgment dismissing the case and ordered that Wheeler take nothing from White by reason of his suit. The Court of Civil Appeals has affirmed the judgment of the trial court. 385 S.W.2d 619. We have concluded that the trial court did not err in sustaining the special exceptions directed at the sufficiency of the contract itself, but that Wheeler's pleadings on the theory of estoppel state a cause of action. Accordingly, we reverse the judgments of the trial court and the Court of Civil Appeals and remand the cause for trial.

Since the trial court sustained White's special exceptions to Wheeler's petition, we necessarily must assume that all the alleged material facts are true. Wheeler alleged that as the owner of a three-lot tract of land in Port Arthur, Texas, he desired to construct a commercial building or shopping center thereon. He and White entered into an agreement, embodied in the written contract involved here, whereby White was to obtain the necessary loan for Wheeler from a third party or provide it himself on or before six months from the date of the contract. The loan as described in the contract, was to be "* * * in the sum of SEVENTY THOUSAND AND 00/100 ($70,000.00) DOLLARS and to be payable in monthly installments over a term of fifteen (15) years and bear interest at a rate of not more than six (6%) per cent per annum." Additionally, under the contract White was to be paid $5,000.00 for obtaining the loan and a five per cent commission on all rentals received from any tenants procured by White for the building. Wheeler alleged that he has been ready and willing to comply with his part of the agreement at all times since the contract was made.

After the contract had been signed by both parties, White assured Wheeler that the money would be available and urged him to proceed with the necessary task of demolishing the buildings presently on the site so as to make way for construction of the new building. The buildings on the site had a reasonable value of $58,500.00 and a rental value of $400.00 per month. By way of reassurance, White stressed the fact that in the event the money was unobtainable elsewhere, he would make the loan himself. Pursuant to such promises Wheeler proceeded to raze the old building and otherwise prepare the land for the new structure; thereafter, he was told by White that there would be no loan. After White's refusal to perform, Wheeler made reasonable efforts to obtain the loan himself but was unsuccessful. In the pleadings[2] Wheeler pleaded the necessary elements of inducement and reliance which entitle him to recover if he can prove the facts alleged.

Where a promisee acts to his detriment in reasonable reliance upon an otherwise unenforceable promise, courts in other jurisdictions have recognized that the disappointed party may have a substantial and compelling claim for relief. The Restatement, Contracts, § 90, says:

> "A promise which the promisor should reasonably expect to induce action or forbearance of a definite and substantial character on the part of the promisee and which does induce such action or forbearance is binding if injustice can be avoided only by enforcement of the promise."

According to Dean Hildebrand's Texas Annotation to the Restatement, Texas follows Section 90, supra. * * *

The binding thread which runs through the cases applying promissory estoppel is the existence of promises designedly made to influence the conduct of the promisee, tacitly encouraging the conduct, which conduct, although not necessarily constituting any actual performance of the contract itself, is something that must be done by the promisee before he could begin to perform, and was a fact known to the promissor. As to the argument that no new cause of action may be created by such a promise regardless of its established applicability as a defense, it has been answered that where one party has by his words or conduct made to the other a promise or assurance which was intended to affect the legal relations between them and to be acted on accordingly, then, once the other party has taken him at his word and acted on it, the party who gave the promise cannot afterward be allowed to revert to the previous relationship as if no such promise had been made. This does not create a contract where none existed before, but only prevents a party from insisting upon his strict legal rights when it would be unjust to allow him to enforce them. See 1 Williston, Contracts, §§ 139–40 (Rev. ed. 1936); and 48 A.L.R.2d 1069 (1956).

The function of the doctrine of promissory estoppel is, under our view, defensive in that it estops a promisor from denying the enforceability of the

---

[2] "Pleading further plaintiff shows the Court that if for any reason said contract is not sufficiently specific and definite, then nevertheless defendant is estopped to so claim and to set up any insufficiency because of the defendant's act in entering into said contract and exhorting plaintiff to clear the premises to make ready for the construction and defendant's representations after the date of said contract to proceed with the demolition of said buildings and clearing the site and that the money would be forthcoming and that defendant would obtain said loan and if for any reason said money could not be obtained elsewhere then said defendant would himself loan the money and plaintiff in reliance on said contract and said exhortations and said representations, both in said contract and given verbally by the defendant after the date of said contract defendant is estopped to claim any deficiency of said contract."

promise. It was said in the case of Dickerson v. Colgrove, 100 U.S. 578, 580, 25 L.Ed. 618, that:

> "The vital principle is that he who by his language or conduct leads another to do what he would not otherwise have done, shall not subject such person to loss or injury by disappointing the expectations upon which he acted. Such a change of position is sternly forbidden * * *. This remedy is always so applied as to promote the ends of justice."

* * * Under this theory, losses of expected profits will not be allowed even if expected profits are provable with certainty. The rule thus announced should be followed in the present case. We agree with the reasoning announced in those jurisdictions that, in cases such as we have before us, where there is actually no contract the promissory estoppel theory may be invoked, thereby supplying a remedy which will enable the injured party to be compensated for his foreseeable, definite and substantial reliance. Where the promisee has failed to bind the promisor to a legally sufficient contract, but where the promisee has acted in reliance upon a promise to his detriment, the promisee is to be allowed to recover no more than reliance damages measured by the detriment sustained. Since the promisee in such cases is partially responsible for his failure to bind the promisor to a legally sufficient contract, it is reasonable to conclude that all that is required to achieve justice is to put the promisee in the position he would have been in had he not acted in reliance upon the promise. * * *

The judgments of the trial court and the Court of Civil Appeals are both reversed and judgment is here entered remanding the cause to the trial court for trial on its merits in accordance with this opinion.

GREENHILL, JUSTICE (concurring).

The Court of Civil Appeals denied a recovery of damages here because the contract, it felt, was too indefinite in its provisions under Bryant v. Clark, 163 Tex. 596, 358 S.W.2d 614 (1962). The holding in Bryant v. Clark was that the contract was not sufficiently definite to be specifically enforceable. The contract here in question, viewed in context, is different in some respects from that in the Bryant case; and I would not extend Bryant v. Clark. See the criticism of that case in 5A Corbin, Contracts 283 (1964).

But assuming that the contract here, under Bryant v. Clark, is not definite enough to be specifically enforced, it is sufficiently definite to support an action for damages. Restatement, Contracts § 370, comment b.

There are Texas cases in which damages have been denied after a holding that the contract was not specifically enforceable. In each of these cases, however, the contracts were held to be within the Statute of Frauds and not enforceable for that reason in a suit for damages. 1 Williston, Contracts § 16 (Rev. ed. 1936). The contract here in question is not within the Statute of Frauds and will support an action for damages.

While I agree with the judgment entered by the Court, it seems to me that the above is a sounder ground upon which to rest our decision.

WHISTLE v. DAVID H. ARRINGTON OIL & GAS INC., 2009 WL 1529819, at *10 (E.D. Ark. 2009). Promissory estoppel is applicable only in the absence of an otherwise enforceable contract.

METZGER AND PHILLIPS, THE EMERGENCE OF PROMISSORY ESTOPPEL AS AN INDEPENDENT THEORY OF RECOVERY

35 Rutgers L. Rev. 472, 550 (1983).

* * * Promisors desirous of limiting estoppel-based liability are, however, not without devices for achieving a measure of protection. Tactics like employing a conditional or indefinite promise, attaching a termination date to the promise, or revoking and promptly communicating this to the promisee can affect the foreseeability and reasonableness of reliance and thus defeat a promissory estoppel claim.

HOFFMAN V. RED OWL STORES

Supreme Court of Wisconsin, 1965.
26 Wis. 2d 683, 133 N.W.2d 267.

Action by Joseph Hoffman (hereinafter "Hoffman") and wife, plaintiffs, against defendants Red Owl Stores, Inc. (hereinafter "Red Owl") and Edward Lukowitz.

The complaint alleged that Lukowitz, as agent for Red Owl, represented to and agreed with plaintiffs that Red Owl would build a store building in Chilton and stock it with merchandise for Hoffman to operate in return for which plaintiffs were to put up and invest a total sum of $18,000; that in reliance upon the above mentioned agreement and representations plaintiffs sold their bakery building and business and their grocery store and business; also in reliance on the agreement and representations Hoffman purchased the building site in Chilton and rented a residence for himself and his family in Chilton; plaintiffs' actions in reliance on the representations and agreement disrupted their personal and business life; plaintiffs lost substantial amounts of income and expended large sums of money as expenses. Plaintiffs demanded recovery of damages for the breach of defendants' representations and agreements.

The action was tried to a court and jury. The facts hereafter stated are taken from the evidence adduced at the trial. Where there was a conflict in the evidence the version favorable to plaintiffs has been accepted since the verdict rendered was in favor of plaintiffs.

Hoffman assisted by his wife operated a bakery at Wautoma from 1956 until sale of the building late in 1961. The building was owned in joint tenancy by him and his wife. Red Owl is a Minnesota corporation having its home office at Hopkins, Minnesota. It owns and operates a number of grocery supermarket stores and also extends franchises to agency stores which are owned by individuals, partnerships and corporations. Lukowitz resides at Green Bay and since September, 1960, has been divisional manager for Red Owl in a territory comprising Upper Michigan and most of Wisconsin in charge of 84 stores. Prior to September, 1960, he was district manager having charge of approximately 20 stores.

In November, 1959, Hoffman was desirous of expanding his operations by establishing a grocery store and contacted a Red Owl representative by the name of Jansen, now deceased. Numerous conversations were had in 1960 with the idea of establishing a Red Owl franchise store in Wautoma. In September, 1960, Lukowitz succeeded Jansen as Red Owl's representative in the negotiations. Hoffman mentioned that $18,000 was all the capital he had available to invest and he was repeatedly assured that this would be sufficient to set him up in business as a Red Owl store. About Christmastime, 1960, Hoffman thought it would be a good idea if he bought a small grocery store in Wautoma and operated it in order that he gain experience in the grocery business prior to operating a Red Owl store in some larger community. On February 6, 1961, on the advice of Lukowitz and Sykes, who had succeeded Lukowitz as Red Owl's district manager, Hoffman bought the inventory and fixtures of a small grocery store in Wautoma and leased the building in which it was operated.

After three months of operating this Wautoma store, the Red Owl representatives came in and took inventory and checked the operations and found the store was operating at a profit. Lukowitz advised Hoffman to sell the store to his manager, and assured him that Red Owl would find a larger store for him elsewhere. Acting on this advice and assurance, Hoffman sold the fixtures and inventory to his manager on June 6, 1961. Hoffman was reluctant to sell at that time because it meant losing the summer tourist business, but he sold on the assurance that he would be operating in a new location by fall and that he must sell this store if he wanted a bigger one. Before selling, Hoffman told the Red Owl representatives that he had $18,000 for "getting set up in business" and they assured him that there would be no problems in establishing him in a bigger operation. The makeup of the $18,000 was not discussed; it was understood plaintiff's father-in-law would furnish part of it. By June, 1961, the towns for the new grocery store had been narrowed down to two, Kewaunee and Chilton. In Kewaunee, Red Owl had an option on a building site. In Chilton, Red Owl had nothing under option, but it did select a site to which plaintiff obtained an option at Red Owl's suggestion. The option stipulated a purchase price of $6,000 with $1,000 to be paid on election to purchase and the balance to be paid within 30 days. On Lukowitz's assurance that everything was all set plaintiff paid $1,000 down on the lot on September 15th.

On September 27, 1961, plaintiff met at Chilton with Lukowitz and Mr. Reymund and Mr. Carlson from the home office who prepared a projected financial statement. Part of the funds plaintiffs were to supply as their investment in the venture were to be obtained by sale of their Wautoma bakery building.

On the basis of this meeting Lukowitz assured Hoffman: "* * * [E]verything is ready to go. Get your money together and we are set." Shortly after this meeting Lukowitz told plaintiffs that they would have to sell their bakery business and bakery building, and that their retaining this property was the only "hitch" in the entire plan. On November 6, 1961, plaintiffs sold their bakery building for $10,000. Hoffman was to retain the bakery equipment as he contemplated using it to operate a bakery in connection with his Red Owl store. After sale of the bakery Hoffman obtained employment on the night shift at an Appleton bakery.

The record contains different exhibits which were prepared in September and October, some of which were projections of the fiscal operation of the business and others were proposed building and floor plans. Red Owl was to procure some third party to buy the Chilton lot from Hoffman, construct the building, and then lease it to Hoffman. No final plans were ever made, nor were bids let or a construction contract entered. Some time prior to November 20, 1961, certain of the terms of the lease under which the building was to be rented by Hoffman were understood between him and Lukowitz. The lease was to be for 10 years with a rental approximating $550 a month calculated on the basis of 1 percent per month on the building cost, plus 6 percent of the land cost divided on a monthly basis. At the end of the 10-year term he was to have an option to renew the lease for an additional 10-year period or to buy the property at cost on an instalment basis. There was no discussion as to what the instalments would be or with respect to repairs and maintenance.

On November 22nd or 23rd, Lukowitz and plaintiffs met in Minneapolis with Red Owl's credit manager to confer on Hoffman's financial standing and on financing the agency. Another projected financial statement was there drawn up entitled, "Proposed Financing For An Agency Store." This showed Hoffman contributing $24,100 of cash capital of which only $4,600 was to be cash possessed by plaintiffs. Eight thousand was to be procured as a loan from a Chilton bank secured by a mortgage on the bakery fixtures, $7,500 was to be obtained on a 5 percent loan from the father-in-law, and $4,000 was to be obtained by sale of the lot to the lessor at a profit.

A week or two after the Minneapolis meeting Lukowitz showed Hoffman a telegram from the home office to the effect that if plaintiff could get another $2,000 for promotional purposes the deal could go through for $26,000. Hoffman stated he would have to find out if he could get another $2,000. He met with his father-in-law, who agreed to put $13,000 into the business provided he could come into the business as a partner. Lukowitz told Hoffman the partnership arrangement "sounds fine" and that Hoffman should not go into the partnership arrangement with the "front office." On January 16, 1962, the Red Owl credit manager teletyped Lukowitz that the father-in-law would have to sign an agreement that the $13,000 was either a gift or a loan subordinate to all general creditors and that he would prepare the agreement. On January 31, 1962, Lukowitz teletyped the home office that the father-in-law would sign one or other of the agreements. However, Hoffman testified that it was not until the final meeting some time between January 26th and February 2nd, 1962, that he was told that his father-in-law was expected to sign an agreement that the $13,000 he was advancing was to be an outright gift. No mention was then made by the Red Owl representatives of the alternative of the father-in-law signing a subordination agreement. At this meeting the Red Owl agents presented Hoffman with the following projected financial statement:

"Capital required in operation:		
"Cash	$ 5,000.00	
"Merchandise	$20,000.00	
"Bakery	$18,000.00	
"Fixtures	$17,500.00	
"Promotional Funds	$1,500.00	
	"TOTAL:	$62,000.00
"Source of funds:		
"Red Owl 7-day terms	$ 5,000.00	
"Red Owl Fixture contract (Term 5 years)	$14,000.00	
"Bank loans (Term 9 years) Union State Bank of Chilton (Secured by Bakery Equipment)	$8,000.00	
"Other loans (Term No-pay) No interest Father-in-law (Secured by None)	$13,000.00	

(Secured by Mortgage on Wautoma Bakery Bldg.)		$2,000.00		
"Resale of land		$6,000.00		
"Equity Capital:	$5,000 Cash			
"Amount owner has $17,500 to invest:	Bakery Equip.	$22,500.00		
			"TOTAL:	$70,500.00

Hoffman interpreted the above statement to require of plaintiffs a total of $34,000 cash made up of $13,000 gift from his father-in-law, $2,000 on mortgage, $8,000 on Chilton bank loan, $5,000 in cash from plaintiff, and $6,000 on the resale of the Chilton lot. Red Owl claims $18,000 is the total of the unborrowed or unencumbered cash, that is, $13,000 from the father-in-law and $5,000 cash from Hoffman himself. Hoffman informed Red Owl he could not go along with this proposal, and particularly objected to the requirement that his father-in-law sign an agreement that his $13,000 advancement was an absolute gift. This terminated the negotiations between the parties.

The case was submitted to the jury on a special verdict with the first two questions answered by the court. This verdict, as returned by the jury, was as follows:

> "Question No. 1: Did the Red Owl Stores, Inc. and Joseph Hoffman on or about mid-May of 1961 initiate negotiations looking to the establishment of Joseph Hoffman as a franchise operator of a Red Owl Store in Chilton? Answer: Yes. (Answered by the Court.)
>
> "Question No. 2: Did the parties mutually agree on all of the details of the proposal so as to reach a final agreement thereon? Answer: No. (Answered by the Court.)
>
> "Question No. 3: Did the Red Owl Stores, Inc., in the course of said negotiations, make representations to Joseph Hoffman that if he fulfilled certain conditions that they would establish him as a franchise operator of a Red Owl Store in Chilton? Answer: Yes.
>
> "Question No. 4: If you have answered Question No. 3 'Yes,' then answer this question: Did Joseph Hoffman rely on said representations and was he induced to act thereon? Answer: Yes.
>
> "Question No. 5: If you have answered Question No. 4 'Yes,' then answer this question: Ought Joseph Hoffman, in the exercise

of ordinary care, to have relied on said representations? Answer: Yes.

"Question No. 6: If you have answered Question No. 3 'Yes' then answer this question: Did Joseph Hoffman fulfill all the conditions he was required to fulfill by the terms of the negotiations between the parties up to January 26, 1962? Answer: Yes.

"Question No. 7: What sum of money will reasonably compensate the plaintiffs for such damages as they sustained by reason of:

"(a) The sale of the Wautoma store fixtures and inventory?

"Answer: $16,735.00.

"(b) The sale of the bakery building?

"Answer: $2,000.00.

"(c) Taking up the option on the Chilton lot?

"Answer: $1,000.00.

"(d) Expenses of moving his family to Neenah?

"Answer: $140.00.

"(e) House rental in Chilton?

"Answer: $125.00."

Plaintiffs moved for judgment on the verdict while defendants moved to change the answers to Questions 3, 4, 5, and 6 from "Yes" to "No", and in the alternative for relief from the answers to the subdivisions of Question 7 or a new trial. On March 31, 1964, the circuit court entered the following order:

"IT IS ORDERED in accordance with said decision on motions after verdict hereby incorporated herein by reference:

"1. That the answer of the jury to Question No. 7(a) be and the same is hereby vacated and set aside and that a new trial be had on the sole issue of the damages for loss, if any, on the sale of the Wautoma store, fixtures and inventory.

"2. That all other portions of the verdict of the jury be and hereby are approved and confirmed and all after-verdict motions of the parties inconsistent with this order are hereby denied."

Defendants have appealed from this order and plaintiffs have cross-appealed from paragraph 1, thereof.

* * *

CURRIE, CHIEF JUSTICE.

The instant appeal and cross-appeal present these questions:

(1) Whether this court should recognize causes of action grounded on promissory estoppel as exemplified by sec. 90 of Restatement, 1 Contracts?

(2) Do the facts in this case make out a cause of action for promissory estoppel?

(3) Are the jury's findings with respect to damages sustained by the evidence?

Recognition of a Cause of Action Grounded on Promissory Estoppel.

* * *

* * * Not only did the trial court frame the special verdict on the theory of sec. 90 of Restatement, 1 Contracts, but no other possible theory has been presented to or discovered by this court which would permit plaintiffs to recover. Of other remedies considered that of an action for fraud and deceit seemed to be the most comparable. An action at law for fraud, however, cannot be predicated on unfulfilled promises unless the promisor possessed the present intent not to perform. Suskey v. Davidoff (1958), 2 Wis.2d 503, 507, 87 N.W.2d 306, and cases cited. Here, there is no evidence that would support a finding that Lukowitz made any of the promises, upon which plaintiffs' complaint is predicated, in bad faith with any present intent that they would not be fulfilled by Red Owl.

Many courts of other jurisdictions have seen fit over the years to adopt the principle of promissory estoppel, and the tendency in that direction continues. * * *

* * *

Because we deem the doctrine of promissory estoppel, as stated in sec. 90 of Restatement, 1 Contracts, is one which supplies a needed tool which courts may employ in a proper case to prevent injustice, we endorse and adopt it.

Applicability of Doctrine to Facts of this Case.

The record here discloses a number of promises and assurances given to Hoffman by Lukowitz in behalf of Red Owl upon which plaintiffs relied and acted upon to their detriment.

Foremost were the promises that for the sum of $18,000 Red Owl would establish Hoffman in a store. After Hoffman had sold his grocery store and paid the $1,000 on the Chilton lot, the $18,000 figure was changed to $24,100. Then in November, 1961, Hoffman was assured that if the $24,100 figure were increased by $2,000 the deal would go through. Hoffman was induced to sell his grocery store fixtures and inventory in June, 1961, on the promise that he would be in his new store by fall. In

November, plaintiffs sold their bakery building on the urging of defendants and on the assurance that this was the last step necessary to have the deal with Red Owl go through.

We determine that there was ample evidence to sustain the answers of the jury to the questions of the verdict with respect to the promissory representations made by Red Owl, Hoffman's reliance thereon in the exercise of ordinary care, and his fulfillment of the conditions required of him by the terms of the negotiations had with Red Owl.

There remains for consideration the question of law raised by defendants that agreement was never reached on essential factors necessary to establish a contract between Hoffman and Red Owl. Among these were the size, cost, design, and layout of the store building; and the terms of the lease with respect to rent, maintenance, renewal, and purchase options. This poses the question of whether the promise necessary to sustain a cause of action for promissory estoppel must embrace all essential details of a proposed transaction between promisor and promisee so as to be the equivalent of an offer that would result in a binding contract between the parties if the promisee were to accept the same.

Originally the doctrine of promissory estoppel was invoked as a substitute for consideration rendering a gratuitous promise enforceable as a contract. See Williston, Contracts (1st ed.), p. 307, sec. 139. In other words, the acts of reliance by the promisee to his detriment provided a substitute for consideration. If promissory estoppel were to be limited to only those situations where the promise giving rise to the cause of action must be so definite with respect to all details that a contract would result were the promise supported by consideration, then the defendants' instant promises to Hoffman would not meet this test. However, sec. 90 of Restatement, 1 Contracts, does not impose the requirement that the promise giving rise to the cause of action must be so comprehensive in scope as to meet the requirements of an offer that would ripen into a contract if accepted by the promisee. Rather the conditions imposed are:

(1) Was the promise one which the promisor should reasonably expect to induce action or forbearance of a definite and substantial character on the part of the promisee?

(2) Did the promise induce such action or forbearance?

(3) Can injustice be avoided only by enforcement of the promise?

We deem it would be a mistake to regard an action grounded on promissory estoppel as the equivalent of a breach of contract action. As Dean Boyer points out, it is desirable that fluidity in the application of the concept be maintained. 98 University of Pennsylvania Law Review (1950), 459, at page 497. While the first two of the above listed three requirements of promissory estoppel present issues of fact which ordinarily will be resolved by a jury, the third requirement, that the remedy can only be invoked where necessary to avoid injustice, is one that involves a policy decision by the court. Such a policy decision necessarily embraces an element of discretion.

We conclude that injustice would result here if plaintiffs were not granted some relief because of the failure of defendants to keep their promises which induced plaintiffs to act to their detriment.

HENDERSON, PROMISSORY ESTOPPEL AND TRADITIONAL CONTRACT DOCTRINE

78 Yale L.J. 343, 358–60 (1969).

Because the doctrine of promissory estoppel imposes liability without regard to expressed intention, its use in pre-agreement negotiations is bound to alter the traditional scheme of offer and acceptance. This is particularly so where, after lengthy and expensive negotiations, no agreement is in fact reached. * * *

* * * The parties in *Hoffman* dealt with each other with the intent of effecting a business exchange without reaching agreement on a contract. In fact, the failure to reach agreement upon essential terms prevented defendant's promises from achieving even the level of an operative offer. * * *

* * * The key to the court's opinion is its apparent belief that the conventional use of promissory estoppel as a "substitute for consideration" in connection with gratuitous promises is now obsolete and that section 90 should serve as a distinct basis of liability without regard to * * * bargain, contract, or consideration. * * *

* * * [T]he use of the doctrine in pre-agreement bargaining is inconsistent with a line of authority * * * [that] maintains that pre-agreement discussions and negotiations can at most constitute an agreement to agree, which is not generally enforceable. * * * With respect to the allocation of the risks of reliance inherent in business negotiations, it would appear that the practical differences between a clearly expressed offer and a promise which contemplates the settling of other matters ought to be taken into account. The original judgment that Section 90 was not to apply to bargains was undoubtedly influenced by doubts about the reasonableness, in bargain situations, of reliance that takes unbargained-for forms. Those same doubts are relevant to the negotiation stages of bargain.

WHITFORD & MACAULAY, HOFFMAN V. RED OWL STORES: THE REST OF THE STORY

61 Hastings L.J. 801, 854–57 (2010).

It is common to interpret a precedent as though the facts of the case are those stated in the opinion. From that perspective, the case stands for enforcement of the "promise" that Hoffman would get a franchise for an investment of $18,000. Scott has referred to *Hoffman* as an unfortunate case that, because of the attention that it has received, has retarded thinking about the precise limits of a rule allowing recovery for precontractual reliance. We agree that because the Court does not explain why Lukowitz' statements about the $18,000 should be considered a promise rather than a mere opinion or enthusiastic encouragement, the opinion does not help explain the limits on precontractual reliance.

In historical context, however, the *Hoffman* case is best known as the leading early American case to allow recovery for precontractual reliance, in a case where the parties clearly contemplated at all relevant times later negotiations and agreement. Though still controversial, a considerable majority of commentators now support a legal remedy for precontractual reliance in some circumstances. It is now widely recognized that when in precontractual bargaining only one party detrimentally relies, the other party is immediately in a stronger bargaining position. The relying party now has an investment it wants to protect, while the other party can walk away from the deal without loss. For reasons of both efficiency and fairness, scholars who advocate various positions are now willing to accept, at least in some circumstances, recovery of reliance loss caused by a failed negotiation. Most are comfortable with such a recovery where the reliance was at the defendant's urging or was a foreseeable and desired response to a strong assurance that a deal would be reached. The efficiency concern is that without some legal protection, the relying party will be reluctant to make a precontractual investment that will likely benefit the parties' prospective project. The fairness concern is that because of its stronger bargaining position, the non-relying party may be able in later negotiations to secure an undue share of the joint benefits from the deal.

* * * *Hoffman v. Red Owl Stores* provides a mainstream example of precontractual liability under any of these rationales. Hoffman relied on Red Owl's assurances in order to benefit the franchise project. He sold the bakery business and the building in order to get his money together and position himself to work on establishing the Chilton store as soon as possible. He was reluctant to do this because he knew that Red Owl had not yet signed a formal franchise contract. Yet he trusted Lukowitz' statement about the position of the home office—sale of the bakery was "the only hitch." Hoffman probably did not think about his legal rights at this point, but he thought that he had a firm commitment from Red Owl. When the deal fell apart, he told the Red Owl representatives that he was

considering seeing a lawyer. Further, once the Hoffmans sold their bakery business, their bargaining position was compromised because they had only less attractive alternatives if the deal collapsed. Red Owl responded by demanding ever increasing investments from Hoffman. If he had made these investments, they would have reduced Red Owl's risks in the joint enterprise.

NOTE:
JOSEPH HOFFMAN'S OBITUARY

Joseph Hoffman died on October 6, 2019. His obituary in Obit Tree, available at https://obittree.com/obituary/us/michigan/st-joseph/starks-family-funeral-homes/joseph-hoffmann/3986611/index.php includes the following passage: "One of the accomplishments he was most proud of was the court case of Hoffman v. Red Owl, where he was the David that slew Goliath, which established the Doctrine[ ] of Promissory Estoppel and Detrimental Reliance. This court case has benefited small businesses everywhere." (The actual spelling of Joseph's last name was Hoffmann. Apparently the case spelling was in error and the secondary sources followed the case spelling.)

ELVIN ASSOCIATES v. FRANKLIN, 735 F. Supp. 1177 (S.D.N.Y. 1990). [A Broadway musical producer, Springer, sought to hire Aretha Franklin for the title role in a musical about Mahalia Jackson. Franklin "expressed her strong interest" and the parties negotiated for several months, working out most details but never executing a final agreement. During negotiations, Springer incurred substantial expenses making arrangements for the production based on Franklin's assurances that the producer's "final proposal" was acceptable and that she would perform. Springer also learned that Franklin had recently canceled several obligations because of a newly developed fear of flying. Franklin never appeared for rehearsals and Springer sued.]

WHITMAN KNAPP, DISTRICT JUDGE.

The central issue pertaining to plaintiff's claim for breach of contract is whether or not the parties to that proposed contract * * * evinced an intent not to be formally bound before execution of a written, integrated contract. Language inserted in a draft of the agreement referring to its validity upon execution has generally been found to be strong (though not conclusive) evidence of intent *not* to be bound prior to execution. * * * Although we based our tentative findings largely on the fact that all of the incidental terms had been worked out by the final draft, and that the understanding was that Franklin would sign the agreement when she came to New York, there remains the obstacle of the preamble that Kramer, [Springer's lawyer], drafted and that remained in every draft, namely: "This letter, when countersigned by you, shall constitute our understanding until a more formal agreement is prepared." After reviewing the above cited authorities and the post-trial submissions, we are constrained to find that such language indicates that [Franklin] was not to be contractually bound to Springer until the draft agreement was executed. * * * The cause of action for breach of contract must therefore be dismissed. * * *

That, however, does not end the case. As above noted, plaintiff has asserted, in the alternative, a right to recover on a theory of promissory estoppel. * * *

It is difficult to imagine a more fitting case for applying the doctrine. * * * We find that Franklin had unequivocally and intentionally committed herself to appear in the production long before the day on which it was intended that the finalized agreement with her corporation would be signed.

First, it is clear from the testimony of all of the witnesses that Franklin was enthusiastic about appearing in the production and that at all times during the relevant period gave it the highest professional priority. She early on stated to Springer: "This is what I am doing." Combined with her oral agreement, through her agents, to the basic financial terms of her engagement, her continued expression of this enthusiasm to Springer more than amply afforded Springer a reasonable basis for beginning to make the various arrangements and expenditures necessary to bring the production to fruition.

Second, Franklin could not possibly have assumed that Springer could have performed his obligations to her—which, among other things, included arranging a complicated schedule of performances to commence shortly after her arrival in New York—without committing himself to and actually spending considerable sums prior to her affixing her signature to the contract on the date of such arrival. Throughout the time that he was making those commitments and advancing the necessary sums, she accepted his performance without any disclaimer of her prior promises to him. Indeed, she actively participated in many aspects of the necessary arrangements.

Third, Franklin's expression to Springer of her fear of flying did not, as she has contended, make her promise conditional or coat it with a patina of ambiguity that should have alerted Springer to suspend his efforts to mount the production. Although Franklin rejected Springer's offer to make alternative ground transportation arrangements, her primary reason for doing so was that she was determined to overcome her fear of flying, and it was reasonable for Springer to rely on her reassurances that she would be able to fly. Moreover, it was also entirely reasonable for him to assume that if she could not overcome her fear she would travel to New York by other means, even if it meant spreading the trip over several days. In short,

Franklin's fear of flying provides no basis whatsoever for avoiding liability for failing to fulfill her promise, reiterated on several occasions, to appear in "Mahalia." If she could not bring herself to fly, she should have traveled by way of ground transportation. It has not been established that she was otherwise unable to come to New York to meet her obligations.

We conclude that under the circumstances as we have outlined them it would be unconscionable not to compensate Springer for the losses he incurred through his entirely justified reliance on Franklin's oral promises. A determination of the exact amount to be awarded has been reserved for a later trial on damages.

R. HILLMAN, PRINCIPLES OF CONTRACT LAW

106 (4th ed. 2019).

Here's an example of a weak promissory estoppel claim that went nowhere. Landowner, a real estate developer, and Wal-Mart negotiated for the lease of real property to Wal-Mart to build a store. The parties signed a "Letter of Intent," which stated in part: "This lease proposal is intended only as an outline of the major provisions of a proposed lease, * * * and as such, whether or not countersigned, is non-binding. Neither party shall have any obligation to the other with respect to this proposal * * * until a mutually acceptable lease agreement is fully executed and delivered by both parties." If that wasn't enough, the letter of intent added that "[t]he provisions of this proposal are subject to withdrawal and modification by either party at any time for any reason." Although the parties produced several draft leases, they never agreed to or signed a "mutually acceptable lease agreement." The deal fell through, but not before the landowner allegedly expended "millions of dollars," including purchasing additional acreage to accommodate Wal-Mart's need for a larger parcel. The landowner claimed that it had relied on the oral statements of Wal-Mart's agents, including that "the deal was important to Wal-Mart Stores to obtain affirmative action goals," that it was "critical that the deal be completed" and that a "closing would occur in a few weeks."

The court first dismissed the landowner's breach of contract claim, calling the letter of intent an unenforceable agreement to agree and noting that the alleged subsequent promises were unenforceable under the Statute of Frauds. However, the landowner also pursued a promissory estoppel claim. The court granted summary judgment to Wal-Mart on this claim, reasoning in part that landowner's reliance was unreasonable in light of the express language of the letter of intent, which distinguishes the case from *Hoffman*, where there was no written preliminary agreement. The vagueness and indefiniteness of the alleged promises also motivated the court, which found that the promises actually amounted only to expressions of future intentions. [Landan v. Wal-Mart Real Estate Bus. Trust, 2016 WL 5253329 (W.D. Pa. 2016.)]

NOTE:
ANOTHER POP STAR'S EXPERIENCE WITH PROMISSORY ESTOPPEL

The *Cochran* case (above) cites Alden v. Presley, 637 S.W.2d 862 (Tenn. 1982). The facts of Alden are colorful. Before his death, Elvis Presley (the "King") promised his fiancé's mother, Jo Laverne Alden, that he would, among other things, pay off the mortgage on her home. In reliance on this promise, Alden filed for divorce from her husband and, in a proposed property settlement, agreed to release her husband from further liability on the mortgage. After the King's untimely death, his estate refused to pay off the mortgage. Subsequently, the divorce court dismissed Alden's divorce action for lack of prosecution but, after she refiled, the divorce court granted Alden a divorce and approved the initial property settlement. Was the King's estate liable to Alden on the ground of promissory estoppel, as Alden claimed? The court hearing that claim held that the King's estate was not liable because Alden had pursued the divorce settlement, including her husband's release on the mortgage, in her second divorce action. By this time, Alden had been notified that the King's estate would not pay off the mortgage. Therefore Alden had not detrimentally relied on the King's promise.

ALFRED V. WALT DISNEY CO., 2015 Del. Ch. Lexis 12. This matter is before me on the Defendants' motions to dismiss a complaint sounding in contract, filed by the Plaintiff, Mr. Alfred, *pro se*. That Complaint is remarkable. It is in my experience a unique example of the pleader's art. It cites to the epic of Gilgamesh, Woody Guthrie, the Declaration of Independence, Noah and The Great Flood, *Game of Thrones*, *Star Wars Episode V: The Empire Strikes Back*, *Star Trek*, President Obama, and Euclid's proof of the Infinity of Primes, among other references. * * * If the Plaintiff needed to sum up this entire case in one sentence, it is this: "Two executives of the Disney Company are stalling the next evolution of human transportation on this planet."

Non-party Terrafugia, Inc. ("TI") is an enterprise that the Plaintiff believes capable of producing a vertical take-off and landing vehicle, which vehicle the user could program for flight to a given destination and which would then be remotely operated by the FAA. * * * In the Plaintiff's conception, this vehicle would be built to resemble the X-wing, which would promote its acceptance by the public. Plaintiff has developed a marketing plan, pursuant to which Disney would license TI the right to use the X-wing name and appearance, TI would develop the previously described short takeoff and landing programmable remotely controlled vehicle in the appearance of an X-wing (the "Flying Car"), and the Plaintiff would raise the necessary funds for development of the Flying Car through internet pledges of $10,000, each entitling the investor to a ride in the Flying Car.

Crucial to the Plaintiff's promotional idea would be the support of Disney, with its extensive existing connections, through its ownership of the *Star Wars* franchise and otherwise, to flying cars. * * * Implied in the Complaint is that the Plaintiff made an unsolicited proposal involving *Star Wars* marketing to Disney. He was then contacted by someone at Disney to arrange a conference call scheduled for July 22, 2014. In anticipation of this call, the Plaintiff sent Disney a slide deck laying out the proposal described above. On July 22, the conference call took place. * * * [O]n July 29, 2014, [an] executive assistant, a Disney paralegal, or a "nameless Disney attorney" called or emailed the Plaintiff and stated that Disney was not interested in his proposal. * * *

The "promise" that plaintiff points to is Disney's willingness to hear his proposal. In reliance on that willingness, the plaintiff sent Disney a slide deck to describe the promotion and licensing that he wanted from Disney. If Disney's promise was to give the plaintiff's ideas an airing, despite its prior policy not to consider unsolicited proposals, they complied with that promise. The promise to hear a proposal out, however, cannot be reasonably relied upon as a promise to consummate a contract. There is simply no basis for the imposition of relief under a rubric of promissory estoppel.

LOCAL 1330, UNITED STEEL WORKERS v. UNITED STATES STEEL CORP.

United States Court of Appeals, Sixth Circuit, 1980.
631 F.2d 1264.

EDWARDS, CHIEF JUDGE.

This appeal represents a cry for help from steelworkers and townspeople in the City of Youngstown, Ohio who are distressed by the prospective impact upon their lives and their city of the closing of two large steel mills. These two mills were built and have been operated by the United States Steel Corporation since the turn of the century. The Ohio Works began producing in 1901; the McDonald Works in 1918. The District Court which heard this cause of action found that as of the notice of closing, the two plants employed 3,500 employees.

The leading plaintiffs are two labor organizations, locals 1330 and 1307 of the United Steel Workers of America. This union has had a collective bargaining contract with the United States Steel Corporation for many years. These local unions represent production and maintenance employees at the Ohio and McDonald Works respectively.

In the background of this litigation is the obsolescence of the two plants concerned, occasioned both by the age of the facilities and machinery involved and by the changes in technology and marketing in steelmaking in the years intervening since the early nineteen hundreds.

For all of the years United States Steel has been operating in Youngstown, it has been a dominant factor in the lives of its thousands of employees and their families, and in the life of the city itself. The contemplated abrupt departure of United States Steel from Youngstown will, of course, have direct impact on 3,500 workers and their families. It will doubtless mean a devastating blow to them, to the business community and to the City of Youngstown itself. While we cannot read the future of Youngstown from this record, what the record does indicate clearly is that we deal with an economic tragedy of major proportion to Youngstown and Ohio's Mahoning Valley. As the District Judge who heard this case put the matter:

> Everything that has happened in the Mahoning Valley has been happening for many years because of steel. Schools have been built, roads have been built. Expansion that has taken place is because of steel. And to accommodate that industry, lives and destinies of the inhabitants of that community were based and planned on the basis of that institution: Steel.

In the face of this tragedy, the steel worker local unions, the Congressman from this district, and the Attorney General of Ohio have sued United States Steel Corporation, asking the federal courts to order the United States Steel Corporation to keep the two plants at issue in operation. * * *

Defendant United States Steel Corporation answered plaintiffs complaints, claiming that the plants were unprofitable and could not be made otherwise due to obsolescence and change in technology, markets, and transportation. The company also asserts an absolute right to make a business decision to discharge its former employees and abandon Youngstown. It states that there is no law in either the State of Ohio or the United States of America which provides either legal or equitable remedy for plaintiffs.

The District Judge, after originally restraining the corporation from ceasing operations as it had announced it would, and after advancing the case for prompt hearing, entered a formal opinion holding that the plants had become unprofitable and denying all relief. We believe the dispositive paragraphs of a lengthy opinion entered by the District Judge are the following:

> This Court has spent many hours searching for a way to cut to the heart of the economic reality—that obsolescence and market forces demand the close of the Mahoning Valley plants, and yet

> the lives of 3500 workers and their families and the supporting Youngstown community cannot be dismissed as inconsequential. United States Steel should not be permitted to leave the Youngstown area devastated after drawing from the lifeblood of the community for so many years.
>
> Unfortunately, the mechanism to reach this ideal settlement, to recognize this new property right, is not now in existence in the code of laws of our nation.
>
> * * *
>
> This Court is mindful of the efforts taken by the workers to increase productivity, and has applauded these efforts in the preceding paragraphs. In view of the fact, however, that this Court has found that no contract or enforceable promise was entered into by the company and that, additionally, there is clear evidence to support the company's decision that the plants were not profitable, the various acts of forebearance taken by the plaintiffs do not give them the basis for relief against defendant.

Plaintiffs-appellants claim that certain of the District Judge's findings of fact are clearly erroneous [and] that he has misconstrued federal and state contract law. * * *

* * *

The primary issue in this case is a claim on the part of the steel worker plaintiffs that United States Steel made proposals to the plaintiffs and/or the membership of the plaintiffs to the general effect that if the workers at the two steel plants concerned put forth their best efforts in terms of productivity and thereby rendered the two plants "profitable," the plants would then not be closed. It is clear that this claimed contract does not rest upon any formal written document, either authorized or signed by the parties to this lawsuit.

* * *

Thus, appellants' contract claim depends essentially upon oral statements and newspaper releases concerning the efforts of the company to secure increased productivity by enlisting the help of the workers of the plant and upon the employee responses thereto. The representations as set forth in the steelworkers' complaint include many oral statements made over the "hotline" employed by management in the plants[1] to advise U.S. Steel employees of company policy. They began in the Fall of 1977 in the midst of much public speculation that the Ohio and McDonald works at Youngstown were to be closed. In general they follow the very first

[1] Telephones were placed strategically in these plants so that employees could hear prerecorded management policy statements.

statement made by William Ashton, then superintendent of Youngstown works of U.S. Steel, on September 1, 1977, which said:

> In response to many rumors, I want to tell you that there are no immediate plans to permanently shut down either the Ohio Works or McDonald Mills.
>
> However, steps will have to be taken to improve these plants' profitability. These steps, which have been and are currently under study, will require the suspension and consolidation of some operations in the months ahead.
>
> Ohio Works and McDonald Mills are faced with very serious profit problems caused by a combination of heavy imports of foreign steel, higher energy costs, higher taxes and, of course, environmental expenditures.
>
> The continued operation of these plants is absolutely dependent upon their being profit-makers.
>
> In the months ahead, we will be calling for the full support of each and every one of you. Your cooperation and assistance is absolutely necessary if our facilities are to continue to operate.

Many similar statements were made by the company and were responded to by the employees. As 1977 and 1978 went by, there began to be statements over similar facilities and sometimes by company press releases indicating improvement in productivity at the two Youngstown facilities. Some of these included reference to "a complete turnaround" and reference to the Youngstown plants as "profitable" and once again viable.

* * *

As we read this lengthy record, and as the District Judge read it, it does not contain any factual dispute over the allegations as to company statements or the responsive actions of steelworkers in relation thereto. It is beyond argument that the local management of U.S. Steel's Youngstown plants engaged in a major campaign to enlist employee participation in an all-out effort to make these two plants profitable in order to prevent their being closed. It is equally obvious that the employees responded wholeheartedly.

The District Judge, however, rejected the promissory estoppel contract theory on three grounds. The first ground was that none of the statements made by officers and employees of the company constituted a definite promise to continue operation of the plants if they did become profitable. The second ground was that the statements relied upon by plaintiffs were made by employees and public relations officers of the company and not by company officers. The third ground was a finding of fact that "The condition precedent of the alleged contract and promise—profitability of the

Youngstown facilities—was never fulfilled, and the actions in contract and for detrimental reliance cannot be found for plaintiffs."

The District Judge's fundamental disposition of plaintiffs-appellants' contract claims is stated in this finding of fact:

> [T]here is clear evidence to support the company's decision that the plants were not profitable, the various acts of forebearance taken by the plaintiffs do not give them the basis for relief against defendant.

Our examination of this record offers no ground for our holding that this finding of fact is "clearly erroneous." *See* Fed.R.Civ.P. 52(a).

* * *

We believe that this record demonstrates without significant dispute that the profitability issue in the case depends in large part upon definition. The plaintiffs wish to employ the direct costs of operating the two plants, compared to the total selling price of their products. The difference, they contend, is "profit." This formula would eliminate such charges as corporate purchasing and sales expense allocable to the Youngstown plants, and allocable corporate management expenses including, but not limited to marketing, engineering, auditing, accounting, advertising. Obviously, any multiplant corporation could quickly go bankrupt if such a definition of profit was employed generally and over any period of time.

Plaintiffs-appellants point out, however, that this version of Youngstown profitability was employed by the Youngstown management in setting a goal for its employees and in statements which described achieving that goal. The standard of Restatement (Second) of Contracts 90, upon which plaintiffs-appellants rely, however, is one of reasonable expectability of the "promise" detrimentally relied upon. The District Judge did not find, nor can we, that reliance upon a promise to keep these plants open on the basis of coverage of plant fixed costs was within reasonable expectability. We cannot hold that the District Judge erred legally or was "clearly erroneous" in his fact finding when he held that the "promise" to keep the plants open had to be read in the context of normal corporate profit accounting and that profitability had not been achieved.

[After affirming the district judge's dismissal of the promissory estoppel claim, the court considered and rejected plaintiffs' theory that their long-term relationship with U.S. Steel established a "property right" in the plaintiffs. The court found no authority for such a theory and stated that only the legislature could deal with the problem. The court remanded the case for further proceedings, however, on the basis of an antitrust claim that U.S. Steel refused to sell the two mills to the plaintiffs, thereby eliminating a potential competitor.]

29 U.S.C. § 2102 (2020).

Notice required before plant closings and mass layoffs

(a) Notice to employees, State dislocated worker units, and local governments

An employer shall not order a plant closing or mass layoff until the end of a 60-day period after the employer serves written notice of such an order—

(1) to each representative of the affected employees as of the time of the notice or, if there is no such representative at that time, to each affected employee; * * *

(b) Reduction of notification period

(1) An employer may order the shutdown of a single site of employment before the conclusion of the 60-day period if as of the time that notice would have been required the employer was actively seeking capital or business which, if obtained, would have enabled the employer to avoid or postpone the shutdown and the employer reasonably and in good faith believed that giving the notice required would have precluded the employer from obtaining the needed capital or business.

(2)(A) An employer may order a plant closing or mass layoff before the conclusion of the 60-day period if the closing or mass layoff is caused by business circumstances that were not reasonably foreseeable as of the time that notice would have been required.

(B) No notice under this chapter shall be required if the plant closing or mass layoff is due to any form of natural disaster, such as a flood, earthquake, or the drought currently ravaging the farmlands of the United States.

(3) An employer relying on this subsection shall give as much notice as is practicable and at that time shall give a brief statement of the basis for reducing the notification period.

HILLMAN, QUESTIONING THE "NEW CONSENSUS" ON PROMISSORY ESTOPPEL: AN EMPIRICAL AND THEORETICAL STUDY

98 Colum. L. Rev. 580, 580–81, 590, 596 (1998).

The purpose of this Article is to present evidence of a fundamental misunderstanding of how courts apply the theory of obligation called promissory estoppel. Contrary to the accepted wisdom, the data and analysis presented here (1) demonstrate that the theory seldom leads to victory in reported decisions, (2) underscore the immense importance of reliance as a substantive element of the theory, and (3) suggest the willingness of courts to grant reliance damages to successful litigants.

The first point, the lack of success of the theory in the courts, contradicts theorists who predicted that promissory estoppel would "swallow up" the bargain theory of contract and become the dominant promissory theory of obligation. Although some writers have questioned the prediction, this Article is the first comprehensive empirical study that demonstrates promissory estoppel's limited role.

* * *

I decided to examine all of the reported decisions in the United States in which a promissory estoppel claim succeeded or failed or in which promissory estoppel was discussed from July 1, 1994 through June 30, 1996. * * * [T]he data demonstrate the remarkable lack of success of promissory estoppel claims in the reported decisions.

* * *

* * * [T]he most accurate measure of success and failure may be gained by comparing success and failure rates on the merits. * * * [O]nly 9.70% of promissory estoppel claims that reached a decision on the merits of the claim were successful.

* * *

The lingering question is, of course, why is promissory estoppel not faring well in the courts? * * * One possible explanation for the low win rate is that parties miscomprehended the nature of promissory estoppel. Although the theory of promissory estoppel still receives wide publicity as a principal basis for promise enforcement, the rhetoric may no longer reflect the reality of judicial attitudes toward the theory. Parties in the mid-1990s simply may not have comprehended a judicial souring on the theory, which is consistent with courts' recent reluctance to intervene in the contracting process on other grounds. Such parties might therefore fail to settle what they should have predicted as likely wins for defendants (but did not).

Another possible explanation for the low win rate is that claimants are bringing weak promissory estoppel claims and not making an effort to settle them. Claimants may bring promissory estoppel claims only as subsidiary theories tacked on to a contract or other claim, sometimes even as an afterthought. The abstract call for "justice" in the second Restatement's definition of promissory estoppel may add to the allure of "throwing in" the claim. Evidence supporting this explanation comes from examining the tenuous nature of many of the claims in the multitude of cases in which promissory estoppel failed.

PROBLEM 2-7

The ABA Journal eReport reported that in the summer of 2005 an associate in a major New York City law firm, whom we shall call Ira, sued the firm for $100 million for breaking a promise to "put him up for partnership." Ira claimed that his evaluations from the firm were excellent, that a partner told him he had "a great future" with the firm, and that several partners promised to "put him up for consideration in a year." Further, they assured Ira that the partnership process was a "rubber stamp, so long as his name was put up." Finally, Ira explained that, at the time of these assurances, the partners thought they might lose certain clients if Ira left the firm. Ira sent an e-mail to the managing partner and other partners outlining his understanding about his candidacy for partnership based on the above facts, which the partnership confirmed. According to Ira, the law firm then reneged on considering him for partnership. The law firm denied these allegations and stated it would "vigorously defend the case."

Assume the facts alleged by Ira are correct. Does he have a claim based on agreement with consideration? Based on promissory estoppel?

NOTE:
EQUITABLE ESTOPPEL STILL IMPORTANT TODAY

Recall that equitable estoppel requires, among other things, conduct amounting to a representation or concealment of facts that the other party reasonably relies on to his or her detriment. The theory is still prominent today although not always successful. Consider the Vintage Rodeo Parent case, which follows:

VINTAGE RODEO PARENT, LLC v. RENT-A-CENTER, INC., 2019 WL 1223026 (Ct. Chancery of Del. 2019). Plaintiff Vintage Capital Management, LLC ("Vintage Capital) indirectly owns stores offering consumer goods to the public under the trade name "Buddy's." Buddy's is a "rent-to-own" retailer. * * * [Plaintiff] entered a merger agreement to acquire defendant Rent-A-Center, Inc., a bigger player in the rent-to-own market. Because of the overlap of these competing retail operations, the parties knew that Federal Trade Commission ("FTC") permission would be required for [their] merger, and that the review process could be lengthy. Therefore, in a vigorously negotiated provision, the merger agreement provided an "End Date," six months from signing, after which either party could terminate the merger agreement. If, however, the FTC review process was still ongoing, each party negotiated for itself the unilateral right to extend the End Date for three months (and a second time for an additional three months), by giving the other side notice of the election to extend before the original End Date. By doing so, the extending party was binding both its counterparty and itself to compliance with the merger terms during the extension period. If neither party chose to extend the End Date, the merger was not terminated once that date had passed—both parties were still bound by the merger agreement, but either could terminate at will, simply by giving notice.

Thus, as the End Date approached, each party had a set of decisions to contemplate. It could give notice of election to extend, in which case both it and its counterparty would be bound to use commercially reasonable efforts to close during the extension period before the new End Date. If it chose not to extend, the party would nonetheless continue to be so bound if the counterparty gave notice of election to extend.

If neither party gave the required notice, the parties were free to proceed to closing, but with the knowledge that either party had the right to terminate at will before closing.

* * *

At a meeting of Rent-A-Center's Board of Directors (the "Board") shortly before the End Date, the Board was given a presentation by corporate counsel. According to counsel, the Board was faced with the decision matrix described above: whether it should unilaterally extend the End Date, and if not—and if Vintage chose not to extend—should it immediately cancel the merger, or proceed towards closing? The Rent-A-Center Board determined that it was, by that point, no longer in the corporate interest to proceed under the terms of the merger agreement. It decided, therefore, not to elect extend the End Date, and, should Vintage not elect to extend, to terminate the merger. The Rent-A-Center Board was told by counsel that it was likely that Vintage would extend, given, I assume, market conditions and [a fee that Vintage would have to pay if the deal did not go through, called "the reverse breakup fee."] In that case, Rent-A-Center would be bound to continue to use commercially reasonable efforts to obtain FTC approval and consummate the merger. If Vintage made the surprising decision not to give notice of an election to extend, Rent-A-Center was ready to exercise its resulting right to terminate, immediately. As it happened, Vintage failed to give notice of an election to extend, and a few hours later, Rent-A-Center gave the notice required to terminate the merger agreement.

Vintage Capital was blindsided. In this litigation, it seeks relief including a declaration that Rent-A-Center's notice of termination was ineffective, and an order that the parties must proceed to obtain FTC approval and merge. * * *

At bottom, the Plaintiffs' argument is that they were working in good faith toward a 2019 closing, which was expected to occur only after the first End Date, and that Rent-A-Center made it abundantly clear that it was working toward the same goal. Both parties had committed much time and effort in that regard, as required by the merger agreement. Under these circumstances, per the Plaintiffs, it is unfair to allow Rent-A-Center to exercise the letter of its bargained-for rights and walk away from the contract, because of a mistaken failure by Vintage to exercise a right that Rent-A-Center must have known Vintage wanted to exercise. I find, however, that the End Date, and the methods to extend it, were matters of importance to the parties, and were heavily negotiated. The parties are bound to their contractual bargain. And a finding that contractually-required expenditures of time and effort made, before the End Date, equated to sufficient notice of election to extend, would fundamentally rewrite the bargain of the parties. I explain my reasoning below.

[In the course of the court's discussion, it considered whether Rent-A-Center was equitably estopped from asserting its right to terminate. Footnotes are omitted.] The Plaintiffs claim that equitable estoppel bars the Defendant from terminating the Merger Agreement. "[E]quitable estoppel is invoked 'when a party by his conduct intentionally or unintentionally leads another, in reliance upon that conduct, to change position to his detriment.' " * * * The Plaintiffs "must demonstrate that: (i) they lacked knowledge or the means of obtaining knowledge of the truth of the facts in question; (ii) they reasonably relied on the conduct of the party against whom estoppel is claimed; and (iii) they suffered a prejudicial change of position as a result of their reliance." This Court does not lightly turn to equitable estoppel to enforce contract rights which cannot be vindicated as the contract is written.

The Plaintiffs claim that they had no reason to doubt the impression they received * * *—that Rent-A-Center remained in enthusiastic support of the merger—and had no way to discover the Board's plan to terminate the Merger Agreement. The Plaintiffs contend that they reasonably relied on Rent-A-Center's "business as usual" act following the December 5 and 6, 2018 Rent-A-Center Board meetings. The Plaintiffs' argument for equitable estoppel suffers from the same flaw as their contractual arguments: an agreement to extend the time of closing into 2019 is not agreement to extend the End Date. Fatal to the Plaintiffs' equitable estoppel claim, though, is the Plaintiffs' own ability to unilaterally extend the End Date and bind Rent-A-Center.

The Plaintiffs argue that they lacked knowledge of, or the means to obtain, the truth that Rent-A-Center did not consider the End Date extended based on * * * conduct between the parties. However, what Rent-A-Center believed about the End Date would have been immaterial had Vintage merely exercised its contractual right and sent a written notice explicitly extending the End Date. Vintage negotiated for this right, and was constructively aware of it. Therefore, the Plaintiffs cannot have reasonably relied on the demeanor of Rent-A-Center's principals. Nor did they change positions based on any reliance. Again, Vintage did not make a *decision* that it need not send notice of election to extend before the End

Date based on some action by Rent-A-Center. It appears that Vintage simply forgot the End Date in the Merger Agreement—and its implications. The estoppel argument is another after-the-fact attempt to excuse Vintage's lack of action: Vintage did not change its position based on Rent-A-Center's actions. Vintage's attenuated claim that an honest lack of enthusiasm on the part of Rent-A-Center might have caused Vintage to read the Merger Agreement and act accordingly is another version of the misplaced duty to warn.

SECTION FOUR: OBLIGATION ARISING FROM UNJUST ENRICHMENT

MOSES v. MACFERLAN, 97 Eng. Rep. 676 (K.B. 1760) (MANSFIELD, J.). If the defendant be under an obligation, from the ties of natural justice, to refund, the law implies a debt, and gives this action, founded in the equity of the plaintiff's case. * * *

This kind of action, to recover back money, which ought not in justice be kept, is very beneficial. * * *

RESTATEMENT (THIRD) OF RESTITUTION § 1.

A person who is unjustly enriched at the expense of another is subject to liability in restitution.

G. PALMER, LAW OF RESTITUTION

§ 1.1 at 1–2 (1978).

It has been traditional to regard tort and contract as the two principal sources of civil liability at common law. * * * There is another category. * * * [T]his is liability based in unjust enrichment. In particularized form this has been a part of our law from an early time, but it has been slow to emerge as a general theory. In present American law, however, the idea of unjust enrichment has been generally accepted and widely applied.

Restitution based upon unjust enrichment cuts across many branches of the law, including contract, tort, and fiduciary relationship, but it also occupies much territory that is its sole preserve.

BLOOMGARDEN V. COYER

United States Court of Appeals, District of Columbia Circuit, 1973.
479 F.2d 201.

SPOTTSWOOD W. ROBINSON, III, CIRCUIT JUDGE.

This appeal follows appellant Bloomgarden's unsuccessful effort in the District Court to recover a $1 million finder's fee. The fee was sought for services leading to the inauguration of an enterprise to extensively develop certain property on the Georgetown waterfront in Washington. The principals in the enterprise are appellees Coyer and Guy, individual real estate developers, and appellee Georgetown-Inland Corporation (Georgetown-Inland), one of five companies organized, with Coyer and Guy as two of the stockholders in each, to effectuate the project. At the center of the controversy is Bloomgarden's assertion that it was he who brought the organizers together in this mutually beneficial venture and who, by the same token, should be rewarded for that contribution.

It is fully conceded that Bloomgarden introduced Coyer and Guy to those with whom they were later to join forces. There was, however, no express agreement, written or oral, pertaining to the part Bloomgarden played or calling for compensation therefor from any of the appellees. Bloomgarden's quest for a finder's fee proceeded on the theory that he was entitled to remuneration by virtue of a contract which should either be factually implied from prevalent custom and usage or recognized as a legal consequence of the transaction when viewed in light of the surrounding circumstances.

After the close of the pleadings and some amount of discovery, Bloomgarden moved for partial summary judgment on the issue of liability and appellees for summary judgment on the entire case. The District Court denied Bloomgarden's motion and granted appellees', in each instance on two separate grounds. The court held that because Bloomgarden did not hold the license required of real estate and business-chance brokers in the District of Columbia he was precluded from charging for what he did. The court further held that Bloomgarden had no enforceable claim for recompense because it appeared without dispute that at the time he introduced the parties he did not expect to be personally compensated for so doing. Without reaching the first ground relied on by the District Court, we affirm for reasons underlying the second.

Bloomgarden's suit traces its origin to a series of events commencing in the fall of 1969 and extending into the spring of 1970. Throughout this period he was serving as president of Socio-Dynamics Industries, Inc. (SDI), a consulting and research firm in the field of urban and environmental affairs. Nearly half of SDI's capital stock was owned by David Carley, president of Public Facilities Associates, Inc. (PFA), which was engaged in the development of public and private housing and the redevelopment of urban areas.[1] Carley had requested Bloomgarden to remain alert to any potentially fruitful investment opportunities for PFA in the Washington area.

At the time, Coyer and Guy held contracts or options on several parcels of real estate on the Georgetown waterfront. Bloomgarden met Coyer in the summer of 1969 while arranging to lease office space in a building in which Coyer had an interest. At one of their meetings, Coyer revealed to Bloomgarden the details of a plan for the assembly and development of a sizeable segment of the waterfront into a multipurpose business complex. Coyer explained that he and Guy lacked the financial resources needed to carry the project through, and Bloomgarden offered to put him in touch with Carley.

Bloomgarden promptly apprised Carley of Coyer's project and set up a meeting between them and others for January 26, 1970. Ideas were then exchanged but no suggestion was made by Bloomgarden to Carley or Coyer that he expected to be paid for bringing them together. By Bloomgarden's arrangement the group attended another meeting, on February 19 in Chicago, with representatives of subsidiaries of Inland Steel Company (Inland Steel). Again the plan was discussed and again Bloomgarden gave no indication that he anticipated a fee for introducing Coyer and Guy to Carley and his Inland associates. On the contrary, during a ride to the airport on the day after the Chicago meeting, Guy inquired of Bloomgarden as to what he hoped to get out of the project, and Bloomgarden responded merely that possibly SDI, his company, might garner some work in implementing the plan.[2] Aside from furnishing three of the principals—Coyer, Guy and Carley—with information about the others, Bloomgarden had no further role in the transaction.

An agreement in principle was reached between Coyer, Guy and the Inland Steel group in early April, 1970. This was formalized by a contract in June and a shareholders' agreement executed in August. Five corporations, among them Georgetown-Inland, were organized to handle

---

[1] In February, 1970, PFA became a subsidiary of Inland Steel Company (Inland Steel), and in April its name was changed to Inland Steel Development Corporation (ISDC).

[2] The conversation, as portrayed by Bloomgarden on deposition, was:

Q. You had discussed the [SDI] role in this project in February with Mr. Coyer, had you not?

A. Yes, I had in the cab coming from the Palmer House to the airport * * * Bill Guy said to me at some point and not in any context—I don't even know what we were discussing—he surprised me with the question, "Hank, if this project goes through, what do you expect out of it?" And I really wasn't prepared for the question because I had not thought it through in detail and I really didn't know in detail what I expected out of it. I expected something out of it and something substantial. I said, "Well, for one thing we have some capability in the environmental field and Chuck Coyer mentioned a possibility of a closed energy system here," and I said "We might be involved in that kind of thing." That was about the whole conversation. We did not at that point discuss a finder's fee or anything else.

the project. It was not until the end of March, 1970, however, that Bloomgarden asserted any monetary claim on behalf of SDI for bringing about the initial contact, and it was not until May that he asked for compensation for himself.[3] After each of these demands was rejected, Bloomgarden, on September 14, wrote to Coyer, again claiming a fee for sparking the business opportunity culminating in the Georgetown project. That likewise failing, Bloomgarden commenced his suit on October 1.

* * *

In the case at bar, the District Court, relying on Bloomgarden's own deposition, as was its prerogative in evaluating the summary-judgment motions made by the parties, concluded that Bloomgarden did not contemplate personal remuneration for his services, and that in consequence he lacked an indispensable prerequisite to recovery on either an implied-in-fact contract or a quasi-contract. Like the District Court, we are unable to perceive any factual basis upon which it could be asserted that, at the time he introduced the parties, Bloomgarden looked forward to any finder's fee for himself, as distinguished from a fee and future business for his company. His silence on the matter at the January meeting in Washington and again at the February meeting in Chicago, followed by his statements on the day after the Chicago meeting and later in his deposition, indicated unequivocally that at most the gain he then anticipated was work and compensation for SDI, of which he was president. Bloomgarden summed it up when in his deposition he said:

> It was always my intention that [SDI] should benefit, not myself personally, from putting Inland and Coyer together. [SDI] should have the credit; that [SDI] should get work assignments and that a finder's fee should be paid to [SDI]. It wasn't until I was told that I could not bring suit in the name of [SDI] and was urged to see if I wanted to sue Coyer as an individual that I began to recognize that I was in a very, very difficult spot.[4]

In addition, the pleadings and depositions reveal that it was not until after Bloomgarden had done his service for the parties that they were put on notice that he had in mind a finder's fee, either for his company or for himself. Both Coyer and Guy avowed in their depositions that they thought Bloomgarden was acting either for SDI or Carley when in January he made the introductions. Their understanding in that regard was buttressed in February by Bloomgarden during the ride to the Chicago airport when,

---

[3] The change from a company to a personal claim resulted from SDI's ultimate decision not to participate in the Georgetown waterfront project. * * *

[4] The events referred to in the last sentence of the quoted material occurred when SDI decided not to take part in the Georgetown project, and that decision was not made until long after the parties had been brought together. See note 3, *supra*. Thus, by Bloomgarden's own statement—which harmonizes with all else in the record—his expectation was at most a benefit for his company, rather than for himself, at the time he introduced the parties.

asked pointedly as to his expectations, he omitted reference to individual recompense and replied simply that he had in view the possibility that his company would receive work assignments flowing from the Georgetown project if it materialized. Moreover, Bloomgarden admitted in his deposition that not until the end of March—long after completion of the services for which remuneration was demanded—did he suggest compensation for SDI, his company, and not until May did he indicate that he anticipated personal compensation.

* * * Our careful examination of the record leads us to concur with the District Court that appellees bore their burden as to the nonexistence of any genuine factual issue, and that Bloomgarden offered nothing substantial to bar their request for summary judgment. It remains for us to determine whether the principles of substantive law governing recovery on contracts implied in fact and quasi-contracts were correctly applied.

Despite the marked dissimilarity of contracts implied in fact to quasi-contracts, their separate characteristics have been blurred by courts and commentators over the years. For any satisfactory understanding of Bloomgarden's twofold legal approach, it is important to keep the two concepts clear and distinct. An implied-in-fact contract is a true contract, containing all necessary elements of a binding agreement; it differs from other contracts only in that it has not been committed to writing or stated orally in express terms, but rather is inferred from the conduct of the parties in the milieu in which they dealt. A quasi-contract, on the other hand, is not a contract at all, but a duty thrust under certain conditions upon one party to requite another in order to avoid the former's unjust enrichment. The principles governing the two remedies differ, though in particular cases they may dictate the same result.

It is well settled that, in order to establish an implied-in-fact contract to pay for services, the party seeking payment must show (1) that the services were carried out under such circumstances as to give the recipient reason to understand (a) that they were performed for him and not for some other person, and (b) that they were not rendered gratuitously, but with the expectation of compensation from the recipient; and (2) that the services were beneficial to the recipient.

Particularly where commission-type fees are sought in business-opportunity transactions, such a contract will not be implied unless the recipient knows or has reasonable grounds to believe that the beneficial acts were performed in anticipation of remuneration therefor. The reasons underlying these requirements are evident. Activities beneficial to a party frequently proceed on behalf of another. Often they are engaged in without thought of remuneration. Not uncommonly, and irrespective of motivation, they are not really helpful to the recipient. An agreement to pay for services defies implication where the recipient not unreasonably fails to realize that the services were rendered for him in contemplation of *quid pro quo* for value conferred. And the point in time at which the elements essential to implication must concur is the time at which the services are rendered.[5]

We may assume on the record before us that Bloomgarden's introductions were valuable to appellees, or that at least there was a genuine issue as to whether they were. Yet, for Bloomgarden to recover on the basis of a contract implied in fact, he would have to show additionally that he looked forward to personal payment for his services, and that the circumstances under which he introduced Coyer and Guy to Carley were such as would reasonably have put them on notice that he had that in mind. From aught that appears from the record, Bloomgarden could not have met these standards at a trial.

* * *

* * * The record establishes without controversy that Bloomgarden introduced appellees on the chance that a coalition to develop the Georgetown waterfront would eventually produce business for SDI, his company, and that appellees reasonably understood that his activities were directed solely to that end. The record further establishes that even if Bloomgarden then entertained the notion of charging a finder's fee, appellees were not alerted to that possibility until long after his activities had ended. On these uncontradicted bases we find ample legal support for the District Court's conclusion that Bloomgarden failed to show an implied-in-fact contract supporting his claim.

We turn finally to examine the sufficiency of Bloomgarden's quasi-contract theory as a basis for recovery of the finder's fee which he sought. At the outset, we again call attention to the need for conceptual clarity. The quasi-contract, as we have said, is not really a contract, but a legal obligation closely akin to a duty to make restitution. There is, of course, no need to resort to it when the evidence sustains the existence of a true contract, either express or implied in fact. For the purpose of preventing unjust enrichment, however, a quasi-contract—an obligation to pay money to another—will be recognized in appropriate circumstances, even though no intention of the parties to bind themselves contractually can be discerned. And where, as here, the essential facts are not in dispute, the question whether a quasi-contract should be erected is one of law, and as such is a proper subject for summary disposition.

---

[5] That is because an implied-in-fact contract to compensate for services arises, if at all, at the time the services are rendered, and only if the then-existing circumstances enable implication of a contract does it come into being. These precepts are elemental, and so much is implicit in the decisions holding that services performed without expectation of remuneration or simply in expectation of a non-monetary business advantage do not warrant implication of a contract to pay. In all of these cases there was at some point a change of heart, and an effort in the suit to recover cash compensation not contemplated when the acts were performed. * * *

Generally, in order to recover on a quasi-contractual claim, the plaintiff must show that the defendant was unjustly enriched at the plaintiff's expense, and that the circumstances were such that in good conscience the defendant should make restitution. Because quasi-contractual obligations rest upon equitable considerations, they do not arise when it would not be unfair for the recipient to keep the benefit without having to pay for it. Thus, to make out his case, it is not enough for the plaintiff to prove merely that he has conferred an advantage upon the defendant, but he must demonstrate that retention of the benefit without compensating the one who conferred it is unjustified. What must be resolved here is whether Bloomgarden made such a showing or evinced his capability of possibly doing so at trial.

By their very nature, the equitable principles of quasi-contracts are more difficult to apply where the court must determine whether services rendered by one person to another are to go unrewarded than where it must make that determination with respect to money or property unjustly retained. But since there is no general responsibility in quasi-contract law to pay for services *irrespective* of the circumstances in which they are carried out, a number of factual criteria have been utilized by courts to ascertain whether in a given case the defendant has undeservedly profited by the plaintiff's efforts. Thus, in situations involving personal services, it has been variously stated that a duty to pay will not be recognized where it is clear that the benefit was conferred gratuitously or officiously, or that the question of payment was left to the unfettered discretion of the recipient. Nor is compensation mandated where the services were rendered simply in order to gain a business advantage. And the courts have reached the same conclusion where the plaintiff did not contemplate a personal fee, or the defendant could not reasonably have supposed that he did. * * * Nor, we add, can an uncommunicated expectation of remuneration serve the plaintiff's purpose where the defendant had no cause to believe that such was the fact.

Thus we come full circle to the identical considerations which were dispositive of Bloomgarden's claim for recovery on an implied-in-fact contract. There simply was no basis on which a jury could rationally find that when he brought the parties together[6] he entertained any thought of a finder's fee for himself, or that those with whom he dealt held the payment of such a fee in prospect. These circumstances defeat Bloomgarden's quasi-contract claim as well. On what emerges clearly and undisputably from the record, we find that the District Court was fully

[6] As in the instance of an implied-in-fact contract, the circumstances allegedly creating a quasi-contractual obligation to pay for services must have existed when the services were performed. No unfairness results from a denial of compensation to the claimant who had no expectation of personal remuneration at the time of performance. On the contrary, it would be unjust to impose a liability for payment on the party who accepts the services without any warning, from the surrounding circumstances or otherwise, that they were rendered for a price.

warranted in holding that, as a matter of law, Bloomgarden was not entitled to recover on either a contract implied-in-fact or a quasi-contract, and its action in so doing is accordingly

Affirmed.

BLACKMON v. IVERSON, 324 F. Supp. 2d 602 (E.D. Pa. 2004). Jamil Blackmon has sued the defendant basketball player Allen Iverson, for idea misappropriation, breach of contract, and quantum meruit (unjust enrichment), all arising out of the defendant's use of "The Answer," both as a nickname and as a logo or slogan.

* * *

The facts according to the amended complaint are as follows. * * *

Mr. Blackmon maintained a close personal friendship and relationship with Mr. Iverson and his family from 1987 forward. At various times in their friendship, Mr. Blackmon provided Mr. Iverson and his family with financial support, allowed Mr. Iverson and his family members to live in Mr. Blackmon's home, and provided other support to Mr. Iverson, such as picking him up from school and providing him with a tutor.

In July of 1994, Mr. Blackmon suggested that Mr. Iverson use "The Answer" as a nickname in the summer league basketball tournaments in which Mr. Iverson would be playing. Mr. Blackmon told Mr. Iverson that Mr. Iverson would be "The Answer" to all of the National Basketball Association's ("NBA's") woes. Mr. Blackmon and Mr. Iverson also discussed the fact that the nickname "The Answer" had immediate applications as a label, brand name, or other type of marketing slogan for use in connection with clothing, sports apparel, and sneakers. The parties also discussed using "The Answer" as a logo.

Later that evening, Mr. Iverson promised to give Mr. Blackmon twenty-five percent of all proceeds the merchandising of products sold in connection with the term "The Answer." * * * Mr. Blackmon thereafter began to invest significant time, money, and effort in the refinement of the concept of "The Answer."

* * *

[The court dismissed the breach of contract claim in part because Blackmon made the suggestion to use "The Answer" as a nickname before Iverson promised to pay so any consideration was past consideration.]

The facts alleged in the complaint do not include an allegation that the plaintiff expected payment if the defendant used the nickname "The Answer." The plaintiff's facts show that he wanted and intended the defendant to use the nickname in summer league basketball tournaments, starting in 1994, without expecting any payment for that use. The plaintiff cannot make out a claim that the defendant was unjustly enriched by the use of a nickname that the plaintiff freely offered.

It is the use of the nickname on products for which the plaintiff claims damages. But the use of the nickname on products came years after the defendant began using the nickname. If the plaintiff concedes, as he does, that the idea of putting a nickname on products is not novel; and if the plaintiff is not claiming any damages for merely suggesting the use of the nickname to the defendant, and he is not, there is no unjust enrichment alleged in the complaint. Any benefit to the defendant from the marketing of products with "The Answer" on them comes from his fame as a basketball player and the investment in marketing the products by Reebok. [The court dismissed the unjust enrichment claim.]

SPARKS V. GUSTAFSON

Supreme Court of Alaska, 1988.
750 P.2d 338.

MATTHEWS, JUSTICE.

Robert J. Sparks, Jr., executor of his father's estate (Estate), appeals from a superior court decision ordering the Estate to pay $65,706.07 to the plaintiff, Ernie Gustafson, in compensation for management services that Gustafson rendered to the Estate and for maintaining and improving Estate property. The central issue presented here is whether it is unjust to allow the Estate to retain these benefits without paying for them. In particular, Sparks argues that Gustafson gave his services to the Estate gratuitously, without the Estate's knowledge or consent.

Facts and Proceedings

The decedent, Robert Sparks, Sr., and the plaintiff, Ernie Gustafson, were personal friends and business associates for many years. In 1980 Sparks purchased a one-half interest in the Nome Center Building. Gustafson managed the building for Sparks without charge until Sparks died on March 1, 1981. Thereafter Gustafson continued to manage the building and collect rents on behalf of Sparks, Sr.'s estate, with the knowledge and approval of the executor, Robert Sparks, Jr. Gustafson did not request any compensation for his services.

Under Gustafson's management, Nome Center operated at a loss. The Estate deposited $10,000 in a Nome Center account to cover operating expenses, but the amount was not sufficient to meet the necessary costs of insurance, mortgage payments, utility bills, and repairs. Gustafson often paid Nome Center expenses out of his own pocket. Maintenance and remodeling work were performed by Gustafson, using in part his own funds. Although he mailed monthly reports of the Nome Center's income and expenses, these reports did not include all of his own expenditures.

In February, 1982, the Estate signed a document entitled "purchase agreement" which indicated that Gustafson had purchased the building from the Estate, and would assume the deed of trust as soon as the purchase details could be worked out. However, no purchase details were ever agreed upon. The Estate sold the building to a third party in February, 1983, and Gustafson ceased to manage the property at that time.

On July 14, 1983, Gustafson and his business corporation, Nome Business Venture, Inc., filed suit against the Estate and the executor in Nome, claiming that the defendants breached an oral agreement to sell the Nome Center Building to Gustafson. Plaintiffs subsequently filed an amended complaint which further alleged that Gustafson was entitled to recover for funds and services that he expended on the building under a statutory or equitable lien theory. Defendants filed an answer and counterclaimed for an accounting of all monies collected and expended on the building.

At trial the superior court found that Gustafson had no enforceable lien. The court also concluded that it would be inequitable to allow the Estate to retain the benefits that Gustafson had conferred upon Nome Center at his own expense. The court ordered the Estate to pay Gustafson $65,706.07 in compensation for the services and improvements that he conferred upon the Estate during his two years of managing the Nome Center Building. This appeal followed.

* * *

Unjust enrichment exists where the defendant has received a benefit from the plaintiff and it would be inequitable for defendant to retain the benefit without compensating plaintiff for its value. * * * Sparks claims that plaintiffs failed to prove either element of unjust enrichment: first, that the Estate received any benefit from plaintiffs, and second, that if a benefit was received then its retention would be unjust.

A person confers a benefit upon another if he gives the other some interest in money, land or possessions; performs services beneficial to or at the request of the other; satisfies a debt of the other; or in any way adds to the other's advantage. *Restatement of the Law of Restitution* § 1, comment b (1937). In this case Gustafson made substantial repairs and improvements to the Nome Center, provided management services that kept Nome Center operating, and paid debts incurred by Nome Center, all arguably on the Estate's behalf. There is no question that Gustafson conferred a benefit upon the Estate.

Even where a person has conferred a benefit upon another, however, he is entitled to compensation only if it would be just and equitable to require compensation under the circumstances. *Restatement of the Law of Restitution* § 1, comment c (1937). Courts will allow the defendant to retain a benefit without compensating plaintiff in several situations, one of which is relevant to the case at hand: where the benefit was given gratuitously without expectation of payment. * * * Appellants argue that this situation is present in the case before us.

This court has not yet addressed the circumstances which give rise to a finding of gratuitous intent. A good discussion of this issue in the context of a decedent's estate can be found in *Kershaw v. Tracy Collins Bank & Trust Co.,* 561 P.2d 683 (Utah 1977). In that case the decedent's best friend provided a variety of services to the decedent's widow, including chauffeuring, buying groceries, running errands, and performing minor repair work. *Id.* at 684. The court looked at the extent of the services provided to the widow, the closeness of the relationship between the parties, and the fact that the plaintiff never sought compensation until after the widow died. The court found that the widow had not been unjustly enriched, since plaintiff's services were not necessary for the widow's existence and were of the sort which could reasonably be expected from a long time friend. *Id.* at 687.

In this case there was a similarly close relationship between the plaintiff and the decedent. It appears that Gustafson managed the Nome Center Building for the decedent without requesting compensation, in recognition of many long years of friendship and business association together. At trial, the executor testified that he thought Gustafson would continue to manage the building for two years after Sparks' death out of the goodness of his heart, without expectation of payment. Gustafson never requested compensation for his services during his tenure as the Nome Center manager for the Estate. The closeness of the parties' relationship and Gustafson's failure to request compensation in a timely manner suggest that Gustafson offered his services to the Estate gratuitously.

However, the services that Gustafson performed for the Estate were not the sort which one would ordinarily expect to receive from a friend as a mere gratuity. Gustafson spent approximately five hours a day for two years collecting rents for Nome Center, soliciting new tenants, making repairs and improvements, paying utility, insurance and mortgage bills out of his own pocket when rental income fell short of expenses, and performing other general maintenance and management services for the Estate. These are the types of extensive business services for which one would ordinarily expect to be paid. We therefore agree with the trial court that Gustafson's services were not offered gratuitously.

* * *

The judgment of the superior court is AFFIRMED.

PROBLEM 2-8

On December 19, 2007, the New York Times reported that a former municipal court judge sued David Chase, the creator of the "Sopranos," for royalties in major part for "arranging meetings Chase had with police and prosecutors during a three-day tour of New Jersey mob sites in 1995." The judge-plaintiff asserted that Chase agreed "to take care of him' if the show was a hit but never discussed a sum." Should the judge's claim succeed?

D. DOBBS, REMEDIES

298–99 (1973).

When one person confers a benefit upon another not required by contract or legal duty, the recipient of the benefit is often unjustly enriched and required to make restitution of the benefit or its value. But this is not always so. He is not unjustly enriched, and therefore not required to make restitution, where the benefit was conferred by a volunteer or intermeddler.

This general rule involves two entirely distinct principles. The first principle is that one who has conferred a benefit upon another with an intention to make a gift, has no equitable claim for relief against the recipient of the benefit in the absence of fraud, mistake, duress or undue influence. In such a case the recipient of the benefit is enriched, but not unjustly, since there is no injustice in retaining a completed gift. This principle holds no matter what form the gift might take. Gratuitously rendered services are within this principle, for example, as are any other benefits.

The second principle is that one who confers a benefit upon another without affording that other the opportunity to reject the benefit, has no equitable claim for relief against the recipient of the benefit in the absence of some special policy that would outweigh the right of free choice in the benefited party. For instance, a house painter cannot paint an owner's home in his absence and then recover for the benefit conferred, even though the house needed paint and is much increased in value. In such a case the recipient of the benefit is enriched, and perhaps unjustly, but such enrichment is preferable to payment of the intermeddler, who should not thus be encouraged to invade another's freedom of choice about his own affairs. There are, as would be expected, situations in which this policy is outweighed by other considerations, * * * but the basic principle is solidly established.

BROWN v. BROWN, 524 A.2d 1184 (D.C. App. 1987). Substantial policy considerations * * * underlie the presumption that services rendered between siblings are gratuitous. We believe that, as a matter of common human experience, such services are usually performed out of a sense of family responsibility, not pursuant to a contractual agreement with the legitimate expectation of payment.

GAY V. MOONEY

Supreme Court of New Jersey, 1901.
67 N.J.L. 27, 50 A. 596, aff'd per curiam, 67 N.J.L. 687, 52 A. 1131.

Action by Michael Gay against Hugh Mooney, administrator of Hugh Mooney, deceased. Judgment for plaintiff, and defendant brings error. Affirmed.

* * *

DIXON, J. The defendant's intestate was the uncle of the plaintiff's wife, and for several years before his death resided in the plaintiff's family. In the present suit the plaintiff sought to recover compensation for the board and lodging furnished to the deceased.

In order to rebut a presumption that the service was rendered and received as a gratuity, the plaintiff put in evidence tending to show an understanding between himself and the deceased that the latter would devise a certain dwelling house to the plaintiff's children in return for what he should receive as a member of the family. For such a purpose this evidence was plainly legitimate. It came within the rule laid down in Disbrow v. Durand, 54 N.J. Law, 343, 24 Atl. 545, 33 Am.St.Rep. 678, that in cases like the present a reasonable and proper expectation that there would be compensation must, and hence may, be shown. The bargain thus exhibited is not one on which an action at law could be maintained, because it related to land, and was not susceptible of such proof as the statute of frauds requires; but when, in pursuance of a bargain for this reason unenforceable, services have been rendered, the legal remedy is by an action on the quantum meruit for the value of the services. McElroy v. Ludlum, 32 N.J.Eq. 828. As was said in Stone v. Todd, 49 N.J.Law, 274, 281, 8 Atl. 300, the intended devise was but the method of paying an admitted obligation, and, if payment in that manner be not made, the creditor is entitled to recover the value of the services.

Although the bargain between the plaintiff and the intestate contemplated payment to be made to the plaintiff's children, and not directly to himself, yet, as that bargain did not take the form of an actionable contract, it falls out of view as a ground of legal remedy, and appears only to give color to the conduct of the parties in furnishing and accepting the service rendered. It affords the means of determining that the service was not a gift, but a sale, and out of that determination the law deduces a right in him who sold the service to be paid its value by him who bought it. These principles sufficiently answer the important exceptions taken at the trial and all the exceptions mentioned in the brief of counsel. The other exceptions, therefore, need not be noticed.

The judgment of the Middlesex pleas is affirmed.

PERILLO, RESTITUTION IN A CONTRACTUAL CONTEXT

73 Colum. L. Rev. 1208, 1215–16 (1973).

We are attuned by custom and long usage to think in terms of a contract action for damages as an action on the contract and therefore based upon agreement. We are also attuned by custom and long usage to think in terms of an action for restitution, even in a contract setting, as an action which is not based on contract. * * * By way of illustration, let us assume the plaintiff performed services under an oral contract which provided for a two year term of employment. An action for damages would require the setting out of the contract in the declaration and would be met by a plea of the Statute of Frauds. Plaintiff, therefore, to avoid the plea would bring an action in general assumpsit for the reasonable value of his services. Such an action required a two act scenario. First, it is pretended that the contract made by the parties never existed. It is either ignored or retroactively avoided. Then the plaintiff must state that he had rendered work, labor and services at the request of the defendant and that the defendant had promised to pay him "so much money as he therefore reasonably deserved to have." The promise is not the contractual promise but a fictional promise. How, then, could one assert that the action was on the unenforceable contract? The answer is to be found not in the pleadings but in the actual trial of the action, where one will find constant reference to the oral contract itself. How does one prove the request for services? By introducing evidence of the oral contract. What if the defendant wishes to show that, although plaintiff has rendered services, plaintiff has breached the oral contract and therefore should not recover? May he raise this defense based upon the terms of the contract? Indeed he may. May the rate of compensation stated in the contract be put into evidence to establish the reasonable value of the services? Yes, say the vast majority of cases. At every step and turn questions of fact and questions of law are definitively or partially resolved by reference to the [unenforceable] contract.

POSNER V. SEDER

Supreme Judicial Court of Massachusetts, 1903.
184 Mass. 331, 68 N.E. 335.

CONTRACT, against manufacturers of clothing, by a foreman and cutter for his services, according to an account annexed. * * *

[After a trial, the judge found for the plaintiff; and the defendants alleged exceptions.]

* * *

HAMMOND, J. Under the contract the defendants were to employ the plaintiff for one year, and pay him for his services $17 a week, "the same to be paid at the end of each and every week." The plaintiff was to report at the shop for duty at 6:30 a.m., and remain there on duty until 6 p.m., with the exception of the hour between noon and 1 p.m., and was "also, without extra pay, to work overtime at said shop * * * not more than two hours in one day and not more than two months in the aggregate for the year." The defendants broke the contract by the discharge of the plaintiff. In such a case the innocent party may either sue on the contract for damages for the breach, or, if he so elects, he may regard the action of the defendants as indicating a purpose on their part to repudiate the contract, may accept the repudiation, and recover upon a quantum meruit the value of his services as if the special contract had not existed. Brown v. Woodbury, 183 Mass. 279, 67 N.E. 327. In this case the plaintiff has sued upon a quantum meruit for the value of only a part of the services, namely, for those rendered in the extra hours named in the contract.

The plaintiff contends that the $17 which he received each week was payment for only the time between 6:30 a.m. and 6 p.m., and not for the extra time; and that, therefore, he may, upon breach of the contract, appropriate the weekly sum to the payment of the services during the regular hours, and recover on quantum meruit for the extra time. The defendants, on the contrary, contend that the $17 was a payment for the services of the week, whatever they were, and therefore that the plaintiff has been fully paid, and so cannot recover.

Neither view seems to us correct. The contract was to continue a year. The weekly hours of labor were variable, and it is fair to assume that there would be a weekly variation in the value of the services. The contract is to be taken as a whole. On the one hand, the defendants could not hold the plaintiff to the work during the extra hours in any week for the sum of $17 except in connection with the other part of the contract, namely, that they were to pay him $17 in other weeks when there was no extra time; nor, on the other hand, could the plaintiff hold the defendants to the payment of $17 for a week in which he did not work extra time, except in connection with the other part of the contract, namely, that in any week in which he did work extra time he should receive only $17. The true construction of the contract is that it was a hiring for a year, payments to be made by weekly installments, without reference to * * * the amount of work done. Since the payments were made during the existence of the contract, they cannot be considered as having no reference to the other parts of the contract.

If the plaintiff desires to proceed upon the theory that the contract has been repudiated, his proper course is to proceed upon quantum meruit for the value of all his services, less what he has received. If he has been paid what they are worth, he can recover nothing; if he has not, he may recover the balance due him. But it is plain that the sum due him is not necessarily the fair price for the extra hours in addition to the sum of $17 per week which he has received. He cannot appropriate the $17 to the payment of the ordinary week's work, and sue only for the balance, because, for the reasons above stated, that is not in accordance with the contract under which the payment was made. Upon quantum meruit the question is, what are his whole services fairly worth, and is there anything due him. Manifestly, under a contract like this, that may be an entirely different sum from the market value of the services during the extra hours. * * *

* * * It is not necessary that the plaintiff, before bringing his action, should return what he has received. It is necessary only that the amount received should be credited upon his claim. Brown v. Woodbury, supra.

Exceptions sustained.

KELLEY V. HANCE

Supreme Court of Errors of Connecticut, 1928.
108 Conn. 186, 142 A. 683.

BANKS, J. In September, 1926, the plaintiff and defendant entered into a contract in which the former agreed to excavate to the proper level and construct a concrete sidewalk and curb in front of the latter's property for the agreed price of $420, being at the rate of $3 per running foot for 140 feet. The plaintiff agreed to start the work within a week and to complete it before cold weather set in. The plaintiff did not start work until December 4, 1926. He removed a strip of earth along the frontage of defendant's premises to a width of 12 feet and a depth of 8 [inches] and then left the premises and has not since done anything further toward the completion of his contract. On March 2, 1927, the defendant notified the plaintiff that he canceled the contract. The reasonable value of the work done by the plaintiff was $158.60. Judgment was rendered in favor of the plaintiff for $133.68 which amount imports an award of nominal damages of $25 to the defendant upon his counterclaim for the value of the earth removed by the plaintiff.

The trial court reached the conclusion that the defendant was justified in canceling the contract because of the failure of the plaintiff to perform, but that the latter was entitled to recover the reasonable value of the benefits accruing to the defendant from the work done by the plaintiff.

While the plaintiff's contract was for the construction of a sidewalk and curb at a unit price per running foot, no section of the walk and curb was completed, and it is not claimed that plaintiff could recover upon the theory of a performance of a divisible portion of the contract; nor was he entitled to recover upon the theory of a substantial performance. This was in the nature of a construction contract as to which class of contracts the rule is liberally applied permitting a recovery where a contractor has deviated slightly from the terms of the contract, not willfully, but in good faith, and there has been a substantial performance of the contract of which the other party has received the benefit. Pinches v. Swedish Lutheran Church, 55 Conn. 183, 10 A. 264; Daly v. New Haven Hotel Co., 91 Conn. 280, 99 A. 853. Here, however, not only is there no finding of substantial performance, but it appears from the finding that no portion of the sidewalk and curb was actually constructed by the plaintiff, who, after making an excavation along the front of defendant's premises, left the work and has not done anything since toward its completion. The court has found that the reasonable worth of the work done by the plaintiff was $158.60, slightly more than a third of the contract price, and that the defendant has benefited to that extent from the plaintiff's work. The case, therefore, is one where a contractor has without justification abandoned his contract before completion, but seeks to recover from the defendant the reasonable worth to the latter of the work done prior to the abandonment.

Though a contractor has failed of performance for reasons which would not excuse a breach, and where there has not been even substantial performance, the breach being merely negligent, many of the more recent decisions have held that he could recover the value of his work, less the damages caused by his default. 3 Williston on Contracts, § 1475, and cases cited. Such recovery is allowed, not upon the original contract, for that has been breached, but in quasi contract upon the theory that, if such recovery were not allowed, the other party would be unjustly enriched at the expense of the contractor. 6 Page on Contracts, § 3262. Some cases have gone so far as to allow an employee who has performed part of his employment to recover reasonable compensation, though his failure to render further performance was due to his willful abandonment of his contract. 3 Williston on Contracts, § 1477. By the weight of authority, however, there can ordinarily be no recovery where the contractor has willfully abandoned his contract without justification. * * *

While the mere fact that part performance has been beneficial to the defendant will not entitle the plaintiff to recover where he has abandoned performance without justification, the defendant may nevertheless make himself liable by his voluntary acceptance of the benefits under circumstances sufficient to raise an implied promise to pay for them notwithstanding the nonperformance of the contract. Where one retains goods received in part performance of a contract, a promise to pay for them is ordinarily implied since he has the option either to pay for or return them. Where, however, work has been done upon one's land, the benefit cannot well be returned and an acceptance of the benefit cannot be implied from the mere retention of possession of the land. In such cases, therefore, the better rule would seem to be that, except where there has been an actual acceptance of the work prior to its abandonment by the plaintiff, mere inaction on the part of the defendant will not be treated as an acceptance of the work from which a promise to pay for it may be implied. * * *

We have held that recovery can be had for partial performance which has been beneficial only when the benefit has been appropriated by the defendant under circumstances sufficient to raise an implied promise to pay for the reasonable value of what has been received. Jones v. Marlborough, 70 Conn. 583, 589, 40 A. 460; Jones & Hotchkiss Co. v. Davenport, 74 Conn. 418, 420, 50 A. 1028.

The finding discloses an abandonment of his contract by the plaintiff after the excavation was made, but before any portion of the sidewalk and curb had been constructed. No justification for this abandonment appears and the plaintiff cannot therefore recover the reasonable value of the work done, unless there has been such an acceptance of it by the defendant as to raise an implied promise on his part to pay for it. No acceptance of the work by the defendant prior to the breach is found and no promise to pay for the benefit received can be implied from the mere fact that he has received a benefit which from the nature of the case he could not avoid receiving and was powerless to return. It follows that the court erred in its conclusion that the plaintiff was entitled to recover the reasonable value of the work done by him in the partial performance of his contract.

In the absence of any evidence of the market value of the dirt which it is found was wrongfully disposed of by the plaintiff, the defendant cannot justly complain of the award to him of nominal damages.

There is error, the judgment is reversed, and the city court of Meriden is directed to enter its judgment in favor of the defendant for nominal damages upon his counterclaim.

All concur.

BRITTON V. TURNER

Supreme Court of Judicature of New Hampshire, 1834.
6 N.H. 481.

Assumpsit, for work and labor, performed by the plaintiff, in the service of the defendant, from March 9, 1831, to December 27, 1831.

The declaration contained the common counts, and among them a count in *quantum meruit,* for the labor, averring it to be worth $100. At the trial in the C. C. Pleas, the plaintiff proved the performance of the labor as set forth in the declaration.

The defense was that it was performed under a special contract; that the plaintiff agreed to work one year, from some time in March, 1831, to March, 1832, and that the defendant was to pay him for said year's labor the sum of $120; and the defendant offered evidence tending to show that such was the contract under which the work was done.

Evidence was also offered to show that the plaintiff left the defendant's service without his consent, and it was contended by the defendant that the plaintiff had no good cause for not continuing in his employment.

There was no evidence offered of any damage arising from the plaintiff's departure, farther than was to be inferred from his nonfulfilment of the entire contract.

The court instructed the jury that, if they were satisfied from the evidence that the labor was performed under a contract to labor a year, for the sum of $120, and if they were satisfied that the plaintiff labored only the time specified in the declaration, and then left the defendant's service, against his consent, and without any good cause, yet the plaintiff was entitled to recover, under his *quantum meruit* count, as much as the labor he performed was reasonably worth, and under this direction the jury gave a verdict for the plaintiff for the sum of $95.

The defendant excepted to the instructions thus given to the jury.

* * *

PARKER, J., delivered the opinion of the court.

* * *

It is clear * * * that [plaintiff] is not entitled to recover upon the contract itself, because the service, which was to entitle him to the sum agreed upon, has never been performed.

But the question arises, can the plaintiff, under these circumstances, recover a reasonable sum for the service he has actually performed, under the count in *quantum meruit?* Upon this, and questions of a similar nature, the decisions to be found in the books are not easily reconciled.

It has been held, upon contracts of this kind for labor to be performed at a specified price, that the party who voluntarily fails to fulfil the contract by performing the whole labor contracted for, is not entitled to recover anything for the labor actually performed, however much he may have done towards the performance, and this has been considered the settled rule of law upon this subject. * * *

That such rule in its operation may be very unequal, not to say unjust, is apparent. A party who contracts to perform certain specified labor, and who breaks his contract in the first instance, without any attempt to perform it, can only be made liable to pay the damages which the other party has sustained by reason of such non-performance, which in many instances may be trifling—whereas a party who in good faith has entered upon the performance of his contract, and nearly completed it, and then abandoned the further performance, although the other party has had the full benefit of all that has been done, and has perhaps sustained no actual damage—is in fact subjected to a loss of all which has been performed, in the nature of damages for the nonfulfilment of the remainder, upon the technical rule, that the contract must be fully performed in order to [sustain] a recovery of any part of the compensation.

By the operation of this rule, then, the party who attempts performance may be placed in a much worse situation than he who wholly disregards his contract, and the other party may receive much more, by the breach of the contract, than the injury which he has sustained by such breach, and more than he could be entitled to were he seeking to recover damages by an action.

The case before us presents an illustration. Had the plaintiff in this case never entered upon the performance of his contract, the damage could not probably have been greater than some small expense and trouble incurred in procuring another to do the labor which he had contracted to perform. But having entered upon the performance, and labored nine and a half months, the value of which labor to the defendant as found by the jury is $95, if the defendant can succeed in this defense, he in fact receives nearly five-sixths of the value of a whole year's labor, by reason of the breach of contract by the plaintiff, a sum not only utterly disproportionate to any probable, not to say possible damage which could have resulted from the neglect of the plaintiff to continue the remaining two and [a] half months, but altogether beyond any damage which could have been recovered by the defendant, had the plaintiff done nothing towards the fulfilment of his contract.

* * *

It is said that in those cases where the plaintiff has been permitted to recover there was an acceptance of what had been done. The answer is that where the contract is to labor from day to day, for a certain period, the party for whom the labor is done in truth stipulates to receive it from day to day, as it is performed, and although the other may not eventually do all he has contracted to do, there has been, necessarily, an acceptance of what has been done in pursuance of the contract, and the party must have understood when he made the contract that there was to be such acceptance.

If, then, the party stipulates in the outset to receive part performance from time to time, with a knowledge that the whole may not be completed, we see no reason why he should not equally be holden to pay for the amount of value received, as where he afterwards takes the benefit of what has been done, with a knowledge that the whole which was contracted for has not been performed. In neither case has the contract been performed. In neither can an action be sustained on the original contract. In both the party has assented to receive what is done. The only difference is that in the one case the assent is prior, with a knowledge that all may not be performed; in the other it is subsequent, with a knowledge that the whole has not been accomplished.

* * *

* * * [W]e think the technical reasoning, that the performance of the whole labor is a condition precedent, and the right to recover anything dependent upon it; that the contract being entire there can be no apportionment—and that there being an express contract no other can be implied, even upon the subsequent performance of service—is not properly applicable to this species of contract, where a beneficial service has been actually performed; for we have abundant reason to believe, that the general understanding of the community is that the hired laborer shall be entitled to compensation for the service actually performed, though he do not continue the entire term contracted for, and such contracts must be presumed to be made with reference to that understanding, unless an express stipulation shows the contrary.

* * *

It is easy, if parties so choose, to provide by an express agreement that nothing shall be earned, if the laborer leaves his employer without having performed the whole service contemplated, and then there can be no pretense for a recovery if he voluntarily deserts the service before the expiration of the time.

The amount, however, for which the employer ought to be charged, where the laborer abandons his contract, is only the reasonable worth, or the amount of advantage he receives upon the whole transaction (*Wadleigh v. Sutton,* 6 N.H. 15), and, in estimating the value of the labor, the contract price for the service cannot be exceeded. * * *

If a person makes a contract fairly, he is entitled to have it fully performed, and if this is not done, he is entitled to damages. He may maintain a suit to recover the amount of damage sustained by the non-performance. The benefit and advantage which the party takes by the labor, therefore, is the amount of value which he receives, if any, after deducting the amount of damage; and if he elects to put this in defense he is entitled so to do, and the implied promise which the law will raise, in such case, is to pay such amount of the stipulated price for the whole labor, as remains after deducting what it would cost to procure a completion of the residue of the service and also any damage which has been sustained by reason of the nonfulfilment of the contract. If in such case it be found that the damages are equal to or greater than the amount of the labor performed, so that the employer, having a right to the full performance of the contract, has not upon the whole case received a beneficial service, the plaintiff cannot recover.

This rule, by binding the employer to pay the value of the service he actually receives, and the laborer to answer in damages where he does not complete the entire contract, will leave no temptation to the former to drive the laborer from his service, near the close of his term, by ill treatment, in order to escape from payment; nor to the latter to desert his service before the stipulated time, without a sufficient reason. * * *

* * *

Applying the principles thus laid down, to this case, the plaintiff is entitled to judgment on the verdict. The defendant sets up a mere breach of the contract in defense of the action, but this cannot avail him. He does not appear to have offered evidence to show that he was damnified by such breach, or to have asked that a deduction should be made upon that account. The direction to the jury was therefore correct, that the plaintiff was entitled to recover as much as the labor performed was reasonably worth, and the jury appear to have allowed a *pro rata* compensation, for the time which the plaintiff labored in the defendant's service.

As the defendant has not claimed or had any adjustment of damages, for the breach of the contract, in this action, if he has actually sustained damage he is still entitled to a suit to recover the amount.

* * *

Judgment on the verdict.

GORDON, *BRITTON V. TURNER*: A SIGNPOST ON THE CROOKED ROAD TO "FREEDOM" IN THE EMPLOYMENT CONTRACT

Contracts Stories 187 (2007).

[Britton is a] seemingly unremarkable little case [that] has had a long and remarkable career. * * * [I]t was cited and debated by state courts throughout the nineteenth century. Writers of treatises on contracts, quasi-contracts, and employment law singled it out for special comment. In the twentieth century—even after legislation mandating regular wage payments had rendered the doctrine of the case mostly irrelevant—jurists like the great contract scholars Samuel Williston and Arthur Corbin continued to fight over the decision and whether the American Law Institute should accept or reject its holding. Starting in the 1970s a half-dozen historians of labor and contract law revived interest in the case and contributed to studies of its origins and significance.

PROBLEM 2-9

Frank Stein is negotiating with Ken's Drugs, Inc. concerning a one-year appointment with Ken's as a chemist. Ken tells you that the first four months of a new chemist's time is mostly in training and that Ken's receives little benefit during this time. Ken therefore asks you to draft a provision in the proposed employment contract ensuring that Frank will receive no compensation unless he completes at least six months work. Draft the provision. Consider N.Y. Labor Law § 191(d) (McKinney Supp. 2009):

> 1. Clerical and other worker.—A clerical and other worker shall be paid the wages earned in accordance with the agreed terms of employment, but not less frequently than semi-monthly, on regular pay days designated in advance by the employer.
>
> 2. No employee shall be required as a condition of employment to accept wages at periods other than as provided in this section.
>
> 3. If employment is terminated, the employer shall pay the wages not later than the regular pay day for the pay period during which the termination occurred, as established in accordance with the provisions of this section. If requested by the employee, such wages shall be paid by mail.

DE LEON v. ALDRETE, 398 S.W.2d 160 (Tex. Civ. App.1965). [Plaintiff Aldrete defaulted after having paid installments of $1,070 out of a total due of $1,500 for the purchase of a tract of land from the De Leons. Aldrete was not in possession of the land. The De Leons thereupon sold the land to another for $1,300. Plaintiff sought the return of the $1,070. The trial court found for plaintiff. On appeal, the court deducted $200 from the $1,070 and affirmed.]

CADENA, JUSTICE.

* * *

What is generally described as the majority rule in this country is that a defaulting purchaser cannot recover any money paid by him under the contract to the vendor even though, as a result of the purchaser's breach, the vendor has abandoned all idea of further performance and retains the money, not for application on the purchase price, but as forfeited. Anno.: 31 A.L.R.2d 8, 11–12 (1953).[1]

* * *

[1] In New York, defaulting purchasers of real estate cannot recover their down payments, at least if they are in the neighborhood of 10%. In *Maxton Builders, Inc. v. Lo Galbo*, 68 N.Y.2d 373, 509 N.Y.S.2d 507, 502 N.E.2d 184 (1986), the court reasoned that down payments of about 10% roughly equal the amount of damages to the seller.

* * * Dogmatic application of the majority rule leads to indefensibly absurd results. Under that rule of forfeiture the amount of the forfeiture will always and necessarily depend simply on the stage to which the purchaser's performance has progressed, with complete disregard of the amount of damages suffered by the vendor. * * *

* * *

In the case before us, plaintiff had paid in excess of 70% of the purchase price. The damages which defendants suffered as a result of plaintiff's breach are definite and ascertainable from the evidence by resort to simple mathematical calculation. Had plaintiff fully performed, defendants would have received $1,500.00 for their land. Because of such breach, they received only $1,300.00. Plaintiff makes no contention that this was not a fair price. Clearly, in order to prevent defendants from suffering as a result of plaintiff's default, it is only necessary to allow them to retain, from the amount paid by plaintiff, the sum of $200.00. To allow them to retain the $1,070.00 paid by plaintiff, after they had received $1,300.00 as a result of their termination of the contract and sale of the land to a third party, would result in a situation where defendants would be unjustly enriched in the amount of $870.00. This result can be justified only if we are prepared to hold that plaintiff must be punished for his breach. Punitive damages are alien to the law of contract. The fundamental principle of our law concerning the liability of one who breaches his contract is the principle of compensation. This principle contemplates that the liability to respond in compensatory, as distinguished from punitive, damages will afford sufficient protection to the innocent party, and this is the only interest, absent extraordinary circumstances which are not present here, which the social welfare demands should be the subject of judicial solicitude. * * *

NOTE:
VARIANT TERMINOLOGY: UNJUST ENRICHMENT, RESTITUTION, QUASI-CONTRACT, QUANTUM MERUIT, COMMON COUNTS

Confucius said:

> Now, if names of things are not properly defined, words will not correspond to facts. When words do not correspond to facts, it is impossible to perfect anything. Where it is impossible to perfect anything, the arts and institutions of civilization cannot flourish. When the arts and institutions of civilization cannot flourish, law and justice do not attain their ends; and when law and justice do not attain their ends, the people will be at a loss to know what to do. (Confucius, THE ANALECTS, xiii, 3.)

In our study of unjust enrichment in Section Four, we have encountered a significant amount of variant terminology. We now offer some clarifying remarks with the caveat that, as to some terms, usage is by no means uniform. The term "unjust enrichment" is ordinarily used as the name of a legally recognized general theory of obligation. The core idea of this theory is that a person who has been unjustly enriched at the claimant's expense incurs a duty to satisfy the claim asserted to the extent of the enrichment (absent a defense). Another name sometimes used for this theory of obligation is "restitution." But restitution is more frequently employed to designate any *remedy*, whether at law or in equity, that redresses unjust enrichment. In addition, restitution may refer to one kind of remedy for breach of contract, as where an aggrieved plaintiff simply seeks to recover money paid to the breaching party. See Chapter Three. In Bloomgarden v. Coyer, we saw that courts also refer to the unjust enrichment theory of obligation as "quasi-contract."

Still another phrase sometimes used to designate the theory of unjust enrichment is "contract implied in law." You should distinguish between contract implied in fact and contract implied in law. A contract implied in fact is one kind of enforceable agreement with consideration—one in which the facts of agreement and consideration are based on implication and inference rather than on explicit assent as in an express contract. Consider again Bloomgarden v. Coyer. But something rather different is meant by a contract implied in law, for this expression ordinarily refers to obligations arising under the theory of unjust enrichment.

The general theory of obligation known as unjust enrichment is applicable in many diverse contexts, promissory and non-promissory. In Section Four, we have seen the relevance of unjust enrichment theory to contract and related areas. But the theory may be invoked in other fields, too. For example, if A uses B's goods for one month, thinking that they belong to A, and then returns them after learning the truth. B is entitled under unjust enrichment theory to the reasonable rental value of the goods for the month involved.

In several cases in this section, we also encountered the expression "quantum meruit." This Latin phrase means, literally, "as much as he deserved." It originally designated a simplified form of pleading used to bring an action at law to obtain payment for services rendered. This form of pleading was called a "common count" in general assumpsit. Two related common counts were "quantum valebant" (for goods sold and delivered) and for "money had and received." Each of these counts included not only an allegation of "services rendered" or the equivalent, but also an allegation of a promise to pay for such. For a case discussing the meaning of quantum meruit, see Paffhausen v. Balano, 708 A.2d 269, 271 (Me. 1998) ("A valid claim in *quantum meruit* requires: 'that (1) services were rendered to the defendant by the plaintiff; (2) with the knowledge and consent of the defendant; and (3) under circumstances that make it reasonable for the plaintiff to expect payment.' Bowden v. Grindle, 651 A.2d 347, 351 (Me.1994)."

WATTS V. WATTS

Supreme Court of Wisconsin, 1987.
137 Wis. 2d 506, 405 N.W.2d 303.

SHIRLEY S. ABRAHAMSON, JUSTICE.

* * *

The case involves a dispute between Sue Ann Evans Watts, the plaintiff, and James Watts, the defendant, over their respective interests in property accumulated during their nonmarital cohabitation relationship which spanned 12 years and produced two children. The case presents an issue of first impression and comes to this court at the pleading stage of the case, before trial and before the facts have been determined.

The plaintiff asked the circuit court to order an accounting of the defendant's personal and business assets accumulated between June 1969 through December 1981 (the duration of the parties' cohabitation) and to determine plaintiff's share of this property. The circuit court's dismissal of plaintiff's amended complaint [for failure to state a claim] is the subject of this appeal. * * *

* * *

The plaintiff commenced this action in 1982. The plaintiff's amended complaint alleges the following facts, which for purposes of this appeal must be accepted as true. The plaintiff and the defendant met in 1967, when she was 19 years old, was living with her parents and was working full time as a nurse's aide in preparation for a nursing career. Shortly after the parties met, the defendant persuaded the plaintiff to move into an apartment paid for by him and to quit her job. According to the amended complaint, the defendant "indicated" to the plaintiff that he would provide for her.

Early in 1969, the parties began living together in a "marriage-like" relationship, holding themselves out to the public as husband and wife. The plaintiff assumed the defendant's surname as her own. Subsequently, she gave birth to two children who were also given the defendant's surname. The parties filed joint income tax returns and maintained joint bank accounts asserting that they were husband and wife. The defendant insured the plaintiff as his wife on his medical insurance policy. He also took out a life insurance policy on her as his wife, naming himself as the beneficiary. The parties purchased real and personal property as husband and wife. The plaintiff executed documents and obligated herself on promissory notes to lending institutions as the defendant's wife.

During their relationship, the plaintiff contributed childcare and homemaking services, including cleaning, cooking, laundering, shopping, running errands, and maintaining the grounds surrounding the parties' home. Additionally, the plaintiff contributed personal property to the relationship which she owned at the beginning of the relationship or acquired through gifts or purchases during the relationship. She served as hostess for the defendant for social and business-related events. The amended complaint further asserts that periodically, between 1969 and 1975, the plaintiff cooked and cleaned for the defendant and his employees while his business, a landscaping service, was building and landscaping a golf course.

From 1973 to 1976, the plaintiff worked 20–25 hours per week at the defendant's office, performing duties as a receptionist, typist, and assistant bookkeeper. From 1976 to 1981, the plaintiff worked 40–60 hours per week at a business she started with the defendant's sister-in-law, then continued and managed the business herself after the dissolution of that partnership. The plaintiff further alleges that in 1981 the defendant made their relationship so intolerable that she was forced to move from their home and their relationship was irretrievably broken. Subsequently, the defendant barred the plaintiff from returning to her business.

The plaintiff alleges that during the parties' relationship, and because of her domestic and business contributions, the business and personal wealth of the couple increased. Furthermore, the plaintiff alleges that she never received any compensation for these contributions to the relationship and that the defendant indicated to the plaintiff both orally and through his conduct that he considered her to be his wife and that she would share equally in the increased wealth.

The plaintiff asserts that since the breakdown of the relationship the defendant has refused to share equally with her the wealth accumulated through their joint efforts or to compensate her in any way for her contributions to the relationship.

* * *

The plaintiff's third legal theory on which her claim rests is that she and the defendant had a contract to share equally the property accumulated during their relationship. The essence of the complaint is that the parties had a contract, either an express or implied in fact contract, which the defendant breached.

The plaintiff has alleged that she quit her job and abandoned her career training upon the defendant's promise to take care of her. A change in one party's circumstances in performance of the agreement may imply an agreement between the parties. * * * In addition, the plaintiff alleges that she performed housekeeping, childbearing, childrearing, and other services related to the maintenance of the parties' home, in addition to various services for the defendant's business and her own business, for which she received no compensation. Courts have recognized that money, property, or services (including housekeeping or childrearing) may constitute adequate consideration independent of the parties' sexual relationship to support an agreement to share or transfer property. * * *

According to the plaintiff's complaint, the parties cohabited for more than twelve years, held joint bank accounts, made joint purchases, filed joint income tax returns, and were listed as husband and wife on other legal documents. Courts have held that such a relationship and "joint acts of a financial nature can give rise to an inference that the parties intended to share equally." Beal v. Beal, 282 Or. 115, 122, 577 P.2d 507, 510 (1978). The joint ownership of property and the filing of joint income tax returns strongly implies that the parties intended their relationship to be in the nature of a joint enterprise, financially as well as personally. * * *

* * * [W]e conclude that the plaintiff in this case has pleaded the facts necessary to state a claim for damages resulting from the defendant's breach of an express or an implied in fact contract to share with the plaintiff the property accumulated through the efforts of both parties during their relationship. Once again, we do not judge the merits of the plaintiff's claim; we merely hold that she be given her day in court to prove her claim.

The plaintiff's fourth theory of recovery involves unjust enrichment. Essentially, she alleges that the defendant accepted and retained the benefit of services she provided knowing that she expected to share equally in the wealth accumulated during their relationship. She argues that it is unfair for the defendant to retain all the assets they accumulated under these circumstances and that a constructive trust should be imposed on the property as a result of the defendant's unjust enrichment. In his brief, the defendant does not attack specifically either the legal theory or the factual allegations made by the plaintiff.

Unlike claims for breach of an express or implied in fact contract, a claim of unjust enrichment does not arise out of an agreement entered into by the parties. Rather, an action for recovery based upon unjust enrichment is grounded on the moral principle that one who has received a benefit has a duty to make restitution where retaining such a benefit would be unjust. Puttkammer v. Minth, 83 Wis.2d 686, 689, 266 N.W.2d 361, 363 (1978).

Because no express or implied in fact agreement exists between the parties, recovery based upon unjust enrichment is sometimes referred to as "quasi contract," or contract "implied in law" rather than "implied in fact." Quasi contracts are obligations created by law to prevent injustice. * * *

In Wisconsin, an action for unjust enrichment, or quasi contract, is based upon proof of three elements: (1) a benefit conferred on the defendant by the plaintiff, (2) appreciation or knowledge by the defendant of the benefit, and (3) acceptance or retention of the benefit by the defendant under circumstances making it inequitable for the defendant to retain the benefit. Puttkammer, supra, 83 Wis.2d at 689, 266 N.W.2d 361; Wis.J.I.Civil No. 3028 (1981).

The plaintiff has cited no cases directly supporting actions in unjust enrichment by unmarried cohabitants, and the defendant provides no authority against it. This court has previously extended such relief to a party to a cohabitation in Estate of Fox, 178 Wis. 369, 190 N.W. 90, 31 A.L.R. 420 (1922). In Fox, the plaintiff was a woman who had believed in good faith that she was married to the decedent, when in fact she was not. The court found that the decedent "husband" had "by fraudulent representations induced the plaintiff to enter into the illicit relationship." Fox, supra, 178 Wis. at 372, 190 N.W. 90. Under those circumstances, the court reasoned that it was "just and logical" to infer "from the nature of the transaction" that "the supposed husband [can be] held to have assumed to pay [for services rendered by his 'spouse'] because in point of law and equity it is just that he should pay." Id.

In Fox, the court expressly refused to consider whether the same result would necessarily follow in other circumstances. Thus, Fox does not supply explicit support for the plaintiff's position here where she does not claim that she thought the parties were actually married.

The Steffes case, [95 Wis.2d 490, 290 N.W.2d 697 (1980)] however, does provide additional support for the plaintiff's position. Although Steffes involved a claim for recovery in contract by an unmarried cohabitant for the value of services she performed for the decedent, the same equitable principles that governed that case would appear to apply in a case where the plaintiff is seeking recovery based upon unjust enrichment. In Steffes, the court cited with approval a statement by the trial judge that "[t]he question I have in mind is why should the estate be enriched when that man was just as much a part of the illicit relationship as she was and not let her have her fair dues. I don't understand that law that would interpret unjust enrichment that way and deprive one and let the other benefit and do it on the basis that there was an illicit relationship but not equally held against the both. * * * " Steffes, supra, 95 Wis.2d at 508, 290 N.W.2d 697.

* * *

* * * Many courts have held, and we now so hold, that unmarried cohabitants may raise claims based upon unjust enrichment following the termination of their relationships where one of the parties attempts to retain an unreasonable amount of the property acquired through the efforts of both.

In this case, the plaintiff alleges that she contributed both property and services to the parties' relationship. She claims that because of these contributions the parties' assets increased, but that she was never compensated for her contributions. She further alleges that the defendant, knowing that the plaintiff expected to share in the property accumulated, "accepted the services rendered to him by the plaintiff" and that it would be unfair under the circumstances to allow him to retain everything while she receives nothing. We conclude that the facts alleged are sufficient to state a claim for recovery based upon unjust enrichment.

The judgment of the circuit court is reversed and the cause remanded.

SANDS v. MENDARD, 904 N.W.2d 789 (Wis. 2017). Properly understood, Watts stands for a very simple proposition: Wisconsin's public policy favoring marriage does not prohibit unmarried formerly cohabitating couples from asserting unjust enrichment claims against one another. Watts, 137 Wis. 2d at 532, 405 N.W.2d 303. In such cases, the focus is on the benefit received by one party from the other party which would be inequitable to retain. Boldt v. State, 101 Wis. 2d 566, 573, 305 N.W.2d 133 (1981). Therefore, the proper focus is on property accumulated, not on the type of personal relationship that existed between the parties. Stated otherwise, a claim for unjust enrichment may lie when two people work together to acquire property "through the efforts of both," regardless of their personal relationship. Watts, 137 Wis. 2d at 533, 405 N.W.2d 303.

That James and Sue Ann Watts were romantic cohabitants is not central to the merits of Sue Ann's unjust enrichment claim. For example, if James, instead, had a joint enterprise to accumulate wealth with his sister, mom or next door neighbor who provided necessary child care, domestic services and part-time office help, an unjust enrichment claim by that person would require the same proof as Watts required of Sue Ann. Watts simply provided that cohabitation between unmarried romantic partners is not a bar to an otherwise valid claim of unjust enrichment. It did not provide that the romantic relationship created the claim for relief. Watts, 137 Wis. 2d at 532–33, 405 N.W.2d 303.

NOTE:
REGULATION OF PRIVATE RELATIONS

Watts v. Watts involved a nonmarital relationship, but suppose the parties were married. Could the parties have contracted for compensation for Sue Ann Evans Watts? For all of her contributions? Some private relations, such as marriage, are heavily regulated by the state, which supplies most of the rules that govern the marriage, including in many states a prohibition against compensation for certain contributions of a spouse. For example, "courts have refused to enforce such agreements between spouses as: payment by one spouse to another for domestic, child care, or other services in the home; planned termination of the marriage after a given period of time; alteration of statutory duties of support; and provision in advance for the eventuality of divorce." Shultz, *Contractual Ordering of Marriage: A New Model for State Policy*, 70 Calif. L. Rev. 204, 231 (1982). (However, spouses are entitled to share in the accumulated property of the marital estate. In addition, many states allow spouses to make certain agreements, such as those concerning property rights and post-separation support.)

Several theorists have argued for greater freedom of contract even within a marriage. They assert the diminished importance of communal and religious standards governing marriage, the greater tolerance of diversity in the form of relationships, and the increasing need and desire for partners to make their own arrangements. Moreover, "[t]he contracting process * * * helps the parties articulate and clarify their goals and expectations. It stimulates straightforward, open communication * * *." L. Weitzman, THE MARRIAGE CONTRACT 232 (1981).

The April 6, 2006 New York Times reported that prenuptial agreements are now "all but routine in some circles as a way for the rich to protect their assets from the ravages of divorce court." Further, postnuptial agreements, "although a novelty" are gaining in popularity and "are often requested by wives who leave the work force to raise children. Many of them are corporate lawyers or investment bankers who 'want to compensate for the loss they'll be taking."

G. GILMORE, THE DEATH OF CONTRACT

95 (2d. ed. 1995).

Speaking descriptively, we might say that what is happening is that "contract" is being reabsorbed into the mainstream of "tort." * * * We have had more than one occasion to notice the insistence of the classical theorists on the sharp differentiation between contract and tort—the [early] refusal to admit any liability in "contract" until the formal requisites of offer, acceptance and consideration had been satisfied, the dogma that only "bargained-for" detriment or benefit could count as consideration, and notably, the limitations on damage recovery. Classical contract theory might well be described as an attempt to stake out an enclave within the general domain of tort. The dykes which were set up to protect the enclave have, it is clear enough, been crumbling at a progressively rapid rate. With the growth of the ideas of quasi-contract and unjust enrichment, classical consideration theory was breached on the benefit side. With the growth of the promissory estoppel idea, it was breached on the detriment side. We are fast approaching the point where, to prevent unjust enrichment, any benefit received by a defendant must be paid for unless it was clearly meant as a gift; where any detriment, reasonably incurred by a plaintiff in reliance on the defendant's assurances must be recompensed. When that point is reached, there is really no longer any viable distinction between liability in contract and liability in tort.

J. DAWSON, GIFTS AND PROMISES

2–4 (1980).

Some of the critics [of the consideration doctrine] condemn it altogether and demand that it be abolished. One of the most ardent of the abolitionists, however, was able recently to report some good news: that bargain consideration, produced only a century ago by that odd couple, Christopher Columbus Langdell and Oliver Wendell Holmes, has recently and quietly expired. No active surgery was needed, it seems, merely a denial of life support. For this coincided with the Death of Contract when Contract was consumed by the law of Tort, an event that was celebrated at a festive funeral not quite ten years ago.

To me it has seemed that the account of both deaths was exaggerated. In these essays the premise will be that bargain consideration has been and will remain for a long time to come a central feature of our law of contract, central in the sense that it provides a strong affirmative reason for enforcing promises, the reason that is by a wide margin the most often used, though it is not the only one. The reason is persuasive: the promisor receives or is assured that he will receive the kind of advantage that he in fact desires and has expressly promised to pay for. * * * Actually, this is not the issue on which battle is joined. Even the most embittered critics of bargain consideration do not really object to the enforcement of bargains. The objection has been to its transformation into a formula of denial, a formula that would deny legal effect to most promises for which there is nothing given or received in exchange.

In our own law of course the negation is not complete. Some promises are enforced for other reasons.

SECTION FIVE: OBLIGATION ARISING FROM PROMISES FOR BENEFIT RECEIVED

MILLS V. WYMAN

Supreme Judicial Court of Massachusetts, 1825.
20 Mass. (3 Pick.) 207.

This was an action of assumpsit brought to recover a compensation for the board, nursing, etc. of Levi Wyman, son of the defendant, from the 5th to the 20th of February, 1821. The plaintiff then lived at Hartford, in Connecticut; the defendant, at Shrewsbury, in this county. Levi Wyman, at the time when the services were rendered, was about 25 years of age, and had long ceased to be a member of his father's family. He was on his return from a voyage at sea, and being suddenly taken sick at Hartford, and being poor and in distress, was relieved by the plaintiff in the manner and to the extent above stated. On the 24th of February, after all the expenses had been incurred, the defendant wrote a letter to the plaintiff, promising to pay him such expenses. There was no consideration for this promise, except what grew out of the relation which subsisted between Levi Wyman and the defendant, and Howe, J., before whom the cause was tried in the court of common pleas, thinking this not sufficient to support the action, directed a nonsuit. To this direction the plaintiff filed exceptions.

* * *

PARKER, C.J. General rules of law established for the protection and security of honest and fair-minded men, who may inconsiderately make promises without any equivalent, will sometimes screen men of a different character from engagements which they are bound in *foro conscientiae* to perform. This is a defect inherent in all human systems of legislation. The rule that a mere verbal promise, without any consideration, cannot be enforced by action, is universal in its application, and cannot be departed from to suit particular cases in which a refusal to perform such a promise may be disgraceful.

The promise declared on in this case appears to have been made without any legal consideration. The kindness and services towards the sick son of the defendant were not bestowed at his request. The son was in no respect under the care of the defendant. He was twenty-five years old, and had long left his father's family. On his return from a foreign country, he fell sick among strangers, and the plaintiff acted the part of the good Samaritan, giving him shelter and comfort until he died. The defendant, his father, on being informed of this event, influenced by a transient feeling of gratitude, promised in writing to pay the plaintiff for the expenses he had incurred. But he has determined to break this promise, and is willing to have his case appear on record as a strong example of a particular injustice sometimes necessarily resulting from the operation of general rules.

It is said a moral obligation is a sufficient consideration to support an express promise; and some authorities lay down the rule thus broadly; but upon examination of the cases we are satisfied that the universality of the rule cannot be supported, and that there must have been some preexisting obligation, which has become inoperative by positive law, to form a basis for an effective promise. The cases of debts barred by the statute of limitations, of debts incurred by infants, of debts of bankrupts, are generally put for illustration of the rule. Express promises founded on such preexisting equitable obligations may be enforced; there is a good consideration for them; they merely remove an impediment created by law to the recovery of debts honestly due, but which public policy protects the debtors from being compelled to pay. In all these cases there was originally a *quid pro quo;* and according to the principles of natural justice the party receiving ought to pay; but the legislature has said he shall not be coerced; then comes the promise to pay the debt that is barred, the promise of the man to pay the debt of the infant, of the discharged bankrupt to restore to his creditor what by the law he had lost. In all these cases there is a moral obligation founded upon an antecedent valuable consideration. These promises therefore have a sound legal basis. They are not promises to pay something for nothing; not naked pacts; but the voluntary revival or creation of obligation which before existed in natural law, but which had been dispensed with, not for the benefit of the party obliged solely, but principally for the public convenience. If moral obligation, in its fullest sense, is a good substratum for an express promise, it is not easy to perceive why it is not equally good to support an implied promise. What a man ought to do, generally he ought to be made to do, whether he promise or refuse. But the law of society has left most of such obligations to the *interior* forum, as the tribunal of conscience has been aptly called. Is there not a moral obligation upon every son who has become affluent by means of the education and advantages bestowed upon him by his father, to relieve that father from pecuniary embarrassment, to promote his comfort and happiness, and even to share with him his riches, if thereby he will be made happy? And yet such a son may, with impunity, leave such a father in any degree of penury above that which will expose the community in which he dwells, to the danger of being obliged to preserve him from absolute want. Is not a wealthy father under strong moral obligation to advance the interest of an obedient, well disposed son, to furnish him with the means of acquiring and maintaining a becoming rank in life, to rescue him from the horrors of debt incurred by misfortune? Yet the law will uphold him in any degree of parsimony, short of that which would reduce his son to the necessity of seeking public charity.

Without doubt there are great interests of society which justify withholding the coercive arm of the law from these duties of imperfect obligation, as they are called; imperfect, not because they are less binding upon the conscience than those which are called perfect, but because the wisdom of the social law does not impose sanctions upon them.

A deliberate promise, in writing, made freely and without any mistake, one which may lead the party to whom it is made into contracts and expenses, cannot be broken without a violation of moral duty. But if there was nothing paid or promised for it, the law, perhaps wisely, leaves the execution of it to the conscience of him who makes it. It is only when the party making the promise gains something, or he to whom it is made loses something, that the law gives the promise validity. And in the case of the promise of the adult to pay the debt of the infant, of the debtor discharged by the statute of limitations or bankruptcy, the principle is preserved by looking back to the origin of the transaction, where an equivalent is to be found. An exact equivalent is not required by the law; for there being a consideration, the parties are left to estimate its value: though here the courts of equity will step in to relieve from gross inadequacy between the consideration and the promise.

These principles are deduced from the general current of decided cases upon the subject as well as from the known maxims of the common law. The general position, that moral obligation is a sufficient consideration for an express promise, is to be limited in its application, to cases where at some time or other a good or valuable consideration has existed.

A legal obligation is always a sufficient consideration to support either an express or an implied promise; such as an infant's debt for necessaries, or a father's promise to pay for the support and education of his minor children. But when the child shall have attained to manhood, and shall have become his own agent in the world's business, the debts he incurs, whatever may be their nature, create no obligation upon the father; and it seems to follow, that his promise founded upon such a debt has no legally binding force.

* * *

For the foregoing reasons we are all of opinion that the nonsuit directed by the court of common pleas was right, and that judgment be entered thereon for costs for the defendant.

NOTE:
MILLS V. WYMAN: ADDITIONAL FACTS

Relying on court records of Mills v. Wyman, Professor Watson has reported that caring for Levi Wyman was no lark. See Watson, In the Tribunal of Conscience: Mills v. Wyman Reconsidered, 71 Tulane L. Rev. 1749 (1997). Levi, "in a dergan'd state * * * leaped out of a chamber window" and required two guards for his safety. *Id.* at 1755 (quoting court records). However, apparently Levi did not die from his illness: "All available evidence suggests that Levi in fact recovered and eventually settled in Springfield, Massachusetts." *Id.* at 1756. Why the court believed Levi died remains a mystery: "Perhaps a stray suggestion of counsel at oral argument influenced the court; only the plaintiff's attorneys appeared in person." *Id.* at 1757–58.

Perhaps most interesting, defendant Wyman's letter to Mills, which the court interpreted as a promise to pay for Levi's *previous* care, may only have pertained to care in the future. The letter stated:

Dear Sir

> I received a line from you relating to my Son Levi's sickness and requesting me to come up and see him, but as the going is very bad I cannot come up at the present, but I wish you to take all possible care of him and if you cannot have him at your house I wish you to remove him to some convenient place and if he cannot satisfy you for it I will.

I want that you should write me again immediately how he does and greatly oblige your most obedient servant.

Seth Wyman
Shrewbury Feb 24th

Id. at 1760–61.

RESTATEMENT (SECOND) OF CONTRACTS § 82(1).

A promise to pay all or part of an antecedent contractual or quasi-contractual indebtedness owed by the promisor is binding if the indebtedness is still enforceable or would be except for the effect of a statute of limitations.

WEBB V. MCGOWIN

Court of Appeals of Alabama, 1935.
27 Ala. App. 82, 168 So. 196.

Action by Joe Webb against N. Floyd McGowin and Joseph F. McGowin, as executors of the estate of J. Greeley McGowin, deceased. From a judgment of nonsuit, plaintiff appeals.

BRICKEN, PRESIDING JUDGE.

This action is in assumpsit. The complaint as originally filed was amended. The demurrers to the complaint as amended were sustained, and because of this adverse ruling by the court the plaintiff took a non-suit, and the assignment of errors on this appeal are predicated upon said action or ruling of the court.

A fair statement of the case presenting the questions for decision is set out in appellant's brief, which we adopt.

> "On the 3d day of August, 1925, appellant while in the employ of the W.T. Smith Lumber Company, a corporation, and acting within the scope of his employment, was engaged in clearing the upper floor of mill No. 2 of the company. While so engaged he was in the act of dropping a pine block from the upper floor of the mill to the ground below; this being the usual and ordinary way of clearing the floor, and it being the duty of the plaintiff in the course of his employment to so drop it. The block weighed about 75 pounds.
>
> "As appellant was in the act of dropping the block to the ground below, he was on the edge of the upper floor of the mill. As he started to turn the block loose so that it would drop to the ground, he saw J. Greeley McGowin, testator of the defendants, on the ground below and directly under where the block would have fallen had appellant turned it loose. Had he turned it loose

it would have struck McGowin with such force as to have caused him serious bodily harm or death. Appellant could have remained safely on the upper floor of the mill by turning the block loose and allowing it to drop, but had he done this, the block would have fallen on McGowin and caused him serious injuries or death. The only safe and reasonable way to prevent this was for appellant to hold to the block and divert its direction in falling from the place where McGowin was standing and the only safe way to divert it so as to prevent its coming into contact with McGowin was for appellant to fall with it to the ground below. Appellant did this, and by holding to the block and falling with it to the ground below, he diverted the course of its fall in such way that McGowin was not injured. In thus preventing the injuries to McGowin appellant himself received serious bodily injuries, resulting in his right leg being broken, the heel of his right foot torn off and his right arm broken. He was badly crippled for life and rendered unable to do physical or mental labor.

"On September 1, 1925, in consideration of appellant having prevented him from sustaining death or serious bodily harm and in consideration of the injuries appellant had received, McGowin agreed with him to care for and maintain him for the remainder of appellant's life at the rate of $15 every two weeks from the time he sustained his injuries to and during the remainder of appellant's life; it being agreed that McGowin would pay this sum to appellant for his maintenance. Under the agreement McGowin paid or caused to be paid to appellant the sum so agreed on up until McGowin's death on January 1, 1934. After his death the payments were continued to and including January 27, 1934, at which time they were discontinued. Thereupon plaintiff brought suit to recover the unpaid installments accruing up to the time of the bringing of the suit.

"The material averments of the different counts of the original complaint and the amended complaint are predicated upon the foregoing statement of facts."

In other words, the complaint as amended averred in substance: (1) That on August 3, 1925, appellant saved J. Greeley McGowin, appellee's testator, from death or grievous bodily harm; (2) that in doing so appellant sustained bodily injury crippling him for life; (3) that in consideration of the services rendered and the injuries received by appellant, McGowin agreed to care for him the remainder of appellant's life, the amount to be paid being $15 every two weeks; (4) that McGowin complied with this agreement until he died on January 1, 1934, and the payments were kept up to January 27, 1934, after which they were discontinued.

The action was for the unpaid installments accruing after January 27, 1934, to the time of the suit.

The principal grounds of demurrer to the original and amended complaint are: (1) It states no cause of action; (2) its averments show the contract was without consideration; (3) it fails to allege that McGowin had, at or before the services were rendered, agreed to pay appellant for them; (4) the contract declared on is void under the statute of frauds.

The averments of the complaint show that appellant saved McGowin from death or grievous bodily harm. This was a material benefit to him of infinitely more value than any financial aid he could have received. Receiving this benefit, McGowin became morally bound to compensate appellant for the services rendered. Recognizing his moral obligation, he expressly agreed to pay appellant as alleged in the complaint and complied with this agreement up to the time of his death; a period of more than 8 years.

Had McGowin been accidentally poisoned and a physician, without his knowledge or request, had administered an antidote, thus saving his life, a subsequent promise by McGowin to pay the physician would have been valid. Likewise, McGowin's agreement as disclosed by the complaint to compensate appellant for saving him from death or grievous bodily injury is valid and enforceable.

Where the promisee cares for, improves, and preserves the property of the promisor, though done without his request, it is sufficient consideration for the promisor's subsequent agreement to pay for the service, because of the material benefit received. * * *

In Boothe v. Fitzpatrick, 36 Vt. 681, the court held that a promise by defendant to pay for the past keeping of a bull which had escaped from defendant's premises and been cared for by plaintiff was valid, although there was no previous request, because the subsequent promise obviated that objection; it being equivalent to a previous request. On the same principle, had the promisee saved the promisor's life or his body from grievous harm, his subsequent promise to pay for the services rendered would have been valid. Such service would have been far more material than caring for his bull. Any holding that saving a man from death or grievous bodily harm is not a material benefit sufficient to uphold a subsequent promise to pay for the service, necessarily rests on the assumption that saving life and preservation of the body from harm have only a sentimental value. The converse of this is true. Life and preservation of the body have material, pecuniary values, measurable in dollars and cents. Because of this, physicians practice their profession charging for services rendered in saving life and curing the body of its ills, and surgeons perform operations. The same is true as to the law of negligence, authorizing the assessment of damages in personal injury cases based upon the extent of the injuries, earnings, and life expectancies of those injured.

In the business of life insurance, the value of a man's life is measured in dollars and cents according to his expectancy, the soundness of his body, and his ability to pay premiums. The same is true as to health and accident insurance.

It follows that if, as alleged in the complaint, appellant saved J. Greeley McGowin from death or grievous bodily harm, and McGowin subsequently agreed to pay him for the service rendered, it became a valid and enforceable contract.

It is well settled that a moral obligation is a sufficient consideration to support a subsequent promise to pay where the promisor has received a material benefit, although there was no original duty or liability resting on the promisor. * * *

The case at bar is clearly distinguishable from that class of cases where the consideration is a mere moral obligation or conscientious duty unconnected with receipt by promisor of benefits of a material or pecuniary nature. * * * Here the promisor received a material benefit constituting a valid consideration for his promise.

Some authorities hold that, for a moral obligation to support a subsequent promise to pay, there must have existed a prior legal or equitable obligation, which for some reason had become unenforceable, but for which the promisor was still morally bound. This rule, however, is subject to qualification in those cases where the promisor, having received a material benefit from the promisee, is morally bound to compensate him for the services rendered and in consideration of this obligation promises to pay. In such cases the subsequent promise to pay is an affirmance or ratification of the services rendered carrying with it the presumption that a previous request for the service was made. * * *

Under the decisions above cited, McGowin's express promise to pay appellant for the services rendered was an affirmance or ratification of what appellant had done raising the presumption that the services had been rendered at McGowin's request.

The averments of the complaint show that in saving McGowin from death or grievous bodily harm, appellant was crippled for life. This was part of the consideration of the contract declared on. McGowin was benefited. Appellant was injured. Benefit to the promisor or injury to the promisee is a sufficient legal consideration for the promisor's agreement to pay. * * *

Under the averments of the complaint the services rendered by appellant were not gratuitous. The agreement of McGowin to pay and the acceptance of payment by appellant conclusively shows the contrary.

The contract declared on was not void under the statute of frauds * * *. The demurrer on this ground was not well taken. * * *

From what has been said, we are of the opinion that the court, below erred in the ruling complained of; that is to say, in sustaining the demurrer, and for this error the case is reversed and remanded.

Reversed and remanded.

SAMFORD, JUDGE (concurring).

The questions involved in this case are not free from doubt, and perhaps the strict letter of the rule, as stated by judges, though not always in accord, would bar a recovery by plaintiff, but following the principle announced by Chief Justice Marshall in Hoffman v. Porter, Fed.Cas. No. 6,577, 2 Brock. 156, 159, where he says, "I do not think that law ought to be separated from justice, where it is at most doubtful," I concur in the conclusions reached by the court.

OBERER, ON LAW, LAWYERING AND LAW PROFESSING: THE GOLDEN SAND

39 J. Legal Educ. 203, 203–05 (1989).

Easy cases are resoluble in lawyers' offices by the application of legal doctrines to provable facts. In such cases, the lawyer tells the client "no" or "yes." Hard cases, by contrast, are hard because the legal doctrines working for the potential plaintiff encounter, head on, the counterdoctrines working for the potential defendant. Where these doctrines meet is in an area of "murk" in which legal and/or factual line drawing must be done; the case is "hard" because reasonable minds may disagree as to the drawing of those lines. In such cases, the lines are not drawn by the "law." They are drawn by human beings called "judges," sometimes aided by other human beings called "jurors."

These human beings decide the case on the totality of the relevant evidence and law, bringing to bear in their search for "justice" ("sense," "fairness") the totality of their life experiences. The case is not (should not be) decided mechanistically on the basis of some doctrinal technicality, even though, in explaining the decision after the fact, that human being, the judge—obeisant to the shortness of life and the longness of the docket—may make it seem so in the written opinion.

In these hard cases, the ones that belong in court, legal doctrine is not irrelevant. There is not, accordingly, any cynicism in my dealing with it. Indeed, the opposite is true; it is the ultimate idealism to declare that justice between and among human beings is the product of the application of human judgment to the totality of the evidence and the arguments rallied in this particular, never before decided, case.

EDSON V. POPPE

South Dakota Supreme Court, 1910.
24 S.D. 466, 124 N.W. 441.

Action by George F. Edson against William Poppe. Judgment for plaintiff, and defendant appeals. Affirmed.

* * *

MCCOY, J. The plaintiff recovered judgment upon the verdict of a jury in the circuit court. The case was tried upon the following complaint: That the defendant at all the times hereinafter named was the owner of the following described premises situated in Turner county, S.D., to wit (describing the land); that at all the times herein named George Poppe was in possession of said premises as the tenant of defendant; that during the year 1904 this plaintiff, at the instance and request of said George Poppe, drilled and dug upon said premises a well 250 feet deep, and obtained water in said well, and placed casing therein; that the reasonable value of the digging and casing of said well was and is the sum of $250; that said well was and is a valuable improvement upon the said premises, and greatly adds to the value thereof, and has been used by the occupants of said premises since the said digging thereof, with the knowledge and consent of defendant; that on or about the 5th day of August, 1905, the defendant, at the said premises, after having examined the said well, and in consideration of the said well to him, and of the improvement it made upon said premises, expressly ratified the acts of his said tenant in having said well drilled, and then and there promised and agreed to pay plaintiff the reasonable value of the digging and casing of the said well as aforesaid; that defendant has since refused, and still refuses, to pay plaintiff anything for said well. Wherefore, etc. To the said complaint defendant made the following answer: Denies generally and specifically each and every allegation in said complaint, except such as is hereinafter specifically admitted. Defendant admits that he is the owner of the said premises as stated in the complaint. At the opening of the trial, and upon the offer of testimony on the part of plaintiff, defendant objected to the introduction of any evidence, for the reason that the complaint did not state a cause of action, in that the consideration alleged in the contract is a past consideration, and no consideration for any promise, if any was made, and no consideration for the promise alleged. The objection was overruled, and defendant excepted. This ruling of the trial court is assigned and now urged as error, but we are of the opinion that the ruling of the learned trial court was correct.

It seems to be the general rule that past services are not a sufficient consideration for a promise to pay therefor, made at a subsequent time, and after such services have been fully rendered and completed; but in some courts a modified doctrine of moral obligation is adopted, and it is held that a moral obligation, founded on previous benefits received by the promisor at the hands of the promisee, will support a promise by him. * * *

The authorities are not so clear as to the sufficiency of past services, rendered without previous request, to support an express promise; but, when proper distinctions are made, the cases as a whole seem to warrant the statement that such a promise is supported by a sufficient consideration if the services were beneficial, and were not intended to be gratuitous. * * * In Drake v. Bell, 26 Misc.Rep. 237, 55 N.Y.Supp. 945, a mechanic, under contract to repair a vacant house, by mistake repaired the house next door, which belonged to the defendant. The repairing was a benefit to the latter, and he agreed to pay a certain amount therefor. It was held that the promise rested upon sufficient consideration. Gaynor, J., says: "The rule seems to be that a subsequent promise, founded on a former enforceable obligation, or on value previously had from the promisee, is binding." * * * In Boothe v. Fitzpatrick, 36 Vt. 681, it is held that if the consideration, even without request, moves directly from the plaintiff to the defendant, and inures directly to the defendant's benefit, the promise is binding though made upon a past consideration. In this case the court held that a promise by defendant to pay for the past keeping of a bull, which had escaped from defendant's premises and been cared for by plaintiff, was valid, although there was no previous request, but that the subsequent promise obviated that objection; it being equivalent to a previous request. The allegation of the complaint here is that the digging and casing of the well in question inured directly to the defendant's benefit, and that, after he had seen and examined the same, he expressly promised and agreed to pay plaintiff the reasonable value thereof. It also appears that said well was made under such circumstances as could not be deemed gratuitous on the part of plaintiff, or an act of voluntary courtesy to defendant. We are therefore of the opinion that under the circumstances alleged, the subsequent promise of defendant to pay plaintiff the reasonable value for digging and casing said well was binding, and supported by sufficient consideration. We are also of the opinion that the instructions based on this complaint, and in particular as to the validity of the subsequent promise of defendant, properly submitted the issues to the jury.

* * *

Finding no error in the record, the judgment of the circuit court is affirmed.

HENDERSON, PROMISES GROUNDED IN THE PAST: THE IDEA OF UNJUST ENRICHMENT AND THE LAW OF CONTRACTS

57 Va. L. Rev. 1115, 1115, 1159–62 (1971).

* * * [R]ecognition of the promise for benefit received has come slowly in our law largely because of the very policy reasons responsible for singling

out gifts for special treatment. Because a price is not presently asked for a promise anchored in the past, the general assumption has been that the promisor is vulnerable to dangers similar to those that threaten donors of gift promises. As a result, policies designed to protect the interests of the makers of unexecuted gifts have been transferred to the moral obligation promisor. The vehicle for implementation of those policies is, of course, consideration doctrine. The question * * * is whether the natural formalities and substantive basis of the promise for benefit received dictate a classification that rejects the policies thought to require a denial of enforcement of gift promises.

Certainly it is settled beyond recall that unjust enrichment, viewed independently or as reinforcement of bargain, itself constitutes a substantive ground for the enforcement of promises. Moreover, one is hard pressed to resist the proposition that the impressiveness of the ground is enhanced when the enrichment factor is coupled with a promissory confession that it has created in the recipient a sense of moral obligation. * * *

Consideration doctrine declares many promises unenforceable because the maker's deliberations are thought to be inadequate to impress upon him the seriousness of the transaction. * * * [C]oncern about ill-considered promise making is largely misplaced. Given the usual sequence in which events unfold—i.e., a performance on one side, resulting in an often identifiable gain in the hands of the other party, followed by the other's promissory response—the transaction itself involves natural safeguards equivalent to those of form or present exchange. The time lag between performance and promise affords an opportunity for deliberation and the exercise of caution, as well as an evaluation of "price," not present in most conventional bargains. * * *

NOTE: THE CONCEPT OF MORAL OBLIGATION

According to Charles Fried,

> "[m]orality is concerned with how people should lead their lives and how they should treat each other. * * * By morality I do not mean what people think is the way they should live and how they should treat each other, nor how some person or group of persons think people should live their lives. Morality does not in the first degree describe attitudes, beliefs, or demands about these things, any more than mathematics in the first degree is about what people think, teach, or ordain about the domain of numbers and abstract relations. In both cases there is a fact of the matter: the gratuitous infliction of pain is wrong; 2 + 2 = 4."

Charles Fried, The Convergence of Contract and Promise, 120 Harv. L. Rev. F.1 (2007).

The concept of moral obligation (or moral consideration) plays a role in most of the cases in this section. The courts using this concept seldom attempt to define it or otherwise subject it to careful analysis. But in Park Falls State Bank v. Fordyce, 206 Wis. 628, 238 N.W. 516 (1931), the Supreme Court of Wisconsin offered these remarks:

> It is true that there are numerous cases holding that a mere moral consideration will not support a promise to pay. But it is equally true that there are numerous cases holding a moral consideration sufficient where the promisor originally received from the promisee something of value sufficient to arouse a moral, as distinguished from a legal obligation. One, ought, in morals, to make return for things of value not intended as a gift that he has accepted, and he ought, in morals to do what he knowingly and advisedly gave one acting for his benefit and to his own hurt to understand he would do.

Do you agree? Consider whether the foregoing analysis of the concept of moral obligation applies to the cases in this section in which the plaintiff prevailed. Consider also the following remarks of Lon L. Fuller:

> When we say the defendant was morally obligated to do the thing he promised, we in effect assert the existence of a substantive ground for enforcing the promise. * * * The court's conviction that the promisor ought to do the thing, plus the promisor's own admission of his obligation, may tilt the scales in favor of enforcement where neither standing alone would be sufficient. If it be argued that moral consideration threatens certainty, the solution would seem to lie, not in rejecting the doctrine, but in taming it by continuing the process of judicial exclusion and inclusion already begun in cases involving infant's contracts, barred debts, and discharged bankrupts.

Fuller, Consideration and Form, 41 Colum. L. Rev. 799, 821–22 (1941).

RESTATEMENT (SECOND) OF CONTRACTS § 86.

Promise for Benefit Received

(1) A promise made in recognition of a benefit previously received by the promisor from the promisee is binding to the extent necessary to prevent injustice.

(2) A promise is not binding under Subsection (1)

(a) if the promisee conferred the benefit as a gift or for other reasons the promisor has not been unjustly enriched; or

(b) to the extent that its value is disproportionate to the benefit.

Comment:

a. "Past consideration"; "moral obligation." Enforcement of promises to pay for benefit received has sometimes been said to rest on "past consideration" or on the "moral obligation" of the promisor, and there are statutes in such terms in a few states. Those terms are not used here: "past consideration" is inconsistent with the meaning of consideration stated in § 71, and there seems to be no consensus as to what constitutes a "moral obligation." The mere fact of promise has been thought to create a moral obligation, but it is clear that not all promises are enforced. Nor are moral obligations based solely on gratitude or sentiment sufficient of themselves to support a subsequent promise.

* * *

b. Rationale. Although in general a person who has been unjustly enriched at the expense of another is required to make restitution, restitution is denied in many cases in order to protect persons who have had benefits thrust upon them. See Restatement of Restitution §§ 1, 2, 112. In other cases restitution is denied by virtue of rules designed to guard against false claims, stale claims, claims already litigated, and the like. In many such cases a subsequent promise to make restitution removes the reason for the denial of relief, and the policy against unjust enrichment then prevails. Compare Restatement, Second, Agency § 462 on ratification of the acts of a person who officiously purports to act as an agent. Enforcement of the subsequent promise sometimes makes it unnecessary to decide a difficult question as to the limits on quasi-contractual relief.

* * * [T]he broader principle [of Section 86] * * * may not be applied if there is doubt whether the objections to restitution are fully met by the subsequent promise. Facts such as the definite and substantial character of the benefit received, formality in the making of the promise, part performance of the promise, reliance on the promise or the probability of such reliance may be relevant to show that no imposition results from enforcement.

* * *

e. Benefit conferred as a gift. In the absence of mistake or the like, there is no element of unjust enrichment in the receipt of a gift, and the rule of this Section has no application to a promise to pay for a past gift. Similarly, when a debt is discharged by a binding agreement, the transaction is closed even though full payment is not made. But marginal cases arise in which both parties understand that what is in form a gift is intended to be reimbursed indirectly, or in which a subsequent promise to pay is expressly contemplated. * * * Enforcement of the subsequent promise is proper in some such cases.

SECTION SIX: OBLIGATION ARISING FROM TORT

W. PROSSER AND W. KEETON ON TORTS

3, 6 (5th ed. 1984).

Included under the head of torts are miscellaneous civil wrongs, ranging from simple, direct interferences with the person, such as assault, battery and false imprisonment, or with property, as in the case of trespass or conversion, up through various forms of negligence, to disturbances of intangible interests, such as those in good reputation, or commercial or social advantage. * * *

* * *

* * * So far as there is one central idea [in tort law], it would seem that it is that liability must be based upon conduct which is socially unreasonable. The common thread woven into all torts is the idea of unreasonable interference with the interests of others.

MCR FEDERAL, LLC v. JB&A, INC., 808 S.E.2d 186 (Va. 2017). "The law of torts provides redress only for the violation of certain common law and statutory duties involving the safety of persons and property, which are imposed to protect the broad interests of society." *Filak v. George*, 267 Va. 612, 618, 594 S.E.2d 610, 613 (2004). In contrast, "the major consideration underlying contract law is the protection of bargained for expectations." *Id.* "Losses suffered as a result of the breach of a duty assumed only by agreement, rather than a duty imposed by law, remain the sole province of the law of contracts." *Id.*

In determining whether a cause of action sounds in tort, contract, or both, "the source of the duty violated must be ascertained." *Richmond Metro. Auth. v. McDevitt Street Bovis, Inc.*, 256 Va. 553, 558, 507 S.E.2d 344, 347 (1998). In certain circumstances, a single act or occurrence can support causes of action for both breach of contract and for breach of a duty arising in tort. "To avoid turning every breach of contract into a tort, however, we have consistently adhered to the rule that, in order to recover in tort, the duty tortiously or negligently breached must be a common law duty, not one existing between the parties solely by virtue of the contract." *Dunn Constr. Co. v. Cloney*, 278 Va. 260, 267, 682 S.E.2d 943, 946 (2009).

R. SPEIDEL, THE BORDERLAND OF CONTRACT

10 N. Ky. L. Rev. 164, 168–71 (1983).

Doctrinal Differences Between Contract and Tort

Despite continuing disputes over historical cause and effect, important doctrinal differences between Contract and Tort emerged from the 19th Century and are still imprinted on American law. * * *

(A) *Conduct.*

In Contract, the actionable conduct is a failure without justification to perform an enforceable promise. A must make and break a promise, but B is not required to prove that the breach was negligent or intentional or otherwise "wrongful." To this extent, Contract is a law of strict rather than fault based liability. The concept of breach also covers a defective promised performance (misfeasance) and a failure to perform as promised (nonfeasance). In Tort, liability is usually imposed for affirmative conduct that causes loss. Unless there are special circumstances, the failure to act is not a tort. In addition, not all conduct which causes loss is actionable. The conduct must be intentional or negligent or, perhaps, that which creates unreasonable danger to others. In short, fault and motive play a greater role in Tort than in Contract. But in both, liability is imposed in a selective process by the courts: not all broken promises are contracts and not all conduct which causes loss is a tort.

MAULDIN V. SHEFFER

Court of Appeals of Georgia, 1966.
113 Ga. App. 874, 150 S.E.2d 150.

FRANKUM, JUDGE.

L. Miles Sheffer, doing business as L. Miles Sheffer & Associates, sued John G. Mauldin, doing business as Coastal Engineering Company, for damages. The original petition did not clearly set forth a cause of action, either ex contractu or ex delicto [tort] but after the defendant had demurred thereto and the petition had been once amended, and the defendant had orally moved to dismiss the petition as amended, the plaintiff filed a redrafted petition in which he set forth the following material facts. Plaintiff was a licensed architect engaged in the practice of his profession. He entered into an oral contract with the defendant, a registered professional mechanical engineer actively engaged in such profession under the terms of which defendant agreed to provide plaintiff with certain engineering designs, plans, drawings and specifications to be drawn, written and produced by defendant who was to serve as consulting engineer for plaintiff's architectural work and projects. Pursuant thereto the defendant did, in June, 1961, undertake to furnish plaintiff with certain engineering designs, plans, drawings, specifications and engineering data for the plaintiff's use in the design and construction of additions to five specified school buildings. In consideration for such services plaintiff agreed to pay defendant $200 per week, and plaintiff did pay to the defendant such sums. Defendant did, in his professional engineering capacity, produce certain designs, drawings, plans, specifications, engineering data, and revisions thereof which he furnished to plaintiff in December, 1961, and in January, April, and May of 1962, all with respect to the aforesaid additions to school buildings. Said plans were incorporated by plaintiff in his overall architectural plans and delivered by plaintiff to the various school boards by whom plaintiff had been employed. Said designs, plans, specifications and engineering data and revisions prepared by the defendant and delivered to plaintiff were in numerous respects erroneous, incorrect and contrary to generally accepted engineering standards, in that they were contrary to and in violation of the fundamental laws of physics and were contrary to and in violation of the promulgated policies, regulations and standards of the Georgia State School Building Authority, the Georgia Department of Education, and the county boards of education by whom plaintiff was employed. The errors in the defendant's work concerned the plumbing, heating and electrical designs of the said projects, a detailed list of said errors being attached as Exhibit A and by reference incorporated in the petition. Plaintiff used defendant's work in his designs and delivered the same to his clients for approval and acceptance, and thereafter, the various projects were advertised for construction bids, but before the contract was let the State School Building Authority recalled the bids and returned the plans to the plaintiff for correction of the engineering errors of defendant. Defendant prepared revisions of his designs which were duly resubmitted by plaintiff, and the same procedure resulted in a rejection of the plans by the State School Building Authority on two subsequent occasions, each revision of defendant being rejected as being unsatisfactory for the various reasons set forth in the petition and the exhibit attached thereto. As the result of the rejection of the plans as aforesaid, plaintiff's clients and the State School Building Authority made certain charges against the plaintiff for expenses incurred in advertising and readvertising the projects for bids, and it was necessary ultimately for plaintiff to employ other engineering personnel to completely redesign, re-engineer, redraw and rewrite the designs, plans, specifications and data which defendant had been employed by plaintiff to prepare, and plaintiff incurred in so doing, specified expenses which are set forth in the petition in detail. Plaintiff also incurred other specified losses and expenses, including the loss of a contract to perform architectural services on certain other school building projects planned by one of the plaintiff's clients who, as a result of the engineering errors and mistakes perpetrated by the defendant, refused to permit plaintiff to serve as architect on said projects, although having previously contracted with plaintiff to so serve. All of plaintiff's special damages alleged to have proximately resulted from the defendant's negligence are set forth in the petition in detail.

* * *

Paragraphs 38 and 39 of the petition are as follows: "38. That the defendant, in the preparation of said designs, drawings, specifications, plans and data did willfully and intentionally utilize designs, drawings, specifications, plans and data from other building projects and other engineering projects on which defendant had worked in the past, which were not suited or in any way reasonabl[y] intended to be suited or adapted to the plaintiff's architectural plans for said five school building projects; that the defendant did frivolously utilize said other and non-related plans, drawings, specifications, designs and data with full knowledge that the same were not usable or adaptable to the plaintiff's architectural plans and the said conduct of the defendant was willful and wanton and was in deliberate disregard of his ethical, moral and legal duties as an engineer registered under the laws of Georgia and was in deliberate and willful disregard of his duty to plaintiff to perform said engineering work in a skilled, conscientious and diligent manner according to his ability and was in willful, deliberate and intentional disregard of his duty to use reasonable and ordinary care in the performance of his engineering duties. 39. That the defendant, in thus frivolously, willfully, deliberately and intentionally failing to exercise ordinary care and reasonable care in the performance of his duties as an engineer in the preparation of said plans, designs, drawings, specifications and data for the plaintiff, did perpetrate an act of aggravated tortious conduct within the meaning and scope of Section 105–2002 of the Code of Georgia and plaintiff taxes punitive and exemplary damages against defendant in the sum of Five Hundred Thousand ($500,000.00) Dollars to deter the defendant from repeating such wrongdoing and sued the defendant for said punitive damages." In paragraph 40 plaintiff alleged that all of his injury and damage was directly and proximately caused by the negligence of the defendant in enumerated particulars therein set out. Exhibit A, referred to in the petition, listed 151 errors alleged to have been committed by the defendant in the preparation of the engineering plans and specifications for the plaintiff. To the redrafted petition the defendant filed general and special demurrers. The trial court overruled the grounds of general demurrer. This judgment is enumerated as error in this appeal.

While it does not appear from the record, counsel for the appellant in their brief before this court state, in effect, that counsel for the plaintiff declared in open court that it was their intention to proceed in tort rather than ex contractu. Counsel for the appellee do not deny this statement or in any way directly refer to it in their brief, but from the tenor of their argument it is apparent that their contention was and is that the petition as finally amended set forth a cause of action ex delicto. We will accordingly treat the case as being one where such an election has been made and will consider the issue of whether or not the petition as finally amended is sufficient to set forth a cause of action ex delicto. * * *

Generally, a mere breach of a valid contract amounting to no more than a failure to perform in accordance with its terms does not constitute a tort or authorize the aggrieved party to elect whether he will proceed ex contractu or ex delicto. * * * Accordingly, under the foregoing authorities, if there is no liability except that arising out of a breach of the express terms of the contract, the action must be in contract, and an action in tort cannot be maintained. Of course, as was said in City & Suburban Ry. Co. of Savannah v. Brauss, 70 Ga. 368, 377, in referring to those situations where from the nature of the breach or the duty violated an election may be made by the aggrieved party "private duties may arise from statute, or flow from relations created by contract, express or implied. The violation of any such specific duty, accompanied with damage, gives a right of action." * * * Thus, if a contract imposes a legal duty upon a party thereto, which duty exists apart from the specific obligation of the contract, the neglect of that duty is a tort founded upon a contract. * * * In such a case the liability arises out of the breach of duty incident to and created by the contract, but is only dependent upon the contract to the extent necessary to raise the duty * * *. So, it is well settled * * * that in some cases the plaintiff may have an election to sue for a breach of contract or for damages in tort. Code § 105–105. * * * From the foregoing authorities it can be seen that it is not in every case where a contract has been breached that a right accrues to the opposite party to make an election. * * *

The rule which affords an election to sue ex delicto or ex contractu in cases involving a breach of a duty implied by reason of a contractual relation has been applied to contractual relations between principal and agent, bailor and bailee, attorney and client, physician and patient, carrier and passenger or shipper, master and servant, and possibly other well recognized relations. * * * As may be seen from a mere casual perusal of the cases * * * the formulation of a definitive rule workable upon application to all cases is most difficult, and the Georgia authorities, numerous as they may be, leave room for considerable doubt as to the proper application of the rule in particular cases. However, one clear distinction seems to have been made which is indicative of the scope and application of the rule, and that is the distinction between nonfeasance or the mere failure to perform the contract at all, and misfeasance or the negligent performance of the contract. * * * As to the former of these the cases have fairly consistently held that it affords no basis for an action ex delicto, even though the failure to perform may have been characterized as negligent * * * while in the latter a cause of action ex delicto may be had. * * * Though some may contend that in cases of misfeasance there is always a right to make such an election, no case expressly so holding has been found and such a holding being patently unnecessary to a decision of the question now before us, we are unwilling to go that far. There may be exceptions to the rule even in misfeasance cases. It is sufficient to say that the opposite appears to be more nearly the true rule, that is, that it is *only* in such cases that the right to elect between a tort action and a contract action exists.

From the authorities to which we have referred and from others which we have examined, the rule may be fairly deduced that in order to maintain an action ex delicto because of a breach of duty growing out of a contractual relation the breach must be shown to have been a breach of a duty imposed by law and not merely the breach of a duty imposed by the contract itself. * * * This is consistent with the definition of a tort set forth in Code § 105–101. "Duty imposed by law" as used in this context means, of course, either a duty imposed by a valid statutory enactment of the legislature or a duty imposed by a recognized common law principle declared in the reported decisions of the appellate courts of the State or jurisdiction involved. The question in this case then resolves itself to whether the petition sufficiently alleges the violation of such a "duty imposed by law."

The law imposes upon persons of professional standing performing medical, architectural, engineering, and those performing other and like skilled services, pursuant to their contracts made with their clients, an obligation to exercise a reasonable degree of care, skill and ability, such as is ordinarily exercised under similar conditions and like circumstances by persons employed in the same or similar professions. * * * This is a duty apart from any express contractual obligation. Therefore, persons of this class performing services pursuant to their contracts with their clients have been held to be liable in tort for their negligence in failing to exercise the required degree of skill, and thus to be liable to a suit ex delicto under the doctrine applicable to the second category above referred to. * * * In a proper case the question of whether the defendant exercised the required degree of skill is, like any other question of fact, to be decided by a jury. * * * We think then that it is clear that the petition in this case does allege the violation of a duty imposed by law under the principles which we have set forth above. Clearly, if the defendant undertook to perform the contract for the plaintiff in the manner alleged, a jury would be authorized to find that he had failed to exercise that reasonable degree of care, skill and ability such as is ordinarily exercised under the same or similar conditions and under like circumstances by engineers generally in practicing their professions. The petition stated a cause of action ex delicto as against the general demurrer interposed, and the trial court did not err in overruling the general demurrer.

Judgment affirmed.

W. PROSSER AND W. KEETON ON TORTS

660–61, 656–57, 664–66 (5th ed. 1984).

[T]he American courts have extended the tort liability for misfeasance to virtually every type of contract where defective performance may injure the promisee. An attorney or an abstractor examining a title, a physician treating a patient, a surveyor, an agent collecting a note or lending money or settling a claim, or a liability insurer defending a suit, all have been held liable in tort for their negligence. The same is true of contractors employed to build a structure, to transport people or goods, to install a windmill or a lightning rod, or to shoot an oil well, or a beauty shop giving a permanent wave, of suppliers of chattels, and of many others. The principle which seems to have emerged from the decisions in the United States is that there will be liability in tort for misperformance of a contract whenever there would be liability for gratuitous performance without the contract—which is to say, whenever such misperformance involves a foreseeable, unreasonable risk of harm to the interests of the plaintiff.

HARGRAVE V. OKI NURSERY, INC.

United States Court of Appeals, Second Circuit, 1980.
636 F.2d 897.

NICKERSON, DISTRICT JUDGE.

Plaintiffs appeal from an order of the United States District Court for the Eastern District of New York dismissing the complaint against defendant Oki Nursery, Inc. for lack of personal jurisdiction.

Plaintiff Long Island Vineyards, Inc., is a New York corporation of which plaintiff Hargrave is president. Plaintiffs operate a vineyard in Suffolk County, New York, and make wine from the grapes they produce. Oki is a California corporation with its main office in Sacramento and grows and sells nursery stocks including wine grape vines. The complaint, brought in the Supreme Court of the State of New York, Suffolk County, asserts six claims against Oki. The first alleges that during 1973 and 1974 Oki represented to plaintiffs that vines purchased from Oki would be healthy, free of disease, and suitable for wine production, that plaintiffs relied on the representations and in May 1974 purchased vines from Oki, that the representations were knowingly false, and that the vines sold to plaintiffs were diseased and incapable of bearing fruit of adequate quality or quantity for plaintiffs' commercial wine production.

The other five claims allege substantially the same facts and assert, respectively, breach of contract, breach of express warranty, breach of implied warranty of merchantability, breach of warranty of fitness for a particular purpose, and negligent performance of the contract.

Asserting diversity of citizenship, Oki removed the action to the District Court and moved to dismiss for lack of personal jurisdiction. The court granted the motion. In this case New York State law determines whether personal jurisdiction over Oki was obtained. Rule 4(e) of the Federal Rules of Civil Procedure. Section 302(a)(3), of the New York Civil Practice Law and Rules recites, in pertinent part, "(a)s to a cause of action arising from any of the acts enumerated in this section, a court may exercise personal jurisdiction over any nondomiciliary, * * * who in person or through an agent: * * * commits a tortious act without the state causing injury to person or property within the state, * * * if he * * * expects or should reasonably expect the act to have consequences in the state and derives substantial revenue from interstate or international commerce."

Plaintiffs say that Oki's false representations constituted fraudulent and tortious acts committed in California and causing injury in New York and that Oki should reasonably have expected its fraudulent representations to have New York consequences, and derived substantial revenue from interstate commerce. Oki does not dispute that it could reasonably have expected its representations to have consequences in New York or that it derives substantial revenue from interstate commerce. Oki argues, however, that no "tortious act" has been alleged in the complaint since plaintiffs, by applying the fraud label, may not convert a claim for breach of a contractual representation into a tort claim * * *.

The law of torts and the law of contracts are said to protect different interests. Albemarle Theatre Inc. v. Bayberry Realty Corp., 27 A.D.2d 172, 277 N.Y.S.2d 505 (1st Dept.1967). A plaintiff may recover in contract because the defendant has made an agreement, and the law thinks it desirable that he be held to that agreement. Tort liability is imposed on the basis of some social policy that disapproves the infliction of a specific kind of harm irrespective of any agreement. Id. Specifically the law of fraud seeks to protect against injury those who rely to their detriment on the deliberately dishonest statements of another.

Thus, it does not follow that because acts constitute a breach of contract they cannot also give rise to liability in tort. Where the conduct alleged breaches a legal duty which exists "independent of contractual relations between the parties" a plaintiff may sue in tort. Channel Master Corporation v. Aluminum Limited Sales, Inc., 4 N.Y.2d 403, 408, 176 N.Y.S.2d 259, 263, 151 N.E.2d 833, 836 (1958). If the only interest at stake is that of holding the defendant to a promise, the courts have said that the plaintiff may not transmogrify the contract claim into one for tort. * * * But if in addition there is an interest in protecting the plaintiff from other kinds of harm, the plaintiff may recover in tort whether or not he has a valid claim for breach of contract.

In the present case the complaint sets forth all the elements of an action in tort for fraudulent representations, namely, "representation of a material existing fact, falsity, scienter, deception and injury." Channel Master Corporation v. Aluminum Limited Sales, Inc., 4 N.Y.2d at 407, 176 N.Y.S.2d 259, 151 N.E.2d 833, and see cases cited. Oki is alleged to have knowingly misrepresented the material existing fact that the vines were healthy. Plaintiffs assert they relied on the misrepresentations, paid for the vines, and sustained injury because they were in fact diseased. These allegations state a claim for fraud, and if Oki indeed made the fraudulent representations it "is subject to liability in tort whether the agreement is enforcible or not." Id. at 408, 176 N.Y.S.2d 259, 151 N.E.2d 833.

* * *

The court need not consider plaintiffs' other contentions.

The order is reversed.

[Section Three of Chapter Five of this book continues the investigation of the doctrine of misrepresentation.]

NOTE:
ADDITIONAL ELABORATION OF OKI NURSERY'S ARGUMENT

Oki Nursery made the following argument in its brief to the Court of Appeals for the Second Circuit:

> * * * [E]ven a cursory review of the complaint reveals [that] the acts constituting the alleged breach of contract and warranties are the same acts which form the basis for the fraud and negligent causes of action and, as such, do not give rise to a tort action.
>
> The true basis of HARGRAVE'S claim against Oki is set forth in paragraph 22 (A. 26a) of the verified complaint, as follows:
>
> > "On or about December, 1973, plaintiffs and Oki entered into an agreement whereby plaintiffs were to purchase from Oki approximately 12,000 grapevines FOB Sacramento, California, for the sum of approximately $7,839.00 plus freight. Said vines were to be free from all disease and infection, suitable for commercial wine production and to be delivered within a reasonable time."
>
> It is clear that the contract entered into between HARGRAVE and Oki provided that the vines were to be free of disease and infection and suitable for commercial wine production. The contract unquestionably fully occupied all of the rights and responsibilities between the parties and specifically encompassed the acts upon which the fraud and negligent causes of action are predicated. The breach of warranty causes of action are nothing more than a restatement of the contractual breaches allegedly committed by Oki.

Under these circumstances, the alleged breach of contract and warranties cannot form the basis for the fraud and negligence claims.

I. AYRES & G. KLASS, INSINCERE PROMISES

4, 6, 7, 9 (2005).

An oft-forgotten corner of the law, the doctrine of promissory fraud, provides an entry into the idea that promises can say things. The doctrine recognizes that a promisor, by the very act of promising, typically communicates that she intends to perform her promise. * * * By saying something about the promisor's present intent, the act of promising creates the opportunity to lie. If a court finds that a defendant-promisor did not intend *ab initio* (at the time of promising) to perform her promise, it can subject her to both compensatory and punitive damages under the doctrine of promissory fraud or even sentence her to prison under the corresponding crime of false promise.

* * *

In order for a court properly to conclude that a promisor made a material promissory misrepresentation for which she should be held liable, it must make three key inferences: first, it must decide what the promisor said with her promise, explicitly or implicitly; second, it must ascertain whether, at the time of promising, that representation was true; and third, it must determine whether the promisor made the promissory misrepresentation in question recklessly or knowingly, that is, with the scienter necessary for punitive sanctions.

FOLEY v. INTERACTIVE DATA CORP., 47 Cal. 3d 654, 254 Cal. Rptr. 211, 765 P.2d 373 (1988). [Foley alleged that Interactive Data fired him because he informed his supervisor that the person hired to succeed the supervisor was under investigation by the FBI for embezzlement in a previous job. One of Foley's causes of action was based on "tortious breach of the implied covenant of good faith and fair dealing." Foley argued that the court "should recognize tort remedies for such a breach in the context of employment termination." Noting that the obligation of good faith performance is a "contract term" and that most courts have excluded tort remedies for breach of the obligation, the court dismissed Foley's cause of action. The court distinguished breach of employment contracts from breach of insurance contracts where courts have allowed tort remedies for bad faith breach. In insurance cases, the court reasoned that the insured "seeks protection against calamity" instead of "commercial advantage" and the insurance company supplies a service of a "quasi-public nature." Moreover the "the relationship of the insurer and insured is inherently unbalanced." The court was "not convinced" that employment contracts merit the same treatment.] "[A] breach in the employment context does not place the employee in the same economic dilemma that an insured faces when an insurer in bad faith refuses to pay a claim to accept a settlement offer within policy limits. When an insurer takes such actions, the insured cannot turn to the marketplace to find another insurance company willing to pay for the loss already incurred. The wrongfully terminated employee, on the other hand, can (and must, in order to mitigate damages * * *) make reasonable efforts to seek alternative employment. Moreover, the role of the employer differs from that of the 'quasi-public' insurance company with whom individuals contract specifically in order to obtain protection from potential specified economic harm. The employer does not similarly 'sell' protection to its employees; it is not providing a public service."

VANLENTE v. UNIV. OF WYOMING RESEARCH CORP., 975 P.2d 594 (Wyo. 1999). [VanLente, an employee-at-will, worked successfully for nine years as Human Resources Manager for the University of Wyoming's Western Research Institute. He claimed the institute's termination of his employment constituted a bad-faith tort because he failed to cooperate in retaliating against another employee who had submitted a complaint under the Equal Employment Opportunity Act. The Wyoming Supreme Court affirmed a summary judgment against VanLente in part because VanLente failed to demonstrate any genuine issues of fact with respect to his claim of a "special relationship between him and the Institute."]

THOMAS, JUSTICE.

* * * [A] breach of the implied covenant of good faith and fair dealing will be the premise for a tort action if a "special relationship of trust and reliance is demonstrated * * *." The situations are rare in which such a special relationship exists when employment is at-will. Up to this time, no case has been presented to this Court in which the facts demonstrate the existence of the requisite special relationship.

* * * In Wilder [v. Cody Country Chamber of Commerce, 868 P.2d 211 (Wyo. 1994)], we held that mere longevity of service does not suffice to create the special relationship leading to the tort remedy. * * * Garcia v. UniWyo Federal Credit Union, 920 P.2d 642, 646 (Wyo.1996), added another factor to the concept of the special relationship. There we ruled that usually such a special relationship can be found only in a "long term employment relationship coupled with a discharge calculated to avoid employer responsibilities to the employee * * *." Id. at 646. * * *

* * * The only point that VanLente presented in his Response in Opposition to Motion for Summary Judgment was that he had a special relationship of trust and confidence that justified the invocation of the tort remedy. VanLente contends that the relationship was one of "trust and

reciprocal confidence with regard to extremely sensitive human resource policy and employment matters * * *." The relationship articulated by VanLente is simply one that is inherent in the duties of a human resources manager. It, therefore, was no more than one of the functions with which he was tasked, and did not arise from any special relationship as we have defined it. Longevity, coupled with performance of job duties, is not sufficient to structure the special relationship required by Wilder. Further, the record does not disclose any effort on the part of VanLente to demonstrate that the termination was driven by some motive to deprive him of the potential benefits. In light of this record, the district court correctly entered summary judgment in favor of the Institute * * * on the alleged tort remedy of breach of the implied covenant of good faith and fair dealing.

SECTION SEVEN: OBLIGATION ARISING SOLELY FROM FORM

The least prominent theory of obligation in contract and related areas is based on a promise made in accordance with a legally prescribed formality. Such a formality may take the form of a promise "under seal" or a written promise of some type.

In the English common law a promise made under seal was binding in an action at law even without consideration. What was a "seal"? According to Comment a to section 96 of the Restatement (Second) of Contracts,

> Originally a seal often consisted of wax bearing the imprint of an individualized signet ring, and in the seventeenth century Lord Coke said that wax without impression was not a seal. But in the United States the courts have not required either wax or impression. Impressions directly on the paper were recognized early and are still common for notarial and corporate seals, and gummed wafers have been widely used. In the absence of statute decisions have divided on the effectiveness of the written or printed word "seal," the printed initials "L.S." (locus sigilli, meaning place of the seal), a scrawl made with a pen (often called a "scroll") and a recital of sealing.

As Comment a intimates, at one time in this country a promise under seal also gave rise to a binding obligation. Today, many state statutes specifically provide that a mere donative promise under seal has no binding effect. Other states recognize the seal, but only as presumptive evidence of consideration. See, e.g., Huff v. Gallagher, 521 B.R. 107 (E.D.N.C. 2014). The presumption, of course, can be rebutted by contrary evidence, but in some circumstances, such as when the promisor has died, this may be difficult. In still other states, there is no statute or other law dealing with the seal, but in the vast majority of these states the defense of lack of consideration is probably available to a donative promisor.

In a few states a binding obligation arises in certain circumstances if a promise is made in writing. For example, the New York General Obligations Law, § 5–1103 to § 5–1115 and § 15–303, provide that certain agreements and promises are enforceable if in writing and signed (for example, agreements involving securities and agreements assigning rights), although without consideration. See also Miss. Code Ann. § 75–19–3. In some states, a promise in writing is merely presumptive evidence of consideration.

Written recitals of consideration ("for good consideration hereby exchanged") are fairly common in real-world agreements. The First Restatement, the Uniform Written Obligations Act (adopted only in Pennsylvania) and, in the last twenty-five years, at least seventeen additional states have explicitly endorsed nominal consideration and recitals. Some courts hold that additional recitals of money (sometimes called "nominal consideration") can make enforceable an otherwise unenforceable naked recital; others treat nominal consideration as at best irrelevant and at worst evidence of the invalidity of the bargain because of the disparity in value exchanged. The latter is especially true when the nominal consideration is not exchanged—in so-called "sham consideration" cases.

Writers frequently lament the demise of the seal and the general failure to recognize a formal substitute, which mean that we have no generally available device for making donative promises binding. Some scholars point to continental models and recommend their adoption here. For example, the German Civil Code recognizes certain formally notarized donative promises as binding (§ 518 BGB), but provides that the promisor may be excused from liability if he was improvident in making the promise or later suffers adversity (§ 519 BGB), or if the donee is guilty of "gross" ingratitude (§ 530 BGB). Consider these reflections by a leading contracts scholar:

EISENBERG, DONATIVE PROMISES

47 U. Chi. L. Rev. 1, 13–18 (1979).

[F]ormalities certainly address the problems of deliberative intent and evidentiary security. Form alone, however, cannot meet the problems of improvidence and ingratitude. * * *

* * * [O]ur legal system could not appropriately follow the lead of the civil law by making donative promises enforceable on the basis of their form * * * unless we are also prepared to [have] a body of rules dealing with the problems of improvidence and ingratitude. Certainly such an enterprise is possible. It may be questioned, however, whether the game would be worth

the candle. * * * Perhaps the civil-law style of adjudication is suited to wrestling with these kinds of inquiries, but they have held little appeal for common-law courts, which have traditionally been oriented toward inquiry into acts rather than into personal characteristics.

* * *

Of course, the result of the common-law regime is that some promises that should be kept—those made with the requisite intention and excused by neither improvidence nor ingratitude—are not enforced, just as some completed gifts that should be returned are permitted to be kept. In contrast, a regime like that of the civil law appears more closely tailored to the morality of donation. The question is whether the social and economic gains of recognizing a formality that will make donative promises enforceable are worth the social and economic costs. The answer seems to be that—except perhaps for categories recognized as involving some special social utility, such as formal promises to charitable institutions—the advantages and disadvantages of an enforcement regime are in rough balance. If the common-law rules cannot be defended as preferable, the arguments for change cannot be regarded as compelling.

1464-EIGHT LTD. & MILLIS V. JOPPICH

Supreme Court of Texas, 2004.
154 S.W.3d 101.

STEVEN WAYNE SMITH, JUSTICE.

The question presented is whether section 87(1)(a) of the Restatement (Second) of Contracts should be incorporated into the common law of Texas.

* * *

In July 1997, Gail Ann Joppich entered into an earnest money contract with 1464-Eight, Ltd. and Millis Management Corporation (collectively "Millis") under which Joppich agreed to buy, and Millis agreed to convey, an undeveloped residential lot located in a subdivision being developed by Millis. The purchase price was $65,000. An addendum attached to the earnest money contract provided:

> All Lots being sold in Shiloh Lake Estates Subdivision are being sold pursuant to an Option Agreement to be executed by Buyer and Seller at closing that shall survive closing and provide Seller with an option to purchase the Property from the Buyer at a price equal to 90% of the sale price herein if Buyer fails to commence construction of a private residence on the Property within 18 months from the date of closing.

At the closing later the same month, Millis executed a special warranty deed conveying the lot to Joppich. In addition, the parties executed a separate four-page document entitled "Option Agreement." The notarized document, which was signed by both Joppich and Millis, provided:

> 1. *Grant of Option.* In consideration of the sum of Ten and No/100 ($10.00) Dollars ("Option Fee") paid in cash by Developer, the receipt and sufficiency of which is hereby acknowledged and confessed, Purchaser hereby grants to Developer the exclusive right and option to purchase [the Property]. This Option may be exercised at any time from and after January 21, 1999.
>
> 2. *Purchase Price.* The total purchase price for the Property shall be [$58,500] and shall be due and payable at closing.
>
> 3. *Expiration Date.* This Option shall automatically expire at 5:00 o'clock p.m. on the date which is five (5) years after the date of execution and recording in the Office of the County Clerk of Fort Bend County, Texas unless prior to the expiration date this Option is exercised by Developer.
>
> 4. *Termination.* This Option shall automatically terminate on the date that Purchaser, or Purchaser's assigns, commence construction of a primary residence which has been approved by [the appropriate committee].

The Option Agreement did not contain an express statement regarding whether the parties intended the offer to sell real property to be revocable or irrevocable.

In October 1999, Joppich filed suit against Millis, seeking a declaratory judgment that the Option Agreement was unenforceable. In her original petition, Joppich asserted that "[a]lthough the Option Agreement states that a sum of Ten and No/100 dollars was given to Plaintiff in consideration for granting the option, this sum was not then nor has it ever been tendered to nor paid to Plaintiff," and she requested that "the Court declare that the Agreement granting the exclusive right and option to purchase [the Property] to the Developer is void and unenforceable for lack of consideration or alternatively, failure of consideration." Millis answered with a general denial.

* * *

[Millis later moved for summary judgment on the consideration issue. The trial court found that the Option Agreement was enforceable. The court of appeals reversed and Millis appealed.]

"[A] promise to give an option is valid if supported by an independent consideration. For example, if a sum of money be paid for the option, the promisee may, at his election, enforce the contract." *Nat'l Oil & Pipe Line Co. v. Teel,* 95 Tex. 586, 68 S.W. 979, 980 (1902); *see also* Restatement

(Second) of Contracts § 25 (1981) ("An option contract is a promise which meets the requirements for the formation of a contract and limits the promisor's power to revoke an offer.").

In addition, under the Restatement (Second) of Contracts, certain promises that lack consideration are enforceable. *See* Restatement (Second) of Contracts §§ 82–94 (1981); *see also* 1 Murray, Murray on Contracts § 61 (4th ed. 2001) ("The *Restatement 2d* expressly adopts the view that a clause reciting nominal consideration in either a guaranty or an option contract should operate as a formalistic validation device, supporting the promise in either type of contract, regardless of the fact that the recited amount was never paid."); 2 Perillo & Bender, Corbin on Contracts § 5.17 (rev. ed. 1995) ("The Restatement (Second) has taken the position that in the commercially important situations of options and credit guaranties, a promise is made binding by a false recital of consideration.").

Section 87(1)(a) of the Restatement (Second) of Contracts provides: "An offer is binding as an option contract" if the offer "is in writing and signed by the offeror, recites a purported consideration for the making of the offer, and proposes an exchange on fair terms within a reasonable time." Restatement (Second) of Contracts § 87(1)(a) (1981). Similarly, section 88(a) provides: "A promise to be surety for the performance of a contractual obligation, made to the obligee, is binding" if the promise "is in writing and signed by the promisor and recites a purported consideration." *Id.* § 88(a)

* * *

The position taken by section 87(1)(a) of the Restatement (Second) of Contracts is admittedly the minority position among the limited number of state supreme courts that have addressed the question. *See, e.g., Lewis v. Fletcher,* 101 Idaho 530, 617 P.2d 834, 835 (1980) (holding that a written option agreement that contains a fictional recital of a nominal consideration is unenforceable for lack of consideration); *Berryman v. Kmoch,* 221 Kan. 304, 559 P.2d 790, 793 (1977) (same); *Am. Handkerchief v. Frannat Realty Co.,* 17 N.J. 12, 109 A.2d 793, 796–97 (1954) (same); *Bard v. Kent,* 19 Cal.2d 449, 122 P.2d 8, 10 (1942) (same); *Kay v. Spencer,* 213 P. 571, 574, 29 Wyo. 382 (1923) (same); *Smith v. Wheeler,* 233 Ga. 166, 210 S.E.2d 702, 704 (1974) (implying an obligation to pay the recited but unpaid nominal consideration); *Real Estate Co. v. Rudolph,* 301 Pa. 502, 153 A. 438, 439 (1930) (employing an estoppel theory to prevent contradiction of a fictional recital of a nominal consideration).

Nevertheless, we are persuaded that the position of the Restatement (Second) of Contracts, which is supported by a well-articulated and sound rationale, represents the better approach. *See, e.g.,* Restatement (Second) of Contracts § 87 cmt. b (1981) ("The fact that the option is an appropriate preliminary step in the conclusion of a socially useful transaction provides a sufficient substantive basis for enforcement, and a signed writing taking a form appropriate to a bargain satisfies the desiderata of form."); Gordon, *Consideration and the Commercial-Gift Dichotomy,* 44 Vand. L.Rev. 283, 293–94 (1991) ("Option contracts are related to economic exchanges—transactions based on self-interest, not altruism. Moreover, people expect that option contracts are serious and binding commitments.").

Based on the foregoing analysis, we reverse the court of appeals's judgment and remand the case to the court of appeals for further proceedings.

CHIEF JUSTICE JEFFERSON filed a concurring opinion, in which JUSTICE BRISTER joined.

[If] the Court enforces option contracts containing fictional recitals of consideration, why mandate such recitals at all? Why recognize and require parties to recite "a lie, a sham"? James D. Gordon III, *Consideration and the Commercial-Gift Dichotomy,* 44 Vand. L.Rev. 283, 294 (1991) (commenting on section 87 of the Restatement (Second) of Contracts); *see also* John P. Dawson, Gifts and Promises 4 (1980) (criticizing consideration requirement as a "needless hindrance to the processes by which agreement is reached and, being artificial as well as needless, was soon made to look silly, so that a dollar, a hairpin, or a false recital would do").

Instead, I agree with the authors of a leading treatise that while the Restatement approach is a step in the right direction, it "fails to lead the way to more progressive reform. Having recognized the value of the enforceability of options as commercial devices, it still insists on the fictional recital of a purported consideration. Such fictional charades should not be part of a mature legal system. Commercial promises such as options and credit guaranties should be enforceable without consideration." Although I am not prepared to advocate elimination of the consideration requirement in all commercial contracts, I believe it is time to acknowledge that the doctrine serves no justifiable purpose in option agreements. * * *

But perhaps Justice Holmes's aphorism that "a page of history is worth a volume of logic" applies here. *New York Trust Co. v. Eisner,* 256 U.S. 345, 349, 41 S.Ct. 506, 65 L.Ed. 963 (1921). A rule known only to lawyers and relied on by parties seeking a technicality by which to avoid contractual obligations, consideration in option contracts is a relic, much like the seal of earlier days. Although Texas eliminated the seal requirement in 1858, our courts continue to insist on a formalistic (even if false) recitation of consideration in an option contract that both parties enter into willingly, fully expecting it to be enforceable, and as part of an underlying transaction that is supported by consideration. It is time to put this "overworked shibboleth" to rest. *Rye v. Phillips,* 203 Minn. 567, 282 N.W. 459, 460 (1938).

For these reasons, I concur in the Court's judgment but not in its reasoning.

RESTATEMENT (SECOND) OF CONTRACTS § 87(1).

Comment:

a. Consideration and form. The traditional common-law devices for making a firm offer or option contract are the giving of consideration and the affixing of a seal. * * * But the firm offer serves a useful purpose even though no preliminary bargain is made: it is often a necessary step in the making of the main bargain proposed, and it partakes of the natural formalities inherent in business transactions. The erosion of the formality of the seal has made it less and less satisfactory as a universal formality. As literacy has spread, the personal signature has become the natural formality and the seal has become more and more anachronistic. The rules stated in this section reflect the judicial and legislative response to this situation.

b. Nominal consideration. Offers made in consideration of one dollar paid or promised are often irrevocable under Subsection (1)(a). The irrevocability of an offer may be worth much or little to the offeree, and the courts do not ordinarily inquire into the adequacy of the consideration bargained for. * * * Hence a comparatively small payment may furnish consideration for the irrevocability of an offer proposing a transaction involving much larger sums. But gross disproportion between the payment and the value of the option commonly indicates that the payment was not in fact bargained for but was a mere formality or pretense. In such a case there is no consideration * * *.

Nevertheless, such a nominal consideration is regularly held sufficient to support a short-time option proposing an exchange on fair terms. The fact that the option is an appropriate preliminary step in the conclusion of a socially useful transaction provides a sufficient substantive basis for enforcement, and a signed writing taking a form appropriate to a bargain satisfies the desiderata of form. In the absence of statute, however, the bargaining form is essential: a payment of one dollar by each party to the other is so obviously not a bargaining transaction that it does not provide even the form of an exchange.

UNIFORM COMMERCIAL CODE § 2–205.

Firm Offers

An offer by a merchant to buy or sell goods in a signed writing which by its terms gives assurance that it will be held open is not revocable, for lack of consideration, during the time stated or if no time is stated for a reasonable time, but in no event may such period of irrevocability exceed three months; but any such term of assurance on a form supplied by the offeree must be separately signed by the offeror.

PROBLEM 2-10

Can you reconcile the following sections of the Restatement (Second) of Contracts?

§ 71 Requirement of Exchange

(1) To constitute consideration, a performance or a return promise must be bargained for. * * *

§ 87 Option Contract

(1) An offer is binding as an option contract if it

(a) is in writing and signed by the offeror, recites a purported consideration for the making of the offer, and proposes an exchange on fair terms within a reasonable time. * * *

SECTION EIGHT: OBLIGATION ARISING FROM A STATUTORY WARRANTY

Our law enforces promises made by sellers, lessors, or others concerning the quality of their performance. Such promises are called "warranties." For example, in many states the seller or lessor of a residence may make a "warranty of habitability." In addition, the seller of goods may warrant that they are fit for the ordinary purposes for which such goods are used. Lessors of goods and providers of services may also make warranties of quality. Some warranties, usually called "express warranties," arise solely from the parties' agreement. Others arise from a combination of agreement and common law or statute. The most pervasive example of the latter involves warranties arising under Article 2 of the Uniform Commercial Code, the sale-of-goods article. Here we merely introduce warranty theory. Most law schools also treat this subject extensively in an upper level commercial law course.

UNIFORM COMMERCIAL CODE § 2–313.

Express Warranties by Affirmation, Promise, Description, Sample

(1) Express warranties by the seller are created as follows:

(a) Any affirmation of fact or promise made by the seller to the buyer which relates to the goods and becomes part of the basis of the bargain creates an express warranty that the goods shall conform to the affirmation or promise.

(b) Any description of the goods which is made part of the basis of the bargain creates an express warranty that the goods shall conform to the description.

(c) Any sample or model which is made part of the basis of the bargain creates an express warranty that the whole of the goods shall conform to the sample or model.

(2) It is not necessary to the creation of an express warranty that the seller use formal words such as "warrant" or "guarantee" or that he have a specific intention to make a warranty, but an affirmation merely of the value of the goods or a statement purporting to be merely the seller's opinion or commendation of the goods does not create a warranty.

UNIFORM COMMERCIAL CODE § 2–314.

Implied Warranty: Merchantability; Usage of Trade

(1) Unless excluded or modified (Section 2–316), a warranty that the goods shall be merchantable is implied in a contract for their sale if the seller is a merchant with respect to goods of that kind. * * *

(2) Goods to be merchantable must be at least such as

(a) pass without objection in the trade under the contract description; and

(b) in the case of fungible goods, are of fair average quality within the description; and

(c) are fit for the ordinary purposes for which such goods are used; and

(d) run, within the variations permitted by the agreement, of even kind, quality and quantity within each unit and among all units involved; and

(e) are adequately contained, packaged, and labeled as the agreement may require; and

(f) conform to the promise or affirmations of fact made on the container or label if any.

UNIFORM COMMERCIAL CODE § 2–315.

Implied Warranty: Fitness for Particular Purpose

When the seller at the time of contracting has reason to know any particular purpose for which the goods are required and that the buyer is relying on the seller's skill or judgment to select or furnish suitable goods, there is unless excluded or modified under the next section an implied warranty that the goods shall be fit for such purpose.

KEITH V. BUCHANAN

California Court of Appeals, 1985.
173 Cal. App. 3d 13, 220 Cal. Rptr. 392.

OCHOA, ASSOCIATE JUSTICE.

This breach of warranty case is before this court after the trial court granted defendants' motion for judgment at the close of plaintiff's case during the trial proceedings. We hold that an express warranty under section 2313 of the California Uniform Commercial Code was created in this matter, and that actual reliance on the seller's factual representation need not be shown by the buyer. The representation is presumed to be part of the basis of the bargain, and the burden is on the seller to prove that the representation was not a consideration inducing the bargain. We affirm all other aspects of the trial court's judgment but reverse in regard to its finding that no express warranty was created and remand for further proceedings consistent with this opinion.

Statement of Facts

Plaintiff, Brian Keith, purchased a sailboat from defendants in November 1978 for a total purchase price of $75,610. Even though plaintiff belonged to the Waikiki Yacht Club, had attended a sailing school, had joined the Coast Guard Auxiliary, and had sailed on many yachts in order to ascertain his preferences, he had not previously owned a yacht. He attended a boat show in Long Beach during October 1978 and looked at a number of boats, speaking to sales representatives and obtaining advertising literature. In the literature, the sailboat which is the subject of this action, called an "Island Trader 41," was described as a seaworthy vessel. In one sales brochure, this vessel is described as "a picture of sure-footed seaworthiness." In another, it is called "a carefully well-equipped, and very seaworthy live-aboard vessel." Plaintiff testified he relied on representations in the sales brochures in regard to the purchase. Plaintiff and a sales representative also discussed plaintiff's desire for a boat which was ocean-going and would cruise long distances.

Plaintiff asked his friend, Buddy Ebsen, who was involved in a boat building enterprise, to inspect the boat. Mr. Ebsen and one of his associates, both of whom had extensive experience with sailboats, observed the boat and advised plaintiff that the vessel would suit his stated needs. A deposit was paid on the boat, a purchase contract was entered into, and optional accessories for the boat were ordered. After delivery of the vessel, a dispute arose in regard to its seaworthiness.

Plaintiff filed the instant lawsuit alleging causes of action in breach of express warranty and breach of implied warranty. The trial court granted defendants' Code of Civil Procedure section 631.8 motion for judgment at the close of plaintiff's case. The court found that no express warranty was established by the evidence because none of the defendants had undertaken in writing to preserve or maintain the utility or performance of the vessel, nor to provide compensation for any failure in utility or performance. It found that the written statements produced at trial were opinions or commendations of the vessel. The court further found that no implied warranty of fitness was created because the plaintiff did not rely on the skill and judgment of defendants to select and furnish a suitable vessel, but had rather relied on his own experts in selecting the vessel.

I. Express Warranty

California Uniform Commercial Code section 2313[1] provides, inter alia, that express warranties are created by (1) any affirmation of fact or promise made by the seller to the buyer which relates to the goods and becomes part of the basis of the bargain, and (2) any description of the goods which is made part of the basis of the bargain. Formal words such as "warranty" or "guarantee" are not required to make a warranty, but the seller's affirmation of the value of the goods or an expression of opinion or commendation of the goods does not create an express warranty.

* * *

California Uniform Commercial Code section 2313, regarding express warranties, was enacted in 1963 and consists of the official text of Uniform Commercial Code section 2–313 without change. In deciding whether a statement made by a seller constitutes an express warranty under this provision, the court must deal with three fundamental issues. First, the court must determine whether the seller's statement constitutes an "affirmation of fact or promise" or "description of the goods" under California Uniform Commercial Code section 2313, subdivision (1)(a) or (b) or whether it is rather "merely the seller's opinion or commendation of the goods" under section 2313, subdivision (2). Second, assuming the court finds the language used susceptible to creation of a warranty, it must then be determined whether the statement was "part of the basis of the bargain." Third, the court must determine whether the warranty was breached. (See *Sessa v. Riegle* (E.D.Pa.1977) 427 F.Supp. 760, 765.)

---

[1] Section 2313: "Express Warranties by Affirmation, Promise, Description, Sample. (1) Express warranties by the seller are created as follows:

"(a) Any affirmation of fact or promise made by the seller to the buyer which relates to the goods and becomes part of the basis of the bargain creates an express warranty that the goods shall conform to the affirmation or promise.

"(b) Any description of the goods which is made part of the basis of the bargain creates an express warranty that the goods shall conform to the description.

"(c) Any sample or model which is made part of the basis of the bargain creates an express warranty that the whole of the goods shall conform to the sample or model.

"(2) It is not necessary to the creation of an express warranty that the seller use formal words such as 'warrant' or 'guarantee' or that he have a specific intention to make a warranty, but an affirmation merely of the value of the goods or a statement purporting to be merely the seller's opinion or commendation of the goods does not create a warranty."

A warranty relates to the title, character, quality, identity, or condition of the goods. The purpose of the law of warranty is to determine what it is that the seller has in essence agreed to sell. (*A. A. Baxter Corp. v. Colt Industries, Inc.* (1970) 10 Cal.App.3d 144, 153, 88 Cal.Rptr. 842.) "Express warranties are chisels in the hands of buyers and sellers. With these tools, the parties to a sale sculpt a monument representing the goods. Having selected a stone, the buyer and seller may leave it almost bare, allowing considerable play in the qualities that fit its contours. Or the parties may chisel away inexactitudes until a well-defined shape emerges. The seller is bound to deliver, and the buyer to accept, goods that match the sculpted form. [Fn. omitted.]" (*Special Project: Article Two Warranties in Commercial Transactions, Express Warranties—Section 2–313* (1978–79) 64 Cornell L.Rev. 30 (hereafter cited as *Warranties in Commercial Transactions*) at pp. 43–44.)

A. *Affirmation of fact, promise or description versus statement of opinion, commendation or value.*

"The determination as to whether a particular statement is an expression of opinion or an affirmation of fact is often difficult, and frequently is dependent upon the facts and circumstances existing at the time the statement is made." (*Willson v. Municipal Bond Co.* (1936) 7 Cal.2d 144, 150, 59 P.2d 974.) Recent decisions have evidenced a trend toward narrowing the scope of representations which are considered opinion, sometimes referred to as "puffing" or "sales talk," resulting in an expansion of the liability that flows from broad statements of manufacturers or retailers as to the quality of their products. Courts have liberally construed affirmations of quality made by sellers in favor of injured consumers. (*Hauter v. Zogarts* (1975) 14 Cal.3d 104, 112, 120 Cal.Rptr. 681, 534 P.2d 377; see also 55 Cal.Jur.3d, Sales, § 74, p. 580.) It has even been suggested "that in an age of consumerism all seller's statements, except the most blatant sales pitch, may give rise to an express warranty." (1 Alderman and Dole, A Transactional Guide to the Uniform Commercial Code (2d ed.1983) p. 89.)

Courts in other states have struggled in efforts to create a formula for distinguishing between affirmations of fact, promises, or descriptions of goods on the one hand, and value, opinion, or commendation statements on the other. The code comment indicates that the basic question is: "What statements of the seller have in the circumstances and in objective judgment become part of the basis of the bargain?" The commentators indicated that the language of subsection (2) of the code section was included because "common experience discloses that some statements or predictions cannot fairly be viewed as entering into the bargain." (See U.Com.Code com. 8 to Cal.U.Com.Code, § 2313, West's Ann.Com.Code (1964) p. 250.)

Statements made by a seller during the course of negotiation over a contract are presumptively affirmations of fact unless it can be demonstrated that the buyer could only have reasonably considered the statement as a statement of the seller's opinion. Commentators have noted several factors which tend to indicate an opinion statement. These are (1) a lack of specificity in the statement made, (2) a statement that is made in an equivocal manner, or (3) a statement which reveals that the goods are experimental in nature. (See *Warranties in Commercial Transactions, supra,* at pp. 61–65.)

It is clear that statements made by a manufacturer or retailer in an advertising brochure which is disseminated to the consuming public in order to induce sales can create express warranties. * * * In the instant case, the vessel purchased was described in sales brochures as "a picture of sure-footed seaworthiness" and "a carefully well-equipped and very seaworthy vessel." The seller's representative was aware that appellant was looking for a vessel sufficient for long distance ocean-going cruises. The statements in the brochure are specific and unequivocal in asserting that the vessel is seaworthy. Nothing in the negotiation indicates that the vessel is experimental in nature. In fact, one sales brochure assures prospective buyers that production of the vessel was commenced "after years of careful testing." The representations regarding seaworthiness made in sales brochures regarding the Island Trader 41 were affirmations of fact relating to the quality or condition of the vessel.

B. *"Part of the basis of the bargain" test.*

Under former provisions of law, a purchaser was required to prove that he or she acted in reliance upon representations made by the seller. (*Grinnell v. Charles Pfizer & Co.* (1969) 274 Cal.App.2d 424, 440, 79 Cal.Rptr. 369.) California Uniform Commercial Code section 2313 indicates only that the seller's statements must become "part of the basis of the bargain." According to official comment 3 to this Uniform Commercial Code provision, "no particular reliance . . . need be shown in order to weave [the seller's affirmations of fact] into the fabric of the agreement. Rather, any fact which is to take such affirmations, once made, out of the agreement requires clear affirmative proof." (See U.Com.Code com. 3 to Cal.U.Com.Code, § 2313, West's Ann.Com.Code (1964) p. 249.)

The California Supreme Court, in discussing the continued viability of the reliance factor, noted that commentators have disagreed in regard to the impact of this development. Some have indicated that it shifts the burden of proving non-reliance to the seller, and others have indicated that the code eliminates the concept of reliance altogether. (*Hauter v. Zogarts, supra,* 14 Cal.3d at pp. 115–116, 120 Cal.Rptr. 681, 534 P.2d 377.) The court did not resolve this issue, but noted that decisions of other states prior to that time had "ignored the significance of the new standard and have held that consumer reliance still is a vital ingredient for recovery based on express warranty." (*Id.*, at p. 116, fn. 13, 120 Cal.Rptr. 681, 534 P.2d 377; see also *Fogo v. Cutter Laboratories, Inc.* (1977) 68 Cal.App.3d 744, 760, 137 Cal.Rptr. 417.)

The shift in language clearly changes the degree to which it must be shown that the seller's representation affected the buyer's decision to enter into the agreement. A buyer need not show that he would not have entered into the agreement absent the warranty or even that it was a dominant factor inducing the agreement. A warranty statement is deemed to be part of the basis of the bargain and to have been relied upon as one of the inducements for the purchase of the product. In other words, the buyer's demonstration of reliance on an express warranty is "not a prerequisite for breach of warranty, as long as the express warranty involved became part of the bargain. See White & Summers, Uniform Commercial Code (2d ed. 1980) § 9–4. If, however, the resulting bargain does not rest at all on the representations of the seller, those representations cannot be considered as becoming any part of the 'basis of the bargain.' * * * " (*Allied Fidelity Ins. Co. v. Pico* (Nev.S.Ct.1983) 656 P.2d 849, 850.)

The official Uniform Commercial Code comment in regard to section 2–313 "indicates that in actual practice affirmations of fact made by the seller about the goods during a bargain are regarded as part of the description of those goods; hence no particular reliance on such statements need be shown in order to weave them into the fabric of the agreement." (*Young & Cooper, Inc. v. Vestring* (1974) 214 Kan. 311, 521 P.2d 281, 291; *Brunner v. Jensen* (1974) 215 Kan. 416, 524 P.2d 1175, 1185.) It is clear from the new language of this code section that the concept of reliance has been purposefully abandoned. * * *

The change of the language in section 2313 of the California Uniform Commercial Code modifies both the degree of reliance and the burden of proof in express warranties under the code. The representation need only be part of the basis of the bargain, or merely a factor or consideration inducing the buyer to enter into the bargain. A warranty statement made by a seller is presumptively part of the basis of the bargain, and the burden is on the seller to prove that the resulting bargain does not rest at all on the representation.

The buyer's actual knowledge of the true condition of the goods prior to the making of the contract may make it plain that the seller's statement was not relied upon as one of the inducements for the purchase, but the burden is on the seller to demonstrate such knowledge on the part of the buyer. Where the buyer inspects the goods before purchase, he may be deemed to have waived the seller's express warranties. But, an examination or inspection by the buyer of the goods does not necessarily discharge the seller from an express warranty if the defect was not actually discovered and waived. * * *

Appellant's inspection of the boat by his own experts does not constitute a waiver of the express warranty of seaworthiness. Prior to the making of the contract, appellant had experienced boat builders observe the boat, but there was no testing of the vessel in the water.[2] Such a warranty (seaworthiness) necessarily relates to the time when the vessel has been put to sea (*Werner v. Montana* (1977) 117 N.H. 721, 378 A.2d 1130, 1134–35) and has been shown to be reasonably fit and adequate in materials, construction, and equipment for its intended purposes. * * *

In this case, appellant was aware of the representations regarding seaworthiness by the seller prior to contracting. He also had expressed to the seller's representative his desire for a long distance ocean-going vessel. Although he had other experts inspect the vessel, the inspection was limited and would not have indicated whether or not the vessel was seaworthy. It is clear that the seller has not overcome the presumption that the representations regarding seaworthiness were part of the basis of this bargain.

II. Implied Warranty

Appellant also claimed breach of the implied warranty of fitness for a particular purpose[3] in regard to the sale of the subject vessel. An implied warranty of fitness for a particular purpose arises when a "seller at the time of contracting has reason to know any particular purpose for which the goods are required and that the buyer is relying on the seller's skill or judgment to select or furnish suitable goods," which are fit for such purpose. (Cal.U.Com.Code, § 2315.) The Consumer Warranty Act makes such an implied warranty applicable to retailers, distributors, and manufacturers. (Civ.Code, §§ 1791.1, 1792.1, 1792.2, subd. (a).) An implied warranty of fitness for a particular purpose arises only where (1) the purchaser at the time of contracting intends to use the goods for a particular purpose, (2) the seller at the time of contracting has reason to know of this particular purpose, (3) the buyer relies on the seller's skill or judgment to select or furnish goods suitable for the particular purpose, and

---

[2] Evidence was presented of examination or inspection of the boat after the making of the contract of sale and prior to delivery and acceptance of the vessel. Such an inspection would be irrelevant to any issue of express warranty. Although it deals with implied warranties as opposed to express warranties, the Uniform Commercial Code comment 8 to section 2–316 (Cal.U.Com.Code, § 2316) is instructive: "Under paragraph (b) of subdivision (3) warranties may be excluded or modified by the circumstances where the buyer examines the goods or a sample or model of them *before entering into the contract. 'Examination' as used in this paragraph is not synonymous with inspection before acceptance or at any other time after the contract has been made. It goes rather to the nature of the responsibility assumed by the seller at the time of the making of the contract.*" (See U.Com.Code com. 8 to Cal.U.Com.Code, § 2316, West's Ann.Com.Code (1964) p. 308, emphasis added.)

[3] No claim of breach of implied warranty of merchantability has been presented in this action.

(4) the seller at the time of contracting has reason to know that the buyer is relying on such skill and judgment. (*Metowski v. Traid Corp.* (1972) 28 Cal.App.3d 332, 341, 104 Cal.Rptr. 599.)

The reliance elements are important to the consideration of whether an implied warranty of fitness for a particular purpose exists. "If the seller had no reason to know that he was being relied upon, his conduct in providing goods cannot fairly be deemed a tacit representation of their suitability for a particular purpose. And if the buyer did not in fact rely, then the principal justification for imposing a fitness warranty disappears." (See *Warranties in Commercial Transactions, supra,* at p. 89.) The major question in determining the existence of an implied warranty of fitness for a particular purpose is the reliance by the buyer upon the skill and judgment of the seller to select an article suitable for his needs. * * *

The trial court found that the plaintiff did not rely on the skill and judgment of the defendants to select a suitable vessel, but that he rather relied on his own experts. "Our sole task is to determine 'whether the evidence, viewed in the light most favorable to [respondent], sustains [these] findings.' [Citations.] Moreover, 'in examining the sufficiency of the evidence to support a questioned finding an appellate court must accept as true all evidence tending to establish the correctness of the finding as made, taking into account, as well, all inferences which might reasonably have been thought by the trial court to lead to the same conclusion.' [Citations.] If appellate scrutiny reveals that substantial evidence supports the trial court's findings and conclusions, the judgment must be affirmed." (*Board of Education v. Jack M.* (1977) 19 Cal.3d 691, 697, 139 Cal.Rptr. 700, 566 P.2d 602.)

A review of the record reveals ample evidence to support the trial court's finding. Appellant had extensive experience with sailboats at the time of the subject purchase, even though he had not previously owned such a vessel. He had developed precise specifications in regard to the type of boat he wanted to purchase. He looked at a number of different vessels, reviewed their advertising literature, and focused on the Island Trader 41 as the object of his intended purchase. He also had friends look at the boat before making the final decision to purchase. The trial court's finding that the buyer did not rely on the skill or judgment of the seller in the selection of the vessel in question is supported by substantial evidence.

The trial court's judgment that no express warranty existed in this matter is reversed. The trial court's judgment is affirmed in all other respects. Since considerable contradictory evidence was elicited at trial relating to the asserted breach of warranty of seaworthiness of the subject vessel, and since the trial court made no finding in regard to that issue, the matter is remanded to the trial court for further proceedings consistent with this opinion. Each party is to bear his own costs on appeal.

SUGAWARA v. PEPSICO, INC., 2009 WL 1439115 (E.D. Cal. 2009). [Sugawara sued PepsiCo for, breach of express warranty, among other things. PepsiCo moved to dismiss the complaint.]

MORRISON C. ENGLAND, JR., DISTRICT JUDGE.

* * * Plaintiff contends that the colorful Crunchberries, combined with use of the word "berry" in the Product name, convey the message that Cap'n Crunch is not all sugar and starch, but contains redeeming fruit. This message is allegedly supplemented and reinforced by additional marketing that represents that "Crunch Berries is a combination of Crunch biscuits and colorful red, purple, teal and green berries." In actuality, the Product contains no berries of any kind. If the consumer takes the box from the shelf and examines the fine print of the ingredient list, he or she will discover that the only fruit content is a touch of strawberry fruit concentrate, twelfth in order on the ingredient list.

* * *

* * * In this case, * * * while the challenged packaging contains the word "berries" it does so only in conjunction with the descriptive term "crunch." This Court is not aware of, nor has Plaintiff alleged the existence of, any actual fruit referred to as a "crunchberry." Furthermore, the "Crunchberries" depicted on the [display panel] are round, crunchy, brightly-colored cereal balls, and the [display panel] clearly states both that the Product contains "sweetened corn & oat cereal" and that the cereal is "enlarged to show texture." Thus, a reasonable consumer would not be deceived into believing that the Product in the instant case contained a fruit that does not exist. * * *

[PepsiCo's motion to dismiss was granted.]

NOTE:
MORE ON (1) THE DIFFERENCES BETWEEN AFFIRMATIONS OF FACT AND OPINION AND (2) THE FITNESS FOR A PARTICULAR PURPOSE WARRANTY

If a seller of Sleep Number Beds advertises that "your Sleep Number is your key to a perfect night's sleep" has the seller created an express warranty? How about if the seller claims that customers will enjoy a "perfect night's sleep"? O.k., if you think neither of these are warranties under the test of Keith v. Buchanan (specificity and lack of equivocation), how about if the seller claims that the bed will be "maintenance free"? The court in Stearns v. Select Comfort Retail Corp., 2009 WL 1635931 (N.D. Cal. 2009) held that all of the above statements were mere opinion (also called "puffing"), adding that "no consumer reasonably could have" expected any product to be "maintenance-free." Do you agree? For a further challenge, according to one court, the label on a cosmetic product that stated, "100% natural mineral advanced protection," was just puffing, but the same court found that "100% natural mineral hydrating defense" survived a motion to dismiss. Do you agree with the distinction? See Gasser v. Kiss My Face, LLC, 93 U.C.C. Rep. Serv. 2d 1403, 2017 WL 4773426 (N.D. Cal., 2017); see also Sebastian v. Kimberly-Clark Corp., 2017 WL 6497675 (S.D. Cal. 2017) (plaintiff's claim that Huggies Natural Care Products made an express warranty when it described its product as "natural, gentle and hypoallergenic" survived a motion to dismiss).

Turning to the fitness for a particular purpose warranty, a claim for breach of the warranty will not be successful if a purchaser buys a product for its ordinary purpose. For example, if a purchaser selects an automobile for ordinary road use, but the car is defective, the purchaser may recover based on the merchantability warranty (see the Webster case that follows), but not based on the fitness for a particular purpose warranty. See, e.g., Watson Quality Ford v. Casanova, 999 So. 2d 830 (Miss. 2008).

WEBSTER V. BLUE SHIP TEA ROOM

Supreme Judicial Court of Massachusetts, 1964.
347 Mass. 421, 198 N.E.2d 309.

REARDON, JUSTICE.

This is a case which by its nature evokes earnest study not only of the law but also of the culinary traditions of the Commonwealth which bear so heavily upon its outcome. It is an action to recover damages for personal injuries sustained by reason of a breach of implied warranty of food served by the defendant in its restaurant. An auditor, whose findings of fact were not to be final, found for the plaintiff. On a retrial in the Superior Court before a judge and jury, in which the plaintiff testified, the jury returned a verdict for her. The defendant is here on exceptions to the refusal of the judge (1) to strike certain portions of the auditor's report, (2) to direct a verdict for the defendant, and (3) to allow the defendant's motion for the entry of a verdict in its favor under leave reserved.

The jury could have found the following facts: On Saturday, April 25, 1959, about 1 P.M., the plaintiff, accompanied by her sister and her aunt, entered the Blue Ship Tea Room operated by the defendant. The group was seated at a table and supplied with menus.

This restaurant, which the plaintiff characterized as "quaint," was located in Boston "on the third floor of an old building on T Wharf which overlooks the ocean."

The plaintiff, who had been born and brought up in New England (a fact of some consequence), ordered clam chowder and crabmeat salad. Within a few minutes she received tidings to the effect that "there was no more clam chowder," whereupon she ordered a cup of fish chowder. Presently, there was set before her "a small bowl of fish chowder." She had previously enjoyed a breakfast about 9 A.M. which had given her no difficulty. "The fish chowder contained haddock, potatoes, milk, water and seasoning. The chowder was milky in color and not clear. The haddock and potatoes were in chunks" (also a fact of consequence). "She agitated it a little with the spoon and observed that it was a fairly full bowl * * *. It was hot when she got it, but she did not tip it with her spoon because it was hot * * * but stirred it in an up and under motion. She denied that she did this because she was looking for something, but it was rather because she wanted an even distribution of fish and potatoes." "She started to eat it, alternating between the chowder and crackers which were on the table with * * * [some] rolls. She ate about 3 or 4 spoonfuls then stopped. She looked at the spoonfuls as she was eating. She saw equal parts of liquid, potato and fish as she spooned it into her mouth. She did not see anything unusual about it. After 3 or 4 spoonfuls she was aware that something had lodged in her throat because she couldn't swallow and couldn't clear her throat by gulping and she could feel it." This misadventure led to two esophagoscopies at the Massachusetts General Hospital, in the second of which, on April 27, 1959, a fish bone was found and removed. The sequence of events produced injury to the plaintiff which was not insubstantial.

We must decide whether a fish bone lurking in a fish chowder, about the ingredients of which there is no other complaint, constitutes a breach of implied warranty under applicable provisions of the Uniform Commercial Code,[1] the annotations to which are not helpful on this point. As the judge put it in his charge, "Was the fish chowder fit to be eaten and wholesome? * * * [N]obody is claiming that the fish itself wasn't wholesome. * * * But the bone of contention here—I don't mean that for a pun—but was this fish bone a foreign substance that made the fish chowder unwholesome or not fit to be eaten?"

The plaintiff has vigorously reminded us of the high standards imposed by this court where the sale of food is involved (see Flynn v. First Natl. Stores Inc., 296 Mass. 521, 523, 6 N.E.2d 814) and has made reference to cases involving stones in beans (Friend v. Childs Dining Hall Co., 231 Mass. 65, 120 N.E. 407, 5 A.L.R. 1100), trichinae in pork (Holt v. Mann, 294 Mass. 21, 22, 200 N.E. 403), and to certain other cases, here and elsewhere, serving to bolster her contention of breach of warranty.

---

[1] "(1) Unless excluded or modified by section 2–316, a warranty that the goods shall be merchantable is implied in a contract for their sale if the seller is a merchant with respect to goods of that kind. Under this section the serving for value of food or drink to be consumed either on the premises or elsewhere is a sale. (2) Goods to be merchantable must at least be such as * * * (c) are fit for the ordinary purposes for which such goods are used * * *." G.L. c. 106, § 2–314.

"* * * (3)(b) [W]hen the buyer before entering into the contract has examined the goods or the sample or model as fully as he desired or has refused to examine the goods there is no implied warranty with regard to defects which an examination ought in the circumstances to have revealed to him * * *." G.L. c. 106, § 2–316.

The defendant asserts that here was a native New Englander eating fish chowder in a "quaint" Boston dining place where she had been before; that "[f]ish chowder, as it is served and enjoyed by New Englanders, is a hearty dish, originally designed to satisfy the appetites of our seamen and fishermen"; that "[t]his court knows well that we are not talking of some insipid broth as is customarily served to convalescents." We are asked to rule in such fashion that no chef is forced "to reduce the pieces of fish in the chowder to miniscule size in an effort to ascertain if they contained any pieces of bone." "In so ruling," we are told (in the defendant's brief), "the court will not only uphold its reputation for legal knowledge and acumen, but will, as loyal sons of Massachusetts, save our world-renowned fish chowder from degenerating into an insipid broth containing the mere essence of its former stature as a culinary masterpiece." Notwithstanding these passionate entreaties we are bound to examine with detachment the nature of fish chowder and what might happen to it under varying interpretations of the Uniform Commercial Code.

Chowder is an ancient dish preexisting even "the appetites of our seamen and fishermen." It was perhaps the common ancestor of the "more refined cream soups, purees, and bisques." Berolzheimer, The American Woman's Cook Book (Publisher's Guild Inc., New York, 1941) p. 176. The word "chowder" comes from the French "chaudière," meaning a "cauldron" or "pot." "In the fishing villages of Brittany * * * 'faire la chaudière' means to supply a cauldron in which is cooked a mess of fish and biscuit with some savoury condiments, a hodge-podge contributed by the fishermen themselves, each of whom in return receives his share of the prepared dish. The Breton fishermen probably carried the custom to Newfoundland, long famous for its chowder, whence it has spread to Nova Scotia, New Brunswick, and New England." A New English Dictionary (MacMillan and Co., 1893) p. 386. Our literature over the years abounds in references not only to the delights of chowder but also to its manufacture. A namesake of the plaintiff, Daniel Webster, had a recipe for fish chowder which has survived into a number of modern cookbooks and in which the removal of fish bones is not mentioned at all. One old time recipe recited in the New English Dictionary study defines chowder as "A dish made of fresh fish (esp. cod) or clams, stewed with slices of pork or bacon, onions, and biscuit. 'Cider and champagne are sometimes added.'" Hawthorne, in The House of the Seven Gables (Allyn and Bacon, Boston, 1957) p. 8, speaks of "[a] codfish of sixty pounds, caught in the bay, [which] had been dissolved into the rich liquid of a chowder." A chowder variant, cod "Muddle," was made in Plymouth in the 1890s by taking "a three or four pound codfish, head added. Season with salt and pepper and boil in just enough water to keep from burning. When cooked, add milk and piece of butter." The recitation of these ancient formulae suffices to indicate that in the construction of chowders in these parts in other years, worries about fish bones played no role whatsoever. This broad outlook on chowders has persisted in more modern cookbooks. "The chowder of today is much the same as the old chowder * * *." The American Woman's Cook Book, supra, p. 176. The all embracing Fannie Farmer states in a portion of her recipe, fish chowder is made with a "fish skinned, but head and tail left on. Cut off head and tail and remove fish from backbone. Cut fish in 2-inch pieces and set aside. Put head, tail, and backbone broken in pieces, in stewpan; add 2 cups cold water and bring slowly to boiling point * * *." The liquor thus produced from the bones is added to the balance of the chowder. Farmer, The Boston Cooking School Cook Book (Little Brown Co., 1937) p. 166.

Thus, we consider a dish which for many long years, if well made, has been made generally as outlined above. It is not too much to say that a person sitting down in New England to consume a good New England fish chowder embarks on a gustatory adventure which may entail the removal of some fish bones from his bowl as he proceeds. We are not inclined to tamper with age old recipes by any amendment reflecting the plaintiff's view of the effect of the Uniform Commercial Code upon them. We are aware of the heavy body of case law involving foreign substances in food, but we sense a strong distinction between them and those relative to unwholesomeness of the food itself, e.g., tainted mackerel (Smith v. Gerrish, 256 Mass. 183, 152 N.E. 318), and a fish bone in a fish chowder. Certain Massachusetts cooks might cavil at the ingredients contained in the chowder in this case in that it lacked the heartening lift of salt pork. In any event, we consider that the joys of life in New England include the ready availability of fresh fish chowder. We should be prepared to cope with the hazards of fish bones, the occasional presence of which in chowders is, it seems to us, to be anticipated, and which, in the light of a hallowed tradition, do not impair their fitness or merchantability. While we are bouyed up in this conclusion by Shapiro v. Hotel Statler Corp., 132 F.Supp. 891 (S.D.Cal.), in which the bone which afflicted the plaintiff appeared in "Hot Barquette of Seafood Mornay," we know that the United States District Court of Southern California, situated as are we upon a coast, might be expected to share our views. We are most impressed, however, by Allen v. Grafton, 170 Ohio St. 249, 164 N.E.2d 167, where in Ohio, the Midwest, in a case where the plaintiff was injured by a piece of oyster shell in an order of fried oysters, Mr. Justice Taft (now Chief Justice) in a majority opinion held that "the possible presence of a piece of oyster shell in or attached to an oyster is so well known to anyone who eats oysters that we can say as a matter of law that one who eats oysters can reasonably anticipate and guard against eating such a piece of shell * * *." (P. 259 of 170 Ohio St., p. 174 of 164 N.E.2d.)

Thus, while we sympathize with the plaintiff who has suffered a peculiarly New England injury, the order must be

Exceptions sustained.

Judgment for the defendant.

IN RE FCA US LLC, 280 F.Supp.3d 975 (E.D. Mich. 2017). This case concerns alleged design defects in certain cars made by defendant FCA US, LLC (commonly referred to as Fiat Chrysler Automotive, or FCA) between 2012 and 2015. The [complaint] alleges * * * various liability theories * * * on behalf of the named plaintiffs and all other persons in the United States "who purchased, leased or own a 2012–2014 Chrysler 300, 2012–2014 Dodge Charger, or 2014–2015 Jeep Grand Cherokee equipped with a monostable electronic gearshift supplied by ZF Friedrichshaffen AG" (the so-called "monostable shifter" or "defective shifter"). This shifter design does not use a lever that moves physically to different positions, but instead is pushed in a direction by the driver, and then springs back to its original position after a gear is selected. The only indication that the car has changed gears or is in a particular gear is from lighted indicators on the dashboard and shifter that change to display letters such as "D" for "Drive" or "P" for "Park." Unlike some other vehicles with similar gearshift designs made by FCA's competitors, the cars at issue in this lawsuit also do not have any mechanism to automatically shift the car to "Park" when the driver exits the car while it is in another gear.

* * *

The defendant contends that it is undisputed that the cars are "minimally fit for the ordinary purpose of providing basic transportation," *Haag v. Hyundai Motor Am.*, 969 F.Supp.2d 313, 317 (W.D.N.Y. 2013), that the only alleged "failure" of the vehicles to provide transportation would be the result of gross misuse of the cars by the plaintiffs, and that the alleged "failure" does not concern anything that happens during "transportation," but only a purported tendency of the cars to "roll away" after they are fully stopped and parked. * * * [Some of the plaintiffs alleged that they experienced "rollaway incidents" with their cars.]

[T]he decisions on point in implied warranty cases concerning defective cars have recognized that merchantability implies not only that a vehicle can provide transportation, but that it can do so in a reasonably safe and controlled manner. In order to plead a viable claim for breach of the implied warranty, the plaintiff must allege that the defect rendered the car "unfit for its intended purpose [by] compromis[ing] the vehicle's safety, render[ing] it inoperable, or drastically reduc[ing] its mileage range." *Troup v. Toyota Motor Corp.*, 545 Fed.Appx. 668, 669 (9th Cir. 2013). Here the allegations of the [complaint] certainly suffice to suggest that the gear shifter defect seriously "compromised the safety" of the class vehicles, and that the defect has resulted in hundreds of accidents and injuries.

It is well recognized, both as a matter of law and common sense, that "a merchantable vehicle under the statute requires more than the mere capability of just getting from point A to point B." *Brand v. Hyundai Motor Am.*, 226 Cal.App.4th 1538, 173 Cal.Rptr.3d 454, 460 (2014). *Brand* involved a car whose sunroof opened and closed without driver input. The car certainly was capable of providing transportation. But the court also emphasized that "an important consideration under the implied warranty is consumer safety." *Ibid.* As the court explained, "[t]his minimum guarantee in the implied warranty of merchantability protects not only the vehicle purchaser, but other motorists, passengers, pedestrians, and the public generally." *Id.* at 461. Applying that rubric, the court agreed that "a vehicle sunroof that opens and closes on its own creates a substantial safety hazard." *Ibid.* * * * In this case, as in *Brand*, the facts alleged in the FACMC would allow a jury reasonably to infer "a multitude of similar unsafe scenarios" that could result from the failure by a class vehicle to select an intended gear, and the "element of surprise and lack of control" that would result from spontaneous and undirected shifts by the vehicle from one gear into another.

J. WHITE & R. SUMMERS, UNIFORM COMMERCIAL CODE

477 (6th ed. 2010).

[O]ne should understand how a warranty lawsuit looks to a plaintiff's lawyer and how it differs from a suit against an "insurer" on the one hand and an allegedly negligent defendant on the other. If an insurance company insures against the loss of an arm, all the claimant need do to recover is show the bloody stump. If the same claimant wishes to recover in warranty from the seller of the offending chain saw, he has a much tougher case to prove. Proof of injury—the loss of his arm—is just the beginning. First, he must prove that the defendant made a warranty, express or implied, under 2–313, 2–314, or 2–315. Second, he must prove that the goods did not comply with the warranty, that is, that they were defective at the time of the sale. Third, he must prove that his injury was caused, proximately and in fact, by the defective nature of the goods (and not, for example, by his careless use of the saw). Fourth, he must prove his damages. Finally, the warranty plaintiff must fight off all sorts of affirmative defenses such as disclaimers, statute of limitations, privity, lack of notice, and assumption of the risk.

* * *

* * * [O]ne should distinguish between warranty (particularly express warranty) and fraud or misrepresentation. Typically, only a naughty seller is guilty of misrepresentation or fraud, but a seller can be Simon pure and yet break an express warranty. The former cases usually require at least that the defendant be negligent in making its representation and in some

cases that it intentionally state a mistruth. There is no such requirement of evil doing on the part of a warranty defendant. A seller can fully believe that the representations he makes are accurate and yet find himself liable for the breach of an express warranty.

CONVENTION ON CONTRACTS FOR THE INTERNATIONAL SALE OF GOODS.

Article 35

(1) The seller must deliver goods which are of the quantity, quality and description required by the contract and which are contained or packaged in the manner required by the contract.

(2) Except where the parties have agreed otherwise, the goods do not conform with the contract unless they:

(a) Are fit for the purposes for which goods of the same description would ordinarily be used;

(b) Are fit for any particular purpose expressly or impliedly made known to the seller at the time of the conclusion of the contract, except where the circumstances show that the buyer did not rely, or that it was unreasonable for him to rely, on the seller's skill and judgment;

(c) Possess the qualities of goods which the seller has held out to the buyer as a sample or model;

(d) Are contained or packaged in the manner usual for such goods or, where there is no such manner, in a manner adequate to preserve and protect the goods.

(3) The seller is not liable under subparagraphs (a) to (d) of the preceding paragraph for any lack of conformity of the goods if at the time of the conclusion of the contract the buyer knew or could not have been unaware of such lack of conformity.

C. GERMAIN, THE UNITED NATIONS CONVENTION ON CONTRACTS FOR THE INTERNATIONAL SALE OF GOODS: GUIDE TO RESEARCH AND LITERATURE

117–18 (1995).

On January 1, 1988, the United Nations Convention on Contracts for the International Sale of Goods (the Convention) became effective in the United States. In general, the Convention * * * applies to contracts for the sale of goods between enterprises having their places of business in different countries, provided these countries have adopted the Convention. Freedom of contract, however, is a fundamental principle of the Convention, and the parties may opt out or modify the effects of its provisions.

A Contracting State now has two sales law: a domestic sales law and the Convention. In the United States, for example, the Uniform Commercial Code (U.C.C.) and the Convention are now both US law. * * *

The Convention simplifies contract negotiation and dispute resolution. With the exception of up to five possible reservations, the Convention is a uniform text governing international sales transactions. * * *

* * *

Not all contracts and contract-related issues are governed by the Convention. For example, sales to consumers, issues of validity, the effect of a sale on third-party claims, and claims for death or personal injury caused by defects in the goods sold are excluded. Likewise, a number of contracts that are ancillary to an international sales contract, e.g., carriage insurance, letters of credit, and dispute resolution are not governed by the Convention.

SECTION NINE: THE STATUTE OF FRAUDS

Unlike other sections of this chapter, this section does not present an additional general theory of obligation. Instead, it concerns a formal requirement for the enforcement of certain agreements with consideration, namely the requirement of a writing. We have already encountered the statute of frauds in cases such as Gay v. Mooney and Kearns v. Andree. We now pause for a more concentrated analysis. The subject is vast. (Corbin devotes an entire volume of his treatise to it.) Here we mainly explore the basic nature of statute of frauds problems and introduce relevant methodology. But first, a brief historical sketch:

> In 1671, in Old Marston, Oxfordshire, England, defendant Egbert was sued by plaintiff John over an alleged oral promise by Egbert to sell to John a fighting [rooster] named Fiste. John's friend, Harold, claimed he overheard the "deal" and by that dubious means John won, though in fact there apparently was no deal. In 1671 courts did not allow parties to a lawsuit to testify so Egbert could not testify to rebut Harold's story. Compounding the problem was the fact that courts then could not throw out jury verdicts manifestly contrary to the evidence. So, in response to the plight of the Egberts of the world and to the recurring mischief of the Johns, as well as to combat possible "Fraude and perjurie" by the Harolds, Parliament passed in 1677 a "Statute of Frauds" which required [among other things] that certain contracts for the sale of goods be in writing to be enforceable.

Thomson Printing Machinery Co. v. B.F. Goodrich Co., 714 F.2d 744, 746 (7th Cir.1983), quoting J. White and R. Summers, The Uniform Commercial Code 50 (2d ed. 1980).

Sections (4) and (17) of the English Statute of Frauds provided as follows:

> § 4. * * * [N]o action shall be brought (1) whereby to charge any executor or administrator upon any special promise, to answer damages out of his own estate; (2) or whereby to charge the defendant upon any special promise to answer for the debt, default or miscarriages of another person; (3) or to charge any person upon any agreement made upon consideration of marriage; (4) or upon any contract or sale of lands, tenements or hereditaments, or any interest in or concerning them; (5) or upon any agreement that is not to be performed within the space of one year from the making thereof; (6) unless the agreement upon which such action shall be brought, or some memorandum or note thereof, shall be in writing, and signed by the party to be charged therewith, or some other person thereunto by him lawfully authorized.
>
> § 17. * * * [N]o contract for the sale of any goods, wares and merchandises, for the price of ten pounds sterling or upwards, shall be allowed to be good, except the buyer shall accept part of the goods sold, and actually receive the same, or give something in earnest to bind the bargain, or in part of payment, or that some note or memorandum in writing of the said bargain be made and signed by the parties to be charged by such contract, or their agents thereunto lawfully authorized.

Although the above statute is no longer in force, some important writing requirements still exist under English law, including for the creation or transfer of certain interests in land and for contracts of suretyship. Observe, too, that the original English Statute of Frauds was far from complete in coverage. For example, it omitted construction contracts and insurance contracts.

Courts have treated the statute of frauds in the United States differently. Almost all states copied or adopted some version of the *general* English Statute of Frauds, set forth above. These state versions, with occasional modification, extensive judicial gloss, and even some judicial revision, are in force today. In addition to the general statute of frauds, one or more *special* statutes imposing additional writing requirements, such as for real estate brokerage agreements and certain contracts to make a will, are also in force in virtually all American jurisdictions. The Uniform Commercial Code embodies several special writing requirements, as well as the modern day sale of goods counterpart to old section 17 of the English statute. See U.C.C. § 2–201.

For illustrative purposes, consider Hawaii's version of the general statute of frauds. Although Hawaii is farther away from England than any other American state, Hawaii's statute tracks the English version rather closely.

HAWAII REVISED STATUTES § 656–1 (2014).

Certain contracts, when actionable. No action shall be brought and maintained in any of the following cases:

(1) To charge a personal representative, upon any special promise to answer for damages out of the personal representative's own estate:

(2) To charge any person upon any special promise to answer for the debt, default, or misdoings of another;

(3) To charge any person, upon an agreement made in consideration of marriage;

(4) Upon any contract for the sale of lands, tenements, or hereditaments, or of any interest in or concerning them;

(5) Upon any agreement that is not to be performed within one year from the making thereof;

(6) To charge any person upon any agreement authorizing or employing an agent or broker to purchase or sell real estate for compensation or commission;

(7) To charge the estate of any deceased person upon any agreement which by its terms is not to be performed during the lifetime of the promisor * * *

unless the promise, contract, or agreement upon which the action is brought, or some memorandum or note thereof, is in writing, and is signed by the party to be charged therewith, or by some person thereunto by the party in writing lawfully authorized.

Compliance with the statute of frauds does not itself prove the existence of a contract. If put to proof, the plaintiff must show all the requirements of an agreement with consideration. Thus, the plaintiff will not prevail merely by satisfying the statute of frauds. Conversely, if the defendant has a statute of frauds defense, i.e., the statute applies, the contract is not in writing and no exception applies, the plaintiff will not recover on the grounds of an agreement with consideration even if the plaintiff proves the contract. But the plaintiff may be able to recover the value of any benefit conferred on a restitution theory. See, e.g., Gay v. Mooney.

A statute of frauds can pose problems of conscience for the practicing lawyer. With the exception of U.C.C. § 2–201(3)(b), involving the sale of goods, the statute unqualifiedly allows a defendant to admit an oral agreement, yet plead the statute as a bar to recovery by the plaintiff. "In the conflict between conscience and judicially approved practice, what is the lawyer to do? Conscience tells * * * that the practice is wrong, but the literature from insurance companies reminds * * * [the lawyer] of liability for malpractice." Stevens, Ethics and the Statute of Frauds, 37 Cornell L.Q. 355, 356 (1952).

The basic problems arising under a statute of frauds and its case law are these: (1) Does the statute apply; or, in legal jargon, is the case "within the statute?" (2) If the case is within the statute, does a memorandum, note, or other writing satisfy the statute? (3) If the case is within the statute and there is no complying writing, does the statute or the case law recognize an exception? And (4) If the case is within the statute, there is no complying writing, and there is no applicable exception, does any other doctrine mitigate what would otherwise be the effect of non-compliance?

The cases below treat several of the most important statute of frauds issues. The cases also reveal the propensity of courts to treat the statute as a "common law" statute subject to judicial revision.

HOWARD M. SCHOOR ASSOCIATES, INC. V. HOLMDEL HEIGHTS CONSTRUCTION CO.

Supreme Court of New Jersey, 1975.
68 N.J. 95, 343 A.2d 401.

MOUNTAIN, J.

Plaintiffs, two engineering and surveying firms with identical or very similar management and ownership, brought this action to recover amounts due for professional services rendered by them to defendant, Holmdel Heights Construction Company. The latter is in receivership and the suit has proceeded, in effect, solely against defendant, Alan Sugarman. Plaintiffs' claim is that Sugarman, an attorney at law of this state, personally undertook to pay for the services rendered. He defends on the factual ground that he made no promises to do so and upon the legal ground that even had he made such a promise, it would be unenforceable under the Statute of Frauds.

The trial judge, sitting without a jury, resolved both the factual and legal issues in favor of plaintiffs and entered judgment against defendant in the amount of $24,105.30, together with interest. On appeal to the Appellate Division the judgment was reversed, with one judge dissenting. Plaintiffs have appealed to this Court as a matter of right.

Holmdel Heights Construction Company was in the process of developing a tract of land upon which it was constructing homes. Defendant, Sugarman, owned slightly more than 18% of the capital stock of this corporation and at all relevant times acted as its attorney. Plaintiff corporations were engaged to do surveying, engineering and professional planning work in connection with the development. The amount of their fees was not fixed by agreement but there has never been any dispute as to the reasonableness of their charges. Some of the invoices they submitted to the developer were paid, but others were not. The total of these unpaid charges continued to increase and plaintiffs became concerned.

On April 14, 1970 an important conference took place in the office of Mr. Sugarman. In addition to Mr. Sugarman there were also present at this meeting Howard M. Schoor, president of the plaintiff corporations, and Lawrence Schwartz, Esq., their attorney. The question of plaintiff's unpaid bills was a principal subject of discussion. Both Mr. Schoor and Mr. Schwartz testified that at this meeting Mr. Sugarman agreed personally to pay all outstanding bills as well as any charges that might be incurred in the future, if plaintiffs would continue with the work they were doing. The developer, Holmdel Heights Construction Company, was then busily engaged in seeking additional financing. Everyone concedes that in order to secure this financing, it was essential that further engineering work be done at once. Mr. Sugarman drew a check on his trust account for $2,000 and gave it to Mr. Schoor. According to the latter, the delivery of the check was accompanied by a statement made by Mr. Sugarman that this was intended to show his good faith in giving his personal guaranty as to payment of the outstanding and continuing obligation. On redirect examination Mr. Schoor again stated,

> At the April 14th meeting Mr. Sugarman very pointedly said that the corporation had no money at this time and was giving me his own money to attempt to satisfy me and have us continue to work on the project.

The testimony of Mr. Schwartz was substantially the same.

Defendant disagreed as to the purport of the conversation. His recollection was that after indicating the corporation's lack of liquidity, he gave Schoor the check for $2,000, indicating that that was the best the corporation could do at that time and that as further funds were received by it, additional payments would be made. At about this period Sugarman seems to have been actively managing many of the corporation's financial affairs; large amounts of corporate funds passed through his trust account.

Schoor and Schwartz left the meeting apparently satisfied, and the needed engineering work went forward. On June 12, 1970, Sugarman wrote a letter to Schoor, enclosing a further check in the sum of $1,000. The letter stated,

> I have enclosed to your order a check in the sum of $1,000.00. The Corporation does not have this money. This is my money being submitted to you in good faith because I promised it to you last week. I certainly hope you don't let us down.

The letter also contained a detailed specification of further engineering work that was needed at once in connection with the proposed new financing. Plaintiffs appear to have done all the work requested, but received no further payment. Shortly thereafter Holmdel Heights Construction Company went into receivership and this suit followed.

The trial judge made the following findings of fact:

> 1. At the April 14, 1970 meeting Sugarman led Schoor and Schwartz to believe:
>
> a. that the corporation was in financial difficulty;
>
> b. that there was a legitimate prospect of securing further financing;
>
> c. that such financing could not be obtained without further work by Schoor's companies;
>
> d. Sugarman knew that if Schoor would not continue, the corporation did not have sufficient funds to secure the essential engineering services from another source;
>
> e. Sugarman believed that the corporation could solve its difficulties as is evidenced by his July 16, 1970 loan of $5,000;[1]
>
> f. Sugarman had a substantial financial interest in seeing to it that Holmdel Heights was a success;
>
> g. to induce Schoor to continue work, Sugarman intentionally led Schoor and Schwartz to believe that he was pledging his personal finances to payment of past and future corporate debt to Schoor's companies;
>
> h. and that this latter finding is corroborated by the language of Sugarman's letter to Schoor on July 16, 1970.[2]

He further concluded that Sugarman

> * * * made an oral promise to Schoor to pay out of his personal finances, if necessary, past and future debts of Holmdel Heights to Schoor's companies in exchange for Schoor's agreement to continue engineering work for the corporation.

The majority of the Appellate Division neither accepted nor rejected these findings, concluding that even if the defendant made a promise to pay, it was unenforceable under the Statute of Frauds. The dissenting member of that Court accepted the findings of the trial judge and also agreed with his resolution of the legal issue.

---

[1] A loan of $5,000 was in fact later made by Sugarman to Holmdel Heights Construction Company on July 16, 1970.

[2] The date should probably be June 12, 1970.

We have carefully examined the trial record. It contains ample support for the findings and factual conclusions reached by the trial judge. He was in a position to observe the witnesses, take note of their demeanor and acquire a "feel of the case" that cannot make its way to a reviewing tribunal. Even on the cold record, however, we would be inclined to reach the same result. We find that the promise was made.

This brings us to the legal issue. Defendant contends that his promise—conceding it to have been made, as we have concluded it was—is unenforceable under the Statute of Frauds. The relevant section of that act reads as follows:

> No action shall be brought upon any of the following agreements or promises, unless the agreement or promise, upon which such action shall be brought or some memorandum or note thereof, shall be in writing, and signed by the party to be charged therewith, or by some other person thereunto by him lawfully authorized:
>
> * * *
>
> b. A special promise to answer for the debt, default or miscarriage of another person; [N.J.S.A. 25:1–5]

It is conceded by everyone that the promise was not in writing, nor was there any written memorandum or note thereof. Defendant contends that the promise—again assuming it to have been made—obligated him only secondarily to pay the debt owed by Holmdel Heights Construction Company in the event it should default, and that as such it comes squarely within the purview of the statute. Plaintiffs argue that the promise was made largely if not principally for defendant's personal benefit, that it did not create a suretyship relationship but rather was an "original" promise resting upon consideration sought by defendant for his personal ends, and that this being so the promise is not controlled by the statute. This latter argument rests upon what is sometimes referred to as the "leading object or main purpose rule." It has been stated as follows:

When the leading object of the promise or agreement is to become guarantor or surety to the promisee for a debt for which a third party is and continues to be primarily liable, the agreement, whether made before or after or at the time with the promise of the principal, is within the statute, and not binding unless evidenced by writing. On the other hand, when the leading object of the promisor is to subserve some interest or purpose of his own, notwithstanding the effect is to pay or discharge the debt of another, his promise is not within the statute. [2 *Corbin on Contracts* § 366, at 273–74 (1950)]

Thus in applying this rule, which we think expresses sound doctrine, it becomes important, and probably decisive, to determine what interest, purpose or object was sought to be advanced by defendant's promise to pay plaintiff's fees. As noted above defendant owned slightly more than 18% of the capital stock of Holmdel Heights Construction Company, for which he had paid $10,000. He was also attorney for the corporation and at the time of trial, January 18, 1973, was still owed $14,000 for legal services. Some part of this, how much we are not specifically told, was already owing to him at the time of the April 14, 1970 conference. Defendant, in the course of his testimony, agreed that had the corporation eventually been successful, the amount he would have received upon his investment, together with reasonably anticipated legal fees, would have been a substantial sum.

On the other hand, defendant was acting as counsel for the development corporation and presumably, in this capacity, was doing all he could to maintain its solvency and to further its best interests. The consideration that was sought and received from plaintiffs took the form of a continuing professional effort on their part to provide the developer with vital materials and data intended to become part of its submission to a finance agency in connection with its application for a substantial loan. Obviously this consideration would be of benefit both to defendant personally, even though indirectly, as well as to the client he served.

Although the leading object or main purpose rule has been widely accepted, neither courts nor commentators have reached agreement as to the analytical method that courts should adopt and follow in determining whether a particular set of facts does or does not come within the scope of the rule. Professor Williston identified eight different tests as having been from time to time applied by various courts. 3 *Williston on Contracts* §§ 467–475 (3d ed. Jaeger 1960).

Recent cases in this state seem to have placed most reliance upon the "original-collateral promise" test and the "credit" test. * * * The former test amounts to little more than a restatement of the rule itself and may be stated thus: where the leading object or main purpose of the promisor is to become surety for another's debt, the promise is a collateral one and within the Statute of Frauds; on the other hand, where the principal purpose is to subserve or promote some interest personal to the promisor, then the promise will be deemed an original one and not controlled by the Statute. In applying this test, as is mentioned below, emphasis is placed upon discovering the *leading* object and the *principal* or *main* purpose of the promisor. A chief reason for this approach is that in most cases the consideration for which the new promise is given will clearly benefit *both* the promisor and the original debtor.

The "credit" test calls upon the court to decide to whom in fact credit was given. While this test is useful, it appears to suffer from two drawbacks. In the first place the inquiry focuses upon the subjective intent and state of mind of the promisee. By the time of trial, either consciously or subconsciously, the promisee will probably have come to the conclusion that he extended credit to that person—generally the promisor—who will be the more readily able to respond in damages. Other evidence in the case may very likely be insufficient to overcome what may too often be essentially a self-serving determination by the promisee. In the second place, it will often if not generally be true that the promisee has in fact relied upon the credit of *both* the promisor and the original debtor.

* * *

The leading object or main purpose rule has been set forth in the *Restatement of Contracts* § 184 (1932) in the following form:

> Where the consideration for a promise that all or part of a previously existing duty of a third person to the promisee shall be satisfied is in fact or apparently desired by the promisor mainly for his own pecuniary or business advantage, rather than in order to benefit the third person, the promise is not within [the Statute of Frauds]. * * * [Emphasis added]

The identical formulation of the rule appears in the *Restatement of Security* § 93 (1941). This statement implicitly recognizes what has been adverted to above, that in many if not most cases the consideration for which the new promise is given will be beneficial *both* to the promisor and to the original debtor. Whether or not the Statute of Frauds will apply is then to depend upon whether this consideration was *mainly* desired for the promisor's benefit or for the benefit of the original debtor. In applying this rule the finder of fact must examine all circumstances bearing upon the transaction, the relationship of the parties to one another and endeavor to discern the intent, purpose and object of the promisor. In undertaking this examination the nature of the consideration will be of great if not paramount importance. To what extent will performance by the promisee benefit the promisor, directly or indirectly?

* * *

* * * A * * * pertinent example appears in the *Restatement of Contracts,* as an illustration under § 184,

> 2. D owes C $1000. C is about to levy an attachment on D's factory. S, who is also a creditor of D's, fearing that the attachment will ruin D's business and thereby destroy his own chance of collecting his claim, orally promises C that if C will forbear to take legal proceedings against D for three months, S will pay D's debt if D fails to do so. S's promise is enforceable.

The interest of defendant, Sugarman, in inducing plaintiffs to undertake the work that they did after the April 14 conference seems obvious. His substantial pecuniary and business interest to be furthered is abundantly clear. On the other hand there is little to support the view that he meant to commit his personal assets to so considerable an extent only to further his client's interest. We have no difficulty in agreeing with the trial court and with the dissenting member of the Appellate Division that the consideration was *mainly* desired for his personal benefit.

Accordingly the judgment of the Appellate Division is reversed and the judgment of the Law Division is hereby reinstated.

For reversal: JUSTICES MOUNTAIN, SULLIVAN, PASHMAN, CLIFFORD and SCHREIBER and JUDGE CONFORD—6.

For affirmance: None.

NOTE: WHAT KIND OF WRITING?

What kind of writing satisfies the statute of frauds? The answer depends on the language of the statute and the case law thereunder. But it is possible to generalize. The Restatement of Contracts (Second), § 131, states:

> Unless additional requirements are prescribed by the particular statute, a contract within the Statute of Frauds is enforceable if it is evidenced by any writing, signed by or on behalf of the party to be charged, which
>
> (a) reasonably identifies the subject matter of the contract,
>
> (b) is sufficient to indicate that a contract with respect thereto has been made between the parties or offered by the signer to the other party, and
>
> (c) states with reasonable certainty the essential terms of the unperformed promises in the contract.

The next case focuses in part on § 131(c).

STERLING V. TAYLOR

Supreme Court of California, 2007.
40 Cal. 4th 757, 152 P.3d 420.

CORRIGAN, J.

The statute of frauds provides that certain contracts "are invalid, unless they, or some note or memorandum thereof, are in writing and subscribed by the party to be charged. * * * " (Civ.Code, § 1624.) In this case, the Court of Appeal held that a memorandum regarding the sale of several apartment buildings was sufficient to satisfy the statute of frauds. Defendants contend the court improperly considered extrinsic evidence to resolve uncertainties in the terms identifying the seller, the property, and the price.

We reverse, but not because the court consulted extrinsic evidence. Extrinsic evidence has long been held admissible to clarify the terms of a memorandum for purposes of the statute of frauds. Statements to the contrary appear in some cases, but we disapprove them. A memorandum serves only an evidentiary function under the statute. If the writing includes the essential terms of the parties' agreement, there is no bar to the admission of relevant extrinsic evidence to explain or clarify those terms. The memorandum, viewed in light of the evidence, must be sufficient to demonstrate with reasonable certainty the terms to which the parties agreed to be bound. Here, plaintiffs attempt to enforce a price term that lacks the certainty required by the statute of frauds.

I. FACTUAL AND PROCEDURAL BACKGROUND

In January 2000, defendant Lawrence Taylor and plaintiff Donald Sterling discussed the sale of three apartment buildings in Santa Monica owned by the Santa Monica Collection partnership (SMC). Defendant was a general partner in SMC. Plaintiff and defendant, both experienced real estate investors, met on March 13, 2000 and discussed a series of transactions including the purchase of the SMC properties. At this meeting, plaintiff drafted a handwritten memorandum entitled "Contract for Sale of Real Property". * * *

The memorandum encompasses the sale of five properties; only the SMC properties are involved here. They are identified in the memorandum as "808 4th St.," "843 4th St.," and "1251 14th St.," with an aggregate price term of "approx. 10.468 X gross income[,] estimated income 1.600.000, *Price $16,750.⁰⁰.*" Although defendant had given plaintiff rent rolls showing the income from the properties, neither man brought these documents to the March 13 meeting. Plaintiff dated and initialed the memorandum as "Buyer," but the line he provided for "Seller" was left blank. Plaintiff contends the omission was inadvertent. Defendant, however, asserts he did not sign the document because he needed approval from a majority of SMC's limited partners.

On March 15, 2000, plaintiff wrote to defendant, referring to the properties by street address only, and stating "[t]his letter will confirm our contract of sale of the above buildings." The letter discussed deposits plaintiff had given to defendant, and noted "our agreement that the depreciation allocation and tax benefits will be given to me no later than April 1, 2000, since I now have equitable tittle [*sic*]." Price terms were not mentioned. Both parties signed the letter, defendant beneath the handwritten notation "Agreed, Accepted, & Approved."

Plaintiff claims the March 13 memorandum was attached to the March 15 letter, which defendant annotated and signed in his presence. Defendant insists nothing was attached to the March 15 letter, which he did not sign until March 30. According to defendant, his signature reflected only an accommodation to acknowledge the deposits he had received from plaintiff.

On April 4, 2000, defendant sent plaintiff three formal purchase agreements with escrow instructions, identifying the properties by their legal descriptions. SMC was named as the seller and the Sterling Family Trust as the buyer. The price terms totalled $16,750,000. Defendant signed the agreements as a general partner of SMC. Plaintiff refused to sign. Defendant claims plaintiff telephoned on April 28, saying the purchase price was unacceptable. Plaintiff asserts that after reviewing the rent rolls, he determined the actual rental income from the SMC buildings was $1,375,404, not $1,600,000 as estimated on the March 13 memorandum. Plaintiff claims he tried to have defendant correct the escrow instructions, but defendant did not return his calls. Plaintiff wanted to lower the price to $14,404,841, based on the actual rental income figure and the 10.468 multiplier noted in the memorandum.[1]

Plaintiff did not ask for the $16,750.00 purchase price stated in the memorandum. He admits that he "accidentally left off one zero" when he wrote down that figure. Defendant also acknowledges that the price recorded on the memorandum was meant to be $16,750,000.[2] Defendant returned plaintiff's uncashed deposit checks on May 23. The parties conducted further negotiations in December 2000 and January 2001. Defendant provided additional rent rolls, but no agreement was reached.

In March 2001 the trustees of the Sterling Family Trust sued Taylor, SMC, and related entities, alleging breach of a written contract to sell the properties for a total price of $14,404,841. The March 13 memorandum and the March 15 letter were attached to the complaint as the "Purchase Agreement." The complaint included causes of action for breach of the implied covenant of good faith and fair dealing, specific performance, declaratory relief, an accounting, intentional misrepresentation, and imposition of a constructive trust.

Defendants sought summary judgment, claiming that no contract was formed, the alleged contract violated the statute of frauds, and plaintiffs could not prove fraud. Defendants contended the memorandum and letter did not satisfy the statute because they established no agreement on price, failed to sufficiently identify either the contracting parties or the properties, and were not signed by Taylor and Christina Development. The trial court granted summary judgment. It ruled that the price term was too

---

1 The formula does not yield the plaintiff's modified price: $1,375,404 multiplied by 10.468 is $14,397,729. In a declaration filed in the trial court, plaintiff explained that he made two mistakes in arriving at the figure of $14,404,841, one in the rental income calculation and another in the multiplier he applied to that figure.

2 Given the superscript notation employed by plaintiff when he wrote "$16,750.^{00}," it might be said that *three* zeros were omitted from the price. However, the characterization of the error is immaterial in light of the parties' agreement that the intended figure was $16,750,000.

uncertain to be enforced and the writings did not comply with the statute of frauds. The court also concluded that the undisputed facts disclosed neither a fraudulent intent on defendant's part nor damages to plaintiff, thus foreclosing the misrepresentation claim.

The Court of Appeal reversed as to the contract causes of action, but remanded for entry of summary adjudication in defendants' favor on the fraud claim. The court held that Taylor's name and signature on the writings submitted by plaintiffs satisfied the statute of frauds. It also deemed the identification of the properties by street address sufficient, in light of extrinsic evidence specifying the city and state. Likewise, the court held that the price terms in the March 13 memorandum, while ambiguous, could be clarified by examining extrinsic evidence. It concluded that defendants' evidence raised a triable issue as to whether the parties had agreed on a formula for determining the purchase price. The court further ruled that the fraud claim failed because plaintiffs could not prove damages. Only the contract claims are at issue in this appeal.

II. DISCUSSION

Defendants contend the Court of Appeal improperly considered extrinsic evidence to establish essential contract terms. They insist the statute of frauds requires a memorandum that, standing alone, supplies all material elements of the contract. Plaintiffs, on the other hand, argue that extrinsic evidence is routinely admitted for the purpose of determining whether memoranda comply with the statute of frauds. * * *

Both sides of this debate find support in California case law, sometimes in the same opinion. Part A of our discussion explains that plaintiffs' view is correct. The statute of frauds does not preclude the admission of evidence in any form; it imposes a writing requirement, but not a comprehensive one. In part B, however, we conclude that defendants are nevertheless entitled to judgment. The Court of Appeal properly considered the parties' extrinsic evidence, but erroneously deemed it legally sufficient under the statute of frauds to establish the price sought by plaintiffs.

A. *The Memorandum Requirement of the Statute of Frauds*

The statute of frauds does not require a written contract; a "note or memorandum * * * subscribed by the party to be charged" is adequate. (Civ.Code, § 1624, subd. (a).) In *Crowley v. Modern Faucet Mfg. Co.* (1955) 44 Cal.2d 321, 282 P.2d 33, we observed that "[a] written memorandum is not identical with a written contract [citation]; it is merely evidence of it and usually does not contain all of the terms." (*Id.* at p. 323, 282 P.2d 33; * * *. Indeed, in most instances it is not even necessary that the parties intended the memorandum to serve a contractual purpose. * * *

A memorandum satisfies the statute of frauds if it identifies the subject of the parties' agreement, shows that they made a contract, and states the essential contract terms with reasonable certainty. (Rest.2d Contracts, § 131; 1 Witkin, Summary of Cal. Law, *supra,* Contracts, § 353, p. 399.) "Only the essential terms must be stated, ' "details or particulars" need not [be]. What is essential depends on the agreement and its context and also on the subsequent conduct of the parties. * * * ' (Rest.2d Contracts, § 131, com. g, p. 338.)" (*Seaman's Direct Buying Service, Inc. v. Standard Oil Co.* (1984) 36 Cal.3d 752, 762–763, 206 Cal.Rptr. 354, 686 P.2d 1158, overruled on another point in *Freeman & Mills, Inc. v. Belcher Oil Co.* (1995) 11 Cal.4th 85, 88, 44 Cal.Rptr.2d 420, 900 P.2d 669.)

This court recently observed that the writing requirement of the statute of frauds " 'serves only to prevent the contract from being unenforceable' [citation]; it does not necessarily establish the terms of the parties' contract." (*Casa Herrera, Inc. v. Beydoun* (2004) 32 Cal.4th 336, 345, 9 Cal.Rptr.3d 97, 83 P.3d 497.) * * * As the drafters of the Second Restatement of Contracts explained: "The primary purpose of the Statute is evidentiary, to require reliable evidence of the existence and terms of the contract and to prevent enforcement through fraud or perjury of contracts never in fact made. The contents of the writing must be such as to make successful fraud unlikely, but the possibility need not be excluded that some other subject matter or person than those intended will also fall within the words of the writing. Where only an evidentiary purpose is served, *the requirement of a memorandum is read in the light of the dispute which arises and the admissions of the party to be charged;* there is no need for evidence on points not in dispute." (Rest.2d Contracts, § 131, com. c, p. 335, italics added; accord, *Seaman's Direct Buying Service, Inc. v. Standard Oil Co., supra,* 36 Cal.3d at pp. 764–765, 206 Cal.Rptr. 354, 686 P.2d 1158.)

Thus, when ambiguous terms in a memorandum are disputed, extrinsic evidence is admissible to resolve the uncertainty. * * * Extrinsic evidence can also support reformation of a memorandum to correct a mistake. (Rest.2d Contracts, § 131, com. g, p. 338; *Calhoun v. Downs* (1931) 211 Cal. 766, 768–770, 297 P. 548; 1 Witkin, Summary of Cal. Law, *supra,* Contracts, §§ 355, 356, pp. 403–404.)

Because the memorandum itself must include the essential contractual terms, it is clear that extrinsic evidence cannot *supply* those required terms. (See, e.g., *Friedman v. Bergin* (1943) 22 Cal.2d 535, 537–539, 140 P.2d 1.) It can, however, be used to *explain* essential terms that were understood by the parties but would otherwise be unintelligible to others. * * *

* * *

To clarify the law on this point, we disapprove the statements in California cases barring consideration of extrinsic evidence to determine the sufficiency of a memorandum under the statute of frauds. The purposes of the statute are not served by such a rigid rule, which has never been a consistent feature of the common law. Corbin observes: "Judicial dicta abound to the effect that the writing must contain all of the 'essential terms and conditions' of the contract, and it is often said that these must be so clear as to be understood 'without any aid from parol testimony.' But the long course of judicial decision shows that 'essential terms and conditions' is itself a term of considerable flexibility and that the courts do not in fact blind themselves by excluding parol testimony when it is a necessary aid to understanding." (4 Corbin on Contracts (rev. ed.1997) § 22.2, pp. 706–707, fns. omitted.)

"Some confusion is attributable to a failure to keep clearly in mind the purpose of the statute and the informal character of the evidence that the actual words of the statute require; some is no doubt due to differences in the attitude of the judges as to the beneficence of the statute and the wisdom of its existence. Further, there are differences in the strictness of judicial requirements as to the contents of the memorandum. It is believed that sometimes these apparent differences can be explained by the degree of doubt existing in the court's mind as to the actual making and performance of the alleged contract. The better and the more disinterested is the oral testimony offered by the plaintiff, the more convincing the corroboration that is found in the surrounding circumstances, and the more limited the disputed issue because of admissions made by the defendant, the less that should be and is required of the written memorandum." (4 Corbin on Contracts, *supra,* § 22.2, p. 709, fn. omitted.) * * *

The governing principle is: "That is certain which can be made certain." (Civ.Code, § 3538; * * *). We hold that if a memorandum includes the essential terms of the parties' agreement, but the meaning of those terms is unclear, the memorandum is sufficient under the statute of frauds if extrinsic evidence clarifies the terms with reasonable certainty and the evidence as a whole demonstrates that the parties intended to be bound. Conflicts in the extrinsic evidence are for the trier of fact to resolve, but whether the evidence meets the standard of reasonable certainty is a question of law for the court. [3]

We emphasize that a memorandum of the parties' agreement is *controlling* evidence under the statute of frauds. Thus, extrinsic evidence cannot be employed to prove an agreement at odds with the terms of the memorandum. This point was made in *Beazell v. Schrader* (1963) 59 Cal.2d

---

[3] We note that a flexible, pragmatic view of the statute of frauds has deep roots in the common law. In 1747, Lord Hardwicke, sitting as Lord Chancellor, observed: "The meaning of the statute is to reduce contracts to a certainty, in order to avoid perjury on the one hand, and fraud on the other, and therefore, both in this court and the courts of common law, when an agreement has been reduced to such a certainty, and the substance of the statute has been complied with in the material part, the forms have never been insisted upon." (*Welford v. Beazely* (1747) 26 Eng.Rep. 1090 (Ch.); * * *.

577, 30 Cal.Rptr. 534, 381 P.2d 390. There, the plaintiff sought to recover a 5 percent real estate broker's commission under an oral agreement. (*Id.* at p. 579, 30 Cal.Rptr. 534, 381 P.2d 390.) The escrow instructions, which specified a 1.25 percent commission, were the "memorandum" on which the plaintiff relied to comply with the statute. However, he contended the instructions incorrectly reflected the parties' actual agreement, as shown by extrinsic evidence. (*Id.* at p. 580, 30 Cal.Rptr. 534, 381 P.2d 390.) The *Beazell* court rejected this argument, holding that under the statute of frauds, "the parol agreement of which the writing is a memorandum must be one whose terms are consistent with the terms of the memorandum." (*Id.* at p. 582, 30 Cal.Rptr. 534, 381 P.2d 390.) Thus, in determining whether extrinsic evidence provides the certainty required by the statute, courts must bear in mind that the evidence cannot contradict the terms of the writing.

B. *The Sufficiency of This Memorandum*

As noted above, it is a question of law whether a memorandum, considered in light of the circumstances surrounding its making, complies with the statute of frauds. * * * Accordingly, the issue is generally amenable to resolution by summary judgment. * * * We independently review the record to determine whether a triable issue of fact might defeat the statute of frauds defense in this case. * * *

A memorandum of a contract for the sale of real property must identify the buyer, the seller, the price, and the property. * * *

* * *

As defendants forthrightly conceded in the trial court, "[t]he problem here is the price term." The Court of Appeal concluded that the lines in the memorandum stating "approx. 10.468 X gross income[,] estimated income 1.600.000, *Price $16,750.00*" were ambiguous, given the use of the modifier "approx." before the multiplier, the omitted zero in the price, and the uncertain meaning of "gross income." The court then considered Sterling's testimony that "approx." was meant to modify the total price, not the multiplier; that the missing zero was merely an error; and that "gross income" was used by the parties to refer to actual gross annual income. It decided that this evidence, if accepted by the trier of fact, could establish an agreement to determine the price based on a formula, which would be binding under *Carver v. Teitsworth* (1991) 1 Cal.App.4th 845, 852, 2 Cal.Rptr.2d 446. In *Carver,* a bid for either a specified price or $1,000 over any higher bid was deemed sufficiently certain. (*Id.* at pp. 849, 852–853, 2 Cal.Rptr.2d 446.)

In this court, plaintiffs also cite *Cal. Lettuce Growers v. Union Sugar Co.* (1955) 45 Cal.2d 474, 289 P.2d 785, to show that a price term may be calculated from a formula. There, a price formula was derived from industry custom and the parties' past practice. (*Id.* at pp. 482–483, 289 P.2d 785.) Plaintiffs contend the parties here negotiated a 10.468 multiplier to be applied to the actual gross rental income from the buildings in March 2000, as indicated by the fact that Taylor gave Sterling rent rolls before their March 13 meeting.

The Court of Appeal erred by deeming Sterling's testimony sufficient to establish his interpretation of the memorandum for purposes of the statute of frauds. Had Taylor testified that the parties meant to leave the price open to determination based on a rental income figure that was yet to be determined, this would be a different case. Then, the "admissions of the party to be charged" might have supported a reasonably certain price term derived from a negotiated formula. (Rest.2d Contracts, § 131, com. c, p. 335.) Here, however, Taylor insists the price was meant to be $16,750,000, and Sterling agrees that was the number he intended to write down, underlined, as the "Price."

$16,750,000 is clearly an approximate product of the formula specified in the memorandum, applied to the income figure stated there.[4] On the other hand, Sterling's asserted price of $14,404,841 cannot reasonably be considered an approximation of $16,750,000. It is instead an approximate product of the formula applied to an actual income figure not found in the memorandum. The writing does not include the term "actual gross income," nor does it state that the price term will vary depending on proof or later agreement regarding the actual rental income from the buildings. In effect, Sterling would employ only the first part of the price term ("approx. 10.468 X gross income") and ignore the last parts ("estimated income 1.600.000, *Price $16,750.00*"). He would hold Taylor to a price that is 10.468 times the actual rental income figure gleaned from the rent rolls, but only "approximately" so because of Sterling's computational errors. * * *

Thus, two competing interpretations of the memorandum were before the court. Taylor's is consistent with the figures provided in the memorandum, requiring only the correction of the price by reference to undisputed extrinsic evidence. Sterling's price is not stated in the memorandum, and depends on extrinsic evidence in the form of his own testimony, disputed by Taylor, that the parties intended to apply the formula to actual gross rental income instead of the estimated income noted in the memorandum. Even if the trier of fact were to accept Sterling's version of the parties' negotiations, the price he seeks is not reflected in the memorandum; indeed, it is inconsistent with the price term that appears in the memorandum. Under these circumstances, we conclude the evidence is insufficient to establish Sterling's price term with the reasonable certainty required by the statute of frauds. * * *

---

[4] The actual product of $1,600,000 multiplied by 10.468 is $16,748,800.

The statute of frauds demands written evidence that reflects the parties' mutual understanding of the essential terms of their agreement, when viewed in light of the transaction at issue and the dispute before the court. The writing requirement is intended to permit the enforcement of agreements actually reached, but "to prevent enforcement through fraud or perjury of contracts never in fact made." (Rest.2d Contracts, § 131, com. c, p. 335.) The sufficiency of a memorandum to fulfill this purpose may depend on the quality of the extrinsic evidence offered to explain its terms. In Preble v. Abrahams, supra, 88 Cal. 245, 26 P. 99, the memorandum failed to describe the property to be sold with any certainty, but extrinsic evidence established that the parties could only have been referring to the portion of a tract that was not sold to another buyer. *Id.* at p. 250, 26 P. 99.) Similarly, in *Brewer v. Horst-Lachmund Co., supra,* 127 Cal. 643, 60 P. 418, telegrams that were otherwise inscrutable demonstrated an ascertainable agreement when the court considered the circumstances of the transaction and the parties' understanding of the terms employed. (*Id.* at pp. 646–647, 60 P. 418.)

Here, unlike in the *Preble* and *Brewer* cases, the extrinsic evidence offered by plaintiffs is at odds with the writing, which states a specific price and does not indicate that the parties contemplated any change based on actual rental income. Therefore, the evidence is insufficient to show with reasonable certainty that the parties understood and agreed to the price alleged by plaintiffs. The price terms stated in the memorandum, considered together with the extrinsic evidence of the contemplated price, leave a degree of doubt that the statute of frauds does not tolerate. The trial court properly granted defendants summary judgment.

III. DISPOSITION

The judgment of the Court of Appeal is reversed with directions to affirm the trial court judgment in its entirety.

GEORGE, C.J., BAXTER, CHIN, and MORENO, JJ., concur. Concurring and Dissenting Opinion by KENNARD, J.

I agree with the majority that extrinsic evidence is admissible to resolve the meaning of an ambiguity in a written memorandum required by the statute of frauds as evidence of an agreement, and that conflicts in the evidence are for the trier of fact to resolve. The majority, however, goes astray when it takes it upon itself to resolve an existing conflict in the evidence. In my view, the ambiguity in the language of the memorandum at issue should be resolved by the trier of fact.

* * *

The issue is whether the document entitled "Contract for the Sale of Real Property" is a memorandum sufficient to satisfy the statute of frauds. That statute provides that contracts for, among other things, the sale of real estate are invalid unless evidenced by a note or memorandum signed by the party to be charged. (Civ.Code, § 1624, subd. (a)(3).) Plaintiff here claims that the memorandum meets the requirements of the statute of frauds because extrinsic evidence he offered clarifies that the agreed price was $14,404,841—determined by applying the formula in the memorandum of multiplying the actual rent times 10.468. Plaintiff's extrinsic evidence includes the "Contract for Sale of Real Property," the letter dated March 15, 2000 confirming the buildings' sale signed by defendant, and defendant's having given plaintiff information showing the actual rent received. Defendant maintains that the price is the figure $16,750,000 expressed in the memorandum.

* * *

The parties' dispute here centers on whether the price description in the memorandum is ambiguous so that extrinsic evidence is admissible to clarify its meaning and satisfy the statute of frauds. Regarding price the memorandum states: "approx. 10.468 X gross income [,] estimated income 1.600.000, *Price $16,750,000.*" Plaintiff claims that the word "approx." modified the entire statement, not just "10.468 X gross income," and that the parties understood the term "gross income" to mean actual annual gross rental income. In other words, plaintiff's position is that the memorandum sets forth a formula for determining the actual price—10.468 multiplied by actual annual gross rental income, which results in a price of $14,404,841—and that the reference to "*Price $16,750,000*" is an estimate of the actual price, determined by application of the formula just mentioned, albeit using a somewhat inaccurate estimate of gross annual rental income. * * *. Defendant disagrees, contending that the memorandum's mention of "*Price $16,750,000*" reflects the actual purchase price agreed upon by the parties. Both have a point.

As the Court of Appeal observed, the language in the memorandum is ambiguous; that is, it can reasonably be read as each party proposes. * * * To accept plaintiff's argument would give meaning to the language in the disputed statement of "10.468 X gross income [,] estimated 1.600.000." To accept defendant's argument would give meaning to the term "*Price $16,750,000.*" Which view should be accepted is a determination to be made by the trier of fact, based on its consideration of the extrinsic evidence presented. * * * Either way, the trier of fact's resolution would result in a specific purchase price: one arrived at through application of a formula expressed in the memorandum, the other through acceptance of the figure $16,750,000 mentioned in the memorandum.

The majority, however, simply adopts defendant's view instead of leaving it to the trier of fact to resolve the conflict in the evidence. In accepting defendant's view, the majority rejects plaintiff's view as attempting to alter rather than explain the terms of the memorandum.

(Maj. opn., *ante,* 55 Cal.Rptr.3d at pp. 129–30, 152 P.3d at pp. 430–31.) I disagree.

Apparently based on its own evaluation of the evidence, which as discussed above is conflicting, the majority takes it upon itself to decide that the agreed price was $16,750,000 and then concludes that any extrinsic evidence presented by plaintiff would be inconsistent with that figure. * * * The majority reasons that plaintiff is looking only to the first part of the memorandum's price description of "approx. 10.468 X gross income," while ignoring the last part stating "estimated income 1.600.000, *Price $16,750,000.*" (*Ibid.*) This is both a misapprehension of plaintiff's view and a failure to appreciate that defendant's view too is not free from ambiguity.

Plaintiff's position that the memorandum sets forth a formula for determining the price does not ignore the memorandum's reference to "estimated income 1.600.000, *Price $16,750,000.*" According to plaintiff, the memorandum's *stated* price is itself an *estimate,* for it is the product of the *estimated* income of 1.600.000 times 10.468, while the *actual* price is to be determined by using the formula 10.468 multiplied by the *actual* gross income, resulting in a price of $14,404,841. Defendant's view that the actual price is $16,750,000 finds support in the memorandum's mention of "*Price $16,750,000*" but it ignores the memorandum's formula that plaintiff relies on. Unlike the majority, I see no reason to reject plaintiff's position as a matter of law when the purchase terms in the memorandum are ambiguous and are as reasonably susceptible to plaintiff's position as to defendant's. I would leave it to the trier of fact to resolve the ambiguity.

Unlike the majority, I would affirm the judgment of the Court of Appeal.

NOTE: MORE ON WHAT KIND OF WRITING?

In addition to the points made in Sterling v. Taylor, several additional propositions (with Restatement Second section references) command wide support either in statutory language or case law:

1. The memorandum may take the form of several writings, provided one of them is signed and the evidence shows that they relate to the same transaction. See § 132.

2. In general, the parties do not have to create the writing specifically to serve as a memorandum of a contract. For example, a letter obliquely referring to the contract may suffice. Even a writing that purports to cancel or repudiate the contract will suffice if the writing is otherwise sufficient. See § 133.

3. The signature need not be handwritten. Any symbol will do if made or adopted with the intent of authenticating the writing as that of the signer. See § 134.

4. The memorandum "may be made or signed at any time before or after the formation of the contract." See § 136.

5. If the original memorandum has been lost or destroyed, its contents may be shown by "an unsigned copy or by oral evidence." See § 137.

See generally E.A. Farnsworth, CONTRACTS 384–389 (4th ed. 2004).

MCINTOSH V. MURPHY

Supreme Court of Hawaii, 1970.
52 Haw. 29, 469 P.2d 177.

LEVINSON, JUSTICE.

This case involves an oral employment contract which allegedly violates the provision of the Statute of Frauds requiring "any agreement that is not to be performed within one year from the making thereof" to be in writing in order to be enforceable. HRS § 656–1(5). In this action the plaintiff-employee Dick McIntosh seeks to recover damages from his employer, George Murphy and Murphy Motors, Ltd., for the breach of an alleged one-year oral employment contract.

While the facts are in sharp conflict, it appears that defendant George Murphy was in southern California during March, 1964 interviewing prospective management personnel for his Chevrolet-Oldsmobile dealerships in Hawaii. He interviewed the plaintiff twice during that time. The position of sales manager for one of the dealerships was fully discussed but no contract was entered into. In April, 1964 the plaintiff received a call from the general manager of Murphy Motors informing him of possible employment within thirty days if he was still available. The plaintiff indicated his continued interest and informed the manager that he would be available. Later in April, the plaintiff sent Murphy a telegram to the effect that he would arrive in Honolulu on Sunday, April 26, 1964. Murphy then telephoned McIntosh on Saturday, April 25, 1964 to notify him that the job of assistant sales manager was open and work would begin on the following Monday, April 27, 1964. At that time McIntosh expressed surprise at the change in job title from sales manager to assistant sales manager but reconfirmed the fact that he was arriving in Honolulu the next day, Sunday. McIntosh arrived on Sunday, April 26, 1964 and began work on the following day, Monday, April 27, 1964.

As a consequence of his decision to work for Murphy, McIntosh moved some of his belongings from the mainland to Hawaii, sold other possessions, leased an apartment in Honolulu and obviously forwent any other employment opportunities. In short, the plaintiff did all those things which were incidental to changing one's residence permanently from Los Angeles to Honolulu, a distance of approximately 2200 miles. McIntosh continued working for Murphy until July 16, 1964, approximately two and one-half months, at which time he was discharged on the grounds that he was unable to close deals with prospective customers and could not train the salesmen.

At the conclusion of the trial, the defense moved for a directed verdict arguing that the oral employment agreement was in violation of the Statute of Frauds, there being no written memorandum or note thereof. The trial court ruled that as a matter of law the contract did not come within the Statute, reasoning that Murphy bargained for acceptance by the actual commencement of performance by McIntosh, so that McIntosh was not bound by a contract until he came to work on Monday, April 27, 1964. Therefore, assuming that the contract was for a year's employment, it was performable within a year exactly to the day and no writing was required for it to be enforceable. Alternatively, the court ruled that if the agreement was made final by the telephone call between the parties on Saturday, April 25, 1964, then that part of the weekend which remained would not be counted in calculating the year, thus taking the contract out of the Statute of Frauds. With commendable candor the trial judge gave as the motivating force for the decision his desire to avoid a mechanical and unjust application of the Statute.[1]

The case went to the jury on the following questions: (1) whether the contract was for a year's duration or was performable on a trial basis, thus making it terminable at the will of either party; (2) whether the plaintiff was discharged for just cause; and (3) if he was not discharged for just cause, what damages were due the plaintiff. The jury returned a verdict for the plaintiff in the sum of $12,103.40. The defendants appeal to this court on four principal grounds, three of which we find to be without merit. The remaining ground of appeal is whether the plaintiff can maintain an action on the alleged oral employment contract in light of the prohibition of the Statute of Frauds making unenforceable an oral contract that is not to be performed within one year.

I. Time of Acceptance of the Employment Agreement

The defendants contend that the trial court erred in refusing to give an instruction to the jury that if the employment agreement was made more than one day before the plaintiff began performance, there could be no recovery by the plaintiff. The reason given was that a contract not to be

---

1 THE COURT: You make the law look ridiculous, because one day is Sunday and the man does not work on Sunday; the other day is Saturday; he is up in Fresno. He can't work down there. And he is down here Sunday night and shows up for work on Monday. To me that is a contract within a year. I don't want to make the law look ridiculous, Mr. Clause, because it is one day later, one day too much, and that one day is a Sunday, and a non-working day.

performed within one year from its making is unenforceable if not in writing.

The defendants are correct in their argument that the time of acceptance of an offer is a question of fact for the jury to decide. But the trial court alternatively decided that even if the offer was accepted on the Saturday prior to the commencement of performance, the intervening Sunday and part of Saturday would not be counted in computing the year for the purposes of the Statute of Frauds. The judge stated that Sunday was a non-working day and only a fraction of Saturday was left which he would not count. In any event, there is no need to discuss the relative merits of either ruling since we base our decision in this case on the doctrine of equitable estoppel which was properly briefed and argued by both parties before this court, although not presented to the trial court.

II. Enforcement by Virtue of Action in Reliance on the Oral Contract

In determining whether a rule of law can be fashioned and applied to a situation where an oral contract admittedly violates a strict interpretation of the Statute of Frauds, it is necessary to review the Statute itself together with its historical and modern functions. The Statute of Frauds, which requires that certain contracts be in writing in order to be legally enforceable, had its inception in the days of Charles II of England. Hawaii's version of the Statute is found in HRS § 656–1 and is substantially the same as the original English Statute of Frauds.

The first English Statute was enacted almost 300 years ago to prevent "many fraudulent practices, which are commonly endeavored to be upheld by perjury and subornation of perjury". 29 Car. 2, c. 3 (1677). Certainly, there were compelling reasons in those days for such a law. At the time of enactment in England, the jury system was quite unreliable, rules of evidence were few, and the complaining party was disqualified as a witness so he could neither testify on direct-examination nor, more importantly, be cross-examined. Summers, The Doctrine of Estoppel and the Statute of Frauds, 79 U.Pa.L.Rev. 440, 441 (1931). The aforementioned structural and evidentiary limitations on our system of justice no longer exist.

Retention of the Statute today has nevertheless been justified on at least three grounds: (1) the Statute still serves an evidentiary function thereby lessening the danger of perjured testimony (the original rationale); (2) the requirement of a writing has a cautionary effect which causes reflection by the parties on the importance of the agreement; and (3) the writing is an easy way to distinguish enforceable contracts from those which are not, thus channelling certain transactions into written form.[2]

---

[2] Fuller, Consideration and Form, 41 Colum.L.Rev. 799, 800–03 (1941); Note: Statute of Frauds—The Doctrine of Equitable Estoppel and the Statute of Frauds. 66 Mich.L.Rev. 170 (1967).

In spite of whatever utility the Statute of Frauds may still have, its applicability has been drastically limited by judicial construction over the years in order to mitigate the harshness of a mechanical application.[3] Furthermore, learned writers continue to disparage the Statute regarding it as "a statute for promoting fraud" and a "legal anachronism."[4]

Another method of judicial circumvention of the Statute of Frauds has grown out of the exercise of the equity powers of the courts. Such judicially imposed limitations or exceptions involved the traditional dispensing power of the equity courts to mitigate the "harsh" rule of law. When courts have enforced an oral contract in spite of the Statute, they have utilized the legal labels of "part performance" or "equitable estoppel" in granting relief. Both doctrines are said to be based on the concept of estoppel, which operates to avoid unconscionable injury. * * *

Part performance has long been recognized in Hawaii as an equitable doctrine justifying the enforcement of an oral agreement for the conveyance of an interest in land where there has been substantial reliance by the party seeking to enforce the contract. * * * Other courts have enforced oral contracts (including employment contracts) which failed to satisfy the section of the Statute making unenforceable an agreement not to be performed within a year of its making. This has occurred where the conduct of the parties gave rise to an estoppel to assert the Statute. * * *

It is appropriate for modern courts to cast aside the raiments of conceptualism which cloak the true policies underlying the reasoning behind the many decisions enforcing contracts that violate the Statute of Frauds. There is certainly no need to resort to legal rubrics or meticulous legal formulas when better explanations are available. The policy behind enforcing an oral agreement which violated the Statute of Frauds, as a policy of avoiding unconscionable injury, was well set out by the California Supreme Court. In Monarco v. Lo Greco, 35 Cal.2d 621, 623, 220 P.2d 737, 739 (1950), a case which involved an action to enforce an oral contract for the conveyance of land on the grounds of 20 years performance by the promisee, the court said:

> The doctrine of estoppel to assert the statute of frauds has been consistently applied by the courts of this state to prevent fraud

---

[3] Thus a promise to pay the debt of another has been construed to encompass only promises made to a creditor which do not benefit the promisor (Restatement of Contracts § 184 (1932); 3 Williston, Contracts § 452 (Jaeger ed. 1960)); a promise in consideration of marriage has been interpreted to exclude mutual promises to marry (Restatement, *supra* § 192; 3 Williston, *supra* § 485); a promise not to be performed within one year means a promise not performable within one year (Restatement, *supra* § 198; 3 Williston, *supra,* § 495); a promise not to be performed within one year may be removed from the Statute of Frauds if one party has fully performed (Restatement, *supra* § 198; 3 Williston, *supra* § 504); and the Statute will not be applied where all promises involved are fully performed (Restatement, *supra* § 219; 3 Williston, *supra* § 528).

[4] Burdick, A Statute for Promoting Fraud, 16 Colum. L. Rev. 273 (1916); Willis, The Statute of Frauds—A Legal Anachronism, 3 Ind.L.J. 427, 528 (1928).

> that would result from refusal to enforce oral contracts in certain circumstances. Such fraud may inhere in the unconscionable injury that would result from denying enforcement of the contract after one party has been induced by the other seriously to change his position in reliance on the contract * * *.

In seeking to frame a workable test which is flexible enough to cover diverse factual situations and also provide some reviewable standards, we find very persuasive section [139] of the Second Restatement of Contracts. That section specifically covers those situations where there has been reliance on an oral contract which falls within the Statute of Frauds. Section [139] states:

> (1) A promise which the promisor should reasonably expect to induce action or forbearance on the part of the promisee or a third person and which does induce the action or forbearance is enforceable notwithstanding the Statute of Frauds if injustice can be avoided only by enforcement of the promise. The remedy granted for breach is to be limited as justice requires.
>
> (2) In determining whether injustice can be avoided only by enforcement of the promise, the following circumstances are significant: (a) the availability and adequacy of other remedies, particularly cancellation and restitution; (b) the definite and substantial character of the action or forbearance in relation to the remedy sought; (c) the extent to which the action or forbearance corroborates evidence of the making and terms of the promise, or the making and terms are otherwise established by clear and convincing evidence; (d) the reasonableness of the action or forbearance; (e) the extent to which the action or forbearance was foreseeable by the promisor.

We think that the approach taken in the Restatement is the proper method of giving the trial court the necessary latitude to relieve a party of the hardships of the Statute of Frauds. Other courts have used similar approaches in dealing with oral employment contracts upon which an employee had seriously relied. See Alaska Airlines, Inc. v. Stephenson, 217 F.2d 295 (9th Cir.1954); Seymour v. Oelrichs, 156 Cal. 782, 106 P. 88 (1909). This is to be preferred over having the trial court bend over backwards to take the contract out of the Statute of Frauds. In the present case the trial court admitted just this inclination and forthrightly followed it.

There is no dispute that the action of the plaintiff in moving 2200 miles from Los Angeles to Hawaii was foreseeable by the defendant. In fact, it was required to perform his duties. Injustice can only be avoided by the enforcement of the contract and the granting of money damages. No other remedy is adequate. The plaintiff found himself residing in Hawaii without a job.

It is also clear that a contract of some kind did exist. The plaintiff performed the contract for two and one-half months receiving $3,484.60 for his services. The exact length of the contract, whether terminable at will as urged by the defendant, or for a year from the time when the plaintiff started working, was up to the jury to decide.

In sum, the trial court might have found that enforcement of the contract was warranted by virtue of the plaintiff's reliance on the defendant's promise. Naturally, each case turns on its own facts. Certainly there is considerable discretion for a court to implement the true policy behind the Statute of Frauds, which is to prevent fraud or any other type of unconscionable injury. We therefore affirm the judgment of the trial court on the ground that the plaintiff's reliance was such that injustice could only be avoided by enforcement of the contract.

Affirmed.

ABE, JUSTICE (dissenting).

The majority of the court has affirmed the judgment of the trial court; however, I respectfully dissent.

I.

Whether alleged contract of employment came within the Statute of Frauds:

As acknowledged by this court, the trial judge erred when as a matter of law he ruled that the alleged employment contract did not come within the Statute of Frauds; however, I cannot agree that this error was not prejudicial as this court intimates.

On this issue, the date that the alleged contract was entered into was all important and the date of acceptance of an offer by the plaintiff was a question of fact for the jury to decide. In other words, it was for the jury to determine when the alleged one-year employment contract was entered into and if the jury had found that the plaintiff had accepted the offer[5] more than one day before plaintiff was to report to work, the contract would have come within the Statute of Frauds and would have been unenforceable. * * *

II.

This court holds that though the alleged one-year employment contract came within the Statute of Frauds, nevertheless the judgment of the trial court is affirmed "on the ground that the plaintiff's reliance was such that injustice could only be avoided by enforcement of the contract."

---

[5] Plaintiff testified that he accepted the offer in California over the telephone.

I believe this court is begging the issue by its holding because to reach that conclusion, this court is ruling that the defendant agreed to hire the plaintiff under a one-year employment contract. The defendant has denied that the plaintiff was hired for a period of one year and has introduced into evidence testimony of witnesses that all hiring by the defendant in the past has been on a trial basis. The defendant also testified that he had hired the plaintiff on a trial basis.

Here on one hand the plaintiff claimed that he had a one-year employment contract; on the other hand, the defendant claimed that the plaintiff had not been hired for one year but on a trial basis for so long as his services were satisfactory. I believe the Statute of Frauds was enacted to avoid the consequences this court is forcing upon the defendant. In my opinion, the legislature enacted the Statute of Frauds to negate claims such as has been made by the plaintiff in this case. But this court holds that because the plaintiff in reliance of the one-year employment contract (alleged to have been entered into by the plaintiff, but denied by the defendant) has changed his position, "injustice could only be avoided by enforcement of the contract." Where is the sense of justice?

Now assuming that the defendant had agreed to hire the plaintiff under a one-year employment contract and the contract came within the Statute of Frauds, I cannot agree, as intimated by this court, that we should circumvent the Statute of Frauds by the exercise of the equity powers of courts. As to statutory law, the sole function of the judiciary is to interpret the statute and the judiciary should not usurp legislative power and enter into the legislative field. A. C. Chock, Ltd. v. Kaneshiro, 51 Haw. 87, 93, 451 P.2d 809 (1969); Miller v. Miller, 41 Ohio Op. 233, 83 N.E.2d 254 (Ct.C.P.1948). Thus, if the Statute of Frauds is too harsh as intimated by this court, and it brings about undue hardship, it is for the legislature to amend or repeal the statute and not for this court to legislate.

DUMAS v. INFINITY BROAD. CORP., 416 F.3d 671 (7th Cir. 2005). [Cliff Dumas, a radio personality, negotiated with Scott Aurand, the program director for US-99, a radio station, regarding employment opportunities. Dumas and Aurand exchanged several e-mails in which they discussed "talking points" for an employment contract. Dumas alleged that during a telephone call the parties agreed to a starting date for his employment, a salary, and a duration of five years. On the same day, Aurand sent Dumas an e-mail in which Aurand stated that "the station was 'moving forward with [the] plan[ ] to bring [him] in.' " A few weeks later Dumas tendered his resignation from another station. After US-99 hired a new operations manager, the station declined to hire Dumas. He then brought an action against the station for breach of contract and promissory estoppel. The District Court granted the station summary judgment based on the Statute of Frauds. The Seventh Circuit affirmed for the same reason, stating in part:] At the outset, Dumas admits that he has no quarrel with the district court's determination that his breach of contract claim is barred by Illinois' statute of frauds because any alleged contract between US-99 and himself could not be established with the paucity of written evidence (e-mails) presented to the district court. * * * In the ordinary course of litigation of this nature it is commonplace for the plaintiff, after having been unsuccessful in producing written documentation of an alleged oral contract as required by the statute of frauds, to seek to recover under the alternate theory of promissory estoppel. * * * In such a case, since the statute of frauds applies with equal force under either a breach of contract or promissory estoppel theory under Illinois law, it is unnecessary for the courts to undertake a separate promissory estoppel analysis, for the statute of frauds *per se* cannot be satisfied. The only substantive difference between that scenario and the situation before us, is Dumas' additional claim that, although the documents he submitted to the district court (admittedly) failed to satisfy the elements of an enforceable contract, they might conceivably constitute an unambiguous promise to employ. We agree with the reasoning employed by the district court and are of the opinion that it is unnecessary for a court, once satisfied that the statute of frauds could not be satisfied concerning a breach of contract claim, to undertake a separate analysis of whether or not an 'unambiguous promise' exists for promissory estoppel purposes, for the outcome would be the same in either instance.

UNIFORM COMMERCIAL CODE § 2–201.

Formal Requirements; Statute of Frauds

(1) Except as otherwise provided in this section a contract for the sale of goods for the price of $500 or more is not enforceable by way of action or defense unless there is some writing sufficient to indicate that a contract for sale has been made between the parties and signed by the party against whom enforcement is sought or by his authorized agent or broker. A writing is not insufficient because it omits or incorrectly states a term agreed upon but the contract is not enforceable under this paragraph beyond the quantity of goods shown in such writing.

(2) Between merchants if within a reasonable time a writing in confirmation of the contract and sufficient against the sender is received and the party receiving it has reason to know its contents, it satisfies the requirements of subsection (1) against such party unless written notice of objection to its contents is given within 10 days after it is received.

(3) A contract which does not satisfy the requirements of subsection (1) but which is valid in other respects is enforceable

(a) if the goods are to be specially manufactured for the buyer and are not suitable for sale to others in the ordinary course of the seller's business and the seller, before notice of repudiation is received and under circumstances which reasonably indicate that the goods are for the buyer, has made either a substantial beginning of their manufacture or commitments for their procurement; or

(b) if the party against whom enforcement is sought admits in his pleading, testimony or otherwise in court that a contract for sale was made, but the contract is not enforceable under this provision beyond the quantity of goods admitted; or

(c) with respect to goods for which payment has been made and accepted or which have been received and accepted (Sec. 2–606).

WALBRO ENGINE MANAGEMENT, LLC v. SURECAN, INC., 2017 WL 6345825 (Mich. Ct. App. 2017). This case arises out of a failed business arrangement between the parties. According to Surecan, it "developed and designed a plastic molded portable [fuel] tank for the consumer market which has unique features, including a flexible rotating nozzle." As the developer of the gas tank, Surecan began discussing a business relationship with Walbro, where Walbro would be the exclusive manufacturer of the fuel tanks. * * * [The parties representatives signed an agreement to this effect, but Walbro's board then rejected the project.] Walbro claims * * * the trial court erred when it held that the Agreement included a valid quantity term, and therefore, complied with the statute of frauds. We disagree. * * * To establish a valid contract under the UCC, a quantity term must be specifically stated. * * * However, it need not be certain because "to require that it be stated with certainty would put most distributorship agreements out of compliance" with [2–201]. Here, the Agreement included a valid quantity term. In paragraph 1 of the Agreement, the parties agreed to a term of five years or 5,000,000 units. While the final quantity of gas tanks to be produced is not certain, the quantity term, which is expressly stated in the agreement, puts a cap on the number of gas tanks that Walbro would be required to manufacture. Therefore, it is valid, and the trial court did not err when it reached the same conclusion in its first opinion and order.

NOTE: *PART PERFORMANCE AND THE STATUTE OF FRAUDS*

Reliance in the form of part performance may be sufficient to bar assertion of the statute of frauds as a defense. McNamee Schmetterer Euro RSCG Inc. v. Aegis Group, 93 N.Y.2d 229, 689 N.Y.S.2d 674, 711 N.E.2d 953 (1999). For example, under § 2–201(3)(c) of the Uniform Commercial Code, an oral agreement for the sale of goods is enforceable "with respect to goods for which payment has been made and accepted or which have been received and accepted." Why this approach? Official Comment 1 to § 2–201 states that "[a]ll that is required is that the writing afford a basis for believing that the offered oral evidence rests on a real transaction." Does part performance, for example, part payment for the goods, provide a reliable substitute for such a writing?

Generally, in an action for damages, part performance of an oral land sale contract does not remove the bar of the statute of frauds. In addition, courts generally hold that a vendee's partial (or sometimes even full) payment of the price in a suit for specific performance does not remove the bar of the statute of frauds. More is required than "something beyond injury adequately compensable in money." Jasmin v. Alberico, 135 Vt. 287, 290, 376 A.2d 32, 33 (1977). For example, if the vendee takes possession with the vendor's assent and makes improvements or pays a portion of the price, the vendee can get specific performance. Review again Seavey v. Drake. Was there part performance in that case?

An employee's part performance of an employment contract with a duration of more than one year generally does not take the contract out of the statute of frauds. Consider, for example, a football coach who accepts a university's seven-year, seven million dollar contract. After four months on the job, but before the parties sign a written contract, the coach is fired for alleged misbehavior. (This is based on a real event.) The coach cannot enforce the seven-year contract even if the firing was wrongful.

PROBLEM 2-11

1. If the requirement of consideration is satisfied, is it necessary to satisfy any otherwise applicable statute of frauds requirement?

2. Is the statute of frauds applicable to each of the theories of obligation studied in this chapter? Answer this question with reference to the Hawaii statute, a common version of the statute of frauds.

FRY, X MARKS THE SPOT: NEW TECHNOLOGIES COMPEL NEW CONCEPTS FOR COMMERCIAL LAW

26 Loy. L.A. L. Rev. 607, 607–609, 611–612, 622 (1993).

Predictions of a paperless society have been around for years—so many years that many of us no longer pay much attention. In spite of all the prophesying, people still write checks, send letters and reduce agreements to paper. Office supply stores and catalogs are filled with pads of standard form purchase orders, invoices, notes and leases, which are ready for the small business to purchase.

While paper has not disappeared—and shows few signs of doing so—some of the prophets' predictions of a paperless society have come and will continue to come to pass. We may not eliminate paper in the foreseeable future, but a constantly increasing stream of transactions are consummated without the use of a single piece of paper. Still more are consummated in reliance on information transmitted electronically, and pieces of paper are generated after the fact only to be placed in overstuffed filing cabinets and forgotten.

NOTE:
THE STATUTE OF FRAUDS AND ELECTRONIC CONTRACTING

The 2003 amendments to Uniform Commercial Code § 2–201 would have dealt with electronic contracting and the statute of frauds, but no state has enacted or likely will enact the amendments. However, revised U.C.C. Article 1, adopted by most states and applicable to Article 2 sales, includes definitions of "signed" ("using any symbol executed or adopted with present intention to adopt or accept a writing.") and "writing" ("includes printing, typewriting, or any other intentional reduction to tangible form."). U.C.C. §§ 1–201(b)(37) & (43). Under these definitions, a click on an "I agree" icon should satisfy the statute of frauds.

Courts considering whether an e-mail is a "writing" find that they are "tangible" because they can be saved on a hard drive and can be printed on paper. In support of this conclusion, courts point to the U.C.C.'s flexible approach to the writing requirement in section 2–201. See, e.g., Bazak Intern. Corp. v. Tarrant Apparel Group, 378 F. Supp. 2d 377 (S.D.N.Y. 2005).

The Electronic Signatures in Global and National Commerce Act, 15 U.S.C. § 7001 (as amended 2006), allows parties to bind themselves to contracts online through electronic signatures. The law governs, among other things, banking, insurance and brokerage contracts made online. For more on this act, see, e.g., Carl, Ciocchetti, Barton & Christensen, Are Online Business Transactions Executed by Electronic Signatures Legally Binding? 2001 Duke LTR 5. In addition, most states have enacted the Uniform Electronic Transactions Act (UETA). UETA makes electronic signatures enforceable, including those found on e-mails.

ST. JOHNS HOLDINGS, LLC v. TWO ELECTRONICS, LLC, 2016 WL 1460477 (Mass. Land Court 2016). Whether text messages qualify as a writing under the Statute of Frauds is a novel issue in the Commonwealth. In general, writings of relative informality and brevity can satisfy the statute. *A.B.C. Auto Parts, Inc. v. Moran,* 359 Mass. 327, 329, 268 N.E.2d 844 (1971) (finding that an endorsement on a check which indicated the nature of the transaction, parties, property, and purchase price satisfied the Statute of Frauds). The writing need not be a formal contract, but the terms of the writing must be sufficiently complete and definite and the writing must reflect a present intent of the parties at the time of formation to be bound. *Id.* (stating that the "fact that the memorandum is on the back of a check is immaterial"); *Targus Group Int'l, Inc.,* 76 Mass.App.Ct. at 428,

922 N.E.2d 841 ("Sufficient completeness depends upon the substance of the terms approved by the parties."). The writing must contain directly, or by implication, all of the essential terms of the parties' agreement. *Michelson v. Sherman,* 310 Mass. 774, 775, 39 N.E.2d 633 (1942). "It is a court's function, therefore, to determine what provisions are essential to an agreement sought to be enforced and whether an omitted provision can be supplied by implication." *Simons v. Simons,* 35 Mass.App.Ct. 705, 709, 625 N.E.2d 564 (1994), citing Restatement (Second) of Contracts § 131, comment g (1979).

To support its position, Two Electronics directs the court to *Singer v. Adamson,* a prior Land Court decision that addressed a similar issue involving emails between real estate agents where the court decided that the emails did not meet the demands of the Statute of Frauds. *Singer v. Adamson,* 11 LCR 338, 342, 2003 WL 23641985 (2003), *aff'd,* 65 Mass.App.Ct. 1103 (2005). In reaching its decision, the court noted that emails "by their quick and casual nature, tend to lack in many instances the cautionary and memorializing functions a traditional signed writing serves under the Statute of Frauds." *Id.* The Land Court judge further acknowledged that "[e]-mails facilitate rapid, almost instantaneous communication, but in many cases they analogize more closely to telephone calls, or at least to voice mail messages, shot back and forth between parties whose chief goal is prompt response. . . . It is far from obvious that average parties launching e-mails to each other appreciate that their quickly-composed electronic missives are contractual in nature, and will constitute, when assembled into one long 'thread' after the fact, a memorandum of a binding and enforceable agreement. In many instances, the e-mails reveal that the parties are really just 'talking' with the help of the internet, and not sitting down across a virtual table to electronically 'write up' a memorandum of any contractual significance." *Id.*

Singer was decided over a decade ago. Since then the use of electronic communications, particularly in the legal field, has advanced immensely and become commonplace. Several more recent decisions acknowledge that emails may be writings that satisfy the Statute of Frauds and create a binding contract. *Feldberg v. Coxall,* No. MICV201201649A, 2012 WL 3854947, at * 6 (Mass.Super. May 22, 2012); *Fecteau Benefits Group, Inc. v. Knox,* 72 Mass.App.Ct. 204, 212–213, 890 N.E.2d 138 (2008) (finding the parties intended to be bound by emails settling a fee dispute where they formed a clear and complete agreement including material terms such as the amount of legal fees, a deadline for acceptance, and acceptance without equivocation); *Slover,* 24 LCR at 5 ("Emails between the parties may create a binding contract that satisfies the Statute of Frauds, provided the emails contain all essential terms"). Moreover, the facts in *Singer* are distinguishable from this case. In *Singer,* the court found that the emails lacked specificity on many key terms including the dates of performance, deposit terms, rights to inspection, mortgage and other contingencies. The parties themselves "had no prior history of contracting, no definitive written agreement had been signed by them previously, and they did not communicate directly, even using e-mail." *Singer,* 11 LCR at 342. These are not the circumstances of the present case.

The facts in *Shattuck v. Klotzbach* are more similar to this matter. *Shattuck v. Klotzbach,* No. 011109A, 2001 WL 1839720, at *3–4 (Mass. Super. Dec. 11, 2001). The court in Shattuck denied a seller's motion to dismiss, holding that email messages exchanged between a prospective buyer and seller satisfied the Statute of Frauds. *Id.* The plaintiff-buyer and defendant-seller had engaged in negotiations concerning the sale of property through their attorneys that were conducted in person, by telephone, and email. Several emails were exchanged addressing specific contractual provisions, including the closing date, purchase price, deposit amount, and waivers of contingencies. *Id.* at *1–2. The court found that these emails reflected detailed attention to many of the provisions that would govern the purchase and sale, and signified a close involvement of the parties' attorneys in forming the transaction. *Id.* at *3–4. On these facts, the court had little difficulty denying the seller's motion to dismiss. *Id.* at *4.

The Superior Court addressed the issue more recently in *Feldberg v. Coxall.* In *Feldberg,* the parties disputed whether a series of emails between their attorneys regarding the sale of property was sufficient to satisfy the Statute of Frauds. *Feldberg,* 2012 WL 3854947, at * 4. The key email at issue was sent by the plaintiffs' attorney with a revised offer attached with changes reflecting conversations between the parties. The draft attached to the email contained a purchase price, described the property, and provided a closing date. *Id.* The defendant's attorney responded asking for a written approval from the bank and ending the email by stating "I think we are ready to go. . . . We are almost there." *Id.* Plaintiffs' attorney did provide a copy of a commitment letter from the bank containing reasonable conditions for plaintiff's mortgage transaction, which the defendant claimed the conditions repudiated the deal. *Id.* The court ultimately concluded that these transactions provided a reasonable and supportable response to the defense of Statute of Frauds. *Id.* at *6. In reaching the decision, the court noted that "[i]n truth, the Courts have not yet set forth rules of the road for 'the intersection between the seventeenth-century Statute of Frauds and twenty-first century electronic mail.' " *Id.,* citing *May Trucking Co. v. Northwest Volvo Trucks, Inc.,* 238 Or.App. 21, 24, 241 P.3d 729 (2010). Relying on existing authority in *Shattuck v. Klotzbach,* the court found that the plaintiffs' response to the Statute of Frauds defense had an arguable basis, which was "not difficult on this issue of first impression." *Id.* at *5.

Based on the undisputed facts and drawing inferences in SJH's favor, the Court finds that the February 3rd text message is a writing and that, read in the context of exchanges between the parties, it contains sufficient terms to state a binding contract between SJH and Two Electronics. * * *

PROBLEM 2-12

Review: Alec had roto-tilled his lawn, readying it for some sorely needed seeding. Unfortunately, he injured his back and was not able to seed the lawn himself. Time was of the essence because it was getting hot. Alec asked his neighbor, Iris, for help. She agreed to help, worked for three days, and completed the job. Nothing was said at the time about payment. Months later, while admiring his lawn, Alec told Iris that it was about time for him to "settle up." He asked her how much he owed her and, after protestations, she replied that $250 would be fine. Later Alec refused to pay anything. Iris consults you about possible causes of action and possible recoveries. Advise! (Before working through this problem, you should reread the introduction and peruse the general contents of this chapter.)

CHAPTER THREE

REMEDIES

■ ■ ■

Different measures of recovery cannot be [explained] without an inquiry into the reasons which underlie the enforcement of promises generally.

FULLER

SECTION ONE: REMEDIES AND THE ROLE OF LAWYERS

We have now studied a variety of theories of obligation that serve as general bases for imposing particular legal duties. Typically, the parties honor their duties and no dispute arises. But when a party fails to perform a duty or repudiates a duty not yet due, the general law of remedies becomes relevant. Of course, the aggrieved party may not seek a remedy even in the face of a significant breach. For example, that party may want to preserve the relationship, hoping to do business with the breacher in the future. But not infrequently, the aggrieved party sees a lawyer, and the lawyer will turn to the general law of remedies at an early stage. This body of law incorporates rules dealing with such topics as: the general availability of damages for breach or repudiation; the different measures of damages; unforeseeability and other limits on recoverable damages; restitutionary relief in promissory contexts; the validity of private remedial clauses in agreements; specific performance and other forms of specific relief; and punitive damages.

The general law of remedies is fundamental and important. Indeed, to fully understand a theory of obligation, one must study the remedies available for breach of a duty arising under the theory. The general law of remedies reveals most of the leading policies of contract and related law, and is worthy of special emphasis for this reason.

Lawyers turn to the general law of remedies as planners, drafters, interpreters, counselors, negotiators, and litigators. While much of this law cannot be varied or displaced by the parties' agreement, the parties do enjoy significant freedom to include their own remedial provisions. When planning an agreement, the lawyer must consider the limits on the power of private parties to create their own remedies. The effective lawyer works within such limits to plan and draft remedial provisions that meet the particular needs of the client.

When planning an arrangement or when helping to settle a dispute, the lawyer is frequently called upon to interpret and apply general law governing available remedies, as well as to interpret and apply contract clauses setting forth remedies. The lawyer also commonly negotiates the settlement of disputes against the background of a particular remedy likely to be available if settlement fails. In addition, the lawyer advises the client concerning appropriate conduct after the other party's breach so the client will not pile up losses that will be uncompensated under the general law of remedies. Of course, when preparing for and litigating lawsuits, lawyers must keep their eyes fixed on the specific judicial remedy or remedies available at the end of the line.

Because of the interplay between theories of obligation and remedies (already explored to a limited extent in the first two chapters), it should be no surprise that this chapter, too, is organized mainly around theories of obligation.

SECTION TWO: REMEDIAL THEORY—SOME FUNDAMENTALS

In a foundational early article, Fuller and Perdue[a] suggested courts advanced three distinct purposes in awarding contract damages.

First, the facts may indicate that "plaintiff has in reliance on the promise of the defendant conferred some value on the defendant." In such cases, courts may require the "defendant to disgorge the value he received from the plaintiff." This advances the *restitution interest.* Second, the "plaintiff has in reliance on the promise of the defendant changed his position." Damages can undo the harm by requiring the defendant to reimburse the plaintiffs losses—"Our object is to put him in as good a position as he was in before the promise was made." This is the *reliance interest.*

Both the *restitution* and *the reliance interests* are familiar and intuitive (insofar as anything about law school is familiar and intuitive). The third interest that contract law advances is singular. Fuller and Perdue, describing the *expectation interest*, proposed that contract law usually aims to put the non-breaching party in "as good a position as he would have occupied had the defendant performed his promise." This expectation interest justifies ordering the defendant to actually render the performance due (called *specific performance*), but also a damages remedy that as nearly as possible approximates that performance. They continued:

[a] The Reliance Interrest in Contract Damages, 46 Yale L. J. 52 (1936).

It is obvious that the three "interests" we have distinguished do not present equal claims to judicial intervention. It may be assumed that ordinary standards of justice would regard the need for judicial intervention as decreasing in the order in which we have listed the three interests. The "restitution interest," involving a combination of unjust impoverishment with unjust gain, presents the strongest case for relief. If, following Aristotle, we regard the purpose of justice as the maintenance of an equilibrium of goods among members of society, the restitution interest presents twice as strong a claim to judicial intervention as the reliance interest, since if A not only causes B to lose one unit but appropriates that unit to himself, the resulting discrepancy between A and B is not one unit but two.

On the other hand, the promisee who has actually relied on the promise, even though he may not thereby have enriched the promisor, certainly presents a more pressing case for relief than the promisee who merely demands satisfaction for his disappointment in not getting what was promised him. In passing from compensation for change of position to compensation for loss of expectancy we pass, to use Aristotle's terms again, from the realm of corrective justice to that of distributive justice. The law no longer seeks merely to heal a disturbed status quo, but to bring into being a new situation. It ceases to act defensively or restoratively, and assumes a more active role. With the transition, the justification for legal relief loses its self-evident quality. It is as a matter of fact no easy thing to explain why the normal rule of contract recovery should be that which measures damages by the value of the promised performance.

What, then, explains and justifies the *expectation interest*? The rest of this chapter (and in some ways entire book) tries to answer that question.

WILKINSON-RYAN AND HOFFMAN, BREACH IS FOR SUCKERS

63 Vand. L. Rev. 1003, 1013–15 (2010).

[Recent] [b]ehavioral research has generally concluded that breach creates in its victims a feeling of injury that cannot be fully remedied with money, but studies have also demonstrated that the quality and valence of commonsense responses to breach are susceptible to changes in experimental setting. * * * [P]eople seem to prefer performance and disdain money damages as a remedy, even when the level of damages appears to be fully or even overly compensatory from an objective standpoint. The first systematic exploration of the moral psychology of contracts found that subjects believed breach was morally objectionable and should, in turn, be punished with supracompensatory damages.

In one experiment from that series of studies, subjects were asked to choose the appropriate level of damages themselves; subjects were then asked to indicate whether breach was morally problematic if the promisor paid the specified damages. On average, subjects asked for damages 2.19 times the expectation value. And, further, on a scale of 1 to 7, where 1 was "not immoral," 4 was "somewhat immoral" and 7 was "extremely immoral," participants thought that breach rated over 5—even though in many cases subjects had chosen supracompensatory awards. As part of the same experiment, subjects were asked to consider specific performance for a fairly run-of-the-mill contract for home renovation services. Not only did 75 percent of participants believe that the promisor ought to perform rather than pay damages, 66.7 percent of subjects believed that the court should enforce specific performance. Subjects thought that even supracompensatory damages were morally inferior to performance.

These experiments yielded two other puzzling findings. First, people treat harms in contract and tort differently, [as they were more likely to demand punishment for breach of promise than for an ordinary tort.] Moreover, subjects chose greater punishment for breachers who breached to make a bigger profit than for breachers who were facing a loss on the existing contract.

SECTION THREE: EXPECTANCY DAMAGES FOR BREACH OF AN AGREEMENT WITH CONSIDERATION—THE RULE, ITS RATIONALES, AND ITS APPLICATION IN VARIOUS CONTEXTS

GROVES V. JOHN WUNDER CO.

Supreme Court of Minnesota, 1939.
205 Minn. 163, 286 N.W. 235.

STONE, JUSTICE.

Action for breach of contract. Plaintiff got judgment for a little over $15,000. Sorely disappointed by that sum, he appeals.

In August, 1927, S.J. Groves & Sons Company, a corporation (hereinafter mentioned simply as Groves), owned a tract of 24 acres of Minneapolis suburban real estate. It was served or easily could be reached by railroad trackage. It is zoned as heavy industrial property. But for lack of development of the neighborhood its principal value thus far may have been in the deposit of sand and gravel which it carried. The Groves company had a plant on the premises for excavating and screening the gravel. Nearby defendant owned and was operating a similar plant.

In August, 1927, Groves and defendant made the involved contract. For the most part it was a lease from Groves, as lessor, to defendant, as lessee; its term seven years. Defendant agreed to remove the sand and gravel and to leave the property "at a uniform grade, substantially the same as the grade now existing at the roadway * * * on said premises, and that in stripping the overburden * * * it will use said overburden for the purpose of maintaining and establishing said grade."

Under the contract defendant got the Groves screening plant. The transfer thereof and the right to remove the sand and gravel made the consideration moving from Groves to defendant, except that defendant incidentally got rid of Groves as a competitor. On defendant's part it paid Groves $105,000. So that from the outset, on Groves' part the contract was executed except for defendant's right to continue using the property for the stated term. (Defendant had a right to renewal which it did not exercise.)

Defendant breached the contract deliberately. It removed from the premises only "the richest and best of the gravel" and wholly failed, according to the findings, "to perform and comply with the terms, conditions, and provisions of said lease * * * with respect to the condition in which the surface of the demised premises was required to be left." Defendant surrendered the premises, not substantially at the grade required by the contract "nor at any uniform grade." Instead, the ground was "broken, rugged, and uneven." Plaintiff sues as assignee and successor in right of Groves.

As the contract was construed below, the finding is that to complete its performance 288,495 cubic yards of overburden would need to be excavated, taken from the premises, and deposited elsewhere. The reasonable cost of doing that was found to be upwards of $60,000. But, if defendant had left the premises at the uniform grade required by the lease, the reasonable value of the property on the determinative date would have been only $12,160. The judgment was for that sum, including interest, thereby nullifying plaintiff's claim that cost of completing the contract rather than difference in value of the land was the measure of damages. The gauge of damage adopted by the decision was the difference between the market value of plaintiff's land in the condition it was when the contract was made and what it would have been if defendant had performed. The one question for us arises upon plaintiff's assertion that he was entitled, not to that difference in value, but to the reasonable cost to him of doing the work called for by the contract which defendant left undone.

1. Defendant's breach of contract was wilful. There was nothing of good faith about it. Hence, that the decision below handsomely rewards bad faith and deliberate breach of contract is obvious. That is not allowable. Here the rule is well settled, and has been since Elliott v. Caldwell, 43 Minn. 357, 45 N.W. 845, 9 L.R.A. 52, that, where the contractor wilfully and fraudulently varies from the terms of a construction contract, he

cannot sue thereon and have the benefit of the equitable doctrine of substantial performance. That is the rule generally. See Annotation, "Wilful or intentional variation by contractor from terms of contract in regard to material or work as affecting measure of damages," 6 A.L.R. 137.

Jacob & Youngs, Inc. v. Kent, 230 N.Y. 239, 243, 244, 129 N.E. 889, 891, 23 A.L.R. 1429, is typical. It was a case of substantial performance of a building contract. (This case is distinctly the opposite.) Mr. Justice Cardozo, in the course of his opinion, stressed the distinguishing features. "Nowhere," he said, "will change be tolerated, however, if it is so dominant or pervasive as in any real or substantial measure to frustrate the purpose of the contract." Again, "the willful transgressor must accept the penalty of his transgression."

2. In reckoning damages for breach of a building or construction contract, the law aims to give the disappointed promisee, so far as money will do it, what he was promised. 9 Am.Jur. Building and Construction Contracts, § 152. It is so ruled by a long line of decisions in this state, beginning with Carli v. Seymour, Sabin & Co., 26 Minn. 276, 3 N.W. 348, where the contract was for building a road. There was a breach. Plaintiff was held entitled to recover what it would cost to complete the grading as contemplated by the contract. * * *

Never before, so far as our decisions show, has it even been suggested that lack of value in the land furnished to the contractor who had bound himself to improve it any escape from the ordinary consequences of a breach of the contract.

A case presently as interesting as any of our own, is Sassen v. Haegle, 125 Minn. 441, 147 N.W. 445, 446, 52 L.R.A.,N.S., 1176. The defendant, lessee of a farm, had agreed to haul and spread manure. He removed it, but spread it elsewhere than on the leased farm. Plaintiff had a verdict, but a new trial was ordered for error in the charge as to the measure of damages. The point was thus discussed by r. Justice Holt [125 Minn. page 443, 147 N.W. page 446, 52 L.R.A.,N.S., 1176]: "But it is also true that the landlord had a perfect right to stipulate as to the disposal of the manure or as to the way in which the farm should be worked, and the tenant cannot evade compliance by showing that the farm became more valuable or fertile by omitting the agreed work or doing other work. Plaintiff's pleading and proof was directed to the reasonable value of performing what defendant agreed but failed to perform. Such reasonable cost or value was the natural and proximate damages. The question is not whether plaintiff made a wise or foolish agreement. He had a right to have it performed as made, and the resulting damage, in case of failure, is the reasonable cost of performance. Whether such performance affects the value of the farm was no concern of defendant."

Even in case of substantial performance in good faith, the resulting defects being remediable, it is error to instruct that the measure of damage is "the difference in value between the house as it was and as it would have been if constructed according to contract." The "correct doctrine" is that the cost of remedying the defect is the "proper" measure of damages. Snider v. Peters Home Building Co., 139 Minn. 413, 414, 416, 167 N.W. 108.

Value of the land (as distinguished from the value of the intended product of the contract, which ordinarily will be equivalent to its reasonable cost) is no proper part of any measure of damages for wilful breach of a building contract. The reason is plain.

The summit from which to reckon damages from trespass to real estate is its actual value at the moment. The owner's only right is to be compensated for the deterioration in value caused by the tort. That is all he has lost.[1] But not so if a contract to improve the same land has been breached by the contractor who refuses to do the work, especially where, as here, he has been paid in advance. The summit from which to reckon damages for that wrong is the hypothetical peak of accomplishment (not value) which would have been reached had the work been done as demanded by the contract.

The owner's right to improve his property is not trammeled by its small value. It is his right to erect thereon structures which will reduce its value. If that be the result, it can be of no aid to any contractor who declines performance. As said long ago in Chamberlain v. Parker, 45 N.Y. 569, 572: "A man may do what he will with his own, * * * and if he chooses to erect a monument to his caprice or folly on his premises, and employs and pays another to do it, it does not lie with a defendant who has been so employed and paid for building it, to say that his own performance would not be beneficial to the plaintiff." To the same effect is Restatement, Contracts, § 346, p. 576, Illustrations of Subsection (1), par. 4.

Suppose a contractor were suing the owner for breach of a grading contract such as this. Would any element of value, or lack of it, in the land have any relevance in reckoning damages? Of course not. The contractor would be compensated for what he had lost, i.e., his profit. Conversely, in such a case as this, the owner is entitled to compensation for what he has lost, that is, the work or structure which he has been promised, for which he has paid, and of which he has been deprived by the contractor's breach.

To diminish damages recoverable against him in proportion as there is presently small value in the land would favor the faithless contractor. It would also ignore and so defeat plaintiff's right to contract and build for the future. To justify such a course would require more of the prophetic vision than judges possess. This factor is important when the subject

[1] So also in condemnation cases, where the owner loses nothing of promised contractual performance.

matter is trackage property in the margin of such an area of population and industry as that of the Twin Cities.

For purposes of measuring damages for breach of construction contracts, those with municipal corporations (see City of St. Paul v. Bielenberg, 164 Minn. 72, 204 N.W. 544) are no exception to the general rule. No sound reason is assigned why they should be. We have seen no case indicating their supposed exceptional character as a factor of decision. If these so-called public contracts were in the suggested special category for measuring damages, a municipal corporation would be dealt with more favorably than the ordinary litigant. But courts cannot be more generous with one class of litigants than with another. Such partiality runs counter to the law's demand for equal treatment of litigants who stand on the same footing both as to right and as to remedy.

The genealogy of the error pervading the argument contra is easy to trace. It begins with Seely v. Alden, 61 Pa. 302, 100 Am.Dec. 642, a tort case for pollution of a stream. Resulting depreciation in value of plaintiff's premises, of course, was the measure of damages. About 40 years later, in Bigham v. Wabash-Pittsburg T. Ry., 223 Pa. 106, 72 A. 318, the measure of damages of the earlier tort case was used in one for breach of contract, without comment or explanation to show why. That case was followed in Sweeney v. Lewis Construction Co., 66 Wash. 490, 119 P. 1108, and Sandy Valley & Elkhorn Ry. Co. v. Hughes, 175 Ky. 320, 194 S.W. 344, with no thought given to the anomaly of using in a case in contract a standard ordinarily applicable only in cases of tort. The Washington case, by the way, is sui generis. The contract was to waive damages for the lowering of a street grade. So it adopted as matter of express contract the measure of damages applicable in cases of trespass.

It is at least interesting to note Morgan v. Gamble, 230 Pa. 165, 79 A. 410, decided two years after the Bigham case. The doctrine of substantial performance is there correctly stated, but plaintiff was denied its benefit because he had deliberately breached his building contract. It was held that: "Where, a building contractor agrees to lay an extra strong lead water pipe, and he substitutes therefor an iron pipe, he will be required to allow to the owners in a suit upon the contract, not the difference [in value] between the iron and lead pipes, but the cost of laying a lead pipe as provided in the agreement."

To show how remote any factors of value were considered, it was also held that: "Where a contractor of a building agrees to construct two gas lines, one for natural gas, and one for artificial gas, he will not be relieved from constructing both lines, because artificial gas was not in use in the town in which the building was being constructed."

The objective of this contract of present importance was the improvement of real estate. That makes irrelevant the rules peculiar to damages to chattels, arising from tort or breach of contract. Crowley v. Burns Boiler & Mfg. Co., 100 Minn. 178, 187, 110 N.W. 969, 973, dealt with a breach of contract for the sale of a steam boiler. The court observed: "If the application of a particular rule for measuring damages to given facts results in more than compensation, it is at once apparent that the wrong rule has been adopted."

That is unquestioned law, but for its correct application there must be ascertainment of the loss for which compensation is to be reckoned. In tort, the thing lost is money value, nothing more. But under a construction contract, the thing lost by a breach such as we have here is a physical structure or accomplishment, a promised and paid for alteration in land. That is the "injury" for which the law gives him compensation. Its only appropriate measure is the cost of performance.

It is suggested that because of little or no value in his land the owner may be unconscionably enriched by such a reckoning. The answer is that there can be no unconscionable enrichment, no advantage upon which the law will frown, when the result is but to give one party to a contract only what the other has promised; particularly where, as here, the delinquent has had full payment for the promised performance.

3. It is said by the Restatement, Contracts, § 346, comment b: "Sometimes defects in a completed structure cannot be physically remedied without tearing down and rebuilding, at a cost that would be imprudent and unreasonable. The law does not require damages to be measured by a method requiring such economic waste. If no such waste is involved, the cost of remedying the defect is the amount awarded as compensation for failure to render the promised performance."

The "economic waste" declaimed against by the decisions applying that rule has nothing to do with the value in money of the real estate, or even with the product of the contract. The waste avoided is only that which would come from wrecking a physical structure, completed, or nearly so, under the contract. The cases applying that rule go no further. Illustrative are Bucholz v. Rosenberg, 163 Wis. 312, 156 N.W. 946; Burmeister v. Wolfgram, 175 Wis. 506, 185 N.W. 517. Absent such waste, as it is in this case, the rule of the Restatement, Contracts, § 346, is that "the cost of remedying the defect is the amount awarded as compensation for failure to render the promised performance." That means that defendants here are liable to plaintiff for the reasonable cost of doing what defendants promised to do and have wilfully declined to do.

It follows that there must be a new trial. The initial question will be as to the proper construction of the contract. Thus far the case has been considered from the standpoint of the construction adopted by plaintiff and acquiesced in, very likely for strategic reasons, by defendants. The question has not been argued here, so we intimate no opinion concerning it, but we put the question whether the contract required removal from the premises of any overburden. The requirement in that respect was that the overburden should be used for the purpose of "establishing and maintaining" the grade. A uniform slope and grade were doubtless required. But whether, if it could not be accomplished without removal and deposit elsewhere of large amounts of overburden, the contract required as a condition that the grade everywhere should be as low as the one recited as "now existing at the roadway" is a question for initial consideration below.

The judgment must be reversed with a new trial to follow.

So ordered.

JULIUS J. OLSON, JUSTICE (dissenting).

* * *

There is no case directly in point in this state. * * *

The involved lease provides that the granted premises were to be used by defendant "for the purpose of removing the sand and gravel therefrom." The cash consideration was $105,000, plus defendant's covenant to level and grade the premises to a specified base. There was no segregation or allocation of the cash consideration made applicable to any of the various items going into the deal, and the instrument does not suggest any sum as being representative of the cost of performance by defendant of the leveling and grading process. Nor is there any finding that the contractor "wilfully and fraudulently" violated the terms of its contract. All that can be said is that defendant did nothing except to mine the sand and gravel purchased by it and deemed best suited to its own interest and advantage. No question of partial or substantial performance of its covenant is involved since it did nothing in that behalf. The sole question here is whether the rule adopted by the court respecting recoverable damages is wrong. The essential facts, not questioned, are that "The fair and reasonable value as of the end of the term of said lease, May 1, 1934, of performing the said work necessary to put the premises in the condition in which they were required by the terms of said lease to be left, is the sum of $60,893.28," and that if defendant "had left said premises at a uniform grade as required by said lease, the fair and reasonable value of said premises on May 1, 1934, would have been the sum of $12,160." In that sum, plus interest from May 1, 1934, plaintiff was awarded judgment, $15,053.58. His sole contention before the trial court and here is that upon these findings the court, as a matter of law, should have allowed him the cost of performance, $60,893.28, plus interest since date of the breach, May 1, 1934, amounting to more than $76,000.

Since there is no issue of fact we should limit our inquiry to the single legal problem presented: What amount in money will adequately compensate plaintiff for his loss caused by defendant's failure to render performance?

When the parties entered into this contract each had a right to rely upon the promise of full and complete performance on the part of the other. And by "performance" is meant "such a thorough fulfillment of a duty as puts an end to obligations by leaving nothing more to be done." McGuire v. J. Neils Lumber Co., 97 Minn. 293, 298, 107 N.W. 130, 132. But the "obligation of the contract does not inhere or subsist in the agreement itself proprio vigore, but in the law applicable to the agreement, that is, in the act of the law in binding the promisor to perform his promise. When it is said that one who enters upon an undertaking assumes the legal duties relating to it, what is really meant is that the law imposes the duties on him. A contract is not a law, nor does it make law. It is the agreement plus the law that makes the ordinary contract an enforceable obligation." 12 Am.Jur., Contracts, § 2.

There is here no room for dispute as to contract obligation; therefore it is the duty of the court to enforce its terms "without a leaning in either direction," the parties being "on an equal footing" and as such "were free to do what they chose." Id. § 226.

Another principle, of universal application, is that a party is entitled to have that for which he contracted, or its equivalent. What that equivalent is depends upon the circumstances of each case. If the effect of performance is such that the defective part "may be remedied without the destruction of any substantial part of the benefit which the owner's property has received by reason of the contractor's work, the equivalent to which the owner is entitled is the cost of making the work conform to the contract." 9 Am.Jur., Building and Construction Contracts, § 152. Here, however, defendant did nothing. As such plaintiff "is entitled to be placed, in so far as this can be done by money, in the same position he would have occupied if the contract had been performed." But "his recovery is limited to the loss he has actually suffered by reason of the breach; he is not entitled to be placed in a better position than he would have been in if the contract had not been broken." 15 Am.Jur., Damages, § 43. * * *

* * *

That the subject matter here involved was one within the proper scope of contractual obligation, and its purpose entirely lawful, is obvious. Plaintiff, as owner of the tract upon which the work was to be done, had the undoubted right to insist upon that kind of contract and to its performance. We are not concerned with whether he exercised economic wisdom or displayed lack thereof. Defendant agreed to do the work for what is conceded to have been legally sufficient consideration. It must either perform or pay plaintiff for all damages by him suffered. * * *

* * *

But to be noted, in none of the cited cases was it made to appear that the cost of completion or construction would exceed the value of the property as and when completed. Public contracts are in a separate class, and as to these comment will be made later.

As the rule of damages to be applied in any given case has for its purpose compensation, not punishment, we must be ever mindful that, "If the application of a particular rule for measuring damages to given facts results in more than compensation, it is at once apparent that the wrong rule has been adopted." Crowley v. Burns Boiler & Mfg. Co., 100 Minn. 178, 187, 110 N.W. 969, 973.

We have here then a situation where, concededly, if the contract had been performed, plaintiff would have had property worth, in round numbers, no more than $12,000. If he is to be awarded damages in an amount exceeding $60,000 he will be receiving at least 500 per cent more than his property, properly leveled to grade by actual performance, was intrinsically worth when the breach occurred. To so conclude is to give him something far beyond what the parties had in mind or contracted for. There is no showing made, nor any finding suggested, that this property was unique, specially desirable for a particular or personal use, or of special value as to location or future use different from that of other property surrounding it. Under the circumstances here appearing, it seems clear that what the parties contracted for was to put the property in shape for general sale. And the lease contemplates just that, for by the terms thereof defendant agreed "from time to time, as the sand and gravel are removed from the various lots * * * leased, it will surrender said lots to the lessor" if of no further use to defendant "in connection with the purposes for which this lease is made."

The theory upon which plaintiff relies for application of the cost of performance rule must have for its basis cases where the property or the improvement to be made is unique or personal instead of being of the kind ordinarily governed by market values. His action is one at law for damages, not for specific performance. As there was no affirmative showing of any peculiar fitness of this property to a unique or personal use, the rule to be applied is, I think, the one applied by the court. The cases bearing directly upon this phase so hold. Briefly, the rule here applicable is this: Damages recoverable for breach of a contract to construct is the difference between the market value of the property in the condition it was when delivered to and received by plaintiff and what its market value would have been if defendant had fully complied with its terms. Bigham v. Wabash-Pittsburg T. Ry. Co., 223 Pa. 106, 72 A. 318 * * *.

* * *

The principle for which I contend is not novel in construction contract cases. It is well stated in McCormick, Damages, § 168, pp. 648, 649, as follows: "In whatever way the issue arises, the generally approved standards for measuring the owner's loss from defects in the work are two: First, in cases where the defect is one that can be repaired or cured without undue expense, so as to make the building conform to the agreed plan, then the owner recovers such amount as he has reasonably expended, or will reasonably have to spend, to remedy the defect. Second, if, on the other hand, the defect in material or construction is one that cannot be remedied without an expenditure for reconstruction disproportionate to the end to be attained, or without endangering unduly other parts of the building, then the damages will be measured not by the cost of remedying the defect, but by the difference between the value of the building as it is and what it would have been worth if it had been built in conformity with the contract."

And the same thought was expressed by Mr. Justice Cardozo in Jacob & Youngs, Inc. v. Kent, 230 N.Y. 239, 244, 129 N.E. 889, 891, 23 A.L.R. 1429, 1433, thus: "The owner is entitled to the money which will permit him to complete, unless the cost of completion is grossly and unfairly out of proportion to the good to be attained. When that is true, the measure is the difference in value." To the same effect is 5 Williston, Contracts (Rev. ed.) § 1363, p. 3825. (The supporting cases are found under note 12.) In 1 Restatement, Contracts, § 346 p. 576, Illustrations of Subsection (1), par. 3, reads: "A contracts with B to sink an oil well on A's own land adjacent to the land of B, for development and exploration purposes. Other exploration wells prove that there is no oil in that region; and A breaks his promise to sink the well. B can get judgment for only nominal damages, not the cost of sinking the well."

* * *

If this were a case to recover damages for tortious injury the applicable rule is the difference in the market value and not the cost of restoring the premises to the former condition if such exceeds the diminution in value. Karst v. St. Paul, S. & T.F.R. Co., 23 Minn. 401; Ziebarth v. Nye, 42 Minn. 541, 547, 44 N.W. 1027. In Heath v. Minneapolis, St. P. & S. Ste. M. Ry. Co., 126 Minn. 470, 475, 148 N.W. 311, 312, L.R.A.1916E, 977, it was held that, "The rental value plus the cost of restoration is the true measure of damages, in cases of continuing trespass, when it appears that this is less than the difference between the value of the premises before and immediately after the wrong."

* * *

No one doubts that a party may contract for the doing of anything he may choose to have done (assuming what is to be done is not unlawful) "although the thing to be produced had no marketable value." 45 N.Y. page 572. In 1 Restatement, Contracts, § 346, pp. 576, 577, Illustrations of

Subsection (1), par. 4, the same thought is thus stated: "A contracts to construct a monumental fountain in B's yard for $5,000, but abandons the work after the foundation has been laid and $2800 has been paid by B. The contemplated fountain is so ugly that it would decrease the number of possible buyers of the place. The cost of completing the fountain would be $4000. B can get judgment for $1800, the cost of completion less the part of price unpaid." But that is not what plaintiff's predecessor in interest contracted for. Such a provision might well have been made, but the parties did not. They could undoubtedly have provided for liquidated damages for nonperformance (2 Dunnell, Minn.Dig., 2d ed. & Supps., §§ 2536, 2537), or they might have determined in money what the value of performance was considered to be and thereby have contractually provided a measure for failure of performance.

The opinion also suggests that this property lies in an area where the owner might rightly look for future development, being in a so-called industrial zone, and that as such he should be privileged to so hold it. This he may of course do. But let us assume that on May 1, 1934, condemnation to acquire this area had so far progressed as to leave only the question of price (market value) undetermined; that the area had been graded in strict conformity with the contract but that the actual market value of the premises was only $12,160, as found by the court and acquiesced in by plaintiff, what would the measure of his damages be? Obviously, the limit of his recovery could be no more than the then market value of his property. In that sum he has been paid with interest and costs; and he still has the fee title to the premises, something he would not possess if there had been condemnation. In what manner has plaintiff been hurt beyond the damages awarded? As to him "economic waste" is not apparent. Assume that defendant abandoned the entire project without taking a single yard of gravel therefrom but left the premises as they were when the lease was made, could plaintiff recover damages upon the basis here established? The trouble with the prevailing opinion is that here plaintiff's loss is not made the basis for the amount of his recovery but rather what it would cost the defendant. No case has been decided upon that basis until now.

Plaintiff asserts that he knows of no rule "giving a different measure of damages for public contracts and for private contracts in case of nonperformance." It seems to me there is a clear distinction to be drawn with respect to the application of the rule for recoverable damages in case of breach of a public works contract from that applicable to contracts between private parties. The construction of a public building, a sewer, drainage ditch, highway, or other public work, permits of no application of the market value doctrine. There simply is and can be no "market value" as to such. And for this cogent reason there can be but one rule of damages to apply, that of cost of completion of the thing contracted to be done.

* * * I think the judgment should be affirmed.

HOLT, J. I join in the foregoing dissent.

PEEVYHOUSE v. GARLAND COAL & MINING CO., 382 P.2d 109 (Okla. 1962), cert. denied, 375 U.S. 906 (1963). [Willie and Lucille Peevyhouse sued the defendant, Garland Coal & Mining Co., for damages for breach of a five-year lease of a farm containing coal deposits. The lease permitted the defendant to do strip mining on the farm and required it to perform certain restorative and remedial work at the end of the lease period. This work involved the moving of many thousands of cubic yards of dirt at a cost estimated by expert witnesses at about $29,000. Plaintiffs sued for $25,000. The evidence showed that the failure of defendants to do the restorative and remedial work reduced the value of the premises no more than $300. The jury returned a verdict for $5000, which was more than the total value of the farm.]

JACKSON, J.

On appeal, the issue is sharply drawn. Plaintiffs contend that the true measure of damages in this case is what it will cost plaintiffs to obtain performance of the work that was not done because of defendant's default. Defendant argues that the measure of damages is the cost of performance "limited, however, to the total difference in the market value before and after the work was performed".

* * *

It may be observed that Groves v. John Wunder Co. is the only case which has come to our attention in which the cost of performance rule has been followed under circumstances where the cost of performance greatly exceeded the diminution in value resulting from the breach. * * *

* * *

* * * The primary purpose of the lease * * * was merely to accomplish the economical recovery and marketing of coal from the premises, to the profit of all parties. The special provisions of the lease contract pertaining to remedial work were incidental to the main object involved.

* * *

23 O.S.1961 §§ 96 and 97 provide as follows:

> "§ 96 * * * Notwithstanding the provisions of this chapter, no person can recover a greater amount in damages for the breach of an obligation, than he would have gained by the full performance thereof on both sides.

* * *

"§ 97 * * * Damages must, in all cases, be reasonable, and where an obligation of any kind appears to create a right to unconscionable and grossly oppressive damages, contrary to substantial justice no more than reasonable damages can be recovered."

Although it is true that the above sections of the statute are applied most often in tort cases, they are by their own terms, and the decisions of this court, also applicable in actions for damages for breach of contract. It would seem that they are peculiarly applicable here where, under the "cost of performance" rule, plaintiffs might recover an amount about nine times the total value of their farm. Such would seem to be "unconscionable and grossly oppressive damages, contrary to substantial justice" within the meaning of the statute. Also, it can hardly be denied that if plaintiffs here are permitted to recover under the "cost of performance" rule, they will receive a greater benefit from the breach than could be gained from full performance, contrary to the provisions of Sec. 96.

* * *

We * * * hold that where * * * the economic benefit which would result to lessor by full performance of the work is grossly disproportionate to the cost of performance, the damages which lessor may recover are limited to the diminution in value resulting to the premises because of the non-performance.

* * * [T]he rule as stated does not interfere with the property owner's right to "do what he will with his own" * * * or his right, if he chooses, to contract for "improvements" which will actually have the effect of reducing his property's value. Where such result is in fact contemplated by the parties, and is a main or principal purpose of those contracting, it would seem that the measure of damages for breach would ordinarily be the cost of performance.

* * *

* * * We are of the opinion that the judgment of the trial court for plaintiffs should be, and it is hereby, modified and reduced to the sum of $300.00, and as so modified it is affirmed.

IRWIN, JUSTICE (dissenting).

* * * Defendant admitted in the trial of the action, that plaintiffs insisted that the * * * [restorative and remedial] provisions be included in the contract and that they would not agree to the coal mining lease unless the above provisions were included.

* * *

* * * [I]n my opinion * * * the proper measure of damages should be the cost of performance. Any other measure of damage would be holding for naught the express provisions of the contract. * * *

EISENBERG, THE RESPONSIVE MODEL OF CONTRACT LAW

36 Stan. L. Rev. 1107, 1163–64 (1984).

It might be argued that since the plaintiff has paid for completion, anything less than cost-of-completion damages would leave the defendant unjustly enriched. For example, assume that prior to its negotiations with Peevyhouse, Garland Coal had decided it was willing to pay royalties to Peevyhouse of one dollar per ton. When Peevyhouse demanded that Garland would have to restore the land, Garland would presumably have calculated the cost of restoration, prorated over the expected tonnage, and agreed to pay Peevyhouse a royalty of a dollar per ton minus the prorated amount. On completion of the mining, Peevyhouse would then in effect have paid Garland an amount equal to the cost of restoration. Limiting damages to diminished value would confer a windfall on Garland equal to that cost. It can also be implied from this argument that instead of measuring damages by diminished value, the court should grant a decree of specific performance: If the plaintiff really wants completion, he will enforce the decree. If he does not, he will make a settlement that divides the windfall at some level between the amount at which he subjectively values the performance and the contractor's cost of completion.

The problem with this argument and its implication is that in many cases the disparity between cost of completion and diminished market value results in large part from circumstances that were not anticipated when the contract was made. In Peevyhouse, for example, Garland's brief suggests that the restoration plan was based on the use of a spoil bank that was to be created by the mining operation. As matters turned out, however, Garland found much less coal than anticipated, the mine was not extended across the entire property, the planned spoil bank was not created, and restoration became much more expensive than originally contemplated. * * * In such [a case], the parties have not factored the cost of completion into the price paid by the plaintiff. Saving that cost would not, therefore, result in a windfall to the defendant, and if the plaintiff has no intent to complete, a decree of specific performance would enable the plaintiff to extract a windfall settlement.

Suppose, however, that the value the plaintiff assigns to the difference between the existing and promised states of the subject matter, although less than the cost of completion, is higher than the market-value differential. In principle, the plaintiff's recovery should be measured by this intermediate figure. (The jury in Peevyhouse may have done just that.)

MAUTE, THE UNEARTHED FACTS OF PEEVYHOUSE v. GARLAND COAL & MINING CO.

Contracts Stories 301 (2007).

Mr. and Mrs. Peevyhouse still live on that land. Time has not healed the wounds inflicted by the mining, which ended nearly fifty years ago. When last visited in 2004, the diversionary channel was badly eroded and overgrown with aggressive bramblebush. Steep embankments on the spoil banks were unstable and muddy. The condition of the land in 2004 was significantly worse than * * * several years ago. Mr. Peevyhouse said he hadn't been on that land in years; about thirty acres is completely useless. * * * Lucille * * * was bitter and distrustful of the legal system. Willie still wants the land fixed.

ROCK ISLAND IMPROVEMENT COMPANY v. HELMERICH & PAYNE, INC.

United States Court of Appeals, Tenth Circuit, 1983.
698 F.2d 1075.

LOGAN, CIRCUIT JUDGE.

In this diversity case Helmerich & Payne, Inc. appeals a jury verdict in favor of Rock Island Improvement Company for breach of contract and appeals the trial court's denial of its motions for judgment notwithstanding the verdict and for a new trial or amendment of the judgment.

From 1968 to 1977 Helmerich & Payne leased two tracts of land in Oklahoma from Rock Island for coal mining purposes. These tracts are referred to as the "Rees-Heavener" and "Rees-Petros" mines. The lease contained a reclamation clause that stated: "Upon the abandonment or completion of any mining operation, or part thereof, including but not limited to any strip operation, the surface shall be restored as nearly as possible to its condition prior to said mining operation. . . ." Helmerich & Payne subleased the land to Sam Sexton, Jr., who used stripmining techniques to remove substantial amounts of coal. When the lease period ended, the tracts were left with two strip pits and were not otherwise reclaimed to Rock Island's satisfaction. Rock Island sued Helmerich & Payne for breach of the lease's reclamation provision, seeking damages equal to the amount necessary to reclaim the land. Helmerich & Payne filed a third party complaint against Sexton, who agreed to pay any judgment won by Rock Island. The jury awarded Rock Island $375,000.

* * *

Helmerich & Payne contends that the trial court improperly applied Oklahoma damages law. In instructing the jury on damages,[1] the trial

[1] The trial court instructed the jury as follows: "The measure of damages is the reasonable cost of performing the contract, or in this case, restoring the land to the same condition it was in

court relied on Peevyhouse v. Garland Coal & Mining Company, 382 P.2d 109 (Okl.), cert. denied, 375 U.S. 906, 84 S.Ct. 196, 11 L.Ed.2d 145 (1963). In Peevyhouse the Oklahoma Supreme Court examined a coal mining lease requiring the lessee to reclaim any land it stripmined. At issue was whether the proper measure of damages for the lessee's failure to reclaim was the cost of performance ($29,000) or the diminution in the fair market value of the land ($300). The court held that the proper measure of damages was the reasonable cost of reclamation, unless the reclamation requirement was incidental to the lease's main purpose and the cost of reclamation would be grossly disproportionate to the diminution in the land's fair market value. In the latter case, the lessor's damages were limited to the diminution in value. Id. at 114.

In the instant case the trial court submitted the issue of the reclamation clause's importance to the jury. We have held that a trial court must submit this issue to the jury when the parties have introduced extrinsic evidence of their intent, Hitchcock v. Peter Kiewit & Sons Co., 479 F.2d 1257 (10th Cir.1973); otherwise, the trial court should treat interpretation of the contract clause as a matter of law. See Walker v. Telex Corp., 583 P.2d 482, 485 (Okl.1978). Neither Rock Island nor Helmerich & Payne introduced evidence establishing the parties' intent in including the restoration clause. Therefore, the trial court should not have submitted interpretation of the contract to the jury.

Helmerich & Payne asserts the trial court should have held that the lease unambiguously focused upon coal mining as its main purpose and that reclamation was merely an incidental purpose. Furthermore, Helmerich & Payne argues that because the parties stipulated the diminution in value of the land was $6,797, and the evidence presented showed that restoring the land would cost $375,000, the court should have held the cost of reclamation was disproportionate to the diminution in land value. Thus, following Peevyhouse, the proper measure of damages would be diminution in market value, an amount the parties stipulated, and thus not a jury issue. Rock Island's response is that Peevyhouse no longer represents Oklahoma law on damages for breach of mining contracts because of subsequent developments in that state's policy toward reclamation.

At the time the parties in Peevyhouse entered into their lease, Oklahoma had no stated policy concerning land reclamation after mining operations. Thus, in Peevyhouse the court considered only the economic

---

before stripmining, unless you find: 1. That the lease provision requiring restoration of Plaintiff's land to the same condition it was in before stripmining was merely incidental to the main purpose of the lease; and 2. That the economic benefit to the Plaintiff by restoring the land would be grossly disproportionate to the cost of restoring the land. Then, if you so find, the amount of damages to which Plaintiff is entitled is the reduced value of Plaintiff's land, that is, the difference between the present fair market value of the land as it is, and the present fair market value of the land restored to the same condition it was in before the stripmining."

benefits to the parties of a situation the court termed "artificial," "unreasonable," and "unrealistic": that a property owner would agree to pay a great deal for "improvements" that would increase the property's value by only a small amount. The court was concerned that if the landowner did not spend the large amount to reclaim the land, he would receive a windfall by recovering the amount from the lessee. 382 P.2d at 112.

However, after the decision in Peevyhouse but before Rock Island leased the tracts to Helmerich & Payne, Oklahoma enacted the Open Cut Land Reclamation Act. 1967 Okla.Sess.Laws Ch. 186 (current version at Okla.Stat.Ann. tit 45, §§ 721–729). The Act stated in part:

> "It is hereby declared to be the policy of this State to provide, after mining operations are completed, for the reclamation and conservation of land subjected to surface disturbance by open cut mining and thereby to preserve natural resources, to aid in the protection of wildlife and aquatic resources, to establish recreational, home and industrial sites, to protect and perpetuate the taxable value of property, and to protect and promote the health, safety and general welfare of the people of this State."

Id. at § 2 (current version at Okla.Stat.Ann. tit 45, § 722).

The statute declares today, as it did in 1967, that the operator of a strip mine has a duty to reclaim the land and that the state may contract for the work to be done if the operator defaults. The statute makes no exception for cases in which the expenditures for reclamation are disproportionate to the resulting increase in value of the land. To be sure the statute looks to the operator as the party responsible for reclamation, and limits the state's recovery to the amount of the bond it has required.[2] Nevertheless, there are many reasons a landowner in Rock Island's position would want a reclamation provision in the lease—to enhance its image in the community, to protect against possible tort liability for conditions on its premises, and to allay any fear that under the recently enacted law it might somehow be held responsible for defaults of the operator. There are reasons a lessee might readily accept such a provision—it already has a duty to reclaim under the state statute.

We are convinced that the Oklahoma Supreme Court would no longer apply the rule it established in Peevyhouse in 1963 if it had the instant dispute before it. Peevyhouse was a 5–4 decision with a strong dissent. More importantly, the public policy of the state has changed, as expressed in its statutes. Although we are bound by decisions of a state supreme court

---

[2] At the time of the Rock Island-Helmerich & Payne contract the maximum bond required was $50 per acre. Today there is no maximum; the bond must cover the estimated reclamation costs. Okla.Stat.Ann. tit. 45, § 728(B).

in diversity cases, we need not adhere to a decision if we think it no longer would be followed.

* * *

* * * When the parties negotiated the contract in question, they expressly included a reclamation clause and required the lessee to bear the cost of reclamation. Given the attention focused by Oklahoma on the importance of reclaiming stripmined lands, it is more logical to assume that the parties meant what they said, calculated their costs and benefits under the contract accordingly, and intended the provision to insure proper reclamation of the land, than it is to assume that they expected the reclamation clause to have no force.[3]

Even though the trial court should not have submitted the issue of the reclamation clause's importance to the jury, we need not reverse. Because we hold that cost of performance is the proper measure of damages, and the jury used this measure in calculating damages, the court's error is harmless.

* * *

AFFIRMED.

PROBLEM 3-1

Pervis Ellington and Acme Construction Company entered a contract for the latter to construct an indoor swimming pool at Ellington's home. The contract provided for the pool to have a depth of 9.5 feet. The construction price was $40,000. Acme constructed the pool, meeting all specifications except that the pool as constructed had a depth of 7.5 feet. Ellington refused to make the final payment of $5000. After fruitless discussions with Acme about the problem, Ellington brought a breach of contract action. He seeks $80,000, the cost of demolishing the existing pool and constructing a new one according to the specifications.

You are the judge in the non-jury trial of Ellington v. Acme Construction Company. You have heard the following testimony: Ellington is a former collegiate diver of some renown. Two experts testified that diving is safe in a pool with a depth of 9.5 feet, but that they "would not recommend" diving in a pool with a depth of less than 8 feet. Ellington testified that he "felt unsafe" diving into the pool as constructed. Ellington failed to produce any evidence that the shortfall in the depth of the pool diminished its market value. Nor did

[3] In Peevyhouse the court relied in part on Oklahoma damages statutes requiring that a party receive no more in damages than it would have gained by full performance. See 382 P.2d at 113 (citing Okla.Stat.Ann. tit 23, §§ 96, 97). Helmerich & Payne contends that these statutes limit the amount of its damages. Because the anticipated cost of reclamation may have affected the contract price, these damages statutes do not preclude use of the cost-of-performance measure of damages.

he testify that he actually intended to arrange for the reconstruction of the pool.

Acme produced testimony of two real estate agents that the pool increased the market value of Ellington's home by $45,000. Acme's president testified that he did not know that Ellington was a diver. He testified that the total cost of constructing the pool was $35,000.

Please decide the case of Ellington v. Acme Construction Company.

NOTE: *THE EXPECTANCY INTEREST IN VARIOUS CONTEXTS*

The next series of cases and materials in this Section illustrates how courts determine the injured party's lost expectancy in several different contexts. These include construction, employment, and sales cases and present claims by building contractors, landowners, employers, employees, and sellers and buyers of goods. The cases have in common an attempt by the court to put the nonbreaching party in as good a position as if there had been no breach. The focus here is on "general damages," which are losses from a breach that arise "naturally or ordinarily," and are often measured by the difference between the contract price and market price. In Section 4, we study "consequential" also called "special" damages because not every aggrieved party in the same circumstances would suffer them.

RESTATEMENT (SECOND) OF CONTRACTS § 347, COMMENT B.

Measure of Damages in General

The first element that must be estimated in attempting to fix a sum that will fairly represent the expectation interest is the loss in the value to the injured party of the other party's performance that is caused by the failure of, or deficiency in, that performance. * * * In principle, this requires a determination of the [value of that performance] * * * to the injured party himself and not [the value] to some hypothetical reasonable person or on some market. * * * [The value of performance] therefore depend[s] on his own particular circumstances or those of his enterprise * * *.

THORNE V. WHITE

District of Columbia Court of Appeals, 1954.
103 A.2d 579.

QUINN, ASSOCIATE JUDGE.

Appellant, hereinafter referred to as Thorne, contracted to put a new roof on appellee's residence and to make certain repairs in connection therewith for the sum of $225. Pursuant to the contract, Thorne delivered certain materials to the job and began work. Within a few hours the work was discontinued because of inclement weather. Thorne never returned to the job and a few days later had his materials hauled away. White then entered into an agreement with the Koons Roofing Company to have the work completed at a cost of $582.26. This was $357.26 more than the amount of Thorne's contract. He sued Thorne for that difference alleging breach of contract. The court, hearing the case without a jury, ruled in favor of White, and Thorne brings this appeal.

We find no error in the trial court's ruling that Thorne had breached the contract. He testified that he had not completed the work because White had ordered him to discontinue, but White denied ever having made such a statement. Thus, the issue as to the breach of contract was clearly one of fact. There was ample support in the evidence to sustain the court's finding.

The aspect of the case which gives us more concern is the question of damages. White was awarded a judgment for $357.26, which amount represents the difference between the contract price with Thorne and the amount paid to the Koons Company for the completion of the work. This sum would be the correct measure of damages, provided the second contract did not call for additional work not contemplated by nor included in the first one. This is in accord with the general rule that a party damaged by a breach may only recover for losses which are the natural consequence and proximate result of that breach. Damages are awarded for the purpose of compensation and the injured party should not be placed in a better position than he would have been in had no breach occurred. In cases such as the present one the successful plaintiff should only be allowed to recover what it has cost him to complete the same work, over and above the original contract price.

In the instant case the trial court found that the two roofing contracts were substantially the same and that the damages were therefore the amount by which Koons' contract exceeded Thorne's price. We rule that such a holding was error. Besides the large difference between the two contract prices, the evidence was that Thorne's contract called for a 4-ply roof, while the second contract was for what was in effect a 5-ply roof; that Thorne was merely to put a new roof over the old one, while the Koons Company entirely removed the old roof; and that several additional items were provided for under the second contract not called for in the first. A representative of the Koons Company testified that these additional items added to the cost of their contract. As the evidence clearly shows that White received more from the Koons Company than he was to receive from Thorne, we think an improper measure of damages was applied.

* * *

Reversed with instructions to grant a new trial on the issue of damages.

MORELLO v. J.H. HOGAN, INC., 1 Conn.App. 150, 468 A.2d 1248 (1984). [A subcontractor contracted to do masonry work for a total price of $44,000. After doing work with a reasonable value of $9,411.87, the subcontractor wrongfully abandoned the job and the prime contractor reasonably spent $54,356.36 to complete the work. The subcontractor sued for $9,411.87 and the prime contractor counterclaimed for the difference between $44,000 and $54,356.36, or $10,356.36. The trial court awarded the prime contractor $944.49, the difference between $9,411.87 and $10,356.56.]

Viewed through a different prism, the court's judgment violated the basic rule of contract damages that the award should place the injured party in the same position as it would have been had the contract been performed. * * * The defendant was required to spend $54,356.36 to complete the work after the plaintiff left the job. Thus the $54,356.36 already took into account the value of the work performed by the plaintiff. Awarding the plaintiff $9,411.87 on the complaint coupled with the award on the counterclaim limiting the defendant to $10,356.36 gave the plaintiff double credit for his work and left the defendant $9411.87 short of the position in which it would have been placed had the contract been performed.

There is error, the judgment on the complaint is set aside and the case remanded with direction to render judgment for the defendant on the complaint.

FREUND v. WASHINGTON SQUARE PRESS, 34 N.Y.2d 379, 357 N.Y.S.2d 857, 314 N.E.2d 419 (1974). [Defendant, Washington Square Press, broke its contract to publish Freund's book. The contract obligated the defendant to pay royalties based upon percentages of sales. The Appellate Division affirmed the trial court's award to Freund of the cost of publication. The Appellate Division "analogized to the construction contract situation where the cost of completion may be the proper measure of damages for a builder's failure to complete a house or for use of wrong materials."]

SAMUEL RABIN, JUDGE.

Since the damages which would have compensated plaintiff for anticipated royalties were not proved with the required certainty, we agree with the dissent in the Appellate Division that nominal damages alone are recoverable. (Cf. Manhattan Sav. Inst. v. Gottfried Baking Co., 286 N.Y. 398, 36 N.E.2d 637.) Though these are damages in name only and not at all compensatory, they are nevertheless awarded as a formal vindication of plaintiff's legal right to compensation which has not been given a sufficiently certain monetary valuation. * * *

In our view, the analogy by the majority in the Appellate Division to the construction contract situation was inapposite. In the typical construction contract, the owner agrees to pay money or other consideration to a builder and expects, under the contract, to receive a completed building in return. The value of the promised performance to the owner is the properly constructed building. In this case, unlike the typical construction contract, the value to plaintiff of the promised performance—publication—was a percentage of sales of the books published and not the books themselves. Had the plaintiff contracted for the printing, binding and delivery of a number of hardbound copies of his manuscript, to be sold or disposed of as he wished, then perhaps the construction analogy, and measurement of damages by the cost of replacement or completion, would have some application.

Here, however, the specific value to plaintiff of the promised publication was the royalties he stood to receive from defendant's sales of the published book. Essentially, publication represented what it would have cost the defendant to confer that value upon the plaintiff, and, by its breach, defendant saved that cost. The error by the courts below was in measuring damages not by the value to plaintiff of the promised performance but by the cost of that performance to defendant. Damages are not measured, however, by what the defaulting party saved by the breach, but by the natural and probable consequences of the breach *to the plaintiff*. In this case, the consequence to plaintiff of defendant's failure to publish is that he is prevented from realizing the gains promised by the contract—the royalties. But, as we have stated, the amount of royalties plaintiff would have realized was not ascertained with adequate certainty and, as a consequence, plaintiff may recover nominal damages only.

Accordingly, the order of the Appellate Division should be modified to the extent of reducing the damage award of $10,000 for the cost of publication to six cents, but with costs and disbursements to the plaintiff.

WARNER V. MCLAY

Supreme Court of Errors, Connecticut, 1918.
92 Conn. 427, 103 A. 113.

Appeal from City Court of New Haven: JOHN R. BOOTH, JUDGE.

Action by Hubert E. Warner, Jr., against James McLay for breach of contract. There was a verdict and judgment for plaintiff, and defendant appeals. Error, and new trial ordered.

The theory of the plaintiff as shown by his complaint and prayer for relief is that he is entitled to recover damages for expenditures and loss of profits occasioned by the breach of a written building contract. It is apparently here conceded that there was an unjust abrogation of this contract, by the defendant. An important question presented by the appeal is as to the measure of damages. Upon this branch of the case the jury were told that:

> "He also claims that he is entitled to 10 per cent profit upon this contract. Of course, in the event of a breach of contract, and the contract was broken, the evidence discloses that, there is no dispute about it. The contract was broken by Mr. McLay's refusal to allow it to proceed, and he does not deny it. Therefore, the contract having been broken, if Mr. Warner was willing and ready to carry out his part of it, but was prevented by Mr. McLay from doing so, he is entitled to any damage he may suffer by reason of the failure of Mr. McLay to allow him to proceed, and he would be entitled to recover any amount of money he was obliged to expend in the securing of materials, but also a reasonable profit upon his contract, which he says is 10 per cent. I haven't the figures. He gave you figures of the different parts of the building showing that there would be a profit."

The jury were also told that:

> "Of course, you will be guided by the evidence submitted before you, and there is no conflict of evidence, because the defendant has offered none, so you will then be obliged to take the evidence as submitted by the plaintiff."

RORABACK, J. (after stating the facts as above). * * *

In the present case the plaintiff had the right to recover such sum in damages as he would have realized in profits if the contract had been fully performed. To ascertain this it was necessary to find the cost and expense of the work and materials necessary to complete the contract. This sum, deducted from the contract price, would have given a balance which would be the profit which would have accrued to the plaintiff out of the contract if it had been fulfilled. This the plaintiff had a right to receive in addition to his expenditures for work and labor supplied towards the completion of the contract. Fox v. Harding, 61 Mass. (7 Cush.) 516; United States v. Behan, 110 U.S. 338, 4 Sup.Ct. 81, 28 L.Ed. 168.

The substance of the instruction to the jury upon this branch of the case was that the plaintiff was entitled to recover for his necessary expenditures and also a reasonable profit upon his contract, which might be, as the plaintiff claimed, 10 per cent. It is apparent that these instructions were not sufficient for the proper guidance of the jury upon the question of profits. There was no attempt to make an application of the principles of law which we have just cited. There was no attempt to define profits, nor any instruction given as to how these profits were to be estimated. The remarks of the court upon this point may have been proper as a statement of the plaintiff's claim for damages, but adopting this claim as the proper rule for damages was making these claims the law for the jury, instead of directing their attention to the correct legal principles applicable to such a situation.

* * *

There is error. The judgment is reversed, and a new trial ordered. The other Judges concurred.

COMMENTS AND QUESTIONS

Why should an aggrieved party recover lost expectancy rather than merely out-of-pocket or other reliance costs? Consider the following views.

FULLER AND PERDUE, THE RELIANCE INTEREST IN CONTRACT DAMAGES

46 Yale L.J. 52, 57, 58, 60–62 (1936).

It is a matter of fact no easy thing to explain why the normal rule of contract recovery should be that which measures damages by the value of the promised performance. Since this "natural rule" throws its shadow across our whole subject it will be necessary to examine the possible reasons for its existence. It may be said parenthetically that the discussion which follows, though directed primarily to the normal measure of recovery where damages are sought, also has relevance to the more general question, why should a promise which has not been relied on ever be enforced at all * * *?

* * *

In seeking justification for the rule granting the value of the expectancy there is no need, however, to restrict ourselves by the assumption, hitherto made, that the rule can only be intended to cure or prevent the loss caused by reliance. A justification can be developed from a less negative point of view. It may be said that there is not only a policy in favor of preventing and undoing the harms resulting from reliance, but also a policy in favor of promoting and facilitating reliance on business agreements. As in the case of the stop-light ordinance we are interested not only in preventing collisions but in speeding traffic. Agreements can accomplish little, either for their makers or for society, unless they are made the basis for action. When business agreements are not only made but are also acted on, the division of labor is facilitated, goods find their way to the places where they are most needed, and economic activity is generally stimulated. These advantages would be threatened by any rule which limited legal protection to the reliance interest. Such a rule would in practice tend to discourage reliance. The difficulties in proving reliance and subjecting it to pecuniary measurement are such that the businessman knowing, or sensing, that these obstacles stood in the way of judicial relief would hesitate to rely on a promise in any case where the legal sanction was of significance to him. To encourage reliance we must therefore dispense with its proof. For this reason it has been found wise to make recovery on a promise independent of reliance, both in the sense that in some cases the promise is enforced though not relied on (as in the bilateral business agreement) and in the sense that recovery is not limited to the detriment incurred in reliance.

HANDICAPPED CHILDREN'S EDUCATION BOARD OF SHEBOYGAN COUNTY V. LUKASZEWSKI

Supreme Court of Wisconsin, 1983.
112 Wis.2d 197, 332 N.W.2d 774.

CALLOW, JUSTICE.

This review arises out of an unpublished decision of the court of appeals which affirmed in part and reversed in part a judgment of the Ozaukee county circuit court, Judge Warren A. Grady.

In January of 1978 the Handicapped Children's Education Board (the Board) hired Elaine Lukaszewski to serve as a speech and language therapist for the spring term. Lukaszewski was assigned to the Lightfoot School in Sheboygan Falls which was approximately 45 miles from her home in Mequon. Rather than move, she commuted to work each day. During the 1978 spring term, the Board offered Lukaszewski a contract to continue in her present position at Lightfoot School for the 1978–79 school year. The contract called for an annual salary of $10,760. Lukaszewski accepted.

In August of 1978, prior to the beginning of the school year, Lukaszewski was offered a position by the Wee Care Day Care Center which was located not far from her home in Mequon. The job paid an annual salary of $13,000. After deciding to accept this offer, Lukaszewski notified Thomas Morrelle, the Board's director of special education, that she intended to resign from her position at the Lightfoot School. Morrelle told her to submit a letter of resignation for consideration by the Board. She did so, and the matter was discussed at a meeting of the Board on August 21, 1978. The Board refused to release Lukaszewski from her contract. On August 24, 1978, the Board's attorney sent a letter to Lukaszewski directing her to return to work. The attorney sent a second letter to the Wee Care Day Care Center stating that the Board would take legal action if the Center interfered with Lukaszewski's performance of her contractual obligations at the Lightfoot School. A copy of this letter was sent to the Department of Public Instruction.

Lukaszewski left the Wee Care Day Care Center and returned to Lightfoot School for the 1978 fall term. She resented the actions of the Board, however, and retained misgivings about her job. On September 8, 1978, she discussed her feeling with Morrelle. After this meeting Lukaszewski felt quite upset about the situation. She called her doctor to make an appointment for that afternoon and subsequently left the school.

Dr. Ashok Chatterjee examined Lukaszewski and found her blood pressure to be high. Lukaszewski asked Dr. Chatterjee to write a letter explaining his medical findings and the advice he had given her. In a letter dated September 11, 1978, Dr. Chatterjee indicated that Lukaszewski had a hypertension problem dating back to 1976. He reported that on the day he examined Lukaszewski she appeared agitated, nervous, and had blood pressure readings up to 180/100. It was his opinion that, although she took hypotensive drugs, her medical condition would not improve unless the situation which caused the problem was removed. He further opined that it would be dangerous for her to drive long distances in her agitated state.

Lukaszewski did not return to work after leaving on September 8, 1978. She submitted a letter of resignation dated September 13, 1978, in which she wrote:

> "I enclose a copy of the doctor's statement concerning my health. On the basis of it, I must resign. I am unwilling to jeopardize my health and I am also unwilling to become involved in an accident. For these reasons, I tender my resignation."

A short time later Lukaszewski reapplied for and obtained employment at the Wee Care Day Care Center.

After Lukaszewski left, the Board immediately began looking for a replacement. Only one qualified person applied for the position. Although this applicant had less of an educational background than Lukaszewski, she had more teaching experience. Under the salary schedule agreed upon by the Board and the teachers' union, this applicant would have to be paid $1,026.64 more per year than Lukaszewski. Having no alternative, the Board hired the applicant at the higher salary.

In December of 1978 the Board initiated an action against Lukaszewski for breach of contract. The Board alleged that, as a result of the breach, it suffered damage in the amount of the additional compensation it was required to pay Lukaszewski's replacement for the 1978–79 school year ($1,026.64). A trial was held before the court. The trial court ruled that Lukaszewski had breached her contract and awarded the Board $1,249.14 in damages ($1,026.64 for breach of contract and $222.50 for costs).

Lukaszewski appealed. The court of appeals affirmed the circuit court's determination that Lukaszewski breached her contract. However, the appellate court reversed the circuit court's damage award, reasoning that, although the Board had to pay more for Lukaszewski's replacement, by its own standards it obtained a proportionately more valuable teacher. Therefore, the court of appeals held that the Board suffered no damage from the breach. We granted the Board's petition for review.

There are two issues presented on this review: (1) whether Lukaszewski breached her employment contract with the Board; and (2) if she did breach her contract, whether the Board suffered recoverable damages therefrom.

* * *

A health danger will not excuse nonperformance of a contractual obligation when the danger is caused by the nonperforming party. *See Jennings v. Lyons,* 39 Wis. at 557–58. Nor will a health condition or danger which was foreseeable when the contract was entered into justify its breach. *Id.* It would be fundamentally unfair to allow a breaching party to escape liability because of a health danger which by his or her own fault has precluded performance.

[The court upheld the trial court's findings that (1) Lukaszewski's medical condition resulted from the "stress condition she had created by an attempted repudiation of her contract," and (2) that Lukaszewski resigned for reasons other than health. The court therefore affirmed the holdings below that Lukaszewski breached her employment contract.]

In the instant case it is undisputed that, as a result of the breach, the Board hired a replacement at a salary exceeding what it had agreed to pay Lukaszewski. There is no question that this additional cost ($1,026.64) necessarily flowed from the breach and was within the contemplation of the parties when the contract was made. Lukaszewski argues and the court of appeals held, however, that the Board was not damaged by this expense. The amount a teacher is paid is determined by a salary schedule agreed upon by the teachers' union and the Board. The more education and experience a teacher has the greater her salary will be. Presumably, then, the amount of compensation a teacher receives reflects her value to the Board. Lukaszewski argues that the Board suffered no net loss because, while it had to pay more for the replacement, it received the services of a proportionately more valuable teacher. Accordingly, she maintains that the Board is not entitled to damages because an award would place it in a better position than if the contract had been performed.

We disagree. Lukaszewski and the court of appeals improperly focus on the objective value of the services the Board received rather than that for which it had bargained. Damages for breach of contract are measured by the expectations of the parties. The Board expected to receive the services of a speech therapist with Lukaszewski's education and experience at the salary agreed upon. It neither expected nor wanted a more experienced therapist who had to be paid an additional $1,026.64 per year. Lukaszewski's breach forced the Board to hire the replacement and, in turn, to pay a higher salary. Therefore, the Board lost the benefit of its bargain. Any additional value the Board may have received from the replacement's greater experience was imposed upon it and thus cannot be characterized as a benefit. We conclude that the Board suffered damages for the loss of its bargain in the amount of additional compensation it was required to pay Lukaszewski's replacement.

This is not to say that an employer who is injured by an employee's breach of contract is free to hire the most qualified and expensive replacement and then recover the difference between the salary paid and the contract salary. An injured party must take all reasonable steps to mitigate damages. *Kuhlman, Inc. v. G. Heileman Brewing Co.,* 83 Wis.2d 749, 752, 266 N.W.2d 382 (1978). Therefore, the employer must attempt to obtain equivalent services at the lowest possible cost. In the instant case the Board acted reasonably in hiring Lukaszewski's replacement even though she commanded a higher salary. Upon Lukaszewski's breach, the Board immediately took steps to locate a replacement. Only one qualified person applied for the position. Having no alternative, the Board hired this applicant. Thus the Board properly mitigated its damages by hiring the least expensive, qualified replacement available.

We hold that the Board is entitled to have the benefit of its bargain restored. Therefore, we reverse that portion of the court of appeals' decision which reversed the trial court's damage award.

The decision of the court of appeals is affirmed in part and reversed in part.

[JUSTICE DAY dissented.]

NOTE: THE CONCEPT OF "EFFICIENT BREACH"— AN INTRODUCTION AND CAVEAT

The concept of "efficient breach of contract" has recently figured prominently in the contract theory of economists and others who stress the importance of economic analysis of contract law. Most of these theorists argue that the concept of efficient breach provides a further justification for granting lost expectancy damages in contract cases. Although the concept applies in theory to any contract setting, it is perhaps most readily grasped in the sale of goods context. The first excerpt that follows introduces the concept, the second offers a caveat. Consider how the Posner excerpt to follow applies to Handicapped Children's Education Bd. v. Lukaszewski. Section 9 of this chapter, in the Dorf excerpt, revisits efficient breach, specific performance, and moral obligation in the context of National Basketball Association star players demanding to be traded despite being under contract to their current team.

R. POSNER, ECONOMIC ANALYSIS OF LAW

89–90 (2d ed. 1977).

[I]n some cases a party would be tempted to breach the contract simply because his profit from breach would exceed his expected profit from completion of the contract. If his profit from breach would also exceed the expected profit to the other party from completion of the contract, and if damages are limited to loss of expected profit, there will be an incentive to commit a breach. There should be. The opportunity cost of completion to the breaching party is the profit that he would make from a breach, and if it is greater than his profit from completion, then completion will involve a loss to him. If that loss is greater than the gain to the other party from completion, breach would be value-maximizing and should be encouraged. And because the victim of the breach is made whole for his loss, he is indifferent; hence encouraging breaches in these circumstances will not deter people from entering into contracts in the future.

An arithmetical illustration may be helpful here. I sign a contract to deliver 100,000 custom-ground widgets at $.10 apiece to A, for use in his boiler factory. After I have delivered 10,000, B comes to me, explains that he desperately needs 25,000 custom-ground widgets at once since otherwise he will be forced to close his pianola factory at great cost, and offers me $.15 apiece for 25,000 widgets. I sell him the widgets and as a result do not complete timely delivery to A, who sustains $1000 in lost profits from my breach. Having obtained an additional profit of $1250 on the sale to B, I am better off even after reimbursing A for his loss. Society is also better off. Since B was willing to pay me $.15 per widget, it must mean that each widget was worth at least $.15 to him. But it was worth only $.14 to A—the $.10 that he paid plus his expected profit of $.04 ($1000 divided by 25,000). Thus the breach resulted in a transfer of the 25,000 widgets from a less to a more valuable use. To be sure, had I refused to sell to B, he could have gone to A and negotiated an assignment of part of A's contract with me to him. But this would have introduced an additional step and so imposed additional transaction costs.

Thus far the emphasis has been on the economic importance of not awarding damages in excess of the lost expectation. It is equally important, however, not to award less than the expectation loss. Suppose A contracts to sell B for $100,000 a machine that is worth $110,000 to B, i.e., that would yield him a profit of $10,000. Before delivery C comes to A and offers him $109,000 for the machine promised B. A would be tempted to breach were he not liable to B for B's loss of expected profit. Given that measure of damages, C will not be able to induce a breach of A's contract with B unless he offers A more than $110,000, thereby indicating that the machine really is worth more to him than to B. The expectation rule thus assures that the machine ends up where it is most valuable.

L. FULLER, THE MORALITY OF LAW

28 (rev. ed. 1969).

Before the principle of marginal utility nothing is sacred; all existing arrangements are subject to being reordered in the interest of increased economic return. The economics of exchange is, in contrast, based on two fixed points: property and contract. While it permits interested calculation to reign everywhere else, such calculation is excluded when the question is fidelity to contract or respect for property. Without a self-sacrificing deference toward these institutions, a regime of exchange would lose its anchorage and no one would occupy a sufficiently stable position to know what he had to offer or what he could count on receiving from another.

PROBLEM 3-2

On January 2, 2015, Edgar Janis entered into a one-year contract of employment at $1500 per month with Addis Corp. The market value of his services was $1200 per month. On January 31, after receiving one month's pay, Janis was wrongfully terminated. Despite a diligent search for a suitable alternative position, Janis remained unemployed until December 1, 2015, when he took a comparable job for comparable pay. You are Janis's lawyer. What will you seek to recover against Addis Corp.?

PROBLEM 3-3

Arvid Anderson contracted at 11:00 a.m. on May 7, 2015 to buy a farm owned by Olaf Norgaard, closing to be July 15, with Anderson to pay a purchase price of $125,000. On the evening of May 7, Anderson changed his mind and telephoned Norgaard to that effect. An average of three appraisals indicated that the fair market value of the farm at all relevant times was about $122,000. Assume that Norgaard tried without success to resell to others for $125,000. Is Norgaard entitled to damages of $3,000? Should Norgaard receive any damages in such a case? Consider these remarks from Karl N. Llewellyn, Our Case-Law of Contract: Offer and Acceptance, II, 48 Yale L.J. 779, 803–04 (1939):

> The case is thus made, in ethics and in policy, for some type of legal remedy when agreement has been expressed, and each party knows of the other's expression, and a bit of time has elapsed. The case remains to be made, in ethics or in policy, for the snapping of the legal trap when the attempted retraction rolls in so quickly that any action taken in reliance becomes questionable, or when the quantity or degree of action taken is patently slight, or even when the retracting side can demonstrate the absence of any such action.

Plainly, in such situations, policy becomes more tenuous; and to my mind only resort to formalism can keep ethics from openly acknowledging "moral" obligation to be here often on slippery footing. * * *

What I think I see here is this: First, and most, a contagion of attitude from deals where there has been no attempt at early retraction, and where it is plain that the deal has been, shall I say, *lived* into, and where men's minds and courts' minds then naturally (though quite without necessity) date the closing as of the easiest time to see and think about: to wit, the time when agreement was expressed. * * * To allow free retraction is uncomfortable and disturbing, both vaguely and demonstrably. It unsettles, and the whole measure of the unsettling is not easy to see in advance. But especially unsettling would free retraction be in regard to * * * the closing of deals for the very purpose of shifting or hedging against the risks of market fluctuation.

UNIFORM COMMERCIAL CODE § 1–305.

Remedies to be Liberally Administered.

(a) The remedies provided by [the Uniform Commercial Code] must be liberally administered to the end that the aggrieved party may be put in as good a position as if the other party had fully performed but neither consequential or special damages nor penal damages may be had except as specifically provided in [the Uniform Commercial Code] or by other rule of law.

UNIFORM COMMERCIAL CODE § 2–713.

Buyer's Damages for Non-delivery or Repudiation.

(1) Subject to the provisions of this Article with respect to proof of market price (Section 2–723), the measure of damages for non-delivery or repudiation by the seller is the difference between the market price at the time when the buyer learned of the breach and the contract price together with any incidental and consequential damages provided in this Article (Section 2–715), but less expenses saved in consequence of the seller's breach.

(2) Market price is to be determined as of the place for tender or, in cases of rejection after arrival or revocation of acceptance, as of the place of arrival.

TONGISH V. THOMAS

Supreme Court of Kansas, 1992.
251 Kan. 728, 840 P.2d 471.

MCFARLAND, J. This case presents the narrow issue of whether damages arising from the nondelivery of contracted-for sunflower seeds should be computed on the basis of *K.S.A. 84–1–106* [now UCC 1–305 above] or *K.S.A. 84–2–713* [UCC 2–713 above]. That is, whether the buyer is entitled to its actual loss of profit or the difference between the market price and the contract price. The trial court awarded damages on the basis of the buyer's actual loss of profit. The Court of Appeals reversed the judgment, holding that the difference between the market price and the contract price was the proper measure of damages. The matter is before us on petition for review.

The pertinent facts are as follows. Denis Tongish entered into a contract on April 28, 1988, with the Decatur Coop Association (Coop) where Tongish agreed to grow 160 acres of sunflower seeds, said crop to be purchased by Coop at $13 per hundredweight for large seeds and $8 per hundredweight for small seeds. By agreement, the acreage was subsequently reduced to 116.8 acres. The crop was to be delivered in increments of one-third by December 31, 1988, March 31, 1989, and May 31, 1989.

Coop had a contract to deliver the seeds purchased to Bambino Bean & Seed, Inc. Coop was to be paid the same price it paid the farmers less a 55 cent per hundredweight handling fee. Coop's only anticipated profit was the handling fee.

In October and November 1988, Tongish delivered sunflower seeds to Coop. In January, a dispute arose over the amount of dockage charged against Tongish's seeds. Tongish's seeds were of higher quality than those of many other farmers selling to Coop, and Coop's practice of commingling seeds prior to sampling was disadvantageous to Tongish. This was resolved by Coop issuing an additional check to Tongish reflecting a lower dockage charge.

Due to a short crop, bad weather, and other factors, the market price of sunflower seeds in January 1989 was double that set forth in the Tongish/Coop contract. On January 13, Tongish notified Coop he would not deliver any more sunflower seeds.

In May 1989, Tongish sold and delivered 82,820 pounds of sunflower seeds to Danny Thomas for approximately $20 per hundredweight. Tongish was to receive $14,714.89, which was $5,153.13 more than the Coop contract price. Thomas paid for approximately one-half of the seeds. Tongish brought this action to collect the balance due. Thomas paid the balance of $7,359.61 into court and was ultimately dismissed from the action.

Meanwhile, Coop intervened in the action, seeking damages for Tongish's breach of their contract. Following a bench trial, the district court held that Tongish had breached the contract with no basis therefor. Damages were allowed in the amount of $455.51, which was the computed loss of handling charges. Coop appealed from said damage award. The Court of Appeals reversed the district court and remanded the case to the district court to determine and award damages pursuant to K.S.A. 84–2–713 (the difference between the market price and the contract price).

The analyses and rationale of the Court of Appeals utilized in resolving the issue are sound and we adopt the following portion thereof:

> * * * Neither party argues that the Uniform Commercial Code is inapplicable. Both agree that the issue to be determined is which provision of the UCC should be applied. As stated by the appellee: 'This is really the essence of this appeal, i.e., whether this general rule of damages controls the measure of damages set forth in K.S.A. 84–2–713 * * *
>
> The cardinal rule of statutory construction, to which all others are subordinate, is that the purpose and intent of the legislature govern. When there is a conflict between a statute dealing generally with a subject and another statute dealing specifically with a certain phase of it, the specific statute controls unless it appears that the legislature intended to make the general act controlling. * * * Therefore, because it appears impractical to make K.S.A. 84–1–106 and K.S.A. 84–2–713 harmonize in this factual situation, K.S.A. 84–2–713 should prevail as the more specific statute according to statutory rules of construction.
>
> As stated, however, Coop protected itself against market price fluctuations through its contract with Bambino. Other than the minimal handling charge, Coop suffered no lost profits from the breach. Should the protection require an exception to the general rule under K.S.A. 84–2–713?
>
> There is authority for appellee's position that K.S.A. 84–2–713 should not be applied in certain circumstances. In *Allied Canners & Packers, Inc. v. Victor Packing Co., 162 Cal. App. 3d 905, 209 Cal. Rptr. 60 (1984)*, Allied contracted to purchase 375,000 pounds of raisins from Victor for 29.75 cents per pound with a 4% discount. Allied then contracted to sell the raisins for 29.75 cents per pound expecting a profit of $4,462.50 from the 4% discount it received from Victor.
>
> Heavy rains damaged the raisin crop and Victor breached its contract, being unable to fulfill the requirement. The market price of raisins had risen to about 80 cents per pound. Allied's buyers agreed to rescind their contracts so Allied was not bound to supply

them with raisins at a severe loss. Therefore, the actual loss to Allied was the $4,462.50 profit it expected, while the difference between the market price and the contract price was about $150,000.

* * *

In *Allied,* the court determined that if the seller knew the buyer had a resale contract for the goods, and the seller did not breach the contract in bad faith, the buyer was limited to actual loss of damages under section 1–106. 162 Cal.App.3d at 915 [209 Cal.Rptr. 60].

The similarities between the present case and *Allied* are that the buyer made a resale contract which the seller knew about. (*Tongish* knew the seeds eventually went to Bambino, although he may not have known the details of the deal.) However, in examining the breach itself, Victor could not deliver the raisins because its crop had been destroyed. Tongish testified that he breached the contract because he was dissatisfied with dockage tests of Coop and/or Bambino. Victor had no raisins to sell to any buyer, while Tongish took advantage of the doubling price of sunflower seeds and sold to Danny Thomas. Although the trial court had no need to find whether Tongish breached the contract in bad faith, it did find there was no valid reason for the breach. Therefore, the nature of Tongish's breach was much different than Victor's in Allied. * * *

The *Allied* decision in 1984 * * * has been sharply criticized. * * * Recently in Scott, *The Case for Market Damages: Revisiting the Lost Profits Puzzle, 57 U. Chi. L. Rev. 1155, 1200 (1990),* the *Allied* result was called 'unfortunate.' Scott argues that section 1–106 is 'entirely consistent' with the market damages remedy of 2–713. 57 U. Chi. L. Rev. at 1201. According to Scott, it is possible to harmonize sections 1–106 and 2–713. Scott states, 'Market damages measure the expectancy ex ante, and thus reflect the value of the option; lost profits, on the other hand, measure losses ex post, and thus only reflect the value of the completed exchange.' 57 U. Chi. L. Rev. at 1174. The author argues that if the nonbreaching party has laid off part of the market risk (like Coop did) the lost profits rule creates instability because the other party is now encouraged to breach the contract if the market fluctuates to its advantage. 57 U. Chi. L. Rev. at 1178.

We are not persuaded that the lost profits view under *Allied* should be embraced. It is a minority rule that has received only nominal support. We believe the majority rule or the market damages remedy as contained in K.S.A. 84–2–713 is more reasoned and should be followed as the preferred measure of damages. While application of the rule may not reflect the actual loss to a buyer, it encourages a more efficient market and discourages the breach of contracts.

At first blush, the result reached herein appears unfair. However, closer scrutiny dissipates this impression. By the terms of the contract Coop was obligated to buy Tongish's large sunflower seeds at $13 per hundredweight whether or not it had a market for them. Had the price of sunflower seeds plummeted by delivery time, Coop's obligation to purchase at the agreed price was fixed. If loss of actual profit pursuant to K.S.A. 84–1–106(1) would be the measure of damages to be applied herein, it would enable Tongish to consider the Coop contract price of $13 per hundredweight plus 55 cents per hundredweight handling fee as the "floor" price for his seeds, take advantage of rapidly escalating prices, ignore his contractual obligation, and profitably sell to the highest bidder. Damages computed under K.S.A. 84–2–713 encourage the honoring of contracts and market stability.

* * *

The judgment of the Court of Appeals reversing the district court and remanding the case for the determination and award of damages pursuant to the provisions of K.S.A. 84–2–713 is affirmed. The judgment of the district court is reversed.

PROBLEM 3-4

1. Assume that Coop was the ultimate purchaser and Tongish repudiated the deal before delivery for large seeds. At this time, the market price was $14 per hundredweight for large seeds and Coop immediately bought seeds in substitution at this price. What are Coop's damages under U.C.C. § 2–712(1) and (2), set forth below? What if Coop bought at $14 per hundredweight and the market price was $15 per hundredweight? Can the buyer still recover under U.C.C. § 2–713?

UNIFORM COMMERCIAL CODE § 2–712.

"Cover"; Buyer's Procurement of Substitute Goods

(1) After a breach within the preceding section the buyer may "cover" by making in good faith and without unreasonable delay any reasonable purchase of or contract to purchase goods in substitution for those due from the seller.

(2) The buyer may recover from the seller as damages the difference between the cost of cover and the contract price together with any incidental or consequential damages as

hereinafter defined (Section 2–715), but less expenses saved in consequence of the seller's breach.

2. Assume Tongish tendered the seeds, but Coop refused to take and pay for them. Assume further at the time and place for tender the market price was $9 per hundredweight and the contract price was $10 per hundredweight. What would the seller recover according to U.C.C. § 1–305(a)? According to U.C.C. § 2–708(1), set forth below?

UNIFORM COMMERCIAL CODE § 2–708.

Seller's Damages for Non-Acceptance or Repudiation

(1) Subject to subsection (2) * * *, the measure of damages for non-acceptance or repudiation by the buyer is the difference between the market price at the time and place for tender and the unpaid contract price together with any incidental damages provided in this Article (Section 2–710), but less expenses saved in consequence of the buyer's breach.

(2) If the measure of damages provided in subsection (1) is inadequate to put the seller in as good a position as performance would have done then the measure of damages is the profit (including reasonable overhead) which the seller would have made from full performance by the buyer, together with any incidental damages provided in this Article (Section 2–710), due allowance for costs reasonably incurred and due credit for payments or proceeds of resale.

3. Again assume that Tongish tendered the seeds, but Coop refused to take and pay for them. At the time and place for tender the market price was $9 per hundredweight and the contract price was $10 per hundredweight. The next day, seller resold at $8 per hundredweight. What are seller's damages under U.C.C. § 2–706(1), set forth below?

UNIFORM COMMERCIAL CODE § 2–706.

Seller's Resale Including Contract for Resale

(1) Under the conditions stated in Section 2–703 on seller's remedies, the seller may resell the goods concerned or the undelivered balance thereof. Where the resale is made in good faith and in a commercially reasonable manner the seller may recover the difference between the resale price and the contract price together with any incidental damages allowed under the provisions of this Article (Section 2–710), but less expenses saved in consequence of the buyer's breach.

4. Assume Tongish agreed to sell to Coop first quality seed and the contract price was $15 per hundredweight. Seller delivered moldy seeds worth

$5 per hundredweight. On the date of delivery, the market price of first quality seeds was $17 per hundredweight. Coop accepted and paid the contract price for the seeds, fed them to its hogs, and sued seller for breach of warranty. What damages under U.C.C. § 2–714, set forth below?

UNIFORM COMMERCIAL CODE § 2–714.

Buyer's Damages for Breach in Regard to Accepted Goods

(1) Where the buyer has accepted goods and given notification (subsection (3) of Section 2–607) he may recover as damages for any non-conformity of tender the loss resulting in the ordinary course of events from the seller's breach as determined in any manner which is reasonable.

(2) The measure of damages for breach of warranty is the difference at the time and place of acceptance between the value of the goods accepted and the value they would have had if they had been as warranted, unless special circumstances show proximate damages of a different amount.

(3) In a proper case any incidental and consequential damages under the next section may also be recovered.

NERI V. RETAIL MARINE CORP.

Court of Appeals of New York, 1972.
30 N.Y.2d 393, 285 N.E.2d 311.

GIBSON, JUDGE.

The appeal concerns the right of a retail dealer to recover loss of profits and incidental damages upon the buyer's repudiation of a contract governed by the Uniform Commercial Code. This is, indeed, the correct measure of damage in an appropriate case and to this extent the code (§ 2–708, subsection [2]) effected a substantial change from prior law, whereby damages were ordinarily limited to "the difference between the contract price and the market or current price". Upon the record before us, the courts below erred in declining to give effect to the new statute and so the order appealed from must be reversed.

The plaintiffs contracted to purchase from defendant a new boat of a specified model for the price of $12,587.40, against which they made a deposit of $40. They shortly increased the deposit to $4,250 in consideration of the defendant dealer's agreement to arrange with the manufacturer for immediate delivery on the basis of "a firm sale", instead of the delivery within approximately four to six weeks originally specified. Some six days after the date of the contract plaintiffs' lawyer sent to defendant a letter rescinding the sales contract for the reason that plaintiff Neri was about to undergo hospitalization and surgery, in consequence of which, according to the letter, it would be "impossible for Mr. Neri to make any payments". The boat had already been ordered from the manufacturer and was delivered to defendant at or before the time the attorneys' letter was received. Defendant declined to refund plaintiffs' deposit and this action to recover it was commenced. Defendant counterclaimed, alleging plaintiffs' breach of the contract and defendant's resultant damage in the amount of $4,250, for which sum defendant demanded judgment. Upon motion, defendant had summary judgment on the issue of liability tendered by its counterclaim; and Special Term directed an assessment of damages, upon which it would be determined whether plaintiffs were entitled to the return of any portion of their down payment.

Upon the trial so directed, it was shown that the boat ordered and received by defendant in accordance with plaintiffs' contract of purchase was sold some four months later to another buyer for the same price as that negotiated with plaintiffs. From this proof the plaintiffs argue that defendant's loss on its contract was recouped, while defendant argues that but for plaintiffs' default, it would have sold two boats and have earned two profits instead of one. Defendant proved, without contradiction, that its profit on the sale under the contract in suit would have been $2,579 and that during the period the boat remained unsold incidental expenses aggregating $674 for storage, upkeep, finance charges and insurance were incurred. Additionally, defendant proved and sought to recover attorneys' fees of $1,250.

The trial court found "untenable" defendant's claim for loss of profit, inasmuch as the boat was later sold for the same price that plaintiffs had contracted to pay; found, too, that defendant had failed to prove any incidental damages; further found "that the terms of section 2–718, subsection 2(b), of the Uniform Commercial Code are applicable and same make adequate and fair provision to place the sellers in as good a position as performance would have done" and, in accordance with paragraph (b) of subsection (2) thus relied upon, awarded defendant $500 upon its counterclaim and directed that plaintiffs recover the balance of their deposit, amounting to $3,750. The ensuing judgment was affirmed, without opinion, at the Appellate Division, 37 A.D.2d 917, 326 N.Y.S.2d 984, and defendant's appeal to this court was taken by our leave.

The issue is governed in the first instance by section 2–718 of the Uniform Commercial Code which provides, among other things, that the buyer, despite his breach, may have restitution of the amount by which his payment exceeds: (a) reasonable liquidated damages stipulated by the contract or (b) absent such stipulation, 20% of the value of the buyer's total performance or $500, whichever is smaller (§ 2–718, subsection [2], pars. [a], [b]). As above noted, the trial court awarded defendant an offset in the amount of $500 under paragraph (b) and directed restitution to plaintiffs of the balance. Section 2–718, however, establishes, in paragraph (a) of subsection (3), an alternative right of offset in favor of the seller, as follows: "(3) The buyer's right to restitution under subsection (2) is subject to offset to the extent that the seller establishes (a) a right to recover damages under the provisions of this Article other than subsection (1)".[b]

Among "the provisions of this Article other than subsection (1)" are those to be found in section 2–708, which the courts below did not apply. Subsection (1) of that section provides that "the measure of damages for non-acceptance or repudiation by the buyer is the difference between the market price at the time and place for tender and the unpaid contract price together with any incidental damages provided in this Article (Section 2–710), but less expenses saved in consequence of the buyer's breach." However, this provision is made expressly subject to subsection (2), providing: "(2) If the measure of damages provided in subsection (1) is inadequate to put the seller in as good a position as performance would have done then the measure of damages is the profit (including reasonable overhead) which the seller would have made from full performance by the buyer, together with any incidental damages provided in this Article (Section 2–710), due allowance for costs reasonably incurred and due credit for payments or proceeds of resale."

* * *

Prior to the code, the New York cases "applied the 'profit' test, contract price less cost of manufacture, only in cases where the seller [was] a manufacturer or an agent for a manufacturer" (1955 Report of N.Y.Law Rev.Comm., vol. 1, p. 693). Its extension to retail sales was "designed to eliminate the unfair and economically wasteful results arising under the older law when fixed price articles were involved. This section permits the recovery of lost profits in all appropriate cases, which would include all standard priced goods." (Official Comment 2, McKinney's Cons.Laws of N.Y., Book 62½, Part 1, p. 605, under Uniform Commercial Code, § 2–708.)

---

[b] Uniform Commercial Code § 2–718 states in part:

§ 2–718. Liquidation or Limitation of Damages; Deposits

(1) Damages for breach by either party may be liquidated in the agreement but only at an amount which is reasonable in the light of the anticipated or actual harm caused by the breach, the difficulties of proof of loss, and the inconvenience or nonfeasibility of otherwise obtaining an adequate remedy. A term fixing unreasonably large liquidated damages is void as a penalty.

(2) Where the seller justifiably withholds delivery of goods because of the buyer's breach, the buyer is entitled to restitution of any amount by which the sum of his payments exceeds

(a) the amount to which the seller is entitled by virtue of terms liquidating the seller's damages in accordance with subsection (1), or

(b) in the absence of such terms, twenty per cent of the value of the total performance for which the buyer is obligated under the contract or $500, whichever is smaller.

(3) The buyer's right to restitution under subsection (2) is subject to offset to the extent that the seller establishes

(a) a right to recover damages under the provisions of this Article other than subsection (1), and

(b) the amount or value of any benefits received by the buyer directly or indirectly by reason of the contract.

Additionally, and "[i]n all cases the seller may recover incidental damages" (*id.,* Comment 3). The buyer's right to restitution was established at Special Term upon the motion for summary judgment, as was the seller's right to proper offsets, in each case pursuant to section 2–718; and, as the parties concede, the only question before us, following the assessment of damages at Special Term, is that as to the proper measure of damage to be applied. The conclusion is clear from the record—indeed with mathematical certainty—that "the measure of damages provided in subsection (1) is inadequate to put the seller in as good a position as performance would have done" (Uniform Commercial Code, § 2–708, subsection [2]) and hence—again under subsection (2)—that the seller is entitled to its "profit (including reasonable overhead) * * * together with any incidental damages * * *, due allowance for costs reasonably incurred and due credit for payments or proceeds of resale."

It is evident, first, that this retail seller is entitled to its profit and, second, that the last sentence of subsection (2), as hereinbefore quoted, referring to "due credit for payments or proceeds of resale" is inapplicable to this retail sales contract.[1] Closely parallel to the factual situation now before us is that hypothesized by Dean Hawkland as illustrative of the operation of the rules: "Thus, if a private party agrees to sell his automobile to a buyer for $2,000, a breach by the buyer would cause the seller no loss (except incidental damages, i.e., expense of a new sale) if the seller was able to sell the automobile to another buyer for $2000. But the situation is different with dealers having an unlimited supply of standard-priced goods. Thus, if an automobile dealer agrees to sell a car to a buyer at the standard price of $2000, a breach by the buyer injures the dealer, even though he is able to sell the automobile to another for $2000. If the dealer has an inexhaustible supply of cars, the resale to replace the breaching buyer costs the dealer a sale, because, had the breaching buyer performed, the dealer would have made two sales instead of one. The buyer's breach, in such a case, depletes the dealer's sales to the extent of one, and the measure of damages should be the dealer's profit on one sale. Section 2–708 recognizes this, and it rejects the rule developed under the Uniform Sales Act by many courts that the profit cannot be recovered in this case." (Hawkland, Sales

---

[1] The concluding clause, "due credit for payments or proceeds of resale", is intended to refer to "the privilege of the seller to realize junk value when it is manifestly useless to complete the operation of manufacture" (Supp. No. 1 to the 1952 Official Draft of Text and Comments of the Uniform Commercial Code, as Amended by the Action of the American Law Institute of the National Conference of Commissioners on Uniform Laws [1954], p. 14). The commentators who have considered the language have uniformly concluded that "the reference is to a resale as scrap under * * * Section 2–704" * * *. Another writer, reaching the same conclusion, after detailing the history of the clause, says that " 'proceeds of resale' previously meant the resale value of the goods in finished form; now it means the resale value of the components on hand at the time plaintiff learns of breach" (Harris, Seller's Damages, 18 Stanf.L.Rev. 66, 104). [Revised U.C.C. Article 2 (April 2000), section 2–708(b) omitted the language "due credit for payments or proceeds of resale," but Revised Article 2 was abandoned.]

and Bulk Sales [1958 ed.], pp. 153–154; and see Comment, 31 Fordham L.Rev. 749, 755–756.)

The record which in this case establishes defendant's entitlement to damages in the amount of its prospective profit, at the same time confirms defendant's cognate right to "any incidental damages provided in this Article (Section 2–710)[2] (Uniform Commercial Code, § 2–708, subsection [2]). From the language employed it is too clear to require discussion that the seller's right to recover loss of profits is not exclusive and that he may recoup his "incidental" expenses as well. * * * Although the trial court's denial of incidental damages in the uncontroverted amount of $674 was made in the context of its erroneous conclusion that paragraph (b) of subsection (2) of section 2–718 was applicable and was "adequate * * * to place the sellers in as good a position as performance would have done", the denial seems not to have rested entirely on the court's mistaken application of the law, as there was an explicit finding "that defendant completely failed to show that it suffered any incidental damages." We find no basis for the court's conclusion with respect to a deficiency of proof inasmuch as the proper items of the $674 expenses (being for storage, upkeep, finance charges and insurance for the period between the date performance was due and the time of the resale) were proven without objection and were in no way controverted, impeached or otherwise challenged, at the trial or on appeal. Thus the court's finding of a failure of proof cannot be supported upon the record and, therefore, and contrary to plaintiffs' contention, the affirmance at the Appellate Division was ineffective to save it.

The trial court correctly denied defendant's claim for recovery of attorney's fees incurred by it in this action. Attorney's fees incurred in an action such as this are not in the nature of the protective expenses contemplated by the statute (Uniform Commercial Code, § 1–106, subd. [1]; § 2–710; § 2–708, subsection [2]) and by our reference to "legal expense" in Procter & Gamble Distr. Co. v. Lawrence Amer. Field Warehousing Corp. (16 N.Y.2d 344, 354–355, 266 N.Y.S.2d 785, 792–793, 213 N.E.2d 873, 878–879, *supra*), upon which defendant's reliance is in this respect misplaced.

It follows that plaintiffs are entitled to restitution of the sum of $4,250 paid by them on account of the contract price less an offset to defendant in the amount of $3,253 on account of its lost profit of $2,579 and its incidental damages of $674.

The order of the Appellate Division should be modified, with costs in all courts, in accordance with this opinion, and, as so modified, affirmed.

---

[2] "Incidental damages to an aggrieved seller include any commercially reasonable charges, expenses or commissions incurred in stopping delivery, in the transportation, care and custody of goods after the buyer's breach, in connection with return or resale of the goods or otherwise resulting from the breach" (Uniform Commercial Code, § 2–710).

* * *

Ordered accordingly.

PROBLEM 3-5

In the excerpt that follows, Professor Melvin A. Eisenberg sets forth several justifications supporting the award of expectancy damages. Consider whether these justifications support the award of such damages in his two "merchant to consumer" hypothetical cases that follow the excerpt. Consider, too, what the plaintiff should recover in such cases. (The excerpt and the problems appear in Eisenberg, The Bargain Principle and Its Limits, 95 Harv. L. Rev. 741, 787, 794, 797 (1982).)

"First, fairness normally requires that a promisee should at least be compensated for the cost he incurred in reasonably relying on a bargain promise. * * * [I]n many transaction-types enforcement of an executory contract to its full extent is desirable on the ground that expectation damages are approximately equal to cost, but much easier to measure. I shall call this justification the surrogate-cost theory.

"Second, a contract for forward delivery typically is made with the purpose of enabling the parties to plan their future conduct reliably. Efficiency normally requires that such planning should be facilitated. The award of expectation damages conduces to that end by making breach unprofitable in the normal case. I shall call this justification the planning theory.

"Third, when a contract is made for forward delivery at a fixed price, it is frequently a purpose of the contract to allocate the risk of price changes. Efficiency normally requires effectuating this allocation, and that is just what is done by expectation damages. Risk allocation also implicates considerations of fairness. As Sharp observed:

> [T]his is not only an industrial and credit economy, but also a risk taking, profit making, more or less gambling economy. This may mean not only that harmful reliance, in fluctuating markets, is best remedied by expectation damages, but also that the profits dependent on good guesses about the future are generally to be assured to the person who is willing to gamble on his judgment.

To put this differently, when parties gamble on market movements and the market does in fact move, the contract is in a sense half-completed rather than executory, and the breaching promisor is like a gambler who welshes on his bet. I shall call this justification the risk theory.

* * *

"*Dance Lessons.* E, an electrical engineer, wants to learn to dance. S operates a dancing school. On May 1, E signs a contract with S to take Dancing I, a group class, which begins on July 1. Dancing I meets two hours a week, runs twenty-six weeks and costs $500. E understands all the provisions of the contract and considered the matter in a deliberative frame of mind, but knows nothing about damage rules. On June 15, E changes his mind and repudiates.

"S incurs little or no incremental out-of-pocket costs for group classes, since its instructors work on full-year contracts and it owns its own studios. S's classes usually don't fill to capacity. The capacity of Dancing I is twenty students. On June 15 sixteen students had enrolled. No additional students enrolled thereafter.

* * *

"*Buick Buyer*. T, a high school teacher, wants to buy a new Buick. After shopping around, T decides to buy at Seller's dealership, since Seller's price matches the lowest price available from competing dealers and Seller has a good reputation for servicing. On October 1, T signs a contract to buy from Seller a new Buick, with specified accessories, for $10,000, delivery on December 1. On November 1, before the factory has begun to fill Seller's order for T's car, T repudiates the contract. Seller's factory cost for the Buick ordered by T is $8,500, and Seller can buy as many new Buicks from the factory as it sells."

NOTE: LOST EXPECTANCY, GENERAL DAMAGES, AND CONSEQUENTIAL DAMAGES

Most of the damage claims asserted by injured parties in the preceding cases and problems were for lost expectancy damages in the form of "general" (also called "direct") damages. General damages are losses from a breach that arise "naturally or ordinarily." For example, a purchaser of a defective stove "naturally or ordinarily" suffers damages measured by the difference between the value of what was accepted and what was promised. Often, however, general damages will be insufficient to make the injured party whole. For example, the stove buyer may have needed the stove to make hamburgers at her new restaurant. She may, therefore, also suffer lost profits at the restaurant due to the defective stove. In this context, the claim for lost profits would be called "special" or "consequential" damages because many aggrieved stove purchasers would not suffer such damages. One can see that to award the aggrieved party full lost expectancy, courts often must award both general and consequential damages.

Is the lost profits claim in Neri v. Retail Marine Corp. general or consequential? The lost profits recovery is general in the sense that it substitutes for the seller's right to the contract-market differential. Still, many sellers of boats will not suffer damages as measured by lost profits. What if the seller in Neri was not a lost-volume seller?

For a case finding that lost profits should be treated as general damages, consider Stern Oil Co. v. Brown, 908 N.W.2d 144 (Sup. Ct. S. D. 2018). Reduced to its essentials, the facts were that Stern Oil Co., a fuel distributor, agreed in two contracts to supply fuel to Brown, an operator of convenience stores. Brown broke the contracts and Stern sought lost profits based in part on a 1.5 cent markup per gallon above the price Stern paid to ExxonMobil for the fuel. After an extended analysis, the court held that the damages were general, not consequential, because they "flowed directly from the contract itself." Further, direct damages "do not have an element of foreseeability because they are, by their very nature, foreseeable by the parties at the time of contracting." The court reasoned that it was foreseeable to Brown that Stern expected a profit and that it was irrelevant that Brown did not know how Stern calculated the expected profit.

While the distinction between general and consequential damages may be blurred in cases such as Neri and Stern Oil (the Restatement (Second) of Contracts § 351, Comment b, states that the terms "general" and "special" damages "are often misleading"), the distinction is still important. Typically, consequential damages are subject to greater qualifications and limits than general damages, as we shall see in the next section.

SECTION FOUR: AVAILABILITY OF LOST EXPECTANCY DAMAGES—QUALIFICATIONS AND LIMITS

A. THE FORESEEABILITY PRINCIPLE

HADLEY V. BAXENDALE

Court of Exchequer, 1854.
9 Exch. 341.

At the trial before CROMPTON, J., at the last Gloucester Assizes, it appeared that the plaintiffs carried on an extensive business as millers at Gloucester; and that, on the 11th of May, their mill was stopped by a breakage of the crank shaft by which the mill was worked. The steam-engine was manufactured by Messrs. Joyce & Co., the engineers, at Greenwich, and it became necessary to send the shaft as a pattern for a new one to Greenwich. The fracture was discovered on the 12th, and on the 13th the plaintiffs sent one of their servants to the office of the defendants, who are the well-known carriers trading under the name of Pickford & Co., for the purpose of having the shaft carried to Greenwich. The plaintiffs' servant told the clerk that the mill was stopped, and that the shaft must be sent immediately; and in answer to the inquiry when the shaft would be taken, the answer was, that if it was sent up by twelve o'clock any day, it would be delivered at Greenwich on the following day. On the following day the shaft was taken by the defendants before noon, for the purpose of being conveyed to Greenwich, and the sum of 2£. 4s. was paid for its carriage for the whole distance; at the same time the defendants' clerk was told that a special entry, if required, should be made to hasten its delivery. The delivery of the shaft at Greenwich was delayed by some neglect; and the consequence was, that the plaintiffs did not receive the new shaft for several days after they would otherwise have done, and the working of their mill was thereby delayed, and they thereby lost the profits they would otherwise have received.

On the part of the defendants, it was objected that these damages were too remote, and that the defendants were not liable with respect to them. The learned Judge left the case generally to the jury, who found a verdict with 25£. damages beyond the amount paid into Court.

Whateley, in last Michaelmas Term, obtained a rule nisi for a new trial, on the ground of misdirection.

* * *

The judgment of the Court was now delivered by ALDERSON, B. We think that there ought to be a new trial in this case; but, in so doing, we deem it to be expedient and necessary to state explicitly the rule which the Judge, at the next trial, ought, in our opinion, to direct the jury to be governed by when they estimate the damages.

It is, indeed, of the last importance that we should do this; for, if the jury are left without any definite rule to guide them, it will, in such cases as these, manifestly lead to the greatest injustice. The Courts have done this on several occasions; and, in Blake v. Midland Railway Company, 18 Q.B. 93, the Court granted a new trial on this very ground, that the rule had not been definitely laid down to the jury by the learned Judge at Nisi Prius.

* * *

Now we think the proper rule in such a case as the present is this:—Where two parties have made a contract which one of them has broken, the damages which the other party ought to receive in respect to such breach of contract should be such as may fairly and reasonably be considered either arising naturally, i.e., according to the usual course of things, from such breach of contract itself,[c] or such as may reasonably be supposed to have been in the contemplation of both parties, at the time they made the contract, as the probable result of the breach of it. Now, if the special circumstances under which the contract was actually made were communicated by the plaintiffs to the defendants, and thus known to both parties, the damages resulting from the breach of such a contract, which they would reasonably contemplate, would be the amount of injury which would ordinarily follow from a breach of contract under these special circumstances so known and communicated. But, on the other hand, if

---

[c] What are the "general" damages for breach of such a contract of carriage? One court answered, much later: "[W]e conclude that [such damages] * * * would be limited to a recovery of the rental value of the shipment for the time of the unreasonable delay." New Orleans & N.E.R. Co. v. J.H. Miner Saw Mfg. Co., 117 Miss. 646, 657, 78 So. 577, 578 (1918).

these special circumstances were wholly unknown to the party breaking the contract, he, at the most, could only be supposed to have had in his contemplation the amount of injury which would arise generally, and in the great multitude of cases not affected by any special circumstances, from such a breach of contract. For, had the special circumstances been known, the parties might have specially provided for the breach of contract by special terms as to the damages in that case; and of this advantage it would be very unjust to deprive them.

Now the above principles are those by which we think the jury ought to be guided in estimating the damages arising out of any breach of contract. It is said, that other cases, such as breaches of contract in the non-payment of money, or in the not making a good title to land, are to be treated as exceptions from this, and as governed by a conventional rule. But as, in such cases, both parties must be supposed to be cognisant of that well-known rule, these cases may, we think, be more properly classed under the rule above enunciated as to cases under known special circumstances, because there both parties may reasonably be presumed to contemplate the estimation of the amount of damages according to the conventional rule. Now, in the present case, if we are to apply the principles above laid down, we find that the only circumstances here communicated by the plaintiffs to the defendants at the time the contract was made, were, that the article to be carried was the broken shaft of a mill, and that the plaintiffs were the millers of that mill. But how do these circumstances shew reasonably that the profits of the mill must be stopped by an unreasonable delay in the delivery of the broken shaft by the carrier to the third person? Suppose the plaintiffs had another shaft in their possession put up or putting up at the time, and that they only wished to send back the broken shaft to the engineer who made it; it is clear that this would be quite consistent with the above circumstances, and yet the unreasonable delay in the delivery would have no effect upon the intermediate profits of the mill. Or, again, suppose that, at the time of the delivery to the carrier, the machinery of the mill had been in other respects defective, then, also, the same results would follow.

Here it is true that the shaft was actually sent back to serve as a model for a new one, and that the want of a new one was the only cause of the stoppage of the mill, and that the loss of profits really arose from not sending down the new shaft in proper time, and that this arose from the delay in delivering the broken one to serve as a model. But it is obvious that, in the great multitude of cases of millers sending off broken shafts to third persons by a carrier under ordinary circumstances, such consequences would not, in all probability, have occurred; and these special circumstances were here never communicated by the plaintiffs to the defendants. It follows, therefore, that the loss of profits here cannot reasonably be considered such a consequence of the breach of contract as could have been fairly and reasonably contemplated by both the parties when they made this contract. For such loss would neither have flowed naturally from the breach of this contract in the great multitude of such cases occurring under ordinary circumstances, nor were the special circumstances, which, perhaps, would have made it a reasonable and natural consequence of such breach of contract, communicated to or known by the defendants. The Judge ought, therefore, to have told the jury that, upon the facts then before them, they ought not to take the loss of profits into consideration at all in estimating the damages. There must therefore be a new trial in this case.

Rule absolute.

PROBLEM 3-6

You represent the miller in Hadley v. Baxendale. On May 12, the day the broken shaft was discovered, you are asked to draft a letter to be handed to the carrier that would assure your client of a consequential damages recovery if the carrier delays carriage of the shaft. Draft the letter. Will the carrier agree to it?

SPANG INDUSTRIES, INC. v. AETNA CASUALTY & SURETY CO., 512 F.2d 365 (2d Cir.1975). In Hadley v. Baxendale a miller sought to recover the profits lost from the closing of the mill as a result of a carrier's failure to make timely delivery of a broken crank shaft to an engineering firm where it was to be used as a model for a replacement. A recovery of those profits was disallowed on the ground that it was not reasonably foreseeable that profits would be lost as a result of the breach of the contract of carriage. Lord Justice Asquith pointed out in Victoria Laundry, Ltd. v. Newman Indus., Ltd., that the headnote in Hadley v. Baxendale is misleading in stating that the clerk of the defendant carrier knew that the mill was stopped and that the broken shaft had to be delivered immediately. The *Victoria* court stated that the Court of Exchequer must have rejected this statement and decided to deny the loss of profits from the closing of the mill because the only knowledge possessed by the defendant was that the mill shaft was broken and that the plaintiffs were the millers. Otherwise, "the court must, one would suppose, have decided the case the other way round * * *." [1949] 2 K.B. at 537. The misleading headnote, however, was considered to reflect the actual facts by at least two scholarly articles on the famous case. Bauer, Consequential Damages in Contract, 80 U.Penn.L.Rev. 687, 689 (1932); McCormick, Damages for Breach of Contract, 19 Minn.L.Rev. 497, 500 (1935).

R. POSNER, ECONOMIC ANALYSIS OF LAW

96 (6th ed.2003).

The task for a court asked to interpret a contract to cover a contingency that the parties did not provide for is to imagine how the parties would have provided for the contingency if they had decided to do so. Often there will be clues in the language of the contract. But often there will not be, and then the court may have to engage in economic thinking—may have to decide what the most efficient way of dealing with the contingency is. For this is the best way of deciding how the parties would have provided for it. Each party, it is true, is interested just in his own profit, and not in the joint profit; but the larger the joint profit is, the bigger the "take" of each party is likely to be. So they have a mutual interest in minimizing the cost of performance. The court can make use of this interest to fill out a contract along lines that the parties would have approved at the time of making the contract.

AYRES AND GERTNER, FILLING GAPS IN INCOMPLETE CONTRACTS: AN ECONOMIC THEORY OF DEFAULT RULES

99 Yale L.J. 87, 101–02 (1989).

The holding in *Hadley* operates as a penalty default. The miller could have informed the carrier of the potential consequential damages and contracted for full damage insurance. The *Hadley* default of denying unforeseeable damages may not be consistent with what fully informed parties would have wanted. The miller's consequential damages were real and the carrier may have been the more efficient bearer of this risk. As a general matter, millers may want carriers to compensate them for consequential damages that carriers can prevent at lower cost. The default can instead be understood as a purposeful inducement to the miller as the more informed party to reveal that information to the carrier. Informing the carrier creates value because if the carrier foresees the loss, he will be able to prevent it more efficiently. At the same time, however, revealing the information to the carrier will undoubtedly increase the price of shipping. Nonetheless, so long as transaction costs are not prohibitive, a miller with high consequential damages will gain from revealing this information and contracting for greater insurance from the carrier because the carrier is the least-cost avoider.

ARMSTRONG V. BANGOR MILL SUPPLY CORP.

Maine Supreme Judicial Court, 1929.
128 Me. 75, 145 A. 741.

STURGIS, J. General motion for a new trial in an action for damages resulting from the defendant's failure to repair a crankshaft from the plaintiff's lath mill in a workmanlike manner.

There is evidence to support the plaintiff's claim that in February, 1927, he sent a broken crankshaft from his lath mill at Vanceboro to the defendant's machine shop in Bangor for repairs, and that in making the repairs the defendant's workmen left the shaft out of alignment, necessitating its return from Vanceboro for realignment. The plaintiff's mill was shut down six days with resultant loss of earnings and expenses of maintenance. For these losses and expenses incidental to the crankshaft repairs he has a verdict.

It is an elementary principle that in the defendant's contract to repair the crankshaft the law implies an undertaking on its part to perform the work in a reasonably skillful and workmanlike manner. * * * Upon the facts here in evidence the jury were justified in finding that this undertaking was not fulfilled.

The damages awarded were not excessive. Wages, fuel, board of men and horses, and other fixed operating charges, continued through the shutdown period. The mill, with an established business yielding regular profits, was "impeded in its efficient operation" by the defendant's failure to fulfill the obligations impliedly imposed by its contract. The jury could properly include this element of loss in their award. * * * The damages awarded do not exceed the losses sustained.

Motion overruled.

NOTE:
THE TACIT AGREEMENT TEST

Although predominant today, Hadley v. Baxendale is not always followed. For example, some courts have permitted a recovery of consequential damages only when the defendant tacitly agreed to assume the risk. In Sunnyland Farms v. Central New Mexico Elec. Coop., Inc., 301 P.3d 387 (N.M. 2013), the New Mexico Supreme Court considered whether to adhere to the tacit agreement rule. Sunnyland involved a fire which destroyed a "hydroponic tomato facility" of a new business. The day before the fire, Central New Mexico had shut off electricity to the farm. Sunnyland alleged that had the electricity not been (wrongfully) shut off, the fire would have been controlled. The trial court awarded over $21 million in lost profit damages (a similar tort verdict was reduced for Sunnyland's comparative fault). The Supreme Court, reviewing the verdict, noted the traditional Hadley rule but continued:

> This Court has cited the *Hadley* standard approvingly and described it as the appropriate rule of analysis in New Mexico cases dealing with consequential damages. *See Camino Real,* 119 N.M. at 446, 891 P.2d at 1200 (describing consequential damages standard as "essentially the rule expressed in the seminal case of *Hadley v. Baxendale*"). However, we have also stated that "the foreseeability rule anticipates an explicit or tacit agreement by the defendant" that he or she will assume particular damages if he or she breaches. * * *

[The court next described the "New Mexico rule" of consequential damages.] This rule is similar to the test in Restatement (Second) of Contracts, but it incorporates the requirement that "the nonperforming party must explicitly or tacitly agree to respond in damages for the particular damages understood to be likely in the event of a breach." This makes the "New Mexico rule * * * more limited and restrictive than the notion of foreseeability in * * * the Restatement or the UCC. * * *

We now abandon the "tacit agreement" test. While we suspect that there may not, in fact, be much space between a "tacit agreement" and the special circumstances required to render a defendant liable for consequential damages, our previous emphasis on the tacit agreement test * * * is confusing and antiquated. We hold that the proper test for consequential damages in New Mexico is the *Hadley* standard as interpreted in Restatement (Second) of Contracts Section 351. In a contract action, a defendant is liable only for those consequential damages that were objectively foreseeable as a probable result of his or her breach when the contract was made. To the extent our earlier cases suggest a different standard, they are overruled. * * *

There were no findings in this case that CNMEC should have known of a particular vulnerability to fire on Sunnyland's part, or that Sunnyland had no backup source of power or water.

Although Professor Farnsworth reports that courts have "generally rejected" the tacit agreement test, E. Farnsworth, Contracts 794 (4th ed. 2004), courts understandably balk at imposing inordinate liability when the breaching party receives relatively insignificant consideration, even if the injured party communicated special circumstances to the breaching party. Do you see why?

PROBLEM 3-7

1. How would the Sunnyland case in the previous note be decided under the provisions that follow?

UNIFORM COMMERCIAL CODE § 2–715(2)(a).

(2) Consequential damages resulting from the seller's breach include

(a) any loss resulting from general or particular requirements and needs of which the seller at the time of contracting had reason to know and which could not reasonably be prevented by cover or otherwise. * * *

Official Comment

* * *

2. Subsection (2) operates to allow the buyer, in an appropriate case, any consequential damages which are the result of the seller's breach. The "tacit agreement" test for the recovery of consequential damages is rejected. * * *

3. In the absence of excuse under the section on merchant's excuse by failure of presupposed conditions, the seller is liable for consequential damages in all cases where he had reason to know of the buyer's general or particular requirements at the time of contracting. * * *

Particular needs of the buyer must generally be made known to the seller while general needs must rarely be made known to charge the seller with knowledge.

RESTATEMENT (SECOND) OF CONTRACTS § 351(3).

A court may limit damages for foreseeable loss by excluding recovery for loss of profits, by allowing recovery only for loss incurred in reliance, or otherwise if it concludes that in the circumstances justice so requires in order to avoid disproportionate compensation.

2. Resolve the following case under all relevant code provisions. WS, a wholesaler, contracts to sell screws to RB, a manufacturer, at $10 per carton. RB intends to use the screws in manufacturing widgets. RB changes its plans and contracts to resell the screws to TB for $20 per carton. WS fails to deliver and the market price is $18 on the date of delivery. RB learns of the breach on the date of delivery. RB is unable to buy substitute screws for delivery to TB. RB sues WS. How much can RB recover?

CONVENTION ON CONTRACTS FOR THE INTERNATIONAL SALE OF GOODS.

Article 74

Damages for breach of contract by one party consist of a sum equal to the loss, including loss of profit, suffered by the other party as a consequence of the breach. Such damages may not exceed the loss which the party in breach foresaw or ought to have foreseen at the time of the conclusion of the contract, in the light of the facts and matters of which he then knew or ought to have known, as a possible consequence of the breach of contract.

B. THE MITIGATION PRINCIPLE

In addition to the foreseeability requirement, another hurdle to the recovery of damages is the "duty" to mitigate damages by making reasonable decisions after breach. We now offer cases and problems that investigate the mitigation principle.

CLARK V. MARSIGLIA

Supreme Court of New York, 1845.
1 Denio 317, 43 Am.Dec. 670.

Error from the New York common pleas. Marsiglia sued Clark in the court below in assumpsit, for work, labor and materials, in cleaning, repairing and improving sundry paintings belonging to the defendant. The defendant pleaded non assumpsit.

The plaintiff proved that a number of paintings were delivered to him by the defendant to clean and repair, at certain prices for each. They were delivered upon two occasions. As to the first parcel, for the repairing of which the price was seventy-five dollars, no defense was offered. In respect to the other, for which the plaintiff charged one hundred and fifty-six dollars, the defendant gave evidence tending to show that after the plaintiff had commenced work upon them, he desired him not to go on, as he had concluded not to have the work done. The plaintiff, notwithstanding, finished the cleaning and repairing of the pictures, and claimed to recover for doing the whole, and for the materials furnished, insisting that the defendant had no right to countermand the order which he had given. The defendant's counsel requested the court to charge that he had the right to countermand his instructions for the work, and that the plaintiff could not recover for any work done after such countermand.

The court declined to charge as requested, but, on the contrary, instructed the jury that inasmuch as the plaintiff had commenced the work before the order was revoked, he had a right to finish it, and to recover the whole value of his labor and for the materials furnished. The jury found their verdict accordingly, and the defendant's counsel excepted. Judgment was rendered upon the verdict.

* * *

PER CURIAM. * * * The plaintiff was allowed to recover as though there had been no countermand of the order; and in this the court erred. The defendant, by requiring the plaintiff to stop work upon the paintings, violated his contract, and thereby incurred a liability to pay such damages as the plaintiff should sustain. Such damages would include a recompense for the labor done and materials used, and such further sum in damages as might, upon legal principles, be assessed for the breach of the contract: but the plaintiff had no right, by obstinately persisting in the work, to make the penalty upon the defendant greater than it would otherwise have been.

To hold that one who employs another to do a piece of work is bound to suffer it to be done at all events, would sometimes lead to great injustice. A man may hire another to labor for a year, and within the year his situation may be such as to render the work entirely useless to him. The party employed cannot persist in working, though he is entitled to the damages consequent upon his disappointment. So if one hires another to build a house, and subsequent events put it out of his power to pay for it, it is commendable in him to stop the work, and pay for what has been done and the damages sustained by the contractor. He may be under a necessity to change his residence; but upon the rule contended for, he would be obliged to have a house which he did not need and could not use. In all such cases the just claims of the party employed are satisfied when he is fully recompensed for his part performance and indemnified for his loss in respect to the part left unexecuted; and to persist in accumulating a larger demand is not consistent with good faith towards the employer. The judgment must be reversed, and a venire de novo awarded.

Judgment reversed.

PROBLEM 3-8

On January 7, 2015, Seller Co. and Buyer Co. agree that Seller will manufacture standard valves for Buyer for delivery on July 1 at a price of $40,000. On January 30, Buyer repudiates. Seller tells you that (1) its cost of manufacture would have been $27,000, and it can (2) cease manufacturing the valves, (3) reallocate the $15,000 worth of labor allocated to the Buyer Co. contract to less skilled tasks to produce goods worth $10,000, and (4) resell for $8,000 components purchased for this contract for $10,000. Overhead of $2,000 allocated to the contract cannot be saved. What can seller recover under U.C.C. § 2–708(2), set forth previously?

Seller wants to know if it can complete manufacture. Assume that Seller tells you that the market for such valves is "firm," and that in July it is "very likely" a buyer could be found for such valves "at $40,000 or above." You advise Seller to complete on the basis of U.C.C. § 2–704(2), which provides:

> Where the goods are unfinished an aggrieved seller may in the exercise of reasonable commercial judgment for the purposes of avoiding loss and of effective realization either complete the manufacture and wholly identify the goods to the contract or cease manufacture and resell for scrap or salvage value or proceed in any other reasonable manner.

On July 1, Seller is able to sell the valves for only $15,000, the market having unexpectedly fallen because of a new technological breakthrough.

What, if anything, can Seller recover from Buyer? Would the recovery conflict with the principle of Clark v. Marsiglia?

CONVENTION ON CONTRACTS FOR THE INTERNATIONAL SALE OF GOODS.

Article 77

A party who relies on a breach of contract must take such measures as are reasonable in the circumstances to mitigate the loss, including loss of profit, resulting from the breach. If he fails to take such measures, the party in breach may claim a reduction in the damages in the amount by which the loss should have been mitigated.

SCHIAVI MOBILE HOMES, INC. V. GIRONDA

Supreme Judicial Court of Maine, 1983.
463 A.2d 722.

NICHOLS, JUSTICE.

The principal issue in this appeal involves a retailer's duty to mitigate damages following a customer's breach of a contract for the purchase from the retailer of a mobile home.

On January 23, 1979, the Defendants, Frank Gironda, Jr., and Patricia Gironda, signed a contract with the Plaintiff, Schiavi Mobile Homes, Inc., for the purchase from that corporation of a yellow, two-bedroom mobile home for a total purchase price of $23,028.69. The Defendants paid a $1,000 deposit.

After undergoing difficulties—medical, financial and marital—the Defendants breached the purchase contract. In September 1979, Howard Palmer, an agent of Schiavi, contacted Frank Gironda, Sr., the father of Frank, Jr. Palmer asked if Frank, Jr., was still planning to purchase the mobile home. Frank Gironda, Sr., responded that because of his son's problems and his son's relocation to the West Coast, he did not know what he planned to do. Frank, Sr., then asked Palmer if he could purchase the home so his son would not lose his deposit. He expressed a willingness to mortgage his own home for this purpose. Palmer responded that this would not be necessary.

On November 7, 1979, the Plaintiff sold this mobile home to a third party for $22,000, and then commenced this action in Superior Court, Oxford County, seeking from the Defendants $4,800 in lost profits and interest expense allegedly incurred as a result of the Defendants' breach. Following a jury-waived trial, the Superior Court awarded the Plaintiff judgment in the amount of $759.45.[1] [Defendants appealed, asserting that the plaintiff failed to mitigate damages.]

The determinative issue in this case concerns the retailer's alleged failure to mitigate damages. At trial only one witness, Frank Gironda, Sr., was called. The father testified as to his conversation with Palmer, in which he expressed his willingness to purchase the mobile home. Although admitting that he did not at that time have ready cash sufficient to cover the cost of the home, he testified that he owned a $30,000 house free and clear and had been ready to mortgage it for that purpose. Questioned by the court as to his willingness to purchase the mobile home in place of his son, the witness testified that he told Palmer that he was willing to buy the mobile home if his son could not be found. He said, "That's the way we operate in our family, Your Honor."

The Plaintiff presented no evidence on the issue of mitigation. After argument by counsel, the Superior Court ruled from the bench that the Plaintiff had not failed to properly mitigate damages, because the offer by the Defendant's father was conditional and vague.[2] In so ruling, the court misapplied the doctrine of mitigation.

It has long been the rule in this state that when a contract is breached, the nonbreaching party has an affirmative duty to take reasonable steps to mitigate his damages. As early as 1830 this Court declared that if a party "has it in his power to take measures, by which his loss may be less aggravated, this will be expected of him." *Miller v. Mariner's Church,* 7 Me. 51, 55 (1830). * * *

* * *

The touchstone of the duty to mitigate is reasonableness. The nonbreaching party need only take reasonable steps to minimize his losses; he is not required to unreasonably expose himself to risk, humiliation or expense.

In the instant case the Superior Court never focused directly on the reasonableness of the Plaintiff's failure to pursue the offer of Frank Gironda, Sr., to purchase the mobile home in the place of his son. Instead

---

[1] This judgment reflected the retention by the Plaintiff of the $1,000 deposit. The Superior Court calculated damages by subtracting the resale price of the home ($22,000) from the contract price ($23,028.69) and then adding in incidental damages for floor-plan interest accruing from the breach ($731.45). We note that these figures yield a damage amount of $1,760.14, which after subtracting the deposit, should have resulted in a judgment of $760.14. The court also awarded the Plaintiff $500 in interest, costs and attorney's fees.

[2] The court ruled:

> I'm going to find for Schiavi on this issue. It is conditional. Even if it weren't, I think this is similar to purchase and sale where you have an actual intent before suing to recover damages. You can't do business on this kind of vague promises and understanding otherwise nobody would know where he stands.

the court solely concerned itself with the legal sufficiency of the father's offer. This approach was fraught with error.

First, the father's announced willingness to purchase the mobile home was conditioned only on his son not being found; that is, upon there being a breach of the son's contractual obligation. That was the same contingency from which arose the Plaintiff's duty to mitigate. As soon as that duty to mitigate arose, the Plaintiff had available to it a then unconditional willingness on the father's part to buy the mobile home.

Second, the father asked the Plaintiff if he could purchase the mobile home in place of his son, and at the time he was ready, willing and able to make the purchase. We cannot agree with the Superior Court's conclusion that the father's offer was too vague to have constituted the foundation for a binding contract when accepted by the Plaintiff.

In any event, the duty to mitigate is more than just a duty to accept legally enforceable offers. Upon learning of the Defendants' breach, the Plaintiff was obligated to take reasonable affirmative measures to keep its losses to a minimum. Palmer's conversation with Frank Gironda, Sr., in September, 1979, revealed that he had a party willing to pay the full price of the mobile home. Regardless of whether the father actually made a valid "offer," the retailer had a duty to pursue this opportunity to minimize the effects of the breach. Instead, the Plaintiff waited another two months and then sold the home for $1,028.69 less than Frank Gironda, Sr., was willing to pay.

There is no evidence in the record that the Plaintiff's failure to sell to its customer's father rested on any legitimate ground. Because the Plaintiff did not take reasonable measures to mitigate its damages, we conclude that the Superior Court erred in awarding it damages based on the ultimate reduction in the selling price of the mobile home. This case must be returned to that court for a recomputation of damages.

* * *

We note * * * that the Plaintiff's failure to sell the home to Frank Gironda, Sr., in September bars recovery of any interest expense incurred after that point in time. * * *

* * *

[Defendants' appeal was granted.]

PROBLEM 3-9

On May 1, 2015 the Illinois Furnace Co. entered into a long-term (6 year) enforceable contract with Ohio Valley Coke, Inc. for the purchase of coke at $40 a ton. Assume that on May 20, 2015, Ohio Valley Coke, Inc. repudiated the contract. At this time, other suppliers were offering long-term contracts at between $50 to $53 a ton. This appreciable increase in price was attributable to flooding in the Ohio Valley that had interfered with the mining of coke during three successive years. Illinois Furnace Co. assumed it could always buy on the spot market and declined to enter into a long-term contract when Ohio Valley repudiated. Six months later, unable to buy sufficient quantities of coke on the spot market, Illinois Furnace was forced to close one of its plants for three weeks at a loss of profit of $450,000. Can Illinois Furnace recover this sum from Ohio Valley Coke, Inc.?

PARKER V. TWENTIETH CENTURY-FOX FILM CORP.

Supreme Court of California, 1970.
3 Cal.3d 176, 474 P.2d 689.

BURKE, JUSTICE.

Defendant Twentieth Century-Fox Film Corporation appeals from a summary judgment granting to plaintiff the recovery of agreed compensation under a written contract for her services as an actress in a motion picture. As will appear, we have concluded that the trial court correctly ruled in plaintiff's favor and that the judgment should be affirmed.

Plaintiff [Shirley MacLaine] is well known as an actress, and in the contract between plaintiff and defendant is sometimes referred to as the "Artist." Under the contract, dated August 6, 1965, plaintiff was to play the female lead in defendant's contemplated production of a motion picture entitled "Bloomer Girl." The contract provided that defendant would pay plaintiff a minimum "guaranteed compensation" of $53,571.42 per week for 14 weeks commencing May 23, 1966, for a total of $750,000. Prior to May 1966 defendant decided not to produce the picture and by a letter dated April 4, 1966, it notified plaintiff of that decision and that it would not "comply with our obligations to you under" the written contract.

By the same letter and with the professed purpose "to avoid any damage to you," defendant instead offered to employ plaintiff as the leading actress in another film tentatively entitled "Big Country, Big Man" (hereinafter, "Big Country"). The compensation offered was identical, as were 31 of the 34 numbered provisions or articles of the original contract.[1] Unlike "Bloomer Girl," however, which was to have been a musical production, "Big Country" was a dramatic "western type" movie. "Bloomer Girl" was to have been filmed in California; "Big Country" was to be produced in Australia. Also, certain terms in the proffered contract varied

---

[1] Among the identical provisions was the following found in the last paragraph of Article 2 of the original contract: "We [defendant] shall not be obligated to utilize your [plaintiff's] services in or in connection with the Photoplay hereunder, our sole obligation, subject to the terms and conditions of this Agreement, being to pay you the guaranteed compensation herein provided for."

from those of the original.[2] Plaintiff was given one week within which to accept; she did not and the offer lapsed. Plaintiff then commenced this action seeking recovery of the agreed guaranteed compensation.

The complaint sets forth two causes of action. The first is for money due under the contract; the second, based upon the same allegations as the first, is for damages resulting from defendant's breach of contract. Defendant in its answer admits the existence and validity of the contract, that plaintiff complied with all the conditions, covenants and promises and stood ready to complete the performance, and that defendant breached and "anticipatorily repudiated" the contract. It denies, however, that any money is due to plaintiff either under the contract or as a result of its breach, and pleads as an affirmative defense to both causes of action plaintiff's allegedly deliberate failure to mitigate damages, asserting that she unreasonably refused to accept its offer of the leading role in "Big Country."

Plaintiff moved for summary judgment under Code of Civil Procedure section 437c, the motion was granted, and summary judgment for $750,000 plus interest was entered in plaintiff's favor. This appeal by defendant followed.

The familiar rules are that the matter to be determined by the trial court on a motion for summary judgment is whether facts have been presented which give rise to a triable factual issue. The court may not pass upon the issue itself. Summary judgment is proper only if the affidavits or declarations[3] in support of the moving party would be sufficient to sustain a judgment in his favor and his opponent does not by affidavit show facts sufficient to present a triable issue of fact. The affidavits of the moving

---

[2] Article 29 of the original contract specified that plaintiff approved the director already chosen for "Bloomer Girl" and that in case he failed to act as director plaintiff was to have approval rights of any substitute director. Article 31 provided that plaintiff was to have the right of approval of the "Bloomer Girl" dance director, and Article 32 gave her the right of approval of the screenplay.

Defendant's letter of April 4 to plaintiff, which contained both defendant's notice of breach of the "Bloomer Girl" contract and offer of the lead in "Big Country," eliminated or impaired each of those rights. It read in part as follows: "The terms and conditions of our offer of employment are identical to those set forth in the 'BLOOMER GIRL' Agreement, Articles 1 through 34 and Exhibit A to the Agreement, except as follows:

"1. Article 31 of said Agreement will not be included in any contract of employment regarding 'BIG COUNTRY, BIG MAN' as it is not a musical and it thus will not need a dance director.

"2. In the 'BLOOMER GIRL' agreement, in Articles 29 and 32, you were given certain director and screenplay approvals and you had preapproved certain matters. Since there simply is insufficient time to negotiate with you regarding your choice of director and regarding the screenplay and since you already expressed an interest in performing the role in 'BIG COUNTRY, BIG MAN,' we must exclude from our offer of employment in 'BIG COUNTRY, BIG MAN' any approval rights as are contained in said Articles 29 and 32; however, we shall consult with you respecting the director to be selected to direct the photoplay and will further consult with you with respect to the screenplay and any revisions or changes therein, provided, however, that if we fail to agree * * * the decision of * * * [defendant] with respect to the selection of a director and to revisions and changes in the said screenplay shall be binding upon the parties to said agreement."

[3] In this opinion "affidavits" includes "declarations under penalty of perjury." (See Code Civ.Proc., § 2015.5.)

party are strictly construed, and doubts as to the propriety of summary judgment should be resolved against granting the motion. Such summary procedure is drastic and should be used with caution so that it does not become a substitute for the open trial method of determining facts. The moving party cannot depend upon allegations in his own pleadings to cure deficient affidavits, nor can his adversary rely upon his own pleadings in lieu or in support of affidavits in opposition to a motion; however, a party can rely on his adversary's pleadings to establish facts not contained in his own affidavits. * * * Also, the court may consider facts stipulated to by the parties and facts which are properly the subject of judicial notice. * * *

As stated, defendant's sole defense to this action which resulted from its deliberate breach of contract is that in rejecting defendant's substitute offer of employment plaintiff unreasonably refused to mitigate damages.

The general rule is that the measure of recovery by a wrongfully discharged employee is the amount of salary agreed upon for the period of service, less the amount which the employer affirmatively proves the employee has earned or with reasonable effort might have earned from other employment. * * * However, before projected earnings from other employment opportunities not sought or accepted by the discharged employee can be applied in mitigation, the employer must show that the other employment was comparable, or substantially similar, to that of which the employee has been deprived; the employee's rejection of or failure to seek other available employment of a different or inferior kind may not be resorted to in order to mitigate damages. * * *

In the present case defendant has raised no issue of *reasonableness of efforts* by plaintiff to obtain other employment; the sole issue is whether plaintiff's refusal of defendant's substitute offer of "Big Country" may be used in mitigation. Nor, if the "Big Country" offer was of employment different or inferior when compared with the original "Bloomer Girl" employment, is there an issue as to whether or not plaintiff acted reasonably in refusing the substitute offer. Despite defendant's arguments to the contrary, no case cited or which our research has discovered holds or suggests that reasonableness is an element of a wrongfully discharged employee's option to reject, or fail to seek, different or inferior employment lest the possible earnings therefrom be charged against him in mitigation of damages.[4]

---

[4] Instead, in each case the reasonableness referred to was that of the *efforts* of the employee to obtain other employment that was not different or inferior: his right to reject the latter was declared as an unqualified rule of law. Thus, Gonzales v. Internat. Assn. of Machinists, 213 Cal.App.2d 817, 823–824, 29 Cal.Rptr. 190, 194, holds that the trial court correctly instructed the jury that plaintiff union member, a machinist, was required to make "such *efforts* as the average [member of his union] desiring employment would make at that particular time and place" (italics added); but, further, that the court *properly rejected* defendant's *offer of proof of* the *availability of other kinds of employment* at the same or higher pay than plaintiff usually received and all outside

Applying the foregoing rules to the record in the present case, with all intendments in favor of the party opposing the summary judgment motion—here, defendant—it is clear that the trial court correctly ruled that plaintiff's failure to accept defendant's tendered substitute employment could not be applied in mitigation of damages because the offer of the "Big Country" lead was of employment both different and inferior, and that no factual dispute was presented on that issue. The mere circumstance that "Bloomer Girl" was to be a musical review calling upon plaintiff's talents as a dancer as well as an actress, and was to be produced in the City of Los Angeles, whereas "Big Country" was a straight dramatic role in a "Western Type" story taking place in an opal mine in Australia, demonstrates the difference in kind between the two employments; the female lead as a dramatic actress in a western style motion picture can by no stretch of imagination be considered the equivalent of or substantially similar to the lead in a song-and-dance production.

Additionally, the substitute "Big Country" offer proposed to eliminate or impair the director and screenplay approvals accorded to plaintiff under the original "Bloomer Girl" contract (see fn. 2, *ante*), and thus constituted an offer of inferior employment. No expertise or judicial notice is required in order to hold that the deprivation or infringement of an employee's rights held under an original employment contract converts the available "other employment" relied upon by the employer to mitigate damages, into inferior employment which the employee need not seek or accept. (See Gonzales v. Internat. Assn. of Machinists, *supra,* 213 Cal.App.2d 817, 823–824, 29 Cal.Rptr. 190 * * *.)

Statements found in affidavits submitted by defendant in opposition to plaintiff's summary judgment motion, to the effect that the "Big Country" offer was not of employment different from or inferior to that under the "Bloomer Girl" contract, merely repeat the allegations of defendant's answer to the complaint in this action, constitute only conclusionary assertions with respect to undisputed facts, and do not give rise to a triable factual issue so as to defeat the motion for summary judgment. * * *

In view of the determination that defendant failed to present any facts showing the existence of a factual issue with respect to its sole defense—plaintiff's rejection of its substitute employment offer in mitigation of

---

the jurisdiction of his union, as plaintiff could not be required to accept different employment or a nonunion job.

In Harris v. Nat. Union, etc., Cooks and Stewards, 116 Cal.App.2d 759, 761, 254 P.2d 673, 676, the issues were stated to be, inter alia, whether comparable employment was open to each plaintiff employee, and if so whether each plaintiff made a *reasonable effort* to secure such employment. It was held that the trial court *properly sustained an objection to an offer to prove a custom of accepting a job in a lower rank* when work in the higher rank was not available, as "The duty of mitigation of damages * * * does not require the plaintiff 'to seek or to accept other employment of a different or inferior kind.' " (p. 764 [5], 254 P.2d p. 676.)

damages—we need not consider plaintiff's further contention that for various reasons, including the provisions of the original contract set forth in footnote 1, *ante,* plaintiff was excused from attempting to mitigate damages.

The judgment is affirmed.

SULLIVAN, ACTING CHIEF JUSTICE (dissenting).

The basic question in this case is whether or not plaintiff acted reasonably in rejecting defendant's offer of alternate employment. The answer depends upon whether that offer (starring in "Big Country, Big Man") was an offer of work that was substantially similar to her former employment (starring in "Bloomer Girl") or of work that was of a different or inferior kind. To my mind this is a factual issue which the trial court should not have determined on a motion for summary judgment. The majority have not only repeated this error but have compounded it by applying the rules governing mitigation of damages in the employer-employee context in a misleading fashion. Accordingly, I respectfully dissent.

The familiar rule requiring a plaintiff in a tort or contract action to mitigate damages embodies notions of fairness and socially responsible behavior which are fundamental to our jurisprudence. Most broadly stated, it precludes the recovery of damages which, through the exercise of due diligence, could have been avoided. Thus, in essence, it is a rule requiring reasonable conduct in commercial affairs. This general principle governs the obligations of an employee after his employer has wrongfully repudiated or terminated the employment contract. Rather than permitting the employee simply to remain idle during the balance of the contract period, the law requires him to make a reasonable effort to secure other employment.[5] He is not obliged, however, to seek or accept any and all types of work which may be available. Only work which is in the same field and which is of the same quality need be accepted.[6]

Over the years the courts have employed various phrases to define the type of employment which the employee, upon his wrongful discharge, is under an obligation to accept. Thus in California alone it has been held that

[5] The issue is generally discussed in terms of a duty on the part of the employee to minimize loss. The practice is long-established and there is little reason to change despite Judge Cardozo's observation of its subtle inaccuracy. "The servant is free to accept employment or reject it according to his uncensored pleasure. What is meant by the supposed duty is merely this: That if he unreasonably reject, he will not be heard to say that the loss of wages from then on shall be deemed the jural consequence of the earlier discharge. He has broken the chain of causation, and loss resulting to him thereafter is suffered through his own act." (McClelland v. Climax Hosiery Mills (1930) 252 N.Y. 347, 359, 169 N.E. 605, 609, concurring opinion.)

[6] This qualification of the rule seems to reflect the simple and humane attitude that it is too severe to demand of a person that he attempt to find and perform work for which he has no training or experience. Many of the older cases hold that one need not accept work in an inferior rank or position nor work which is more menial or arduous. This suggests that the rule may have had its origin in the bourgeois fear of resubmergence in lower economic classes.

he must accept employment which is "substantially similar" * * * "comparable employment" * * * employment "in the same general line of the first employment" * * * "equivalent to his prior position" * * * "employment in a similar capacity" * * * employment which is "not * * * of a different or inferior kind. * * * "

* * *

For reasons which are unexplained, the majority cite several of these cases yet select from among the various judicial formulations which contain one particular phrase, "Not of a different or inferior kind," with which to analyze this case. I have discovered no historical or theoretical reason to adopt this phrase, which is simply a negative restatement of the affirmative standards set out in the above cases, as the exclusive standard. Indeed, its emergence is an example of the dubious phenomenon of the law responding not to rational judicial choice or changing social conditions, but to unrecognized changes in the language of opinions or legal treatises. However, the phrase is a serviceable one and my concern is not with its use as the standard but rather with what I consider its distortion.

The relevant language excuses acceptance only of employment which is of a *different kind.* * * * It has never been the law that the mere existence of *differences between two jobs in the same field* is sufficient, as a matter of law, to excuse an employee wrongfully discharged from one from accepting the other in order to mitigate damages. Such an approach would effectively eliminate any obligation of an employee to attempt to minimize damage arising from a wrongful discharge. The only alternative job offer an employee would be required to accept would be an offer of his former job by his former employer.

Although the majority appear to hold that there was a difference "in kind" between the employment offered plaintiff in "Bloomer Girl" and that offered in "Big Country" * * * an examination of the opinion makes crystal clear that the majority merely point out differences between the two *films* (an obvious circumstance) and then apodically assert that these constitute a difference in the *kind* of *employment.* [Eds. note: a student pointed out to us that Justice Sullivan meant "apodictically"—pretty impressive, don't you think?] The entire rationale of the majority boils down to this: that the *"mere circumstances"* that "Bloomer Girl" was to be a musical review while "Big Country" was a straight drama "demonstrates the difference in kind" since a female lead in a western is not "the equivalent of or substantially similar to" a lead in a musical. This is merely attempting to prove the proposition by repeating it. It shows that the vehicles for the display of the star's talents are different but it does not prove that her employment as a star in such vehicles is of necessity different *in kind* and either inferior or superior.

I believe that the approach taken by the majority (a superficial listing of differences with no attempt to assess their significance) may subvert a valuable legal doctrine.[7] The inquiry in cases such as this should not be whether differences between the two jobs exist (there will always be differences) but whether the differences which are present are substantial enough to constitute differences in the *kind* of employment or, alternatively, whether they render the substitute work employment of an *inferior kind.*

It seems to me that *this* inquiry involves, in the instant case at least, factual determinations which are improper on a motion for summary judgment. Resolving whether or not one job is substantially similar to another or whether, on the other hand, it is of a different or inferior kind, will often (as here) require a critical appraisal of the similarities and differences between them in light of the importance of these differences to the employee. This necessitates a weighing of the evidence, and it is precisely this undertaking which is forbidden on summary judgment. (Garlock v. Cole (1962) 199 Cal.App.2d 11, 14, 18 Cal.Rptr. 393.)

This is not to say that summary judgment would never be available in an action by an employee in which the employer raises the defense of failure to mitigate damages. No case has come to my attention, however, in which summary judgment has been granted on the issue of whether an employee was obliged to accept available alternate employment. Nevertheless, there may well be cases in which the substitute employment is so manifestly of a dissimilar or inferior sort, the declarations of the plaintiff so complete and those of the defendant so conclusionary and inadequate that no factual issues exist for which a trial is required. This, however, is not such a case.

It is not intuitively obvious, to me at least, that the leading female role in a dramatic motion picture is a radically different endeavor from the leading female role in a musical comedy film. Nor is it plain to me that the rather qualified rights of director and screenplay approval contained in the first contract are highly significant matters either in the entertainment industry in general or to this plaintiff in particular. Certainly, none of the declarations introduced by plaintiff in support of her motion shed any light on these issues. Nor do they attempt to explain why she declined the offer of starring in "Big Country, Big Man." Nevertheless, the trial court granted the motion, declaring that these approval rights were "critical" and that their elimination altered "the essential nature of the employment."

---

[7] The values of the doctrine of mitigation of damages in this context are that it minimizes the unnecessary personal and social (e.g., nonproductive use of labor, litigation) costs of contractual failure. If a wrongfully discharged employee can, through his own action and without suffering financial or psychological loss in the process, reduce the damages accruing from the breach of contract, the most sensible policy is to require him to do so. I fear the majority opinion will encourage precisely opposite conduct.

The plaintiff's declarations were of no assistance to the trial court in its effort to justify reaching this conclusion on summary judgment. Instead, it was forced to rely on judicial notice of the definitions of "motion picture," "screenplay" and "director" (Evid.Code, § 451, subd. (e)) and then on judicial notice of practices in the film industry which were purportedly of "common knowledge." (Evid.Code, § 451, subd. (f) or § 452, subd. (g).) This use of judicial notice was error. Evidence Code section 451, subdivision (e) was never intended to authorize resort to the dictionary to solve essentially factual questions which do not turn upon conventional linguistic usage. More important, however, the trial court's notice of "facts commonly known" violated Evidence Code section 455, subdivision (a). Before this section was enacted there were no procedural safeguards affording litigants an opportunity to be heard as to the propriety of taking judicial notice of a matter or as to the tenor of the matter to be noticed. Section 455 makes such an opportunity (which may be an element of due process, see Evid.Code, § 455, Law Revision Com. Comment (a)) mandatory and its provisions should be scrupulously adhered to. "Judicial notice can be a valuable tool in the adversary system for the lawyer as well as the court" (Kongsgaard, Judicial Notice (1966) 18 Hastings L.J. 117, 140) and its use is appropriate on motions for summary judgment. Its use in this case, however, to determine on summary judgment issues fundamental to the litigation without complying with statutory requirements of notice and hearing is a highly improper effort to "cut the Gordion knot of involved litigation." (Silver Land & Dev. Co. v. California Land Title Co. (1967) 248 Cal.App.2d 241, 242, 56 Cal.Rptr. 178, 179.)

The majority do not confront the trial court's misuse of judicial notice. They avoid this issue through the expedient of declaring that neither judicial notice nor expert opinion (such as that contained in the declarations in opposition to the motion) is necessary to reach the trial court's conclusion. *Something,* however, clearly *is* needed to support this conclusion. Nevertheless, the majority make no effort to justify the judgment through an examination of the plaintiff's declarations. Ignoring the obvious insufficiency of these declarations, the majority announce that "the deprivation or infringement of an employee's rights held under an original employment contract" changes the alternate employment offered or available into employment of an inferior kind.

I cannot accept the proposition that an offer which eliminates *any* contract right, regardless of its significance, is, as a matter of law, an offer of employment of an inferior kind. Such an absolute rule seems no more sensible than the majority's earlier suggestion that the mere existence of differences between two jobs is sufficient to render them employment of different kinds. Application of such per se rules will severely undermine the principle of mitigation of damages in the employer-employee context.

I remain convinced that the relevant question in such cases is whether or not a particular contract provision is so significant that its omission create employment of an inferior kind. This question is, of course, intimately bound up in what I consider the ultimate issue: whether or not the employee acted reasonably. This will generally involve a factual inquiry to ascertain the importance of the particular contract term and a process of weighing the absence of that term against the countervailing advantages of the alternate employment. In the typical case, this will mean that summary judgment must be withheld.

In the instant case, there was nothing properly before the trial court by which the importance of the approval rights could be ascertained, much less evaluated. Thus, in order to grant the motion for summary judgment, the trial court misused judicial notice. In upholding the summary judgment, the majority here rely upon per se rules which distort the process of determining whether or not an employee is obliged to accept particular employment in mitigation of damages.

I believe that the judgment should be reversed so that the issue of whether or not the offer of the lead role in "Big Country, Big Man" was of employment comparable to that of the lead role in "Bloomer Girl" may be determined at trial.

Rehearing denied; SULLIVAN, J., dissenting.

HILLMAN, KEEPING THE DEAL TOGETHER AFTER MATERIAL BREACH—COMMON LAW MITIGATION RULES, THE UCC, AND THE RESTATEMENT (SECOND) OF CONTRACTS

47 U. Colo. L. Rev. 553, 559–60 (1976).

Under the rule of avoidable consequences, the injured party must, when reasonable, make substitute agreements with third parties to avoid loss from the breach. The extent to which the injured party must deal with the breaching party to avoid loss is less clear. Many courts are mindful that upon material breach an injured party is entitled to cease performance, treat the contract as ended, and seek damages. These courts, perhaps unwilling to allow the breaching party to "escape" full liability, are reluctant to apply the avoidable consequences rule when the only alternative, or the least damaging alternative for the injured party, is to accept a new offer from the breaching party. These courts have, in effect, taken the fact-finding function away from the jury by deciding that it is *never* reasonable to deal further with the breacher.

Such decisions often view the contract breaker as one who should not be "rewarded" for the breach by "requiring" the injured party to accept the new offer. They focus on the "bad" actions of the contract breaker rather than on making the injured party whole. * * *

PROBLEM 3-10

Alan Turlway calls your law office and tells you that Arlo Electronics has wrongfully fired him from his job as a television salesperson. Alan had a contract for one more year of employment, but Arlo's business was slow. Alan was earning $275 per week. He tells you that he has been offered employment at Teale Electronics as a computer salesperson for $300 per week for one year. Teale Electronics is 20 miles from Alan's home, however, whereas Arlo Electronics is only five miles away, and Alan is reluctant to accept. He asks you whether he should take the job, and what the consequences will be if he does not. Advise Alan. What further information would you seek?

IN RE WORLDCOM, INC.

United States Bankruptcy Court, Southern District of New York, 2007.
361 B.R. 675.

Opinion Regarding Cross-Motions for Summary Judgment Brought Separately by Michael Jordan and Worldcom, Inc.

ARTHUR J. GONZALEZ, BANKRUPTCY JUDGE.

Introduction

Before the Court are cross-motions for summary judgment separately brought by Michael Jordan ("Jordan") and WorldCom, Inc. (hereafter referred to as the "Debtors" or "MCI").

Background

On or about July 10, 1995, Jordan and the Debtors entered into an endorsement agreement (the "Agreement"). At that time, Jordan was considered to be one of the most popular athletes in the world. The Agreement granted MCI a ten-year license to use Jordan's name, likeness, "other attributes," and personal services to advertise and promote MCI's telecommunications products and services beginning in September 1995 and ending in August 2005. The Agreement did not prevent Jordan from endorsing most other products or services, although he could not endorse the same products or services that MCI produced. In addition to a $5 million signing bonus, the Agreement provided an annual base compensation of $2 million for Jordan. The Agreement provided that Jordan would be treated as an independent contractor and that MCI would not withhold any amount from Jordan's compensation for tax purposes. The Agreement provided that Jordan was to make himself available for four days, not to exceed four hours per day, during each contract year to produce television commercials and print advertising and for promotional appearances. The parties agreed that the advertising and promotional materials would be submitted to Jordan for his approval, which could not be unreasonably withheld, fourteen days prior to their release to the general public. From 1995 to 2000, Jordan appeared in several television commercials and a large number of print ads for MCI.

On July 1, 2002, MCI commenced a case under chapter 11 of title 11 of the United States Code (the "Bankruptcy Code") in the Bankruptcy Court for the Southern District of New York. On January 16, 2003, Jordan filed Claim No. 11414 in the amount of $2 million plus contingent and unliquidated amounts allegedly due under the Agreement. On July 18, 2003, the Debtors rejected the Agreement as of that date, pursuant to § 365(a) of the Bankruptcy Code. Following that rejection of the Agreement, Jordan filed Claim No. 36077 (the "Claim") in the amount of $8 million-seeking $2 million for each of the payments that were due in June of 2002, 2003, 2004, and 2005. MCI does not object to the Claim to the extent Jordan seeks $4 million for the 2002 and 2003 payments under the Agreement. As of the rejection in July 2003, two years remained under the Agreement.

The Parties' Contentions

MCI asserts two bases for disallowance of the Claim. One, MCI contends that the Agreement is an "employment contract" within the meaning of section 502(b)(7) of the Bankruptcy Code and that Jordan's claim is "capped" pursuant to that section. [Discussion of this contention is omitted.] Second, MCI argues that Jordan had an obligation to mitigate his damages and failed to do so. MCI argues that these two bases entitle it to summary judgment with respect to its objection to the Claim * * *.

Jordan argues for summary judgment allowing the Claim in full and overruling and dismissing MCI's objections to the Claim. * * *. Regarding MCI's mitigation argument, Jordan argues that the objection should be overruled and dismissed for three independent reasons (1) Jordan was a "lost volume seller" and thus mitigation does not apply, (2) there is no evidence that Jordan could have entered into a "substantially similar" endorsement agreement, and (3) Jordan acted reasonably when he decided not to pursue other endorsements after MCI's rejection of the Agreement.

Discussion

* * *

C. *Mitigation*

* * *

Whether Jordan Was a "Lost Volume Seller"

Jordan argues that MCI's mitigation defense does not apply here because Jordan is akin to a "lost volume seller." Jordan points to testimony demonstrating that he could have entered into additional endorsement contracts even if MCI had not rejected the Agreement. Thus, he argues, any additional endorsement contracts would not have been substitutes for the Agreement and would not have mitigated the damages for which MCI is liable.

"A lost volume seller is one who has the capacity to perform the contract that was breached in addition to other potential contracts due to unlimited resources or production capacity." *Precision Pine & Timber, Inc. v. United States,* 72 Fed.Cl. 460, 490 (Fed.Cl.2006). A lost volume seller does not minimize its damages by entering into another contract because it would have had the benefit of both contracts even if the first were not breached. * * * The lost volume seller has two expectations, the profit from the breached contract and the profit from one or more other contracts that it could have performed at the same time as the breached contract. * * *

This case offers a twist on the typical lost volume seller situation. In what the Court regards as the typical situation, the non-breaching seller has a near-inexhaustible supply of inventory. *See, e.g., Katz Commc'ns, Inc. v. Evening News Ass'n,* 705 F.2d 20, 26 (2d Cir.1983). In the typical situation, when a buyer breaches an agreement to buy a good or service from the seller, the item is returned to inventory and the lost volume seller continues in its efforts to sell its goods or services. However, the transactions that occur following the breach are not necessarily the result of the breach but fundamentally the result of the seller continuing efforts to market its goods and services. It is this continuous effort coupled with a virtually limitless supply that warrants the lost volume exception to mitigation. As stated above, the transactions that may occur after the breach would in the context of the lost volume seller have occurred independent of the breach. Here, Jordan lacked a nearly limitless supply and had no intention of continuing to market his services as a product endorser.

* * *

To claim lost volume seller status, Jordan must establish that he would have had the benefit of both the original and subsequent contracts if MCI had not rejected the Agreement. * * * Although there is no definitive set of elements that the non-breaching party must show, many cases seem to follow the language from the Restatement (2d), Section 347, that the non-breaching party must show that it "could and would have entered into" a subsequent agreement. *See, e.g.,* * * * Green Tree Financial, 2002 WL 31163072, at *9 ("[t]o recover lost profits under this theory, a non-breaching party must prove three things: (1) that the seller of services had the capability to perform both contracts simultaneously; (2) that the second contract would have been profitable; and (3) that the seller of service would have entered into the second contract if the first contract had not been terminated").

In his arguments, Jordan focuses primarily on his *capacity* to enter subsequent agreements, arguing that the loss of MCI's sixteen-hour annual time commitment hardly affected his ability to perform additional endorsement services. On this prong alone, Jordan likely would be considered a lost volume seller of endorsement services because he had sufficient time to do multiple endorsements. Although he does not have the "infinite capacity" that some cases discuss, a services provider does not need unlimited capacity but must have the requisite capacity and intent to perform under multiple contracts at the same time. * * *

Contrary to Jordan's analysis, courts do not focus solely on the seller's capacity. The seller claiming lost volume status must also demonstrate that it *would* have entered into subsequent transactions. * * *). Jordan has not shown he could and *would have* entered into a subsequent agreement. Rather, the evidence shows that Jordan did not have the "subjective intent" to take on additional endorsements. * * * The testimony from Jordan's representatives establishes that although Jordan's popularity enabled him to obtain additional product endorsements in 2003, Jordan desired to scale back his level of endorsements. Jordan's financial and business advisor, Curtis Polk ("Polk"), testified that at the time the Agreement was rejected, Jordan's desire was "not to expand his spokesperson or pitchman efforts with new relationships." *See* Debtors' Mot. Summ. J., App. 5, at 32. Polk testified that had Jordan wanted to do additional endorsements after the 2003 rejection, he could have obtained additional deals. *See id.* at 64–65. Jordan's agent, David Falk ("Falk"), testified that "there might have been twenty more companies that in theory might have wanted to sign him" but that Jordan and his representatives wanted to avoid diluting his image. *See* Debtors' Mot. Summ J., App. 6, at 24. Jordan's Memorandum for Summary Judgment stated that at the time the Agreement was rejected, Jordan had implemented a strategy of not accepting new endorsements because of a belief that new deals would jeopardize his ability to achieve his primary goal of National Basketball Association ("NBA") franchise ownership.

One of the classic examples of the lost volume seller is found in *Neri v. Retail Marine Corp.,* 30 N.Y.2d 393, 399–400, 334 N.Y.S.2d 165, 169–70, 285 N.E.2d 311 (N.Y.1972):

> [I]f a private party agrees to sell his automobile to a buyer for $2,000, a breach by the buyer would cause the seller no loss (except incidental damages, i.e., expense of a new sale) if the seller was able to sell the automobile to another buyer for $2,000. But the situation is different with dealers having an unlimited supply or standard-priced goods. Thus, if an automobile dealer agrees to sell a car to a buyer at the standard price of $2,000, a breach by the buyer injures the dealer, even though he is able to sell the automobile to another for $2,000. If the dealer has an inexhaustible supply of cars, the resale to replace the breaching buyer costs the dealer a sale, because, had the breaching buyer

> performed, the dealer would have made two sales instead of one. The buyer's breach, in such a case, depletes the dealer's sales to the extent of one, and the measure of damages should be the dealer's profit on one sale.

This example would surely have a different result if the car dealership was winding down its business and had agreed to sell one of its last cars to a buyer. If that buyer subsequently breached the contract and did not purchase the car, the dealership could hardly be expected to recover lost profits damages if the dealer put the car back onto a deserted car lot, made no attempts to sell it, and kept the dealership shuttered to new customers. Those modifications are analogous to Jordan's situation, with his stated desire to withdraw his services from the endorsement marketplace, and the lost volume seller theory accordingly does not apply to his circumstances.

Jordan states that it is a "red herring" to speculate under the lost volume analysis on what he *would* have done because that

> ignores the central point of the lost volume principle: if Jordan had * * * accepted a substantially similar endorsement opportunity—exactly what [MCI] argues he was required to do to mitigate damages—the damages for which [MCI] is liable would not have been reduced by one penny because the lost volume principle would allow Jordan to retain the benefits of both the [MCI] Agreement and the hypothetical additional endorsement.

See Michael Jordan's Reply Brief, at 14–15.

Jordan overlooks an important point about the lost volume seller theory-that the "original sale and the second sale are independent events," *Snyder,* 380 A.2d at 625, because the lost volume seller's intent to enter into new contracts is the same before and after a purchaser's breach. The lost volume seller's desire to sell more units of goods or services is virtually unaffected by the loss of a single sale or agreement.

Next, even if Jordan had mitigated damages by entering one subsequent endorsement agreement, this, without more, does not mean that Jordan was a lost volume seller. The lost volume seller has the intent and capacity to sell multiple units despite the breach of a contract for one transaction.

Finally, if Jordan had entered into a subsequent agreement or agreements, and if he had showed both the capacity and the intent to make subsequent sales, that might have had the effect of helping him to establish his status as a lost volume seller, which generally would relieve him of the duty to mitigate. This would not be a novel situation but it ignores the fact that he did not do so. * * *

Because the evidence establishes, among other things, that Jordan would not have entered into subsequent agreements, Jordan has not established that he is a lost volume seller. This theory thus does not relieve Jordan from the duty to mitigate damages.

[The court went on to find that Jordan "did not take affirmative steps to mitigate damages." In part, the court reasoned as follows:] In arguing that Jordan acted reasonably by avoiding further endorsements based on a belief that those efforts would harm his business interests or reputation, Jordan argues essentially that he would be harmed by doing precisely what he originally contracted to do under the Agreement and what he has been doing for other clients for a number of years—endorsing products and services. The Court recognizes the possibility of Jordan's market saturation being a valid concern but Jordan's argument that he wanted to get out of endorsements to pursue other ventures does not relieve the duty to mitigate. Furthermore, MCI's expert stated that an additional endorsement agreement would not have harmed Jordan's reputation by either diminishing Jordan's image in the endorsement marketplace or harming Jordan's goal of becoming an NBA team owner. *See* Debtors' Reply Memo, Exh. C. at 91, 58 (pointing out that other NBA franchise owners have multiple business interests). Jordan has not asserted any facts to refute those assertions nor did he undermine the credibility of the expert making such assertions. Based on the foregoing, there is a no genuine issue of material fact as to whether reasonable endorsement efforts done to mitigate damages would have harmed Jordan's reputation. The Court notes that even if there were a genuine issue of material fact as to whether another endorsement would negatively impact his becoming an NBA team owner * * * such would be irrelevant to the issue of mitigation regarding his endorsement contract.

* * *

Conclusion

* * * MCI's motion for summary judgment is granted in part and denied in part. * * * To the extent MCI claimed that Jordan failed to mitigate damages, MCI's motion is granted in part. The Court finds that Jordan failed to mitigate damages but a further evidentiary hearing is necessary to determine what Jordan could have received had he made reasonable efforts to mitigate, a determination that consequently will affect the Claim.

The Debtors are to settle an order consistent with this opinion.

C. THE CERTAINTY PRINCIPLE

EVERGREEN AMUSEMENT CORP. V. MILSTEAD

Court of Appeals of Maryland, 1955.
206 Md. 610, 112 A.2d 901.

HAMMOND, JUDGE.

The Evergreen Amusement Corporation, the appellant, operator of a drive-in movie theater, was held liable by the court, sitting without a jury, to Harold D. Milstead, the appellee, a contractor, for the balance due on a written contract for the clearing and grading of the site of the theater and certain extras, less the cost of completing a part of the work and damages for delay in completion, based on rental value of the theater property during the period of delay and out-of-pocket costs for that time.

The appellant, by counterclaim, sought recovery of lost profits for the period of delay. The court held the amount claimed to have been so lost to be too uncertain and speculative, and refused evidence proffered to support appellant's theory. * * *

* * *

The real reliance of the Evergreen Amusement Corporation is on the slowness of the contractor in completing the work. It says that the resulting delay in the opening of the theater from June first to the middle of August cost it twelve thousand five hundred dollars in profits. It proffered a witness to testify that he had built and operated a majority of the drive-in theaters in the area, that he is in the theater equipment business and familiar with the profits that drive-in theaters make in the area, that a market survey was made in the area before the site of the theater was selected, and that it had shown the need for such a theater in the neighborhood. It was said he would testify as to the reasonably anticipated profits during the months in question by comparing the months in its second year of operation with those in which it could not operate the year before, and would say that the profits would have been the same. His further testimony would be, it was claimed, that weather conditions, the population, and competition were all approximately the same in the year the theater opened and the following year.

We think the court did not err in refusing the proffered evidence. Under the great weight of authority, the general rule clearly is that loss of profit is a definite element of damages in an action for breach of contract or in an action for harming an established business which has been operating for a sufficient length of time to afford a basis of estimation with some degree of certainty as to the probable loss of profits, but that, on the other hand, loss of profits from a business which has not gone into operation may not be recovered because they are merely speculative and incapable of being ascertained with the requisite degree of certainty. Restatement, Contracts, Sec. 331, states the law to be that damages are recoverable for profits prevented by breach of contract "only to the extent that the evidence affords a sufficient basis for estimating their amount in money with reasonable certainty", and that where the evidence does not afford a sufficient basis, "damages may be measured by the rental value of the property." Comment "d" says this: "If the defendant's breach has prevented the plaintiff from carrying on *a well-established business,* the amount of profits thereby prevented is often capable of proof with reasonable certainty. On the basis of its past history, a reasonable prediction can be made as to its future." (Italics supplied.) * * * See also The Requirement of Certainty for Proof of Lost Profits, 64 Harvard Law 317. The article discusses the difficulties of proving with sufficient certainty the profits which were lost, and then says: "These difficulties have given rise to a rule in some states that no new business can recover for its lost profits." While this Court has not laid down a flat rule (and does not hereby do so), nevertheless, no case has permitted recovery of lost profits under comparable circumstances. In Abbott v. Gatch, 13 Md. 314, the claim for loss of profits arose because of delay in completion of a flour mill. The Court held that the mill owner's loss was to be established by fair rental value for the time of the delay resulting from failure to complete it according to contract, that he could not recover estimated profits, because it was dependent, as they were, upon the quality of flour available, the fluctuation of prices of flour, continuance of the mill in running order and other variants. The Court labelled the damages claimed speculative and refused to follow a Vermont case which had allowed them to be shown. The rule laid down in this case has been followed in a number of others. In Winslow Elevator & Machine Co. v. Hoffman, 107 Md. 621, 69 A. 394, 17 L.R.A., N.S., 1130, an elevator was not installed within the specified time and was defective. The owner sought to recover loss of rents because of the refusal of prospective tenants to lease offices and the moving out of others. The Court followed Abbott v. Gatch, supra, and held that the claim for loss of rentals must be denied as too uncertain and remote. * * *

* * *

We think that the case below was tried and decided without reversible error.

Judgment affirmed, with costs.

NOTE:
THE NEW BUSINESS RULE TODAY

The "new business rule" of Evergreen Amusement Corp. is in decline. See, e.g., Tilley v. Malvern National Bank, 532 S.W.3d 570, 579 (Ark. 2017) (overturning a *per se* new-business rule preventing recovery of lost profits).

Some courts find it "grossly unfair" to deny recovery of lost profits where the defendant's breach prevented the plaintiff from establishing the amount of lost profits. See, e.g., Drews Co. v. Ledwith-Wolfe Assoc., Inc., 296 S.C. 207, 371 S.E.2d 532 (1988). Other courts are wary of denying recovery of lost profits to a new business because doing so would encourage parties contracting with such businesses to breach. Vickers v. Wichita State University, 213 Kan. 614, 518 P.2d 512 (1974). Many courts allow for the recovery of a new business's lost profits when there is "a reasonably certain factual basis for computation of probable losses." Earle M. Jorgensen Co. v. Tesmer Mfg. Co., 10 Ariz.App. 445, 450, 459 P.2d 533, 538 (1969); see also Act II Jewelry, LLC v. Wooten, 318 F.Supp.3d 1073 (N.D. Ill. 2018) (Illinois follows the new businesses rule, but the presumption may be overcome if the party claiming lost profits can prove them to a reasonable degree of certainty); American Heritage, Inc. v. Nevada Gold & Casino, Inc., 259 S.W.3d 816, 825 (Tex.App. 2008) ("The mere fact that the breached agreement contemplated a new business with no prior history of profits * * * does not bar recovery under a lost profits measure as too speculative, uncertain, or remote."); Kenford Company, Inc. v. County of Erie, 108 A.D.2d 132, 141, 489 N.Y.S.2d 939, 946 (1985) (no strict rule against new business recovering lost profits; only a rule of evidence "permitting recovery of lost profits if there is some rational basis on which to calculate such an award"). For cases enforcing the new business rule, see Kinesoft Dev. Corp. v. Softbank Holdings, Inc., 139 F. Supp. 2d 869 (N.D. Ill. 2001); Hunters Intl. Man. Corp. v. Christiana Metals Corp., 561 F. Supp. 614 (E.D.Mich.1982). For a more thorough discussion of the new business rule today, see Kinesoft Dev. Corp. v. Softbank Holdings, Inc., 139 F. Supp. 2d 869 (N.D. Ill. 2001).

PIER 1 CRUISE EXPERTS V. REVELEX CORP.

U.S. Court of Appeals, 11th Cir., 2019.
929 F.3d 1334.

[Pier 1, a travel agency, sought breach of contract damages from Revelex, a software contractor, for failing to complete delivery of software to enhance Pier 1's booking capabilities. One issue was whether the district court correctly denied Pier 1's claim for lost profits.]

NEWSOM, CIRCUIT JUDGE:

Pier 1's lost-profits claim rested on the testimony of its financial manager, Mariana Peres, who was not tendered as an expert but rather appeared as a lay witness. Peres projected that if Revelex's software had worked, Pier 1 would "actually [have] double[d] the number of cruises" sold through online channels alone, which would have meant selling about one additional cruise per month either directly or through its sub-agents. Peres further testified that Pier 1 brings in revenue, on average, of $1,000 per cruise. She also predicted a 10% increase in Pier 1's expenses. Peres based her calculation on Pier 1's historical sales and its experience in the Brazilian cruise industry. When Revelex objected that Peres, as a lay witness, was attempting to offer expert testimony, the district court agreed and cut off her testimony. Pier 1 presented no other evidence pertaining to lost profits, and the district court later granted judgment as a matter of law against its lost-profits claim.

We agree with the district court's determination that Pier 1's lost-profits calculation was too speculative to proceed and that, without it, the evidence regarding lost profits was legally insufficient. The district court correctly concluded that Peres seemed to have "decided to pick a number out of thin air" to conclude that Pier 1 could have sold "double[ ]" the number of cruises that sold through conventional means. Peres's lone justification for her assertion that Pier 1 would have doubled its sales was that "[she] considered [it] a very reasonable [estimate] because [Pier 1] would have a new market" and "other distribution channels" with the new software. To be sure, she testified that she did some "market research" on "e-commerce in Brazil," but she never explained why it was reasonably certain that Pier 1 would sell twice as many cruises online as it had sold offline.

Peres's calculation of Pier 1's increased expenses—10%—was also impermissibly speculative. She projected that expenses would grow as a result of both the costs of marketing the software's benefits and inflation in Brazil. With respect to her particular number, she testified that she "went ahead and added ten percent to all of [Pier 1's] expenses" because it "would be reasonable to have an additional ten percent in order to include all of the different market variations"—meaning "inflation and anything else that might come up." Peres testified that "it was [her] intent to be conservative with respect to the calculations," but her choice to peg the expense increase at 10% also seems to have come out of "thin air."

Because the district court cut Peres's testimony short, Pier 1's only surviving evidence of lost profits was its historical revenues and expenses. But from Pier 1's past *offline* sales the jury could only speculate about the profits it might have lost from missed *online* opportunities. For example, Pier 1 didn't establish how the jury could have concluded that the hypothetical individuals who would have bought cruises online were new customers, rather than old customers who had switched from offline to online purchasing. And because Pier 1 acknowledged that no comparable businesses existed—it said that it would have been the first Brazilian travel agency to offer online bookings in Portuguese—it provided no "yardstick" by which the jury could calculate lost online sales. Finally, as the district court explained, unlike the ordinary lost-profits case, "[i]n this case, we're not talking about losing business; we're talking about not gaining business." Pier 1, that is, wasn't being denied existing sales as a result of Revelex's failure to deliver the customized software; customers could continue to book cruises over the phone or in person. Instead, Pier 1 had hoped to add a new method of distribution through online bookings, which it claimed Revelex had failed to deliver. Again, though, Pier 1 didn't present sufficient evidence by which the jury could calculate the resulting lost profits with reasonable certainty.

The district court correctly granted Revelex judgment as a matter of law on Pier 1's lost-profits claim.

BEN-SHAHAR AND BERNSTEIN, THE SECRECY INTEREST IN CONTRACT LAW

109 Yale L.J. 1885, 1886–89 (2000).

* * * When a breach occurs and expectation damages are sought, the expectation measure will often include lost profit. Lost profit is typically calculated on the basis of business information related to the promisee's operations, such as materials and labor costs, inventory size, availability of alternative suppliers, the identity of her downstream contracting partners (customers), and, in the case of newer businesses, her business plan. This and other information revealed during the discovery process may be information that the promisee would prefer to keep private. [For example] revealing the information might damage her bargaining position in future contract negotiations with this or another transactor and might lead to her having to pay a higher price in future transactions. The promisee's weakened bargaining position arises not only because the promisor will know that, in the event of breach, he will have to pay higher damages, but also, and more importantly, because he will learn the true value of performance to the promisee. Knowing the value of performance to the promisee should enable the promisor to extract a greater share of the bargaining surplus in subsequent transactions. * * * More generally, to the extent that the value of a firm is based on the value of the private information it possesses—whether this information takes the form of a customer list or any of a variety of forms of intellectual property—legal rules that require the revelation of this information in order to obtain a remedy for breach of contract or to enforce any other substantive legal right, may be undesirable.

Recognizing that an aggrieved party will often prefer to keep the information necessary to establish the magnitude of expectation damages private suggests that while the traditional literature on remedies has focused on the aggrieved party's interest in being made whole (her "compensatory interest"), there is another, potentially conflicting interest that needs to be taken into account, namely her desire to keep information private (her "secrecy interest"). Although the secrecy interest and the compensatory interest are often in direct conflict, they cannot be reconciled simply by elevating one over the other ex post. When the secrecy interest is sufficiently strong, the cost of revealing the underlying private information may well exceed the aggrieved party's expected recovery at trial. As a consequence, the aggrieved party may not file suit and may therefore receive no compensation. Because the existence of the promisee's secrecy interest will often be known to a promisor who has either breached or is contemplating breach, the secrecy interest may undermine the credibility of the promisee's threat to sue.

D. EMOTIONAL DISTRESS AND OTHER DAMAGES ISSUES

CHRUM V. CHARLES HEATING AND COOLING, INC.

Court of Appeals of Michigan, 1982.
121 Mich. App. 17, 327 N.W.2d 568.

GILLESPIE, JUDGE.

In November 1978, Mr. and Mrs. Chrum (hereinafter plaintiffs) purchased a furnace from the defendant, Charles Heating & Cooling, Inc., which the defendant agreed to, and did, install.

On April 11, 1979, the furnace caused a fire which destroyed the plaintiffs' home and its contents. There were no physical injuries. Mr. and Mrs. Chrum were insured by plaintiff State Farm Fire & Casualty Company, who paid the Chrums $43,782.49 as a result of the loss.

State Farm Fire & Casualty Company commenced an action against Charles Heating & Cooling, Inc. on October 17, 1979, seeking subrogation. On December 10, 1979, Mr. and Mrs. Chrum filed a separate action seeking additional compensation for economic loss, alleging negligence in installation. The complaint alleged that the defendant "carelessly, recklessly and negligently" installed the furnace and:

> "9. That as a direct and proximate result of Defendant's negligence and breach of implied warranties, Plaintiffs have suffered loss of their home, household effects and personal belongings. In addition, Plaintiffs have suffered emotional distress, fright, mental anguish and loss of income."

The action brought by the Chrums was consolidated with the action brought by State Farm. Defendant moved for partial summary judgment, pursuant to GCR 1963, 117.2(1), with respect to plaintiffs' emotional distress claim. The trial court denied defendant's motion, stating:

> "It would be the Court's opinion that it is more personal to the purchasers than it would be commercial. We're not talking about a contract to pay money. We're talking about a thing—at least in Michigan—which is essential for life—at least in the months of November through March. Without it, we could not live. It therefore becomes noncommercial, and not in any way commercial to the pecuniary interests of the purchasers.

> "It is likely that if—most reasonable people, at least, would likely conclude that a furnace is a potentially dangerous item. It can blow up. It can cause fires. I'm sure there's all sorts of other things that can happen as a result of a defective furnace, which not only could cause total destruction of what could be a married couple's property, but it could be their total economic picture—their total marital estate—which, today, normally is a home and all their furniture; and it would be reasonable for this Court to conclude that someone selling a furnace understands the potential and foresees the fact that if there are problems or difficulties with the furnace, they could be totally disruptive to the purchaser's life; and if someone were to lose their home, all their contents, all their personal belongings, that certainly would be likely to cause a great deal of emotional distress, and mental anguish would have to necessarily result."

The remaining claims against defendant were dismissed following a settlement, leaving only the mental distress claim. By order entered August 7, 1981, defendant's application for leave to appeal the trial court's denial of the motion for partial summary judgment was granted.

The law governing damages for mental distress in contract cases was enunciated by the Michigan Supreme Court in the case of *Kewin v. Massachusetts Mutual Life Ins. Co.,* 409 Mich. 401, 295 N.W.2d 50 (1980), *reh. den.,* 409 Mich. 1116 (1980). In that case, the Supreme Court relied upon the rule of *Hadley v. Baxendale,* 9 Exch. 341, 156 Eng.Rep. 145 (1854), and held that damages recoverable for breach of contract are generally limited to damages arising naturally from the breach or contemplated by the parties at the time the contract is made. Where an action is for a breach of a commercial contract, damages for mental distress are not recoverable.

The Supreme Court in *Kewin* recognized a general exception to the above rule, developed in *Stewart v. Rudner,* 349 Mich. 459, 84 N.W.2d 816 (1957). In *Stewart,* plaintiff sued her doctor for breach of an agreement to deliver her child by Caesarean section, alleging that his breach resulted in the stillbirth of her child. The Court allowed damages for mental distress, holding that where the contract breached is a personal agreement involving matters of "mental concern and solicitude", damages for emotional suffering are recoverable. 349 Mich. at 471, 84 N.W.2d 816. See also *Avery v. Arnold Home, Inc.,* 17 Mich.App. 240, 169 N.W.2d 135 (1969), allowing damages for failure of a nursing home to notify plaintiff of his mother's impending death, and *Allinger v. Kell,* 102 Mich.App. 798, 302 N.W.2d 576 (1981), allowing damages for a funeral director's mutilation of the body of plaintiffs' murdered daughter. * * *

Generally, and as evidenced by the above-cited cases, damages for mental distress are allowed where the injury suffered is to the person. This

Court has considered another line of cases, where damages for mental distress in breach of contract actions were sought for injuries to property. Plaintiffs in these cases have been uniformly unsuccessful. See *Jankowski v. Mazzotta,* 7 Mich.App. 483, 152 N.W.2d 49 (1967), where damages for mental distress were sought for defendant's failure to conform a house to specifications; *Caradonna v. Thorious,* 17 Mich.App. 41, 169 N.W.2d 179 (1969), involving damages for mental distress in a dispute over rebuilding a tornado damaged home; *Scott v. Hurd-Corrigan Moving & Storage Co., Inc.,* 103 Mich.App. 322, 302 N.W.2d 867 (1981), *lv. den.* 412 Mich. 881 (1981), where damages for mental distress were sought for a storage company's wrongful sale of plaintiff's household goods.

Still another line of cases denying damages for mental distress in breach of contract cases involve intangible claims such as failure to pay insurance claims and breach of employment contracts. See *Van Marter v. American Fidelity Fire Ins. Co.,* 114 Mich.App. 171, 318 N.W.2d 679 (1982) * * *.

These illustrative cases demonstrate that the rule of *Stewart* applies where deep, personal human relations are involved. Where property loss is involved, the courts have generally not allowed recovery for mental distress in breach of contract actions. One's property can be lost on a public carrier, in a fire, or as the result of a bailment and, under *Kewin,* damages for mental distress will not be recoverable. Other than the *Stewart* exception, the only grounds upon which damages for mental distress are recoverable in a breach of contract case is where plaintiff alleges tortious conduct, independent of any breach of the commercial contract.

* * *

In this case, plaintiffs seek to bring their mental distress claim for damages within the purview of the *Stewart* exception. However, the installation of a furnace as well as other home improvements clearly arise by commercial contract and do not involve matters of mental concern and solicitude. The injury suffered by plaintiffs was to property and not person. Neither the *Stewart* exception nor the general rule of *Kewin* authorize damages for mental distress in this case.

We must next examine whether plaintiffs' complaint sufficiently pleads an independent tort, allowing for damages for mental distress under a theory of tort rather than contract.

In *Hart v. Ludwig,* 347 Mich. 559, 564–565, 79 N.W.2d 895 (1956), the Supreme Court held that the unskilled performance of a contract may give rise to an independent tort action and may be a basis for damages for mental distress.

The case of *Daley v. LaCroix,* 384 Mich. 4, 179 N.W.2d 390 (1970), clarifies the law of Michigan governing damages for mental distress in tort actions, as *Kewin* does in contract actions. In that case, the defendant's vehicle ran off the road, shearing a utility pole which snapped a number of high voltage lines. These voltage lines, in turn, tangled with electrical lines leading to the plaintiffs' house, causing an electrical explosion in their home. Plaintiffs sued for mental distress resulting from the accident though no direct physical injury occurred to either of them, except for emotional disturbance and traumatic neurosis.

The Court in *Daley* overturned the rule previously recognized in Michigan which required some impact on the plaintiff before damages for mental distress could be recovered. The Court prospectively laid down the rule as follows:

> "We hold that where a definite and objective physical injury is produced as a result of emotional distress proximately caused by defendant's negligent conduct, the plaintiff in a properly pleaded and proved action may recover in damages for such physical consequences to himself notwithstanding the absence of any physical impact upon plaintiff at the time of the mental shock.
>
> "The rule we adopt today is, of course, subject to familiar limitations.
>
> "Generally, defendant's standard of conduct is measured by reactions to be expected of normal persons. Absent specific knowledge of plaintiff's unusual sensitivity, there should be no recovery for hypersensitive mental disturbance where a normal individual would not be affected under the circumstances." 384 Mich. at 12–13, 179 N.W.2d 390.

The complaint in the case before us was designed to fall under the rule of *Stewart,* acknowledged and accepted in *Kewin* as an exception to the rule that damages for mental distress are not allowed in contract cases. This pleading is inadequate to support an independent claim for mental distress in tort. However, under GCR 1963, 117.3, "[e]ach party shall be given opportunity to amend his pleadings as provided by Rule 118 unless the evidence then before the court shows amendment would not be justified".

Reversed and remanded for further proceedings in light of this opinion.

NOTE:
MENTAL DISTRESS DAMAGES AND JURY INSTRUCTIONS

The Chrum case articulates a general proscription against mental distress damages, with some exceptions. However, an empirical study, excerpted below, suggests that this general rule isn't always translated into the actual courtroom jury instructions. Only New Hampshire specifically tells its juries in contracts cases *not* to award mental distress. The others, as described, instruct on the proper measure of damages using various incantations and ignore the issue of mental harm. Do you think that these differing approaches mean that in particular jurisdictions mental distress damages are more or less commonly awarded?

HOFFMAN AND RADUS, INSTRUCTING JURIES ON NONECONOMIC CONTRACT DAMAGES

81 Fordham L Rev 1221, 1238–39, 1241, 1243–44 (2013).

[Hoffman and Radus surveyed pattern instructions and found four approaches to noneconomic contract damages. The first is looking at the issue case-by-case. The others follow:]

1. [Ten jurisdictions] instruct juries using a formulaic, traditional expectation damages approach. * * * The District of Columbia's instruction exemplifies a "pure" expectation calculation: "The measure of damages for a breach of contract is that amount of money necessary to place the injured party in the same economic position [he] [she] would have been in if the contract had not been breached. To calculate the damages, first determine the amount of money the plaintiff would have received had the contract not been breached. Next, add both incidental damages and consequential damages, if any. Lastly, subtract from that any money [he] [she] saved because [he] [she] did not have to complete the contract."

2. [Fifteen jurisdictions instruct juries that] "[t]he underlying rationale on a breach of contract action is to place the innocent party in the position he/she would have been in if the contract had been fully performed." * * * Unlike the destination and road map approach of Expectation Formula instructions, [such] instructions merely state the destination, leaving the jury to find its way. Alabama is representative: "If you decide that (name of plaintiff) proved [his/her/its] claim against (name of defendant) for breach of contract, you also must decide how much money will reasonably compensate (name of plaintiff) for the harm caused by the breach. * * * The purpose of such damages is to put (name of plaintiff) in as good a position as [he/she/it] would have been if (name of defendant) had not broken the contract."

3. [Eight jurisdictions] use abstract language that grants juries considerable discretion and provides little guidance on how to measure damages. * * * Virginia's instruction is representative: "If you find your verdict for the plaintiff, then he is entitled to recover as damages all of the losses he sustained [, including gains prevented,] that are a natural

> and ordinary result of the breach and that he has proved by the greater weight of the evidence."

NOTE:
PUNITIVE DAMAGES IN CONTRACT CASES

Recall the approach to punitive damages in White v. Benkowski, set forth in Chapter One. In the following excerpt from Thyssen, Inc. v. S.S. Fortune Star, 777 F.2d 57, 63 (2d Cir.1985), Judge Friendly set forth the prevailing view as reflected in the Restatement, and then offered some reasons for this view.

> Restatement (Second) of Contracts § 355 (1979) [states]:
>
> Punitive damages are not recoverable for a breach of contract unless the conduct constituting the breach is also a tort for which punitive damages are recoverable.

See also 11 *Williston on Contracts* § 1340, at 209–11 (W. Jaeger 3d ed. 1968); 5 *Corbin on Contracts* § 1077, at 438–39 (1964); Sullivan, *Punitive Damages in the Law of Contract*, 61 Minn. L. Rev. 207, 207 (1977). This rule applies although the breach is intentional or even when it has been affected with malicious intent. Simpson, *Punitive Damages for Breach of Contract*, 20 Ohio St. L.J. 284, 284 (1959); Farnsworth, *Contracts* § 12.8, at 874 [(2d ed. 1990).] Under Holmes' theory that a contract is simply a set of alternative promises either to perform or to pay damages for nonperformance, Holmes, *The Common Law* 235–36 (M. Howe ed. 1963), the rule would require no other explanation. Nevertheless, a good many have been offered. One is that the law of contracts governs primarily commercial relationships, where the amount required to compensate for loss is easily fixed, in contrast to the law of torts, which compensates for injury to personal interests that are more difficult to value, thus justifying noncompensatory recovery. Sullivan, *supra*, at 222. Another, given by Corbin, *supra* § 1077, at 438, is that breaches of contract do not cause the kind of "resentment or other mental and physical discomfort as do the wrongs called torts and crimes," and no retributive purpose would be served by punitive damages in contract cases. A third explanation, offered by economists, is the notion that breaches of contract that are in fact efficient and wealth-enhancing should be encouraged, and that such "efficient breaches" occur when the breaching party will still profit after compensating the other party for its "expectation interest." The addition of punitive damages to traditional contract remedies would prevent many such beneficial actions from being taken. *See* Farnsworth, *supra*, § 12.3, at 848; *Restatement (Second) of Contracts* ch. 16 reporter's note. In any event the general rule is well established, although certain exceptions have been adopted.

The most common exception, which is specifically incorporated in the general rule in the *Restatement* and comprehends several other exceptions listed below, is where the breach constitutes an independent, wilful tort in addition to being a breach of contract, 5 Corbin, *supra*, § 1077, at 445; Farnsworth, *supra*, § 12.8, at 875–76. Others include breach of a contract to marry, Sullivan, *supra*, at 222–23; Corbin, *supra*, § 1077, at 440–43; failure of a public service company enjoying monopoly or quasi-monopoly power to discharge its obligations to the public, Sullivan, *supra*, at 223–26; Corbin, *supra*, § 1077, at 443–44; breach of a fiduciary duty, Sullivan, *supra*, at 226–29; breach of contract accompanied by fraudulent conduct (where, for example, the defendant conveys to a third party property given as security for the plaintiff's debt when the defendant has promised to reconvey the property to the plaintiff upon repayment of the debt), *id.* at 229–36; and the bad faith refusal by an insurer to settle an insurance claim for which it is liable, *id.* at 844 * * *.

NOTE: *OTHER QUALIFICATIONS AND LIMITS ON LOST EXPECTANCY RECOVERY*

There are many additional qualifications and limits on the recovery of lost expectancy damages. Some of the most noteworthy of these are identified below.

Denial of lost expectancy recovery in medical contexts. As we saw in Sullivan v. O'Connor in Chapter One, a court may deny lost expectancy in a medical context. As Judge Kaplan pointed out, "considering the uncertainties of medical science and the variations in the physical and psychological conditions of individual patients, doctors can seldom in good faith promise specific results." For a case entertaining a contract theory for enforcement in the medical context, see, e.g., Murphy v. Implicito, 920 A.2d 678 (N.J. Super. Ct. App. Div. 2007) (doctor wrongly used a cadaver bone in a spinal surgery).

Denial of recovery for loss of reputation or goodwill. According to some courts, the measure of damages for lost expectancy does not include compensation for loss of reputation or loss of goodwill. Stancil v. Mergenthaler Linotype Co., 589 F. Supp. 78, 84 (D.Hawaii 1984); Quinn v. Straus Broadcasting Group, Inc., 309 F. Supp. 1208 (S.D.N.Y.1970). But in AM/PM Franchise Assoc. v. Atlantic Richfield Co., 526 Pa. 110, 584 A.2d 915 (1990), the court approved, as a general proposition, the award of damages for loss of goodwill. The court defined goodwill as "the reputation that businesses have built over the course of time that is reflected by the return of customers to purchase goods and the attendant profits that accompanies such sales." The court noted that many of the cases denying damages for loss of goodwill "were written in a time * * * where market studies and economic forecasting were unexplored," and that "a significant majority of the cases have allowed for the recovery of lost goodwill in proper circumstances." Finally, the court held that the party claiming damages for loss of goodwill must "provide the trier of fact with a reasonable basis from which to calculate damages." In addition, see Klayman v. Judicial Watch, Inc., 255 F.Supp.3d 161 (D.C. Cir. 2017) (reputation damages awardable if subject to calculation and certainty); Hangzhou Silk Import & Export Corp. v. P.C.B. Intern. Indus., 2002 WL 2031591 at *7 (S.D.N.Y. 2002). ("Under New York law, consequential damages for a breach of contract or warranty claim can include loss of goodwill, including the loss of customers, future profits, and harm to business reputation. * * * To succeed on a claim for consequential damages in the form of loss of goodwill, a party must make three showings: 1) that a loss of goodwill did in fact occur; 2) objective proof of the amount of that loss; and 3) that the loss was caused by the opposing party's breach.").

Denial of lost expectancy to attorneys. Some courts allow wrongfully discharged lawyers only the reasonable value of their services up to the date of discharge. Barwick, Dillian, & Lambert, P.A. v. Ewing, 646 So.2d 776 (Fla.App.1994); Rosenberg v. Levin, 409 So.2d 1016 (Fla. 1982); Hardman v. Snyder, 183 W. Va. 34, 393 S.E.2d 672 (1990).

Denial of attorneys' fees and interest. Typically, the largest, although not the only type of litigation cost, is attorneys' fees. The general rule is that a victorious party cannot recover attorneys' fees from the losing party. D. Dobbs, Remedies 276 (2d ed.1993). Thus, even though a plaintiff may receive a judgment for expectancy damages, the fees that a party may have to pay may consume a large part of the award. One rationale for the rule often heard is that taxing the losing party for attorney's fees would discourage the poor from litigating possibly meritorious claims.

Courts and legislatures have created some exceptions to the rule against recovery of attorneys' fees. The most important exception is that courts will generally enforce a specific contract clause providing for recovery of attorneys' fees *to the extent the fees are reasonable.* Trustees of the Prince Condominium Trust v. Prosser, 412 Mass. 723, 592 N.E.2d 1301 (1992); Leventhal v. Krinsky, 325 Mass. 336, 90 N.E.2d 545 (1950). A plaintiff also may recover attorneys' fees as reliance damages if the plaintiff wasted the fees due to the defendant's breach. For example, a plaintiff can recover attorneys' fees to pay for a title search if the vendor of land later repudiates the contract of sale. The latter fees, of course, are not a litigation expense.

A few state legislatures authorize the award of attorneys' fees to the prevailing party. Alaska Stat. § 09.60.010 (Supp.1991); Nev. Rev. Stat. § 18.010 (Michie 1986). Some federal statutes also provide for the award of attorneys' fees, usually to induce private enforcement of public policies. One such statute is the Truth in Lending Act, 15 U.S.C.A. § 1640(a) (1982).

Among academic commentators critical of the general rule against the award of attorneys' fees are Ehrenzweig, Reimbursement of Counsel Fees and the Great Society, 54 Cal. L. Rev. 792 (1966); McLaughlin, The Recovery of Attorney's Fees: A New Method of Financing Legal Services, 40 Ford. L. Rev. 761 (1972); Sands, Attorney's Fees as Recoverable Costs, 63 A.B.A.J. 510 (1977).

Denial of pre-judgment interest. Now we turn briefly to a further major limitation on the general principle of expectancy recovery. Plaintiffs generally cannot recover pre-judgment interest unless the amount of damages is ascertained or liquidated prior to entry of judgment. See, e.g., World Classic

Productions, Inc. v. RFD-TV The Theater, LLC, 498 S.W.3d 874, 879–880 (Tenn. Ct. App. 2016) (prejudgment interest recoverable only if damages are liquidated); Coulter v. Asten Group, Inc., 155 Wash. App. 1, 230 P.3d 169 (2010) ("A prevailing party is generally entitled to prejudgment interest, provided the damages are liquidated. The interest is awardable 'when the amount claimed is liquidated,' or 'when the amount claimed is unliquidated but is determinable by computation with reference to a fixed standard in a contract.' A claim is liquidated if 'data in the evidence makes it possible to compute the amount with exactness, without reliance on opinion or discretion.' "); Waukesha Concrete Prods. Co., Inc. v. Capitol Indemnity Corp., 127 Wis.2d 332, 379 N.W.2d 333 (1985); D. Dobbs, Remedies 246–48 (2d ed. 1993). For example, if a contractor breaches his agreement to build a structure, the owner, who sues two years later and recovers a judgment against the contractor, receives interest not from the date of breach but only from the date of judgment. (Most states have statutes prescribing the rate of post-judgment interest.) One reason often given for denying pre-judgment interest on unliquidated claims is that it would unfairly penalize the defendant, who could not pay the sum owed and thus end the accrual of interest because of the uncertainty of how much the defendant owed. But is such an approach fair to the plaintiff?

HILLMAN, CONTRACT LORE

27 J. Corp. L. 505, 507–508 (2002).

* * * Whatever the reasons behind the expectancy approach, contracts people continue to report that the goal of expectancy damages is to make injured parties whole. The reality is dramatically different. A large set of remedial rules often limits the recovery of injured parties to well below expectancy. For example, in our legal system, parties usually must pay their own lawyers and can rarely recover prejudgment interest. These impediments, of course, constitute costs of litigation and apply across all areas of the law. More specific to contract law, injured parties cannot recover unforeseeable or difficult-to-prove damages, even though often real and large. In addition, courts typically compute damages objectively, thereby ignoring a party's special circumstances, including emotional distress and sentimental value.

Of course, the failure of expectancy damages to make injured parties whole is not the world's best kept secret, and many theorists have recognized this reality and have discussed reasons for it. One obvious reason is that the expectancy goal runs into institutional counter policies. We do not want to discourage parties from exercising their right to a day in court for fear of having to pay the other party's legal fees. We do not want to license courts to award baseless recoveries, so we require injured parties to prove their damages with some precision.

Another reason is the existence of contradictory substantive policies. For example, we want to avoid discouraging people from making contracts based on a fear (rational or not) of inordinate liability. We also want to encourage promisees to disclose special circumstances, so we deny them consequential damages when the breaching promisor could not reasonably foresee a particular loss and the injured promisee did not disclose its possibility. In addition, contract law's actual remedial goal may be to protect an injured party from reliance losses, which are often more difficult to prove than expectancy damages. Expectancy damages therefore may serve as a surrogate for reliance damages, thereby diminishing concern when the former fails to give the injured party the full value of her promise.

SECTION FIVE: REIMBURSEMENT OF RELIANCE COSTS AS AN ALTERNATIVE REMEDY WHERE THERE IS A BREACH OF AN AGREEMENT WITH CONSIDERATION

NURSE V. BARNS

Kings Bench, 1664.
Raym. Sir T. 77, 83 Eng. Rep. 43.

The plaintiff declares, that the defendant in consideration of [10£] promised to let him enjoy certain iron mills for six months; and it appeared that the iron mills were worth but [20£] per annum, and yet damages were given [in the amount of 500£] by reason of the loss of stock laid in; and *per Curiam* the jury may well find such damages, for they are not bound to give only the [10£] but also all the special damages.

CHICAGO COLISEUM CLUB V. DEMPSEY

Appellate Court of Illinois, 1932.
265 Ill. App. 542.

MR. JUSTICE WILSON delivered the opinion of the court.

Chicago Coliseum Club, a corporation, as plaintiff, brought its action against William Harrison Dempsey, known as Jack Dempsey, to recover damages for breach of a written contract executed March 13, 1926, but bearing date of March 6 of that year.

Plaintiff was incorporated as an Illinois corporation for the promotion of general pleasure and athletic purposes and to conduct boxing, sparring and wrestling matches and exhibitions for prizes or purses. The defendant William Harrison Dempsey was well known in the pugilistic world and, at the time of the making and execution of the contract in question, held the title of world's Champion Heavy Weight Boxer.

Under the terms of the written agreement, the plaintiff was to promote a public boxing exhibition in Chicago, or some suitable place to be selected by the promoter, and had engaged the services of one Harry Wills, another well known boxer and pugilist, to engage in a boxing match with the defendant Dempsey for the championship of the world. By the terms of the agreement Dempsey was to receive $10, receipt of which was acknowledged, and the plaintiff further agreed to pay to Dempsey the sum of $300,000 on the 5th day of August 1926,—$500,000 in cash at least 10 days before the date fixed for the contest, and a sum equal to 50 per cent of the net profits over and above the sum of $2,000,000 in the event the gate receipts should exceed that amount. In addition the defendant was to receive 50 per cent of the net revenue derived from moving picture concessions or royalties received by the plaintiff, and defendant agreed to have his life and health insured in favor of the plaintiff in a manner and at a place to be designated by the plaintiff. Defendant further agreed not to engage in any boxing match after the date of the agreement and prior to the date on which the contest was to be held. * * *

March 6, 1926, the plaintiff entered into an agreement with Harry Wills, in which Wills agreed to engage in a boxing match with the Jack Dempsey named in the agreement hereinbefore referred to. Under this agreement the plaintiff, Chicago Coliseum Club was to deposit $50,000 in escrow in the National City Bank of New York City, New York, to be paid over to Wills on the 10th day prior to the date fixed for the holding of the boxing contest. Further conditions were provided in said contract with Wills, which, however, are not necessary to set out in detail. There is no evidence in the record showing that the $50,000 was deposited nor that it has ever been paid, nor is there any evidence in the record showing the financial standing of the Chicago Coliseum Club, a corporation, plaintiff in this suit. This contract between the plaintiff and Wills appears to have been entered into several days before the contract with Dempsey.

March 8, 1926, the plaintiff entered into a contract with one Andrew C. Weisberg, under which it appears that it was necessary for the plaintiff to have the services of an experienced person skilled in promoting boxing exhibitions and that the said Weisberg was possessed of such qualifications and that it was necessary for the plaintiff to procure his help in the promoting of the exhibition. It appears further from the agreement that it was necessary to incur expenditures in the way of traveling expenses, legal services and other costs in and about the promotion of the boxing match, and Weisberg agreed to investigate, canvass and organize the various hotel associations and other business organizations for the purpose of securing accommodations for spectators and to procure subscriptions and others for the erection of an arena and other necessary expense in order to carry out the enterprise and to promote the boxing match in question. Under these agreements Weisberg was to furnish the funds for such purposes and was to be reimbursed out of the receipts from the sale of tickets for the expenses incurred by him, together with a certain amount for his services.

Both the Wills contract and the Weisberg contract are referred to at some length, inasmuch as claims for damages by plaintiff are predicated upon these two agreements. Under the terms of the contract between the plaintiff and Dempsey and the plaintiff and Wills, the contest was to be held during the month of September, 1926.

July 10, 1926, plaintiff wired Dempsey at Colorado Springs, Colorado, stating that representatives of life and accident insurance companies would call on him for the purpose of examining him for insurance in favor of the Chicago Coliseum Club, in accordance with the terms of his contract, and also requesting the defendant to begin training for the contest not later than August 1, 1926. In answer to this communication plaintiff received a telegram from Dempsey, as follows:

"BM Colorado Springs Colo July 10th 1926

B.E. Clements

President Chicago Coliseum Club Chgo Entirely too busy training for my coming Tunney match to waste time on insurance representatives stop as you have no contract suggest you stop kidding yourself and me also

JACK DEMPSEY."

We are unable to conceive upon what theory the defendant could contend that there was no contract, as it appears to be admitted in the proceeding here and bears his signature and the amounts involved are sufficiently large to have created a rather lasting impression on the mind of anyone signing such an agreement. It amounts, however, to a repudiation of the agreement and from that time on Dempsey refused to take any steps to carry out his undertaking. It appears that Dempsey at this time was engaged in preparing himself for a contest with Tunney to be held at Philadelphia, Pennsylvania, sometime in September, and on August 3, 1926, plaintiff, as complainant, filed a bill in the superior court of Marion county, Indiana, asking to have Dempsey restrained and enjoined from engaging in the contest with Tunney, which complainant was informed and believed was to be held on the 16th day of September, and which contest would be in violation of the terms of the agreement entered into between the plaintiff and defendant at Los Angeles, March 13, 1926.

Personal service was had upon the defendant Dempsey in the proceeding in the Indiana court and on August 27, 1926, he entered his general appearance, by his attorneys, and filed his answer in said cause. September 13, 1926, a decree was entered in the superior court of Marion county, finding that the contract was a valid and subsisting contract between the parties, and that the complainant had expended large sums of money in carrying out the terms of the agreement, and entering a decree that Dempsey be perpetually restrained and enjoined from in any way, wise, or manner, training or preparing for or participating in any contracts or engagements in furtherance of any boxing match, prize fight or any exhibition of like nature, and particularly from engaging or entering into any boxing match with one Gene Tunney, or with any person other than the one designated by plaintiff.

It is insisted among other things that the costs incurred by the plaintiff in procuring the injunctional order in Marion county, Indiana, were properly chargeable against Dempsey for his breach of contract and recoverable in this proceeding. Under the evidence in the record in this proceeding there appears to have been a valid subsisting agreement between the plaintiff and Dempsey, in which Dempsey was to perform according to the terms of the agreement and which he refused to do, and the plaintiff, as a matter of law, was entitled at least to nominal damages. For this reason, if for no other, judgment should have been for the plaintiff.

During the proceeding in the circuit court of this county it was sought to introduce evidence for the purpose of showing damages, other than nominal damages, and in view of the fact that the case has to be retried, this court is asked to consider the various items of expense claimed to have been incurred and various offers of proof made to establish damages for breach of the agreement. Under the proof offered, the question of damages naturally divides itself into the four following propositions:

1st. Loss of profits which would have been derived by the plaintiff in the event of the holding of the contest in question;

2nd. Expenses incurred by the plaintiff prior to the signing of the agreement between the plaintiff and Dempsey;

3rd. Expenses incurred in attempting to restrain the defendant from engaging in other contests and to force him into a compliance with the terms of his agreement with the plaintiff; and

4th. Expenses incurred after the signing of the agreement and before the breach of July 10, 1926.

Proposition 1. Plaintiff offered to prove by one Mullins that a boxing exhibition between Dempsey and Wills held in the City of Chicago on September 22, 1926, would bring a gross receipt of $3,000,000, and that the expense incurred would be $1,400,000, leaving a net profit to the promoter of $1,600,000. The court properly sustained an objection to this testimony. The character of the undertaking was such that it would be impossible to produce evidence of a probative character sufficient to establish any amount which could be reasonably ascertainable by reason of the character of the undertaking. The profits from a boxing contest of this character, open to the public, is dependent upon so many different circumstances that they are not susceptible of definite legal determination. The success or failure of such an undertaking depends largely upon the ability of the promoters, the reputation of the contestants and the conditions of the weather at and prior to the holding of the contest, the accessibility of the place, the extent of the publicity, the possibility of other and counter attractions and many other questions which would enter into consideration. Such an entertainment lacks utterly the element of stability which exists in regular organized business. This fact was practically admitted by the plaintiff by the allegation of its bill filed in the Marion county court of Indiana asking for an injunction against Dempsey. Plaintiff in its bill in that proceeding charged, as follows:

"That by virtue of the premises aforesaid, the plaintiff will, unless it secures the injunctive relief herein prayed for, suffer great and irreparable injury and damages, not compensable by any action at law in damages, the damages being incapable of commensuration, and plaintiff, therefore, has no adequate remedy at law."

Compensation for damages for a breach of contract must be established by evidence from which a court or jury are able to ascertain the extent of such damages by the usual rules of evidence and to a reasonable degree of certainty. We are of the opinion that the performance in question is not susceptible of proof sufficient to satisfy the requirements and that the damages, if any, are purely speculative. * * *

Proposition 2: Expenses incurred by the plaintiff prior to the signing of the agreement between the plaintiff and Dempsey.

The general rule is that in an action for a breach of contract a party can recover only on damages which naturally flow from and are the result of the act complained of. *O'Conner v. Nolan,* 64 Ill.App. 357. The Wills contract was entered into prior to the contract with the defendant and was not made contingent upon the plaintiff's obtaining a similar agreement with the defendant Dempsey. Under the circumstances the plaintiff speculated as to the result of his efforts to procure the Dempsey contract. It may be argued that there had been negotiations pending between plaintiff and Dempsey which clearly indicated an agreement between them, but the agreement in fact was never consummated until sometime later. The action is based upon the written agreement which was entered into in Los Angeles. Any obligations assumed by the plaintiff prior to that time are not chargeable to the defendant. Moreover, an examination of the record discloses that the $50,000 named in the contract with Wills, which was to be payable upon a signing of the agreement, was not and never has been paid. There is no evidence in the record showing that the plaintiff is responsible financially, and, even though there were, we consider that it is not an element of damage which can be recovered for breach of the contract in question.

Proposition 3: Expenses incurred in attempting to restrain the defendant from engaging in other contests and to force him into a compliance with the terms of his agreement with the plaintiff.

After the repudiation of the agreement by the defendant, plaintiff was advised of defendant's match with Tunney which, from the evidence, it appears, was to take place in Philadelphia in the month of September and was in direct conflict with the terms of the agreement entered into between plaintiff and defendant. Plaintiff's bill, filed in the superior court of Marion county, Indiana, was an effort on the part of the plaintiff to compel defendant to live up to the terms of his agreement. The chancellor in the Indiana court entered his decree, which apparently is in full force and effect, and the defendant in violating the terms of that decree, after personal service, is answerable to that court for a violation of the injunctional order entered in said proceeding. The expenses incurred, however, by the plaintiff in procuring that decree are not collectible in an action for damages in this proceeding; neither are such similar expenses as were incurred in the trips to Colorado and Philadelphia, nor the attorney's fees and other expenses thereby incurred. *Cuyler Realty Co. v. Teneo Co., Inc.,* 188 N.Y.S. 340. The plaintiff having been informed that the defendant intended to proceed no further under his agreement, took such steps at its own financial risk. There was nothing in the agreement regarding attorney's fees and there was nothing in the contract in regard to the services of the defendant from which it would appear that the action for specific performance would lie. After the clear breach of contract by the defendant, the plaintiff proceeded with this character of litigation at its own risk. We are of the opinion that the trial court properly held that this was an element of damages which was not recoverable.

Proposition 4: Expenses incurred after the signing of the agreement and before the breach of July 10, 1926.

After the signing of the agreement plaintiff attempted to show expenses incurred by one Weisberg in and about the furtherance of the project. Weisberg testified that he had taken an active part in promoting sports for a number of years and was in the employ of the Chicago Coliseum Club under a written contract during all of the time that his services were rendered in furtherance of this proposition. This contract was introduced in evidence and bore the date of March 8, 1926. Under its terms Weisberg was to be reimbursed out of the gate receipts and profits derived from the performance. His compensation depended entirely upon the success of the exhibition. Under his agreement with the plaintiff there was nothing to charge the plaintiff unconditionally with the costs and expenses of

Weisberg's services. The court properly ruled against the admissibility of the evidence.

We find in the record, however, certain evidence which should have been submitted to the jury on the question of damages sustained by the plaintiff. The contract on which the breach of the action is predicated shows a payment of $10 by the plaintiff to the defendant and the receipt acknowledged. It appears that the stadium located in the South Park District, known as Soldier's Field, was considered as a site for the holding of the contest and plaintiff testified that it paid $300 to an architect for plans in the event the stadium was to be used for the performance. This item of damage might have been made more specific and may not have been the best evidence in the case but, standing alone, it was sufficient to go to the jury. There were certain elements in regard to wages paid assistant secretaries which may be substantiated by evidence showing that they were necessary in furtherance of the undertaking. If these expenses were incurred they are recoverable if in furtherance of the general scheme. The defendant should not be required to answer in damages for salaries paid regular officials of the corporation who were presumed to be receiving such salaries by reason of their position, but special expenses incurred are recoverable. The expenses of Hoffman in going to Colorado for the purpose of having Dempsey take his physical examination for insurance, if before the breach and reasonable, are recoverable. The railroad fares for those who went to Los Angeles for the purpose of procuring the signing of the agreement are not recoverable as they were incurred in a furtherance of the procuring of the contract and not after the agreement was entered into. The services of Shank in looking after railroad facilities and making arrangements with the railroad for publicity and special trains and accommodations were items which should be considered and if it develops that they were incurred in a furtherance of the general plan and properly proven, are items for which the plaintiff should be reimbursed.

The items recoverable are such items of expense as were incurred between the date of the signing of the agreement and the breach of July 10, 1926, by the defendant and such as were incurred as a necessary expense in furtherance of the performance. Proof of such items should be made subject to the usual rules of evidence.

For the reasons stated in this opinion the judgment of the circuit court is reversed and the cause remanded for a new trial.

Judgment reversed and cause remanded.

NOTE:
SUBSEQUENT DEVELOPMENTS: DEMPSEY V. TUNNEY

Perhaps Dempsey should have honored his contract to fight Wills. On September 23, 1926, Dempsey fought Tunney in Philadelphia and lost on points. When asked by his wife why he lost, he responded: "Honey, I guess I forgot to duck." In a rematch a year later, Dempsey knocked Tunney down, but continued to stand over him instead of going to a neutral corner. This delayed the referee's count and allowed Tunney over 14 seconds to recover. Tunney subsequently won the fight. © 1983 Reuters, Ltd.; Reuters North European Service.

ANGLIA TELEVISION LTD. v. REED, 3 All Eng. Rep. 690 (C.A.1971). [Plaintiff Anglia sued Reed for expenditures incurred by Anglia prior to contracting with Reed. Anglia had been preparing to make a film and had spent money to hire a director and other key persons. Reed then agreed to play the lead role. Later, Reed repudiated, and Anglia, unable to find another lead actor, abandoned the film. The Court of Appeal, per Lord Denning, held for Anglia.] [Plaintiff] * * * can claim also the expenditures incurred *before* the contract, provided that it was such as would reasonably be in the contemplation of the parties as likely to be wasted if the contract was broken. Applying that principle here, it is plain that, when Mr. Reed entered into this contract, he must have known perfectly well that much expenditure had already been incurred * * *. He must have contemplated—or, at any rate, it is reasonable to be imputed to him—that if he broke his contract, all that expenditure would be wasted, whether or not it was incurred before or after the contract. He must pay damages for all the expenditures so wasted * * *.

MERRY GENTLEMAN, LLC V. GEORGE & LEONA PRODS., INC.

United States Court of Appeals, Seventh Circuit, 2015.
799 F.3d 827.

HAMILTON, CIRCUIT JUDGE.

Merry Gentleman, LLC produced the motion picture *The Merry Gentleman,* which was released in 2009. Despite some critical acclaim, the film was a commercial flop. Merry Gentleman blames Michael Keaton, the film's lead actor and director, for the bust. It brought this breach of contract action against Keaton and George and Leona Productions, Inc., Keaton's "loan-out company" that he uses for professional contracting, alleging that Keaton violated his directing contract by (1) failing to prepare the first cut of the film in a timely fashion, (2) submitting a first cut that was incomplete, (3) submitting a revised cut that was not ready for the producers to watch, (4) communicating directly with officials at the Sundance Film Festival and threatening to boycott the festival if they did not accept his director's cut instead of the producers' preferred cut, (5) failing to cooperate with the producers during the post-production process, and (6) failing to promote the film adequately.

If the case were to go to trial, one might expect Keaton to dispute that any of these alleged breaches actually violated the directing contract. After all, Keaton completed the movie. It was accepted at the prestigious Sundance Film Festival. It received critical praise—Roger Ebert, for example, gave it 3.5 stars out of 4 and called it "original, absorbing and curiously moving." And the film's executive producer, Paul Duggan, admitted during his deposition that he was unaware of any director who did more publicity than Keaton did for a movie with a comparable budget.

Keaton moved for summary judgment, however, on the narrow ground that Merry Gentleman had failed to produce sufficient evidence that his alleged breaches of the directing contract caused it damages. For purposes of deciding this appeal, we must therefore assume as the district court did that Keaton in fact breached the contract.

Illinois law governs the directing contract. Under Illinois law, a "party injured by another's breach or repudiation of a contract usually seeks recovery in the form of damages based on his 'expectation interest,' which involves obtaining the 'benefit of the bargain,' or his 'reliance interest,' which involves reimbursement for loss caused by reliance on a contract." *MC Baldwin Financial Co. v. DiMaggio, Rosario & Veraja, LLC,* 364 Ill.App.3d 6, 300 Ill.Dec. 601, 845 N.E.2d 22, 30 (2006), quoting Restatement (Second) of Contracts § 344 (1981). The district court granted Keaton's motion for summary judgment, concluding that Merry Gentleman had failed to present a genuine issue of material fact on either damages theory.

First, the district court held that Merry Gentleman forfeited the expectation damages theory by not addressing it sufficiently in its response to summary judgment. *Merry Gentleman, LLC v. George & Leona Productions, Inc.,* 76 F.Supp.3d 756, 761 (N.D.Ill.2014). Merry Gentleman does not dispute this conclusion on appeal, so expectation damages are out.

Second, the district court held that Merry Gentleman failed to produce evidence from which a reasonable trier of fact could find that Keaton's alleged breaches caused the damages Merry Gentleman seeks: all $5.5 million it spent producing the movie. *Id.* at 761–66. This holding is the focus of Merry Gentleman's appeal.

We review the grant of summary judgment *de novo*, reviewing the record in the light most favorable to Merry Genetleman, as the non-moving party, and drawing all reasonable inferences in its favor. * * *

Illinois follows the approach of § 349 of the Restatement (Second) of Contracts (1981), which provides that as an alternative to expectation damages, "the injured party has a right to damages based on his reliance interest, including expenditures made in preparation for performance or in performance, less any loss that the party in breach can prove with reasonable certainty the injured party would have suffered had the contract been performed." See, e.g., *Herbert W. Jaeger & Associates v. Slovak American Charitable Ass'n,* 156 Ill.App.3d 106, 107 Ill.Dec. 710, 507 N.E.2d 863, 868 (1987) (discussing § 349). Reliance damages are designed to put the injured party "in as good a position as [the injured party] would have been in had the contract not been made." Restatement (Second) of Contracts § 344; *MC Baldwin Financial,* 300 Ill.Dec. 601, 845 N.E.2d at 30 (discussing § 344); *Designer Direct, Inc. v. DeForest Redevelopment Auth.,* 313 F.3d 1036, 1049 (7th Cir.2002) (same).

Merry Gentleman argues that the district court required too much when it held that Merry Gentleman failed to establish a causal connection between its expenditures on the film and Keaton's alleged breaches. The causation standard is minimal when the injured party seeks reliance damages under § 349, Merry Gentleman contends, and it cleared this low hurdle when it submitted an affidavit from Duggan stating that the production company spent over $5 million in reliance on the directing contract. Once it produced that evidence, Merry Gentleman continues, the burden shifted to Keaton to prove that the production company would have suffered the alleged losses even if Keaton had fully performed. And because Keaton did not submit evidence with his motion for summary judgment showing beyond reasonable dispute that these losses were inevitable, summary judgment against Merry Gentleman was improper. Or so goes the argument.

We agree with Merry Gentleman that a party seeking reliance damages under § 349 has a relatively low bar to clear to establish causation and that once it makes this showing, the burden shifts to the breaching party to prove any reduction in those damages. This causation threshold is low because the injured party is forced to prove a counterfactual: what would have happened if the contract had not been signed in the first place. See *Autotrol Corp. v. Continental Water Systems Corp.,* 918 F.2d 689, 695 (7th Cir.1990). Proving this kind of counterfactual is difficult because the value of performance can be so difficult to establish. That is especially true in cases where the injured party is seeking reliance damages. If damages were easy to calculate, the injured party likely would have sought expectation damages to begin with on a benefit-of-the-bargain theory under § 347. Reliance damages are appropriate precisely because the injured party is at an evidentiary disadvantage. Cf. Restatement (Second) of Contracts § 349, cmt. a (1981) (reliance damages are appropriate where the injured party "cannot prove his profit with reasonable certainty"). That is why courts use the burden-shifting framework of § 349. As Judge Hand explained long ago:

> It is often very hard to learn what the value of the performance would have been; and it is a common expedient, and a just one, in such situations to put the peril of the answer upon that party who by his wrong has made the issue relevant to the rights of the other.

> On principle therefore the proper solution would seem to be that the promisee may recover his outlay in preparation for the performance, subject to the privilege of the promisor to reduce it by as much as he can show that the promisee would have lost, if the contract had been performed.

L. Albert & Son v. Armstrong Rubber Co., 178 F.2d 182, 189 (2d Cir.1949) (footnote omitted).

The burden does not shift to the breaching party until the injured party first satisfies this threshold showing of causation, however. And just because the causation threshold under § 349 is low does not mean it is not there, as Merry Gentleman seems to suggest. To oppose summary judgment on this point, the injured party must still produce evidence sufficient to permit a reasonable trier of fact to find that the losses claimed were caused by the breach * * *.

In the typical case where reliance damages are sought, the defendant has simply repudiated the contract and walked away from the deal. This causal link will be straightforward in those cases. As the district court explained, in such cases the non-breaching plaintiff is left "holding the bag after having made its expenditures." *Merry Gentleman,* 76 F.Supp.3d at 763. In those cases, it is appropriate for the injured party to claim as damages all expenditures it made in preparation for performance because the other side failed to perform at all. In such cases, the complete loss of investment will often be the proximate result of the breach.

But in cases like this one, where the breaching party has substantially performed and the alleged breaches have to do with the quality of the final product, the causal link between reliance damages and the breach is not so direct. An injured party cannot reasonably claim that *all* of its expenditures were caused by the other party's breach without some reason to think the breach destroyed the entire value of the breaching party's performance. In this context, the breach does not cause the complete loss of investment.

Take this case, for example. Who can say why a critically praised movie did not make money? Merry Gentleman claims as damages all $5.5 million it spent to produce the movie. If Keaton had somehow prevented completion of the movie, Merry Gentleman might well have been entitled to all expenditures made in preparation for his performance (subject, of course, to the "losing contract" limitation in § 349). But here, Keaton actually made the movie. Merry Gentleman complains that Keaton slowed down the production process and failed to publicize the movie adequately after it was finished. No doubt, these services have economic value and, on a proper showing, Merry Gentleman might have been entitled to recover damages for these shortcomings. (Imagine, for instance, if Keaton's tardiness in submitting the first cut forced Merry Gentleman to pay the film editors for a longer period. Or, to take a more extreme example, imagine if Keaton had publicly criticized the film released to theaters so harshly that no one bought tickets to see it.) But no reasonable trier of fact could find that Merry Gentleman lost its entire investment of $5.5 million because Keaton failed to submit his first cut on time or failed to publicize the movie better. Merry Gentleman entered the directing contract to have Keaton deliver a finished movie, and he delivered one that showed well at Sundance and won some critical praise. The breaches by Keaton that Merry Gentleman alleges cannot reasonably be said to have rendered the investment completely worthless.

The fundamental problem we have been describing is that Merry Gentleman's damages theory is completely insensitive to the importance and severity of Keaton's alleged breaches. * * *

* * *

* * * Merry Gentleman made no effort to establish any causal connection between the particular breaches asserted—the failure to submit a first cut on time, submitting a revised cut that was incomplete, failing to publicize the film better, etc.—and the $5.5 million that Merry Gentleman spent on the production process as a whole.[1]

We agree with the district court that Merry Gentleman, in seeking $5.5 million in reliance damages, "effectively wants to shift the entire cost—and risk—of producing *The Merry Gentleman* to Keaton for his alleged breaches, giving it a windfall and placing it in a *better* position than it would have been in had the contract never been signed." *Merry Gentleman,* 76 F.Supp.3d at 766. Reliance damages are not insurance. Courts "will not 'knowingly put the plaintiff [receiving a reliance recovery] in a better position than he would have occupied had the contract been fully performed.'" *Bausch & Lomb Inc. v. Bressler,* 977 F.2d 720, 729 (2d Cir.1992), quoting L.L. Fuller & William R. Perdue, Jr., *The Reliance Interest in Contract Damages: 1,* 46 Yale L.J. 52, 79 (1936); see also, e.g., *V.S. Int'l, S.A. v. Boyden World Corp.,* 862 F.Supp. 1188, 1198 (S.D.N.Y.1994) (assuming for sake of argument that defendant breached contract but declining to award reliance damages: "Based on plaintiffs continued running of a successful business, any compensation for these initial expenses would not place plaintiffs in the same position as they were

[1] One of the most troubling aspects of Merry Gentleman's theory here is evident from the disparity between the price Merry Gentleman agreed to pay Keaton under the directing contract ($100,000) and the damages Merry Gentleman seeks ($5,500,000). Comment a to § 349 of the Restatement (Second) of Contracts (1981) teaches: "If the injured party's expenditures exceed the contract price, it is clear that at least to the extent of the excess, there would have been a loss. For this reason, recovery for expenditures under the rule stated in this section may not exceed the full contract price." The relevant contract price here would seem to be the price for the contract that was breached, which would be $100,000. Nevertheless, we do not need to depend on that theory to affirm here.

prior to the execution of the contract, as reliance damages are intended to do, but would instead constitute a windfall for plaintiffs.").

As noted, we must assume here that Keaton breached the $100,000 contract as alleged, but these alleged breaches did not render his performance completely worthless. He directed the movie, it was accepted by Sundance, and it was released to the public. Reimbursing Merry Gentleman for all $5.5 million it spent, even though it received from Keaton a finished film praised by critics, would put it in a better position than if the contract had not been made. Perhaps Merry Gentleman might have been able to present a genuine issue for trial on a more modest damages theory, but it decided to shoot for the moon and missed. A reasonable trier of fact could not find that Keaton's alleged breaches caused Merry Gentleman to sustain $5.5 million in damages.

The district court's judgment is AFFIRMED.

COPPOLA v. KRAUSHAAR, 102 App. Div. 306, 92 N.Y.S. 436 (N.Y. App. Div. 1905). [Plaintiff alleged that he was engaged to be married, had ordered two gowns for his fiancée from defendant on January 3, 1902, to be delivered on January 18, and had told defendant he was incurring great expense for the wedding to be held on January 19. Plaintiff alleged further that the defendant failed to deliver the gowns on January 18, that as a result the wedding "was broken off" by his fiancée, and that $500 in expenses for "presents, wines, clothes" etc. were expended uselessly. Plaintiff claimed $500 damages. Held, plaintiff could recover $10 allegedly paid on the price of the gowns, but not the $500. The court stated that the latter expenses were "too remote," citing Hadley v. Baxendale, 9 Exch. 341 (1854).]

FULLER AND PERDUE, THE RELIANCE INTEREST IN CONTRACT DAMAGES

46 Yale L.J. 52, 75–80 (1936).

It is obvious that we need a distinction between two kinds of reliance. Certain acts of reliance are in a loose sense the "price" of whatever benefits the contract may involve for the plaintiff. This type of reliance we shall call "essential reliance". Under this heading would be included the performance of * * * [the agreed exchange], preparations to perform, * * * and the losses involved in entering the contract itself, as, for instance, in foregoing the opportunity to enter other profitable contracts. As to this kind of reliance ("essential reliance") if we do not limit recovery by the "contract price" we are permitting the plaintiff to shift to the defendant his own contractual losses, when the defendant is guilty of nothing more reprehensible than breach of contract.

In contrast to "essential reliance" is the kind of reliance involved in *Nurse v. Barns,* which we shall call "incidental reliance." The plaintiff's reliance there (laying in a stock of goods) followed naturally, and, we may assume, foreseeably, from the contract. It did not, however, consist of acts necessary to the perfection of the plaintiff's rights on the contract; it cannot be regarded as the "price" of the defendant's performance. To shift the burden of such reliance to the defendant in an amount exceeding "the full contract price" is not to shift to the defendant the plaintiff's contractual losses. In such a case therefore there appears no valid reason to limit the plaintiff's recovery by the expectation interest measured "objectively." If there is to be any limit at all it must be according to some standard more generous than the "contract price."

* * *

* * * All of these points are contained by implication in a very simple formula: *We will not in a suit for reimbursement for losses incurred in reliance on a contract knowingly put the plaintiff in a better position than he would have occupied had the contract been fully performed.*

AUTOTROL CORP. V. CONTINENTAL WATER SYSTEMS CORP.

United States Court of Appeals, Seventh Circuit, 1990.
918 F.2d 689.

POSNER, CIRCUIT JUDGE.

This is a diversity suit, primarily for breach of contract. The suit was tried to a jury, and the plaintiff, Autotrol Corporation, obtained a judgment of more than $1.5 million. The appeal raises a large number of issues, only a handful of which require discussion. * * *

* * *

The contract, signed in May 1986, established a joint venture between Autotrol's controls division and Continental Water Systems Corporation to create a system for water purification based on a patented new technology, known as "electrodiarese," that Continental owned the exclusive right to exploit. Autotrol was to manufacture the control for the system and Continental the rest and both companies would sell the completed systems—Autotrol the large systems, Continental the small ones. There was an ambiguity, later to prove critical, about the dividing line between large and small.

Before production could begin, there had to be product specifications. These had not been completed when the contract was signed. Anticipating this possibility, the contract provided that when approved by both parties the specifications would be attached to, and thereby made a part of, the contract; and should the parties be "unable, in good faith, to agree upon the contents of the Products Specifications Schedule by June 30, 1986, either party hereto may elect to terminate this Agreement." On June 25 the parties agreed to extend this deadline to July 17. July 17 came and went and the product specifications had not been agreed upon but neither party exercised its right of termination. It was almost a year later, with the product specifications still not having been agreed upon, that Continental declared the contract terminated. That is the alleged breach. * * *

* * *

[Judge Posner held in part that the] jury was entitled to find that the parties had modified the contract to forbid termination on this ground at least until such time as the need to agree on product specifications was urgent and agreement impossible. That deadline had not been reached when the defendants terminated—on a ground, moreover, that had nothing to do with *product* specifications, but rather with the division of the market for the product. * * *

The remaining issues relate to damages. During the year in which the contract was in force, Autotrol incurred $245,000 in out-of-pocket costs of performance. There is no quarrel over the appropriateness of awarding these costs as damages for breach of the contract. But in addition the jury awarded Autotrol more than $700,000 in overhead expenses. If, for example, a salaried engineer spent 25 percent of his time on the project, then 25 percent of his salary and benefits during the period he was working on the project were considered to be damages from the breach. The defendants object, pointing out that it is merely a conjecture that if the contract had never been made in the first place Autotrol would have replaced it with a project that would have covered the engineer's salary and benefits.

Economists distinguish between a firm's fixed and variable costs. The former, as the name implies, are the same whether or not the firm does anything; a good example is the fee that a state charges for a corporate charter. The fee is paid before the firm begins operations and is utterly invariant to the firm's fortunes. It would be an improper item of damages for the breach of a contract because the breach could not have caused the expense to be incurred.

Variable costs are those that vary with the firm's activity—more precisely that are caused by fluctuations in that activity. It is easy to see how the out-of-pocket expenses that Autotrol incurred in the joint venture were variable costs—specifically, variable costs of the joint venture, that is, of the contract. Had it not been for the contract, those expenses would not have been incurred. They are recoverable as damages because the breach deprived Autotrol of the opportunity to recover them by making and selling the water-purification systems envisaged by the contract.

It is more difficult to see how any part of the salary of the engineer in our illustration is a variable cost of the contract. His salary would presumably have been paid, for a time anyway, whether or not he worked on the electrodiarese project or, for that matter, on some substitute project. His salary was an expense but not an expense "caused" even in part by the project and hence, it might seem, was not a loss when the project collapsed because of Continental's breach and Autotrol was as a consequence unable to recoup the money that it had expended on the project.

But this analysis is superficial. * * * If the contract had never been signed, the engineer would have had more time to devote to some other project of Autotrol's. If we assume that the project would have been sufficiently profitable (which does not mean grandly profitable) to cover the salary and benefits of Autotrol's salaried employees who worked on it, it follows that the electrodiarese project turned this expense into a loss by preempting the substitute project that would have enabled the expense to be covered. Autotrol was left at the end of the day—thanks to Continental's breach—with no customer to charge 25 percent of the engineer's salary and benefits to.

It is a question of fact whether, as the example assumes, salary and other overhead items allocated as a bookkeeping matter to a broken contract would in fact have been recovered in a substitute contract. If the victim of the breach of contract is a growing firm—as Autotrol was—it is quite likely that they will be recovered. Growth implies alternative uses for the company's workforce. If not this contract there would have been another, and it would not have been broken—or if it would have been broken, there would have been the same entitlement to damages. But if the firm is declining, then it might well have had to pay its overhead expenses out of its own pocket had this contract not been signed, although before concluding this one would have to consider the possibility that the firm could have economized on those expenses by layoffs and other adjustments.

It might be a useful simplification of the law of damages to have a flat rule that any firm whose business was growing in real (i.e., inflation-adjusted) terms over the period of the contract is entitled to recover the overhead on the contract that was broken; for in all likelihood the firm could have substituted another contract profitable enough to cover that overhead. But this we need not decide; and naturally we are reluctant to speculate about the course of Texas law, let alone try to influence it. It is enough that a reasonable jury could conclude that Autotrol probably would have recouped its overhead expenses on other projects had the contract with Continental never been signed, instead of wasting a year of its employees' time on this barren contract. There was testimony that Autotrol's controls division was consistently overbooked with new projects and that its new projects had a consistent record of profitability—and remember that any project that Autotrol would have substituted for the electrodiarese project, had the latter never existed, need only have been profitable enough to cover the overhead expenses that Autotrol would have incurred in the substitute project, using the inputs that instead it wasted on electrodiarese, in order to justify an award of those overhead expenses to Autotrol as damages.

Of course if this substitute project were the last of Autotrol's promising projects, then the only thing the breach would have done was to accelerate Autotrol's having to swallow its overhead expenses. But this is merely a variant of the declining-firm scenario, one in which the award of overhead expenses will sometimes be inappropriate. Sometimes, perhaps often, but not always. To repeat a previous point, a declining firm may be able to slash its overhead expenses; and if it did not do so because they were necessary to the performance of the contract, and now it is left holding the bag because the contract has been broken, then those expenses are a loss caused by the breach and are recoverable as contract damages.

The question of the proper treatment of overhead expenses arises more frequently in cases in which the plaintiff is seeking not the expenses themselves—they have not been incurred—but the price of a contract that has not yet been fully performed, and the defendant asks that the overhead expenses assigned by the plaintiff on the uncompleted portion of the contract be deducted, on the theory that they were saved by the breach and therefore that their inclusion would exaggerate the plaintiff's loss. The proper analysis of that case is symmetrical with the proper analysis of our case. * * * If the plaintiff can either cut his overhead expenses or recover them in a substitute contract, then he indeed has not lost them as a result of the breach and they should not be figured in his damages. But if he cannot do either of these things—if in other words these really are fixed costs—then the breach gives him no scope to economize and there should be no deduction.

The breach in this case of course occurred *after* the overhead expenses were incurred. This sequence meant that the breach, far from enabling those expenses to be covered in a substitute contract, converted them from a bookkeeping entry into a loss, because it was too late for the plaintiff to make the substitute contract that would have enabled the plaintiff to recover the expenses. If there had been a contract price, therefore, the jury would not have been entitled to subtract the overhead expenses from it in figuring Autotrol's damages. The only thing to be subtracted would be expenses not yet incurred, and therefore saved by the breach. But there was no contract price. Autotrol was not selling something to Continental; they were joint venturers. That made figuring profits difficult and the implicit theory of the damages award is that Autotrol would have had zero profits on the venture, and is thus conservative. The defendants do not deny that Autotrol would have done well enough on the contract to cover the overhead expenses allocated to it, and with that concession Autotrol's case is complete.

The assumption of zero profits is based on the rule of Texas law "that the loss of anticipated profits from a new business is too speculative and conjectural to support a recovery of damages." *Universal Commodities, Inc. v. Weed,* 449 S.W.2d 106, 113 (Tex.Civ.App.1969); see also *Southwest Battery Corp. v. Owen,* 131 Tex. 423, 427, 115 S.W.2d 1097, 1099 (1938). Were it not for that rule Autotrol would not be seeking reliance damages, but instead expectation damages, and the issue of overhead expenses to which we have been devoting such complex attention would be simplified. Autotrol would have presented an estimate of the price at which it would have sold the water-purification systems envisaged by the contract and would have subtracted the costs that it would have incurred to complete the systems after the breach. The difference would be its damages. Suppose that the overhead and other expenses that Autotrol incurred before the breach were $1 million, the costs it would have (but had not yet) incurred to complete the systems after the breach $2 million, and the price it would have obtained for the systems $4 million. Then its damages would be $2 million ($4 million−$2 million), and this would cover the overhead expenses plus an allowance for profit. Since Autotrol was not in fact a new business, and had an established track record on new projects from which a projection could have been made of the likely success of the joint venture with Continental, we are far from certain that the Texas "new business" rule should apply to this case; but that is a matter for the Texas courts to think about; it is not an issue for us.

The defendants place great weight on a passage in *Kansas City Bridge Co. v. Kansas City Structural Steel Co.,* 317 S.W.2d 370, 377 (Mo.1958), from which we quote the gist: "prerequisite to plaintiff's recovery of this general overhead item as part of its damages, some evidence was essential from which the jury reasonably could have found that such general overhead was not only an *expense* but also represented a *loss* to plaintiff * * * [E]ven though a percentage of that fixed overhead was properly allocable to the Leavenworth job during the period of delay, nevertheless any amount so allocated could not represent a *loss* or *damage* to plaintiff unless plaintiff would have, but for the delay, obtained other work (which it did not have or which it did not in fact obtain) sufficient in amount to have absorbed the allocated portion of general overhead." (Italics in original.) We have no quarrel with this; it is our analysis in a nutshell. But since the plaintiff is being asked to prove a counterfactual (what would have happened had the contract in suit *not* been signed in the first place), he should not be subjected to too demanding a burden of proof. The degree of precision that can reasonably be demanded of a litigant, unless you want to doom his case from the outset, depends on the nature of the issue. The most that can fairly be asked of a plaintiff in Autotrol's shoes is to establish a reasonable probability that it would have covered its overhead expenses by means of another contract had the contract in suit never been made. A higher burden would not only be unrealistic but reward people who break their contracts. A lower burden might, as noted earlier, be justified by a desire to simplify litigation to the ultimate benefit of both plaintiffs and defendants.

* * *

Affirmed

SECTION SIX: VALIDITY OF TERMS PROVIDING FOR A SPECIFIC MONETARY REMEDY IN THE EVENT OF BREACH OR REPUDIATION OF AN AGREEMENT WITH CONSIDERATION

Within certain limits, contract law enforces contract terms that set forth the damages liability of a party should that party breach the contract. Such a term is called a "stipulated" or "agreed" damages provision. The parties may want to include such a term to save the costs of proving damages in litigation and to create incentives for a party to perform the contract. An agreed damages term may also assure a recovery for an injured party if damages would be too difficult to prove.

Not all stipulated damages provisions are enforceable. Courts will enforce them—deem them "liquidated damages"—only when they are reasonable. They will refuse to enforce them—labelling them "penalty" provisions—when they bear no relationship to actual damages. One challenge in this area is distinguishing enforceable liquidated damages from unenforceable penalties.

TRUCK RENT-A-CENTER, INC. V. PURITAN FARMS 2ND, INC.

Court of Appeals of New York, 1977.
41 N.Y.2d 420, 361 N.E.2d 1015.

JASEN, JUDGE.

The principal issue on this appeal is whether a provision in a truck lease agreement which requires the payment of a specified amount of money to the lessor in the event of the lessee's breach is an enforceable liquidated damages clause, or, instead, provides for an unenforceable penalty.

Defendant Puritan Farms 2nd, Inc. (Puritan), was in the business of furnishing milk and milk products to customers through home delivery. In January, 1969, Puritan leased a fleet of 25 new milk delivery trucks from plaintiff Truck Rent-A-Center for a term of seven years commencing January 15, 1970. Under the provisions of a truck lease and service agreement entered into by the parties, the plaintiff was to supply the trucks and make all necessary repairs. Puritan was to pay an agreed upon weekly rental fee. It was understood that the lessor would finance the purchase of the trucks through a bank, paying the prime rate of interest on the date of the loan plus 2%. The rental charges on the trucks were to be adjusted in the event of a fluctuation in the interest rate above or below specified levels. The lessee was granted the right to purchase the trucks, at any time after 12 months following commencement of the lease, by paying to the lessor the amount then due and owing on the bank loan, plus an additional $100 per truck purchased.

Article 16 of the lease agreement provided that if the agreement should terminate prior to expiration of the term of the lease as a result of the lessee's breach, the lessor would be entitled to damages, "liquidated for all purposes", in the amount of all rentals that would have come due from the date of termination to the date of normal expiration of the term less the "re-rental value" of the vehicles, which was set at 50% of the rentals that would have become due. In effect, the lessee would be obligated to pay the lessor, as a consequence of breach, one half of all rentals that would have become due had the agreement run its full course. The agreement recited that, in arriving at the settled amount of damage, "the parties hereto have considered, among other factors, Lessor's substantial initial investment in purchasing or reconditioning for Lessee's service the demised motor vehicles, the uncertainty of Lessor's ability to re-enter the said vehicles, the costs to Lessor during any period the vehicles may remain idle until re-rented, or if sold, the uncertainty of the sales price and its possible attendant loss. The parties have also considered, among other factors, in so liquidating the said damages, Lessor's saving in expenditures for gasoline, oil and other service items."[1]

The bulk of the written agreement was derived from a printed form lease which the parties modified by both filling in blank spaces and typing in alterations. The agreement also contained several typewritten

---

[1] The text of article 16 of the lease, in pertinent part, reads as follows:

"16. Upon termination of this agreement, * * * Lessor * * * shall be entitled to damages, herein liquidated for all purposes * * * as follows:

"(a) The sum of all rents designated as 'Fixed Rental Charges' which would have become due under the normal operation of this agreement from the date of the said termination * * * including any effective renewal period; less

"(b) The re-rental value of said motor vehicles which is hereby agreed upon as fifty per cent (50%) of the sum of such 'Fixed Rental Charges' as are set forth in subdivision '(a)' of this article.

"In arriving at said liquidated damages, the parties hereto have considered, among other factors, Lessor's substantial * * * investment in purchasing or reconditioning for Lessee's service the demised motor vehicles, the uncertainty of Lessor's ability to re-enter the said vehicles, the costs to Lessor during any period the vehicles may remain idle until re-rented, or if sold, the uncertainty of the sales price and its possible attendant loss. The parties have also considered, among other factors, in so liquidating the said damages, Lessor's saving in expenditures for gasoline, oil and other service items."

indorsements which also made changes in the provisions of the printed lease. The provision for lessee's purchase of the vehicles for the bank loan balance and $100 per vehicle was contained in one such indorsement. The liquidated damages clause was contained in the body of the printed form.

Puritan tendered plaintiff a security deposit, consisting of four weeks' rent and the lease went into effect. After nearly three years, the lessee sought to terminate the lease agreement. On December 7, 1973, Puritan wrote to the lessor complaining that the lessor had not repaired and maintained the trucks as provided in the lease agreement. Puritan stated that it had "repeatedly notified" plaintiff of these defaults, but plaintiff had not cured them. Puritan, therefore, exercised its right to terminate the agreement "without any penalty and *without purchasing the trucks*". (Emphasis added.) On the date set for termination, December 14, 1973, plaintiff's attorneys replied to Puritan by letter to advise it that plaintiff believed it had fully performed its obligations under the lease and, in the event Puritan adhered to the announced breach, would commence proceedings to obtain the liquidated damages provided for in article 16 of the agreement. Nevertheless, Puritan had its drivers return the trucks to plaintiff's premises, where the bulk of them have remained ever since. At the time of termination, plaintiff owed $45,134.17 on the outstanding bank loan.

Plaintiff followed through on its promise to commence an action for the payment of the liquidated damages. Defendant counterclaimed for the return of its security deposit. At the nonjury trial, plaintiff contended that it had fully performed its obligations to maintain and repair the trucks. Moreover, it was submitted, Puritan sought to cancel the lease because corporations allied with Puritan had acquired the assets, including delivery trucks, of other dairies and Puritan believed it cheaper to utilize this "shadow fleet". The home milk delivery business was on the decline and plaintiff's president testified that efforts to either re-rent or sell the truck fleet to other dairies had not been successful. Even with modifications in the trucks, such as the removal of the milk racks and a change in the floor of the trucks, it was not possible to lease the trucks to other industries, although a few trucks were subsequently sold. The proceeds of the sales were applied to the reduction of the bank balance. The other trucks remained at plaintiff's premises, partially protected by a fence plaintiff erected to discourage vandals. The defendant countered with proof that plaintiff had not repaired the trucks promptly and satisfactorily.

At the close of the trial, the court found, based on the evidence it found to be credible, that plaintiff had substantially performed its obligations under the lease and that defendant was not justified in terminating the agreement. Further, the court held that the provision for liquidated damages was reasonable and represented a fair estimate of actual damages which would be difficult to ascertain precisely. "The parties, at the time the agreement was entered into, considered many factors affecting damages, namely: the uncertainty of the plaintiff's ability to re-rent the said vehicles; the plaintiff's investment in purchasing and reconditioning the vehicles to suit the defendant's particular purpose; the number of man hours not utilized in the non-service of the vehicles in the event of a breach; the uncertainty of reselling the vehicles in question; the uncertainty of the plaintiff's savings or expenditures for gasoline, oil or other service items, and the amount of fluctuating interest on the bank loan." The court calculated that plaintiff would have been entitled to $177,355.20 in rent for the period remaining in the lease and, in accordance with the liquidated damages provision, awarded plaintiff half that amount, $88,677.60. The resulting judgment was affirmed by the Appellate Division, with two Justices dissenting. (51 A.D.2d 786, 380 N.Y.S.2d 37.)

The primary issue before us is whether the "liquidated damages" provision is enforceable. Liquidated damages constitute the compensation which, the parties have agreed, should be paid in order to satisfy any loss or injury flowing from a breach of their contract. (*Wirth & Hamid Fair Booking v. Wirth,* 265 N.Y. 214, 223, 192 N.E. 297, 301.) In effect, a liquidated damage provision is an estimate, made by the parties at the time they enter into their agreement, of the extent of the injury that would be sustained as a result of breach of the agreement. (5 Williston, Contracts [3d ed.], § 776, p. 668.) Parties to a contract have the right to agree to such clauses, provided that the clause is neither unconscionable nor contrary to public policy. (*Mosler Safe Co. v. Maiden Lane Safe Deposit Co.,* 199 N.Y. 479, 485, 93 N.E. 81, 83.) Provisions for liquidated damage have value in those situations where it would be difficult, if not actually impossible, to calculate the amount of actual damage. In such cases, the contracting parties may agree between themselves as to the amount of damages to be paid upon breach rather than leaving that amount to the calculation of a court or jury. (14 N.Y.Jur., Damages, § 155, pp. 4–5.)

On the other hand, liquidated damage provisions will not be enforced if it is against public policy to do so and public policy is firmly set against the imposition of penalties or forfeitures for which there is no statutory authority. (*City of Rye v. Public Serv. Mut. Ins. Co.,* 34 N.Y.2d 470, 472–473, 358 N.Y.S.2d 391, 392–393, 315 N.E.2d 458, 459.) It is plain that a provision which requires, in the event of contractual breach, the payment of a sum of money grossly disproportionate to the amount of actual damages provides for penalty and is unenforceable. * * * A liquidated damage provision has its basis in the principle of just compensation for loss. (Cf. Restatement, Contracts, § 339, and Comment thereon.) A clause which provides for an amount plainly disproportionate to real damage is not intended to provide fair compensation but to secure performance by the compulsion of the very disproportion. A promisor would be compelled, out of fear of economic devastation, to continue performance and his promisee, in the event of default, would reap a windfall well above actual harm sustained. * * *

The rule is now well established. A contractual provision fixing damages in the event of breach will be sustained if the amount liquidated bears a reasonable proportion to the probable loss and the amount of actual loss is incapable or difficult of precise estimation. * * * If, however, the amount fixed is plainly or grossly disproportionate to the probable loss, the provision calls for a penalty and will not be enforced. * * * In interpreting a provision fixing damages, it is not material whether the parties themselves have chosen to call the provision one for "liquidated damages", as in this case, or have styled it as a penalty. * * * Such an approach would put too much faith in form and too little in substance. Similarly, the agreement should be interpreted as of the date of its making and not as of the date of its breach. * * *

In applying these principles to the case before us, we conclude that the amount stipulated by the parties as damages bears a reasonable relation to the amount of probable actual harm and is not a penalty. Hence, the provision is enforceable and the order of the Appellate Division should be affirmed.

Looking forward from the date of the lease, the parties could reasonably conclude, as they did, that there might not be an actual market for the sale or re-rental of these specialized vehicles in the event of the lessee's breach. To be sure, plaintiff's lost profit could readily be measured by the amount of the weekly rental fee. However, it was permissible for the parties, in advance, to agree that the re-rental or sale value of the vehicles would be 50% of the weekly rental. Since there was uncertainty as to whether the trucks could be re-rented or sold, the parties could reasonably set, as they did, the value of such mitigation at 50% of the amount the lessee was obligated to pay for rental of the trucks. This would take into consideration the fact that, after being used by the lessee, the vehicles would no longer be "shiny, new trucks", but would be used, possibly battered, trucks, whose value would have declined appreciably. The parties also considered the fact that, although plaintiff, in the event of Puritan's breach, might be spared repair and maintenance costs necessitated by Puritan's use of the trucks, plaintiff would have to assume the cost of storing and maintaining trucks idled by Puritan's refusal to use them. Further, it was by no means certain, at the time of the contract, that lessee would peacefully return the trucks to the lessor after lessee had breached the contract.

With particular reference to the dissent at the Appellate Division, it is true that the lessee might have exercised an option to purchase the trucks. However, lessee would not be purchasing 25 "shiny, new trucks" for a mere $2,500. Rather, lessee, after the passage of one year from the commencement of the term, could have purchased trucks that had been used for at least one year for the amount outstanding on the bank loan, in addition to the $2,500. Of course, the purchase price would be greater if the option were exercised early in the term rather than towards the end of the term since plaintiff would be making payments to the bank all the while.[2] More fundamental, the existence of the option clause has absolutely no bearing on the validity of the discrete, liquidated damages provision. The lessee could have elected to purchase the trucks but elected not to do so. In fact, the lessee's letter of termination made a point of the fact that the lessee did not want to purchase the trucks. The reality is that the lessee sought, by its wrongful termination of the lease, to evade all obligations to the plaintiff, whether for rent or for the agreed upon purchase price. Its effort to do so failed. That lessee could have made a better bargain for itself by purchasing the trucks for $48,134.17[3] pursuant to the option, instead of paying $92,341.79 in damages for wrongful breach of the lease is not availing to it now. Although the lessee might now wish, with the benefit of hindsight, that it had purchased the trucks rather than default on its lease obligations, the simple fact is that it did not do so.

We attach no significance to the fact that the liquidated damages clause appears on the preprinted form portion of the agreement. The agreement was fully negotiated and the provisions of the form, in many other respects, were amended. There is no indication of any disparity of bargaining power or of unconscionability. The provision for liquidated damages related reasonably to potential harm that was difficult to estimate and did not constitute a disguised penalty. We also find no merit in the claim of trial error advanced by Puritan.

Accordingly, the order of the Appellate Division should be affirmed, with costs.

PROBLEM 3-11

In a number of cases in Section Four, losses of the type involved were not recoverable under the general law of damages. Would a properly drafted liquidated damages clause have made recovery possible in any of these cases? For example, would a liquidated damages provision compensating for mental distress damages be enforceable in Chrum v. Charles Heating & Cooling, Inc.?

---

[2] According to the lease agreement, the amount of plaintiff's bank loan payments were not to vary and interest and amortization were to be constant.

[3] This sum represents the $45,634.17 still owed by plaintiff on the bank loan, plus $2,500 ($100 for each of the 25 trucks).

NOTE: POSSIBLE RECOVERY UNDER A STIPULATED DAMAGES CLAUSE WHEN THERE ARE NO ACTUAL DAMAGES

Can a party recover under a stipulated damages clause even though the other party's breach caused no actual damages? There are cases suggesting or holding in the affirmative. An example is Southwest Engineering Co. v. United States, 341 F.2d 998 (8th Cir.1965). There the court stated:

> We believe that the cases holding that the situation existing at the time of the contract is controlling in determining the reasonableness of liquidated damages are based upon sound reasoning and represent the weight of authority. Where parties have by their contract agreed upon a liquidated damage provision as a reasonable forecast of just compensation for breach of contract and damages are difficult to estimate accurately, such provision should be enforced. If in the course of subsequent developments, damages prove to be greater than those stipulated, the party entitled to damages is bound by the liquidated damage agreement. It is not unfair to hold the contractor performing the work to such agreement if by reason of later developments damages prove to be less or nonexistent. Each party by entering into such contractual provision took a calculated risk and is bound by reasonable contractual provisions pertaining to liquidated damages.

Do you agree with the court? If the parties assume that the breach will cause some damages when they draft a stipulated damages provision, should the court interpret the clause to deny recovery when there are no damages? See also Ladco Properties XVII, LLC v. Jefferson-Pilot Life Ins. Co., 523 F. Supp. 2d 940, 952 (S.D. Iowa 2007) (quoting Knutton v. Cofield, 273 N.C. 355, 160 S.E.2d 29, 35 (S.C. 1968) ("The general rule in North Carolina, however, is that 'the amount stipulated in a contract as liquidated damages for a breach, if not a penalty, may be recovered in the event of a breach even though no actual damages are suffered.' "); Guiliano v. Cleo, Inc., 995 S.W.2d 88 (Tenn.1999); California and Hawaiian Sugar Co. v. Sun Ship, Inc., 794 F.2d 1433 (9th Cir.1986).

Not all courts enthusiastically award stipulated damages in the absence of actual damages. For example, in Massman Construction Co. v. City Council of Greenville, 147 F.2d 925 (5th Cir.1945), Massman failed to complete certain bridge construction within the time specified. Nonetheless, the delay caused no damages because, among other things, Massman completed the bridge before the construction of a road to the bridge. The court refused to enforce the damages clause. To the same effect, see Garden Ridge, L.P. v. Advance Int'l, Inc., 403 S.W.3d 432 (Tex. App. 2013); Mihlfeld & Assocs., Inc. v. Bishop & Bishop, LLC, 295 S.W.3d 163, 172 (Mo. Ct. App. 2009). In the Garden Ridge case, the court noted that Garden Ridge, a purchaser for resale of inflatable holiday snowmen, "made all the money it would have made if the snowmen were delivered exactly as ordered." The court then found that "both the common law and the UCC allow courts to determine the reasonableness of a liquidated-damages clause by considering whether the defendant has shown that the stipulated amount was unreasonably large compared to the actual damages."

PROBLEM 3-12

According to Dunbar, Drafting The Liquidated Damage Clause—When And How, 20 Ohio State L.J. 221, 234–35 (1959):

> The draftsman should:
>
> (1) Make sure that the damages stipulated will fall within the range between the upper and lower limits of potential actual damages foreseeable at the time of the making of the contract. Otherwise, the provision is likely to be held to be invalid as prescribing a penalty.
>
> (2) See to it that the parties actually, seriously negotiate on the question of the amount of measure of the liquidated damages, with full consideration of all foreseeable consequences of breach. Then, for added protection, incorporate in the contract recitals which will show that they have done so.
>
> (3) If the contemplated breach is of a covenant which requires the party to perform a particular act within a time limit, provide suitable machinery for reasonable extensions to adjust for delays which may result from actions or derelictions of the other party or of third parties. Especially do so in construction contracts.
>
> (4) Make the amount of damages agreed upon vary with extent of the breach, such as duration of the delay or period of default.
>
> (5) Incorporate a suitable recital indicating that it was the intention of the parties to provide for liquidated damages; at least, characterize by using the words "liquidated damages." Before some courts, it may help.
>
> (6) Recite the facts which caused the parties to incorporate the provision in the contract, such as that, for stated reasons, the amount of damages upon the breach will be very difficult to ascertain with precision.

VANDERBILT UNIVERSITY v. DINARDO

United States Court of Appeals, Sixth Circuit, 1999.
174 F.3d 751.

GIBSON, CIRCUIT JUDGE.

Gerry DiNardo resigned as Vanderbilt's head football coach to become the head football coach for Louisiana State University. As a result, Vanderbilt University brought this breach of contract action. The district court entered summary judgment for Vanderbilt, awarding $281,886.43

pursuant to a damage provision in DiNardo's employment contract with Vanderbilt. DiNardo appeals, arguing that the district court erred in concluding: (1) that the contract provision was an enforceable liquidated damage provision and not an unlawful penalty under Tennessee law; (2) that Vanderbilt did not waive its right to liquidated damages; (3) that the Addendum to the contract was enforceable; and (4) that the Addendum applied to the damage provision of the original contract. DiNardo also argues that there are disputed issues of material fact precluding summary judgment. We affirm the district court's ruling that the employment contract contained an enforceable liquidated damage provision and the award of liquidated damages under the original contract. We conclude, however, that there are genuine issues of material fact as to whether the Addendum was enforceable. We therefore reverse the judgment awarding liquidated damages under the Addendum and remand the case to the district court.

On December 3, 1990, Vanderbilt and DiNardo executed an employment contract hiring DiNardo to be Vanderbilt's head football coach. Section one of the contract provided:

> The University hereby agrees to hire Mr. DiNardo for a period of five (5) years from the date hereof with Mr. DiNardo's assurance that he will serve the entire term of this Contract, a long-term commitment by Mr. DiNardo being important to the University's desire for a stable intercollegiate football program. * * *

The contract also contained reciprocal liquidated damage provisions. Vanderbilt agreed to pay DiNardo his remaining salary should Vanderbilt replace him as football coach, and DiNardo agreed to reimburse Vanderbilt should he leave before his contract expired. Section eight of the contract stated:

> Mr. DiNardo recognizes that his promise to work for the University for the entire term of this 5-year Contract is of the essence of this Contract to the University. Mr. DiNardo also recognizes that the University is making a highly valuable investment in his continued employment by entering into this Contract and its investment would be lost were he to resign or otherwise terminate his employment as Head Football Coach with the University prior to the expiration of this Contract. Accordingly, Mr. DiNardo agrees that in the event he resigns or otherwise terminates his employment as Head Football Coach (as opposed to his resignation or termination from another position at the University to which he may have been reassigned), prior to the expiration of this Contract, and is employed or performing services for a person or institution other than the University, he will pay to the University as liquidated damages an amount equal

> to his Base Salary, less amounts that would otherwise be deducted or withheld from his Base Salary for income and social security tax purposes, multiplied by the number of years (or portion(s) thereof) remaining on the Contract.

During contract negotiations, section eight was modified at DiNardo's request so that damages would be calculated based on net, rather than gross, salary.

Vanderbilt initially set DiNardo's salary at $100,000 per year. DiNardo received salary increases in 1992, 1993, and 1994.

[The court's discussion of the facts surrounding the contract Addendum, which purported to extend the terms of the contract by two years, are omitted.]

In November 1994, Louisiana State University contacted Vanderbilt in hopes of speaking with DiNardo about becoming the head football coach for L.S.U. Hoolahan gave DiNardo permission to speak to L.S.U. about the position. On December 12, 1994, DiNardo announced that he was accepting the L.S.U. position.

Vanderbilt sent a demand letter to DiNardo seeking payment of liquidated damages under section eight of the contract. Vanderbilt believed that DiNardo was liable for three years of his net salary: one year under the original contract and two years under the Addendum. DiNardo did not respond to Vanderbilt's demand for payment.

Vanderbilt brought this action against DiNardo for breach of contract. DiNardo removed the action to federal court, and both parties filed motions for summary judgment. The district court held that section eight was an enforceable liquidated damages provision, not an unlawful penalty, and that the damages provided under section eight were reasonable. *Vanderbilt University v. DiNardo,* 974 F.Supp. 638, 643 (M.D.Tenn.1997). The court held that Vanderbilt did not waive its contractual rights under section eight when it granted DiNardo permission to talk to L.S.U. and that the Addendum was enforceable and extended the contract for two years. *Id.* at 643–45. The court entered judgment against DiNardo for $281,886.43. *Id.* at 645. DiNardo appeals.

I.

DiNardo first claims that section eight of the contract is an unenforceable penalty under Tennessee law. DiNardo argues that the provision is not a liquidated damage provision but a "thinly disguised, overly broad non-compete provision," unenforceable under Tennessee law.

We review the district court's summary judgment de novo, using the same standard as used by the district court. * * * We view the evidence in the light most favorable to the non-moving party to determine whether there is a genuine issue as to any material fact. * * * Summary judgment is proper if the record shows that "there is no genuine issue as to any material fact and that the moving party is entitled to judgment as a matter of law." Fed.R.Civ.P. 56(c).

Contracting parties may agree to the payment of liquidated damages in the event of a breach. *See Beasley v. Horrell,* 864 S.W.2d 45, 48 (Tenn.Ct.App.1993). The term "liquidated damages" refers to an amount determined by the parties to be just compensation for damages should a breach occur. *See id.* Courts will not enforce such a provision, however, if the stipulated amount constitutes a penalty. *See id.* A penalty is designed to coerce performance by punishing default. *See id.* In Tennessee, a provision will be considered one for liquidated damages, rather than a penalty, if it is reasonable in relation to the anticipated damages for breach, measured prospectively at the time the contract was entered into, and not grossly disproportionate to the actual damages. *See Beasley,* 864 S.W.2d at 48; *Kimbrough & Co. v. Schmitt,* 939 S.W.2d 105, 108 (Tenn.Ct.App.1996). When these conditions are met, particularly the first, the parties probably intended the provision to be for liquidated damages. However, any doubt as to the character of the contract provision will be resolved in favor of finding it a penalty. *See Beasley,* 864 S.W.2d at 48.

The district court held that the use of a formula based on DiNardo's salary to calculate liquidated damages was reasonable "given the nature of the unquantifiable damages in the case." 974 F.Supp. at 642. The court held that parties to a contract may include consequential damages and even damages not usually awarded by law in a liquidated damage provision provided that they were contemplated by the parties. *Id.* at 643. The court explained:

> The potential damage to [Vanderbilt] extends far beyond the cost of merely hiring a new head football coach. It is this uncertain potentiality that the parties sought to address by providing for a sum certain to apply towards anticipated expenses and losses. It is impossible to estimate how the loss of a head football coach will affect alumni relations, public support, football ticket sales, contributions, etc. * * * As such, to require a precise formula for calculating damages resulting from the breach of contract by a college head football coach would be tantamount to barring the parties from stipulating to liquidated damages evidence in advance.

Id. at 642.

DiNardo contends that there is no evidence that the parties contemplated that the potential damage from DiNardo's resignation would go beyond the cost of hiring a replacement coach. He argues that his salary has no relationship to Vanderbilt's damages and that the liquidated damage amount is unreasonable and shows that the parties did not intend the provision to be for liquidated damages.

DiNardo's theory of the parties' intent, however, does not square with the record. The contract language establishes that Vanderbilt wanted the five-year contract because "a long-term commitment" by DiNardo was "important to the University's desire for a stable intercollegiate football program," and that this commitment was of "essence" to the contract. Vanderbilt offered the two-year contract extension to DiNardo well over a year before his original contract expired. Both parties understood that the extension was to provide stability to the program, which helped in recruiting players and retaining assistant coaches. Thus, undisputed evidence, and reasonable inferences therefrom, establish that both parties understood and agreed that DiNardo's resignation would result in Vanderbilt suffering damage beyond the cost of hiring a replacement coach.

This evidence also refutes DiNardo's argument that the district court erred in presuming that DiNardo's resignation would necessarily cause damage to the University. That the University may actually benefit from a coaching change (as DiNardo suggests) matters little, as we measure the reasonableness of the liquidated damage provision at the time the parties entered the contract, not when the breach occurred, *Kimbrough & Co.,* 939 S.W.2d at 108, and we hardly think the parties entered the contract anticipating that DiNardo's resignation would benefit Vanderbilt.

The stipulated damage amount is reasonable in relation to the amount of damages that could be expected to result from the breach. As we stated, the parties understood that Vanderbilt would suffer damage should DiNardo prematurely terminate his contract, and that these actual damages would be difficult to measure. *See Kimbrough & Co.,* 939 S.W.2d at 108.

* * *

* * * Vanderbilt hired DiNardo for a unique and specialized position, and the parties understood that the amount of damages could not be easily ascertained should a breach occur. Contrary to DiNardo's suggestion, Vanderbilt did not need to undertake an analysis to determine actual damages, and using the number of years left on the contract multiplied by the salary per year was a reasonable way to calculate damages considering the difficulty of ascertaining damages with certainty. *See Kimbrough & Co.,* 939 S.W.2d at 108. The fact that liquidated damages declined each year DiNardo remained under contract, is directly tied to the parties' express understanding of the importance of a long-term commitment from DiNardo. Furthermore, the liquidated damages provision was reciprocal and the result of negotiations between two parties, each of whom was represented by counsel.

We also reject DiNardo's argument that a question of fact remains as to whether the parties intended section eight to be a "reasonable estimate" of damages. The liquidated damages are in line with Vanderbilt's estimate of its actual damages. *See Kimbrough & Co.,* 939 S.W.2d at 108–09. Vanderbilt presented evidence that it incurred expenses associated with recruiting a new head coach of $27,000.00; moving expenses for the new coaching staff of $86,840; and a compensation difference between the coaching staffs of $184,311. The stipulated damages clause is reasonable under the circumstances, and we affirm the district court's conclusion that the liquidated damages clause is enforceable under Tennessee law.

[Next, the court found that (1) Vanderbilt did not waive its right to liquidated damages by allowing DiNardo to talk to L.S.U. and (2) an issue of fact remained concerning the enforcement of the Addendum.]

Accordingly, we affirm the district court's judgment that the contract contained an enforceable liquidated damage provision, and we affirm the portion of the judgment reflecting damages calculated under the original five-year contract. We reverse the district court's judgment concluding that the Addendum was enforceable as a matter of law. * * *

We affirm in part, reverse in part, and remand the case to the district court for further proceedings consistent with this opinion.

DAVID A. NELSON, CIRCUIT JUDGE, concurring in part and dissenting in part.

If section eight of the contract was designed primarily to quantify, in an objectively reasonable way, damages that the university could be expected to suffer in the event of a breach, such damages being difficult to measure in the absence of an agreed formula, the provision is enforceable as a legitimate liquidated damages clause. If section eight was designed primarily to punish Coach DiNardo for taking a job elsewhere, however, the provision is a penalty unenforceable under Tennessee law. My colleagues on the panel and I are in agreement, I believe, on both of these propositions. We disagree, however, as to section eight's primary function.

It seems to me that the provision was designed to function as a penalty, not as a liquidation of the university's damages. Insofar as the court holds otherwise, I am constrained to dissent. In all other respects, I concur in Judge Gibson's opinion and in the judgment entered pursuant to it.

My principal reasons for viewing section eight as a penalty are these: (1) although the damages flowing from a premature resignation would normally be the same whether or not Coach DiNardo took a job elsewhere, section eight does not purport to impose liability for liquidated damages unless the coach accepts another job; (2) the section eight formula incorporates other variables that bear little or no relation to any reasonable approximation of anticipated damages; and (3) there is no evidence that the parties were attempting, in section eight, to come up with a reasonable estimate of the university's probable loss if the coach left. I shall offer a few words of explanation on each of these points.

Section eight does not make Coach DiNardo liable for any liquidated damages at all, interestingly enough, unless, during the unexpired term of his contract, he "is employed or performing services for a person or institution other than the University * * *." But how the coach spends his post-resignation time could not reasonably be expected to affect the university's damages; should the coach choose to quit in order to lie on a beach somewhere, the university would presumably suffer the same damages that it would suffer if he quit to coach for another school. The logical inference, therefore, would seem to be that section eight was intended to penalize the coach for taking another job, and was not intended to make the university whole by liquidating any damages suffered as a result of being left in the lurch.

This inference is strengthened, as I see it, by a couple of other anomalies in the stipulated damages formula. First, I am aware of no reason to believe that damages arising from the need to replace a prematurely departing coach could reasonably be expected to vary in direct proportion to the number of years left on the coach's contract. Section eight, however, provides that for every additional year remaining on the contract, the stipulated damages will go up by the full amount of the annual take-home pay contemplated under the contract. Like the "other employment" proviso, this makes the formula look more like a penalty than anything else.

Second, the use of a "take-home pay" measuring stick suggests that the function of the stick was to rap the coach's knuckles and not to measure the university's loss. Such factors as the number of tax exemptions claimed by the coach, or the percentage of his pay that he might elect to shelter in a 401(k) plan, would obviously bear no relation at all to the university's anticipated damages.

Finally, the record before us contains no evidence that the contracting parties gave any serious thought to attempting to measure the actual effect that a premature departure could be expected to have on the university's bottom line. On the contrary, the record affirmatively shows that the university did not attempt to determine whether the section eight formula would yield a result reasonably approximating anticipated damages. The record shows that the university could not explain how its anticipated damages might be affected by the coach's obtaining employment elsewhere, this being a subject that the draftsman of the contract testified he had never thought about. And the record shows that the question of why the number of years remaining on the contract would have any bearing on the amount of the university's damages was never analyzed either.

In truth and in fact, in my opinion, any correspondence between the result produced by the section eight formula and a reasonable approximation of anticipated damages would be purely coincidental. What section eight prescribes is a penalty, pure and simple, and a penalty may not be enforced under Tennessee law. On remand, therefore, in addition to instructing the district court to try the factual questions identified in Judge Gibson's opinion, I would instruct the court to determine the extent of any actual damages suffered by the university as a result of Coach DiNardo's breach of his contract. Whether more than the section eight figure or less, I believe, the university's actual damages should be the measure of its recovery.

NOTE: *MORE ON DINARDO*

Consider the following additional points about the DiNardo case. First, the case record shows the contract's stipulated damages were bilateral, meaning that if DiNardo were terminated without fault, he would have received his salary for the remainder of the contracts' term with no obligation to mitigate. Does that fact cut in Vanderbilt's favor (the contract wasn't one-sided and oppressive) or DiNardo's (both parties sought to discourage breach). Second, as the court points out, non-compete clauses are unenforceable under Tennessee law. But is that really why the parties chose a stipulated payment? Professors Randall Thomas and Lawrence Van Horn, in a recent article studying 429 college football coach contracts, found only 23 that included a noncompete instead of a termination payment. If you were advising one of the parties, how would you weigh the advantages and disadvantages of liquidated damage clauses in this context?

RINALDI AND SONS, INC. v. WELLS FARGO ALARM SERVICE, INC., 39 N.Y.2d 191, 197, 383 N.Y.S.2d 256, 259, 347 N.E.2d 618, 620 (1976). A limitation of damages to $50 must be distinguished from a liquidated damages clause, "analytically a different category with different governing rules."

PROBLEM 3-13

Fran Burns and Blanken Construction Company are negotiating for the construction of a house. You are a senior partner in Truman & Budweiser and Blanken is an important client. Blanken's president, Alice Drake, asks the firm to draft a clause that will protect the company from unlimited liability in case it is late in completing the house. You ask your associate, Darlene Brown, to draft the provision. Brown gives you the following proposed provision:

> The Owner will suffer financial loss if the Project is not completed by the above date. The Contractor shall be liable for and shall pay to the

> Owner, on an actual expense basis as established by receipts, not more than $1,000 for packing and storage of furnishings and $30 per day for temporary accommodation.

Evaluate the provision. What additional language would you include, if any? What changes would you make, if any? Is the provision one for liquidated damages or is it a limitation of consequential damages? Does it matter? (For the rule governing the latter type of clause in the sale of goods setting, see U.C.C. § 2–719(3), which states in part: "Consequential damages may be limited or excluded unless the limitation or exclusion is unconscionable.").

UNIFORM COMMERCIAL CODE § 2–718(1).

Damages for breach by either party may be liquidated in the agreement but only at an amount which is reasonable in the light of the anticipated or actual harm caused by the breach, the difficulties of proof of loss, and the inconvenience or nonfeasibility of otherwise obtaining an adequate remedy. A term fixing unreasonably large liquidated damages is void as a penalty.

HEMLOCK SEMICONDUCTOR CORP. V. KYOCERA CORP.

United States Court of Appeals, Sixth Circuit, 2018.
747 Fed.Appx. 285.

THAPAR, CIRCUIT JUDGE.

Kyocera Corporation is locked in a long-running bout with Hemlock Semiconductor Corporation and Hemlock Semiconductor, LLC, which supply Kyocera with polysilicon that it uses to make solar panels. Kyocera is fighting to get out of certain obligations under the parties' contracts. Below, the district court declared victory for Hemlock. But at this stage, Hemlock has earned only a partial victory. We therefore reverse in part and affirm in part.

I.

In the mid-2000s, the market for solar panels was taking off. Kyocera needed a steady supply of quality polysilicon. So it entered into four contracts with Hemlock, in which Kyocera promised to purchase specified amounts of polysilicon from Hemlock at specified prices over the course of the next ten years or so.

Those contracts contain so-called "take-or-pay" provisions. Under these provisions, the contracts require Kyocera to "take" a specified quantity of polysilicon from Hemlock each year. But if Kyocera does not want to take the polysilicon in a given year, Kyocera still has to "pay" full price for it. This means that Kyocera is on the hook for a certain quantity of polysilicon annually, whether it takes the polysilicon or not.

The contracts also contain so-called "acceleration" provisions. If Kyocera defaults under the contracts, these provisions accelerate the amount it owes Hemlock, such that Hemlock can demand *all* remaining sums owed. For these acceleration provisions to take effect, Kyocera must default, Hemlock must serve notice of default, and Hemlock must give Kyocera 180 days to cure its default. But if Kyocera does not cure, Hemlock can elect to terminate, at which point Kyocera becomes liable for all remaining payments due—effectively, the sum of the take-or-pay provisions.

Several years into Kyocera and Hemlock's deal, the Chinese government disrupted the solar-panel market by subsidizing Chinese solar-panel companies. This intervention reduced the market price of polysilicon such that the price Kyocera agreed to pay Hemlock was far greater than the going rate. And so Kyocera sought to renegotiate. Initially, the parties came to a compromise, temporarily lowering the price of polysilicon under the parties' deal. But eventually, Hemlock signaled that it would begin insisting that Kyocera take or pay for polysilicon at the original (and now inflated) price.

This litigation ensued. Hemlock sought a declaratory judgment that Kyocera had repudiated the parties' contracts by indicating that it would not take or pay at the original price. In response, Kyocera counterclaimed, seeking a declaratory judgment that the "pay" portion of the take-or-pay provisions is an unlawful penalty, and thus that the acceleration provisions are too. Kyocera also counterclaimed for breach of contract, alleging that three of the parties' contracts obligated Hemlock to expand certain production facilities, which Hemlock had not done. Hemlock moved to dismiss Kyocera's counterclaims, and the district court agreed. Kyocera now appeals.

II.

Kyocera first appeals the dismissal of its challenge to the take-or-pay provisions. We review the district court's decision de novo. * * *

In assessing Kyocera's claim, we apply Michigan law—the law of the forum state and that designated in the parties' contracts. * * * As it happens, Michigan's courts provide little guidance here. The thrust of Kyocera's claim is that the take-or-pay provisions are unlawful penalties in disguise. But there is no case in which a Michigan court has considered such a claim. * * *

With no Michigan authority on point, we must look elsewhere to attempt to discern what path the Michigan Supreme Court might take. * * * Under the approach followed in other jurisdictions, the key question is whether the take-or-pay provisions offer Kyocera two viable performance options, on the one hand, or one performance option coupled with a liquidated damages provision, on the other. * * * If the former, the take-or-pay provisions are enforceable as written. If the latter, the question becomes whether the "pay" option quantifies lawful liquidated damages or an unlawful penalty. If the payment obligation is a penalty, it is unenforceable—regardless of what the parties' contract labels it. And at least on this point, Michigan law certainly agrees. * * *

Alternative Performance v. Liquidated Damages. First, we ask whether the take-or-pay provisions offer Kyocera two viable performance options, or one option coupled with liquidated damages. To make this call, courts consider whether, at the time of contracting, it appears that the parties intended that the "pay" option present a relatively equivalent (and thus desirable) mode of performance—and not, as Kyocera claims, a measure to coerce compliance with the "take" option. * * * And at the outset, common sense points to coercion: Why would Kyocera opt to pay for polysilicon and get nothing in return? * * *

Hemlock offers three suggestions. First, Hemlock reasons that Kyocera must have seen the pay option as a viable alternative, because Kyocera is a big, smart corporation and would never have agreed to the deal otherwise. But the fact that a sophisticated entity has agreed to pay a sum does not necessarily mean that the law will always enforce its promise, *see, e.g., Lake River Corp. v. Carborundum Co.*, 769 F.2d 1284, 1289 (7th Cir. 1985), and Hemlock points to no Michigan authority holding otherwise. Kyocera's sophistication at the bargaining table may later become relevant, but in this posture, it does not doom Kyocera's claim as a matter of law. So Hemlock's first argument swings and misses. Second, Hemlock hypothesizes that Kyocera might have thought that in certain circumstances it would be willing to pay for polysilicon one year (but not take it) as a way to keep the contract alive in the event it still wanted polysilicon in the future. But if Kyocera wanted to keep the contract alive, it could simply purchase polysilicon *and take delivery*. It would not need to pay and get nothing in return. So here again, Hemlock swings and misses.

Hemlock saves its best swing for last. Moving and storing polysilicon is not free. And so Hemlock theorizes that, if the price of polysilicon tanks [falls] (as it did here), it might make sense for Kyocera to pay for polysilicon without taking it in order to avoid transportation and storage costs. If the math is right, and the parties intended for the "pay" provision to account for this possibility, Hemlock may have a point. But nothing in the pleadings suggests that this math influenced the parties' negotiations. In fact, Kyocera alleges that there were no such negotiations. Nor do the pleadings suggest that the price of polysilicon has fallen so much that transportation and storage costs would justify paying for polysilicon without taking it. At this stage, we consider only Kyocera's allegations, viewed in a light most favorable to Kyocera, construing all reasonable inferences in Kyocera's favor. * * * Accepting Hemlock's transportation-and-storage argument at this juncture would disregard those precepts. So we are left with the common-sense conclusion that paying a lot of money for nothing in return is not a real performance option under a contract. To be sure, if discovery bears out Hemlock's point, Kyocera's claim may later fail. But for now, Hemlock goes down swinging.

Moreover, two additional allegations further support the conclusion that paying something for nothing is not a valid performance option. Both have to do with the kind of provisions that normally appear in lawful take-or-pay contracts. First, the take-or-pay provisions do not contain "make-up rights" that would credit any money advanced under the "pay" option to Kyocera's purchase of polysilicon in future years. Make-up-rights are common in enforceable take-or-pay arrangements. * * * Although the absence of make-up rights may not be dispositive, *see World Fuel Servs., Inc. v. John E. Retzner Oil Co., Inc.*, 234 F.Supp.3d 1234, 1241 (S.D. Fla. 2017), their absence nevertheless pushes Kyocera's claim further into the realm of plausibility, * * *. Second, while lawful take-or-pay arrangements often involve the *seller* (here, Hemlock) bearing construction costs and associated risks at the outset of a contract, *see, e.g., Diamond Shamrock Expl. Co. v. Hodel*, 853 F.2d 1159, 1167 (5th Cir. 1988), the contracts at issue required *Kyocera* to front Hemlock money for construction and expansion. So Kyocera—not Hemlock—bore these costs and risks from the start. True, the contracts do require Hemlock to repay this money to Kyocera over time, as a credit against purchases of polysilicon—meaning that eventually, Hemlock internalizes these costs. But it is far from clear that the parties envisioned that the pay option would compensate Hemlock for these costs this late in the duration of the contracts, when construction and expansion are long over and Hemlock has been providing Kyocera with polysilicon for over a decade. Thus, these allegations further belie any conceivable purpose for the pay option other than to liquidate damages.

Liquidated Damages v. Penalty. The fact that the pay option might not be a valid mode of performance is not the end of the inquiry. If the pay option is a lawful measure of liquidated damages, then it is nevertheless enforceable. * * * But if not, it is a penalty, and Hemlock can seek only its actual damages. * * *

Under Michigan law, damages can be liquidated, "but only at an amount which is reasonable in the light of the anticipated or actual harm caused by the breach, the difficulties of proof of loss, and the inconvenience or nonfeasibility of otherwise obtaining an adequate remedy." Mich. Comp. Laws § 440.2718(1). Otherwise, the clause is "void as a penalty." *Id.* Demanding full price for nothing in return seems unreasonable for one of two reasons. First, if Hemlock has already produced Kyocera's polysilicon, requiring Kyocera to pay the full contract price fails to account for Hemlock's ability to resell the polysilicon elsewhere. Or, if Hemlock can avoid producing the polysilicon at all—as Kyocera alleges happened here—requiring Kyocera to pay full price fails to account for any costs Hemlock would save. Here again, common-sense points to a problem: Under the pay option, Hemlock can get all the money promised under the contract but do nothing, thereby making a *greater* profit than if the parties performed as envisioned. * * *

* * *

[T]the district court dismissed Kyocera's claim at the pleading stage—without the benefit of expert testimony or other record information that might justify the amount owing under the pay provisions. So in this posture, we cannot say that requiring Kyocera to pay full price for nothing is a reasonable measure of damages. This is particularly so in light of Kyocera's allegations that Hemlock could have adjusted the amount due under the "pay" option to account for cost savings at the time of contracting, but did not. Down the road, the record may develop in this case such that Kyocera's claim falters * * *. But for now, Kyocera's claim passes muster, and the district court erred by dismissing it on the pleadings.

[The dissenting opinion (on other grounds) of Circuit Judge Clay is omitted.]

HILLMAN, THE LIMITS OF BEHAVIORAL DECISION THEORY IN LEGAL ANALYSIS: THE CASE OF LIQUIDATED DAMAGES

85 Cornell L. Rev. 717, 718–719, 726–728, 738 (2000).

Based on society's respect for individual freedom, its moral view that people should keep their promises, and its perspective that private exchange best allocates and distributes resources, freedom of contract enjoys a predominant role as a justificatory principle of contract law. Contract law allows parties to agree on contract terms as they choose and, in the absence of demonstrable market failures such as unequal bargaining power or concrete infirmities such as diminished capacity, evaluates the validity of their choices largely based on their objective manifestation of assent. Courts operating within this conceptual framework rarely intercede in parties' agreements to test the adequacy of consideration.

On the other hand, courts readily impinge on freedom of contract when assessing the validity of agreed (also called liquidated) damages clauses. Regardless of the quality of bargaining and the type of parties, if a court determines that an agreed damages provision is a "penalty," the court will refuse to enforce the provision. Why do judges single out liquidated damages provisions for special treatment? * * *

* * *

* * * Courts and commentators offer several explanations related to either the substance of agreed damages provisions, the bargaining process that produced them, or both. None of these explanations seems wholly

satisfactory. For example, some analysts explain the modern judicial antipathy for agreed damages provisions as a holdover from the equity court's practice of refusing to enforce penal bonds, in which a party promised to pay a certain sum if that party broke a contract. The equity court believed that contract remedies were designed to compensate the injured party for the loss, not to punish or coerce the breaching party into performing, even when the parties had agreed to the penal bond precisely for those latter purposes.

Modern courts apparently have greeted with open arms the equity court's response to penal bonds. Indeed, courts now seem to have a curiously heightened sensitivity to any agreed damages provision, whether penal or not. Courts have also accepted the equity court's estimation of the coercive and punitive effect of penal bonds without seriously investigating the accuracy and validity of that position. Whether courts should consider an agreed remedy that is incommensurate with actual damages to be punitive and coercive, however, depends on the nature of the bargaining that produced the clause. After all, if the promisee paid a premium for an agreed damages provision that is greater than actual damages and the promisor understood the significance of agreeing to the term, "just compensation" arguably would entail enforcing the provision. In fact, in the context of fair bargaining between business people, courts sometimes find palatable (and enforceable) provisions that amount to penalties, such as "take or pay" contracts in which purchasers of natural gas agree to pay regardless of whether they take the gas.

Modern courts therefore reinforce their antipathy to penalties by finding the bargaining process deficient. For example, courts generalize that parties do not negotiate agreed remedies provisions. Instead, courts believe that promisors share an " 'illusion[ ] of hope' " that nothing will go wrong and consequently fail to bargain adequately over remedial provisions. But even if this is an empirically accurate and otherwise persuasive explanation, why have courts singled out liquidated damages provisions for special treatment on this ground? For example, why do courts fail to police the parties' purported allocation of risk of unanticipated but calamitous circumstances with the same vigor to determine whether the parties were too optimistic that nothing would go wrong?

In addition, courts apparently believe that promisors are peculiarly susceptible to being coerced into agreeing to penalty provisions. Little evidence from actual cases supports this assertion and nothing about the nature of agreed remedies explains why promisees would have more leverage with respect to these clauses than any other clause.

Another alleged deficiency in the bargaining process with respect to agreed remedies is "the limits of cognition" of contracting parties in this context. Professor Eisenberg asserts that although parties can easily understand terms "such as subject matter, quantity, and price," they cannot comprehend "the scenarios of breach" and the "application of a liquidated damages provision" to these scenarios. In addition, parties discount the probability of breach based on a cost-benefit analysis tainted by optimism about performance. For these reasons, parties may fail to focus on liquidated damages provisions when agreeing to a contract, thereby supplying courts with a justification for scrutinizing these provisions more closely.

As with the other explanations for the policing of liquidated damages, the "limits of cognition" approach depends on the speculative assertion that parties' planning and bargaining of liquidated damages provisions are less effective than their planning and bargaining of other provisions. * * *

* * *

* * *[P]erhaps courts should abandon the special tests for agreed damages and simply apply traditional policing doctrines, such as unconscionability and duress. Courts employing this approach would strike an agreed damages provision only if they found it "oppressive" or the product of "unfair surprise." In short, agreed damages provisions probably should be treated like any other contract term.

NOTE:
PETE DAVIDSON'S NONDISCLOSURE AGREEMENT

Pete Davidson, of Saturday Night Live fame, sought to require fans attending his shows to sign a $1 million nondisclosure agreement (NDA) in order to deter fans from divulging the jokes in his show. Would the NDA be enforceable or would the joke be on Davidson?

SECTION SEVEN: MONETARY REMEDIES WHERE THE THEORY OF OBLIGATION IS PROMISSORY ESTOPPEL

Recall that § 90 of the Restatement (First) of Contracts provides:

> A promise which the promisor should reasonably expect to induce action or forbearance of a definite and substantial character on the part of the promisee and which does induce such action or forbearance is binding if injustice can be avoided only by enforcement of the promise.

In 1926 at an American Law Institute meeting devoted in part to proposed § 90, the Reporter, Professor Samuel Williston, put the following hypothetical case: Suppose Johnny says to his uncle: "I want to buy a Buick car." The uncle responds: "I will give you $1000." A member of the ALI, Mr. Frederick Coudert, asked Professor Williston whether, if Johnny thereafter bought the car in reliance on his uncle's promise but paid only $500 for it, Uncle would still be liable for $1000. The exchange below ensued. Consider who is right.

> *Mr. Williston:* "If Johnny had done what he was expected to do, or is acting within the limits of his uncle's expectation, I think the uncle would be liable for $1000; but not otherwise."
>
> *Mr. Coudert:* "In other words, substantial justice would require that uncle should be penalized in the sum of $500."
>
> *Mr. Williston:* "Why do you say 'penalized'?"
>
> * * *
>
> *Mr. Coudert:* "Because substantial justice there would require, it seems to me, that Johnny get his money for his car, but should he get his car and $500 more? * * * "
>
> *Mr. Williston:* "Either the promise is binding or it is not. If the promise is binding it has to be enforced as it is made. As I said to Mr. Coudert, I could leave this whole thing to the subject of quasi contracts so that the promisee under the circumstances shall never recover on the promise but he shall recover such an amount as will fairly compensate him for any injury incurred; but it seems to me you have to take one leg or the other. You have either to say the promise is binding or you have to go on the theory of restoring the *status quo.*" American Law Institute Proceedings, vol. IV, Appendix 98–99, 103–04 (1926).

RESTATEMENT (SECOND) OF CONTRACTS § 90.

Promise Reasonably Inducing Action or Forbearance

(1) A promise which the promisor should reasonably expect to induce action or forbearance on the part of the promisee or a third person and which does induce such action or forbearance is binding if injustice can be avoided only by enforcement of the promise. The remedy granted for breach may be limited as justice requires.

* * *

Comment:

> b. *Character of Reliance Protected.* The principle of this Section is flexible. The promisor is affected only by reliance which he does or should foresee, and enforcement must be necessary to avoid injustice. Satisfaction of the latter requirement may depend on the reasonableness of the promisee's reliance, on its definite and substantial character in relation to the remedy sought, on the formality with which the promise is made, on the extent to which the

evidentiary, cautionary, deterrent and channeling functions of form are met by the commercial setting or otherwise, and on the extent to which such other policies as the enforcement of bargains and the prevention of unjust enrichment are relevant. * * *

* * *

d. *Partial Enforcement.* A promise binding under this section is a contract, and full-scale enforcement by normal remedies is often appropriate. But the same factors which bear on whether any relief should be granted also bear on the character and extent of the remedy. In particular, relief may sometimes be limited to restitution or to damages or specific relief measured by the extent of the promisee's reliance rather than by the terms of the promise. * * *

* * *

Reporter's Note.

The principal change from former sec. 90 is the recognition of the possibility of partial enforcement. See Fuller and Perdue, The Reliance Interest in Contract Damages, 46 Yale L.J. 52, 63–65 (1936). * * *

GOODMAN V. DICKER

U.S. Court of Appeals, District of Columbia Circuit, 1948.
169 F.2d 684.

PROCTOR, ASSOCIATE JUSTICE.

This appeal is from a judgment of the District Court in a suit by appellees for breach of contract.

Appellants are local distributors for Emerson Radio and Phonograph Corporation in the District of Columbia. Appellees, with the knowledge and encouragement of appellants, applied for a "dealer franchise" to sell Emerson's products. The trial court found that appellants by their representations and conduct induced appellees to incur expenses in preparing to do business under the franchise, including employment of salesmen and solicitation of orders for radios. Among other things, appellants represented that the application had been accepted; that the franchise would be granted, and that appellees would receive an initial delivery of thirty to forty radios. Yet, no radios were delivered, and notice was finally given that the franchise would not be granted.

The case was tried without a jury. The court held that a contract had not been proven but that appellants were estopped from denying the same by reason of their statements and conduct upon which appellees relied to their detriment. Judgment was entered for $1500, covering cash outlays of $1150 and loss of $350, anticipated profits on sale of thirty radios.

The main contention of appellants is that no liability would have arisen under the dealer franchise had it been granted because, as understood by appellees, it would have been terminable at will and would have imposed no duty upon the manufacturer to sell or appellees to buy any fixed number of radios. From this it is argued that the franchise agreement would not have been enforceable (except as to acts performed thereunder) and cancellation by the manufacturer would have created no liability for expenses incurred by the dealer in preparing to do business. Further, it is argued that as the dealer franchise would have been unenforceable for failure of the manufacturer to supply radios appellants would not be liable to fulfill their assurance that radios would be supplied.

We think these contentions miss the real point of this case. We are not concerned directly with the terms of the franchise. We are dealing with a promise by appellants that a franchise would be granted and radios supplied, on the faith of which appellees with the knowledge and encouragement of appellants incurred expenses in making preparations to do business. Under these circumstances we think that appellants cannot now advance any defense inconsistent with their assurance that the franchise would be granted. Justice and fair dealing require that one who acts to his detriment on the faith of conduct of the kind revealed here should be protected by estopping the party who has brought about the situation from alleging anything in opposition to the natural consequences of his own course of conduct. Dair v. United States, 1872, 16 Wall. 1, 4, 21 L.Ed. 491. In Dickerson v. Colgrove, 100 U.S. 578, 580, 25 L.Ed. 618, the Supreme Court, in speaking of equitable estoppel, said: "The law upon the subject is well settled. The vital principle is that he who by his language or conduct leads another to do what he would not otherwise have done, shall not subject such person to loss or injury by disappointing the expectations upon which he acted. Such a change of position is sternly forbidden. * * * This remedy is always so applied as to promote the ends of justice." * * *

In our opinion the trial court was correct in holding defendants liable for moneys which appellees expended in preparing to do business under the promised dealer franchise. These items aggregated $1150. We think, though, the court erred in adding the item of $350 for loss of profits on radios promised under an initial order. The true measure of damage is the loss sustained by expenditures made in reliance upon the assurance of a dealer franchise. As thus modified, the judgment is

Affirmed.

WALTERS V. MARATHON OIL CO.

United States Court of Appeal, Seventh Circuit, 1981.
642 F.2d 1098.

SPEARS, DISTRICT JUDGE.

This action arose as a result of the Iranian revolution and the uncertainty of oil supplies. Marathon Oil Company, the appellant, is engaged in the business of reselling and distributing petroleum products. The appellee, Dennis E. Walters, contacted appellant in late December, 1978, about the possibility of locating a combination foodstore and service station on a vacant gasoline service station site in Indianapolis. Appellees (husband and wife) purchased the service station in February, 1979, and continued to make improvements upon it, based upon promises made, and the continuing negotiations with representatives from appellant. Paper work apparently proceeded normally, and appellees' proposal was delivered to appellant along with a three-party agreement, signed by appellees and Time Oil Company, the previous supplier to the service station site appellees had purchased. Before appellees' proposal was accepted by appellant, but after it was received at the office, appellant placed a moratorium on the consideration of new applications for dealerships and seller arrangements, and refused to sign the three-party agreement.

After a bench trial, the court found for appellees and against appellant on the theory of promissory estoppel. This finding has not been challenged. The two issues presented for review in this appeal pertain only to the award of damages in the form of lost profits, and the alleged failure of appellees to take reasonable steps to mitigate their damages. We affirm the judgment of the district court.

The appellant first argues that the trial court committed error by ignoring evidence that appellees failed to take reasonable steps to mitigate their damages. The record clearly reflects, however, the appellees contacted Shell Oil Company, Standard Oil of Indiana, and Texaco with respect to becoming a new supplier of their service station, after appellant notified them it would not provide them with gasoline. Appellee, Dennis E. Walters, testified that he had telephoned the president of Time Oil, to seek a supply, but his request was declined. Appellees did not contact appellant, but they could hardly have been expected to do so, considering the treatment appellant had already given them. There are ample facts in the record to support the finding of the trial court that appellees exercised the ordinary care of a person in the same circumstances to mitigate their damages. That finding, under the evidence, was not clearly erroneous. Furthermore, the trial court found that the plaintiffs "had no gasoline market experience and were not familiar with the marketing practices of gasoline companies." Thus, the fact that alternative suppliers may have existed if appellees had asserted legal rights, and complied with Department of Energy regulations, does not alone impose the duty to mitigate damages by searching for additional sources, if appellees lacked the sophistication with which to conduct such a search.

The appellant next argues that the trial court's computation of damages is clearly erroneous and contrary to the law. The trial court found that appellees lost anticipated profits of six cents per gallon for the 370,000 gallons they were entitled to receive under their allocation for the first year's gasoline sales, totaling $22,200.00, and awarded this amount in damages. The appellant insists that since appellees succeeded at trial solely on a promissory estoppel theory, and the district court so found, loss of profits is not a proper measure of damages. It contends that appellees' damages should have been the amount of their expenditures in reliance on the promise, measured by the difference between their expenditures and the present value of the property. Using this measure of damages, appellees would have received no award, for the present value of the real estate and its improvements is slightly more than the amount expended by appellees in reliance upon the promise. As a consequence, the appellant says that because appellees can recoup all they spent in reliance on appellant's promise, they would be in the same position they would have been in had the promise not been made.

However, in reliance upon appellant's promise to supply gasoline supplies to them, appellees purchased the station, and invested their funds and their time. It is unreasonable to assume that they did not anticipate a return of profits from this investment of time and funds, but, in reliance upon appellant's promise, they had foregone the opportunity to make the investment elsewhere. As indicated, the record reflects that had appellant performed according to its promise, appellees would have received the anticipated net profit of $22,200.00. The findings of the trial court in this regard were fully supported by the evidence. For example, it was shown that the [1977/78] base period for this particular station was 375,450 gallons. The appellant's own exhibit reflected the same amount. The testimony of the previous owner showed that the location pumped 620,000 gallons in 1972, and that he pumped 375,450 gallons in 1978. Furthermore, an expert witness testified that the site would pump 360,000 gallons a year. Appellant's own witness testified that all of its dealers received 100% of their base period allocation for the time in question. Thus, the trial court was not clearly erroneous in its finding that appellees would have sold 370,000 gallons of gasoline had appellant's promise been performed.

An equity court possesses some discretionary power to award damages in order to do complete justice. * * * Furthermore, since it is the historic purpose of equity to secure complete justice, the courts are able to adjust the remedies so as to grant the necessary relief, * * * and a district court sitting in equity may even devise a remedy which extends or exceeds the terms of a prior agreement between the parties, if it is necessary to make the injured party whole. *Levitt Corp. v. Levitt,* 593 F.2d 463 (2d Cir.1979).

Since promissory estoppel is an equitable matter, the trial court has broad power in its choice of a remedy, and it is significant that the ancient maxim that "equity will not suffer a wrong to be without a remedy" has long been the law in the State of Indiana. * * *

In this case the promissory estoppel finding of the district court is not challenged. Moreover, it is apparent that the appellees suffered a loss of profits as a direct result of their reliance upon the promise made by appellant, and the amount of the lost profits was ascertained with reasonable certainty.[1] In addition, appellees took reasonable steps to mitigate their damages, and an award of damages based upon lost profits was appropriate in order to do complete justice.

Under the circumstances, and concluding, as we do, that the findings of the district court are not clearly erroneous, we affirm the judgment which awards damages to appellees based upon lost profits.

AFFIRMED.

PROBLEM 3-14

Alice White worked for Federal Aviation for 40 years as an airplane mechanic. Federal Aviation then promised White a lifetime pension of $200 per week when she retires. After hearing the promise, Alice turned down an offer of employment for 3 years at $175 per week from American Aviation, a competitor of Federal, and she retired. Federal then withdrew the promise of a pension before paying Alice anything. Alice comes to your law office and asks you what her rights are against Federal. Please explain.

NOTE:
RELIANCE RECOVERY WHEN THE AGREEMENT HAS BEEN DISRUPTED

In Chapter Eight, we will see that a contracting party occasionally may rightfully cease performance because of the occurrence of an unforeseen contingency that makes performance unfairly onerous or impossible or even

---

[1] In *Goodman v. Dicker,* 169 F.2d 684 (D.C.Cir.1948), relied upon by appellant, the court held that the true measure of damages in that equitable estoppel case was the loss in the sum of $1150 sustained by expenditures made in reliance on assurances given to the injured parties, and that the trial court had erred in *adding* the item of $350 for lost profits. No reasons were assigned or authorities cited by the court for the action it took, and there was no suggestion that in an appropriate case loss of profits could not be a true measure of damages. In any event, it is apparent that the award of double damages was rejected and the higher figure of $1150 was chosen in order to do complete justice. In this connection, it is interesting to note that in *National Savings and Trust Company v. Kahn,* 300 F.2d 910 (D.C.Cir.1962), the same circuit commented that "(T)he cost of performance may be the proper measure of damages where plaintiff renders part performance *and it is impossible to estimate the profits he would have received but for defendant's breach.* (Citing authorities). That is not this case." (Emphasis supplied). *See id.* at 914 n. 7.

because of a shared mistaken assumption about the facts existing at the time of contracting. Upon such a rightful cessation, we will see that the Restatement (Second) of Contracts and some modern courts suggest that a party may be entitled to recover reliance expenses.

SECTION EIGHT: RESTITUTIONARY RELIEF AND THEORIES OF OBLIGATION

Courts use the term "restitutionary relief" to refer both to monetary remedies and to certain forms of specific relief, such as an order requiring the defendant to return a specific item. In this section, we concentrate on monetary remedies. A monetary remedy is restitutionary in nature insofar as it requires A to pay B the monetary value of any benefit B conferred on A. Courts often base the measure of relief on either Restatement (Second) of Contracts, § 371(a) or (b), below. In addition, we will encounter additional measures of restitutionary relief. For example, courts sometimes award B its full outlay in preparing to perform or in performing, even if this measure exceeds A's gain.

In this section, we focus not only on restitutionary remedies but also on theories of obligation that justify the remedies. Sometimes the theory of obligation is unjust enrichment. Sometimes it is breach of an agreement with consideration. Sometimes the theory is quite obscure.

RESTATEMENT (SECOND) OF CONTRACTS § 371.

Measure of Restitution Interest

If a sum of money is awarded to protect a party's restitution interest, it may as justice requires be measured by either

(a) the reasonable value to the other party of what he received in terms of what it would have cost him to obtain it from a person in the claimant's position, or

(b) the extent to which the other party's property has been increased in value or his other interests advanced.

Comment:

a. *Measurement of benefit.* * * * An especially important choice is that between the reasonable value to a party of what he received in terms of what it would have cost him to obtain it from a person in the claimant's position and the addition to the wealth of that party as measured by the extent to which his property has been increased in value or his other interests advanced. In practice, the first measure is usually based on the market price of such a substitute. Under the rule stated in this Section, the court has considerable discretion in making the choice between these two measures of benefit. Under either choice, the court may properly consider the purposes of the recipient of the benefit when he made the contract, even if those purposes were later frustrated or abandoned.

b. *Choice of measure.* * * * [A] party seeking restitution for part performance is commonly allowed the more generous measure of reasonable value, unless that measure is unduly difficult to apply, except when he is in breach.

REALMARK DEVELOPMENTS, INC. v. RANSON, 214 W.Va. 161, 588 S.E.2d 150 (W. Va. 2003). In Robertus v. Candee, 205 Mont. 403, 670 P.2d 540 (1983), the Supreme Court of Montana explained why the measure of damages in this type of case can be either the quantum meruit value of the plaintiff's labor and materials or the value of the enhancement to the defendant's property. The Court stated:

> There may be cases where the enhancement to the defendant's property will be far less than the quantum meruit value of the plaintiff's efforts. For example, where the improvement did not enhance the value of the property but did result in a pecuniary saving to the defendant, the enhancement measure would not reflect the unjust enrichment. Conversely, there may be cases where the value of the enhancement greatly exceeds the cost of the improvement, as in this case.
>
> Thus the rule has evolved that the proper measure of damages in unjust enrichment should be the greater of the two measures. Restatement of Law, Contracts 2d § 371 comment b [(1981)]; 12 Williston, Contracts § 1480.

205 Mont. at 408–09, 670 P.2d at 543.

CRASWELL, AGAINST FULLER AND PERDUE

67 U. Chi. L. Rev. 99, 142 (2000).

* * * [T]here are actually many different remedial measures—some more generous to the promisee, some less so—that could plausibly pass under the name of restitution. If, for example, a builder finishes building half of a house before the homeowner unjustifiably repudiates the contract, and the builder then sues for the reasonable value of the half-completed house, that value could be measured in several different ways. To name just four, the builder might collect (a) any increase in the market value of the home-owner's land resulting from having a half-completed house on it; (b) whatever price the home-owner would have to pay another builder, at current construction rates, to build that half-completed house; (c) half of the price the home-owner originally agreed to pay this builder, for the fully completed house; or even (d) whatever this builder spent to build the first

half of the house, taking the builder's actual costs as a rough measure of the house's value. Depending on how favorable the original contract was, and also on what has happened to property values and construction costs since the original contract was signed, any one of these measures could (in a particular case) be larger or smaller than the others. They could also be either larger or smaller than any of the ways in which expectation damages might be measured, and so could exceed or fall short of the builder's expectation interest. As a result, it is highly misleading to speak of "restitution" as though it were a single unified remedy.

Of course, if these excesses and shortfalls were randomly distributed, there would be little reason to comment on them. But * * * there is some evidence that courts are influenced in their choice of measurement by how well or badly the breaching party behaved. For example, if the breach was particularly egregious, the courts may be more inclined to measure the nonbreacher's services in a way that gives him a particularly generous measure of recovery (or to measure the breacher's services in a way that minimizes their value). The egregiousness of the breacher's behavior may also be one factor in deciding whether the breach was "total" or "material," which is the doctrinal prerequisite for the nonbreacher to have the option of figuring his damages in restitution.

A. WHERE A NON-BREACHING PLAINTIFF CONFERRED A BENEFIT AND ELECTS A RESTITUTIONARY RECOVERY

In Posner v. Seder (Chapter 2), we saw that a party injured by the breach of an agreement with consideration may elect to recover the benefit conferred on the breacher under the theory of unjust enrichment, instead of expectancy damages for breach of contract. Here we focus on the problem of measurement of the benefit conferred when an injured party seeks restitution in this context.

UNITED STATES FOR USE OF SUSI CONTRACTING CO. v. ZARA CONTRACTING CO.

United States Court of Appeals, Second Circuit, 1944.
146 F.2d 606.

CLARK, CIRCUIT JUDGE.

Plaintiffs, Susi Contracting Co., Inc., and D'Agostino & Cuccio, Inc., brought this action under the provisions of the Miller Act, 40 U.S.C.A. § 270a et seq., in the name of the United States against Zara Contracting Co., Inc., and American Bonding Company of Baltimore, the surety on its bond, to recover for work performed for and equipment supplied Zara in the performance of its contract with the United States, dated March 4, 1941, for the extension of Tri-Cities Airport, Endicott, New York. On April

2, 1941, Zara entered into a subcontract with plaintiffs, wherein plaintiffs agreed, except for one $100 item, to perform the entire work called for by the main contract with the United States. This work involved the excavation of material and placing, manipulating, rolling, and compacting it as a base and surface course for landing strips or runways. During the course of the excavation plaintiffs encountered unexpected soil conditions, mostly due to the presence of a great deal of clay material, which made progress of their work extremely difficult, caused the breakdown of their tools, and, according to their allegations, generally required the performance of work not called for by the contract. Consequently on several occasions they made demands on Zara for extra money; and eventually the dispute arose which led to mutual claims of breach of contract and, by easy stages, to the opposing claims for monetary solace of this action. At any rate, defendant Zara took over the completion of the contract about July 12, 1941, or two months after plaintiffs had begun work. It also took possession of and for some three months utilized the equipment furnished by plaintiffs at the contract site.

In this action plaintiffs alleged that Zara wrongfully terminated the subcontract, and sought recovery for the reasonable cost and value of the actual work performed, and the fair and reasonable rental value of the equipment for the period of its retention and use. Defendant Zara put in issue the material allegations of the complaint and also filed a counterclaim wherein it alleged that it was compelled to terminate the contract by plaintiffs' refusal to perform it, and demanded damages for its breach against plaintiffs. Defendant American also put in issue the material allegations of the complaint and asserted further that plaintiffs had failed to state a claim against it upon which relief could be granted. The District Court found generally for the plaintiffs, holding that Zara had wrongfully terminated the contract and that there was due them $39,107.10 for work done at the contract rate, $18,600 for increased cost of excavation due to the soil conditions encountered, and $5,157.75 as rental allowance for plaintiffs' equipment, less $43,345.20, the amount advanced by Zara during the course of the work, or a net of $19,519.65, together with interest from the date of the filing of the suit. * * *

* * *

[The court affirmed the district court's decision that Zara "wrongfully prevented plaintiffs from completing the project."] This * * * disposes of Zara's claim for damages and leaves for consideration the amount of recovery due the plaintiffs. In their complaint originally plaintiffs had a second count claiming an accounting of profits; but this they abandoned, and they have made no claim for damages for breach of contract. Their only claim, therefore, is for the value of the work performed and of the rental of equipment retained by Zara on the job. Taking up, first, the value of the work performed, three theories are suggested to justify the additional award made below—in addition to that made at the regular contract rate—of $18,600 for the increased cost of excavating the clay material. The first, apparently most favored by the plaintiffs, is that this excavating (as well as the separate mixing of materials to form the airport runways made necessary by the soil condition) was extra work, not covered by the contract figures, and hence was separately compensable. * * * The second, relied on by the trial court, is that, since the subcontract made the provisions of the main contract determinative and applicable to the subparties, except where otherwise provided, the plaintiffs should have the advantage of the provisions of the main contract under which Zara successfully sought additional compensation against the United States. And the third is that, in view of Zara's default, they may waive the contract entirely and sue in quantum meruit for the reasonable value of the work performed.

Defendants contend, however, that under the terms of the subcontract plaintiffs were not entitled to any allowance for extra costs over and above the contract price, even though entailed in consequence of the misrepresentations as to the subsoil conditions. They rely principally on Article 5 of the subcontract, reprinted in the margin,[1] wherein plaintiffs agreed that no representations as to subsurface conditions have been made, nor have they been induced to enter into the contract in reliance upon the drawings or plans, and they promised to make no claim for damages for unknown conditions. In support of their contention they cite such cases as T.J.W. Corporation v. Board of Higher Education of City of New York, 251 App.Div. 405, 296 N.Y.S. 693, affirmed 276 N.Y. 644, 12 N.E.2d 800, and Niewenhous Co. v. State, 248 App.Div. 658, 288 N.Y.S. 22, affirmed 272 N.Y. 484, 3 N.E.2d 880. But these cases are limited to claims for extra work, where the contract has not been wrongfully terminated by the employer. The situation is quite otherwise where, as here, defendants have breached the agreement. We agree that the definite commitment which the plaintiffs have made in Article 5 is one they must stand by so long as they must rely upon their contract; and hence we find it difficult to see why the first two theories presented above, that particularly pressed by the plaintiffs and that relied on by the trial court, do not conflict directly with this agreement, which seems to contemplate the very situation to which it would then be held inapplicable. No such infirmity attaches to the third theory, however.

---

[1] "No representations have been made to the Sub-Contractor as to any sub-surface or latent conditions at the site; nor has the Sub-Contractor been induced to enter into this sub-contract in reliance upon any representations shown on the drawings or indicated in the specifications as to any sub-surface or latent conditions at the site. The Sub-Contractor agrees that it will make no claim against the Contractor for damages in the event that, during the progress of the work, the Sub-Contractor encounters sub-surface and/or latent conditions at the site materially differing from those shown on the drawings or indicated in the specifications, or unknown conditions of an unusual nature differing materially from those ordinarily encountered and generally recognized as inhering in work of the character provided for in the plans and specifications."

For it is an accepted principle of contract law, often applied in the case of construction contracts, that the promisee upon breach has the option to forego any suit on the contract and claim only the reasonable value of his performance. * * *

It also appears to be the general view, save for an occasional case viewed as illogical by the text writers, who are solidly in support of the doctrine. * * *

These authorities make it quite clear that under the better rule the contract price or the unit price per cubic yard of a construction or excavation contract does not limit recovery. * * * This doctrine is particularly applicable to unit prices in construction contracts; as Professor Patterson points out, 31 Col.L.Rev. at page 1303, a plaintiff may well have completed the hardest part of a job for which an average cost had been set. But it seems settled now in New York that with the breach fall all the other parts of the contract. * * * Hence it is clear that plaintiffs are not limited to the contract prices in the situation disclosed here.

As we have noted, the trial court granted recovery for $39,107.10 for the work done at the contract price, together with an additional sum of $18,600 for the extra cost of excavation of the clay, computed as 62,000 cubic yards at the additional expense of 30 cents per cubic yard. * * * As to the monetary amounts, these are based on the cost of the work to Zara, as well as expert testimony for plaintiffs, and are not seriously disputed. Indeed, in fixing the additional allowance at 30 cents per cubic yard, the judge relied particularly on Zara's claim to the United States wherein it stated that its records showed an actual cost to it of the extra work, amounting to 28.7 cents per cubic yard for the excavating, and 2½ cents per cubic yard for placing the excavated material in the runways. Professor Williston points out that the measure of recovery by way of restitution, though often confused with recovery on the contract, should not be measured or limited thereby; but he does point out that the contract may be important evidence of the value of the performance to the defendant, as may also the cost of the labor and materials. 5 Williston on Contracts, Rev.Ed., §§ 1482, 1483, 1485. It is therefore appropriate here, particularly in default of any challenging evidence, to base recovery on proper expenditures in performance * * * and to make use of the contract as fixing the basic price. * * *

It is to be noted that, since it is the defendant who is in default, and plaintiffs' performance here is "part of the very performance" for which the defendant had bargained, "it is to be valued, not by the extent to which the defendant's total wealth has been increased thereby, but by the amount for which such services and materials as constituted the part performance could have been purchased from one in the plaintiff's position at the time they were rendered." Restatement, Contracts, § 347, comment c. * * * It is to be noted that in fact defendant Zara did receive benefits most substantial from plaintiffs' performance. Plaintiffs had actually excavated 211,390 cubic yards, for which Zara's profit, as determined by the spread between the main and the subcontract of 5½ cents per cubic yard as a minimum, with higher amounts for a part, would be around $12,000; it had already collected $17,115.79 from the United States for the additional cost of removing the "cohesive silt," of which most was done by plaintiffs, and it had pending a claim against the United States for $18,840.10 more; and what is perhaps most important, it had received a performance which it needed to make to ensure recovery of these profits and sums from the United States and avoid the danger of being in default, and which it would have had to do itself or purchase in the market. Hence the allowance made by the District Court is justified on the evidence and the law, and we find no error, therefore, in this item of recovery.

* * *

[The Court's discussion of measurement of the rental value of the equipment retained by Zara is omitted.]

The judgment is modified by increasing the allowance for the fair rental value of equipment furnished from $5,157.75 to $7,227.50, and as so modified is affirmed.

B. WHERE A NON-BREACHING PLAINTIFF CONFERRED A BENEFIT BUT HAD A NEGATIVE EXPECTANCY (A "LOSING" CONTRACT)

RESTATEMENT (SECOND) OF CONTRACTS § 373.

Comment d.

An injured party who has performed in part will usually prefer to seek damages based on his expectation interest (§ 347) instead of a sum of money based on his restitution interest because such damages include his net profit and will give him a larger recovery. Even if he cannot prove what his net profit would have been, he will ordinarily seek damages based on his reliance interest * * *, since this will compensate him for all of his expenditures, regardless of whether they resulted in a benefit to the party in breach. * * * In the case of a contract on which he would have sustained a loss instead of having made a profit, however, his restitution interest may give him a larger recovery than would damages on either basis. The right of the injured party under a losing contract to a greater amount in restitution than he could have recovered in damages has engendered much controversy. The rules stated in this Section give him that right. He is entitled to such recovery even if the contract price is stated in terms of a rate per unit of work and the recovery exceeds that rate.

CITY OF PHILADELPHIA v. TRIPPLE, 230 Pa. 480, 79 A. 703 (Pa. 1911). [Contractor Dietrich was hired by the city of Philadelphia to construct the foundations and superstructure for a fire engine house. For the sum of $34,500 to be paid in monthly cash payments as the work progressed, Dietrich engaged subcontractor McMenamy to perform necessary excavation work and to construct the main conduit from the Delaware River to the engine house. The contract provided that the work was to be completed within 125 working days from its date. Difficulties arose in the course of the excavation work resulting in flooding and delays.

Although the period of 125 days specified in the contract had expired, no action was taken by Dietrich in view of the non-completion of the work at that time, and McMenamy continued work under his contract with the knowledge and acquiescence of Dietrich. Subsequently, however, Dietrich became dissatisfied with the rate of progress and requested McMenamy to discontinue further work on the conduit.

McMenamy ceased work and brought suit in "indebitatus assumpsit"[d] to recover the actual cost of his labor and materials. The lower court found that Dietrich had broken the contract and was equitably estopped from asserting the failure to complete within the specified time as a defense, since he had known of and acquiesced in McMenamy's further performance after the lapse of the time period. The referee awarded McMenamy the actual cost of his labor and material. The referee held that a plaintiff may recover from a defaulting defendant the cost of labor and materials less payments made, although such cost exceeds the price fixed in the contract. The court affirmed per curiam. Excerpts from the referee's report follow.]

* * * Let it be assumed that, in an extreme case, a builder has actually expended in the course of his work a sum in excess of the contract price and has not yet completed performance. If, under such circumstances, the builder finishes his work, the owner, upon paying the contract price, will receive the benefit of a large expenditure actually made, in return for the payment of a smaller sum of money. This result, which may well involve a hardship upon the builder, is made necessary by a proper regard for the contractual rights of the owner. The owner has made a valid contract, and this contract must be protected and enforced, even if the builder suffers.

Let it further be supposed, however, that the owner, who finds himself in this position of advantage, voluntarily puts an end to his contract rights

---

[d] Indebitatus assumpsit is analogous to quantum meruit. However, in indebitatus assumpsit the claim is for a specific sum, whereas in quantum meruit the claim is for reasonable value. See Appendix B.

in the premises. This in legal effect he does if he himself breaks the contract or discharges the builder from his obligation to perform it. The situation which then presents itself is one in which the builder has in good faith expended money in the course of work done for the benefit of the owner, and has, in the absence of contract, an equitable claim to be reimbursed. The owner, on the other hand, has deprived himself of the legal right which would have sufficed to defeat the equity. He accordingly stands defenseless in the presence of the builder's claim.

Such, it is submitted, is the legal analysis of the situation in which the parties to this action find themselves. It may, of course, be contended that Dietrich did not receive an actual benefit coextensive with McMenamy's expenditure. It is a sufficient answer to this contention to observe that (upon the facts as heretofore found) McMenamy expended the money in good faith and in the course of attempted performance. That is sufficient to give him an equitable claim for reimbursement.

JOHNSON v. BOVEE, 40 Colo. App. 317, 574 P.2d 513 (Colo. Ct. App. 1978). [Plaintiff agreed in a written contract to build a house for defendants according to a specified set of plans for $47,176. During the course of construction, plaintiff and defendants orally agreed to many deviations from the original plans, resulting in both additions ("extras") and deletions.

Defendants became dissatisfied with the quality of the construction and stopped making required payments to plaintiff. Plaintiff therefore stopped work on the house and filed suit to foreclose on his mechanics lien.

The lower court found that plaintiff had substantially performed his obligations under the contract and that defendants' refusal to make payments constituted a breach. It also found that the house was 90% complete when construction was stopped. Plaintiff was awarded damages calculated as follows:

Contract Price	$ 47,176.00
Net Value of Agreed Extras	$ 7,700.78
Payments Made by Defendants	$ − 49,485.18
Cost to Plaintiff had he Completed the House (10% of $47,176)	$ − 4,717.60
Total	$ 674.00

Plaintiff appealed as to damages, arguing that he was entitled to recover in *quantum meruit* for the reasonable value of the services he rendered, which he claimed exceeded the original contract price and agreed extras by $9,000. Held, where the owners breached the contract by refusing to make required payments to builder, builder was entitled to recover the reasonable value of his services, but the contract price constituted a ceiling on his recovery of restitution.] Courts and commentators are divided over the question of whether restitution should be limited by the contract. * * *

We believe using the contract price as a ceiling on restitution is the better-reasoned resolution of this question. Had Johnson fully performed, his recovery would be limited to the contract price, since he would be suing for specific performance of the liquidated debt obligation under the contract. * * * It is illogical to allow him to recover the full cost of his services when, if he completed the house, he would be limited to the contract price plus the agreed upon extras.

OLIVER v. CAMPBELL, 43 Cal.2d 298, 273 P.2d 15 (Cal. 1954). [Plaintiff Oliver, a lawyer, agreed to represent defendant Campbell in a divorce proceeding for a flat sum of $850, including $100 for costs etc. The trial lasted 29 days, with the trial judge finally indicating an intention to grant a divorce, so that Oliver's services were worth far more than the agreed flat sum. When Oliver's services were essentially complete (according to the appellate court), Campbell discharged Oliver, who had at that point been paid $550. Oliver then sued upon a *quantum meruit* for the reasonable value of his services and the court below found this to be $5,000. Held, reversed.]

It is well settled that one who is wrongfully discharged and prevented from further performance of his contract may elect as a general rule to treat the contract as rescinded, may sue upon a quantum meruit as if the special contract of employment had never been made and may recover the reasonable value of the services performed even though such reasonable value exceeds the contract price. * * * Under [the] * * * circumstances [of this case] it would appear that in effect, plaintiff had completed the performance of his service and the rule would apply that "[t]he remedy of restitution in money is not available to one who has fully performed his part of a contract, if the only part of the agreed exchange for such performance that has not been rendered by the defendant is a sum of money constituting a liquidated debt" * * *.

CHILDRES & GARAMELLA, THE LAW OF RESTITUTION AND THE RELIANCE INTEREST IN CONTRACT

64 Nw. U. L. Rev. 433, 439–40 (1969).

There is no justification for the position that the terms of the promise do not regulate the recovery of reliance damages in some cases which may be twisted into an "action in *quantum meruit*." A promise excites expectations and causes reliance, for both of which the law should justly give protection. The crucial question, then, is whether or not the promise which was relied upon, being the *provocateur* of the reliance, will regulate the damages recoverable in event of a breach.

It may be thought undesirable to admit that *quantum meruit* restitution, insofar as it rests not on unjust enrichment but upon abuse of a contracting party's reliance interest, is merely a variant of the contract reliance claim. However, sufficient reason exists for the admission.

By way of example, a firm agrees to manufacture X number of rifles for the government at Y unit price. After the government requires that performance cease, the firm seeks five times Y for each rifle delivered, saying that this was the reasonable value of what it did. The argument is an attempt to entirely upset the parties' original business arrangement. If freedom of contract means freedom to deviate from the standards of reasonable men, fully informed, and enjoying levels of knowledge and intelligence to be expected in the situation, it can have no more fertile field than that of allocating market and other relevant risks in a business transaction. Specifically, the parties' own allocation of the market or other risks should be upset, if at all, by substantive doctrine and not by whether one chooses the label "*quantum meruit*" or "common count" on the one hand, or "reliance damages" on the other.

KULL, RESTITUTION AS A REMEDY FOR BREACH OF CONTRACT

67 S. Cal. L. Rev. 1465, 1482–83 (1994).

* * * If our moral condemnation of promise-breakers were strenuous enough, the social judgment underlying the remedy of restitution for breach might indeed be that any advantage conferred by the contractual exchange upon one who later defaults becomes, ipso facto, unjust enrichment in the defaulter's hands. Yet the explanation seems strained at best. A more straightforward way of putting the same proposition would be to say that courts in some circumstances favor a punitive remedy for breach of contract, and that stripping a defendant of the benefits secured by a contract he has failed to perform has seemed to judges, in some circumstances, to be no more than poetic justice. If promise-breakers are wrongdoers we can, of course, choose to punish them any way we see fit: Forcing them to surrender a favorable bargain may be an appropriate form of punishment, however rarely and haphazardly applied. But the argument at this point involves contract remedies, not unjust enrichment by any useful definition.

PROBLEM 3-15

Ajax Construction Company agreed to construct a restaurant for Hal Evans on his land for $350,000. After Ajax had spent $105,000 in preparation and part performance, only $5,000 of which was salvageable, Hal repudiated the contract because of a lack of funds. The cost of completing construction after the repudiation would have been $255,000. The partial performance increased the value of Hal's land by $100,000. Hal can hire another contractor to complete the work for $270,000. Ajax received no progress payments. Ajax's president, Turlway, has asked you how much the company can recover from Hal Evans. Turlway tells you that he has received a settlement offer of $60,000. Should he accept the offer?

C. WHERE A NON-BREACHING PLAINTIFF CONFERRED A BENEFIT BUT CANNOT PROVE LOST EXPECTANCY

BAUSCH & LOMB, INC. V. BRESSLER

United States Court of Appeals, Second Circuit, 1992.
977 F.2d 720.

WALKER, CIRCUIT JUDGE.

This case involves Bausch & Lomb, Inc.'s ("B & L") claims for damages arising from the alleged breach by Sonomed Technology, Inc. ("Sonomed") of a contract whereby B & L agreed to purchase and distribute ophthalmic diagnostic instruments manufactured and supplied by Sonomed. The district court, after a bench trial, entered judgment in favor of B & L in the amount of $555,000 in damages plus interest. On appeal, Sonomed attacks the judgment by challenging: (1) the finding that Sonomed, not B & L, breached the purchase and distribution agreement [and] (2) the damage award to B & L * * *. For reasons that will be discussed, we affirm the district court's * * * determination that Sonomed is liable to B & L for breach of contract. * * * However, we vacate in part the district court's damage award.

Background

* * *

Sonomed develops, manufactures and markets ultrasound devices used for ophthalmologic diagnosis. Sonomed makes two complementary products, the "A-Scan"—which measures distances in the eye—and the "B-Scan"—which provides a two-dimensional image of the eye. B & L is engaged in the optical products business, including the purchase and distribution of ophthalmic devices manufactured by other companies. On December 21, 1984, Sonomed and B & L entered into a sale and distribution agreement (the "1984 Agreement"). Under the terms of the 1984 Agreement, B & L was to become the exclusive world-wide distributor of Sonomed's A-Scan and B-Scan products for a period of three years. In return for the exclusive distributorship rights, B & L paid $500,000 to Sonomed and agreed to make annual minimum purchases of Sonomed's products beginning in 1985.

On July 1, 1986, the parties rescinded the 1984 Agreement and entered into a new contract (the "1986 Agreement" or the "Agreement"). Among other things, the 1986 Agreement reduced the size of B & L's exclusive distributorship to a territory including the United States, Puerto Rico and Canada and extended the expiration date of the distributorship until December 31, 1989, two years beyond the expiration date of the 1984 Agreement. It is the 1986 Agreement that is largely at issue in this case. Unless otherwise indicated, the contract provisions we refer to are those of the 1986 Agreement.

* * *

Section 12.07 stated that the $500,000 payment made by B & L to Sonomed in connection with the 1984 Agreement constituted a "prepaid royalty" and that "[i]n the event of any dispute with respect to this Agreement, such payment shall be deemed to be payment for exclusive distribution rights."

* * *

[In 1987, after disputes over Sonomed's violation of the terms of the agreement by selling its products in B & L's territory and over whether Sonomed could supply on time], Sonomed stated that it would no longer accept or fill product orders from B & L and intended to market Sonomed products itself. * * *

* * *

On November 30, 1987, B & L commenced this action, asserting claims for * * * breach of contract against Sonomed. * * *

Following trial, the district court entered judgment for B & L [for $555,000 in damages and interest] on * * * its breach of contract claims * * *. Specifically, the court found two separate breaches by Sonomed.

First, the court determined that Sonomed breached the Agreement by selling products in B & L's exclusive territory. This claim was not challenged at trial. Sonomed's agents admitted that Sonomed sold products in B & L's territory.

Second, the district court determined that Sonomed wrongfully terminated the Agreement. * * *

* * *

Discussion

* * *

1. Breach of Contract

Sonomed accepts the district court's finding that, by selling Sonomed products in B & L's exclusive territory, it breached the Agreement.

However, Sonomed challenges the finding that it materially breached the Agreement by wrongfully refusing to perform its contractual duties and terminating the Agreement.

* * *

[W]e affirm the district court's finding that Sonomed, not B & L, is liable for breach of the Agreement * * *.

2. Damages

* * * Sonomed challenges the $500,000 damage award to B & L. * * *

a. The $500,000 Award

At trial, B & L made claims for lost profits, and sought to prove these alleged damages by pointing to the profits Sonomed realized through its violative sales before and after Sonomed terminated the Agreement. However, B & L offered no evidence tending to prove that it would have made the same sales—or realized the same profits—as Sonomed absent Sonomed's breaches of the Agreement. New York law requires that a plaintiff prove with a reasonable degree of certainty that any claimed loss of profits was caused by the defendant's breach. * * * The district court thus denied these claims as speculative, a determination B & L does not challenge on appeal.

The district court found, as an alternative, non-speculative measure of B & L's loss the $500,000 "prepaid royalty" paid by B & L under the 1984 Agreement in return for the right to purchase and serve as exclusive distributor of Sonomed's products. The court stated that B & L was denied its full rights to exclusive distribution, first, because of Sonomed's sales in B & L's territory while the Agreement was still in force, and, second, because of Sonomed's repudiation of the Agreement. Thus, the district court reasoned, "in fairness and in accordance with the law of contract damages, the defendant Sonomed should return the $500,000."

In granting B & L the $500,000 award, the district court may have been seeking to apply the doctrine of expectation damages. This doctrine gives force to the provisions of a contract by placing the aggrieved party in the same economic position it would have been in had both parties fully performed. * * * If it awarded the $500,000 as expectation damages, we think the district court erred. Although to be sure B & L did not receive the full benefits of the distribution rights it contracted for, it does not follow that B & L would have realized a $500,000 return if the contract had been fully performed. There is simply no evidence connecting this $500,000 to any profit that B & L would have received had Sonomed fully performed the Agreement. Thus, the district court's award cannot be sustained pursuant to an expectation theory of recovery.

The district court suggested that its award of the $500,000 payment might alternatively be appropriate pursuant to the doctrine of reliance damages. Under this doctrine, a plaintiff may recover "his expenses of preparation and of part performance, as well as other foreseeable expenses incurred in reliance upon the contract." J. Calimari & J. Perillo, Contracts § 14–9, at 603 (3d ed. 1987); see also L. Albert & Son v. Armstrong Rubber Co., 178 F.2d 182, 190–91 (2d Cir.1949). However, the alternative reliance "measure of damages rests on the premise that the injured party's reliance interest is no greater than the party's expectation interest." 3 E.A. Farnsworth, Farnsworth on Contracts § 12.16, at 265 (2d ed. 1990). And courts will not "knowingly put the plaintiff [receiving a reliance recovery] in a better position than he would have occupied had the contract been fully performed." Fuller & Perdue, The Reliance Interest in Contract Damages (Pt. 1), 46 Yale L.J. 52, 59 (1936); see L. Albert & Son, 178 F.2d at 191. Thus, a reliance recovery will be offset by the amount of "any loss that the party in breach can prove with reasonable certainty the injured party would have suffered had the contract been fully performed." Restatement (Second) of Contracts § 349 (1979); see Farash v. Sykes Datatronics, Inc., 59 N.Y.2d 500, 504, 465 N.Y.S.2d 917, 919, 452 N.E.2d 1245, 1247 (1983). If the breaching party establishes that the plaintiff's losses upon full performance would have equalled or exceeded its reliance expenditures, the plaintiff will recover nothing under a reliance theory.

The district court did not address the "losing contract" limitation upon awards of reliance damages, and thus, as far as we can tell, did not examine what revenues B & L would have received absent Sonomed's breach. Portions of the district court opinion, in fact, seem to offer support for Sonomed's contention on appeal that the Agreement was a losing contract for B & L, entitling Sonomed to an offset of all or part of the $500,000 payment under a reliance theory. The district court found that during 1987 B & L was having difficulty selling Sonomed products, was engaged in a "massive crash sales operation" and was discounting its prices by as much as 40 percent. We see no justification on this record for an award of the $500,000 as reliance damages.

We believe, however, that B & L may be entitled to a damage award by way of restitution, a remedies doctrine not addressed by the district court. * * * The doctrine of restitution is premised upon the equitable principle that "[a] person who has been unjustly enriched at the expense of another is required to make restitution to the other." Restatement of Restitution § 1 (1937). Upon a demonstration that a defendant is liable for material breach, the plaintiff may recover "the reasonable value of services rendered, goods delivered, or property conveyed less the reasonable value of any counter-performance received by him." Calimari & Perillo, supra, § 15–4, at 651; see United States v. Zara Contracting Co., 146 F.2d 606, 610 (2d Cir.1944); Farash, 59 N.Y.2d at 506, 465 N.Y.S.2d at 920, 452

N.E.2d at 1248. Because the doctrine of restitution looks to the reasonable value of any benefit conferred upon the defendant by the plaintiff, and is not governed by the terms of the parties' agreement, restitution is available even if the plaintiff would have lost money on the contract if it had been fully performed. * * *

Following a restitution theory, B & L would be entitled to recover as much of the $500,000 payment it made to Sonomed as it can show unjustly enriched Sonomed. We reject Sonomed's contention that an award of any portion of the $500,000 payment is precluded by the terms of the Agreement which states that the prepaid royalty "under no circumstances is refundable to B & L". The terms of the Agreement do not control an award of restitution.

However, restitution does not permit B & L to recover the entire $500,000 payment. B & L paid the $500,000 for the right to distribute Sonomed products over the duration of both agreements and it had that right from early 1985 (under the rescinded 1984 Agreement) until Sonomed's termination of the Agreement in 1987. These several years of distribution rights constitute a benefit the value of which must be offset against the $500,000 paid.

In order to determine how much of the $500,000 payment Sonomed must pay to B & L under a restitution theory, the district court must ascribe a value to the distribution right B & L enjoyed for the years preceding the Agreement's termination and then use it as an offset to the $500,000. As set forth above, the reasonable value of the benefit unjustly received, not the contract price, determines the amount of an award in restitution. However, the contract may provide probative evidence of the value of the benefit. See United States v. Western States Mechanical Contractors, Inc., 834 F.2d 1533, 1552 (10th Cir.1987); Constantino v. American S/T Achilles, 580 F.2d 121, 122–23 (4th Cir.1978); Calimari & Perillo, supra, § 15–4, at 652. Indeed, in the absence of a readily available market price, the value that the parties ascribed to a benefit in their contract may be the best valuation measure available to the court. See, e.g., 12 S. Williston & W.H.E. Jaeger, Williston on Contracts §§ 1480, 1482 (3d ed. 1970) (contract price is important evidence of value of performance to defendant).

It may be that the $500,000 price that B & L agreed to pay and Sonomed agreed to accept for the exclusive right to distribute Sonomed products for an approximately five year period—from the commencement of the 1984 Agreement until the date set for termination of the Agreement—offers the best evidence available of the reasonable value of the right. If the district court on remand determines this to be the case, it would then be appropriate to pro-rate the $500,000 to determine the value of the right actually received and exercised by B & L.

The district court should also take into account the fact that B & L did not receive the exclusive distributorship promised by Sonomed in the Agreement. As set forth above, Sonomed sold its products in various parts of B & L's exclusive territory even before it terminated the Agreement. These violative sales may have diminished the value of the benefit B & L received, although it may be difficult to calculate the amount of the diminution. The profits Sonomed obtained through its violative sales may, however, provide some evidence of the diminished value of the distribution right.

We thus vacate this portion of the district court's award and direct the court on remand to grant a restitutionary award to B & L consistent with this opinion.* * *

Conclusion

For the reasons set forth above, the judgment of the district court is affirmed in part and vacated in part and remanded for further proceedings consistent with this opinion.

OSTEEN V. JOHNSON

Colorado Court of Appeals, 1970.
473 P.2d 184.

DUFFORD, JUDGE. * * *

This was an action for breach of an oral contract. Trial was to the court, which found that the plaintiffs had paid the sum of $2,500. In exchange, the defendant had agreed to "promote" the plaintiffs' daughter, Linda Osteen, as a singer and composer of country-western music. More specifically, it was found that the defendant had agreed to advertise Linda through various mailings for a period of one year; to arrange and furnish the facilities necessary for Linda to record several songs; to prepare two records from the songs recorded; to press and mail copies of one of the records to disc jockeys throughout the country; and, if the first record met with any success, to press and mail out copies of the second record.

The trial court further found that the defendant did arrange for several recording sessions, at which Linda recorded four songs. A record was prepared of two of the songs, and 1,000 copies of the record were then pressed. Of the pressed records, 340 copies were mailed to disc jockeys, 200 were sent to the plaintiffs, and the remainder were retained by the defendant. Various mailings were made to advertise Linda; flyers were sent to disc jockeys throughout the country; and Linda's professional name was advertised in trade magazines. The record sent out received a favorable review and a high rating in a trade magazine.

Upon such findings the trial court concluded that the defendant had substantially performed the agreement. However, a judgment was entered in favor of the plaintiffs in the sum of $1.00 and costs on the basis that the defendant had wrongfully caused the name of another party to appear on the label of the record as co-author of a song which had been written solely by Linda. The trial court also ordered the defendant to deliver to the plaintiffs certain master tapes and records in the defendant's possession.

1. Right of Restitution

Although plaintiffs' reasons are not clearly defined, they argue here that the award of damages is inadequate, and that the trial court erred in concluding that the defendant had substantially performed the agreement. However, no evidence was presented during the trial of the matter upon which an award of other than nominal damages could be based. In our opinion, the remedy which plaintiffs proved and upon which they can rely is that of restitution. See 5 A. Corbin, Contracts § 996. This remedy is available where there has been a contract breach of vital importance, variously defined as a substantial breach or a breach which goes to the essence of the contract. See 5 A. Corbin, Contracts § 1104, where the author writes:

> "In the case of a breach by non-performance, * * * the injured party's alternative remedy by way of restitution depends upon the extent of the non-performance by the defendant. The defendant's breach may be nothing but a failure to perform some minor part of his contractual duty. Such a minor non-performance is a breach of contract and an action for damages can be maintained. The injured party, however, can not maintain an action for restitution of what he has given the defendant unless the defendant's non-performance is so material that it is held to go to the 'essence'; it must be such a breach as would discharge the injured party from any further contractual duty on his own part. Such a vital breach by the defendant operates, with respect to the right of restitution, in the same way that a repudiation of the contractual obligation would operate. A minor breach by one party does not discharge the contractual duty of the other party; and the latter being still bound to perform as agreed can not be entitled to the restitution of payments already made by him or to the value of other part performances rendered."

This rule is modified somewhat where the damages which might have been awarded would be difficult or impossible to determine or inadequate. * * *

2. Breach of Contract

The essential question here then becomes whether any breach on the part of the defendant is substantial enough to justify the remedy of restitution. Plaintiffs argue that the defendant breached the contract in the following ways: First, the defendant did not promote Linda for a period of one year as agreed; secondly, the defendant wrongfully caused the name of another party to appear on the label as co-author of the song which had been composed solely by Linda; and thirdly, the defendant failed to press and mail out copies of the second record as agreed.

The first argument is not supported by the record. Plaintiffs brought the action within the one-year period for which the contract was to run. There was no evidence that during this period the defendant had not continued to promote Linda through the use of mailings and advertisements. Quite obviously the mere fact that the one-year period had not ended prior to the commencement of the action does not justify the conclusion that the defendant had breached the agreement. Plaintiffs' second argument overlooks the testimony offered on behalf of the defendant that listing the other party as co-author of the song would make it more likely that the record would be played by disc jockeys.

The plaintiffs' third argument does, however, have merit. It is clear from the record and the findings of the trial court that the first record had met with some success. It is also clear that copies of the second record were neither pressed nor mailed out. In our opinion the failure of the defendant to press and mail out copies of the second record after the first had achieved some success constituted a substantial breach of the contract and, therefore, justifies the remedy of restitution. * * * Both parties agree that the essence of their contract was to publicize Linda as a singer of western songs and to make her name and talent known to the public. Defendant admitted and asserted that the primary method of achieving this end was to have records pressed and mailed to disc jockeys. * * *

* * *

3. Determining Damages

It is clear that the defendant did partially perform the contract and, under applicable law, should be allowed compensation for the reasonable value of his services. See 5 A. Corbin, Contracts § 1114, where the author writes:

> "[A]ll courts are in agreement that restitution by the defendant will not be enforced unless the plaintiff returns in some way what he has received as a part performance by the defendant."

It shall, therefore, be the ultimate order of this court that prior to restoring to the plaintiffs the $2,500 paid by them to the defendant further proceedings be held during which the trial court shall determine the reasonable value of the services which the defendant rendered on plaintiffs' behalf.

The judgment is reversed, and this case is remanded with directions that a new trial be held to determine the one issue of the amount to which the plaintiffs are entitled by way of restitution. Such amount shall be the $2,500 paid by plaintiffs to defendant less the reasonable value of the services which the defendant performed on behalf of plaintiffs.

NOTE:
THE IMPORTANCE OF FORMAL WRITTEN CONTRACTS

The Osteens paid $500 to Johnson in advance and $2000 at Linda's first rehearsal. The Osteens' brief to the Supreme Court of Colorado reports that at the time the Osteens paid Johnson (also known as "Little Richie Johnson") they requested a written contract. Little Richie told them that "he did not write out contracts and that if his word was not as good as a contract, he didn't even want to make one." How should the Osteens have responded?

D. WHERE THE PLAINTIFF HAS CONFERRED A BENEFIT BUT THE CONTRACT IS INVALID, FRUSTRATED, OR OTHERWISE UNENFORCEABLE

Restitutionary relief may be granted to a party whose agreement is unenforceable. For example, suppose B agrees to convey certain land to A, and, in anticipation, A, who is in possession, improves the land. Even if the parties' agreement is unenforceable, for example, for lack of consideration or a required writing or for indefiniteness, and even if A cannot recover on the theory of promissory estoppel (assume, for example, that B should not reasonably have expected A to rely on B's promise to convey), A may be able to recover on unjust enrichment grounds. Section Four of Chapter Two presents the substantive requirements for recovery.

In Chapter Eight, we will see that restitution is also sometimes available after still other grounds of disruption. Grounds of disruption studied in Chapter Eight include mistake, impossibility, impracticability and frustration. The chapter also considers restitutionary and other remedies available for such grounds of disruption.

WILLIS v. RUSSEL, 315 S.E.2d 91 (N.C. Ct. App. 1984). Plaintiff offered to perform certain architectural design services for defendants in exchange for certain compensation; their discussions dealt with both the entire condominium project and the schematic design, and the fees to be paid therefor were clearly stated. Defendants told plaintiff to begin the work, approved his work as it proceeded, and approved the fee and profit schedules received. A jury could properly find therefrom that defendants expressly contracted with plaintiff for either the schematic design work or for the entire project on the fee basis that plaintiff testified was discussed. Defendants' refusal to execute a written contract so providing does not necessarily establish that plaintiff's services were not accepted, as defendants contend; the intent of the parties controls such matters, and acceptance may be manifested orally or by conduct, as well as by a signature. * * * In our view this evidence was sufficient to support the claim that the defendants engaged plaintiff upon express terms to either design and supervise the entire condominium project or just do the schematic design phase.

Upon retrial, therefore, it will be for the jury to determine whether the parties contracted at all, and, if so, whether for the entire project or just the schematic design. If the jury finds that there was a contract for the entire project based on the fee schedule referred to and defendants breached it, the measure of damages would include plaintiff's prospective profits, as well as the fees for work performed. The general rule in this state is that prospective profits prevented or interrupted by breach of contract are recoverable when it appears:

> (1) that it is reasonably certain that such profits would have been realized except for the breach of the contract, (2) that such profits can be ascertained and measured with reasonable certainty, and (3) that such profits may be reasonably supposed to have been within the contemplation of the parties, when the contract was made, as the probable result of a breach.

Perkins v. Langdon, 237 N.C. 159, 171, 74 S.E.2d 634, 644 (1953). But, of course, if the jury finds that the parties had no express contract, it would then be appropriate for them to consider issues of implied contract and *quantum meruit.* In which event, of course, the measure of damages will be the reasonable value of the services rendered, less any benefits received, *Doub v. Hauser,* 256 N.C. 331, 123 S.E.2d 821 (1962) * * *. But, since damages, at least beyond a nominal amount, are never presumed, for plaintiff to recover any substantial sum under a *quantum meruit* theory, evidence will be required as to the reasonable value or market value of his services and those of any of his assistants or employees that contributed to the work that was done for the defendants. *Harrell v. W.B. Lloyd Construction Co.,* 41 N.C.App. 593, 255 S.E.2d 280 (1979). The value of plaintiff's services will not have to be determined, however, if the jury first decides that the parties had an express contract and defendants breached it; for, with minor exceptions irrelevant to this appeal, our law permits people to contract as they see fit and enforces agreements so made according to their terms.

E. WHERE THE PLAINTIFF HAS MATERIALLY BROKEN THE CONTRACT AFTER CONFERRING A BENEFIT

A plaintiff who has committed an uncured material breach of contract (see Chapter Seven) cannot recover on a contract theory (agreement with consideration). Nevertheless, the plaintiff may have conferred a benefit on the defendant and it may be unjust for the defendant to retain the benefit, in whole or in part. In a proper case, our law permits such a plaintiff to have restitutionary relief premised on the prevention of unjust enrichment.

PROBLEM 3-16

Assume that A contracts to make repairs to B's building in exchange for a promise by B to pay $10,000 for this work. A expends $8,000 making repairs but inadvertently fails to follow the specifications so that he does not substantially perform and therefore cannot recover his expectancy "in contract." Assume that to correct the defects a large portion of the repairs would have to be redone. Nevertheless, A's work has increased the value of the building by $4,000. B can hire another contractor for $9,000 to complete the work promised by A. B has not yet paid A anything. How much should A recover? $8,000? $4,000? $1,000? Nothing? Does the unjust enrichment theory for imposing liability on B suggest an answer? Comment b to § 374 of the Restatement (Second) Contracts, on restitution in favor of a party in breach, states:

> Since the party seeking restitution is responsible for posing the problem of measurement of benefit, doubts will be resolved against him, and his recovery will not exceed the less generous of the two measures stated in [§ 371], that of the other party's increase in wealth. * * * If no value can be put on this, he cannot recover. * * * Although the contract price is evidence of the benefit, it is not conclusive. However, in no case will the party in breach be allowed to recover more than a ratable portion of the total contract price where such portion can be determined.

Do you agree with the approach of the Restatement?

SECTION NINE: SPECIFIC PERFORMANCE

KITCHEN V. HERRING

Supreme Court of North Carolina, 1851.
42 N.C. 190.

PEARSON, J. In December 1846, the defendant, Herring, executed a contract in writing in these words, "Rec'd. of John L. Kitchen payment in full for a certain tract of land lying on the southwest side of Black River, adjoining the lands of William Haffland and Martial, for which I am to give him a good deed etc." The defendant Pridgen wrote the contract and is a subscribing witness. The plaintiff was put into possession in March 1847. Pridgen united with him; and the other defendant, Musgrove, under a contract with Pridgen, with a large number of hands, commenced cutting down the timber, which constitutes the chief value of the land. Pridgen was the surety of the plaintiff, to a note of $325, given payable at three months for the price of the land. In January, Herring executed a deed for the land to Pridgen, and under this title the plaintiff was turned out of possession.

The prayer of the Bill is for a specific performance, for an account of the profits and for an injunction. After the Bill was filed, an arrangement was made, by which Musgrove continued his operations in getting timber, and agreed to account with the successful party. * * *

* * *

It was * * * insisted, that, as it appears by the plaintiff's own showing, that "the land is chiefly valuable on account of the timber," this case does not come within the principle, on which a specific performance is decreed.

The position is new, and the Counsel admitted, that there was no authority to sustain it, but he contended with earnestness, that it was so fully sustained by "the reason of the thing," as to justify a departure from a well settled rule of this Court, under the maxim, *cessante ratione cessat lex.*

The argument failed wholly to prove, that "the reason of the thing" called for an exception. The principle in regard to land was adopted, not because it was fertile or rich in minerals or *valuable for timber,* but simply because it was land—a favorite and favored subject in England, and every country of Anglo Saxon origin. Our constitution gives to land preeminence over every other species of property; and our law, whether administered in Courts of law or of equity, gives to it the same preference. Land, whether rich or poor, cannot be taken to pay debts until the personal property is exhausted. Contracts concerning land must be in writing. Land must be sold at the Court House, must be conveyed by deeds duly registered, and other instances "too tedious to mention." The principle is, that land is *assumed* to have a peculiar value, so as to give an equity for a specific performance, without reference to its quality or quantity. * * * [I]n regard to other property, less favored, a specific performance will not be decreed, unless there be peculiar circumstances; for, if with the money, an article of the same description can be bought in market—corn, cotton, etc., the remedy at law is adequate.

There must be a decree for the plaintiff with costs.

NOTE: *REMEDIAL RIGHTS UNDER A CONTRACT FOR THE SALE OF LAND*

According to the general view today (stated in Kitchen v. Herring), a vendee of land is entitled to specific performance (absent a defense). The theory is that land is inherently unique and thus damages cannot be an adequate remedy. (But see the Marsh excerpt that follows this Note.) In addition to specific performance, the vendee can also recover money damages for any delay. Daves v. Potter, 92 Wash. App. 1047 (1998)). There are some qualifications to the vendee's right to specific performance, however. For example, suppose after contracting with Kitchen, but before performance, Herring contracted to convey the same land to a bona fide purchaser. (Pridgen was not a bona fide purchaser because of his knowledge and participation in the contract between Kitchen and Herring.) Generally, Kitchen would recover only damages and the subsequent bona fide purchaser would receive specific performance. But the court may impose a "constructive trust" in favor of Kitchen on Herring's proceeds from the second sale.

Disappointed vendors of land also may receive specific performance for the unpaid purchase price of the land (through "money decrees"). Metro Holdings One, LLC v. Flynn Creek Partner, LLC, 25 N.E.3d 141 (Ind. Ct. App. 2014) (noting that specific performance may be granted to the seller when the purchaser breaches an agreement to purchase real property); Steiner v. Wisconsin Am. Mut. Ins. Co., 281 Wis.2d 395, 697 N.W.2d 452, 458 n.16 (Wis. 2005) ("If specific performance is chosen, the land contract vendor recovers only the purchase price plus costs and disbursements."). Money is not inherently unique, of course, so courts had to derive other theories for granting specific performance. One theory (now largely discredited) was that "equality is equity"; since the vendee of land is entitled to specific performance, the vendor should have the same right. See, e.g., TLC Hospitality, LLC v. Pillar Income Asset Management, Inc., 570 S.W.3d 749, 771 (Tex. App. 2018) (specific performance is not barred by absence of mutuality of remedy). Another theory is that land values are too speculative and the vendor cannot prove precise damages. When a vendor is successful, the court may condition specific performance on the vendor's tender of the deed or the vendor's deposit of the deed with the clerk of the court for delivery to the vendee. In this way, the court may secure "mutuality of performance."

In addition to specific performance, the vendor in most states can instead pursue an action at law for the unpaid balance of the purchase price. The court can ensure that the vendor tenders a deed before payment by issuing a conditional stay of execution.

Suppose the vendor grants possession to the vendee under a land sale contract in which the vendee is to make periodic payments of the price. After making some payments, the vendee breaches the agreement. In many states, the vendor can both retake possession of the land and retain the payments already made. It should be obvious that this remedy of the vendor may produce harsh results if the payments exceed the rental value.

MARSH, SOMETIMES BLACKACRE IS A WIDGET: RETHINKING COMMERCIAL REAL ESTATE CONTRACT REMEDIES

88 Neb. L. Rev. 635, 670–73 (2010).

[I]t becomes clear that none of the historical rationales for giving real property special treatment apply to all land. Romantic notions of the presumed uniqueness of land seem quaint when applied to a strip shopping center, a cookie-cutter suburban office building, or a non-descript lot in a subdivision. Yet recent decisions have found the following types of real property to be unique: a new condominium unit, a mobile home park intended for a quick resale, unimproved lots, and farmland. A few courts have clearly stated that the actual uniqueness of a parcel of real property is irrelevant because of the strength of the common law presumption: "Our holding rests . . . upon a broader ground: that a contract of sale of a designated condominium unit like any real property is specifically enforceable by the purchaser irrespective of any special proof of its uniqueness."

CURTICE BROTHERS CO. V. CATTS

Court of Chancery of New Jersey, 1907.
72 N.J. Eq. 831, 66 A. 935.

Complainant is engaged in the business of canning tomatoes and seeks the specific performance of a contract wherein defendant agreed to sell to complainant the entire product of certain land planted with tomatoes. Defendant contests the power of this court to grant equitable relief.

LEAMING, V.C. The fundamental principles which guide a court of equity in decreeing the specific performance of contracts are essentially the same whether the contracts relate to realty or to personalty. By reason of the fact that damages for the breach of contract for the sale of personalty are, in most cases, easily ascertainable and recoverable at law, courts of equity in such cases withhold equitable relief. Touching contracts for the sale of land, the reverse is the case. But no inherent difference between real estate and personal property controls the exercise of the jurisdiction. Where no adequate remedy at law exists, specific performance of a contract touching the sale of personal property will be decreed with the same freedom as in the case of a contract for the sale of land. Prof. Pomeroy, in referring to the distinction, says: "In applying these principles, taking into account the discretionary nature of the jurisdiction an agreement for the sale of land is prima facie presumed to come within their operation, so as to be subject to specific performance, but a contrary presumption exists in regard to agreements concerning chattels." Pomeroy on Contracts, Specific Performance, § 11.

Judge Story urges that there is no reasonable objection to allowing the party who is injured by the breach of any contract for the sale of chattels to have an election either to take damages at law or to have a specific performance in equity. 2 Story's Eq. Juris. (13th Ed.) § 717a. While it is probable that the development of this branch of equitable remedies is decidedly toward the logical solution suggested by Judge Story, it is entirely clear that his view cannot at this time be freely adopted without violence to what has long been regarded as accepted principles controlling the discretion of a court of equity in this class of cases. The United States Supreme Court has probably most nearly approached the view suggested by Judge Story. In Mechanics' Bank of Alexandria v. Seton, 1 Pet. (U.S.) 229, 305, 7 L.Ed. 152, Mr. Justice Thompson, delivering the opinion of that court, says: "But, notwithstanding this distinction between personal contracts for goods and contracts for lands is to be found laid down in the books, as a general rule; yet there are many cases to be found where specific performance of contracts, relating to personalty, have been enforced in chancery; and courts will only view with greater nicety contracts of this description than such as relate to land." See, also, Barr v. Lapsley, 1 Wheat. (U.S.) 151, 4 L.Ed. 58. In our own state contracts for the sale of chattels have been frequently enforced and the inadequacy of the remedy at law, based on the characteristic features of the contract or peculiar situation and needs of the parties, have been the principal grounds of relief. * * *

I think it clear that the present case falls well within the principles defined by the cases already cited from our own state. Complainants' factory has a capacity of about 1,000,000 cans of tomatoes. The season for packing lasts about six weeks. The preparations made for this six weeks of active work must be carried out in all features to enable the business to succeed. These preparations are primarily based upon the capacity of the plant. Cans and other necessary equipments, including labor, must be provided and secured in advance with reference to the capacity of the plant during the packing period. With this known capacity and an estimated average yield of tomatoes per acre the acreage of land necessary to supply the plant is calculated. To that end, the contract now in question was made, with other like contracts, covering a sufficient acreage to insure the essential pack. It seems immaterial whether the entire acreage is contracted for to insure the full pack, or whether a more limited acreage is contracted for and an estimated available open market depended upon for the balance of the pack. In either case a refusal of the parties who contract to supply a given acreage to comply with their contracts leaves the factory helpless, except to whatever extent an uncertain market may perchance supply the deficiency. The condition which arises from the breach of the contracts is not merely a question of the factory being compelled to pay a higher price for the product. Losses sustained in that manner could, with some degree of accuracy, be estimated. The condition which occasions the irreparable injury by reason of the breaches of the contracts is the inability to procure at any price at the time needed and of the quality needed, the necessary tomatoes to insure the successful operation of the plant. If it should be assumed as a fact that upon the breach of contracts of this nature other tomatoes of like quality and quantity could be procured in the open market without serious interference with the economic arrangements of the plant, a court of equity would hesitate to assume to interfere; but the very existence of such contracts proclaims their necessity to the economic management of the factory. The aspect of the situation bears no resemblance to that of an ordinary contract for the sale of merchandise in the course of an ordinary business. The business and its needs are extraordinary in that the maintenance of all of the conditions prearranged to secure the pack are a necessity to insure the successful operation of the plant. The breach of the contract by one planter differs but in degree from a breach by all.

The objection that to specifically perform the contract personal services are required will not divest the court of its powers to preserve the benefits of the contract. Defendant may be restrained from selling the crop to others, and, if necessary, a receiver can be appointed to harvest the crop.

A decree may be advised pursuant to the prayer of the bill.

By reason of the manner in which the facts on which this opinion is based were stipulated, no costs will be taxed.

CURRAN v. BAREFOOT, 183 N.C. App. 331, 645 S.E. 2d 187 (2007).

TYSON, JUDGE.

Robert M. Barefoot, as trustee for the Robert M. Barefoot Revocable Trust, ("defendant") appeals from judgment entered which ordered defendant to specifically perform a contract to convey real and personal property to Thomas L. Curran and Josephine Curran (collectively "plaintiffs"). Defendant also appeals from order entered denying his Rule 59 motion for a new trial and Rule 60(b) motion for relief from judgment. We affirm in part, reverse in part, and remand.

I. Background

Defendant owns a house ("the lake house") on Lake Tillery in Mt. Gilead, North Carolina. On 19 November 2003, plaintiffs and defendant executed an Offer to Purchase and Contract ("the contract"). Defendant agreed to convey the lake house to plaintiffs. An addendum accompanying the contract listed certain items of personal property defendant agreed to convey with the lake house: (1) "[a]ll furniture, linens, window treatments, appliances, pictures, towels, flatware, dishes, and all other items currently in the [lake] house" except "clothes and personal items;" (2) "[o]ne antique wardrobe located in an upstairs bedroom;" (3) "[o]ne small table located in [the] downstairs hallway;" and (4) "[a]ll watercraft and accessories." Defendant refused to tender and convey on the scheduled closing date.

On 29 January 2004, plaintiffs filed suit against defendant seeking specific performance of the contract. After a bench trial, the trial court found and concluded as a matter of law: (1) an enforceable contract existed between plaintiffs and defendant; (2) the contract should be reformed to correct draftsman's errors and mutual mistakes of the parties; (3) defendant repudiated the contract in late December 2003, refused to close the transaction, and breached the contract; (4) the subject real property is unique such that money damages are not an adequate remedy; and (5) plaintiffs are entitled to specific performance of their contract with defendant for conveyance of the subject real property and the associated personal property listed in the addendum, including watercraft. The trial court entered judgment on 30 December 2005.

On 9 January 2006, defendant moved for relief from the trial court's 30 December 2005 judgment, or alternatively for a new trial. The trial court denied defendant's motions on 13 February 2006. Defendant appeals from the judgment and this order.

* * *

"As a general rule, the remedy for a breach of contract for the sale of personal property is an action at law, where damages are awarded." Bell v. Concrete Products, Inc., 263 N.C. 389, 390, 139 S.E.2d 629, 630 (1965). However, our Supreme Court has stated "there are recognized exceptions." Trust Co. v. Webb, 206 N.C. 247, 250, 173 S.E. 598, 600 (1934). "Jurisdiction to enforce specific performance rests, not on the distinction between real and personal property, but on the ground that damages at law will not afford a complete remedy." Id. (citing Paddock v. Davenport, 107 N.C. 710, 12 S.E. 464 (1890); Tobacco Association v. Battle, 187 N.C. 260, 121 S.E. 629 (1924)).

Here, the plain language of the contract, defendant's admissions, and other competent evidence in the record clearly proves defendant intended to convey to plaintiffs a furnished lake house with three watercraft for $550,000.00. The trial court's judgment ordering specific performance of both the real and personal property provides "a complete remedy" to plaintiffs. Id. The trial court did not err as a matter of law by awarding plaintiffs specific performance of a sales contract for the purchase of the real property, that included incidental personal property, as a consideration for and part of the conveyance.

UNIFORM COMMERCIAL CODE § 2–716.

Buyer's Right to Specific Performance or Replevin

(1) Specific performance may be decreed where the goods are unique or in other proper circumstances.

(2) The decree for specific performance may include such terms and conditions as to payment of the price, damages, or other relief as the court may deem just.

IN RE DORSEY TRAILER CO., INC., 2009 WL 764572 (Bankr. M. D. Ala., 2009). One of the ways a buyer may recover goods is specific performance which "may be decreed where the goods are unique or in other proper circumstances." [§ 2–716.] "Under the U.C.C. a more liberal test in determining entitlement to specific performance has been established than the test one must meet for classic equitable relief." Eastern Air Lines, Inc. v. Gulf Oil Corp., 415 F. Supp. 429, 442–43 (S.D.Fla.1975) appeal dismissed per curiam 443 F.2d 1364 (9th Cir.1971). The comments explains that "uniqueness is not the sole basis of the remedy under this section for the relief may also be granted in other proper circumstances and inability to cover is strong evidence of other proper circumstances." "The scarcity of a chattel has been recognized as an important factor in determining whether specific performance of a contract for its sale will be granted." Madariaga v. Morris, 639 S.W.2d 709, 711 (Tex.App.1982) (citing 71 Am.Jur.2d,

Specific Performance §§ 153 and 156). One court has restated the test for specific performance as follows: "[b]asically courts now determine whether goods are replaceable as a practical matter-for example, whether it would be difficult to obtain similar goods on the open market." Magellan Int'l Corp. v. Salzgitter Handel GmbH, 76 F.Supp.2d 919, 926 (N.D.Ill.1999).

STEPHAN'S MACHINE & TOOL, INC. v. D & H MACHINERY CONSULTANTS, INC., 65 Ohio App. 2d 197, 417 N.E.2d 579 (Ohio Ct. App. 1979). [Plaintiff bought a unique machine from defendant, borrowing $96,000 to pay for it. The machine failed to function. Defendant agreed to replace the machine but failed to do so. Plaintiff was unable to raise the money to buy a replacement elsewhere, although such machines were available. Was plaintiff entitled to specific performance of defendant's agreement to replace? Held, yes.] The inoperable condition of machine no. 1, for which plaintiff borrowed $96,000 from Toledo Trust Company, placed an unsurmountable financial strain on plaintiff, causing a default on plaintiff's note to the bank, followed by a judgment on the renewal note. The financial circumstances of plaintiff were such that [it] is folly to contend that plaintiff could have avoided his business losses by buying a comparable boring machine from a source other than the defendant. Plaintiff, therefore, did suffer irreparable harm and had no adequate remedy at law.

I.LAN SYS v. NETSCOUT SERV. LEVEL CORP., 183 F. Supp. 2d 328 (D. Mass. 2002). The plaintiff, i.LAN Systems, Inc. ("i.LAN"), helps companies monitor their computer networks. The defendant, NetScout Service Level Corp., formerly known as NextPoint Networks, Inc. ("NextPoint"), sells sophisticated software that monitors networks. In 1998, i.LAN and NextPoint signed a detailed Value Added Reseller ("VAR") agreement whereby i.LAN agreed to resell NextPoint's software to customers. [A dispute arose over whether i.LAN] purchased the unlimited right to use NextPoint's software, replete with perpetual upgrades and support, whereby it effectively could rent, rather than sell, NextPoint's software to customers. * * * i.LAN [moved] for summary judgment, argu[ing] that it should be awarded specific performance—in particular, perpetual upgrades of NextPoint's software and unlimited support. [One issue was whether the software was "unique."]

* * *

* * * i.LAN makes three arguments why NextPoint's software is unique. First, i.LAN argues that the software is copyrighted and took years to design. The same could be said of any mass-produced item, however, and certainly a mass-produced item is the antithesis of the word "unique." More

importantly, NextPoint's software is one of several competing software packages in the market; all run on ordinary computers and perform substantially the same functions. Although these software packages may be copyrighted and the product of intense labor, they are interchangeable as a practical matter and thus none is unique. Second, i.LAN argues that *it* has tailored its business around NextPoint's software, thus making the software unique to *it*. The UCC is sensitive to this consideration, but at the same time this Court will not conflate reliance with uniqueness. Much as i.LAN may not want to, it certainly *could* purchase comparable software on the open market and reconfigure its systems to run that software, just as any person could buy such software and run it. Finally, i.LAN argues that it does not know the number of software licenses it will need in the future to provide its rental services, so money damages would not adequately compensate it. This argument is not that NextPoint's goods are unique, but that i.LAN had struck what it thought to be a unique contract: for a mere $85,231.42 it would have unlimited copies of all of NextPoint's software forever. The UCC, however, looks to the uniqueness of the goods, not the contract.

In sum, even if the clickwrap license agreement permits specific performance, and even if the Court were to enter judgment in favor of i.LAN, NextPoint's software is not unique or irreplaceable as a practical matter, so the Court would not award specific performance.

NOTE: *ENFORCEMENT OF SPECIFIC PERFORMANCE DECREES*

Decrees for specific performance are enforced differently from decrees or judgments for damages. If a defendant against whom a judgment for damages has been entered refuses to pay the judgment, the clerk of the court will issue to the plaintiff a writ of execution, which empowers the sheriff to take custody of property of the defendant, sell it, and apply the proceeds to satisfy the judgment. This process is in accordance with an elaborate scheme of rules, mostly statutory.

What if a court enters a decree of specific performance against a defendant and the defendant fails to perform as ordered? If the performance calls for a ministerial act, such as the execution of a deed, statutes in most states provide either that the decree will *automatically operate* as if the defendant had performed or that an officer of the court, such as a sheriff, will carry out the act required of the defendant (e.g., execution of the deed). Such statutes thus modify the traditional doctrine that a decree of specific performance operates only "in personam" to coerce the defendant personally to perform upon threat of imprisonment or fine for "contempt" of the decree.

Even when the decree calls for the defendant to perform an act that is not ministerial, the court's procedures of enforcement may go beyond coercing the defendant. Thus, the plaintiff may ignore the defendant's failure to perform and ask the court to appoint a "receiver" or other officer of the court to carry out the contract. See, again, the reference to a receiver in Curtice Brothers Co. v. Catts.

In still other cases, the act involved will be neither ministerial nor one that can otherwise be performed satisfactorily by an actor, such as a receiver, substituting for the defendant. What if the defendant refuses to obey such a decree? The plaintiff may then initiate a "show-cause" proceeding in which the defendant must show cause why he or she should not be cited for contempt of the court's decree and subjected to imprisonment or a fine. In such a show-cause proceeding, the defendant may assert various defenses such as that he complied with the decree, or that the decree was too vague, or that he could not comply because of changed circumstances. The risk of non-persuasion in such a proceeding typically rests on the defendant, who sometimes must meet a standard of proof that is somewhat higher than "a preponderance of the evidence," yet is below "beyond a reasonable doubt." If the court finds the defendant to be in contempt of the decree, the court has power to imprison the defendant. The usual theory of such imprisonment is not punitive. Rather, it is to coerce the defendant to comply with the decree. As the United States Supreme Court has said, when such a defendant goes to jail, he "carries the keys to his freedom in his willingness to comply with the court's directive." Uphaus v. Wyman, 360 U.S. 72 (1959). One (of several) important limitations on a court's power to imprison for contempt is the constitutional or statutory prohibition (in most states) against imprisonment for nonpayment of debt.

A second sanction for contempt is a fine. Again, the usual theory of this sanction is not to punish, but rather to coerce compliance or to provide direct reparation to the plaintiff (in which case the amount will be measured by the injury caused by the failure to satisfy the decree). A court may, for example, impose a fine of so many dollars per day, until the defendant complies.

The foregoing uses of imprisonment and fines to bring about compliance with the decree are classic illustrations of the ancient maxim that a decree of specific performance may be enforced "in personam"—against the person of the defendant. The enforcement of decrees is treated in D. Dobbs, Remedies 130–62 (1993).

IN RE IBP, INC. SHAREHOLDERS LITIGATION

Delaware Chancery Court, 2001.
789 A.2d 14.

STRINE, VICE CHANCELLOR.

This post-trial opinion addresses a demand for specific performance of a "Merger Agreement" by IBP, Inc., the nation's number one beef and number two pork distributor. By this action, IBP seeks to compel the "Merger" between itself and Tyson Foods, Inc., the nation's largest chicken distributor, in a transaction in which IBP stockholders will receive their choice of $30 a share in cash or Tyson stock, or a combination of the two.

The IBP-Tyson Merger Agreement resulted from a vigorous auction process that pitted Tyson against the nation's number one pork producer, Smithfield Foods. To say that Tyson was eager to win the auction is to slight its ardent desire to possess IBP. During the bidding process, Tyson was anxious to ensure that it would acquire IBP, and to make sure Smithfield did not. By succeeding, Tyson hoped to create the world's preeminent meat products company—a company that would dominate the meat cases of supermarkets in the United States and eventually throughout the globe.

During the auction process, Tyson was given a great deal of information that suggested that IBP was heading into a trough in the beef business. Even more, Tyson was alerted to serious problems at an IBP subsidiary, DFG, which had been victimized by accounting fraud to the tune of over $30 million in charges to earnings and which was the active subject of an asset impairment study. Not only that, Tyson knew that IBP was projected to fall seriously short of the fiscal year 2000 earnings predicted in projections prepared by IBP's Chief Financial Officer in August, 2000.

By the end of the auction process, Tyson had come to have great doubts about IBP's ability to project its future earnings, the credibility of IBP's management, and thought that the important business unit in which DFG was located—Foodbrands—was broken.

Yet, Tyson's ardor for IBP was such that Tyson raised its bid by a total of $4.00 a share after learning of these problems. Tyson also signed the Merger Agreement, which permitted IBP to recognize unlimited additional liabilities on account of the accounting improprieties at DFG. It did so without demanding any representation that IBP meet its projections for future earnings, or any escrow tied to those projections.

After the Merger Agreement was signed on January 1, 2001, Tyson trumpeted the value of the merger to its stockholders and the financial community, and indicated that it was fully aware of the risks that attended the cyclical nature of IBP's business. In early January, Tyson's stockholders ratified the merger agreement and authorized its management to take whatever action was needed to effectuate it.

During the winter and spring of 2001, Tyson's own business performance was dismal. Meanwhile, IBP was struggling through a poor first quarter. Both companies' problems were due in large measure to a severe winter, which adversely affected livestock supplies and vitality. As these struggles deepened, Tyson's desire to buy IBP weakened.

This cooling of affections first resulted in a slow-down by Tyson in the process of consummating a transaction, a slow-down that was attributed to IBP's on-going efforts to resolve issues that had been raised about its financial statements by the Securities and Exchange Commission ("SEC").

The most important of these issues was how to report the problems at DFG, which Tyson had been aware of at the time it signed the Merger Agreement. Indeed, all the key issues that the SEC raised with IBP were known by Tyson at the time it signed the Merger Agreement. The SEC first raised these issues in a faxed letter on December 29, 2000 to IBP's outside counsel. Neither IBP management nor Tyson learned of the letter until the second week of January, 2001. After learning of the letter, Tyson management put the Merger Agreement to a successful board and stockholder vote.

But the most important reason that Tyson slowed down the Merger process was different: it was having buyer's regret. Tyson wished it had paid less especially in view of its own compromised 2001 performance and IBP's slow 2001 results. By March, Tyson's founder and controlling stockholder, Don Tyson, no longer wanted to go through with the Merger Agreement. He made the decision to abandon the Merger. His son, John Tyson, Tyson's Chief Executive Officer, and the other Tyson managers followed his instructions. Don Tyson abandoned the Merger because of IBP's and Tyson's poor results in 2001, and not because of DFG or the SEC issues IBP was dealing with. Indeed, Don Tyson told IBP management that he would blow DFG up if he were them.

After the business decision was made to terminate, Tyson's legal team swung into action. They fired off a letter terminating the Agreement at the same time they filed suit accusing IBP of fraudulently inducing the Merger that Tyson had once so desperately desired.

This expedited litigation ensued, which involved massive amounts of discovery and two weeks of trial. In this opinion, I address IBP's claim that Tyson had no legal basis to avoid its obligation to consummate the Merger Agreement, as well as Tyson's contrary arguments.

* * *

Having determined that the Merger Agreement is a valid and enforceable contract that Tyson had no right to terminate, I now turn to the question of whether the Merger Agreement should be enforced by an order of specific performance. Although Tyson's voluminous post-trial briefs argue the merits fully, its briefs fail to argue that a remedy of specific performance is unwarranted in the event that its position on the merits is rejected.

This gap in the briefing is troubling. A compulsory order will require a merger of two public companies with thousands of employees working at facilities that are important to the communities in which they operate. The impact of a forced merger on constituencies beyond the stockholders and top managers of IBP and Tyson weighs heavily on my mind. The prosperity of IBP and Tyson means a great deal to these constituencies. I therefore approach this remedial issue quite cautiously and mindful of the interests of those who will be affected by my decision.

I start with a fundamental question: is this is a truly unique opportunity that cannot be adequately monetized? If the tables were turned and Tyson was seeking to enforce the contract, a great deal of precedent would indicate that the contract should be specifically enforced. In the more typical situation, an acquiror argues that it cannot be made whole unless it can specifically enforce the acquisition agreement, because the target company is unique and will yield value of an unquantifiable nature, once combined with the acquiring company. In this case, the sell-side of the transaction is able to make the same argument, because the Merger Agreement provides the IBP stockholders with a choice of cash or Tyson stock, or a combination of both. Through this choice, the IBP stockholders were offered a chance to share in the upside of what was touted by Tyson as a unique, synergistic combination. This court has not found, and Tyson has not advanced, any compelling reason why sellers in mergers and acquisitions transactions should have less of a right to demand specific performance than buyers, and none has independently come to my mind.

In addition, the determination of a cash damages award will be very difficult in this case. And the amount of any award could be staggeringly large. No doubt the parties would haggle over huge valuation questions, which (Tyson no doubt would argue) must take into account the possibility of a further auction for IBP or other business developments. A damages award can, of course, be shaped; it simply will lack any pretense to precision. An award of specific performance will, I anticipate, entirely eliminate the need for a speculative determination of damages.

Finally, there is no doubt that a remedy of specific performance is practicable. Tyson itself admits that the combination still makes strategic sense. At trial, John Tyson was asked by his own counsel to testify about whether it was fair that Tyson should enter any later auction for IBP hampered by its payment of the Rawhide Termination Fee. This testimony indicates that Tyson Foods is still interested in purchasing IBP, but wants to get its original purchase price back and then buy IBP off the day-old goods table. I consider John Tyson's testimony an admission of the feasibility of specific performance.

Probably the concern that weighs heaviest on my mind is whether specific performance is the right remedy in view of the harsh words that have been said in the course of this litigation. Can these management teams work together? The answer is that I do not know. [Executives from IBP] say they can. I am not convinced, although Tyson's top executives continue to respect the managerial acumen of [IBP's executives], if not that of their financial subordinates.

What persuades me that specific performance is a workable remedy is that Tyson will have the power to decide all the key management questions itself. It can therefore hand-pick its own management team. While this may be unpleasant for the top level IBP managers who might be replaced, it was a possible risk of the Merger from the get-go and a reality of today's M & A market.

The impact on other constituencies of this ruling also seems tolerable. Tyson's own investment banker thinks the transaction makes sense for Tyson, and is still fairly priced at $30 per share. One would think the Tyson constituencies would be better served on the whole by a specific performance remedy, rather than a large damages award that did nothing but cost Tyson a large amount of money.

In view of these factors, I am persuaded that an award of specific performance is appropriate, regardless of what level of showing was required by IBP. That is, there is clear and convincing evidence to support this award. Such an award is decisively preferable to a vague and imprecise damages remedy that cannot adequately remedy the injury to IBP's stockholders.

Conclusion

For all the foregoing reasons, IBP's claim for specific performance is granted. Tyson's claims for relief are dismissed. The parties shall collaborate and present a conforming partial final order no later than June 27. In addition, the parties shall schedule an office conference with the court to occur later that same week.

E. FARNSWORTH, CONTRACTS

746–47 (4th ed. 2004).

The tendency is, however, to liberalize the granting of specific performance and injunction by enlarging the classes of cases in which damages are regarded as an inadequate remedy. The contemporary approach is to compare remedies to determine which is more effective in affording suitable protection to the injured party's legally recognized interest, which is usually that party's expectation interest. The concept of adequacy has thus tended to become relative, and the comparison more often leads to granting equitable relief than was historically the case.

NOTE:
DEFENSES TO AND LIMITATIONS ON AVAILABILITY OF SPECIFIC PERFORMANCE

We have seen that specific performance is available only if the remedy at law is inadequate. In addition, there are numerous other defenses to and limitations on specific performance. We will consider most of the major ones here. Although such a defense or limitation is applicable to bar specific performance, the plaintiff may still usually recover any damages for contract breach.

Courts of equity, from which the remedy of specific performance emerged, were said to be "courts of conscience." Accordingly, those courts evolved a number of defenses to specific performance based on unfairness. The grounds of unfairness (many of which overlap) include sharp practice, unfair advantage taking, non-disclosure, post-contractual unconscionability, inadequacy of consideration, mistake, misrepresentation, duress, undue influence, and the like. Suppose, for example, that F is an old, ill, and illiterate farmer "who moves in a small circle." B is an experienced businessman who is acquainted with a real estate developer, D. B knows that D wishes to buy F's farm in anticipation of a general rise in the market value of real estate likely to occur because a railway is planned for the area, and that D is willing to pay above current market price for the farm. F is unaware of these facts. B offers to buy F's farm at the current market price, and persuades F not to seek advice from others. F agrees to sell to B at this price, which is much below the price D subsequently agrees to pay B for the land. F learns all the facts and refuses to perform. B sues for specific performance and F defends on the ground of unfairness. In a leading case, Wollums v. Horsley, 93 Ky. 582, 20 S.W. 781 (1892), this defense carried the day on facts similar to those posed.

A second defense is sometimes called "lack of mutuality of performance." The essence of this defense is that a court will not grant specific performance to P unless D can be reasonably assured of receiving P's return performance. Suppose D contracts to build custom-made logging equipment for P in accord with detailed specifications, P to pay $5,000 down, $10,000 at the halfway point, and $25,000 on completion. After P has paid $5,000 and D has begun work, D repudiates and P seeks specific performance. D defends on the ground that P's financial position is shaky. The court may grant P a decree of specific performance on condition that P post a bond satisfactory to the court. If P cannot post the bond, the court will not grant specific performance. The Restatement (Second) of Contracts deals with this defense in § 363; see also Hogan v. Goldsmith, 533 S.W.3d 921, 925 (Tex. App. 2017) (reversing lower court grant of summary judgement for Plaintiff because a genuine material issue of fact existed as to whether plaintiff was ready, willing, and able to perform at the relevant times).

Still another important defense is based on indefiniteness of the agreement. See, e.g., Offerman v. Granada LLC, 418 P.3d 921, 924 (Ariz. Ct. App. 2017) ("given the absence of essential terms in the * * * language agreed to by the parties, an order of specific performance [is] not a proper remedy"); Boardwalk at Daytona Development, LLC v. Paspalakis, 220 So.3d 457, 463 (Fla. Dist. Ct. App. 2016) (holding that specific performance was not available where the agreement's description of the property to be conveyed described three potential properties). A contract may not be invalid on this ground, yet be too indefinite to serve as the basis for a decree of specific performance. If a contract is too indefinite, the court cannot draft with precision a decree ordering performance of the contract. It would, of course, be unfair to hold a party in contempt for failing to abide by an imprecise decree of specific performance. For example, B contracts to build a "first class theater" on land he is to buy from P, which theater will enhance the value of P's land. P cannot get specific performance of this promise, although he may get damages for B's failure to enhance P's land value.

A related defense is sometimes called "impracticability of performance," or "difficulty in enforcement or supervision." Some of the flavor of this defense is captured in the following quotation from a case in which the court denied specific performance: "It must, I think, be conceded that the items of renovation and construction work are numerous and noticeably diversified. Moreover, by their nature they are such as to render their actual performance and accomplishment provocative of frequent disputes. The difficulty in supervision that would be necessary is obvious." Lester's Home Furnishers, Inc. v. Modern Furniture Co., 1 N.J.Super. 365, 370–71, 61 A.2d 743, 746 (1948).

Courts will not grant specific performance of a contract to provide personal services. Pingley v. Brunson, 272 S.C. 421, 252 S.E.2d 560 (1979) (specific performance of contract to play music at plaintiff's restaurant denied). What reasons might be given to justify this limitation? If, however, the plaintiff can show that a party has agreed to provide "unique" personal services, this party may be enjoined from providing those services to a third person, at least where the contract includes a covenant not to render such services to a third person. Dallas Cowboys Football Club, Inc. v. Harris, 348 S.W.2d 37 (Tex.Civ.App.1961) (injunction prohibiting James B. Harris from playing for Dallas Texans of newly organized American Football League).

In the employer-employee context, the personal services limitation generally operates to preclude granting specific performance to either party. Felch v. Findlay College, 119 Ohio App. 357, 200 N.E.2d 353 (1963) (employer could not be forced to reinstate faculty member even if discharged in breach of contract). However, labor law statutes, cases, and collective bargaining agreements may provide that an employer must grant reinstatement on request after wrongful dismissal. Such agreements may be specifically enforceable. 12 Corbin on Contracts § 1204 at 445 (rev. ed.1993). In addition, courts can reinstate an employee when an employer intentionally engages in an "unlawful employment practice" under 42 U.S.C. § 2000e–5(g) (2006).

Suppose the seller of real estate is unable to convey precisely what was promised. For example, suppose an acreage deficiency or an encumbrance on the title. Many courts will grant specific performance to the purchaser with an abatement in the purchase price corresponding to the value of the defect. However, if the deficiency is sufficiently material so that the abatement would be a large portion of the contract price, specific performance may be denied. Ide v. Joe Miller & Co., 703 P.2d 590 (Colo. App. 1984).

DORF, DO CONTRACTS IMPOSE MORAL OBLIGATIONS?

Justia Verdict, August 7, 2019.

[W]hat are we to make of [National Basketball Association] players leaving their teams by demanding to be traded while they remain contractually obligated to those teams? [In 2019, Kawhi] Leonard will be joined on the [Los Angeles] Clippers by one of last season's three MVP finalists, Paul George, who demanded and received a trade from the Oklahoma City Thunder with three of the four years remaining on the contract he signed just last year. And the Clippers will share an arena with the Los Angeles Lakers, who will team all-time great Lebron James with newly acquired perennial all-star Anthony Davis after Davis demanded and received a trade from the New Orleans Pelicans.

In light of the successful trade demands by George, Davis, and others * * * Golden State Warriors head coach Steve Kerr recently objected. Moves like these, Kerr said, are "bad for the league."

* * *

* * * Kerr did not mean that moves by the likes of Davis and George are bad for competition. After all, the salary cap and revenue sharing constrain large-market teams' ability to stockpile superstars. No, Kerr drew a sharp distinction between free agents moving teams and players under contract demanding to be traded. He said: "When you sign on that dotted line, you owe your effort and your play to that team, to that city, to the fans. And then it's completely your right to leave as a free agent. But if you sign the contract, then you should be bound to that contract."

Kerr thus expressed the view that contracts create a kind of moral obligation. I suspect that many people hold a similar view. And yet, [some have] recognized a quite different view. Under the doctrine of "efficient breach," a contract does not create an obligation to perform; it only creates an obligation to pay damages if one chooses not to perform. Kerr certainly knows basketball, but did he get the law of contracts wrong?

Efficient Breach and Damages

Suppose Jane makes a contract with Bob for Bob to sell Jane his 2011 Honda Civic sedan. Based on the car's mileage, condition, and Bluebook value, they agree on a price of $10,000, with Jane to take delivery in a week. However, two days before Bob plans to deliver the car to Jane, Elaine sends him an email. She saw Bob's ad and she thinks the car he is selling, which he himself bought used in 2017, was Elaine's first car. It has sentimental value to her. She offers Bob $12,000 for it. What should Bob do?

Steve Kerr might say that Bob has to forgo the extra $2,000 and sell the car to Jane, because he signed on the dotted line with Jane. But putting aside various special regulations that states may enact, that's not what contract law traditionally says. Contract law allows Bob to breach his contract with Jane and sell to Elaine.

Isn't that unfair to Jane? Not really. Bob's 2011 Honda Civic is not special, except to Elaine. Jane can now buy a different version of it. Indeed, she has a duty to do so. In contract law, we say that Jane has a duty to "cover," i.e., to mitigate the loss. If Jane gets an even better deal than she made with Bob, then Bob has no contract liability to her. If she gets a worse deal—perhaps the best price she can find for a comparable car is the $10,500 that Joe wants for his Civic—then Bob needs to pay damages to put Jane in the same position she would have been in had Bob performed the contract. In this example, that means Bob would pay Jane $500. Jane ends up just where she would have been, while Bob nets an extra $1,500.

To be sure, in the foregoing example, you might still think the result is unfair to Jane. Bob could have sold his particular Civic to Jane for the $10,000 and then Jane could have turned around and resold it to Elaine for $12,000, whereupon she would pay $10,500 for Joe's Civic. Everyone would end up with (and without) the same cars, but Jane rather than Bob would pocket the $1,500 surplus.

That is a fair criticism. It shows why the idea of "efficient breach" is "efficient" only in the sense of so-called Kaldor-Hicks efficiency, which does not pay attention to distributional questions like the one just raised. And, as I shall explain momentarily, in some circumstances, when goods are considered unique, specific performance will be required. In those cases, efficient breach does not apply. Nevertheless, the very concept of efficient breach—and its widespread availability in contract—shows that in general the law does not impose an obligation to carry out one's end of a bargain; it imposes only an obligation to make the other party whole if you do not.

From Basketball to Opera

But wait. What has any of this to do with star professional athletes, whose services surely are unique? Although statistical analyses of sports now routinely include such categories as the number of wins a particular player adds above an average replacement player, professional athletes are not simply packages of statistical production. It might be possible to replace Anthony Davis's scoring, rebounding, and defense with some combination of above-average players, but star players bring other qualities, like leadership and excitement. As Kerr observed, fans form emotional connections with particular players, not just with the WAR (wins above replacement) such players provide.

Accordingly, the law might treat the services of a star player as unique, in the same way that the law treats a particular parcel of real estate as unique. Whereas the breach of a contract for the sale of interchangeable commodities gives rise only to a claim for money damages—because the disappointed buyer can simply purchase replacement commodities on the market and sue for the difference in price—courts will order specific performance for unique goods.

But now we encounter a further wrinkle. A basketball player's contract is not a contract for goods. It is a contract to provide a kind of personal services—making use of the player's body and skill. Even apart from concerns about involuntary servitude that arise under the Thirteenth Amendment, courts typically do not order specific performance of such contracts. The leading case involved an opera singer.

In the 1852 English decision of *Lumley v. Wagner*, the court acknowledged that it lacked the power to order Johanna Wagner to sing for three months at Her Majesty's Theatre, notwithstanding her contractual obligation to do so. Nonetheless, the judge explained that he could do the next best thing, by forbidding her to perform at the rival Royal Italian Opera, Covent Garden during the period of the contract. Although the contract with Her Majesty's Theatre contained an express non-compete clause, the judge said that if Wagner "had attempted, even in the absence of any negative stipulation, to perform at another theatre, she would have broken the spirit and true meaning of the contract . . . ." For generations since, first-year contracts professors have used *Lumley v. Wagner* to illustrate the proposition that while courts cannot typically require people to perform personal services, *negative* injunctions are permissible.

If, instead of acceding to Davis's trade demands, the Pelicans had gone to court, they could have obtained an order forbidding Davis to play for a rival team and/or to pay them back his salary for games he refused to play.

Good Faith and Fair Dealing

Yet everyone knew all along that Davis was not going to just start playing for the Lakers or any other team but the Pelicans without a trade. And even if a judge issued an order to Davis forbidding him from taking his talents to another team, that would not ensure that Davis would play well for the Pelicans. The very factors that lead courts not to order specific performance of personal services contracts also limit the utility of negative injunctions. Forbidden to sing at Covent Garden for more money, Wagner might have resented the owners of Her Majesty's Theatre and given each aria less than her best effort.

Something like that happened with Davis. Looking to the post-Davis future, the Pelicans reduced Davis's minutes. Davis, in turn, may have been grateful for the reduced risk of injury. Once it was clear that Davis wanted to leave, his continuing to be under contract with the Pelicans was at best awkward.

To be clear, the problem that arises when a star player with substantial time remaining on his contract demands to be traded is not a question of the player's legal obligation. Contracts come with an implicit obligation of good faith and fair dealing, so even a player who wants out must provide his best effort for the team.

The problem is that the law does not and cannot fully enforce the obligation of good faith and fair dealing during an ongoing contract for personal services. If a star player's scoring average dips, who can say whether he is tanking or just in a slump? And even if he is tanking, his current team will have an impossible time proving it in court and then getting a damages remedy. The only sure remedy available—an order barring the player from joining a competing team, as in the opera singer case—is unnecessary and therefore unhelpful.

Accordingly, it looks like Kerr was right after all. Although he was perhaps confusing the issue by using moralistic language, Kerr might have meant that because the legal remedies for enforcing sports contracts are inadequate, the NBA and its fans must rely on the consciences of individual players to honor the obligation of good faith.

SECTION TEN: ALTERNATIVE DISPUTE RESOLUTION: AN INTRODUCTION

LIEBERMAN & HENRY, LESSONS FROM THE ALTERNATIVE DISPUTE RESOLUTION MOVEMENT

53 U. Chi. L .Rev. 424, 424–426 (1986).

The ADR roster includes such well-known processes as arbitration, mediation, conciliation, and, perhaps, negotiation. These processes can be used to settle existing disputes or to prevent disputes from developing. There are also new hybrid devices that borrow from courtroom procedure—including, most prominently, the mini-trial. The roster may also be expanded to include the roles played by certain officials and quasi-officials (such as court appointed masters, special masters, and neutral experts), by private persons retained as neutrals, by ombudsmen, and by private judges. Changes in procedural rules to provide incentives to the parties to settle (for example, further penalizing parties who turn down reasonable settlement offers) and the greater use of partial summary judgment might also be viewed as ADR techniques.

It is easier to point to discrete practices than to discern the entire direction of the new movement. ADR has no generally accepted abstract or theoretical definition. But it does have a fundamental premise: it is worthwhile both to reduce the costs of resolving disputes, however this can be accomplished, and to improve the quality of the final outcome. We offer a working definition of ADR as a starting point for analysis: ADR is a set of practices and techniques that aim (1) to permit legal disputes to be resolved outside the courts for the benefit of all disputants; (2) to reduce the cost of conventional litigation and the delays to which it is ordinarily subject; or (3) to prevent legal disputes that would otherwise likely be brought to the courts.

SHAVELL, ALTERNATIVE DISPUTE RESOLUTION: AN ECONOMIC ANALYSIS

24 J. Leg. Studies 1, 2–3 (1994).

* * * ADR may be adopted because it is to the mutual benefit of the parties to a contract or to those who have some other relationship with each other. * * * First, ADR may lower the cost of resolving disputes or risk. Second, ADR may engender superior incentives through greater accuracy of result or other characteristics. Suppose, for instance, that substandard performance of a contract would be correctly assessed by expert arbitrators under ADR but not by courts. Then the parties to the contract might well prefer to adopt ADR because it would induce good performance, thereby raising the willingness of the promisee to pay for the contract. Third, ADR may result in improved incentives to engage in disputes or to refrain from that. For example, it may be that the number of disputes brought under the legal process would be excessive, dissipating substantial resources of the parties without instigating mutually desirable changes in behavior; thus an ADR agreement that would serve to limit the number of disputes would be advantageous.

COLE, THE LOST PROMISE OF ARBITRATION

70 SMU L. Rev. 849, 857–58, 860–64 (2017).

As originally envisioned * * * arbitration was an informal, speedy, and flexible process that enabled a disputant to avoid slow court processes and achieve a final, binding result. Merchants, in particular, preferred arbitration because they were interested in a system that would resolve disputes quickly and in a manner consistent with industry standards (to facilitate relationships among the parties). * * * Judicial review of arbitration awards was unwanted because the timetable for such review was inconsistent with the parties' need for immediate resolution. Opinion writing was equally unnecessary because the principles the arbitrator applied were based on customs and norms that the parties generally understood. Speed and efficiency of award issuance took precedence over accuracy and reasoning.

* * *

[T]he arbitration process has changed in the context of arbitrations among one-shot players like consumers and employees on the one hand, and repeat players, like businesses and employers, on the other. As most readers know, businesses and employers dramatically increased their use of pre-dispute arbitration agreements in the 1980s and 1990s. Looking for less expensive and speedier methods for resolving disputes, these entities turned toward arbitration. The Supreme Court facilitated the move to arbitration by sanctioning agreements that mandated arbitration of the vast majority of statutory claims. Not surprisingly, some of the businesses adopting arbitral processes overreached, attempting to bias the arbitration process heavily in their favor by, for example, skewing the arbitrator selection process, choosing inconvenient locations for the arbitration, or charging disputants excessive fees to participate in arbitration. Courts and policy makers intervened, though, establishing parameters for businesses interested in using arbitration to resolve disputes with consumers and employees. In addition to ensuring fair arbitrator selection processes, courts and policy makers circumscribed businesses' ability to require consumers and employees to pay administrative and arbitrator fees, curtail discovery, and bind only consumers and employees to arbitration, rather than both parties. * * *

* * *

Whether proceeding pursuant to institutional rules or their own arbitration agreement, most businesses continue to confer significant discretion on the arbitrators to run the hearing. Though prone to err on the side of admitting evidence, arbitrators carefully consider hearsay, relevancy, and duplicative testimony objections. Moreover, arbitrators routinely refer to the rules of evidence as guidelines to assist them in running the hearing. Although not held in a courtroom, arbitral hearings are quite formal, with opening statements, direct and cross-examination, and swearing in of witnesses, together with ruling on evidentiary objections. In many ways, both substantively and procedurally, modern arbitration resembles a bench trial or a hearing before an administrative law judge. Arbitrators also write reasoned opinions more frequently today than they did in the 1970s and 1980s. These opinions look much like judicial opinions. Moreover, arbitrators deciding legal issues often seek out "precedent," like court decisions or other arbitral opinions, to help guide their decision-making. Like judges, law-trained arbitrators prefer to decide cases consistent with the law and with other arbitrators' decisions.

STIPANOWICH, ARBITRATION: THE "NEW LITIGATION"

2010 U. Ill. L. Rev. 1, 6–7.

In the United States * * * three significant developments are subjecting business arbitration processes to unprecedented stress and strain, and subjecting arbitration to swelling criticism. First, it appears that as arbitration has been called upon to assume the burden of resolving virtually every kind of civil dispute, it has taken on more and more features of a court trial. Today, for example, proceedings under standard arbitration rules are likely to include prehearing motion practice and extensive discovery. Hearings may go on for extended periods of time in order to avoid charges of procedural injustice, and there is evidence that the much-vaunted finality of arbitral awards is eroding. The higher costs associated with these developments is a leading cause for complaint about arbitration among business users. At the same time, paradoxically, it appears that an increasing number of lawyers are seeking ways of eliminating the remaining differences between arbitration and court trial, most notably through contractual provisions for expanded judicial review of arbitration awards.

A second, concurrent phenomenon is the explosion of mediation and other competing dispute resolution alternatives to "extended adjudication." Just as alternative dispute resolution (ADR) has played a prominent role in changing the landscape of civil litigation, the use of mediation and other "thin-slicing" approaches is dramatically altering the environment of private dispute resolution. Such approaches are generally perceived as doing a better job of accomplishing many of the benefits traditionally associated with arbitration, and they often better serve and resonate with various business goals. As a result, if changes to recent standard contracts are any indication, arbitration usage may be diminishing in some commercial arenas such as construction; some suggest that we have passed the zenith of commercial arbitration in America—at least in anything similar to its present form. * * *

A third momentous trend is the broad enforcement of binding arbitration provisions in standardized adhesion contracts that govern employment relationships and consumer transactions. This evolution has fueled a continuing debate over the need for regulation of arbitration agreements—regulation that sometimes "spills over" into the business-to-business arena in ways that increase related costs without enhancing the value of the process. It has also contributed to a generally negative image of arbitration, as evidenced in first-year contracts casebooks.

PART TWO

THE AGREEMENT PROCESS

■ ■ ■

CHAPTER FOUR

AGREEMENTS AND PROMISES

▪ ▪ ▪

> *Whereas tradition has [the lawyer] as a participant in specific controversies, today he has the added major role of planner who seeks not only to avoid controversy but affirmatively to advance his client's interests.*
>
> DICKERSON

SECTION ONE: THE AGREEMENT PROCESS AND THE ROLE OF LAWYERS

Lawyers frequently play major roles in the process whereby parties reach and formulate an agreement. They are often asked to advise on the general law applicable to an agreement, to find facts that bear on prospective terms, to ascertain and particularize the goals of the parties, to plan and draft the overall agreement, and to negotiate with the other side. These tasks are introduced in Sections Two and Three.

After considering these lawyer roles, we turn to the requirements of a valid agreement. By previewing lawyer planning and drafting first, you can develop a planner's perspective from which to view the agreement stage and all that follows in this book.

SECTION TWO: AN INTRODUCTION TO CONTRACT PLANNING

Most contract planning occurs at the agreement stage. We introduced this topic in the White-Benkowski episode in Chapter One. The Macneil excerpt and the Note that follows set forth two main types of planning, namely performance and risk planning. These are followed by three excerpts that consider the influences of technology on planning and drafting agreements. Needless to say, these topics demand entire courses in your upper-class curriculum.

MACNEIL, A PRIMER OF CONTRACT PLANNING

48 S. Cal. L. Rev. 627, 639–41 & 641 n. 31 (1975).

Parties enter contracts to achieve particular known goals at the expense of incurring particular known costs. These particular goals and costs may or may not be planned specifically at the time of making a contract. For example, one goes to a doctor for an examination knowing that the doctor's fee will have to be paid, but often not knowing just what the fee will be. Goals and costs of this nature are central to party purposes in making the contract, and planning for them can usefully be called performance planning. A shorthand way of identifying performance planning is to ask: Will what is planned almost certainly have to be carried out if this contract is to go through to a successful conclusion as planned? An affirmative answer identifies performance planning.

Like any other human activity, engaging in contractual behavior involves risks of loss. Sometimes dealing with risks of loss is the central purpose of the contract, as in the case of insurance. Where this is the case, planning for those risks is performance planning. In many circumstances, however, risks of loss exist which are peripheral to the main purposes of the parties in making the contract in the sense that the contract may be carried to a completely successful conclusion without the cost of such loss ever being incurred. Planning for such risks can usefully be distinguished from performance planning and called risk planning. * * *

* * *

The goal of performance planning must always be the smoothly efficient accomplishment of the aims of the parties. (Since contract planning reflects the lack of identity of interests of the parties, the performance planning goal of one party is the smoothly efficient accomplishment of that party's aims; this may or may not correspond to goals the other party would favor.) Except respecting application of legal knowledge, this often involves many subjects in which the lawyer has little or no expertise. Whole courses and sequences of courses at business, engineering, technical, and many other schools are devoted to the development of understanding of planning and coordinating such expertise. Major portions of the commercial and financial world devote their energies to contract performance planning of this nature. * * *

NOTE:
RISK PLANNING

The lawyer must consider what could go wrong when planning an agreement in order to avoid bad outcomes, such as disputes or even contract breakdown. Lawyer skills such as knowledge of the applicable rules, business expertise, and even imagination help the lawyer anticipate the types of events or risks that must be avoided. Such risks include federal, state, or local law, or agency regulations that conflict with the goals of the agreement, complaints from third parties that interfere with performance of the agreement, and unanticipated events such as strikes, fire, flood, or epidemics that make performance impossible or impractical. (Chapter Eight covers this last set of risks that have led to almost countless days in court for unfortunate parties.)

LARRY E. RIBSTEIN, DELAWYERING THE CORPORATION

2012 Wis. L. Rev. 305, 314–16.

Technology facilitates combining past experience with customization and learning. Firms have developed software that revises a basic template based on the client's responses to a questionnaire. For example, ContractExpress DealBuilder uses web-based templates, questionnaires, and other materials. Kiiac can analyze a database of contracts and create a "Reference Standard" that firms can use to create new agreements.

* * *

Corporate adoption of transactional software will affect in-house lawyers' routine corporate work. Rather than starting each contract from scratch, the contracting process increasingly will be automated. Although there will still be a role for individual judgments, particularly in large deals or deals calling for new types of structures, corporations may be able to automate enough of their contracting to trim their dedicated legal staffs. Firms could assign the work to law-trained people embedded in firms' operational departments, such as human resources or purchasing, rather than in a "legal" department. These employees could make basically business judgments about deal terms, using their legal skills to choose and use the appropriate template; then they could refer out to lawyers for quality control. They also could collaborate with non-law-trained technicians to develop new templates for recurring situations.

HRICIK, MORGAN & WILLIAMS, THE ETHICS OF USING ARTIFICIAL INTELLIGENCE TO AUGMENT DRAFTING LEGAL DOCUMENTS

4 Tex. A&M J. Prop. L. 465, 466–67 (2018).

Because technology may be able to do some tasks better, or at a lower cost, or both, lawyers should use technology when it will, considering the risks, benefit clients. That obligation requires lawyers to "keep abreast of changes in . . . practice, including the benefits and risk associated with relevant technology . . . ." Assessing the benefits and risks of a particular technology obviously requires due diligence into the practical and legal risks of the technology, and comparing that to the benefits it brings to a representation. That assessment requires applying existing ethical rules in a process that can best be analyzed as comprising two stages.

The first step requires determining whether the technology does what it is supposed to do in a reasonably competent manner. For example, just as a lawyer could not use a paralegal to use a form to create the first draft of a contract for a client if the paralegal's work was known to be unreliable or unreasonably expensive, a lawyer cannot use an automated contract drafting service with the same shortcomings. The first step, in other words, requires reasonable efforts by the lawyer to determine the competency of the service. If the service does not provide competent assistance, the lawyer obviously cannot use it.

The second step requires determining whether a competent service can be used while complying with the ethical obligations of the lawyer, beyond competency. Just as a lawyer must ensure that non-lawyer employees and agents maintain the confidentiality of client information consistent with the lawyer's ethical obligations, he must do so with all services provided by third parties, including automated services. Likewise, lawyers must ensure non-lawyer assistants—even those who are independent contractors hired for a particular matter, and not firm employees—must not have conflicts of interest or violations of other ethical rules.

JEREMY M. SKLAROFF, SMART CONTRACTS AND THE COST OF INFLEXIBILITY

166 U. Pa. L. Rev. 263, 273–74 (2017).

The appeal of "smart contracts," agreements built in computer code and stored on a blockchain, is in many ways similar to that of Bitcoin and other early blockchain applications, harnessing the same critical features like decentralized consensus, instantaneous exchange, and complex computational states. A smart contract is immutable and unmodifiable once created, since its logic is seeded into a blockchain spread across multiple points. This prevents powerful parties from opportunistically breaching the contract or extracting a beneficial modification that disadvantages weaker counterparties. It is written and executed without the need for expensive intermediating institutions; by interacting with devices that monitor states of the world and with firms' internal information systems, it can check whether conditions are satisfied and then instantaneously provide the bargained-for goods or money. And it can exist either in isolation or be nested within multiple sets of other smart contracts, so that its complexity can scale up to meet whatever transaction logic the parties desire.

A seminal smart contract example is an automated car lease. Suppose that Bob has a fleet of cars, one of which he wants to lease to Alice. Further suppose that in this world, cars can be operated by a digitally-enabled "key" such as a smartphone app, QR code, or fingerprint, which can be activated and terminated remotely. According to the smart contract, Alice provides down payment to Bob in exchange for use of his car for a set amount of time. Both Alice and Bob have pre-specified a bargaining logic based on their desired terms, such as lease length, interest rate, size of down payment, and car specification. Bob runs a blockchain program that monitors his accounts and inventory, analyzes Alice's proposed terms, and then autonomously negotiates terms acceptable to both. Alice runs a similar blockchain program that monitors her personal accounts to ensure sufficient funds to pay for the lease. Both applications are authorized to bargain and enter into a smart contract for their respective owners. Once the agreement is formed, Bob's smart contract discovers Alice's payment, chooses a car that matches her desired specifications, and instructs that car to accept her digital key.

Now, imagine that Alice fails to make an interest payment and falls into default. Not only could the smart contract respond by terminating her digital key, but it could activate a variety of other complex actions. It could terminate the key only until Alice cures her default. It could activate a bank's key so that the car can be repossessed. And it could monitor the car's activity once the breach is discovered, such that the car is not disabled while driving down the highway.

PROBLEM 4-1

What is gained—and lost—when lawyers rely on standardization and computer-aided drafting techniques?

PROBLEM 4-2

Although limitations on successful planning and drafting are unavoidable the goal of the attorney is to eliminate or minimize as many problems as possible at the least cost to the client. Consider the following language from a force majeure clause unearthed by Professor Robert Anderson:

> Each Party shall be excused from liability for the failure or delay in performance under this Agreement (other than failure to make a payment when due) by reason of any event beyond such Party's reasonable control including Acts of God, fire, flood, explosion, earthquake, pandemic flu, or other natural forces, war, civil unrest, acts of terrorism, accident, destruction or other casualty . . . or any other event similar to those enumerated above."

Covid-19, the cause of the 2020 pandemic, is not an influenza virus. Is it covered by this clause? Why or why not?

SECTION THREE: THE LIMITS OF PLANNING

Even the able lawyer who works hard at planning and drafting will not always achieve success. Too many hurdles stand in the way. Indeed, the parties might not even believe in the efficacy of lawyers and the law!

MACAULAY, THE USE AND NON-USE OF CONTRACT IN THE MANUFACTURING INDUSTRY

9 Practical Lawyer, Nov. 1963 at 14, 17–18.

Most businessmen I have talked to have an attitude toward contracts that can be best described as indifferent or even hostile to the whole idea. They remark, "Contracts are a waste of time. We've never had any trouble, because we know our customers and our suppliers. If we needed a contract with a man, we wouldn't deal with him." "Lawyers are overprotective and just get in the way of buying or selling. If business had to be done by lawyers as buyers and sellers, the economy would stop. No one would buy or sell anything; they'd just negotiate forever."

Yet, some businessmen look at things differently: "We've been sued (or our competitor has been sued), and one ought to be careful. There is no need to skate on thin ice legally. We've learned the hard way." "If you get the intent spelled out, you won't have any trouble. People perform commitments they understand. It's worth a little extra time to make sure everyone is talking about the same thing."

* * *

Why Business Can and Does Ignore Contract

Businessmen can deal without contract for obvious reasons. They have little, if any, trouble, even if they run risks of trouble. It is in the interest of everyone to perform agreements. There are personal relationships between buyers and sellers on all levels of the two corporations. Purchasing agents know salesmen, corporate presidents know corporate presidents, and so forth. This creates an incentive to get along in a continuing relationship. Most importantly, the two businesses want to do business in the future. You don't get repeat orders from unsatisfied customers, and one's reputation can influence future business if word gets around. And word does get around.

Time constraints also explain why, in some cases, the conscientious lawyer's efforts at planning and drafting may not be successful. Sometimes clients "must" have an agreement "at the end of today"—or even "yesterday." Similarly, the costs of planning, drafting, and negotiating an agreement may, on some points, simply be too high. Weidemaier and Gulati, exploring boilerplate terms in sovereign bond contracts, explain that "situational constraints include time pressure, lawyers' natural reluctance to change contract boilerplate, and concern on the part of bankers, investors, and issuers over the pricing implications of new contract language. Given these constraints, blind copying might be a perfectly rational strategy."[a]

NOTE:
CONTRACTS IN RUSSIA IN THE 1990S

In the early- to mid-1990s, few laws governing private exchange existed in Russia. Nonetheless, the New York Times reported that the "free market [was] not waiting for a legal system." (New York Times, January 17, 1992, page A1.) Private parties increasingly made contracts to exchange goods and services and the legal system tried to catch up. What kinds of deals take place in the absence of a mature contract-law system? First, parties attempted to account for everything in detail because there were no "default rules" to fill in the gaps in their contracts. Second, the parties tried to ensure that each of them profited from the deal so that there would be no incentive to break the contract. (The parties could not count on help from a court.) Third, the parties sought immediate returns from their deal. They could not plan long term because they could not predict the future law. Fourth, many transactions were performed by both parties at the same time.

SECTION FOUR: THE NATURE OF ASSENT

The lawyer must plan for the legal enforceability of the agreement. In order to do this, the lawyer must understand the legal requirements of a valid agreement. Of course, this body of law is also a concern of lawyers consulted for the first time after a dispute has arisen. Indeed, as we will see, this body of law has very largely grown out of cases in which lawyers seem to have played little or no role until after the beginning of a dispute.

The law governing the validity of an agreement that you study here, and the law of consideration that you already studied in Chapter Two, specify the principal requirements of an "agreement with consideration." Nevertheless, remember that even if a party's contract claim fails because of the absence of a valid agreement, another theory of obligation may still apply.

EMBRY V. HARGADINE, MCKITTRICK DRY GOODS CO.

St. Louis Court of Appeals, Missouri, 1907.
127 Mo. App. 383, 105 S.W. 777.

Action by Charles R. Embry against the Hargadine, McKittrick Dry Goods Company. From a judgment for defendant, plaintiff appeals. Reversed and remanded.

---

[a] W. Mark C. Weidemaier & Mitu Gulati, *How Markets Work: The Lawyer's Version*, in FROM ECONOMY TO SOCIETY? PERSPECTIVES ON TRANSACTIONAL RISK REGULATION 107–137 (Bettina Lange et al. eds, 2013).

* * *

GOODE, J. * * * The appellant was an employé of the respondent company under a written contract to expire December 15, 1903, at a salary of $2,000 per annum. His duties were to attend to the sample department of respondent, of which he was given complete charge. It was his business to select samples for the traveling salesmen of the company, which is a wholesale dry goods concern, to use in selling goods to retail merchants. Appellant contends that on December 23, 1903, he was re-engaged by respondent, through its president, Thos. H. McKittrick, for another year at the same compensation and for the same duties stipulated in his previous written contract. On March 1, 1904, he was discharged, having been notified in February that, on account of the necessity of retrenching expenses, his services and that of some other employés would no longer be required. The respondent company contends that its president never re-employed appellant after the termination of his written contract, and hence that it had a right to discharge him when it chose. The point with which we are concerned requires an epitome of the testimony of appellant and the counter testimony of McKittrick, the president of the company, in reference to the alleged re-employment. Appellant testified: That several times prior to the termination of his written contract on December 15, 1903, he had endeavored to get an understanding with McKittrick for another year, but had been put off from time to time. That on December 23d, eight days after the expiration of said contract, he called on McKittrick, in the latter's office, and said to him that as appellant's written employment had lapsed eight days before, and as there were only a few days between then and the 1st of January in which to seek employment with other firms, if respondent wished to retain his services longer he must have a contract for another year, or he would quit respondent's service then and there. That he had been put off twice before and wanted an understanding or contract at once so that he could go ahead without worry. That McKittrick asked him how he was getting along in his department, and appellant said he was very busy, as they were in the height of the season getting men out—had about 110 salesmen on the line and others in preparation. That McKittrick then said: "Go ahead, you're all right. Get your men out, and don't let that worry you." That appellant took McKittrick at his word and worked until February 15th without any question in his mind. It was on February 15th that he was notified his services would be discontinued on March 1st. McKittrick denied this conversation as related by appellant, and said that, when accosted by the latter on December 23d, he (McKittrick) was working on his books in order to get out a report for a stockholders' meeting, and, when appellant said if he did not get a contract he would leave, that he (McKittrick) said: "Mr. Embry, I am just getting ready for the stockholders' meeting tomorrow. I have no time to take it up now. I have told you before I would not take it up until I had these matters out of the way. You will have to see me at a later time. I said: 'Go back upstairs and get your men out on the road.' I may have asked him one or two other questions relative to the department, I don't remember. The whole conversation did not take more than a minute."

Embry also swore that, when he was notified he would be discharged, he complained to McKittrick about it, as being a violation of their contract, and McKittrick said it was due to the action of the board of directors, and not to any personal action of his, and that others would suffer by what the board had done as well as Embry. Appellant requested an instruction to the jury setting out, in substance, the conversation between him and McKittrick according to his version, and declaring that those facts, if found to be true, constituted a contract between the parties that defendant would pay plaintiff the sum of $2,000 for another year, provided the jury believed from the evidence that plaintiff commenced said work believing he was to have $2,000 for the year's work. This instruction was refused, but the court gave another embodying in substance appellant's version of the conversation, and declaring it made a contract "if you (the jury) find both parties thereby intended and did contract with each other for plaintiff's employment for one year from and including December 23, 1903, at a salary of $2,000 per annum." Embry swore that, on several occasions when he spoke to McKittrick about employment for the ensuing year, he asked for a renewal of his former contract, and that on December 23d, the date of the alleged renewal, he went into Mr. McKittrick's office and told him his contract had expired, and he wanted to renew it for a year, having always worked under year contracts. Neither the refused instruction nor the one given by the court embodied facts quite as strong as appellant's testimony, because neither referred to appellant's alleged statement to McKittrick that unless he was re-employed he would stop work for respondent then and there.

It is assigned for error that the court required the jury, in order to return a verdict for appellant, not only to find the conversation occurred as appellant swore, but that both parties intended by such conversation to contract with each other for plaintiff's employment for the year from December, 1903, at a salary of $2,000. If it appeared from the record that there was a dispute between the parties as to the terms on which appellant wanted re-employment, there might have been sound reason for inserting this clause in the instruction; but no issue was made that they split on terms; the testimony of McKittrick tending to prove only that he refused to enter into a contract with appellant regarding another year's employment until the annual meeting of stockholders was out of the way. Indeed, as to the proposed terms McKittrick agrees with Embry, for the former swore as follows: "Mr. Embry said he wanted to know about the renewal of his contract. Said if he did not have the contract made he would leave." As the two witnesses coincided as to the terms of the proposed re-employment, there was no reason for inserting the above-mentioned clause in the instruction in order that it might be settled by the jury whether or not plaintiff, if employed for one year from December 23, 1903, was to be paid $2,000 a year. Therefore it remains to determine whether or not this part of the instruction was a correct statement of the law in regard to what was necessary to constitute a contract between the parties; that is to say, whether the formation of a contract by what, according to Embry, was said, depended on the intention of both Embry and McKittrick. Or, to put the question more precisely: Did what was said constitute a contract of re-employment on the previous terms irrespective of the intention or purpose of McKittrick?

Judicial opinion and elementary treatises abound in statements of the rule that to constitute a contract there must be a meeting of the minds of the parties, and both must agree to the same thing in the same sense. Generally speaking, this may be true; but it is not literally or universally true. That is to say, the inner intention of parties to a conversation subsequently alleged to create a contract cannot either make a contract of what transpired, or prevent one from arising, if the words used were sufficient to constitute a contract. In so far as their intention is an influential element, it is only such intention as the words or acts of the parties indicate; not one secretly cherished which is inconsistent with those words or acts. * * * In Smith v. Hughes, L.R. 6 Q.B. 597, 607, it was said: "If, whatever a man's real intention may be, he so conducts himself that a reasonable man would believe that he was assenting to the terms proposed by the other party, and that other party upon that belief enters into the contract with him, the man thus conducting himself would be equally bound as if he had intended to agree to the other party's terms." And that doctrine was adopted in Phillip v. Gallant, 62 N.Y. 256. In 9 Cyc. 245, we find the following text: "The law imputes to a person an intention corresponding to the reasonable meaning of his words and acts. It judges his intention by his outward expressions and excludes all questions in regard to his unexpressed intention. If his words or acts, judged by a reasonable standard, manifest an intention to agree in regard to the matter in question, that agreement is established, and it is immaterial what may be the real, but unexpressed, state of his mind on the subject." * * * In view of those authorities, we hold that, though McKittrick may not have intended to employ Embry by what transpired between them according to the latter's testimony, yet if what McKittrick said would have been taken by a reasonable man to be an employment, and Embry so understood it, it constituted a valid contract of employment for the ensuing year.

The next question is whether or not the language used was of that character, namely, was such that Embry, as a reasonable man, might consider he was re-employed for the ensuing year on the previous terms, and act accordingly. We do not say that in every instance it would be for the court to pronounce on this question, because, peradventure, instances might arise in which there would be such an ambiguity in the language relied on to show an assent by the obligor to the proposal of the obligee that it would be for the jury to say whether a reasonable mind would take it to signify acceptance of the proposal. * * * With [this rule] in mind, let us recur to the conversation of December 23d between Embry and McKittrick as related by the former. Embry was demanding a renewal of his contract, saying he had been put off from time to time, and that he had only a few days before the end of the year in which to seek employment from other houses, and that he would quit then and there unless he was re-employed. McKittrick inquired how he was getting along with the department, and Embry said they, i.e., the employés of the department, were very busy getting out salesmen. Whereupon McKittrick said: "Go ahead, you are all right. Get your men out, and do not let that worry you." We think no reasonable man would construe that answer to Embry's demand that he be employed for another year, otherwise than as an assent to the demand, and that Embry had the right to rely on it as an assent. The natural inference is, though we do not find it testified to, that Embry was at work getting samples ready for the salesmen to use during the ensuing season. Now, when he was complaining of the worry and mental distress he was under because of his uncertainty about the future, and his urgent need, either of an immediate contract with respondent, or a refusal by it to make one, leaving him free to seek employment elsewhere, McKittrick must have answered as he did for the purpose of assuring appellant that any apprehension was needless, as appellant's services would be retained by the respondent. The answer was unambiguous, and we rule that if the conversation was according to appellant's version, and he understood he was employed, it constituted in law a valid contract of re-employment, and the court erred in making the formation of a contract depend on a finding that both parties intended to make one. It was only necessary that Embry, as a reasonable man, had a right to and did so understand. * * *

The judgment is reversed, and the cause remanded. All concur.

HOTCHKISS v. NATIONAL CITY BANK OF NEW YORK, 200 Fed. 287, 293 (S.D.N.Y. 1911) (LEARNED HAND, DISTRICT JUDGE). A contract has, strictly speaking, nothing to do with the personal, or individual, intent of the parties. A contract is an obligation attached by the mere force of law to certain acts of the parties, usually words, which ordinarily accompany and represent a known intent. If, however, it were proved by twenty bishops that either party, when he used the words, intended something else than the usual meaning which the law imposes upon them, he would still be held, unless there were some mutual mistake, or something else of the sort.

PROBLEM 4-3

The Kabil Development Corporation negotiated with Inland Helicopters for the latter to provide helicopter services needed by Kabil for a construction job. Munroe, Kabil's vice president, discussed with Inland's agent, Honeycutt, the proposed job, the helicopter equipment, the time required and Inland's rates. Kabil then used the information in preparing its bid for the construction job. At a subsequent meeting, Munroe told Honeycutt that Kabil's bid had been accepted and Honeycutt said that Inland would do the job. After Inland refused to perform Kabil brought an action for contract breach. During the trial the following exchange took place:

> Q. Mr. Munroe, going back to the meeting of June 25th, that was where you and Mr. Klovstad and Mr. Honeycutt were all present, after your meeting did you feel at that time in your mind that Kabil Development Corporation was obligated to give the helicopter work to Inland Helicopter?
>
> MR. COULTER: Objection, Your Honor. What he felt in his mind wouldn't be at all probative of whether a contract was or was not formed.
>
> THE COURT: I think he can testify as to what his feelings as to whether or not he was bound. As I understand it, the question was whether or not Kabil Development Company felt that they were bound by the contract.
>
> MR. HAMPTON: That's correct, Your Honor.
>
> MR. COULTER: And it wouldn't make any difference, your honor. I think it is the objective manifestations of the contract that are the only elements that are involved in this case. What is subjective in the mind of an offeror or an offeree and not expressed or communicated does not have probative weight of establishing a contract.
>
> THE COURT: He may answer.
>
> A. Yes, I felt that we were obligated to Inland Helicopter, and equally I felt they were obligated to us.

Was the court correct in permitting Mr. Munroe to answer? In light of the Embry case, evaluate the following argument made by the court: Although the "manifestations of a party's intention, rather than the actual or real intention is controlling," the testimony is admissible because "a factfinder might well believe that what a party thought he was doing would show in fact what he did."

LUCY V. ZEHMER

Supreme Court of Appeals of Virginia, 1954.
196 Va. 493, 84 S.E.2d 516.

BUCHANAN, JUSTICE.

This suit was instituted by W.O. Lucy and J.C. Lucy, complainants, against A.H. Zehmer and Ida S. Zehmer, his wife, defendants, to have specific performance of a contract by which it was alleged the Zehmers had sold to W.O. Lucy a tract of land owned by A.H. Zehmer in Dinwiddie county containing 471.6 acres, more or less, known as the Ferguson farm, for $50,000. * * *

The instrument sought to be enforced was written by A.H. Zehmer on December 20, 1952, in these words: "We hereby agree to sell to W.O. Lucy the Ferguson Farm complete for $50,000.00, title satisfactory to buyer," and signed by the defendants, A.H. Zehmer and Ida S. Zehmer.

The answer of A.H. Zehmer admitted that at the time mentioned W.O. Lucy offered him $50,000 cash for the farm, but that he, Zehmer, considered that the offer was made in jest; that so thinking, and both he and Lucy having had several drinks, he wrote out "the memorandum" quoted above and induced his wife to sign it; that he did not deliver the memorandum to Lucy, but that Lucy picked it up, read it, put it in his pocket, attempted to offer Zehmer $5 to bind the bargain, which Zehmer refused to accept, and realizing for the first time that Lucy was serious, Zehmer assured him that he had no intention of selling the farm and that the whole matter was a joke. Lucy left the premises insisting that he had purchased the farm.

Depositions were taken and the decree appealed from was entered holding that the complainants had failed to establish their right to specific performance, and dismissing their bill. The assignment of error is to this action of the court.

W.O. Lucy, a lumberman and farmer, thus testified in substance: He had known Zehmer for fifteen or twenty years and had been familiar with the Ferguson farm for ten years. Seven or eight years ago he had offered Zehmer $20,000 for the farm which Zehmer had accepted, but the agreement was verbal and Zehmer backed out. On the night of December 20, 1952, around eight o'clock, he took an employee to McKenney, where Zehmer lived and operated a restaurant, filling station and motor court. While there he decided to see Zehmer and again try to buy the Ferguson farm. He entered the restaurant and talked to Mrs. Zehmer until Zehmer came in. He asked Zehmer if he had sold the Ferguson farm. Zehmer replied that he had not. Lucy said, "I bet you wouldn't take $50,000.00 for that place." Zehmer replied, "Yes, I would too; you wouldn't give fifty." Lucy said he would and told Zehmer to write up an agreement to that effect. Zehmer took a restaurant check and wrote on the back of it, "I do hereby agree to sell to W.O. Lucy the Ferguson Farm for $50,000 complete." Lucy told him he had better change it to "We" because Mrs. Zehmer would have to sign it too. Zehmer then tore up what he had written, wrote the agreement quoted above and asked Mrs. Zehmer, who was at the other end of the counter ten or twelve feet away, to sign it. Mrs. Zehmer said she would for $50,000 and signed it. Zehmer brought it back and gave it to Lucy, who offered him $5 which Zehmer refused, saying, "You don't need to give me any money, you got the agreement there signed by both of us."

The discussion leading to the signing of the agreement, said Lucy, lasted thirty or forty minutes, during which Zehmer seemed to doubt that Lucy could raise $50,000. Lucy suggested the provision for having the title examined and Zehmer made the suggestion that he would sell it "complete, everything there," and stated that all he had on the farm was three heifers.

Lucy took a partly filled bottle of whiskey into the restaurant with him for the purpose of giving Zehmer a drink if he wanted it. Zehmer did, and he and Lucy had one or two drinks together. Lucy said that while he felt the drinks he took he was not intoxicated, and from the way Zehmer handled the transaction he did not think he was either.

December 20 was on Saturday. Next day Lucy telephoned to J.C. Lucy and arranged with the latter to take a half interest in the purchase and pay half of the consideration. On Monday he engaged an attorney to examine the title. The attorney reported favorably on December 31 and on January 2 Lucy wrote Zehmer stating that the title was satisfactory, that he was ready to pay the purchase price in cash and asking when Zehmer would be ready to close the deal. Zehmer replied by letter, mailed on January 13, asserting that he had never agreed or intended to sell.

Mr. and Mrs. Zehmer were called by the complainants as adverse witnesses. Zehmer testified in substance as follows:

He bought this farm more than ten years ago for $11,000. He had had twenty-five offers, more or less, to buy it, including several from Lucy, who had never offered any specific sum of money. He had given them all the same answer, that he was not interested in selling it. On this Saturday night before Christmas it looked like everybody and his brother came by there to have a drink. He took a good many drinks during the afternoon and had a pint of his own. When he entered the restaurant around eight-thirty Lucy was there and he could see that he was "pretty high." He said to Lucy, "Boy, you got some good liquor, drinking, ain't you?" Lucy then offered him a drink. "I was already high as a Georgia pine, and didn't have any more better sense than to pour another great big slug out and gulp it down, and he took one too."

After they had talked a while Lucy asked whether he still had the Ferguson farm. He replied that he had not sold it and Lucy said, "I bet you wouldn't take $50,000.00 for it." Zehmer asked him if he would give $50,000 and Lucy said yes. Zehmer replied, "You haven't got $50,000.00 in cash." Lucy said he did and Zehmer replied that he did not believe it. They argued "pro and con for a long time," mainly about "whether he had $50,000 in cash that he could put up right then and buy that farm."

Finally, said Zehmer, Lucy told him if he didn't believe he had $50,000, "you sign that piece of paper here and say you will take $50,000.00 for the farm." He, Zehmer, "just grabbed the back off of a guest check there" and wrote on the back of it. At that point in his testimony Zehmer asked to see what he had written to "see if I recognize my own handwriting." He examined the paper and exclaimed, "Great balls of fire, I got 'Firgerson' for Ferguson. I have got satisfactory spelled wrong. I don't recognize that writing if I would see it, wouldn't know it was mine."

After Zehmer had, as he described it, "scribbled this thing off," Lucy said, "Get your wife to sign it." Zehmer walked over to where she was and she at first refused to sign but did so after he told her that he "was just needling him [Lucy], and didn't mean a thing in the world, that I was not selling the farm." Zehmer then "took it back over there * * * and I was still looking at the dern thing. I had the drink right there by my hand, and I reached over to get a drink, and he said, 'Let me see it.' He reached and picked it up, and when I looked back again he had it in his pocket and he dropped a five dollar bill over there, and he said, 'Here is five dollars payment on it.' * * * I said, 'Hell no, that is beer and liquor talking. I am not going to sell you the farm. I have told you that too many times before.' "

* * *

On examination by her own counsel [Mrs. Zehmer testified] that her husband laid this piece of paper down after it was signed; that Lucy said to let him see it, took it, folded it and put it in his wallet, then said to Zehmer, "Let me give you $5.00," but Zehmer said, "No, this is liquor talking. I don't want to sell the farm, I have told you that I want my son to have it. This is all a joke." Lucy then said at least twice, "Zehmer, you have sold your farm," wheeled around and started for the door. He paused at the door and said, "I will bring you $50,000.00 tomorrow. * * * No, tomorrow is Sunday. I will bring it to you Monday." She said you could tell definitely that he was drinking and she said to her husband, "You should have taken him home," but he said, "Well, I am just about as bad off as he is."

* * *

The defendants insist that the evidence was ample to support their contention that the writing sought to be enforced was prepared as a bluff or dare to force Lucy to admit that he did not have $50,000; that the whole matter was a joke; that the writing was not delivered to Lucy and no binding contract was ever made between the parties.

It is an unusual, if not bizarre, defense. When made to the writing admittedly prepared by one of the defendants and signed by both, clear evidence is required to sustain it.

In his testimony Zehmer claimed that he "was high as a Georgia pine," and that the transaction "was just a bunch of two doggoned drunks bluffing to see who could talk the biggest and say the most." That claim is inconsistent with his attempt to testify in great detail as to what was said and what was done. It is contradicted by other evidence as to the condition of both parties, and rendered of no weight by the testimony of his wife that when Lucy left the restaurant she suggested that Zehmer drive him home. The record is convincing that Zehmer was not intoxicated to the extent of being unable to comprehend the nature and consequences of the instrument he executed, and hence that instrument is not to be invalidated on that ground. * * * It was in fact conceded by defendants' counsel in oral argument that under the evidence Zehmer was not too drunk to make a valid contract.

The evidence is convincing also that Zehmer wrote two agreements, the first one beginning "I hereby agree to sell." Zehmer first said he could not remember about that, then that "I don't think I wrote but one out." Mrs. Zehmer said that what he wrote was "I hereby agree," but that the "I" was changed to "We" after that night. The agreement that was written and signed is in the record and indicates no such change. Neither are the mistakes in spelling that Zehmer sought to point out readily apparent.

The appearance of the contract, the fact that it was under discussion for forty minutes or more before it was signed; Lucy's objection to the first draft because it was written in the singular, and he wanted Mrs. Zehmer to sign it also; the rewriting to meet that objection and the signing by Mrs. Zehmer; the discussion of what was to be included in the sale, the provision for the examination of the title, the completeness of the instrument that was executed, the taking possession of it by Lucy with no request or suggestion by either of the defendants that he give it back, are facts which furnish persuasive evidence that the execution of the contract was a serious business transaction rather than a casual, jesting matter as defendants now contend.

* * *

If it be assumed, contrary to what we think the evidence shows, that Zehmer was jesting about selling his farm to Lucy and that the transaction was intended by him to be a joke, nevertheless the evidence shows that Lucy did not so understand it but considered it to be a serious business transaction and the contract to be binding on the Zehmers as well as on himself. The very next day he arranged with his brother to put up half the money and take a half interest in the land. The day after that he employed an attorney to examine the title. The next night, Tuesday, he was back at

Zehmer's place and there Zehmer told him for the first time, Lucy said, that he wasn't going to sell and he told Zehmer, "You know you sold that place fair and square." After receiving the report from his attorney that the title was good he wrote to Zehmer that he was ready to close the deal.

Not only did Lucy actually believe, but the evidence shows he was warranted in believing, that the contract represented a serious business transaction and a good faith sale and purchase of the farm.

In the field of contracts, as generally elsewhere, "We must look to the outward expression of a person as manifesting his intention rather than to his secret and unexpressed intention. 'The law imputes to a person an intention corresponding to the reasonable meaning of his words and acts.' " First Nat. Exchange Bank of Roanoke v. Roanoke Oil Co., 169 Va. 99, 114, 192 S.E. 764, 770.

At no time prior to the execution of the contract had Zehmer indicated to Lucy by word or act that he was not in earnest about selling the farm. They had argued about it and discussed its terms, as Zehmer admitted, for a long time. Lucy testified that if there was any jesting it was about paying $50,000 that night. The contract and the evidence show that he was not expected to pay the money that night. Zehmer said that after the writing was signed he laid it down on the counter in front of Lucy. Lucy said Zehmer handed it to him. In any event there had been what appeared to be a good faith offer and a good faith acceptance, followed by the execution and apparent delivery of a written contract. Both said that Lucy put the writing in his pocket and then offered Zehmer $5 to seal the bargain. Not until then, even under the defendants' evidence, was anything said or done to indicate that the matter was a joke. Both of the Zehmers testified that when Zehmer asked his wife to sign he whispered that it was a joke so Lucy wouldn't hear and that it was not intended that he should hear.

* * *

An agreement or mutual assent is of course essential to a valid contract but the law imputes to a person an intention corresponding to the reasonable meaning of his words and acts. If his words and acts, judged by a reasonable standard, manifest an intention to agree, it is immaterial what may be the real but unexpressed state of his mind. 17 C.J.S., Contracts, § 32, p. 361; 12 Am.Jur., Contracts, § 19, p. 515.

So a person cannot set up that he was merely jesting when his conduct and words would warrant a reasonable person in believing that he intended a real agreement. * * *

Whether the writing signed by the defendants and now sought to be enforced by the complainants was the result of a serious offer by Lucy and a serious acceptance by the defendants, or was a serious offer by Lucy and an acceptance in secret jest by the defendants, in either event it constituted a binding contract of sale between the parties.

Defendants contend further, however, that even though a contract was made, equity should decline to enforce it under the circumstances. These circumstances have been set forth in detail above. They disclose some drinking by the two parties but not to an extent that they were unable to understand fully what they were doing. There was no fraud, no misrepresentation, no sharp practice and no dealing between unequal parties. The farm had been bought for $11,000 and was assessed for taxation at $6,300. The purchase price was $50,000. Zehmer admitted that it was a good price. There is in fact present in this case none of the grounds usually urged against specific performance.

* * *

The complainants are entitled to have specific performance of the contract sued on. The decree appealed from is therefore reversed and the cause is remanded for the entry of a proper decree requiring the defendants to perform the contract in accordance with the prayer of the bill.

Reversed and remanded.

NOTE:
QUITE AN INFORMAL CONTRACT

You have learned in Chapter 2 that enforceable contracts can be quite informal so long as they satisfy consideration and Statute of Frauds requirements. This chapter adds the requirement of an agreement. If, like many law students, you have not had the opportunity to buy or sell real estate, a facsimile of the receipt on which Lucy and Zehmer concluded their deal (below) may be unusual, but not wildly so.

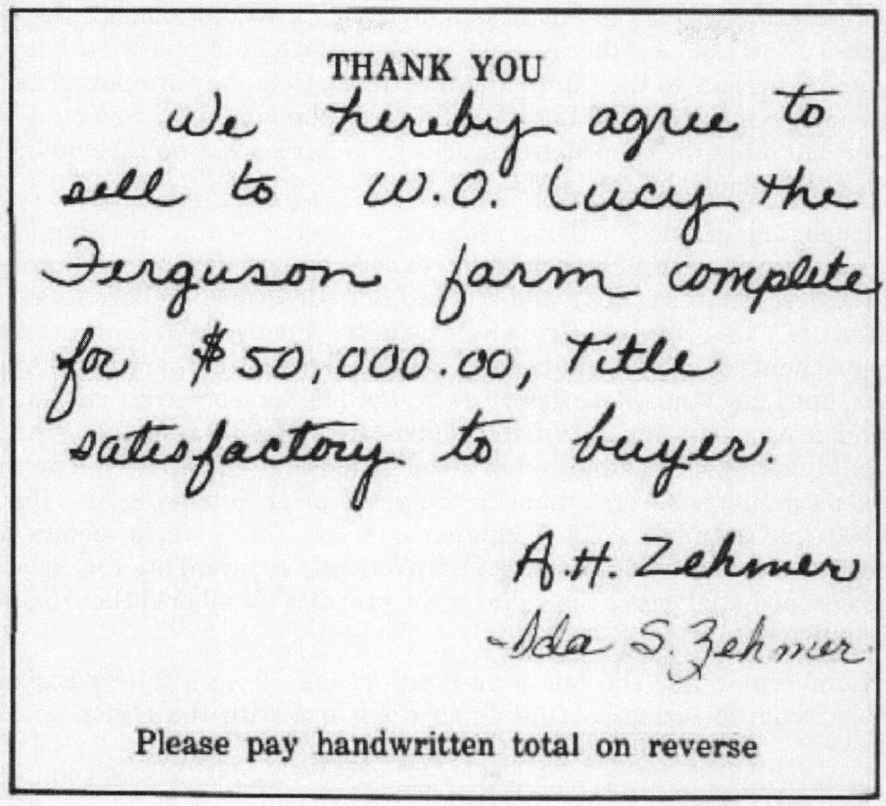
THANK YOU

We hereby agree to sell to W.O. Lucy the Ferguson farm complete for $50,000.00, title satisfactory to buyer.

A.H. Zehmer

Ida S. Zehmer

Please pay handwritten total on reverse

But consider that most normal real estate deals are concluded with contracts running tens of thousands of words. They typically describe the property with precision, detail the personal possessions that come with the land, the price and how it is to be paid (including a deposit and the form of currency that will work), conditions on sale, details about the mortgage and title, how the price may be adjusted at closing, what to do about tenants, the date and place of closing, and what the seller is representing about the land's condition.

Given the difference between the receipt and the normal sale of land contract, do you think the Lucy-Zehmer contract is sufficient to constitute an enforceable contract?

RICHMAN AND SCHMELZER, WHEN MONEY GREW ON TREES: LUCY V. ZEHMER AND CONTRACTING IN A BOOM MARKET

61 DUKE L.J. 1511, 1552–55 (2012).

A. The Secret to the Lucys' Success

Property records reveal that the Lucy brothers signed dozens of land and timber deeds between the 1930s and the 1960s. Though generally involving properties smaller than the 471.6-acre Ferguson farm, these deeds reflect a pattern of business activity in Dinwiddie and Brunswick Counties: The Lucy brothers would purchase farmland and then harvest the timber for sale to the Camp Manufacturing Company or another large paper mill. Sometimes the Lucys would resell the land after removing the timber, but often the immediate returns from harvesting would enable the Lucys to keep much of the land.

Engaging in such activity required a keen eye for "cruising," the process of strolling through a property to determine the value of its timber, and the descendants of John and Welford Lucy described Welford as a true master of the trade. Cruising usually involved taking careful measurements of a land's timber and making calculations based on market prices, but Lucy family lore describes Welford as someone who could stroll around a property and intuitively make an accurate assessment of its value. In fact, Welford admitted in a deposition that he had driven around Zehmer's property several times in the years prior to making his offer of $50,000 in December 1952, including one trip three weeks before the disputed sale. Those trips suggest that Welford's eventual offer was based on a reasoned analysis of the value of the property's timber rather than on an impulsive wager.

Lumbermen like the Lucys profited not only from intuitive cruising but also from fostering continuing relationships with the region's mills. * * *

B. Answering the $50,000 Question

Both the region's economic history and the parties' personal histories clarify the events that surrounded Lucy's meeting with Zehmer shortly before Christmas in 1952. They also help illuminate the court's determination that $50,000 was a fair price for the Ferguson farm. Timber prices, and thus timberland prices, were skyrocketing, and neither historic prices nor the tax assessment values relied upon by the court accurately reflected appropriate timberland values. In fact, the Ferguson farm's history [allowing the farm's forests to grow unharvested for decades] leading up to 1952 had contributed to its growing value.

* * *

Viewing the conversation between Zehmer and Lucy through this lens, one can understand why Zehmer might have thought that $50,000 was an attractive price at first but changed his mind after realizing that it was so agreeable to Lucy. Zehmer likely became aware of his land's potential value only after Lucy walked out of Zehmer's restaurant excitedly waving the restaurant receipt-cum-contract. Lucy's zeal in enforcing the contract and Zehmer's strong resistance to selling are in tension with Justice Buchanan's proclamation that $50,000 was, if not a windfall for Zehmer, a fair price for the land. A careful examination of Dinwiddie property records provides reason to question the accuracy of Justice Buchanan's valuation.

NOTE: THEORIES OF OBLIGATION REVISITED

Did the court adopt the wrong theory of obligation in Lucy v. Zehmer? Instead of agreement with consideration, should the court have found that the Zehmers' careless use of language constituted a tort? Consider these views:

WHITTIER, THE RESTATEMENT OF CONTRACTS AND MUTUAL ASSENT

17 Cal. L. Rev. 441, 442–43 (1929).

It would have simplified our law of contracts if actual meeting of the minds mutually communicated had remained essential. The liability for carelessly misleading the other party into the reasonable belief that there was assent might well have been held to be in tort. With such a liability in tort the danger that one could falsely claim that he did not assent and so escape the contract would be rendered insubstantial. In most cases the triers of the fact would not be misled by his false evidence of non-assent. If they concluded that he truly did not assent then there would be liability in tort unless his mistake was also found to have been non-negligent or to have resulted in no damage. Under the present law the non-consenting party is liable on the contract itself if careless. The chief unfortunate result of this state of law is that he is bound to the contract though the other party is notified of the mistake before the latter has changed his position or suffered any damage. To hold one for the merely careless use of language which causes no damage whatever to the party to whom the language is addressed is certainly inconsistent with principles generally applied. If D drives down Michigan Avenue, Chicago, in a careless manner but no one is hurt, can any of those who might have been hurt sue D?

But taking the law as settled that one is liable on the contract where he carelessly misleads the other party to reasonably believe there was assent, is it wise to state the entire law of mutual assent in terms of these admittedly exceptional cases? Why not say that actual assent communicated is the basis of "mutual assent" except where there is careless misleading which induces a reasonable belief in assent? The writer thinks that this approach to the problems involved is more likely to lead one to just conclusions.

PROBLEM 4-4

Assume that Edgar Denny was counsel for Lucy. During the early stages of preparation for trial, the following exchange took place in Denny's office. Consider whether Denny acted contrary to Opinion No. 79 of the Committee on Legal Ethics of the District of Columbia bar, below (which we will assume to be applicable).

> Denny: You know, don't you, that you will not win this case unless you understood, and reasonably so, that Zehmer was making a present offer to sell to you when you were together there in the restaurant.
>
> Lucy: Well, it was Saturday night before Christmas, and we were in Zehmer's restaurant drinking together, and it all started out we were joking around * * *.
>
> Denny: What's that?
>
> Lucy: We were a drinking and a joking around.
>
> Denny: Well, when did you get serious?
>
> Lucy: Oh, not until I got home and started sobering up a bit did I really think how much I wanted that farm, and I got the piece of paper out of my pocket, and those words on there looked real good to me.
>
> Denny: Do you mean you never, for a moment, thought Zehmer was really serious while you were at the restaurant?
>
> Lucy: Oh, well, I guess I did. A little. That's right, when we started writing everything down. Then I thought maybe it was a little serious.
>
> Denny: Well, now how do you plan to testify?
>
> Lucy: I'll say I was serious midway through and that is the way Zehmer looked to me.
>
> Denny: Only midway?
>
> Lucy: Well maybe even earlier, when we started talking figures.

OPINION NO. 79, LEGAL ETHICS COMMITTEE OPINION 169.

Committee on Legal Ethics, District of Columbia Bar (1980)

[A] lawyer may not prepare, or assist in preparing, testimony that he or she knows, or ought to know, is false or misleading. So long as this prohibition is not transgressed, a lawyer may properly suggest language as well as the substance of testimony, and may—indeed, should—do whatever is feasible to prepare his or her witnesses for examination.

* * *

It follows, therefore * * * that the fact that the particular words in which testimony, whether written or oral, is cast originated with a lawyer rather than the witness whose testimony it is has no significance so long as the substance of that testimony is not, so far as the lawyer knows or ought to know, false or misleading. If the particular words suggested by the lawyer, even though not literally false, are calculated to convey a misleading impression, this would be equally impermissible from the ethical point of view. Herein, indeed, lies the principal hazard (leaving aside outright subornation of perjury) in a lawyer's suggesting particular forms of language to a witness instead of leaving the witness to articulate his or her thought wholly without prompting: there may be differences in nuance among variant phrasings of the same substantive point, which are so significant as to make one version misleading while another is not. Yet it is obvious that by the same token, choice of words may also improve the clarity and precision of a statement: even subtle changes of shading may as readily improve testimony as impair it. The fact that a lawyer suggests particular language to a witness means only that the lawyer may be affecting the testimony as respects its clarity and accuracy; and not necessarily that the effect is to debase rather than improve the testimony in these respects. It is not, we think, a matter of undue difficulty for a reasonably competent and conscientious lawyer to discern the line of impermissibility, where truth shades into untruth, and to refrain from crossing it.

PROBLEM 4-5

1. Assume Zehmer phoned you prior to the restaurant episode and said that Lucy wanted to buy the Ferguson farm. Zehmer asks you to draft a proposed agreement and you suggest a meeting first in your office. Make a list of the major questions you would want to ask Zehmer at such a meeting. In preparing your list, consider West's Legal Form that follows the case.

2. According to the Associated Press, Jay Arsenault caught Barry Bonds' 600th home run. A friend had given Arsenault tickets to the game, the friend alleges, in exchange for Arsenault's promise to split the value of the ball if he caught it. The Associated Press reports that "[u]nder California law, oral promises are contracts under most circumstances * * *. But is there a chitchat exception—an allowance that friends shooting the breeze might not always be serious?" If the reporter had called you to explain whether Arsenault's promise was enforceable (if true), what would you have said?

MORROW V. MORROW

Court of Appeals of Oklahoma, 1980.
612 P.2d 730.

ROMANG, JUDGE.

The Plaintiffs-Appellants, Warren and Betty Morrow (husband and wife), brought this action to recover for services rendered to the decedent Maude Morrow, mother of Warren and Defendant-Appellee Woodye Morrow. They also sought to set aside a conveyance of certain mineral interests from Woodye to Defendant-Appellee Dennis M. Morrow, Woodye's son. This conveyance was made without consideration. Woodye had acquired title from Maude by warranty deed.

At trial the District Court, sitting without a jury as chancellor, found the evidence insufficient to support the Plaintiffs' claim for services and ordered the mineral conveyance set aside and the proceeds of the surface sale (less certain expenses) and mineral rights be evenly distributed to 8 surviving children of Maude.

* * *

The Plaintiffs' theory was that after receiving title to Maude's real property, Woodye orally agreed with Plaintiffs that if they would care for Maude that on her death Woodye would sell the property and first pay the Plaintiffs for the care of Maude and divide the remainder equally among her heirs.

* * *

* * * [T]he findings of the trial court, sitting without a jury, are entitled to the weight of a jury's verdict, i. e. they must be affirmed if supported by any probative evidence.

* * *

Whether there was a contract is a matter as to which the party asserting the contract has the burden. * * * As part of the fact finders process, courts are convinced that in our society the vast majority of family arrangements are not expected to be attended with contractual consequences. * * * This expectation may be upset by any facts showing the parties expected to be bound legally an element not normally relevant in agreements between nonfamily members. As Corbin says:

> The following statements may be of assistance in distinguishing between non-enforceable social engagements and contractual agreements: 1. If the subject matter and terms of a transaction are such as customarily have affected legal relations and there is nothing to indicate that the one now asserting their existence had reasons to know that the other party intended not to affect his legal relations, thus the transaction will be operative legally. 2. If the subject matter and terms are not such as customarily have affected legal relations, the transaction is not legally operative unless the expressions of the parties indicate an intention to make it so. (Footnotes omitted.) 1 Corbin on Contracts s 34. See also Restatement of Contracts (Second) s 21B comment c (T.D. 1973).

Nothing in our cases hold that family members may not make their arrangements contractual in nature. * * * Rather the point of our cases and scholarly comment is that there is a norm of societal expectation. The subject matter here involved is care for an invalid mother. Such arrangements are frequently gratuitous, founded in love and affection. But where there are a number of children, it is also frequently the case that one child and spouse will undertake primary care and the others will contribute financially in agreed amounts or as they can. Whether these arrangements are contractual or not depends on the intent of the parties. But in such cases the party asserting the contract has the burden of setting aside our belief that most such arrangements are not contractual.

* * *

In this case the trier of fact was unpersuaded. Based on the record evidence we cannot say as a matter of law he was wrong. Accordingly, we affirm.

AFFIRMED.

TILBERT V. EAGLE LOCK CO.

Supreme Court of Errors of Connecticut, 1933.
116 Conn. 357, 165 A. 205.

Action by Annie Tilbert against the Eagle Lock Company to recover upon a "certificate of benefit" issued by the defendant to the husband of the plaintiff brought to the court of common pleas and reserved for the advice of this court.

Judgment in favor of plaintiff.

* * *

HINMAN, JUSTICE.

The crucial question reserved is whether the demurrer to the amended complaint should be sustained; it being stipulated that, if the facts alleged entitle the plaintiff to recover, judgment shall be rendered accordingly. The complaint as amended alleged, in substance, that the plaintiff's husband, Kasimierz Tilbert, entered the employ of the defendant corporation prior to January 1, 1922, and continued therein until his death on August 28, 1931. On or about June 29, 1923, the defendant canceled the group insurance which covered the plaintiff's intestate and issued a so-called "Certificate of Benefit" to him, a copy of which and of a letter attached thereto are annexed to the complaint as schedules A and B. It is alleged that "in accordance with the terms of said certificate the plaintiff's intestate remained in the employ of the defendant more than five years and at the time of his death was employed by said defendant and was not notified of any attempted cancellation of said certificate." By the terms of the certificate the plaintiff as beneficiary is entitled to $1,000, with interest. The plaintiff notified the defendant of the death of her husband and demanded payment, which the defendant refused.

It is further alleged that on or before August 22, 1931, the officers of the defendant corporation decided to withdraw the certificates of benefit and on August 24th the treasurer caused notices to be printed, dated August 28, 1931, stating, "Effective immediately, all certificates of benefit are hereby canceled and the benefit plan discontinued." Notice of a reduction in wages was also included. The treasurer inserted in each printed notice the number of a particular employee, and these were put in the pay envelopes given by the paymaster to the employees on August 28, 1931, which was the regular pay day at the defendant's factory. Among said notices was one bearing the factory number of Tilbert and the amount of the hourly pay which he was thereafter to receive. The plaintiff's intestate had been ill for about four weeks and died about 2 o'clock in the morning of August 28th. Schedule A, above mentioned, reads as follows:

"Certificate of Benefit

"Certificate No. 970

"From Eagle Lock Co., Terryville, Conn.

"Accruing to Kasimierz Tilbert (Hereinafter called the Employee) the sum of Seven Hundred (700) Dollars,

"Payable to Annie Tilbert, wife as Beneficiary so named by above employee should death of said employee occur while in the employ of said Eagle Lock Co.

"The schedule below indicates the rate of increase of this benefit as determined by continuous service. [Schedule of increases yearly, up to $1,000 for term of service of five years and over.]

"This certificate automatically is made void when the holder ceases to be an employee. [Provision for payment of full benefit then effective if any employee holding certificate shall before attaining the age of 60, become wholly and permanently disabled by bodily injuries or disease.]

"Eagle Lock Co.
"O.B. Hough, Treasurer.

"Dated June 29th, 1923."

Schedule B, which was printed on the same sheet as schedule A, reads in part as follows:

"To Our Employees:

"The success of this Company depends in a large degree on the efficiency and loyalty of its Employees and, of course, just as truly does the prosperity of the community and our Employees and their families depend upon the success of the Company.

"Desiring to show our appreciation of the continuing service and the efficiency and loyalty of the Employees, in a substantial manner which will aid each Employee to provide for his dependents in the event of death or permanent disability, we offer the following plan of benefits, grading the amounts according to term of continuous service."

An explanation of the plan and its operation is then given, followed by:

"This benefit plan being voluntary on the part of Eagle Lock Co., it is understood that it constitutes no contract with any Employee or any beneficiary, and confers no legal rights on him or them. It in no way interferes with his freedom to leave our employ whenever he pleases, nor on the other hand, does it take away our right as Employer to dismiss any Employee.

"We fully expect and hope that this benefit plan as outlined above will continue indefinitely and will be appreciated by the Employees to the extent that we feel justified in continuing the plan indefinitely. We must, however, and do reserve to ourselves the right to discontinue these benefits at any time without any liability on our part to any employee or any beneficiary, either or both.

"We trust every Employee will appreciate the value of these benefits to those he leaves behind should death occur, as it does often unexpectedly and very often prematurely, and not sacrifice these benefits to his dependents by hastily making a change of employment, thus making void the certificate.

"Respectfully,
"Eagle Lock Co."

* * *

As to the claimed lack of consideration, it appears clearly enough from schedule B that a prime purpose of the granting of the benefits was to secure the good will, loyalty, and efficiency of the defendant's employees, and especially, through the progressive premium placed on long-continued service, to minimize labor turnover and obtain the advantages of experienced operatives. The attainment of these purposes constituted a benefit or advantage received by the defendant, who must be assumed to have requested, because it desired it and regarded it as beneficial to its interests. Tilbert remained in the employ of the defendant more than seven years after receiving the certificate. By so doing he manifested his acceptance of the promise, forbore his right to terminate the employment and engage elsewhere, and conferred the benefit which the defendant sought. * * *

The declaration in schedule B, above quoted, that the plan constitutes no contract and confers no legal rights, when read, as it must be, with due regard to the other provisions, may and should be construed as preserving the right of the employer to discharge the employee and of the latter to leave the employment at any time, and the right of the employer to discontinue the benefits without liability for such discontinuance or for benefits for death occurring subsequent thereto. To construe it as meaning, further, that, notwithstanding acceptance by an employee and compliance therewith, no obligation whatever was imposed upon the defendant, and that, without exercise of the reserved right of discontinuance or other action terminating the agreement, it might refuse to perform it, would ascribe to the defendant an intention to mislead its employees, to its advantage, by an inducement which was known and intended by it to be entirely nugatory, and which this record does not require us to attribute to it. Surely Exhibits A and B constitute more than an offer or promise made with an understood intention that, even if accepted and acted on, it was not to be legally binding at any time but only expressive of a present intention, and therefore not a contract. Wellington v. Apthorp, 145 Mass. 69, 74, 13 N.E. 10; Page, Contracts, § 77. It is by no means analogous to the illustrations cited by the defendant—an intention announced by a corporation to open a social center for its workmen, or an announcement by an individual of a purpose to give a Christmas present to a friend. Nor is the situation of the employee comparable with that of a person who voluntarily renders occasional services merely in the expectation of receiving gratuities therefor. Gibbs v. Downs, 94 Conn. 487, 490, 109 A. 170. It amounted to and constituted a promise, unless and until it was withdrawn, to employees who accepted and acted upon it, and the beneficiaries of those who died while it was in effect.

It is clear that the defendant reserved the right to discontinue the benefit system at any time, without the consent of the employees or any notice to them expressly provided for. Its action, as alleged in the complaint, in withdrawing the certificates of benefit, was in line with this reservation and authorized by it. The only inference to be drawn from the facts alleged is that, on or before August 22, 1931, it was decided to do so, the withdrawal to take effect when the next pay envelopes were distributed, which would be on the 28th. The allegations as to the preparations made and the sending of the notice so indicate. The plaintiff's decedent died on that date, but long before the commencement of the working day, and therefore before the notice could be or was intended to be distributed and the withdrawal put into effect. The general rule that the law knows no fractions of a day is not allowed to operate against right and justice, and these fractions will be taken into account when, as here, from the nature of the case, justice requires that it be done or when necessary to save a vested right. * * * Also, under the general rule, the entire day upon which a contract expires is open for compliance with it. * * * As the termination of the agreement was not complete until the end of the day of August 28th, Tilbert's death at any time on that date entitled his beneficiary to the designated benefit.

Our answers to the questions reserved are that the demurrer should be overruled, and that, on the facts stated in the amended complaint, judgment should be rendered for the plaintiff. No costs will be taxed in this court.

In this opinion the other Judges concurred, except MALTBIE, C.J., who dissented.

1 CORBIN ON CONTRACTS

§ 2.13 (2019).

It should be noted that when the subject matter of an agreement is of a kind that is customarily dealt with in enforceable contracts, and the parties have in fact acted under the agreement, a court is likely to look with some distaste at provisions that seem to exclude all sanction and remedy.

PROBLEM 4-6

If Eagle Lock Co. had asked you to draft its "Certificate of Benefit" and had told you it did not want to be bound under any circumstances, what would you have told the company? If you represented Mrs. Tilbert and the case arose today, what additional theories of obligation, if any, would you pursue?

CARGILL COMMISSION CO. v. MOWERY, 99 Kan. 389, 161 P. 634 (1916). [Through a series of telegrams, Cargill negotiated with the Hutchinson Grain Company for the purchase of wheat. Seller Hutchinson used the wrong "code word" concerning the number of bushels it was offering to sell so that, while it intended to sell only 3,000 to 3,500 bushels, Cargill reasonably believed Hutchinson had agreed to sell 35,000 bushels. Thinking it had bought 35,000 bushels from Hutchinson, Cargill immediately resold 35,000 bushels of wheat on the market. Cargill later received a letter and telegram from Hutchinson correcting its error. Cargill brought an action against Hutchinson for its refusal to deliver more than 3,500 bushels of wheat.

Cargill appealed from an order denying its motion for judgment on the pleadings, and from an order sustaining a demurrer to its evidence.]

WEST, J.

* * *

The telegrams themselves consist of a bid for 30,000 to 35,000 bushels, a direction to book that amount, and a reply that it had been booked. Had the correspondence ended here no question could arise as to its meaning or obligation. When the additional fact appears that pursuant thereto the plaintiff at once sold 35,000 bushels of wheat in reliance upon this contract, the final and binding character of the deal is accentuated. When the news of the defendant's position and intention reached the plaintiff the sale of the 35,000 bushels had already been made. Had the contract contained in the messages of June 29th been in the form of a written agreement signed by the parties, and the plaintiff relying thereon had acted as it did, the defendant could not then have been heard to say at the expense of the plaintiff that he had made a mistake in the number of bushels he wrote into the contract, and therefore was not bound.

Had the mistake been discovered and made known to the plaintiff before acting on the contract the error could have been corrected, but it was not the plaintiff's mistake nor was it the plaintiff's fault that the defendant used the wrong word in the contract, and did not make this known until the plaintiff had obligated itself to furnish the amount of wheat which the written contract or written evidence of the contract—the telegrams—between the parties called for. * * *

* * *

The order sustaining the demurrer to the evidence of plaintiff is reversed, and the cause is remanded, with directions to render judgment for the plaintiff in accordance herewith. All the Justices concurring.

RAFFLES V. WICHELHAUS

Court of Exchequer, 1864.
2 H. & C. 906, 159 Eng. Rep. 376.

Declaration. For that it was agreed between the plaintiff and the defendants, to wit, at Liverpool, that the plaintiff should sell to the defendants, and the defendants buy of the plaintiff, certain goods, to wit, 125 bales of Surat cotton, guaranteed middling fair merchant's Dhollorah, to arrive ex "Peerless" from Bombay; and that the cotton should be taken from the quay, and that the defendants would pay the plaintiff for the same at a certain rate, to wit, at the rate of 17¼d. per pound, within a certain time then agreed upon after the arrival of the said goods in England.—Averments: that the said goods did arrive by the said ship from Bombay in England, to wit, at Liverpool, and the plaintiff was then and there ready, and willing and offered to deliver the said goods to the defendants, & c. Breach: that the defendants refused to accept the said goods or pay the plaintiff for them.

Plea. That the said ship mentioned in the said agreement was meant and intended by the defendants to be the ship called the "Peerless," which sailed from Bombay, to wit, in October; and that the plaintiff was not ready and willing and did not offer to deliver to the defendants any bales of cotton which arrived by the last mentioned ship, but instead thereof was only ready and willing and offered to deliver to the defendants 125 bales of Surat cotton which arrived by another and different ship, which was also called the "Peerless," and which sailed from Bombay, to wit, in December.

Demurrer, and joinder therein.

Milward, in support of the demurrer.—The contract was for the sale of a number of bales of cotton of a particular description, which the plaintiff was ready to deliver. It is immaterial by what ship the cotton was to arrive, so that it was a ship called the "Peerless." The words "to arrive ex 'Peerless,'" only mean that if the vessel is lost on the voyage, the contract is to be at an end. [POLLOCK, C.B.—It would be a question for the jury whether both parties meant the same ship called the "Peerless."] That would be so if the contract was for the sale of a ship called the "Peerless;" but it is for the sale of cotton on board a ship of that name. [POLLOCK, C.B.—The defendant only bought that cotton which was to arrive by a particular ship. It may as well be said, that if there is a contract for the purchase of certain goods in warehouse A, that is satisfied by the delivery of goods of the same description in warehouse B.] In that case there would be goods in both warehouses; here it does not appear that the plaintiff had any goods on board the other "Peerless."

[MARTIN, B. It is imposing on the defendant a contract different from that which he entered into. POLLOCK, C.B. It is like a contract for the purchase of wine coming from a particular estate in France or Spain, where there are two estates of that name.] The defendant has no right to contradict by parol evidence a written contract good upon the face of it. He does not impute misrepresentation or fraud, but only says that he fancied the ship was a different one. Intention is of no avail, unless stated at the time of the contract. [POLLOCK, C.B.—One vessel sailed in October and the other in December.] The time of sailing is no part of the contract.

Mellish (Cohen with him), in support of the plea.—There is nothing on the face of the contract to shew that any particular ship called the "Peerless" was meant; but the moment it appears that two ships called the "Peerless" were about to sail from Bombay there is a latent ambiguity, and parol evidence may be given for the purpose of shewing that the defendant meant one "Peerless" and the plaintiff another. That being so, there was no consensus ad idem, and therefore no binding contract.—He was then stopped by the Court.

PER CURIAM—There must be judgment for the defendants.

Judgment for the defendants.

RESTATEMENT (SECOND) OF CONTRACTS § 20.

Effect of Misunderstanding

(1) There is no manifestation of mutual assent to an exchange if the parties attach materially different meanings to their manifestations and

(a) neither party knows or has reason to know the meaning attached by the other; or

(b) each party knows or each party has reason to know the meaning attached by the other.

(2) The manifestations of the parties are operative in accordance with the meaning attached to them by one of the parties if

(a) that party does not know of any different meaning attached by the other, and the other knows the meaning attached by the first party; or

(b) that party has no reason to know of any different meaning attached by the other, and the other has reason to know the meaning attached by the first party.

RESTATEMENT (SECOND) OF CONTRACTS § 201.

Illustration

4. "A agrees to sell and B to buy a quantity of eviscerated 'chicken.' A tenders 'stewing chicken' or 'fowl'; B rejects on the ground that the contract calls for 'broilers' or 'fryers.' Each party makes a claim for damages against the other. It is found that each acted in good faith and that neither had reason to know of the difference in meaning. Both claims fail."

A.W.B. SIMPSON, LEADING CASES IN THE COMMON LAW

154 (1995).

Assuming that there had been a genuine misunderstanding when the contract was made, what harm had this done to Wichelhaus and Busch? Surely none. Given the way prices had fallen, whichever ship they took delivery from they had made a losing contract, and if cotton had been delivered to them from *Peerless* (Major), the October ship they said they had in mind, they would have suffered a *larger* loss than they would incur by accepting delivery from *Peerless* (Flavin), the December ship. In common sense they had nothing to complain about. * * *

Had the matter been handled by arbitrators, they might well have decided that the sensible and decent way to handle the problem, the equitable solution, would be to require Wichelhaus and Busch to take delivery from Raffles, and consider themselves lucky not to have lost more. * * * What they would surely never have countenanced would be for them to escape all liability on their losing contract. * * *

DICKEY v. HURD, 33 F.2d 415 (1st Cir.1929). [Dickey in Georgia sent a letter to Hurd in Massachusetts requesting the price of Hurd's land in

Georgia. On July 8, 1926, Hurd offered to sell the land at "$15 per acre cash" and stated that he would give Dickey "till July 18, 1926 including that day to accept this offer." Dickey telegraphed an acceptance on July 17 and promised to send a $500 down payment. Although Hurd received the telegram on July 17, he claimed his offer required Dickey to pay the cash price by July 18.]

BINGHAM, C.J.

A * * * difficult question is whether the offer calls for payment of the purchase price, an act of acceptance, on or before July 18; or whether it simply calls for a notice of acceptance. The language of the offer is: "I will sell the same to you for [having named the price] cash and give you till July 18, 1926, including that day to accept this offer." Standing alone and apart from the surrounding circumstances, the words "to accept this offer" are equivocal. They may mean that he would give through July 18 to accept the offer by paying the price fixed; or would give him through that date to accept the offer by giving him notice to that effect. But two letters were put in evidence, written by Mr. Dickey to Mr. Hurd between the 8th and the 17th of July. The first is dated July 12th and the second July 15th. In both of these letters Mr. Dickey clearly discloses that he understood the offer did not require him to pay the purchase price on or before July 18, but to give an answer, notice of acceptance, on or before that day. In the letter of the 12th he says: "Answering your favor of the 8th inst., I thank you for giving me through the 18th of July to give you an *answer* about your property. * * * I expect to give you a *definite answer* about your property before that time," and later on in the same letter he states: "I will give you an *answer* within the time you were kind enough to allow me." And in the letter of July 15th, after explaining difficulties he was having, he stated: "If possible I am going to give you an *answer* within the time you have allowed me." When Mr. Hurd received these communications, he was fully apprised of how Mr. Dickey understood the language of his offer, and, if that was not the meaning which he intended to give to it, it was his duty to have at once informed him that the offer called for payment of the price on or before the 18th of July, and not simply for a notice of acceptance. It was not open to him to lie quietly by until after the time of acceptance had expired and then say my offer called for payment of the price on or before July 18, and you have not met the requirements.

COLFAX ENVELOPE CORP. v. LOCAL NO. 458–3M, CHICAGO GRAPHIC COMMUNICATIONS INTERN, 20 F.3d 750, 754 (7th. Cir. 1994) (POSNER, CHIEF JUDGE). When parties agree to a patently ambiguous term, they submit to have any dispute over it resolved by interpretation. That is what courts and arbitrators are *for* in contract cases—to resolve interpretive questions founded on ambiguity. It is when parties agree to terms that reasonably appear to each of them to be unequivocal but are not, cases like that of the ship *Peerless* where the ambiguity is buried, that the possibility of rescission on grounds of mutual misunderstanding, or, the term we prefer, latent ambiguity, arises.

SECTION FIVE: THE OFFER

1 CORBIN ON CONTRACTS

§ 1.11 (2019).

An offer is an expression by one party of assent to certain definite terms, provided that the other party involved in the bargaining transaction will likewise express assent to the same terms.

LEFKOWITZ V. GREAT MINNEAPOLIS SURPLUS STORE, INC.

Supreme Court of Minnesota, 1957.
251 Minn. 188, 86 N.W.2d 689.

MURPHY, JUSTICE.

This is an appeal from an order of the Municipal Court of Minneapolis denying the motion of the defendant for amended findings of fact, or, in the alternative, for a new trial. The order for judgment awarded the plaintiff the sum of $138.50 as damages for breach of contract.

This case grows out of the alleged refusal of the defendant to sell to the plaintiff a certain fur piece which it had offered for sale in a newspaper advertisement. It appears from the record that on April 6, 1956, the defendant published the following advertisement in a Minneapolis newspaper:

"Saturday 9 A.M. Sharp 3 Brand New Fur Coats Worth to $100.00. First Come First Served $1 Each."

On April 13, the defendant again published an advertisement in the same newspaper as follows:

"Saturday 9 A.M. 2 Brand New Pastel Mink 3-Skin Scarfs Selling for $89.50 Out they go Saturday. Each . . . $1.00. 1 Black lapin Stole Beautiful, worth $139.50 . . . $1.00. First Come First Served."

The record supports the findings of the court that on each of the Saturdays following the publication of the above-described ads the plaintiff was the first to present himself at the appropriate counter in the defendant's store and on each occasion demanded the coat and the stole so advertised and indicated his readiness to pay the sale price of $1. On both occasions, the defendant refused to sell the merchandise to the plaintiff, stating on the first occasion that by a "house rule" the offer was intended for women only and sales would not be made to men, and on the second visit that plaintiff knew defendant's house rules.

The trial court properly disallowed plaintiff's claim for the value of the fur coats since the value of these articles was speculative and uncertain. The only evidence of value was the advertisement itself to the effect that the coats were "Worth to $100.00," how much less being speculative especially in view of the price for which they were offered for sale. With reference to the offer of the defendant on April 13, 1956, to sell the "1 Black Lapin Stole * * * worth $139.50 * * * " the trial court held that the value of this article was established and granted judgment in favor of the plaintiff for that amount less the $1 quoted purchase price.

1. The defendant contends that a newspaper advertisement offering items of merchandise for sale at a named price is a "unilateral offer" which may be withdrawn without notice. He relies upon authorities which hold that, where an advertiser publishes in a newspaper that he has a certain quantity or quality of goods which he wants to dispose of at certain prices and on certain terms, such advertisements are not offers which become contracts as soon as any person to whose notice they may come signifies his acceptance by notifying the other that he will take a certain quantity of them. Such advertisements have been construed as an invitation for an offer of sale on the terms stated, which offer, when received, may be accepted or rejected and which therefore does not become a contract of sale until accepted by the seller; and until a contract has been so made, the seller may modify or revoke such prices or terms. * * *.

The defendant relies principally on Craft v. Elder & Johnston Co., 38 N.E.2d 416. In that case, the court discussed the legal effect of an advertisement offering for sale, as a one-day special, an electric sewing machine at a named price. The view was expressed that the advertisement was (38 N.E.2d 417) "not an offer made to any specific person but was made to the public generally. Thereby it would be properly designated as a unilateral offer and not being supported by any consideration could be withdrawn at will and without notice." It is true that such an offer may be withdrawn before acceptance. Since all offers are by their nature unilateral because they are necessarily made by one party or on one side in the negotiation of a contract, the distinction made in that decision between a unilateral offer and a unilateral contract is not clear. On the facts before us we are concerned with whether the advertisement constituted an offer, and, if so, whether the plaintiff's conduct constituted an acceptance.

There are numerous authorities which hold that a particular advertisement in a newspaper or circular letter relating to a sale of articles may be construed by the court as constituting an offer, acceptance of which would complete a contract. * * *

The test of whether a binding obligation may originate in advertisements addressed to the general public is "whether the facts show that some performance was promised in positive terms in return for something requested." 1 Williston, Contracts (Rev. ed.) § 27.

The authorities above cited emphasize that, where the offer is clear, definite, and explicit, and leaves nothing open for negotiation, it constitutes an offer, acceptance of which will complete the contract. The most recent case on the subject is Johnson v. Capital City Ford Co., La.App., 85 So.2d 75, in which the court pointed out that a newspaper advertisement relating to the purchase and sale of automobiles may constitute an offer, acceptance of which will consummate a contract and create an obligation in the offeror to perform according to the terms of the published offer.

Whether in any individual instance a newspaper advertisement is an offer rather than an invitation to make an offer depends on the legal intention of the parties and the surrounding circumstances. Annotation, 157 A.L.R. 744, 751; 77 C.J.S., Sales, § 25b; 17 C.J.S., Contracts, § 389. We are of the view on the facts before us that the offer by the defendant of the sale of the Lapin fur was clear, definite, and explicit, and left nothing open for negotiation. The plaintiff having successfully managed to be the first one to appear at the seller's place of business to be served, as requested by the advertisement, and having offered the stated purchase price of the article, he was entitled to performance on the part of the defendant. We think the trial court was correct in holding that there was in the conduct of the parties a sufficient mutuality of obligation to constitute a contract of sale.

2. The defendant contends that the offer was modified by a "house rule" to the effect that only women were qualified to receive the bargains advertised. The advertisement contained no such restriction. This objection may be disposed of briefly by stating that, while an advertiser has the right at any time before acceptance to modify his offer, he does not have the right, after acceptance, to impose new or arbitrary conditions not contained in the published offer. * * *

Affirmed.

FORD MOTOR CREDIT CO. v. RUSSELL, 519 N.W.2d 460 (1994). [Monticello Ford advertised a 1988 Ford Escort Pony in the *Monticello Shopper* for $7,826. The monthly payments set forth were "$159.29, based on a 60-month loan at 11% A.P.R." The Russells sought to purchase a Ford Escort as advertised but Monticello Ford could not obtain financing for them at 11%. The parties signed a contract at 13.75%. When the Russells defaulted on "numerous payments," Ford Credit Company, Monticello Ford's assignee, repossessed and resold the car. Ford Credit Company then sought to recover a deficiency judgment. The Russells counterclaimed, contending that they had accepted an offer in the *Monticello Shopper* and the failure of Ford to obtain 11% financing was a breach of contract.] Generally, if goods are advertised for sale at a certain price, it is not an offer and no contract is formed; such an advertisement is merely an invitation to bargain rather than an offer. 1 Samuel Williston, *A Treatise on the Law of Contracts* § 4:7 (4th ed. 1990); Restatement (Second) of Contracts § 26 (1981). The test of whether a binding obligation may originate in advertisements addressed to the general public is "whether the facts show that some performance was promised in positive terms in return for something requested." *Lefkowitz v. Great Minneapolis Surplus Store, Inc.,* 251 Minn. 188, 191, 86 N.W.2d 689, 691 (1957) (quoting 1 Samuel Williston, *A Treatise on the Law of Contracts* § 27) (3rd ed. 1957)).

We conclude that the advertisement here did not constitute an offer of sale to the general public. *See id.* (an advertisement may constitute an offer where it is clear, definite, explicit, and leaves nothing open for negotiation). Because not everyone qualifies for financing and Monticello Ford does not have an unlimited number of Ford Escorts to sell, it was unreasonable for appellants to believe that the advertisement was an offer binding the advertiser.

KEARNEY v. EQUILON ENTERPRISES, LLC, ET AL., 65 F. Supp. 3d 1033 (D. Or. 2014). At the heart of Plaintiffs' claims is an advertisement allegedly displayed by Defendant at Shell-brand service stations. * * * Plaintiffs allege the advertisement looked like this:

This advertisement was part of Defendant's "Ski Free" promotion. Under this promotion, after individuals purchased ten gallons of fuel and requested a voucher for a free lift ticket, they received a voucher with their purchase receipt. This voucher could not be exchanged directly for a free lift ticket, but rather was a "two for one" coupon that allowed the individual to obtain a free lift ticket only after purchasing a lift ticket at full price at a participating ski resort. Moreover, the voucher contained various other restrictions. Plaintiffs assert that Defendant's advertisement created a contract, the terms of which entitled Plaintiffs to a free ski resort lift ticket in exchange for buying ten gallons of gas at a participating Shell station. Plaintiffs argue Defendant breached the terms of the contract, and also violated state unlawful trade practices, when Defendant failed to provide a voucher that could be directly exchanged for a free lift ticket at a participating resort, but instead provided a "two for one" voucher that required the purchase of a second lift ticket in order to receive a "free" lift ticket.

* * *

Construing the alleged facts in the light most favorable to Plaintiffs, the *only* advertisement the consumer saw was the sign stating, "buy 10 gallons of fuel, get a voucher for a free lift ticket!" Based on this allegation, Defendant, in clear and positive terms, promised to render performance in exchange for the purchase of ten gallons of fuel. Namely, if one purchases ten gallons of fuel at a Shell Station participating in the "Ski Free" promotion, then the purchaser is rewarded with a voucher for a free lift ticket. Additionally, Plaintiff, as the recipient of the advertisement, "reasonably might have concluded that by acting in accordance with the request a contract would be formed." The clear offer in the advertisement established a unilateral contract, and Plaintiffs accepted the offer through performance by purchasing ten gallons of fuel at a Shell station participating in the "Ski Free" promotion.

NOTE: CLICKING "PAY NOW" DOES NOT MEAN YOU HAVE A CONTRACT!

It looks like Margaret Schultz does not have a claim for damages after she saw a flight listed for $197 on American Airline's website, clicked on the necessary links to purchase the flight, and wound up on the "Review and Pay" screen, where she clicked "Pay now," only to read a new screen that said that the flight would cost $297. The court dealing with this miserable bait and switch strategy held in part that "[b]ecause the absence of a seat selection contemplates further action and renders total price uncertain, the 'offer' fails to overcome the presumption that an advertisement is not an offer." Ouch. Schultz v. American Airlines, Inc., 2018 WL 7287194 (S.D.Fla. 2018).

AUGSTEIN V. LESLIE

United States District Court, S.D.N.Y., 2012.
2012 WL 4928914.

HON. HAROLD BAER, JR., DISTRICT JUDGE.

Armin Augstein brought this action to collect a reward from Ryan Leslie upon the return of Leslie's stolen laptop computer. The laptop was stolen and recovered in Germany and returned to Leslie in New York. * * * Augstein now moves for summary judgment * * *. The motion is GRANTED * * *.

Background

Leslie is a musician and NextSelection a company that owns the trademark to Leslie's name and performances. While on tour in Germany, Leslie's laptop computer, external hard drive, and certain other belongings were stolen. The laptop contained valuable intellectual property, including music and videos related to Leslie's records and performances. In videos, news articles, and online postings, Leslie stated that he would pay $20,000—later increased to $1 million—to anyone who returned his property. After Augstein returned the laptop and hard drive, Leslie refused to pay the reward because, Leslie alleges, the intellectual property for which he valued the laptop was not present on the hard drive when it was returned. Leslie claims that he and several staff members tried to access the data on the hard drive but were unable to do so. Leslie sent the hard drive to the manufacturer, Avastor, which ultimately deleted the information prior to sending Leslie a replacement. The circumstances of the return of the hard drive and the meaning of Leslie's communications with Avastor are disputed. Augstein claims that Leslie, after he received correspondence from Augstein regarding the collection of the reward, caused the hard drive to be erased. Augstein now argues the Court should grant him summary judgment on the issues of the validity of the offer and of the reward and its subsequent acceptance and performance by Augstein when he returned the laptop to the police in Germany. * * *

Discussion

Augstein argues that Leslie made an offer of a reward for the return of his property and that Augstein accepted and fully performed when he presented the property to the police in Germany. Leslie responds that a reasonable person would not have understood the mention of the reward to be an offer of a unilateral contract, but instead would have understood it to be an advertisement—in essence, an invitation to negotiate. And even if it was an offer, Leslie continues, Augstein did not perform because he did not return the *intellectual* property, only the *physical* property. Whether or not the external hard drive, which was subsequently destroyed by Avastor, contained Leslie's intellectual property is a heavily disputed issue in this case. * * *

Summary Judgment

A district court may not grant summary judgment if there exists a genuine issue of material fact. * * * "For summary judgment purposes, a 'genuine issue' exists where the evidence is such that a reasonable jury could decide in the non-moving party's favor." *Cambridge Realty Co., LLC v. St. Paul Fire & Marine Ins. Co.,* 421 F. App'x 52, 53 (2d Cir.2011) (internal citations omitted). "An offer is the manifestation of willingness to enter into a bargain, so made as to justify another person in understanding that his assent to that bargain is invited and will conclude it." Restatement

(Second) of Contracts § 24 (1981). To evaluate the legitimacy of this offer, the court should consider "what an objective, reasonable person would have understood [Leslie's conduct] to convey." *Leonard v. Pepsico, Inc.,* 88 F.Supp.2d 116, 127 (S.D.N.Y.1999).

Leslie mentioned the $20,000 reward for the return of his property in a YouTube video on October 24, 2010. In the video, Leslie says, "I am offering a reward of $20,000." * * * He also implied that the lost property was worth much more than $20,000. On November 6, 2010, a video was posted increasing the reward to $1,000,000. At the end of the video, a message reads, "In the interest of retrieving the invaluable intellectual property contained on his laptop & hard drive, Mr. Leslie has increased the reward offer from $20,000 to $1,000,000 USD." * * * The increase of the reward was publicized on Leslie's Facebook and Twitter accounts, including a post on Twitter which read, "I'm absolutely continuing my Euro tour. I raised the reward for my intellectual property to $1mm" and included a link to the video on YouTube. * * * News organizations also published reports on Leslie's reward offer, both in print and online. Finally, Leslie was interviewed on MTV on November 11, 2010, and reiterated the $1,000,000 reward, saying "I got a million dollar reward for anybody that can return all my intellectual property to me." * * *

Leslie's videos and other activities together are best characterized as an offer for a reward. Leslie "sought to induce performance, unlike an invitation to negotiate [often an advertisement], which seeks a reciprocal promise." *Leonard,* 88 F.Supp.2d at 125 (discussing *Carlill v. Carbolic Smoke Ball Co.,* [1892] 1 Q.B. 256 (Eng.). Offers of reward are "intended to induce a potential offeree to perform a specific action." *Id.* at 126. A reasonable person viewing the video would understand that Leslie was seeking the return of his property and that by returning it, the bargain would be concluded. The increase of the reward from $20,000 to $1,000,000, the value of the property lost (in particular the unreleased album) and the news reports regarding the reward offer would lead a reasonable person to believe that Leslie was making an offer. As such, the video constitutes a valid offer and summary judgment is granted as to that issue. "[I]f a person chooses to make extravagant promises . . . he probably does so because it pays him to make them, and, if he has made them, the extravagance of the promises is no reason in law why he should not be bound by them." *Id.* at 125 (quoting *Carbolic Smoke Ball,* 1 Q.B. at 268 (Bowen, L.J.)).

Leslie attempts to persuade the court that the video is not an offer but an advertisement. Because advertisements, Leslie argues, are not generally considered offers, there is no contract. * * * He cites *Leonard v. Pepsico,* where the court did find an advertisement rather than an offer, to support that argument. However, unlike the television commercial in *Leonard,* Leslie's conduct in this case was meant to induce performance. Leslie was not seeking a promise from an individual who would return his belongings, rather he was seeking performance—the actual return of his property. In addition, his videos and other commentary cannot be reasonably understood as an invitation to negotiate because, similarly, Leslie was not soliciting help in finding his property, but the actual return itself. Leslie also relies on the fact that the offer was conveyed over YouTube (a website where many advertisements and promotional videos are shared, along with any number of other types of video) to undermine the legitimacy of the offer. * * * I do not find this reasoning persuasive. The forum for conveying the offer is not determinative, but rather, the question is whether a reasonable person would have understood that Leslie made an offer of a reward. I conclude that they would.

[The court also found that "Leslie and his team were at least negligent in their handling of the hard drive," and that "it shall be assumed that the desired intellectual property was present on the hard drive when Augstein returned it to the police."]

* * * Augstein's motion for summary judgment is GRANTED insofar as he seeks a declaration that the reward was an offer * * *."

STELLUTI KERR, L.L.C. v. MAPEI CORP., 703 Fed. Appx. 214 (5th Cir. 2017). This case involves a dispute between Stelluti Kerr, L.L.C. (SK) and Mapei Corporation (Mapei) over the Arovac, a machine used to package the cement-based powders that, when mixed with water, become the mortars and grouts used in tile installation. Historically, these powders have been packaged in paper bags, which are prone to leaking and breaking open. The Arovac, however, packages these powders in plastic bags, which are less prone to leak and break. The Arovac is manufactured by Arodo BVBA (Arodo), a Belgian company. In early 2006, SK and Arodo entered into an agreement for SK to distribute the Arovac in North America on a non-exclusive basis (the Distributorship Agreement). The Distributorship Agreement was for an indefinite duration. At the time, the Arovac was only a prototype, but the parties believed the Arovac would soon be perfected and decided to exhibit the plastic bags that the prototype was producing at a trade show in May 2006. Mapei, a Florida-based manufacturer of (among other things) cement-based tile adhesives, saw the plastic bags at that show and was immediately interested. Mapei had recently lost a major multi-million dollar contract with a big-box retailer, which had contracted with a competitor using a cleaner bag than Mapei. To win back that contract, Mapei was actively searching for a cleaner package, which Mapei believed the Arovac could ultimately produce.

SK and Mapei agree that, after their introduction at the 2006 trade show, they formed a contract, but do not agree on much beyond that, including whether the contract was for the sale of one Arovac or 14 Arovacs. * * *

[The court affirmed the jury's "implied finding" that a price quotation prepared by SK was an offer.] First, the Price Quotation was highly detailed, totaling more than 50 pages and containing all the necessary elements for a contract. Second, the Price Quotation was not the initial substantive contact between the parties. Rather, as detailed, * * * the Price Quotation followed numerous meetings and communications between the parties over the nearly ten-month period between August 2006 and June 2007, which resulted in two separate sets of revisions. Finally, the Price Quotation was not a generalized quote sent to a number of potential customers, "such as one appearing in a brochure or on a flyer." *J.D. Fields*, 426 Fed.Appx. at 276. It was prepared and revised twice specifically for Mapei, at Mapei's request.

The home office acceptance clause in the Price Quotation's lengthy terms and conditions section—stating that "[a]ll quotations, orders and agreements made between [Mapei] and [SK]'s [agent] shall be subject to the acceptance and approval of [SK]'s headquarters"—certainly does undermine the jury's implied finding that the quotation was an offer. * * * But we cannot say, as Mapei urges, that it prevented the Price Quotation from constituting an offer as a matter of law. *See Crest Ridge Constr. Grp., Inc. v. Newcourt Inc.*, 78 F.3d 146, 150 (5th Cir. 1996) (concluding that a clause in a price quotation stating it was subject to credit department approval did not prevent it from being an offer as a matter of law). "[I]n light of the extensive dealings and preparations between these two parties, the jury could conclude this [home office approval] clause at most created a condition precedent on [SK]'s obligation to perform and did not prevent the formation of a contract." *Id.* Indeed, the evidence showed that the Price Quotation was already approved by SK's "corporate headquarters"; it was prepared by SK's co-owner at, and sent directly from, SK's Texas headquarters.

UNIFORM COMMERCIAL CODE § 2–204(3).

Even though one or more terms are left open a contract for sale does not fail for indefiniteness if the parties have intended to make a contract and there is a reasonably certain basis for giving an appropriate remedy.

UNIFORM COMMERCIAL CODE § 2–311(1).

An agreement for sale which is otherwise sufficiently definite (subsection (3) of section 2–204) to be a contract is not made invalid by the fact that it leaves particulars of performance to be specified by one of the parties. Any such specification must be made in good faith and within limits set by commercial reasonableness.

PROBLEM 4-7

People sometimes make unusual offers. But sometimes people try to take advantage of others by claiming to "accept" what they know or should know are not offers. For an example of the latter, in Leonard v. Pepsico, Inc., 210 F.3d 88 (2d Cir. 2000), the court described the so-called offer and then rendered its brief decision:

> In 1995, defendant-appellee Pepsico, Inc. conducted a promotion in which it offered merchandise in exchange for "points" earned by purchasing Pepsi Cola. A television commercial aired by Pepsico depicted a teenager gloating over various items of merchandise earned by Pepsi points, and culminated in the teenager arriving at high school in a Harrier Jet, a fighter aircraft of the United States Marine Corps. For each item of merchandise sported by the teenager (a T shirt, a jacket, sunglasses), the ad noted the number of Pepsi points needed to get it. When the teenager is shown in the jet, the ad prices it as 7 million points.
>
> Plaintiff-appellant John D.R. Leonard alleges that the ad was an offer, that he accepted the offer by tendering the equivalent of 7 million points, and that Pepsico has breached its contract to deliver the Harrier jet. Pepsico characterizes the use of the Harrier jet in the ad as a hyperbolic joke ("zany humor"), cites the ad's reference to offering details contained in the promotional catalog (which contains no Harrier fighter plane), and argues that no objective person would construe the ad as an offer for the Harrier jet.
>
> The United States District Court for the Southern District of New York (Wood, *J.*) agreed with Pepsico and granted its motion for summary judgment on the grounds (1) that the commercial did not amount to an offer of goods; (2) that no objective person could reasonably have concluded that the commercial actually offered consumers a Harrier Jet; and (3) that the alleged contract could not satisfy the New York statute of frauds.
>
> We affirm for substantially the reasons stated in Judge Wood's opinion. *See* 88 F.Supp.2d 116 (S.D.N.Y.1999).

Here are some true additional examples of possible offers. In which cases, if any, do you think the "offeror" should be held to the "offer?"

1. Radio disk jockey Ben Stone announced that anyone who got a permanent "93 Rock" tattoo on his or her forehead would receive $30,000 per year for five years. Two men have sued Stone and his station for failing to pay after they received the tattoos. They also seek consequential damages because they have been unable to get jobs with the tattoos on their foreheads.

2. During the height of the Monica Lewinsky scandal, on his television program, Geraldo Rivera promised to pay $10,000 to anyone who could find a case in which someone was criminally prosecuted for lying about a sexual

matter. The National Law Journal reported on November 9, 1998 that Marc Bogatin, a criminal defense lawyer, claimed payment for finding several such cases. On February 22, 1999, the same newspaper reported that NBC Television agreed to pay Bogatin (and two other lawyers who also submitted examples), although NBC "continues to believe that none of the claims have satisfied the challenge."

3. Nationwide Mutual Insurance Company offered "his-and-her" Mercedes to the person who wrote the best slogan for its 1994 regional convention. David Mears' eight-word slogan won the contest, but Nationwide claimed the promotion was "just a joke."

4. In an advertisement in USA Today in December 1995, Haley Barbour, Republican National Chairman, promised $1 million "to the first American who can prove the following statement is false: 'In November 1995, the U.S. House and Senate passed a balanced budget bill. It increases total federal spending on Medicare by more than 50% from 1995 to 2002, pursuant to Congressional Budget Office standards.' " Eighteen people claimed to have proven the assertion false. The RNC claimed that the advertisement was not a "bona fide offer."

5. A lawyer appearing on TV's "Dateline," who was defending a condemned client, offered $1 million to anyone who could prove that it was possible to get to a motel five miles from the Atlanta airport in less than 30 minutes. The client's alibi for murder depended on this being impossible. A lawyer made the trip in 28 minutes and demanded the money. See Kolodzie v. Mason, 774 F.3d 736 (11th Cir. 2014).

6. Julian Assange, the founder of WikiLeaks, tweeted an offer agreeing to be extradited to the U.S. if President Obama commuted Chelsea Manning's sentence. Manning had leaked classified information to WikiLeaks, which had published the information. President Obama later commuted Manning's sentence, but the White House denied that the motive was to accept Assange's "offer."

7. A man awaiting Powerball results tweeted that if he won he would give 10 people $1 million each if they retweeted his tweet. The man then deleted his tweet.

8. In early May, Disney tweeted from its corporate account and encouraged users of the platform to use the #MayThe4th Hashtag. But, it tweeted, "By sharing your message with us using #MayThe4th, you agree to our use of the message and your account name in all media and our terms of use here." Does using the hashtag constitute acceptance of all of Disney's terms? A few hours later, after facing blowback, it tweeted, "The above legal language applies ONLY to replies to this tweet using #MayThe4th and mentioning @DisneyPlus." Is this sufficiently definite to be an offer?

SECTION SIX: THE ACCEPTANCE

CORBIN, OFFER AND ACCEPTANCE, AND SOME OF THE RESULTING LEGAL RELATIONS

26 Yale L.J. 169, 199–200 (1917).

An acceptance is a voluntary act of the offeree whereby he exercises the power conferred upon him by the offer, and thereby creates the set of legal relations called a contract. What acts are sufficient to serve this purpose? We must look first to the terms in which the offer was expressed, either by words or by other conduct. The offeror is the creator of the power and at the time of its creation he has full control over both the fact of its existence and its terms. The offeror has, in the beginning, full power to determine the acts that are to constitute acceptance. After he has once created the power, he may lose his control over it, and may become disabled to change or to revoke it; but the fact that, in the beginning, the offeror has full control of the immediately succeeding relation called a power, is the characteristic that distinguishes contractual relations from non-contractual ones. After the offeror has created the power, the legal consequences thereof are out of his hands, and he may be brought into numerous consequential relations of which he did not dream, and to which he might not have consented. These later relations are nevertheless called contractual.

ARDENTE V. HORAN

Supreme Court of Rhode Island, 1976.
117 R.I. 254, 366 A.2d 162.

DORIS, JUSTICE.

Ernest P. Ardente, the plaintiff, brought this civil action in Superior Court to specifically enforce an agreement between himself and William A. and Katherine L. Horan, the defendants, to sell certain real property. The defendants filed an answer together with a motion for summary judgment * * *. [J]udgment was entered by a Superior Court justice for the defendants. The plaintiff now appeals.

In August 1975, certain residential property in the city of Newport was offered for sale by defendants. The plaintiff made a bid of $250,000 for the property which was communicated to defendants by their attorney. After defendants' attorney advised plaintiff that the bid was acceptable to defendants, he prepared a purchase and sale agreement at the direction of defendants and forwarded it to plaintiff's attorney for plaintiff's signature. After investigating certain title conditions, plaintiff executed the agreement. Thereafter plaintiff's attorney returned the document to defendants along with a check in the amount of $20,000 and a letter dated September 8, 1975, which read in relevant part as follows:

> "My clients are concerned that the following items remain with the real estate: a) dining room set and tapestry wall covering in dining room; b) fireplace fixtures throughout; c) the sun parlor furniture. I would appreciate your confirming that these items are a part of the transaction, as they would be difficult to replace."

The defendants refused to agree to sell the enumerated items and did not sign the purchase and sale agreement. They directed their attorney to return the agreement and the deposit check to plaintiff and subsequently refused to sell the property to plaintiff. This action for specific performance followed.

In Superior Court, defendants moved for summary judgment on the ground that the facts were not in dispute and no contract had been formed as a matter of law.[1] The trial justice ruled that the letter quoted above constituted a conditional acceptance of defendants' offer to sell the property and consequently must be construed as a counteroffer. Since defendants never accepted the counteroffer, it followed that no contract was formed, and summary judgment was granted.

* * *

The trial justice proceeded on the theory that the delivery of the purchase and sale agreement to plaintiff constituted an offer by defendants to sell the property. Because we must view the evidence in the light most favorable to the party against whom summary judgment was entered, in this case plaintiff, we assume as the trial justice did that the delivery of the agreement was in fact an offer.[2]

The question we must answer next is whether there was an acceptance of that offer. The general rule is that where, as here, there is an offer to form a bilateral contract, the offeree must communicate his acceptance to the offeror before any contractual obligation can come into being. A mere mental intent to accept the offer, no matter how carefully formed, is not sufficient. The acceptance must be transmitted to the offeror in some overt manner. * * * A review of the record shows that the only expression of acceptance which was communicated to defendants was the delivery of the executed purchase and sale agreement accompanied by the letter of

---

1 Although the contract would appear to be within the statute of frauds, defendants did not raise this defense in the trial court, nor do they raise it here. Where a party makes no claim to the benefit of the statute, the court sua sponte will not interpose it for him. *Conti v. Fisher,* 48 R.I. 33, 36, 134 A. 849, 850 (1926).

2 The conclusion that the delivery of the agreement was an offer is not unassailable in view of the fact that defendants did not sign the agreement before sending it to plaintiff, and the fact that plaintiff told defendants' attorney *after* the agreement was received that he would have to investigate certain conditions of title before signing the agreement. If it was not an offer, plaintiff's execution of the agreement could itself be no more than an offer, which defendants never accepted.

September 8. Therefore it is solely on the basis of the language used in these two documents that we must determine whether there was a valid acceptance. Whatever plaintiff's unexpressed intention may have been in sending the documents is irrelevant. We must be concerned only with the language actually used, not the language plaintiff thought he was using or intended to use.

There is no doubt that the execution and delivery of the purchase and sale agreement by plaintiff, without more, would have operated as an acceptance. The terms of the accompanying letter, however, apparently conditioned the acceptance upon the inclusion of various items of personalty. In assessing the effect of the terms of that letter we must keep in mind certain generally accepted rules. To be effective, an acceptance must be definite and unequivocal. "An offeror is entitled to know in clear terms whether the offeree accepts his proposal. It is not enough that the words of a reply justify a probable inference of assent." 1 Restatement *Contracts* § 58, comment *a* (1932). The acceptance may not impose additional conditions on the offer, nor may it add limitations. "An acceptance which is equivocal or upon condition or with a limitation is a counteroffer and requires acceptance by the original offeror before a contractual relationship can exist." * * *

However, an acceptance may be valid despite conditional language if the acceptance is clearly independent of the condition. Many cases have so held. Williston states the rule as follows:

> "Frequently an offeree, while making a positive acceptance of the offer, also makes a request or suggestion that some addition or modification be made. So long as it is clear that the meaning of the acceptance is positively and unequivocally to accept the offer whether such request is granted or not, a contract is formed." 1 Williston, *Contracts* § 79 at 261–62 (3d ed. 1957).

Corbin is in agreement with the above view. 1 Corbin, * * * § 84 at 363–65. Thus our task is to decide whether plaintiff's letter is more reasonably interpreted as a qualified acceptance or as an absolute acceptance together with a mere inquiry concerning a collateral matter.

In making our decision we recognize that, as one text states, "The question whether a communication by an offeree is a conditional acceptance or counter-offer is not always easy to answer. It must be determined by the same common-sense process of interpretation that must be applied in so many other cases." 1 Corbin, *supra* § 82 at 353. In our opinion the language used in plaintiff's letter of September 8 is not consistent with an absolute acceptance accompanied by a request for a gratuitous benefit. We interpret the letter to impose a condition on plaintiff's acceptance of defendants' offer. The letter does not unequivocally state that even without the enumerated items plaintiff is willing to complete the contract. In fact, the letter seeks "confirmation" that the listed items "are a part of the transaction". Thus, far from being an independent, collateral request, the sale of the items in question is explicitly referred to as a part of the real estate transaction. Moreover, the letter goes on to stress the difficulty of finding replacements for these items. This is a further indication that plaintiff did not view the inclusion of the listed items as merely collateral or incidental to the real estate transaction.

A review of the relevant case law discloses that those cases in which an acceptance was found valid despite an accompanying conditional term generally involved a more definite expression of acceptance than the one in the case at bar. * * *

Accordingly, we hold that since the plaintiff's letter of acceptance dated September 8 was conditional, it operated as a rejection of the defendants' offer and no contractual obligation was created.

The plaintiff's appeal is denied and dismissed, the judgment appealed from is affirmed and the case is remanded to the Superior Court.

PROBLEM 4-8

Howard Wade executed an offer to purchase certain real estate. The offer contained a provision in which the seller agreed that it had no verbal agreements with others to give them a right of first refusal on the particular land. This language was added to the offer because Wade knew that the present tenant on the land had requested from the seller a right of first refusal. The seller signed the purchase offer after adding the following provision: "It is understood and agreed that the present tenant, Robert Tank, has first right of refusal on this offer." (1) Is a contract formed? (2) If the seller wants Tank to have a right of first refusal, but does not want to lose the possible sale to Wade, what advice would you give the seller? (3) Is there a contract if Wade's offer did not contain the provision concerning the right of first refusal?

BERGEY V. HSBC BANK USA

Court of Appeals of Ohio, 2010.
2010 WL 2395506.

MOORE, J. Richard Bergey tried to purchase a home at 652 Orlando Road in Akron, Ohio, from the owner of record, HSBC Bank. Tracy Jones and Remax were HSBC's broker and agent for the sale of the property (collectively referred to as "Jones"). The home was eventually sold to someone else. On July 11, 2008, Richard Bergey filed a complaint for damages, an injunction, and specific performance against HSBC Bank, Tracy Jones, and Remax Realty for breach of contract and interference with a contract.

On June 22, 2008, Bergey, through his real-estate agent, submitted to Jones a proposed purchase agreement for the property. Jones received multiple offers, and, as a result, requested that all the potential buyers submit their highest and best offer by June 24, 2008. On June 24, 2008, Bergey modified his proposed purchase price from $45,151 to $55,101. Jones submitted all the offers to HSBC's servicer and attorney-in-fact. The highest offer was from John and Susan Randolph for $56,000, but it was contingent upon financing. Although Bergey's offer of $55,101 was not the highest, it was a cash offer, and HSBC's servicer authorized Jones to accept the $55,101. Jones emailed Bergey's real-estate agent to inform him that the offer had been accepted and that she would send addenda and instructions.

Subsequently, the Randolphs, who had offered $56,000 contingent upon financing, contacted Jones to remove the contingency. Jones relayed the modification to HSBC's servicer, who then authorized Jones to accept the $56,000 cash offer. Jones informed Bergey's real-estate agent that she had "jumped the gun" when she previously emailed him to accept Bergey's offer. On July 3, 2008, Jones informed Bergey's real-estate agent that another offer had been accepted. HSBC completed the sale of the property to the Randolphs. Eventually, Bergey purchased the property from the Randolphs.

HSBC and Jones filed motions for summary judgment. The trial court granted the motions, concluding that because HSBC did not accept Bergey's offer, no contract was formed, thus there could be no breach of contract or interference with the contract. Bergey timely appealed from this decision, raising one assignment of error for our review.

* * *

In the instant case, HSBC and Jones moved for summary judgment arguing, in part, that Bergey and HSBC never entered into a written purchase agreement. The trial court agreed, concluding that "[t]here is no evidence that HSBC ever accepted the B[e]rgey Offer." Accordingly, the trial court held that because there was never a contract, there could be no breach of contract or interference with the contract. We do not agree.

* * *

After Bergey submitted his $55,101 price modification, Jones, as agent for HSBC submitted the offer to HSBC, via its loan servicing agent, for consideration. HSBC's servicer emailed Jones, informing her that she was "[a]pproved to accept the $55,101 cash offer." Jones then emailed Bergey and informed him that "[y]our offer has been accepted, I need to get a few things out of the way, then I will send you addendums and instructions, thanks."

HSBC initially contends that Bergey "ignores the fact that the email itself indicates that other requirements must be satisfied before the deal is final. In other words, there was no contract." The trial court agreed, referring to this email as "conditional acceptance[.]" "A conditional acceptance is a statement that the offeree is willing to enter into a bargain differing in some respect from that proposed in the original offer; the conditional acceptance is, aside from cases involving the Uniform Commercial Code, itself a counteroffer and operates to reject the original offer." *Purdin v. Hitchcock* (Jan. 21, 1993), 4th Dist. No. CA 531, at *3, citing 2 Lord, Williston on Contracts (4 Ed.1991) 104–105, Section 6:13.

Jones' emailed acceptance simply stated that she would send Bergey the addenda and instructions. "Addendum" is defined as "[s]omething to be added, esp. to a document; a supplement." Black's Law Dictionary (8th ed.2004) 41. Thus, at most, Jones' email contained a request to add something to the contract. "An acceptance which requests a change or addition to the terms of the offer is not thereby invalidated unless the acceptance is made to depend on an assent to the changed or added terms." Restatement of the Law 2d, Contracts, (1981), Formation of Informal Contract[s], Section 6[1]. HSBC's acceptance of Bergey's offer was not made to depend upon Bergey's assent to the "addendums and instructions[.]" HSBC's acceptance, via Jones, was not a conditional acceptance. HSBC accepted Bergey's offer.

HSBC and Jones further argue that Bergey's offer was never accepted under the terms of the offer itself. They pointed the trial court to the section of the offer entitled "Acceptance" with blanks for the seller's signature, address, phone number, date, etc. They contend that "[a]ccording to the Offer's own terms, it became a legally binding contract only upon acceptance in writing. * * * The 'Acceptance' section is blank, and has not been completed by HSBC." Therefore, according to HSBC, there was no valid acceptance. It appears that HSBC and Jones contend that the only manner of acceptance, pursuant to the terms of the offer, was to fill in the blanks in the offer form. We do not agree.

"[T]he general rule is that, where an offer prescribes the place, time, or manner of acceptance, those terms must be strictly complied with by the offeree (here, the buyer)." * * * Here, Bergey's offer prescribed that the acceptance must be in writing ("Upon written acceptance and then either written or verbal notice of such acceptance to the last-offering party, this offer and any addenda listed below shall become a LEGALLY BINDING AGREEMENT UPON BUYER AND SELLER"). It did not, however, prescribe *how* that written acceptance was to be made. In other words, the terms did not require HSBC to fill in the blank "Acceptance" section of the offer in order to constitute a written acceptance. By stating in writing that HSBC, through its agent, accepted Bergey's offer, HSBC complied with the term of Bergey's offer requiring the acceptance to be in writing. HSBC, Jones, and the trial court's reliance upon the fact that the "Acceptance" section of the offer was blank is therefore without merit

We conclude that, as a matter of law, HSBC accepted Bergey's offer in writing. Accordingly, the trial court erred when it granted summary judgment, concluding that HSBC did not accept Bergey's offer.

UNIFORM COMMERCIAL CODE § 2–206(1)(a).

(1) Unless otherwise unambiguously indicated by the language or circumstances

(a) an offer to make a contract shall be construed as inviting acceptance in any manner and by any medium reasonable in the circumstances.

RESTATEMENT (SECOND) OF CONTRACTS § 32.

Invitation of Promise or Performance

In case of doubt an offer is interpreted as inviting the offeree to accept either by promising to perform what the offer requests or by rendering the performance, as the offeree chooses.

WHITE V. CORLIES

New York Court of Appeals, 1871.
46 N.Y. 467.

Appeal from judgment of the General Term of the first judicial district, affirming a judgment entered upon a verdict for plaintiff.

The action was for an alleged breach of contract.

The plaintiff was a builder, with his place of business in Fortieth street, New York city.

The defendants were merchants at 32 Dey street.

In September, 1865, the defendants furnished the plaintiff with specifications, for fitting up a suit of offices at 57 Broadway, and requested him to make an estimate of the cost of doing the work.

On September twenty-eighth the plaintiff left his estimate with the defendants, and they were to consider upon it, and inform the plaintiff of their conclusions.

On the same day the defendants made a change in their specifications and sent a copy of the same, so changed, to the plaintiff for his assent under his estimate, which he assented to by signing the same and returning it to the defendants.

On the day following the defendants' book-keeper wrote the plaintiff the following note:

"New York, *September 29th.*

"*Upon an agreement* to finish the fitting up of offices 57 Broadway in two weeks from date, you can begin at once.

"The writer will call again, probably between five and six this P.M.

"W.H.R.,
"For J.W. Corlies & Co.,
"32 Dey street."

No reply to this note was ever made by the plaintiff; and on the next day the same was countermanded by a second note from the defendants.

Immediately on receipt of the note of September twenty-ninth, and before the countermand was forwarded, the plaintiff commenced a performance by the purchase of lumber and beginning work thereon.

And after receiving the countermand, the plaintiff brought this action for damages for a breach of contract.

The court charged the jury as follows: "From the contents of this note which the plaintiff received, was it his duty to go down to Dey street (meaning to give notice of assent), before commencing the work?"

"In my opinion it was not. He had a right to act upon this note and commence the job, *and that was a binding contract between the parties.*"

To this defendants excepted.

* * *

FOLGER, J. We do not think that the jury found, or that the testimony shows, that there was any agreement between the parties, before the written communication of the defendants of September thirtieth was received by the plaintiff. This note did not make an agreement. It was a proposition, and must have been accepted by the plaintiff before either party was bound, in contract, to the other. The only overt action which is claimed by the plaintiff as indicating on his part an acceptance of the offer, was the purchase of the stuff necessary for the work, and commencing work, as we understand the testimony, upon that stuff.

We understand the rule to be, that where an offer is made by one party to another when they are not together, the acceptance of it by that other must be manifested by some appropriate act. It does not need that the acceptance shall come to the knowledge of the one making the offer before he shall be bound. But though the manifestation need not be brought to his knowledge before he becomes bound, he is not bound, if that manifestation is not put in a proper way to be in the usual course of events, in some reasonable time communicated to him. Thus a letter received by mail containing a proposal, may be answered by letter by mail, containing the acceptance. And in general, as soon as the answering letter is mailed, the contract is concluded. Though one party does not know of the acceptance, the manifestation thereof is put in the proper way of reaching him.

In the case in hand, the plaintiff determined to accept. But a mental determination not indicated by speech, or put in course of indication by act to the other party, is not an acceptance which will bind the other. Nor does an act, which, in itself, is no indication of an acceptance, become such, because accompanied by an unevinced mental determination. Where the act uninterpreted by concurrent evidence of the mental purpose accompanying it, is as well referable to one state of facts as another, it is no indication to the other party of an acceptance, and does not operate to hold him to his offer.

Conceding that the testimony shows, that the plaintiff did resolve to accept this offer, he did no act which indicated an acceptance of it to the defendants. He, a carpenter and builder, purchased stuff for the work. But it was stuff as fit for any other like work. He began work upon the stuff, but as he would have done for any other like work. There was nothing in his thought formed but not uttered, or in his acts that indicated or set in motion an indication to the defendants of his acceptance of their offer, or which could necessarily result therein.

But the charge of the learned judge was fairly to be understood by the jury as laying down the rule to them, that the plaintiff need not indicate to the defendants his acceptance of their offer; and that the purchase of stuff and working on it after receiving the note, made a binding contract between the parties. In this we think the learned judge fell into error.

* * *

Judgment reversed, and new trial ordered.

KNUTSON v. SIRIUS XM RADIO, INC., 771 F.3d 559 (9th Cir. 2014). [The purchaser of a Toyota that came with Sirius XM radio received a Sirius XM consumer agreement one month after purchasing the car. One issue was whether the consumer agreement was enforceable.] Sirius XM argues * * * that although there was a delay between the activation of the service and Knutson's receipt of the Customer Agreement, Knutson's continued use of its service after that receipt constituted his assent to be bound to the Customer Agreement. Sirius XM cites *Golden Eagle Ins. Co. v. Foremost Ins. Co.,* which states that "[a]s a general rule, silence or inaction does not constitute acceptance of an offer. There are several well-recognized exceptions to this rule. Acceptance of an offer may be inferred from inaction in the face of a duty to act . . . and from retention of the benefit offered." 20 Cal.App.4th 1372, 1385–86, 25 Cal.Rptr.2d 242 (1993) (citations omitted); *see also* Cal. Civ.Code § 1589 ("A voluntary acceptance of the benefit of a transaction is equivalent to a consent to all the obligations arising from it, so far as the facts are known, or ought to be known, to the person accepting.").

Nothing in the record, however, indicates that Sirius XM's offer was clearly and effectively communicated to Knutson by mailing him the Customer Agreement. Knutson would only have had notice of his opportunity to cancel his subscription, or the effect of his continued use of the service, if he opened the Welcome Kit from Sirius and read all of the documents therein, which—in view of his lack of awareness of any contractual relationship with Sirius—he had no reason to do. He could not be obligated to act where there was no effective notice that action was required. Accordingly, Knutson's continued use of the service after his receipt of the Customer Agreement did not manifest his assent to the provisions in the Customer Agreement.

PROBLEM 4-9

On April 1, Edgar receives a Mozart album in the mail, sent by Nifty Records, with an attached cover letter stating: "We hereby offer you these records at the bargain price of $21. Please remit payment by the end of the month to our business office noted above." Edgar opens the package and letter and plays one piece, Mozart's 21st piano concerto (Rubinstein). Thereafter Edgar, dissatisfied with the rendition, puts the record to one side and forgets about it. What are Nifty Records' rights, if any, under the Restatement (Second) and U.S. Code sections set forth below? What if the album had arrived by United Parcel Service?

RESTATEMENT (SECOND) OF CONTRACTS § 69.

Acceptance by Silence or Exercise of Dominion

(1) Where an offeree fails to reply to an offer, his silence and inaction operate as an acceptance in the following cases only:

(a) Where an offeree takes the benefit of offered services with reasonable opportunity to reject them and reason to know that they were offered with the expectation of compensation.

(b) Where the offeror has stated or given the offeree reason to understand that assent may be manifested by silence or inaction, and the offeree in remaining silent and inactive intends to accept the offer.

(c) Where because of previous dealings or otherwise, it is reasonable that the offeree should notify the offeror if he does not intend to accept.

(2) An offeree who does any act inconsistent with the offeror's ownership of offered property is bound in accordance with the offered terms unless they are manifestly unreasonable. But if the act is wrongful as against the offeror it is an acceptance only if ratified by him.

39 U.S.C. § 3009 (2006).

Mailing of Unordered Merchandise

(a) Except for (1) free samples clearly and conspicuously marked as such, and (2) merchandise mailed by a charitable organization soliciting contributions, the mailing of unordered merchandise * * * constitutes an unfair method of competition and an unfair trade practice * * *.

(b) Any merchandise mailed in violation of subsection (a) of this section, or within the exceptions contained therein, may be treated as a gift by the recipient, who shall have the right to retain, use, discard, or dispose of it in any manner he sees fit without any obligation whatsoever to the sender. All such merchandise shall have attached to it a clear and conspicuous statement informing the recipient that he may treat the merchandise as a gift to him and has the right to retain, use, discard, or dispose of it in any manner he sees fit without any obligation whatsoever to the sender.

(c) No mailer of any merchandise mailed in violation of subsection (a) of this section, or within the exceptions contained therein, shall mail to any recipient of such merchandise a bill for such merchandise or any dunning communications.

(d) For the purposes of this section, "unordered merchandise" means merchandise mailed without the prior expressed request or consent of the recipient.

NOTE:
INDEPENDENT SIGNIFICANCE OF AGREEMENT AND CONSIDERATION

What is the relation between agreement and consideration? Reflect on the remarks of Professor Patterson:

> Wherein does the requirement of "agreement" by the promisee differ from the requirement of "consideration"? * * * It does seem that the promisee's manifested assent to accept a gift from the promisor does not constitute an "agreement" in Anglo-American law, and probably not in some other legal systems. At all events it does not constitute a "consideration." Aside from this case it is hard to think of a case in which the promisee has "agreed" to anything unless he has given consideration. Possibly such a case is the one in which a father promised to discharge his son's obligation on a promissory note in return for the son's agreeing not to importune his father any more. However, an English court held the father's promise unenforceable on the ground that the father and son did not at the time intend to create a legal obligation. While the decision seems questionable, it may be taken to mean that there was no agreement, or no *exchange* of promise for promise. It has recently been argued that the English

doctrine of consideration is merely another aspect of the requirement of offer and acceptance. * * * (Patterson, An Apology for Consideration, 58 Colum.L.Rev. 929, 944 (1958).)

SECTION SEVEN: DURATION OF OFFERS

RESTATEMENT (SECOND) OF CONTRACTS § 36.

Methods of Termination of the Power of Acceptance

(1) An offeree's power of acceptance may be terminated by

(a) rejection or counter-offer by the offeree, or

(b) lapse of time, or

(c) revocation by the offeror, or

(d) death or incapacity of the offeror or offeree.

(2) In addition, an offeree's power of acceptance is terminated by the non-occurrence of any condition of acceptance under the terms of the offer.

AKERS V. J.B. SEDBERRY, INC.

Court of Appeals of Tennessee, 1955.
39 Tenn. App. 633, 286 S.W.2d 617.

FELTS, JUDGE.

These two consolidated causes are before us upon a writ of error sued out by J.B. Sedberry, Inc., and Mrs. M.B. Sedberry, defendants below, to review a decree of the Chancery Court, awarding a recovery against them in favor of each of the complainants, Charles William Akers and William Gambill Whitsitt, for damages for breach of a contract of employment.

The principal question presented is whether complainants resigned their employment, or were wrongfully discharged by defendants; and if there was a breach of contract for which complainants are entitled to recover, there are some further questions as to the measure or extent of the recovery.

J.B. Sedberry, Inc., was a Tennessee corporation with its principal place of business at Franklin, Tennessee. Mrs. M.B. Sedberry owned practically all of its stock and was its president and in active charge of its affairs. It was engaged in the business of distributing "Jay Bee" hammer mills, which were manufactured for it under contract by Jay Bee Manufacturing Company, a Texas corporation, whose plant was in Tyler, Texas, and whose capital stock was owned principally by L.M. Glasgow and B.G. Byars.

On July 1, 1947, J.B. Sedberry, Inc., by written contract, employed complainant Akers as Chief Engineer for a term of five years at a salary of

$12,000 per year, payable $1,000 per month, plus 1% of its net profits for the first year, 2% the second, 3% the third, 4% the fourth, and 5% the fifth year. His duties were to carry on research for his employer, and to see that the Jay Bee Manufacturing Company, Tyler, Texas, manufactured the mills and parts according to proper specifications. Mrs. M.B. Sedberry guaranteed the employer's performance of this contract.

On August 1, 1947, J.B. Sedberry, Inc., by written contract, employed complainant Whitsitt as Assistant Chief Engineer for a term of five years at a salary of $7,200 per year, payable $600 per month, plus 1% of the corporation's net profits for the first year, 2% for the second, 3% for the third, 4% for the fourth, and 5% for the fifth year. His duties were to assist in the work done by the Chief Engineer. Mrs. M.B. Sedberry guaranteed the employer's performance of this contract.

Under Mrs. Sedberry's instructions, Akers and Whitsitt moved to Tyler, Texas, began performing their contract duties in the plant of the Jay Bee Manufacturing Company, continued working there, and were paid under the contracts until October 1, 1950, when they ceased work, under circumstances hereafter stated.

In 1947, when these employment contracts were made, Mrs. Sedberry owned no stock in the Jay Bee Manufacturing Company. In 1948 she purchased the shares of stock in this company which were owned by the Glasgow interests, and in 1949 she purchased the 750 shares owned by her brother, B.G. Byars, and gave him her note therefor in the sum of $157,333.93, pledging the 750 shares with him as collateral to her note.

Glasgow had been general manager of the Jay Bee Manufacturing Company, but when he sold his stock, he was succeeded by A.M. Sorenson as manager. There soon developed considerable friction between Sorenson and complainants Akers and Whitsitt. The Jay Bee Manufacturing Company owed large sums to the Tyler State Bank & Trust Co.; and the bank's officers, fearing the company might fail under Sorenson's management, began talking to Akers and Whitsitt about the company's financial difficulties.

One of the bank's vice-presidents, J. Harold Stringer, made a trip to Franklin to see Mrs. Sedberry about the company's indebtedness to the bank. He told her that they could not get along with Sorenson and did not agree with the way he was managing the company's affairs. Mrs. Sedberry asked Stringer as soon as he got back to Tyler to see Akers and Whitsitt and discuss with them plans for the refinancing and the operation of the company; and thereafter the bank's officers had a number of conferences with Akers and Whitsitt about these matters.

While these matters were pending, Akers and Whitsitt flew to Nashville and went to Franklin to talk with Mrs. Sedberry about them. They had a conference with her at her office on Friday, September 29, 1950, lasting from 9:30 a.m. until 4:30 p.m. As they had come unannounced, and unknown to Sorenson, they felt Mrs. Sedberry might mistrust them; and at the outset, to show their good faith, they offered to resign, but she did not accept their offer. Instead, she proceeded with them in discussing the operation and refinancing of the business.

Testifying about this conference, Akers said that, at the very beginning, to show their good faith, he told Mrs. Sedberry that they would offer their resignations on a ninety-day notice, provided they were paid according to the contract for that period; that she pushed the offers aside—"would not accept them", but went into a full discussion of the business; that nothing was thereafter said about the offers to resign; and that they spent the whole day discussing the business. Akers making notes of things she instructed him to do when he got back to Texas.

Whitsitt testified that at the beginning of the meeting Akers stated the position for both of them, and told Mrs. Sedberry, as evidence of their good faith, "we would resign with ninety-days notice if she paid us the monies that she owed us to that date, and on the other hand, if she did not accept that resignation, we would carry forth the rest of our business." He said that she did not accept the offer, but proceeded with the business, and nothing further was said about resigning.

Mrs. Sedberry testified that Akers and Whitsitt came in and "offered their resignations"; that they said they could not work with Sorenson and did not believe the bank would go along with him; and that "they said if it would be of any help to the organization they would be glad to tender their resignation and pay them what was due them." She further said that she "did not accept the resignation", that she "felt it necessary to contact Mr. Sorenson and give consideration to the resignation offer." But she said nothing to complainants about taking the offer under consideration.

On cross-examination she said that in the offer to resign "no mention was made of any ninety-day notice". Asked what response she made to the offer she said, "I treated it rather casually because I had to give it some thought and had to contact Mr. Sorenson." She further said she excused herself from the conference with complainants, went to another room, tried to telephone Sorenson in Tyler, Texas, but was unable to locate him.

She then resumed the conference, nothing further was said about the offers to resign, nothing was said by her to indicate that she thought the offers were left open or held under consideration by her. But the discussion proceeded as if the offers had not been made. She discussed with complainants future plans for refinancing and operating the business, giving them instructions, and Akers making notes of them.

Following the conference, complainants, upon Mrs. Sedberry's request, flew back to Texas to proceed to carry out her instructions. * * *

On Monday, October 2, 1950, Mrs. Sedberry sent to complainants similar telegrams, signed by "J.B. Sedberry, Inc., by M.B. Sedberry, President", stating that their resignations were accepted, effective immediately. We quote the telegram to Akers, omitting the formal parts:

> "Account present unsettled conditions which you so fully are aware we accept your kind offer of resignation effective immediately. Please discontinue as of today with everyone employed in Sedberry, Inc., Engineering Department, discontinuing all expenses in this department writing."

While this said she was "writing", she did not write. * * *

* * * Akers (then wrote) that he was amazed to get her telegram, and called her attention to the fact that no offer to resign by him was open or outstanding when she sent the telegram; that while he had made a conditional offer to resign at their conference on September 29, she had immediately rejected the offer, and had discussed plans for the business and had instructed him and Whitsitt as to things she wanted them to do in the business on their return to Tyler.

This letter further stated that Akers was expecting to be paid according to the terms of his contract until he could find other employment that would pay him as much income as that provided in his contract, and that if he had to accept a position with less income, he would expect to be paid the difference, or whatever losses he suffered by her breach of the contract. Whitsitt's letter contained a similar statement of his position.

On November 10, 1950, Mrs. Sedberry wrote a letter addressed to both Akers and Whitsitt in which she said that "no one deplored the action taken more than the writer", but she did not recede from her position as expressed in the telegram. She stated her contention that the offers to resign had been without condition; and though she also said she would like to make an amicable settlement, no settlement was made.

As it takes two to make a contract, it takes two to unmake it. It cannot be changed or ended by one alone, but only by mutual assent of both parties. A contract of employment for a fixed period may be terminated by the employee's offer to resign, provided such offer is duly accepted by the employer. * * *

An employee's tender of his resignation, being a mere offer is, of course, not binding until it has been accepted by the employer. Such offer must be accepted according to its terms and within the time fixed. The matter is governed by the same rules as govern the formation of contracts. * * *

An offer may be terminated in a number of ways, as, for example, where it is rejected by the offeree, or where it is not accepted by him within the time fixed, or, if no time is fixed, within a reasonable time. An offer terminated in either of these ways ceases to exist and cannot thereafter be accepted. * * *

The question what is a reasonable time, where no time is fixed, is a question of fact, depending on the nature of the contract proposed, the usages of business and other circumstances of the case. Ordinarily, an offer made by one to another in a face to face conversation is deemed to continue only to the close of their conversation, and cannot be accepted thereafter.

The rule is illustrated by Restatement of Contracts, section 40, Illustration 2, as follows:

> "2. While A and B are engaged in conversation, A makes B an offer to which B then makes no reply, but a few hours later meeting A again, B states that he accepts the offer. There is no contract unless the offer or the surrounding circumstances indicate that the offer is intended to continue beyond the immediate conversation."

* * *

Professor Corbin says:

> "When two negotiating parties are in each other's presence, and one makes an offer to the other without indicating any time for acceptance, the inference that will ordinarily be drawn by the other party is that an answer is expected at once. * * * If, when the first reply is not an acceptance, the offeror turns away in silence, the proper inference is that the offer is no longer open to acceptance." 1 Corbin on Contracts (1950), section 36, p. 111.

The only offer by Akers and Whitsitt to resign was the offer made by them in their conversation with Mrs. Sedberry. They made that offer at the outset, and on the evidence it seems clear that they expected an answer at once. Certainly, there is nothing in the evidence to show that they intended the offer to continue beyond that conversation; and on the above authorities, we think the offer did not continue beyond that meeting.

Indeed, it did not last that long, in our opinion, but was terminated by Mrs. Sedberry's rejection of it very early in that meeting. While she did not expressly reject it, and while she may have intended, as she says, to take the offer under consideration, she did not disclose such an intent to complainants; but, by her conduct, led them to believe she rejected the offer, brushed it aside, and proceeded with the discussion as if it had not been made.

> "An offer is rejected when the offeror is justified in inferring from the words or conduct of the offeree that the offeree intends not to accept the offer or to take it under further advisement (Rest. Contracts sec. 36)." 1 Williston on Contracts, section 51.

So, we agree with the Trial Judge that when defendants sent the telegrams, undertaking to accept offers of complainants to resign, there was no such offer in existence; and that this attempt of defendants to terminate their contract was unlawful and constituted a breach for which they are liable to complainants. * * *

* * *

Finally, defendants contend that if complainants are entitled to any recovery at all, such recovery should have been limited to the ninety-day period from and after October 2, 1950, because complainants themselves admitted that they had offered to resign upon ninety days notice with pay for that period.

The answer to this contention is that their offer to resign on ninety days notice was not accepted, but had terminated, and there was no offer in existence when Mrs. Sedberry undertook to accept their offers of resignation. Such attempt by defendants to terminate their contract was unlawful and was a breach for which they become liable for the measure of recovery as above stated.

* * *

All of the assignments of error are overruled and the decree of the Chancellor is affirmed. * * * The causes are remanded to the Chancery Court for further proceedings not inconsistent with this opinion.

E. FARNSWORTH, CONTRACTS

160 (4th ed. 2004).

Rejection by the offeree terminates the power of acceptance. If a seller offers to deliver goods to a buyer for $10,000, and the buyer replies, "I don't want your goods," the buyer's power of acceptance is terminated—the buyer cannot later accept. (If the buyer tried to, the purported acceptance might itself be an offer to the seller.) The rationale is that the offeror may rely on the rejection, by action (such as selling the goods elsewhere) or by inaction (such as failing to prepare to deliver them) or by merely failing to revoke the offer. The possibility of reliance is enough, and no actual reliance is required. * * * Rejection has this effect even though the offerer has fixed a longer time after which the offer lapses.

VASKIE V. WEST AMERICAN INSURANCE CO.

Superior Court of Pennsylvania, 1989.
383 Pa. Super. 76, 556 A.2d 436.

BECK, JUDGE.

This is an appeal from a grant of summary judgment in favor of plaintiff-appellee Anne Marie Vaskie in her breach of contract action against defendant-appellant West American Insurance Company.

On January 1, 1985, Ms. Vaskie was involved in an automobile accident with a vehicle owned and operated by persons who were insured by West American. Ms. Vaskie retained Harold Murnane, Esquire, to represent her in connection with obtaining recovery for the personal injuries she sustained as a result of this accident. At some point prior to December 1986 Mr. Murnane and West American began negotiations aimed at settling Ms. Vaskie's claim. The parties' correspondence reveals that as of November 1986, West American had offered $25,000. Apparently after continuing negotiations by telephone, on December 1, 1986 West American addressed a letter to Mr. Murnane which concluded by stating that West American had carefully reviewed Ms. Vaskie's claim and that West American's "offer will remain $25,000." This letter did not specify a date on which the offer would terminate. On January 9, 1987, Mr. Murnane sent a mailgram to West American in which he, on behalf of Ms. Vaskie, unconditionally accepted West American's $25,000 offer.

West American refused to pay, arguing that there was no contract between the parties because the statute of limitations on Ms. Vaskie's personal injury claim had run on January 1, 1987, eight days before she accepted West American's offer.

Ms. Vaskie then instituted this suit for breach of the alleged settlement agreement. Both parties filed motions for summary judgment. The trial court granted Ms. Vaskie's motion, awarding her $25,000, and denied West American's motion.

West American appealed, arguing alternatively that either judgment should have been entered in its favor or that at a minimum factual disputes requiring resolution by a jury should have prevented the entry of summary judgment for Ms. Vaskie. Ms. Vaskie cross-appealed solely on the ground that the trial court erred in failing to award her pre-judgment interest and costs.

On review of a grant of summary judgment, we must remain mindful that summary judgment is appropriate only where, viewing all the facts in the light most favorable to the non-moving party and resolving all doubts as to the existence of issues of material fact against the moving party, the moving party is nevertheless entitled to judgment as a matter of law. *Mariscotti v. Tinari,* 335 Pa.Super. 599, 485 A.2d 56 (1984).

The central question to be decided is whether the parties entered into an enforceable contract for the payment of $25,000 to Ms. Vaskie in exchange for her relinquishment of her claim for damages for personal injuries. On their face, the facts reveal just such an agreement. West American made a written unconditional offer to pay $25,000 to settle Ms. Vaskie's claim and Ms. Vaskie responded with a written unconditional acceptance, thereby indicating her willingness to accept $25,000 in exchange for her surrender of her claim and forbearance from suing thereon.

However, West American offers several possible impediments to enforcing this apparent agreement. First, West American argues that no agreement was formed by Ms. Vaskie's acceptance because the offer had lapsed as a matter of law when the statute of limitations on personal injury claims, i.e. two years, had expired. As a variation on this theme, West American argues that there is at least a factual issue as to whether the offer had lapsed by the time of Ms. Vaskie's acceptance. Since the offer itself did not specify an expiration date, West American argues that the offer is legally deemed to expire within a reasonable time and what is a reasonable time is a factual question. * * *

There is no doubt on this record that West American made an offer of $25,000 to settle Ms. Vaskie's claim in a letter dated December 1, 1986. There is also no doubt that this offer did not contain any express expiration date. Moreover, there were no further oral or written communications between the parties in which any expiration date was set, nor was the offer ever withdrawn. Under such circumstances, i.e. where an offer does not specify an expiration date or otherwise limit the allowable time for acceptance, it is both hornbook law and well established in Pennsylvania that the offer is deemed to be outstanding for a reasonable period of time. * * * What is a reasonable time is ordinarily a question of fact to be decided by the jury and is dependent upon the numerous circumstances surrounding the transaction. * * * Such circumstances as the nature of the contract, the relationship or situation of the parties and their course of dealing, and usages of the particular business are all relevant. * * *

However, there are situations where the question of what is a reasonable time for acceptance may be decided by the court as a matter of law. As stated in *Boyd* [*v. Merchants and Farmers Peanut Co.*, 25 Pa.Super. 199 (1904)]:

> What is a reasonable time for acceptance is a question of law for the court in such commercial transactions as happen in the same way, day after day, and present the question upon the same data in continually recurring instances; and where the time taken is so clearly reasonable or unreasonable that there can be no question of doubt as to the proper answer to the question. Where the

> answer to the question is one dependent on many different circumstances, which do not continually recur in other cases of like character, and with respect to which no certain rule of law could be laid down, the question is one of fact for the jury.

Boyd, 25 Pa.Super. at 205.

The trial court in the instant matter decided that this was a case where the issue of reasonableness could be decided as a matter of law and found that Ms. Vaskie's acceptance on January 9, 198[7] was tendered within a reasonable time.

We reject West American's contention that its offer of December 1, 1986 lapsed as a matter of law two years after Ms. Vaskie suffered her injuries. However, we do agree with West American insofar as it argues that the trial court erred in deciding as a matter of law that Ms. Vaskie's acceptance was tendered within a reasonable time. We find that under the circumstances of this case, the question of reasonableness is a disputed material issue of fact that should not have been resolved as a matter of law on summary judgment.

There is no merit in the argument that offers of settlement of personal injury claims automatically terminate two years after the injuries were sustained. West American has offered no precedent that so holds, we have located none and the reasons for the dearth of authority supporting such an argument are clear. First, the argument is based on the incorrect assumption that in every personal injury case the statute of limitations will run precisely two years from the date of the accident. In fact, the statute may be tolled due to the inability of the plaintiff to discover his or her injuries or their cause, *Pocono International Raceway, Inc. v. Pocono Produce, Inc.*, 503 Pa. 80, 86, 468 A.2d 468, 471 (1983), or due to fraud or concealment of material information by the defendant. *Molineux v. Reed,* 516 Pa. 398, 532 A.2d 792, 794 (1987). Thus, in each particular case the date on which the statute would be deemed to have run may vary. Given this variation, we cannot fashion a rule that creates an implied-in-law termination date, fixed on the expiration of the statute of limitations, in all settlement offers. To do so would leave the plaintiff-offeree in the untenable position of having to predict and, for purposes of settlement negotiations, accept the defendant-offeror's view of when the statute should be deemed to have run.

Moreover, to hold that every such offer contains an implied-in-law termination date would be to dictate a term of such offers which the parties themselves can and should decide upon. If an offering defendant wishes to limit the duration of his offer to a certain time, whether a date two years from the accident or otherwise, he need only so state in the offer itself. He is the master of his offer. There is no need for us to provide such a term where, as here, the defendant has not done so.

This is not to say, however, that the passing of the statute of limitations is irrelevant to a determination of whether an offer of settlement of a personal injury claim has been accepted within a reasonable time. The reasonableness of the time an offeree takes to accept an offer is measured from the perspective of the offeree. As the explanatory comment to the pertinent section of the Restatement (Second) of Contracts states:

> In general, the question is what time would be thought satisfactory to the offeror by a reasonable man in the position of the offeree. * * *

Restatement (Second) of Contracts, § 41 comment b (1981).

The fact that the statute of limitations may already have run by the time Ms. Vaskie accepted is unquestionably relevant to a determination of the reasonableness of her conduct in waiting until January 9, 1987 to accept. Further, this is only one of many circumstances surrounding the parties' negotiations and the status of Ms. Vaskie's claim that may be relevant to a determination of reasonableness. This is certainly not a case such as that described above in *Boyd* where the reasonableness question can be decided as a matter of law. It is not a commercial transaction continually occurring in like manner day after day. The course and nature of settlement negotiations varies greatly from case to case. This is very unlike the situation of a merchant who offers goods for sale on a daily basis at a price that changes daily, where it is clear beyond cavil that an offer made at one day's price is not intended to continue to the next day. In settlement negotiations the reasonable duration of an offer is not fixed at a particular time because of clear and uniform courses of dealing and usages of the trade that invariably arise from the very nature of the transaction.

Thus, we conclude that the trial court erred in holding that Ms. Vaskie's January 9th acceptance was tendered within a time that was reasonable as a matter of law. Therefore, the entry of summary judgment in Ms. Vaskie's favor was in error on this ground.

* * *

The judgment is reversed. Jurisdiction is relinquished.

BRIEF OF WEST AMERICAN INSURANCE CO. IN THE SUPERIOR COURT OF PENNSYLVANIA.

It was completely unreasonable for the Court below to implicitly require the Defendant to hold open its settlement offer after the Statute of Limitations had expired for the commencement of a personal injury action against its insured. In other words, although the Defendant's settlement offer did not specify a time for acceptance, the nature of the proposed settlement agreement, the purposes of the parties thereto, and the relevant usages of trade all dictate that Plaintiff's counsel could not have reasonably expected that the settlement offer would be held open after the expiration of the Statute of Limitations, unless a timely action for Plaintiff's personal injuries had been commenced.

DEPOSITION OF PLAINTIFF'S LAWYER BY WEST AMERICAN INSURANCE CO.

Q. You further indicated that your understanding at all times relevant to your representation of Anne Marie Vaskie that you were aware that an action against the Krenitskys would have to be brought within two years after the date of the accident?

A. Under ordinary circumstances.

Q. So, therefore, wasn't it, in fact, the case that an action—

A. Let me just interrupt you. You're not, I don't believe, cross-examining me. You're starting your question by telling me, was it not a fact. Why don't you ask me a question instead of stating facts unless these are additional premises in the question that you're going to ask me.

Q. Let me ask the question, and maybe you can answer it.

Isn't it, then, a fact under what you've just said, under ordinary circumstances, that any lawsuit to be brought on behalf of Anne Marie Vaskie against the Krenitskys should have been brought on or before January 1 of '87?

THE WITNESS: I don't think that's an appropriate question. I think the question is objectionable. You know, I think, as I said before, if you want to make that conclusion, the Superior Court of the State of Pennsylvania does not agree with you; and they've already ruled so in this case.

So I'm certainly not going to answer a question that they've already made a decision on that requires a legal conclusion, that they're the ones that are charged with making that conclusion * * *.

* * *

Q. I'm asking you what was your belief, as her counsel, as to what actions, if any, you should have taken to conclude the acceptance on or before January 1 of '87?

A. It was my belief that there was an offer of $25,000 that would remain. And, as a matter of fact, there was a discussion—and I don't know precisely when that discussion took place—at some time between Mr. Hudak and myself in the Fall of 1986. And I believe it was before the end of November of 1986 as to when the statute of limitations would run.

He specifically asked me, when does the statute run in this case, in one of those conversations. And there was no indication from Mr. Hudak in any conversation that we had or in any letter that was sent to me that the offer of $25,000 would not remain open for some period of time after January 1st of 1987.

So it was my belief that since my client wanted to accept the $25,000, that the offer should be accepted within a reasonable period of time, which it was.

NOTE:
STILL FURTHER ASPECTS OF VASKIE V. WEST AMERICAN INSURANCE CO.

In a letter to the editors, West American's lawyer wrote:

> Please be advised that this case was settled towards the end of 1989 for the sum of $15,000, in compromise of the full claim of $25,000. I believe that [plaintiff's lawyer] made up the remaining $10,000 to his client, Anne Marie Vaskie, who was also his cousin.
>
> * * * We have since advised West American and a number of our other insurance company clients that they should set a definite date when their settle-offers would expire, rather than leaving them open-ended, as was the case in the instant matter.

CALDWELL V. CLINE

Supreme Court of Appeals of West Virginia, 1930.
109 W. Va. 553, 156 S.E. 55.

LIVELY, P.

In this chancery suit for the specific performance for a contract for the sale and exchange of real estate, the chancellor sustained a demurrer to plaintiff's bill of complaint and dismissed the bill. Plaintiff appeals.

According to the allegations contained in the bill, W.D. Cline, residing at Valls Creek, McDowell county, W. Va., owner of a tract of land on Indian creek, McDowell county, addressed a letter, dated January 29, 1929, to W.H. Caldwell, at Peterstown, Monroe county, W. Va., in which Cline proposed to pay to Caldwell the sum of $6,000 cash and to deed to Caldwell his land on Indian creek in exchange for Caldwell's land known as the McKinsey farm. The letter further provided that Cline "will give you (Caldwell) eight days in which" to accept or reject the offer. Caldwell received the letter at Peterstown on February 2, 1929. On February 8, 1929, the offeree wired Cline as follows: "Land deal is made. Prepare deed to me. See letter." The telegram reached Cline on February 9, 1929. Upon Cline's refusal to carry out the terms of the alleged agreement, plaintiff instituted this suit for specific performance: the titles to the farms remaining unchanged.

* * *

Defendant's main contention is that the offer was not accepted within the time limit specified in the offer, and counsel for defendant, in his brief, states the law to be as "the time for acceptance runs from the date of the offer and not from the date of its delivery." * * * [C]ourts and text-writers have recognized the rule that, where a person uses the post to make an offer, the offer is not made when it is posted, but when it is received. * * * The reason for such a rule is clear. When contracting parties are present, words spoken by one party must strike the ear of the other before there can be mutual assent. So inter absentes, letters, which perform the office of words, must come to the knowledge of the party to whom they are addressed before they are accorded legal existence. "The distinction between contracts inter presentes and those inter absentes has no metaphysical existence, for even inter presentes some appreciable time must elapse between the offer on the one hand and the acceptance on the other. As the parties withdraw from each other this time increases, and when they are so far apart that they are obliged to resort to writing to communicate their thoughts to each other, it is none the less true of the communications made by this medium, than of those made by means of spoken words, that in law they are allowed no existence until they reach the intelligence of the person to whom they are addressed." 7 Amer.Law Rev. 434, 456.

* * *

The letter, proposing that Cline "will give you eight days" to accept or reject the offer, is, without more, conclusive of the offeror's intention; and, the unconditional acceptance having been received by Cline within the specified time limit, the result was a concurrence of the minds of the contracting parties upon the subject-matter of their negotiations; in other words, a consummated contract * * *.

* * *

Decree reversed; bill reinstated; cause remanded.

RESTATEMENT (SECOND) OF CONTRACTS § 39(2).

An offeree's power of acceptance is terminated by his making of a counter-offer, unless the offeror has manifested a contrary intention or unless the counter-offer manifests a contrary intention of the offeree.

NOTE:
COUNTER-OFFERS

Recall Ardente v. Horan. The court found that the purchaser's response to the sellers' offer of real estate was a counter-offer and not an acceptance because, according to the court, the purchaser indicated that he would not go through with the sale if he did not receive the dining room set and other items with the real estate. But the court noted that it is possible to accept and yet include a "request" dealing with additional matters. Consider also the following illustrative case, drawn from a rather special context:

COLLINS v. THOMPSON, 679 F.2d 168 (9th Cir. 1982). [The State of Washington proposed a consent decree to end litigation with inmates of the Washington State Reformatory over the appropriate population of the prison. The consent decree included the wrong date for initial reduction of the population (March 1, 1981) and the state therefore submitted on February 13, 1981, an amended decree including the correct date (April 1, 1981). The inmates moved for approval of the decree with the March 1, 1981 date, or alternatively, for a notice to the class of inmates reflecting the modification to the April 1 date. The magistrate denied both requests and found no contract in light of the absence of "a meeting of the minds" on the date for initial reduction. The inmates' appeal was denied. On May 15, 1981, the inmates filed a notice of acceptance of the offer of settlement with the April 1, 1981 date for initial reduction. Both the magistrate and the district court on appeal held that the inmates had not rejected the state's settlement offer with the April 1, 1981 date and the state had not revoked the offer. They therefore approved the consent decree. The state appealed.]

SKOPIL, C.J.

General contract principles apply to questions of interpretation of consent decrees. *United States v. ITT Continental Baking Co.,* 420 U.S. 223, 236–37, 95 S.Ct. 926, 934–35, 43 L.Ed.2d 148 (1975). * * * Questions regarding formation of consent decrees likewise are to be resolved by general contract principles. A consent decree is essentially an agreement of the parties to resolve their dispute, and the facets of agreement are analyzed by applying contract principles.

* * *

The state argues that the prisoners' actions in strenuously pursuing the enforcement of the proposed consent decree with the March 1, 1981 date constituted a rejection of the February 13, 1981 offer.

Generally, a rejection or counteroffer ordinarily terminates the power to accept the previously-made offer. 1 Jaeger, *Williston on Contracts* § 51 (3d ed. 1957); 1 Corbin, *Contracts* § 90 (1963 & Supp.1980). However,

> "The offeree [has] the power to prevent his counteroffer (or even a rejection) from terminating his power of acceptance. Suppose he should say: 'I am still considering your offer; but meantime I am now willing to buy the property you offer if you will reduce your price by $500.' There is no reason why this should lead the offeror into a change of position, or why it should operate to terminate the power of accepting the original offer still under consideration."

1 Corbin, *Contracts* § 92. The *Restatement* also agrees with the above contract principle:

> "A manifestation of intention not to accept an offer is a rejection *unless the offeree manifests an intention to take it under further advisement.*"
>
> *Restatement (Second) of Contracts* § 38 (1981) (emphasis added).

On February 26, 1981 the prisoners moved for either (1) approval of the consent decree with the March 1, 1981 date, or, in the alternative (2) a notice to the class to reflect the change in the decree to April 1, 1981.

The district court found that

> "The plaintiff's alternative motion on February 26, 1981 for a new notice to the class clearly indicated that the plaintiffs were not rejecting the entire settlement and that they fully intended settlement even if the date were the April 1st date."

There is sufficient evidence such that this finding cannot be held clearly erroneous. As stated above, the objective test is used to determine questions of contract formation. The February 26th motion would not clearly indicate to a reasonable person that the prisoners were rejecting the proposed settlement offer with the April 1st date. In point of fact, the prisoners in this motion specifically indicated they were still considering the April 1st date.

* * *

Affirmed.

DICKINSON v. DODDS, 2 Ch. Div. 463 (1876). [Dodds gave Dickinson a signed memo on Wednesday, June 10, 1874, offering to sell certain real estate "to Mr. George Dickinson." The memo included a postscript that read: "This offer to be left over until Friday, 9 o'clock a.m. J.D. (the twelfth), 12th June, 1874." The bill alleged that the plaintiff, Dickinson, decided to accept the offer on the morning of Thursday, the 11th of June, but did not at once signify his acceptance to Dodds, thinking he could do so until 9 a.m. on Friday. But later that Thursday afternoon, a Mr. Berry told Dickinson that Dodds "had been offering or agreeing to sell the property to Thomas

Allen." Thereafter Dickinson immediately attempted to communicate his acceptance to Dodds, who took the position that his offer had been revoked. Held, for Dodds.] "[I]t is said that the only mode in which Dodds could assert * * * [the power to revoke] was by actually and distinctly saying to Dickinson, 'Now I withdraw my offer.' It appears to me that there is neither principle nor authority [for that assertion] * * *. [I]n this case, beyond all question, the plaintiff knew that Dodds was no longer minded to sell the property to him."

J. DAWSON, GIFTS AND PROMISES

212–13 (1980).

[Dickinson v. Dodds] concluded with great confidence that a time limit fixed by the offeror could not prevent revocation before the time limit had expired, for in the absence of consideration any restriction on the power to revoke was simply *nudum pactum.* American decisions have dutifully followed this line ever since and thereby made the consideration test a still more prominent target of public ridicule * * *.

NOTE: THE OFFEROR'S POWER TO REVOKE

The approach of Dickinson v. Dodds is still generally followed today. See Restatement (Second) of Contracts § 42 ("An offeree's power of acceptance is terminated when the offeree receives from the offeror a manifestation of an intention not to enter into the proposed contract."). One explanation for this result is that a representation that an offer will remain open is a bare promise, unsupported by consideration, and therefore unenforceable. Another explanation, plausible at the time of decision, was that:

> An offer is merely one of the elements of a contract; and it is indispensable to the making of a contract that the wills of the contracting parties do, in legal contemplation, concur at the moment of making it. An offer, therefore, which the party making it has no power to revoke, is a legal impossibility.

Langdell, A Summary of the Law of Contracts, § 178 at 240 (2d ed. 1880).

We have seen in our study of the nature of mutual assent that contract law no longer adheres to Langdell's subjective will theory. In the following materials we will see a variety of devices utilized by courts to bar revocation of offers. In fact, in the 1464-Eight Ltd. & Millis v. Joppich case in Chapter 2, you already saw that courts enforce real estate options without consideration. You should consider why contract law has moved in this direction.

Note that the general rule, according to Restatement (Second) section 42, is that a revocation must be *received* before the offeree's power of acceptance is terminated. One exception to this rule is found in Shuey v. United States, 92 U.S. (2 Otto) 73 (1875). There, the U.S. War Department had published an offer of a reward of $25,000 for the apprehension of a criminal, but then revoked the offer through a similar publication. The claimant saw the reward offer but not the revocation. Five months after the revocation, the claimant, unaware of the withdrawal, gave information that led to the arrest of the criminal. The court held, *inter alia,* that the claimant was not entitled to recover because the revocation was effective. It had been given the same notoriety as the offer and "the offer of the reward not having been made to [the claimant] directly, but by means of a publicized proclamation, he should have known that it could be revoked in the manner in which it was made."

DAVIS V. JACOBY

Supreme Court of California, 1934.
1 Cal. 2d 370, 34 P.2d 1026.

PER CURIAM.

Plaintiffs appeal from a judgment refusing to grant specific performance of an alleged contract to make a will. The facts are not in dispute and are as follows:

The plaintiff Caro M. Davis was the niece of Blanche Whitehead, who was married to Rupert Whitehead. Prior to her marriage in 1913 to her coplaintiff Frank M. Davis, Caro lived for a considerable time at the home of the Whiteheads, in Piedmont, Cal. The Whiteheads were childless and extremely fond of Caro. The record is replete with uncontradicted testimony of the close and loving relationship that existed between Caro and her aunt and uncle. During the period that Caro lived with the Whiteheads, she was treated as and often referred to by the Whiteheads as their daughter. In 1913, when Caro was married to Frank Davis, the marriage was arranged at the Whitehead home and a reception held there. After the marriage Mr. and Mrs. Davis went to Mr. Davis' home in Canada, where they have resided ever since. During the period 1913 to 1931 Caro made many visits to the Whiteheads, several of them being of long duration. The Whiteheads visited Mr. and Mrs. Davis in Canada on several occasions. After the marriage and continuing down to 1931 the closest and most friendly relationship at all times existed between these two families. They corresponded frequently, the record being replete with letters showing the loving relationship.

By the year 1930 Mrs. Whitehead had become seriously ill. She had suffered several strokes and her mind was failing. Early in 1931 Mr. Whitehead had her removed to a private hospital. The doctors in attendance had informed him that she might die at any time or she might linger for many months. Mr. Whitehead had suffered severe financial reverses. He had had several sieges of sickness and was in poor health. The record shows that during the early part of 1931 he was desperately in need of assistance with his wife, and in his business affairs, and that he did not trust his friends in Piedmont. On March 18, 1931, he wrote to Mrs. Davis telling her of Mrs. Whitehead's condition and added that Mrs. Whitehead was very wistful. "Today I endeavored to find out what she wanted. I finally asked her if she wanted to see you. She burst out crying and we had great difficulty in getting her to stop. Evidently, that is what is on her mind. It is a very difficult matter to decide. If you come it will mean that you will have to leave again, and then things may be serious. I am going to see the doctor, and get his candid opinion and will then write you again. * * * Since writing the above, I have seen the doctor, and he thinks it will help considerably if you come." Shortly thereafter, Mr. Whitehead wrote to Caro Davis further explaining the physical condition of Mrs. Whitehead and himself. On March 24, 1931, Mr. Davis, at the request of his wife, telegraphed to Mr. Whitehead as follows: "Your letter received. Sorry to hear Blanche not so well. Hope you are feeling better yourself. If you wish Caro to go to you can arrange for her to leave in about two weeks. Please wire me if you think it advisable for her to go." On March 30, 1931, Mr. Whitehead wrote a long letter to Mr. Davis, in which he explained in detail the condition of Mrs. Whitehead's health and also referred to his own health. He pointed out that he had lost a considerable portion of his cash assets but still owned considerable realty, that he needed some one to help him with his wife and some friend he could trust to help him with his business affairs and suggested that perhaps Mr. Davis might come to California. He then pointed out that all his property was community property; that under his will all the property was to go to Mrs. Whitehead; that he believed that under Mrs. Whitehead's will practically everything was to go to Caro. Mr. Whitehead again wrote to Mr. Davis under date of April 9, 1931, pointing out how badly he needed some one he could trust to assist him, and giving it as his belief that if properly handled he could still save about $150,000. He then stated: "Having you [Mr. Davis] here to depend on and to help me regain my mind and courage would be a big thing." Three days later, on April 12, 1931, Mr. Whitehead again wrote, addressing his letter to "Dear Frank and Caro," and in this letter made the definite offer, which offer it is claimed was accepted and is the basis of this action. In this letter he first pointed out that Blanche, his wife, was in a private hospital and that "she cannot last much longer * * * my affairs are not as bad as I supposed at first. Cutting everything down I figure 150,000 can be saved from the wreck." He then enumerated the values placed upon his various properties and then continued:

"My trouble was caused by my friends taking advantage of my illness and my position to skin me.

"Now if Frank could come out here and be with me, and look after my affairs, we could easily save the balance I mention, provided I don't get into another panic and do some more foolish things.

"The next attack will be my end, I am 65 and my health has been bad for years, so, the Drs. dont give me much longer to live. So if you can come, Caro will inherit everything and you will make our lives happier and see Blanche is provided for to the end.

"My eyesight has gone back on me, I cant read only for a few lines at a time. I am at the house alone with Stanley [the chauffeur] who does everything for me and is a fine fellow. Now, what I want is some one who will take charge of my affairs and see I dont lose any more. Frank can do it, if he will and cut out the booze.

"Will you let me hear from you as soon as possible, I know it will be a sacrifice but times are still bad and likely to be, so by settling down you can help me and Blanche and gain in the end. If I had you here my mind would get better and my courage return, and we could work things out."

This letter was received by Mr. Davis at his office in Windsor, Canada, about 9:30 a.m. April 14, 1931. After reading the letter to Mrs. Davis over the telephone, and after getting her belief that they must go to California, Mr. Davis immediately wrote Mr. Whitehead a letter, which, after reading it to his wife, he sent by air mail. This letter was lost, but there is no doubt that it was sent by Davis and received by Whitehead; in fact, the trial court expressly so found. Mr. Davis testified in substance as to the contents of this letter. After acknowledging receipt of the letter of April 12, 1931, Mr. Davis unequivocally stated that he and Mrs. Davis accepted the proposition of Mr. Whitehead and both would leave Windsor to go to him on April 25. This letter of acceptance also contained the information that the reason they could not leave prior to April 25 was that Mr. Davis had to appear in court on April 22 as one of the executors of his mother's estate. The testimony is uncontradicted and ample to support the trial court's finding that this letter was sent by Davis and received by Whitehead. In fact, under date of April 15, 1931, Mr. Whitehead again wrote to Mr. Davis and stated:

"Your letter by air mail received this a.m. Now, I am wondering if I have put you to unnecessary trouble and expense, if you are making any money dont leave it, as things are bad here. * * * You know your business and I dont and I am half crazy in the bargain, but I dont want to hurt you or Caro.

"Then on the other hand if I could get some one to trust and keep me straight I can save a good deal, about what I told you in my former letter."

This letter was received by Mr. Davis on April 17, 1931, and the same day Mr. Davis telegraphed to Mr. Whitehead: "Cheer up—we will soon be there, we will wire you from the train."

Between April 14, 1931, the date the letter of acceptance was sent by Mr. Davis, and April 22, Mr. Davis was engaged in closing out his business affairs, and Mrs. Davis in closing up their home and in making other arrangements to leave. On April 22, 1931, Mr. Whitehead committed suicide. Mr. and Mrs. Davis were immediately notified and they at once came to California. From almost the moment of her arrival Mrs. Davis devoted herself to the care and comfort of her aunt, and gave her aunt constant attention and care until Mrs. Whitehead's death on May 30, 1931. * * *

* * * In fact the record shows that after their arrival in California Mr. and Mrs. Davis fully performed their side of the agreement.

After the death of Mrs. Whitehead, for the first time it was discovered that the information contained in Mr. Whitehead's letter of March 30, 1931, in reference to the contents of his and Mrs. Whitehead's wills was incorrect. By a duly witnessed will dated February 28, 1931, Mr. Whitehead, after making several specific bequests, had bequeathed all of the balance of his estate to his wife for life, and upon her death to respondents Geoff Doubble and Rupert Ross Whitehead, his nephews. Neither appellant was mentioned in his will. It was also discovered that Mrs. Whitehead by a will dated December 17, 1927, had devised all of her estate to her husband. The evidence is clear and uncontradicted that the relationship existing between Whitehead and his two nephews, respondents herein, was not nearly as close and confidential as that existing between Whitehead and appellants.

After the discovery of the manner in which the property had been devised was made, this action was commenced upon the theory that Rupert Whitehead had assumed a contractual obligation to make a will whereby "Caro Davis would inherit everything"; that he had failed to do so; that plaintiffs had fully performed their part of the contract; that damages being insufficient, quasi specific performance should be granted in order to remedy the alleged wrong, upon the equitable principle that equity regards that done which ought to have been done. The requested relief is that the beneficiaries under the will of Rupert Whitehead, respondents herein, be declared to be involuntary trustees for plaintiffs of Whitehead's estate.

It should also be added that the evidence shows that as a result of Frank Davis leaving his business in Canada he forfeited not only all insurance business he might have written if he had remained, but also forfeited all renewal commissions earned on past business. According to his testimony this loss was over $8,000.

* * *

The theory of the trial court and of respondents on this appeal is that the letter of April 12 was an offer to contract, but that such offer could only be accepted by performance and could not be accepted by a promise to perform, and that said offer was revoked by the death of Mr. Whitehead before performance. In other words, it is contended that the offer was an offer to enter into a unilateral contract, and that the purported acceptance of April 14 was of no legal effect.

The distinction between unilateral and bilateral contracts is well settled in the law. It is well stated in section 12 of the American Institute's Restatement of the Law of Contracts as follows: "A unilateral contract is one in which no promisor receives a promise as consideration for his promise. A bilateral contract is one in which there are mutual promises between two parties to the contract; each party being both a promisor and a promisee." This definition is in accord with the law of California. * * *

* * *

Although the legal distinction between unilateral and bilateral contracts is thus well settled, the difficulty in any particular case is to determine whether the particular offer is one to enter into a bilateral or unilateral contract. Some cases are quite clear cut. Thus an offer to sell which is accepted is clearly a bilateral contract, while an offer of a reward is a clear-cut offer of a unilateral contract which cannot be accepted by a promise to perform, but only by performance. * * * Between these two extremes is a vague field where the particular contract may be unilateral or bilateral depending upon the intent of the offer and the facts and circumstances of each case. The offer to contract involved in this case falls within this category. By the provisions of the Restatement of the Law of Contracts it is expressly provided that there is a *presumption* that the offer is to enter into a bilateral contract. Section 31 provides: "In case of doubt it is presumed that an offer invites the formation of a bilateral contract by an acceptance amounting in effect to a promise by the offeree to perform what the offer requests, rather than the formation of one or more unilateral contracts by actual performance on the part of the offeree."

Professor Williston, in his Treatise on Contracts, volume 1, § 60, also takes the position that a presumption in favor of bilateral contracts exists.

In the comment following section 31 of the Restatement the reason for such presumption is stated as follows: "It is not always easy to determine whether an offerer requests an act or a promise to do the act. As a bilateral contract immediately and fully protects both parties, the interpretation is favored that a bilateral contract is proposed."

* * *

Keeping these principles in mind, we are of the opinion that the offer of April 12 was an offer to enter into a bilateral as distinguished from a unilateral contract. Respondents argue that Mr. Whitehead had the right as offerer to designate his offer as either unilateral or bilateral. That is undoubtedly the law. It is then argued that from all the facts and circumstances it must be implied that what Whitehead wanted was performance and not a mere promise to perform. We think this is a non sequitur, in fact the surrounding circumstances lead to just the opposite conclusion. These parties were not dealing at arm's length. Not only were they related, but a very close and intimate friendship existed between them. The record indisputably demonstrates that Mr. Whitehead had confidence in Mr. and Mrs. Davis, in fact that he had lost all confidence in every one else. The record amply shows that by an accumulation of occurrences Mr. Whitehead had become desperate, and that what he wanted was the promise of appellants that he could look to them for assistance. He knew from his past relationship with appellants that if they gave their promise to perform he could rely upon them. The correspondence between them indicates how desperately he desired this assurance. Under these circumstances he wrote his offer of April 12, above quoted, in which he stated, after disclosing his desperate mental and physical condition, and after setting forth the terms of his offer: "*Will you let me hear from you as soon as possible*—I know it will be a sacrifice but times are still bad and likely to be, so by settling down you can help me and Blanche and gain in the end." By thus specifically requesting an immediate reply Whitehead expressly indicated the nature of the acceptance desired by him, namely, appellants' promise that they would come to California and do the things requested by him. This promise was immediately sent by appellants upon receipt of the offer, and was received by Whitehead. It is elementary that when an offer has indicated the mode and means of acceptance, an acceptance in accordance with that mode or means is binding on the offerer.

Another factor which indicates that Whitehead must have contemplated a bilateral rather than an unilateral contract, is that the contract required Mr. and Mrs. Davis to perform services until the death of both Mr. and Mrs. Whitehead. It is obvious that if Mr. Whitehead died first some of these services were to be performed after his death, so that he would have to rely on the promise of appellants to perform these services. It is also of some evidentiary force that Whitehead received the letter of acceptance and acquiesced in that means of acceptance.

* * *

For the foregoing reasons we are of the opinion that the offer of April 12, 1931, was an offer to enter into a bilateral contract which was accepted by the letter of April 14, 1931. Subsequently appellants fully performed their part of the contract. Under such circumstances it is well settled that damages are insufficient and specific performance will be granted. * * *

* * *

For the foregoing reasons the judgment appealed from is reversed.

WORMSER, THE TRUE CONCEPTION OF UNILATERAL CONTRACTS

26 Yale L.J. 136, 136–38 (1916).

Suppose A says to B, "I will give you $100 if you walk across the Brooklyn Bridge," and B walks—is there a contract? It is clear that A is not asking B for B's *promise* to walk across the Brooklyn Bridge. What A wants from B is the *act* of walking across the bridge. When B has walked across the bridge there is a contract, and A is then bound to pay to B $100. At that moment there arises a unilateral contract. A has bartered away his volition for B's act of walking across the Brooklyn Bridge.

When an act is thus wanted in return for a promise, a unilateral contract is created when the act is done. It is clear that only one party is bound. B is not bound to walk across the Brooklyn Bridge, but A is bound to pay B $100 if B does so. Thus, in unilateral contracts, on one side we find merely an act, on the other side a promise. On the other hand, in bilateral contracts, A barters away his volition in return for another promise; that is to say, there is an exchange of promises or assurances. In the case of the bilateral contract both parties, A and B, are bound from the moment that their promises are exchanged. Thus, if A says to B, "I will give you $100 if you will promise to walk across the Brooklyn Bridge," and B then promises to walk across the bridge, a bilateral contract is created at the moment when B promises, and both parties are thereafter bound. * * *

It is plain that in the Brooklyn Bridge case as first put, what A wants from B is the act of walking across the Brooklyn Bridge. A does not ask for B's promise to walk across the bridge and B has never given it. B has never bound himself to walk across the bridge. A, however, has bound himself to pay $100 to B, if B does so. Let us suppose that B starts to walk across the Brooklyn Bridge and has gone about one-half of the way across. At that moment A overtakes B and says to him, "I withdraw my offer." Has B then any rights against A? Again, let us suppose that after A has said "I withdraw my offer," B continues to walk across the Brooklyn Bridge and completes the act of crossing. Under these circumstances, has B any rights against A?

* * *

The objection is made, however, that it is very "hard" upon B that he should have walked half-way across the Brooklyn Bridge and should get no compensation. This suggestion, invariably advanced, might be dismissed with the remark that "hard" cases should not make bad law. But going a step further, by way of reply, the pertinent inquiry at once suggests itself, "Was B bound to walk across the Brooklyn Bridge?" The answer to this is obvious. By hypothesis, B was not bound to walk across the Brooklyn Bridge. B had never surrendered his volition with regard to walking across the bridge. B had never promised A that he would walk across the bridge.

There had been no interchange of promises. A was bound to pay B $100 in the event that B should walk across the bridge, but B had not bound himself to walk. It follows that at the moment when A overtook B, after B had walked half-way across the bridge, that B was not then bound to complete the crossing of the bridge. B, on his side, could have refused at that time, or at any other time, to continue to cross the bridge without making himself in any way legally liable to A. If B is not bound to continue to cross the bridge, if B is will-free, why should not A also be will-free?

BRACKENBURY V. HODGKIN

Supreme Judicial Court of Maine, 1917.
116 Me. 399, 102 A. 106.

CORNISH, C.J. The defendant Mrs. Sarah D. P. Hodgkin on the 8th day of February, 1915, was the owner of certain real estate—her home farm, situated in the outskirts of Lewiston. She was a widow and was living alone. She was the mother of six adult children, five sons, one of whom, Walter, is the codefendant, and one daughter, who is the coplaintiff. The plaintiffs were then residing in Independence, Mo. Many letters had passed between mother and daughter concerning the daughter and her husband returning to the old home and taking care of the mother, and finally on February 8, 1915, the mother sent a letter to the daughter and her husband which is the foundation of this bill in equity. In this letter she made a definite proposal, the substance of which was that if the Brackenburys would move to Lewiston, and maintain and care for Mrs. Hodgkin on the home place during her life, and pay the moving expenses, they were to have the use and income of the premises, together with the use of the household goods, with certain exceptions, Mrs. Hodgkin to have what rooms she might need. The letter closed, by way of postscript, with the words, "you to have the place when I have passed away."

Relying upon this offer, which was neither withdrawn nor modified, and in acceptance thereof, the plaintiffs moved from Missouri to Maine late in April, 1915, went upon the premises described and entered upon the performance of the contract. Trouble developed after a few weeks, and the relations between the parties grew most disagreeable. The mother brought two suits against her son-in-law on trifling matters, and finally ordered the plaintiffs from the place, but they refused to leave. Then on November 7, 1916, she executed and delivered to her son, Walter C. Hodgkin, a deed of the premises, reserving a life estate in herself. Walter, however, was not a bona fide purchaser for value without notice, but took the deed with full knowledge of the agreement between the parties and for the sole purpose of evicting the plaintiffs. On the very day the deed was executed he served a notice to quit upon Mr. Brackenbury, as preliminary to an action of forcible entry and detainer which was brought on November 13, 1916. This bill in equity was brought by the plaintiffs to secure a reconveyance of the farm from Walter to his mother, to restrain and enjoin Walter from further prosecuting his action of forcible entry and detainer, and to obtain an adjudication that the mother holds the legal title impressed with a trust in favor of the plaintiffs in accordance with their contract.

The sitting justice made an elaborate and carefully considered finding of facts and signed a decree, sustaining the bill with costs against Walter C. Hodgkin, and granting the relief prayed for. The case is before the law court on the defendants' appeal from this decree.

Four main issues are raised.

1. As to the completion and existence of a valid contract.

A legal and binding contract is clearly proven. The offer on the part of the mother was in writing, and its terms cannot successfully be disputed. There was no need that it be accepted in words, nor that a counter promise on the part of the plaintiffs be made. The offer was the basis, not of a bilateral contract, requiring a reciprocal promise, a promise for a promise, but of a unilateral contract requiring an act for a promise. "In the latter case the only acceptance of the offer that is necessary is the performance of the act. In other words, the promise becomes binding when the act is performed." 6 R.C.L. 607. This is elementary law.

The plaintiffs here accepted the offer by moving from Missouri to the mother's farm in Lewiston and entering upon the performance of the specified acts, and they have continued performance since that time so far as they have been permitted by the mother to do so. The existence of a completed and valid contract is clear.

2. The creation of an equitable interest.

This contract between the parties, the performance of which was entered upon by the plaintiffs, created an equitable interest in the land described in the bill in favor of the plaintiffs. The letter of February 8, 1915, signed by the mother, answered the statutory requirement that "there can be no trust concerning lands, except trusts arising or resulting by implication of law, unless created or declared by some writing signed by the party or his attorney." R.S. 1903, c. 75, § 14. No particular formality need be observed; a letter or other memorandum is sufficient to establish a trust provided its terms and the relations of the parties to it appear with reasonable certainty. * * * The equitable interest of the plaintiffs in these premises is obvious, and they are entitled to have that interest protected.

3. Alleged breach of duty on the part of the plaintiffs.

The defendants contend that, granting an equitable estate has been established, the plaintiffs have failed of performance because of their improper and unkind treatment of Mrs. Hodgkin, and therefore have forfeited the right to equitable relief which they might otherwise be entitled to. The sitting justice decided this question of fact in favor of the plaintiffs, and his finding is fully warranted by the evidence. Mrs. Hodgkin's temperament and disposition, not only as described in the testimony of others, but as revealed in her own attitude, conduct, and testimony as a witness, as they stand out on the printed record, mark her as the provoking cause in the various family difficulties. She was "the one primarily at fault."

* * *

The plaintiffs are entitled to the remedy here sought, and the entry must be:

Appeal dismissed.

NOTE:
AN EVEN TRUER CONCEPTION OF UNILATERAL CONTRACTS

Section 45 of the Restatement (First) of Contracts (1932) provided:

> If an offer for a unilateral contract is made, and part of the consideration requested in the offer is given or tendered by the offeree in response thereto, the offeror is bound by a contract, the duty of immediate performance of which is conditional on the full consideration being given or tendered within the time stated in the offer, or, if no time is stated therein, within a reasonable time.

In 1950, Professor Wormser changed his view to conform to this rule:

> Since that time I have repented, so that now, clad in sackcloth, I state frankly that my point of view has changed. I agree, at this time, with the rule set forth in the Restatement of the Law of Contracts of the American Law Institute, § 45.

Wormser, Book Review, 3 J. of Legal Educ. 145, 146 (1950) (reviewing E. Patterson and G. Goble, Cases on Contracts (1949)).

The Restatement (Second) of Contracts § 45 now provides:

> **Option Contract Created By Part Performance Or Tender**
>
> (1) Where an offer invites an offeree to accept by rendering a performance and does not invite a promissory acceptance, an option contract is created when the offeree tenders or begins the invited performance or tenders a beginning of it.
>
> (2) The offeror's duty of performance under any option contract so created is conditional on completion or tender of the invited performance in accordance with the terms of the offer.
>
> Comment:
>
> (a) *Offer limited to acceptance by performance only.* This Section is limited to cases where the offer does not invite a promissory

acceptance. Such an offer has often been referred to as an "offer for a unilateral contract."

PROBLEM 4-10

1. What result in Brackenbury v. Hodgkin under Wormser's original conception of unilateral contracts set forth in 1916? What result under the Restatement (First) of Contracts? Under Restatement (Second)? What are the differences between the two sections?

2. Does Brackenbury v. Hodgkin actually support either version of section 45?

PETTERSON V. PATTBERG

New York Court of Appeals, 1928.
248 N.Y. 86, 161 N.E. 428.

KELLOGG, J. The evidence given upon the trial sanctions the following statement of facts: John Petterson, of whose last will and testament the plaintiff is the executrix, was the owner of a parcel of real estate in Brooklyn, known as 5301 Sixth avenue. The defendant was the owner of a bond executed by Petterson, which was secured by a third mortgage upon the parcel. On April 4, 1924, there remained unpaid upon the principal the sum of $5,450. This amount was payable in installments of $250 on April 25, 1924, and upon a like monthly date every three months thereafter. Thus the bond and mortgage had more than five years to run before the entire sum became due. Under date of the 4th of April, 1924, the defendant wrote Petterson as follows:

> "I hereby agree to accept cash for the mortgage which I hold against premises 5301 6th Ave., Brooklyn, N.Y. It is understood and agreed as a consideration I will allow you $780 providing said mortgage is paid on or before May 31, 1924, and the regular quarterly payment due April 25, 1924, is paid when due."

On April 25, 1924, Petterson paid the defendant the installment of principal due on that date. Subsequently, on a day in the latter part of May, 1924, Petterson presented himself at the defendant's home, and knocked at the door. The defendant demanded the name of his caller. Petterson replied: "It is Mr. Petterson. I have come to pay off the mortgage." The defendant answered that he had sold the mortgage. Petterson stated that he would like to talk with the defendant, so the defendant partly opened the door. Thereupon Petterson exhibited the cash, and said he was ready to pay off the mortgage according to the agreement. The defendant refused to take the money. Prior to this conversation, Petterson had made a contract to sell the land to a third person free and clear of the mortgage to the defendant. Meanwhile, also, the defendant had sold the bond and mortgage to a third party. It therefore became necessary for Petterson to pay to such person the full amount of the bond and mortgage. It is claimed that he thereby sustained a loss of $780 the sum which the defendant agreed to allow upon the bond and mortgage, if payment in full of principal, less that sum, was made on or before May 31, 1924. The plaintiff has had a recovery for the sum thus claimed, with interest.

Clearly the defendant's letter proposed to Petterson the making of a unilateral contract, the gift of a promise in exchange for the performance of an act. The thing conditionally promised by the defendant was the reduction of the mortgage debt. The act requested to be done, in consideration of the offered promise, was payment in full of the reduced principal of the debt prior to the due date thereof. "If an act is requested, that very act, and no other, must be given." Williston on Contracts, § 73. "In case of offers for a consideration, the performance of the consideration is always deemed a condition." Langdell's Summary of the Law of Contracts, § 4. It is elementary that any offer to enter into a unilateral contract may be withdrawn before the act requested to be done has been performed. * * * The offer of a reward in consideration of an act to be performed is revocable before the very act requested has been done. * * *

An interesting question arises when, as here, the offeree approaches the offeror with the intention of proffering performance and, before actual tender is made, the offer is withdrawn. Of such a case Williston says:

> "The offeror may see the approach of the offeree and know that an acceptance is contemplated. If the offeror can say 'I revoke' before the offeree accepts, however brief the interval of time between the two acts, there is no escape from the conclusion that the offer is terminated." Williston on Contracts, § 60b.

In this instance Petterson, standing at the door of the defendant's house, stated to the defendant that he had come to pay off the mortgage. Before a tender of the necessary moneys had been made, the defendant informed Petterson that he had sold the mortgage. That was a definite notice to Petterson that the defendant could not perform his offered promise, and that a tender to the defendant, who was no longer the creditor, would be ineffective to satisfy the debt. "An offer to sell property may be withdrawn before acceptance without any formal notice to the person to whom the offer is made. It is sufficient if that person has actual knowledge that the person who made the offer has done some act inconsistent with the continuance of the offer, such as selling the property to a third person." Dickinson v. Dodds, 2 Ch. Div. 463, headnote. * * * Thus it clearly appears that the defendant's offer was withdrawn before its acceptance had been tendered. It is unnecessary to determine, therefore, what the legal situation might have been had tender been made before withdrawal. It is the individual view of the writer that the same result would follow. This would be so, for the act requested to be performed was the completed act of payment, a thing incapable of performance, unless assented to by the person to be paid. Williston on Contracts, § 60b. Clearly an offering party has the right to name the precise act performance of which would convert his offer into a binding promise. Whatever the act may be until it is performed, the offer must be revocable. However, the supposed case is not before us for decision. We think that in this particular instance the offer of the defendant was withdrawn before it became a binding promise, and therefore that no contract was ever made for the breach of which the plaintiff may claim damages.

The judgment of the Appellate Division and that of the Trial Term should be reversed, and the complaint dismissed, with costs in all courts.

LEHMAN, J. (dissenting). The defendant's letter to Petterson constituted a promise on his part to accept payment at a discount of the mortgage he held, provided the mortgage is paid on or before May 31, 1924. Doubtless, by the terms of the promise itself, the defendant made payment of the mortgage by the plaintiff, before the stipulated time, a condition precedent to performance by the defendant of his promise to accept payment at a discount. If the condition precedent has not been performed, it is because the defendant made performance impossible by refusing to accept payment, when the plaintiff came with an offer of immediate performance. "It is a principle of fundamental justice that if a promisor is himself the cause of the failure of performance either of an obligation due him or of a condition upon which his own liability depends, he cannot take advantage of the failure." Williston on Contracts, § 677. The question in this case is not whether payment of the mortgage is a condition precedent to the performance of a promise made by the defendant, but, rather, whether, at the time the defendant refused the offer of payment, he had assumed any binding obligation, even though subject to condition.

The promise made by the defendant lacked consideration at the time it was made. Nevertheless, the promise was not made as a gift or mere gratuity to the plaintiff. It was made for the purpose of obtaining from the defendant something which the plaintiff desired. It constituted an offer which was to become binding whenever the plaintiff should give, in return for the defendant's promise, exactly the consideration which the defendant requested.

Here the defendant requested no counter promise from the plaintiff. The consideration requested by the defendant for his promise to accept payment was, I agree, some act to be performed by the plaintiff. Until the act requested was performed, the defendant might undoubtedly revoke his offer. Our problem is to determine from the words of the letter, read in the light of surrounding circumstances, what act the defendant requested as consideration for his promise.

The defendant undoubtedly made his offer as an inducement to the plaintiff to "pay" the mortgage before it was due. Therefore, it is said, that "the act requested to be performed was the completed act of payment, a thing incapable of performance, unless assented to by the person to be paid." In unmistakable terms the defendant agreed to accept payment, yet we are told that the defendant intended, and the plaintiff should have understood, that the act requested by the defendant, as consideration for his promise to accept payment, included performance by the defendant himself of the very promise for which the act was to be consideration. The defendant's promise was to become binding only when fully performed; and part of the consideration to be furnished by the plaintiff for the defendant's promise was to be the performance of that promise by the defendant. So construed, the defendant's promise or offer, though intended to induce action by the plaintiff, is but a snare and delusion. The plaintiff could not reasonably suppose that the defendant was asking him to procure the performance by the defendant of the very act which the defendant promised to do, yet we are told that, even after the plaintiff had done all else which the defendant requested, the defendant's promise was still not binding because the defendant chose not to perform.

I cannot believe that a result so extraordinary could have been intended when the defendant wrote the letter. "The thought behind the phrase proclaims itself misread when the outcome of the reading is injustice or absurdity." See opinion of Cardozo, C.J., in Surace v. Danna, 248 N.Y. 18, 161 N.E. 315. If the defendant intended to induce payment by the plaintiff and yet reserve the right to refuse payment when offered he should have used a phrase better calculated to express his meaning than the words: "I agree to accept." A promise to accept payment, by its very terms, must necessarily become binding, if at all, not later than when a present offer to pay is made.

I recognize that in this case only an offer of payment, and not a formal tender of payment, was made before the defendant withdrew his offer to accept payment. Even the plaintiff's part in the act of payment was then not technically complete. Even so, under a fair construction of the words of the letter, I think the plaintiff had done the act which the defendant requested as consideration for his promise. The plaintiff offered to pay, with present intention and ability to make that payment. A formal tender is seldom made in business transactions, except to lay the foundation for subsequent assertion in a court of justice of rights which spring from refusal of the tender. If the defendant acted in good faith in making his offer to accept payment, he could not well have intended to draw a distinction in the act requested of the plaintiff in return, between an offer which, unless refused, would ripen into completed payment, and a formal tender. Certainly the defendant could not have expected or intended that the plaintiff would make a formal tender of payment without first stating that he had come to make payment. We should not read into the language of the defendant's offer a meaning which would prevent enforcement of the defendant's promise after it had been accepted by the plaintiff in the very way which the defendant must have intended it should be accepted, if he acted in good faith.

The judgment should be affirmed.

CARDOZO, C.J. and POUND, CRANE and O'BRIEN, JJ., concur with KELLOGG, J.

LEHMAN, J., dissents in an opinion in which ANDREWS, J. concurs.

PROBLEM 4-11

Suppose you were consulted by Petterson after Pattberg made his offer, but before the events of late May. Petterson wanted advice concerning how to accept Pattberg's offer. How would you have advised Petterson?

NOTE: ADDITIONAL FACTS IN PETTERSON V. PATTBERG

A student note in the Cornell Law Quarterly (now the Cornell Law Review) reported that the record in Petterson v. Pattberg revealed that Pattberg was prevented from testifying that he had sent a letter to Petterson revoking the offer. The testimony was barred under the rule excluding the testimony of an interested party when the other was dead. In addition, the note writer believed the record suggested that Petterson knew of the sale of the mortgage, since he brought $4,000 cash, his wife, and a notary public to Pattberg's home in "anticipation" of Pattberg's refusal. See Note, 14 Cornell L.Q. 81, 84 n. 18 (1928).

PETTIT, MODERN UNILATERAL CONTRACTS

63 B.U. L. Rev. 551, 551–52, 559–61, 564–65 (1983).

Why would anyone write about unilateral contracts today? After all, Karl Llewellyn argued convincingly more than forty years ago that unilateral contracts are rare and unimportant and should be relegated to the "freak tent." Academics, he said, created the "Great Dichotomy" between unilateral and bilateral contracts; lack of support for the unilateral contract idea in the cases required those academics to illustrate the concept with ridiculous hypotheticals about climbing greased flagpoles and crossing the Brooklyn Bridge. The drafters of the *Second Restatement of Contracts* thus considered it a step forward when they not only minimized the importance of the unilateral-bilateral distinction but sought to eliminate the term "unilateral contract" from the lexicon of the law.[1] Today, those commentators who still deem the subject worthy of mention applaud the burial of the unilateral contract. Why unearth the decaying corpse?

This Article suggests that in fact unilateral contract never died, but is alive and thriving as never before. An examination of American cases, decided since the first tentative draft of the *Second Restatement* was published in 1964, reveals not only that lawyers and judges continue to employ unilateral contract analysis in traditional areas, but that they find the concept useful for expanding contractual analysis into new areas. Of particular importance is the use of unilateral contract to establish one-way obligations of such institutions as employers, governments, and schools toward individuals with whom they deal. Unilateral contract has become an important concept in defining relationships that arise in our increasingly organized society. Despite the efforts of Llewellyn and the drafters of the *Second Restatement* unilateral contracts are overcrowding the freak tent and spilling over into the Big Top.

* * * In *Sylvestre v. State,* six retired Minnesota state district judges brought an action seeking a declaration that the state could not reduce their retirement benefits by amending the judges' retirement statute. The Supreme Court of Minnesota characterized the retirement statute that was in effect when the plaintiffs began their judicial careers as an offer for a unilateral contract. The court stated the offer as follows: "If you will stay on the job for at least 15 years and then retire after having reached the specified retirement age, we will pay you a part of your salary for the remainder of your life."

HILLMAN, MARK PETTIT'S CLASSIC: MODERN UNILATERAL CONTRACTS

28 B. U. Public Interest L. J. 295, 295–296 (2019).

[T]he primary reason the Public Interest Law Journal asked me to write this dedication, was to introduce the reprinting of Mark's remarkable 1983 article, "Modern Unilateral Contracts." In unilateral contract cases, offerors require acceptance by return performance instead of return promise. I say "remarkable" because the common wisdom at the time Mark wrote, supported by such luminaries as Llewellyn and by the prestigious Restatement (Second) of Contracts, was that unilateral contracts were anomalous, unimportant, and functionally obsolete, primarily because the vast majority of contracts included a return promise by the offeree. Mark's article demonstrated that this perception was entirely wrongheaded. Mark

[1] The Restatement (Second) dispensed with the unilateral-bilateral contract terminology because of "doubt as to the utility of the distinction." Reporter's Note to Restatement (Second) of Contracts § 1, comment f.

showed in detail the importance and proliferation of modern unilateral contracts in various transactions, especially in those important employment cases where employers promise pensions, bonuses, and the like in return for faithful performance of service by the employee. Mark thoughtfully explained that the continued recognition and expansion of the use of unilateral contract demonstrate "a movement toward increased contractual obligation."

A brief survey of cases since 1983 more than substantiates Mark's insight that unilateral contract remains a significant and growing construct in the legal lexicon. Rather than falling out of favor, unilateral contract continues to provide a useful framework for analyzing a whole series of modern contract cases. Perhaps that insight is even more important now than when Mark contributed this marvelous article. "Modern Unilateral Contracts" is, therefore, a classic well worth reading again.

ROLEY V. GOOGLE, LLC

N.D. Cal. 2019.
2019 WL 1779974.

BETH LABSON FREEMAN, UNITED STATES DISTRICT JUDGE.

Before the Court is Defendant Google LLC's ("Google") motion to dismiss Plaintiff Andrew Roley's ("Roley") First Amended Complaint [FAC] in this consumer class action case. The Court held a hearing on the motion on April 17, 2019. For the reasons stated on the record and as discussed below, Google's motion is DENIED.

I. BACKGROUND

In early 2015, Google created its "Local Guides" program to improve its Google Maps and Google Earth products. Individuals who sign up to be local guides share photographs, comments, reviews, and the like about various establishments and locations in their communities, which benefits Google through increased page views and advertising revenue. In return for these benefits and to encourage enrollment in and participation in the program, Google offers local guides various benefits for their participation. One such benefit Google offered was a free terabyte of data storage for those local guides who achieved "Level 4 status" in the program.

On April 4, 2016, Roley, who had previously uploaded pictures to Google, received an email from Google inviting him to join the Local Guides program. Specifically, the email provided, in part:

> **Get rewards for the photos you shared**
>
> When you become a local guide you earn power points for your photos and other contributions to Google maps. These points can unlock cool benefits like:

1 TB of Google Drive storage

Invitations to exclusive events

Early access to new Google products

Local guides badge

You've already earned points with your photos. Why not join our community of explorers today?

Get started.

Relying on the perceived promise of a terabyte of free data storage, Roley joined the Local Guides Program and thereafter received an email acknowledging his enrollment.

In order to enroll, Roley had to agree to the program's rules—the Local Guides Program Terms and Conditions ("Terms"). The Terms state that "[b]y signing up to be a member of the Local Guides Program . . . you agree to be bound" by the Terms. As is relevant here, the Terms purport to give Google wide discretion with respect to providing benefits to local guides. Specifically, the Terms state the following: (1) "Level requirements and descriptions are subject to change, at Google's sole discretion;" (2) "Benefits are offered at the discretion of Google and its affiliates;" and (3) "Benefits are subject to change."

Throughout the next several months, Roley uploaded photos, business information, and other content to Google as part of the Local Guides program. During this time, Google sent several emails to Roley, who started as a Level 3 local guide, encouraging him to continue to post photos and reviews through Local Guides and, at least on one occasion, to "[l]evel up now and get more exclusive benefits." On July 7, 2016, Google emailed Roley stating that it would be "adjust[ing] [its] Level 4 benefit to 100 GB of free Google Drive storage," but that "Local Guides who reach Level 4 in the next 2 weeks can still unlock the original offer of 1TB of free Drive storage." On July 14, 2016, within the two-week time frame Google provided, Roley achieved Level 4 status, and Google notified him that he could redeem his Google Drive storage. Roley alleges that Google believes that at the time Roley claimed his free storage, Google informed him that his free storage would last only two years, but Roley alleges this is not true.

Two years later, in April 2018, Google notified Roley that his free Drive storage was expiring and that he would have to begin paying monthly for his terabyte of storage. Roley was surprised to learn that his free storage was ending because none of the offers or information he had received relating to the terabyte of storage ever included a time limitation. Roley alleges that through these actions Google "convert[ed] the offer of a 'free terabyte' of data to a service that cost $ 10/month." Roley was then forced to either delete some of his data or pay $ 10/month to continue using the terabyte of storage. He ultimately was shut out of some Google services until he deleted some of his data.

Roley alleges that no reasonable consumer would have understood that the offer of free storage was time-limited to two years. And he alleges that Google intentionally failed to disclose this time limit (and thus misrepresented the benefit) in an effort to induce Roley and members of the putative class to sign up for Local Guides to the benefit of Google. Based on these alleged actions, Roley brings the following claim[ ] against Google: [B]reach of contract [other claims omitted].

The breach of contract claim is premised on the allegation that Google "promised Plaintiff and Class members a free terabyte of data storage if they achieved 'Level 4' status as a Local Guide" in exchange for Roley's and the class's performance of certain services for Google, like uploading photos and reviews. Roley alleges that he "accepted the terms of the contract through performance." * * *

* * *

[II]. DISCUSSION

Roley alleges that he entered into a unilateral contract with Google. Read in the light most favorable to Roley, Roley alleges that Google's emails to Roley beginning in April 2016 and continuing through July 7, 2016 constituted a binding offer for a free terabyte of storage if Roley reached Level 4 status. Roley alleges he accepted this offer by fully performing—that is, by reaching Level 4 status.

Recognizing that Roley's allegations are somewhat imprecise with respect to whether the April 2016 email alone or in tandem with the subsequent emails through July 7, 2016 constitutes the alleged binding offer, Google argues that the April email was not a binding offer because (1) it did not include essential terms necessary to tell the recipients how they could accept the offer through performance, including how many points were needed to earn the terabyte benefit; (2) recipients were required to take additional steps before they could start performing as local guides, including clicking "Get Started" and enrolling in the program; and (3) the Terms, to which Roley agreed, expressly allowed Google to change the free storage benefit. Indeed, Google argues that the Terms, not the "advertising" email, constitutes the relevant contract here.

The Court agrees with Roley that on the facts alleged, he states a valid claim for breach of contract.

* * *

[T]he Court concludes that, at the motion to dismiss stage, the offer here was a binding offer that Roley accepted through full performance. As an initial matter, the Court takes as true Roley's allegation that Google's offer was for storage for an indefinite period of time and that Google changed the benefit to a two-year time-limited benefit *after* Roley fully performed (*i.e.*, reached Level 4). On the facts alleged, the question of whether the offer was for storage that would last forever or that was implicitly time-limited is a question of fact not appropriate for resolution on a motion to dismiss.

Here, Google offered Roley a free terabyte of storage in exchange for his earning points through the Local Guides program. Once Roley enrolled in the program, Google continued to encourage his performance, specifically encouraging him toward the benefit of one terabyte of storage. Indeed, on July 7, 2016, Google promised Roley that if he reached Level 4 status within two weeks, he would receive one terabyte of free storage. Roley fully performed in accordance with Google's terms. As such, the "totality of the circumstances" demonstrate that Google "in clear and positive terms, promised to render performance"—provision of a terabyte of storage—"in exchange for something requested by the advertiser"—achievement of Level 4 status—and that Roley "reasonably might have concluded that by acting in accordance with the request a contract would be formed." * * * [T]hat Roley had to enroll in the program does not render the offer non-binding. And contrary to Google's argument, at least as of the July 7 email, the essential terms of the agreement were set—Google promised the terabyte of data in exchange for Level 4 status if reached within two weeks.

* * * The April 4 email directed Roley to "start now" but did not indicate that Roley would be required to take additional steps (such as providing credit card information) beyond mere enrollment in the program. * * * Likewise, the Terms here do not expressly provide for a time-limited storage benefit, * * *. Moreover, though the FAC is not entirely clear as to when the binding offer was made (be it April or July 7, 2016, or otherwise), Roley clearly does not allege that the contract was formed at the time of enrollment.

Roley's agreement to the Terms does not change this conclusion. Google is correct that * * * the Terms can be considered part of the offer and contract here. But these provisions do not help Google because Roley alleges that Google promised as late as July 7, 2016 to provide the terabyte of storage for the next two weeks. * * * Google did not live up to this promise. Moreover, by this point Roley had fully performed—he had reached Level 4 status. * * *

Perhaps most importantly, * * * the Terms here do not give Google such blanket discretion. They say only that Google has the discretion to change level requirements and offer benefits; they do not say it can terminate the offer of benefits without any notice whatsoever to individuals who have fully performed. Absent an express provision to the contrary, the

Court cannot read the contract to give Google such broad discretion. Indeed, reading such broad discretion into the contract could render the contract illusory. If Google could simply choose not to confer promised benefits after full performance by the consumer, it would have no duty to perform under the contract. * * * At this stage, on these facts, the Court interprets Google's discretion to be limited at least by the implied duty of good faith and fair dealing. * * * Especially in light of the fact that Google allegedly continued to promise that Roley could earn the terabyte by performing, there is a question of fact as to how to interpret the discretionary provision of the Terms.

Thus, on the facts as alleged in the FAC, Roley has successfully alleged the existence of a binding offer from Google that Roley fully accepted through performance, such that Google allegedly breached by failing to satisfy said offer.

* * *

IV. ORDER

Based on the foregoing, Google's motion to dismiss Roley's FAC is DENIED.

GARBER V. HARRIS TRUST & SAV. BANK

Appellate Court of Illinois, 1982.
104 Ill. App. 3d 675, 432 N.E.2d 1309.

WHITE, PRESIDING JUSTICE.

Plaintiffs, Gary L. Blank and Sheldon Garber, purporting to represent a class of credit cardholders, brought this action in chancery against defendants Harris Trust and Savings Bank (Harris Trust), Sears Roebuck and Co. (Sears), J.C. Penney Co., Inc. (Penney), and First National Bank of Chicago (FNB). The amended complaint alleges that Blank is the holder of credit cards issued by the defendants Sears, Penney and FNB. It also alleges that Garber is the holder of Master Charge credit cards issued by Harris Trust. In essence, the amended complaint asserts that each defendant had breached the provisions of its "cardholder agreement" document by changing the terms on which that defendant would offer to extend credit and that the alleged changes in the cardholder agreements were void for lack of consideration. These cardholder agreements are alleged to be contracts. In their prayer for relief, plaintiffs sought injunctive relief against the changes, money damages, and other relief. Defendants moved to dismiss the amended complaint. After hearing oral argument, the circuit court entered an order granting the motions to dismiss and dismissing the cause of action with prejudice. Plaintiffs appeal from this order.

The alleged modifications of the cardholder agreements at issue are as follows. In Spring, 1980, FNB announced that, effective July 1, 1980, it would begin charging a twenty dollar annual fee for its VISA cards and would increase the minimum monthly payment from four percent to five percent on the outstanding balance in any VISA account. The changed terms only became effective if cardholders used their cards after June 30, 1980.

[The alleged modifications made by the other defendants are omitted.]

Plaintiffs assert that the cardholder agreements between the defendant credit card issuers and the plaintiff credit cardholders are binding contracts to continue to extend credit on the same terms and that there was no consideration to support the alleged modifications since a promise to do something which one is already obligated to do, *i.e.,* to extend credit, does not constitute a valid consideration. Plaintiffs find the existence of a contract in the following manner. The applications and brochures, displayed and advertised by defendants, are invitations for an offer. The credit application submitted by a potential cardholder to one of the defendant credit card issuers constitutes an offer. Acceptance of this offer occurs when the issuer issues a credit card to the cardholder. A cardholder furnishes consideration to the issuer by providing the issuer with requested credit information and by allowing the issuer to commence a credit check prior to the issuance of the card.

Conversely, the card issuers argue that the issuance of a card constitutes an offer to extend credit, and that this offer is accepted by use of the card. Upon such use, the cardholder agrees to all provisions in the cardholder agreement, and the agreement becomes a binding contract between the cardholder and the issuer. In other words, each use of the credit card constitutes a separate contract between the parties.

For the reasons stated below, we conclude that a contract was not formed at the time of the issuance of the credit card; that a separate contract is created each time the card is used according to the terms of the cardholder agreement at the time of such use; that the cardholder agreements were subject to modification at will; and that in any event, consideration was given for the modifications.

Although the parties do not refer us to any Illinois cases to support the position that cardholder agreements are standing offers to extend credit, support for this position is found in the case law of other jurisdictions. In *City Stores Co. v. Henderson* (1967), 116 Ga.App. 114, 156 S.E.2d 818, plaintiffs brought an action for tortious misconduct based upon an alleged refusal, without prior notice of credit revocation, of defendant's clerk to extend further credit to one of the plaintiffs when she sought to charge purchases made at its store. In discussing the nature of the relationship between a cardholder and the issuer of the card, the court stated:

> "The issuance of a credit card is but an offer to extend a line of open account credit. It is unilateral and supported by no consideration. The offer may be withdrawn at any time, without prior notice, for any reason or, indeed, for no reason at all, and its withdrawal breaches no duty—for there is no duty to continue it—and violates no rights. Acceptance or use of the card by the offeree makes a contract between the parties according to its terms, but we have seen none which prevents a termination of the arrangement at any time by either party." (156 S.E.2d at 823.) * * *

* * * [T]he prevailing view in this country is that the issuance of a credit card is only an offer to extend credit. There is no persuasive reason, under the circumstances presented in the instant appeal, for swaying from the accepted position that the issuance of a credit card does not create a contract. We therefore conclude that defendant credit card issuers could terminate or modify the terms of their offers to extend credit as to future transactions. Once a credit card issuer withdraws its offer, a cardholder cannot compel it to extend credit to him in accordance with the terms of that offer.

* * *

For the aforementioned reasons, the judgment of the circuit court of Cook County is affirmed.

Affirmed.

NOTE:
MORE ON CREDIT CARD OFFER AND ACCEPTANCE

One court recited the credit card formation issue as follows:

> The issuance of a credit card is only an offer to extend credit; acceptance of the credit offer occurs each time a credit purchase is made by the cardholder. Consistent with the treatment of each credit card purchase as a separate offer and acceptance, modifications to credit card terms are binding between the parties when, after notice of the modifications, the cardholder uses his credit card. Accordingly each time a credit card is used, a new contract exists between the parties according to the terms in effect (*i.e.*, having been communicated to the defendant in a reasonable manner) at the time of the use. * * * [M]odified terms of an agreement, once communicated to the cardholder, are deemed accepted when the card is used after the modifications.

Midland Funding, LLC v. Raney, 93 N.E.3d 724 (App. Ct. Ill. 2018) (citations omitted).

Some banks charge an annual fee for a credit card. One such bank includes the following provision when changing the terms of credit card arrangements. Why did the bank include this provision?

Non-acceptance Instructions

> If you do not wish to accept the change in terms, send us a letter by * * * stating your non-acceptance. Include your name, address and account number on this correspondence and mail it to Citibank. If you notify us that you do not accept the new terms, you can continue to use your card under the existing terms until the end of your current membership year or the expiration date on your card, whichever is later. At that time, your account will be closed and you can pay off your remaining balance under your current terms.

NOTE:
THE DUTY OF THE OFFEREE OF A UNILATERAL CONTRACT WHO HAS BEGUN PERFORMANCE TO NOTIFY THE OFFEROR

In Carlill v. Carbolic Smoke Ball Co., 1 Q.B. 256 (1893), the Carbolic Smoke Ball Co. offered £100 to any person who contracted influenza after using its product. In such a setting, unlike Petterson v. Pattberg, the offeror will not know when the offeree has begun performance or has completed it. When must notice of acceptance be given to the offeror? In Carlill, the court stated that the offeror "does not expect and does not require notice of the acceptance apart from notice of the performance. * * * " Id. at 263. Similarly, under the Restatement (Second) of Contracts section 54(1), a contract is formed by performance without any notice, "unless the offer requests" a notice. Under section 54(2), however, the offeror is discharged if the offeree "has reason to know that the offeror has no adequate means of learning of the performance" promptly, unless the offeree "exercises reasonable diligence" to notify the offeror, or the "offeror learns of the performance within a reasonable time," or "the offeror indicates that notification of acceptance is not required." The Uniform Commercial Code in section 2–206(2) states:

> Where the beginning of a requested performance is a reasonable mode of acceptance an offeror who is not notified of acceptance within a reasonable time may treat the offer as having lapsed before acceptance.

What is the rationale for these rules? Why should an offeror for a unilateral contract receive notice?

DRENNAN V. STAR PAVING CO.

Supreme Court of California, 1958.
51 Cal. 2d 409, 333 P.2d 757.

TRAYNOR, JUSTICE.

Defendant appeals from a judgment for plaintiff in an action to recover damages caused by defendant's refusal to perform certain paving work according to a bid it submitted to plaintiff.

On July 28, 1955, plaintiff, a licensed general contractor, was preparing a bid on the "Monte Vista School Job" in the Lancaster school district. Bids had to be submitted before 8:00 p.m. Plaintiff testified that it was customary in that area for general contractors to receive the bids of subcontractors by telephone on the day set for bidding and to rely on them in computing their own bids. Thus on that day plaintiff's secretary, Mrs. Johnson, received by telephone between fifty and seventy-five subcontractors' bids for various parts of the school job. As each bid came in, she wrote it on a special form, which she brought into plaintiff's office. He then posted it on a master cost sheet setting forth the names and bids of all subcontractors. His own bid had to include the names of subcontractors who were to perform one-half of one per cent or more of the construction work, and he had also to provide a bidder's bond of ten per cent of his total bid of $317,385 as a guarantee that he would enter the contract if awarded the work.

Late in the afternoon, Mrs. Johnson had a telephone conversation with Kenneth R. Hoon, an estimator for defendant. He gave his name and telephone number and stated that he was bidding for defendant for the paving work at the Monte Vista School according to plans and specifications and that his bid was $7,131.60. At Mrs. Johnson's request he repeated his bid. Plaintiff listened to the bid over an extension telephone in his office and posted it on the master sheet after receiving the bid form from Mrs. Johnson. Defendant's was the lowest bid for the paving. Plaintiff computed his own bid accordingly and submitted it with the name of defendant as the subcontractor for the paving. When the bids were opened on July 28th, plaintiff's proved to be the lowest, and he was awarded the contract.

On his way to Los Angeles the next morning plaintiff stopped at defendant's office. The first person he met was defendant's construction engineer, Mr. Oppenheimer. Plaintiff testified: "I introduced myself and he immediately told me that they had made a mistake in their bid to me the night before, they couldn't do it for the price they had bid, and I told him I would expect him to carry through with their original bid because I had used it in compiling my bid and the job was being awarded them. And I would have to go and do the job according to my bid and I would expect them to do the same."

Defendant refused to do the paving work for less than $15,000. Plaintiff testified that he "got figures from other people" and after trying for several months to get as low a bid as possible engaged L & H Paving Company, a firm in Lancaster, to do the work for $10,948.60.

The trial court found on substantial evidence that defendant made a definite offer to do the paving on the Monte Vista job according to the plans and specifications for $7,131.60, and that plaintiff relied on defendant's bid in computing his own bid for the school job and naming defendant therein as the subcontractor for the paving work. Accordingly, it entered judgment for plaintiff in the amount of $3,817.00 (the difference between defendant's bid and the cost of the paving to plaintiff) plus costs.

Defendant contends that there was no enforceable contract between the parties on the ground that it made a revocable offer and revoked it before plaintiff communicated his acceptance to defendant.

There is no evidence that defendant offered to make its bid irrevocable in exchange for plaintiff's use of its figures in computing his bid. Nor is there evidence that would warrant interpreting plaintiff's use of defendant's bid as the acceptance thereof, binding plaintiff, on condition he received the main contract, to award the subcontract to defendant. In sum, there was neither an option supported by consideration nor a bilateral contract binding on both parties.

Plaintiff contends, however, that he relied to his detriment on defendant's offer and that defendant must therefore answer in damages for its refusal to perform. Thus the question is squarely presented: Did plaintiff's reliance make defendant's offer irrevocable?

Section 90 of the Restatement of Contracts states: "A promise which the promisor should reasonably expect to induce action or forbearance of a definite and substantial character on the part of the promisee and which does induce such action or forbearance is binding if injustice can be avoided only by enforcement of the promise." This rule applies in this state. * * *

Defendant's offer constituted a promise to perform on such conditions as were stated expressly or by implication therein or annexed thereto by operation of law. (See 1 Williston, Contracts [3rd. ed.], § 24A, p. 56, § 61, p. 196.) Defendant had reason to expect that if its bid proved the lowest it would be used by plaintiff. It induced "action * * * of a definite and substantial character on the part of the promisee."

Had defendant's bid expressly stated or clearly implied that it was revocable at any time before acceptance we would treat it accordingly. It was silent on revocation, however, and we must therefore determine whether there are conditions to the right of revocation imposed by law or reasonably inferable in fact. In the analogous problem of an offer for a unilateral contract, the theory is now obsolete that the offer is revocable at any time before complete performance. Thus section 45 of the Restatement of Contracts provides: "If an offer for a unilateral contract is made, and part of the consideration requested in the offer is given or tendered by the offeree in response thereto, the offeror is bound by a contract, the duty of immediate performance of which is conditional on the full consideration being given or tendered within the time stated in the offer, or, if no time is stated therein, within a reasonable time." In explanation, comment *b* states that the "main offer includes as a subsidiary promise, necessarily implied, that if part of the requested performance is given, the offeror will not revoke his offer, and that if tender is made it will be accepted. Part performance or tender may thus furnish consideration for the subsidiary promise. Moreover, merely acting in justifiable reliance on an offer may in some cases serve as sufficient reason for making a promise binding (see § 90)."

Whether implied in fact or law, the subsidiary promise serves to preclude the injustice that would result if the offer could be revoked after the offeree had acted in detrimental reliance thereon. Reasonable reliance resulting in a foreseeable prejudicial change in position affords a compelling basis also for implying a subsidiary promise not to revoke an offer for a bilateral contract.

The absence of consideration is not fatal to the enforcement of such a promise. It is true that in the case of unilateral contracts the Restatement finds consideration for the implied subsidiary promise in the part performance of the bargained-for exchange, but its reference to section 90 makes clear that consideration for such a promise is not always necessary. The very purpose of section 90 is to make a promise binding even though there was no consideration "in the sense of something that is bargained for and given in exchange." (See 1 Corbin, Contracts 634 et seq.) Reasonable reliance serves to hold the offeror in lieu of the consideration ordinarily required to make the offer binding. In a case involving similar facts the Supreme Court of South Dakota stated that "we believe that reason and justice demand that the doctrine [of section 90] be applied to the present facts. We cannot believe that by accepting this doctrine as controlling in the state of facts before us we will abolish the requirement of a consideration in contract cases, in any different sense than an ordinary estoppel abolishes some legal requirement in its application. We are of the opinion, therefore, that the defendants in executing the agreement [which was not supported by consideration] made a promise which they should have reasonably expected would induce the plaintiff to submit a bid based thereon to the Government, that such promise did induce this action, and that injustice can be avoided only by enforcement of the promise." Northwestern Engineering Co. v. Ellerman, 69 S.D. 397, 408, 10 N.W.2d 879, 884; * * * cf. James Baird Co. v. Gimbel Bros., 2 Cir., 64 F.2d 344.

When plaintiff used defendant's offer in computing his own bid, he bound himself to perform in reliance on defendant's terms. Though defendant did not bargain for this use of its bid neither did defendant make it idly, indifferent to whether it would be used or not. On the contrary it is reasonable to suppose that defendant submitted its bid to obtain the subcontract. It was bound to realize the substantial possibility that its bid would be the lowest, and that it would be included by plaintiff in his bid. It was to its own interest that the contractor be awarded the general contract; the lower the subcontract bid, the lower the general contractor's bid was likely to be and the greater its chance of acceptance and hence the greater defendant's chance of getting the paving subcontract. Defendant had reason not only to expect plaintiff to rely on its bid but to want him to. Clearly defendant had a stake in plaintiff's reliance on its bid. Given this interest and the fact that plaintiff is bound by his own bid, it is only fair that plaintiff should have at least an opportunity to accept defendant's bid after the general contract has been awarded to him.

It bears noting that a general contractor is not free to delay acceptance after he has been awarded the general contract in the hope of getting a better price. Nor can he reopen bargaining with the subcontractor and at the same time claim a continuing right to accept the original offer. See, R.J. Daum Const. Co. v. Child, Utah, 247 P.2d 817, 823. In the present case plaintiff promptly informed defendant that plaintiff was being awarded the job and that the subcontract was being awarded to defendant.

Defendant contends, however, that its bid was the result of mistake and that it was therefore entitled to revoke it. * * * Plaintiff, however, had no reason to know that defendant had made a mistake in submitting its bid, since there was usually a variance of 160 per cent between the highest and lowest bids for paving in the desert around Lancaster. He committed himself to performing the main contract in reliance on defendant's figures. Under these circumstances defendant's mistake, far from relieving it of its obligation, constitutes an additional reason for enforcing it, for it misled plaintiff as to the cost of doing the paving. Even had it been clearly understood that defendant's offer was revocable until accepted, it would not necessarily follow that defendant had no duty to exercise reasonable care in preparing its bid. It presented its bid with knowledge of the substantial possibility that it would be used by plaintiff; it could foresee the harm that would ensue from an erroneous underestimate of the cost. Moreover, it was motivated by its own business interest. Whether or not these considerations alone would justify recovery for negligence had the case been tried on that theory (see Biakanja v. Irving, 49 Cal.2d 647, 650, 320 P.2d 16), they are persuasive that defendant's mistake should not defeat recovery under the rule of section 90 of the Restatement of Contracts. As between the subcontractor who made the bid and the general contractor who reasonably relied on it, the loss resulting from the mistake should fall on the party who caused it.

* * *

The judgment is affirmed.

LANGDELL, A SUMMARY OF THE LAW OF CONTRACTS

§ 178 at 240–41 (2d ed. 1880).

An offer which contains no stipulation as to how long it shall continue, as it confers no right on the offeree, is in its nature revocable at any moment. * * * An offer, therefore, which the party making it has no power to revoke, is a legal impossibility.

RESTATEMENT (SECOND) OF CONTRACTS § 87(2).

An offer which the offeror should reasonably expect to induce action or forbearance of a substantial character on the part of the offeree before acceptance and which does induce such action or forbearance is binding as an option contract to the extent necessary to avoid injustice.

PROBLEM 4-12

Dan offers to sell his car to Adrienne if she promises to buy it for $400. Before accepting, Adrienne runs out to the store and buys accessories for the car worth hundreds of dollars. Dan then decides not to sell his car. He asks whether he is bound to sell the car to Adrienne and, if so, if he is liable for her lost expectancy or the amount of her purchases.

NOTE:
RELIANCE IN THE BARGAINING CONTEXT

Recall Hoffman v. Red Owl Stores, Inc. in Chapter Two. The case illustrates that a prospective offeror may be liable for the other party's reasonable reliance on promises and representations made during pre-offer negotiations. Although few cases have faced this issue, many courts and analysts have cited Hoffman, and the case presages future developments.

Like many such "advances" in the law, Hoffman raises more questions than it answers. For example, what is the appropriate remedy for the relying party, lost expectancy or reliance damages? See Chapter Three. If you represent a party like Red Owl Stores, what advice can you give your client to ensure that the client will not incur liability during the bargaining process? What is the nature of the reliance that is actionable?

It is worthwhile to contrast the Anglo-American approach with the general approach in German and French law:

KESSLER AND FINE, CULPA IN CONTRAHENDO, BARGAINING IN GOOD FAITH, AND FREEDOM OF CONTRACT: A COMPARATIVE STUDY

77 Harv. L. Rev. 401, 420–21 (1964).

Once negotiations have reached the stage where one of the parties has made an offer, contract law is confronted with delicate problems of adjusting the possibly conflicting interests of the parties. Should an offeree be entitled to rely on an offer or should the offeror, according to the bargain (reciprocity) principle, be free to revoke with impunity so long as the other party has not committed himself by acceptance? Should a middle position be taken? This would mean that a mere offer cannot be relied upon. The offeree who changes his position before acceptance has himself to blame if the offeror changes his mind. But a firm offer, *i.e.,* an offer coupled with a promise to keep it open for a stated period, might be treated differently. All of these solutions have at one time or another been adopted by the various legal systems. Considerations of tradition, of logic, and of utility have been given different weight.

The German law, in its solicitude for the interests of the offeree and in order "to speed up transactions," has gone farthest in breaking with the bargain principle. Unless the offeror by appropriate language has given fair warning to the offeree that the offer is not binding, any offer once communicated is binding. [Ed. note: See the German Civil Code § 145.] But an offer lapses if there is no timely acceptance and the risk of loss or delay of an acceptance is on the offeree and not, as under common law, on the offeror. The French law has not gone quite so far. An ordinary offer is revocable until accepted. On the other hand, the firm offer, which may set a period for reply either expressly or "by implication," is binding. There is considerable controversy with regard to the consequences of revocation. According to one view revocation is ineffective; according to another it entitles the offeree to reliance damages.

SECTION EIGHT: BARGAINING AT A DISTANCE

ADAMS V. LINDSELL

King's Bench, 1818.
1 Barn. & Ald. 681.

Action for non-delivery of wool according to agreement. At the trial at the last Lent Assizes for the county of Worcester, before Burrough J. it appeared that the defendants, who were dealers in wool, at St. Ives, in the county of Huntingdon, had, on Tuesday the 2d of September 1817, written the following letter to the plaintiffs, who were woollen manufacturers residing in Bromsgrove, Worcestershire. "We now offer you eight hundred tods of wether fleeces, of a good fair quality of our country wool, at 35s. 6d.

per tod, to be delivered at Leicester, and to be paid for by two months' bill in two months, and to be weighed up by your agent within fourteen days, receiving your answer in course of post."

This letter was misdirected by the defendants, to Bromsgrove, Leicestershire, in consequence of which it was not received by the plaintiffs in Worcestershire till 7 P.M. on Friday, September 5th. On that evening the plaintiffs wrote an answer, agreeing to accept the wool on the terms proposed. The course of the post between St. Ives and Bromsgrove is through London, and consequently this answer was not received by the defendants till Tuesday, September 9th. On the Monday September 8th, the defendants not having, as they expected, received an answer on Sunday September 7th, (which in case their letter had not been misdirected, would have been in the usual course of the post,) sold the wool in question to another person. Under these circumstances, the learned Judge held, that the delay having been occasioned by the neglect of the defendants, the jury must take it, that the answer did come back in due course of post; and that then the defendants were liable for the loss that had been sustained: and the plaintiffs accordingly recovered a verdict.

Jervis having in Easter term obtained a rule nisi for a new trial, on the ground that there was no binding contract between the parties,

Dauncey, Puller, and Richardson, shewed cause. They contended, that at the moment of the acceptance of the offer of the defendants by the plaintiffs, the former became bound. And that was on the Friday evening, when there had been no change of circumstances. They were then stopped by the Court, who called upon

Jervis and Campbell in support of the rule. They relied on *Payne v. Cave (a),* and more particularly on *Cooke v. Oxley (b).* In that case, Oxley, who had proposed to sell goods to Cooke, and given him a certain time at his request, to determine whether he would buy them or not, was held not liable to the performance of the contract, even though Cooke, within the specified time, had determined to buy them, and given Oxley notice to that effect. So here the defendants who have proposed by letter to sell this wool, are not to be held liable, even though it be now admitted that the answer did come back in due course of post. Till the plaintiffs' answer was actually received, there could be no binding contract between the parties; and before then, the defendants had retracted their offer, by selling the wool to other persons. But

The Court said, that if that were so, no contract could ever be completed by the post. For if the defendants were not bound by their offer when accepted by the plaintiffs till the answer was received, then the plaintiffs ought not to be bound till after they had received the notification that the defendants had received their answer and assented to it. And so it might go on ad infinitum. The defendants must be considered in law as making, during every instant of the time their letter was travelling, the same identical offer to the plaintiffs; and then the contract is completed by the acceptance of it by the latter. Then as to the delay in notifying the acceptance, that arises entirely from the mistake of the defendants, and it therefore must be taken as against them, that the plaintiffs' answer was received in course of post.

Rule discharged.

MORRISON v. THOELKE, 155 So. 2d 889 (1963). [Owners of real estate accepted an offer to sell the land by signing a written contract and sending it to purchasers' lawyer. Owners called the lawyer and repudiated their agreement, however, before the written contract arrived in the mail. The issue before the court was whether this repudiation was effective. Owners argued that the right to recall mail according to modern postal regulations makes the Post Office the sender's agent. Thus acceptance could occur only upon receipt. The court, however, adhered to the rule in Adams v. Lindsell and held that the repudiation was invalid. The court based its decision on "traditional acceptance" of the rule of Adams v. Lindsell, and on the need for a definite and certain rule. The court also noted that the equities in this situation favored neither party.]

LEWIS v. BROWNING, 130 Mass. 173 (Mass. 1881).

GRAY, C.J.

In *M'Culloch* v. *Eagle Ins. Co.* 18 Mass. 278, 1 Pick. 278, this court held that a contract made by mutual letters was not complete until the letter accepting the offer had been received by the person making the offer; and the correctness of that decision is maintained, upon an able and elaborate discussion of reasons and authorities, in Langdell on Contracts (2d ed.) 989–996. In England, New York and New Jersey, and in the Supreme Court of the United States, the opposite view has prevailed, and the contract has been deemed to be completed as soon as the letter of acceptance has been put into the post-office duly addressed. *Adams v. Lindsell,* 1 B. & Ald. 681. * * *

But this case does not require a consideration of the general question; for, in any view, the person making the offer may always, if he chooses, make the formation of the contract which he proposes dependent upon the actual communication to himself of the acceptance. * * * And in the case at bar, the letter written in the plaintiff's behalf by her husband as her agent on July 8, 1878, in California, and addressed to the defendant at Boston, appears to us clearly to manifest such an intention. After proposing the terms of an agreement for a new lease, he says: "If you agree to this plan, and will telegraph me on receipt of this, I will forward power of attorney to Mr. Ware," the plaintiff's attorney in Boston. "Telegraph me 'yes' or 'no.' If 'no,' I will go on at once to Boston with my wife, and between us we will try to recover our lost ground. If I do not hear from you by the 18th or 20th, I shall conclude 'no.'" Taking the whole letter together, the offer is made dependent upon an actual communication to the plaintiff of the defendant's acceptance on or before the 20th of July, and does not discharge the old lease, nor bind the plaintiff to execute a new one, unless the acceptance reaches California within that time. Assuming, therefore, that the defendant's delivery of a despatch at the telegraph office had the same effect as the mailing of a letter, he has no ground of exception to the ruling at the trial.

Exceptions overruled.

PROBLEM 4-13

The New York Times, reporting the death of Mel Hein, the star football player for the New York Giants in the 1930s and 1940s, mentioned the following facts: After finishing his collegiate football career at Washington State, Hein sent letters to several National Football League teams, announcing his availability. The Providence Steamrollers responded affirmatively, offering Hein a contract for $125 per game. Hein signed the contract and mailed it to the Steamrollers. As luck would have it, the Giants offer of $150 per game reached Hein the next day. Hein wired the postmaster in Providence and asked him to locate the Steamroller letter and to send it back to him. The postmaster complied with Hein's request and he then accepted the Giants' offer. Suppose the Steamrollers learned of these facts. Would they have had any legal rights against Hein?

NOTE: ELECTRONIC CONTRACT ISSUES

In the twenty-first century, parties are forming many contracts electronically, for example, via the internet or via e-mail. Such conduct raises questions concerning the appropriate nature and content of contract formation rules to facilitate electronic contracting. For cases and materials on some of the issues raised by this mode of communication, see Chapter 5. Several statutory responses to electronic contracting have been drafted, such as the Uniform Computer Information Transactions Act (UCITA), which deals with "information" licensing, and the Uniform Electronic Transactions Act (UETA), which "remove[s] barriers to electronic commerce by validating and effectuating electronic records and signatures. [UETA] is NOT a general contracting statute—the substantive rules of contracts remain unaffected by UETA." UETA, Prefatory Note. For more on these and other laws, see Winn and Pullen, Despatches From the Front: Recent Skirmishes Along the Frontiers of Electronic Contracting Law, 55 Business Lawyer 455 (1999). The Electronic Signatures in Global and National Commerce Act, 15 U.S.C. § 7001 (as amended 2006), enforces electronic signatures, but is limited in scope. For more on this act, see, e.g., Carl, Ciocchetti, Barton & Christensen, Are Online Business Transactions Executed by Electronic Signatures Legally Binding? 2001 Duke L. & Tech. Rev. 5.

NOTE:
CONTRACT FORMATION REVISITED

Is contract law on formation consistent with when parties typically *believe* themselves to be bound? Consider a recent paper by Wilkinson-Ryan and Hoffman, *The Common Sense of Contract Formation,* 67 Stanford L. Rev. 1269 (2015). Wilkinson-Ryan and Hoffman, studying lay subjects, posed a series of hypotheticals mirroring the kinds of cases you have read. They found that, generally, subjects believed formation happened when parties *signed documents* or *paid for the goods*, not when they communicated assent verbally. For example, the authors asked subjects when a binding contract existed in the following mailbox-rule scenario:

> "Janine is looking to hire a general contractor to rehab her house. She interviews Jayson, who makes a good impression. He gives her a standard form contract, which he has signed, that lays out the terms and conditions of the job. She decides to take it home to think over the deal. At home, she signs the form. The next day, she puts it in the mail. Two days later, he receives it"

Subjects (recruited online) responded:

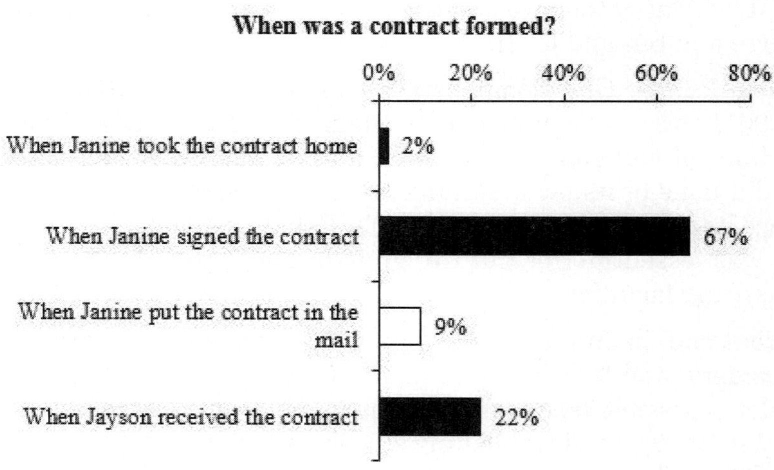

Wilkinson-Ryan and Hoffman conclude that "individuals privilege particular behavioral moments—signature, payment, and possession—above the verbal communication of assent. * * * We surmise that the prototypical contract implicates the vernacular of 'doing the paperwork,' 'getting it in writing,' and 'signing on the dotted line.' " What implications do these findings have for policy—particularly, regarding firms' ability to manipulate lay views of formation to their benefit?

SECTION NINE: AGREEMENTS TO AGREE AND RELATED MATTERS

After some negotiations, contracting parties often decide to draft a preliminary writing of some kind. They may want to clarify their respective bargaining positions or to record points on which they have reached agreement. The writing thus facilitates further negotiation of the ultimate agreement. Sometimes the parties may even intend to be bound by their preliminary agreement, leaving for future negotiation an issue on which they cannot presently agree or a term dependent on some future development, such as a change in market rates of interest. The challenge of the law is to determine when agreements preliminary in some sense should be enforced and, when enforced, to determine the appropriate remedy for breach.

ARNOLD PALMER GOLF CO. V. FUQUA INDUS., INC.

United States Court of Appeals, Sixth Circuit, 1976.
541 F.2d 584.

MCCREE, CIRCUIT JUDGE.

This is an appeal from the district court's grant of summary judgment in favor of defendant Fuqua Industries, Inc. (Fuqua) in an action for breach of contract. The district court determined that a document captioned "Memorandum of Intent" and signed by both parties was not a contract because it evidenced the intent of the parties not to be contractually bound. We reverse and remand for trial.

Arnold Palmer Golf Company (Palmer) was incorporated under Ohio law in 1961, and has been primarily engaged in designing and marketing various lines of golf clubs, balls, bags, gloves, and other golf accessories. Palmer did none of its own manufacturing, but engaged other companies to produce its products. In the late 1960's, Palmer's management concluded that it was essential for future growth and profitability to acquire manufacturing facilities.

To that end, in January, 1969, Mark McCormack, Palmer's Executive Vice-President, and E.D. Kenna, Fuqua's President, met in New York City to consider a possible business relationship between the two corporations. The parties' interest in establishing a business relationship continued and they held several more meetings and discussions where the general outline of the proposed relationship was defined. In November 1969, Fuqua, with Palmer's assistance and approval, acquired Fernquest and Johnson, a California manufacturer of golf clubs. The minutes of the Fuqua Board of Directors meeting on November 3, 1969, reveal that Fuqua:

> proposed that this Corporation participate in the golf equipment industry in association with Arnold Palmer Golf Co. and Arnold

Palmer Enterprises, Inc. The business would be conducted in two parts. One part would be composed of a corporation engaged in the manufacture and sale of golf clubs and equipment directly related to the playing of the game of golf. This Corporation would be owned to the extent of 25% by Fuqua and 75% by the Arnold Palmer interests. Fuqua would transfer the Fernquest & Johnson business to the new corporation as Fuqua's contribution.

In November and December of 1969 further discussions and negotiations occurred and revised drafts of a memorandum of intent were distributed.

The culmination of the discussions was a six page document denominated as a Memorandum of Intent. It provided in the first paragraph that:

> This memorandum will serve to confirm the general understanding which has been reached regarding the acquisition of 25% of the stock of Arnold Palmer Golf Company ("Palmer") by Fuqua Industries, Inc. ("Fuqua") in exchange for all of the outstanding stock of Fernquest and Johnson Golf Company, Inc. ("F & J"), a wholly-owned California subsidiary of Fuqua, and money in the amount of $700,000; and for the rendition of management services by Fuqua.

The Memorandum of Intent contained detailed statements concerning, *inter alia,* the form of the combination, the manner in which the business would be conducted, the loans that Fuqua agreed to make to Palmer, and the warranties and covenants to be contained in the definitive agreement.

Paragraph 10 of the Memorandum of Intent stated:

> (10) *Preparation of Definitive Agreement.* Counsel for Palmer and counsel for Fuqua will proceed as promptly as possible to prepare an agreement acceptable to Palmer and Fuqua for the proposed combination of businesses. Such agreement will contain the representations, warranties, covenants and conditions, as generally outlined in the example submitted by Fuqua to Palmer * * *.

In the last paragraph of the Memorandum of Intent, the parties indicated that:

> (11) *Conditions.* The obligations of Palmer and Fuqua shall be subject to fulfillment of the following conditions:
>
> > (i) preparation of the definitive agreement for the proposed combination in form and content satisfactory to both parties and their respective counsel;

(ii) approval of such definitive agreement by the Board of Directors of Fuqua; * * *.

The Memorandum of Intent was signed by Palmer and by the President of Fuqua. Fuqua had earlier released a statement to the press upon Palmer's signing that "Fuqua Industries, Inc., and The Arnold Palmer Golf Co. have agreed to cooperate in an enterprise that will serve the golfing industry, from the golfer to the greens keeper."

In February, 1970, the Chairman of Fuqua's Board of Directors, J.B. Fuqua, told Douglas Kenna, Fuqua's President, that he did not want to go through with the Palmer deal. Shortly thereafter Kenna informed one of Palmer's corporate officers that the transaction was terminated.

Palmer filed the complaint in this case on July 24, 1970. Nearly three and one-half years later, on January 14, 1974, the defendant filed a motion for summary judgment. More than one year after the briefs had been filed by the parties, on May 30, 1975, the district court granted defendant's motion.

The district court determined that:

> The parties were not to be subject to any obligations until a definitive agreement satisfactory to the parties and their counsel had been prepared. The fact that this agreement had to be "satisfactory" implies necessarily that such an agreement might be unsatisfactory. * * * The parties by the terms they used elected not to be bound by this memorandum and the Court finds that they were not bound.

The primary issue in this case is whether the parties intended to enter into a binding agreement when they signed the Memorandum of Intent, and the primary issue in this appeal is whether the district court erred in determining this question on a motion for summary judgment. The substantive law of Ohio applies.

We agree with the district court that both parties must have a clear understanding of the terms of an agreement and an intention to be bound by its terms before an enforceable contract is created. As Professor Corbin has observed:

> The courts are quite agreed upon general principles. The parties have power to contract as they please. They can bind themselves orally or by informal letters or telegrams if they like. On the other hand, they can maintain complete immunity from all obligation, even though they have expressed agreement orally or informally upon every detail of a complex transaction. The matter is merely one of expressed intention. If their expressions convince the court that they intended to be bound without a formal document, their contract is consummated, and the expected

> formal document will be nothing more than a memorial of that contract. 1 Corbin on Contracts, § 30 (1963). [Footnote omitted.]

The decision whether the parties intended to enter a contract must be based upon an evaluation of the circumstances surrounding the parties' discussions. The introduction of extrinsic evidence does not violate the parol evidence rule because that rule applies only after an integrated or a partially integrated agreement has been found. *Itek Corp. v. Chicago Aerial,* 248 A.2d 625 (Del.1968) * * *.

At bottom, the question whether the parties intended a contract is a factual one, not a legal one, and, except in the clearest cases, the question is for the finder of fact to resolve. * * *

* * *

The Delaware Supreme Court considered a case similar to this one in *Itek Corp. v. Chicago Aerial, supra.* Like the district court here, the trial court in *Itek* granted defendants' motion for summary judgment in a breach of contract action based upon a letter of intent. The letter of intent provided that the parties:

> [S]hall make every reasonable effort to agree upon and have prepared as quickly as possible a contract providing for the foregoing purchase by Itek and sale by CAI, subject to the approval of CAI stockholders, embodying the above terms and such other terms and conditions as the parties shall agree upon. If the parties fail to agree upon and execute such a contract they shall be under no further obligations to one another. 248 A.2d at 627.

The trial judge decided in favor of the defendants because of the last sentence quoted above. The Delaware Supreme Court, considering the entire document and other evidence submitted by the plaintiff, reversed, determining that:

> there is evidence which, if accepted by the trier of fact, would support the conclusion that * * * Itek and CAI intended to be bound * * *. There is also evidence which, if accepted by the trier of fact, would support the conclusion that subsequently, * * * CAI willfully failed to negotiate in good faith and to make "every reasonable effort" to agree upon a formal contract, as it was required to do. 248 A.2d at 629.

In a Third Circuit opinion, *Melo-Sonics Corp. v. Cropp,* 342 F.2d 856 (1965), the court reversed a district court's judgment in favor of defendants on a motion to dismiss a complaint. The plaintiffs contended that they had a contract with defendants which the latter had breached. Plaintiffs relied on a telegram they sent to defendants, and defendants' subsequent acceptance, as constituting a contractual agreement. The telegram provided in pertinent part:

> My three clients are willing to sell their capital stock in said corporations for the total price of one million five hundred thousand ($1,500,000) dollars subject to formalizing a preliminary agreement along lines previously discussed. Will be in your office at 10:00 A.M. on February 15, 1960 with my clients for purpose of formalizing such an agreement. 342 F.2d at 858.

The defendants eventually notified plaintiffs that they would not sign the agreement, whereupon plaintiffs filed suit.

The reviewing court pointed out that it would be permissible for the district court to make a finding of fact that no contract existed after it had conducted a full hearing, but that where no trial had been conducted and no findings of fact had been made it was improper to grant the defendants' motion to dismiss because plaintiffs' claim, if proved, entitled them to recovery.

Considering this appeal in the light of these authorities, we determine that our proper course is to remand this case to the district court for trial because we believe that the issue of the parties' intention to be bound is a proper one for resolution by the trier of fact. Upon first blush it may appear that the Memorandum of Intent is no more than preliminary negotiation between the parties. A cursory reading of the conditions contained in paragraph 11, by themselves, may suggest that the parties did not intend to be bound by the Memorandum of Intent.

Nevertheless, the memorandum recited that a "general understanding [had] been reached." And, as the *Itek* court noted, the entire document and relevant circumstances surrounding its adoption must be considered in making a determination of the parties' intention.[1] In this case we find an extensive document that appears to reflect all essential terms concerning the transfer of Arnold Palmer stock to Fuqua in exchange for all outstanding stock in Fernquest and Johnson. The form of combination, the location of the principal office of Palmer, the license rights, employment contracts of Palmer personnel and the financial obligations of Fuqua are a few of the many areas covered in the Memorandum of Intent, and they are all described in unqualified terms. The Memorandum states, for instance, that "Fuqua *will* transfer all of the * * * stock," that the "principal office of Palmer *will* be moved to Atlanta," that "Palmer * * * *shall* possess an exclusive license," and that "Fuqua *agrees* to advance to Palmer up to an aggregate of $700,000 * * *." [Emphasis added.]

---

[1] Parties may orally or by informal memoranda, or by both, agree upon all essential terms of the contract and effectively bind themselves, if that is their intention, even though they contemplate the execution, at a later time, of a formal document to memorialize their undertaking. *Comerata v. Chaumont, Inc.,* 52 N.J.Super. 299, 145 A.2d 471 (1958).

Paragraph 10 of the Memorandum states, also in unqualified language, that counsel for the parties "will proceed as promptly as possible to prepare an agreement acceptable to [the parties] * * *." We believe that this paragraph may be read merely to impose an obligation upon the parties to memorialize their agreement. We do not mean to suggest that this is the correct interpretation. The provision is also susceptible to an interpretation that the parties did not intend to be bound.

As we have indicated above, it is permissible to refer to extrinsic evidence to determine whether the parties intended to be bound by the Memorandum of Intent. In this regard, we observe that Fuqua circulated a press release in January 1970 that would tend to sustain Palmer's claim that the two parties intended to be bound by the Memorandum of Intent. Fuqua's statement said that the two companies "have agreed to cooperate in an enterprise that will serve the golfing industry."

Upon a review of the evidence submitted in connection with the motion for summary judgment, we believe that there is presented a factual issue whether the parties contractually obligated themselves to prepare a definitive agreement in accordance with the understanding of the parties contained in the Memorandum of Intent. * * * Because the facts and the inferences from the facts in this case indicate that the parties may have intended to be bound by the Memorandum of Intent, we hold that the district court erred in determining that no contract existed as a matter of law.

We reject appellee's argument that summary judgment was appropriate because the obligations of the parties were subject to an express condition that was not met. We believe a question of fact is presented whether the parties intended the conditions in paragraph 11 to operate only if the definitive agreement was not in conformity with the general understanding contained in the Memorandum of Intent. * * * The parties may well have intended that there should be no binding obligation until the definitive agreement was signed, but we regard this question as one for the fact finder to determine after a consideration of the relevant evidence.

* * *

Accordingly, the judgment of the district court is reversed and the case is remanded for proceedings not inconsistent with this opinion.

RESTATEMENT (SECOND) OF CONTRACTS § 27.

Existence of Contract Where Written Memorial is Contemplated

Manifestations of assent that are in themselves sufficient to conclude a contract will not be prevented from so operating by the fact that the parties also manifest an intention to prepare and adopt a written memorial thereof; but the circumstances may show that the agreements are preliminary negotiations.

Comment:

a. Parties who plan to make a final written instrument as the expression of their contract necessarily discuss the proposed terms of the contract before they enter into it and often, before the final writing is made, agree upon all the terms which they plan to incorporate therein. This they may do orally or by exchange of several writings. It is possible thus to make a contract the terms of which include an obligation to execute subsequently a final writing which shall contain certain provisions. If parties have definitely agreed that they will do so, and that the final writing shall contain these provisions and no others, they have then concluded the contract.

b. On the other hand, if either party knows or has reason to know that the other party regards the agreement as incomplete and intends that no obligation shall exist until other terms are assented to or until the whole has been reduced to another written form, the preliminary negotiations and agreements do not constitute a contract.

c. Among the circumstances which may be helpful in determining whether a contract has been concluded are the following: the extent to which express agreement has been reached on all the terms to be included, whether the contract is of a type usually put in writing, whether it needs a formal writing for its full expression, whether it has few or many details, whether the amount involved is large or small, whether it is a common or unusual contract, whether a standard form of contract is widely used in similar transactions, and whether either party takes any action in preparation for performance during the negotiations. Such circumstances may be shown by oral testimony or by correspondence or other preliminary or partially complete writings.

d. Even though a binding contract is made before a contemplated written memorial is prepared and adopted, the subsequent written document may make a binding modification of the terms previously agreed to.

MILLER V. GLEGENHEIMER

Supreme Court of Vermont, 2016.
161 A.3d 524.

REIBER, C.J.

This is an appeal from the trial court's decision on the merits. The case requires us to determine whether a series of e-mails exchanged between two business partners who jointly own a document shredding company constituted an enforceable contract to sell one partner's interest in the company to the other partner. The defendant (seller) appeals the trial court's determination that the partners had an enforceable contract and that seller is obligated to negotiate the remaining terms of the deal in good faith. He argues that there were too many open terms to produce an enforceable contract and that the partners had no intent to be bound to a contract by their e-mails. The plaintiff (buyer) cross-appeals and argues that the e-mails do demonstrate intent to be bound and that we should enforce the contract. We reject buyer's argument that the parties had entered into a fully completed contract, agree with seller that there was no enforceable contract at all, and accordingly reverse and enter judgment for defendant.

Buyer and seller are joint owners and two of three cofounders of a document shredding company (the company). Each partner currently owns half of the stock in the company. The company has been successful. The same cannot be said of its partners' working relationship. By 2010, it had become apparent to the partners that they were not working well together, so they hired an outside CEO and put in place a three-person advisory board to resolve their disputes independently. They also considered selling the company to an interested outside purchaser but could not agree on the price. The following year, the outside CEO left and seller became CEO. Buyer withdrew from day-to-day operations for both business and personal reasons.

The partners then conducted months of negotiations in an attempt to include a buy-sell agreement in their shareholders' agreement. The buy-sell agreement would create a process for one partner to buy out the other. The partners engaged counsel and exchanged numerous drafts of the proposed agreement. They spent over $30,000 of company money on the effort. In the end, buyer refused to sign the final draft of the agreement, and negotiations fell apart on December 9, 2013.

The buy-sell agreement drafts had several features that mirrored seller's eventual offer to buyer. These included a "claw-back provision," which provided that if one partner bought out the other and then sold the company for a higher price within two years, the partner who was bought out would receive half of the difference between the value at which he sold the company and the value his partner received when he resold it. The buy-sell agreement drafts did not name a fixed price for the company, and they did not include a non compete agreement or a non solicitation agreement.

On December 26, fifteen days after negotiations had broken down over the buy-sell agreement, seller sent buyer an e-mail offering terms of sale for his stock in the company. In the e-mail, seller offered to sell the company to buyer at a price reflecting the average of two appraisals they had previously commissioned and also with the claw-back provision in place:

> Your decision not to sign the buy/sell agreement on the day of our last Board meeting on December 9, 2013, an agreement that the Board had endorsed and we had previously agreed to sign, has made me realize that our goals for the company are inconsistent and incompatible with each other.
>
> Accordingly, I am offering you the option to purchase my share of [the company] for a price [which] . . . reflects the average of the 2 professional appraisals we had done in the fall of 2012. I extend this offer to you in a good faith attempt to allow you to purchase the entire company with 1 condition, namely, if you sell the company within 2 years of acquiring my shares, you will agree to equally split with me all proceeds in excess of [twice the price above]. This offer will remain open until Friday, January 10, 2014 at which point it will be withdrawn.
>
> Likewise, I am prepared to purchase all of your shares on the same terms and conditions as outlined above.

Five days later, on December 31, buyer replied by e-mail that "I will accept" the offer, acknowledged the claw-back, and that seller should expect "definitive documents" with "customary provisions" within about two weeks:

> Thank you for your e-mail of December 26, 2013. I will accept your offer to purchase your shares of [the company] for a price of [same as proposed]. I also agree that the definitive documents evidencing this sale will contain a claw-back in the event that I sell the company within two years of the closing in excess of [twice the price above] . . . You should expect to see drafts of the definitive documents containing customary provisions for transactions of this type prior to January 10th.

On January 9, 2014, buyer sent a short e-mail to seller and attached a twelve-page Stock Purchase Agreement and a six-page Confidentiality, Non-Competition, and Non-Solicitation Agreement (Non-Compete Agreement). In the Non-Compete Agreement, seller would agree not to compete with the company or solicit employees or customers of the company for three years. The Non-Compete Agreement referred to itself as "a condition precedent" of the Stock Purchase Agreement. The agreements also lowered the price buyer offered seller for his shares by $50,000, assigning that consideration to the Non-Compete Agreement. Five days later, on January 14, seller responded that he had reviewed the Stock Purchase Agreement and Non-Compete Agreement and would be withdrawing his offer to sell his shares:

> I am in receipt of the draft Stock Purchase Agreement and Non-compete. . . . After reviewing the documents with my counsel, and after further contemplation of the terms of the sale as well as my

> own personal investment in the company, I have determined that it is not in my best interest to move forward with the transaction at this time. Accordingly, I am withdrawing my offer to sell my shares.

In the same e-mail, seller also told buyer that he would be stepping away from the day-to-day operations of the company by March 31.

Buyer brought suit against seller, requesting specific performance of the contract. Seller moved for summary judgment. The court, in its ruling on the motion for summary judgment, adopted a framework from New York law in which there are two categories of preliminary agreements: Type I and Type II. See Teachers Ins. & Annuity Ass'n of Am. v. Tribune Co., 670 F.Supp. 491, 498 (S.D.N.Y. 1987). The court defined a Type I agreement as "essentially a done deal that merely needs follow-up documentation" and a Type II agreement as "a preliminary agreement that obligates the partners to negotiate further terms in good faith." The court later used the same framework in its ruling on the merits of the case. In its ruling on the merits, the court found that buyer and seller had entered into a Type II agreement by exchanging their December e-mails. It found that buyer's January 9 e-mail and draft documents constituted a proposal of additional terms that did not invalidate the original acceptance of the offer. Further, the court ordered that the partners were obligated to negotiate the remaining terms of the contract in good faith.

On appeal, seller argues that the court erred in its ruling on the merits when it found an enforceable contract to negotiate the remaining terms of the contract in good faith, specifically a Type II agreement. Buyer cross-appeals and argues that the court erred in not finding a Type I agreement. We conclude that there was no enforceable contract between buyer and seller and accordingly reverse the judgment for buyer.

We first address whether a series of e-mails exchanged between two business partners constitutes an enforceable contract, either for the terms of the contract or as a preliminary agreement to negotiate further terms in good faith. * * *

Our review is concerned with the "legal interpretation of whatever hazy agreement existed," namely whether there was an enforceable contract to negotiate the remaining terms in good faith, which is a question of law. Kellogg v. Shushereba, 2013 VT 76, ¶ 17, 194 Vt. 446, 82 A.3d 1121. We therefore review de novo whether there was an enforceable contract as a matter of law.

Preliminary agreements are not a novel concept. Courts have long acknowledged that there is a range of preliminary agreements, some of which are enforceable and some of which are not. * * *

Here, whether the series of e-mails constituted an enforceable contract or—instead—a preliminary agreement depends on two factors: the parties' intent to be bound and the definiteness of terms in the communications between the parties. * * * We therefore * * * begin our analysis by examining whether the parties intended to be bound by their e-mails. In doing so we recognize the paramount right of each party to determine the exact moment at which it becomes bound to an agreement. * * *

* * *

[W]e determine intent to be bound using an objective test. Evarts v. Forte, 135 Vt. 306, 310, 376 A.2d 766, 769 (1977) ("It is never enough that the parties think they have made a contract; they must express their subjective intent in a manner that is capable of understanding."). * * * Parties can show that they intend to be bound through their words or through their actions. See Restatement (Second) of Contracts § 18 (1981) . * * *

* * *

[W]e apply a four-factor test to determine whether parties intended to be bound:

> "(1) whether there has been an express reservation of the right not to be bound in the absence of a writing; (2) whether there has been partial performance of the contract; (3) whether all of the terms of the alleged contract have been agreed upon; and (4) whether the agreement at issue is the type of contract that is usually committed to writing."

Winston v. Mediafare Entm't Corp., 777 F.2d 78, 80 (2d Cir. 1985).

The first factor is "whether there has been an express reservation of the right not to be bound." When determining whether the partners expressly reserved the right not to be bound, we look first at the "parties' correspondence and other documentary evidence." Catamount Slate Prods., Inc. v. Sheldon, 2003 VT 112, ¶ 18. Here, the most relevant pieces of documentary evidence are the e-mails between the partners. A party's intent to be bound must be shown by his or her actions at the time of agreement. * * * The Second Circuit, from which we have adopted the four-factor * * * test, has found that a reference to a future writing shows an intent not to be bound. * * * This factor therefore weighs against enforceability.

* * *

The second factor is whether there has been partial performance of the contract. As the court found and as both buyer and seller acknowledge, there was no partial performance of the purported contract. We agree with the court that "[t]his factor weighs against enforceability."

The third factor is whether all the terms have been agreed on. As the court recognized by requiring the partners to negotiate the remaining terms in good faith, not all the terms were agreed on here. Several large and material terms were not decided. These include whether or not the contract includes a form of non compete or non solicitation agreement, the price to be paid for the shares (as opposed to the Non-Compete Agreement), and the structure of the claw-back provision. While it is true that "not all terms of a contract need to be fixed with absolute certainty," it is also true that an agreement "in which a material term is left for future negotiations, is unenforceable." Tractebel Energy Mktg., 487 F.3d at 95 (quotations omitted). Therefore, terms left open for negotiation must be minor terms, so buyer's argument that "they are not unimportant or fine details, but also they're not . . . insurmountable" is flawed.

* * *

The fourth * * * factor has two aspects: first, whether the agreement at issue is of a type that is usually committed to writing and, second, whether the agreement is so complex that the parties could not reasonably have expected to be bound without a writing." Willey v. Willey, 2006 VT 106, ¶ 18, 180 Vt. 421, 912 A.2d 441 (quotation omitted). We address the first aspect of this factor first. * * * [W]e construe this factor to ask whether this is the type of contract usually reduced to a formal writing of the type that seller contends it must be reduced to in order to be enforceable. The short answer is yes. The court likewise found that this is the type of contract that is usually reduced to a writing, and we agree. The court found that "[t]he parties agree they intended a written document to follow their emails."

* * *

We finally address the second aspect of the fourth factor: whether the potential contract is so complex that the partners could not reasonably have expected to be bound without a writing. Here, we conclude that it was. The contract the buyer prepared included a twelve-page Stock Purchase Agreement and a separate six-page Non-Compete Agreement. The court found that "there is no evidence presented that there was anything complicated about this deal." However, seller presented evidence that this contract contained numerous complicated provisions, including the claw-back and the Non-Compete Agreement. Seller testified, "[n]othing's simple about a 3.6-million dollar deal." While the court did not find this evidence credible, and while that determination lies with the court, the court erred in stating that there was "no evidence" of complexity. Further, the fact that the partners were considering a very similar agreement—the buy-sell agreement—to which they both agreed they were not bound without a signed writing also demonstrates that this potential contract was so complex that the partners could not reasonably have expected to be bound without a writing. This factor therefore weighs against enforceability.

[The court also discussed whether the alleged contract was sufficiently definite and concluded that the two e-mails that "framed" the terms of the agreement were unclear because they did not refer to the non-compete agreement and the reduction of the price by $50,000, and because they did not spell out the "particulars" of the claw-back provision.]

Reversed; judgment entered for defendant. [ROBINSON, J.'s concurrence is omitted.]

LLEWELLYN, ON WARRANTY OF QUALITY, AND SOCIETY

37 Colum. L. Rev. 341, 375, 379 (1937).

Our contract-law has yet built no tools to really cope with this vexing and puzzling situation of fact. The standing relation is not only real in business fact, it is also vibrant with legal implication. The trouble is that the legal implication is still—legally—inarticulate. It is felt—no question about that. It is felt—but it is not felt with any clarity. * * *

* * *

The problem, though wholly unsolved, is there, and is in ferment. It is not a theorist's creation; it is a fact, at work in the courts, warping the older, inadequate theory of the single deal. * * * The job is to give direction to the fermentation.

WHITFORD, IAN MACNEIL'S CONTRIBUTION TO CONTRACTS SCHOLARSHIP

1985 Wis. L. Rev. 545, 546–48.

Briefly, relational contracts emerge in the context of ongoing relationships. They are to be contrasted with what Macneil calls discrete contracts. Although all contracts have relational elements, contracts occurring between parties who have little interaction other than the contract itself tend to fall on the discrete end of the relational-discrete continuum. Macneil gives as an example of a mostly discrete transaction the purchase of gasoline at a service station along a superhighway.

The more generally accepted of Macneil's messages is that relational contracts differ from discrete contracts in that typically there is no single moment at which the parties confirm a meeting of the minds respecting the important terms of the contract. Rather, to quote Macneil:

> The exercise of choice [about contract content] is * * * an incremental process in which parties gather increasing information and gradually agree to more and more as they proceed. Indeed, the very process of exercising choice in such

circumstances, such as through engineering studies, may entail major parts of the total costs of the whole project as finally agreed.

Both economists and lawyers have come to acknowledge this behavioral reality. There is a growing body of economics literature explaining that in relational contracting it is commonly more in the parties' perceived self-interest to reach agreement gradually rather than all at one time, allowing much performance to occur while important terms remain to be negotiated. This economics literature speculates about what kinds of contracting strategies might be expected in these circumstances. * * *

If relational contracts lacking a grand meeting of the minds are to be enforced, there is no way to explain the results reached within the structure of classical contract law because that body of law provides only the parties' agreement as a reference point for determining contractual content. If the results of cases purporting to enforce such contracts are not to appear unpredictable and ad hoc, some basis outside the framework of classical contract law must be established for determining when liability begins, defining the terms of relationship, and setting the remedy upon breach.

JOSEPH MARTIN, JR., DELICATESSEN, INC. V. SCHUMACHER

Court of Appeals of New York, 1981.
52 N.Y.2d 105, 417 N.E.2d 541.

FUCHSBERG, JUDGE.

This case raises an issue fundamental to the law of contracts. It calls upon us to review a decision of the Appellate Division, 70 A.D.2d 1, 419 N.Y.S.2d 558 which held that a realty lease's provision that the rent for a renewal period was "to be agreed upon" may be enforceable.

The pertinent factual and procedural contexts in which the case reaches this court are uncomplicated. In 1973, the appellant, as landlord, leased a retail store to the respondent for a five-year term at a rent graduated upwards from $500 per month for the first year to $650 for the fifth. The renewal clause stated that "[t]he Tenant may renew this lease for an additional period of five years at annual rentals to be agreed upon; Tenant shall give Landlord thirty (30) days written notice, to be mailed certified mail, return receipt requested, of the intention to exercise such right". It is not disputed that the tenant gave timely notice of its desire to renew or that, once the landlord made it clear that he would do so only at a rental starting at $900 a month, the tenant engaged an appraiser who opined that a fair market rental value would be $545.41.

The tenant thereupon commenced an action for specific performance in Supreme Court, Suffolk County, to compel the landlord to extend the lease for the additional term at the appraiser's figure or such other sum as the court would decide was reasonable. For his part, the landlord in due course brought a holdover proceeding in the local District Court to evict the tenant. On the landlord's motion for summary judgment, the Supreme Court, holding that a bald agreement to agree on a future rental was unenforceable for uncertainty as a matter of law, dismissed the tenant's complaint. Concordantly, it denied as moot the tenant's motion to remove the District Court case to the Supreme Court and to consolidate the two suits.

It was on appeal by the tenant from these orders that the Appellate Division, expressly overruling an established line of cases in the process, reinstated the tenant's complaint and granted consolidation. In so doing, it reasoned that "a renewal clause in a lease providing for future agreement on the rent to be paid during the renewal term is enforceable if it is established that the parties' intent was not to terminate in the event of a failure to agree". It went on to provide that, if the tenant met that burden, the trial court could proceed to set a "reasonable rent". One of the Justices, concurring, would have eliminated the first step and required the trial court to proceed directly to the fixation of the rent. Each party now appeals by leave of the Appellate Division pursuant to CPLR 5602 (subd. [b], par. 1). The tenant seeks only a modification adopting the concurrer's position. The question formally certified to us by the Appellate Division is simply whether its order was properly made. Since we conclude that the disposition at the Supreme Court was the correct one, our answer must be in the negative.

We begin our analysis with the basic observation that, unless otherwise mandated by law (e.g., residential emergency rent control statutes), a contract is a private "ordering" in which a party binds himself to do, or not to do, a particular thing (*Fletcher v. Peck,* 6 Cranch [10 U.S.] 87, 136; 3 L.Ed. 162. Hart and Sachs, Legal Process, 147–148 [1958]). This liberty is no right at all if it is not accompanied by freedom not to contract. The corollary is that, before one may secure redress in our courts because another has failed to honor a promise, it must appear that the promisee assented to the obligation in question.

It also follows that, before the power of law can be invoked to enforce a promise, it must be sufficiently certain and specific so that what was promised can be ascertained. Otherwise, a court, in intervening, would be imposing its own conception of what the parties should or might have undertaken, rather than confining itself to the implementation of a bargain to which they have mutually committed themselves. Thus, definiteness as to material matters is of the very essence in contract law. Impenetrable vagueness and uncertainty will not do (1 Corbin, Contracts, § 95, p. 394 * * *).

Dictated by these principles, it is rightfully well settled in the common law of contracts in this State that a mere agreement to agree, in which a material term is left for future negotiations, is unenforceable. * * * This is especially true of the amount to be paid for the sale or lease of real property. * * * The rule applies all the more, and not the less, when, as here, the extraordinary remedy of specific performance is sought (11 Williston, Contracts [Jaeger 3d ed.], § 1424; Pomeroy, Equity Jurisprudence, § 1405).

This is not to say that the requirement for definiteness in the case before us now could only have been met by explicit expression of the rent to be paid. The concern is with substance, not form. It certainly would have sufficed, for instance, if a methodology for determining the rent was to be found within the four corners of the lease, for a rent so arrived at would have been the end product of agreement between the parties themselves. Nor would the agreement have failed for indefiniteness because it invited recourse to an objective extrinsic event, condition or standard on which the amount was made to depend. All of these, *inter alia,* would have come within the embrace of the maxim that what can be made certain is certain. * * *

But the renewal clause here in fact contains no such ingredients. Its unrevealing, unamplified language speaks to no more than "annual rentals to be agreed upon". Its simple words leave no room for legal construction or resolution of ambiguity. Neither tenant nor landlord is bound to any formula. There is not so much as a hint at a commitment to be bound by the "fair market rental value" which the tenant's expert reported or the "reasonable rent" the Appellate Division would impose, much less any definition of either. Nowhere is there an inkling that either of the parties directly or indirectly assented, upon accepting the clause, to subordinate the figure on which it ultimately would insist, to one fixed judicially, as the Appellate Division decreed be done, or, for that matter, by an arbitrator or other third party.

Finally, in this context, we note that the tenant's reliance on *May Metropolitan Corp. v. May Oil Burner Corp.,* 290 N.Y. 260, 49 N.E.2d 13 is misplaced. There the parties had executed a franchise agreement for the sale of oil burners. The contract provided for annual renewal, at which time each year's sales quota was "to be mutually agreed upon". In holding that the defendant's motion for summary judgment should have been denied, the court indicated that the plaintiff should be given an opportunity to establish that a series of annual renewals had ripened into a course of dealing from which it might be possible to give meaning to an otherwise uncertain term. * * *

For all these reasons, the order of the Appellate Division should be reversed, with costs, and the orders of the Supreme Court, Suffolk County, reinstated. The certified question, therefore, should be answered in the negative. * * *

* * *

JASEN, JUDGE (dissenting in part).

While I recognize that the traditional rule is that a provision for renewal of a lease must be "certain" in order to render it binding and enforceable, in my view the better rule would be that if the tenant can establish its entitlement to renewal under the lease, the mere presence of a provision calling for renewal at "rentals to be agreed upon" should not prevent judicial intervention to fix rent at a reasonable rate in order to avoid a forfeiture. Therefore, I would affirm the order of the Appellate Division for the reasons stated in the opinion * * * at the Appellate Division.

UNIFORM COMMERCIAL CODE § 2–204(3).

Even though one or more terms are left open a contract for sale does not fail for indefiniteness if the parties have intended to make a contract and there is a reasonably certain basis for giving an appropriate remedy.

KLEINSCHMIDT DIVISION OF SCM CORP. v. FUTURONICS CORP., 41 N.Y.2d 972, 973, 395 N.Y.S.2d 151, 152, 363 N.E.2d 701, 702 (1977). The basic philosophy of the sales article of the Uniform Commercial Code is simple. Practical business people cannot be expected to govern their actions with respect to nice legal formalisms. Thus, when there is basic agreement, however manifested and whether or not the precise moment of agreement may be determined, failure to articulate that agreement in the precise language of a lawyer, with every difficulty and contingency considered and resolved, will not prevent formation of a contract.

SECTION TEN: LIMITS ON THE SCOPE OF TRADITIONAL OFFER-ACCEPTANCE ANALYSIS—A SUMMARY

The excerpt that follows, written by Professor Rudolf Schlesinger, a distinguished professor at Cornell Law School for much of his career, summarizes a number of the limits on the application of traditional offer and acceptance analysis. We return to this theme again in Section Twelve of this chapter on contract formation in the form-contract setting.

SCHLESINGER, MANIFESTATION OF ASSENT WITHOUT IDENTIFIABLE SEQUENCE IN OFFER AND ACCEPTANCE

II Formation of Contracts 1583–1587, 1591–92 (R. Schlesinger ed., 1968).

There seems to be no doubt in American law that a contract can be formed without an identifiable sequence of offer and acceptance * * *.

Especially when large deals are concluded among corporations and individuals of substance, the usual sequence of events is not that of offer and acceptance; on the contrary, the businessmen who originally conduct the negotiations, often will consciously refrain from ever making a binding offer, realizing as they do that a large deal tends to be complex and that its terms have to be formulated by lawyers before it can be permitted to become a legally enforceable transaction. Thus the original negotiators will merely attempt to ascertain whether they see eye to eye concerning those aspects of the deal which seem to be most important from a business point of view. Once they do, or think they do, the negotiation is then turned over to the lawyers, usually with instructions to produce a document which all participants will be willing to sign. * * * When the lawyers take over, again there is no sequence of offer and acceptance, but rather a sequence of successive drafts. These drafts usually will not be regarded as offers, for the reason, among others, that the lawyers acting as draftsmen have no authority to make offers on behalf of their clients. After a number of drafts have been exchanged and discussed, the lawyers may finally come up with a draft which meets the approval of all of them, and of their clients. It is only then that the parties will proceed to the actual formation of the contract, and often this will be done by way of a formal "closing" * * * or in any event by simultaneous execution or delivery, in the course of a more or less ceremonial meeting, of the document or documents prepared by the lawyers.

In the usual negotiation of a large-scale transaction there is thus no room for offer and acceptance (except where options are involved). If the writers on contract law nevertheless continue to analyze the formation of contracts almost exclusively in terms of offer and acceptance, they may be right insofar as they speak of the majority of personal and business transactions of modest or medium size; but in the world of truly large-scale dealings, the traditional analysis is no longer in tune with present-day practice.

SECTION ELEVEN: INTRODUCTION TO CONTRACT FORMATION IN THE FORM CONTRACT SETTING

Much of what you have learned about the formation of contracts pursuant to the general theory of obligation "agreement with consideration" does not apply in any direct way to modern "form-pad" transactions. For one thing, the terminology you have learned is not the language used by merchants employing modern forms. Instead of talk about offer, acceptance, revocation, and rejection, the purchasing manager of a company usually speaks of purchase orders, acknowledgments, and invoices. Furthermore, today's merchants often do not bargain and reach agreement in the relatively logical and orderly fashion portrayed in some of the materials in this chapter. Instead, a seller or buyer sends a form to the other; the other typically does not read the form, but instead, sends a second form back to the first party. The second form may differ substantially from the first. During or after the exchange of forms that neither party reads, the seller frequently ships the goods and the buyer accepts and uses them. Is there a contract between these parties? What are its terms?

The drafters of Article 2 of the Uniform Commercial Code sought to recognize the foregoing complexities in form-pad transactions. Accordingly, they modified the common law of offer and acceptance in the sale of goods context. Consider the White and Summers excerpt as you read the Code provisions that follow the excerpt.

J. WHITE & R. SUMMERS, THE UNIFORM COMMERCIAL CODE

38, 53–54 (6th ed. 2010).

[I]t is a mistake to think of 2–207 as a law dealing principally with contract formation. Parties to sales much more often call on courts to use 2–207 to decide the terms of their contract after they exchange documents, perform, or start to perform and then fall into dispute. Here the courts are not deciding whether there is a contract. They are answering a different question: what are its terms?

* * *

Under the present state of the law we believe that there is no language that a lawyer can put on a form that will always assure the client of forming a contract on the client's own terms. These efforts will be frustrated by a responsive document that is expressly conditional on assent to that document's terms, by prior oral agreement or by the document's use as an acceptance, not an offer. If one must have a term, that party should bargain with the other party for the term; a client should not get it by a lawyer's sleight of hand. If a seller must have the term to reduce its liability, but cannot strike a bargain for it, the only answer may be to raise the price [or] buy insurance * * *.

UNIFORM COMMERCIAL CODE § 2–204(2).

An agreement sufficient to constitute a contract for sale may be found even though the moment of its making is undetermined.

UNIFORM COMMERCIAL CODE § 2–207.

Additional Terms in Acceptance or Confirmation

(1) A definite and seasonable expression of acceptance or a written confirmation which is sent within a reasonable time operates as an acceptance even though it states terms additional to or different from those offered or agreed upon, unless acceptance is expressly made conditional on assent to the additional or different terms.

(2) The additional terms are to be construed as proposals for addition to the contract. Between merchants such terms become part of the contract unless:

(a) the offer expressly limits acceptance to the terms of the offer;

(b) they materially alter it; or

(c) notification of objection to them has already been given or is given within a reasonable time after notice of them is received.

(3) Conduct by both parties which recognizes the existence of a contract is sufficient to establish a contract for sale although the writings of the parties do not otherwise establish a contract. In such case the terms of the particular contract consist of those terms on which the writings of the parties agree, together with any supplementary terms incorporated under any other provisions of this Act.

Official Comment

1. This section is intended to deal with two typical situations. The one is the written confirmation, where an agreement has been reached either orally or by informal correspondence between the parties and is followed by one or both of the parties sending formal memoranda embodying the terms so far as agreed upon and adding terms not discussed. The other situation is offer and acceptance, in which a wire or letter expressed and intended as an acceptance or the closing of an agreement adds further minor suggestions or proposals such as "ship by Tuesday," "rush," "ship draft against bill of lading inspection allowed," or the like. A frequent example of the second situation is the exchange of printed purchase order and acceptance (sometimes called "acknowledgment") forms. Because the forms are oriented to the thinking of the respective drafting parties, the terms contained in them often do not correspond. Often the seller's form contains terms different from or additional to those set forth in the buyer's form. Nevertheless, the parties proceed with the transaction. [Comment 1 was amended in 1966.]

2. Under this Article a proposed deal which in commercial understanding has in fact been closed is recognized as a contract. Therefore, any additional matter contained in the confirmation or in the acceptance falls within subsection (2) and must be regarded as a proposal

for an added term unless the acceptance is made conditional on the acceptance of the additional or different terms. [Comment 2 was amended in 1966.]

3. Whether or not additional or different terms will become part of the agreement depends upon the provisions of subsection (2). If they are such as materially to alter the original bargain, they will not be included unless expressly agreed to by the other party. If, however, they are terms which would not so change the bargain they will be incorporated unless notice of objection to them has already been given or is given within a reasonable time.

4. Examples of typical clauses which would normally "materially alter" the contract and so result in surprise or hardship if incorporated without express awareness by the other party are: a clause negating such standard warranties as that of merchantability or fitness for a particular purpose in circumstances in which either warranty normally attaches; a clause requiring a guaranty of 90% or 100% deliveries in a case such as a contract by cannery, where the usage of the trade allows greater quantity leeways; a clause reserving to the seller the power to cancel upon the buyer's failure to meet any invoice when due; a clause requiring that complaints be made in a time materially shorter than customary or reasonable.

5. Examples of clauses which involve no element of unreasonable surprise and which therefore are to be incorporated in the contract unless notice of objection is seasonably given are: a clause setting forth and perhaps enlarging slightly upon the seller's exemption due to supervening causes beyond his control, similar to those covered by the provision of this Article on merchant's excuse by failure of presupposed conditions or a clause fixing in advance any reasonable formula of proration under such circumstances; a clause fixing a reasonable time for complaints within customary limits, or in the case of a purchase for sub-sale, providing for inspection by the sub-purchaser; a clause providing for interest on overdue invoices or fixing the seller's standard credit terms where they are within the range of trade practice and do not limit any credit bargained for; a clause limiting the right of rejection for defects which fall within the customary trade tolerances for acceptance "with adjustment" or otherwise limiting remedy in a reasonable manner (see Sections 2–718 and 2–719).

6. If no answer is received within a reasonable time after additional terms are proposed, it is both fair and commercially sound to assume that their inclusion has been assented to. Where clauses on confirming forms sent by both parties conflict each party must be assumed to object to a clause of the other conflicting with one on the confirmation sent by himself. As a result the requirement that there be notice of objection which is found in subsection (2) is satisfied and the conflicting terms do not become a part

of the contract. The contract then consists of the terms originally expressly agreed to, terms on which the confirmations agree, and terms supplied by this Act, including subsection (2). The written confirmation is also subject to Section 2–201. Under that section a failure to respond permits enforcement of a prior oral agreement; under this section a failure to respond permits additional terms to become part of the agreement. * * *

NOTE: BASIC ROUTES TO CONTRACT FORMATION UNDER SECTION 2–207

Section 2–207 contemplates contract formation by at least four routes. Route A consists of that part of subsection 1 up to the comma, closing a contract via a "definite and seasonable expression of acceptance." Route A1 consists of that part of subsection 1 up to the comma, recognizing a contract via "a written confirmation" of terms "agreed upon." Route B consists of that part of subsection 1 after the comma. Route C consists of subsection 3. Be prepared to explain how the terms of the resulting contract may differ depending on which route controls contract formation.

STEMCOR USA, INC. V. TRIDENT STEEL CORP.

United States District Court, Southern District of New York, 2006.
471 F. Supp. 2d 362.

OPINION AND ORDER

KOELTL, DISTRICT JUDGE.

The petitioner, Stemcor USA, Inc. ("Stemcor"), filed a petition to compel arbitration under Sections 3 and 4 of the Federal Arbitration Act ("FAA"), 9 U.S.C. §§ 3, 4. Stemcor also moved for a preliminary injunction to stay three third-party actions filed against it by the respondent, Trident Steel Corporation ("Trident"), that are pending in the state courts of Texas. The parties agreed at a hearing on March 10, 2006 that the preliminary injunction motion and the underlying petition could be consolidated after supplemental briefing.

The Court today dispenses with both actions by denying Stemcor's petition to compel arbitration.

I.

The disputes at issue in the Texas actions arose out of Stemcor's sale of steel products to Trident between October 2000 and April 2002. During that period, the two companies entered into a series of twelve sales agreements for steel casings, or hollow steel pipe. Pursuant to those sales agreements, Stemcor delivered steel casings to Trident.

The parties do not dispute that their sales agreements constituted valid contracts. Trident initiated each purchase by sending to Stemcor a purchase order including the basic specifications of the steel casings desired. Each of Trident's purchase order forms included the following clause:

> 1. No terms or conditions, other than those stated herein, and no agreement or understanding in any way modifying the terms and conditions herein stated shall be binding upon purchaser, unless mutually agreed upon in writing.

(Ex. A to Decl. of Wendy C. Michael, Feb. 14, 2006.)

In response to Trident's purchase orders, Stemcor sent two subsequent documents to Trident: an acknowledgement form, alternately labeled a "Sales Contract" or a "Sale Note," sent prior to delivery of the goods, and a "Sales Invoice," sent following the delivery of goods. Each acknowledgement form included the following paragraph:

> This contract is made between the buyer and the seller whereby the buyer agrees to buy and the seller agrees to sell the undermentioned goods subject to the terms and conditions as stipulated hereafter. This contract reflects in its entirety all details as agreed between the parties thereto. Any changes must be in writing and accepted by both parties. Any contract disputes are to be resolved through friendly negotiations. If no settlement can be reached then either party may submit the dispute to arbitration as per the rules of the American Arbitration Association in New York.

(Ex. A to Aff. of Alec Sauchik, Jan. 24, 2006.) Some of the acknowledgement forms also altered other terms contained in Trident's purchase orders, including changes in the length of the payment term and minor variations in the price and the amount of steel casing to be delivered. * * *

After sending each acknowledgement form to Trident, Stemcor delivered the requested steel casings to Trident at Houston, Texas. * * * Trident accepted each delivery of casings, but it failed to pay Stemcor $144,690.74 of the amount due under various invoices. * * *

After it received the steel casings, Trident modified them by threading the ends and in turn re-sold them to a number of companies that operate oil wells. (Pet. to Compel Arbitration ¶ 7.) Three of those oil well operators brought suit against Trident in Texas state courts alleging that the steel casings were defective * * *. In each of these three actions, the oil well operators asserted claims against Trident alleging that the steel casings delivered by Trident were defective, and in each case Trident filed a third-party complaint against Stemcor seeking indemnification for any damages it might owe to the oil well operators. (*See* Petition to Compel Arbitration ¶¶ 8–17.)

* * *

On December 15, 2005, Stemcor filed a demand for arbitration with the American Arbitration Association ("AAA"), claiming that Trident was bound to arbitrate any disputes arising out of the sales agreements. * * * Trident's answer to the demand for arbitration, filed with the AAA on January 16, 2006, asserted that the AAA was without jurisdiction to arbitrate the disputes because no valid agreement to arbitrate existed between Stemcor and Trident. * * * The parties agreed to place the matter before the AAA in abeyance. * * *

Stemcor initiated this action by filing its petition to compel arbitration and for injunctive relief on January 24, 2006.

II.

A.

Federal courts, in ruling on a petition to compel arbitration under the FAA, are to determine "two issues: i) whether a valid agreement or obligation to arbitrate exists, and ii) whether one party to the agreement has failed, neglected, or refused to arbitrate." *PaineWebber, Inc. v. Bybyk,* 81 F.3d 1193, 1198 (2d Cir.1996). It has long been settled that arbitration is a matter of contract and that, therefore, a party cannot be compelled to submit to arbitration any matter that party has not agreed to arbitrate. * * * Whether a valid agreement exists to submit certain issues to binding arbitration is determined by state law principles governing the formation of contracts. * * * In applying those state law principles, however, the FAA requires that arbitration agreements be treated no more harshly than other contractual provisions. * * *

B.

In this case, there is no dispute that Stemcor and Trident entered into a series of binding sales contracts, and the parties agree that those contracts are governed by New York law, and in particular by the Uniform Commercial Code ("UCC") as adopted by New York. The parties do not, however, agree on the answer to the central question under the FAA analysis: whether those contracts included an agreement to submit disputes between Stemcor and Trident to arbitration. An arbitration clause appears in the acknowledgement forms Stemcor used to confirm Trident's orders, but not in Trident's purchase orders. Trident contends that its purchase orders constituted offers, and that Stemcor's acknowledgement forms constituted acceptances of those offers. Stemcor argues that its acknowledgement forms were not acceptances of Trident's offers, but were instead counter-offers that Trident accepted by performance when it took delivery of the steel casings.

Under New York law, section 2–207 of the UCC governs the formation of contracts when the terms of the parties' writings are not identical. This provision was adopted to alter the common law rule requiring perfect symmetry between the terms of an offer and an acceptance and to resolve the "battle of the forms" problem in a way that better conforms to modern business practices. * * *

Under paragraph (1) of section 2–207, a seller's form response to a buyer's purchase order normally constitutes a "definite and seasonable expression of acceptance" if it repeats the terms of the buyer's order. * * * According to the proviso at the end of paragraph (1), if the seller's response does not state that acceptance is "expressly made conditional" on the buyer's assent to additional terms the seller included, that response operates as an acceptance and a contract is formed. * * * When a contract is formed under paragraph (1), paragraph (2) applies to determine whether the additional or different terms become part of the contract * * *

If, however, the seller's response is "expressly made conditional on assent" to the divergent terms, then the proviso in paragraph (1) provides that no contract is formed, and instead the seller's response constitutes a counter-offer. * * * When the paragraph (1) proviso applies to prevent contract formation, the parties' conduct may nonetheless recognize the existence of a contract, and in that case paragraph (3) of section 2–207 defines the terms of the agreement as those upon which the parties agree together with any supplemental default terms provided elsewhere in the U.C.C. N.Y. U.C.C. § 2–207(3) & cmt. 7 * * *.

Stemcor argues that its acknowledgement forms were "expressly made conditional on assent" to their additional terms, including the arbitration clause, and thus that they could not have operated as acceptances under section 2–207(1). Stemcor asserts that its acknowledgement forms therefore constituted counter-offers, which were subsequently accepted by Trident's performance. Stemcor does not, however, point to specific language indicating unambiguously that its sales were "expressly made conditional on assent" to its additional terms. The following two sentences from Stemcor's forms are the only likely candidates for Stemcor's alleged "express" condition:

> This contract reflects in its entirety all details as agreed between the parties thereto. Any changes must be in writing and accepted by both parties.

But these sentences merely purport to characterize the acknowledgement forms as final versions of an agreement that the parties had already reached, rather than expressly requiring assent to additional terms. Stemcor's acknowledgement forms thus were not "expressly made conditional" on assent to their additional terms, and in particular to the arbitration clause they included.

This finding is consistent with decisions of other courts that have determined whether a responsive form contained a sufficient "express condition" to avoid operating as an acceptance. The language in Stemcor's acknowledgements differs markedly from the express language that courts have found sufficient to establish an "express condition." In *C. Itoh & Co. v. Jordan Int'l Co.*, for example, a seller of steel coils replied to a buyer's purchase order with an acknowledgement form including the following statement, along with an added arbitration provision:

> Seller's acceptance is, however, *expressly conditional on Buyer's assent* to the additional or different terms and conditions set forth below and printed on the reverse side. If the terms and conditions are not acceptable, Buyer should notify seller at once.

552 F.2d at 1230 (emphasis added). The Court of Appeals for the Seventh Circuit found that because the seller's condition tracked the language of section 2–207(1) precisely, it prevented the seller's form from operating as an acceptance. *Id.* at 1235–36 * * *.

The boilerplate language Stemcor included in its acknowledgement forms is more analogous to * * * attempts to characterize a writing as the final expression of terms * * * than to the clear, explicitly conditional language used in *Itoh* * * *. Hence the proviso discussed above does not apply, and Stemcor's acknowledgement forms operated as acceptances under section 2–207(1).[1]

Because Stemcor's responsive forms did form a contract under section 2–207(1) despite proposing additional terms, section 2–207(2) applies to determine whether those additional terms became part of the contract. Section 2–207(2) provides that when both the buyer and seller are merchants, the proposed additional terms become binding unless any one of three exceptions applies. The first exception, which is relevant here, excludes additional terms when "the offer expressly limits acceptance to the terms of the offer." N.Y. U.C.C. § 2–207(2)(a).

In each of its purchase orders, Trident included the clause: "No terms or conditions, other than those stated herein, and no agreement or understanding in any way modifying the terms and conditions herein stated shall be binding upon purchaser, unless mutually agreed upon in writing." This clause contains clear language expressly limiting acceptance to the terms contained in the purchase order. Stemcor's acknowledgement forms thus could not unilaterally impose additional terms without Trident's written assent. * * *

---

[1] It should be noted that even if Stemcor's forms constituted counter-offers as it has argued, Stemcor could not succeed in incorporating its arbitration clause into the contract. Where, as here, the conduct of the parties indicates that a contract was formed, but the parties' writings do not themselves form the contract, section 2–207(3) applies to provide the terms of the agreement. N.Y. U.C.C. § 2–207(3) & cmt. 7. The parties' writings do not agree on the arbitration clause, and it does not fall under any default provision of the UCC, so section 2–207(3) would exclude the arbitration clause. Stemcor's arguments that its forms included some different terms regarding the price and specifications for the steel casings ordered and that Trident never objected to these variations upon delivery are unhelpful, because Trident's conduct in accepting the goods only evidences the formation of a contract and Trident's agreement to certain undisputed terms.

Stemcor argues that its arbitration clause was not a "material alteration" and hence should not be excluded from the agreement. N.Y. U.C.C. 2–207(2)(b) * * *. This argument addresses the applicability of section 2–207(2)(b), but fails to account for the independent exception in 2–207(2)(a), discussed above. The fact that arbitration agreements may no longer be considered "material" alterations as a matter of law, is thus unavailing for Stemcor.

* * *

The Court has considered all of Stemcor's remaining arguments and finds each to be without merit in light of the application of UCC section 2–207 described above. The Court thus finds that the contracts between Stemcor and Trident did not incorporate an arbitration provision.

C.

Because the Court finds that the parties' contracts included no valid arbitration clause, Stemcor's petition to compel arbitration under the FAA is denied.

CONCLUSION

For all of the foregoing reasons, Stemcor's petition to compel arbitration is denied. Because there is no agreement to arbitrate, Stemcor's outstanding application for preliminary injunction is also denied. The Clerk is directed to enter judgment and to close this case.

SO ORDERED.

NOTE: MORE ON THE "EXPRESSLY MADE CONDITIONAL" LANGUAGE OF SECTION 2–207(1)

In Micor Industries, Inc. v. Mazak Corp., 2018 WL 804303 (N.D. Ala. 2018), Micor purchased from Mazak industrial equipment that was allegedly defective. Mazak, had sent a "sales order confirmation" (SOC) with a forum selection clause. Micor sent back a purchase order acceptance (PO) with a conflicting forum selection clause. The PO also stated in part that "different or additional terms * * * are hereby rejected and your acceptance of this order is expressly limited to the specific terms and conditions contained herein." The court held that this (and similar) language did not trigger the "acceptance is expressly made conditional on assent to the additional or different terms" language of 2–207(1). The court reasoned:

> Plaintiff's POs do not contain any provision that expressly conditions acceptance on Defendant's assent to additional or different terms. The closest the POs come are in two clauses that state: "Different or additional terms or conditions in your quotation and/or acknowledgement are hereby rejected and your acceptance of this order is expressly limited to the specific terms and conditions

> contained herein." The POs likewise refer to the terms and conditions displayed at www.micorind.com, which include the following "DIFFERENT OR ADDITIONAL TERMS OR SELLER'S RESPONSES ARE HEREBY REJECTED AND NO PRIOR OR SUBSEQUENT CONDUCT OF [Plaintiff] SHALL BE DEEMED TO BE AN ACCEPTANCE OF DIFFERENT OR ADDITIONAL TERMS." Neither of these terms contain a clear, express conditioning of *acceptance* on Defendant's assent to Plaintiff's different terms. Instead, they purport to only accept terms that are consistent with the terms or conditions in Plaintiff's POs. Expressly conditioning acceptance amounts to the offeree saying there is no deal if the offeror does not assent to the additional terms. *Dorton*, 453 F.2d at 1168 ("we believe that [Section 2–207] was intended to apply only to an acceptance which clearly reveals that the offeree is unwilling to proceed with the transaction unless he is assured of the offeror's assent to the additional or different terms therein"). What Defendant has done here is to recognize the existence of a contract, but dictate what terms are or are not part of that contract. Thus, the Court holds that Defendant's SOCs constituted an offer, which the Plaintiff accepted by sending the POs back to Defendant under [2–207].

Micor focuses on interpreting the language of Micor's PO. Other courts focus on the substance of the disagreement itself, applying a "knock out" rule for conflicting terms where conflicting terms are knocked out and not included in the resulting contract. See Ultraflex Systems of Florida, Inc. v. Veritev Operating Co., 100 U.C.C. Rep Serv 2d 1200, 2019 WL 7207483 (D. N. J. 2019). There, the electronic purchase order indicated venue for a lawsuit was in Delaware. The confirmation named New Jersey. The court applied the "majority" knock out rule where the second form contained a different term than the first. The court then assigned the venue according to federal law. See also Hydraulics International, Inc. v. Amalga Composites, Inc., 101 U.C.C. Rep Serv 2d 233, 2020 WL 586867 (D. Utah, 2020).

PAUL GOTTLIEB & CO., INC. V. ALPS SOUTH CORP.

District Court of Appeal of Florida, 2007.
985 So. 2d 1.

CASANEUVA, JUDGE.

I. FACTUAL BACKGROUND

Gottlieb is a fabric converter based in New York City. Gottlieb supplies its customers specialty knitted fabrics that are shipped directly from third-party knitting and finishing mills. Alps is a manufacturer of medical devices located in St. Petersburg, Florida. Alps produces various types of liners that amputees use to attach prosthetic devices. In January 2000, Alps used liners that consisted of a specially designed gel material covered in spandex fabric that stretched to allow the liner to be placed over the appendage and then compressed to provide stability.

Alps began testing a number of new fabrics in February 2000 hoping to develop a new product possessed of enhanced durability and stability. Gottlieb was a source of the new fabrics. After some initial testing, Alps settled on a specialty fabric provided by Gottlieb identified as TL2646 Coolmax fabric which outperformed the other fabrics. Alps began incorporating the new fabric into its liners. Alps received positive feedback from its customers that the new liners had increased comfort. The commercial relationship between Alps and Gottlieb started out in a promising fashion.

Unfortunately, six months later, in August 2000, the relationship began showing signs of a downturn. Alps rejected some fabric samples Gottlieb submitted because of unacceptable inconsistencies in both color and texture. On August 29, 2000, Alps sent a letter promptly notifying Gottlieb of the product deficiencies and stating that any future commercial relationship mandated that Gottlieb provide a more consistent product. However, the letter did not inform Gottlieb of the possibility that Alps could incur substantial additional costs as a result of using a different fabric. Also Alps did not disclose the specialized use of the fabric to Gottlieb. Gottlieb agreed to rework the fabric before delivering it to Alps.

Later events resulted in a worsening of the situation. Gottlieb exhausted its supply of the yarn used to produce the specialized high-tech fabric. It substituted a similar, but not identical, yarn without notifying Alps of the substitution. The trial court found this substitution caused a defect that was not easily discoverable by Alps. The new fabric did not stretch nearly as well as the original fabric that had been designated, tested, and approved by Alps. In early December of that same year, Alps began receiving complaints from customers that the fabric in the liners was less comfortable. The problems were so severe that Alps recalled the liners it had placed on the market and destroyed the devices in its inventory.

When Alps and Gottlieb discovered that the cause of the defective products was the undisclosed substitute yarn, the parties' business relationship further deteriorated. The business relationship ended when Gottlieb failed to receive payment for a submitted bill. Gottlieb then brought an action to collect damages due to the nonpayment. In turn, Alps counterclaimed for damages it asserted were caused by Gottlieb's breach of warranty. Of importance to the damage claim is the language set forth on the back of Gottlieb's finished goods contract which purports to limit its liability. The trial court ultimately considered this language to be an affirmative defense to the counterclaim.

Following a nonjury trial, the trial court awarded damages to Gottlieb on its claim totaling $28,846.29; awarded damages to Alps on its counterclaim of $694,640.04; and determined that under Florida's U.C.C. provisions, the limitation of liability clause was a material alteration of the parties' contract. The trial court declined to enforce the provision concluding that by operation of law, it was not a part of the contract.

II. LIMITATION OF LIABILITY CLAUSE

This dispute arises from the common, but risky, commercial practice where the seller and buyer negotiate a contract involving goods by exchanging each others' standardized forms. The transactions of this type involved here are governed by section 2–207 of the U.C.C., codified in section 672.207, Florida Statutes (2000).

Here, Gottlieb first contends that the trial court erred by failing to enforce the limitation of liabilities clause found on the back of its finished goods contract. The clause in contention reads:

> BUYER SHALL NOT IN ANY EVENT BE ENTITLED TO, AND SELLER SHALL NOT BE LIABLE FOR INDIRECT OR CONSEQUENTIAL DAMAGES OF ANY NATURE, INCLUDING, WITHOUT BEING LIMITED TO, LOSS OF PROFIT, PROMOTIONAL OR MANUFACTURING EXPENSES, INJURY TO REPUTATION OR LOSS OF CUSTOMER.

In its analysis, the trial court determined the clause constituted a material alteration under [2–207(2)] and as such it did not become part of the contract. * * * For the following reasons, we conclude the trial court erred. * * *

Procedurally, in determining whether a term constitutes a material alteration, other courts have placed the burden of proof upon the party seeking the term's exclusion. * * * We conclude that this rule is appropriate and hold that a party seeking the exclusion of a contractual term or provision pursuant to section 672.207(2), as constituting a material alteration, has the burden of proof. In doing so, we align this court with the great majority of this nation's courts. * * *

Having determined which party appropriately bears the burden of proof, we next address the nature of proof that a party must offer to meet its burden. Unfortunately, the law in this area is not yet clearly developed. For example, Official Comment 4 to U.C.C. § 2–207 offers examples of "typical clauses which would normally 'materially alter' the contract" and that would "result in surprise or hardship if incorporated without express awareness by the other party." * * *

In contrast, Official Comment 5 to U.C.C. § 2–207 offers "[e]xamples of clauses which involve no element of *unreasonable surprise* and which therefore are to be incorporated in the contract unless notice of objection is seasonably given." (Emphasis added.) Relying on this language and common law principles, some courts have removed hardship from the analysis and look solely for surprise. *See Union Carbide Corp. v. Oscar Mayer Foods Corp.,* 947 F.2d 1333 (7th Cir.1991). There, Judge Posner explained:

> What is expectable, hence unsurprising, is okay; what is unexpected, hence surprising, is not. Not infrequently the test is said to be "surprise or hardship," but this appears to be a misreading of Official Comment 4 to UCC § 2–207. The comment offers examples of "typical clauses which would normally 'materially alter' the contract *and so result in surprise or hardship* if incorporated without express awareness by the other party" (emphasis added). Hardship is a consequence, not a criterion. (Surprise can be either.) You cannot walk away from a contract that you can fairly be deemed to have agreed to, merely because performance turns out to be a hardship for you, unless you can squeeze yourself into the impossibility defense or some related doctrine of excuse.

Union Carbide, 947 F.2d at 1336 (citations omitted). Today, we continue to follow this rationale.

Turning first to the surprise prong, Alps must prove "that, under the circumstances, it cannot be presumed that a reasonable merchant would have consented to the additional term." *See Bayway Refining* [*Co. v. Oxygenated Mktg. & Trading,* 215 F.3d 219, 224 (2d Cir. 2000)]. The finished goods contract at issue was the sixth in a series between the two parties and each contract included the limitation of liability term. Each proposed contract contained the terms which were visible on its face. The sole evidence presented at trial to establish surprise was that Alps had not read the contract before the dispute arose. Florida law has never excused a party from a contract simply because it failed to read the contract terms. *See* Allied Van Lines, Inc. v. Bratton, 351 So.2d 344 (Fla.1977); *Kinko's, Inc. v. Payne,* 901 So.2d 354 (Fla. 2d DCA 2005). Additionally, Official Comment 5 to UCC § 2–207 includes clauses which limit remedies in a reasonable manner among the examples of terms which do not involve unreasonable surprise. The record in this case does not allow a conclusion that Gottlieb's limitation of liability clause was an unreasonable surprise to Alps.

The record is similarly lacking with respect to hardship as a result of surprise. Courts that consider hardship look to whether the term would "impose substantial economic hardship on the non-assenting party." [*Dale R. Horning Co. v. Falconer Glass Indus., Inc.,* 730 F.Supp. 962, 962 (S.D. Ind. 1990] (quoting *Trans-Aire Int'l, Inc. v. N. Adhesive Co., Inc.,* 882 F.2d 1254 (7th Cir.1989).) The *Horning* court reviewed a clause that provided "the buyer's exclusive and sole remedy for defective goods shall be to secure replacement." Id. at 963. In that case, the supplier was aware that the buyer could incur substantial liability if a breach occurred. Id. at 967. Further, the supplier's actions, in offering to work with the buyer, caused the buyer to believe that its costs would be reimbursed because of the breach. Id. at 963–64. The *Horning* court concluded that "[i]n this situation, where [the supplier] knew or had reason to know that [the buyer] could incur substantial liability for delays in finishing its subcontract, there can be no doubt that a limitation of consequential damages would work a hardship on the buyer." Id. at 963.

Here, the facts do not permit a result identical to that of *Horning*. Gottlieb never represented that, in the event of a breach, it would reimburse Alps for any or all consequential damages it sustained resulting from the breach. Instead, the evidence showed that Alps previously had returned a sample of nonconforming fabric to Gottlieb with a letter insisting on conforming goods. This letter did not mention or make claim for additional costs or damages resulting from Gottlieb's prior breach of performance. The evidence shows that Alps never informed Gottlieb of any consequences other than discontinuing their relationship. Alps did not inform Gottlieb of the specific manner in which the subject fabric would be used or what product would be crafted. Thus, Gottlieb could not foresee the *greater extent* of its potential liability, should a subsequent breach occur. Because Alps neglected to inform Gottlieb of the larger consequences of the breach, we conclude that Alps cannot maintain that incorporating the limitation of liability clause would result in a severe economic hardship. Thus, Alps failed to carry the burden of proof on hardship.

For these reasons, we conclude that the trial court erred by not enforcing the limitation of consequential damages clause. The award of consequential damages must be stricken.

Finally, we note that enforcing of the clause at issue only bars consequential damages. The limitation in this clause does not exclude other damages available under the law. *See* § 672.719; *Council Bros., Inc. v. Ray Burner Co.,* 473 F.2d 400 (5th Cir.1973) (interpreting Florida law). We observe that section 671.106(1), Florida Statutes (2000), suggests that an injured party should not be worse off because the other party breached:

> The remedies provided by this code shall be liberally administered to the end that the aggrieved party may be put in as good as a position as if the other party had fully performed but neither consequential or special nor penal damages may be had except as specifically provided in this Act or by other rule of law.

Thus, Alps is still able to recover some of its direct and incidental damages, although it is precluded from receiving consequential damages. *See* § 672.714–.715. Comment (a) of the Restatement of Contracts (Second) section 347 echoes this sentiment in that expectation damages are intended to give the injured party "the benefit of his bargain by putting him in as good as a position as he would have been had the contract been performed." The code also provides for incidental damages arising from the breach. These "include expenses reasonably incurred in inspection, receipt, transportation and care and custody of goods rightfully rejected, any commercially reasonable charges, expenses or commissions in connection with effecting cover and any other reasonable expense incident to the delay or other breach." § 672.715(1). Therefore, the trial court may award Alps its direct and incidental damages. *See Adam Metal Supply, Inc. v. Electrodex, Inc.,* 386 So.2d 1316 (Fla. 2d DCA 1980) (holding a buyer's expenses incurred before discovering a defect are recoverable as incidental damages).

* * * Reversed and remanded with instructions.

NOTE: TERMS AND THEIR PACKAGING

Suppose a buyer in an oral conversation agrees to order goods from a seller and the seller agrees to deliver them. Consider two possibilities:

> First, suppose that the seller and buyer exchange forms simultaneously by email (or by text message or other electronic means). What does 2–207 tell you to do in that case? To the extent that 2–207 does not define which of the forms is the "offer," how are you to start your analysis? Does it matter?
>
> Alternatively, what if neither party immediately sends a form, and instead the seller includes additional or different terms on or in the packaging of the goods and the buyer accepts the goods. Do the new terms become part of the contract? Does section 2–207 apply to this problem? The following two cases shed light on these questions.

HILL V. GATEWAY 2000

United States Court of Appeals, Seventh Circuit, 1997.
105 F.3d 1147.

EASTERBROOK, CIRCUIT JUDGE.

A customer picks up the phone, orders a computer, and gives a credit card number. Presently a box arrives, containing the computer and a list of terms, said to govern unless the customer returns the computer within 30 days. Are these terms effective as the parties' contract, or is the contract term-free because the order-taker did not read any terms over the phone and elicit the customer's assent?

One of the terms in the box containing a Gateway 2000 system was an arbitration clause. Rich and Enza Hill, the customers, kept the computer more than 30 days before complaining about its components and performance. They filed suit in federal court arguing, among other things, that the product's shortcomings make Gateway a racketeer (mail and wire fraud are said to be the predicate offenses), leading to treble damages under RICO for the Hills and a class of all other purchasers. Gateway asked the district court to enforce the arbitration clause; the judge refused, writing that "[t]he present record is insufficient to support a finding of a valid arbitration agreement between the parties or that the plaintiffs were given adequate notice of the arbitration clause." Gateway took an immediate appeal, as is its right. 9 U.S.C. § 16(a)(1)(A).

The Hills say that the arbitration clause did not stand out: they concede noticing the statement of terms but deny reading it closely enough to discover the agreement to arbitrate, and they ask us to conclude that they therefore may go to court. Yet an agreement to arbitrate must be enforced "save upon such grounds as exist at law or in equity for the revocation of any contract." 9 U.S.C. § 2. Doctor's Associates, Inc. v. Casarotto, 116 S.Ct. 1652, 134 L.Ed.2d 902 (1996), holds that this provision of the Federal Arbitration Act is inconsistent with any requirement that an arbitration clause be prominent. A contract need not be read to be effective; people who accept take the risk that the unread terms may in retrospect prove unwelcome. * * * Terms inside Gateway's box stand or fall together. If they constitute the parties' contract because the Hills had an opportunity to return the computer after reading them, then all must be enforced.

ProCD, Inc. v. Zeidenberg, 86 F.3d 1447 (7th Cir.1996), holds that terms inside a box of software bind consumers who use the software after an opportunity to read the terms and to reject them by returning the product. Likewise, Carnival Cruise Lines, Inc. v. Shute, 499 U.S. 585, 111 S.Ct. 1522, 113 L.Ed.2d 622 (1991), enforces a forum-selection clause that was included among three pages of terms attached to a cruise ship ticket. ProCD and Carnival Cruise Lines exemplify the many commercial transactions in which people pay for products with terms to follow; ProCD discusses others. 86 F.3d at 1451–52. The district court concluded in ProCD that the contract is formed when the consumer pays for the software; as a result, the court held, only terms known to the consumer at that moment are part of the contract, and provisos inside the box do not count. Although this is one way a contract could be formed, it is not the only way: "A vendor, as master of the offer, may invite acceptance by conduct, and may propose limitations on the kind of conduct that constitutes acceptance. A buyer may accept by performing the acts the vendor proposes to treat as acceptance." Id. at 1452. Gateway shipped computers with the same sort of accept-or-return offer ProCD made to users of its software. ProCD relied on the Uniform Commercial Code rather than any peculiarities of Wisconsin law; both Illinois and South Dakota, the two states whose law might govern relations between Gateway and the Hills, have adopted the UCC; neither side has pointed us to any atypical doctrines in those states that might be pertinent; ProCD therefore applies to this dispute.

Plaintiffs ask us to limit ProCD to software, but where's the sense in that? ProCD is about the law of contract, not the law of software. Payment preceding the revelation of full terms is common for air transportation, insurance, and many other endeavors. Practical considerations support allowing vendors to enclose the full legal terms with their products. Cashiers cannot be expected to read legal documents to customers before ringing up sales. If the staff at the other end of the phone for direct-sales operations such as Gateway's had to read the four-page statement of terms before taking the buyer's credit card number, the droning voice would anesthetize rather than enlighten many potential buyers. Others would hang up in a rage over the waste of their time. And oral recitation would not avoid customers' assertions (whether true or feigned) that the clerk did not read term X to them, or that they did not remember or understand it. Writing provides benefits for both sides of commercial transactions. Customers as a group are better off when vendors skip costly and ineffectual steps such as telephonic recitation, and use instead a simple approve-or-return device. Competent adults are bound by such documents, read or unread. For what little it is worth, we add that the box from Gateway was crammed with software. The computer came with an operating system, without which it was useful only as a boat anchor. See Digital Equipment Corp. v. Uniq Digital Technologies, Inc., 73 F.3d 756, 761 (7th Cir.1996). Gateway also included many application programs. So the Hills' effort to limit ProCD to software would not avail them factually, even if it were sound legally—which it is not.

For their second sally, the Hills contend that ProCD should be limited to executory contracts (to licenses in particular), and therefore does not apply because both parties' performance of this contract was complete when the box arrived at their home. This is legally and factually wrong: legally because the question at hand concerns the formation of the contract rather than its performance, and factually because both contracts were incompletely performed. ProCD did not depend on the fact that the seller characterized the transaction as a license rather than as a contract; we treated it as a contract for the sale of goods and reserved the question whether for other purposes a "license" characterization might be preferable. 86 F.3d at 1450. All debates about characterization to one side, the transaction in ProCD was no more executory than the one here: Zeidenberg paid for the software and walked out of the store with a box under his arm, so if arrival of the box with the product ends the time for revelation of contractual terms, then the time ended in ProCD before Zeidenberg opened the box. But of course ProCD had not completed performance with delivery of the box, and neither had Gateway. One element of the transaction was the warranty, which obliges sellers to fix defects in their products. The Hills have invoked Gateway's warranty and are not satisfied with its response, so they are not well positioned to say that Gateway's obligations were fulfilled when the motor carrier unloaded the box. What is more, both ProCD and Gateway promised to help customers to use their products. Long-term service and information obligations are common in the computer business, on both hardware and software sides. Gateway offers "lifetime service" and has a round-the-clock telephone hotline to fulfil this promise. Some vendors spend more money helping customers use their products than on developing and manufacturing them. The document in Gateway's box includes promises of future performance that some consumers value highly; these promises bind Gateway just as the arbitration clause binds the Hills.

Next the Hills insist that ProCD is irrelevant because Zeidenberg was a "merchant" and they are not. Section 2–207(2) of the UCC, the infamous battle-of-the-forms section, states that "additional terms [following acceptance of an offer] are to be construed as proposals for addition to a contract. Between merchants such terms become part of the contract unless . . .". Plaintiffs tell us that ProCD came out as it did only because Zeidenberg was a "merchant" and the terms inside ProCD's box were not excluded by the "unless" clause. This argument pays scant attention to the opinion in ProCD, which concluded that, when there is only one form, "sec. 2–207 is irrelevant." 86 F.3d at 1452. The question in ProCD was not whether terms were added to a contract after its formation, but how and when the contract was formed—in particular, whether a vendor may propose that a contract of sale be formed, not in the store (or over the phone) with the payment of money or a general "send me the product," but after the customer has had a chance to inspect both the item and the terms. ProCD answers "yes," for merchants and consumers alike. * * *

At oral argument the Hills propounded still another distinction: the box containing ProCD's software displayed a notice that additional terms were within, while the box containing Gateway's computer did not. The difference is functional, not legal. Consumers browsing the aisles of a store can look at the box, and if they are unwilling to deal with the prospect of additional terms can leave the box alone, avoiding the transactions costs of returning the package after reviewing its contents. Gateway's box, by contrast, is just a shipping carton; it is not on display anywhere. Its function is to protect the product during transit, and the information on its sides is for the use of handlers rather than would-be purchasers.

Perhaps the Hills would have had a better argument if they were first alerted to the bundling of hardware and legal-ware after opening the box and wanted to return the computer in order to avoid disagreeable terms, but were dissuaded by the expense of shipping. What the remedy would be in such a case—could it exceed the shipping charges?—is an interesting question, but one that need not detain us because the Hills knew before they ordered the computer that the carton would include some important terms, and they did not seek to discover these in advance. Gateway's ads state that their products come with limited warranties and lifetime support. How limited was the warranty—30 days, with service contingent on shipping the computer back, or five years, with free onsite service? What sort of support was offered? Shoppers have three principal ways to discover these things. First, they can ask the vendor to send a copy before deciding whether to buy. The Magnuson-Moss Warranty Act requires firms to distribute their warranty terms on request, 15 U.S.C. § 2302(b)(1)(A); the Hills do not contend that Gateway would have refused to enclose the remaining terms too. Concealment would be bad for business, scaring some customers away and leading to excess returns from others. Second, shoppers can consult public sources (computer magazines, the Web sites of vendors) that may contain this information. Third, they may inspect the documents after the product's delivery. Like Zeidenberg, the Hills took the third option. By keeping the computer beyond 30 days, the Hills accepted Gateway's offer, including the arbitration clause.

* * * The decision of the district court is vacated, and this case is remanded with instructions to compel the Hills to submit their dispute to arbitration.

NORCIA v. SAMSUNG TELECOMMUNICATIONS AMERICA, 845 F.3d 1279 (9th Cir. 2017). Daniel Norcia purchased a Samsung Galaxy S4 phone in a Verizon Wireless store. The receipt, entitled "Customer Agreement" included a term in capital letters stating "I understand that I am agreeing to . . . settlement of disputes by arbitration and other means instead of jury trials . . . ." The phone was in a package stating that the "Package Contains . . . Product Safety & Warranty Brochure." The 101-page brochure in the box contained warranty information and also an arbitration clause. Norcia signed the Customer Agreement, but then took the box to a table, opened it, and with an employee's help transferred his contacts from his old phone. Norcia then left the store without the box. The court stated that "[t]here is no dispute that Norcia did not expressly assent to any agreement in the brochure. Nor did Norcia sign the brochure or otherwise act in a manner that would show 'his intent to use his silence or failure to opt out, as a means of accepting the arbitration agreement.' " In addition, "the outside of the box did not notify the consumer that opening the box would be considered agreement to the terms set forth in the brochure." Further, a consumer must be put on notice "of the existence of a term before he or she can be legally held to have assented to it." The court concluded that

> [a] reasonable person in Norcia's position would not be on notice that the brochure contained a freestanding obligation outside the scope of the warranty. Nor would a reasonable person understand that receiving the seller's warranty and failing to opt out of an arbitration provision contained within the warranty constituted assent to a provision requiring arbitration of all claims against the

> seller, including claims not involving the warranty. * * * Norcia was not bound by the arbitration provision even if the in-the-box contract were otherwise enforceable under California law. * * * Because California courts have not adopted the principle set forth in *Hill*, but have made clear that silence alone does not constitute assent, * * * we reject Samsung's argument that Norcia reasonably assented to the arbitration provision because he failed to opt out of the arbitration provision contained in the product box.

The court also dismissed Samsung's argument that the Customer Agreement also formed an agreement to arbitrate because the Agreement was with Verizon not Samsung. The court refused to enforce the agreement to arbitrate.

CHAPTER FIVE

POLICING AGREEMENTS AND PROMISES

■ ■ ■

A legal order can indeed be characterized by the agreements which it does or does not enforce.

WEBER

SECTION ONE: POLICING DOCTRINES AND THE ROLE OF LAWYERS

When the parties satisfy the requirements of a theory of obligation, prima facie duties arise. But a party with such a duty may have one or more defenses, and thus ultimately owe no duty at all (or only a lesser duty). Such defenses may be grouped into two broad categories: (1) those arising pursuant to "policing doctrines"—defenses involving either grossly unfair terms or overreaching by one party at the bargaining or promising stage (or both), and (2) other full or partial defenses such as those based on changed circumstances after making an agreement or promise.

In this chapter, we study only those defenses arising pursuant to policing doctrines. (We study other defenses in Chapters Seven and Eight.) We focus mainly on policing doctrines that generate defenses to prima facie duties arising under an agreement with consideration because courts most often apply these doctrines in this context.

Policing doctrines fall into two basic categories: those addressed to the existence and quality of assent, and those concerned with the content of the agreement or promise. Assent oriented defenses such as duress, misrepresentation, and nondisclosure, if successful, show the lack of a valid agreement or promise. A buyer of a briefcase, for example, can invoke the defense of misrepresentation if the buyer can show that the seller claimed the briefcase was genuine leather when it was actually imitation. Although the buyer did not agree to purchase an imitation leather case, contract law commonly treats the buyer as having incurred a prima facie duty to pay, a duty the buyer can defeat by showing a misrepresentation.

Other policing defenses focus on the substantive content of an agreement or promise rather than on the quality of assent. For an extreme example, consider a builder who agrees that the owner can cut off the builder's toes if he does not finish construction of a house by a certain date.

Obviously the courts will refuse to enforce this term. Doctrines such as inequality of the exchange, public policy, mutuality of obligation and substantive unconscionability all focus on the substantive terms of the exchange.

Today, in addition to case law, numerous statutes set forth policing doctrines. For example, section 2–302 of the Uniform Commercial Code authorizes courts to police for unconscionable agreements for the sale of goods. The Code also includes other provisions designed to protect parties from overreaching, which provisions are not variable by agreement. For example, section 2–316(2) provides that a disclaimer of the warranty of merchantability must include the term merchantability.

Policing doctrines sometimes generate affirmative claims for damages, as well as serve as defenses. For example, a misrepresentation may not only provide a defense to a breach of contract claim, but may also generate a cause of action for damages in tort.

We explore various themes in this chapter. First, the lawyer must understand the relationship between policing doctrines and the principle of freedom of contract. Professor Friedrich Kessler discussed freedom of contract in these terms:

> [F]reedom of contract does not commend itself for moral reasons only; it is also an eminently practical principle. It is the inevitable counterpart of a free enterprise system. As a result, our legal lore of contracts reflects a proud spirit of individualism and of *laissez faire*. This is particularly true for the axioms and rules dealing with the formation and interpretation of contracts, the genuineness and reality of consent. Contract—the language of the cases tells us—is a private affair and not a social institution. The judicial system, therefore, provides only for their interpretation, but the courts cannot make contracts for the parties. There is no contract without assent, but once the objective manifestations of assent are present, their author is bound. * * * Either party is supposed to look out for his own interests and his own protection. Oppressive bargains can be avoided by careful shopping around. Everyone has complete freedom of choice with regard to his partner in contract, and the privity-of-contract principle respects the exclusiveness of this choice. Since a contract is the result of the free bargaining of parties who are brought together by the play of the market and who meet each other on a footing of social and approximate economic equality, there is no danger that freedom of contract will be a threat to the social order as a whole. Influenced by this optimistic creed, courts are extremely hesitant to declare contracts void as against public policy "because if there is one thing which more than another public policy requires it is

> that men of full age and competent understanding shall have the utmost liberty of contracting, and that their contracts when entered into freely and voluntarily shall be held sacred and shall be enforced by Courts of justice."[a]

Policing doctrines define the boundaries of freedom of contract. If the parties in our earlier example actually agreed to cut off the builder's toes for late performance, why should a court refuse to enforce this agreement? After all, freedom of contract includes freedom not to contract, and the builder did not have to agree to such a term. Of course, such an agreement is abhorrent, and the courts will not enforce it. To consider a less extreme example, what if the penalty for late performance were only a sum of money out of proportion to the harm caused? Should *this* penalty be enforced? We saw in Chapter Three that courts will not enforce penalty claims either. Yet vast scope remains for the exercise of contractual freedom, and one challenge for the lawyer is to draw the often fine line between what is permissible and what is not.

Another theme of this chapter is that courts are mindful of the interplay between factors that may diminish the quality of assent on the one hand and the possibly objectionable character of the *content* of the agreement on the other. May a court bar enforcement of a contract solely on the basis of bargaining improprieties, or must the exchange itself be substantively objectionable as well? Conversely, in the absence of bargaining unfairness, may a court refuse to enforce terms based on substantive objections alone? We have already suggested that some policing doctrines focus primarily on the quality of assent and others primarily on the resulting terms, but the two problems are often closely related. If an agreement really calls for toe amputation in the event performance is delayed, it is likely that something was wrong with the bargaining process as well!

A further theme for study relates to the objective theory of "mutual assent" studied in Chapter Four. Except in the field of insurance contracts and in relation to certain form-pad transactions, most courts today generally adhere to the common law doctrine that a party who signs a contract, understandable to a reasonable person, is bound by its terms regardless of whether he or she read or understood those terms. By signing the agreement, a party manifests assent to the agreement. This so-called "duty to read" rule has been explained in the following way:

> If A sends an offer to B who, without opening it and without suspecting that it is an offer, decides to confuse A by sending a letter which states "I accept," there is a contract because A reasonably believed that B assented to the deal. It is not

[a] Kessler, Contracts of Adhesion—Some Thoughts About Freedom of Contract, 43 Colum.L.Rev. 629, 629–31 (1943).

> important to decide whether B has acted intentionally or negligently, because under the objective theory of contracts a party is bound by the impression he reasonably creates. The same principle supplies the basic rule relating to questions of duty to read: a party who signs an instrument manifests assent to it and may not later complain that he did not read the instrument or that he did not understand its contents. A leading case has stated that "one having the capacity to understand a written document who reads it, or, without reading it or having it read to him, signs it, is bound by his signature." The feeling is that no one could rely on a signed document if the other party could avoid the transaction by saying that he had not read or did not understand the writing.
>
> The same rule applies even without a signature if the acceptance of a document which purports to be a contract implies assent to its terms. Thus, for example, the acceptance of documents such as bills of lading, passenger tickets, insurance policies, bank books and warehouse receipts may give rise to contracts based upon the provisions contained therein.[b]

Of course, if a party was the victim of fraud, or was unfairly induced to sign an agreement, or if certain terms of the agreement were not truly understandable, courts usually have no difficulty finding an exception to the "duty to read." But the line between cases falling under the duty and those qualifying for exceptional treatment may be difficult to draw. Is a poor consumer with limited education bound to a complex clause the consumer has not read that disclaims or excludes all warranties concerning the quality of the goods? How does a court differentiate between lawful market pressure and unfair coercion? When is a written agreement understandable and when not?

A final theme for study is that courts apply policing doctrines in light of the nature of the transaction involved. For example, the problem of policing fully-negotiated agreements is very different from policing standardized form contracts. And policing a transaction between a merchant and a consumer is very different from policing between two business entities. Courts also apply policing doctrines in light of the remedy sought by the aggrieved party. For example, we will see that a court's policing response may differ dramatically depending on whether a party seeks the return of money, or damages, or the equitable remedy of specific performance, etc.

Policing doctrines are important to the lawyer as planner, drafter, counselor, negotiator and litigator. As we will see, by careful planning and drafting the lawyer can greatly reduce the risk that policing doctrines will be invoked adversely. For example, by determining prior to contracting

---

[b] Calamari, Duty to Read—A Changing Concept, 43 Fordham L.Rev. 341, 341–42 (1974).

whether a particular remedy for breach is enforceable, lawyers can help contracting parties avoid litigation over the issue later. In fulfilling this planning role, the lawyer often must identify and apply various standards of fairness generally accepted in the community. Typically, the lawyer must study court decisions dealing with the scope and requirements of relevant policing doctrines. Often the lawyer must engage in careful fact finding about the nature of business practices. The lawyer must draw on similar sources of information to counsel clients who request information on the validity of proposed agreements, or on whether they can avoid agreements already made.

The lawyer must also utilize negotiating skills in dealing with policing problems. For example, a client may ask the lawyer to renegotiate the terms of an agreement in light of perceived problems with the original agreement. In Section Nine of this chapter, we briefly consider some of the special negotiating tactics required of the lawyer.

SECTION TWO: DURESS

STANDARD BOX CO. V. MUTUAL BISCUIT CO.

Court of Appeal, Third District, 1909.
10 Cal.App. 746, 103 P. 938.

[Defendant, Mutual Biscuit Co., had purchased a number of boxes pursuant to a 1905 contract with plaintiff, Standard Box Co. On September 1, 1905, plaintiff offered defendant an option, beginning on July 25, 1906, to buy boxes for one year at the 1905 price. Before defendant exercised the option, San Francisco suffered a serious earthquake on April 18, 1906, which resulted in a very short supply of boxes. On July 25, 1906, defendant sought to exercise the option. Plaintiff refused to sell further boxes to defendant at the 1905 price promised in the option, but was willing to sell at market value. Plaintiff knew that defendant sold bakery products, needed boxes to pack its goods, and would go out of business without the boxes, and that it was "practically impossible" for defendant to get boxes elsewhere. After objecting to plaintiff's refusal to sell at the 1905 price, defendant accepted some boxes on plaintiff's terms in October and November, 1906, but then refused to pay for some of them. Plaintiff brought an action for the price of those boxes. Defendant counterclaimed in part to recover the excess paid for some boxes and in part for damages for plaintiff's refusal to deliver additional boxes at the 1905 price. Defendant appealed a jury verdict in favor of plaintiff.

The court first held that the defendant had not accepted the offered option within a reasonable time, so that by July 25, 1906, it had expired.]

CHIPMAN, P.J.

* * *

As there were no contract relations between plaintiff and defendant by which defendant had any right to demand the merchandise, all considerations of contract obligations on the part of plaintiff must be eliminated from the case. When, therefore, defendant solicited the goods, it stood to plaintiff as a stranger seeking to make purchases. It was told the prices it must pay, and the evidence was, and it is not alleged otherwise, that these prices were the market rates charged to other customers. However pressing defendant's need and whatever consequences to its trade should it fail to get the articles, plaintiff had a clear right to make its own prices and having made them, and defendant having accepted the goods under the agreement then made, its action, it seems to us, was voluntary as was its subsequent payment for the goods. Defendant, in fact, when its averments are reduced to their last analysis, alleged no more than that plaintiff refused to recognize the existence of any contract, demanded the current market prices, and that in order to secure the much needed articles defendant paid to plaintiff the higher price demanded. We fail to discover in the transaction the elements of duress.

* * *

* * * As was said in Phelan v. San Francisco, 120 Cal. 1, 52 P. 38: "There must be some compulsion or coercion which controls the conduct of the party making the payment, * * * some threatened exercise of power or authority over his person or property which can be avoided only by making the payment." In Huddleston v. Washington, the court said: "A payment is not to be regarded as compulsory unless made to emancipate the person or property from an actual and existing duress imposed upon it by the party to whom the money is paid." A threat to refuse performance of a contract cannot be made the predicate of legal duress. * * * In Cable v. Foley, 45 Minn. 421, 47 N.W. 1135, certain contracts were sought to be avoided as having been executed under duress. The evidence offered for that purpose, said the court, "amounted to no more than that, the plaintiff being without means to pay his men, the defendants refused to pay what was then due him, unless he executed the contracts. The mere threat to withhold from a party a legal right, which he has an adequate remedy to enforce, is not, in the eyes of the law, duress; certainly not such as will avoid the execution of a contract." Defendant's duty here was to seek aid of the courts to enforce his rights under the contract. He could not receive the goods under the terms upon which they were delivered, afterwards pay for them, and then claim that the payment was compulsory, and recover the difference between the price thus paid and the prices mentioned in the contract. The payment must be regarded as voluntary. Regan v. Baldwin, 126 Mass. 485, 30 Am.Rep. 689.

Appellant says that it seeks relief "on the line of the complaint" in Rowland v. Watson, 4 Cal.App. 476, 88 Pac. 495. The circumstances there were very different from the facts here, and that case furnishes no guide for us here. Burke v. Gould, 105 Cal. 277, 38 Pac. 733, is cited. Without stating the facts in that case, suffice it to quote from the opinion: "The unvarying principle of them all [the cited cases] is that by the performance or threat to perform some unlawful act whereby plaintiff will suffer loss the defendant has induced the plaintiff, under circumstances sufficient to control the action of a reasonable man, to pay money which he otherwise would not have paid." The court then proceeds to show that all that defendant threatened was to foreclose the mortgage which plaintiff had executed, and that this was not an unlawful act; that it was the exercise of a right which the law conferred upon him, and was neither in law nor in morals reprehensible. We fail to see how this case can avail defendant. Here there were no contractual relations, as we have held, and plaintiff did no more than to require defendant to pay for the merchandise its market value. Refusing to sell more goods unless defendant would pay for what it had bought was but an act of common business prudence. There was absolutely nothing unlawful in plaintiff's action in the matter. * * * Conceding that the courts recognize what may be termed moral duress under some circumstances, there is always some element of illegality in the demand complained of, some denial of a right, some unfounded claim, some extortion, as was said by Justice Cooley in Hackley v. Headley, 45 Mich. 569, 8 N.W. 511, "as a condition to the exercise by the party of a legal right." Here defendant had no legal right to demand the goods at his own prices or at all for that matter. On the contrary, plaintiff had the legal right to fix the price upon his own goods. It was no concern of plaintiff that defendant could not get the goods elsewhere. Plaintiff was under no obligation to see that defendant's business was safeguarded. It is not pretended that defendant was treated differently from other customers of plaintiff's or that more than market rates were charged for the goods or that those rates were excessive or burdensome.

* * *

The order is affirmed.

MACHINERY HAULING, INC. v. STEEL OF WEST VIRGINIA, 181 W.Va. 694, 384 S.E.2d 139 (1989). [Plaintiff, Machinery Hauling, a freight transporter, contracted to transport defendant Steel's steel product to a third party, who rightfully rejected it for defects. Steel instructed Machinery Hauling to pay Steel $31,000, the price of the undelivered product, "or else [Steel] would cease to do business with the plaintiff." Machinery Hauling refused.]

MILLER, JUSTICE.

While we recognize the concept of business or economic duress, we do not find it exists in this case. There was no continuing contract between the plaintiff and the defendants. Thus, the demand by the defendants that the plaintiff pay $31,000 for the defective steel was not coupled with a threat to terminate an existing contract. Furthermore, the plaintiff did not accede to the defendants' demand and pay over the money.

The plaintiff's claim, stripped to its essentials, is that it has been deprived of its future prospects of doing business with the defendants. However, this future expectancy is not a legal right on which the plaintiff can anchor a claim of economic duress. * * *

Finally, there appears to be general acknowledgement that duress is not shown because one party to the contract has driven a hard bargain or that market or other conditions now make the contract more difficult to perform by one of the parties or that financial circumstances may have caused one party to make concessions. * * *

The questions certified to us by the Cabell County Circuit Court are, therefore, answered, and this case is dismissed from the docket.

DALZELL, DURESS BY ECONOMIC PRESSURE I

20 N.C.L.Rev. 237, 237 (1942).

Some economic pressures have for centuries been treated in our courts as requiring restraint, but for the most part our habitual Anglo-Saxon individualism has been in control of the common law, so as to make any such curb exceptional. We have been proud of our "freedom of contract," confident that the maximum of social progress will result from encouragement of each man's initiative and ambition by giving him the right to use his economic powers to the full. One of the most frequently and emphatically declared axioms of contract law is that our courts are not concerned with the equivalence of the consideration given for a promise. But doubts are growing of late years.

* * *

We are not yet ready to allow the idea of individual initiative to be completely swallowed up in the "wave of the future," as has been done in some recently organized societies, but some limitation on economic duress seems inevitable.

S.P. DUNHAM & COMPANY V. KUDRA

Superior Court of New Jersey, Appellate Division, 1957.
44 N.J.Super. 565, 131 A.2d 306.

CLAPP, S.J.A.D.

Plaintiff, S.P. Dunham & Company, sued defendants for the restitution of $3,232.55 paid them allegedly under business compulsion. The trial court, sitting without a jury, gave judgment for the plaintiff in the amount stated. Defendants appeal.

Plaintiff has for over a century operated a department store in Trenton. For some three years it had leased its fur department to a concessionaire, Elmer A. Hurwitz & Co., but the business of the department was so conducted as to appear to customers to have been a part of plaintiff's operations. During these three years fur coats, left by customers with Hurwitz for storage and cleaning were turned over by him to the defendants Kudra who stored and cleaned them pursuant to an agreement with Hurwitz. Plaintiff knew something of Hurwitz' arrangement with Kudra.

In November 1955 Hurwitz went bankrupt and Dunham thereupon cancelled his concession. However, winter was coming on, and Dunham's customers wanted their coats. On November 23, 1955 Kudra had possession of 412 garments, on which Hurwitz owed Kudra $622.50. This sum plaintiff offered to pay Kudra in return for the garments. But Hurwitz owed Kudra an additional $3,232.55 with respect to other garments that had been delivered back to customers during the preceding two years; and on November 23, Kudra announced that the 412 coats would not be turned over unless plaintiff paid the total sum of $3,855.05. One of the owners of Dunham, much upset, asked Kudra for a few days to think the matter over and consult with counsel. Apparently at about that time, the temperature had dropped to 15°; many substantial customers of the store demanded their coats. When both owners of Dunham then sought to negotiate further, Kudra came up with the proposition that it would deliver the garments directly to plaintiff's customers without charge to the plaintiff, if plaintiff would turn over their names; not only would plaintiff thus place the names of customers in the hands of a competitor in the fur business, but Kudra apparently purposed to bill them directly for Hurwitz' total charges on the coats, which totaled some $4,000. Plaintiff flatly rejected this proposition and on November 29 yielded to Kudra's original demand, paying the $3,855.05. Allegedly, three days later it sought the return of $3,232.55 and on December 15 commenced this action.

Plaintiff seeks the restitution of the $3,232.55 on the ground that the money was paid to defendants, not voluntarily, but under a species of duress, sometimes known as "business compulsion." It claims that defendants, taking advantage of its plight, sought to squeeze it between their own improper demands and the complaints of its customers. Indeed, the predicament in which it was placed was so embarrassing a matter that one of the owners of the store, apprehensive of a serious impairment in its good will, himself spent hours in the fur department talking to customers. There is little doubt but that the pressure which defendants brought to bear upon the plaintiff was an inducing (Restatement, Contracts, § 492f), indeed the sole cause of its payment of the $3,232.55.

A slight examination of the subject will demonstrate that the law of duress is in the process of development. * * * Thus in New Jersey, after some conflicting decisions on the point, our courts have finally rejected the objective test, namely, that duress is irremediable unless it is of such severity as to overcome the will of a person of ordinary firmness; the test now is simply this—has the person complaining been constrained to do what he otherwise would not have done? * * *

Apropos of this, attention may be directed to a point brought up by the respondent. It has repeatedly been held in our cases that a person cannot claim to have made a payment under duress if, before he made the payment, there was available to him an immediate and adequate remedy in the courts to test or resist it. * * * This harsh rule has been rejected by the Restatement, Contracts, § 493, Illustrations 8, 9, and also by Williston. Williston points out that

> "the only reason which could be given for such a rule is that a threat of this sort should not terrify a person of" ordinary firmness. "But, though such statements are still repeated, the rule is artificial and, so far as it would require a person threatened with injury necessarily to endure the injury because the law provides a remedy for it, cannot be accepted." § 1620, at p. 4529.

* * * Now that New Jersey has definitely repudiated the standard of "ordinary firmness," there may be little reason to retain the other rule; the criterion perhaps should be solely whether the will of the victim was really overborne. An attempt has been made to justify the rule stated, upon the ground that the person exerting the duress has relied on the payment made to him by the victim, and having relied, he should be protected. * * * But why should the law have such a tender regard for a wrongdoer? Relief by way of restitution puts no undue burden upon him; he is not subjected to damages for his wrong, but merely called upon to give back that which he forced from his victim. The court granting restitution should have an easy conscience in the matter.

However, we need not pass upon this more fundamental question. If we accept the rule as stated in our cases, we must still ask ourselves whether the plaintiff had a "complete and adequate remedy" * * * enabling it to recover the coats for its customers and avoid the payment of the $3,232.55. * * * [W]e come to plaintiff's third contention, namely, that there was no adequate remedy here through any form of litigation. Plaintiff, faced with the clamoring demands of its customers, plainly did not want it brought home to each of them at that juncture that its competitors, the defendants, were in fact attending to the storing and cleaning of her coat. We think a public suit at that time did not constitute adequate relief.

We turn now to defendants' principal argument, which seems to be that they should not be chargeable by plaintiff with "the duress * * * it itself had long ago prepared." They rely on the fact that plaintiff for three years during the summer months had lent Hurwitz money "in the neighborhood of $2,000, $1,500"; and they claim that, though these amounts were paid back in September each year, plaintiff should have known of Hurwitz' financial difficulties. The argument seems to be that plaintiff itself caused defendants to exert the duress. The point is without the slightest substance.

Next, defendants seem to argue, referring to the early common-law doctrine of "duress of goods," that under our present concepts of "business compulsion" redress could be had by the plaintiff here only if it had been compelled to pay out money in order to recover *its own* property. There is nothing to this point either. The law today does not take such a narrow view of the matter, if indeed it ever did.

Further, defendants contend that the plaintiff cannot have been under duress since, for six days, it had an opportunity to deliberate and consult with its own counsel. These are matters which should be taken into account in determining whether in fact the plaintiff made the payment voluntarily and whether the pressure of defendants' demands still subsisted after deliberation and consultation; but they do not of themselves preclude relief. Restatement, Contracts, § 492, comment c.

Again it is urged that one person (Dunham) cannot claim to have been placed under duress if he pays money to the defendants for the relief of another person (i.e., its customers). We need not refer to the law on the subject, cf. Williston, supra, § 1621, because it is apparent that Dunham paid the $3,232.55 for the relief of itself from an injury to its own good will.

* * *

* * * [W]e might refer to the trial court's concluding remarks below: "it [defendant's conduct] is one of the things I prefer not to * * * have to live within the community. I couldn't justify it."

* * *

Affirmed.

DALZELL, DURESS BY ECONOMIC PRESSURE I

20 N.C.L.Rev. 237, 238 (1942).

We have talked of contracts signed under duress as lacking "real consent." This seems to be a manner of speech rather than a reasoned conclusion. When I feel that I must choose between having a bullet lodged in my head and signing a contract, my desire to escape the bullet would hardly be described as unreal or merely apparent; and the signing of the contract is simply the expression of that fear of death. To call such a consent "unreal" is to characterize the normal human desire to continue alive as mere pretense. The father who pays a ransom to his daughter's kidnappers does so because he fears he will lose his daughter. Of the only two developments which he then foresees with assurance, his choice is for payment; and, *on the assumption on which he acts,* that he must choose between payment and tragedy, his choice is certainly an expression of the most genuine, heartfelt consent—and often a very happy consent indeed.

What we meant by calling such consent unreal, was that it would not have been given except for the unpleasant alternative.

DAWSON, ECONOMIC DURESS AND THE FAIR EXCHANGE IN FRENCH AND GERMAN LAW

11 Tul.L.Rev. 345, 345 (1937).

The system of "free" contract described by nineteenth century theory is now coming to be recognized as a world of fantasy, too orderly, too neatly contrived, and too harmonious to correspond with reality. As welcome fiction is slowly displaced by sober fact, the regime of "freedom" can be visualized as merely another system, more elaborate and more highly organized, for the exercise of economic pressure. With new vision has come a more conscious and sustained effort to select the forms of permissible pressure and to control the manner of its exercise. In law, as in politics, the control of economic power has emerged as the central problem of modern times.

M. TREBILCOCK, THE LIMITS OF FREEDOM OF CONTRACT

242–43 (1993).

Difficult questions arise as to when a transaction can be regarded as voluntary or, conversely, coerced. It has proven difficult to construct an autonomy-based theory of coercion without first constructing a moral baseline (or set of rights) for the party choosing to accept a proposal under constrained circumstances, against which the proposal can be evaluated. Similarly, difficulties arise in determining when a contracting party has sufficient information about the contract subject matter or future course of events affecting the value of the contract subject matter for a conclusion to be sustained that the choices in question were autonomous. Although contracting choices made with false information or in the absence of highly material information may, at one level, be regarded as non-autonomous, at another level the decision to forgo opportunities to acquire further information may itself be an autonomous choice. * * *

* * *

[I]t can be argued that a rich conception of individual autonomy entails not only a negative theory of liberty—that is, freedom from external constraint on the individual right of self-determination—but also a positive theory of liberty, which holds that an autonomous ability to choose one's own conception of the good life entails access to economic opportunities and resources that makes non-demeaning, self-fulfilling life choices a realistic possibility. * * * For example with respect to the question of coercion, it might be argued that deliberate exploitation by one party of another party's lack of choices to exact returns that exceed those normally realizable in a more competitive environment should be viewed as suspect.

PROBLEM 5-1

In which of the following factual situations, if any, would you advise the party subject to the "pressure" that he or she could make out a case of duress?

A. The vendors at Yankee Stadium, realizing that they have a captive audience, mark up the cost of refreshments 200%.

B. Vendors sell water in the middle of the desert for $50 per glass more than otherwise realizable to persons literally "dying" of thirst.

C. Gasoline stations during an oil supply shortage mark up the price of gasoline 200%.

D. A supplier of construction materials, with knowledge that X has entered into a contract with Y to build a warehouse and that X cannot get supplies in time from anyone but the supplier, marks up the price 200%.

NOTE:
"PRICE GOUGING" STATUTES

Many states have enacted "price gouging" statutes. Generally these apply only if the state has declared a "state of emergency" and a vendor charges an "unconscionable" or "excessive and unjustified price." The latter is often defined as a particular percentage markup of the price from the price before the emergency (for example, 10% or 25%).

NOTE:
UNDUE INFLUENCE

A policing doctrine related to duress is undue influence. Undue influence has been defined as "undue susceptibility" of one party and "excessive pressure" placed on that party by another. Olam v. Congress Mortg. Co., 68 F. Supp.2d 1110 (N.D. Cal. 1999). The pressure must be exerted by a person enjoying a special relationship with the victim that makes the victim especially susceptible to the pressure. For example, if a lawyer convinces an aged and infirm client to sign over his stocks to the lawyer, the "agreement" may be voidable by the client. Or, if a maternity home persuades an emotionally distraught mother of an illegitimate child to give up the child, the mother's agreement may be voidable. Methodist Mission Home v. NAB, 451 S.W.2d 539 (Tex.Civ.App.1970). For more discussion, see Myerchin v. Family Benefits, Inc., 162 Cal.App.4th 1526, 1540, 76 Cal.Rptr.3d 816 (2008) ("overpersuasion is generally accompanied by certain characteristics which tend to create a pattern. The pattern usually involves several of the following elements: (1) discussion of the transaction at an unusual or inappropriate time, (2) consummation of the transaction in an unusual place, (3) insistent demand that the business be finished at once, (4) extreme emphasis on untoward consequences of delay, (5) the use of multiple persuaders by the dominant side against a single servient party, (6) absence of third-party advisers to the servient party, (7) statements that there is no time to consult financial advisers or attorneys. If a number of these elements are simultaneously present, the persuasion may be characterized as excessive.") (quoting Odorizzi v. Bloomfield Sch. Dist., 246 Cal.App.2d 123, 132–33, 123, 54 Cal.Rptr. 533 (1966)).

SECTION THREE: MISREPRESENTATION, CONCEALMENT, AND THE DUTY TO DISCLOSE

One contracting party has a duty not to mislead the other. But what are the parameters of that duty? Obviously one may not lie. But how do we differentiate "seller's talk," sometimes called "puffing" ("this is an A-1 Used Car") from misrepresentation ("this is genuine leather"). In addition, in what circumstances (if any) will remaining silent about known defects constitute an actionable wrong or a basis for rescission? When, in other words, does a duty to disclose arise?

BATES V. CASHMAN

Supreme Judicial Court of Massachusetts, 1918.
230 Mass. 167, 119 N.E. 663.

RUGG, C.J. This is a suit to recover for the breach of a written contract to buy the stocks and bonds of the Newburyport Cordage Company. The securities were the means by which to convey control of land with a factory and machinery. There is no controversy that the contract was made. The defendant contends that he was induced to sign it by such false representations by the plaintiff as release him from obligation to perform. This case was referred to a master. It is reserved upon his report with exceptions thereto and the pleadings. There is no report of evidence.

It has been found that during the negotiations preceding the contract the plaintiff represented that a right of way, which was a substantial factor of value in the real estate, was owned by the Newburyport Cordage Company and could not be interfered with. This representation was untrue. The plaintiff did not know that it was untrue. The defendant relied upon it and would not have signed the contract if he had known that it was false. A person seasonably may rescind a contract to which he has been induced to become a party in reliance upon false though innocent misrepresentations respecting a cognizable material fact made as of his own knowledge by the other party to the contract * * *.

* * *

Bill dismissed with costs.

GIBB V. CITICORP MORTGAGE, INC.

Supreme Court of Nebraska, 1994.
246 Neb. 355, 518 N.W.2d 910.

CAPORALE, J.

I. Statement of Case

Through his operative petition, the plaintiff-appellant, Patrick B. Gibb, seeks, under a variety of theories, to recover damages resulting from the termite infestation of the house he purchased through an agent acting for the seller, the defendant-appellee, Citicorp Mortgage, Inc. After Citicorp successfully demurred, Gibb elected to stand on his pleading; the district court thereupon dismissed his action. Gibb then appealed to the Nebraska Court of Appeals, assigning the dismissal as error, claiming in effect that the district court erred in concluding he had failed to state a cause of action. We, on our own motion, removed the matter to this court in order to regulate the caseloads of the two appellate tribunals. We now reverse and remand for further proceedings.

* * *

III. Factual Allegations

According to the operative petition, Citicorp acquired the house through the foreclosure of a mortgage when the mortgagee abandoned the property because of extensive termite infestation and damage and defaulted on his mortgage obligation. Citicorp's selling agent had been informed through a report of a termite service that the property in question was infested with termites and appeared to have extensive damage. The service recommended that a qualified building inspector assess the damage. However, Citicorp chose to ignore the recommendation and instead hired the service to treat the termites and "[shore] up" the visible damage to the house.

Prior to the purchase, Citicorp's selling agent showed Gibb a single area where termite damage had occurred and assured Gibb that this was the only termite-damaged area and that all necessary repairs and treatments had been made to eliminate the termite problem.

Although neither the agent nor Citicorp made any effort to determine the full extent of the damage, the agent knew that the nonvisible termite damage had not been repaired and that it was much greater than the visible evidence indicated; nonetheless, the agent represented that the damage had been repaired and the termite problem alleviated. Citicorp knew the agent's representations to be false but failed to repudiate them; rather, Citicorp and the agent concealed and suppressed all evidence of termite damage, failed to disclose that the termite damage extended beyond those areas said to be repaired, and concealed and suppressed the fact that the additional " 'wood destroying insect inspection' " required by the purchase agreement to be made at Gibb's cost had not in fact been obtained. In point of fact, at the closing of the transaction, Citicorp provided Gibb with a copy of a 5-month-old report prepared by the termite service after it had submitted its recommendation that the damage be assessed, which indicated that visible evidence of infestation was noted and proper control measures were performed.

The purchase agreement recited that the transaction was "based upon [Gibb's] personal inspection or investigation of the Property and not upon any representation or warranties of condition by [Citicorp] or [its] agent." The agreement further provided that the property was "sold strictly in 'AS IS' condition. [Citicorp] does not make any warranties regarding the condition of the property at the time of sale and thereafter."

Nonetheless, Gibb claims to have relied on the misrepresentations made to him and asserts he has suffered damage as a consequence.

IV. Analysis

Gibb seeks recovery under any one of two fraud theories, a negligence theory, or a contract theory.

1. Fraud Theories

Gibb first avers he was deceived by the fraudulent misrepresentations and fraudulent concealment made by Citicorp through its agent.

(a) Fraudulent Misrepresentation

In order to maintain an action for fraudulent misrepresentation, the plaintiff must allege and prove the following elements: (1) that a representation was made; (2) that the representation was false; (3) that when made, the representation was known to be false or made recklessly without knowledge of its truth and as a positive assertion; (4) that it was made with the intention that the plaintiff should rely upon it; (5) that the plaintiff reasonably did so rely; and (6) that he or she suffered damage as a result. *Nielsen v. Adams,* 223 Neb. 262, 388 N.W.2d 840 (1986).

Gibb has pled all the essential elements for recovery based on fraudulent misrepresentation. He has claimed that Citicorp's selling agent represented that the only termite damage was the visible damage and further represented that all the necessary repairs and treatments had been made. Therefore, a representation was alleged. In addition, Gibb avers that the representation was false because the report from the termite service reveals extensive damage and recommends that a qualified building inspector assess the damage.

Moreover, it can reasonably be inferred that the representation was made with the intention that Gibb rely on it because it relates to a material fact, and Gibb asserts he did in fact rely on the misrepresentations and that he suffered damage as a consequence.

(b) Fraudulent Concealment

In order to maintain an action based on fraudulent concealment, the plaintiff must allege and prove the following elements: (1) that the defendant concealed or suppressed a material fact; (2) that the defendant had knowledge of this material fact; (3) that this material fact was not within the reasonably diligent attention, observation, and judgment of the plaintiff; (4) that the defendant suppressed or concealed this fact with the intention that the plaintiff be misled as to the true condition of the property; (5) that the plaintiff was reasonably so misled; and (6) that the plaintiff suffered damage as a result. *Nelson v. Cheney,* 224 Neb. 756, 401 N.W.2d 472 (1987).

Gibb's operative petition states sufficient facts to allege all the elements for recovery based on fraudulent concealment. He avers that Citicorp concealed or suppressed the fact that the termite damage was more extensive than the visible damage. In addition, by asserting that Citicorp's agent informed it of the termite service's initial report and recommendations, Gibb claims that Citicorp knew the extent of the damage.

Furthermore, Gibb alleges that the material facts regarding the termite damage were not within his diligent attention or observation because he was misled as to the true condition of the house.

Gibb also charges that Citicorp concealed the extent of the termite damage to intentionally mislead him as to the true condition of the house.

In addition, the petition states that Gibb was misled and suffered damage as a result.

(c) Citicorp's Contentions

Notwithstanding that Gibb has pled all of the elements of those two bases of recovery, Citicorp asserts that where an agreement for the sale of real estate contains a disclaimer and an "as is" clause such as those present here, the seller should not be held liable for the fraudulent misrepresentations or concealments of its agent. Citicorp further urges that Gibb had as much access to the relevant information as did Citicorp.

(i) Effect of "As Is" and Disclaimer Clauses

In so arguing, Citicorp acknowledges that under our law, a principal may be liable for the fraudulent actions of its agent, *Corman v. Musselman,* 232 Neb. 159, 439 N.W.2d 781 (1989), but urges that we adopt the position of New York's highest court in *Danann Realty Corp. v. Harris,* 5 N.Y.2d 317, 157 N.E.2d 597, 184 N.Y.S.2d 599 (1959). Therein, the New York Court of Appeals held that a purchaser had no cause of action against a seller for false representation when the contract for the purchase of a lease contained disclaimer, "as is," and merger clauses as follows:

> "The Purchaser has examined the premises agreed to be sold and is familiar with the physical condition thereof. The Seller has not made and does not make any representations as to the physical condition, rents, leases, *expenses, operation* or any other matter or thing affecting or related to the aforesaid premises, except as herein specifically set forth, and the Purchaser hereby *expressly acknowledges that no such representations have been made, and the Purchaser further acknowledges that it has inspected the premises and agrees to take the premises 'as is'* * * * It is understood and agreed that all understandings and agreements heretofore had between the parties hereto are merged in this contract, which alone fully and completely expresses their agreement, *and that the same is entered into after full investigation, neither party relying upon any statement or representation,* not embodied in this contract. . . ."

(Emphasis in original.) *Danann Realty Corp.,* 5 N.Y.2d at 320, 157 N.E.2d at 598, 184 N.Y.S.2d at 601.

The *Danann Realty Corp.* purchaser nonetheless claimed that he had been induced to enter into a contract for the purchase of a lease by the sellers' false oral representations regarding the building's operating expenses. The purchaser sought to affirm the contract and recover damages for fraud.

The *Danann Realty Corp.* majority concluded that the specific disclaimer clause, in conjunction with the merger clause, declared that the parties did not rely on representations not embodied in the contract and thus prevented the purchaser from adducing parol evidence to establish otherwise, thereby destroying the purchaser's allegations of reliance.

However, on several occasions we have addressed whether a disclaimer clause within a contract will bar a purchaser's fraud-based claim. * * *

* * * In *Flakus v. Schug,* 213 Neb. 491, 494–95, 329 N.W.2d 859, 863 (1983), *overruled on other grounds, Nielsen v. Adams,* 223 Neb. 262, 388 N.W.2d 840 (1986), we emphasized:

> It is true that in discussing the elements of fraud we said a disclaimer clause is relevant in determining whether a claimant relied on a false representation disclaimed in the clause. We also said, however, that the disclaimer is ineffective to preclude the trier of fact from considering whether fraud induced formation of the bargain.

We have also concluded that an "as is" clause does not necessarily bar a purchaser's fraud-based claim, writing in *Wolford v. Freeman,* 150 Neb. 537, 547, 35 N.W.2d 98, 103 (1948), that " '[a] provision that the buyer takes the article in the condition in which it is, or in other words, "as is," does not prevent fraudulent representations relied on by the buyer from constituting fraud. . . .' "

Claiming fraud, the *Wolford* plaintiff sought to rescind a contract for the purchase of a house, which recited that he had " 'been advised as to settling of structure and is buying same as is.' " 150 Neb. At 546, 35 N.W.2d at 101. He asserted that the vendor's agent represented that the cracks in the foundation of the house had been repaired and that the damage had been corrected, so that the purchaser should have no fear of further cracking.

After the purchaser took possession, the cracks in the foundation became progressively worse and eventually appeared in the outer walls and the foundation. The purchaser learned that the house had been built on filled ground, in violation of the city building code, and asserted the vendor knew the house had been built on filled ground, rendering the foundation faulty, yet had concealed those facts.

We determined that the purchaser was entitled to prevail unless the vendor was relieved by the "as is" clause. We then reasoned that while the clause disclosed the purchaser's knowledge of the cracking, it did not disclose or suggest the cause of that condition. We accordingly ruled that the clause did not bind the purchaser to buying a house with the undisclosed or concealed condition which caused the visible cracking. Thus, a clause that an article is taken in the condition in which it is, or in other words, "as is," is relevant in determining whether a claimant relied on a false representation concerning the condition of the article, but is not controlling.

In like fashion here, Gibb agreed to purchase a house with visible termite damage, which Citicorp's agent misrepresented as being the extent of the termite destruction. Like the purchaser in *Wolford,* Gibb was aware of the repair to the visible damage to the structure, but, according to his allegations, was unaware of the extent of the damage. Thus, just as the disclaimer does not necessarily prevent Gibb from stating causes of action for fraudulent misrepresentation or fraudulent concealment, neither does the "as is" clause, nor do the two clauses together prevent him from doing so. Under these circumstances, the question as to whether Gibb acted reasonably is one of fact.

(ii) Principal's Responsibility for Agent

[The court rejected Citicorp's argument that because the house was sold with a disclaimer and an "as is" clause, Gibb necessarily knew that Citicorp's agent had no authority to make any representations. Instead, the court held that such contract terms do not limit the scope of an agent's "ostensible authority."]

* * *

2. Negligence Theory

Gibb next asserts that Citicorp negligently misrepresented the situation, declaring that Citicorp, through its agent, failed to use reasonable care when he represented that the property was free of termites. Furthermore, Gibb charges that the representations by Citicorp's agent were false, that he relied upon the representations, and that as a result he suffered damage. And it can be inferred from the setting in which the transaction allegedly arose that both the agent and Citicorp had a pecuniary interest in it.

* * * [W]e, in St. Paul Fire & Marine Ins. Co. v. Touche Ross & Co., 244 Neb. 408, 507 N.W.2d 275 (1993), noted the position of Restatement (Second) of Torts § 552 (1977) regarding negligent misrepresentation as a basis of liability. Thereunder, liability for negligent misrepresentation is based upon the failure of the actor to exercise reasonable care or competence in supplying correct information. Id., § 552, comment a. Section 552 specifies at 126–27:

> (1) One who, in the course of his business, profession or employment, or in any other transaction in which he has a pecuniary interest, supplies false information for the guidance of others in their business transactions, is subject to liability for pecuniary loss caused to them by their justifiable reliance upon the information, if he fails to exercise reasonable care or competence in obtaining or communicating the information.

* * * The Restatement further observes that the liability for negligent misrepresentation is more restricted than for fraudulent misrepresentation, explaining that the reason for the narrower scope of liability fixed for negligent misrepresentation is the difference between the obligations of honesty and of care.

> Honesty requires only that the maker of a representation speak in good faith and without consciousness of a lack of any basis for belief in the truth or accuracy of what he says. * * * Any user of commercial information may reasonably expect the observance of this standard by a supplier of information to whom his use is reasonably foreseeable.
>
> On the other hand, it does not follow that every user of commercial information may hold every maker to a duty of care. Unlike the duty of honesty, the duty of care to be observed in supplying information for use in commercial transactions implies an undertaking to observe a relative standard, which may be defined only in terms of the use to which the information will be put, weighed against the magnitude and probability of loss that might attend that use if the information proves to be incorrect.

§ 552, comment a. at 128. Therefore, the difference between fraudulent misrepresentation and negligent misrepresentation is the duty required in each claim. In fraudulent misrepresentation, one becomes liable for breaching the general duty of good faith or honesty. However, in a claim of negligent misrepresentation, one may become liable even though acting honestly and in good faith if one fails to exercise the level of care required under the circumstances.

* * *

We * * * specifically adopt the definition of the negligent misrepresentation cause of action found in § 552, supra.

As we have established * * * that a principal may be liable for the representations of its agent, it follows that Gibb's negligence theory does not fail merely because he alleges that Citicorp's liability arises from its agent's negligent misrepresentations.

The rule that a principal is liable for the contracts of its agent applies even though the agent, in contracting, acts in his or her own interests and adversely to the principal, where the party with whom the agent contracts has no knowledge of the agent's dereliction and is not cognizant of any fact charging him or her with knowledge thereof. The principal, having selected its representative and vested him or her with apparent authority, should be the loser in such case, and not the innocent party who relied thereon. Draemel v. Rufenacht, Bromagen & Hertz, Inc., 223 Neb. 645, 392 N.W.2d 759 (1986).

Other jurisdictions have recognized a purchaser's claim against a vendor based on the negligent misrepresentations of the vendor's agent. * * *

* * *

Thus, as was the case with respect to Gibb's fraud theories, the reasonableness of Gibb's reliance on the agent's misrepresentations under these circumstances is a factual question.

* * *

[The court also sustained Gibb's contract theory.]

V. Judgment

For the foregoing reasons, the judgment of the district court is reversed and the cause remanded for further proceedings.

DUSHANE v. BENEDICT, 120 U.S. 630 (1887). This was an action of *assumpsit* by a rag-dealer against papermakers to recover $813.03 for rags sold and delivered by him to them. The plea was in the peculiar form used in Pennsylvania, with a counter-claim. The plaintiff had a verdict and judgment, and the case comes before us on a writ of error sued out by the defendants.

* * *

Before proceeding to consider the rulings and instructions at the trial as applied to the facts of the case, it will be convenient to refer to the general rules of law * * *. When a dealer contracts to sell goods which he deals in, to be applied to a particular purpose, and the buyer has no opportunity to inspect them before delivery, there is an implied warranty that they shall be reasonably fit for that purpose. * * * If the seller falsely represents to the buyer that the goods are of a certain quality, or fit for a certain purpose, he is liable to an action for the fraudulent representations * * * and must be supported by proof that he knew the representations to be false when he made them. * * *

The damages recoverable for a breach of warranty, or for a false representation, include all damages which, in the contemplation of the parties, or according to the natural or usual course of things, may result from the wrongful act. For instance, if a man sells hay or grain for the purpose of being fed to cattle, or such as is ordinarily used to feed cattle, and it contains a substance which poisons the buyer's cattle, the seller is responsible for the injury. * * *

* * *

The special matter stated in the affidavits of defense was that the plaintiff came to the defendants' mill, and there solicited and obtained an order for good merchantable rags, free from infection; that the defendants had no opportunity to inspect the rags before delivery; that the rags sent were infected with the small-pox before the plaintiff shipped them; that when some of them were unpacked, and used at the defendant's mill, the infection in the rags caused the small-pox to break out in the mill, in consequence of which some of the workmen died, others were disabled from working, it became impossible to hire new ones at the usual rates, and customers were deterred from buying the defendants' paper; that by reason of the interruption and injury to the defendants' business thereby occasioned, and the money paid by the defendants to those disabled by the disease, they were put to loss and expense far exceeding the amount of the plaintiff's bill; that the plaintiff shipped the rags knowing them to be infected, and intending to deceive, cheat, and defraud the defendants; and that the defendants, as soon as they discovered the infection, informed the plaintiff of the fact, and held those which had not been consumed subject to his order, until their foreman, by mistake, used them up. The affidavits concluded by submitting that the defendants ought not to pay the prices charged, but such amount only as the rags were reasonably worth, if anything; and by asking for a certificate for the amount of their damages in excess of what the plaintiff might be entitled to. In short, the matter stated in the affidavits of defense was a sale of rags upon a warranty or a fraudulent representation that they were clean and free from infection, and a delivery by the plaintiff, under that contract of sale, of rags infected with the small-pox, causing the breaking out of the disease in the defendants' mill, and consequent injuries to their workmen and their business. The plaintiff, by counter-affidavit of claim, met all the issues so notified to him by the defendant's plea and affidavits.

At the trial, the defendants, as appears by the answer of their counsel to an inquiry of the court after the arguments to the jury, and by the statement thereupon made by the court in its charge, did not deny the sale and delivery of the rags at the prices sued for, but relied on their counter-claim for damages on the cause of action growing out of the infected condition of the rags, both by way of a full defense to the plaintiff's action, and also as a ground for obtaining a certificate and judgment for the damages sustained by them in excess of his claim. The defendants offered evidence tending to show that the contract was for clean rags; that the rags delivered were filthy, and infected with the small-pox; and that their infected condition caused the breaking out of the disease in the defendants' mill. This was of itself sufficient evidence to be submitted to the jury of a warranty, and a breach of it. A warranty, express or implied, that rags sold are fit to be manufactured into paper, is broken not only if they will not make good paper, but equally if they cannot be made into paper at all without killing or sickening those employed in the manufacture.

Upon the question whether the plaintiff, when he shipped the rags, knew them to be infected with the small-pox, and fraudulently represented to the defendants that they were clean and free from infection, the evidence was as follows: The plaintiff, having been called as a witness in his own behalf, admitted on cross-examination that the rags were collected by him in Pittsburgh and Allegheny City and the country round about, where he knew that the small-pox was then epidemic, and that he bought rags from any and all dealers, not knowing where they were collected; and further testified that the rags were assorted and baled up under his instructions in his establishment, and had been baled up and laid in his warehouse for a year or more before; that to the best of his knowledge and belief they were clean and free from infection, and there was no sulphur, carbolic acid, or other disinfectant in the bales; and that he never used disinfectants in his establishment. In contradiction of this testimony the defendants produced a letter sent to them by him with the first invoice of rags, showing that he did not then have all the rest on hand; and introduced the testimony of three work-women in the mill that the rags, when opened, smelt strongly of sulphur and carbolic acid. This evidence, taken in connection with that already mentioned, was, in our opinion, sufficient to be submitted to the jury as tending to prove that the plaintiff knew that the rage which he sold and shipped as clean rags, fit to be used in the manufacture of paper, were in fact infected with the small-pox, and that he fraudulently represented them to be clean, intending to deceive and defraud the defendants.

* * *

[W]e are of opinion that the court erred in instructing the jury that the evidence admitted would not justify them in finding that the plaintiff knowingly and fraudulently shipped to the defendants rags infected with the small-pox, as well as in instructing them that there was no evidence which would enable the jury to estimate the amount of damage, if any, which the defendants had sustained, and in directing the jury to return a verdict for the plaintiff for the whole amount of his claim. The defendants' exceptions to these instructions must therefore be sustained, and a new trial had.

* * *

Judgment reversed, and case remanded to the circuit court, with directions to set aside the verdict, and to order a new trial.

HOLCOMB V. HOFFSCHNEIDER

Supreme Court of Iowa, 1980.
297 N.W.2d 210.

UHLENHOPP, JUSTICE.

This appeal involves a claim [in tort for] fraudulent misrepresentations by a realtor regarding the number of acres in irregularly shaped real estate it sold * * *. A jury awarded the purchasers $6000 actual damages. The realtor appealed * * *.

The realtor contends in this appeal that the purchasers did not rely on any representations as to the size of the property and that because the purchasers knew the actual boundaries of the property they bought, they did not sustain damages.

* * *

We view the evidence in the light most favorable to the purchasers who prevailed before the jury. * * *

I. *Reliance.* Dorothea A. and John Hoffschneider listed their house and lots for sale with defendant C.B. Property Sales. The price was $65,000 and the size of the lots, numbers 6 and 7, was stated as 6.8 acres. Dean Olson, a salesman for C.B. Property, placed advertisements in two local newspapers on several days in May through July 1975. The ads stated the property contained six acres.

The purchasers, plaintiffs James R. and Jacquelyn Holcomb, first saw the property in July 1975. They attended an open house of the property hosted by Olson. Subsequently Olson walked the boundaries of the property with them. He also showed them the listing before they made their offer to buy, and stated at various times prior to the sale that he would guarantee the property contained at least 6.6 acres. Actually it contained 4.6 acres.

The parties dispute whether the Holcombs saw the newspaper ads before they offered to buy. Without question the Holcombs saw the listing contract prior to their offer. James R. Holcomb testified on direct examination:

> Q. Was the question of acreage of property that was for sale ever brought up? A. Yes, before we made an offer to buy the property we stopped at Dean's office and he gave us like a listing agreement and it showed the amount of acres. It showed 6.8 and this was on his original copy and before he Xeroxed it he says, I don't know, Jim, I guarantee at least 6.6 acres of ground here. So I put a check by the 6.8 acres and put a question mark and wrote 6.6.

He run a Xerox copy and we took it home and that's what we made the offer to buy off of; that sheet of paper.

Q. How many times prior to the closing of the transaction—how many times did the question of acreage come up? A. Probably 10, 15 times at least.

Q. Was it brought up by you or how? A. By me because it just didn't appear to me that there was that much ground there and he says we sell 90% of the acreages out here and Mr. Herzberg used to live in this house and there is a plat on our wall down in the office and I know that there is that much ground there. So, I took his word for it.

Q. Did he make an explanation? A. He said because it was pie shaped and that hills is deceiving because it is along from the one point to the top of the hill is a long ways. It does look, you know, the distance is deceiving of just how far it is.

Q. What was the terrain like? A. Well, the road comes around like this and it goes, the property goes down like this and goes up like this, you know, it's like that (indicating).

Q. So behind your house there is first a valley and then a hill; is that what you are saying? A. Yeah.

Holcomb reasserted on cross-examination that Olson represented the property contained 6.6 acres and that the Holcombs relied on those statements:

Q. And every time you asked Dean Olson he said about six acres. A. No, he said, I guarantee at least 6.6.

Q. And you asked him the same question 15 to 20 times and every time he said, I guarantee the size to be 6.8 acres. A. He said Mr. Herzberg lived in here. There is a plat of this on our wall. And he said, no, if there was any difference they would catch it.

Q. Why did you ask him 15 to 20 times? A. Because it didn't look like there was that much property there.

Q. Why didn't you check a little further on it? [Objection, overruled.] A. Because Dean guaranteed me there was that much ground there.

Q. Did you walk the boundaries of the land you were talking about? A. Yes.

Q. You went out and looked at it? A. Yes.

Herzberg was president of C.B. Property and also the general contractor who constructed the house in question. He lived in the house prior to its sale to Hoffschneiders.

The Holcombs eventually offered $54,000 for the house and lots, and purchased the property for that price.

As to C.B. Property's contention that the Holcombs did not rely on the misrepresentations, the evidence does show that the Holcombs examined the property. This court has said, however, that a buyer cannot generally be held to be able to judge the contents of a parcel of land by the eye. *Boddy v. Henry,* 126 Iowa 31, 42, 101 N.W. 447, 451 (1904). Even though a buyer examines land before purchasing, he may normally rely upon the representations of the seller as to measurement. *Id.* At 42, 101 N.W. at 450–51.

C.B. Property argues that if the Holcombs really wanted to know the exact acreage, they should have obtained a survey. On cross-examination Holcomb had this to say on that subject:

> Q. Do you know what a survey is? A. Yes.
>
> Q. Would you tell the jury what a survey is? A. Well, that's when you have a surveyor come out and tell you how much ground is in there.
>
> Q. And a surveyor would also tell you how many acres you are buying. A. Correct.
>
> Q. And you knew what a survey was at that time you were purchasing this property. A. Yes, but I didn't feel it was necessary to have it surveyed since C.B. Property was engaged in the whole transaction out there in the Rolling Hill Addition.
>
> Q. So you didn't ask for a survey because of that, is that correct? A. Correct.

This court stated in *McGibbons v. Wilder,* 78 Iowa 531, 535, 43 N.W. 520, 522 (1889):

> This court has repeatedly held, in effect, that a party may rely upon representations as to the ownership of property, its location, and the like; and that, to entitle him to recover for fraudulent representations, he is not bound to show that he instituted inquiry by consulting records or plats, or employing a surveyor, or the like. * * *

Under the testimony and these pronouncements, we hold the Holcombs generated a jury issue on reliance. The jury could say that although the Holcombs doubted the representations as to acreage were right, after Olson's repeated assurances they took his word.

II. Damages. Iowa follows the benefit-of-the-bargain rule, that is, a defrauded purchaser is entitled to the difference between the value the property would have had as represented and the value of the property he actually received. * * *

* * *

The gist of C.B. Property's argument on damages is that the Holcombs saw the property they bought, from visual inspection they knew its actual size, and they bid and bought that exact tract for $54,000—they were willing to pay that amount for what they saw. C.B. Property urges that the Holcombs got what they paid for and they therefore sustained no damage.

Involved in an issue of this kind are two kinds of cases: those in which a purchaser intends to purchase a tract, not a quantity in acres or by dimensions, * * * as distinguished from those in which the purchaser intends to purchase a number of acres or by dimensions. In the latter situation the purchaser is damaged if the seller fraudulently misrepresents the acreage or dimensions. * * * The jury could reasonably find on the evidence that this case was of the latter sort. C.B. Property makes a cogent jury argument that the case was of the former kind, but the decision was ultimately for the jury. We do not find merit in this claim of error.

[Although the jury found the misrepresentations to be fraudulent, the trial court refused to submit the issue of punitive damages to the jury and the Supreme Court affirmed, holding that Holcomb's case involved at best "ordinary" or "simple fraud." The court relied on 37 Am.Jur.2d Fraud and Deceit section 347, at 466 (1968), which states in part:

Generally speaking, a recovery of exemplary or punitive damages in an action based on a fraudulent sale will be allowed only where the fraud is an aggravated one, as where it is malicious, deliberate, gross, or wanton.]

AFFIRMED.

PORRECO v. PORRECO, 571 Pa. 61, 811 A.2d 566 (2002). [Before their marriage, Louis Porreco gave Susan Porreco an engagement ring. At least in part because Louis had showered Susan with other valuable presents prior to giving her the ring, including expensive jewelry, Susan believed the ring was a diamond. Susan later found out the ring was a fake, but not before signing an unfavorable prenuptial agreement granting her only $3500 per month upon a divorce. Louis' net worth was over $3 million. The prenuptial agreement included a personal financial statement, prepared by Louis, that listed the ring as an engagement ring, without further identification, with a value of $21,000. Apparently, it was worth far less. At the divorce proceeding in which Susan sought to avoid the prenuptial agreement, she testified that "she would not have signed the prenuptial agreement if she knew that Louis had given her a fake ring and lied about it and 'would not have married the man.' "]

MADAME JUSTICE NEWMAN.

[W]e cannot agree that Susan's alleged reliance on Louis' misrepresentation of the value of the ring on the schedule of her assets was justifiable. Susan had possession of the ring and was not impeded from doing what she ultimately did when the parties separated: obtain an appraisal of the ring. She had sufficient opportunity to inform herself fully of the nature and extent of her own assets, rather than rely on Louis' statements concerning the valuation of her holdings. We find her failure to do this simple investigation to be unreasonable. Although we do not excuse Louis' actions we will not sanction the avoidance of an entire prenuptial agreement—the consequences of which Susan admittedly understood—on the basis of fraud in these circumstances.

WEINTRAUB V. KROBATSCH

Supreme Court of New Jersey, 1974.
64 N.J. 445, 317 A.2d 68.

JACOBS, J.

The [summary judgment] * * * directed that the appellants Donald P. Krobatsch and Estella Krobatsch, his wife, pay the sum of $4,250 to the plaintiff Natalie Weintraub and the sum of $2,550 to the defendant The Serafin Agency, Inc. We granted certification on the application of the appellants. * * *

* * * [W]e must resolve doubts in favor of the appellants and must accept their factual allegations, along with the inferences most favorable to them. * * *

Mrs. Weintraub owned and occupied a six-year-old Englishtown home which she placed in the hands of a real estate broker (The Serafin Agency, Inc.) for sale. The Krobatsches were interested in purchasing the home, examined it while it was illuminated and found it suitable. On June 30, 1971 Mrs. Weintraub, as seller, and the Krobatsches, as purchasers, entered into a contract for the sale of the property for $42,500. The contract provided that the purchasers had inspected the property and were fully satisfied with its physical condition, that no representations had been made and that no responsibility was assumed by the seller as to the present or future condition of the premises. A deposit of $4,250 was sent by the purchasers to the broker to be held in escrow pending the closing of the transaction. The purchasers requested that the seller have the house fumigated and that was done. A fire after the signing of the contract caused damage but the purchasers indicated readiness that there be adjustment at closing.

During the evening of August 25, 1971, prior to closing, the purchasers entered the house, then unoccupied, and as they turned the lights on they were, as described in their petition for certification, "astonished to see roaches literally running in all directions, up the walls, drapes, etc." On the following day their attorney wrote a letter to Mrs. Weintraub, care of her New York law firm, advising that on the previous day "it was discovered that the house is infested with vermin despite the fact that an exterminator has only recently serviced the house" and asserting that "the presence of vermin in such great quantities, particularly after the exterminator was done, rendered the house as unfit for human habitation at this time and therefore, the contract is rescinded." On September 2, 1971 an exterminator wrote to Mr. Krobatsch advising that he had examined the premises and that "cockroaches were found to have infested the entire house." He said he could eliminate them for a relatively modest charge by two treatments with a twenty-one day interval but that it would be necessary to remove the carpeting "to properly treat all the infested areas."

Mrs. Weintraub rejected the rescission by the purchasers and filed an action in the Law Division joining them and the broker as defendants. Though she originally sought specific performance she later confined her claim to damages in the sum of $4,250, representing the deposit held in escrow by the broker. The broker filed an answer and counterclaim seeking payment of its commission in the sum of $2,550. There were opposing motions for summary judgment by the purchasers and Mrs. Weintraub, along with a motion for summary judgment by the broker for its commission. At the argument on the motions it was evident that the purchasers were claiming fraudulent concealment or nondisclosure by the seller as the basis for their rescission. Thus at one point their attorney said: "Your honor, I would point out, and it is in my clients' affidavit, every time that they inspected this house prior to this time every light in the place was illuminated. Now, these insects are nocturnal by nature and that is not a point I think I have to prove through someone. I think Webster's dictionary is sufficient. By keeping the lights on it keeps them out of sight. These sellers had to know they had this problem. You could not live in a house this infested without knowing about it."

The Law Division denied the motion by the purchasers for summary judgment but granted Mrs. Weintraub's motion and directed that the purchasers pay her the sum of $4,250. It further directed that the deposit monies held in escrow by the broker be paid to Mrs. Weintraub in satisfaction of her judgment against the purchasers. * * * It denied the broker's summary judgment motion for its commission but held that matter for trial. On appeal, the Appellate Division sustained the summary judgment in Mrs. Weintraub's favor but disagreed with the Law Division's holding that the broker's claim must await trial. It considered that since the purchasers were summarily held to have been in default in rescinding rather than in proceeding with the closing, they were responsible for the commission. Accordingly, it modified the Law Division's judgment to the end that the purchasers were directed to pay not only the sum of $4,250 to Mrs. Weintraub but also the sum of $2,550 to the broker.

Before us the purchasers contend that they were entitled to a trial on the issue of whether there was fraudulent concealment or nondisclosure entitling them to rescind; if there was, then clearly they were under no liability to either the seller or the broker and would be entitled to the return of their deposit held by the broker in escrow. See Keen v. James, 39 N.J.Eq. 527, 540 (E. & A. 1885) where Justice Dixon, speaking for the then Court of last resort, pointed out that "silence may be fraudulent" and that relief may be granted to one contractual party where the other suppresses facts which he, " 'under the circumstances, is bound in conscience and duty to disclose to the other party, and in respect to which he cannot, innocently, be silent.' " * * *

Mrs. Weintraub asserts that she was unaware of the infestation and the Krobatsches acknowledge that, if that was so, then there was no fraudulent concealment or nondisclosure on her part and their claim must fall. But the purchasers allege that she was in fact aware of the infestation and at this stage of the proceedings we must assume that to be true. She contends, however, that even if she were fully aware she would have been under no duty to speak and that consequently no complaint by the purchasers may legally be grounded on her silence. She relies primarily on cases such as Swinton v. Whitinsville Sav. Bank, 311 Mass. 677, 42 N.E.2d 808, 141 A.L.R. 965 (1942) * * *. *Swinton* is pertinent but, as Dean Prosser has noted [Prosser, Torts 695, 696 (4th ed. 1971)], it is one of a line of "singularly unappetizing cases" which are surely out of tune with our times.

In *Swinton* the plaintiff purchased a house from the defendant and after he occupied it he found it to be infested with termites. The defendant had made no verbal or written representations but the plaintiff, asserting that the defendant knew of the termites and was under a duty to speak, filed a complaint for damages grounded on fraudulent concealment. The Supreme Judicial Court of Massachusetts sustained a demurrer to the complaint and entered judgment for the defendant. In the course of its opinion the court acknowledged that "the plaintiff possesses a certain appeal to the moral sense" but concluded that the law has not "reached the point of imposing upon the frailties of human nature a standard so idealistic as this." 42 N.E.2d at 808–809. That was written several decades ago and we are far from certain that it represents views held by the current members of the Massachusetts court. * * * In any event we are certain that it does not represent our sense of justice or fair dealing and it has understandably been rejected in persuasive opinions elsewhere. * * *

In Obde v. Schlemeyer, 56 Wash.2d 449, 353 P.2d 672, [1960] the defendants sold an apartment house to the plaintiff. The house was termite infested but that fact was not disclosed by the sellers to the purchasers who later sued for damages alleging fraudulent concealment. The sellers contended that they were under no obligation whatever to speak out and they relied heavily on the decision of the Massachusetts court in *Swinton* * * * The Supreme Court of Washington flatly rejected their contention, holding that though the parties had dealt at arms length the sellers were under "a duty to inform the plaintiffs of the termite condition" of which they were fully aware. 353 P.2d at 674. * * * In the course of its opinion the court quoted approvingly from Dean Keeton's article [Keeton, Fraud—Concealment and Nondisclosure, 15 Tex. 1 (1936)]. There the author first expressed his thought that when Lord Cairns suggested in Peek v. Gurney, L.R. 6 H.L. 377 (1873), that there was no duty to disclose facts, no matter how "morally censurable" (at 403), he was expressing nineteenth century law as shaped by an individualistic philosophy based on freedom of contracts and unconcerned with morals. He then made the following comments which fairly embody a currently acceptable principle on which the holding in *Obde* may be said to be grounded:

> In the present stage of the law, the decisions show a drawing away from this idea, and there can be seen an attempt by many courts to reach a just result in so far as possible, but yet maintaining the degree of certainty which the law must have. The statement may often be found that if either party to a contract of sale conceals or suppresses a material fact which he is in good faith bound to disclose then his silence is fraudulent.
>
> The attitude of the courts toward nondisclosure is undergoing a change and contrary to Lord Cairns' famous remark it would seem that the object of the law in these cases should be to impose on parties to the transaction a duty to speak whenever justice, equity, and fair dealing demand it. This statement is made only with reference to instances where the party to be charged is an actor in the transaction. This duty to speak does not result from an implied representation by silence, but exists because a refusal to speak constitutes unfair conduct. 15 Tex.L.Rev. at 31.

* * *

In Simmons v. Evans, [185 Tenn. 282, 206 S.W.2d 295 (1947)] the defendants owned a home which was serviced by a local water company. The company supplied water during the daytime but not at night. The defendants sold their home to the plaintiffs but made no mention of the limitation on the water service. The plaintiffs filed an action to rescind their purchase but the lower court dismissed it on the ground that the defendants had not made any written or verbal representations and the plaintiffs had "inspected the property, knew the source of the water supply, and could have made specific inquiry of these defendants or ascertained from other sources the true situation and, therefore, are estopped." 206 S.W.2d at 296. The dismissal was reversed on appeal in an opinion which took note of the general rule that " 'one may be guilty of fraud by his silence, as where it is expressly incumbent upon him to speak concerning material matters that are entirely within his own knowledge.' " 206 S.W.2d at 296. With respect to the plaintiffs' failure to ascertain the water situation before their purchase the court stated that the plaintiffs were surely not required "to make a night inspection in order to ascertain whether the water situation with reference to this residence was different from what it was during the day." 206 S.W.2d at 297.

* * *

* * * The purchasers here were entitled to withstand the seller's motion for summary judgment. They should have been permitted to proceed with their efforts to establish by testimony that they were equitably entitled to rescind because the house was extensively infested in the manner described by them, the seller was well aware of the infestation, and the seller deliberately concealed or failed to disclose the condition because of the likelihood that it would defeat the transaction. The seller may of course defend factually as well as legally and since the matter is primarily equitable in nature the factual as well as legal disputes will be for the trial judge alone.

If the trial judge finds such deliberate concealment or nondisclosure of the latent infestation not observable by the purchasers on their inspection, he will still be called upon to determine whether, in the light of the full presentation before him, the concealment or nondisclosure was of such significant nature as to justify rescission. Minor conditions which ordinary sellers and purchasers would reasonably disregard as of little or no materiality in the transaction would clearly not call for judicial intervention. While the described condition may not have been quite as major as in the termite cases which were concerned with structural impairments, to the purchasers here it apparently was of such magnitude and was so repulsive as to cause them to rescind immediately though they had earlier indicated readiness that there be adjustment at closing for damage resulting from a fire which occurred after the contract was signed. We are not prepared at this time to say that on their showing they acted either unreasonably or without equitable justification.

* * *

Reversed and Remanded.

AMERICAN LAW INSTITUTE PRINCIPLES OF THE LAW OF SOFTWARE CONTRACTS

§ 3.05(b).

A transferor that receives money or a right to payment of a monetary obligation in exchange for the software warrants to any party in the normal chain of distribution that the software contains no material hidden defects of which the transferor was aware at the time of the transfer. This warranty may not be excluded. In addition, this warranty does not displace an action for misrepresentation or its remedies.

* * *

Comment b. Hidden defects. Subsection (b) creates a nonexcludable implied warranty that the software "contains no material hidden defects of which the transferor was aware at the time of the transfer." The section memorializes existing law, including the contract obligation of good faith, the contract duty to disclose, and fraudulent concealment law. * * * The nature of software means that end users should not expect perfection. Several Sections of these Principles shield software providers from inordinate liability, such as by enforcing disclaimers and remedy limitations. However, software transferors should have a duty to disclose known material hidden defects in order to allocate those risks to the party best able to accommodate or avoid them. Hidden material defects, known to the software transferor but not disclosed, shift costs to the transferee who cannot learn of the defects until it is too late and therefore cannot protect itself.

Section 3.05(b) requires that the transferor know of the defect at the time of the transfer, the defect is material, and it is hidden. The *time of the transfer* is the time of conveyance of rights in the software or of authorization to access software. * * *

A *material* defect consists of a software error serious enough to constitute a material breach of the contract. Section 3.11 of these Principles and the well-established common-law material-breach doctrine, which ask whether the injured party received substantially what it bargained for and reasonably expected, inform the court's decision on whether a defect is material. Software that requires major workarounds to achieve contract-promised functionality and that causes long periods of downtime or never achieves promised functionality ordinarily would constitute a material defect.

A *hidden* material defect means that the defect would not surface upon any testing that was or should have been performed by the transferee. * * * Negligence on the part of transferors in failing to discover defects is not covered by the Section and is the subject of products-liability law. Nor does the subsection displace the law of misrepresentation, which applies to affirmative statements meant to deceive. As with fraudulent concealment law, ordinarily § 3.05(b) should require an intent to deceive, which may be inferred if a transferor licenses software it knows is materially defective and knows the user cannot discover it upon an inspection.

Disclosure of a material hidden defect occurs when a reasonable transferee would understand the existence and basic nature of the defect. Disclosure ordinarily should involve a direct communication to the transferee, if feasible. A mere posting of defects on the transferor's website may be insufficient depending on the circumstances. Ultimately, the type of disclosure that would make a reasonable transferee aware of the defect is heavily context dependent and should be developed by the courts.

Putting together the requirements of transferor actual knowledge of the defect at the time of the transfer, transferee reasonable lack of knowledge, and a defect that constitutes a material breach means that a transferor would not be liable if the transferor has received reports of problems but reasonably has not had time to investigate them, if the transferee's problems are caused by uses of which the transferor is unaware, if the transferor learns of problems only after the transfer, and if the problems are benign or require reasonable workarounds to achieve functionality.

KRONMAN, MISTAKE, DISCLOSURE, INFORMATION AND THE LAW OF CONTRACTS

7 J. Legal Stud. 1, 13, 18 (1978).

As it is used here, the term "deliberately acquired information" means information whose acquisition entails costs which would not have been incurred but for the likelihood, however great, that the information in question would actually be produced. These costs may include, of course, not only direct search costs (the cost of examining the corporation's annual statement) but the costs of developing an initial expertise as well (for example, the cost of attending business school). If the costs incurred in acquiring the information * * * would have been incurred in any case—that is, whether or not the information was forthcoming—the information may be said to have been casually acquired.

* * *

The distinction between deliberately and casually acquired information helps us to understand the pattern exhibited by the cases in which a duty to disclose is asserted by one party or the other. By and large, the cases requiring disclosure involve information which is likely to have been casually acquired (in the sense defined above). The cases permitting nondisclosure, on the other hand, involve information which, on the whole, is likely to have been deliberately produced. Taken as a group, the disclosure cases give at least the appearance of promoting allocative efficiency by limiting the assignment of property rights to those types of information which are likely to be the fruit of a deliberate investment (either in the development of expertise or in actual searching).

C. FRIED, CONTRACT AS PROMISE

79, 83 (Rev. ed. 2015).

An oil company has made extensive geological surveys seeking to identify possible oil and gas reserves. These surveys are extremely expensive. Having identified one promising site, the oil company (acting through a broker) buys a large tract of land from its prosperous farmer owner, revealing nothing about its survey, its purposes, or even its identity. The price paid is the going price for farmland of that quality in that region.

* * *

Anthony Kronman has recently written that [the] arguments in terms of encouraging investment in information show that the results in such cases do and should just depend on a policy of efficiency and redistribution. The decisions favor the oil company because even the sellers will be better off in the long run under a rule that encourages such investments in knowledge. And in general, argues Kronman, what contracts are enforced is (or should be) always just a function of what will make the least advantaged party to the particular kind of transaction better off. But this misconceives the argument. The oil company wins not because we want to encourage its future investments but because it would be unfair to defeat its past reasonable expectations. To be sure, our determination to be fair even in the face of sentimental pressures to favor a weaker party (the farmer) will encourage investment—that is, rational planning for the future. But Kronman gets the arguments exactly the wrong way around. Indeed, if we played fair with the oil company only because (and only so far as) this led to greater economic productivity or improved the situation of the least advantaged party, then our playing fair on a particular occasion would not create confidence and so would not even procure these supposed general benefits. In general we can get the social, collective benefits of trust only if we are faithful for the sake of trust itself, not just for the sake of the resulting benefits.

HILLMAN AND O'ROURKE, DEFENDING DISCLOSURE IN SOFTWARE LICENSING

78 U. Chi. L. Rev. 95, 98 (2011).

One prominent issue in the literature of disclosure law is the effect of disclosure on the incentives to "generate and utilize * * * information in the first place." Kronman argues that the law does not require disclosure of deliberately acquired information in order to create an incentive to acquire the information. For example, a company might not look for oil if it had to disclose its findings to a prospective seller of the land, who obviously would raise the price if it knew of the oil. Requiring the disclosure of casually acquired information, on the other hand, does not discourage the production of information.

Analysts are almost unanimous in concluding that disclosure of important information by sellers is desirable notwithstanding Kronman's analysis. For example, Trebilcock urges that sellers must disclose adverse information because nondisclosure would "substantially impair the expected value of the transaction to the buyer," whereas the adverse information is a "sunk cost" for the seller. The role of the law is to deter "further misallocat[ion]" of the resources. In addition, sellers would likely acquire information about their assets even if required to disclose the information. This certainly is likely in the case of software licensors, who inevitably uncover problems with their software in the process of engineering, debugging, and manufacturing it.

PROBLEM 5-2

1. The Stambovskys, residents of New York City, call you because they want to recover their $32,500 down-payment on the purchase of the Ackleys' home in Nyack, New York. The Stambovskys tell you that the Ackleys did not disclose their belief that the house is haunted by ghosts. Ms. Ackley had shared her view with the public by publishing articles about the house in the Reader's Digest and in local newspapers. In fact, two months after signing the contract, a local newspaper described the house as a "riverfront Victorian (with ghosts)." Assume that the market value of the house and its resale potential are materially affected by its reputation. Please advise the Stambovskys.

2. The following facts are also based on an actual episode. Eddie Crowe signed a twelve-year lease for a bar and restaurant on Second Avenue on the upper east side of New York City. He then invested over $350,000 in renovations. Unfortunately, he was not aware at the time that New York City was about to begin construction of a Second Avenue subway literally in front of his bar. Assume construction would continue for the first four years of Crowe's lease and that it would decrease income from the bar by about one third. Did Crowe's landlord have a duty during negotiations to disclose New York City's plans assuming the landlord was aware of them?

NOTE:
DUTY TO DISCLOSE THE LEGAL EFFECT OF AN AGREEMENT

Some courts have required a party to disclose, not only factual circumstances surrounding a transaction, such as in Weintraub v. Krobatsch, but also information about the legal effect of contract terms. The duty arises when the contract contains fine print or otherwise hidden terms, but it also arises in the absence of these infirmities when one party enjoys superior knowledge or a superior position. Such superior knowledge or position may be based on a discernible weakness of the other party, such as lack of education, or it may be based on the type of transaction, such as a form contract offered on a take-it-or-leave-it basis.

The American Law Institute's "Principles of the Law of Software Contracts" does not create a duty to disclose the terms of software licenses prior to a particular transaction. However, the Principles set forth a safe harbor that licensors can follow to ensure enforcement of their forms (provided the terms are not unconscionable or against public policy). To satisfy the safe harbor, software licensors must publish their forms on the Internet prior to any transaction so that a licensee can shop around for terms if so inclined. Admittedly, few people read electronic standard forms (or paper ones, for that matter) even when they commit to a contract, so it is also unlikely they will search for terms or compare them. Nevertheless, the cost of such disclosure is negligible and may lead to the creation of effective "watchdog" websites that collect unfavorable terms. To date, alternative proposals to increase reading of standard forms seem unrealistic and expensive or can easily supplement the disclosure safe harbor.

WEAVER v. AMERICAN OIL CO., 257 Ind. 458, 276 N.E.2d 144 (1971). [A lease between American Oil and station-owner Weaver exculpated American Oil from liability for its own negligence and required Weaver to indemnify American Oil for any liability for American Oil's negligence. The litigation arose when American Oil's employee sprayed gasoline over Weaver and his assistant, causing them to be burned and American Oil sought a declaratory judgment determining the extent of *Weaver's* liability. The court first highlighted Weaver's lack of education (he had left high school) and his failure to read the lease (each year a salesman from American Oil brought the lease for Weaver to sign and he did so without reading it or without a warning from the salesman about the indemnification clause).]

When a party can show that the contract, which is sought to be enforced, was in fact an unconscionable one, due to a prodigious amount of bargaining power on behalf of the stronger party, which is used to the stronger party's advantage and is unknown to the lesser party, causing a great hardship and risk on the lesser party, the contract provision, or the contract as a whole, if the provision is not separable, should not be enforceable on the grounds that the provision is contrary to public policy. The party seeking to enforce such a contract has the burden of showing that the provisions were explained to the other party and *came to his knowledge* and there was in fact *a real and voluntary meeting of the minds and not merely an objective meeting.*

* * *

We do not mean to say or infer that parties may not make contracts exculpating one of his negligence and providing for indemnification, but it must be done *knowingly* and *willingly* as in insurance contracts made for that very purpose.

[A dissenting judge took a different view:]

The facts as found, are that although the defendant never read the lease, he had ample opportunity to do so and to obtain counsel. A general rule in effect not only in Indiana but elsewhere, is that a person who signs a contract, without bothering to read the same, will be bound by its terms. * * *

P. SIVIGLIA, WRITING CONTRACTS

51 (1996).

Too often lawyers—or, perhaps, just too many lawyers—believe that when they draft an agreement, they must prepare the document to reflect only the interests of their client. They pay little, if any, attention to the legitimate concerns of the other party.

* * *

Highhanded drafting * * * is not only offensive, antagonizing the other party and his or her lawyer, but it needlessly prolongs the negotiating and drafting process, thereby adding to the legal costs of both parties and to the mounting deficit in respect that clients and the general public have for lawyers.

SECTION FOUR: PUBLIC POLICY

Freedom of contract is itself a public policy. One court, applying Texas contract law, but quite representative of a more general approach, makes the point as follows: "Texas's public policy strongly favors freedom of contract. * * * [C]ompetent parties have the utmost liberty of contract, and that, when entered freely and voluntarily, contracts shall be held sacred * * *. This 'paramount public policy' mandates that * * * courts not lightly interfere with freedom of contract. * * * Absent compelling reasons, courts must respect and enforce the terms of a contract the parties have entered freely and voluntarily." Fairfield Ind., Inc. v. EP Energy F&P Co., 531 S.W.3d 234, 249 (Tex. App. 2017). But sometimes freedom of contract clashes with other public policies. The materials that follow illustrate in various contexts how courts deal with this dilemma.

HANFORD V. CONNECTICUT FAIR ASSOCIATION

Connecticut Supreme Court, 1918.
103 A. 838.

SHUMWAY, J.

This is a civil action wherein the plaintiffs count upon a written contract and claim damages for its breach. The complaint alleges that the plaintiffs agreed to promote and manage a baby show at Charter Oak Park, in Hartford, on September 6th, 7th and 8th, 1916. The contract annexed to the complaint discloses that the plaintiffs agreed to supply one hundred and twenty prizes, certain printed matter for advertising the show, and to do certain other things not material to the present inquiry. The defendant agreed to furnish a room in which to hold the show and to pay the plaintiffs $600.

The defendant in its answer alleged that during the middle and latter part of August and early in September, 1916, a disease popularly known as infantile paralysis was epidemic in the city of Hartford, and throughout the State of Connecticut, which disease attacked children, and particularly babies and young children, in large number. Said disease proved fatal in a large proportion of the cases, and permanently crippled many of those afflicted with it; and for some time prior to, and at the time of the proposed baby show referred to in said alleged contract, was so widespread and so serious as to make assemblies of children, and especially young children, highly dangerous to the health of the children of the community; and by reason of said facts it was contrary to public policy to hold a baby show of the nature and at the time provided for in said alleged contract. The answer further alleged that the defendant notified the plaintiffs about the middle of August that it wished to cancel the contract for the reason above set forth, and thereafter the contract was definitely and finally cancelled for the reason named.

To this answer the plaintiffs demurred. The court overruled the demurrer, and this ruling furnishes the only reason of appeal.

It appears that the contract was a joint undertaking by the plaintiffs and defendant. Each of them was to furnish and do such things as were deemed essential to attract a number of babies to the grounds and buildings controlled by the Fair Association. Presumably the babies were in some manner to be exhibited, and it was expected that at least one hundred and twenty prizes would be awarded for such excellent and desirable traits as the babies might be adjudged to possess upon an inspection and comparison. Such an assembly of children it is alleged would be "highly dangerous" to the health of the community, and against public policy. For the present purpose it must be assumed that it would be dangerous to the public health. However, it seems that whenever all the facts bearing upon the question of public policy in any given case are undisputed, whether or not the acts or contracts are contrary to public policy in any given case are undisputed, whether or not the acts or contracts are contrary to public policy, is a question of law. *Connors* v. *Connolly*, 86 Conn. 641, 86 A. 600. Then the allegation in the answer, that the performance of this contract was contrary to public policy, must be treated as a statement of a legal conclusion, and not a fact which is admitted by the demurrer. In the case of *Connors* v. *Connolly, supra*, the court quotes with approval this passage from Greenwood on Public Policy, page 5: "The question of the validity of the contract does not depend upon the circumstance whether it can be shown that the public has, in fact, suffered any detriment, but whether the contract is, in its nature, such as might have been injurious to the public. . . . The law looks to the general tendency of such contracts."

It is conceded that if a contract is contrary to public policy it is void. As it is admitted that the holding of a baby show under the circumstances narrated would be highly dangerous to the health of the community, it must follow that such a show would be contrary to public policy. This court is now considering the sufficiency of an allegation, not how that allegation can be proved. The allegation that the baby show would be dangerous to public health might be avoided by the plaintiff by alleging, if such is the fact, that effectual precautions had been taken to prevent the communication of the disease from one child to another, or by setting up any other fact making it clear that no harm could result to the public from the show. But the court cannot regard the averment that the assemblage of a number of children as proposed would be "highly" dangerous to the public health, other than as a fact which the plaintiff must answer, either by denial or matter in avoidance.

The court will not require the performance, or award damages for a breach, of a contract in which the public have so great an interest as the preservation of health, if the health is in fact endangered, any more than it would require one to be performed the tendency of which was immoral or one which interfered with the right of everyone to earn a livelihood by a lawful occupation. *Connors* v. *Connolly*, 86 Conn. 641, 86 A. 600. The plaintiffs in their brief rely upon these cases: *Libby* v. *Inhabitants of Douglas*, 175 Mass. 128, 55 N.E. 808; *Dewey* v. *Alpena School District*, 43 Mich. 480, 5 N.W. 646; and *Gear* v. *Gray*, 10 Ind. App. 428, 37 N.E. 1059. These appear to be actions brought by school teachers to recover salary when the schools had been closed by reason of the prevalence of some contagious or infectious disease in the community. There is a difference between a contract to teach school, and one to promote and manage a baby show. Teaching proper subjects can never be unlawful or contrary to public policy, though the assemblage of a number of children in one room might become very harmful. The teacher has usually no control over the attendance in his school. The baby show, however, would be highly dangerous to health, and this is just what the parties have agreed to promote and carry out for their mutual profit.

The plaintiffs contend that the defendant's undertaking was absolute and unqualified, and they cite in their brief the case of *School District No. 1* v. *Dauchy*, 25 Conn. 530. The trial court appears to have had this case in mind in overruling the demurrer, and applied the principle there enunciated. Even though in this case the promise was absolute and unqualified, yet neither party contemplated that the show would be held if the public health would be endangered thereby, and therefore the contract impliedly contains a provision to that effect. The trial court so held.

BEACH, J. (dissenting).

I dissent from the broad proposition that whenever an otherwise lawful act becomes dangerous to the public health, it automatically becomes contrary to public policy and therefore unlawful, without any statute or order intervening to make it so.

Confining the statement to things which are inherently lawful,—such as a baby show—but which may become dangerous to public health because of an external temporary condition, the public policy of Connecticut as regards the taking of prophylactic measures, appears to me to be manifested by the establishment of a complete system of State, county and municipal health officials armed with all necessary powers. It is our public policy, I think, that a determination of the preliminary question whether the public health is endangered, should be left to the responsible medical experts appointed for that purpose, and not to the *judicium rusticum* of a jury; also that these official experts should determine in advance what, if any, preventive measures ought to be taken, instead of leaving that question to be determined, after the event, by a jury.

For these reasons I think the demurrer to the answer ought to have been sustained, on the ground that it did not appear that the holding of this baby show had been prohibited by an order of the county or State health officials.

In this opinion PRENTICE, C. J., concurred.

NOTE:
COVID-19 AND PUBLIC POLICY

As we write this note, in the first iteration of the Great Pause of 2020 due to the pandemic, millions of contracts, ranging from residential leases to billion dollar mergers between corporate giants, are not being performed. The particular circumstances of such failures will obviously make a difference to the litigation tidal wave that is coming. Under what circumstances, if any, will *Hanford*-like public policy defenses serve defendants to avoid obligation?

One of your authors (Hoffman) has recently written about this issue with Professor Cathy Hwang. In *The Social Cost of Contract*, Columbia Law Review (2021), Hoffman and Hwang write:

> There is no general public health exception to contract enforcement—but the court found one. And while the cases on how to adjudicate excuse based on public health risks are rare, Hanford is not the only example of its kind. Cases considering public health distortions of ordinary contractual doctrine have resulted from nearly every epidemic of the last two centuries.
>
> Hanford and other cases excusing, reinterpreting, and reforming performance obligations on public policy grounds show how the public's interest interacts with private contracting. On a daily basis, private parties enter into contracts—to use a website, to lease an apartment, to host a family reunion, or to merge two companies into one. And while seats at the contract-negotiation table are primarily occupied by the contracting parties themselves, one place is always implicitly reserved for another party: the public.

* * *

Consider this 1915 letter from Babyland Amusement Company, which discusses the Fair to come. Does it strengthen or weaken the firm's claim for recovery?

"THE CARNIVAL OF THE BABE"

L. M. RICH
MANAGER

W. J. HANFORD
TREASURER

M. L. RICH
SECRETARY

WE PROMOTE
SHOWS FOR
PARKS
FAIRS
THEATRES
CARNIVALS

Babyland Amusement Co.

HOME OFFICE
874 SEAVIEW AVENUE

AMUSEMENT PROMOTERS TO THE
KINGS AND QUEENS OF BABYLAND

N. Y. REPRESENTATIVE
JAMES E. CLANCY
PUTNAM BUILDING
1493 BROADWAY

BRIDGEPORT, CONN. Aug. 17, 1915.

Mr. G.M. Rundle,
Sec. Danbury Fair,
Danbury, Conn.

Dear Sir;-

I would be pleased to take up with you the proposition, which we side-tracked, last year. I am promoting the big Conn. Fair Show and they are now making this attraction one of thier leading events and are using three days this season for the baby show.

I would be glad to come to Danbury during next week, after our Springfield show, and go over the details. You can make a regular leading feature of the baby show, as conducted by our company, each season,and your committee ought to do so, because the baby is the biggest kind of a drawing card.

I will be glad to hear from you and will come up to see you if you say so.

Very truly,

Babyland Amusement Co.

per L.M. Rich Mgr.

LMR/M.

MCCUTCHEON V. UNITED HOMES CORP.

Washington Supreme Court, 1971.
79 Wn.2d 443, 486 P.2d 1093.

STAFFORD, ASSOCIATE JUSTICE.

The two cases involved herein were considered separately by the trial court. Since the issues presented are identical, they have been consolidated on appeal.

Plaintiff Norma McCutcheon, a tenant of defendant United Homes Corporation, was injured one evening when she fell down an unlighted flight of stairs leading from her apartment. She [sued in tort and] alleged the defendant was negligent because the lights at the top and bottom of the stairwell were not operative.

Plaintiff Douglas R. Fuller, also defendant's tenant, was injured as he descended the outside stairs of his apartment on his way to work. A step pulled loose causing him to fall. He, too, alleged negligence on the part of defendant.

Defendant's answer alleged each plaintiff had executed a form "Month to Month Rental Agreement" which contained the following exculpatory clause:

> neither the Lessor, nor his Agent, shall be liable for any injury to Lessee, his family, guests or employees or any other person entering the premises or the building of which the demised premises are a part.

In each case the trial court granted a summary judgment of dismissal.

The question is one of first impression. The issue is whether the lessor of a residential unit within a multi-family dwelling complex may exculpate itself from liability for personal injuries sustained by a tenant, which injuries result from the lessor's own negligence in maintenance of the approaches, common passageways, stairways and other areas under the lessor's dominion and control, but available for the tenants' use. (Hereinafter called the "common areas".)

Basic to the entire discussion is the common law rule that one who leases a portion of his premises but retains control over the approaches, common passageways, stairways and other areas to be used in common by the owner and tenants, has a duty to use reasonable care to keep them in safe condition for use of the tenant in his enjoyment of the demised premises. * * * The landlord is required to do more than passively refrain from negligent acts. He has a duty of affirmative conduct, an affirmative obligation to exercise reasonable care to inspect and repair the previously mentioned portions of the premises for protection of the lessee. * * *

It is readily apparent that the exculpatory clause was inserted in defendant's form "Month to Month Rental Agreement" to bar its tenants from asserting actions for personal injuries sustained through the landlord's own negligence. It was adopted to negative the result of the lessor's failure to comply with its affirmative duty to the tenants.

The defendant asserts that a lessor may contract, in a rental agreement, to exculpate itself from liability to its lessee, for personal injuries caused by lessor's own negligence. 49 Am.Jur.2d Landlord and Tenant § 869, p. 837 (1970). It contends such exculpatory clauses are not contrary to public policy because the landlord-tenant relationship *is not a matter of public interest, but relates exclusively to the private affairs of the parties concerned and that the two parties stand upon equal terms. Thus, there should be full freedom to contract.* * * *

* * *

The importance of "freedom of contract" is clear enough. However, the use of such an argument for avoiding the affirmative duty of a landlord to its residential tenant is no longer compelling in light of today's multi-family dwelling complex wherein a tenant merely rents some space with appurtenant rights to make it more usable or livable. Under modern circumstances the tenant is almost wholly dependent upon the landlord to provide reasonably for his safe use of the "common areas" beyond the four walls demised to him. Quinn and Phillips, The Law of Landlord-Tenant, 38 Fordham L.Rev. 225, 231 (1969).

As early as 1938 Williston recognized that while such exculpatory clauses were recognized as "legal", many courts had shown a reluctance to enforce them. Even then, courts were disposed to interpret them strictly so they would not be effective to discharge liability for the consequences of negligence in making or failing to make repairs. 6 Williston, A Treatise on the Law of Contracts § 1751C p. 4968 (Rev. ed. 1938). * * *

The key to our problem is found in Restatement of Contracts § 574, p. 1079 (1932) which reads:

> A bargain for exemption from liability for the consequences of negligence *not falling greatly below the standard established by law* for the protection of others against unreasonable risk of harm, is legal * * *

(Italics ours.) In other words, such an exculpatory clause may be legal, when considered in the abstract. However, when applied to a specific situation, one may be exempt from liability for his own negligence *only when the consequences thereof do not fall greatly below the standard established by law.*

In the landlord-tenant relationship it is extremely meaningful to require that a landlord's attempt to exculpate itself, from liability for the result of its own negligence, *not fall greatly below the standard of negligence set by law.* As indicated earlier, a residential tenant who lives in a modern multi-family dwelling complex is almost wholly dependent upon the landlord for the reasonably safe condition of the "common areas". However, a clause which exculpates the lessor from liability to its lessee, for personal injuries caused by lessor's own acts of negligence, not only lowers the standard imposed by the common law, it effectively *destroys* the landlord's affirmative obligation or duty to keep or maintain the "common areas" in a reasonably safe condition for the tenant's use.

When a lessor is no longer liable for the failure to observe standards of affirmative conduct, or for *any* conduct amounting to negligence, by virtue of an exculpatory clause in a lease, *the standard ceases to exist.* In short, such a clause *destroys* the concept of negligence in the landlord-tenant relationship. Neither the standard nor negligence can exist in abstraction.

It is no answer to argue that the rental agreement relates exclusively to the "personal and private affairs of two parties on equal footing" and thus is "not a matter of public interest." Such a concept had its origin in contracts entered into between *indemnitors* and *indemnitees.* * * * In Cannon v. Bresch, 307 Pa. 31, 35, 160 A. 595 (1932), the court first used the language now relied on by defendant, applying it to an exculpatory clause concerned with *property damage* arising out of a lease for business purposes:

> It is a contract between persons conducting a strictly private business, and relates entirely to their personal and private affairs, and so cannot be opposed to public policy. It would seem to be a matter of no interest to the public or the state.

The foregoing case and its progeny actually forms the basis for the so-called "majority rule" cited in 49 Am.Jur.2d Landlord and Tenant § 870 p. 839 (1970) and Annot., 175 A.L.R. 8, 83–92 (1948). It is safe to say, however, that there is no true majority rule. There are only numerous conflicting decisions, decisions concerned with contracts of indemnity, cases relating to property damage under business leases, and a disposition of the courts to emasculate such exculpatory clauses by means of strict construction. * * * From this, one can reasonably infer that even though such clauses are recognized by some courts, a great number have regarded them with disfavor. * * *

It is inaccurate to characterize the foregoing as a "majority rule". Furthermore, one must ignore present day realities to say that such an exculpatory clause, which relieves a lessor of liability for personal injuries caused by its own negligence, is purely a "personal and private affair" and "not a matter of public interest."

We no longer live in an era of the occasional rental of rooms in a private home or over the corner grocery. In the relatively short span of 30 years the public's use of rental units in this state has expanded dramatically. In the past 10 years alone, in the state of Washington, there has been an increase of over 77,000 rental units. It takes no imagination to see that a business which once had a minor impact upon the living habits of the citizenry has developed into a major commercial enterprise directly touching the lives of hundreds of thousands of people who depend upon it for shelter.

Thus, we are not faced merely with the theoretical duty of construing a provision in an isolated contract specifically bargained for by *one landlord and one tenant* as a "purely private affair". Considered realistically, we are asked to construe an exculpatory clause, the generalized use of which may have an impact upon thousands of potential tenants.

Under these circumstances it cannot be said that such exculpatory clauses are "purely a private affair" or that they are "not a matter of public interest." The real question is whether we should sanction a technique of immunizing lessors of residential units within a multi-family dwelling complex, from liability for personal injuries sustained by a tenant, which injuries result from the lessor's own negligence in maintaining the "common areas"; particularly when the technique employed destroys the concept of negligence and the standard of affirmative duty imposed upon the landlord for protection of the tenant.

An exculpatory clause of the type here involved contravenes long established common law rules of tort liability that exist in the landlord-tenant relationship. As so employed, it offends the public policy of the state and will not be enforced by the courts. It makes little sense for us to insist, on the one hand, that a workman have a safe place in which to work, but, on the other hand, to deny him a reasonably safe place in which to live.

The trial court is reversed and the cause is remanded for trial.

ABACUS FEDERAL SAVINGS BANK V. ADT SECURITY SERVICES, INC.

New York Court of Appeals, 2012.
18 N.Y.3d 675, 967 N.E.2d 666, 944 N.Y.S.2d 443.

CIPARICK, J.

Plaintiff Abacus Federal Savings Bank (Abacus) commenced this action against defendants ADT Security Services, Inc. (ADT) and Diebold, Incorporated (Diebold) to recover damages under tort and contract theories for losses incurred during a burglary of the bank. We affirm the dismissal of the complaint with one exception. We conclude that Abacus has adequately stated a cause of action for breach of contract as against ADT for its alleged losses other than losses allegedly sustained by its safe deposit box customers.

Abacus is a federally chartered savings and loan association with a branch located in Lower Manhattan (the branch). It provides a variety of deposit services, including the leasing of safe deposit boxes to its customers. Following the close of business on Saturday, March 20, 2004, burglars forced their way into the branch through a back entrance door and a second interior door. According to security camera images taken during the course of the incident, the burglars located the vault inside and, during a several hour period, used large acetylene gas tanks as blow torches to break down one of the vault's concrete and metal walls. Once in the vault, the burglars gained access to a safe storing the branch's overnight cash and over 20 safe deposit boxes belonging to Abacus' customers. The amended complaint alleges that the burglars stole $589,749.55 in cash from the safe and property valued at $926,512 from the safe deposit boxes. The police were not notified during the course of the burglary. Rather, an Abacus employee discovered what had occurred when the branch opened for business on Monday morning, March 22, 2004.

Prior to the burglary, each defendant had separately contracted with Abacus to supply security services for the branch. Specifically, ADT's contract with Abacus obligated ADT to install and maintain a 24-hour industry-certified central station security system to protect the branch premises and the vault. Within the vault, ADT purported to utilize certain detectors that would identify intruder movement and the presence of smoke. ADT's security system was supposedly designed to transmit any alarm signals triggered in the vault to ADT's central monitoring system. Diebold's contract with Abacus required Diebold to provide a backup alarm system that included additional central station monitoring, another form of telephone line security and "signal monitoring," which would activate an alarm if ADT's alarm system failed to operate properly.

The gravamen of Abacus' amended complaint is that defendants violated their contractual obligations by installing woefully inadequate security systems, which they failed to inspect. Abacus further alleges that defendants knew for weeks, if not months, that the security systems in place were not working in that they were generating a series of flaws, malfunctions and false alarms. For example, in the three months preceding the burglary there were, according to an expert's affidavit Abacus submitted in opposition to defendants' motions, 17 phone line failures and a number of other occurrences that were "consistent with an intruder cutting the phone line" and "should have created an alarm event." Abacus asserts that not only did defendants fail to investigate these malfunctions, but they failed to notify anyone at the branch of the problem.

Both contracts contained clauses that exculpated defendants from liability for their own negligence and limited their liability, under all circumstances, to $250. Diebold's contract contained a clause entitled "Property Insurance and Waiver of Subrogation" where Abacus agreed to obtain insurance coverage to cover its losses in the event of a theft. The agreement between Diebold and Abacus provided that Abacus "shall look solely to its insurer for recovery of its loss and hereby waives any and all claims for such loss against Diebold" and that Abacus' insurance policy would contain a clause providing that such waiver would not invalidate the coverage. There was no similar waiver-of-subrogation clause in the contract between Abacus and ADT. Instead, their contract merely provided "that insurance, if any, covering personal injury and property loss or damage" was Abacus' responsibility to obtain.

In addition to the losses incurred during the weekend of the burglary, Abacus seeks money damages for not less than $5 million for lost business as a result of the burglary, not less than $5 million for a loss of reputation in the community and not less than $1 million in punitive damages. Abacus also seeks $85,436 in costs to repair the vault and $30,000 in added security costs it absorbed. Defendants moved to dismiss the complaint, 10 causes of action in all, in its entirety. Supreme Court denied defendants' motion to dismiss the breach of contract cause of action and the gross negligence cause of action, but dismissed the remainder of the amended complaint.

Addressing the breach of contract claim, Supreme Court observed that while New York courts regularly enforce contractual provisions absolving a party from acts of its own ordinary negligence, public policy prohibits waivers of liability for gross negligence. The court concluded that since the pleadings adequately alleged that defendants were grossly negligent in their failure to respond to the burglary, Abacus could proceed to discovery on the breach of contract cause of action. Supreme Court likewise denied the motion to dismiss the tort cause of action. It further opined that Abacus has standing to assert claims based upon losses suffered by its safe deposit box customers. Defendants appealed.

The Appellate Division reversed the order of Supreme Court and granted defendants' motions to dismiss the amended complaint in its entirety * * *. In dismissing the breach of contract cause of action, the court held that the allegations in the amended complaint "amount to nothing more than claims of ordinary negligence as opposed to gross negligence." The court similarly found no basis for tort liability in the complaint). Furthermore, the court concluded that, in any event, the waiver-of-subrogation provision contained in the contract between Abacus and Diebold serves as "a defense to all of plaintiff's claims" against Diebold. We granted Abacus leave to appeal and now modify.

As a general rule, parties are free to enter into contracts that absolve a party from its own negligence * * * or that limit liability to a nominal sum * * *. However, it is New York's public policy that a party cannot "insulate itself from damages caused by grossly negligent conduct" (*Sommer v Federal Signal Corp.*, 79 NY2d 540, 554 [1992]). Therefore, exculpatory clauses and liquidated damages clauses in contracts are not enforceable against allegations of gross negligence (*see id.*). We have observed that "[g]ross negligence, when invoked to pierce an agreed-upon limitation of liability in a commercial contract, must 'smack[ ] of intentional wrongdoing'" (*id.*, quoting *Kalisch-Jarcho, Inc. v City of New York*, 58 NY2d 377, 385 [1983]). "It is conduct that evinces a reckless indifference to the rights of others" (*id.*).

We applied this standard in *David Gutter Furs v Jewelers Protection Servs.* (79 NY2d 1027 [1992]). In that case, the "plaintiff, a fur dealer, contracted with [the] defendant to design, install and monitor a burglar alarm system" (*id.* At 1028). Several weeks after plaintiff occupied its premises, furs were stolen in a nighttime burglary, but the alarm did not sound. Plaintiff commenced an action against the defendant for breach of contract and further claimed that the exculpatory and limitation of liability clauses in their contract were unenforceable because the defendant was grossly negligent (*see id.* At 1028–1029). We concluded that the plaintiff's allegations—"that there should have been two motion detectors, instead of one, on each level; a shock sensor should have been installed; defendant should have ascertained how the inventory would be arranged; and a post-occupancy inspection should have been undertaken"—only amounted to ordinary negligence as there was no issue of fact that the "defendant performed its duties with reckless indifference to [the] plaintiff's rights" (*id.* At 1029).

Here, in contrast, we conclude that the allegations in the amended complaint sufficiently allege conduct on the part of the defendants that, if true, constitutes gross negligence. Indeed, unlike the plaintiff in *David Gutter Furs*, Abacus has alleged much more than mere failure to install a proper working alarm system and inspect it. Abacus alleges that both defendants had knowledge—for weeks, if not months—that the equipment had been malfunctioning. Moreover, Abacus asserts that defendants not only failed to investigate the source of their equipment malfunction, but they failed to put anyone at the branch on notice of the potential security breach. Of course, these allegations may not be proved, or may be shown by defendants' evidence to be less significant than they seem; but on this record, plaintiffs have alleged the type of conduct that smacks of intentional wrongdoing and evinces a reckless indifference to the rights of others * * *.

Nevertheless, Diebold argues that the waiver-of-subrogation clause in its contract with Abacus acts as a total defense to the claims asserted by

Abacus in its complaint. We agree. In *Board of Educ., Union Free School Dist. No. 3, Town of Brookhaven v Valden Assoc.* (46 NY2d 653 [1979]), we upheld a similar waiver-of-subrogation clause. There, we observed that the contract between the plaintiffs and the defendants required the plaintiffs to obtain insurance to cover 100% of any losses incurred on the plaintiff's property (*see id.* At 656). Further, the plaintiffs expressly "waive[d] all rights" to seek damages as against the defendants covered by such insurance (*id.*). In upholding the validity of this contract, we recognized that "[a] distinction must be drawn between contractual provisions which seek to exempt a party from liability . . . and contractual provisions . . . which in effect simply require one of the parties to the contract to provide insurance for all of the parties" (*id.* At 657; * * *. We discern no basis to depart from this rule here. Thus, we affirm the dismissal of the complaint as against Diebold.

ADT's contract with Abacus does not contain a similar waiver-of-subrogation clause that would act as a total defense to Abacus' claim. We note that the contract between Abacus and ADT did not require Abacus to obtain insurance to cover losses stemming from ADT's gross negligence. The decision to obtain insurance, "if any," was discretionary as to Abacus. Moreover, the contract did not contain an express waiver by Abacus to waive all rights for damages covered by insurance it may have obtained as against ADT. Thus, we reinstate the breach of contract cause of action as against ADT. In so doing, we note that the complaint only adequately states a basis upon which Abacus can recover for its own losses. As pleaded, Abacus fails to allege sufficient facts to confer standing to pursue the losses allegedly sustained by its safe deposit box customers.

Finally, we conclude that the complaint did not allege conduct that would give rise to separate liability in tort. Here, the allegations that a breach of contract occurred as a result of gross negligence does not give rise to a duty independent of the contractual relationship (*see Clark-Fitzpatrick, Inc. v. Long Is. R.R. Co.,* 70 N.Y.2d 382, 389, 521 N.Y.S.2d 653, 516 N.E.2d 190 [1987]; *cf. Sommer,* 79 N.Y.2d at 551–553, 583 N.Y.S.2d 957, 593 N.E.2d 1365 [the plaintiff's breach of contract claim against the defendant fire alarm company may also sound in tort where the defendant's alleged failure to act with due care affected a significant public interest independent of its contractual obligations]).

Accordingly, the order of the Appellate Division should be modified, without costs, by reinstating so much of plaintiff's cause of action for breach of contract as against ADT Security Services, Inc. that does not assert claims on behalf of plaintiff's safe deposit box customers and, as so modified, affirmed.

CHIEF JUDGE LIPPMAN and JUDGES GRAFFEO, READ, SMITH, PIGOTT and JONES concur.

NOTE: INTERPLAY BETWEEN PROCESS AND SUBSTANCE

In the squib case above, Weaver v. American Oil Co., the court invalidated the exculpatory clause in part because American Oil failed to explain it to Weaver, an unsophisticated contracting party. But even "arms-length" transactions without any duty of explanation may be unenforceable on public policy grounds. A decision overturning contract terms because of their content alone tests the limits of freedom of contract and, if carried too far, threatens the sanctity of contract. A decision based not only on objectionable content but also on insufficiency of assent is therefore generally more acceptable. While the following materials in this section and the next focus primarily on the possibly objectionable content of the exchange, you should also attempt to isolate any bargaining infirmities that may be involved and should consider whether the decision would be the same without those infirmities. You should also consider whether a clear line can be drawn between those terms that should be enforceable and those that are simply too objectionable to enforce even when there is "full assent."

HENDERSON V. QUEST EXPEDITIONS

Tennessee Court of Appeals, 2005.
174 S.W.3d 730.

HERSCHEL PICKENS FRANKS, P.J.

In this action for personal injuries allegedly due to defendant's negligence, the Trial Court granted defendant summary judgment on the grounds that plaintiffs had executed a Waiver and Release of Liability which was required by defendant prior to plaintiffs' participation in white water rafting. Plaintiffs have appealed, insisting the Release is void as against the public policy of this State. We affirm.

Plaintiffs' Complaint alleged that Henderson was injured while on a white water rafting expedition operated by defendant. The Complaint alleged that defendant "ferries rafters to and from the Ocoee River by means of a series of dilapidated school buses.", and that after Henderson had completed his rafting trip, he and other rafters were put on a bus, and then told to get on another bus, and when disembarking from the first bus he slipped and fell, sustaining severe personal injuries. Plaintiffs further alleged that defendant's negligence was the proximate cause of his injuries.

Defendant in its Answer admitted that Henderson had participated in a rafting trip sponsored by defendant, and among its defenses raised was waiver, because plaintiff had signed a "Waiver and Release of Liability", which defendant attached to its Answer. [The Waiver and Release specifically released Quest from liability for its negligence.]

In their Answers to Requests for Admissions, plaintiffs admitted that the waiver in question had been signed by Henderson. Defendant then filed a Motion for Summary Judgment, which plaintiffs opposed and Henderson filed his Affidavit which stated that Henderson had no previous white-water rafting experience, and was given a pre-printed document to sign prior to the excursion which was not reviewed with him by an employee of defendant. He further stated that he was not advised whether there were any other rafting companies who would allow him to go rafting without having to sign a waiver, or whether he could pay additional money to not have to sign the waiver.

The Trial Court determined that the waiver in this case did not affect the public interest, and thus the waiver was not void as against public policy. The court noted that *Olson v. Molzen,* 558 S.W.2d 429 (Tenn.1977) did not apply to this situation and he was guided by the rule adopted in California, which states that "exculpatory agreements in the recreational sports context do not implicate the public interest." Citing *Allan v. Snow Summit, Inc.,* 51 Cal.App.4th 1358, 59 Cal.Rptr.2d 813, 823 (Ca.App.1996).

Plaintiffs on appeal insist the Waiver is void against public policy, and in the alternative, that the Waiver was void on the grounds it was too excessive in scope.

Plaintiffs concede that if the Waiver is enforceable then this action is barred, but argue the waiver violates the public policy of this State.

As our Supreme Court has explained:

> It is well settled in this State that parties may contract that one shall not be liable for his negligence to another but that such other shall assume the risk incident to such negligence. . . . Further, it is not necessary that the word 'negligence' appear in the exculpatory clause and the public policy of Tennessee favors freedom to contract against liability for negligence.

Empress Health and Beauty Spa, Inc. v. Turner, 503 S.W.2d 188 (Tenn.1973).

An exception to this rule was recognized by the Supreme Court in *Olson v. Molzen,* wherein the Court held that certain relationships required greater responsibility which would render such a release "obnoxious". *Olson,* at p. 430. The Court adopted the opinion of the California Supreme Court in *Tunkl v. Regents of University of California,* 60 Cal.2d 92, 32 Cal.Rptr. 33, 383 P.2d 441 (Ca.1963), which held that where the public interest would be affected by an exculpatory provision, such provision could be held invalid. *Olson,* at p. 431.

Our Supreme Court adopted the six criteria set forth in *Tunkl* as useful in determining when an exculpatory provision should be held invalid as contrary to public policy. *See Olson.* These criteria are:

(a.) It concerns a business of a type generally thought suitable for public regulation.

(b.) The party seeking exculpation is engaged in performing a service of great importance to the public, which is often a matter of practical necessity for some members of the public.

(c.) The party holds himself out as willing to perform this service for any member of the public who seeks it, or at least for any member coming within certain established standards.

(d.) As a result of the essential nature of the service, in the economic setting of the transaction, the party invoking exculpation possesses a decisive advantage of bargaining strength against any member of the public who seeks his services.

(e.) In exercising a superior bargaining power the party confronts the public with a standardized adhesion contract of exculpation, and makes no provision whereby a purchaser may pay additional reasonable fees and obtain protection against negligence.

(f.) Finally, as a result of the transaction, the person or property of the purchaser is placed under the control of the seller, subject to the risk of carelessness by the seller or his agents.

Olson, at p. 431.

In *Olson,* the Supreme Court invalidated a contract between a doctor and patient which attempted to release the doctor from liability for his negligence in the performance of medical services. *Also see Carey v. Merritt,* 148 S.W.3d 912 (Tenn.Ct.App.2004) and *Russell v. Bray,* 116 S.W.3d 1 (Tenn.Ct.App.2003). In *Russell,* this Court refused to enforce an exculpatory contract between home buyers and the home inspectors who were hired by the buyers, because the Court found that the home inspectors were professionals whose services affected the public interest, and thus the contracts were offensive to public policy, based on the factors enumerated in *Olson.* In *Carey,* this Court made clear that not all of the factors had to be present in order to invalidate an exculpatory agreement, but generally, the factors were limited to circumstances involving "a contract with a profession, as opposed to 'tradesmen in the marketplace'." *Carey,* at p. 916; *cf. Parton v. Mark Pirtle Oldsmobile-Cadillac-Isuzu, Inc.,* 730 S.W.2d 634 (Tenn.Ct.App.1987) (auto repair shop is not "professional" as would qualify it as service affecting public interest in order to invalidate exculpatory contract).

This case is factually different from *Olson, Carey,* and *Parton* because the white-water rafting service offered by defendant is not a "professional" trade, which affects the public interest. As discussed in factor number two quoted above, this is not a service of "great importance to the public, which is often a matter of practical necessity for some members of the public." *See*

Olson. There is no necessity that one go white-water rafting. In fact, many jurisdictions have recognized that such recreational sporting activities are not activities of an essential nature which would render exculpatory clauses contrary to the public interest. *See Seigneur v. National Fitness Institute, Inc.,* 132 Md.App. 271, 752 A.2d 631 (2000) (health club services not essential for purposes of holding exculpatory clause unenforceable as offensive to public interest); *Allan v. Snow Summit, Inc.,* 51 Cal.App.4th 1358, 59 Cal.Rptr.2d 813 (1996) ("voluntary participation in recreational and sports activities [skiing] does not implicate the public interest"); *Schutkowski v. Carey,* 725 P.2d 1057 (Wyo.1986) (sky diving and other private recreational businesses generally do not involve services which are necessary to the public such that exculpatory contract would be invalidated).

* * *

Accordingly we affirm the Trial Court's determination that the exculpatory contract in this case does not affect the public interest such that it should be invalidated pursuant to the *Olson* criteria.

Finally, appellants argue that the Release in this case should not operate as a bar to their claims because the injury suffered by Henderson was not within the "inherent risks" of the sport of white water rafting, and thus was not within the contemplation of the parties when the release was signed. [The court followed the "majority view" that "an exculpatory provision which specifically and expressly releases a defendant from its own negligence will be upheld, without regard to whether the injury sustained is one typically thought to be 'inherent in the sport.' " The court also noted the "split of authority among the states regarding whether the word 'negligence' is even required to be present in the exculpation clause for the provision to be construed as releasing the defendant from its own negligence" but added that this was not an issue in this case because "the Release in question does specifically and expressly release defendant from any liability for its negligence or that of any employees, owners, agents, etc."]

* * *

The Contract under consideration is clear and unambiguous, and states that plaintiffs agreed to release defendant from any and all liability, including defendant's own negligence. Moreover, the Contract specifically mentions that plaintiffs are being furnished and participating in white water rafting and "bus or van transportation" provided by the defendant. The Contract states that plaintiffs realize that they could be injured due to dangers from the rafting as well as the use of white water equipment, forces of nature, or even due to the negligence of defendant's employees and other rafters. The Contract states that defendant is being relieved of any liability caused by its own negligence in no less than four places, the last of which is in bold print above the signature line. This Contract is plain, and enforceable as written. We conclude the Trial Court properly granted summary judgment to defendant on plaintiffs' negligence claims.

The Trial Court's Judgment is affirmed, and the cost of the appeal is assessed to plaintiffs Nathan and Brandy Henderson.

PROBLEM 5-3

Garretson, an experienced ski jumper and a college student, read the following entry blank necessary to compete in an amateur ski-jumping tournament:

ENTRY BLANK

Please fill out this entry blank properly and return immediately.

NAME ______________________ ADDRESS ______________________

CITY ______________________ STATE ______________________

CLUB & CARD NO. ______________________

ACCIDENT INSURANCE CO. ______________________

JUMPING CLASS:

Choose one.

( ) Junior Novice ( ) B Class

( ) Junior Expert ( ) Veteran

( ) Cross country (if any)

In consideration of the acceptance of my application, I hereby release the Leavenworth Winter Sports Club, U.S. Ski Association, Ski Patrol, U.S. Forest Service, their members or agents and any person officially connected with this competition from all liability for any injuries or damages whatsoever arising from participation in or presence at this competition.

SIGNED ______________________

APPROVED ______________________

(parent or guardian)

Mail to: Ralph E. Steele Box 158 Leavenworth, Wash.

Garretson had signed similar entry blanks with releases in other "competitions." He added "A" to the jumping classifications, checked it and signed the form. Garretson was seriously injured in attempting his jump. He sued all the organizations listed in the exculpatory clause on the theory that they were negligent in failing to warn him of unsafe conditions for jumping.

What result? If the Leavenworth Winter Sports Club asked you to revise the entry blank, what changes would you make, if any?

BASS v. FACEBOOK, INC., 394 F.Supp. 3d 1024 (N.D. Cal. (2019). [Facebook, an online social network (in case anyone doesn't know), discovered that it had a coding vulnerability that caused a data breach, in which over 90 million accounts were potentially affected. Facebook's terms of service contained an "as is" and limited-liability term. The latter portion of the term stated, "[O]ur liability shall be limited to the fullest extent permitted by applicable law." When plaintiffs sued, one of the theories was breach of contract. Facebook moved to dismiss the claim. The court found that Facebook's disclosure of the "as is" and limitation-of-liability term was "fair." "The clause was not buried. The clause was plainly above board and contained clear enough language. True, it is an adhesion contract, but there is no 'rule that an adhesion contract is per se unconscionable.' No one is forced to enroll in Facebook's social media service." However, the court also considered whether the "as is" and limitation-of-liability terms insulated Facebook from its alleged negligence.]

"An agreement insulating one from liability for his own negligence must specifically so provide and is strictly construed against the party asserting the exemption, especially where he is the author of the agreement." *Viotti v. Giomi*, 230 Cal. App. 2d 730, 739, 41 Cal.Rptr. 345 (1964). "An agreement which seeks to limit generally without mentioning negligence is construed to shield a party only for passive negligence, not for active negligence." *Burnett v. Chimney Sweep*, 123 Cal. App. 4th 1057, 1066, 20 Cal.Rptr.3d 562 (2004) (quotations omitted). "Whereas passive negligence involves mere nonfeasance, such as the failure to discover a dangerous condition or to perform a duty imposed by law, active negligence involves an affirmative act, *knowledge of or acquiescence in negligent conduct*, or failure to perform specific duties." *Frittelli, Inc. v. 350 N. Canon Drive, LP*, 202 Cal. App. 4th 35, 48, 135 Cal.Rptr.3d 761 (2011) (quotation omitted) (emphasis added). In other words, Facebook's mere failure to discover the vulnerability might be barred by the clause, but if it had acquiesced to, or known of the vulnerability, the claim would certainly be allowed through.

Here, the limitation-of-liability clause does not mention "negligence" at all, let alone unequivocally preclude liability for negligence. At this early stage, no facts have been teased out. Precluding the claims for negligence pursuant to the liability clause is therefore impossible. They remain for now.

PROBLEM 5-4

Pier 1, a travel agency, sought breach of contract damages from Revelex, a software contractor, for failing to complete delivery of software in part to enhance Pier 1's booking capabilities. The contract contained the following exculpatory clause:

> Revelex shall not be liable . . . for any direct, special, indirect, incidental, consequential, punitive, exemplary or any other damages regardless of kind or type (whether in contract, tort (including negligence), or otherwise), including but not limited to loss of profits, data, or goodwill, regardless of whether Revelex knew or should have known of the possibility of such damages. . . . Customer waives any and all claims, now known or later discovered, that it may have against Revelex and its licensors and vendors arising out of this agreement and the services.

Is the clause enforceable? Is the entire contract unenforceable on the ground that, in light of this clause, the promise of the software is illusory? See Pier 1 Cruise Experts v. Revelex Corp., 929 F.3d 1331 (11th Cir. 2019). For more on this case, see Chapter Three.

KARPINSKI V. INGRASCI

Court of Appeals of New York, 1971.
28 N.Y.2d 45, 268 N.E.2d 751.

FULD, CHIEF JUDGE.

This appeal requires us to determine whether a covenant by a professional man not to compete with his employer is enforceable and, if it is, to what extent.

The plaintiff, Dr. Karpinski, an oral surgeon, had been carrying on his practice alone in Auburn—in Cayuga County—for many years. In 1953, he decided to expand and, since nearly all of an oral surgeon's business stems from referrals, he embarked upon a plan to "cultivate connections" among dentists in the four nearby Counties of Tompkins, Seneca, Cortland and Ontario. The plan was successful, and by 1962 twenty per cent of his practice consisted of treating patients referred to him by dentists located in those counties. In that year, after a number of those dentists had told him that some of their patients found it difficult to travel from their homes to Auburn, the plaintiff decided to open a second office in centrally-located Ithaca.[c] He began looking for an assistant and, in the course of his search, met the defendant, Dr. Ingrasci, who was just completing his training in oral surgery at the Buffalo General Hospital and was desirous of entering private practice. Dr. Ingrasci manifested an interest in becoming

[c] Located on scenic Cayuga Lake in beautiful central New York, Ithaca is one of the world's centers of learning. It is the home of Cornell University, with over 700 students at a great law school.

associated with Dr. Karpinski and, after a number of discussions, they reached an understanding; the defendant was to live in Ithaca, a locale with which he had no prior familiarity, and there work as an employee of the plaintiff.

A contract, reflecting the agreement, was signed by the defendant in June, 1962. It was for three years and, shortly after its execution, the defendant started working in the office which the plaintiff rented and fully equipped at his own expense. The provision of the contract with which we are concerned is a covenant by the defendant not to compete with the plaintiff. More particularly, it recited that the defendant

> "promises and covenants that while this agreement is in effect and forever thereafter, he will never practice dentistry and/or Oral Surgery in Cayuga, Cortland, Seneca, Tompkins or Ontario counties except: (a) In association with the [plaintiff] or (b) If the [plaintiff] terminates the agreement and employs another oral surgeon".

In addition, the defendant agreed, "in consideration of the * * * terms of employment, and of the experience gained while working with" the plaintiff, to execute a $40,000 promissory note to the plaintiff, to become payable if the defendant left the plaintiff and practiced "dentistry and/or Oral Surgery" in the five enumerated counties.[1]

When the contract expired, the two men engaged in extended discussions as to the nature of their continued association—as employer and employee or as partners. Unable to reach an accord, the defendant, in February, 1968, left the plaintiff's employ and opened his own office for the practice of oral surgery in Ithaca a week later. The dentists in the area thereupon began referring their patients to the defendant rather than to the plaintiff, and in two months the latter's practice from the Ithaca area dwindled to almost nothing and he closed the office in that city. In point of fact, the record discloses that about 90% of the defendant's present practice comes from referrals from dentists in the counties specified in the restrictive covenant, the very same dentists who had been referring patients to the plaintiff's Ithaca office when the defendant was working there.[2]

The plaintiff, alleging a breach of the restrictive covenant, seeks not only an injunction to enforce it but also a judgment of $40,000 on the note. The Supreme Court, after a nonjury trial, decided in favor of the plaintiff and granted him both an injunction and damages as requested. On appeal,

---

[1] Either party was privileged to terminate the agreement on 60 days' notice within the three-year period and, if the plaintiff were to do so, the contract recited, the defendant was released from the restrictive covenant and the note.

[2] There are two other oral surgeons, in addition to the plaintiff and the defendant, serving the Ithaca area.

however, the Appellate Division reversed the resulting judgment and dismissed the complaint; it was that court's view that the covenant was void and unenforceable on the ground that its restriction against the practice of both dentistry and oral surgery was impermissibly broad.

There can be no doubt that the defendant violated the terms of the covenant when he opened his own office in Ithaca. But the mere fact of breach does not, in and of itself, resolve the case. Since there are "powerful considerations of public policy which militate against sanctioning the loss of a man's livelihood," the courts will subject a covenant by an employee not to compete with his former employer to an "overriding limitation of 'reasonableness' ". (Purchasing Assoc. v. Weitz, 13 N.Y.2d 267, 272, 246 N.Y.S.2d 600, 603, 196 N.E.2d 245 * * *.) Such covenants by physicians are, if reasonable in scope, generally given effect. * * * "It is a firmly established doctrine", it has been noted, "that a member of one of the learned professions, upon becoming assistant to another member thereof, may, upon a sufficient consideration, bind himself not to engage in the practice of his profession upon the termination of his contract of employment, within a reasonable territorial extent, as such an agreement is not in restraint of trade or against public policy" (Ann., Restriction on Practice of Physician, 58 A.L.R. 156, 162).

Each case must, of course, depend, to a great extent, upon its own facts. It may well be that, in some instances, a restriction not to conduct a profession or a business in two counties or even in one, may exceed permissible limits. But, in the case before us, having in mind the character and size of the counties involved, the area restriction imposed is manifestly reasonable. The five small rural counties which it encompasses comprise the very area from which the plaintiff obtained his patients and in which the defendant would be in direct competition with him. Thus, the covenant's coverage coincides precisely with "the territory over which the practice extends", and this is proper and permissible. (6A Corbin, Contracts [1962], § 1393, p. 87 * * *.) In brief, the plaintiff made no attempt to extend his influence beyond the area from which he drew his patients, the defendant being perfectly free to practice as he chooses outside the five specified counties.

Nor may the covenant be declared invalid because it is unlimited as to time, forever restricting the defendant from competing with the plaintiff. It is settled that such a covenant will not be stricken merely because it "contains no time limit or is expressly made unlimited as to time". (37 N.Y.Jur., Master and Servant § 179, p. 60 * * *). * * * In the present case, the defendant opened an office in Ithaca, in competition with the plaintiff, just one week after his employment had come to an end. Under the circumstances presented, we thoroughly agree with the trial judge that it is clear that nearly all of the defendant's practice was, and would be, directly attributable to his association with his former employer.

This brings us to the most troublesome part of the restriction imposed upon the defendant. By the terms of the contract, he agreed not to practice "dentistry and/or Oral Surgery" in competition with the plaintiff. Since the plaintiff practices only "oral surgery," and it was for the practice of that limited type of "dentistry" that he had employed the defendant, the Appellate Division concluded that the plaintiff went beyond permissible limits when he obtained from the defendant the covenant that he would not engage in any "dentistry" whatsoever. The restriction, *as formulated,* is, as the Appellate Division concluded, too broad; it is not reasonable for a man to be excluded from a profession for which he has been trained when he does not compete with his former employer by practicing it.

The plaintiff seeks to justify the breadth of the covenant by urging that, if it had restricted only the defendant's practice of oral surgery and permitted him to practice "dentistry"—that is, to hold himself out as a dentist generally—the defendant would have been permitted, under the Education Law (§ 6601, subd. 3), to do all the work which an oral surgeon could. We have no sympathy with this argument; the plaintiff was not privileged to prevent the defendant from working in an area of dentistry in which he would not be in competition with him. The plaintiff would have all the protection he needs if the restriction were to be limited to the practice of oral surgery, and this poses the question as to the court's power to "sever" the impermissible from the valid and uphold the covenant to the extent that it is reasonable.

Although we have found no decision in New York directly in point, cases in this court support the existence of such a power. * * * Moreover, a number of out-of-state decisions, and they are supported by authoritative texts and commentators, explicitly recognize the court's power of severance and divisibility in order to sustain the covenant insofar as it is reasonable. As Professor Blake put it (73 Harv.L.Rev., at pp. 674–675), "If in balancing the equities the court decides that his [the employee's] activity would fit within the scope of a reasonable prohibition, it is apt to make use of the tool of severance, paring an unreasonable restraint down to appropriate size and enforcing it." In short, to cull from the Washington Supreme Court's opinion in Wood v. May, 73 Wash.2d 307, 314, 438 P.2d 587, 591, "we find it just and equitable to protect appellant [employer] by injunction to the extent necessary to accomplish the basic purpose of the contract insofar as such contract is reasonable." Accordingly, since his practice is solely as an oral surgeon, the plaintiff gains all the injunctive protection to which he is entitled if effect be given only to that part of the covenant which prohibits the defendant from practicing oral surgery.

The question arises, however, whether injunctive relief is precluded by the fact that the defendant's promissory note for $40,000 was to become payable if he breached the agreement not to compete. We believe not. The mere inclusion in a covenant of a liquidated damages provision does not automatically bar the grant of an injunction. (See Rubinstein v. Rubinstein, 23 N.Y.2d 293, 298, 296 N.Y.S.2d 354, 358, 244 N.E.2d 49, 51; Wirth & Hamid Fair Booking v. Wirth, 265 N.Y. 214, 224, 192 N.E. 297, 301; * * *.) The covenant under consideration in this case may not reasonably be read to render "the liquidated damages provision * * * the sole remedy." (Rubinstein v. Rubinstein, 23 N.Y.2d 293, 298, 296 N.Y.S.2d 354, 358, 244 N.E.2d 49, 51, *supra.*) On the other hand, it would be grossly unfair to grant the plaintiff, in addition to an injunction, the full amount of damages ($40,000) which the parties apparently contemplated for a total breach of the covenant, since the injunction will halt any further violation. The proper approach is that taken in *Wirth* (265 N.Y. 214, 192 N.E. 297, *supra*). The court, there faced with a similar situation, granted the injunction sought and, instead of awarding the amount of liquidated damages specified, remitted the matter for determination of the *actual* damages suffered during the period of the breach.

The hardship necessarily imposed on the defendant must be borne by him in view of the plaintiff's rightful interest in protecting the valuable practice of oral surgery which he built up over the course of many years. The defendant is, of course, privileged to practice "dentistry" generally in Ithaca or continue to practice "oral surgery" anywhere in the United States outside of the five small rural counties enumerated. The covenant, part of a contract carefully negotiated with no indication of fraud or overbearing on either side, must be enforced, insofar as it reasonably and validly may, according to its terms. In sum, then, the plaintiff is entitled to an injunction barring the defendant from practicing oral surgery in the five specified counties and to damages actually suffered by him in the period during which the defendant conducted such a practice in Ithaca after leaving the plaintiff's employ.

The order appealed from should be reversed, with costs, and the case remitted to Supreme Court, Cayuga County, for further proceedings in accordance with this opinion.

DWYER V. JUNG

Superior Court of New Jersey, 1975.
133 N.J.Super. 343, 336 A.2d 498, aff'd per curiam, 137 N.J.Super. 135, 348 A.2d 208.

KIMMELMAN, J.S.C.

[Plaintiffs, Dwyer and Lisbona, two lawyers from a dissolved law firm, claimed that the following term from their partnership agreement was void as against public policy:

> Should the partnership terminate, all clients listed in exhibit "A" shall be designated to certain individual partners. Upon termination, and by virtue of this Agreement, all partners shall

be restricted from doing business with a client designated as that of another partner for a period of 5 (five) years.

The agreement also contained the following provision:

Exhibit A, annexed thereto, contained a list of insurance carriers; 154 were designated to defendant Jung as his clients, 5 were designated to plaintiff Dwyer as his clients, and none was ascribed to plaintiff Lisbona.]

In this action brought for an accounting defendant, by way of counterclaim, contends that plaintiffs have violated the restrictive covenant contained in the partnership agreement which designates or assigns certain clients to partners in the event of dissolution. Specifically, plaintiffs are charged with attempting to pirate defendant's clients and undermining his relationship with certain named insurance carriers. These charges are denied.

* * *

Initially, it must be recognized that lawyer restrictive covenants are to be distinguished from noncompetitive covenants incident to the sale of a business where the covenants are designed to protect the good will of the business for the benefit of the buyer. * * * A lawyer's clients are neither chattels nor merchandise, and his practice and good will may not be offered for sale. * * * In this regard Abraham Lincoln's sage observation (slightly paraphrased) is particularly appropriate: A lawyer's time and advice are his stock in trade.

Nor may lawyer restrictive covenants, whether contained in a partnership agreement or an agreement of employment, be classified within the general category of agreements restricting post-employment competition. The usual employee restrictive covenant is a legitimate business device to protect the business and good will of an employer against various forms of unfair competition. Although not freely as enforceable as a seller's noncompetitive agreement, such restrictive covenant will nevertheless be given effect if it is reasonable under all of the circumstances. "It will generally be found to be reasonable where it simply protects the legitimate interests of the employer, imposes no undue hardship on the employee, and is not injurious to the public." *Solari, supra,* 55 N.J. at 576, 264 A.2d at 56; *Whitmyer, supra,* 58 N.J. at 32, 274 A.2d 577.

Commercial standards may not be used to evaluate the reasonableness of lawyer restrictive covenants. Strong public policy considerations preclude their applicability. In that sense lawyer restrictions are injurious to the public interest. A client is always entitled to be represented by counsel of his own choosing.[1] See Marshall v. Romano, 10 N.J.Misc. 113,

[1] Except, perhaps, in cases of indigency.

114, 158 A. 751, 752 (C.P.1932). The attorney-client relationship is consensual, highly fiduciary on the part of counsel, and he may do nothing which restricts the right of the client to repose confidence in any counsel of his choice. *Drinker, supra* at 89 et seq. No concept of the practice of law is more deeply rooted. The lawyer's function is to serve, but serve he must with fidelity, devotion and erudition in the highest traditions of his noble profession.

These principles underlie DR 2–108(A) of the Disciplinary Rules of the Code of Professional Responsibility of the American Bar Association which provide:

> A lawyer shall not be a party to or participate in a partnership or employment agreement with another lawyer that restricts the right of a lawyer to practice law after the termination of a relationship created by the agreement except as may be provided in a bona fide retirement plan and then only to the extent reasonably necessary to protect the plan.

Opinion No. 147 of the Supreme Court's Advisory Committee on Professional Ethics, 92 N.J.L.J. 177 (March 20, 1969), applied these precepts in dealing with a restrictive covenant in a law partnership agreement. The agreement provided that a withdrawing partner shall not open an office or associate with or be employed by any attorney engaged in the practice of law in the county for a period of five years from the date of withdrawal.

In deciding that the provision was unethical, the committee said:

> We recognize in the legal profession the existence of a "client market" which is divided among lawyers within a particular locality. But the division of that "market" can be ethically achieved only through individual performance and the "establishment of a well-merited reputation for professional capacity and fidelity to trust." (Original Canon 27, August 27, 1908 (33 A.B.A. Reports 85)) It cannot be achieved by active competition and solicitation of professional employment. The insertion of a restrictive covenant in a law partnership agreement is an attempt to control and divide the "client market" by means other than individual performance. Therefore, it is the opinion of this Committee that the instant restrictive covenant is improper, unworthy of the legal profession, and unethical. See Disciplinary Rule 2–108(A) of the Preliminary Draft of the Code of Professional Responsibility of the American Bar Association Committee on Evaluation of Ethical Standards, dated January 15, 1969.

Question No. 621 (73–9) posed to the New York County Lawyers' Association Committee on Professional Ethics and reported at 97 N.J.L.J. 199 (March 21, 1974) involved the following issue:

> Is it proper for a lawyer to agree that upon his withdrawal from membership in a partnership he will not for a period of two years thereafter accept professional employment from any person who was a client of the partnership at the time he ceased being a member?
>
> The committee concluded as follows:
>
> It is not proper for a lawyer to enter into what is in effect a restrictive covenant. DR 2–108(A) provides in substance that a lawyer shall not be a party to or participate in a partnership agreement with another lawyer that restricts the right of a lawyer to practice law after the termination of the partnership, except as a condition to payment of retirement benefits.
>
> In this connection EC 2–26 provides in substance that in furtherance of the objective of the bar to make legal services fully available, a lawyer should not lightly decline proffered employment; and EC 2–31 provides in substance that full availability of legal counsel requires both that persons be able to obtain counsel and that lawyers who undertake representation, complete the work involved.
>
> Reading these provisions together leads to the conclusions that a covenant restricting a lawyer after leaving a partnership from accepting employment by persons who were theretofore clients of the partnership, or from otherwise fully practicing his profession, is an unwarranted restriction on the right of the lawyer to choose his clients in the event they seek his services, and an unwarranted restriction on the right of the client to choose the lawyer he wishes to represent him. [N.Y. State 129 (1970)]

Reported cases in this area are almost nonexistent. Only one warrants mention. Hicklin v. O'Brien, 11 Ill.App.2d 541, 138 N.E.2d 47 (App.Ct.1956), upheld a noncompetitive covenant incidental to the sale of a law practice limiting the geographical area in which the selling attorney could practice. While not binding upon this court, it is not at all persuasive. That case, in this court's opinion, incorrectly proceeded upon the theory that the restrictive covenant imposed no undue burden upon the attorney and completely ignored the effect the covenant might have upon potential clients. The court there viewed the matter as a business proposition and failed to respect the underlying ethical considerations affecting the practice of law.

In view of the foregoing it is apparent that an agreement dividing the client market and prohibiting attorneys from representing certain insurance carriers in the defense of negligence cases has the effect of restricting those carriers in their unlimited choice of counsel. Accordingly, the restrictive covenant contained in the partnership agreement of the former law firm of "Jung, Dwyer and Lisbona" is declared to be void as against public policy. All counts of the pleadings relating thereto will be stricken and the case will continue solely for the purpose of effecting a proper accounting amongst the parties.

QUANDT'S WHOLESALE DISTRIBUTORS, INC. v. GIARDINO, 87 A.D.2d 684, 448 N.Y.S.2d 809 (1982). [Plaintiff, a wholesale distributor of institutional and restaurant food and supplies, hired defendant to service accounts in a three-county area. The employment contract contained a restrictive covenant providing that, for a period of six months immediately following termination of his employment, defendant would not compete with plaintiff in the area to which he had been assigned. After about nine months, defendant resigned and went to work for plaintiff's competitor. Plaintiff sued immediately to enforce the restrictive covenant and sought a preliminary injunction enjoining defendant for six months from competing in the three counties involved. On appeal from the trial court's grant of the preliminary injunction, held for defendant.] Such covenants will be enforced only if reasonably limited temporally and geographically * * * and then only to the extent necessary to protect the employer from the employee's use or disclosure of trade secrets or confidential customer lists. * * * Plaintiff alleges no trade secrets or confidential customer lists. Certainly the names of plaintiff's institutional and restaurant customers are readily available from directories.

NOTE:
ADDITIONAL COVENANTS NOT TO COMPETE

Jeopardy's contract with contestants contains the following clause:

> "I agree not to participate in any manner on any other game show or reality show until six (6) months after the initial broadcast of each and any of my appearances on the program. * * * I recognize that a breach by me of any part of this paragraph would cause Producer irreparable injury and damage that cannot be reasonably or adequately compensated by damages in an action at law and, therefore, I hereby expressly agree that Producer shall be entitled to injunctive and other equitable relief to prevent and/or cure any breach or threatened breach of this paragraph by me."

Is the clause enforceable? By injunctive relief?

In another context, Above the Law reported on 9/22/14 that members of a law school study group were required to sign the following agreement:

> "Each Study Group member hereby agrees that at all times during their participation in the Study Group thereafter, to hold this in the strictest confidence, and to not disclose confidential information as

> defined herein to anyone who is not also a current member of the study group, without unanimous agreement, memorialized in writing, from the other Study Group members. "Confidential information" shall mean any intellectual property, trade secrets or the study group's private information, including, but not limited to, organizational techniques, processes, formulas, shared documents, outlines, notes from discussions, either written or memorized; research projects, operating methods, information the study group receives in confidence from any other party, or any other secret or confidential matters of the study group. * * * The penalty for breach in the foregoing agreement shall be the sum of $5000 to be rendered in cash, checks, or ACH transfers wherein the penalty sum is distributed equally among non-breaching members."

Enforceable? Ridiculous? For the full story, see "The Worst Study Group Ever," Above the Law, 9/22/2014, available at http://abovethelaw.com/2014/09/the-worst-study-group-ever/.

Finally, the Huffington Post reported on 10/13/14 that Jimmy John's sandwich shop requires its sandwich makers to agree to a "non-competition" clause with a surprisingly broad scope:

> "Employee covenants and agrees that, during his or her employment with the Employer and for a period of two (2) years after . . . he or she will not have any direct or indirect interest in or perform services for . . . any business which derives more than ten percent (10%) of its revenue from selling submarine, hero-type, deli-style, pita and/or wrapped or rolled sandwiches and which is located with three (3) miles of either [the Jimmy John's location in question] or any such other Jimmy John's Sandwich Shop."

The covenant was the subject of a class action lawsuit, which was resolved in favor of Jimmy John's (on other grounds) in May, 2015. If it hadn't been, what legal arguments against the enforceability of the clause could you make? Would it turn on whether the employee was a manager or an entry-level maker of turkey subs? Why do you think Jimmy John's included this clause in its standard employment agreements?

R. HILLMAN, PRINCIPLES OF CONTRACT LAW

245–246 (4th ed. 2019).

Not surprisingly, contracts to perform illegal acts under a state's criminal law, such as prostitution or embezzlement, are not enforceable. This principle sometimes makes courts uncomfortable because defendants, who have willingly engaged in an illegal scheme and gained from it, can then use the illegality as a shield against contractual liability. Nonetheless, most courts follow the admonition to "leave the parties where it finds them," meaning that courts will not enforce illegal contracts even if defendants have already gained from them.

NOTE:
ON NONDISCLOSURE AGREEMENTS AND SEXUAL HARASSMENT

As you are probably aware, the social movement embodied by the hashtag #metoo concerned itself in part with the hiding of allegations of sexual harassment and abuse behind nondisclosure agreements. Victims of harassment, ranging from Olympic gymnasts to television anchors to low-wage workers, were paid for their silence, leaving nonsignatories vulnerable to predatory behavior. In response, several states passed laws that in effect made such contracts unenforceable as violative of public policy. New Jersey's—NJ S–121 (2019)—is particularly interesting. It makes any nondisclosure agreement about sexual harassment generated within an employment relationship unenforceable. It also states that any settlement agreement regarding claims of discrimination, retaliation, or harassment must include the following language in a prominent place:

> ALTHOUGH THE PARTIES MAY HAVE AGREED TO KEEP THE SETTLEMENT AND UNDERLYING FACTS CONFIDENTIAL, SUCH A PROVISION IN AN AGREEMENT IS UNENFORCABLE AGAINST THE EMPLOYER IF THE EMPLOYEE PUBLICALLY REVEALS SUFFICIENT DETAILS OF THE CLAIM SO THAT THE EMPLOYER IS REASONABLY IDENTIFIABLE

Violators of the New Jersey law are subject to tort remedies, including punitive remedies. Consider whether common law courts ought to follow this approach to nondisclosure agreements that enable harms to nonparties, either within or outside of the employment relationship. For an argument that they should, *see* David A. Hoffman and Eric Lampmann, *Hushing Contracts*, 97 WASH U. L. REV. 165 (2019).

SECTION FIVE: INEQUALITY OF THE EXCHANGE

1 J. STORY, COMMENTARIES ON EQUITY JURISPRUDENCE AS ADMINISTERED IN ENGLAND AND AMERICA

337 (14th ed. 1918).

[E]very person who is not from his peculiar condition or circumstances under disability is entitled to dispose of his property in such a manner and upon such terms as he chooses; and whether his bargains are wise and discreet or profitable or unprofitable or otherwise, are considerations not for courts of justice but for the party himself to deliberate upon.

FRIENDLY ICE CREAM CORP. V. BECKNER

Supreme Court of Virginia, 2004.
268 Va. 23, 597 S.E.2d 34.

ELIZABETH B. LACY, JUSTICE.

In this appeal we review the chancellor's decree rescinding an amendment to a lease because the lease amendment was the result of undue influence.

Facts

Beatrice Beckner and her husband entered into a commercial lease with Friendly Ice Cream Corporation (Friendly) allowing Friendly to build and operate a retail store on property owned by the Beckners. The lease commenced in 1976 with an original term of 15 years. Friendly could exercise five renewal options of five years each. If all five options were exercised, the lease would terminate in 2016. In addition to a monthly base rent, the lease required an annual payment of two percent of the store's annual gross sales exceeding $275,000 (percentage rent). FriendCo Restaurants, Inc. (FriendCo) operated the retail ice cream store through a sublease with Friendly. In 2001, the lease generated a base rent of $1,105.00 per month and a percentage rent of $7,984.68, for a total income of approximately $21,200.00.

In December 2001, Friendly and FriendCo decided to close the retail store. Fourteen years remained on the lease if the renewal option were fully exercised. Riggs Bank, N.A. (Riggs), among others, expressed an interest in acquiring Friendly's interest in the lease. Riggs planned to demolish the existing retail building and build a bank building on the property. Riggs was willing to pay Friendly approximately $800,000 for terminating the sublease and assigning the lease to Riggs if the lease were amended to relieve Riggs from payment of the percentage rent.

On December 26, 2001, Sandra L. Hughes, Vice-President and Deputy General Counsel for FriendCo, wrote to the Beckners seeking their consent to the assignment of the lease to Riggs, to the proposed redevelopment of the property, and to an agreement that the percentage rent requirement would not apply to Riggs' use of the property as a bank. On January 3, 2002, in response to a telephone call from Mrs. Beckner, Hughes went to Mrs. Beckner's home and discussed the provisions of a proposed amendment to the lease that would meet Riggs' conditions for the lease assignment. At that meeting Mrs. Beckner, then widowed and 80 years old, told Hughes that her lawyer was Norman Hammer.

Hughes contacted Hammer and, at Hammer's request, sent him a letter dated January 25, 2002, setting out the history of payments made on the percentage rent, offering to increase the base rate by $5,000 a year, and proposing an amendment to the lease eliminating the percentage rent.

Hammer replied on February 20, stating that he had no counter offer and that he wanted to confer with Mrs. Beckner's son, Robert O. Beckner.

In a February 27 telephone call to Hughes, Mrs. Beckner stated that Hammer was no longer her attorney and that she wanted to meet with Hughes to discuss the amendment to the lease. Hughes went to Mrs. Beckner's home and discussed the terms of the proposed amendment to the lease, including the offer to increase the annual base rent by $5,000. Mrs. Beckner replied that she wanted the base rate increased by $8,940 a year, from $1,105 per month to $1,850 per month. Hughes agreed to submit Mrs. Beckner's proposal to Friendly.

On February 28, Hammer sent a facsimile to Hughes instructing Hughes not to contact Mrs. Beckner directly and terming the "present offer" unacceptable. Hughes replied by facsimile on March 1, telling Hammer that she had met with Mrs. Beckner at Mrs. Beckner's request; that Mrs. Beckner stated that Hammer no longer represented Mrs. Beckner; that Hughes was a principal of FriendCo, the subtenant; and that "principals may talk to one another at any time, without going through lawyers if they so choose."

Hammer met with Mrs. Beckner on March 7, 2002 to discuss the amendment to the lease and his representation of her. Also present at the meeting were Robert Beckner, Clyde R. Christopherson—a lawyer who had also represented Mrs. Beckner, and Leroy Jackson, Mrs. Beckner's long-time friend and insurance agent. Mrs. Beckner agreed that Hammer should negotiate with Friendly on her behalf regarding the proposed amended lease. Christopherson drafted a letter reflecting this decision and, after reviewing the letter with Mrs. Beckner on March 8, sent the letter to Hughes' superior, David J. Norman.

Mrs. Beckner telephoned Hughes on Friday, March 8, reiterated her desire to deal directly with Hughes, and asked if Friendly had responded to the increase in base rent that Mrs. Beckner had requested. Hughes told Mrs. Beckner that Friendly had agreed to the increase. Although Mrs. Beckner wanted to sign the amendment to the lease immediately, Hughes could not meet with her until Monday, March 11. Hughes sent Mrs. Beckner a copy of the amendment to the lease along with a copy of Christopherson's March 8 letter and the facsimile exchanges between Hammer and Hughes on February 28 and March 1.

On March 11, Hughes arrived at Mrs. Beckner's home, reviewed the amendment to the lease with her, and then, at Mrs. Beckner's direction, went with her to the bank where a bank employee with whom Mrs. Beckner had dealt in the past notarized her signature on the documents. Hughes then presented Mrs. Beckner with a letter Hughes had drafted for Mrs. Beckner's signature stating that Mrs. Beckner wanted to deal directly with Hughes. Mrs. Beckner signed the letter.

Shortly thereafter, Robert Beckner informed Hughes and Norman that he was concerned about his mother's actions. After receiving copies of the documents Mrs. Beckner had signed, Christopherson wrote Norman indicating Christopherson considered the documents to be invalid and that the documents should be resubmitted to Mrs. Beckner for further consideration.

* * *

[The court concluded that that Mrs. Beckner was not subject to undue influence in part because she did not have a confidential relationship with Hughes and in part because the consideration she received was not "grossly inadequate." The portion of the opinion dealing with the latter argument follows.]

* * * Mrs. Beckner first claims that under the original or amended lease, the base rent was "significantly below prevailing market rates." Mrs. Beckner claimed that the rental value of the property "had risen dramatically" and, according to her expert witness, the current fair market rental value would be between approximately $5,000 and $8,000 a month. However, Mrs. Beckner's expert did not consider the impact the outstanding lease would have on the fair market rental value of the property. The chancellor, while refusing to strike the testimony of this expert, considered it "weightless." We agree with the chancellor that evidence of current fair market rental value without consideration of the existence of the lease or its conditions is not probative of whether the consideration for the amendment to the lease is grossly inadequate.

Next, Mrs. Beckner argues that the consideration was grossly inadequate because the increase in base rent contained in the amendment did not significantly increase the annual amount she received compared to the aggregate amount of base and percentage rent she received under the lease before the amendment. The base rent in the amended lease produced only $80 a month more than she received in 2001 from the combined base and percentage rents, thereby making the consideration received grossly inadequate, according to Mrs. Beckner.

We disagree. The increase in the base rate was in an amount Mrs. Beckner specifically requested. Over the likely lifetime of the amended lease, Mrs. Beckner would receive $310,800 in base rent, $125,160 more than she would have received in base rent without the amendment. The record also shows that the percentage rent in 2001 declined from the prior year. There is no evidence in the record that the value of percentage rent would remain at 2001 levels or would increase. Although Mrs. Beckner labels as speculative the suggestion that Friendly's would or could close the retail store, thereby discontinuing the obligation to pay percentage rent, the uncontradicted evidence was that Friendly's had decided to close the store and that Mrs. Beckner was aware of that decision. Mrs. Beckner testified that she understood that, if the store closed, she would no longer receive any percentage rent. Thus, the increase in base rent was not grossly inadequate in light of the additional income it would produce and the uncertainty of the amount or continuation of revenue from the percentage rent.

Mrs. Beckner next argues that the possibility that she might own a bank building valued at $800,000 at the end of the lease period should not be included as part of the consideration because it also was speculative. Here again the uncontradicted evidence was that, if the lease was amended, Riggs planned to build such a building. This potential asset was a known part of the business transaction and, in the absence of fraud, may be considered as part of the benefit Mrs. Beckner received from agreeing to the lease amendment.

Finally, Mrs. Beckner asserts that the appropriate comparison of "value exchanged" is to compare the additional $80 per month Mrs. Beckner would receive under the amendment with the $800,000 Friendly's would receive for the assignment of the lease to Riggs. This disparity, she maintains, shows that the consideration she received was grossly inadequate. The amount Friendly's would receive from Riggs to assign the lease is irrelevant to the adequacy of the consideration Mrs. Beckner received. Mrs. Beckner could not recover any amount from Riggs because she could not assign the lease to Riggs. The lease had, at a minimum, four years remaining, with the potential to extend, if the tenant so desired, to fourteen years, and contained no provisions for termination by the landlord other than for nonpayment of rent or insolvency of the tenant. Therefore, the value of Mrs. Beckner's consideration must be measured not simply in the amount of increase in base rent but also in light of the rights that she possessed regarding the property and her options at the time of the amendment.

Consideration is grossly inadequate when the " 'inequality [is] so strong, gross and manifest that it must be impossible to state it to a [person] of common sense without producing an exclamation at the inequality of it. * * * ' " *Jackson,* 193 Va. At 741, 71 S.E.2d at 185 (quoting *Gwynne v. Heaton,* 1 Bro. Ch. 1, 9, 28 Eng. Rep. 949 (1778)). That others could have bargained for a higher base rent or secured more favorable terms for the execution of the lease amendment does not affect the determination of grossly inadequate consideration. In this case, by executing the amendment to the lease, Mrs. Beckner received an annual increase of $8,940 in base rent regardless of whether the lease was assigned to another party and whether any business was operating on the property. She also acquired the possibility of owning the new bank building at the end of the lease. This record does not support a finding that the consideration Mrs. Beckner received was grossly inadequate.

Mrs. Beckner also asserts the chancellor was justified in finding that the transaction occurred under suspicious circumstances because Hughes did not further investigate whether Mrs. Beckner was represented by counsel following Christopherson's March 8 letter and because Hughes drafted a letter for Mrs. Beckner's signature stating that Mrs. Beckner wanted to deal with Hughes directly. As noted above, the record clearly shows that Mrs. Beckner herself initiated all but two of the contacts with Hughes. Mrs. Beckner's active participation in the negotiations regarding the lease amendment belies the existence of circumstances that would give rise to a level of suspicion sufficient to support the presumption of undue influence and rescission of the amendment.

We need not address the chancellor's finding that Mrs. Beckner suffered from great weakness of mind because even assuming that the finding is supported by the record, weakness of mind alone will not entitle Mrs. Beckner to rescission. *McGrue,* 202 Va. At 426, 117 S.E.2d at 707; *Fishburne,* 84 Va. At 111, 4 S.E. at 582.

Because the record is insufficient to support the chancellor's findings that Mrs. Beckner had a confidential relationship with Hughes and that the consideration she received was grossly inadequate or the transaction occurred under suspicious circumstances, Mrs. Beckner was not entitled to a presumption of undue influence. Therefore, the chancellor erred in rendering judgment in favor of Mrs. Beckner on Count IV, Undue Influence.

The chancellor also entered judgment in Mrs. Beckner's favor on Count II of her Bill of Complaint—grossly inadequate consideration. Substantial failure of consideration is a recognized ground for rescission of a contract because such gross inadequacy is clear evidence of fraud. *Texas Co. v. Northup,* 154 Va. 428, 442–45, 153 S.E. 659, 663–64 (1930); *Broaddus v. Broaddus,* 144 Va. 727, 750, 130 S.E. 794, 801 (1925). The standard for this claim is the same as claims of undue influence based on grossly inadequate consideration: "[a]n inequality so strong, gross and manifest that it must be impossible to state it to a man of common sense without producing an exclamation at the inequality of it." *Texas Co.,* 154 Va. At 443, 153 S.E. at 663, (quoting *Gwynne,* 1 Bro. Ch. At 9). Finally, because gross inadequacy is based on fraud, it must be shown by clear and convincing evidence. *Id.*

We have already determined in considering Mrs. Beckner's claim of undue influence that the record did not support a finding of grossly inadequate compensation. Applying the same standard to her claims in this Count, we conclude that the chancellor erred in entering judgment in favor of Mrs. Beckner on Count II because the consideration was not grossly inadequate.

Accordingly, for the reasons stated, we will reverse the trial court's decree rescinding the amendment to the lease and requiring repayment of funds by Mrs. Beckner.

JACKSON V. SEYMOUR

Supreme Court of Appeals of Virginia, 1952.
193 Va. 735, 71 S.E.2d 181.

[Lucy Jackson brought this action for rescission of a deed by which she conveyed to her brother, Benjamin Seymour, a tract of land for $275. She also sought an accounting. She alleged that she was induced to sell the land as the result of the representations of her brother, in whom she had "complete confidence" concerning the management of her property, that the land was of "no value except for a pasture," and that she later discovered the land contained merchantable timber worth $3,200 to $5,000. Jackson further alleged that certain statements of her brother were "false" and "fraudulent."]

EGGLESTON, JUSTICE.

* * *

Since 1931 Mrs. Jackson had been the owner of a farm of 166 acres in Brunswick county which adjoined lands owned by her brother, Benjamin J. Seymour, the defendant. After the death of her husband (the date of which is not shown in the record) Mrs. Jackson sought and obtained the assistance of her brother, who is a successful farmer and business man, in renting the farm for her. He rented the tillable portions of the farm, collected the rents, and made settlements with her which she never questioned. Up to the time of the transaction with which we are concerned they were devoted to each other and she had, as she says, "the utmost confidence in him."

In 1946 Tazewell Wilkins approached Seymour about the purchase of a tract of Seymour's land containing 30.46 acres for a pasture. He also wanted to buy the adjoining tract of 31 acres, which was a part of the land owned by Mrs. Jackson. Seymour told Wilkins that while he was willing to take $275 for his (Seymour's) land, he did not own the 31-acre tract and suggested that Wilkins see Mrs. Jackson about buying it. While Seymour also conveyed this information to Mrs. Jackson the record discloses no negotiations between Wilkins and Mrs. Jackson for the purchase of her land.

In February, 1947, Mrs. Jackson approached her brother, saying that she was in need of funds and was anxious to sell the 31-acre tract in which Wilkins had shown interest. Seymour did not want to buy the property, but because of his sister's need for money he agreed to purchase it at $275, which was the price which had been mentioned in his negotiations with

Wilkins. The brother was then unaware that there was valuable timber on the land and contemplated using it for a pasture. Seymour gave his sister a check for $275 and she signed a receipt therefor. On the next day Mrs. Jackson executed and delivered a deed conveying the property to her brother. The deed was prepared by a local attorney at Seymour's request and expense.

A short while after Seymour had acquired the property it came to his attention that some trees had been cut from the tract. Upon investigation he discovered for the first time that there was valuable timber on the land.

The evidence does not disclose the exact quantity and value of this timber. It shows that in 1948 Seymour cut from the land which he had purchased from his sister and from adjoining lands owned by him, 148,055 feet of lumber and that the greater portion of this came from the Jackson tract. This timber had a stumpage value of approximately $20 per 1,000 feet.

The land in controversy is located in an isolated section and it is undisputed that Mrs. Jackson had never been on it and knew nothing of its character. While Seymour had hunted in the vicinity and been within sight of the property he had never actually been on the land. To use his own words, "I was positive that it was just naked land" and worth $8 or $9 an acre. Thus, neither vendor nor vendee knew that there was valuable timber growing on the land.

On cross-examination Seymour admitted that the presence of timber on the land "was not within the contemplation" of him and his sister at the time the sale was consummated. He testified that if he had known of this timber he would not have bought the property from her for $275.

After Mrs. Jackson discovered that her brother had cut and marketed valuable timber from the land she demanded an accounting from him of the profits derived therefrom. When this demand was refused the present litigation followed.

Upon the conclusion of the evidence the lower court dictated from the bench an opinion holding that the plaintiff's allegations of *actual* fraud had not been sustained by the evidence and that consequently she was not entitled to rescission of the deed on that ground. It took under advisement whether under the allegations of the bill the plaintiff was entitled to relief on the ground of *constructive* fraud because of the "confidential relationship" of the parties and the "gross inadequacy in price."

[While the constructive fraud allegation was under advisement, Jackson attempted to "amend her bill" to include a count based on her "honest and material" mistake of fact, which would make enforcement of the deed a "fraud" upon her rights. The lower court rejected the amendment because it was "tendered too late." Since Jackson's case was based on actual fraud, the lower court denied Jackson any relief. She appealed.]

* * *

* * * We are of opinion that under the evidence, viewed in the light of the trial court's determination of the issues of fact favorable to the defendant, the plaintiff is entitled to equitable relief on the ground of constructive fraud, and that such relief is within the scope of the allegations of the original bill of complaint.

The undisputed evidence shows that shortly after the defendant had acquired this tract of land from his sister for the sum of $275, he cut and marketed therefrom timber valued at approximately ten times what he had paid for the property. A mere statement of the matter shows the gross and shocking inadequacy of the price paid.

This is not the ordinary case in which the parties dealt at arm's length and the shrewd trader was entitled to the fruits of his bargain. The parties were brother and sister. He was a successful business man and she a widow in need of money and forced by circumstances, according to the defendant's own testimony, to sell a part of the lands which she had inherited. Because of their friendly and intimate relations she entrusted to him and he assumed the management and renting of a portion of this very land. He engaged tenants for such of the land as could be cultivated and collected the rents. She accepted his settlements without question.

Moreover, it is undisputed that neither of the parties knew of the timber on the land and we have from the defendant's own lips the admission that as it turned out "afterwards" he had paid a grossly inadequate price for the property and that he would not have bought it from her for the small amount paid if he had then known of the true situation.

To hold that under these circumstances the plaintiff is without remedy would be a reproach to the law. Nor do we think that a court of equity is so impotent.

The controlling principles were thus stated in Planters Nat. Bank v. Heflin Co., 166 Va. 166, 173, 174, 184 S.E. 216, 219:

> "* * * Mere failure of consideration or want of consideration will not ordinarily invalidate an executed contract. The owner of the historic estate of 'Blackacre' can give it away, and he can sell it for a peppercorn. Courts, though they have long arms, cannot relieve one of the consequences of a contract merely because it was unwise. They are not guardians in general to the people at large, but where inadequacy of price is such as to shock their conscience equity is alert to seize upon the slightest circumstance indicative of fraud, either actual or constructive." * * *

In Texas Co. v. Northrup, [154 Va. 428, 153 S.E. 659] we quoted with approval this definition by Lord Thurlow of the gross inadequacy of consideration as indicating constructive fraud: " 'An inequality so strong, gross and manifest that it must be impossible to state it to a man of common sense without producing an exclamation at the inequality of it.' * * * Gwynne v. Heaton, 1 Bro.Ch. 1, 9; 28 Rep. 949." 154 Va., at page 443, 153 S.E., at page 663.

Clearly the inadequacy of consideration here meets that definition.

In addition to the gross inadequacy of consideration we have the confidential relation of the parties, the pecuniary distress of the vendor, and the mutual mistake of the parties as to the subject matter of the contract. Unquestionably, we think, to permit the transaction to stand would result in constructive fraud upon the rights of the plaintiff. Hence, she is entitled to relief in equity.

To grant a rescission of the deed, under the circumstances here, does no violence to the principle that the relief granted must conform to the case made out in the bill of complaint. While the bill alleges actual fraud, it also contains allegations of these constituent elements of constructive fraud: The confidential relation of the parties; the reliance by the plaintiff upon the advice and judgment of the defendant in her business affairs; the gross inadequacy of the price paid; her offer to restore the purchase price and rescind the transaction, and his rejection of the offer.

In Moore v. Gregory, 146 Va. 504, 131 S.E. 692, we quoted with approval this definition of constructive fraud as written in 26 C.J., Fraud, § 4, p. 1061, now found in 37 C.J.S., Fraud, § 2–c, pp. 211, 212: " 'Constructive fraud is a breach of legal or equitable duty, which irrespective of the moral guilt of the fraud feasor, the law declares fraudulent, because of its tendency to deceive others, to violate public or private confidence, or to injure public interests. Neither actual dishonesty of purpose nor intent to deceive is an essential element of constructive fraud. An intent to deceive is an essential element of actual fraud. The presence or absence of such an intent distinguishes actual fraud from constructive fraud.' " 146 Va., at page 523, 131 S.E., at page 697.

In the same case we said: "Constructive fraud may be inferred from the intrinsic nature and subject of the bargain itself." 146 Va., at page 527, 131 S.E., at page 698.

It is true that there is no specific allegation in the bill here that the circumstances under which the defendant acquired the property amounted to constructive fraud, but such allegation would have been merely the conclusion of the pleader which necessarily flows from the facts alleged. * * *

* * *

We are, therefore, of opinion that the lower court should have entered a decree granting the plaintiff's prayer for a rescission of the conveyance and restoring the parties to the *status quo* in so far as practicable. By way of incidental relief the plaintiff is entitled to recover of the defendant the fair stumpage value of the timber removed by the latter from the land, with interest from the date of such removal, and the fair rental value of the property during the time the defendant was in possession. The defendant is entitled to a return of the purchase price paid by him, with interest from the date that the plaintiff offered to rescind the transaction, and taxes paid by him on the land since the date of the conveyance, with interest.

The decree appealed from is reversed and the cause remanded for further proceedings in conformity with the views here expressed.

Reversed and remanded.

IN RE LAMEY, 2020 WL 1671550 (Bankr. D.N.M. 2020). [T]he tort of constructive fraud: "*is a breach of legal* or equitable *duty* which, *irrespective of the moral guilt of the fraud feasor*, the law declares fraudulent because of its tendency to *deceive others*, to violate public or private confidence, or to injure public interests. Neither actual dishonesty of purpose nor intent to deceive is an essential element of constructive fraud." *Scudder v. Hart*, 110 P.2d 536, 539 (N.M. 1941) (emphasis in original).

ATIYAH, BOOK REVIEW: C. FRIED, CONTRACT AS PROMISE

95 Harv.L.Rev. 509, 527 (1981).

The proposition that a person is always the best judge of his own interests is a good starting point for laws and institutional arrangements, but as an infallible empirical proposition it is an outrage to human experience. The parallel moral argument, that to prevent a person, even in his own interests, from binding himself is to show disrespect for his moral autonomy, can ring very hollow when used to defend a grossly unfair contract secured at the expense of a person of little bargaining skill. If a smart operator makes a highly advantageous deal with a person of low intelligence or skill, does the former really show "respect" for the latter's moral autonomy by exploiting his advantage in this way?

* * * Promises ought to be treated as prima facie binding rather than absolutely and conclusively binding. Exchanges of benefits are likely to be in the interests of those who make them, and there is therefore a strong prima facie case for upholding them. Promises are likely to be relied upon and those who rely would suffer loss from breach; these too are prima facie good reasons for upholding the binding nature of a promise.

On the other hand, to say that such results are likely to follow is not to say that they are certain to follow; the presumption must be rebuttable.

SECTION SIX: UNCONSCIONABILITY

A. ORIGINS

In the Middle Ages, the English Chancery Court introduced equitable rules and remedies partly in response to the inflexibility of English courts of law. Eventually the Chancellors began to follow their own precedents, and principles such as mistake, misrepresentation, estoppel, unclean hands, and unconscionability emerged. These principles reflected the general allegiance of equity courts to various ideas of fairness. Equity courts in the United States came to recognize most of the same general principles.

Unconscionability was frequently invoked in equity as a defense to specific performance of contracts for the sale of land, and conflicting authority developed on the precise elements necessary for a finding of unconscionability. Some decisions required not only bargaining improprieties, such as concealment of facts or trickery, but substantive unfairness of terms as well. Other decisions required only one or the other.

Today, the Uniform Commercial Code in section 2–302 incorporates the unconscionability doctrine and makes it available as a defense in all sale of goods cases, not just those in which an equitable remedy such as specific performance is sought. Moreover, many courts today apply the unconscionability doctrine in non-sales cases as well. A detailed history of the drafting of U.C.C. § 2–302 is found in Leff, Unconscionability and the Code—The Emperor's New Clause, 115 U.Pa.L.Rev. 485 (1967).

At the outset, students should think about the difference between unconscionability and public policy issues. One court stated the distinction in the following way: "A refusal to enforce a contract on the grounds of public policy may be distinguished from a finding of unconscionability. Rather than focus on the relationship between the parties and the effect of the agreement upon them, public policy analysis requires the court to consider the impact of such arrangements upon society as a whole." Eagle v. Fred Martin Motor Co., 157 Ohio App.3d 150, 809 N.E.2d 1161, 1180 (2004).

RYAN V. WEINER

Court of Chancery of Delaware, 1992.
610 A.2d 1377.

ALLEN, CHANCELLOR.

In this action Robert Ryan seeks, *inter alia,* an order canceling a deed to his house that he gave to Norman Weiner in May 1984. Ryan asserts that in making that transfer he was deceived by Weiner and only recently came to understand that the deed in question was not simply a security interest. Mr. Weiner denies all aspects of the complaint. The case has been through a brief trial.

While I do not reach the question whether Weiner in fact deceived Ryan by making false statements to him upon which Ryan relied, I do conclude that the transfer in question represents a shocking and oppressive transaction; that Mr. Weiner took the grossest advantage of Mr. Ryan, who found himself in weakened and distressed circumstances, and that Weiner manipulated their dealings to accomplish that result. In short, for the reasons set forth below, I conclude, that this represents that unusual case in which a court of equity cannot let stand an executed contract but is obligated to grant the remedy of rescission.

I.

Mr. Ryan is a 69 year old man with a ninth grade education. He retired about ten years ago from his work as a laborer and subsists on a small pension and social security benefits. In 1971, Ryan and his now deceased wife purchased a modest house located at 928 Pine Street in Wilmington, Delaware to live in. The price was $8,600. Most of that was borrowed and repayment was secured by a first mortgage.

After about 12 years of mortgage payments, Mr. Ryan (who had become a widower in the interim) fell badly behind in his mortgage payments. The monthly payment was $98 per month at that time. By April 1984, he owed in excess of $1,000 in arrearages.

It is agreed that Ryan's house had a fair market value at that time of $19,800. (Stip. Facts ¶ 18). The balance of the loan secured by the mortgage was less than $8,000. In March 1984, the mortgage lender instituted foreclosure proceedings. Mr. Ryan did not answer the complaint and, on April 16, 1984, a default judgment in the amount of $7,843.26 was entered. A sheriff's sale was scheduled for June 12, 1984.

Ryan testified that throughout this period he was an active alcoholic.

Defendant, Norman Weiner, was (and is) a licensed real estate broker who engages in the business, *inter alia,* of buying and leasing inner-city houses. On Sunday, May 13, 1984, Weiner arrived at Ryan's home unannounced and informed Ryan that he could help him keep his house.

The parties had not met prior to that. They disagree about what was said at that meeting. Ryan reports that he understood that Weiner offered to lend him the money to make up the back payments and to take a deed to secure repayment. Weiner reports that he offered to buy the house and to let Ryan continue to live in it as a tenant. They agree, however, that Weiner did not offer to make a cash payment to Ryan.

Weiner showed Ryan no papers but told him he would pick him up the following morning to complete the transaction. When Weiner left that afternoon, he took Ryan's original deed to the property which he said he would hold in his safe deposit box.

At 8:00 a.m. the following day, Weiner picked Ryan up at his house and drove him to the office of Harold Green, a Delaware lawyer, who represented Weiner in real estate transactions and is also a close personal friend and relative. At Green's office, Ryan was asked to sign several documents which Weiner explained were necessary. Green did not explain any of the documents to Ryan, nor did he speak to him during their ten-minute meeting. Neither Weiner nor Green advised Ryan of his right to seek independent legal advice concerning the transaction. (Tr. 26–27, 182). At trial, Green testified that he had no specific recollection of his meeting with Ryan and was unable to confirm any of the alleged conversations or events that took place between the parties. Ryan says that he signed the documents without reading them because he trusted the defendant's statements that the papers were loan documents. (Tr. 19, 28).

In fact, Ryan did not sign loan documents on May 14, 1984, but signed a deed transferring the Pine Street property to Weiner. (Pl.'s Exh. 1). According to Ryan, he did not see the front page of the deed containing the property description when he signed the back of the deed and neither Weiner nor Green told him that he was signing a deed. (Tr. 20, 82). He also claims that he did not understand a one-sentence document that he signed in Green's office, assigning all money held in escrow to Weiner. (Pl.'s Exh. 9). Ryan also signed a document which he later learned was a settlement sheet. He testified that when he signed the document on May 14, 1984, it contained no figures and only had about two inches of writing on it. The document now bears the date May 15, 1984 and contains many figures. (Pl.'s Exh. 2 & Tr. 23). Ryan was not given any copies of documents that he had signed. (Tr. 26, 234).

Before Weiner had gone to Ryan's house, Mr. Green had requested and received from the mortgagee two documents: a "Sale Subject to Mortgage" document (now dated May 14, 1984) and an "Insurance Information and Assignment of Escrow." The assignment form required Ryan's signature and required that Seller's address be set forth. (Pl.'s Exhs. 8 & 16). But, Weiner, not Ryan, signed the Assignment of Escrow form, completing the section which requested the seller's forwarding address with Weiner's own

P.O. box number. The forms were then sent back to the mortgage company as an enclosure with a letter from Green of May 15, 1984. (Pl.'s Exh. 14). Ryan never saw the Sale Subject to Mortgage Statement or Insurance Information and Assignment of Escrow form.

The May 14, 1984 deed signed by Ryan recites that $7,000 in consideration was paid to him. He did not, however, receive any cash, nor did Mr. Weiner ever pay off the balance of the outstanding mortgage on the property or satisfy the default judgment entered against Ryan. Weiner did thereafter pay the mortgage company $1,898.30 in order to bring the loan current. But Weiner did not sign any documents assuming the legal obligations of the mortgage. (Tr. 113–115).

The result of the transaction was that Ryan transferred ownership of his property to Weiner without receiving any part of the financial value of the then equity in the property of approximately $12,000. Ryan has remained personally liable for paying off the mortgage balance under the mortgage bond and note.

* * *

Following the May 13 and 14 meetings with Weiner, Ryan continued to live in the house. A lease was executed with an effective date of May 14, 1984. (Pl.'s Exh. 3). Weiner steadily increased Ryan's monthly payments over intervening seven years from $100 a month to $310 per month. (Stip. Facts ¶¶ 20–25). During the same period the mortgage payment also increased, but only from $93 in 1984 to $120 in 1991. (Stip. Facts ¶¶ 13 & 14). Over the course of this arrangement Ryan paid Weiner the following amounts:

Time Period	Number of Monthly Payments	Amount	Total
July 1984	1	$100	$ 100
Aug. 1984—June 1985	11	160	1,760
July 1985—Oct. 1985	4	260	1,040
Nov. 1985—Dec. 1988	38	270	10,260
Jan. 1989—June 1990	18	290	5,220
July 1990—Apr. 1991	10	310	3,100
	Total:		$21,480

Over the years, while Ryan paid him a total of $21,480, Mr. Weiner expended $12,149.27 on the mortgage, insurance, taxes, sewer and water charges, including the amount paid to bring the mortgage up to date in 1984.[1]

* * *

Before his May, 1991 payment was due, Ryan concluded that he had paid Weiner a total amount in excess of the amount of the mortgage on the property and the amount of Weiner's "loan." He refused to make any more monthly payments to Weiner in May, 1991. Weiner promptly commenced a summary action in the justice of peace court to evict Ryan. On Ryan's motion, this court stayed that proceeding, concluding that issues of the quality of Weiner's title itself and Ryan's alleged right to have Weiner's deed canceled were remedies not available in the justice of peace court.

II.

The right of competent persons to make contracts and thus privately to acquire rights and obligations is a basic part of our general liberty. This ability to enter and enforce contracts is universally thought not only to reflect and promote liberty, but as well to promote the production of wealth. Thus, the right to make and enforce contracts is elemental in our legal order. But not every writing purporting to contain a promise or every document purporting to make a transfer will be given legal effect. A large body of law defines when valid contracts are formed and when and how they can be enforced.

Contracts or transfers induced by fraudulent misrepresentations, for example, can be avoided. Similarly, a lack of legal capacity or the existence of duress can lead a court to declare a promise unenforceable or a transfer voidable. *See, e.g.,* A. Farnsworth, *Contracts* §§ 4.1–4.20 (1982). Ordinarily, an evaluation of relative values of the bargain to the parties will not provide a basis for such judicial action.

It is general rule, recited by courts for well over a century, that the adequacy or fairness of the consideration that adduces a promise or a transfer is not alone grounds for a court to refuse to enforce a promise or to give effect to a transfer. *See, e.g.,* 1 A. Corbin, *Corbin on Contracts* § 127 (1963 & Supp.1991) (adequacy of consideration); 3 J. Pomeroy, *A Treatise on Equity Jurisprudence* § 926 n. 7 (citing numerous federal and state cases). This rule, present in 17th and 18th century cases, achieved its greatest dignity in the jurisprudence of 19th century classical liberalism. *See, e.g.,* P. Atiyah, *The Rise and Fall of Freedom of Contract* 146–152 & 169–180 (Clarendon Press Oxford 1979). Thus, the classical liberal's premise concerning the subjectivity (and thus non-reviewability) of value[2]

[1] Ryan asked Weiner to make repairs to the property since it was in a deteriorated condition. Weiner apparently purchased material for repairs to the property but left the repair work to be completed by Ryan or his friends. (Tr. 41–42).

[2] An early statement of this view of the subjective and relative nature of value is Hobbes', in *The Leviathan:*

has plainly been a dominant view in our contract law for a very long time. Countless cases from the 19th and 20th centuries could be cited for the proposition that "mere inadequacy of price" will not invalidate a contract or a transfer. But as standard as that generalization is, it has not precluded courts, on occasion, from striking down contracts or transfers in which inadequacy of price is coupled with some circumstance that amounts to inequitable or oppressive conduct. That is, the "rule" that courts will not weigh consideration or assess the wisdom of bargains, has not fully excluded the opposite proposition, that at some point courts will do so even in the absence of actual fraud, duress or incapacity. *See* 2 Devlin, *Real Property and Deeds* § 814 (1911); Story, *Commentaries on Equity Jurisprudence,* (Cambridge Press 1835), (Arno Press Reprint 1972) §§ 238, 244–247.

The notion that a court can and will review contracts for fairness is apt for good reason to strike us as dangerous, subjecting negotiated bargains to the loosely constrained review of the judicial process. Perhaps for this reason, courts have evoked this doctrine with extreme reluctance and then only when all of the facts suggest a level of unfairness that is unconscionable.

The applicable principle is ancient. It was old when Justice Story summarized it in 1835:

> Of a kindred nature, to the cases already considered, are cases of bargains of such an unconscionable nature, and of such gross inequality, as naturally lead to the presumption of fraud, imposition, or undue influence. This is the sort of fraud, to which Lord Hardwicke alluded in the passage already cited, when he said, that they were such bargains, as no man in his senses and not under delusion would make on the one hand, and as no honest and fair man would accept on the other, being inequitable and unconscientious bargains. Mere inadequacy of price, or any other inequality in the bargain, is not, however, to be understood as constituting *per se* a ground to avoid a bargain in Equity. * * *
>
> * * *

Story, *Commentaries on Equity Jurisprudence, supra,* §§ 244–246 (footnotes omitted).

* * *

[Real estate] cases give a flavor for the application of this judicial nullification of contract. *Lampley v. Pertuit,* Miss.Supr., 199 So.2d 452 (1967), for example, involved an alleged sale of a house, valued in excess of

---

The value of all things contracted for is measured by the Appetites of the Contractors; and therefore just value, is that which they be content to give.

The Leviathan (Pelican edition) Part I, Chp. 15, at 208 (Harmondsworth 1974).

$1600, for $400. While plaintiffs had given a deed absolute, they testified that they had intended a loan not a sale and had intended the deed as security. In canceling the deed, the court concluded that the parties must have entered a loan transaction, reasoning that, a $400 purchase price would represent "grossly inadequate" consideration for the plaintiffs' house. The court gave weight to the trial court's finding that the defendant had a far superior education and understanding of the intricacies of real estate transactions than the plaintiffs. *Id.* At 454.

* * *

Statutory developments over the last thirty years reflect an explicit legislative endorsement of this ancient equitable doctrine. The most important example of this mid-twentieth century codification is the unconscionability provision contained in Section 2–302 of the Uniform Commercial Code. That provision has, of course, been adopted in almost all of the states and applies to sale of all goods. Section 2–302 provides, in part:

> (1) If the court as a matter of law finds the contract or any clause * * * to have been unconscionable [when] * * * made the court may refuse to enforce the contract. * * *

6 *Del.C.* § 2–302 (Michie 1975). The drafters' comments note that "the basic test is whether, in light of the general commercial background and the commercial needs of the particular trade or case, the clauses involved are so one-sided as to be unconscionable under the circumstances existing at the time of the making of the contract." *Id.*

While the UCC does not, of course, apply to sales of land, there is good reason to assume that the legislature's solicitude for parties who are disadvantaged by bargains that are unconscionably oppressive should not be entirely ignored where sales of land are concerned. Such transactions are obviously enormously more significant than a purchase of goods to the average person. They will occur rarely in the typical life and will often involve a person's largest single asset. *See* Leff, *Unconscionability and the Code—The Emperor's New Clause,* 115 U.Pa.L.Rev. 485, 537 (1967).[3]

* * *

[The court found the contract to be unconscionable:]

(a) *The substance:* the financial aspects of the sale are shocking. Mr. Ryan had lived for more than 13 years in this modest house and had until relatively shortly before the sale regularly made his mortgage payment. The house had a fair market value of $19,800 and a mortgage of about $7,800.00. Thus, at the time it represented some $12,000 of equity which,

[3] "* * * real property is likely to be the only thing that relatively unsophisticated people have which is worth tricking them out of * * * the equity cases are replete with factual patterns involving the old being bilked and farmers sweet-talked into ruinous trades." 115 U.Pa.L.Rev. at 536.

one can safely assume, represented all of the assets that Ryan had acquired over a long life as an employed laborer.

In exchange for the conveyance of this asset, Ryan received no cash, and no release of liability. He received only a promise to be able to occupy the same house at a market-rate rent. That rent was, at first, modestly in excess of the mortgage payment ($100) but within 15 months it had been raised twice, first to $160 (60% increase) then to $260 per month (additional 62% increase). *See* * * * (table) above.

What, on the other hand, did Mr. Weiner get from the transaction and what did he give? He received, of course, the value of the property net of the mortgage. He paid out some cash (about $1,900) but that amount, in large measure, reduced the amount of the mortgage lien on the property and thus immediately accrued to the financial interest, not of Ryan, but of the new equity owner—Weiner himself. Therefore if the transaction is valid all that Weiner extended as consideration to Ryan was the right to be a tenant in his house at a fair market rate in excess of the mortgage amortization cost.

From a financial perspective this transaction is as close to a gift as one is likely to encounter.

(b) *The process:* the process that lead to this one-sided bargain, in part, appears to explain and account for it. Ryan was, of course, vulnerable, and unsophisticated, but those facts do not prevent him from making valid contracts. But Ryan's circumstances—his age, his obvious lack of sophistication, his poverty, his distress and his fear of being dispossessed—are factors that one who initiates a transaction concerning transfer of the other's home should take into account, in order to offer some assurance that whatever deal may be made is made knowingly and with due consideration. But instead of offering Ryan sufficient time to consider his proposal (and to perhaps consult with others), Mr. Weiner moved with urgent speed. He did not give Ryan time to consider the matter, perhaps to seek advice from a Legal Aid lawyer or to consider alternatives. Weiner rushed Ryan. He picked him up at his home early the next day and took Ryan to Weiner's lawyer to sign papers. I am convinced that Ryan did not understand the nature and effect of the papers he signed.

* * *

[The Court also considered Ryan's fault in agreeing to the transaction:] It is hard to say that Ryan exercised ordinary care of a prudent man in entering this transaction. He did not understand the transaction and appears to have naively placed himself entirely into Mr. Weiner's hands. But while Ryan appears as a financial innocent upon whom Mr. Weiner could practice his skills, Weiner appears a manipulative and skillful predator. When one with substantially greater knowledge, experience, and resources himself seeks out the powerless to deal with them directly on matters of vital importance, he assumes some responsibility to assure, to the extent circumstances permit, that they do understand the nature of the transaction proposed. If he does not do this and if the transaction he initiates is oppressive and shockingly one-sided, he cannot retain the bargain. Even if Weiner did not affirmatively deceive Mr. Ryan (as to which I make no finding), he did not assure that the party from whom he attempted to extract so much understood the nature of this transaction. It was this fact more than Ryan's lack of care that accounts for Mr. Ryan's unilateral mistake of thinking he was signing a secured loan.

It is possible to restore the status quo. On one level, the transaction was entirely financial. Ryan never moved out of his house. The mortgage was not paid off by Mr. Weiner; rather he made monthly payments from the payments that Ryan made to him. Thus it is not difficult to return the parties to the status quo as of May, 1984. All that is required is for Mr. Weiner to establish what he paid on account of the house: mortgage, taxes, insurance, heat, utilities and maintenance. These amounts, including the expenditures necessary to bring the mortgage up to date in May 1984 appear to total $12,149.27. They will be credited to him. On the other hand the $21,480.00 paid by Mr. Ryan to Mr. Weiner should be credited to him. After this operation is gone through (and tax adjusted) a net amount will be owing to Mr. Ryan. Interest is a matter upon which the parties should be heard, if they cannot resolve it. Surely Mr. Weiner is entitled to a fair rate of interest on any amounts of credit that he had extended, for so long as he was a net lender into the transaction. It is, however, not clear in the record how long a time passed before all net expenditures were fully recovered from "rental" payments in excess of mortgage payments. Counsel can work out those details. The significant point is that there is no factor that would preclude the entry of an order that will return defendant, financially speaking, to the position he occupied when he went to Mr. Ryan's home to induce a transaction.

* * *

Thus I conclude that this transaction is one that, under principles applied for more than two hundred years, cannot in equity be allowed to stand.[4] I conclude that it involves shockingly unconscionable financial terms, coupled with innocent failure to understand the transaction on one side and sharp and predatory practices on the other. I am satisfied that

[4] I accept the evidence that Ryan has only recently realized that he sold his house absolutely to Norman Weiner in 1984 and that he has proceeded promptly thereafter to adjudicate his rights. More importantly I cannot conclude that any delay in asserting this claim has substantially prejudiced Mr. Weiner. He has made no such claim with respect to his defense of this lawsuit and with respect to his financial position, the rescission to be afforded to plaintiff contemplates that defendant will be restored to the May 1984 status quo financially. Thus, I find no detriment to defendant from the passage of time.

these facts clearly are the equivalent of cases in which courts have set aside land transfers as fraudulent or constructively fraudulent.

The plaintiff may submit a form of order consistent with the foregoing, on notice.

UNIFORM COMMERCIAL CODE § 2–302.

Unconscionable Contract or Clause

(1) If the court as a matter of law finds the contract or any clause of the contract to have been unconscionable at the time it was made the court may refuse to enforce the contract, or it may enforce the remainder of the contract without the unconscionable clause, or it may so limit the application of any unconscionable clause as to avoid any unconscionable result.

(2) When it is claimed or appears to the court that the contract or any clause thereof may be unconscionable the parties shall be afforded a reasonable opportunity to present evidence as to its commercial setting, purpose and effect to aid the court in making the determination.

B. PROCEDURAL AND SUBSTANTIVE UNCONSCIONABILITY

INDUSTRALEASE AUTOMATED & SCIENTIFIC EQUIPMENT CORP. V. R.M.E. ENTERPRISES, INC.

New York Supreme Court, Appellate Division, 1977.
58 A.D.2d 482, 396 N.Y.S.2d 427.

HOPKINS, JUSTICE PRESIDING.

The primary issue before us is whether disclaimers of express and implied warranties in a lease of industrial equipment are unconscionable under the circumstances where the equipment never operated (see Uniform Commercial Code [UCC], §§ 2–302, 2–316). * * *

* * *

The defendant R.M.E. Enterprises, Inc. (Enterprises) owned a 40-acre picnic grove in Warren, New Jersey. The operation of the grove necessarily generated considerable refuse during the season, which begins in May. Prior to the events involved in this litigation, the trash was piled in 40-foot open-top steel containers and disposed of by a rubbish collector. Enterprises was wholly owned by the defendant Max Evans who, with his wife, the defendant Irene Evans, managed the picnic grove.

Max Evans became interested in disposing of the rubbish through nonpollutant burning on the premises. He visited Farmingdale, New York, at the invitation of Clean Air Controls, Inc. (Clean Air) to inspect equipment in operation which, Clean Air informed him, would meet the requirements of Enterprises. Impressed with what he saw, he told Clean Air that he would take two units, one to be in reserve if the other broke down. Eventually, on February 24, 1971, a lease between Clean Air and Enterprises was executed, providing for 60 monthly payments of $322.58 in return for the use of the two units. The lease also contained a clause generally disclaiming any warranties, except that it preserved the warranties if the lessor were the manufacturer of the equipment.[1] As Clean Air was the manufacturer of the leased equipment, under the language of the lease the usual warranties were thus in force for the benefit of Enterprises.

Thereafter, acting under instructions, Evans installed a concrete slab, underground wiring and a fuel tank. Evans testified that on May 13, 1971 (and this is not contested by the plaintiff) he was visited by a representative of Clean Air and a representative of the plaintiff who presented him with a set of new papers which "were like the other papers I signed but with a different company's name on the top", that he was told that the lease he had signed before was "no good", and that the new papers had to be signed "so we can get our money so you can get your incinerator." Evans testified that he signed the new papers, which were a lease between Enterprises and the plaintiff for the same equipment, providing for 60 monthly rental payments of $319.70, plus sales tax, and a guaranty by Max and Irene Evans of the lease. That lease contained an unqualified disclaimer of express and implied warranties.[2] It also contained an option which granted the right to Enterprises to acquire the equipment at the end of the lease by a payment to the plaintiff in the sum of $1,390.

On May 14, 1971, the next day, the incinerators were delivered and installed. Evans testified (and his testimony was not contested by the plaintiff) that they did not then or thereafter work, although he complained to both Clean Air and to the plaintiff, which tried in vain to make the equipment operative. Enterprises during this period made four rental payments to the plaintiff. By letters dated September 16, 1971 and

---

1 The lease provided, in bold print:

"9. Lessor makes no warranties with respect to the fitness or suitability of the Leased Property for any purpose or use or with respect to its durability. Lessee acknowledges that the Leased Property is of a size, design and capacity selected by Lessee as suitable for its purposes. Lessor makes no warranties, expressed or implied, with respect to the Leased Property other than that, if new, the standard manufacturer's warranty of new equipment is in effect and Lessor will exercise its rights thereunder for the mutual benefit of Lessor and Lessee (or if Lessor be the manufacturer, it will comply with the terms and conditions of its warranty)."

2 The lease provided, in bold print:

"2.C. (12) Representations. And Lessee does hereby agree that each unit is of a size, design, capacity, and material selected by Lessee, and that Lessee is satisfied that each such unit is suitable for Lessee's purposes, and sufficiently durable under the conditions of usage thereof by Lessee, and that Lessor has made no representations or warranties with respect to the suitability or durability of any unit for the purposes or uses of Lessee, or with respect to the permissible load thereof, or any other representation or warranty, express or implied, with respect thereto."

December 30, 1971, Enterprises demanded the removal of the incinerators from its premises, but the plaintiff did not accede and required the continuance of the monthly payments.

This litigation then ensued.

The plaintiff's complaint sought $17,936.76, representing the balance of the payments due under the lease, together with the sum of $2,500 for legal expenses. The defendants denied liability, claiming that the plaintiff had breached its warranty that the equipment was properly constructed, free of operational defects, and capable of meeting the need of disposing of the rubbish accumulated as the result of its business: and the defendants counterclaimed in addition for the sum of $5,000, alleged to have been incurred as expenses by them in installing the equipment and attempting to make it function properly.

At the trial the court held that the disclaimer of warranties contained in the lease was not unconscionable as a matter of law. The court left to the jury the determination of the issue whether the plaintiff had made express warranties concerning the capacity of the incinerators to function properly, instructing the jury that if in fact the warranties had been made, and the incinerators had not worked properly, the plaintiff had breached its contract.

The jury returned a verdict on the complaint in favor of the defendants and awarded the defendants $1,342.76 on their counterclaim.

[The court first concluded that the U.C.C. applied to the lease because the lease "assumed the true model of a sale."]

* * *

The UCC plainly recognizes the validity of disclaimers of warranties in sales agreements under certain circumstances (UCC, § 2–316). Here, pursuant to the statute, the exclusion of warranties was accomplished by conspicuous and bold print and thus complied with the statute in that respect. The question whether in this case the disclaimer is unconscionable remains.

The defendants had raised the issue of unconscionability at the trial. Trial Term held that the disclaimer was not unconscionable, but submitted to the jury the issues whether the plaintiff had made express warranties concerning the capacity and operating ability of the incinerators and whether the warranties had been breached by the plaintiff. The submission of these issues was, however, in direct conflict with the language of the disclaimer, which excluded reliance by the defendant on any such warranties. Hence, a reversal of the judgment must be directed, unless, on examination of the facts and the language of the disclaimer, we conclude that the disclaimer is unenforceable because of its unconscionability, in which event the issues of the making of express warranties and their breach would survive and hence were properly submitted to the jury. We turn, accordingly, to the question whether under the circumstances of this case the disclaimer is unconscionable.

Section 2–302 of the UCC provides that the court may refuse to enforce a contract clause once it finds the clause to have been unconscionable at the time it was made. The determination of unconscionability is a matter of law for the court to decide * * * and thus subject to our review. The Official Comment to section 2–302 states that it "is intended to allow the court to pass directly on the unconscionability of the contract or particular clause therein and to make a conclusion of law as to its unconscionability", and that "[t]he basic test is whether, in the light of the general commercial background and the commercial needs of the particular trade or case, the clauses involved are so one-sided as to be unconscionable under the circumstances existing at the time of the making of the contract". * * * The term "unconscionable" is thus flexible, to be applied within the framework of the transaction under scrutiny, and considered in the light of the commercial climate then existing and the common law.

Though unconscionability, as an element in the enforcement of contracts, is equitable in origin, there is evidence to sustain the conclusion that the common-law courts as well were moved by the doctrine to invalidate contracts under certain circumstances (1 Corbin on Contracts, § 128, p. 551). The original concept was broad: An unconscionable contract was one "such as no man in his senses and not under delusion would make on the one hand, and as no honest and fair man would accept on the other" (*Earl of Chesterfield v. Janssen,* 2 Ves.Sen. 125, 155, 28 Eng.Reprint 82, 100; cf. *Hume v. United States,* 132 U.S. 406, 411, 10 S.Ct. 134, 33 L.Ed. 393). The test has been more sharply defined "to include an absence of meaningful choice on the part of one of the parties together with contract terms which are unreasonably favorable to the other party", and characterized "by a gross inequality of bargaining power" (*Williams v. Walker-Thomas Furniture Co.,* 121 U.S.App.D.C. 315, 350 F.2d 445, 449). In dealing with the doctrine, commentators have differentiated between procedural and substantive unconscionability. * * *[3] We need not treat that distinction here, for we think that components of both aspects are present. Moreover, in considering the question, we have put aside the cases holding disclaimers of warranties invalid as against public policy in which damages arising from personal injuries were sought to be recovered * * * for we think different considerations are there present. * * *

[3] Procedural unconscionability in general is involved with the contract formation process, and focuses on high pressures exerted on the parties, fine print of the contract, misrepresentation, or unequal bargaining position. Substantive unconscionability, on the other hand, is involved with the content of the terms of the contract per se, such as inflated prices, unfair disclaimers or termination clauses (see *Nu Dimensions Figure Salons v. Becerra,* 73 Misc.2d 140, 143, 340 N.Y.S.2d 268, 272).

We must begin the examination of the facts underlying the contract with the awareness that "[p]arties to a contract are given broad latitude within which to fashion their own remedies for breach of contract" * * * and that under the UCC "the obligations of good faith, diligence, reasonableness and care prescribed by this Act may not be disclaimed" (UCC. § 1–102, subd. [3] * * *). Here the evidence is that shortly before the incinerators were to be delivered, the defendants were told that the contract in existence between themselves and Clean Air could not be performed for not clearly communicated reasons, and that a new contract had to be executed to insure delivery of the equipment. The new contract eliminated the warranties which the Clean Air contract had preserved, since Clean Air was the manufacturer of the equipment. The atmosphere of haste and pressure on the defendants is clearly pervasive. In addition, at this point of the bargaining, with the beginning of the season for the defendants' operations at hand, the defendants were clearly at a disadvantage to bargain further and, indeed, did not profess to understand the size and mechanism of the equipment which would satisfy their needs.

Thus, the defendants did not pretend to have equal expertise in the field; they had dealt with Clean Air as purchasers seeking a means to meet a necessity arising in the business, and Clean Air undertook to design and build equipment to achieve the desired result. The interposition of the plaintiff in the transaction served only the purpose of Clean Air and not of the defendants.

Although the statute prescribes that we are to determine unconscionability as of the time of the making of the contract (UCC, § 2–302), we cannot divorce entirely the events which occur later. In this case, the evidence plainly establishes that the equipment did not work at all, that it achieved none of the purposes of the parties. This is a result so "one-sided", in the words of the authors of the Official Comment to the UCC, that the disclaimer in good conscience should not be enforced. In effect, the equipment was worthless. * * *

We therefore hold that the disclaimer of warranties is unconscionable under the circumstances and may not be enforced.

We thus conclude that as the jury found that the plaintiff had made express warranties to the defendants concerning the incinerators and that the warranties had been breached, the judgment should be affirmed.

NOTE: *PROCEDURAL AND SUBSTANTIVE UNCONSCIONABILITY*

In his leading article on unconscionability,[d] Professor Arthur Leff suggested a framework that many courts have followed. He wrote that the

[d] Leff, Unconscionability and the Code—The Emperor's New Clause, 115 U.Pa.L.Rev. 485 (1967).

paradigm case for finding unconscionability involves both "bargaining naughtiness," which he characterized as procedural unconscionability, and grossly unfair terms, which he called substantive unconscionability. One can see Professor Leff's analysis at work in the Industralease case.

Because of remaining ambiguities about the proper "mix" of procedural and substantive unconscionability required for a finding of unconscionability and because of the widespread view that the "best" case for finding unconscionability will include a healthy sprinkling of both, courts may go to some lengths to find both. Can an argument be made that Industralease really did *not* involve substantive unconscionability? Consider first sections 2–313 and 2–314 of the Uniform Commercial Code (involving the creation of warranties) and section 2–316 (involving exclusion or modification of warranties), all of which also applied to the case. (You should also review Section 8 of Chapter 2.) Compare, too, the Dillman case, which follows the UCC provisions:

UNIFORM COMMERCIAL CODE § 2–316.

Exclusion or Modification of Warranties

(1) Words or conduct relevant to the creation of an express warranty and words or conduct tending to negate or limit warranty shall be construed wherever reasonable as consistent with each other; but * * * negation or limitation is inoperative to the extent that such construction is unreasonable.

(2) Subject to subsection (3), to exclude or modify the implied warranty or merchantability or any part of it the language must mention merchantability and in case of a writing must be conspicuous, and to exclude or modify any implied warranty of fitness the exclusion must be by a writing and conspicuous. Language to exclude all implied warranties of fitness is sufficient if it states, for example, that "There are no warranties which extend beyond the description on the face hereof."

(3) Notwithstanding subsection (2)

(a) unless the circumstances indicate otherwise, all implied warranties are excluded by expressions like "as is", "with all faults" or other language which in common understanding calls the buyer's attention to the exclusion of warranties and makes plain that there is no implied warranty; and

(b) when the buyer before entering into the contract has examined the goods or the sample or model as fully as he desired or has refused to examine the goods there is no implied warranty with regard to defects which an examination ought in the circumstances to have revealed to him; and

(c) an implied warranty can also be excluded or modified by course of dealing or course of performance or usage of trade.

DILLMAN & ASSOCIATES, INC. v. CAPITOL LEASING CO., 110 Ill.App.3d 335, 66 Ill.Dec. 39, 442 N.E.2d 311 (1982). [In an equipment lease, the lessor disclaimed all responsibility for the performance of the leased equipment. Plaintiff, in the income tax return preparation business, complained that a copying machine it had leased from defendant was defective and that the defendant's disclaimer of all warranties on the preprinted lease was unconscionable. The disclaimer included the following language:

> "THERE ARE NO WARRANTIES, EXPRESSED OR IMPLIED OF MERCHANTABILITY, FITNESS, OR OTHERWISE WHICH EXTEND BEYOND THE ABOVE DESCRIPTION OF THE EQUIPMENT. LESSOR ASSUMES NO RESPONSIBILITY FOR PERFORMANCE OR MAINTENANCE. EQUIPMENT WILL BE INSURED BY LESSEE."
>
> " * * * Lessee acknowledges and agrees (1) that each unit is of a size, design, capacity and manufacture selected by Lessee, (2) that Lessee is satisfied that the same is suitable for its purpose, (3) that LESSOR IS NOT A MANUFACTURER THEREOF NOR A DEALER IN PROPERTY OF SUCH KIND, and (4) that LESSOR HAS NOT MADE, AND DOES NOT HEREBY MAKE, ANY REPRESENTATION OR WARRANTY OR COVENANT WITH RESPECT TO THE MERCHANTABILITY, CONDITION, QUALITY, DURABILITY OR SUITABILITY OF ANY SUCH UNIT IN ANY RESPECT OR IN CONNECTION WITH OR FOR THE PURPOSES AND USES OF LESSEE, OR ANY OTHER REPRESENTATION OR WARRANTY OR COVENANT OF ANY KIND OF CHARACTER, EXPRESS OR IMPLIED, WITH RESPECT THERETO.
>
> * * * AS BETWEEN LESSOR AND LESSEE, THE EQUIPMENT SHALL BE ACCEPTED AND LEASED BY LESSEE 'AS IS' AND IF ANY FAULTS PREVAIL LESSEE AGREES TO SETTLE ALL SUCH CLAIMS DIRECTLY WITH THE SUPPLIER AND WILL NOT ASSERT ANY SUCH CLAIMS AGAINST LESSOR OR LESSOR'S ASSIGNEE."
>
> "NO REPRESENTATION REGARDING THE EQUIPMENT HEREIN LEASED HAS BEEN MADE BY CAPITOL LEASING COMPANY. LESSEE HAS SELECTED THE PROPERTY TO BE LEASED AND IT IS ORDERED BY CAPITOL LEASING

COMPANY FOR THIS LESSEE AND AT LESSEE'S ENTIRE DIRECTION AND RISK."

The court stated:]

The lease before us, was * * * entered into by businessmen of equal sophistication. This is not the case of an experienced businessman taking unfair advantage of a poorly educated consumer. Although plaintiff was under no compulsion to lease the equipment and could presumably have purchased it either outright or through the use of conventional financing, it chose to obtain a new copying machine by leasing one for reasons which do not appear in the record. After deciding to lease a new copier, the plaintiff was free to select the machine which would best suit its needs and circumstances. Upon making its selection, the plaintiff signed a lease which contained conspicuous, and thus legally binding * * * disclaimers of warranty in not one, but in three locations. The defendant fulfilled its contractual obligations by purchasing and delivering to plaintiff the machine which plaintiff chose. Apparently, the copier which plaintiff received was either defectively manufactured or was inadequate to handle plaintiff's volume of copying. Plaintiff now asks us to declare the lease unconscionable because it is unable to assert against the lessor claims as to the equipment's inadequacy, for which the lessor bears no responsibility whatsoever. We cannot accede to this request. Courts should not assume an overly paternalistic attitude toward the parties to a contract by relieving one or another of them of the consequences of what is at worst a bad bargain * * *, and in declaring the lease in issue here unconscionable, we would be doing exactly that.

DAVIS v. KOLB, 263 Ark. 158, 563 S.W.2d 438 (1978).

BYRD, JUSTICE.

Appellant Ronnie Davis obtained a timber deed to a 294 acre tract from the appellees, Joseph E. Kolb, et al. The consideration recited in the timber deed was: "First $10,500 to [appellees]; next $2,000 to [appellant], all remaining to be divided fifty/fifty after payment of costs of removal of timber." The chancellor set aside the timber deed on the basis that appellant had misrepresented his experience and knowledge as a timber buyer to the appellees and that since appellant was not an experienced timber buyer, the deed was not supported by consideration. For reversal appellant contends:

I. The chancellor's finding of no consideration is clearly against the preponderance of the evidence.

II. The particular misrepresentation found was not a sufficient ground for cancellation of the timber deed because it was not material to the execution of the deed.

The record shows that during the negotiations, appellant led the appellees to believe that appellant was knowledgeable about the value of timber and that appellant was going to cut and remove the timber. Appellant does not deny that he told appellees during the negotiations that the timber was worth $18,000 to $20,000. After obtaining the contract, appellant started trying to sell his contract to someone else and readily admits that he was shocked to find out that the timber had a value in excess of $50,000.

While we do not disagree with the reasoning of the chancellor, and without intending to indicate that his findings are not sufficient to affirm the setting aside of the deed, we affirm upon the basis of Ark.Stat.Ann. § 85–2–302 (Add.1961), which provides: [the Court set forth U.C.C. § 2–302].

The Uniform Commercial Code is made applicable to timber sales by Ark.Stat.Ann. § 85–2–107 (Add.1961).

When we add to the undisputed facts the further fact that appellant had no capital invested and no risk, it would be unconscionable for any court to enforce the contract. See Annotation 18 A.L.R.3d 1305.

Affirmed.

HILLMAN, DEBUNKING SOME MYTHS ABOUT UNCONSCIONABILITY: A NEW FRAMEWORK FOR U.C.C. SECTION 2–302

67 Cornell L.Rev. 1, 19 (1981).

Simply stated, the application of unconscionability to cases involving bargaining problems without reference to the common law [policing] doctrines causes confusion by increasing the level of abstraction in judicial reasoning. For example, instead of determining whether the specific elements of fraud or duress exist, a court using the current unconscionability approach may merely list the many factors influencing its decision—*e.g.*, age, status, intelligence, business sophistication, bargaining power, explanation (or the lack thereof) of terms, firmness of the seller's position (the take-it-or-leave-it approach), and availability of alternative sources of supply—and then simply conclude that the contract is or is not unconscionable. The court need not make any effort to show which factors are essential, which are sufficient, and which are superfluous. Consequently, factors previously subsumed under appropriate common law categories simply may be lumped together without consideration of their weight and effect.

JONES V. STAR CREDIT CORP.

Supreme Court of New York, Special Term, Nassau County, 1969.
59 Misc.2d 189, 298 N.Y.S.2d 264.

SOL M. WACHTLER, JUSTICE.

On August 31, 1965 the plaintiffs, who are welfare recipients, agreed to purchase a home freezer unit for $900 as the result of a visit from a salesman representing Your Shop At Home Service, Inc. With the addition of the time credit charges, credit life insurance, credit property insurance, and sales tax, the purchase price totaled $1,234.80. Thus far the plaintiffs have paid $619.88 toward their purchase. The defendant claims that with various added credit charges paid for an extension of time there is a balance of $819.81 still due from the plaintiffs. The uncontroverted proof at the trial established that the freezer unit, when purchased, had a maximum retail value of approximately $300. The question is whether this transaction and the resulting contract could be considered unconscionable within the meaning of Section 2–302 of the Uniform Commercial Code * * *.

There was a time when the shield of "caveat emptor" would protect the most unscrupulous in the marketplace—a time when the law, in granting parties unbridled latitude to make their own contracts, allowed exploitive and callous practices which shocked the conscience of both legislative bodies and the courts.

The effort to eliminate these practices has continued to pose a difficult problem. On the one hand it is necessary to recognize the importance of preserving the integrity of agreements and the fundamental right of parties to deal, trade, bargain, and contract. On the other hand there is the concern for the uneducated and often illiterate individual who is the victim of gross inequality of bargaining power, usually the poorest members of the community.

Concern for the protection of these consumers against overreaching by the small but hardy breed of merchants who would prey on them is not novel. The dangers of inequality of bargaining power were vaguely recognized in the early English common law when Lord Hardwicke wrote of a fraud, which "may be apparent from the intrinsic nature and subject of the bargain itself; such as no man in his senses and not under delusion would make." The English authorities on this subject were discussed in Hume v. United States, 132 U.S. 406, 411, 10 S.Ct. 134, 136, 33 L.Ed. 393 (1889) where the United States Supreme Court characterized (p. 413, 10 S.Ct. p. 137) these as "cases in which one party took advantage of the other's ignorance of arithmetic to impose upon him, and the fraud was apparent from the face of the contracts."

The law is beginning to fight back against those who once took advantage of the poor and illiterate without risk of either exposure or interference. From the common law doctrine of intrinsic fraud we have, over the years, developed common and statutory law which tells not only the buyer but also the seller to beware. This body of laws recognizes the importance of a free enterprise system but at the same time will provide the legal armor to protect and safeguard the prospective victim from the harshness of an unconscionable contract.

Section 2–302 of the Uniform Commercial Code enacts the moral sense of the community into the law of commercial transactions. It authorizes the court to find, as a matter of law, that a contract or a clause of a contract was "unconscionable at the time it was made", and upon so finding the court may refuse to enforce the contract, excise the objectionable clause or limit the application of the clause to avoid an unconscionable result. "The principle", states the Official Comment to this section, "is one of the prevention of oppression and unfair surprise". It permits a court to accomplish directly what heretofore was often accomplished by construction of language, manipulations of fluid rules of contract law and determinations based upon a presumed public policy.

There is no reason to doubt, moreover, that this section is intended to encompass the price term of an agreement. In addition to the fact that it has already been so applied (State by Lefkowitz v. ITM, Inc., 52 Misc.2d 39, 275 N.Y.S.2d 303; Frostifresh Corp. v. Reynoso, 52 Misc.2d 26, 274 N.Y.S.2d 757, revd. 54 Misc.2d 119, 281 N.Y.S.2d 964; American Home Improvement, Inc. v. MacIver, 105 N.H. 435, 201 A.2d 886, 14 A.L.R.3d 324), the statutory language itself makes it clear that not only a clause of the contract, but the contract in toto, may be found unconscionable as a matter of law. Indeed, no other provision of an agreement more intimately touches upon the question of unconscionability than does the term regarding price.

Fraud, in the instant case, is not present; nor is it necessary under the statute. The question which presents itself is whether or not, under the circumstances of this case, the sale of a freezer unit having a retail value of $300 for $900 ($1,439.69 including credit charges and $18 sales tax) is unconscionable as a matter of law. The court believes it is.

Concededly, deciding the issue is substantially easier than explaining it. No doubt, the mathematical disparity between $300, which presumably includes a reasonable profit margin, and $900, which is exorbitant on its face, carries the greatest weight. Credit charges alone exceed by more than $100 the retail value of the freezer. These alone, may be sufficient to sustain the decision. Yet, a caveat is warranted lest we reduce the import of Section 2–302 solely to a mathematical ratio formula. It may, at times, be that; yet it may also be much more. The very limited financial resources of the purchaser, known to the sellers at the time of the sale, is entitled to weight in the balance. Indeed, the value disparity itself leads inevitably to the felt conclusion that knowing advantage was taken of the plaintiffs. In addition, the meaningfulness of choice essential to the making of a contract, can be negated by a gross inequality of bargaining power. (Williams v. Walker-Thomas Furniture Co., 121 U.S.App.D.C. 315, 350 F.2d 445.)

There is no question about the necessity and even the desirability of instalment sales and the extension of credit. Indeed, there are many, including welfare recipients, who would be deprived of even the most basic conveniences without the use of these devices. Similarly, the retail merchant selling on instalment or extending credit is expected to establish a pricing factor which will afford a degree of protection commensurate with the risk of selling to those who might be default prone. However, neither of these accepted premises can clothe the sale of this freezer with respectability.

Support for the court's conclusion will be found in a number of other cases already decided. In American Home Improvement, Inc. v. MacIver, supra, the Supreme Court of New Hampshire held that a contract to install windows, a door and paint, for the price of $2,568.60, of which $809.60 constituted interest and carrying charges and $800 was a salesman's commission was unconscionable as a matter of law. In State by Lefkowitz v. ITM, Inc., supra, a deceptive and fraudulent scheme was involved, but standing alone, the court held that the sale of a vacuum cleaner, among other things, costing the defendant $140 and sold by it for $749 cash or $920.52 on time purchase was unconscionable as a matter of law. Finally, in Frostifresh Corp. v. Reynoso, supra, the sale of a refrigerator costing the seller $348 for $900 plus credit charges of $245.88 was unconscionable as a matter of law.

* * *

Having already paid more than $600 toward the purchase of this $300 freezer unit, it is apparent that the defendant has already been amply compensated. In accordance with the statute, the application of the payment provision should be limited to amounts already paid by the plaintiffs and the contract be reformed and amended by changing the payments called for therein to equal the amount of payment actually so paid by plaintiffs.

JAMES v. NATIONAL FINANCIAL, LLC, 132 A.3d 799 (Ct. Chancery of Del. 2016). [James borrowed $200 from a finance company with the trade name "Loan Till Payday." James was to make twenty-six, bi-weekly, interest-only payments of $60. In addition to still another payment of $60, Jones was to pay the original principal of $200. "The total repayments added up to $1820, representing a cost of credit of $1620." The annual percentage rate for the loan was 838.45%. James defaulted and sought to rescind the loan. The court found that the terms of the loan were unconscionable. The surprise was that it took about 30 pages of discussion for the court to reach that conclusion. The court discussed ten factors that are probative of an unconscionability decision:]

This court has identified ten factors to guide the analysis of unconscionability. *See Fritz v. Nationwide Mut. Ins. Co.,* 1990 WL 186448 (Del. Ch. Nov. 26, 1990). In the language of the *Fritz* decision, they are:

> (1) The use of printed form or boilerplate contracts drawn skillfully by the party in the strongest economic position, which establish industry wide standards ***815** offered on a take it or leave it basis to the party in a weaker economic position[;]
>
> (2) a significant cost-price disparity or excessive price;
>
> (3) a denial of basic rights and remedies to a buyer of consumer goods[;]
>
> (4) the inclusion of penalty clauses;
>
> (5) the circumstances surrounding the execution of the contract, including its commercial setting, its purpose and actual effect[;]
>
> (6) the hiding of clauses which are disadvantageous to one party in a mass of fine print trivia or in places which are inconspicuous to the party signing the contract[;]
>
> (7) phrasing clauses in language that is incomprehensible to a layman or that divert his attention from the problems raised by them or the rights given up through them;
>
> (8) an overall imbalance in the obligations and rights imposed by the bargain;
>
> (9) exploitation of the underprivileged, unsophisticated, uneducated and the illiterate[;] and
>
> (10) inequality of bargaining or economic power.

GIESEL, A NEW LOOK AT CONTRACT MISTAKE DOCTRINE AND PERSONAL INJURY RELEASES

19 Nv.L. J. 535, 577–78 (2018).

Unfortunately, the typical personal injury releasor likely will not find the unconscionability doctrine to be a friendly port in the storm. Such a plaintiff must illustrate that the release was procedurally unconscionable. The typical release and settlement that the release is a part of is not a complex transaction. The plaintiff gets money in exchange for ceasing to pursue any claim against the other party. The actual release document is often one or two pages and the language used is relatively clear that the injured party is releasing his or her claim for all injuries related to the event, whether or not the injuries are known at the time of the release. The release is often the product of some negotiation over time with the actual amount to be paid changing in the midst of the back-and-forth. While it is certainly true that in most cases the injured party does not create the language of the release and simply accepts that language, it is also true that the injured party could refuse to enter into the agreement if the terms are unacceptable or could demand more in exchange for the executed release. Often, the releasor has the benefit of an attorney's assistance as well. In such circumstances it is difficult to find that the release is the product of procedural unconscionability.

An injured party might have an easier time illustrating that the deal is substantively unconscionable but only if the determination of unconscionability is made after the injuries have all come to light. Yet, the unconscionability doctrine requires that the determination of unconscionability be a determination that the agreement was unconscionable at the time of the formation of the release, not as it later appears with the benefit of hindsight. Thus, the unconscionability doctrine, if properly applied, will rarely be the basis for a refusal to enforce a personal injury release.

CHALK v. T-MOBILE USA, INC., 560 F.3d 1087 (9th Cir. 2009). [Consumers, including Stewart and Chalk, brought a class action lawsuit in federal court against T-Mobile for selling a defective wireless card. The trial court upheld a class action waiver in an arbitration provision and dismissed the action. On appeal, the Ninth Circuit, applying Oregon law, held that the class-action waiver was not procedurally unconscionable because

> "[t]he take-it-or-leave-it nature of T-Mobile's agreement is insufficient to render it unenforceable. Stewart's signature appears on the Service Agreement below the arbitration clause and class action waiver—both of which are featured in boldface and uppercase text. * * * Under these circumstances, there is insufficient evidence of oppression or surprise to render the agreement procedurally unconscionable under Oregon law."

However, the court found the class-action waiver to be substantively unconscionable and struck the provisions on that ground alone.]

REINHARDT, CIRCUIT JUDGE.

The arbitration agreement, while not procedurally unconscionable, was adhesive and therefore reflected an underlying inequality in the parties' ability to bargain. * * * Because Oregon law does not *require* that a contract exhibit procedural unconscionability in order to be invalid * * * we must still determine whether the terms of T-Mobile's arbitration agreement are unfairly onesided. [Based on *Vasquez-Lopez v. Beneficial Oregon, Inc.*, 152 P.3d 940 (Or. 2007)], we conclude that the class action waiver in the present case is substantively unconscionable and unenforceable under Oregon law.

The *Vasquez-Lopez* court explained that a class action waiver in a consumer contract is unreasonably favorable to a company like T-Mobile for two distinct reasons. First, such a waiver is inherently one-sided when contained in a consumer contract. *Id.* Even if the waiver on its face applies equally to both parties, it is entirely unilateral in effect. Wryly noting the well-known literary passage that " 'the majestic equality of the laws * * * forbid[s] rich and poor alike to sleep under the bridges, to beg in the streets, and to steal their bread,' " the Oregon Court of Appeals observed, "Although the arbitration rider with majestic equality forbids lenders as well as borrowers from bringing class actions, the likelihood of the lender seeking to do so against its own customers is as likely as the rich seeking to sleep under bridges." *Id.* (quoting Anatole France, *The Red Lily* 95 (Winifred Stephens trans., Frederic Chapman ed., 1894)).

Second, a consumer class action waiver frequently prevents individuals from vindicating their rights. A ban on class action denies plaintiffs a crucial opportunity "without which many meritorious claims would simply not be filed" because the cost of pursuing each claim individually outweighs the potential relief. *Id.* At 950. " 'The policy at the very core of the class action mechanism is to overcome the problem that small recoveries do not provide the incentive for any individual to bring a solo action prosecuting his or her rights.' " *Id.* (quoting *Amchem Products Inc. v. Windsor,* 521 U.S. 591, 617, 117 S.Ct. 2231, 138 L.Ed.2d 689 (1997)). As *Vasquez-Lopez* explained, by preventing consumers from pursuing small but meritorious claims a class action waiver "gives defendant[s] a virtual license to commit, with impunity, millions of dollars' worth of small-scale fraud." *Id.* At 951.

Like the Supreme Courts of California and Washington, * * * the *Vasquez-Lopez* court declared that a class action waiver in a contract where individual damages are likely to be small is substantively unconscionable as a matter of state contract law. Because Defendants have presented no convincing evidence that Oregon's Supreme Court would disagree with *Vasquez-Lopez,* we must follow *Vasquez-Lopez* in determining whether T-Mobile's waiver is substantively unconscionable. * * *

The class action waiver in T-Mobile's Service Agreement presents the same problems that led the *Vasquez-Lopez* court to find substantive unconscionability in that case. First, like the class action waiver in *Vasquez-Lopez,* T-Mobile's waiver is unilateral in effect: It can hardly be imagined that T-Mobile or its suppliers would ever want or need to bring a class action against T-Mobile's customers.

Second, the class action waiver here creates the same disincentive to litigate recognized in *Vasquez-Lopez.* The actual damages alleged by Plaintiffs do not exceed $693.63, which includes the monthly service fee over the one-year contract duration and the cost of the card. * * * Moreover, many of the customer claims covered by the class action waiver will be much smaller than Plaintiffs' claim, because they will involve something less than a total hardware failure resulting in a complete loss of service. We must evaluate unconscionability "under the circumstances existing at the time of the making of the contract," *W.L. May Co., Inc. v. Philco-Ford Corp.,* 273 Or. 701, 543 P.2d 283, 286 (1975), and it is impossible to know at the time of formation whether a customer's future claims against T-Mobile will involve a total failure or something far less costly. These latter potential claims are as relevant to our analysis of the waiver's unconscionability as Plaintiffs' actual claim. * * *

* * *

Because T-Mobile's class action waiver is identical in effect to the class action waiver in *Vasquez-Lopez,* it is substantively unconscionable as a matter of Oregon law. We recognize that, under Oregon law, "every case [involving an allegedly unconscionable contract] is decided on its own facts," *id.* At 948, and, as in *Shroyer,* "[w]e do not hold that all class action waivers are necessarily unconscionable." 498 F.3d at 983. Instead, our decision simply applies the holding of *Vasquez-Lopez*—that a class action waiver in a consumer contract involving small claims is substantively unconscionable—to the virtually identical class action waiver in T-Mobile's arbitration agreement.

Conclusion

Under Oregon law, "only substantive unconscionability is absolutely necessary" to find that an agreement is unenforceable. *Vasquez-Lopez,* 152 P.3d at 948. Because Oregon courts have declared that class action waivers in consumer contracts where individual damages are likely to be small are substantively unconscionable and the waiver here was contained in a contract of adhesion, the class action waiver in T-Mobile's arbitration agreement is not enforceable. *Id.* At 950. Because the arbitration agreement prohibits severance of the waiver, the agreement as a whole is unenforceable. We therefore reverse the district court's decision to dismiss the case pending arbitration.

REVERSED and REMANDED.

R. HILLMAN, PRINCIPLES OF CONTRACT LAW

252–53 (4th ed. 2019).

[A] recent U.S. Supreme Court case appears to have overturned or at least placed severe limits on the holding in Chalk and other cases finding unconscionable terms in consumer contracts that waive class-action arbitration. In AT&T Mobility LLC v. Concepcion, [563 U.S. 333 (2011)] a 5–4 decision, the Court considered the effect of the Federal Arbitration Act (FAA) on such decisions. The FAA states in part that a written agreement to arbitrate "shall be valid, irrevocable, and enforceable, save upon such grounds as exist at law or in equity for the revocation of any contract." [9 U.S.C. § 2] You can see that this provision promotes arbitration and, as federal law [under the Supremacy Clause of the Constitution], it "preempts" (replaces) state law that would contradict it. At this point you might think that unconscionability is a ground that "exist[s] at law or in equity for the revocation of any contract." Therefore you would think that cases finding unconscionable waivers of class-action arbitration would be unaffected by the FAA. But the Supreme Court in Concepcion created confusion by finding that the FAA did preempt the California rule of Discover Bank v. Superior Court, [113 P.3d 1100 (Cal. 2005)] which rule barred such class action waivers if (1) they were in a standard-form consumer contract presented on a take-it-or-leave-it basis (an "adhesion" contract), (2) a small sum of money was at stake, and (3) the consumer alleged fraud. The Supreme Court reasoned that, contrary to the policies of the FAA, the Discover Bank rule narrows the freedom of parties to construct their own rules of arbitration and adds to the complexity of dispute resolution. [In part, the court reasoned that

> California's *Discover Bank* rule * * * interferes with arbitration. Although the rule does not *require* classwide arbitration, it allows any party to a consumer contract to demand it *ex post*. The rule is limited to adhesion contracts. *Discover Bank*, 36 Cal.4th, at 162–163, 30 Cal.Rptr.3d 76, 113 P.3d, at 1110, but the times in which consumer contracts were anything other than adhesive are long past. * * * The rule also requires that damages be predictably small, and that the consumer allege a scheme to cheat consumers. *Discover Bank, supra,* at 162–163, 30 Cal.Rptr.3d 76, 113 P.3d, at 1110. The former requirement, however, is toothless and malleable (the Ninth Circuit has held that damages of $4,000 are sufficiently small, see *Oestreicher v. Alienware Corp.*, 322 Fed.Appx. 489, 492 (2009) (unpublished)), and the latter has no limiting effect, as all that is required is an allegation. Consumers remain free to bring and resolve their disputes on a bilateral basis under *Discover Bank,* and some may well do so; but there is little incentive for lawyers to arbitrate on behalf of individuals when they may do so for a class and reap far higher fees in the process. And faced with inevitable class arbitration, companies would have less incentive to continue resolving potentially duplicative claims on an individual basis.]

According to the court, such law therefore has a "disproportionate impact on arbitration agreements," contrary to Congress's intent in enacting the FAA, and is therefore preempted.

The decision casts into doubt whether waivers of class-action arbitration in consumer contracts can ever be unconscionable, although some commentators and courts reason that Concepcion merely "precludes courts from *categorically* denying effect to waivers of class-wide arbitration in consumer contracts on grounds of unconscionability under state contract law." [George A. Bermann, Arbitration in the Roberts Supreme Court, 2012 Am. U. Int. L. Rev. 893, 908 and cases cited therein (emphasis added).] Indeed, the Concepcion case can be read narrowly to preclude a finding of unconscionability only under the factors enumerated in Discover Bank (listed above). However, a consumer often will be challenged to find additional factors that will convince a court to hold a waiver of class-action arbitration unconscionable. Cases involving evidence of strong procedural unconscionability, such as an Internet agreement in which the waiver is difficult to locate on the site, may provide an example of a "ground[ ] * * * at law or in equity for the revocation of any contract." At any rate, one can argue with some conviction that Concepcion simply reveals five justices' preference for enforcing standard terms, even if presented on a take-it-or-leave-it basis and under the cloud of fraud, and their quite passionate dislike of class actions.

CULLINANE v. UBER TECHNOLOGIES, 893 F.3d 53 (1st. Cir. 2018). [The court held that an arbitration clause was unenforceable in part because plaintiffs did not receive reasonable notice of Uber's terms of use that contained the clause. The hyperlink sending the plaintiffs to the terms of use "did not have the common appearance of a hyperlink." In addition, the hyperlink was surrounded by other terms with "more noticeable attributes."]

NEHF, WRITING CONTRACTS IN THE CLIENT'S INTEREST

51 S.C. L. Rev. 153, 169–70 (1999).

The drafting lawyer is put in a difficult position if the client insists on including a provision that is likely to be unenforceable. * * * The better course will usually be to explain to the client the legal principles involved and the potential ramifications for both lawyer and client if an unenforceable provision is included. Explanation of the exposure risks often persuades the client that the provision is not in her best interest.

KADENS, CHEATING PAYS

119 Colum. L. Rev. 527, 529–32 (2019).

Private-ordering theories * * * hold that merchants have an incentive to act honestly because they will get a bad reputation if they act dishonestly, and this will damage their future business prospects. This Essay argues that reputation-based private-ordering theories predict the wrong outcome [involving] low-level cheating * * * because they fail to recognize that not all opportunistic behavior is the same. Reputation-based private ordering that creates a disincentive for individuals or firms to commit big cheats may not effectively prevent * * * small cheats * * *.

The difference between big and small cheats lies primarily in the difficulty of discovery, the cheater's plausible deniability, and the victim's willingness to suffer the flawed performance in silence. The big cheat—failure to deliver or to pay, delivery of unusable goods, hold-up, or significant misrepresentation—will rarely pass unnoticed. But victims of small cheats—the chiseling, shirking, and taking advantage at the margins—may never detect the cheating. And if victims discover the breach, the cheat may be minor enough that they may not be sure whether a trading partner had merely made a mistake she will happily correct, committed an inadvertent breach that will never happen again, or deliberately wronged them. In addition, even if victims discover what they believe is low-level cheating, they may still prefer not to publicize it. Doing so may be too much effort; victims may want to continue to do business with the cheater; or they may not be certain that others will believe their claims that the cheater cheated. If victims do not realize they have been cheated or prefer not to impugn the cheater's reputation, they cannot leverage either private ordering or the courts to discipline the cheater.

* * *

Small cheats thus appear to raise governance challenges that neither public nor reputation-based private ordering can solve. Today, firms with bargaining power can put monitoring and verification terms into their contracts to try to prevent shirking and punish small cheats with liquidated damages. Consumers, by contrast, facing contracts of adhesion and unable to monitor the performance of the companies with which they transact, have limited options. They used to be able to use class actions to aggregate the small wrongs done to large numbers of individuals, but the Supreme Court has narrowed that avenue for redress. Those trying to leverage the power of reputation by posting complaints on social media could find themselves slapped with a commercial disparagement suit. The problem of consumer impotence in the face of low-level cheating has particular salience now that the American Law Institute is considering a draft Restatement of Consumer Contracts.

IN RE LISA FAY ALLEN, 174 B.R. 293 (Bkrtcy.Or.1994). [Lisa Allen leased a washer and dryer from Affordable Rent-to-Own. One week later, Allen filed a voluntary petition for Chapter 13 bankruptcy relief. One issue before the court was whether the lease was unconscionable. The court found neither procedural nor substantive unconscionability. First, Affordable did not engage in "oppressive bargaining practices." After having been denied credit to purchase a washer and dryer at two stores, Allen saw Affordable's television advertisements and contacted it about leasing the equipment. Affordable approved her application on the telephone. Two delivery people from Affordable then delivered the equipment and gave her the lease to sign, which was "written in understandable terms." The lease disclosed the weekly payments, Allen's right to terminate, and her right to purchase for half the total weekly payments. Allen also "had the opportunity to read the lease before signing it."

Second, the terms of the lease were also not unreasonably favorable to Affordable. Affordable guaranteed that the equipment would work for the duration of the lease. Allen agreed to lease for a minimum of three months with the right to terminate thereafter. Although the lease payments for the duration of the lease would have been $1558.96 and Affordable had purchased the equipment for $523, Allen had the right to purchase it at any time for $779.48 (half of the total rental obligation). The court termed the purchase price as "not a shocking price."]

NOTE: UNCONSCIONABILITY AND REMEDY LIMITATIONS

Section 2–719 of the Uniform Commercial Code deals with remedy limitations. It provides:

> (1) Subject to the provisions of subsections (2) and (3) of this section and of the preceding section on liquidation and limitation of damages,
>
> > (a) the agreement may provide for remedies in addition to or in substitution for those provided in this Article and may limit or alter the measure of damages recoverable under this Article, as by limiting the buyer's remedies to return of the goods and repayment of the price or to repair and replacement of non-conforming goods or parts; and
> >
> > (b) resort to a remedy as provided is optional unless the remedy is expressly agreed to be exclusive, in which case it is the sole remedy.

> (2) Where circumstances cause an exclusive or limited remedy to fail of its essential purpose, remedy may be had as provided in this Act.
>
> (3) Consequential damages may be limited or excluded unless the limitation or exclusion is unconscionable. Limitation of consequential damages for injury to the person in the case of consumer goods is prima facie unconscionable but limitation of damages where the loss is commercial is not.
>
> Official Comment
>
> 1. Under this section parties are left free to shape their remedies to their particular requirements and reasonable agreement limiting or modifying remedies are to be given effect.
>
> However, it is of the very essence of a sales contract that at least minimum adequate remedies be available. * * *

Section 2–719 permits parties to "shape" their own remedies, and reflects the principle of freedom of contract. Nevertheless, because merchant sellers often can dictate terms to consumers, these sellers can often severely limit the remedies of the buyers. For example, although section 2–719(1)(b) states that an agreed remedy is presumed to be optional, sellers need only state that a remedy is exclusive to rebut the presumption.

In two respects, section 2–719 provides some protection for a buyer, however. First, we briefly encountered section 2–719(3), which tests the exclusion of consequential damages against the standard of unconscionability. Courts also often invoke the procedural-substantive analysis in this regard. An example is A & M Produce Co. v. FMC Corp., 135 Cal.App.3d 473, 186 Cal.Rptr. 114 (1982). In that case, certain machinery purchased by the buyer to harvest a tomato crop proved unsatisfactory. The buyer sought consequential damages despite an exclusion of such damages in the agreement. The court found the exclusion unconscionable because it was buried on the back page of a long form contract and not disclosed. In addition, consequential damages were "explicitly obvious" if the machinery was defective and the seller was the only party reasonably able to prevent the loss. But see Anderson v. Newmar Corp., 319 F. Supp. 2d 943 (D. Minn. 2004), where the court held that a consequential damages disclaimer in a sales contract for a mobile home was not unconscionable because the buyer had bought at least five prior mobile homes.

The second measure of protection for the buyer is the "failure of essential purpose" test of section 2–719(2). An agreed remedy may fail of its essential purpose for many reasons. For example, when the exclusive remedy calls for the seller to repair or replace defective parts, the remedy may fail of its essential purpose when the product causes damages to the buyer before it could be repaired or the parts replaced. The remedy also may fail of its essential purpose when the repairs or parts are unsatisfactory. See, e.g., Liberty Truck Sales, Inc. v. Kimbrel, 548 So.2d 1379 (Ala.1989); Riley v. Ford Motor Co., 442 F.2d 670 (5th Cir.1971).

The close connection between the failure of essential purpose test and the unconscionability standard should be obvious. In fact, in some cases, the court invokes both tests to invalidate a clause limiting the remedy to repair or replacement. For example, in Bosway Tube & Steel Corp. v. McKay Machine Co., 65 Mich.App. 426, 237 N.W.2d 488 (1975), the buyer purchased a machine for manufacturing both round and square metal tubing but the machine did not satisfactorily produce square tubing, which was the buyer's primary purpose in purchasing the machine. After some attempts at repair, the seller gave up. The remedy was limited to repair or replacement (although there was some question as to whether the limitation was part of the contract). The court stated, "[t]here is no question that the machine on delivery was grossly defective. Not only does the limitation of remedies provision fail of its essential purpose, but its application in this case would be unconscionable." *Id.* At 430, 237 N.W.2d at 490.

You should be careful not to confuse the concept of warranty disclaimer with the concept of remedy limitation. The former deals with a seller's attempts to limit its *liability* for defects, while the latter involves a seller's efforts to limit the *remedies* available to a buyer, assuming liability is established. This distinction is important for various reasons. For example, the requirements for a valid remedy limitation are not identical with the requirements for a valid disclaimer. Compare section 2–316 with section 2–719.

PRAIRIE RIVER HOME CARE, INC. V. PROCURA, LLC

United States District Court, District of Minnesota, 2019.
2019 WL 3021253.

JOHN R. TUNHEIM, CHIEF JUDGE.

* * *

Prairie River [a family-owned, unsophisticated (according to the court) company that performed in-home medical services for elderly and disabled people] contracted to buy a license to Procura's software, which never functioned properly on Prairie River's systems. * * *

* * *

* * * Because Prairie River has alleged facts sufficient to show that the contractual clauses limiting remedies and disclaiming consequential damages are invalid, the Court will deny Procura's motion to dismiss Prairie River's claims for consequential damages. * * *

* * *

The Agreement includes a "Warranty of Performance," warranting that the Software would "be capable of functioning substantially in accordance with its related [D]ocumentation" and "in a manner consistent with industry standards." It also required the Software to be substantially functional within 90 days of the Agreement's execution. Finally, it explicitly limits remedies to a refund and disclaims consequential damages and all implied warranties:

> **8.1 Basic Disclaimer.** EXCEPT AS EXPRESSLY PROVIDED IN SECTION 7, THE SOFTWARE . . . AND ALL MAINTENANCE SUPPORT AND PROFESSIONAL SERVICES ARE PROVIDED ON AN "AS IS" BASIS WITH NO OTHER WARRANTIES OF ANY KIND, AND, UNLESS OTHERWISE PRECLUDED BY LAW, LICENSOR DISCLAIMS ALL OTHER WARRANTIES, EXPRESS OR IMPLIED, INCLUDING WITHOUT LIMITATION ANY WARRANTY OF MERCHANTABILITY OR FITNESS FOR A PARTICULAR PURPOSE.
>
> **9.1 Disclaimer of Consequential Damages.** EXCEPT WITH RESPECT TO A PARTY'S INDEMNIFICATION OBLIGATOINS AS SET FORTH IN THIS AGREEMENT, NEITHER PARTY . . . SHALL BE LIABLE UNDER THIS TO THE OTHER PARTY OR ANY THIRD PARTY FOR ANY INDIRECT, SPECIAL, INCIDENTAL, PUNITIVE OR CONSEQUENTIAL LOSS OR DAMAGES OR ANY OTHER SIMILAR DAMAGES UNDER ANY THEORY OF LIABILITY.
>
> **9.2 Limitation of Liability.** EXCEPT WITH RESPECT TO LICENSOR'S INDEMNIFICATION OBLIGATION PURSUANT TO SECTION 11.1, BELOW, LICENSOR'S . . . TOTAL AGGREGATE LIABILITY TO CUSTOMER FOR ANY LOSS, COST, CLAIM OR DAMAGES OF ANY KIND ARISING OUT OF OR RELATED TO THIS AGREEMENT SHALL NOT EXCEED IN THE AGGREGATE THE AMOUNT OF FEES ACTUALLY PAID TO THE LICENSOR IN THE PREVIOUS TWELVE (12) MONTH PERIOD PRIOR TO THE INITIATION OF THE CLAIM BY CUSTOMER.

* * *

Software Failures at Prairie River

Although Procura had delivered a database to Prairie River by November 2015—within the 90-day window established by the Agreement—the Software wasn't functional at any Prairie River office until June 2016. Prairie River alleges that six major categories of software failures occurred after the Software was implemented. * * *

* * *

Prairie River's Claims for Consequential Damages

Procura moves to dismiss Prairie River's claims for consequential damages, citing the Agreement's damages and remedies limitation clauses.

Because contractual limitations on remedies and exclusions of consequential damages are independent inquiries under Illinois law, the Court will assess the validity of the clauses separately. * * *

i. Limitation on Remedies

Section 9.2 of the Agreement limits Procura's liability to the amount of fees paid by Prairie River in the twelve months preceding the notice of dispute. If valid, the effect of the section is to limit Prairie River's available remedies to a refund of the price paid for the Software (if paid in the preceding twelve months) and, accordingly, to exclude consequential damages. But if, as Prairie River argues, the limitation "fails of its essential purpose, it is as if that limitation of remedy does not exist for the purposes of the damages to which [Prairie River] is entitled."

"[W]hen a contract limits [a buyer's] remedy to return of the purchase price, the limited remedy fails of its essential purpose 'when goods have latent defects which are not discoverable upon receipt and reasonable inspection.'" *PDC Laboratories, Inc. v. Hach Co.*, 2009 WL 2605270, at *4 (C.D. Ill. Aug. 25, 2009) (citing *Leprino v. Intermountain Brick Co.*, 759 P.2d 835, 836 (Colo. App. 1988)). When the underlying good is "readily amenable to being returned to the seller before being used in a way that either consumed [the good] or involved [its] irreversible integration into something else," a refund remedy is less likely to fail of its essential purpose because the buyer has recourse to protect the value of her bargain. *BAE Systems Info. & Electronics Systems Integration, Inc. v. SpaceKey Components, Inc.*, 2013 WL 149656, at *4 (D.N.H. Jan. 11, 2013).

Here, the Software's defects were only discoverable after the Software was incorporated into Prairie River's computer systems, which occurred between eight and ten months after execution of the Agreement. The defects were not only latent, but of such a nature that Prairie River could not discover them until after it had spent considerable time, money, and other resources integrating the Software into its systems. Moreover, Procura repeatedly assured Prairie River that it could fix the problems with the Software, leaving Prairie River with no way of knowing that new problems would arise with each update and attempted fix. By the time Prairie River determined that it could not operate with the Software and abandoned it, more than twelve months had passed since it had paid Procura, which—under the limitation on remedies provision in the contract—would leave Prairie River with no remedy whatsoever. Considering all the circumstances, the Court finds that Prairie River has alleged facts sufficient to show that the limitation of remedy fails of its essential purpose.

ii. Damages Limitation Clause

The Court must next decide whether the Agreement's damages limitation clause requires dismissal of Prairie River's claims for consequential damages. Procura argues that the clause is unambiguous and enforceable, thus requiring dismissal of the claims. Prairie River counters that * * * the clause is invalid as unconscionable * * *.

a. Unconscionability

A contractual exclusion of consequential damages "is to be enforced unless unconscionable." *Razor* [v. *Hyundai Motor America,* 854 N.E.2d 607, 618 (Sup. Ct. Ill. 2006)] (citing 810 ILCS 5/2–719(3)). "If the court as a matter of law finds the contract or any clause of the contract to have been unconscionable at the time it was made the court may refuse to enforce the contract, or it may enforce the remainder of the contract without the unconscionable clause." 810 ILCS 5/2–302.

* * *

Prairie River argues that the Agreement's consequential damages exclusion is both procedurally and substantively unconscionable. With respect to procedural unconscionability, Prairie River argues that it entered the contract in an unfair bargaining position. Prairie River points to several factors, including Procura's sophistication relative to Prairie River, the pressure that Procura placed on Prairie River to enter the contract by September 30, and Prairie River's inability to discover defects in the Software prior to entering the contract due to Procura's alleged concealment of issues the Software had already caused for another company. Prairie River also argues that the clause is substantively unconscionable because, when implemented alongside the limitation on remedy, it would deprive Prairie River of any remedy for Procura's breach.

Viewing the facts in the light most favorable to Prairie River, the Court finds that Prairie River has pleaded facts sufficient to show that the Agreement's consequential damages exclusion is procedurally and substantively unconscionable. Considered together, the circumstances surrounding the execution of the Agreement suggest that Prairie River may not have had a reasonable opportunity to fully understand what it was agreeing to, including the nature of the product it contracted to buy, rendering the clause procedurally unconscionable. Of particular concern are the allegations that Procura placed pressure on Prairie River to enter the Agreement by September 30, 2015, and that Procura concealed known defects from Prairie River. Had Prairie River had more time to learn about the Software, explore references, and become informed of possible defects, it may have been in a different—and fairer—bargaining position. Additionally, because the consequential damages exclusion could leave Prairie River without any remedy, the Court finds it plausible that the clause is unreasonably favorable to Procura, and thus substantively unconscionable.

Lefebvre Intergraphics v. Sanden Machine Limited, which Procura asks the Court to rely on, does not compel a different conclusion. 946 F. Supp. 1358 (N.D. Ill. 1996). In that case, the plaintiff, a commercial printer, bought a printing press from the defendant pursuant to a contract. *Id.* At 1361. Prior to the sale, the defendant had represented that the printing press would operate in a "commercially reasonable manner," but failed to disclose that another customer had encountered problems with the same model in the past. *Id.* At 1363. The printer did not function properly, and the defendant's attempted repairs were unsuccessful. *Id.* At 1361–62. There, as here, the parties' contract included a consequential damages exclusion. *Id.* At 1370. The defendant moved to dismiss the plaintiff's claims for consequential damages. *Id.*

The *Lefebvre* court held that the contract's consequential damages exclusion was not unconscionable. *Id.* At 1372. The court noted that both parties were sophisticated businesses and that "nothing in [the] complaint indicate[d] any disparity in bargaining power." *Id.* The court also found it implausible that the plaintiff did not foresee the possibility of the printer's malfunction and expressed doubt as to the claim that the defendant acted in bad faith. *Id.*

As an initial matter, *Lefebvre* is not binding on this Court. Moreover, it is distinguishable from the present case in key respects. The plaintiff in *Lefebvre* did not allege facts showing a disparity in bargaining power. *See id.* Here, Prairie River **has** alleged facts showing that it was in an unfair bargaining position, including that Procura intentionally concealed information about the Software that it had no way of uncovering on its own. And unlike Prairie River, the plaintiff in *Lefebvre* was as commercially sophisticated as the seller. *Id.* At 1372. Finally, there is no indication that the *Lefebvre* plaintiff was under any undue pressure to contract within a certain time frame, as Prairie River alleges it was in 2015.

Accordingly, the Court will deny Procura's motion to dismiss Prairie River's claims for consequential damages.

SECTION SEVEN: POLICING THE STANDARD FORM CONTRACT

Most contracts today involve paper or electronic standard forms. You have already encountered cases in Chapter Five that deal with standard forms. Section Seven focuses on these transactions and considers the special problems associated with standard forms because of the absence of bargaining and their take-it-or leave it nature. The Section also presents additional policing solutions, such as the reasonable expectations doctrine and section 211 of the Restatement (Second) of Contracts. Finally, the Section introduces contract law's response to standard forms in the Internet retail setting.

KESSLER, CONTRACTS OF ADHESION—SOME THOUGHTS ABOUT FREEDOM OF CONTRACT

43 Colum.L.Rev. 629, 631–33, 640–41 (1943).

The development of large scale enterprise with its mass production and mass distribution made a new type of contract inevitable—the standardized mass contract. A standardized contract, once its contents have been formulated by a business firm, is used in every bargain dealing with the same product or service. The individuality of the parties which so frequently gave color to the old type contract has disappeared. The stereotyped contract of today reflects the impersonality of the market. It has reached its greatest perfection in the different types of contracts used on the various exchanges. Once the usefulness of these contracts was discovered and perfected in the transportation, insurance, and banking business, their use spread into all other fields of large scale enterprise, into international as well as national trade, and into labor relations. It is to be noted that uniformity of terms of contracts typically recurring in a business enterprise is an important factor in the exact calculation of risks. Risks which are difficult to calculate can be excluded altogether. Unforeseeable contingencies affecting performance, such as strikes, fire, and transportation difficulties can be taken care of. The standard clauses in insurance policies are the most striking illustrations of successful attempts on the part of business enterprises to select and control risks assumed under a contract. The insurance business probably deserves credit also for having first realized the full importance of the so-called "juridical risk", the danger that a court or jury may be swayed by "irrational factors" to decide against a powerful defendant. Ingenious clauses have been the result. Once their practical utility was proven, they were made use of in other lines of business. * * * Standardized contracts have thus become an important means of excluding or controlling the "irrational factor" in litigation. In this respect they are a true reflection of the spirit of our time with its hostility to irrational factors in the judicial process, and they belong in the same category as codifications and restatements.

In so far as the reduction of costs of production and distribution thus achieved is reflected in reduced prices, society as a whole ultimately benefits from the use of standard contracts. And there can be no doubt that this has been the case to a considerable extent. The use of standard contracts has, however, another aspect which has become increasingly important. Standard contracts are typically used by enterprises with strong bargaining power. The weaker party, in need of the goods or services, is frequently not in a position to shop around for better terms, either because the author of the standard contract has a monopoly (natural or artificial) or because all competitors use the same clauses. His contractual intention is but a subjection more or less voluntary to terms dictated by the stronger party, terms whose consequences are often understood only in a vague way, if at all. Thus, standardized contracts are frequently contracts of adhesion; they are *à prendre ou à laisser.*[e] * * *

And yet the tremendous economic importance of contracts of adhesion is hardly reflected in the great texts on contracts or in the Restatement. As a matter of fact, the term "contract of adhesion" or a similar symbol has not even found general recognition in our legal vocabulary. This will not do any harm if we remain fully aware that the use of the word "contract" does not commit us to an indiscriminate extension of the ordinary contract rules to all contracts. But apparently the realization of the deepgoing antinomies in the structure of our system of contracts is too painful an experience to be permitted to rise to the full level of our consciousness. Consequently, courts have made great efforts to protect the weaker contracting party and still keep "the elementary rules" of the law of contracts intact. As a result, our common law of standardized contracts is highly contradictory and confusing, and the potentialities inherent in the common law system for coping with contracts of adhesion have not been fully developed. The law of insurance contracts furnishes excellent illustrations. Handicapped by the axiom that courts can only interpret but cannot make contracts for the parties, courts had to rely heavily on their prerogative of interpretation to protect a policy holder. To be sure many courts have shown a remarkable skill in reaching "just" decisions by construing ambiguous clauses against their author even in cases where there was no ambiguity. * * *

FAIRFIELD LEASING CORPORATION V. TECHNI-GRAPHICS, INC.

Superior Court of New Jersey, 1992.
256 N.J.Super. 538, 607 A.2d 703.

DONALD S. COBURN, J.S.C.

In this civil action for breach of contract, the primary issue posed today is whether the court should enforce a waiver of the constitutional right of trial by jury contained in a standardized mass contract, commonly referred to as a contract of adhesion.

On January 30, 1991, defendant Techni-Graphics, Inc., a New Jersey corporation (TGI) signed a 39-month lease for a coffee machine at a rental of $209.50 per month with third-party defendant U-Vend, Inc., a New York corporation (U-Vend). Defendant Robin Umstead guaranteed performance of the lease for TGI. U-Vend assigned the lease to plaintiff, Fairfield Leasing Corporation, a New Jersey corporation (FLC). Under the contract only U-Vend is responsible to TGI for failures with respect to the leased equipment, and payment to the assignee of the monthly rent must continue despite any breach of contract by U-Vend.

---

[e] The word "contract of adhesion" was introduced into the legal vocabulary by Patterson, The Delivery of a Life Insurance Policy, 33 Harv.L.Rev. 198, 222 (1919).

TGI alleged that the machine was defective and infested with cockroach larvae. Because U-Vend refused to take corrective action, TGI stopped making the rental payments to FLC in March, 1991. FLC instituted suit and TGI brought in U-Vend by way of a third-party complaint based on breach of contract. TGI demanded a trial by jury on all issues.

This matter is now before the court on the joint motion of plaintiff FLC and third-party defendant U-Vend to strike the jury demand based on the following provision contained in the lease and in the guarantee:

> The undersigned does further waive trials by jury in any action or proceeding brought by the leasing Company, or its assignee, against the undersigned on any matters whatsoever arising out of, under or by virtue of the terms of the Agreement or of this Guarantee.

The agreement is a standardized form contract containing 23 paragraphs. U-Vend prepared it. The jury waiver provision is contained in the last part of the twenty-second paragraph, which also contains a merger clause and a no-modification clause. The guarantee, which is part of the agreement, contains the jury waiver clause on lines 21 to 23 of a 25-line paragraph. The letters of the single-spaced contract and guarantee are 1/10 of a centimeter in height, or approximately one-half the size of the letters produced by the typical typewriter. It is a classic example of a document which has been prepared with the intent that it neither be negotiated nor read.

Two New Jersey cases have directly considered the question of waiver of trial by jury in civil cases based upon a provision of the contract in litigation: *Sexton v. Newark Dist. Telegraph Co.,* 84 *N.J.L.* 85, 101, 86 *A.* 451 (Sup.Ct.1913) and *Franklin Discount Co. v. Ford,* 27 *N.J.* 473, 492–493, 143 *A.*2d 161 (1958). Although both cases accept that such a waiver can be made, neither case involved a contract of adhesion.

In *Henningsen v. Bloomfield Motors, Inc.,* 32 *N.J.* 358, 161 *A.*2d 69 (1960), the Supreme Court identified the problem with commercial adhesion contracts in these words:

> The traditional contract is the result of free bargaining of parties who are brought together by the play of the market, and who meet each other on a footing of approximate economic equality. In such a society there is no danger that freedom of contract will be a threat to the social order as a whole. But in present-day commercial life the standardized mass contract has appeared. It is used primarily by enterprises with strong bargaining power and position. "The weaker party, in need of the goods or services, is frequently not in a position to shop around for better terms, either because the author of the standard contract

> has a monopoly (natural or artificial) or because all competitors use the same clauses. His contractual intention is but a subjection more or less voluntary to terms dictated by the stronger party, terms whose consequences are often understood in a vague way, if at all." Such standardized contracts have been described as those in which one predominant party will dictate its law to an undetermined multiple rather than to an individual. They are said to resemble a law rather than a meeting of the minds. (at 389–390, 161 *A.*2d 69) (Citations omitted).

Since *Henningsen,* our courts have invalidated unconscionable or unfair terms of such contracts in a variety of contexts. * * *

The federal courts have been appropriately sensitive to the dangers posed to the public by jury waiver provisions in contracts of adhesion. * * * For example, in *National Equipment Rental, Ltd. V. Hendrix,* 565 *F.*2d 255 (2d Cir.1977), the court was concerned with an equipment leasing arrangement similar to the one involved in this case. The waiver of jury trial was "literally buried in the eleventh paragraph of a fine-print sixteen clause agreement." *Id.* At 258. The court said:

> It is elementary that the Seventh Amendment right to a jury is fundamental and that its protection can only be relinquished knowingly and intentionally. * * * Indeed, a presumption exists against its waiver. *Aetna Insurance Co. v. Kennedy,* 301 *U.S.* 389, 393, 57 *S.Ct.* 809 [811], 81 *L.Ed.* 1177 (1937). There is little doubt that the provision relied on by NER fails to overcome this presumption. The waiver clause was set deeply and inconspicuously in the contract, and Justice Black, dissenting in *National Equipment Rental, Ltd. v. Szukhent,* 375 *U.S.* 311, 332–3, 84 *S.Ct.* 411, 423, 11 *L.Ed.*2d 354 (1964) aptly characterized the nature of NER's form agreements:
>
> > this printed form provision buried in a multitude of words is too weak an imitation of a genuine agreement to be treated as a waiver of so important a constitutional safeguard . . . it exhausts credulity to think that they or any other layman reading these legalistic words would have known or even suspected that they amounted to [such] an agreement . . . (*Id.*)

In *Dreiling v. Peugeot Motors of America, Inc.,* 539 *F.Supp.* 402, 403 (D.Col.1982), the court, in refusing to enforce a contractual jury waiver, observed:

> Jury trial may be waived if done knowingly and intentionally, but courts will indulge every reasonable presumption against waiver. *Aetna Insurance Co. v. Kennedy,* 301 *U.S.* 389, 393, 57 *S.Ct.* 809, 811, 81 *L.Ed.* 1177 (1937); *Rodenbur v. Kaufmann,* 320

> *F.*2d 679, 683 (D.C.Cir.1963). In view of this strong presumption the defendants have a very heavy burden of proving that the plaintiffs knowingly, voluntarily and intentionally agreed upon the jury waiver provision in the 1978 Agreement. A constitutional guarantee so fundamental as the right to jury trial cannot be waived unknowingly by mere insertion of a waiver provision on the twentieth page of a twenty-two page standardized form contract.
>
> Defendants have presented no evidence that the waiver provision was a bargained for term of the contract, was mentioned during negotiations, or was even brought to the plaintiffs' attention. In fact, the defendants have failed to show that the plaintiffs had any choice other than to accept the contract as written. The 1978 Agreement appears to be Peugeot's standardized printed dealer contract, drafted by Peugeot. Obviously, the plaintiffs had little, if any, opportunity to negotiate the provisions. Absent proof to the contrary, such an inequality in relative bargaining positions suggests that the asserted waiver was neither knowing nor intentional.

By contrast, where the parties have been represented by counsel or there was evidence of negotiation without substantial inequality in bargaining positions, or the waiver provision was conspicuous, the tendency has been to enforce the waiver. * * *

Since this case comes within the province of the Uniform Commercial Code, *N.J.S.A.* 12A:1 *et seq.,* analysis is further aided by reference to *Herbstman v. Eastman Kodak Co.,* 131 *N.J.Super.* 439, 330 *A.*2d 384 (App.Div.1974), where the court applied the Code's requirement of conspicuousness for warranty disclaimers under *N.J.S.A.* 12A:2–316 to the limitations of remedy provision found in *N.J.S.A.* 12A:2–719, even though the latter section did not expressly require conspicuousness for such disclaimers. Significantly, the Code defines conspicuousness in these terms:

> "Conspicuous": A term or clause is conspicuous when it is so written that a reasonable person against whom it is to operate ought to have noticed it. A printed heading in capitals (as: NON-NEGOTIABLE BILL OF LADING) is conspicuous. Language in the body of a form is "conspicuous" if it is in larger or other contrasting type or color. But in a telegram any stated term is "conspicuous." Whether a term or clause is "conspicuous" or not is for decision by the court. *N.J.S.A.* 12A:1–201(10).

By that definition, and any other, the jury waiver in the instant case is utterly inconspicuous.

Since the inestimable right to civil jury trial is preserved in Article 1, paragraph 9, of the New Jersey Constitution, it is fit that the courts protect that right as a matter of public policy at least to the extent that the Uniform Commercial Code protects against waivers of warranties and limitations of remedy. Therefore, where, as here, a non-negotiated jury waiver clause appears inconspicuously in a standardized form contract entered into without assistance of counsel, the waiver should not be enforced.

* * *

In accordance with the law of New Jersey, the motion to strike the jury demand is denied.

STEINER v. MOBIL OIL CORP., 20 Cal.3d 90, 100, 141 Cal.Rptr. 157, 164, 569 P.2d 751, 758 (1977). [A]dhesion contract analysis teaches us not to enforce contracts until we look behind the I of the formalistic standardized agreement in order to determine whether any inequality of bargaining power between the parties renders contractual terms unconscionable, or causes the contract to be interpreted against the more powerful party.

C & J FERTILIZER, INC. v. ALLIED MUTUAL INSURANCE CO. 227 N.W.2d 169 (Iowa 1975). [C & J Fertilizer, a fertilizer manufacturer, negotiated with an agent of Allied for the purchase of burglary insurance. The agent told an officer of C & J that visible evidence of burglary was required to recover under the burglary policy. When the policy arrived, the president of C & J, a 37-year-old farmer with a high school education, did not read the definition of burglary, which required visible marks of entry on the *exterior* of the building. C & J suffered a loss of chemicals in an interior room of its warehouse, but Allied asserted that it was not liable because of the absence of exterior signs of forced entry. The trial court, noting the definition of burglary in the policy, found for Allied and C & J appealed.]

REYNOLDSON, JUSTICE.

* * *

Reasonable expectations.

This court adopted the doctrine of reasonable expectations in Rodman v. State Farm Mutual Ins. Co., 208 N.W.2d 903, 905–908 (Iowa 1973). The Rodman court approved the following articulation of that concept:

> " 'The objectively reasonable expectations of applicants and intended beneficiaries regarding the terms of insurance contracts

> will be honored even though painstaking study of the policy provisions would have negated those expectations.' "
>
> —208 N.W.2d at 906. * * *

* * *

Nor can it be asserted the above doctrine does not apply here because plaintiff knew the policy contained the provision now complained of and cannot be heard to say it reasonably expected what it knew was not there. A search of the record discloses no such knowledge.

The evidence does show, as above noted, a "dicker" for burglary insurance coverage on chemicals and equipment. The negotiation was for what was actually expressed in the policies' "Insuring Agreements": the insurer's promise "To pay for loss by burglary or by robbery of a watchman, while the premises are not open for business, of merchandise, furniture, fixtures and equipment within the premises * * *."

In addition, the conversation included statements from which the plaintiff should have understood defendant's obligation to pay would not arise where the burglary was an "inside job." Thus the following exclusion should have been reasonably anticipated:

> "Exclusions
>
> "This policy does not apply:
>
> " * * *
>
> "(b) to loss due to any fraudulent, dishonest or criminal act by any Insured, a partner therein, or an officer, employee, director, trustee or authorized representative thereof * * *."

But there was nothing relating to the negotiations with defendant's agent which would have led plaintiff to reasonably anticipate defendant would bury within the definition of "burglary" another exclusion denying coverage when, no matter how extensive the proof of a third-party burglary, no marks were left on the exterior of the premises. This escape clause, here triggered by the burglar's talent (an investigating law officer, apparently acquainted with the current modus operandi, gained access to the steel building without leaving any marks by leaning on the overhead plexiglas door while simultaneously turning the locked handle), was never read to or by plaintiff's personnel, nor was the substance explained by defendant's agent.

Moreover, the burglary "definition" which crept into this policy comports neither with the concept a layman might have of that crime, nor with a legal interpretation. See State v. Murray, 222 Iowa 925, 931, 270 N.W. 355, 358 (1936) ("We have held that even though the door was partially open, by opening it farther, in order to enter the building, this is a sufficient breaking to comply with the demands of the statute"); State v. Ferguson, 149 Iowa 476, 478–479, 128 N.W. 840, 841–842 (1910) ("It need not appear that this office was an independent building, for it is well known that it is burglary for one to break and enter an inner door or window, although the culprit entered through an open outer door * * * "); see State v. Hougland, 197 N.W.2d 364, 365 (Iowa 1972).

The most plaintiff might have reasonably anticipated was a policy requirement of visual evidence (abundant here) indicating the burglary was an "outside" not an "inside" job. The exclusion in issue, masking as a definition, makes insurer's obligation to pay turn on the skill of the burglar, not on the event the parties bargained for: a bona-fide third party burglary resulting in loss of plaintiff's chemicals and equipment.

The "reasonable expectations" attention to the basic agreement, to the concept of substance over form, was appropriately applied by this court for the insurer's benefit in Central Bearings Co. v. Wolverine Insurance Company, 179 N.W.2d 443 (Iowa 1970), a case antedating Rodman. We there reversed a judgment for the insured which trial court apparently grounded on a claimed ambiguity in the policy. In denying coverage on what was essentially a products liability claim where the insured purchased only a "Premises-Operations" policy (without any misrepresentation, misunderstanding or overreaching) we said at page 449 of 179 N.W.2d:

> "In summation we think the insured as a reasonable person would understand the policy coverage purchased meant the insured was not covered for loss if the 'accident' with concomitant damage to a victim occurred away from the premises and after the operation or sale was complete."

The same rationale of reasonable expectations should be applied when it would operate to the advantage of the insured. Appropriately applied to this case, the doctrine demands reversal and judgment for plaintiff. [The court also held that "the liability avoiding provision in the definition of the burglary is, in the circumstances of this case, unconscionable."]

* * *

We reverse and remand for judgment in conformance herewith.

Reversed and remanded.

LEGRAND, JUSTICE (dissenting).

* * *

Crucial to a correct determination of this appeal is the disputed provision of each policy defining burglary as "the felonious abstraction of insured property * * * by a person making felonious entry * * * by actual force and violence, of which force and violence there are visible marks made by tools, explosives, electricity or chemicals upon, or physical damage to, the exterior of the premises at the place of such entry * * *." The starting point of any consideration of that definition is a determination whether it is ambiguous. Yet the majority does not even mention ambiguity.

The purpose of such a provision, of course, is to omit from coverage "inside jobs" or those resulting from fraud or complicity by the assured. The overwhelming weight of authority upholds such provisions as legitimate in purpose and unambiguous in application. * * *

Once this indisputable fact is recognized, plaintiff's arguments virtually collapse. We may not—at least we *should* not—by any accepted standard of construction meddle with contracts which clearly and plainly state their meaning simply because we dislike that meaning, even in the case of insurance policies. * * *

* * * [T]he * * * doctrine of reasonable expectations [should not] be applied here. We adopted that rule in Rodman v. State Farm Mutual Automobile Insurance Company, 208 N.W.2d 903, 906, 907 (Iowa 1973). We refused, however to apply it in that case, where we said:

> "The real question here is whether the principle of reasonable expectations should be extended to cases where an ordinary layman would not misunderstand his coverage from a reading of the policy and where there are no circumstances attributable to the insurer which foster coverage expectations. Plaintiff does not contend he misunderstood the policy. He did not read it. He now asserts in retrospect that if he had read it he would not have understood it. He does not say he was misled by conduct or representations of the insurer. He simply asked trial court to rewrite the policy to cover his loss because if he had purchased his automobile insurance from another company the loss would have been covered, he did not know it was not covered, and if he had known it was not covered he would have purchased a different policy. Trial court declined to do so. We believe trial court correctly refused in these circumstances to extend the principle of reasonable expectations to impose liability."

Yet here the majority would extend the doctrine far beyond the point of refusal in *Rodman*. Here we have affirmative and unequivocal testimony from an officer and director of the plaintiff corporation that he knew the disputed provision was in the policies because "it was just like the insurance policy I have on my farm."

I cannot agree plaintiff may now assert it reasonably expected from these policies something it knew was not there.

MOORE, C.J., and REES and UHLENHOPP, JJ., join this dissent.

MARKLINE CO., INC. v. TRAVELERS INSURANCE CO., 384 Mass. 139, 424 N.E.2d 464 (1981). [Markline purchased a store-owners policy covering "burglary" from defendant. Burglary was defined to require "visible marks." Because of the lack of such marks, defendant refused to indemnify Markline for the loss of inventory, even though a burglar alarm had gone off and the fact of loss was undisputed. The court held, *inter alia,* that the doctrine of reasonable expectations did not apply in Massachusetts, but if it did Markline did not have reasonable expectations of coverage for the loss. According to the court, Markline's president's testimony that it was his understanding that "coverage was complete fire, theft, and liability insurance" "fell fatally short" of sufficient evidence to satisfy the reasonable expectations standard.]

NOLAN, JUSTICE.

* * *

* * * In the Restatement (Second) of Contracts, § 237, Comment f (Tent. Draft Nos. 1–7, 1973), the following description of "reasonable expectation" appears: "Although customers typically adhere to standardized agreements and are bound by them without even appearing to know the standard terms in detail, they are not bound to unknown terms which are beyond the range of reasonable expectation. A debtor who delivers a check to his creditor with the amount blank does not authorize the insertion of an infinite figure. Similarly, a party who adheres to the other party's standard terms does not assent to a term if the other party has reason to believe that the adhering party would not have accepted the agreement if he had known that the agreement contained the particular term. Such a belief or assumption may be shown by the prior negotiations or inferred from the circumstances. Reason to believe may be inferred from the fact that the term is bizarre or oppressive, from the fact that it eviscerates the nonstandard terms explicitly agreed to, or from the fact that it eliminates the dominant purpose of the transaction. The inference is reinforced if the adhering party never had an opportunity to read the term, or if it is illegible or otherwise hidden from view. This rule is closely related to the policy against unconscionable terms and the rule of interpretation against the draftsman." There is nothing in the record before us to bring this case within the sweep of this language.

* * *

LIACOS, JUSTICE (dissenting).

* * *

* * * I feel that the court pays short shrift to the claim of reasonable expectations and the notions of unconscionability inherent therein. * * *

It is patently inconsistent for this court to acknowledge on the one hand that the doctrine lacks precedent in our case law and at the same time to declare that the evidence on record falls short of a reasonable expectation standard. The majority, quoting § 237 of the Restatement (Second) of Contracts, chooses to ignore the clear parallel between this case and the Restatement: "Similarly, a party who adheres to the other party's standard terms does not assent to a term if the other party has reason to believe that the adhering party would not have accepted the agreement if he had known that the agreement contained the particular term. Such a belief or assumption may be shown by the prior negotiations or inferred from the circumstances." Also, "[r]eason to believe may be inferred from the fact that the term * * * eliminates the dominant purpose of the transaction." *Supra* at 466. Restatement (Second) of Contracts, comment f at 541 (Tent. Draft Nos. 1–7, 1973). The evidence here was that the plaintiff expected "comprehensive coverage," having been assured of such coverage by the insurer's agent. The interpretation of the circumstances of the plaintiff's entering the contract are highly material under the general principle that the intent and reasonable expectations of the parties govern the construction of insurance contracts. *Ayres v. Prudential Ins. Co. of America,* 602 F.2d 1309 (9th Cir.1979); see 12 Couch, Insurance § 45:5 at 107 (2d ed. 1964) (basic guide to insurance contract construction is that "parties apparently intended there should be effective coverage with respect to a particular kind or kinds of risk").

The Restatement informs us that "courts in construing and applying a standardized contract seek to effectuate the reasonable expectations of the average member of the public who accepts it." Restatement (Second) of Contracts § 237, comment e at 540 (Tent. Draft Nos. 1–7 1973). Cf. *Ayres, supra* at 1313 ("the exclusion fails only if the insured can reasonably believe [burglary] is not excluded in light of what is publicly known of such exclusions"). Here, the judge found the plaintiff complied with the insurer's requirement that he install a burglar alarm. As soon as he received notice of the alarm's activation he notified the insurer. These facts, along with the agent's precontract assurances, bespeak the plaintiff's reasonable expectation that if the alarm was activated and a loss of inventory occurred, which was otherwise unexplainable, the loss was covered by the burglary provisions of his policy. The issue of reasonable expectation and the unconscionability of defeating those expectations by obscure exclusionary language was adequately raised in the plaintiff's trial brief requesting findings and rulings, and by the evidence at trial. If the judge did utilize these theories in reaching his conclusion, then the question of the plaintiff's reasonable expectation has been placed squarely before us. Rather than put our own gloss on the unclear rulings of the judge, I would remand for a more specific statement of the reasons underlying the judgment. I dissent.

RESTATEMENT (SECOND) OF CONTRACTS § 211.

Standardized Agreements

(1) Except as stated in Subsection (3), where a party to an agreement signs or otherwise manifests assent to a writing and has reason to believe that like writings are regularly used to embody terms of agreements of the same type, he adopts the writing as an integrated agreement with respect to the terms included in the writing.

(2) Such a writing is interpreted wherever reasonable as treating alike all those similarly situated, without regard to their knowledge or understanding of the standard terms of the writing.

(3) Where the other party has reason to believe that the party manifesting such assent would not do so if he knew that the writing contained a particular term, the term is not part of the agreement.

WHITE, FORM CONTRACTS UNDER REVISED ARTICLE 2

75 Wash.U. Law Q. 315, 346–47 (1997).

* * * [A]ppellate courts in Arizona have not been rigorous in following the letter of section 211(3) * * *. In most cases, the Arizona Supreme Court has interpreted section 211(3) as though it does not require a look at the "drafter's" intent, and the court has paid little heed to the requirement that a signer be freed of a term only if he would not have signed had he known of the term. The court has made mincemeat out of [the] requirement that a signer "take the good with the bad." Generally, the court has looked directly at the state of mind of the "party manifesting assent," not at the belief of the drafter about what a hypothetical signer might think. Indeed, the Arizona courts often describe this approach as the doctrine of "reasonable expectations"—meaning the reasonable expectations of the signer, not of the drafter. The Arizona Supreme Court itself has paid only lip service to the notion that one must show that he, or a hypothetical signer, could not have been expected to sign a form containing the offending term.

PROBLEM 5-5

Sally Williams comes to your law office and tells you that during the last five years she purchased over $1,800 worth of household items from Thomas Appliances for which payments were to be made in installments. Williams' balance at Thomas Appliance was now only $164, but she was in default, and could not pay. Thomas Appliances has just told Williams that it is going to take back *all* of the items she has purchased from the store, not just the most recently purchased one which cost more than $164. The terms of each purchase were contained in a printed form contract. Each form contained the following clause:

> [T]he amount of each periodical installment payment to be made by purchaser to the Company under this present agreement shall be inclusive of and not in addition to the amount of each installment payment to be made by purchaser under such prior agreements or accounts; and all payments now and hereafter made by purchaser shall be credited pro rata on all outstanding agreements and accounts due to the Company by purchaser at the time each such payment is made.

Ms. Williams was not well-educated; she had completed only the eighth grade. Before checking your state's consumer protection legislation, are there any common law approaches to Ms. Williams' problem? Do *you* understand the above provision?

GLADDEN v. CADILLAC MOTOR CAR DIVISION, GENERAL MOTORS CORP., 83 N.J. 320, 416 A.2d 394 (1980). [The Court concluded that the term of a tire manufacturer's guarantee that limited the buyer's remedy to replacement or purchase price refund was unenforceable because the guarantee was a "linguistic maze" of contradictory provisions inducing the purchaser into believing "that he was obtaining a guarantee of performance."]

NEW YORK GENERAL OBLIGATIONS LAW § 5–702.

a. Every written agreement entered into after November first, nineteen hundred seventy-eight, for the lease of space to be occupied for residential purposes, for the lease of personal property to be used primarily for personal, family or household purposes, or to which a consumer is a party and the money, property or service which is the subject of the transaction is primarily for personal, family or household purposes must be:

1. Written in a clear and coherent manner using words with common and every day meanings;

2. Appropriately divided and captioned by its various sections.

Any creditor, seller or lessor who fails to comply with this subdivision shall be liable to a consumer who is a party to a written agreement governed by this subdivision in an amount equal to any actual damages sustained plus a penalty of fifty dollars. The total class action penalty against any such creditor, seller or lessor shall not exceed ten thousand dollars in any class action or series of class actions arising out of the use by a creditor, seller or lessor of an agreement which fails to comply with this subdivision. No action under this subdivision may be brought after both parties to the agreement have fully performed their obligation under such agreement, nor shall any creditor, seller or lessor who attempts in good faith to comply with this subdivision be liable for such penalties. This subdivision shall not apply to agreements involving amounts in excess of two hundred and fifty thousand dollars nor prohibit the use of words or phrases or forms of agreement required by state or federal law, rule or regulation or by a governmental instrumentality.

b. A violation of the provisions of subdivision a of this section shall not render any such agreement void or voidable nor shall it constitute:

1. A defense to any action or proceeding to enforce such agreement; or

2. A defense to any action or proceeding for breach of such agreement.

NOTE: *ONE ATTEMPT TO USE PLAIN ENGLISH*

CodePen blog, available at http://blog.codepen.io/legal/terms-of-service/, translated its terms of service into plain English as follows (is such an approach advisable?):

Our License to You

Official legally binding stuff

CodePen hereby grants you a non-exclusive, non-transferable, worldwide right to access and use the CodePen Site, solely with supported browsers through the Internet for your own internal purposes, subject to these Terms of Service. You may not permit the CodePen Site to be used by or for the benefit of unauthorized third parties. Nothing in the Terms of Service shall be construed to grant you any right to transfer or assign rights to access or use the CodePen Site. All rights not expressly granted to you are reserved by CodePen and its licensors. You shall not (i) modify or make derivative works based upon the CodePen Site; (ii) reverse engineer or access the CodePen Site in order to (a) build a competitive product or service, (b) build a product using similar features, functions or graphics of the CodePen Site, or (c) copy any features, functions or graphics of the CodePen Site. You further acknowledge and agree that, as between the parties, CodePen owns all right, title, and interest in and to the CodePen Site, including all intellectual property rights therein.

Plain English

Don't copy CodePen itself.

CASPI V. THE MICROSOFT NETWORK

Superior Court of New Jersey, 1999.
323 N.J.Super. 118, 732 A.2d 528.

KESTIN, J.A.D.

We are here called upon to determine the validity and enforceability of a forum selection clause contained in an on-line subscriber agreement of the Microsoft Network (MSN), an on-line computer service. The trial court granted defendants' motion to dismiss the complaint on the ground that the forum selection clause in the parties' contracts called for plaintiffs' claims to be litigated in the State of Washington. Plaintiffs appeal. We affirm.

The amended class action complaint in eighteen counts sought diverse relief against two related corporate entities, The Microsoft Network, L.L.C. and Microsoft Corporation (collectively, Microsoft). Plaintiffs asserted various theories including breach of contract, common law fraud, and consumer fraud in the way Microsoft had "rolled over" MSN membership into more expensive plans. Among the claims was an accusation that Microsoft had engaged in "unilateral negative option billing," a practice condemned by the attorneys general of twenty-one states, including New Jersey's, with regard to a Microsoft competitor, America Online, Inc. Under the practice as alleged, Microsoft, without notice to or permission from MSN members, unilaterally charged them increased membership fees attributable to a change in service plans.

The four named plaintiffs are members of MSN. Two reside in New Jersey; the others in Ohio and New York. Purporting to represent a nationwide class of 1.5 million similarly aggrieved MSN members, plaintiffs, in May 1997, moved for multi-state class action certification. See R. 4:32.

Shortly thereafter, defendants moved to dismiss the amended complaint for lack of jurisdiction and improper venue by reason of the forum selection clause which, defendants contended was in every MSN membership agreement and bound all the named plaintiffs and all members of the class they purported to represent. That clause, paragraph 15.1 of the MSN membership agreement, provided:

> This agreement is governed by the laws of the State of Washington, USA, and you consent to the exclusive jurisdiction and venue of courts in King County, Washington in all disputes arising out of or relating to your use of MSN or your MSN membership.

* * *

On November 13, 1997, Judge Fitzpatrick, in a written opinion, expressed his reasons for dismissing the complaint based upon the forum selection clause. Given that conclusion * * * plaintiffs' motion to certify the class was denied as moot. Conforming orders were entered on the same date. * * *

The background of the matter was depicted in the * * * opinion:

Before becoming an MSN member, a prospective subscriber is prompted by MSN software to view multiple computer screens of information, including a membership agreement which contains the above clause. MSN's membership agreement appears on the computer screen in a scrollable window next to blocks providing the choices "I Agree" and "I Don't Agree." Prospective members assent to the terms of the agreement by clicking on "I Agree" using a computer mouse. Prospective members have the option to click "I Agree" or "I Don't Agree" at any point while scrolling through the agreement. Registration may proceed only after the potential subscriber has had the opportunity to view and has assented to the membership agreement, including MSN's forum selection clause. No charges are incurred until after the membership agreement review is completed and a subscriber has clicked on "I Agree."

* * *

Judge Fitzpatrick correctly discerned that New Jersey follows the logic of the United States Supreme Court decision in Carnival Cruise Lines v. Shute, 499 U.S. 585, 111 S.Ct. 1522, 113 L.Ed.2d 622 (1991). * * * In Carnival, cruise ship passengers were held to a forum selection clause which appeared in their travel contract. The clause enforced in Carnival was very similar in nature to the clause in question here, the primary difference being that the Carnival clause was placed in small print in a travel contract while the clause in the case sub judice was placed on-line on scrolled computer screens.

* * *

[Judge Fitzpatrick held that] plaintiffs and the class which they purport to represent were given ample opportunity to affirmatively assent to the forum selection clause. Like Carnival, plaintiffs here "retained the option of rejecting the contract with impunity." 499 U.S. 585, 111 S.Ct. 1522, 113 L.Ed.2d 622. * * *

* * *

After reviewing the record in the light of the arguments advanced by the parties, we are in substantial agreement with the reasons for decision articulated by Judge Fitzpatrick. * * * New Jersey's interest in assuring consumer fraud protection will not be frustrated by requiring plaintiffs to proceed with a lawsuit in Washington as prescribed by the plain language of the forum selection clause. * * * If a forum selection clause is clear in its purport and has been presented to the party to be bound in a fair and forthright fashion, no consumer fraud policies or principles have been violated. * * *

The only viable issues that remain bear upon the argument that plaintiffs did not receive adequate notice of the forum selection clause, and therefore that the clause never became part of the membership contract which bound them. A related, alternative argument is that the question of notice is a factual matter that should be submitted to a jury. Defendants respond by arguing that 1) in the absence of fraud, a contracting party is bound by the provisions of a form contract even if he or she never reads them; 2) this clause met all reasonable standards of conspicuousness; and 3) the sign-up process gave plaintiffs ample opportunity to review and reject the agreement. Defendants also contend that notice is a question of law, decidable by a court, not a jury.

The holding in Carnival Cruise Lines v. Shute, 499 U.S. 585, 111 S.Ct. 1522, 113 L.Ed.2d 622 (1991), does not dispose of the notice question because the plaintiffs there had "essentially . . . conceded that they had notice of the forum-selection provision[,]" by stating that they " '[did] not contest . . . that the forum selection clause was reasonably communicated to [them], as much as three pages of fine print can be communicated.' " Id. At 590, 111 S.Ct. at 1525, 113 L.Ed.2d at 630. The dissenting justices described the format in which the forum selection clause had been presented as "in the fine print on the back of the [cruise] ticket." Id. At 597, 111 S.Ct. at 1529, 113 L.Ed.2d at 634 (Stevens, J., dissenting).

The scenario presented here is different because of the medium used, electronic versus printed; but, in any sense that matters, there is no significant distinction. The plaintiffs in Carnival could have perused all the fine-print provisions of their travel contract if they wished before accepting the terms by purchasing their cruise ticket. The plaintiffs in this case were free to scroll through the various computer screens that presented the terms of their contracts before clicking their agreement.

Also, it seems clear that there was nothing extraordinary about the size or placement of the forum selection clause text. By every indication we have, the clause was presented in exactly the same format as most other provisions of the contract. It was the first item in the last paragraph of the electronic document. We note that a few paragraphs in the contract were presented in upper case typeface, presumably for emphasis, but most provisions, including the forum selection clause, were presented in lower case typeface. We discern nothing about the style or mode of presentation, or the placement of the provision, that can be taken as a basis for concluding that the forum selection clause was proffered unfairly, or with a design to conceal or de-emphasize its provisions. To conclude that plaintiffs are not bound by that clause would be equivalent to holding that they were bound by no other clause either, since all provisions were identically presented. Plaintiffs must be taken to have known that they were entering into a contract; and no good purpose, consonant with the dictates of reasonable reliability in commerce, would be served by permitting them to disavow particular provisions or the contracts as a whole. See Rudbart v. North Jersey Dist. Water Supply Comm'n, 127 N.J. 344, 351–53, 605 A.2d 681 (referring to the principle that a contracting party may be bound by the terms of a form contract even if he or she has never read them), cert. denied, 506 U.S. 871, 113 S.Ct. 203, 121 L.Ed.2d 145 (1992).

The issue of reasonable notice regarding a forum selection clause is a question of law for the court to determine. * * * We agree with the trial court that, in the absence of a better showing than has been made, plaintiffs must be seen to have had adequate notice of the forum selection clause. The resolution of this notice issue, at this stage of the litigation between plaintiffs and defendants must, of course, be seen to be without prejudice to any showing either party may have the opportunity to make in another jurisdiction in a plenary proceeding on the contract regarding issues apart from the validity and enforceability of the forum selection clause.

Affirmed.

NOTE:
SOME EVIDENCE OF THE LACK OF READING OF E-STANDARD FORMS

Several law review articles document that consumers fail to read e-standard forms and debate what to do about the problem. See, e.g., Robert A. Hillman & Jeffrey J. Rachlinski, Standard Form Contracting in the Electronic Age, 77 N.Y.U. L. Rev. 429 (2002); Robert A. Hillman, On-line Consumer Standard-Form Contracting Practices: A Survey and Discussion of Legal Implications, in Consumer Protection in the Age of the "Information Economy," 283 (2006); Omri Ben-Shahar, The Myth of the 'Opportunity to Read' in Contract Law, 5 European Review of Contract Law 1 (2009); Yannis Bakos, Florencia Marotta-Wurgler, and David R. Trossen, Does Anyone Read the Fine Print? Consumer Attention to Standard Form Contracts, 43 J. Legal. Stud. 1 (2014). Here's more proof of the lack of reading. Bit-tech.net reported on April 15, 2010, that on April 1 GameStation added a term to its online terms and conditions of sale called the "Immortal Soul" clause that transferred the soul of the purchaser to GameStation. GameStation reported that only 12 percent of its customers opted out of the clause, but that it would decline to enforce it.

NICOSIA V. AMAZON.COM, INC.

United States Court of Appeals, Second Circuit, 2016.
834 F.3d 220.

CHIN, CIRCUIT JUDGE:

In 2013, plaintiff-appellant Dean Nicosia purchased *1 Day Diet*, a weight loss product containing sibutramine, a controlled substance that had been removed from the market in October 2010, on the website of defendant-appellee Amazon.com, Inc. ("Amazon"). Nicosia brought this action below, asserting claims under the Consumer Product Safety Act (the "CPSA"), 15 U.S.C. § 2051 *et seq.*, and state law.

The district court (Townes, *J.*) dismissed the complaint on the ground that the parties are bound by the mandatory arbitration provision in Amazon's Conditions of Use. It found that Nicosia was on constructive notice of the terms and that he assented to mandatory arbitration when he placed his order on the website. * * *

We * * * vacate the dismissal for failure to state a claim, and remand for further proceedings.

BACKGROUND

* * *

Alleged in the Complaint

Nicosia is an Amazon customer. On both January 30 and April 19, 2013, he used the Amazon website to purchase *1 Day Diet (One Day Diet) Best Slimming Capsule 60 Pills* ("*1 Day Diet*"), a weight loss drug containing sibutramine. Sibutramine is a Schedule IV stimulant that was withdrawn from the market in October 2010 by the Food and Drug Administration (the "FDA") because its association with cardiovascular risks and strokes outweighed its limited weight loss value. Prior to the FDA's removal of sibutramine from the market, it was only available to consumers with a doctor's prescription. After its removal, the FDA advised physicians to stop prescribing sibutramine and to advise patients to cease its consumption due to its risks, including "major adverse cardiovascular events."

At the time of his purchase, Nicosia did not know that *1 Day Diet* contained sibutramine and he did not have a doctor's prescription. Sibutramine was not listed as an ingredient on Amazon's website or on the *1 Day Diet* packaging, and Amazon sold the product without requiring a prescription. It was only revealed in November 2013 by the FDA that *1 Day Diet* contained sibutramine.

Amazon has since stopped selling *1 Day Diet* but never notified Nicosia that *1 Day Diet* contained the stimulant or offered to refund his purchases. As of the filing of the complaint in July 2014, Amazon continued to sell other weight loss products identified by the FDA as containing undisclosed amounts of sibutramine.

* * *

[Amazon's] Registration Page and the Order Page both included a link to Amazon's "Conditions of Use." The Amazon declaration provided a copy of the conditions of use apparently in effect in 2013, when Nicosia made his purchases, as they were last updated December 5, 2012 ("2012 Conditions of Use"). They included the following mandatory arbitration provision:

> Any dispute or claim relating in any way to your use of any Amazon Service, or to any products or services sold or distributed by Amazon or through Amazon.com will be resolved by binding arbitration, rather than in court. . . . We each agree that any dispute resolution proceedings will be conducted only on an

individual basis and not in a class, consolidated or representative action.

* * *

The district court granted Amazon's motion to dismiss, concluding that Nicosia failed to state a claim because he was on constructive notice of Amazon's conditions of use. In doing so, the district court relied on the Order Page and the 2012 Conditions of Use as well as Amazon's assertion that Nicosia created an Amazon account in 2008 by signing on through the Registration Page, and used that account to make his purchases of *1 Day Diet*. The district court then concluded that Nicosia was given reasonable notice of the conditions of use given: (1) the conspicuousness of the hyperlink to the 2012 Conditions of Use on the Order Page; and (2) the fact that Nicosia signed up for an Amazon account via the Registration Page in 2008, which required assent to the 2008 Conditions of Use that named King County as the forum for suit but provided that the conditions were subject to change.

The district court also concluded that questions as to the validity of the agreement as a whole had to be submitted to arbitration. * * *

This appeal followed.

DISCUSSION

* * *

Substantive Law

State law principles of contract formation govern the arbitrability question. * * * The district court applied Washington law on the question of contract formation, and the parties do not challenge that decision on appeal. * * *

[The court noted that Washington courts had not yet addressed the issue of reasonable notice in the online setting, but that general contract principles applied.] Under Washington law, contract formation requires an objective manifestation of mutual assent. * * * "The existence of mutual assent may be deduced from the circumstances. . . ." *Jacob's Meadow Owners Ass'n v. Plateau 44 II, LLC*, 139 Wash.App. 743, 765, 162 P.3d 1153 (2007). Where a party has signed a contract without reading it, she can argue that mutual assent was lacking if she was "deprived of the opportunity to read the contract" or if the contract was not " 'plain and unambiguous.' " *Yakima Cty. (W. Valley) Fire Prot. Dist. No. 12 v. City of Yakima*, 122 Wash.2d 371, 389, 858 P.2d 245 (1993) (quoting *Skagit State Bank v. Rasmussen*, 109 Wash.2d 377, 381–84, 745 P.2d 37 (1987)). "So long as a[n] [offeree] could have seen a reasonably conspicuous reference to the . . . Agreement . . . a jury could conclude that [she] manifested assent." *Spam Arrest*, 2013 WL 4675919, at *8 (citing *M.A. Mortenson Co. v.*

Timberline Software Corp., 140 Wash.2d 568, 998 P.2d 305 (2000) (en banc)).

Washington has also upheld the validity of shrinkwrap agreements, endorsing the view that "[n]otice on the outside, terms on the inside, and a right to return the software for a refund if the terms are unacceptable . . . may be a means of doing business valuable to buyers and sellers alike." *M.A. Mortenson*, 140 Wash.2d at 582–83, 998 P.2d 305 (quoting *ProCD, Inc. v. Zeidenberg*, 86 F.3d 1447, 1451 (7th Cir. 1996)). The validity of shrinkwrap agreements assumes that buyers have notice of the *existence* of standard adhesion terms, even if they are not read or understood. *See id.* At 584, 998 P.2d 305 (enforcing terms of adhesion where text of terms were "set forth explicitly or referenced in numerous locations"); *Hill v. Gateway 2000, Inc.*, 105 F.3d 1147, 1148 (7th Cir. 1997) (relying on fact that plaintiffs "concede[d] noticing the statement of terms [on the box], but den[ied] reading it"); * * *

Manifestation of assent to an online contract is not meaningfully different, and can be accomplished by "words or silence, action or inaction," so long as the user " 'intends to engage in the conduct and knows or has reason to know that the other party may infer from his conduct that he assents.' " *Schnabel*, 697 F.3d at 120 (footnote omitted) (quoting *Restatement (Second) of Contracts* § 19(2) (1981)). As with paper contracts or shrinkwrap agreements, to be bound, an internet user need not actually read the terms and conditions or click on a hyperlink that makes them available as long as she has notice of their existence. * * *

* * * Where there is no actual notice of contract terms, "an offeree is still bound by the provision if he or she is on *inquiry* notice of the term and assents to it through the conduct that a reasonable person would understand to constitute assent." *Schnabel*, 697 F.3d at 120; * * *.

One common way of alerting internet users to terms and conditions is via a "clickwrap" agreement, which typically requires users to click an "I agree" box after being presented with a list of terms or conditions of use. *See Register.com*, 356 F.3d at 402–03, 429. Clickwraps force users to "expressly and unambiguously manifest either assent or rejection prior to being given access to the product." *Id.* At 429. In contrast, "browsewrap" agreements involve terms and conditions posted via hyperlink, commonly at the bottom of the screen, and do not request an express manifestation of assent. *See Specht*, 306 F.3d [17], 31–32 [2d Cir. 2002] (describing what would later be termed "browsewrap"). In determining the validity of browsewrap agreements, courts often consider whether a website user has actual or constructive notice of the conditions. * * *

Whether there was notice of the existence of additional contract terms presented on a webpage depends heavily on whether the design and content of that webpage rendered the existence of terms reasonably conspicuous. *See Nguyen*, 763 F.3d at 1177–78 * * *. Thus, when terms are linked in obscure sections of a webpage that users are unlikely to see, courts will refuse to find constructive notice. * * *

Application

We conclude that the district court erred in granting Amazon's motion to dismiss. * * * Nicosia has plausibly stated a claim, as we are not convinced at this stage that he is bound by the arbitration clause.

* * *

Whether Nicosia Plausibly Stated That There Was No Constructive Notice of the 2012 Conditions of Use

Considering only the allegations in the complaint, the Order Page, and the 2012 Conditions of Use linked thereto, we conclude that Nicosia plausibly stated a claim for relief.

Nicosia argues that the 2012 Conditions of Use were a browsewrap agreement. Amazon, like the district court, maintains that the agreement here was neither a clickwrap agreement nor a browsewrap agreement; rather, it was something in between. An Amazon purchaser was not required to click an "I agree" box after being presented with a list of terms and conditions. Nor was the purchaser simply left to browse the page, as she was asked to click on a "Place your order" button after being told elsewhere on the page that "By placing your order, you agree to Amazon.com's privacy notice and conditions of use," with the latter phrase hyperlinked to the 2012 Conditions of Use. * * * For purposes of this appeal, we assume without deciding that the agreement was a hybrid between a clickwrap and a browsewrap agreement. In making this assumption, we do not mean to suggest that a "hybrid" agreement is a type of agreement that Washington law would recognize as such. The question is whether a reasonably prudent offeree would know that the 2012 Conditions of Use governed, such that her purchase manifested implied assent to the additional terms. * * *

Turning to the Order Page, we are not convinced that notice was sufficient as a matter of Washington law. Near the top of the page, below the "Review your order" heading, the critical sentence appears in smaller font: "By placing your order, you agree to Amazon.com's privacy notice and conditions of use." * * * The phrases "privacy notice" and "conditions of use" appear in blue font, indicating that they are clickable links to separate webpages. The body of the page summarizes the user's purchase and delivery information. Among other things, users are shown their shipping address, billing address, and payment method, and given the option to edit that information or "try Amazon Locker." Users are also given the opportunity to change the delivery date, enter gift cards and promotional codes, and sign up for "FREE Two-Day Shipping with a free trial of Amazon

Prime." The Amazon Prime promotion features the words "FREE Two-Day Shipping" four times in the center of the page, appearing in orange, green, and black fonts, and in white font against an orange banner. On the right side of the page appears a "Place your order" button above a box with the heading "Order Summary." The Order Summary box lists the cost of the items to be purchased, shipping and handling costs, total price before tax, estimated tax to be collected, purchase total, gift card amount, and order total. The words "Order total" appear in bold, red font. A large area in the center of the page has been redacted, but presumably features a picture of the product being purchased, its name, price, quantity, stock and seller information, and gifting options. Near the bottom of the page, there are a number of sentences in faint, black font directing users to links to other Amazon webpages for additional information, such as tax and seller information, customer assistance pages, and product return policies. At the very bottom of the page, links to the Conditions of Use and Privacy Policy appear again in blue, next to Amazon's copyright notice.

Notably, unlike typical "clickwrap" agreements, clicking "Place your order" does not specifically manifest assent to the additional terms, for the purchaser is not specifically asked whether she agrees or to say "I agree." * * * Nothing about the "Place your order" button alone suggests that additional terms apply, and the presentation of terms is not directly adjacent to the "Place your order" button so as to indicate that a user should construe clicking as acceptance. *Cf. Fteja v. Facebook, Inc.*, 841 F.Supp.2d 829, 835, 840 (S.D.N.Y. 2012) (finding Facebook user was "informed of the consequences of his assenting click" because he was shown, immediately below the "Sign Up" button, a notice stating, "By clicking Sign Up, you are indicating that you have read and agree to the Terms and Service").

The message itself—"By placing your order, you agree to Amazon.com's . . . conditions of use"—is not bold, capitalized, or conspicuous in light of the whole webpage. * * * Proximity to the top of a webpage does not necessarily make something more likely to be read in the context of an elaborate webpage design. *See Nguyen*, 763 F.3d at 1179 ("[E]ven close proximity of the hyperlink to relevant buttons users must click on—without more—is insufficient to give rise to constructive notice."). There are numerous other links on the webpage, in several different colors, fonts, and locations, which generally obscure the message. *See Zappos.com*, 893 F.Supp.2d at 1064 ("The Terms of Use is inconspicuous, buried in the middle to bottom of every Zappos.com webpage among many other links, and the website never directs a user to the Terms of Use."). Although it is impossible to say with certainty based on the record, there appear to be between fifteen and twenty-five links on the Order Page, and various text is displayed in at least four font sizes and six colors (blue, yellow, green, red, orange, and black), alongside multiple buttons and promotional advertisements. Further, the presence of customers' personal address, credit card information, shipping options, and purchase summary are sufficiently distracting so as to temper whatever effect the notification has. *See Nguyen*, 763 F.3d at 1179 ("Given the breadth of the range of technological savvy of online purchasers, consumers cannot be expected to ferret out hyperlinks to terms and conditions to which they have no reason to suspect they will be bound.").

To draw on Judge Leval's analogy in *Register.com*, it is as if an apple stand visitor walks up to the shop and sees, above the basket of apples, a wall filled with signs. Some of those signs contain information necessary for her purchase, such as price, method of payment, and delivery details, and are displayed prominently in the center of the wall. Others she may quickly disregard, including advertisements for other fruit stands. Among them is a sign binding her to additional terms as a condition of her purchase. Has the apple stand owner provided reasonably conspicuous notice?

We think reasonable minds could disagree.

In a seeming effort to streamline customer purchases, Amazon chose not to employ a clickwrap mechanism. While clickwrap agreements that display terms in a scrollbox and require users to click an icon are not necessarily required, *see Register.com*, 356 F.3d at 403 (an offeree need not specifically assent to certain terms by clicking an "I agree" icon so long as the offeree "makes a decision to take the benefit with knowledge of the terms of the offer"), they are certainly the easiest method of ensuring that terms are agreed to, *see Starkey*, 796 F.3d at 197 n.3 (noting that it would have been "simpler to resolve" this question had a clickwrap mechanism been used).

To be clear, we do not hold that there was no objective manifestation of mutual assent here as a matter of law. Rather, we conclude simply that reasonable minds could disagree on the reasonableness of notice. *See Cascade Auto Glass, Inc. v. Progressive Cas. Ins. Co.*, 135 Wash.App. 760, 767, 145 P.3d 1253 (2006) ("Whether particular notice was reasonable is ordinarily a question of fact for the jury."). We therefore hold that Amazon has failed to show that Nicosia was on notice and agreed to mandatory arbitration as a matter of law. The district court thus erred in concluding that Nicosia had failed to state a claim under Rule 12(b)(6).

* * *

CONCLUSION

For the reasons set forth above, the order of the district court is * * * VACATED in part, and the case is REMANDED for further proceedings.

NICOSIA v. AMAZON.COM, INC., 384 F.Supp. 3d 254 (E.D.N.Y. 2019). The conclusion that arbitration should prevail was arrived at within the legal framework set forth by the Court of Appeals, namely, whether a reasonably prudent internet user would have notice of Amazon's Conditions of Use. The conclusion is reached after substantial research and discussion of the cases and relevant literature summoned in the struggle created by the advent of the internet—the struggle to make the common law of contracts applicable when people interacted with people in the commercial world, fit comfortably in a time when people interact with machines in that world and with each other.

* * *

The puzzle * * * is this. On the one hand, the law cannot countenance an environment where unscrupulous merchants are able to insert any contractual term they wish into the [wrap] agreement and expect automatic enforcement. On the other hand, a legal rule which merely exalts the *form* and *visual layout* of the [wrap] agreement, incentivizing merchants to adopt some judicially-favored website designs while foregoing others, is unlikely to have more than a negligible impact on the way buyers and sellers contract over the internet.

This Court suggests that Llewellyn had the answer: rather than scrutinizing [wrap] agreements for contract formation issues, courts should recognize that such agreements, like other adhesive contracts, represent in substance a "blanket assent" to any terms that are not objectively unreasonable. Llewellyn, *Common Law Tradition* * * * at 370; *see also* Restatement (Second) of Contracts § 211 cmt. F. Accepting this framework, such terms should be rigorously scrutinized for substantive unreasonableness, perhaps to a greater degree than they have been subjected thus far. * * * True, where an arbitration agreement is concerned, a court's latitude to declare certain provisions unconscionable, such as class arbitration waivers, is heavily circumscribed by the [Federal Arbitration Act], as interpreted by the nation's highest Court. * * * But as a general principle, a judicial approach which shifts the inquiry away from the formal trappings of the contract, *e.g.,* notice and acceptance, to the substance of its terms, will much more readily honor the merchant's legitimate commercial expectations while safeguarding the consumer from abuse.

FAGERSTROM v. AMAZON.COM, INC., 141 F.Supp.3d 1051 (S.D. Cal. 2016). [Fagerstrom and others purchased products from Amazon, but claimed that Amazon engaged in false advertising by setting forth discounted prices that actually were the retail price offered by other retailers. Amazon sought to enforce an arbitration clause that was available to consumers

> by reviewing a final checkout page and clicking a 'Place your order' button located on that page. At the top of the checkout page, under the heading 'Review your order,' there is a notice to customers stating that 'By placing your order, you agree to Amazon.com's *privacy notice* and *conditions of* use.' The phrases 'privacy notice' and 'conditions of use' (COUs) are set off in blue-color text that hyperlinks to the full text of the privacy notice and COUs, respectively. The COUs include the Arbitration Agreement at issue here.

One issue was whether the arbitration provision was procedurally unconscionable because the plaintiffs did not have a meaningful choice. The court held that notwithstanding that the arbitration agreement was a contract of adhesion, the agreement was not procedurally unconscionable because the website provided reasonable notice of the provision to the plaintiffs. The court distinguished the facts from those in Specht v. Netscape Communications Corp., 306 F.3d 17 (2d Cir. 2002) because plaintiffs did not have to "scroll to another part of the checkout page or click on any additional link to be put on notice that they are bound by the COUs when they place an order."]

HILLMAN, ONLINE BOILERPLATE: WOULD MANDATORY WEBSITE DISCLOSURE OF E-STANDARD TERMS BACKFIRE?

104 Mich. L. Rev. 837, 837–840, 854–856 (2006).

A law backfires when it produces results opposite from those its drafters intended. Lots of laws may have backfired. For example, people opposed to hate crimes legislation think that the laws "inflame prejudice rather than eradicate it." The Endangered Species Act, according to some analysts, has helped destroy rather than preserve the creatures listed by the Act. Even consumer protection laws, some believe, increase prices and confuse consumers instead of protecting them.

This Article analyzes whether mandatory website disclosure of e-standard terms, advocated by some as a potential solution to market failures when consumers contract over the Internet, is another potential legal backfire. By mandatory website disclosure, I do not mean a "clickwrap" presentation of terms, in which a consumer must click "I agree" or the like on a screen presenting the terms prior to the completion of a transaction in progress. Mandatory website disclosure would require a business to maintain an Internet presence and to post its terms prior to any particular transaction so that a consumer could read and compare terms without making a purchase at all.

The problem is not that mandatory website disclosure would increase the cost of doing business, which would be passed on to consumers in the form of higher prices. Businesses have been unable to demonstrate that displaying their terms on their websites would be costly. Nor should drafting rules that implement the law be too difficult. Businesses could be required to display their terms on their homepage or on another page reachable directly through a clearly identified hyperlink. Further, businesses could be required to prove the availability of their terms by furnishing relatively inexpensive archival records of their websites. Mandatory website disclosure may backfire, however, because it may not increase reading or shopping for terms or motivate businesses to draft reasonable ones, but instead, may make heretofore suspect terms more likely enforceable.

* * *

* * * My preliminary empirical work on e-consumer reading of standard forms, as well as studies of e-shopping behavior suggests that advance disclosure of terms likely will fail to increase reading or shopping for terms. This should be no surprise. Despite the opportunity to read, most e-consumers may still have ample rational reasons for not reading and cognitive processes that deter reading and processing terms. In addition, e-consumers, drawn to the speed and novelty of the Internet, are unlikely to have the patience or discipline to compare terms regardless of when the terms become available. Further, watchdog groups may not positively motivate businesses because they may lack influence and because businesses may conclude that the benefits of particular terms outweigh any potential costs in adverse publicity.

In light of the potential failure of mandatory website disclosure to increase reading and to discipline businesses, the only effects of the proposal may be to insulate businesses from claims of procedural unconscionability and to create a safe harbor for businesses to draft suspect terms. My goal is not to claim that mandatory website disclosure will certainly backfire so that the proposal should be taken off the table. In fact, I conclude that mandatory website disclosure ultimately may be the most viable alternative. I simply want to elaborate on the reasons that the possibility of backfire should be taken seriously before moving in the direction of mandatory website disclosure.

* * *

If courts rarely strike a contract or term based solely on one or the other kind of unconscionability, but use a sliding scale of procedural and substantive unconscionability, what will be the outcome of mandatory website disclosure? Perhaps marginal terms, insufficiently outlandish to motivate a court to strike them on substantive unconscionability grounds alone, will be enforceable because of their early disclosure on the website.

For example, consider the term * * * allowing a software vendor to "collect[ ] certain non-personally identifiable information about [a consumer's] Web surfing and computer usage." If such authorization to "follow around" the consumer is fully disclosed on the vendor's webpage, I doubt that a court would strike it on substantive unconscionability grounds alone. The result of mandatory website disclosure would constitute a legal backfire.

* * *

Despite all that has been said, mandatory website disclosure may still be the best strategy for dealing with the problem of e-standard forms. As mentioned, other solutions present significant problems of their own. Further, mandatory website disclosure is cheap, substantiates the claim of consumer assent, and constitutes a symbolic victory for those advocating greater fairness in e-standard-form contracting.

Of course, mandatory website disclosure is attractive for these reasons only if my fear of a legal backfire proves exaggerated because the benefits of disclosure outweigh the costs of the enforcement of some questionable terms. And perhaps I am being unduly pessimistic about the possibility that disclosure will backfire. After all, if disclosure were a good strategy for businesses to avoid unconscionability claims and of little concern because consumers do not read their standard forms, one would expect to see lots of precontract disclosure of e-standard forms already. Businesses tempted to draft unfair terms must therefore believe that disclosure benefits consumers. But I am not convinced by this argument. Business decisionmakers may themselves fail to make rational decisions for much the same reasons as consumers. For example, businesses may be unduly risk averse concerning the outcome of disclosure and therefore prefer to hide their marginal terms, even though disclosing them actually would work to their advantage.

Ultimately, optimism about disclosure may depend on one's time frame for measuring the law's effects. Even if disclosure backfires in the short term, perhaps eventually the word will get out about a business's unsavory terms. Consider the experience of cigarette manufacturers who, in response to legislation, put warning labels on their packages. For a considerable period of time, these labels helped manufacturers " 'fend[ ] off smokers' suits' " based on smokers' assumption of the risk. As a result, "[w]hat was intended as a burden on tobacco became a shield instead." In the long run, however, the package warnings, along with the many revelations about cigarette manufacturers' attempts to hide other adverse facts about their products, led to a massive change in public opinion and, ultimately, to serious legal sanctions against the cigarette companies. Perhaps mandatory website disclosure will also have a long-term beneficial effect.

NOTE: INTERNET RETAIL STRATEGIES

In a survey of over 500 of the top-selling retailers doing business on the Internet in 2005, Ronald J. Mann and Travis Siebeneicher report that only about 6% use interfaces that would make their contracts enforceable by giving sufficient notice of terms. Further, their standard terms are far more benign than analysts would predict: "[T]he contracts found on internet retailers' websites contain the standard, pro-seller boilerplate provisions—arbitration, disclaimers of consequential damages, and the like—much less frequently than would be expected. No such clauses appear in the contracts for more than half of the retailers that we studied." Mann and Siebeneicher speculate that "[F]or the great majority of internet retailers, the ease of the shopping experience is more important than concerns about possible future liability." Further, they suggest that retailers have conflicting desires "to have terms that appear to be benign and * * * to have terms (albeit not in a binding form) to which consumers will accede in the event of a dispute." Finally, the authors reflect more broadly on their findings:

> In our view, the data we present here suggest that businesses often can succeed in altering the practical terms of their relations with customers without obtaining enforceable contracts. The apparent use of unenforceable terms to guide customer behavior provides a provocative addition to the debate about whether assent should be the focus of doctrinal rules on contract formation. Among other things, it suggests that doctrinal rules that make pro-seller terms unenforceable will have considerably less impact in the real interactions of customers and merchants than scholars have surmised.

Ronald J. Mann & Travis Siebeneicher, Just One Click: The Reality of Internet retail Contracting, 108 Colum. L. Rev. 984, 1011 (2008).

In April, 2014, the New York Times reported on a change to the terms and conditions on General Mills' website, maker of Cheerios, Chex, and other brands. The terms on their face purported to bind customers to arbitration (and other terms) if they downloaded coupons, liked any of the brands on Facebook, or even purchased product at a brick-and-mortar store. The newspaper's account created a furor among consumers. General Mills then withdrew the term and announced that "we have reverted back to our prior legal terms, which contain no mention of arbitration." This and other such incidents suggest that public opinion can play an important role in shaping the nature of retailers' terms.

For more on unenforceable contract terms and the role of lawyers, see Charles A. Sullivan, The Puzzling Persistence of Unenforceable Contract Clauses, 70 Ohio St. L.J. 1127, 1169 (2009); Paul Carrington, Unconscionable Lawyers, 19 Ga. St. U.L. Rev. 361 (2002).

SECTION EIGHT: SOME ADDITIONAL POLICING DOCTRINES

We now identify some additional policing doctrines. The doctrine of mutuality of obligation studied in Chapter Two is also sometimes employed to police agreements. For example, in Oscar Schlegel Manufacturing Co. v. Peter Cooper's Glue Factory, 231 N.Y. 459, 132 N.E. 148 (1921), the seller agreed to sell to the buyer all buyer's "requirements" of special glue" for 9 cents per pound. The buyer was a jobber selling glue to such customers as it might find. In an action by the buyer, after the seller refused to make deliveries, the court held the agreement invalid for lack of consideration. The opinion contained this telling passage:

> The price of glue having risen during the year 1916 from 9 to 24 cents per pound, it is quite obvious why orders for glue increased correspondingly. Had the price dropped below 9 cents, it may fairly be inferred such orders would not have been given. In that case * * * plaintiff would not have been liable to the defendant for damages for a breach, since he had not agreed to sell any glue.

According to the court, the buyer had no obligation to buy any glue from the seller, and, thus, the agreement was technically unenforceable under the mutuality doctrine. But what appears to have been the true concern of the court in finding lack of mutuality?

We have also studied how courts invalidate certain agreed damages provisions as penalties. This too is a policing response. Would it be fair to say that courts seem more willing to strike such provisions as penalties, even without evidence of bargaining improprieties, than to strike provisions such as exculpatory clauses? What do you suppose accounts for this?

As Problem 5-5 illustrates, contract interpretation can serve a policing function. Recall Professor Llewellyn's criticism of this policing approach.

In addition to these doctrines that you have seen before, you should also be acquainted with doctrines addressed to problems of mental illness and infancy. Not all forms of mental illness invalidate assent. The Restatement (Second) of Contracts in section 15 posits the following rule:

> **Mental Illness or Defect**
>
> (1) A person incurs only voidable contract duties by entering into a transaction if by reason of mental illness or defect
>
> (a) he is unable to understand in a reasonable manner the nature and consequences of the transaction, or

(b) he is unable to act in a reasonable manner in relation to the transaction and the other party has reason to know of his condition.

(2) Where the contract is made on fair terms and the other party is without knowledge of the mental illness or defect, the power of avoidance under Subsection (1) terminates to the extent that the contract has been so performed in whole or in part or the circumstances have so changed that avoidance would be unjust. In such a case a court may grant relief as justice requires.

People who have not reached the age of majority (those under a certain age, which varies from state to state) may disaffirm their contracts. E. Farnsworth, Contracts 220–22 (4th ed. 2004). But as you may have already observed in other contexts, absolute rules tend to generate exceptions. One prime candidate for an exception involves the purchase of "necessaries" by "infants" (people under the state age of majority). Contract law typically takes the position that infants should be presumed capable of contracting with respect to some necessaries so that people will be willing to sell such items to them. For example, would you want to sell a car to an infant if the infant could disaffirm the deal? But what if the infant needs a car for work? To ensure that infants can contract for necessaries the law excepts such contracts from the disaffirmance rule. But what is a necessary? What if the infant could take a bus to work? As you can see, exceptions to rules, carved out for policing or other reasons in particular cases, may "cloud" doctrine and cause confusion.

One court's novel approach to the infancy defense is A.V. v. iParadigms, LLC, 544 F. Supp. 2d 473 (E.D. Va. 2008). There, high school students, required to submit their work for plagiarism review to iParadigm's portal, sued the firm for copyright infringement after it kept copies of the work for its database. iParadigms defended by pointing to a waiver of intellectual property rights that the students had agreed to by clicking "I agree" upon submission. The students (children of lawyers?) had written disclaimers on each submitted paper denying intent to be bound to such waivers. But the court said the clickwrap contract was formed when the students clicked I agree and the disclaimer attempts had no legal effect. The students also relied on the infancy doctrine. The District Court judge, denying the application of the doctrine, concluded that the students could not at once use the doctrine as a sword (getting a grade and being granted contractual "standing to bring the present suit") and a shield (denying the validity of the terms of use.) This decision seems deeply confused (and wrong on the infancy defense), though the role of infancy doctrine online is in flux. See generally Cheryl Preston, Cyberinfants, 39 Pepperdine Law Review 225 (2012).

Finally, courts frequently invoke the general obligation of good faith as a policing tool. In Section Five of Chapter Six we will see that good faith is highly fertile in this regard. No lawyer concerned with a policing problem should fail to consider it.

SECTION NINE: POLICING CONTRACT MODIFICATIONS

Contracting parties may desire to modify their agreements if they change their minds or the circumstances change. Suppose, for example, the Benkowskis decided soon after signing their agreement with the Whites that they had not received a fair price for their water service. The Whites might be willing to agree to a price increase for many reasons. They might concede that the deal was too favorable to them. Or they might be willing to pay more to keep their relationship with the Benkowskis harmonious. After all, the Whites may desire to modify the agreement in their own favor sometime in the future.

Because people are relatively free to enter contracts, and to shape the terms of contracts, they should be free to modify their agreements as well. Rules precluding free adjustment, in fact, might even deter some parties from entering contracts (at least long-term ones). Enforcing freely made modifications thus supports the principle of contractual freedom and facilitates economic exchange.

Although freedom to modify should be encouraged, parties must also be able to rely on their agreements so they can plan for the future. They must have some confidence that if they choose to insist on performance as originally agreed, the law will support them. Parties who have made plans in reliance on their contracts may be vulnerable to coercion, however. Planning tends to limit future choices and thus to increase the possibility that the planner will be forced to agree to an unwelcome modification if faced with a threat of nonperformance. The primary rationale for policing contract modifications, then, is to deny enforcement of modifications whereby one party takes undue advantage of the other.

ALASKA PACKERS' ASSOCIATION V. DOMENICO

United States Court of Appeals, Ninth Circuit, 1902.
117 Fed. 99.

ROSS, CIRCUIT JUDGE. The libel in this case was based upon a contract alleged to have been entered into between the libelants and the appellant corporation on the 22d day of May, 1900, at Pyramid Harbor, Alaska, by which it is claimed the appellant promised to pay each of the libelants, among other things, the sum of $100 for services rendered and to be rendered. In its answer the respondent denied the execution, on its part, of the contract sued upon, averred that it was without consideration, and for a third defense alleged that the work performed by the libelants for it was performed under other and different contracts than that sued on, and that, prior to the filing of the libel, each of the libelants was paid by the respondent the full amount due him thereunder, in consideration of which each of them executed a full release of all his claims and demands against the respondent.

The evidence shows without conflict that on March 26, 1900, at the city and county of San Francisco, the libelants entered into a written contract with the appellant, whereby they agreed to go from San Francisco to Pyramid Harbor, Alaska, and return, on board such vessel as might be designated by the appellant, and to work for the appellant during the fishing season of 1900, at Pyramid Harbor, as sailors and fishermen, agreeing to do "regular ship's duty, both up and down, discharging and loading; and to do any other work whatsoever when requested to do so by the captain or agent of the Alaska Packers' Association." By the terms of this agreement, the appellant was to pay each of the libelants $50 for the season, and two cents for each red salmon in the catching of which he took part.

On the 15th day of April, 1900, 21 of the libelants signed shipping articles by which they shipped as seamen on the Two Brothers, a vessel chartered by the appellant for the voyage between San Francisco and Pyramid Harbor, and also bound themselves to perform the same work for the appellant provided for by the previous contract of March 26th; the appellant agreeing to pay them therefor the sum of $60 for the season, and two cents each for each red salmon in the catching of which they should respectively take part. Under these contracts, the libelants sailed on board the Two Brothers for Pyramid Harbor, where the appellant had about $150,000 invested in a salmon cannery. The libelants arrived there early in April of the year mentioned, and began to unload the vessel and fit up the cannery. A few days thereafter, to wit, May 19th, they stopped work in a body, and demanded of the company's superintendent there in charge $100 for services in operating the vessel to and from Pyramid Harbor, instead of the sums stipulated for in and by the contracts; stating that unless they were paid this additional wage they would stop work entirely, and return to San Francisco. The evidence showed, and the court below found, that it was impossible for the appellant to get other men to take the places of the libelants, the place being remote, the season short and just opening; so that, after endeavoring for several days without success to induce the libelants to proceed with their work in accordance with their contracts, the company's superintendent, on the 22d day of May, so far yielded to their demands as to instruct his clerk to copy the contracts executed in San Francisco, including the words "Alaska Packers' Association" at the end, substituting, for the $50 and $60 payments, respectively, of those contracts, the sum of $100, which document, so prepared, was signed by the libelants before a shipping commissioner whom they had requested to be brought from Northeast Point; the superintendent, however, testifying that he at the time told the libelants that he was without authority to enter into any such contract, or to in any way alter the contracts made between them and the company in San Francisco. Upon the return of the libelants to San Francisco at the close of the fishing season, they demanded pay in accordance with the terms of the alleged contract of May 22d, when the company denied its validity, and refused to pay other than as provided for by the contracts of March 26th and April 5th, respectively. Some of the libelants, at least, consulted counsel, and, after receiving his advice, those of them who had signed the shipping articles before the shipping commissioner at San Francisco went before that officer, and received the amount due them thereunder, executing in consideration thereof a release in full, and the others being paid at the office of the company, also receipting in full for their demands.

On the trial in the court below, the libelants undertook to show that the fishing nets provided by the respondent were defective, and that it was on that account that they demanded increased wages. On that point, the evidence was substantially conflicting, and the finding of the court was against the libelants. * * *

The evidence being sharply conflicting in respect to these facts, the conclusions of the court, who heard and saw the witnesses, will not be disturbed. * * *

The real questions in the case as brought here are questions of law, and, in the view that we take of the case, it will be necessary to consider but one of those. Assuming that the appellant's superintendent at Pyramid Harbor was authorized to make the alleged contract of May 22d, and that he executed it on behalf of the appellant, was it supported by a sufficient consideration? From the foregoing statement of the case, it will have been seen that the libelants agreed in writing, for certain stated compensation, to render their services to the appellant in remote waters where the season for conducting fishing operations is extremely short, and in which enterprise the appellant had a large amount of money invested; and, after having entered upon the discharge of their contract, and at a time when it was impossible for the appellant to secure other men in their places, the libelants, without any valid cause, absolutely refused to continue the services they were under contract to perform unless the appellant would consent to pay them more money. Consent to such a demand, under such circumstances, if given, was, in our opinion, without consideration, for the reason that it was based solely upon the libelants' agreement to render the exact services, and none other, that they were already under contract to render. The case shows that they willfully and arbitrarily broke that obligation. As a matter of course, they were liable to the appellant in damages, and it is quite probable, as suggested by the court below in its opinion, that they may have been unable to respond in damages. But we are unable to agree with the conclusions there drawn, from these facts, in these words:

> "Under such circumstances, it would be strange, indeed, if the law would not permit the defendant to waive the damages caused by the libelants' breach, and enter into the contract sued upon,—a contract mutually beneficial to all the parties thereto, in that it gave to the libelants reasonable compensation for their labor, and enabled the defendant to employ to advantage the large capital it had invested in its canning and fishing plant."

Certainly, it cannot be justly held, upon the record in this case, that there was any voluntary waiver on the part of the appellant of the breach of the original contract. The company itself knew nothing of such breach until the expedition returned to San Francisco, and the testimony is uncontradicted that its superintendent at Pyramid Harbor, who, it is claimed, made on its behalf the contract sued on, distinctly informed the libelants that he had no power to alter the original or to make a new contract; and it would, of course, follow that, if he had no power to change the original, he would have no authority to waive any rights thereunder. The circumstances of the present case bring it, we think, directly within the sound and just observations of the supreme court of Minnesota in the case of King v. Railway Co., 61 Minn. 482, 63 N.W. 1105:

> "No astute reasoning can change the plain fact that the party who refuses to perform, and thereby coerces a promise from the other party to the contract to pay him an increased compensation for doing that which he is legally bound to do, takes an unjustifiable advantage of the necessities of the other party. Surely it would be a travesty on justice to hold that the party so making the promise for extra pay was estopped from asserting that the promise was without consideration. A party cannot lay the foundation of an estoppel by his own wrong, where the promise is simply a repetition of a subsisting legal promise. There can be no consideration for the promise of the other party, and there is no warrant for inferring that the parties have voluntarily rescinded or modified their contract. The promise cannot be legally enforced, although the other party has completed his contract in reliance upon it."

[Judgment reversed.]

THREEDY, A FISH STORY: ALASKA PACKERS' ASSOCIATION V. DOMENICO

Contracts Stories 361 (2007).

Crucial to seeing this case as one of coercion is the assumption that if the men had refused to work, Alaska Packers had no other means of obtaining salmon and would have lost its investment in the cannery. The substantial contributions of the Native American fishermen to the cannery's operation, as well as the resources of the fish trust are not seen.

SCHWARTZREICH V. BAUMAN-BASCH, INC.

Court of Appeals of New York, 1921.
231 N.Y. 196, 131 N.E. 887.

CRANE, J. On the 31st day of August, 1917, the plaintiff entered into the following employment agreement with the defendant:

"Bauman-Basch, Inc.
"Coats & Wraps
"31–33 East 32d Street
"New York

"Agreement entered into this 31st day of August, 1917, by and between Bauman-Basch, Inc., a domestic corporation, party of the first part, and Louis Schwartzreich, of the borough of Bronx, city of New York, party of the second part, witnesseth:

"The party of the first part does hereby employ the party of the second part, and the party of the second part agrees to enter the services of the party of the first part as a designer of coats and wraps.

"The employment herein shall commence on the 22d day of November, 1917, and shall continue for twelve months thereafter. The party of the second part shall receive a salary of ninety ($90.00) per week, payable weekly.

"The party of the second part shall devote his entire time and attention to the business of the party of the first part, and shall use his best energies and endeavors in the furtherance of its business.

"In witness whereof, the party of the first part has caused its seal to be affixed hereto and these presents to be signed, and the party of the second part has hereunto set his hand and seal the day and year first above written.

"BAUMAN-BASCH, INC.,
"S. BAUMAN.
"LOUIS SCHWARTZREICH.

"In the presence of."

In October the plaintiff was offered more money by another concern. Mr. Bauman, an officer of the Bauman-Basch, Inc., says that in that month he heard that the plaintiff was going to leave and thereupon had with him the following conversation:

> "A. I called him in the office, and I asked him, 'Is that true that you want to leave us?' and he said 'Yes,' and I said, 'Mr. Schwartzreich, how can you do that; you are under contract with us?' He said, 'Somebody offered me more money.' * * * I said, 'How much do they offer you?' He said, 'They offered him $115 a week.' * * * I said, 'I cannot get a designer now, and, in view of the fact that I have to send my sample line out on the road, I will give you a hundred dollars a week rather than to let you go.' He said, 'If you will give me $100, I will stay.' "

Thereupon Mr. Bauman dictated to his stenographer a new contract, dated October 17, 1917, in the exact words of the first contract and running for the same period, the salary being $100 a week, which contract was duly executed by the parties and witnessed. Duplicate originals were kept by the plaintiff and defendant.

Simultaneously with the signing of this new contract the plaintiff's copy of the old contract was either given to or left with Mr. Bauman. He testifies that the plaintiff gave him the paper but that he did not take it from him. The signatures to the old contract plaintiff tore off at the time according to Mr. Bauman.

The plaintiff's version as to the execution of the new contract is as follows:

> "A. I told Mr. Bauman that I have an offer from Scheer & Mayer of $110 a week, and I said to him: 'Do you advise me as a friendly matter—will you advise me as a friendly matter what to do; you see I have a contract with you, and I should not accept the offer of $110 a week, and I ask you, as a matter of friendship, do you advise me to take it or not.' At the minute he did not say anything, but the day afterwards he came to me in and he said, 'I will give you $100 a week, and I want you to stay with me.' I said: 'All right, I will accept it; it is very nice of you that you do that, and I appreciate it very much.' "

The plaintiff says that on the 17th of October, when the new contract was signed, he gave his copy of the old contract back to Mr. Bauman, who said: "You do not want this contract any more because the new one takes its place."

The plaintiff remained in the defendant's employ until the following December, when he was discharged. He brought this action under the contract of October 17th for his damages.

The defense, insisted upon through all the courts, is that there was no consideration for the new contract as the plaintiff was already bound under his agreement of August 31, 1917, to do the same work for the same period at $90 a week.

The trial justice submitted to the jury the question whether there was a cancellation of the old contract and charged as follows:

> "If you find that the $90 contract was prior to or at the time of the execution of the $100 contract canceled and revoked by the parties by their mutual consent, then it is your duty to find that there was a consideration for the making of the contract in suit, viz., the $100 contract, and, in that event, the plaintiff would be entitled to your verdict for such damages as you may find resulted proximately, naturally, and necessarily in consequence of the plaintiff's discharge prior to the termination of the contract period of which I shall speak later on."

Defendant's counsel thereupon excepted to that portion of the charge in which the court permitted the jury to find that the prior contract may have been canceled simultaneously with the execution of the other agreement. Again the court said:

> "The test question is whether by word or by act, either prior to or at the time of the signing of the $100 contract, these parties mutually agreed that the old contract from that instant should be null and void."

The jury having rendered a verdict for the plaintiff, the trial justice set it aside and dismissed the complaint on the ground that there was not sufficient evidence that the first contract was canceled to warrant the jury's findings.

The above quotations from the record show that a question of fact was presented and that the evidence most favorable for the plaintiff would sustain a finding that the first contract was destroyed, canceled, or abrogated by the consent of both parties.

The Appellate Term was right in reversing this ruling. Instead of granting a new trial, however, it reinstated the verdict of the jury and the judgment for the plaintiff. [The Appellate Division affirmed the decision of the Appellate Term.] The question remains, therefore, whether the charge of the court, as above given, was a correct statement of the law or whether on all the evidence in the plaintiff's favor a cause of action was made out.

Can a contract of employment be set aside or terminated by the parties to it and a new one made or substituted in its place? If so, is it competent to end the one and make the other at the same time?

It has been repeatedly held that a promise made to induce a party to do that which he is already bound by contract to perform is without consideration. But the cases in this state, while enforcing this rule, also recognize that a contract may be canceled by mutual consent and a new one made. * * *

* * *

Any change in an existing contract, such as a modification of the rate of compensation, or a supplemental agreement, must have a new consideration to support it. In such a case the contract is continued, not ended. Where, however, an existing contract is terminated by consent of both parties and a new one executed in its place and stead, we have a different situation and the mutual promises are again a consideration. Very little difference may appear in a mere change of compensation in an existing and continuing contract and a termination of one contract and the making of a new one for the same time and work, but at an increased compensation. There is, however, a marked difference in principle. Where the new contract gives any new privilege or advantage to the promisee, a consideration has been recognized, though in the main it is the same contract. Triangle Waist Co., Inc. v. Todd, 223 N.Y. 27, 119 N.E. 85.

If this which we are now holding were not the rule, parties having once made a contract would be prevented from changing it no matter how willing and desirous they might be to do so, unless the terms conferred an additional benefit to the promisee.

All concede that an agreement may be rescinded by mutual consent and a new agreement made thereafter on any terms to which the parties may assent. Prof. Williston, in his work on Contracts, says (volume 1, § 130a):

> "A rescission followed shortly afterwards by a new agreement in regard to the same subject-matter would create the legal obligations provided in the subsequent agreement."

The same effect follows in our judgment from a new contract entered into at the same time the old one is destroyed and rescinded by mutual consent. The determining factor is the rescission by consent. Provided this is the expressed and acted upon intention, the time of the rescission, whether a moment before or at the same time as the making of the new contract, is unimportant.

* * *

As before stated, in this case we have an express rescission and a new contract.

There is no reason that we can see why the parties to a contract may not come together and agree to cancel and rescind an existing contract, making a new one in its place. We are also of the opinion that reason and authority support the conclusion that both transactions can take place at the same time.

For the reasons here stated, the charge of the trial court was correct, and the judgments of the Appellate Division and the Appellate Term should be affirmed, with costs.

* * *

Judgments affirmed.

CHASE, J., dissents.

PROBLEM 5-6

Suppose Schwartzreich came to your law office after receiving the offer of additional compensation elsewhere, and asked you to represent him in negotiations with Bauman-Basch. Prepare a short outline of the strategy you would propose for conducting those negotiations. Are the divergent views of the parties as to what happened in the actual negotiations surprising?

NOTE: THE PREEXISTING DUTY RULE TODAY

As in Schwartzreich v. Bauman-Basch, Inc., the language of many court opinions is still today concerned with whether modifications were supported by new consideration and with the intricacies of mutual rescission theory and the like, rather than with whether the modification was voluntarily and fairly made. For example, in the case of Recker v. Gustafson, 279 N.W.2d 744 (Iowa 1979), the Reckers and Gustafsons had agreed that the Reckers would pay $290,000 for a tract of land. Subsequent to the agreement, the Reckers, without legal representation, were told by the Gustafsons' attorney that the Gustafsons were "willing to go to court to get out of their agreement and that litigation was expensive," but that the Gustafsons would agree to perform if the Reckers would pay an additional $10,000. The Reckers, in their early twenties, agreed to the price increase.

Was the Reckers' agreement enforceable? Instead of focusing frontally on the issues of voluntariness and fairness, the Iowa court found that there was no consideration in support of the Reckers' promise of an extra $10,000. The court even stated that if the parties had mutually rescinded the original agreement first, the second agreement would have been enforceable, but found no evidence of a rescission.

If parties freely and fairly enter a modification agreement, should it matter whether they formally rescinded their prior agreement first (or rescinded simultaneously)? By the same token, if the modification agreement was not freely and fairly entered, should the presence of formal consideration make the agreement enforceable? For example, suppose the Gustafsons were clearly guilty of coercion but to make their modification enforceable they agreed to convey one day earlier. Should the agreement be enforced?

A recent empirical study, examining the preponderance of modification clauses in 500 online consumer contracts, found that over 95% incorporated a term that allowed modification, 98% of those permitting unilateral changes, and essentially none requiring notice to the consumer. See Shmuel I. Becher & Uri Benoliel, Sneak In Contracts: An Empirical Perspective, 55 Georgia. L. Rev. ___ (forthcoming 2020). The authors argue that such clauses create the risk that "hidden contract changes that harm consumers will go under their radar and be left unnoticed. In such cases, consumers who have read the original contract, or parts of it, may have a false impression of what their contracts say."

UNIFORM COMMERCIAL CODE § 2–209.

Modification, Rescission and Waiver

(1) An agreement modifying a contract within this Article needs no consideration to be binding.

* * *

Official Comment

1. This section seeks to protect and make effective all necessary and desirable modifications of sales contracts without regard to the technicalities which at present hamper such adjustments.

2. Subsection (1) provides that an agreement modifying a sale contract needs no consideration to be binding.

However, modifications made thereunder must meet the test of good faith imposed by this Act. The effective use of bad faith to escape performance on the original contract terms is barred, and the extortion of a "modification" without legitimate commercial reason is ineffective as a violation of the duty of good faith. Nor can a mere technical consideration support a modification made in bad faith.

The test of "good faith" between merchants or as against merchants includes "observance of reasonable commercial standards of fair dealing in the trade" (Section 2–103), and may in some situations require an objectively demonstrable reason for seeking a modification. But such matters as a market shift which makes performance come to involve a loss may provide such a reason even though there is no such unforeseen difficulty as would make out a legal excuse from performance under Sections 2–615 and 2–616.

UNITED STATES v. STUMP HOME SPECIALTIES MFG., INC., 905 F.2d 1117 (7th Cir.1990).

POSNER, CIRCUIT JUDGE.

* * * The cautionary, evidential, and other policies behind the requirement of consideration do not apply, or apply only with much attenuated strength, in the context of written modification. By hypothesis the parties already have a contract, so that the danger of mistaking casual promissory language for an intention to be legally bound is slight; moreover, we deal here with a written, not an oral, modification, so fabrication of a promise is harder.

The requirement of consideration has, however, a distinct function in the modification setting—although one it does not perform well—and that is to prevent coercive modifications. Since one of the main purposes of contracts and of contract law is to facilitate long-term commitments, there is often an interval in the life of a contract during which one party is at the mercy of the other. A may have ordered a machine from B that A wants to place in operation on a given date, specified in their contract; and in expectation of B's complying with the contract, A may have made commitments to his customers that it would be costly to renege on. As the date of scheduled delivery approaches, B may be tempted to demand that A agree to renegotiate the contract price, knowing that A will incur heavy expenses if B fails to deliver on time. A can always refuse to renegotiate, relying instead on his right to sue B for breach of contract if B fails to make delivery by the agreed date. But legal remedies are costly and uncertain, thereby opening the way to duress. Considerations of commercial reputation will deter taking advantage of an opportunity to exert duress on a contract partner in many cases, but not in all: For examples of duress in the contract-modification setting, see *Austin Instrument, Inc. v. Loral Corp.,* 29 N.Y.2d 124, 324 N.Y.S.2d 22, 272 N.E.2d 533 (1971), and *Alaska Packers' Ass'n v. Domenico,* 117 F. 99 (9th Cir.1902); and for general discussion see *Selmer Co. v. Blakeslee-Midwest Co.,* 704 F.2d 924 (7th Cir.1983); *Richards Construction Co. v. Air Conditioning Co. of Hawaii,* 318 F.2d 410, 413–14 (9th Cir.1963) * * *.

The rule that modifications are unenforceable unless supported by consideration strengthens A's position by reducing B's incentive to seek a modification. But it strengthens it feebly, as we pointed out in *Wisconsin Knife Works v. National Metal Crafters, supra,* 781 F.2d at 1285. The law does not require that consideration be adequate—that it be commensurate with what the party accepting it is giving up. Slight consideration, therefore, will suffice to make a contract or a contract modification enforceable. * * * And slight consideration is consistent with coercion. To surrender one's contractual rights in exchange for a peppercorn is not functionally different from surrendering them for nothing.

The sensible course would be to enforce contract modifications (at least if written) regardless of consideration and rely on the defense of duress to prevent abuse. *Wisconsin Knife Works v. National Metal Crafters, supra,* 781 F.2d at 1286; UCC § 2–209, official comment 2; Hillman, *Contract Modification Under the Restatement (Second) of Contracts,* 67 Cornell L.Rev. 680 (1982). All coercive modifications would then be unenforceable, and there would be no need to worry about consideration, an inadequate safeguard against duress.

ANGEL V. MURRAY

Supreme Court of Rhode Island, 1974.
113 R.I. 482, 322 A.2d 630.

[The city of Newport agreed to pay its refuse collector, Maher, an additional $10,000 per year over and above the amount previously agreed upon. Maher had requested the additional money because of a substantial increase in the cost of collection due to an unexpected increase in the number of dwelling units. Angel brought an action claiming that the city had illegally paid $20,000 to Maher for two years service and requested that the collector be ordered to repay it. The lower court ordered the repayment and the city and Maher appealed.]

ROBERTS, C.J.

* * *

The primary purpose of the preexisting duty rule is to prevent what has been referred to as the "hold-up game." * * *

[An] example of the "hold-up game" is found in the area of construction contracts. Frequently, a contractor will refuse to complete work under an unprofitable contract unless he is awarded additional compensation. The courts have generally held that a subsequent agreement to award additional compensation is unenforceable if the contractor is only performing work which would have been required of him under the original contract. *See, e.g.,* Lingenfelder v. Wainwright Brewing Co., 103 Mo. 578, 15 S.W. 844 (1891), which is a leading case in this area. * * *

[This example] clearly illustrate[s] that the courts will not enforce an agreement that has been procured by coercion or duress and will hold the parties to their original contract regardless of whether it is profitable or unprofitable. However, the courts have been reluctant to apply the preexisting duty rule when a party to a contract encounters unanticipated difficulties and the other party, not influenced by coercion or duress, voluntarily agrees to pay additional compensation for work already required to be performed under the contract. For example, the courts have found that the original contract was rescinded, Linz v. Schuck, 106 Md.

220, 67 A. 286 (1907); abandoned, Connelly v. Devoe, 37 Conn. 570 (1871), or waived, Michaud v. McGregor, 61 Minn. 198, 63 N.W. 479 (1895).

Although the preexisting duty rule has served a useful purpose insofar as it deters parties from using coercion and duress to obtain additional compensation, it has been widely criticized as a general rule of law. * * *

The modern trend appears to recognize the necessity that courts should enforce agreements modifying contracts when unexpected or unanticipated difficulties arise during the course of the performance of a contract, even though there is no consideration for the modification, as long as the parties agree voluntarily.

Under the Uniform Commercial Code, § 2–209(1), which has been adopted by 49 states, "[a]n agreement modifying a contract [for the sale of goods] needs no consideration to be binding." *See* G.L.1956 (1969 Reenactment) § 6A–2–209(1). Although at first blush this section appears to validate modifications obtained by coercion and duress, the comments to this section indicate that a modification under this section must meet the test of good faith imposed by the Code, and a modification obtained by extortion without a legitimate commercial reason is unenforceable.

The modern trend away from a rigid application of the preexisting duty rule is reflected by § 89D(a) of the American Law Institute's Restatement Second of the Law of Contracts, [now section 89(a)] which provides: "A promise modifying a duty under a contract not fully performed on either side is binding (a) if the modification is fair and equitable in view of circumstances not anticipated by the parties when the contract was made * * *."

We believe that § 89D(a) is the proper rule of law and find it applicable to the facts of this case. It not only prohibits modifications obtained by coercion, duress, or extortion but also fulfills society's expectation that agreements entered into voluntarily will be enforced by the courts. *See generally* Horwitz, The Historical Foundations of Modern Contract Law, 87 Harv.L.Rev. 917 (1974). Section 89D(a), of course, does not compel a modification of an unprofitable or unfair contract; it only enforces a modification if the parties voluntarily agree and if (1) the promise modifying the original contract was made before the contract was fully performed on either side, (2) the underlying circumstances which prompted the modification were unanticipated by the parties, and (3) the modification is fair and equitable.

The evidence, which is uncontradicted, reveals that in June of 1968 Maher requested the city council to pay him an additional $10,000 for the year beginning on July 1, 1968, and ending on June 30, 1969. This request was made at a public meeting of the city council, where Maher explained in detail his reasons for making the request. Thereafter, the city council voted to authorize the Mayor to sign an amendment to the 1964 contract which provided that Maher would receive an additional $10,000 per year for the duration of the contract. Under such circumstances we have no doubt that the city voluntarily agreed to modify the 1964 contract.

Having determined the voluntariness of this agreement, we turn our attention to the three criteria delineated above. First, the modification was made in June of 1968 at a time when the five-year contract which was made in 1964 had not been fully performed by either party. Second, although the 1964 contract provided that Maher collect all refuse generated within the city, it appears this contract was premised on Maher's past experience that the number of refuse-generating units would increase at a rate of 20 to 25 per year. Furthermore, the evidence is uncontradicted that the 1967–1968 increase of 400 units "went beyond any previous expectation." Clearly, the circumstances which prompted the city council to modify the 1964 contract were unanticipated. Third, although the evidence does not indicate what proportion of the total this increase comprised, the evidence does indicate that it was a "substantial" increase. In light of this, we cannot say that the council's agreement to pay Maher the $10,000 increase was not fair and equitable in the circumstances.

The judgment appealed from is reversed, and the cause is remanded to the Superior Court for entry of judgment for the defendants.

HILLMAN, CONTRACT MODIFICATION UNDER THE RESTATEMENT (SECOND) OF CONTRACTS

67 Cornell L.Rev. 680, 699–700 (1982).

The Inadequacy of Section 89(a)

Perhaps the greatest shortcoming of section 89(a) is not its ambiguity but its underinclusiveness. As an exception to the preexisting-duty rule of section 73, section 89(a) simply may not extend to many situations in which modifications, because they are voluntary, should be enforced. As noted earlier, despite the presence of the "unanticipated circumstances" test, the real thrust of section 89(a) may involve an application of the "fair and equitable" requirement to determine whether a modification was voluntarily made. Nevertheless, the "in view of" connective phrase between "fair and equitable" and "unanticipated circumstances" indicates that some "unanticipated circumstance" must be found before the court can proceed to the voluntariness issue. A host of reasons exist, however, for voluntarily agreeing to a modification in the absence of any unanticipated event. For example, in Illustration 3 to section 89(a), loosely based on *Schwartzreich v. Bauman-Basch, Inc.*, a promise to increase an employee's salary is enforceable when a third party has made the employee a better offer. In *Schwartzreich,* the court did not rest its decision to enforce the modification on the basis of "unanticipated circumstances"; perhaps it did not believe that the third-party offer constituted "unanticipated circumstances."

Instead, it found that a rescission-replacement had occurred. Nevertheless, the court's enforcement of the modification does suggest a belief that the modification was "fair and equitable" under the circumstances.

Requiring either additional consideration or an "unanticipated" event to validate modifications presupposes that contracting parties always act with economic rationality in relation to a particular transaction. This assumption simply is not accurate because a particular contract may be only one part of a much more extensive relationship between the parties. When such a complex relationship exists, there may be excellent reasons for one party to give up something in the short term with the expectation of a return in the future. The party actually may be acting with perfect economic rationality, but only a much broader examination of the overall relationship of the parties will make such a conclusion possible.

MACNEIL, ECONOMIC ANALYSIS OF CONTRACTUAL RELATIONS: ITS SHORTFALLS AND THE NEED FOR A "RICH CLASSIFICATORY APPARATUS"

75 N.W.U.L.Rev. 1018, 1048 (1981).

If there is anything plain in the real economic world it is that seldom do participants in contractual relations go for the jugular when trouble arises. The high transaction costs of fighting are undoubtedly one explanation, but even discounting for that factor, a huge residue of nonassertiveness remains explainable only by the willingness to sacrifice immediate exchange-gains to increase relational security.

FLOWERS V. DIAMOND SHAMROCK CORP.

United States Court of Appeals, Fifth Circuit, 1982.
693 F.2d 1146.

TATE, CIRCUIT JUDGE.

In this Texas diversity suit, the plaintiffs (the Flowers), lessors of the mineral rights of Texas oil and gas fields, seek additional royalties under a market value royalty provision contained in their leases with the defendant, Diamond Shamrock Corporation (Shamrock). The Flowers contend that Shamrock did not base royalty payments on the "market value" of subsequent sales of the gas from the leased properties, but rather only on the lower amount of the actual proceeds from Shamrock's long-term sales contract with an intrastate distributor. The plaintiffs Flowers' cause of action is founded upon the Texas jurisprudential holdings that a landowner-lessor is entitled to royalty payment for gas sold off his premises based upon the market value at the time of sale after production, not upon the price established between the producer and the distributor under an earlier long term contract. *Texas Oil & Gas Corporation v. Vela,* 429 S.W.2d 866, 870–71 (Tex.1968).

The district court set aside parts of favorable jury determinations that justified an award to the Flowers of increased royalties. In so doing, the court held * * * that the endorsement of royalty checks as a matter of law constituted an accord and satisfaction as to some of the earlier royalty payments * * *.

* * * [W]e hold * * * that the jury could properly find on the evidence before it that, when the Flowers endorsed the royalty checks, there was no bona fide dispute as to the amount thereof (an essential prerequisite under Texas law to an accord and satisfaction), so that the district court therefore erred in granting judgment notwithstanding the jury verdict. We remand for the determination of additional royalties therefore due * * *.

The Facts

The plaintiffs Flowers have royalty interests under an oil and gas lease on lands in Ochiltree County, Texas. The defendant Shamrock, as lessee, agreed to pay the plaintiffs royalties based on the "market value" of the natural gas produced from a well it drilled on the property.[1] Gas was discovered on the property in 1963 and since that date has been sold and used solely within the state of Texas.

Shamrock pipes the natural gas from the well to its refinery, where the liquid contents of the gas are stripped, and the residue is sold at the plant "tailgate" to a distributor. Although it commingles the gas from many wells at the refinery, Shamrock measures at each well the volume (by thousand cubic feet, or MCF) and the heating value (by British Thermal Unit, or BTU) of the gas. In 1965 Shamrock committed the gas from the Flowers' well, in addition to that produced from other leased properties, to a twenty-year sales contract with the Southwestern Public Service Company (Southwestern), setting a beginning price at 19.5 cents per thousand cubic feet of gas containing 1000 BTU per cubic foot, escalating over the life of the contract to 22.5 cents. Shamrock has paid the Flowers a royalty based on this contract price, or at times a slightly higher price.

Shamrock tendered to the plaintiffs monthly checks for royalty payments calculated upon the contract price, and the plaintiffs endorsed and cashed these checks. A stub was attached to each check which showed lease numbers, a number that presumably showed the volume of production, the amount of severance tax deducted, and an amount labelled

---

[1] The gas royalty clause of the lease provides that:

The royalties to be paid by lessee are: * * * on gas, including casinghead gas or other gaseous substances, produced from said land and sold or used off the premises or for the extraction of gasoline or other product therefrom, the market value at the well of one-eighth of the gas so sold or used. * * *

Shamrock is the corporate successor to Shamrock Oil and Gas Corporation, the lessee by assignment of the mineral interests in the Flowers' properties. For convenience, use of the Shamrock name includes the predecessor in title or corporate entity.

"Your Part," which was the amount of the check. The following small print appeared on the back of the check itself:

Endorsements

> This check is issued in full settlement of the account stated and the payee accepts it as such by his endorsement. If not correct, return without alteration and state difference.

On February 15, 1974, Shamrock sent a form letter to its royalty owners, including the Flowers, offering to pay higher royalties if the lessor executed a contract agreeing to accept royalties directly based on the sales contract proceeds from the lessee-distributor sales contracts rather than on the market value method of computation set forth in the original leases. On July 29, 1974, Marvin Flowers, for the Flowers, replied that there was no reason to execute an agreement to obtain a rate increase to which the lessors were entitled, and requested payment of "deficit funds" from February.[2] Shamrock acknowledged receipt of that letter in a response attached to the plaintiffs' original pleading, but not introduced into evidence, informing the Flowers that it would continue to pay the royalty in accordance with the lease provisions.

The plaintiffs did not express further dissatisfaction with the amount of royalties received, but stopped endorsing and cashing the checks in February, 1977, and eventually brought this lawsuit.

The plaintiff-lessors sued for the difference in the royalties due them under *Vela* since December, 1973. Trial was to a jury, which found the market values for the applicable months and failed to find for the defendant on its affirmative defense of accord and satisfaction. The trial court granted Shamrock's motion for judgment notwithstanding the verdict. * * * [T]he

---

[2] The July 29, 1974 letter by Marvin Flowers stated:

I have your letter of February 15, 1974, written to me stating that you wished to offer an immediate and substantial increase in my royalty rate pending the signing of an enclosed royalty agreement. The June 1974 gas payment reflected this rate increase.

I am not aware of any previous agreement with you which makes it a requirement for me to sign any document prior to receiving a rate increase on natural gas production from the aforesaid leases.

With this understanding, I am requesting that you pay deficit funds due for the months of February, March, April, and May.

Marvin Flowers testified that he wasn't "sure what the implications" of the communication received by him from Shamrock were, that "he was dissatisfied with what I was getting for my gas," that he thought from Shamrock's letter that he "was due more money going back to February, 1974," but that he was "not technically sharp enough to know what he was getting for my gas." The evidence reveals that the Flowers did not at that time consult a lawyer and that they were completely unaware of their right under *Vela* to receive royalties at all times after the initial production in 1965 that were based on the actual market value of the gas rather than upon the price received by Shamrock from its sales under the contract with the distributor. The purport of Marvin Flowers' testimony, rather, is that he suspected for reason unknown, but probably related to the measurement of the gas or to the price actually received by Shamrock from the distributor, that since February 1974 the gas royalties paid to the Flowers were insufficient—otherwise Shamrock would not have offered the new contract in February 1974.

court held that the defendant had established its accord and satisfaction defense as a matter of law as to those months from 1973 to 1977 when royalty checks were cashed by the plaintiffs. No recovery was therefore awarded for those months. * * *

* * *

I. Accord and Satisfaction

The district court held that the evidence adduced in trial showed, as a matter of law, that the royalty checks cashed by the plaintiffs were accepted in satisfaction of an unliquidated claim. Any dispute over the market value of the gas on which the Flowers' royalties were based was therefore conclusively resolved in an accord and satisfaction with Shamrock that foreclosed recovery of additional amounts.

The plaintiffs Flowers point out that judgment notwithstanding a jury verdict should not be granted by the trial court unless "the facts and inferences point so strongly and overwhelmingly in favor of one party that * * * reasonable men could not arrive at a contrary verdict." *Boeing v. Shipman,* 411 F.2d 365, 374 (5th Cir.1969) (en banc). In ruling upon such a motion, the court must consider all the evidence "in the light and with all reasonable inferences most favorable to the party opposed to the motion." *Id.* Tested by this standard, we agree with the plaintiffs Flowers' contention that the evidence before the jury reasonably permitted a determination, as a factual matter, that at the time the Flowers perfunctorily endorsed their royalty checks, they were not aware of any bona fide dispute between themselves and Shamrock as to the amount of gas royalties due to them under the lease. The jury could thus find under the evidence that, by their endorsements, the Flowers could not have intended to relinquish their rights under *Vela* to additional gas royalties based upon the market value of the gas at the time of production and sale (rather than upon the much lower price received by Shamrock as a result of its long-term contract entered into years earlier with the intrastate distributor).

Shamrock argues that the Flowers' endorsement of the checks conclusively indicates that they relinquished claims to a greater amount. Shamrock contends that this amount was disputed by the Flowers at least as early as July, 1974, the date of the plaintiffs' letter to Shamrock indicating their belief that there may have been a deficit in royalty amounts paid. *See* note 2 *supra.*

The Supreme Court of Texas set out the requirements of an accord and satisfaction in *Jenkins v. Henry C. Beck Co.,* 449 S.W.2d 454, 455 (Tex.1969):

> This defense rests upon a new contract, express or implied, in which the parties agree to the discharge of the existing obligation

> by means of the lesser payment tendered and accepted. * * * The minds must meet and where resting in implication the facts proved must irresistibly point to such conclusion. * * * There must be an unmistakable communication to the creditor that tender of the lesser sum is upon the condition that acceptance will constitute satisfaction of the underlying obligation. It has been said that the conditions must be made plain, definite and certain * * *; that the statement accompanying the tender of a sum less than the contract price must be so clear, full and explicit that it is not susceptible of any other interpretation * * *; that the offer must be accompanied with acts and declarations which the creditor is "bound to understand". * * *

* * *

The consideration for the new contract establishing a discharge of the prior obligation is the settlement of a bona fide dispute between the parties.[3] *See Roylex, Inc. v. S & B Engineers, Inc.,* 592 S.W.2d 59, 60 (Tex.Civ.App.1979) (*see also* " 'The condition that the tender is in full settlement must be brought home to the creditor' ", *id.*) * * *. In the absence of a bona fide dispute as to the obligation owed by the debtor, the acceptance and endorsement of a check marked, "This check is in full settlement of account as shown hereon. Acceptance by endorsement constitutes receipt in full," does not prevent the creditor from collecting the balance of the obligation. *See Ortiz Oil Co. v. Geyer,* 159 S.W.2d 494, 497 (Tex.1942). The requirement of a bona fide dispute presupposes both parties' knowledge that there exists a particular issue as to a greater liability that is settled by the accord. *See Firestone Tire & Rubber Co. v. White,* 274 S.W.2d 452, 455 (Tex.Civ.App.1954), where, even though there was a dispute between the parties as to the debt owed on the purchase of certain merchandise, a judgment for the debtor was reversed because it had not been shown that the money paid was with full knowledge that it was intended to be in full settlement of all matters, including purchases of merchandise the creditor overlooked in preparing the bill.

Mutual assent of the parties to settlement of a dispute is a requirement for an accord and satisfaction, and the creditor must fully understand that the amount tendered is conditioned as full disposition of the underlying obligation. "[I]f the creditor is to be held to have surrendered his claim against the debtor, it must be shown that he understood or should have understood that he was doing so when he received the consideration

[3] Although Texas law continues to distinguish between accord and satisfaction of liquidated claims for a set amount, and of unliquidated claims (where the amount or extent of the obligation is disputed), sufficient consideration for an accord arises out of the settlement of a dispute as to the existence or amount of liability. *See Burgamy v. Davis,* 313 S.W.2d 365, 367 (Tex.Civ.App.1958); *Firestone Tire & Rubber Co. v. White,* 274 S.W.2d 452, 455 (Tex.Civ.App.1954). A bona fide dispute is a prerequisite to an accord of either type of claim. *Id.*

claimed therefor." *Call of Houston, Inc. v. Mulvey,* 343 S.W.2d 522, 524 (Tex.Civ.App.1961). In *Call of Houston,* an employee with a 90-day notice of termination clause in his employment contract was not aware at the time he received payment covering thirty days of the notice period with a check marked "Account in Full" that there was a dispute with his employer as to the necessity of providing ninety days notice or that he accepted the check in settlement of the employer's breach of contract. Because of lack of knowledge and mutual assent, there was no accord and satisfaction.

The parties may refer to past duties or future liabilities between them to prove or disprove the existence of an accord and satisfaction. Such factual issues are to be determined by the jury. *See Call of Houston, supra,* 343 S.W.2d at 525. The Texas cases reiterate the requirement that the minds of creditor and debtor must be found to have met in the making of the new contract "in which the parties agree to the discharge of the existing obligation by means of the lesser payment tendered and accepted." *Industrial Life Insurance Co. v. Finley,* 382 S.W.2d 100, 104 (Tex.1964).

In the present instance, no evidence whatsoever shows that the Flowers had or should have had any knowledge, at the time, that negotiation of these checks would affect or settle a disagreement as to the market value of the gas on which royalties were based. Shamrock's position at all times was that plaintiffs were being paid in accordance with the lease, and there is no evidence in the record that any of the plaintiffs were aware of the incorrectness of that position under *Vela.* The endorsement says that the "account stated" is fully paid and, indeed, the "your part" amount shown on the stub was paid by each check. No issue or dispute relative to value is suggested on the check or stub, and the statement above the place for the endorsement is far from the unequivocal notice to plaintiffs that the checks were conditionally tendered in full and final satisfaction of a disputed obligation, which Texas law requires for there to be an accord and satisfaction. The Flowers' endorsement of the royalty checks signified to them nothing more than acceptance of their part of the gas measured and the account computed at the rate being paid by Shamrock. There is no unequivocal statement here that the endorsement compromises and settles a disputed rate issue; it just as plainly, if not only, purports to make the endorsement an acceptance of Shamrock's arithmetic.[4]

[4] No evidence shows that any of the plaintiffs knew of the holding of *Texas Oil & Gas Corp. v. Vela,* 429 S.W.2d 866 (Tex.1968), and what it meant to their rights in the settlement of the gas royalty. There, as noted, the Texas Supreme Court held that market value should be determined as of the time of delivery of the gas to the purchaser, rather than as of the time of the making of the contract between the lessee and purchaser, and Shamrock undoubtedly knew four years later of the effect of that holding upon its obligation to these plaintiffs. No other logical reason appears for its attempt to get the plaintiffs to amend the lease in this respect. No explanation was made to the plaintiffs of their *Vela* claim under the existing lease, or of the nature of Shamrock's breach of contract in the payment of royalties on the basis of the 1965 contract.

Nor is there evidence that the trial jury was conclusively required to accept to the effect that the Flowers knew that there was a dispute as to the amount of gas royalties due to them, let alone knew that they were indisputably entitled under *Vela* to receive the market value price at the time of sale after production, as opposed to the below-market-value price determined by the contract between Shamrock and *its* purchasor. It is true that in 1974 the Flowers wrote a letter requesting payment of any deficit royalties, but the letter seems to be a response to Shamrock's offer to amend the contract, not acknowledgement of a dispute concerning calculation of market value. At most, any inferences to be drawn from the letter concerning the Flowers' knowledge of a dispute and of the Flowers' intent to reach an accord and satisfaction, were factual issues to be determined by the jury. Under this record, it cannot be said as a matter of law that with the endorsement of these royalty checks the minds of the royalty owners and Shamrock met to change the market value basis for royalty payment to that of the lesser rate which Shamrock had chosen.

The district court therefore erred in granting summary judgment to Shamrock in contradiction of the jury verdict in favor of the Flowers. The evidence before the jury permitted it to find that there was no factual basis upon which to base an accord and satisfaction between the Flowers and Shamrock, as allegedly resulting from their endorsement of gas royalty payment checks between December 197[3] and March 1977. Accordingly, we reverse that part of the district court's order that denied the Flowers' recovery of additional royalties for this period, and we remand for further calculation of the award due for such royalties. The award is to be based on the jury's month-to-month determination of market value for gas production until March, 1977.

FOAKES v. BEER, 9 App.Cas. 605 (House of Lords 1884). [Foakes owed Beer over £2,000 on a judgment. The parties agreed, according to the Court of Appeal, that if Foakes would pay Beer £500 at once and the rest over a certain period in installments, then Beer would give up the right to interest on the debt. Nevertheless, Beer then sued for the interest. Held for Beer because the agreement lacked consideration. One of the judges, however, pointed out that "all men of business, whether merchants or tradesmen, do every day recognise and act on the ground that prompt payment of a part of their demand may be more beneficial to them than it would be to insist on their rights and enforce payment of the whole."]

CONSOLIDATED EDISON CO. OF NEW YORK, INC. V. ARROLL

Civil Court of the City of New York, 1971.
66 Misc.2d 816, 322 N.Y.S.2d 420.

MILTON SANDERS, JUDGE.

This is an action by Consolidated Edison Company of New York, Inc., ("Con Edison,") to recover a balance alleged to be due from defendant on five electric bills for the summer periods of 1968, 1969, and 1970. Defendant disputed the amounts of these bills on the basis that they exceeded past bills for comparable periods, including the summer of 1967, by too great an amount to have any validity. He questioned the accuracy of the meter and/or the readings taken, as well as Con Edison's statements as to the amount of electricity consumed. After a considerable amount of correspondence had taken place between the parties, defendant sent a letter on December 6, 1969 to the attention of the president of Con Edison, with carbon copies to the company at their local office and to the post office box designated for the payment of bills. The letter stated again defendant's disagreement with the amounts of the first three bills, and advised that he had arbitrarily picked the sum of $35.00 as the proper amount due on each bill, as that sum reflected his past experience, and stated further that he was sending three checks for $35.00 each to the office designated for collection. Each check would bear the legend:

> "This check is in full payment and satisfaction of the bill of Consolidated Edison Company of New York, Inc., to Mark Arroll, Account Number 26–2726–0191–002 for the period of ______ to ______ and negotiation of this check constitutes release of any bills or claims of Consolidated Edison Company of New York, Inc., sometimes known as Con Edison, against Mark Arroll."

The letter went on to state that it is the law that the cashing or mere retention of the checks beyond a reasonable length of time constitutes an accord and satisfaction. On September 25, 1970, defendant took the same action with respect to the remaining two bills in dispute, sending a similar letter to the president of the company, and carbon copies to the same offices. Con Edison subsequently replied to defendant's letters, but it merely re-stated in its replies that the meter and the readings thereof had been found to be accurate, and that the electricity billed for had actually been consumed. The letters made no mention of and completely ignored the paragraphs advising about the checks. Five checks in the amount of $35.00 each were mailed by defendant to the address designated by Con Edison for the payment of bills. Each check bore the legend previously stated on the back thereof. On the face of each check the words "paid in full" were written, together with an identification of the bill to which it related, the defendant's account number, and a reference to the letter of either December 6, 1969 or September 25, 1970. All five checks were received and deposited and Con Edison has retained the proceeds thereof. Con Edison now seeks the difference between the payments received and the full amounts of the bills rendered. The customer's defense is accord and satisfaction.

After considering all of the competent and credible evidence presented, I am satisfied that the meter and the readings taken thereof by Con Edison were accurate, and that the electricity billed for was actually consumed, since defendant failed to submit any evidence to the contrary. I find, therefore, that the disputed bills reflected the proper charges for defendant's use of electricity. We are concerned, however, with whether or not the defense of accord and satisfaction has been established in the light of the facts and circumstances described.

The law is well settled that where an amount due is in dispute, and the debtor sends a check for less than the amount claimed, and clearly expresses his intention that the check has been sent as payment in full, and not on account or in part payment, the cashing or retention of the check by the creditor is deemed an acceptance by the creditor of the conditions stated, and operates as an accord and satisfaction of the claim. * * * Con Edison's contention that there was no *bona fide* dispute as to the amount due has no merit. As the Court stated in Schuttinger v. Woodruff, 259 N.Y.2d 212, 181 N.E. 361, in order for the rule to apply, "the debtor must honestly hold the opinion either that he owes nothing or that he is bound only to the extent of paying less than his adversary seeks to exact. * * * The dispute need not rest upon factors arising from sound reasons. The debtor may be wrong in his contention. That he honestly believes in the correctness of his position is enough." (See also Simons v. Supreme Council American Legion of Honor, 178 N.Y. 263, 70 N.E. 776). It is evident, and I so find, from the testimony and the documents and correspondence offered in evidence, that the defendant honestly and in good faith believed that he owed less than the amount Con Edison claimed. Under the circumstances it cannot be said that a *bona fide* dispute did not exist.

* * *

This brings us to the question as to whether the retention of the proceeds of the checks by Con Edison bound the company to an accord and satisfaction. Evidence was presented by Con Edison that the address designated for mailing payment of bills was a post office box from which all payments were picked up directly by employees of the bank in which the company maintained its account. The company argues that the nature and volume of its operations does not allow for an examination by bank employees of each and every check it receives for language written thereon which could bind it to an accord and satisfaction. What Con Edison is really saying is that because it conducts such a large operation, it should be exempted from the application of well settled principles of law which would bind individuals and all smaller business organizations. I cannot accept this conclusion. To permit Con Edison to follow one set of rules while everyone else is following another would cast an intolerable burden on the orderly functioning of the community. The fact remains that Con Edison accepted the benefits of defendant's checks. Con Edison cannot, by arranging for someone else to accept payment of bills for its own convenience, avoid the consequences of the law.

It should be noted that even if Con Edison had written to defendant and expressly rejected the condition that the checks were to be accepted as full payment, the depositing and retention of the proceeds of the checks would nevertheless operate as an accord and satisfaction. As the court stated in Carlton Credit Corp. v. Atlantic Refining Co., [12 A.D.2d 613, 208 N.Y.S.2d 622, *aff'd* 10 N.Y.2d 723, 219 N.Y.S.2d 269, 176 N.E.2d 837] "The plaintiff could not accept the payment and reject the condition (citations omitted). It was fully aware of the attempt to satisfy the amount claimed with a lesser payment but despite that it accepted the check with the condition imposed. True, it is stated that there was no intention to accept the check in full satisfaction and protest was registered. However, such protest is unavailing." (See also Rosenblatt v. Birnbaum, 16 N.Y.2d 212, 264 N.Y.S.2d 521, 212 N.E.2d 37). It is not the creditor's intent that controls. "What is said is overridden by what is done, and assent is imputed as an inference of law" (CARDOZO, Ch. J., in Hudson v. Yonkers Fruit Co., 258 N.Y. 168, 179 N.E. 373).

There is no question that Con Edison was given sufficient notification that the checks were to be considered as payment in full. Defendant's letters to Con Edison's president clearly indicated defendant's intent. In Carlton Credit Corp. v. Atlantic Refining Co., [supra] a case quite similar to this one, it was said that: "The acceptance and negotiation by the plaintiff of the defendant's check constituted an accord and satisfaction. The covering letter to which the check was annexed, itemizing in detail the deductions claimed, makes it clear that the payment made was conditioned upon its acceptance as payment in full for the larger amount claimed by the plaintiff to be due it from the defendant."

The affirmative defense of accord and satisfaction is sustained. Judgment for defendant.

UNIFORM COMMERCIAL CODE § 3–311(c)(1).

Accord and Satisfaction by Use of Instrument

* * * [A] claim is not discharged * * * if * * * [t]he claimant, if an organization, proves that (i) within a reasonable time before the tender, the claimant sent a conspicuous statement to the person against whom the claim is asserted that communication concerning disputed debts, including an instrument tendered as full satisfaction of a debt, are to be sent to a

designated person, office, or place, and (ii) the instrument or accompanying communication was not received by that designated person, office, or place.

PROBLEM 5-7

James Geis, a physicist, and his associate, Cofek, were attempting to develop a laser scanning inspection system (LSIS). They formed a corporation, Geisco, Inc., which contracted with Honeywell Radiation Center through a series of "purchase orders" for Geisco to supply services to design and develop the LSIS. The original purchase order provided that the parties' agreement terminated on June 11, 2004; although no clear duration was set forth, supplemental purchase orders suggested that the parties regarded the original contract as extending beyond June 11, 2004.

On August 29, 2004, James Geis received the following letter from Sheldon Busansky, general manager of Honeywell:

> "James D. Geis, President GEISCO
> 128 Pleasant Drive
> Cheshire, Conn. 07410
>
> Dear Jim:
>
> In light of the corporate decision not to proceed with the LSIS Project, this is your notification of termination of all agreements between Honeywell and GEISCO effective 31 August 2004. We will, of course, honor the terms of the nondisclosure of information agreements. As recognition of our original intent to participate in a long term relationship we are offering you the 60 day termination notice which was in the licensing agreement you signed earlier. The termination compensation will be in the form of a lump sum payment of $9,300 covering yourself and Henry Cofek for the 60 day period.
>
> No expenses beyond 31 August will be paid by Honeywell.
>
> Sincerely yours,
> Sheldon Busansky"

A few days later Geis received a check made out to Geisco, Inc. for the sum of $9,300. At this time, Geis and Cofek believed that Honeywell had wrongfully terminated Geisco, that Honeywell had failed to use "best efforts" under the agreement to market the LSIS, and that Honeywell had fraudulently induced Geisco to enter the agreements.

Geis has come to your law office and has asked for advice. Can he cash the check without surrendering his rights against Honeywell? If so, must he endorse the check in any special way or send Honeywell any notice? If not, why not?

NOTE:
EXECUTORY ACCORD, ACCORD AND SATISFACTION, AND SUBSTITUTED CONTRACT UNDER THE RESTATEMENT (SECOND) OF CONTRACTS

Section 281(1) defines an accord as "a contract under which an obligee promises to accept a stated performance in satisfaction of the obligor's existing duty." Suppose a creditor and a debtor reasonably disagree as to the amount owed. Suppose further that in a settlement, devoid of foul play, made on July 1, the parties agree that on August 1 the debtor will pay 80% of the amount claimed by the creditor. This is called an executory accord. If the debtor pays the 80% on August 1 the executory accord ripens into an "accord and satisfaction." Can the creditor later change his or her mind and recover on the original obligation? No. The accord and satisfaction is a defense to such a claim.

Now suppose the debtor repudiates the July 1 agreement on July 10 so that the executory accord is never performed by the debtor and thus does not become an "accord and satisfaction." In these circumstances, the creditor can pursue the claim for the full amount, not just the 80%.

Section 279 of the Restatement (Second) defines a "substituted contract" as "one that is itself accepted by the obligee in satisfaction of the original duty and thereby discharges it." According to Comment a, "[i]f the parties intend the new contract to replace all of the provisions of the earlier contract, the contract is a substituted contract." Thus, in our example, if the parties intended their July 1 agreement to be a substitute for the original agreement out of which the creditor's claim arose, then the debtor's duty to pay such a claim is discharged even though the debtor repudiates on July 10. That is, despite the repudiation, the creditor can sue only for breach of the July 1 settlement agreement, not for breach of the original agreement. Of course, the intentions of the parties frequently will be unclear on whether the new agreement is an executory accord or a substituted contract. Section 281 of the Restatement (Second) presumes that a new agreement is merely an accord unless the parties make clear that it is a substituted contract. Why? Would a reasonable creditor agree to accept a mere promise to pay 80% of a debt in substitution for a duty to pay 100%? Comment c to section 279 suggests not.

UNIFORM COMMERCIAL CODE § 1–308.

Performance or Acceptance Under Reservation of Rights

(1) A party who with explicit reservation of rights performs or promises performance or assents to performance in a manner demanded or offered by the other party does not thereby prejudice the rights reserved. Such words as "without prejudice," "under protest" or the like are sufficient.

(2) Subsection (1) does not apply to an accord and satisfaction.

PROBLEM 5-8

On February 20, Sayles, a manufacturer and seller of appliances, and Borden enter a written agreement for the sale to Borden of a freezer to be delivered on March 20. On February 25, however, Sayles notifies Borden in writing that it cannot deliver the freezer until April 15 because of delays in the receipt of materials from its suppliers. Borden responds in writing on February 26 that the delay in delivery will cause Borden substantial losses because it will result in a slowdown of its production of ice cream. Borden accepts the freezers on April 15 and pays the contract price. Borden later brings an action against Sayles for lost profits due to the delay in delivery.

1. What is the legal effect of Borden's letter of February 26? If you were consulted by Borden prior to the letter, how would you have drafted it?

2. What is the legal effect of the acceptance of the goods on April 15? If you had been consulted by Borden prior to the acceptance, what advice would you have given?

R. HILLMAN, PRINCIPLES OF CONTRACT LAW

153 (4th ed. 2019).

Suppose * * * you agree to sell your piano to Alice for $2000. Delivery will be in two weeks. Before delivery you and Alice orally and voluntarily agree to change the price to $1800. However, your original signed contract included what we in the know call a NOM clause (No Oral Modification clause). Is the price of the piano now $2000 or $1800?

You may think that, of course, the price is still $2000. The parties agreed that oral modifications would not be enforceable by agreeing to a NOM clause in the original contract. You could cite authority as well. UCC section 2–209(2) states in part that "[a] signed agreement which excludes modification or rescission except by a signed writing cannot be otherwise modified or rescinded * * *." But would I discuss this issue if it were so easy? You have to worry about subsection (4) of 2–209, which states: "Although an attempt at modification or rescission does not satisfy the requirements of subsection (2) * * * it can operate as a waiver." A waiver is an intentional and voluntary relinquishment of a right. Didn't you agree to give up your right to $200 of the purchase price?

As you can guess, subsections (2) and (4) are hard to harmonize. The "can operate as a waiver" language causes headaches because it doesn't tell us *when* an oral modification *does* operate as a waiver. If always, there is nothing left of subsection 2. In addition, what exactly is an "attempt at modification"? Does it simply require an oral agreement to modify? Does it require reliance?[f] Ultimately, subsections (2) and (4) raise issues involving freedom of contract.

[f] UCC § 2–209(5) lets you retract a waiver "unless the retraction would be unjust in view of a material change of position in reliance on the waiver."

Does freedom of contract mean that parties should have the power to bind themselves only to written modifications or does freedom of contract mean that parties have the power to change their minds about requiring only written modifications? Subsections (2) and (4) evidence the UCC's drafters ambivalence about these issues, leading, of course, to lots of litigation and confusion.

PART THREE

THE PERFORMANCE PROCESS

■ ■ ■

Chapter Six

SUBSTANTIVE CONTENT OF THE DUTY TO PERFORM

Chapter Seven

CONDITIONAL NATURE OF THE DUTY TO PERFORM, AND PERMISSIBLE RESPONSES TO FAILURE OF CONDITION AND BREACH OF DUTY

CHAPTER SIX

SUBSTANTIVE CONTENT OF THE DUTY TO PERFORM

■ ■ ■

In a civilized society people must be able to assume that those with whom they deal will act in good faith, and will carry out their undertakings according to the expectations which the moral sentiment of the community attaches thereto.

POUND

SECTION ONE: THE PERFORMANCE STAGE AND THE ROLE OF LAWYERS

Contracting parties create their own governing law by making an agreement with consideration. The parties' agreement (not general law) specifies most of the content of their duties. In the usual case, privately created law of this kind, often with the help of lawyers, serves its purposes well. When the performance stage arrives, the parties perform their duties without dispute.

Sometimes, however, questions arise about the content of a valid agreement or promise, and these questions may even generate a serious dispute and litigation. A party may consult a lawyer for advice on a course of action, to negotiate a settlement, or even to litigate. To do these things well, the lawyer must understand how courts resolve disputes involving the content and meaning of agreements and promises. This is the subject of the present chapter and the next. These chapters are relevant to the lawyer not only at the performance stage, but at earlier stages as well. As you study the material, consider how a lawyer could have done a better job of planning and drafting to avoid the problem that arose.

Assuming that, for better or worse, the parties or their lawyers have already drafted the contract, one of the lawyer's roles at the performance stage may be to counsel the client. For example, consider again the plight of the Whites and the Benkowskis. Their agreement imposed a duty of performance calling for the Benkowskis to supply "water." Assume Ruth

Benkowski phoned a lawyer after the agreement had been drafted, but before it became effective, and asked whether they must supply potable water. To answer this, the lawyer would have to interpret the agreement.

The lawyer as counselor is also often called on to render advice after the other party's non-performance or even after performance. This, too, usually requires close study of the agreement. For example, suppose the Benkowskis supplied water that was discolored at least once a day for an average of from one to two hours. Would this be a breach?

The lawyer may have to interpret not only the law of the agreement, but communications sent between the parties as well. Suppose the Benkowskis received a letter from the Whites on June 10, indicating that they could not pay on time in July. The Benkowskis might ask their lawyer whether they could cut off the water supply at any time, whether they could cut it off only as of July 1, or whether they could cut it off at all.

The lawyer may have other roles at the performance stage in addition to that of counselor. The lawyer might be asked to negotiate a contract modification to resolve a dispute caused by unforeseen circumstances or by a gap in the parties' agreement. For example, the Whites and the Benkowskis might decide to specify whether the Benkowskis must supply potable water. In such negotiations, the lawyer can seldom ignore the original agreement because it may give bargaining leverage to one party or the other.

When a dispute arises at the performance stage and informal dispute resolution fails, the lawyer may be asked to litigate the "law of the contract" in court.

SECTION TWO: CONTRACT TERMS AND PAROL EVIDENCE RULES

In every jurisdiction, a "parol evidence" rule governs the extent to which a party may introduce in court evidence of a claimed prior or contemporaneous agreement, understanding, or negotiation to explain, supplement, or vary a written agreement. The rule favors written agreements largely on the theory that writings are more reliable than oral agreements. According to *one* version of the parol evidence rule,

> [w]hen two parties have made a contract and have expressed it in a writing to which they have both assented as to the complete and accurate integration of that contract, evidence, whether parol or otherwise, of antecedent understandings and negotiations will not be admitted for the purpose of varying or contradicting the writing.[a]

[a] 3 Corbin on Contracts § 573 at 357 (1960). Prior or contemporaneous terms are "integrated" in a writing, according to Professor Corbin, to the extent that the writing embodies

Observe that we refer to parol evidence *rules* in the title to this section. This is not a typographical error! Scholars, judges, legislatures, and Restatement drafters have recommended or adopted a number of different parol evidence rules and exceptions to the rules. Indeed, one may even find more than one parol evidence rule or exception applicable to the same kind of contract. But all variations and exceptions have this in common: they seek some middle position between blind adherence to the language of a written agreement and total willingness to give binding effect to all extrinsic evidence of antecedent agreements, understandings, or negotiations that may affect the writing. You will see how this challenge helps shape the parol evidence rule and its exceptions. (As to the latter, we focus on the collateral contract and ambiguity exceptions to the rule.)

Observe also that no matter what version of the parol evidence rule that applies, the rule does not govern post-contract statements or conduct. As one court has put it, "[b]y its express * * * language, the rule does not apply to conduct and statements taking place *after* a contract has been executed. Thus, evidence of negotiations occurring after a written agreement will not be excluded by the parol evidence rule. * * * Indeed, contractual rights and remedies may be modified or waived by subsequent conduct." Hofeldt v. Mehling, 658 N.W.2d 783, 787 (S.D. Sup. Ct. 2003).

MITCHILL V. LATH

Court of Appeals of New York, 1928.
247 N.Y. 377, 160 N.E. 646.

Appeal from Supreme Court, Appellate Division, Second Department.

Action by Catherine C. Mitchill against Charles Lath and another. Judgment of Special Term in plaintiff's favor, directing specific performance of an agreement to remove an icehouse, was affirmed by the Appellate Division (220 App.Div. 776, 221 N.Y.S. 864), and defendants appeal. Judgments of Appellate Division and Trial Term reversed, and complaint dismissed.

ANDREWS, J. In the fall of 1923 the Laths owned a farm. This they wished to sell. Across the road, on land belonging to Lieutenant Governor Lunn, they had an icehouse which they might remove. Mrs. Mitchill looked over the land with a view to its purchase. She found the icehouse objectionable. Thereupon "the defendants orally promised and agreed, for and in consideration of the purchase of their farm by the plaintiff, to remove the said icehouse in the spring of 1924." Relying upon this promise, she made a written contract to buy the property for $8,400, for cash and a mortgage and containing various provisions usual in such papers. Later receiving a deed, she entered into possession, and has spent considerable

them. A writing is "complete" if it integrates all such terms. A "partial" integration only incorporates some of the terms.

sums in improving the property for use as a summer residence. The defendants have not fulfilled their promise as to the icehouse, and do not intend to do so. We are not dealing, however, with their moral delinquencies. The question before us is whether their oral agreement may be enforced in a court of equity.

This requires a discussion of the parol evidence rule—a rule of law which defines the limits of the contract to be construed. Glackin v. Bennett, 226 Mass. 316, 115 N.E. 490. It is more than a rule of evidence, and oral testimony, even if admitted, will not control the written contract (O'Malley v. Grady, 222 Mass. 202, 109 N.E. 829), unless admitted without objection (Brady v. Nally, 151 N.Y. 258, 45 N.E. 547). It applies, however, to attempts to modify such a contract by parol. It does not affect a parol collateral contract distinct from and independent of the written agreement. It is, at times, troublesome to draw the line. Williston, in his work on Contracts (section 637) points out the difficulty. "Two entirely distinct contracts," he says, "each for a separate consideration, may be made at the same time, and will be distinct legally. Where, however, one agreement is entered into wholly or partly in consideration of the simultaneous agreement to enter into another, the transactions are necessarily bound together. * * * Then if one of the agreements is oral and the other in writing, the problem arises whether the bond is sufficiently close to prevent proof of the oral agreement." That is the situation here. It is claimed that the defendants are called upon to do more than is required by their written contract in connection with the sale as to which it deals.

The principle may be clear, but it can be given effect by no mechanical rule. As so often happens, it is a matter of degree, for, as Prof. Williston also says, where a contract contains several promises on each side it is not difficult to put any one of them in the form of a collateral agreement. If this were enough, written contracts might always be modified by parol. Not form, but substance, is the test.

In applying this test, the policy of our courts is to be considered. We have believed that the purpose behind the rule was a wise one, not easily to be abandoned. Notwithstanding injustice here and there, on the whole it works for good. Old precedents and principles are not to be lightly cast aside, unless it is certain that they are an obstruction under present conditions. New York has been less open to arguments that would modify this particular rule, than some jurisdictions elsewhere. Thus in Eighmie v. Taylor, 98 N.Y. 288, it was held that a parol warranty might not be shown, although no warranties were contained in the writing.

Under our decisions before such an oral agreement as the present is received to vary the written contract, at least three conditions must exist: (1) The agreement must in form be a collateral one; (2) it must not contradict express or implied provisions of the written contract; (3) it must be one that parties would not ordinarily be expected to embody in the writing, or, put in another way, an inspection of the written contract, read in the light of surrounding circumstances, must not indicate that the writing appears "to contain the engagements of the parties, and to define the object and measure the extent of such engagement." Or, again, it must not be so clearly connected with the principal transaction as to be part and parcel of it.

The respondent does not satisfy the third of these requirements. It may be, not the second. We have a written contract for the purchase and sale of land. The buyer is to pay $8,400 in the way described. She is also to pay her portion of any rents, interest on mortgages, insurance premiums, and water meter charges. She may have a survey made of the premises. On their part, the sellers are to give a full covenant deed of the premises as described, or as they may be described by the surveyor, if the survey is had, executed, and acknowledged at their own expense; they sell the personal property on the farm and represent they own it; they agree that all amounts paid them on the contract and the expense of examining the title shall be a lien on the property; they assume the risk of loss or damage by fire until the deed is delivered; and they agree to pay the broker his commissions. Are they to do more? Or is such a claim inconsistent with these precise provisions? It could not be shown that the plaintiff was to pay $500 additional. Is it also implied that the defendants are not to do anything unexpressed in the writing?

That we need not decide. At least, however, an inspection of this contract shows a full and complete agreement, setting forth in detail the obligations of each party. On reading it, one would conclude that the reciprocal obligations of the parties were fully detailed. Nor would his opinion alter if he knew the surrounding circumstances. The presence of the icehouse, even the knowledge that Mrs. Mitchill thought it objectionable, would not lead to the belief that a separate agreement existed with regard to it. Were such an agreement made it would seem most natural that the inquirer should find it in the contract. Collateral in form it is found to be, but it is closely related to the subject dealt with in the written agreement—so closely that we hold it may not be proved.

Where the line between the competent and the incompetent is narrow the citation of authorities is of slight use. Each represents the judgment of the court on the precise facts before it. How closely bound to the contract is the supposed collateral agreement is the decisive factor in each case. * * *

We do not ignore the fact that authorities may be found that would seem to support the contention of the appellant. * * * A line of cases in Massachusetts, of which Durkin v. Cobleigh, 156 Mass. 108, 30 N.E. 474, 17 L.R.A. 270, 32 Am.St.Rep. 436, is an example, have to do with collateral contracts made before a deed is given. But the fixed form of a deed makes it inappropriate to insert collateral agreements, however closely connected with the sale. This may be cause for an exception. Here we deal with the contract on the basis of which the deed to Mrs. Mitchill was given subsequently, and we confine ourselves to the question whether its terms may be modified.

* * *

Our conclusion is that the judgment of the Appellate Division and that of the Special Term should be reversed and the complaint dismissed, with costs in all courts.

LEHMAN, J. (dissenting). I accept the general rule as formulated by JUDGE ANDREWS. I differ with him only as to its application to the facts shown in the record. The plaintiff contracted to purchase land from the defendants for an agreed price. A formal written agreement was made between the sellers and the plaintiff's husband. It is on its face a complete contract for the conveyance of the land. It describes the property to be conveyed. It sets forth the purchase price to be paid. All the conditions and terms of the conveyance to be made are clearly stated. I concede at the outset that parol evidence to show additional conditions and terms of the conveyance would be inadmissible. There is a conclusive presumption that the parties intended to integrate in that written contract every agreement relating to the nature or extent of the property to be conveyed, the contents of the deed to be delivered, the consideration to be paid as a conditions precedent to the delivery of the deeds, and indeed all the rights of the parties in connection with the land. The conveyance of that land was the subject-matter of the written contract, and the contract completely covers that subject.

The parol agreement which the court below found the parties had made was collateral to, yet connected with, the agreement of purchase and sale. It has been found that the defendants induced the plaintiff to agree to purchase the land by a promise to remove an icehouse from land not covered by the agreement of purchase and sale. No independent consideration passed to the defendants for the parol promise. To that extent the written contract and the alleged oral contract are bound together. The same bond usually exists wherever attempt is made to prove a parol agreement which is collateral to a written agreement. Hence "the problem arises whether the bond is sufficiently close to prevent proof of the oral agreement." See Judge ANDREWS' citation from Williston on Contracts, § 637.

JUDGE ANDREWS has formulated a standard to measure the closeness of the bond. Three conditions, at least, must exist before an oral agreement may be proven to increase the obligation imposed by the written agreement. I think we agree that the first condition that the agreement "must in form be a collateral one" is met by the evidence. I concede that this condition is met in most cases where the courts have nevertheless excluded evidence of the collateral oral agreement. The difficulty here, as in most cases, arises in connection with the two other conditions.

The second condition is that the "parol agreement must not contradict express or implied provisions of the written contract." JUDGE ANDREWS voices doubt whether this condition is satisfied. The written contract has been carried out. * * * By the oral agreement the plaintiff seeks to hold the defendants to other obligations to be performed by them thereafter upon land which was not conveyed to the plaintiff. The assertion of such further obligation is not inconsistent with the written contract, unless the written contract contains a provision, express or implied, that the defendants are not to do anything not expressed in the writing. Concededly there is no such express provision in the contract, and such a provision may be implied, if at all, only if the asserted additional obligation is "so clearly connected with the principal transaction as to be part and parcel of it," and is not "one that the parties would not ordinarily be expected to embody in the writing." * * * In this case, therefore, the problem reduces itself to the one question whether or not the oral agreement meets the third condition.

I have conceded that upon inspection the contract is complete. * * * That engagement was on the one side to convey land; on the other to pay the price. The plaintiff asserts further agreement based on the same consideration to be performed by the defendants after the conveyance was complete, and directly affecting only other land. It is true, as Judge ANDREWS points out, that "the presence of the icehouse, even the knowledge that Mrs. Mitchill thought it objectionable, would not lead to the belief that a separate agreement existed with regard to it"; but the question we must decide is whether or not, *assuming* an agreement was made for the removal of an unsightly icehouse from one parcel of land as an inducement for the purchase of another parcel, the parties would ordinarily or naturally be expected to embody the agreement for the removal of the icehouse from one parcel in the written agreement to convey the other parcel. Exclusion of proof of the oral agreement on the ground that it varies the contract embodied in the writing may be based only upon a finding or presumption that the written contract was intended to cover the oral negotiations for the removal of the icehouse which lead up to the contract of purchase and sale. To determine what the writing was intended to cover, "the document alone will not suffice. What it was intended to cover cannot be known till we know what there was to cover. The question being whether certain subjects of negotiation were intended to be covered, we must compare the writing and the negotiations before we can determine whether they were in fact covered." Wigmore on Evidence (2d Ed.) § 2430.

The subject-matter of the written contract was the conveyance of land. The contract was so complete on its face that the conclusion is inevitable that the parties intended to embody in the writing all the negotiations covering at least the conveyance. The promise by the defendants to remove the icehouse from other land was not connected with their obligation to convey except that one agreement would not have been made unless the other was also made. The plaintiff's assertion of a parol agreement by the defendants to remove the icehouse was completely established by the great weight of evidence. It must prevail unless that agreement was part of the agreement to convey and the entire agreement was embodied in the writing.

The fact that in this case the parol agreement is established by the overwhelming weight of evidence is, of course, not a factor which may be considered in determining the competency or legal effect of the evidence. Hardship in the particular case would not justify the court in disregarding or emasculating the general rule. It merely accentuates the outlines of our problem. The assumption that the parol agreement was made is no longer obscured by any doubts. The problem, then, is clearly whether the parties are presumed to have intended to render that parol agreement legally ineffective and nonexistent by failure to embody it in the writing. Though we are driven to say that nothing in the written contract which fixed the terms and conditions of the stipulated conveyance suggests the existence of any further parol agreement, an inspection of the contract, though it is complete on its face in regard to the subject of the conveyance, does not, I think, show that it was intended to embody negotiations or agreements, if any, in regard to a matter so loosely bound to the conveyance as the removal of an icehouse from land not conveyed.

The rule of integration undoubtedly frequently prevents the assertion of fraudulent claims. Parties who take the precaution of embodying their oral agreements in a writing should be protected against the assertion that other terms of the same agreement were not integrated in the writing. The limits of the integration are determined by the writing, read in the light of the surrounding circumstances. A written contract, however complete, yet covers only a limited field. I do not think that in the written contract for the conveyance of land here under consideration we can find an intention to cover a field so broad as to include prior agreements, if any such were made, to do other acts on other property after the stipulated conveyance was made.

In each case where such a problem is presented, varying factors enter into its solution. Citation of authority in this or other jurisdictions is useless, at least without minute analysis of the facts. The analysis I have made of the decisions in this state leads me to the view that the decision of the courts below is in accordance with our own authorities and should be affirmed.

CARDOZO, C.J., and POUND, KELLOGG and O'BRIEN, JJ., concur with ANDREWS, J.

LEHMAN, J., dissents in opinion in which CRANE, J., concurs.

Judgment accordingly.

MASTERSON V. SINE

Supreme Court of California, 1968.
68 Cal.2d 222, 436 P.2d 561.

TRAYNOR, CHIEF JUSTICE.

Dallas Masterson and his wife Rebecca owned a ranch as tenants in common. On February 25, 1958, they conveyed it to Medora and Lu Sine by a grant deed "Reserving unto the Grantors herein an option to purchase the above described property on or before February 25, 1968" for the "same consideration as being paid heretofore plus their depreciation value of any improvements Grantees may add to the property from and after two and a half years from this date." Medora is Dallas' sister and Lu's wife. Since the conveyance Dallas has been adjudged bankrupt. His trustee in bankruptcy and Rebecca brought this declaratory relief action to establish their right to enforce the option.

The case was tried without a jury. Over defendants' objection the trial court admitted extrinsic evidence that by "the same consideration as being paid heretofore" both the grantors and the grantees meant the sum of $50,000 and by "depreciation value of any improvements" they meant the depreciation value of improvements to be computed by deducting from the total amount of any capital expenditures made by defendants grantees the amount of depreciation allowable to them under United States income tax regulations as of the time of the exercise of the option.

The court also determined that the parol evidence rule precluded admission of extrinsic evidence offered by defendants to show that the parties wanted the property kept in the Masterson family and that the option was therefore personal to the grantors and could not be exercised by the trustee in bankruptcy.

The court entered judgment for plaintiffs, declaring their right to exercise the option, specifying in some detail how it could be exercised, and reserving jurisdiction to supervise the manner of its exercise and to determine the amount that plaintiffs will be required to pay defendants for their capital expenditures if plaintiffs decide to exercise the option.

Defendants appeal. They contend that the option provision is too uncertain to be enforced and that extrinsic evidence as to its meaning should not have been admitted. The trial court properly refused to frustrate the obviously declared intention of the grantors to reserve an option to repurchase by an overly meticulous insistence on completeness and clarity of written expression. * * * It properly admitted extrinsic evidence to explain the language of the deed * * * to the end that the consideration for the option would appear with sufficient certainty to permit specific enforcement * * *. The trial court erred, however, in excluding the extrinsic evidence that the option was personal to the grantors and therefore nonassignable.

When the parties to a written contract have agreed to it as an "integration"—a complete and final embodiment of the terms of an agreement—parol evidence cannot be used to add to or vary its terms. * * * When only part of the agreement is integrated, the same rule applies to that part, but parol evidence may be used to prove elements of the agreement not reduced to writing. * * *

The crucial issue in determining whether there has been an integration is whether the parties intended their writing to serve as the exclusive embodiment of their agreement. The instrument itself may help to resolve that issue. It may state, for example, that "there are no previous understandings or agreements not contained in the writing," and thus express the parties' "intention to nullify antecedent understandings or agreements." (See 3 Corbin, Contracts (1960) § 578, p. 411.) Any such collateral agreement itself must be examined, however, to determine whether the parties intended the subjects of negotiation it deals with to be included in, excluded from, or otherwise affected by the writing. Circumstances at the time of the writing may also aid in the determination of such integration. * * *

California cases have stated that whether there was an integration is to be determined solely from the face of the instrument * * * and that the question for the court is whether it "appears to be a complete * * * agreement * * *." * * * Neither of these strict formulations of the rule, however, has been consistently applied. The requirement that the writing must appear incomplete on its face has been repudiated in many cases where parol evidence was admitted "to prove the existence of a separate oral agreement as to any matter on which the document is silent and which is not inconsistent with its terms"—even though the instrument appeared to state a complete agreement. * * * Even under the rule that the writing alone is to be consulted, it was found necessary to examine the alleged collateral agreement before concluding that proof of it was precluded by the writing alone. (See 3 Corbin, Contracts (1960) § 582, pp. 444–446.) It is therefore evident that "The conception of a writing as wholly and intrinsically self-determinative of the parties' intent to make it a sole memorial of one or seven or twenty-seven subjects of negotiation is an impossible one." (9 Wigmore, Evidence (3d ed. 1940) § 2431, p. 103.) For example, a promissory note given by a debtor to his creditor may integrate all their present contractual rights and obligations, or it may be only a minor part of an underlying executory contract that would never be discovered by examining the face of the note.

In formulating the rule governing parol evidence, several policies must be accommodated. One policy is based on the assumption that written evidence is more accurate than human memory. (Germain Fruit Co. v. J.K. Armsby Co. (1908) 153 Cal. 585, 595, 96 P. 319.) This policy, however, can be adequately served by excluding parol evidence of agreements that directly contradict the writing. Another policy is based on the fear that fraud or unintentional invention by witnesses interested in the outcome of the litigation will mislead the finder of facts. (Germain Fruit Co. v. J.K. Armsby Co., supra, 153 Cal. 585, 596, 96 P. 319; Mitchill v. Lath (1928) 247 N.Y. 377, 388, 160 N.E. 646, 68 A.L.R. 239 [dissenting opinion by Lehman, J.] * * *). McCormick has suggested that the party urging the spoken as against the written word is most often the economic underdog, threatened by severe hardship if the writing is enforced. In his view the parol evidence rule arose to allow the court to control the tendency of the jury to find through sympathy and without a dispassionate assessment of the probability of fraud or faulty memory that the parties made an oral agreement collateral to the written contract, or that preliminary tentative agreements were not abandoned when omitted from the writing. (See McCormick, Evidence (1954) § 210.) He recognizes, however, that if this theory were adopted in disregard of all other considerations, it would lead to the exclusion of testimony concerning oral agreements whenever there is a writing and thereby often defeat the true intent of the parties. (See McCormick, op. cit. supra, § 216, p. 441.)

Evidence of oral collateral agreements should be excluded only when the fact finder is likely to be misled. The rule must therefore be based on the credibility of the evidence. One such standard, adopted by section 240(1) (b) of the Restatement of Contracts, permits proof of a collateral agreement if it "is such an agreement as might *naturally* be made as a separate agreement by parties situated as were the parties to the written contract." (Italics added; see McCormick, Evidence (1954) § 216, p. 441; see also 3 Corbin, Contracts (1960) § 583, p. 475, § 594, pp. 568–569; 4 Williston, Contracts (3d ed. 1961) § 638, pp. 1039–1045.) The draftsmen of the Uniform Commercial Code would exclude the evidence in still fewer instances: "If the additional terms are such that, if agreed upon, they would *certainly* have been included in the document in the view of the court, then evidence of their alleged making must be kept from the trier of fact." (Com. 3, § 2–202, italics added.)[1]

---

[1] Corbin suggests that, even in situations where the court concludes that it would not have been natural for the parties to make the alleged collateral oral agreement, parol evidence of such an agreement should nevertheless be permitted if the court is convinced that the unnatural actually happened in the case being adjudicated. (3 Corbin, Contracts, § 485, pp. 478, 480; cf. Murray, The Parol Evidence Rule: A Clarification (1966) 4 Duquesne L.Rev. 337, 341–342.) This suggestion may be based on a belief that judges are not likely to be misled by their sympathies. If the court believes that the parties intended a collateral agreement to be effective, there is no reason to keep the evidence from the jury.

The option clause in the deed in the present case does not explicitly provide that it contains the complete agreement, and the deed is silent on the question of assignability. Moreover, the difficulty of accommodating the formalized structure of a deed to the insertion of collateral agreements makes it less likely that all the terms of such an agreement were included. * * * The statement of the reservation of the option might well have been placed in the recorded deed solely to preserve the grantors' rights against any possible future purchasers and this function could well be served without any mention of the parties' agreement that the option was personal. There is nothing in the record to indicate that the parties to this family transaction, through experience in land transactions or otherwise, had any warning of the disadvantages of failing to put the whole agreement in the deed. This case is one, therefore, in which it can be said that a collateral agreement such as that alleged "might naturally be made as a separate agreement." *A fortiori,* the case is not one in which the parties "would certainly" have included the collateral agreement in the deed.

It is contended, however, that an option agreement is ordinarily presumed to be assignable if it contains no provisions forbidding its transfer or indicating that its performance involves elements personal to the parties. * * * The fact that there is a written memorandum, however, does not necessarily preclude parol evidence rebutting a term that the law would otherwise presume. * * *

In the present case defendants offered evidence that the parties agreed that the option was not assignable in order to keep the property in the Masterson family. The trial court erred in excluding that evidence.

The judgment is reversed.

PETERS, TOBRINER, MOSK, and SULLIVAN, JJ., concur.

DISSENTING OPINION

BURKE, JUSTICE.

I dissent. The majority opinion:

(1) Undermines the parol evidence rule as we have known it in this state since at least 1872 by declaring that parol evidence should have been admitted by the trial court to show that a written option, absolute and unrestricted in form, was intended to be limited and nonassignable;

(2) Renders suspect instruments of conveyance absolute on their face;

(3) Materially lessens the reliance which may be placed upon written instruments affecting the title to real estate; and

(4) Opens the door, albeit unintentionally to a new technique for the defrauding of creditors.

The opinion permits defendants to establish by parol testimony that their grant to their brother (and brother-in-law) of a written option, absolute in terms, was nevertheless agreed to be nonassignable by the grantee (now a bankrupt), and that therefore the right to exercise it did not pass, by operation of the bankruptcy laws, to the trustee for the benefit of the grantee's creditors.

And how was this to be shown? By the proffered testimony of the bankrupt optionee himself! Thereby one of his assets (the option to purchase defendants' California ranch) would be withheld from the trustee in bankruptcy and from the bankrupt's creditors. Understandably the trial court, as required by the parol evidence rule, did not allow the bankrupt by parol to so contradict the unqualified language of the written option.

The court properly admitted parol evidence to explain the intended meaning of the "same consideration" and "depreciation value" phrases of the written option to purchase defendants' land, as the intended meaning of those phrases was not clear. However, there was nothing ambiguous about the *granting* language of the option and not the slightest suggestion in the document that the option was to be nonassignable. Thus, to permit such words of limitation to be added by parol is to *contradict* the absolute nature of the grant, and to directly violate the parol evidence rule.

Just as it is unnecessary to state in a deed to "lot X" that the house located thereon goes with the land, it is likewise unnecessary to add to "I grant an option to Jones" the words *"and his assigns"* for the option to be assignable. As hereinafter emphasized in more detail, California statutes expressly declare that it *is* assignable, and only if I add language in writing showing my intent to withhold or restrict the right of assignment may the grant be so limited. Thus, to seek to restrict the grant by parol is to *contradict* the written document in violation of the parol evidence rule.

The majority opinion arrives at its holding via a series of false premises which are not supported either in the record of this case or in such California authorities as are offered.

* * *

At the outset the majority in the present case reiterate that the rule against contradicting or varying the terms of a writing remains applicable when only part of the agreement is contained in the writing, and parol evidence is used to prove elements of the agreement not reduced to writing. But having restated this established rule, the majority opinion inexplicably proceeds to subvert it.

* * *

Options are property, and are widely used in the sale and purchase of real and personal property. One of the basic incidents of property ownership is the right of the owner to sell or transfer it. * * * These rights of the owner of property to transfer it, confirmed by the cited code sections, are elementary rules of substantive law and not the mere disputable presumptions which the majority opinion in the present case would make of them. Moreover, the right of transferability applies to an option to purchase, unless there are words of limitation in the option forbidding its assignment or showing that it was given because of a peculiar trust or confidence reposed in the optionee. * * *

The right of an optionee to transfer his option to purchase property is accordingly one of the basic rights which accompanies the option unless limited under the language of the option itself. To allow an optionor to resort to parol evidence to support his assertion that the written option is not transferable is to authorize him to limit the option by attempting to restrict and reclaim rights with which he has already parted. A clearer violation of two substantive and basic rules of law—the parol evidence rule and the right of free transferability of property—would be difficult to conceive.

* * *

* * * [D]espite the law which until the advent of the present majority opinion has been firmly and clearly established in California and relied upon by attorneys and courts alike, that parol evidence may *not* be employed to vary or contradict the terms of a written instrument, the majority now announce * * * that such evidence "should be excluded only when the fact finder is *likely to be misled*," and that "The rule must therefore be based on the *credibility of the evidence*." (Italics added.) But was it not, inter alia, to avoid misleading the fact finder, and to further the introduction of only the evidence which is most likely to *be* credible (the written document), that the Legislature adopted the parol evidence rule as a part of the substantive law of this state?

Next, in an effort to implement this newly promulgated "credibility" test, the majority opinion offers a choice of two "standards": one, a "certainty" standard, quoted from the Uniform Commercial Code * * * and the other a "natural" standard found in the Restatement of Contracts * * * and concludes * * * that at least for purposes of the present case the "natural" viewpoint should prevail.

This new rule, not hitherto recognized in California, provides that proof of a claimed collateral oral agreement is admissible if it is such an agreement as might *naturally* have been made a separate agreement by the parties under the particular circumstances. I submit that this approach opens the door to uncertainty and confusion. Who can know what its limits are? Certainly I do not. For example, in its application to this case who could be expected to divine as "natural" a separate oral agreement between the parties that the assignment, absolute and unrestricted on its face, was intended by the parties to be limited to the Masterson family?

Or, assume that one gives to his relative a promissory note and that the payee of the note goes bankrupt. By operation of law the note becomes an asset of the bankruptcy. The trustee attempts to enforce it. Would the relatives be permitted to testify that by a separate oral agreement made at the time of the execution of the note it was understood that should the payee fail in his business the maker would be excused from payment of the note, or that, as here, it was intended that the benefits of the note would be *personal* to the payee? I doubt that trial judges should be burdened with the task of conjuring whether it would have been "natural" under those circumstances for such a separate agreement to have been made by the parties. Yet, under the application of the proposed rule, this is the task the trial judge would have, and in essence the situation presented in the instant case is no different.

Under the application of the codes and the present case law, proof of the existence of such an agreement would not be permitted, "natural" or "unnatural." But conceivably, as loose as the new rule is, one judge might deem it natural and another judge unnatural. And in each instance the ultimate decision would have to be made ("naturally") on a case-by-case basis by the appellate courts.

In an effort to provide justification for applying the newly pronounced "natural" rule to the circumstances of the present case, the majority opinion next * * * attempts to account for the silence of the writing in this case concerning assignability of the option, by asserting that "the difficulty of accommodating the formalized structure of a deed to the insertion of collateral agreements makes it less likely that all the terms of such an agreement were included." What difficulty would have been involved here, to add the words "this option is nonassignable"? The asserted "formalized structure of a deed" is no formidable barrier. * * *

* * *

Comment hardly seems necessary on the convenience to a bankrupt of such a device to defeat his creditors. He need only produce parol testimony that any options (or other property, for that matter) which he holds are subject to an oral "collateral agreement" with family members (or with friends) that the property is nontransferable "in order to keep the property in the family" or in the friendly group. In the present case the value of the ranch which the bankrupt and his wife held an option to purchase has doubtless increased substantially during the years since they acquired the option. The initiation of this litigation by the trustee in bankruptcy to establish his right to enforce the option indicates his belief that there is substantial value to be gained for the creditors from this asset of the bankrupt. Yet the majority opinion permits defeat of the trustee and of the creditors through the device of an asserted collateral oral agreement that the option was "personal" to the bankrupt and nonassignable "in order to keep the property in the family"!

* * *

I would hold that the trial court ruled correctly on the proffered parol evidence, and would affirm the judgment.

MCCOMB, J., concurs.

N.Y. REAL PROP. LAW § 258

Sched. A (McKinney 2006).

Deed With Full Covenants.

Statutory Form A.

(Individual)

This indenture, made the ______ day of ______ nineteen hundred and ______, between ______ (insert residence) party of the first part, and ______ (insert residence) party of the second part,

Witnesseth, that the party of the first part, in consideration of ______ dollars, lawful money of the United States, paid by the party of the second part, does hereby grant and release unto the party of the second part, ______ and assigns forever, all ______ (description), together with the appurtenances and all the estate and rights of the party of the first part in and to said premises,

To have and to hold the premises herein granted unto the party of the second part ______ and assigns forever. And said ______ covenants as follows:

First. That said ______ is seized of said premises in fee simple, and has good right to convey the same;

Second. That the party of the second part shall quietly enjoy the said premises;

Third. That the said premises are free from incumbrances;

Fourth. That the party of the first part will execute or procure any further necessary assurance of the title to said premises;

Fifth. That said ______ will forever warrant the title to said premises.

In witness whereof, the party of the first part has hereunto set his hand and seal the day and year first above written.

In presence of:

BAKER v. BAILEY, 782 P.2d 1286 (Mont. 1989). In June of 1976, Arthur and Elma Bailey moved a mobile home onto property owned by their daughter and son-in-law. With their permission, the Baileys hooked onto the water line which serviced their daughter's home and installed a pipeline which would provide water for their trailer.

Approximately six years later, in the spring of 1982, the Baileys' daughter and son-in-law made the decision to sell their residence and the surrounding property. Because they were concerned about taking care of their parents, however, they transferred one acre of the property to the Baileys. This one acre surrounded the mobile home. The remaining property, consisting of forty-five acres, was sold to the Bakers.

In order to insure that the Baileys continued to have access to water, a Water Well Use Agreement was prepared. Mrs. Baker was concerned about future ownership of the one-acre plot. In particular, she was worried that "a bunch of hippies" would move in next to her and consequently she wanted some control over the type of person who may, in the future, buy the Bailey's land. In order to address this concern, the well agreement specifically provided that the right to use water would only extend to the Baileys. In the event the Baileys conveyed the property, the Bakers were under no obligation to provide the new owners with water.

Despite the plain language used in the agreement, the Baileys believed that although not specifically set forth, the Bakers would transfer the right to use the water well to a subsequent "reasonable purchaser" of the Bailey property. The language of the agreement, according to testimony of both the Baileys and the Bakers, was included for the purpose of addressing Mrs. Baker's concern over potentially undesirable neighbors. This purpose was not, however, articulated within the contract.

In addition to the water well use agreement, the Bakers, at the time of purchase, asked for and received a right of first refusal in the event the Baileys received an offer to purchase their property. If an offer was received, the Baileys were to notify the Bakers of the offer in writing. The Bakers would then have the opportunity to exercise their "right of first refusal" within fifteen days of the offer.

* * *

Shortly after the [Baileys decided] to sell the property, the water system developed several problems. As a result of these problems pressure in the line was reduced and the Baileys were unable to obtain sufficient water to meet their needs. As a result, they found it necessary to bring water to their residence in plastic jugs. [Editors' note: In the words of Yogi Berra, are you experiencing "deja vu all over again?"]

The Bakers were not as significantly affected by the problems. The Bakers always had sufficient water. In fact, during the entire period the

Baileys were deprived of water, the Bakers had enough water to irrigate their lawn. Despite the fact this use adversely affected the Baileys' water supply, the Bakers refused to reduce their consumption. This problem persisted until August when the water system was finally repaired.

After the problems with the water well surfaced, the Bakers informed the Baileys that they would not share the water supply with any new purchaser. Consequently, the property would have to be sold without access to water from the well.

The Baileys searched for alternative sources of water, but unfortunately none was available. They approached the Bakers and offered to purchase joint use of the well. This offer was refused.

Recognizing that they would not be able to provide water for the property, the Baileys realized that the property was virtually without value. They, therefore, agreed to sell it for $8,000.00, which was the fair market value of the trailer and other improvements on the land.

After the Baileys made the decision to accept the $8,000.00 offer, they gave the Bakers notice of its terms in compliance with the right of first refusal provisions in the contract. On August 20, 1984, the Bakers exercised their option and purchased the property for $8,000.00. The transaction was closed on September 10, 1984. At that time, the Bakers acquired the Baileys' one-acre parcel which, if supplied with water, allegedly could be marketed for $40,000.00–$47,500.00.

* * *

The facts of this case present a classic parol evidence problem. The parol evidence rule, briefly stated, requires that in the absence of fraud, duress, or mutual mistake, all extrinsic evidence must be excluded if the parties have reduced their agreement to an integrated writing. Under this rule, all prior and contemporaneous negotiations or understandings of the contract are merged, once that contract is reduced to writing. Williston on Contracts, Third Edition § 631.

As this case illustrates, application of the rule can work to create harsh results. However, the policies behind the rule compel its consistent, uniform application. Commercial stability requires that parties to a contract may rely upon its express terms without worrying that the law will allow the other party to change the terms of the agreement at a later date.

The Baileys maintain that all of the parties to the Water Well Use Agreement shared a common understanding that the Bakers would continue to share the well water with subsequent purchasers provided that the purchasers were acceptable to the Bakers. This contention may be true; however it is not found within the terms of the contract.

The Water Well Use Agreement is very explicit concerning the rights and obligations of the parties. Its terms provide: "it being specifically understood that this Agreement is solely for the benefit of [the Baileys] and shall terminate in the event [the Baileys] no longer occupy [the land]." It further provides that "it is the intent of the parties to fully set forth their understanding concerning the utilization of the domestic water supplies for the respective tracts * * *." There are no terms within the contract which state that the Bakers will provide water to subsequent "reasonable" purchasers.

Therefore, the fact there may have been further oral understandings between the parties is not admissible. The language of the Water Well Use Agreement is clear. Where the language of a written contract is clear and unambiguous, there is nothing for the court to construe. Rather, the duty of the court is simply to apply the language as written to the facts of the case and decide the case accordingly. The lower court's reliance upon evidence of the parties' oral negotiations was therefore in error, and there was no breach of contract.

BAKER v. BAILEY

DEFENDANTS' AMENDED FINDINGS OF FACT AND CONCLUSIONS OF LAW

MONTANA FOURTH JUDICIAL DISTRICT COURT

* * *

* * * The Bakers wanted more control in the event the Baileys were to sell the property to a third person. Specifically, the Bakers represented that they did not want "hippie type" individuals moving on the property. They would, however, be willing to transfer the use of the water well to a "reasonable" purchaser. While not set forth in the Water Well Use Agreement, each of the parties (both Bakers and both Baileys) testified that this was an essential term of their Agreement. Further, the parties had the reasonable expectation that the Bakers would be willing to transfer the use of the well to a "reasonable" third party purchaser. * * *

4 S. WILLISTON AND W. JAEGER, A TREATISE ON THE LAW OF CONTRACTS

§ 633 at 1014–16 (3d ed. 1957).

Since it is only the intention of the parties to adopt a writing as a memorial which makes that writing an integration of the contract, and makes the parol evidence rule applicable, any expression of their intention in the writing in regard to the matter will be given effect. If they provide in terms that the writing shall be a complete integration of their agreement or that it shall be but a partial integration, or no integration at all, the expressed intention will be effectuated.

The parties, however, rarely express their intention upon this point in the writing, and if the court may seek this intention from extrinsic circumstances, the very fact that the parties made a contemporaneous oral agreement will of itself prove that they did not intend the writing to be a complete memorial. The only question open would be whether such a contemporaneous oral agreement was in fact made.

Even if the oral agreement is repugnant to the writing, what was orally agreed would be of equal importance with what was written, since its existence would prove that there was no complete integration of the contract in regard to the matter to which it related. The parol evidence rule would then be of importance only as establishing a presumption that prior and contemporaneous oral agreements and negotiations were merged in the writing, but the practical value of the rule would be much impaired if either party to a writing were allowed to rebut the presumption by proof of any contemporaneous oral agreement. Certainly the law does not permit this. The question arises chiefly where it is asserted not that there is no integration at all, but only a partial integration. It is generally held that the contract must appear on its face to be incomplete in order to permit parol evidence of additional terms.

Frequently, it is not a necessary inference from the writing itself either that it is a statement of the whole agreement, or that it is not. In such a case it has been held that parol evidence is admissible to show which is the fact. The difficulty with such a principle lies in its application. No written contract which does not in terms state that it contains the whole agreement (and few do so provide though it would be generally a wise provision) precludes the possible supposition of additional parol clauses, not inconsistent with the writing.

6 CORBIN ON CONTRACTS

§ 581 at 145–146 (1993).

How is it to be determined whether or not a specific writing is an "integration" or a mere "partial integration"? The "parol evidence rule" does not itself purport to establish the fact of "integration"; and until that fact is established the "rule" does not purport to have any legal operation. Section 228 of the Restatement tells us that "an agreement is integrated where the parties thereto adopt a writing or writings as the final and complete expression of the agreement." But the writing can in no case prove its own "adoption" as such; and in proving the extrinsic expressions of adoption, those expressions are subject to no "parol evidence rule." The alleged "adoption" may be shown to be no adoption at all, or to be a qualified and limited adoption.

From this it appears that it can never be determined by mere interpretation of the words of a writing whether it is an "integration" of anything, whether it is "the final and complete expression of the agreement" or is a mere partial expression of "the agreement." * * * Since the "parol evidence rule" is applicable exclusively to "integrations" and a writing can be shown to be an "integration" only by evidence of adoption and assent, the admissibility of this evidence can not be determined by the "parol evidence rule." Also, the question whether a writing is a complete or a partial integration of "the agreement" can not be determined by mere interpretation of the words of the writing; and relevant evidence in the process of that interpretation can not be excluded by the "parol evidence rule."

CALAMARI & PERILLO, A PLEA FOR A UNIFORM PAROL EVIDENCE RULE AND PRINCIPLES OF CONTRACT INTERPRETATION

42 Ind.L.J. 333, 341 (1967).

The debate [between Williston and Corbin] involves the question: is the public better served by giving effect to the parties' entire agreement written and oral, even at the risk of injustice caused by the possibility of perjury and the possibility that superseded documents [or oral promises] will be treated as operative, or does the security of transactions require that, despite occasional injustices, persons adopting a formal writing be required, on the penalty of voidness of their oral and written side agreements, to put their entire agreement in the formal writing?

PROBLEM 6-1

The Matsons agreed to sell their farm to the Greens for $185,000. The parties entered into a comprehensive contract of sale prepared largely by the Matsons' attorney. On the date of the closing, after inspection of the farm, the Greens refused to tender payment. They claimed that the Matsons had withdrawn all of the furniture from the farmhouse despite the parties' oral agreement (prior to signing the written purchase agreement) that the price included all of the furniture. The contract was silent on the issue. After being sued by the Matsons for breach of contract, the Greens have retained you to defend them at trial. Will you attempt to introduce evidence of the claimed oral agreement, assuming, of course, that you believe your clients are telling the truth? On what grounds? Whom will you cite in your argument, Williston or Corbin? Why? How would the New York Court of Appeals have resolved the issue in 1929? The California Supreme Court in 1969?

UNIFORM COMMERCIAL CODE § 2–202.

Final Written Expression: Parol or Extrinsic Evidence

Terms with respect to which the confirmatory memoranda of the parties agree or which are otherwise set forth in a writing intended by the parties as a final expression of their agreement with respect to such terms as are included therein may not be contradicted by evidence of any prior agreement or of a contemporaneous oral agreement but may be explained or supplemented

(a) by course of dealing or usage of trade (Section 1–205) or by course of performance (Section 2–208); and

(b) by evidence of consistent additional terms unless the court finds the writing to have been intended also as a complete and exclusive statement of the terms of the agreement.

J. WHITE AND R. SUMMERS, UNIFORM COMMERCIAL CODE

117–118 (6th ed. 2010).

As Professor McCormick taught, the division of functions between judge and jury in administering the [parol evidence] rule can "give preference" to written evidence over oral evidence of contract terms. So, too, can allocations of burden of proof. Section 2–202 does not state very clearly what the division of functions is supposed to be. But the way the rule is worded, the trial is certainly not to be a free-wheeling affair in which the parties may introduce before the jury all evidence of terms, including the writing, with the jury then to decide on terms. Rather, it is plain from the rule and from prior history of similar rules that some of the evidence is to be heard initially only by the judge and that the judge may invoke the rule to keep this evidence from the jury. The evidence that is in this way subject to exclusion will usually be oral evidence. Indeed, before a judge can invoke a parol evidence rule at all, the judge must first admit a writing into evidence before the jury. If the judge thereafter excludes oral evidence of terms on the basis of the parol evidence rule, the judge gives preference to the writing already in evidence by prohibiting the jury from considering the oral evidence.

But when can the judge invoke 2–202 to exclude oral evidence of terms? First, the judge may exclude the evidence on finding that the parties intended the writing to be a *complete and exclusive* statement of the terms of the agreement (unless it be evidence of course of dealing, usage of trade, or course of performance introduced only to explain or supplement the writing). Code and comments both state that the question of completeness and exclusivity is for the judge. Second, the judge may exclude evidence extrinsic to terms set forth in the writing if he or she decides that the writing is a final written expression as to these terms and that the other evidence contradicts these terms. The Code does not say that this question is for the judge, but if "completeness and exclusivity" is for the judge, then whether a writing is a final written expression as to the terms it does include would be for the judge, for the greater ordinarily includes the lesser. The issue of contradictoriness is also generally for the judge. Third, in passing on any parol evidence rule objection, the judge may decide that the proffered evidence of terms extrinsic to the writing is not credible, and he or she may exclude it on that ground alone. Section 2–202 is silent on this, but Professor McCormick thought that the "real service" of the parol evidence rule was here.

The foregoing division of functions between judge and jury in the administration of 2–202 inevitably operates to favor written evidence of terms. Yet there is no necessary identity between a writing and the actual deal. Some commentators and at least a few courts conclude that 2–202 abolishes any presumption that a writing apparently complete on its face is complete and exclusive. We are uncertain. One of us (White) would be quite quick to find completeness from elaborate writings and quite comfortable in stilling the tongues of parties claiming other terms or innovative interpretations. The other (Summers) trusts the jury more and is more suspicious of the drafter.

NOTE:
THE AMBIGUITY EXCEPTION TO THE PAROL EVIDENCE RULE

To determine whether evidence of prior understandings and negotiations contradicts or varies a writing, we must first know what the writing means. If the writing is ambiguous, courts admit evidence to ascertain its meaning. Accordingly, apart from whether a writing is fully or partially integrated, much parol evidence rule litigation involves whether or not a writing is ambiguous. The next few cases involve different approaches to the ambiguity exception to the parol evidence rule.

GOLD KIST, INC. V. CARR

Court of Appeals of Texas, 1994.
886 S.W.2d 425.

MCCLOUD, CHIEF JUSTICE.

Edward C. Carr, Jr., entered into a written agreement with Gold Kist, Inc. to purchase trucks and peanut hauling equipment from Gold Kist. Carr later sued Gold Kist for damages alleging breach of contract * * *. The central issue in Carr's suit was whether or not Carr had "exclusive hauling rights." Trial was to the jury who found that:

(1) Gold Kist agreed that Carr would have exclusive hauling of Gold Kist' peanut commodities in the State of Texas during the term of the promissory note.

(2) Carr was able to perform in accordance with that agreement.

* * *

[The trial court entered a judgment for Carr pursuant to the jury's finding of damages.]

Gold Kist appeals challenging the judgment * * *. Gold Kist contends that Carr's breach of contract claim is barred by the parol evidence rule * * *. We sustain [this challenge.]

Background Facts

The record reflects that, in August of 1986, Walter Dan Holland was the manager of Gold Kist' peanut shelling plant in Comyn, Texas. Peanuts were transported to the Comyn plant from statewide "buying points" where farmers sold their peanuts. Some of the buying points were owned by Gold Kist; and others, known as "commissioned buying points," were independently owned. Holland contacted Carr and offered to sell Carr Gold Kist' trucks and hauling equipment at the Comyn plant. Holland and Carr began to negotiate the terms of the sale, and both men were aware that any agreement they reached would have to be approved by Gold Kist' corporate headquarters in Atlanta, Georgia.

They first agreed that Carr would purchase the trucks and equipment and that Carr would have the exclusive right to haul peanuts for Gold Kist in Texas. This agreement was submitted to Michael Stimpert, a vice-president for Gold Kist at the Atlanta corporate headquarters. Some of the commissioned buying points wanted to use their own trucks and equipment to haul the peanuts. Gold Kist did not want to risk losing business from these buying points. Stimpert objected to granting Carr exclusive hauling rights and requested that the final contract be drafted so as to exclude any hauling rights. Holland told Carr that Gold Kist would not grant him the exclusive right to haul all of Gold Kist' peanuts.

A contract was drafted under which Carr would purchase Gold Kist' trucks and hauling equipment for $60,000.00 paying $20,000.00 in cash and executing a five-year promissory note for the remaining $40,000.00. The contract stated: "Gold Kist, from time to time, may, but shall be under no obligation to, engage you to haul commodities on its behalf." Stimpert signed the contract as Gold Kist' "Group Vice President—Agricommodities." On September 24, 1986, Carr signed the contract.

Exclusive Hauling Rights

The central issue in Carr's suit is whether or not Gold Kist granted him the exclusive right to haul its peanuts. Carr testified that, after the original agreement was rejected by Gold Kist' corporate headquarters, he renegotiated the agreement with Holland. Under this second agreement, Carr testified that he was to have exclusive hauling rights with the exception that, during the first year of operation, he would not haul peanuts from the buying points that had protested. After the first year, those buying points would be "educated and straightened out"; and Carr would then have the exclusive right to haul from those buying points as well. Because Carr's hauling during the first year would be reduced under the new agreement, the purchase price of the trucks and equipment was reduced from $100,000.00 to $60,000.00.

When he received the written contract signed by Stimpert, Carr questioned the sentence that stated that Gold Kist had no obligation to use Carr because the sentence did not conform with what he thought was the agreement. Carr asked Holland what it meant. Holland called Ron Clark, the Atlanta-based manager of Gold Kist' peanut division, who told Holland that he thought Gold Kist did not have to use Carr if his performance did not meet Gold Kist' expectations. Holland relayed this information to Carr who signed the agreement.

Parol Evidence Rule

The parol evidence rule precludes consideration of extrinsic evidence to contradict, vary, or add to the terms of an unambiguous written agreement absent fraud, accident, or mistake. * * * Whether a contract is ambiguous is "a question of law for the court to decide by looking at the contract as a whole in light of the circumstances present when the contract was entered." *Coker v. Coker,* 650 S.W.2d 391, 393–94 (Tex.1983). A contract is ambiguous when its meaning is genuinely uncertain and doubtful or when it is reasonably susceptible to more than one meaning. *Coker v. Coker, supra.* If a contract can be given a certain or definite legal meaning or interpretation, it is not ambiguous; and the court will construe the contract as a matter of law.

The Gold Kist-Carr contract provided that "Gold Kist, from time to time, may, but shall be under no obligation to, engage you to haul commodities on its behalf." Considering this sentence in light of the contract as a whole and in light of the surrounding circumstances, we conclude that the contract is not ambiguous. The meaning is not genuinely uncertain and doubtful. The contract clearly states that Gold Kist has "no obligation" to use Carr's hauling services. This provision in the contract is not reasonably susceptible to the interpretation suggested by Carr: that Carr would have exclusive hauling rights for the term of the promissory note. Carr's interpretation contradicts the express language of the contract. The mere fact that Gold Kist and Carr take conflicting views of the agreement or that they differ in their expectations is not sufficient to render the contract ambiguous. *Forbau v. Aetna Life Insurance Company,* 876 S.W.2d 132, 134 (Tex.1994).

Because the contract is unambiguous, we must give effect to the objective intention of the parties as expressed or as is apparent in the written agreement. * * * Under the plain language of the contract, Gold Kist had no obligation to engage Carr's services for the hauling of peanuts.

* * *

Carr also contends that Gold Kist' alleged promise to give Carr exclusive hauling rights is enforceable because the promise was an independent, collateral agreement. * * * We disagree.

The contract clearly contemplated the subject matter of hauling and specifically excluded any obligation to use Carr. Any prior or contemporaneous agreement giving Carr exclusive hauling rights would not be an independent or collateral agreement. Rather, such an agreement would have been inconsistent with and would have contradicted the express terms of the written agreement.

* * *

The judgment of the trial court is reversed, and judgment is rendered that Carr take nothing against Gold Kist. * * *

PACIFIC GAS AND ELECTRIC CO. v. G.W. THOMAS DRAYAGE & RIGGING CO.

Supreme Court of California, 1968.
69 Cal.2d 33, 442 P.2d 641.

TRAYNOR, CHIEF JUSTICE.

Defendant appeals from a judgment for plaintiff in an action for damages for injury to property under an indemnity clause of a contract.

In 1960 defendant entered into a contract with plaintiff to furnish the labor and equipment necessary to remove and replace the upper metal cover of plaintiff's steam turbine. Defendant agreed to perform the work "at [its] own risk and expense" and to "indemnify" plaintiff "against all loss, damage, expense and liability resulting from * * * injury to property, arising out of or in any way connected with the performance of this contract." Defendant also agreed to procure not less than $50,000 insurance to cover liability for injury to property. Plaintiff was to be an additional named insured, but the policy was to contain a cross-liability clause extending the coverage to plaintiff's property.

During the work the cover fell and injured the exposed rotor of the turbine. Plaintiff brought this action to recover $25,144.51, the amount it subsequently spent on repairs. During the trial it dismissed a count based on negligence and thereafter secured judgment on the theory that the indemnity provision covered injury to all property regardless of ownership.

Defendant offered to prove by admissions of plaintiff's agents, by defendant's conduct under similar contracts entered into with plaintiff, and by other proof that in the indemnity clause the parties meant to cover injury to property of third parties only and not to plaintiff's property. Although the trial court observed that the language used was "the classic language for a third party indemnity provision" and that "one could very easily conclude that * * * its whole intendment is to indemnify third parties," it nevertheless held that the "plain language" of the agreement also required defendant to indemnify plaintiff for injuries to plaintiff's property. Having determined that the contract had a plain meaning, the court refused to admit any extrinsic evidence that would contradict its interpretation.

When a court interprets a contract on this basis, it determines the meaning of the instrument in accordance with the " * * * extrinsic evidence of the judge's own linguistic education and experience." (3 Corbin on Contracts (1960 ed.) [1964 Supp. § 579, p. 225, fn. 56].) The exclusion of testimony that might contradict the linguistic background of the judge reflects a judicial belief in the possibility of perfect verbal expression. (9 Wigmore on Evidence (3d ed. 1940) § 2461, p. 187.) This belief is a remnant of a primitive faith in the inherent potency[1] and inherent meaning of words.[2]

The test of admissibility of extrinsic evidence to explain the meaning of a written instrument is not whether it appears to the court to be plain and unambiguous on its face, but whether the offered evidence is relevant to prove a meaning to which the language of the instrument is reasonably susceptible. * * *

A rule that would limit the determination of the meaning of a written instrument to its four-corners merely because it seems to the court to be clear and unambiguous, would either deny the relevance of the intention of the parties or presuppose a degree of verbal precision and stability our language has not attained.

Some courts have expressed the opinion that contractual obligations are created by the mere use of certain words, whether or not there was any intention to incur such obligations.[3] Under this view, contractual obligations flow, not from the intention of the parties but from the fact that they used certain magic words. Evidence of the parties' intention therefore becomes irrelevant.

---

1 E.g., "The elaborate system of taboo and verbal prohibitions in primitive groups; the ancient Egyptian myth of Khern, the apotheosis of the word, and of Thoth, the Scribe of Truth, the Giver of Words and Script, the Master of Incantations; the avoidance of the name of God in Brahmanism, Judaism and Islam; totemistic and protective names in mediaeval Turkish and Finno-Ugrian languages; the misplaced verbal scruples of the 'Précieuses'; the Swedish peasant custom of curing sick cattle smitten by witchcraft, by making them swallow a page torn out of the psalter and put in dough. * * * " from Ullman, The Principles of Semantics (1963 ed.) 43. (See also Ogden and Richards, The Meaning of Meaning (rev.ed.1956) pp. 24–47.)

2 " 'Rerum enim vocabula immutabilia sunt, homines mutabilia,' " (Words are unchangeable, men changeable) from Dig. XXXIII, 10, 7, § 2, de sup. leg. as quoted in 9 Wigmore on Evidence, op. cit. supra, § 2461, p. 187.

3 "A contract has, strictly speaking, nothing to do with the personal, or individual, intent of the parties. A contract is an obligation attached by the mere force of law to certain acts of the parties, usually words, which ordinarily accompany and represent a known intent." (Hotchkiss v. National City Bank of New York (S.D.N.Y.1911) 200 F. 287, 293. * * *

In this state, however, the intention of the parties as expressed in the contract is the source of contractual rights and duties.[4] A court must ascertain and give effect to this intention by determining what the parties meant by the words they used. Accordingly, the exclusion of relevant, extrinsic evidence to explain the meaning of a written instrument could be justified only if it were feasible to determine the meaning the parties gave to the words from the instrument alone.

If words had absolute and constant referents, it might be possible to discover contractual intention in the words themselves and in the manner in which they were arranged. Words, however, do not have absolute and constant referents. "A word is a symbol of thought but has no arbitrary and fixed meaning like a symbol of algebra or chemistry, * * *." (Pearson v. State Social Welfare Board (1960) 54 Cal.2d 184, 195, 5 Cal.Rptr. 553, 559, 353 P.2d 33, 39.) The meaning of particular words or groups of words varies with the "* * * verbal context and surrounding circumstances and purposes in view of the linguistic education and experience of their users and their hearers or readers (not excluding judges). * * * A word has no meaning apart from these factors; much less does it have an objective meaning, one true meaning." (Corbin, The Interpretation of Words and the Parol Evidence Rule (1965) 50 Cornell L.Q. 161, 187.) Accordingly, the meaning of a writing "* * * can only be found by interpretation in the light of all the circumstances that reveal the sense in which the writer used the words. The exclusion of parol evidence regarding such circumstances merely because the words do not appear ambiguous to the reader can easily lead to the attribution to a written instrument of a meaning that was never intended. * * *" Universal Sales Corp. v. Cal. Press Mfg. Co., supra, 20 Cal.2d 751, 776, 128 P.2d 665, 679 (concurring opinion) * * *.

Although extrinsic evidence is not admissible to add to, detract from, or vary the terms of a written contract, these terms must first be determined before it can be decided whether or not extrinsic evidence is being offered for a prohibited purpose. The fact that the terms of an instrument appear clear to a judge does not preclude the possibility that the parties chose the language of the instrument to express different terms. That possibility is not limited to contracts whose terms have acquired a particular meaning by trade usage,[5] but exists whenever the parties'

---

[4] "A contract must be so interpreted as to give effect to the mutual intention of the parties as it existed at the time of contracting, so far as the same is ascertainable and lawful." (Civ.Code, § 1636; see also Code Civ.Proc. § 1859; Universal Sales Corp. v. Cal. Press Mfg. Co. (1942) 20 Cal.2d 751, 760, 128 P.2d 665; Lemm v. Stillwater Land & Cattle Co. (1933) 217 Cal. 474, 480, 19 P.2d 785.)

[5] Extrinsic evidence of trade usage or custom has been admitted to show that the term "United Kingdom" in a motion picture distribution contract included Ireland (Ermolieff v. R.K.O. Radio Pictures (1942) 19 Cal.2d 543, 549–552, 122 P.2d 3); that the word "ton" in a lease meant a long ton or 2,240 pounds and not the statutory ton of 2,000 pounds (Higgins v. Cal. Petroleum, etc., Co. (1898) 120 Cal. 629, 630–632, 52 P. 1080); that the word "stubble" in a lease included not only stumps left in the ground but everything "left on the ground after the harvest time" (Callahan v. Stanley (1881) 57 Cal. 476, 477–479); that the term "north" in a contract dividing mining claims

understanding of the words used may have differed from the judge's understanding.

Accordingly, rational interpretation requires at least a preliminary consideration of all credible evidence offered to prove the intention of the parties.[6] (Civ.Code, § 1647; Code Civ.Proc. § 1860; see also 9 Wigmore on Evidence, op. cit. supra, § 2470, fn. 11, p. 227.) Such evidence includes testimony as to the "circumstances surrounding the making of the agreement * * * including the object, nature and subject matter of the writing * * * " so that the court can "place itself in the same situation in which the parties found themselves at the time of contracting." (Universal Sales Corp. v. Cal. Press Mfg. Co., supra, 20 Cal.2d 751, 761, 128 P.2d 665, 671 * * *). If the court decides, after considering this evidence, that the language of a contract, in the light of all the circumstances, is "fairly susceptible of either one of the two interpretations contended for * * * ", extrinsic evidence relevant to prove either of such meanings is admissible.[7]

In the present case the court erroneously refused to consider extrinsic evidence offered to show that the indemnity clause in the contract was not intended to cover injuries to plaintiff's property. Although that evidence was not necessary to show that the indemnity clause was reasonably susceptible of the meaning contended for by defendant, it was nevertheless relevant and admissible on that issue. Moreover, since that clause was reasonably susceptible of that meaning, the offered evidence was also admissible to prove that the clause had that meaning and did not cover injuries to plaintiff's property.[8] Accordingly, the judgment must be reversed.

---

indicated a boundary line running along the "magnetic and not the true meridian" (Jenny Lind Co. v. Bower & Co. (1858) 11 Cal. 194, 197–199) and that a form contract for purchase and sale was actually an agency contract (Body-Steffner Co. v. Flotill Products (1944) 63 Cal.App.2d 555, 558–562, 147 P.2d 84).

[6] When objection is made to any particular item of evidence offered to prove the intention of the parties, the trial court may not yet be in a position to determine whether in the light of all of the offered evidence, the item objected to will turn out to be admissible as tending to prove a meaning of which the language of the instrument is reasonably susceptible or inadmissible as tending to prove a meaning of which the language is not reasonably susceptible. In such case the court may admit the evidence conditionally by either reserving its ruling on the objection or by admitting the evidence subject to a motion to strike. (See Evid.Code, § 403.)

[7] Extrinsic evidence has often been admitted in such cases on the stated ground that the contract was ambiguous (e.g., Universal Sales Corp. v. Cal. Press Mfg. Co., supra, 20 Cal.2d 751, 761, 128 P.2d 665). This statement of the rule is harmless if it is kept in mind that the ambiguity may be exposed by extrinsic evidence that reveals more than one possible meaning.

[8] The court's exclusion of extrinsic evidence in this case would be error even under a rule that excluded such evidence when the instrument appeared to the court to be clear and unambiguous on its face. The controversy centers on the meaning of the word "indemnify" and the phrase "all loss, damage, expense and liability." The trial court's recognition of the language as typical of a third party indemnity clause and the double sense in which the word "indemnify" is used in statutes and defined in dictionaries demonstrate the existence of an ambiguity. (Compare Civ.Code, § 2772, "Indemnity is a contract by which one engages to save another from a legal consequence of the conduct of one of the parties, or of some other person," with Civ.Code, § 2527, "Insurance is a contract whereby one undertakes to indemnify another against loss, damage, or liability, arising from an unknown or contingent event." Black's Law Dictionary (4th ed. 1951)

PETERS, MOSK, BURKE, SULLIVAN and PEEK, JJ., concur. MCCOMB, J., dissents. [no opinion]

TRIDENT CENTER v. CONNECTICUT GENERAL LIFE INS. CO., 847 F.2d 564 (9th Cir.1988).

KOZINSKI, CIRCUIT JUDGE.

* * * Two decades ago the California Supreme Court in *Pacific Gas & Electric Co. v. G.W. Thomas Drayage & Rigging Co.,* 69 Cal.2d 33, 442 P.2d 641, 69 Cal.Rptr. 561 (1968), turned its back on the notion that a contract can ever have a plain meaning discernible by a court without resort to extrinsic evidence. The court reasoned that contractual obligations flow not from the words of the contract, but from the intention of the parties. * * *

Under *Pacific Gas,* it matters not how clearly a contract is written, nor how completely it is integrated, nor how carefully it is negotiated, nor how squarely it addresses the issue before the court: the contract cannot be rendered impervious to attack by parol evidence. If one side is willing to claim that the parties intended one thing but the agreement provides for another, the court must consider extrinsic evidence of possible ambiguity. If that evidence raises the specter of ambiguity where there was none before, the contract language is displaced and the intention of the parties must be divined from self-serving testimony offered by partisan witnesses whose recollection is hazy from passage of time and colored by their conflicting interests. *See Delta Dynamics, Inc. v. Arioto,* 69 Cal.2d 525, 532, 446 P.2d 785, 72 Cal.Rptr. 785 (1968) (Mosk, J., dissenting). We question whether this approach is more likely to divulge the original intention of the parties than reliance on the seemingly clear words they agreed upon at the

---

defines "indemnity" as "A collateral contract or assurance, by which one person engages to secure another against an anticipated loss or to prevent him from being damnified by the legal consequences of an act or forbearance on the part of one of the parties or of some third person." Stroud's Judicial Dictionary (2d ed. 1903) defines it as a "Contract * * * to indemnify against a liability. * * * " One of the definitions given to "indemnify" by Webster's Third New Internat. Dict. (1961 ed.) is "to exempt from incurred penalties or liabilities.")

Plaintiff's assertion that the use of the word "all" to modify "loss, damage, expense and liability" dictates an all inclusive interpretation is not persuasive. If the word "indemnify" encompasses only third-party claims, the word "all" simply refers to all such claims. The use of the words "loss," "damage," and "expense" in addition to the word "liability" is likewise inconclusive. These words do not imply an agreement to reimburse for injury to an indemnitee's property since they are commonly inserted in third-party indemnity clauses, to enable an indemnitee who settles a claim to recover from his indemnitor without proving his liability. * * *

The provision that defendant perform the work "at his own risk and expense" and the provisions relating to insurance are equally inconclusive. By agreeing to work at its own risk defendant may have released plaintiff from liability for any injuries to defendant's property arising out of the contract's performance, but this provision did not necessarily make defendant an insurer against injuries to plaintiff's property. Defendant's agreement to procure liability insurance to cover damages to plaintiff's property does not indicate whether the insurance was to cover all injuries or only injuries caused by defendant's negligence.

time. *See generally Morta v. Korea Ins. Co.,* 840 F.2d 1452, 1460 (9th Cir.1988).

Pacific Gas casts a long shadow of uncertainty over all transactions negotiated and executed under the law of California. As this case illustrates, even when the transaction is very sizeable, even if it involves only sophisticated parties, even if it was negotiated with the aid of counsel, even if it results in contract language that is devoid of ambiguity, costly and protracted litigation cannot be avoided if one party has a strong enough motive for challenging the contract. While this rule creates much business for lawyers and an occasional windfall to some clients, it leads only to frustration and delay for most litigants and clogs already overburdened courts.

It also chips away at the foundation of our legal system. By giving credence to the idea that words are inadequate to express concepts, *Pacific Gas* undermines the basic principle that language provides a meaningful constraint on public and private conduct. If we are unwilling to say that parties, dealing face to face, can come up with language that binds them, how can we send anyone to jail for violating statutes consisting of mere words lacking "absolute and constant referents"? How can courts ever enforce decrees, not written in language understandable to all, but encoded in a dialect reflecting only the "linguistic background of the judge"? Can lower courts ever be faulted for failing to carry out the mandate of higher courts when "perfect verbal expression" is impossible? Are all attempts to develop the law in a reasoned and principled fashion doomed to failure as "remnant[s] of a primitive faith in the inherent potency and inherent meaning of words"?

* * * It may not be a wise rule we are applying, but it is a rule that binds us. *Erie R.R. Co. v. Tompkins,* 304 U.S. 64, 78, 58 S.Ct. 817, 822, 82 L.Ed. 1188 (1938).

ESKIMO PIE CORP. V. WHITELAWN DAIRIES, INC.

United States District Court, Southern District of New York, 1968.
284 F.Supp. 987.

MANSFIELD, DISTRICT JUDGE.

* * *

The [consolidated] actions arise out of written contracts between Eskimo Pie Corporation ("Eskimo" herein), Whitelawn Dairies, Inc.[1] ("Whitelawn" herein) and Supermarket Advisory Sales, Inc. ("SAS" herein) (Whitelawn and SAS are collectively referred to herein as "Whitelawn-SAS") entered into on or about December 30, 1960, and modified in various

[1] Whitelawn and SAS are subsidiaries of Allstate Dairies, Inc. ("Allstate" herein), also named as a party in these proceedings.

respects in 1961 and 1962. These contracts are referred to by the parties as the "Package Deal." All parties agree that the Package Deal is an integrated agreement setting forth in several writings all of the essential terms agreed upon by Eskimo and Whitelawn-SAS. Under the terms of the Package Deal Eskimo granted to Whitelawn, an ice cream manufacturer, the right to manufacture certain ice cream products bearing "Eskimo" wrappers and labels and to SAS the right to purchase such Eskimo-branded products from Eskimo or an Eskimo-authorized manufacturer for sale in the New York City Metropolitan Area as follows:

> "During the term of this Agreement [SAS] shall have the *non-exclusive* right to purchase the Eskimo stock and stickless products listed in Exhibit A hereto, which may be amended from time to time by addition or deletion, from Eskimo or from a manufacturer authorized by Eskimo to manufacture such products within the New York City metropolitan area * * *." (emphasis supplied).

The present lawsuits were instituted after Eskimo, beginning sometime in 1962 and 1963, sold its Eskimo-branded products to others in the New York City Metropolitan Area, and entered into agreements with M.H. Renken Dairy Co. ("Renken" herein) to manufacture, and with Food Enterprises, Inc. ("Food Enterprises" herein) to sell, such products, and assisted Harry L. Darnstaedt and Imperial Ice Cream Novelties, Inc. ("Imperial" herein) in selling such products in the New York City Metropolitan Area. This led to a deterioration in the relationship between the parties to the Package Deal; a purported termination by Whitelawn and SAS of purchases and sales thereunder; and mutual claims of breach of contract, since Whitelawn and SAS appear to have refused to accept and pay for certain products.

* * *

A threshold question, which appears to be central to the entire dispute between the parties, arises out of the meaning of the word "non-exclusive" as used in the above quotation from the Package Deal, and the proposal of Whitelawn-SAS to offer parol evidence with respect to its meaning. Whitelawn and SAS contend that the word "non-exclusive" as used in the Package Deal meant that Eskimo would have the right to continue existing licenses granted by it to others in the New York City Metropolitan Area and to grant new licenses to national companies (such as the Borden Company, National Dairy Products Corporation), but not to grant licenses to so-called "independent" companies unless required to do so by order of a court or governmental agency, and that Eskimo itself was not to compete with Whitelawn and SAS in the sale of Eskimo-branded ice cream products. Eskimo denies such contentions as to the meaning of the word "non-exclusive" and asserts that it plainly meant that Eskimo was granting a bare non-exclusive right to Whitelawn and SAS to manufacture and sell Eskimo products, while retaining the unfettered right to license others as it saw fit to manufacture and sell Eskimo-branded ice cream products.

Whitelawn-SAS proposes, upon the jury trial of the issues of liability raised by the two lawsuits, to introduce not only the written agreements constituting the Package Deal, but also parol and extrinsic evidence as to what the parties understood and intended the term "non-exclusive" to mean, including earlier drafts of the Package Deal, correspondence and conversations between the parties leading up to its execution, and subsequent conduct of the parties, including a letter written by Darnstaedt on February 12, 1963 stating that the parties "had a gentlemen's agreement that Eskimo would not solicit any stick franchises in New York City except any of the national companies that Eskimo is serving around the country." More specifically, Whitelawn-SAS would offer testimony of its lawyers and others who negotiated the Package Deal on its behalf to the effect that earlier drafts, including one submitted by an Eskimo official named Gunn (now deceased) contained a clause which would have obligated Eskimo not to license or franchise the Eskimo mark, or sell Eskimo-branded ice cream products, to anyone in the New York City Metropolitan Area other than existing licensees or national dairy organizations, unless Eskimo should be required to do so by court or governmental order; that thereafter Eskimo refused to sign an agreement containing the express clause because of a fear expressed by Eskimo's counsel that the proposed clause might violate the federal antitrust laws; and that accordingly, after a series of conferences, the proposed clause was deleted on the understanding that its meaning would be deemed incorporated into the word "non-exclusive" used in the above-quoted license to Whitelawn-SAS.

Although Eskimo, if such parol evidence were admitted at the trial, would offer testimony of its officials contradicting that of the Whitelawn-SAS negotiators, it argues that such evidence is barred by the parol evidence rule, and seeks preliminary rulings before trial is commenced.

* * *

The question of whether parol evidence should be admitted at trial is one of law to be determined and ruled upon by the Court. * * * Normally such rulings are made when the evidence is offered during trial, with the party offering the evidence, should objection be sustained, preserving his rights through an offer of proof out of the jury's presence. In this case, however, Eskimo asserts that since the parol evidence to be offered is extensive (both parties agreeing that if the evidence is admitted several witnesses will be required to testify for at least a few days), Eskimo would be forced to engage in multiple and continuous objections to, and/or motions to strike, testimony as to each of the numerous conversations between the negotiators, and proof of each item of correspondence, drafts, etc., with the result that even if the evidence should ultimately be excluded, Eskimo would be unduly prejudiced before the jury. This argument has much merit and is supported by those who follow the practice in such cases of holding a preliminary hearing for the purpose of ruling on the admissibility of such evidence. Wigmore on Evidence § 1808 at 275–76 (3d ed.). Whitelawn-SAS contends, however, that since the parol evidence should be admitted at trial, a preliminary hearing would result in needless waste and expense occasioned by duplication in testimony and proof. In view of these opposing contentions, consideration by the Court at this time of the applicable evidentiary principles seems appropriate.

* * *

Whitelawn-SAS argues that parol evidence should be admitted on the ground that the term "non-exclusive" is ambiguous, and that even if it in fact lacks ambiguity such evidence may be received to show that the parties gave the term special or particular meaning not to be gathered from the language by a reasonably intelligent person having knowledge of the custom, usage and surrounding circumstances. In support of their position, Whitelawn-SAS relies principally on § 2–202 of the Uniform Commercial Code ("UCC" herein). * * *

* * *

Since the Package Deal predated the effective date of the UCC, and since the UCC was not intended to have retroactive effect, § 2–202 does not apply and the Court must look to prior law. * * *

In any event even if § 2–202 of the UCC were applicable to the written contract here at issue, much of the proof which Whitelawn-SAS would offer to show what the parties intended the word "non-exclusive" to mean would not be admissible. Section 2–202 limits the parties, in explaining the meaning of language in a written integrated contract, to proof of a "course of dealing," "usage of the trade," and a "course of performance." None of these terms encompass testimony or other proof as to the subjective intent of the parties. The term "course of dealing" as defined in § 1–205(1) refers to "previous conduct between the parties" indicating a common basis for interpreting expressions used by them. In short, proof of such conduct is limited to objective facts as distinguished from oral statements of agreement. Likewise the term "usage of trade" is defined in § 1–205(2) as:

> "any practice or method of dealing having such regularity of observance in a place, vocation or trade as to justify an expectation that it will be observed with respect to the transaction in question. The existence and scope of such a usage are to be proved as facts. If it is established that such a usage is embodied in a written trade

code or similar writing the interpretation of the writing is for the court."

The comments of the drafters as well as those of independent commentators make it clear that "usage of the trade" refers to evidence of generalized industry practice or similar recognized custom, as distinguished from particular conversations or correspondence between the parties with respect to the terms of the agreement. UCC § 1–205, Official Comment 5. * * * The same general conclusions must be reached with respect to proof of a "course of performance."

* * *

* * * The courts of New York have never subscribed to the view that, in the absence of ambiguity, evidence as to the subjective intent of the parties may be substituted for the plain meaning that would otherwise be ascribed to the language of a written agreement by a reasonably intelligent person having knowledge of the surrounding circumstances, customs and usages. On the contrary, prior New York law adhered to time-honored objective standards to determine the meaning of language found in writings which represent as did the Package Deal here the final and complete integrated agreement reached by the parties. * * * The cardinal principles forming the cornerstone of those standards are (1) that the meaning to be attributed to the language of such an instrument is that which a reasonably intelligent person acquainted with general usage, custom and the surrounding circumstances would attribute to it; and (2) that in the absence of ambiguity parol evidence will not be admitted to determine the meaning that is to be attributed to such language. * * *

Thus the oral statements of the parties as to what they intended unambiguous language in an integrated document to mean are excluded by the parol evidence rule, because the very purpose and essence of the rule is to avoid fraud that might be perpetrated if testimony as to subjective intent could be substituted for the plain meaning, objectively interpreted in the light of surrounding circumstances, customs and usage. The effect of admitting such testimony in the absence of some showing of ambiguity would be to permit a party to substitute his view of his obligations for those clearly stated. Where—as in the present case—some of the negotiators of the written agreement have died or are unavailable, the door could be opened to fraud. Accordingly, the view of the New York courts has been that an objective standard is essential to maintain confidence in the written integrated agreement as the medium for conducting commercial relations.

The first question to be determined in the present case, therefore, is whether the term "non-exclusive" as used in the Package Deal is ambiguous, which must be decided by the Court. * * * An "ambiguous" word or phrase is one capable of more than one meaning when viewed objectively by a reasonably intelligent person who has examined the context of the entire integrated agreement and who is cognizant of the customs, practices, usages and terminology as generally understood in the particular trade or business. * * * In the absence of proof that the term "non-exclusive" could possibly have the meaning, among others, attributed to it by Whitelawn-SAS, parol evidence must be excluded.

Applying the foregoing principles, the word "non-exclusive" when used—as was the case here—in an integrated license agreement drafted by legal counsel, has an established legal meaning that is usually accepted in the absence of a qualifying context, custom, usage or similar surrounding circumstance. The term has repeatedly been defined as meaning that the licensee is granted a bare right to use the trademark or patent being licensed without any right to exclude others, including other licensees taking from the grantor, from utilizing the mark or invention involved. * * *

Despite the meaning thus usually ascribed by the law to the term "non-exclusive" Whitelawn-SAS urge that here the legal draftsmen intended it to have a contrary meaning, i.e., that subject to certain detailed and specific exceptions (The Borden Company, National Dairy Products Corporation, existing licensees and existing written commitments to others), and except to the extent that Eskimo might be required to deviate therefrom by court or governmental order, the term meant "exclusive." In a business world not noted for its economy of language (the Package Deal covers 70 typewritten pages, including amendments) no business reason, custom or usage is advanced for attaching such an elaborate and paradoxical meaning to the term "non-exclusive," when legal counsel negotiating for both sides could easily have spelled out such specifics in comprehensible terms. Whitelawn-SAS's assertion that the term was used to conceal a detailed secret "gentlemen's agreement" that was feared by Eskimo to violate the antitrust laws hardly comports with the word's having a secondary meaning as a matter of generalized trade usage or custom. On the contrary, such evidence would indicate that the term, despite the definite and plain meaning usually attributed to it, was being used to express a particular, subjective meaning initially conceived by the parties solely for the purpose at hand, and not because the term would be recognized by others as having such a special meaning. Unless the language is meaningless on its face (e.g. "abracadabra") or ambiguous, however, the test for admission of parol evidence is not a secret code meaning given to it by the parties but whether it might objectively be recognized by a reasonably intelligent person acquainted with applicable customs, usages and the surrounding circumstances as having such a special meaning. For instance, would an executive in the ice cream business, who was not privy to the secret oral "gentlemen's agreement," recognize the term "non-exclusive" in this context and setting as granting an "exclusive" right, subject to certain exceptions or as having a meaning other than that usually attributed to it? If so, parol evidence would be admissible. If the law were otherwise, not only the term "non-exclusive" but every apparently clear term in a written agreement, such as a specific purchase price (e.g., "$10,000") could be changed by secret oral agreement to mean something different (e.g., "$25,000").

Nevertheless, although the term "non-exclusive" as used in the Package Deal does not on its face appear to be ambiguous, Whitelawn-SAS will be afforded the opportunity to offer proof showing that the term is ambiguous, and Eskimo the opportunity to rebut such proof. In accordance with the principles hereinabove outlined, proof on the issue of ambiguity may encompass the terms of the Package Deal itself, the surrounding circumstances, common usage and custom as to the meaning attributed to it, and subsequent conduct of the parties under the Package Deal, but evidence of the subjective understanding of the parties as to the meaning attributed by them to the term "non-exclusive" will not be received.

Since the issue of ambiguity must be determined by the Court before ruling on the admission of parol evidence and since Eskimo might suffer prejudice if such rulings were made in the jury's presence, the proof with respect to ambiguity will be received at a preliminary hearing by the Court. Upon conclusion of the preliminary hearing, the Court will rule upon the issue of ambiguity, and the admissibility of the evidence at trial will be governed accordingly. Thereupon, pursuant to Rule 42(b), F.R.C.P., the Court will hold a separate jury trial of the issue of liability, to be followed by trial before the same jury of the damage issues. * * *

So ordered.

JOY v. HAY GROUP, INC., 403 F.3d 875 (7th Cir. 2005).

POSNER, CIRCUIT JUDGE.

[E]ven if a contract is clear "on its face"—which is to say, even if someone who knew nothing of the contract's background or commercial context would think its meaning clear—extrinsic evidence, which is to say evidence besides just the written contract itself, is admissible to demonstrate that the contract may not mean what it says, provided the evidence used to show this is "objective" in the sense of not being merely self-serving, unverifiable testimony. * * *

When * * * the written contract is unclear, *any* evidence admissible under the rules of evidence is usable to establish the contract's meaning.

RIVERISLAND COLD STORAGE, INC. v. FRESNO-MADERA PRODUCTION CREDIT ASSOCIATION

Supreme Court of California, 2013.
55 Cal.4th 1169, 291 P.3d 316.

CORRIGAN, J.

The parol evidence rule protects the integrity of written contracts by making their terms the exclusive evidence of the parties' agreement. However, an established exception to the rule allows a party to present extrinsic evidence to show that the agreement was tainted by fraud. Here, we consider the scope of the fraud exception to the parol evidence rule.

I. BACKGROUND

Plaintiffs Lance and Pamela Workman fell behind on their loan payments to defendant Fresno-Madera Production Credit Association (Credit Association or Association). They restructured their debt in an agreement, dated March 26, 2007, which confirmed outstanding loans with a total delinquency of $776,380.24 * * *. In the new agreement, the Credit Association promised it would take no enforcement action until July 1, 2007, if the Workmans made specified payments. As additional collateral, the Workmans pledged eight separate parcels of real property. They initialed pages bearing the legal descriptions of these parcels * * *.

The Workmans did not make the required payments. On March 21, 2008, the Credit Association recorded a notice of default. Eventually, the Workmans repaid the loan and the Association dismissed its foreclosure proceedings. The Workmans then filed this action, seeking damages for fraud and negligent misrepresentation, and including causes of action for rescission and reformation of the restructuring agreement. They alleged that the Association's vice president, David Ylarregui, met with them two weeks before the agreement was signed, and told them the Association would extend the loan for two years in exchange for additional collateral consisting of two ranches. The Workmans further claimed that when they signed the agreement Ylarregui assured them its term was two years and the ranches were the only additional security. As noted, the contract actually contemplated only three months of forbearance by the Association, and identified eight parcels as additional collateral. The Workmans did not read the agreement, but simply signed it at the locations tabbed for signature.

The Credit Association moved for summary judgment. It contended the Workmans could not prove their claims because the parol evidence rule barred evidence of any representations contradicting the terms of the written agreement. In opposition, the Workmans argued that Ylarregui's misrepresentations were admissible under the fraud exception to the parol evidence rule. Relying on [*Bank of America v. Pendergrass,* 4 Cal.2d 258, 48 P.2d 659 (1935)], the trial court granted summary judgment, ruling that the fraud exception does not allow parol evidence of promises at odds with the terms of the written agreement.

The Court of Appeal reversed. It reasoned that *Pendergrass* is limited to cases of promissory fraud. The court considered false statements about the contents of the agreement itself to be factual misrepresentations beyond the scope of the *Pendergrass* rule. We granted the Credit Association's petition for review * * *.

II. DISCUSSION

A. *The Parol Evidence Rule and the* Pendergrass *Limitation*

The parol evidence rule is codified in Code of Civil Procedure section 1856 and Civil Code section 1625. It provides that when parties enter an integrated written agreement, extrinsic evidence may not be relied upon to alter or add to the terms of the writing. * * * "An integrated agreement is a writing or writings constituting a final expression of one or more terms of an agreement." (Rest.2d Contracts, § 209, subd. (1) * * *.) There is no dispute in this case that the parties' agreement was integrated.

Although the parol evidence rule results in the exclusion of evidence, it is not a rule of evidence but one of substantive law. * * * It is founded on the principle that when the parties put all the terms of their agreement in writing, the writing itself becomes the agreement. The written terms supersede statements made during the negotiations. Extrinsic evidence of the agreement's terms is thus *irrelevant,* and cannot be relied upon. * * * "[T]he parol evidence rule, unlike the statute of frauds, does not merely serve an evidentiary purpose; it determines the enforceable and incontrovertible terms of an integrated written agreement." (Casa Herrera, Inc. v. Beydoun, 32 Cal.4th 336, 345, 9 Cal.Rptr.3d 97, 83 P.3d 497 (2004); * * *. The purpose of the rule is to ensure that the parties' final understanding, deliberately expressed in writing, is not subject to change. (*Casa Herrera,* at p. 345, 9 Cal.Rptr.3d 97, 83 P.3d 497.)

Section 1856, subdivision (f) establishes a broad exception to the operation of the parol evidence rule: "Where the validity of the agreement is the fact in dispute, this section does not exclude evidence relevant to that issue." This provision rests on the principle that the parol evidence rule, intended to protect the *terms* of a valid written contract, should not bar evidence challenging the *validity* of the agreement itself. "Evidence to prove that the instrument is void or voidable for mistake, fraud, duress, undue influence, illegality, alteration, lack of consideration, or another invalidating cause is admissible. This evidence does not contradict the terms of an effective integration, because it shows that the purported instrument has no legal effect." (2 Witkin, Cal. Evidence (5th ed. 2012) Documentary Evidence, § 97, p. 242. The fraud exception is expressly stated in section 1856, subdivision (g): "This section does not exclude other evidence . . . to establish . . . fraud."

Despite the unqualified language of section 1856, which broadly permits evidence relevant to the validity of an agreement and specifically allows evidence of fraud, the *Pendergrass* court decided to impose a limitation on the fraud exception. * * * The facts of *Pendergrass* are similar in certain respects to those here. Borrowers fell behind on their payments. They and the bank executed a new promissory note, which was secured by additional collateral and payable on demand. Soon after it was signed, the bank seized the encumbered property and sued to enforce the note. In defense, the borrowers claimed the bank had promised not to interfere with their farming operations for the remainder of the year, and to take the proceeds of those operations in payment. They alleged that the bank had no intention of performing these promises, but made them for the fraudulent purpose of obtaining the new note and additional collateral. (*Pendergrass, supra,* 4 Cal.2d at pp. 259–262, 48 P.2d 659.)

The *Pendergrass* court concluded that further proceedings were required to determine whether the lender had pursued the proper form of action. (*Pendergrass, supra,* 4 Cal.2d at pp. 262–263, 48 P.2d 659.) However, the court also considered whether oral testimony would be admissible to establish the lender's alleged promise not to require payment until the borrowers sold their crops. "This promise is in direct contravention of the unconditional promise contained in the note to pay the money on demand. The question then is: Is such a promise the subject of parol proof for the purpose of establishing fraud as a defense to the action or by way of cancelling the note, assuming, of course, that it can be properly coupled with proof that it was made without any intention of performing it?" (*Id.* At p. 263, 48 P.2d 659.)

[The Pendergrass court further stated]:

> Our conception of the rule which permits parol evidence of fraud to establish the invalidity of the instrument is that it must tend to establish some independent fact or representation, some fraud in the procurement of the instrument or some breach of confidence concerning its use, and not a promise directly at variance with the promise of the writing. We find apt language in *Towner v. Lucas' Exr.* [(1857)] 54 Va. (13 Gratt.) 705, 716, in which to express our conviction: 'It is reasoning in a circle, to argue that fraud is made out, when it is shown by oral testimony that the obligee contemporaneously with the execution of a bond, promised not to enforce it. Such a principle would nullify the rule: for conceding that such an agreement is proved, or any other contradicting the written instrument, the party seeking to enforce the written agreement according to its terms, would always be guilty of fraud. The true question is, Was there any such agreement? And this can only be established by legitimate testimony. For reasons founded in wisdom and to prevent frauds and perjuries, the rule of the

common law excludes such oral testimony of the alleged agreement; and as it cannot be proved by legal evidence, the agreement itself in legal contemplation, cannot be regarded as existing in fact.'

(*Pendergrass, supra,* 4 Cal.2d at pp. 263–264, 48 P.2d 659.)

B. *Reactions to* Pendergrass

Despite some criticism, *Pendergrass* has survived for over 75 years and the Courts of Appeal have followed it, albeit with varying degrees of fidelity. Until now, this court has not revisited the *Pendergrass* rule.

The primary ground of attack on *Pendergrass* has been that it is inconsistent with the principle, reflected in the terms of section 1856, that a contract may be invalidated by a showing of fraud. Evidence is deemed admissible for the purpose of proving fraud, without restriction, in the Restatements. (Rest.2d Contracts, § 214, subd. (d), and coms. C & d, pp. 134–135; see also *id.,* § 166, com. C, p. 452; Rest.2d Torts, § 530, com. C, p. 65.) Most of the treatises agree that evidence of fraud is not affected by the parol evidence rule. The majority of other jurisdictions follow this traditional view.

Underlying the objection that *Pendergrass* overlooks the impact of fraud on the validity of an agreement is a more practical concern: its limitation on evidence of fraud may itself further fraudulent practices. * * *

Pendergrass has been criticized on other grounds as well. The distinction between promises deemed consistent with the writing and those considered inconsistent has been described as "tenuous." The distinction between false promises and misrepresentations of fact has been called "very troublesome." It has also been noted that some courts have resisted applying the *Pendergrass* limitation by various means, leading to uncertainty in the case law.

* * *

On the other hand, *Pendergrass* has had its defenders. Its limitation on evidence of fraud has been described as "an entirely defensible decision favoring the policy considerations underlying the parol evidence rule over those supporting a fraud cause of action." (*Price v. Wells Fargo Bank, supra,* 213 Cal.App.3d at p. 485, 261 Cal.Rptr. 735; * * *) The *Price* court observed that "[a] broad doctrine of promissory fraud may allow parties to litigate disputes over the meaning of contract terms armed with an arsenal of tort remedies inappropriate to the resolution of commercial disputes." (*Price, supra,* at p. 485, 261 Cal.Rptr. 735; see also *Banco Do Brasil,* at pp. 1010–1011, 285 Cal.Rptr. 870.)

* * *

C. Pendergrass *Reconsidered*

There are multiple reasons to question whether *Pendergrass* has stood the test of time. It has been criticized as bad policy. Its limitation on the fraud exception is inconsistent with the governing statute, and the Legislature did not adopt that limitation when it revised section 1856 based on a survey of California case law construing the parol evidence rule. *Pendergrass*'s divergence from the path followed by the Restatements, the majority of other states, and most commentators is cause for concern, and leads us to doubt whether restricting fraud claims is necessary to serve the purposes of the parol evidence rule. Furthermore, the functionality of the *Pendergrass* limitation has been called into question by the vagaries of its interpretations in the Courts of Appeal.

We respect the principle of stare decisis, but reconsideration of a poorly reasoned opinion is nevertheless appropriate. It is settled that if a decision departed from an established general rule without discussing the contrary authority, its weight as precedent is diminished. Accordingly, we review the state of the law on the scope of the fraud exception when *Pendergrass* was decided, to determine if it was consistent with California law at that time.

Earlier cases from this court routinely stated without qualification that parol evidence was admissible to prove fraud. * * * As the *Ferguson* court declared, "Parol evidence is always admissible to prove fraud, and it was never intended that the parol evidence rule should be used as a shield to prevent the proof of fraud." (*Ferguson v. Koch,* 204 Cal. 342, 347, 268 P. 342.)

Historically, this unconditional rule was applied in cases of promissory fraud. For instance, in *Langley v. Rodriguez* (1898) 122 Cal. 580, 55 P. 406, the trial court excluded evidence of an oral promise by a packing company agent to make an advance payment to a grower. This court reversed, stating:

> The oral promise to pay part of the agreed price in advance of the curing of the crop was in conflict with the provision of the written contract that payment would be made on delivery of the raisins at the packing-house, and if the promise was honestly made it was undoubtedly within the rule forbidding proof of a contemporaneous or prior oral agreement to detract from the terms of a contract in writing. The rule cannot be avoided by showing that the promise outside the writing has been broken; such breach in itself does not constitute fraud. [Citations.] But a promise made without any intention of performing it is one of the forms of actual fraud (Civ.Code, sec.1572); and cases are not infrequent where relief against a contract reduced to writing has been granted on the ground that its execution was procured by

> means of oral promises fraudulent in the particular mentioned, however variant from the terms of the written engagement into which they were the means of inveigling the party. [Citations.] (*Langley, supra,* 122 Cal. At pp. 581–582, 55 P. 406.)

Interestingly, two years after *Pendergrass* this court fell back on the old rule in *Fleury v. Ramacciotti* (1937) 8 Cal.2d 660, 67 P.2d 339, a promissory fraud case. Ramacciotti, a mortgage debtor, claimed he had signed a renewal note without reading it, relying on a false promise that the note included a provision barring a deficiency judgment. (*Id.* At p. 661, 67 P.2d 339.) The trial court ruled in Ramacciotti's favor. The *Fleury* court affirmed, stating summarily: "Plaintiff's contention that the evidence was admitted in violation of the parol evidence rule is of course untenable, for although a written instrument may supersede prior negotiations and understandings leading up to it, fraud may always be shown to defeat the effect of an agreement." (*Id.* At p. 662, 67 P.2d 339; see also *Stock v. Meek* (1950) 35 Cal.2d 809, 815–816, 221 P.2d 15 [mistake of law case, quoting old rule and language from Rest. Of Contracts permitting extrinsic evidence of mistake or fraud].)

Thus, *Pendergrass* was plainly out of step with established California law. * * *

* * *

Accordingly, we conclude that *Pendergrass* was an aberration. It purported to follow section 1856 (*Pendergrass, supra,* 4 Cal.2d at p. 264, 48 P.2d 659), but its restriction on the fraud exception was inconsistent with the terms of the statute, and with settled case law as well. *Pendergrass* failed to account for the fundamental principle that fraud undermines the essential validity of the parties' agreement. When fraud is proven, it cannot be maintained that the parties freely entered into an agreement reflecting a meeting of the minds. Moreover, *Pendergrass* has led to instability in the law, as courts have strained to avoid abuses of the parol evidence rule. The *Pendergrass* court sought to " 'prevent frauds and perjuries' " (*id.* At p. 263, 48 P.2d 659), but ignored California law protecting against promissory fraud. The fraud exception has been part of the parol evidence rule since the earliest days of our jurisprudence, and the *Pendergrass* opinion did not justify the abridgment it imposed. For these reasons, we overrule *Pendergrass,* and its progeny, and reaffirm the venerable maxim stated in *Ferguson v. Koch, supra,* 204 Cal. At page 347, 268 P. 342: "[I]t was never intended that the parol evidence rule should be used as a shield to prevent the proof of fraud."

Here * * * we stress that the intent element of promissory fraud entails more than proof of an unkept promise or mere failure of performance. We note also that promissory fraud, like all forms of fraud, requires a showing of justifiable reliance on the defendant's misrepresentation. The Credit

Association contends the Workmans failed to present evidence sufficient to raise a triable issue on the element of reliance, given their admitted failure to read the contract. However, we decline to decide this question in the first instance. The trial court did not reach the issue of reliance in the summary judgment proceedings below, nor did the Court of Appeal address it.

III. DISPOSITION

We affirm the Court of Appeal's judgment.

CANTIL-SAKAUYE, C.J., KENNARD, BAXTER, WERDEGAR, CHIN, and LIU, JJ., CONCURS.

PROBLEM 6-2

What is the purpose of a "merger" ("full integration") clause?

(a) to indicate unmistakably that the parties intended their written agreement to be a complete and exclusive embodiment of all *terms* of the agreement?

(b) to foreclose issues of interpretation as to the meaning of the agreement?

(c) to put persons on notice that an agent has only limited authority as to the terms of a contract?

(d) other?

Did the clause serve its purpose?

NOTE:
THE PAROL EVIDENCE RULE AND OTHER THEORIES OF OBLIGATION

In the Riverisland case above, could the plaintiffs have recovered on a reliance theory of obligation (promissory estoppel)? Assume the plaintiffs sued based on the theory of promissory estoppel. Does the parol evidence rule bar admissibility of the evidence? Should it?

Please evaluate the following arguments: (1) The parol evidence rule only bars evidence offered to vary or contradict written *contracts,* i.e. agreements with consideration, and therefore does not apply to the proof of a different theory of obligation. (2) Admitting evidence of an oral promise to prove promissory estoppel does not frustrate the policies behind the parol evidence rule because the promissory estoppel remedy differs from the breach of contract remedy. (3) The parol evidence rule deters fraudulent assertion of the existence of agreements. Proof of reliance on a promise tends to show that a promise was made; therefore the parol evidence rule should not apply. (4) The problem of the relationship between the parol evidence rule and promissory estoppel is very similar to the problem of the relationship between the statute of frauds and promissory estoppel (see Chapter 2), and should be handled in the same way. For a case holding that the parol evidence rule bars evidence of promissory estoppel, see Kinn v. Coast Catamaran Corp., 582 F.Supp. 682 (E.D.Wis.1984).

CROWELL V. CAMPBELL SOUP COMPANY

United States Court of Appeals, Eighth Circuit, 2001.
264 F.3d 756.

HANSEN, CIRCUIT JUDGE.

When Herider Farms, Inc. (Herider), a wholly owned subsidiary of Campbell Soup Company (Campbell), decided to terminate its poultry production contracts with the above-named appellant farmers (Growers), the Growers brought suit alleging breach of contract [and] fraudulent inducement and misrepresentation * * *.

I. Background

Beginning in 1987 and continuing until the mid-1990s, several Growers in southwest Minnesota and northwest Iowa entered into broiler chicken production contracts with Herider. The arrangement called for the Growers to construct, equip, and operate poultry barns in return for Herider's agreement to regularly place newborn chicks with the Growers. An average barn cost roughly $250,000 to construct and had a 40,000 chick capacity with an approximate 60-day turnaround time for feeding the chicks to processing weight. Each Grower signed a written Growing Agreement and an accompanying Poultry House Financing Addendum, the interpretation of which are in dispute. On May 19, 1997, Herider sent a letter to each of its Growers informing them that Campbell would be shutting down its processing plant in Worthington, Minnesota and that Herider would cease placing flocks of chickens with the Growers.

The Growers' main argument is that Herider breached the terms of the contract by terminating the contracts without cause. The Growers base their wrongful termination claim on allegations that Herider made several precontract oral promises, namely that Herider was committed to placing chicks with the Growers during the useful lives of the barns, that Herider would only terminate the Growing Agreements "for cause," and that Herider promised certain profit projections which never came to fruition. The Growers claim they entered into the now-disputed written contracts based on these alleged promises. Addenda to the contracts provided that the Growers were entitled to "the reasonable cost of financing construction of a poultry house," according to an attached schedule, in the event that Herider elected to terminate the placement of flocks with Growers prior to the placement of 35 flocks (for contracts entered into prior to 1989) or of 40 flocks (for contracts entered into thereafter). (Appellees' Supp.App. at 52.) We refer to such a termination elsewhere in this opinion as a "premature termination."

The district court, ruling on motions in limine, prohibited parol evidence of any precontract oral promises made by Herider because it found that neither the main contracts nor the accompanying addenda were ambiguous as to Herider's right to terminate the contract without cause at any time, provided no flocks were present or scheduled to be present in the barns. The district court, therefore, dismissed the Growers' misrepresentation, fraudulent inducement, and rescission claims by holding, as a matter of law, that the Growers' reliance on the alleged oral promises was unreasonable because any such reliance was completely contradictory to the termination-at-any-time provisions of the written contracts. The district court then granted summary judgment in favor of Herider on the Growers' wrongful termination claims, finding that Herider had the contractual right to terminate the contracts without cause. * * *

II. Analysis

* * *

Breach of Contract

The Growers argue that Herider breached its contract with the Growers by terminating the contracts without cause. Herider admits that the contracts were not terminated due to any failure on the Growers' part to perform adequately under the contracts, but argues that it had the right to terminate the placements of flocks with the Growers at any time and for any reason.

Once the Growers filed the present lawsuit, Herider refused to make payments for the reasonable cost of financing the construction of the poultry houses on the ground that the Growers' filing of the lawsuit was a material breach of the contract on the part of the Growers. The district court held that the Growers did not breach the contract by filing the lawsuit—a ruling Herider does not directly challenge in this appeal—and therefore properly found Herider to be in breach of its contractual obligation to reimburse the Growers for their costs of financing the construction of the poultry houses.

The Growing Agreements contain the following relevant language:

> *D. 2. Future Flocks:* Termination: Fee Changes. That this Agreement shall apply to any flocks that may be placed on GROWER'S premises from time to time at HERIDER'S election. . . . In addition to GROWER'S right to terminate under the preceding sentence, either party may elect to terminate this Agreement by written notice received by the other party at any time that no flock is placed or scheduled to be placed with GROWER.
>
> *D. 3. Default: Remedies.* That in the event any of the following occurs: (i) GROWER for any reason removes or attempts to

> remove from GROWER'S premises any of HERIDER'S birds, feed, medicines, or other supplies; or (ii) GROWER in any manner encumbers, sells, or assigns any of HERIDER'S birds, feed, medicines, or other supplies, or attempts or permits the same; or (iii) HERIDER determines that GROWER is not following the HERIDER Management Guide or is otherwise improperly or neglectfully feeding, watering, or otherwise caring for said birds; then in any such event HERIDER may at its option immediately terminate this Agreement .... Upon termination of this Agreement for breach as provided herein, GROWER will not be entitled to any fee.

The contractual right contained in D.2. to terminate at any time there is no flock in the barn is restated with even more clarity in the Poultry House Financing Addendum signed by each Grower.

> GROWER acknowledges that HERIDER may terminate the placement of flocks with GROWER at any time when no flock is currently placed or scheduled to be placed, as provided in Section D, paragraph 2, of the foregoing Agreement. HERIDER nevertheless agrees that, if it elects to terminate placements prior to having placed a total of [35 or 40] flocks with GROWER (at a rate of approximately 5 flocks per year), HERIDER will continue to make payments to GROWER at 10-week intervals under the attached Schedule, which payments are intended to reimburse GROWER for the reasonable cost of financing the construction of a poultry house. GROWER acknowledges that GROWER will have no other claim against HERIDER for damages of any kind as a result of such permitted termination prior to the placement of the number of flocks stated in the preceding sentence.

Thus, under Section D.3. of the Growing Agreements, Herider has the right, while flocks are in the Growers' barns, to immediately terminate the contracts without any penalty to Herider based on any breach by a Grower of the specified terms of the contract. Under Section D.2. and the Financing Addendum, Herider has the right to terminate the contracts at any time and for any reason if no flocks are present in the poultry buildings, subject only to the obligation of paying the reasonable costs of financing the construction of the poultry houses if termination occurs prior to the placement of either 35 or 40 flocks. We therefore find no error in the district court's granting of summary judgment in favor of Herider for any damages beyond those which may be due the Growers for the reasonable costs of financing construction of the poultry houses.

Fraud, Misrepresentation, and Rescission

The Growers argue that the district court erred by failing to submit to a jury their fraud, misrepresentation, and rescission claims, which were based on three allegedly false precontract promises made by Herider. The district court found that the alleged promises were completely contradicted by the terms of the written contract, thereby rendering any reliance by the Growers on those promises unreasonable. See Commercial Prop. Invs., Inc. v. Quality Inns Int'l, Inc., 938 F.2d 870, 876 (8th Cir.1991) (interpreting Minnesota law as follows: "When a promise is not in plain contradiction of a contract, or if contradictory, when it is accompanied by misrepresentations of other material facts in addition to the contradictory intent[,] the question of reliance is for the trier of fact.") Based on Minnesota's parol evidence rules, the district court therefore prohibited the introduction of any evidence of the alleged oral promises and granted summary judgment in favor of Herider on the Growers' claims. See Hruska v. Chandler Assoc., Inc., 372 N.W.2d 709, 713 (Minn.1985) ("parol evidence is ordinarily inadmissible to vary, contradict, or alter the written agreement").

We agree with the district court that any reliance by the Growers on the three alleged oral promises made by Herider was unreasonable as a matter of law because each of the alleged oral promises plainly contradicted the terms of the written contract. We also note that besides contradicting the substance of the written contract, the oral promises also plainly contradict Section D.7. of the contract, which states that "this Agreement constitutes the entire agreement between the parties relating to the subject matter hereof and no oral agreement shall alter or add to any part thereof." (Clifford Crowell Growing Agreement, Appellees' Supp.App. at 49.)

First, the alleged overriding oral promise to terminate the Growers only "for cause" plainly contradicts the written contract provisions granting Herider the right to terminate the placement of flocks essentially at any time when flocks are not in the barns. Section D.3. does permit immediate termination only for cause and then explicitly lists the grounds justifying such an immediate termination. Section D.2., however, does not place any limitations on Herider's right to terminate the contract when there are not any flocks present in the barns. In order to accept the Growers' interpretation of the termination provisions of the contract, a court or jury would have to read into Section D.2. not only the words "for cause only" but would have to determine the grounds constituting "cause." The Growers' proposed interpretation would also lead to the odd result that Herider could immediately terminate a contract for cause without incurring any obligation to pay the reasonable cost of financing the construction when flocks were actually in the barns according to Section D.3., but when no flocks were in the barns, Herider could likewise only terminate the contracts for cause and still would be subject to paying the reasonable cost of financing the construction of the barn. We also do not agree with the Growers that the term "permitted termination" in the financing addendum is ambiguous. We agree with the district court that "permitted termination" specifically refers to the between-flock termination authorized in Section D.2. and as explained in the financing addendum, which we have already held permits termination without cause. We therefore agree with the district court that the clear language of the contract permits termination at any time and for any reason, provided no flocks are in the Growers' barns or scheduled to be placed therein, and that any reliance on an alleged, oral, overriding, for-cause-only termination promise is unreasonable because it is plainly contradicted by the written contracts. See Vint v. Nelson, 267 Minn. 490, 127 N.W.2d 177, 181 (1964) (affirming dismissal of fraudulent misrepresentation claim on grounds that oral promise related to matters known to be covered in the written contract and oral promise contradicted the written contract terms); Dorso Trailer Sales, Inc. v. Am. Body and Trailer, Inc., 372 N.W.2d 412, 415 (Minn.Ct.App.1985) (holding that a contract with its only restriction on termination being a 90-day notice requirement, and otherwise silent as to termination for cause or at will, is unambiguously terminable at will under Minnesota law); cf. Cederstrand v. Lutheran Bhd., 263 Minn. 520, 117 N.W.2d 213, 221 (1962) (explaining that a hiring contract for an indefinite term is in reality terminable at will, and thus the contract may be terminated at any time and for any reason).

Second, we likewise find Herider's alleged promise of a long-term commitment to continue placing flocks with the Growers beyond 35 or 40 flocks to be in plain contradiction of the written contract provisions granting to Herider the express right to terminate the contracts prior to the placement of 35 or 40 flocks. We therefore agree with the district court that any reliance by the Growers on this alleged promise would also be unreasonable as a matter of law.

Finally, Herider's alleged revenue misrepresentations over the course of the useful lives of the poultry buildings are not enough to defeat the district court's grant of summary judgment in favor of Herider on the Growers' misrepresentation, fraud, and rescission claims. To begin with, any promise of a certain amount of profits per year for the useful life of the buildings beyond the first seven or eight years (35 to 40 flocks) plainly contradicts the termination-at-any-time provisions of the contract and the limited nature (35 to 40 flocks) of the guarantee to reimburse the reasonable costs of financing construction of the buildings. In addition, any revenue predictions for the first seven or eight years of the contract are plainly contradicted by the fact that each Grower signed a payment schedule specifying the price per pound it would be paid for the finished chickens. That price, generally ranging from 4 to 4.2 cents per pound, was known by the Growers at the time the contracts were signed. Thus, the Growers were well aware of the likely revenues under the contract, and any other alleged oral or written misrepresentations as to revenues are plainly contradicted by the terms of the written contract.

* * *

In sum, we agree with the district court that most of Herider's alleged promises are plainly contradicted by the written terms of the contracts, and the remaining portions which are not plainly contradicted by the written contract nevertheless do not sufficiently allege the necessary misrepresentation of a past or present material fact to save the underlying claims of fraud, misrepresentation, and rescission from dismissal at the summary judgment stage. Any reliance on the alleged promises by the Growers is therefore unreasonable as a matter of law.

* * *

III. Conclusion

For the foregoing reasons, we affirm in all respects the judgment of the district court.

HIELD V. THYBERG

Supreme Court of Minnesota, 1984.
347 N.W.2d 503.

SIMONETT, JUSTICE.

Although the trial court properly allowed plaintiff to use parol evidence to explain the purpose and vary the term of a written contract, we conclude, on the facts of this case, that plaintiff should have been required to prove his case by clear and convincing evidence. We reverse for a new trial.

On June 10, 1977, plaintiff-respondent Willard R. Hield sold his half interest in a corporation, Beauticians Supply, Inc., to defendant-appellant Edwin R. Thyberg, owner of the other half interest. The sale was accomplished by a written document entitled "Assignment," signed by Hield, which provided in part:

> For and in consideration of *Fifteen Thousand* Dollars ($*15,000.00*), Willard R. Hield, of Minneapolis, Minnesota, does hereby assign, order and transfer to Edwin R. Thyberg, of Sioux Falls, South Dakota, all of my right, title and interest in Beauticians Supply, Inc., a corporation, including but not limited to any and all advances made by me to the said corporation and all of my common shares of capital stock * * *.
>
> * * *
>
> The undersigned assignor hereby acknowledges that the assignee assumes no other personal liability toward assignor * * *.

The $15,000 was paid at the time the assignment was signed by Hield. Sometime thereafter, Hield transferred his stock certificates to Thyberg.

In January 1979, plaintiff Hield sued defendant Thyberg, alleging in his complaint that he had sold his corporate shares "for a total consideration of $50,000, $15,000 cash at closing and $35,000 in a promissory note." Plaintiff further alleged that Thyberg, by agreeing to pay $50,000 and then refusing to perform, had committed fraud. The case was tried to a jury. Over defendant's objections, plaintiff was permitted to testify that defendant, indeed, had agreed to pay an additional $35,000 for the corporate stock. Defendant denied any such agreement. The trial court dismissed the fraud allegations, but submitted the contract issue to the jury. The jury resolved the fact issues in favor of plaintiff and, pursuant to the verdict, judgment was entered in favor of plaintiff and against defendant for $35,000 plus 6% interest from June 10, 1977. Defendant Thyberg appeals from the judgment.

The issue is whether the parol evidence rule applies. If it does, plaintiff is bound by the $15,000 agreed consideration set out in the written document and can collect no more. If the parol evidence rule does not apply, there is evidence to sustain the jury's verdict that the true consideration was $50,000, not $15,000. We conclude that parol evidence may be used here but under a higher burden of proof.

When the case was called for trial, the trial court denied defendant's motion to exclude parol evidence and allowed plaintiff's evidence to be received.[1] At the close of all the testimony, defendant's motion for a directed verdict was denied, the trial court observing, "I have grave reservations about this particular lawsuit and I have no hesitancy about stating it."

[Negotiations between the parties began in the spring of 1977. At that time a bank was threatening to foreclose a mortgage on the corporation. Hield had personally guaranteed the loan. On April 18, 1977, Thyberg said he would purchase Hield's stock for ten or fifteen thousand dollars plus an additional sum paid over five years, not to exceed $72,000.]

The key date is June 10, 1977. On that day defendant Thyberg came to Minneapolis to close the deal with plaintiff Hield. Thyberg brought with him the typed "Assignment" paper previously mentioned, which had been drafted by his attorney in Sioux Falls with a blank space provided for insertion of the amount of consideration. Thyberg and Hield held three meetings on that day—at 8 a.m., then about 11 a.m., and finally again at 5 p.m. Hield testified that Thyberg agreed to pay $50,000, $15,000 down and the balance by a demand note which Thyberg would send as soon as he got back to Sioux Falls. Hield testified that Thyberg was intending to get an

[1] "The evidence that the rule seems to exclude must sometimes be heard and weighed before it can be excluded by the rule." 3 Corbin, Contracts § 582 at 450 (1960). Much is left to the trial court's discretion in the particular case. Rather than say that the parol evidence rule prohibits "admission" or "allowance" of certain evidence, it may be better to say that the rule, if it applies, prevents the "use" of parol evidence.

SBA loan and consequently did not want the $35,000 to show on his balance sheet. With this understanding, Hield says he had his secretary type in the blank space a $15,000 consideration, plus an indemnity provision at the bottom of the paper. He then signed the assignment and accepted Thyberg's check for $15,000. Thyberg testified that at the 8 a.m. meeting, he did, indeed, say that payment of a sum in addition to $15,000 "might be a possibility," and that "[i]f there was any other way I could raise any more money, I would,"—but that this depended on whether the business would be profitable and would be able to use the tax loss carryover. It was Thyberg's position that after these preliminaries, however, he offered to pay only $15,000 plus agreeing to save Hield harmless on his personal guarantee of the bank mortgage. Thyberg said he would have elected to liquidate the company if these terms had not been agreeable to Hield.

[Another witness, Flaten, an attorney for Beauticians Supply, Inc., testified that his notes of two conversations with Hield on June 10 indicated that Hield thought the company if liquidated might net $70,000 to $90,000 subject to a $20,000 advance owed Thyberg, that Flaten suggested that Hield should negotiate for more money to be paid on an installment basis, and that the parties were concerned that any additional consideration over $15,000 might prejudice the SBA loan and that it might be better to defer this aspect of their deal. Flaten also told Hield that "camouflaging" additional consideration might be fraudulent and that the "proper procedure" would be a note subordinated to the SBA loan.]

* * * Flaten testified that he explained to Hield that the assignment document "purported to be a complete sale of his entire interest both debt and equity in the corporation *for whatever sum was to be inserted in the contract* if it was executed and I told him that the contract would be effective for that purpose." (Emphasis added.)

We have, then, a classic fact dispute. Thyberg and Hield were alone together when they concluded their agreement, and each has a different version of the purchase price finally agreed upon. Both parties were vague in their recollections in important respects and uncertain what the business was really worth. Did Hield and Thyberg, notwithstanding the attorney's warning, agree to another $35,000 undocumented consideration? Or did Thyberg, knowing Hield's need for cash, simply drive a hard bargain, and Hield, not willing to risk a corporate liquidation, accept $15,000 as payment in full?

The parol evidence rule encourages parties to put their agreements in writing so that there may be fewer, not more, lawsuits. Thus the rule, as generally stated, is that evidence outside a written document is not to be used to vary or contradict the plain terms of the document. The sometimes harsh effect of this rule is, however, ameliorated by a host of exceptions. This is not, however, a case of subsequent modification of the written contract. Nor is it a case of ambiguity in the terms of the written agreement itself. Nor is it a case of the written contract itself being incomplete or silent on a term to which the written contract might not normally be expected to speak. Nor is this a case of no enforceable contract ever being made. If there is an exception to the rule, we must look elsewhere.

Plaintiff Hield argues that while he assented to the written assignment he did not assent to it as a document setting out the complete understanding of the parties. In other words, Hield contends that the written document did not "integrate" the parties' complete understanding and so the jury should be free to use parol evidence to determine the true, entire agreement. This seems to be an attempt to show a written contract is incomplete by introducing through parol evidence a term flatly contradictory to the written contract. Hield seems to imply that he would never have signed the written document if Thyberg had not promised to pay an additional $35,000. The trial court, however, held as a matter of law, there was no fraud in the inducement. Rather, it appears that Hield is claiming that the written assignment is, in part, illusory; that the written assignment containing the $15,000 stated consideration was executed for the purpose of showing it to the Small Business Administration so that an SBA loan could be obtained—a loan, incidentally, which would be used to pay off the bank mortgage which Hield had personally guaranteed; and that the separate oral agreement for Thyberg to give Hield a $35,000 demand note was, together with the note itself, to be kept secret from the SBA.

Hield wants to show that he intended the consideration to be $50,000 even though he himself wrote in the figure $15,000. In other words, he really wants to show the *purpose* of the written contract is other than as stated in the writing. * * *

This case has a curious twist to it. Hield denies any deceit on his part and stops short of claiming that Thyberg intended to use the written contract to deceive. Hield says only that he assumed Thyberg would tell SBA about the undocumented $35,000 debt.[2] The record indicates that Thyberg got his SBA loan. Presumably he did not disclose to SBA any $35,000 debt to Hield or Hield would surely have put such an admission in

---

[2] On direct examination, Hield testified:

Q. Well, were you involved in some scheme to defraud the Small Business Administration?

A. No, sir.

Q. Well, if you weren't going to show this in a written form so that would not affect his balance sheet, why isn't that doing something improper?

A. Well, at this point he—whether he was the president of the company he, in effect, then became the owner. I guess this was up to him at that point.

After absolving himself of any responsibility for whatever use the $15,000 written assignment would be put to, Hield went on to testify that he assumed Thyberg would arrange for the $35,000 debt to be subordinated to the SBA loan.

evidence. In other words, the net impact of Hield's claim is that Thyberg defrauded the SBA with the written assignment. * * *

We hold, * * * that where the parties have entered into a written contract, complete and unambiguous on the consideration to be paid, but it is claimed that the consideration was not as stated so that the contract might be used to mislead or deceive a third party, parol evidence is usable; but the party seeking to vary the terms of the written contract in this situation has the burden of establishing his claim by clear and convincing evidence.

Here the jury was not instructed on the clear and convincing evidence standard. While defendant Thyberg did not request the instruction, he did strenuously throughout the trial claim the benefit of the parol evidence rule. We believe the case should be retried with the appropriate burden of proof instruction.

Reversed and remanded for a new trial.

MODEL RULES OF PROFESSIONAL CONDUCT

R. 1.2(d) (2007).

A lawyer shall not counsel a client to engage, or assist a client, in conduct that the lawyer knows is criminal or fraudulent, but a lawyer may discuss the legal consequences of any proposed course of conduct with a client and may counsel or assist a client to make a good faith effort to determine the validity, scope, meaning, or application of the law.

PROBLEM 6-3

A letter to the editors from counsel for Thyberg, dated April 30, 1985, states:

> As a result of this case, we have concluded that virtually no written contract is safe from attack regardless of the clarity of its wording. It appears that anyone wishing to escape the consequences of a written contract can get to the jury with an argument that there was a parol agreement for something which is directly at variance with the terms of the written contract since it does not seem difficult to be able to show some latent ambiguity or lack of integration.

Do you agree with counsel?

NOTE: THE "CONDITION PRECEDENT" EXCEPTION TO THE PAROL EVIDENCE RULE

Courts sometimes hold that parol evidence is admissible to prove a condition precedent to the legal enforcement of a written agreement. For example, where the parties to a written agreement merging their two corporations orally agreed that the merger was conditioned on the prior accumulation of $672,500 "equity expansion funds," evidence of this oral agreement and of failure of the condition was held admissible to prove a defense of the party resisting the merger. Hicks v. Bush, 10 N.Y.2d 488, 225 N.Y.S.2d 34, 180 N.E.2d 425 (1962). The court stated that evidence of an oral condition precedent is admissible where the evidence does not "directly" or "explicitly" contradict the writing. See also Brown Dev. Corp. v. Hemond, 956 A.2d 104, 108–09 (Me. 2008). In MCM Partners v. Andrews-Bartlett & Assoc., 161 F.3d 443, 447 (7th Cir.1998), on the other hand, the court held that the parol evidence rule barred evidence of a condition precedent because the contract was clear and the evidence would "alter unilaterally the terms of the agreement." See also Morgan Stanley High Yield Secs., Inc. v. Seven Circle Gaming Corp., 269 F. Supp. 2d 206, 220 (S.D.N.Y. 2003) ("It is clear that any provision in a contract characterizing a party's obligations as 'unconditional' would be directly contradicted by any condition, whether established orally or otherwise. Similarly, it is generally accepted that any provision in a contract expressly requiring modifications and amendments to be in writing would be contradicted by an oral condition precedent.").

This discussion suggests the similarities between the condition precedent exception and the issue of whether an agreement is integrated. For example, some courts applying the condition precedent exception have inquired whether the written contract was detailed and contained an integration clause. See, e.g., Whirlpool Corp. v. Regis Leasing Corp., 29 A.D.2d 395, 288 N.Y.S.2d 337 (1st Dept.1968).

6 CORBIN ON CONTRACTS

§ 25.2 (2019).

The statute of frauds and the "parol evidence rule" are sometimes both applied in a single case. To promote clear thinking and correct decision, they should be compared and contrasted. They appear to have a similar purpose, at least when we regard the latter rule as in truth a rule of admissibility; that purpose is the prevention of successful fraud and perjury. In each case, this purpose is only haltingly attained; and if attained at all it is at the expense and to the injury of many honest contractors. Both the statute and the rule may have caused more litigation than they have prevented. Both may have done more harm than good. Both have been convenient hooks on which a judge can support a decision actually reached on other grounds. Both are attempts to determine justice and the truth by a mechanistic device, alike evidencing a distrust of the capacity of courts and juries to weigh human credibility. And both alike have forced the courts, in the effort to prevent them from doing gross injustice to honest men, to make numerous exceptions and fine distinctions, with such resulting complexity and inconsistency that a reasoned statement of their operations requires volumes instead of pages and the case must be rare in which a plausible argument can not be made for deciding either way.

So much for the apparent similarities of the statute and the rule, these similarities being found in their social aims and practical effects. In the means that they employ and in their juristic effects, they are very different.

The statute makes certain oral contracts unenforceable by action, if not evidenced by a signed memorandum; the "parol evidence rule" protects a completely integrated writing from being varied and contradicted by parol.

SECTION THREE: GENERAL PRINCIPLES OF INTERPRETATION

We have already studied some important aspects of the interpretation of written contracts in the preceding section on parol evidence. For example, in Pacific Gas and Electric Co. v. G.W. Thomas Drayage and Rigging Co., Inc., we saw how a court may disregard the "plain meaning" rule and admit extrinsic evidence to interpret an agreement. In Eskimo Pie Corp. v. Whitelawn Dairies, Inc., we saw how a court may resort to extrinsic evidence of a course of dealing, course of performance, or trade custom when interpreting an agreement. But you should not assume that the problem of the admissibility of parol evidence is the same as the problem of interpretation. Parol evidence of an alleged extrinsic term may be clearly admissible although the evidence may pose a problem of interpretation. Conversely, a problem of the admissibility of parol evidence may arise although the parties do not dispute the meaning of the alleged extrinsic term. Even when both problems arise together, the parol evidence rule operates to identify the admissible evidence of an agreement to which the court may then apply the principles of interpretation.

Before considering the following materials, you should review Sections Two and Three of Chapter Four on planning and drafting. Those sections help explain why the interpretation process is often fraught with difficulties for lawyers and courts.

PATTERSON, THE INTERPRETATION AND CONSTRUCTION OF CONTRACTS

64 Colum.L.Rev. 833, 833–34 (1964).

What is interpretation? It is the process of endeavoring to ascertain the meaning or meanings of symbolic expressions used by the parties to a contract, or of their expressions in the formative stage of arriving at the creation of one or more legally obligatory promises. Since most contracts are temporary in their effects, the process of interpretation often consists merely of the direct application of the symbols used to the factual situation that gives rise to controversy.

BERKE MOORE CO. V. PHOENIX BRIDGE CO.

Supreme Court of New Hampshire, 1953.
98 N.H. 261, 98 A.2d 150.

[The defendant, Phoenix Bridge Company, a general contractor, entered a contract with New Hampshire to build a bridge with concrete surfaces. According to the contract, Phoenix Bridge was to receive $12.60 per square yard of "concrete surface included in the bridge deck." The state's printed estimate of the quantity of concrete necessary was "3,933 S.Y." (3,933 square yards). Phoenix Bridge entered a subcontract with the plaintiff, Berke Moore, in which Phoenix Bridge agreed to pay Berke Moore $12.00 per square yard of "concrete surface included in the bridge deck." Berke Moore was aware at the time of contracting of the general contract's printed estimate of 3,933 square yards.

Berke Moore performed the concrete work and ultimately claimed that, according to the above contract language and estimate, it should be paid for the amount of concrete it placed on all of the deck's outer surfaces, including the top, bottom and sides. This totaled 8100 square yards, which at $12.00 per square yard came to $97,200. Phoenix Bridge responded that the contract obligated it to pay at a rate measured only by the amount of concrete in the upper surface area, i.e. 4184 square yards at $12.00 per square yard, or $50,208.

The trial court found that the words "concrete surface included in the bridge deck" were "not so plain and clear that reasonable men could not differ as to their meaning." The Supreme Court of New Hampshire upheld this ruling, although noting that in light of the specifications, which indicated that several surfaces of the deck were of concern to the state, "a strong argument (could) be made" that the parties meant more than "the upper surface alone."

The Supreme Court also affirmed the trial court's finding that both Phoenix Bridge and Berke Moore believed at the time of the execution of the contract that Berke Moore was to be paid only at a rate measured by the top surface, and that this view "was opposed to (Berke Moore's) understanding at the time of trial." The Supreme Court's decision was based both on Berke Moore's knowledge of the general contract quantity estimate and unit price and on the parties' subsequent negotiations to modify a portion of the subcontract. The court was not persuaded by Berke Moore's insistence that the quantity estimate was inconsequential "since payment was to be made for 'actual quantities.' "]

DUNCAN, JUSTICE.

* * * The rule which precludes the use of the understanding of one party alone is designed to prevent imposition of his private understanding upon the other party to a bilateral transaction. * * * But when it appears that the understanding of one is the understanding of both, no violation of the rule results from determination of the mutual understanding according to that of one alone.

Where the understanding is mutual, it ceases to be the "private" understanding of one. Having thus determined the mutual understanding of the parties, the Court properly interpreted the contract accordingly.

RESTATEMENT (SECOND) OF CONTRACTS § 201.

Whose Meaning Prevails

(1) Where the parties have attached the same meaning to a promise or agreement or a term thereof, it is interpreted in accordance with that meaning.

(2) Where the parties have attached different meanings to a promise or agreement or a term thereof, it is interpreted in accordance with the meaning attached by one of them if at the time the agreement was made

> (a) that party did not know of any different meaning attached by the other, and the other knew the meaning attached by the first party; or
>
> (b) that party had no reason to know of any different meaning attached by the other, and the other had reason to know the meaning attached by the first party.

(3) Except as stated in this Section, neither party is bound by the meaning attached by the other, even though the result may be a failure of mutual assent.

PROBLEM 6-4

Charles Leslie agreed to manufacture 7500 humidifiers for Pennco, Inc. The purchase order drafted by Pennco included the following provision:

> PLEASE NOTE THE ABOVE RELEASE SCHEDULE TO BE REVIEWED QUARTERLY

The order specified certain dates for production and delivery. After 3946 humidifiers were delivered to Pennco, it refused to accept further delivery. Pennco claimed that the release schedule provision permitted it to cancel at quarterly intervals. Evaluate the following examination of witnesses at the trial of Leslie v. Pennco, Inc. by Leslie's lawyer.

Direct Examination of Charles Leslie

Q. Now, in capital letters down at the bottom of the page [of the purchase order] would you read to the Court and the jury what it says?

A. "Please note the above release schedule to be reviewed quarterly."

Q. What is the, quotes, above release schedule? What is that?

A. Release schedule is up above here. There's—in capital letters it says, "Released as follows." This is following the amount of humidifiers that were ordered within the designated amount of time, and this was merely the rate at which we would—we are asked to produce and deliver the humidifiers.

Q. Now, was that acceptable to you to permit the review of the release schedule as you went along?

A. Yes, sir, it was.

Q. And what was the background discussion that led to the insertion of that phraseology?

A. It was posed to me that this was the start and that they would—they anticipated wanting a greater number or wanted them faster than seven-hundred-and-fifty a month as the sales program took off.

Q. When you say "they," would you identify the person with whom you discussed this matter?

A. Tom Fadale.

Q. And at any time did you and Mr. Fadale talk about the contingency of reducing that monthly release schedule?

A. No, sir.

Q. Was there ever any hint or indication at any time that at a given quarter the whole deal could be canceled?

A. No, sir.

Cross Examination of Thomas Fadale of Pennco, Inc.

Q. My question is this: Did you and Mr. Haas at any time discuss the idea that you could terminate this contract and not buy seventy-five-hundred units?

A. [by Fadale]: No, sir.

Q. Then you agree with me that what was contemplated here was that [Leslie] would supply seventy-five-hundred in the—in the monthly projections and you would ultimately buy seventy-five hundred.

A. No, sir, I don't agree with you on that.

Q. You don't agree?

A. No.

Q. Well, I thought a moment ago you said that you were obligated to buy the seventy-five-hundred. Did you talk about buying fewer than that and terminating?

A. We did not discuss buying fewer, but on the bottom of the purchase order we did put the statement that we could review quarterly, which meant that we could increase our production—or his production or decrease his production.

Q. Mr. Fadale, I'm going to ask you the question again because obviously I didn't make it clear. I'm going to make it very simple. Recognizing you could increase or decrease by a quarterly review the monthly deliveries, recognizing that, did you ever with Mr. Haas discuss the idea that you could walk in and say stop, we are not going to buy the full seventy-five-hundred?

A. No.

Q. Now, when that matter—When it came time for a purchase order to be given to L & W, this matter never even came up, did it?

A. No, sir.

Q. It was never even discussed between you and Mr. Leslie.

A. No.

Q. The only discussions of rescheduling were with Mr. Haas at Iroquois and neither with Mr. Haas nor indeed with Mr. Leslie was there any suggestion that you could buy fewer than seventy-five-hundred units. Do you agree with me?

A. Yes.

---

1. Was Pennco right that it could cancel?

2. Is the interpretation question here a question of law for the court or fact for the jury? Consider Restatement (Second) of Contracts § 212(2):

> A question of interpretation of an integrated agreement is to be determined by the trier of fact if it depends on the credibility of extrinsic evidence or on a choice among reasonable inferences to be drawn from extrinsic evidence. Otherwise a question of interpretation of an integrated agreement is to be determined as a question of law.

E.M.M.I. INC. V. ZURICH AMERICAN INSURANCE COMPANY

Supreme Court of California 2004.
32 Cal.4th 465, 84 P.3d 385.

Opinion

MORENO, J.

We are called upon in this case to interpret the scope of an exception to a provision excluding coverage in a "jeweler's block" insurance policy. The provision at issue exempted from coverage jewelry stolen from a vehicle unless the insured was "actually in or upon such vehicle at the time of the theft." The question presented is whether the exception to that exclusion applies when the insured is not in the vehicle but is in close proximity to the vehicle and is attending to it when the theft occurs. We conclude the vehicle theft exclusion, as a whole, is ambiguous and fails to plainly and clearly alert insureds that there is no coverage if a theft occurs when the insured has stepped out of the vehicle but remains in close proximity and is attending to it. We therefore hold that coverage is not precluded as a matter of law and reverse the judgment of the Court of Appeal.

I. FACTUAL AND PROCEDURAL BACKGROUND

The facts in this case are simple and essentially undisputed. On February 17, 2000, Brian Callahan, a jewelry salesman, left his home with two "hard cloth garment bags" containing jewelry (some of which belonged to E.M.M.I. Inc., a manufacturer and marketer of jewelry) in the trunk of his vehicle. Shortly after driving away from his home, he heard a clanking noise emanating from the rear of the vehicle. Callahan stopped on the side of the road to investigate the source of the noise, got out of the car and closed the car door but left the engine running. He walked to the rear of the vehicle and, as he crouched down to visually inspect the exhaust pipes, he felt someone pass quickly by him. When he looked up, he saw an individual get into his car and drive away. Callahan was no more than approximately two feet from the car during the entire time he was outside the vehicle until the time of the theft. The police subsequently found the vehicle, but the jewelry was missing.

E.M.M.I. was insured under a jeweler's block insurance policy issued by Zurich American Insurance Company (Zurich). The policy insured E.M.M.I. against "risks of direct physical 'loss' to the covered [jewelry] except those causes of 'loss' listed in the Exclusions." Under "Exclusions" the policy provided that Zurich would "not pay for 'loss' caused or resulting from . . . [t]heft from any vehicle unless, you, an employee, or other person whose only duty is to attend to the vehicle are actually in or upon such vehicle at the time of the theft." (Italics added.) Callahan was specifically designated to carry E.M.M.I.'s jewelry.

E.M.M.I. submitted a claim to Zurich under the policy. Zurich's field adjuster was instructed to ascertain whether Callahan had been physically touching the car when the theft occurred, and therefore had been "in or upon" the car. Because E.M.M.I. was unable to show that Callahan had been physically touching the vehicle when the theft occurred, Zurich denied the claim * * *

The parties, E.M.M.I. [and] Zurich * * * subsequently filed cross motions for summary judgment and summary adjudication. The superior court granted Zurich's motion for summary judgment and denied E.M.M.I.'s * * * motions. The court found that "where the insured was outside the car, crouched down, inspecting the underneath exhaust pipes, before the sequence of events of theft commenced, there unequivocally is no coverage under terms requiring the insured to be in or upon the vehicle at the time of theft."

The Court of Appeal affirmed the resulting judgment. It ruled that "[a]lthough [the salesman] was in close proximity to the car, he was not actually in or upon it." We granted review.

II. DISCUSSION

* * *

A. Rules Governing Interpretation of Insurance Policies

As a question of law, the interpretation of an insurance policy is reviewed de novo under well-settled rules of contract interpretation. (Waller v. Truck Ins. Exchange, Inc. (1995) 11 Cal.4th 1, 18, 44 Cal.Rptr.2d 370, 900 P.2d 619 (Waller).) "The fundamental rules of contract interpretation are based on the premise that the interpretation of a contract must give effect to the 'mutual intention' of the parties. 'Under statutory rules of contract interpretation, the mutual intention of the parties at the time the contract is formed governs interpretation. (Civ.Code, § 1636.) Such intent is to be inferred, if possible, solely from the written provisions of the contract. (Id., § 1639.) The "clear and explicit" meaning of these provisions, interpreted in their "ordinary and popular sense," unless "used by the parties in a technical sense or a special meaning is given to them by usage" (id., § 1644), controls judicial interpretation. (Id., § 1638.)' " (Ibid.)

A policy provision is ambiguous when it is susceptible to two or more reasonable constructions. (Waller, supra, 11 Cal.4th at p. 18, 44 Cal.Rptr.2d 370, 900 P.2d 619.) Language in an insurance policy is "interpreted as a whole, and in the circumstances of the case, and cannot be found to be ambiguous in the abstract." "The proper question is whether the [provision or] word is ambiguous in the context of this policy and the circumstances of this case. 'The provision will shift between clarity and ambiguity with changes in the event at hand." (Bay Cities Paving &

Grading, Inc. v. Lawyers' Mutual Ins. Co. (1993) 5 Cal.4th 854, 868, 21 Cal.Rptr.2d 691, 855 P.2d 1263.) Ambiguity " ' "is resolved by interpreting the ambiguous provisions in the sense the [insurer] believed the [insured] understood them at the time of formation. If application of this rule does not eliminate the ambiguity, ambiguous language is construed against the party who caused the uncertainty to exist." "This rule, as applied to a promise of coverage in an insurance policy, protects not the subjective beliefs of the insurer but, rather, 'the objectively reasonable expectations of the insured.' " 'Any ambiguous terms are resolved in the insureds' favor, consistent with the insureds' reasonable expectations.' " (Safeco Ins. Co. v. Robert S. (2001) 26 Cal.4th 758, 763, 110 Cal.Rptr.2d 844, 28 P.3d 889.)

Furthermore, policy exclusions are strictly construed, * * * while exceptions to exclusions are broadly construed in favor of the insured. * * * " '[A]n insurer cannot escape its basic duty to insure by means of an exclusionary clause that is unclear. As we have declared time and again "any exception to the performance of the basic underlying obligation must be so stated as clearly to apprise the insured of its effect." Thus, "the burden rests upon the insurer to phrase exceptions and exclusions in clear and unmistakable language." The exclusionary clause "must be conspicuous, plain and clear." ' This rule applies with particular force when the coverage portion of the insurance policy would lead an insured to reasonably expect coverage for the claim purportedly excluded." (MacKinnon, supra, at p. 648, 3 Cal.Rptr.3d 228, 73 P.3d 1205.)

B. Interpretation of the Vehicle Theft Exclusion and Exception

E.M.M.I. does not contend that Callahan, E.M.M.I.'s designated salesperson, was "in" the vehicle at the time of the theft, but instead argues that he was "upon" the vehicle. The controversy therefore centers on the meaning of the term "upon" as it is used in the exception to the vehicle theft exclusion. While the parties contend that the term "upon" is unambiguous as applied to the facts of this case, they disagree on how that term should be defined.

Preliminarily, we reject Zurich's contention that an ordinary and reasonable person would understand the phrase "actually in or upon" only in a legal sense or as a "legalism, used only for distinctly legal purposes." We reject this construction because it runs afoul of elementary rules of contract interpretation that policy language is interpreted in its ordinary and popular sense (Waller, supra, 11 Cal.4th at p. 18, 44 Cal.Rptr.2d 370, 900 P.2d 619) and as a "layman would read it and not as it might be analyzed by an attorney or an insurance expert." * * * The policy at issue in this case defines certain words, such as "we" and "us" and further provides that "[o]ther words and phrases that appear in quotation marks have special meaning." Neither the phrase "actually in or upon" nor the term "upon" is enclosed in quotation marks. Thus, nothing in the policy indicates or suggests that the exception to the vehicle theft exclusion is to be construed in a specialized or technical manner, or as Zurich contends—as used in statutes and ordinances. Absent evidence that the parties intended the provision to have a specialized meaning, we must reject Zurich's contention and construe the term in question as would a layperson.

E.M.M.I. contends the exception to the vehicle theft exclusion applies in this case because its salesman was in close proximity to the automobile when the theft occurred. It rests on the fact that the word "upon" is interchangeable with "on" and that the definition of "on" includes "in close proximity." (Merriam-Webster's 10th New Collegiate Dict. (1995) pp. 811, 1298 ["a village [on] the sea"]; Black's Law Dict. (6th ed.1990) p. 1088 [defining "on" as "upon; as soon as; near to; along; along side of; adjacent to; contiguous to; at the time of; following upon; during; at or in contact with the upper surface of a thing"].) Zurich disagrees that close proximity is sufficient and implicitly relies on the definition of "on" "indicat[ing] means of conveyance" (Merriam-Webster's 10th New Collegiate Dict., supra, at p. 811; Random House College Dict. (rev. ed.1980) p. 1444), such as "on a ship" or "on a train" and the definition of "upon" meaning "up and on; upward so as to get or be on" (Random House College Dict., supra, at p. 1444), such as "upon" a motorcycle.

Of course, the fact that a word carries multiple meanings does not by itself render it ambiguous. (Bay Cities Paving & Grading, Inc. v. Lawyers' Mutual Ins. Co., supra, 5 Cal.4th at 868, 21 Cal.Rptr.2d 691, 855 P.2d 1263.) The context in which the word "upon" appears in this policy and under the circumstances of this case, however, renders its meaning ambiguous. Generally, one does not use the phrase "upon the vehicle" in ordinary usage, especially in the sense of "traveling upon the vehicle." Nor is the phrase "upon the vehicle" generally used to mean in close proximity to a vehicle, as E.M.M.I. contends. It is true that "upon" could refer to someone riding upon a motorcycle or the running board of an antique car, such as: "the salesman must be on or upon the motorcycle." Along this line the Court of Appeal observed that when the jeweler's block policy was conceived in the early 1900's, the words "on" or "upon" would have unambiguously applied to a horse or a horse-drawn carriage, and today, the same holds true with respect to motorcycles. But there is no indication that motorcycles are widely used by jewelry salespeople as a means of transporting jewelry; thus an insured would not reasonably expect that "upon" was intended to apply to motorcycles, as opposed to offering an alternative to the requirement that the insured actually be in the vehicle.[1]

---

[1] Justice Chin, in dissent, agrees with the Court of Appeal, and argues the words "on" and "upon," viewed from a "historical perspective" unambiguously referred to a "horse or horse-drawn carriage," when first used more than a century ago, to support his conclusion that in contemporary usage those words refer only to vehicles such as motorcycles. This historical meaning of the words used in a policy, however, does not illuminate the meaning of the policy language to a reasonable

Moreover, the language in the policy does not clearly alert the insured to Zurich's restricted meaning, and it is improbable that a reasonable insured would interpret the language to apply to motorcycles, as opposed to automobiles. In short, neither definition squarely supports the parties' respective arguments. We therefore conclude the language in the vehicle theft exception is ambiguous.

Although the main culprit for this ambiguity is the use of the word "upon" to refer to a vehicle, the ambiguity is exacerbated by the use of the word "or." The exception to the vehicle theft exclusion is phrased in the disjunctive—"actually in or upon"—and therefore a reasonable insured would likely interpret the exception to mean that the insured must be either inside the vehicle, or in some other location relative to the vehicle. (See, e.g., Houge v. Ford (1955) 44 Cal.2d 706, 712, 285 P.2d 257 ["In its ordinary sense, the function of the word 'or' is to mark an alternative such as 'either this or that' "].) Presented with such an alternative, we do not believe a reasonable insured would construe the exception to the vehicle theft exclusion to mean that the insured must be either inside or on top of the vehicle, or that the term "upon" applies solely to motorcycles. An insured using an automobile would not expect coverage to vanish when engaged in routine and necessary activity such as stepping out of the car to retrieve the jewelry from the backseat or trunk. Had the insurer intended the phrase "or upon" to apply solely to the use of motorcycles or other means of transportations such as ships and trains, it could, and should, have made this intention clear to the insured. The insurer could have, for example, defined the meaning of "upon" in the context of the policy language. This is a burden that rests squarely with Zurich, as the insurer. (MacKinnon v. Truck Ins. Exchange, supra, 31 Cal.4th at p. 648, 3 Cal.Rptr.3d 228, 73 P.3d 1205.)

Finding the vehicle theft exclusion and its exception ambiguous, we must resolve the ambiguity in favor of the insured, consistent with the insured's reasonable expectations. (Kazi v. State Farm Fire & Casualty Co. (2001) 24 Cal.4th 871, 879, 103 Cal.Rptr.2d 1, 15 P.3d 223.) As noted above, the jeweler's block policy at issue here provided broad coverage against loss of the insured jewelry. Given that broad coverage language, an insured would have a reasonable expectation that coverage would be provided in this context—when the insured is in close proximity to the vehicle and attending to it when the theft occurs. To construe the exception to the vehicle theft exclusion, and specifically the word "upon," as applying only to situations in which the insured is inside or physically touching the

---

layperson in contemporary times, who may well be unaware of this historical meaning. Even accepting that the words once unambiguously referred to horses and horse-drawn carriages, that clarity loses its luster when applied to "vehicles" in a modern insurance policy. That is, words that may once have been unambiguous, are not necessarily so when the context of their usage has changed. In interpreting policy language, we construe it as would a reasonable layperson, not an expert, attorney, or a historian.

vehicle would upset the reasonable expectations of the insured. Such a narrow construction would unreasonably preclude coverage when the insured exits the vehicle and walks a short distance to retrieve the insured merchandise from either the backseat or the trunk of the vehicle, unless the salesperson keeps constant contact with the car while walking toward the rear of the vehicle. The broad coverage language—providing coverage for all losses except those expressly excluded—along with the ambiguous language in the exclusionary provision, does not support this construction. * * *

Because the exclusionary clause as a whole is ambiguous, it cannot be said to be clear and plain in limiting coverage. (MacKinnon v. Truck Ins. Exchange, supra, 31 Cal.4th at p. 649, 3 Cal.Rptr.3d 228, 73 P.3d 1205.) In no way does the policy language alert a reasonable insured that coverage is lost by simply stepping outside of the vehicle. In such a case, the insured is in close proximity to the jewelry and is providing some protection against theft. That Zurich's position is counterintuitive to what a reasonable insured would expect is partly borne out by its response to a question posed at oral argument. In that response, Zurich maintained that an insured traveling by train would come within the exception to the vehicle theft exclusion if the insured left the jewelry in one compartment while he or she walked to a different compartment, such as the dining car, because such insured would be "upon" the train. Thus, according to Zurich, an insured who remains in close proximity to an automobile and is paying attention to it, providing a theft deterrent, would not be covered under the policy, but an insured traveling by train who leaves the jewelry completely unattended, thus providing no deterrence to theft, would be covered. This outcome cannot be said to be consistent with an insured's reasonable expectations.

Zurich further contends that the exception to the vehicle theft exclusion does not apply in the present case because the purpose of the exception is "to insure against theft by force or intimidation, but not by stealth." * * * We disagree. Nothing in the language of the policy suggests such limitation. Rather, reading the exclusionary clause and the exception in light of the broad coverage language, * * * it appears most reasonable to read the exclusion as applying when the vehicle and the insured jewelry were left unattended and, hence, more vulnerable to thievery. Given the high incidence and relative ease of car theft, it is reasonable that an insurer would exclude coverage for thefts from unattended vehicles. (See, e.g., Ruvelson, supra, 50 N.W.2d at p. 634 [exclusion "obviously intended to cover any situation where a loss occurred when the property was not protected by the presence of someone in or upon the car"].) Coverage for thefts from unattended vehicles might well command an increased premium. But if the insured is "in or upon" the vehicle when the theft occurs, the loss is covered whether or not the theft is accomplished by force or by stealth. A thief, for example, may stealthily break into the trunk of a car while the insured is sitting in the car. * * *

Our conclusion that the exception to the vehicle theft exclusion is not limited to thefts accomplished by force or intimidation is bolstered by the fact that the language in the exception uses the term "theft" as opposed to "robbery." Robbery requires the use of force or intimidation, while theft does not. (See, e.g., 2 Witkin and Epstein, Cal.Criminal Law (3d ed. 2000) Crimes Against Property, § 94, p. 125 [explaining that for a robbery to occur, "the property must be taken by either force (violence) or fear (intimidation)]; People v. Ramkeesoon (1985) 39 Cal.3d 346, 351, 216 Cal.Rptr. 455, 702 P.2d 613 ["Theft is a lesser included offense of robbery; robbery has the additional element of a taking by force or fear."].) The common dictionary definition of these terms also supports this distinction. For instance, Merriam-Webster's 10th New Collegiate Dictionary, supra, at page 1222, defines theft as "the felonious taking and removing of personal property with intent to deprive the rightful owner of it," while robbery is defined as " larceny from the person or presence of another by violence or threat" (id. At p. 1013).

Significantly, the word "theft" is used both in the vehicle theft exclusion and its exception. Despite this, Zurich would have us find that the vehicle theft exclusion applies generally to all thefts from a vehicle, while the exception applies only to the greater crime of robbery. Accepting Zurich's interpretation would require that we give different meanings to the same term used in the same policy paragraph. This would run afoul of the rule of contract interpretation that the same word used in an instrument is generally given the same meaning unless the policy indicates otherwise. * * * Had Zurich intended the exception to apply only to situations involving force or intimidation, i.e., robbery, while the exclusion applied to theft, it should have used the more accurate term "robbery" to put the insured on notice. As written, a reasonable insured would not interpret the language as Zurich contends.

Construing the ambiguous language in favor of the insured, in a manner consistent with the insured's reasonable expectations, and keeping in mind that exclusionary provisions are narrowly interpreted while exceptions are broadly construed, we hold that the exception to the vehicle theft exclusion applies when an insured is in close proximity to the vehicle and is attending to it.

* * *

III. DISPOSITION

Accordingly, we reverse the judgment of the Court of Appeal affirming summary judgment in favor of Zurich.

We concur: GEORGE, C.J., BAXTER AND WERDEGAR, JJ.

Dissenting Opinion by KENNARD, J. [Omitted]

Dissenting Opinion by CHIN, J.

* * *

Jeweler's block insurance was conceived by Lloyds of London at the turn of the previous century. (JMP Associates, Inc. v. St. Paul Fire & Marine Ins. Co. (1997) 345 Md. 630, 693 A.2d 832, fn. 1.) The "all risk" insurance is different from other property or "named peril" insurance because the policy insures all risks of loss or damage to the jewelry subject to certain exclusions. The policy contains an exclusion for all jewelry theft as follows: "We will not pay for 'loss' caused by or resulting from any of the following: * * * Theft from any vehicle unless you, an employee, or other person whose sole duty is to attend the vehicle are actually in or upon such vehicle at the time of the theft." The exclusion and exception for thefts that occur when the employee is "actually in or upon [the insured's] vehicle" has long been included in the policy. Although exceptions to exclusions are construed broadly in the insured's favor, courts will not strain to create an ambiguity where none exists and unambiguous policy language controls. (Waller v. Truck Ins. Exchange (1995) 11 Cal.4th 1, 18, 44 Cal.Rptr.2d 370, 900 P.2d 619.)

* * *

Standard dictionary definitions * * * undermine the majority's strained approach to insurance policy interpretation. As the Court of Appeal observed, "upon" is interchangeable with the word "on." (See, e.g., Webster's Collegiate Dict. (10th ed.1995) p. 1298.) Whereas "on" can mean "in close proximity with," as in "a village on the sea" or as a function word to mean "presence within," as in "rode on a train" there is no definition of "on" or "upon" that includes in close proximity to a car. The majority's hypothetical, in response to a comment made during oral argument involving an insured who carelessly leaves jewelry in one train compartment while walking to a different compartment, strains the policy's application and ignores the standard rules of word usage and function.

In addition, as the Court of Appeal also noted, if we view the terms "on" or "upon" from a historical perspective, those words "logically and unambiguously apply to a horse or a horse-drawn carriage. One would be upon rather than in a horse or carriage. In modern times, the words 'on' or 'upon' would apply to a motorcycle. In the ordinary sense of the words, whether one is 'on' or 'upon' a vehicle means the same thing; the usage varies with the object."

* * *

According to the clear and explicit words used in the jeweler's block policy before us, the insurer reasonably decided that actual presence of the insured or its representative in the car would likely deter a thief, while the absence of an actual presence offers the thief an opportunity to steal. As one court noted, "opportunity makes the thief. If [the insured] had been in the automobile, probably the thief would not have entered." (Princess Ring Co., Inc. v. Home Ins. Co. (1932) 52 R.I. 481, 161 A. 292, 293.) Long ago, insurance companies decided to insure against the theft of jewelry in vehicles only if the insured or its representative took basic precautions to guard against the theft. When the insured or its representative leaves the car for any reason, the risk of theft increases. That is what happened here. When Callahan left the car, with its engine running, to inspect a potential problem, he was not "actually in or upon such vehicle at the time of the theft" as the exception to the theft exclusion requires. He left the vehicle and its contents exposed to theft. The policy's clear language excludes this theft from its coverage.

BROWN, J. concurred with the dissent.

NOTE:
MAXIMS OF CONTRACT INTERPRETATION

In E.M.M.I, the majority thought it important to rely on a maxim of contract interpretation that contracts are to be interpreted "against the drafter," at least where the parties are vastly different in wealth, power, and sophistication. This principle, also known as *contra proferentem,* has particular resonance in the insurance context. Other important rules on interpretation similarly are deployed in cases, usually festooned in Latin, and are an important part of the arsenal of a practicing contract lawyer. Consider the Albrecht and Sutter cases that follow for examples.

ALBRECHT v. FETTIG, 99 U.C.C. Rep Serv 2d 663, 2019 WL 3115493 (Neb. Ct. App. 2019). [The case involved a cattle purchaser entitled to reject delivery because the seller did not deliver the correct percentage of red-hided and black hided steers as required in the contract.] "In the present case, the parties' purchase agreement provides that Albrecht, as the buyer, may reject any cattle that are not in a merchantable condition. However, the agreement does not describe this remedy as the sole remedy under the contract. In the absence of such clear expression of exclusivity, a remedy is presumed cumulative—not exclusive—under § 2–719(1)(b). Nevertheless, Fettig contends that the Latin phrase 'expressio unius est exclusio alterius,' which means 'the expression of one thing is the exclusion of the other,' ought to be applied here to show that Albrecht was limited under their agreement to rejecting the delivery only if the cattle were unmerchantable. * * * Our codified adoption of the U.C.C. supplants general principles of interpretation, and we will adhere to the presumption that remedies are cumulative unless exclusivity is clearly expressed.

Therefore, like the district court, we will not read into the contract the addition of terms that do not appear, and thus, we find that Albrecht was entitled to reject the cattle delivered for reasons beyond their merchantable condition."

SUTTER INSURANCE CO. v. APPLIED SYSTEMS, INC., 393 F.3d 722 (7th Cir. 2004) Commercial reasonableness is a useful guide to the interpretation of an ambiguous contract. * * * "Generally the contract price is roughly equivalent to the value of the contractual performance * * *. An enormous disparity between price and value is a clue that something may be amiss." *PMC, Inc. v. Sherwin-Williams Co.,* 151 F.3d 610, 615 (7th Cir.1998) * * *. Or as the Illinois Appellate Court put it in the *NutraSweet* case, "where a contract is susceptible to one of two constructions, one of which makes it fair, customary, and such as prudent men would naturally execute, while the other makes it inequitable, unusual, or such as reasonable men would not be likely to enter into, the interpretation which makes a rational and probable agreement must be preferred." 635 N.E.2d at 445.

PROBLEM 6-5

David Yarbell, president of Pear Computers, sought to purchase a surge protector to protect Pear Computers' floor models from surges of electrical current. Yarbell researched surge protectors on the Internet and found a range of units priced between $30 and $500. None were suitable for Pear's needs. Yarbell then contacted K-3 Computer Equipment by telephone and spoke with a K-3 salesperson who recommended a certain unit that seemed perfect for Pear's needs. Yarbell asked the price and the salesperson replied, "thirty-six thirty." The salesperson meant $3630, but Yarbell believed the salesperson meant $36.30. Unfortunately, the informal written contract of sale, drafted by K-3's salesperson and signed by Yarbell and the K-3 salesperson, also set forth the price as "thirty-six thirty." The fair market value of the surge protector was $3500. After taking delivery of the surge protector and seeing the invoice for $3630, Yarbell comes to your law office and asks you to explain his rights.

UNIFORM COMMERCIAL CODE § 1–201(b)(3).

"Agreement" * * * means the bargain of the parties in fact as found in their language or inferred from other circumstances, including course of performance, course of dealing, or usage of trade * * *.

UNIFORM COMMERCIAL CODE § 2–208.

Course of Performance or Practical Construction

(1) Where the contract for sale involves repeated occasions for performance by either party with knowledge of the nature of the

performance and opportunity for objection to it by the other, any course of performance accepted or acquiesced in without objection shall be relevant to determine the meaning of the agreement.

(2) The express terms of the agreement and any such course of performance, as well as any course of dealing and usage of trade, shall be construed whenever reasonable as consistent with each other; but when such construction is unreasonable, express terms shall control course of performance and course of performance shall control both course of dealing and usage of trade (Section 1–205).

(3) Subject to the provisions of the next section on modification and waiver, such course of performance shall be relevant to show a waiver or modification of any term inconsistent with such course of performance.

UNIFORM COMMERCIAL CODE § 1–303(b)–(e).

(b) A "course of dealing" is a sequence of conduct concerning previous transactions between the parties to a particular transaction that is fairly to be regarded as establishing a common basis of understanding for interpreting their expressions and other conduct.

(c) A "usage of trade" is any practice or method of dealing having such regularity of observance in a place, vocation, or trade as to justify an expectation that it will be observed with respect to the transaction in question. The existence and scope of such a usage must be proved as facts. If it is established that such a usage is embodied in a trade code or similar record, the interpretation of the record is a question of law.

(d) A course of performance or course of dealing between the parties or usage of trade in the vocation or trade in which they are engaged or of which they are or should be aware is relevant in ascertaining the meaning of the parties' agreement, may give particular meaning to specific terms of the agreement, and may supplement or qualify the terms of the agreement. A usage of trade applicable in the place in which part of the performance under the agreement is to occur may be so utilized as to that part of the performance.

(e) * * * [T]he express terms of an agreement and any applicable course of performance, course of dealing, or usage of trade must be construed whenever reasonable as consistent with each other. If such a construction is unreasonable:

(1) express terms prevail over course of performance, course of dealing, and usage of trade;

(2) course of performance prevails over course of dealing and usage of trade; and

(3) course of dealing prevails over usage of trade.

NANAKULI PAVING AND ROCK CO. V. SHELL OIL CO., INC.

United States Court of Appeals, Ninth Circuit, 1981.
664 F.2d 772.

HOFFMAN, DISTRICT JUDGE.

Appellant Nanakuli Paving and Rock Company (Nanakuli) initially filed this breach of contract action against appellee Shell Oil Company (Shell) in Hawaiian State Court in February, 1976.[1] Nanakuli, the second largest asphaltic paving contractor in Hawaii, had bought all its asphalt requirements from 1963 to 1974 from Shell under two long-term supply contracts; its suit charged Shell with breach of the later 1969 contract. The jury returned a verdict of $220,800 for Nanakuli on its first claim, which is that Shell breached the 1969 contract in January, 1974, by failing to price protect Nanakuli on 7200 tons of asphalt at the time Shell raised the price for asphalt from $44 to $76. Nanakuli's theory is that price-protection, as a usage of the asphaltic paving trade in Hawaii, was incorporated into the 1969 agreement between the parties, as demonstrated by the routine use of price protection by suppliers to that trade, and reinforced by the way in which Shell actually performed the 1969 contract up until 1974. Price protection, appellant claims, required that Shell hold the price on the tonnage Nanakuli had already committed because Nanakuli had incorporated that price into bids put out to or contracts awarded by general contractors and government agencies. The District Judge set aside the verdict and granted Shell's motion for judgment n.o.v., which decision we vacate. We reinstate the jury verdict because we find that, viewing the evidence as a whole, there was substantial evidence to support a finding by reasonable jurors that Shell breached its contract by failing to provide protection for Nanakuli in 1974. * * *

Nanakuli * * * argues [that] all material suppliers to the asphaltic paving trade in Hawaii followed the trade usage of price protection and thus it should be assumed, under the U.C.C., that the parties intended to incorporate price protection into their 1969 agreement. This is so, Nanakuli continues, even though the written contract provided for price to be "Shell's Posted Price at time of delivery," F.O.B. Honolulu. Its proof of a usage that was incorporated into the contract is reinforced by evidence of the commercial context, which under the U.C.C. should form the background for viewing a particular contract. The full agreement must be examined in light of the close, almost symbiotic relations between Shell and Nanakuli on the island of Oahu, whereby the expansion of Shell on the island was intimately connected to the business growth of Nanakuli. The U.C.C. looks to the actual performance of a contract as the best indication of what the parties intended those terms to mean. Nanakuli points out that Shell had

---

[1] Shell removed the suit to United States District Court for the District of Hawaii on March 2 of that year.

price protected it on the two occasions of price increases under the 1969 contract other than the 1974 increase. In 1970 and 1971 Shell extended the old price for four and three months, respectively, after an announced increase. This was done, in the words of Shell's agent in Hawaii, in order to permit Nanakuli's to "chew up" tonnage already committed at Shell's old price.[2]

* * *

Shell presents three arguments for upholding the judgment n.o.v. or, on cross appeal, urging that the District Judge erred in admitting certain evidence. First, it says, the District Court should not have denied Shell's motion *in limine* to define trade, for purposes of trade usage evidence, as the sale and purchase of asphalt in Hawaii, rather than expanding the definition of trade to include other suppliers of materials to the asphaltic paving trade. Asphalt, its argument runs, was the subject matter of the disputed contract and the only product Shell supplied to the asphaltic paving trade. Shell protests that the judge, by expanding the definition of trade to include the other major suppliers to the asphaltic paving trade, allowed the admission of highly prejudicial evidence of routine price protection by all suppliers of aggregate. Asphaltic concrete paving is formed by mixing paving asphalt with crushed rock, or aggregate, in a "hot-mix" plant and then pouring the mixture onto the surface to be paved. Shell's second complaint is that the two prior occasions on which it price protected Nanakuli, although representing the only other instances of price increases under the 1969 contract, constituted mere waivers of the contract's price term, not a course of performance of the contract. A course of performance of the contract, in contrast to a waiver, demonstrates how the parties understand the terms of their agreement. Shell cites two U.C.C. Comments in support of that argument: (1) that, when the meaning of acts is ambiguous, the preference is for the waiver interpretation, and (2) that one act alone does not constitute a relevant course of performance. Shell's final argument is that, even assuming its prior price protection constituted a course of performance and that the broad trade definition was correct and evidence of trade usages by aggregate suppliers was admissible, price protection could not be construed as reasonably consistent with the express price term in the contract, in which case the Code provides that the express term controls.

We hold that the judge did not abuse his discretion in defining the applicable trade, for purposes of trade usages, as the asphaltic paving trade in Hawaii, rather than the purchase and sale of asphalt alone. * * * Additionally, we hold that, under the facts of this case, a jury could

---

[2] Price protection was practiced in the asphaltic paving trade by either extending the old price for a period of time after a new one went into effect or charging the old price for a specified tonnage, which represented work committed at the old price. In addition, several months' advance notice was given of price increases.

reasonably have found that Shell's acts on two occasions to price protect Nanakuli were not ambiguous and therefore indicated Shell's understanding of the terms of the agreement with Nanakuli rather than being a waiver by Shell of those terms.

Lastly we hold that, although the express price terms of Shell's posted price of delivery may seem, at first glance, inconsistent with a trade usage of price protection at time of increases in price, a closer reading shows that the jury could have reasonably construed price protection as consistent with the express term. * * *

[The court first discussed the negotiations prior to the 1969 contract, and, specifically, testimony of Nanakuli's president and vice president that they "understood" they would receive price protection despite the absence of a written provision to that effect. This testimony was not "flatly contradicted" by Shell.]

Trade Usage Before and After 1969

The key to price protection being so prevalent in 1969 that both parties would intend to incorporate it into their contract is found in one reality of the Oahu asphaltic paving market: the largest paving contracts were let by government agencies and none of the three levels of government—local, state, or federal—allowed escalation clauses for paving materials. If a paver bid at one price and another went into effect before the award was made, the paving company would lose a great deal of money, since it could not pass on increases to any government agency or to most general contractors. Extensive evidence was presented that, as a consequence, aggregate suppliers routinely price protected paving contractors in the 1960's and 1970's, as did the largest asphaltic supplier in Oahu, Chevron. Nanakuli presented documentary evidence of routine price protection by aggregate suppliers as well as two witnesses: Grosjean, Vice-President for Marketing of Ameron H.C. & D., and Nihei, Division Manager of Lone Star Industries for Pacific Cement and Aggregate (P.C. & A.). Both testified that price protection to their knowledge had always been practiced: at H.C. & D. for many years prior to Grosjean's arrival in 1962 and at P.C. & A. routinely since Nihei's arrival in 1960. Such protection consisted of advance notices of increases, coupled with charging the old price for work committed at that price or for enough time to order the tonnage committed. The smallness of the Oahu market led to complete trust among suppliers and pavers. H.C. & D. did not demand that Nanakuli or other pavers issue purchase orders or sign contracts for aggregate before incorporating its aggregate prices into bids. Nanakuli would merely give H.C. & D. a list of projects it had bid at the time H.C. & D. raised its prices, without documentation. "Their word and letter is good enough for us," Grosjean testified. Nihei said P.C. & A. at the time of price increases would get a list of either particular projects bid by a paver or simply total tonnage bid at the old price. "We take either one. We take their word for it." None of the aggregate companies had a contract with Nanakuli expressly stating price protection would be given; Nanakuli's contract with P.C. & A. merely set out that P.C. & A. would not charge Nanakuli more than it charged its other customers.

* * *

Shell's Course Of Performance Of The 1969 Contract

The Code considers actual performance of a contract as the most relevant evidence of how the parties interpreted the terms of that contract. In 1970 and 1971, the only points at which Shell raised prices between 1969 and 1974, it price protected Nanakuli by holding its old price for four and three months, respectively, after announcing a price increase. In the late summer of 1970, Shell had announced a price increase from $35 to $40 a ton effective September 1, 1970. When Nanakuli protested to Bohner [Shell's Hawaiian representative] that it should be price protected on work already committed, Blee [a "top Shell asphalt official"] wrote Bohner an in-house memo that, if Bohner could not "convince" Nanakuli to go along with the price increase on September 1, he should try to "bargain" to get Nanakuli to accept the price raise by at least the first of the year, which was what was finally agreed upon. During that four-month period, Nanakuli bought 3,300 tons. Shell announced a second increase in October, 1970, from $40 to $42 effective December 31st. Before that increase went into effect, on November 25 Shell increased the raise to $4, making the price $44 as of the first of the year. Shell again agreed to price protect Nanakuli by holding the price at $40, which had been the official price since September 1, for three months from January to March, 1971. Shell did not actually raise prices again until January, 1974, but at several points it believed that increases would be necessary and gave several months' advance notice of those possible increases. Those actions were in accord with Shell's own policy, as professed by Bohner, and that of other asphalt and aggregate suppliers: to give at least several months' advance notice of price increases. On January 14, 1971, Shell wrote its asphalt customers that the maximum 1971 increase would be to $46. On July 9, 1971, another letter promised the price would not go over $50 in 1972. In addition, Bohner volunteered on direct the information that Shell price protected Nanakuli on the only two occasions of price increases after 1974 by giving 6 months' advance notice in 1977 and 3 or 4 months' advance notice in 1978, a practice he described as "in effect carryover pricing," his term for price protection. By its actions, Bohner testified, Shell allowed Nanakuli time to make arrangements to buy up tonnage committed at the old price, that is, to "chew up" tonnage bid or contracted. Shell apparently offered this testimony to impress the jury with its subsequent good faith toward Nanakuli. In fact, it also may have reinforced the impression of the universality of price protection in the asphaltic paving trade on Oahu and, by showing Shell's adherence to that practice on every relevant occasion except 1974, have highlighted for the jury what was the commercially reasonable standard of fair dealing in effect on Oahu in 1974.

[The court next referred to "structural changes" at Shell in 1973, which left Shell with no one with knowledge about the "peculiarities of the Hawaiian market or about Shell's long-time relations with Nanakuli or its 1969 agreement, beyond the printed contract."]

We conclude that the decision to deny Nanakuli price protection was made by new Houston management without a full understanding of Shell's 1969 agreement with Nanakuli or any knowledge of its past pricing practices toward Nanakuli. If Shell did commit itself in 1969 to price protect Nanakuli, the Shell officials who made the decisions affecting Nanakuli in 1974 knew nothing about that commitment. Nor did they make any effective effort to find out. They acted instead solely in reliance on the 1969 contract's express price term, devoid of the commercial context that the Code says is necessary to an understanding of the meaning of the written word. Whatever the legal enforceability of Nanakuli's right, Nanakuli officials seem to have acted in good faith reliance on its right, as they understood it, to price protection and rightfully felt betrayed by Shell's failure to act with any understanding of its past practices toward Nanakuli.

Scope Of Trade Usage

The validity of the jury verdict in this case depends on four legal questions. First, how broad was the trade to whose usages Shell was bound under its 1969 agreement with Nanakuli: did it extend to the Hawaiian asphaltic paving trade or was it limited merely to the purchase and sale of asphalt, which would only include evidence of practices by Shell and Chevron? Second, were the two instances of price protection of Nanakuli by Shell in 1970 and 1971 waivers of the 1969 contract as a matter of law or was the jury entitled to find that they constituted a course of performance of the contract? Third, could the jury have construed an express contract term of Shell's posted price at delivery as reasonably consistent with a trade usage and Shell's course of performance of the 1969 contract of price protection, which consisted of charging the old price at times of price increases, either for a period of time or for specific tonnage committed at a fixed price in non-escalating contracts? [The fourth issue involving commercial reasonableness is omitted.]

* * *

The Code defines usage of trade as "any practice or method of dealing having such regularity of observance in a *place, vocation or trade* as to justify an expectation that it will be observed with respect to the transaction in question." *Id.* [U.C.C. §] 1–205(2) (emphasis supplied). [Here and in the rest of the opinion, the court applies sections from the forerunner to revised Article 1.] We understand the use of the word "or" to mean that parties can be bound by a usage common to the *place* they are in business, even if it is not the usage of their particular vocation or trade. That reading is borne out by the repetition of the disjunctive "or" in subsection 3, which provides that usages "in the vocation or trade in which they are engaged *or* of which they are or should be aware give particular meaning to and supplement or qualify terms of an agreement." *Id.* [U.C.C. §] 1–205(3). The drafters' Comments say that trade usage is to be used to reach the "* * * commercial meaning of the agreement * * *" by interpreting the language "as meaning what it may fairly be expected to mean to parties involved in the particular transaction *in a given locality or* in a given *vocation or trade.*" *Id.,* Comment 4 (emphasis supplied). The inference of the two subsections and the Comment, read together, is that a usage need not necessarily be one practiced by members of the party's own trade or vocation to be binding *if* it is so commonly practiced in a locality that a party should be aware of it. Subsection 5 also shows the importance of the place where the usage is practiced: "An applicable usage of trade in the place where any part of performance is to occur shall be used in interpreting the agreement as to that part of the performance." The validity of this interpretation is additionally demonstrated by the Comment of the drafters: "Subsection (3), giving the prescribed effect to usages of which the parties 'are or should be aware', reinforces the provision of subsection (2) requiring not universality but only the described 'regularity of observance' of the practice or method. This subsection also reinforces the point of subsection (2) that such usages may be either *general to trade or particular to a special branch of trade.*" *Id.,* Comment 7 (emphasis supplied). This language indicates that Shell would be bound not only by usages of sellers of asphalt but by more general usages on Oahu, as long as those usages were so regular in their observance that Shell should have been aware of them. This reading of the Code, in our opinion, achieves an equitable result. A party is always held to conduct generally observed by members of his chosen trade because the other party is justified in so assuming unless he indicates otherwise. He is held to more general business practices to the extent of his actual knowledge of those practices or to the degree his ignorance of those practices is not excusable: they were so generally practiced he should have been aware of them.

No U.C.C. cases have been found on this point, but the court's reading of the Code language is similar to that of two of the best-known commentators on the U.C.C.:

> Under pre-Code law, a trade usage was not operative against a party who *was not a member of the trade unless* he actually knew of it or *the other party could reasonably believe he knew of it.*

J. White & R. Summers, *Uniform Commercial Code,* § 12–6 at 371 (1972) (emphasis supplied) (citing 3 A. Corbin, *Corbin on Contracts* § 557 at 248 (1960)). * * * White and Summers add (emphasis supplied):

> This view has been carried forward by 1–205(3). * * * [U]sage of the trade is only binding on *members of the trade* involved *or persons* who know or *should know about it.* Persons who should be aware of the trade usage doubtless *include those who regularly deal with members of the relevant trade,* and also members of a second trade that commonly deals with members of a relevant trade (for example, farmers should know something of seed selling).

White & Summers, *supra,* § 12–6 at 371. Using that analogy, even if Shell did not "regularly deal" with aggregate supplies, it did deal constantly and almost exclusively on Oahu with one asphalt paver. It therefore should have been aware of the usage of Nanakuli and other asphaltic pavers to bid at fixed prices and therefore receive price protection from their materials suppliers due to the refusal by government agencies to accept escalation clauses. Therefore, we do not find the lower court abused its discretion or misread the Code as applied to the peculiar facts of this case in ruling that the applicable trade was the asphaltic paving trade in Hawaii. An asphalt seller should be held to the usages of trade in general as well as those of asphalt sellers and common usages of those to whom they sell. Certainly, under the unusual facts of this case it was not unreasonable for the judge to extend trade usages to include practices of other material suppliers toward Shell's primary and perhaps only customer on Oahu. He did exclude, on Shell's motion *in limine,* evidence of cement suppliers. He only held Shell to routine practices in Hawaii by the suppliers of the two major ingredients of asphaltic paving, that is, asphalt and aggregate. Those usages were only practiced towards two major pavers. It was not unreasonable to expect Shell to be knowledgeable about so small a market. In so ruling, the judge undoubtedly took into account Shell's half-million dollar investment in Oahu strictly because of a long-term commitment by Nanakuli, its actions as partner in promoting Nanakuli's expansion on Oahu, and the fact that its sales on Oahu were almost exclusively to Nanakuli for use in asphaltic paving. The wisdom of the pre-trial ruling was demonstrated by evidence at trial that Shell's agent in Hawaii stayed in close contact with Nanakuli and was knowledgeable about both the asphaltic paving market in general and Nanakuli's bidding procedures and economics in particular.

Shell argued not only that the definition of trade was too broad, but also that the practice itself was not sufficiently regular to reach the level of a usage and that Nanakuli failed to show with enough precision how the usage was carried out in order for a jury to calculate damages. The extent of a usage is ultimately a jury question. The Code provides, "The existence and scope of such a usage are to be proved as facts." [U.C.C. §] 1–205(2). The practice must have "such regularity of observance . . . as to justify an expectation that it will be observed. . . ." *Id.* The Comment explains:

> The ancient English tests for "custom" are abandoned in this connection. Therefore, it is not required that a usage of trade be "ancient or immemorial," "universal" or the like. * * * [F]ull recognition is thus available for new usages and for usages currently observed by the great majority of decent dealers, even though dissidents ready to cut corners do not agree.

Id., Comment 5. The Comment's demand that "not universality but only the described 'regularity of observance' " is required reinforces the provision only giving "effect to usages of which the parties 'are or should be aware'. * * * " *Id.,* Comment 7. A "regularly observed" practice of protection, of which Shell "should have been aware," was enough to constitute a usage that Nanakuli had reason to believe was incorporated into the agreement.

Nanakuli went beyond proof of a regular observance. It proved and offered to prove that price protection was probably a universal practice by suppliers to the asphaltic paving trade in 1969. It had been practiced by H.C. & D. since at least 1962, by P.C. & A. since well before 1960, and by Chevron routinely for years, with the last specific instance before the contract being March, 1969, as shown by documentary evidence. The only usage evidence missing was the behavior by Shell, the only other asphalt supplier in Hawaii, prior to 1969. That was because its only major customer was Nanakuli and the judge ruled prior course of dealings between Shell and Nanakuli inadmissible. Shell did not point in rebuttal to one instance of failure to price protect by any supplier to an asphalt paver in Hawaii before its own 1974 refusal to price protect Nanakuli. Thus, there clearly was enough proof for a jury to find that the practice of price protection in the asphaltic paving trade existed in Hawaii in 1969 and was regular enough in its observance to rise to the level of a usage that would be binding on Nanakuli and Shell.

* * *

[The court also upheld the jury's decision that Shell's two instances of price protection of Nanakuli in 1970 and 1971 were a "course of performance" under U.C.C. Section 2–208. Further, the court concluded that the jury's finding in favor of Nanakuli was consistent with U.C.C. Section 1–205(4) (current 1–303(e)), which provides that express terms "control" usage of trade. In the court's view, the price protection trade usage did not completely negate the express term "Shell's Posted Price at time of delivery," but formed an exception to it that the jury could find was "incorporated into the 1969 agreement." The court stated:] Here, the express price term was "Shell's Posted Price at time of delivery." A total negation of that term would be that the buyer was to set the price. It is a less than complete negation of the term that an unstated exception exists at times of price increases, at which times the old price is to be charged, for a certain period or for a specified tonnage, on work already committed at the lower price on nonescalating contracts. Such a usage forms a broad and important exception to the express term, but does not swallow it entirely. Therefore, we hold that, under these particular facts, a reasonable jury could have found that price protection was incorporated into the 1969 agreement between Nanakuli and Shell and that price protection was reasonably consistent with the express term of seller's posted price at delivery.

* * * [W]e reverse the judgment of the District Court and reinstate the jury verdict for Nanakuli in the amount of $220,800, plus interest according to law.

REVERSED AND REMANDED WITH DIRECTIONS TO ENTER FINAL JUDGMENT.

KENNEDY, CIRCUIT JUDGE, concurring specially:

The case involves specific pricing practices, not an allegation of unfair dealing generally. Our opinion should not be interpreted to permit juries to import price protection or a similarly specific contract term from a concept of good faith that is not based on well-established custom and usage or other objective standards of which the parties had clear notice. Here, evidence of custom and usage regarding price protection in the asphaltic paving trade was not contradicted in major respects, and the jury could find that the parties knew or should have known of the practice at the time of making the contract. In my view, these are necessary predicates for either theory of the case, namely, interpretation of the contract based on the course of its performance or a finding that good faith required the seller to hold the price. With these observations, I concur.

HURST v. W.J. LAKE & CO., 141 Or. 306, 16 P.2d 627 (1932). The flexibility of or multiplicity in the meaning of words is the principal source of difficulty in the interpretation of language. Words are the conduits by which thoughts are communicated, yet scarcely any of them have such a fixed and single meaning that they are incapable of denoting more than one thought. In addition to the multiplicity in meaning of words set forth in the dictionaries, there are the meanings imparted to them by trade customs, local uses, dialects, telegraphic codes, etc. One meaning crowds a word full of significance, while another almost empties the utterance of any import. The various groups above indicated are constantly amplifying our language; in fact, they are developing what may be called languages of their own. Thus one is justified in saying that the language of the dictionaries is not the only language spoken in America. For instance, the word "thousand" as commonly used has a very specific meaning; it denotes ten hundreds or fifty scores, but the language of the various trades and localities has assigned to it meanings quite different from that just mentioned. Thus in the bricklaying trade a contract which fixes the bricklayer's compensation at "$5.25 a thousand" does not contemplate that he need lay actually 1,000 bricks in order to earn $5.25, but that he should build a wall of a certain size. Brunold v. Glasser, 25 Misc. 285, 53 N.Y.S. 1021; Walker v. Syms, 118 Mich. 183, 76 N.W. 320. In the lumber industry a contract requiring the delivery of 4,000 shingles will be fulfilled by the delivery of only 2,500 when it appears that by trade custom two packs of a certain size are regarded as 1,000 shingles, and that hence the delivery of eight packs fulfills the contract, even though they contain only 2,500 shingles by actual count. Soutier v. Kellerman, 18 Mo. 509. * * * Numerous other instances could readily be cited showing the manner in which the meaning of words has been contracted, expanded, or otherwise altered by local usage, trade custom, dialect influence, code agreement, etc. In fact, it is no novelty to find legislative enactments preceded by glossaries or brief dictionaries defining the meaning of the words employed in the act. Technical treatises dealing with aeronautics, the radio, engineering, etc., generally contain similar glossaries defining the meaning of many of the words employed by the craft. A glance at these glossaries readily shows that the different sciences and trades, in addition to coining words of their own, appropriate common words and assign to them new meanings. Thus it must be evident that one cannot understand accurately the language of such sciences and trades without knowing the peculiar meaning attached to the words which they use. It is said that a court in construing the language of the parties must put itself into the shoes of the parties. That alone would not suffice; it must also adopt their vernacular.

SCOTT, IS ARTICLE 2 THE BEST WE CAN DO?

52 Hastings L. J. 677, 686–688 (2001).

The statutory direction that a given outcome holds if the action was "reasonable" urges courts to do what Llewellyn asked them to do—to find the imminent law embedded in the particular commercial context and then incorporate that practice as part of the legal, contractual relationship.

* * * While the meaning of particular contract terms might vary from context to context, no contractors would be surprised by subsequent interpretations since incorporation would only embrace those usages that were known (or should have been known) to both parties at the time of contract. Thus, within each interpretive community, the contractual terms—both written and implied from context—would be predictable and transparent and, thus, uniform.

This is a great idea. But unhappily, judicial practice has not followed the theory. * * * A systematic examination of the litigated cases interpreting the "commercial reasonableness" standards of Article 2 shows that courts have consistently viewed their job as requiring deductive speculations about "Code policy" rather than the incorporation of particular commercial norms and prototypes. When this occurs, the result from the parties' perspective is not uniform at all. At least it's not uniform in the sense of the same contract terms being interpreted in the same way both across jurisdictions and over time. * * *

* * *

One who argues for a return to acontextual modes of interpretation has to concede, and I do, that there are real costs to a return to the common law approach. Common law plain meaning interpretation ignores the commercial context except where the parties have expressly written relevant customs and usages into their contracts. Writing contracts in a formalist world becomes very much more laborious and error prone. Moreover, textualist interpretation imposes a social cost on future contracting parties because formal modes of interpretation reduce the stock of tried and true understandings, customs and usages that can be incorporated from the context and thereafter announced by courts as useful defaults for other contacting parties. Llewellyn's fundamental insight was to recognize the benefits that could potentially flow from this incorporation process. * * * [T]he theoretical possibility of those benefits should be acknowledged straightforwardly.

PROBLEM 6-6

On February 7, 2004, Evelyn Faquar sold the Faquar Photographic Studio of Grant County, Hampshire to Bart W. Savage III for $55,000. Grant County contains five sizeable towns: Oldham, Bestwick, Ontario, Westin, and Weiser. The studio's only source of income was photographic work for four public high schools and twelve elementary and junior high schools. Weiser, the smallest of the towns, had no public schools; Weiser children were bused to nearby Westin. However, Marion College, a two-year junior college, was located on the outer edge of Weiser.

The Faquar-Savage contract drafted by Savage's lawyer, Ed Harmore, included the following provisions:

* * *

> (2) Evelyn Faquar hereby sells and conveys to Bart Weatherford Savage III her business known as Photographic Studio of Grant Co., Hampshire, together with all equipment (list appended), supplies (list appended), and goodwill.

> (3) Faquar hereby leases to Savage all four rooms in the Westwood building in Oldham now occupied by said business for a term of five years at a rental of $500 a month, Savage to have an option on a fifth (adjoining room) in said premises in case he decides to expand the business.
>
> * * *
>
> (5) Savage to pay $25,000 down at date of closing and $10,000 a year on July 1 (beginning this year) for three years until the total sale price of $55,000 is paid.
>
> (6) Faquar hereby agrees not to compete with Savage for school photography work in Oldham, Bestwick, Ontario, Westin and Weiser for a period of ten years. * * *

On February 14, 2006, Evelyn Faquar photographed Marion College students for their yearbook. Savage wants to "stop this," and he wants damages as well. He retains you to represent him in this matter. You learn that Hampshire photography businesses rarely deal both with public schools and institutions of higher learning. Savage will testify that the parties intended that "schools" included colleges. The Hampshire general education act defines schools in section 1:

> The word "school" is a generic term, denoting an institution or place for instruction or education, or the collective body of instructors and pupils in any such place or institution. In its ordinary meaning, a school is a place where instruction is imparted to the young. It is an institution of a lower grade, below a college or a university; a place of primary instruction.

You also find nine definitions of "school," some of which include college, in Webster's New Collegiate Dictionary.

What further investigations, if any, would you make? What evidence would you introduce at any trial to lay a foundation for interpreting the word school and related words? What specific interpretational arguments would you make? Do you think you would prevail?

NOTE:
THE IMPORTANCE OF CLEAR DRAFTING

The following contract language illustrates the importance of clear drafting. It led the parties into litigation instead of performance. Do you see why? Could you have drafted more clearly?

> "In consideration of the performance by the said contractor of all of the covenants and conditions contained in this agreement and contained in the plans and specifications the owners agree to pay to the contractor an amount equal to the amount of all material furnished by the contractor and the labor furnished by the contractor together with payroll taxes and Insurance, also together with the sum

> total of the net amount due the subcontractors performing work or furnishing work for said construction. *The Owners also agree to pay to the contractor, in addition to the amount specified hereinabove, a fee equal to 10% of the actual cost of the said residence, said fee to be paid after completion of said residence and acceptance thereof by the Owners. It is specifically agreed by and between the parties that notwithstanding the agreement hereinabove by the owners shall not be required, under the terms of this agreement, to pay to the contractor any amount in excess of the sum of Thirty-Four Thousand, Five Hundred Dollars ($34,500.00) which is the estimated cost of construction, plus the fee provided for herein."* (Emphasis added).

The court in Lewis v. Carnaggio, 257 S.C. 54, 183 S.E.2d 899 (1971), stated in regard to this matter:

> Plaintiff contends that the foregoing language establishes the contract price as the cost of construction plus ten percent, with the cost of construction not to exceed $34,500.00. Defendant, on the other hand, construes the above provision as providing that the total cost of the building, including the ten percent fee, could not under any circumstances exceed the sum of $34,500.00.
>
> * * *
>
> * * * In the first sentence of the emphasized portion of paragraph 3 the parties agree that the contract price would be the cost of construction plus ten percent. The following sentence provides that, notwithstanding the previous agreement, the owners (defendants) were not required "to pay to the contractor (plaintiff) any amount in excess of the sum of thirty-four thousand, five hundred dollars ($34,500.00) which is the estimated cost of construction, plus the fee (10%) provided herein." The clause reading "which is the estimated cost of construction" clearly modifies the antecedent figure of $34,500.00 and restricts its meaning. The phrase "plus the fee provided for herein" is separated from the preceding clause by a comma, showing that it was not included in the preceding clause but was in addition thereto. The fee was therefore recognized as being in addition to the cost of construction. This is the plain grammatical effect of the use of the comma to separate the above phrase from the preceding clause.
>
> When read as punctuated, the present contract is not ambiguous and its meaning is clear. The provisions in question placed a limit of $34,500.00 on the cost of construction of the building and required the defendants to pay, in addition, the contractor's fee of ten percent.

A dissenting judge pointed out:

> * * * I am of the opinion that there is an ambiguity, and accordingly, parol testimony should be considered to determine the true intent of the parties. The evidence shows that the home owner

sought fixed-figure bids for the construction of the house involved. He testified that among the fixed-figure bids he received was one submitted by the plaintiff for $34,500. The contract actually signed came about through discussions growing out of the $34,500 fixed-figure bid. It indicated an effort on the part of the home owner to possibly end up paying less than $34,500, and a willingness on the part of the contractor to give the home owner an advantage.

* * * The punctuation mark relied upon * * * should not be used to defeat what I conceive to be the true intent of the parties.

Actually, the contractor testified that he copied the paragraph in dispute (No. 3) out of a form book. There is nothing in the record to indicate that any of the parties attached significance to the controversial comma until after the dispute arose. Nor is there evidence that either party at the time the contract was signed, had any understanding of the impact of the comma.

For more misery caused by a misplaced comma, consider the following contract clause: The agreement "shall continue in force for a period of five years from the date it is made, and thereafter for successive five year terms, unless and until terminated by one year prior notice in writing by either party." Canada's Globe and Mail reported that Rogers Communications Inc. believed it had a guaranteed five-year contract with Aliant Inc. for the latter to construct cable lines. But Canadian regulators took the position that, because of the second comma in the clause, Aliant Inc. could cancel at any time on one year's notice. This decision cost Rogers more than two million dollars because it was subject to significant rate increases after Aliant's cancellation.

Finally, a recent dispute of some import involved Miramax LLC, as plaintiff, and New Line Cinema and Warner Brothers as defendants. The complaint alleged that Miramax sold the rights to Tolkien's "Lord of the Rings" trilogy and to "The Hobbit" to New Line in exchange for 5 percent of the gross receipts of the "first motion picture" based on the books, but the contract excluded compensation for "remakes." After New Line and Warner Brothers produced three separate and distinct movies based on the Hobbit, they claimed that they owed Miramax only for the first movie, with the second and third movies being "remakes." New Line and Warner prevailed in a private arbitration in December, 2014.

SECTION FOUR: GAP FILLERS

A contract may simply fail to deal with some matter—it may have a gap. Recall, for example, the Whites' and the Benkowskis' failure to deal with the issue of the quality of the water the Benkowskis were to supply. Did it have to be potable? Recall also the materials on planning and the limits of planning in Chapter Four. When a gap exists, a court may turn to a variety of sources and methods to fill it. We study these matters in this section.

A sharp line between gap filling and interpretation of contracts cannot be drawn. First, a court may fill an apparent gap by interpreting written contract language in light of extrinsic evidence and the circumstances. The court may correctly conclude that the parties intended a particular approach to the apparent gap so that there really is no gap at all. Second, a court may purport to ascertain the intentions of the parties even though the parties clearly had no intentions concerning the matter. For example, a court may fill a gap as to the time for performance by finding that the parties "intended" performance in a reasonable time, although the parties did not in fact address the issue. Here the court is actually filling a gap, not interpreting the contract in light of the parties' intentions. Even when a court does acknowledge that it must fill a gap, the court may seek to determine what the parties probably would have intended had they addressed the contingency. Why do courts strive so hard to find the "intentions of the parties"?

COHEN, THE BASIS OF CONTRACT

46 Harv.L.Rev. 553, 584 (1933).

Just as the process of interpreting a statute is really a process of subsidiary legislation, so is the interpretation of a contract really a method of supplementing the original agreement by such provisions as are necessary to determine the point at issue.

HAINES V. CITY OF NEW YORK

Court of Appeals of New York, 1977.
41 N.Y.2d 769, 364 N.E.2d 820.

GABRIELLI, JUDGE.

In the early 1920's, respondent City of New York and intervenors Town of Hunter and Village of Tannersville embarked upon negotiations for the construction of a sewage system to serve the village and a portion of the town. These negotiations were prompted by the city's need and desire to prevent the discharge of untreated sewage by residents of the area into Gooseberry Creek, a stream which fed a reservoir of the city's water supply system in the Schoharie watershed.

In 1923, the Legislature enacted enabling legislation authorizing the city to enter into contracts with municipalities in the watershed area "for the purpose of providing, maintaining [and] operating systems and plants for the collection and disposal of sewage" (L.1923, ch. 630, § 1). The statute further provided that any such contracts would be subject to the approval of the New York City Board of Estimate and Apportionment.

The negotiations culminated in an agreement in 1924 between the city and intervenors. By this agreement, the city assumed the obligation of constructing a sewage system consisting of a sewage disposal plant and sewer mains and laterals, and agreed that "all costs of construction and subsequent operation, maintenance and repair of said sewerage system with the house connections thereof and said disposal works shall be at the expense" of the city. The agreement also required the city to extend the sewer lines when "necessitated by future growth and building constructions of the respective communities". The village and town were obligated to and did obtain the necessary easements for the construction of the system and sewage lines.

The Board of Estimate, on December 9, 1926, approved the agreement and authorized the issuance of $500,000 of "corporate stock" of the City of New York for construction of the system by appropriate resolution. It is interesting to here note that a modification of the original agreement occurred in 1925 wherein the village agreed to reimburse the city for a specified amount representing the expense of changing the location of certain sewer lines. The plant was completed and commenced operation in 1928. The city has continued to maintain the plant through the ensuing years and in 1958 expended $193,000 to rehabilitate and expand the treatment plant and facilities.

Presently, the average flow of the plant has increased from an initial figure of 118,000 gallons per day to over 600,000 gallons daily and the trial court found that the plant "was operating substantially in excess of design capacity". The city asserts, and it is not disputed by any of the parties in this action, that the system cannot bear any significant additional "loadings" because this would result in inadequate treatment of all the sewage and consequently harm the city's water supply. The instant controversy arose when plaintiff, who is the owner of a tract of unimproved land which he seeks to develop into 50 residential lots, applied to the city for permission to connect houses, which he intends to construct on the lots, to existing sewer lines. The city refused permission on the ground that it had no obligation to further expand the plant, which is presently operating at full capacity, to accommodate this new construction.

Plaintiff then commenced this action for declaratory and injunctive relief, in which intervenors town and village joined as plaintiffs, maintaining that the 1924 agreement is perpetual in duration and obligates the city to expend additional capital funds to enlarge the existing plant or build a new one to accommodate the present and future needs of the municipalities. Both the trial court and the Appellate Division, by a divided court, held in favor of plaintiff and intervenors concluding, that, while the contract did not call for perpetual performance, the city was bound to construct additional facilities to meet increased demand until such time as the village or town is legally obligated to maintain a sewage disposal system. Two members of the court dissented in part stating that the agreement should not be construed as requiring the city to construct new or additional facilities.

We conclude that the city is presently obligated to maintain the existing plant but is not required to expand that plant or construct any new facilities to accommodate plaintiff's substantial, or any other, increased demands on the sewage system. The initial problem encountered in ascertaining the nature and extent of the city's obligation pursuant to the 1924 agreement, is its duration. We reject, as did the courts below, the plaintiff's contention that the city is perpetually bound under the agreement. The contract did not expressly provide for perpetual performance and both the trial court and the Appellate Division found that the parties did not so intend. Under these circumstances, the law will not imply that a contract calling for continuing performance is perpetual in duration. * * *

On the other hand, the city's contention that the contract is terminable at will because it provides for no express duration should also be rejected. In the absence of an express term fixing the duration of a contract, the courts may inquire into the intent of the parties and supply the missing term if a duration may be fairly and reasonably fixed by the surrounding circumstances and the parties' intent * * *. It is generally agreed that where a duration may be fairly and reasonably supplied by implication, a contract is not terminable at will * * *.

While we have not previously had occasion to apply it, the weight of authority supports the related rule that where the parties have not clearly expressed the duration of a contract, the courts will imply that they intended performance to continue for a reasonable time * * *. For compelling policy reasons, this rule has not been, and should not be, applied to contracts of employment or exclusive agency, distributorship, or requirements contracts which have been analogized to employment contracts * * *. The considerations relevant to such contracts do not obtain here. Thus, we hold that it is reasonable to infer from the circumstances of the 1924 agreement that the parties intended the city to maintain the sewage disposal facility until such time as the city no longer needed or desired the water, the purity of which the plant was designed to insure. The city argues that it is no longer obligated to maintain the plant because State law now prohibits persons from discharging raw sewage into streams such as Gooseberry Creek. However, the parties did not contemplate the passage of environmental control laws which would prohibit individuals or municipalities from discharging raw, untreated sewage into certain streams. Thus, the city agreed to assume the obligation of assuring that its water supply remained unpolluted and it may not now avoid that obligation for reasons not contemplated by the parties when the agreement was executed, and not within the purview of their intent, expressed or implied.

Having determined the duration of the city's obligation, the scope of its duty remains to be defined. By the agreement, the city obligated itself to build a specifically described disposal facility and to extend the lines of that facility to meet future increased demand. At the present time, the extension of those lines would result in the overloading of the system. Plaintiff claims that the city is required to build a new plant or expand the existing facility to overcome the problem. We disagree. The city should not be required to extend the lines to plaintiffs' property if to do so would overload the system and result in its inability to properly treat sewage. In providing for the extension of sewer lines, the contract does not obligate the city to provide sewage disposal services for properties in areas of the municipalities not presently served or even to new properties in areas which are presently served where to do so could reasonably be expected to significantly increase the demand on present plant facilities.

Thus, those paragraphs of the judgment which provide that the city is obligated to construct any additional facilities required to meet increased demand and that plaintiff is entitled to full use of the sewer lines should be stricken.

* * *

Order modified. * * *

NOTE:
DISTINGUISHING INTERPRETATION FROM GAP FILLING

Did the court fill a gap in the Haines case or did it simply determine the meaning of the contract based on the parties' intentions? The distinction between gap filling and interpretation is often blurred.

For example, in Yonkers v. Otis Elevator Co., 844 F.2d 42 (2d Cir. 1988), Yonkers and Otis Elevator agreed that Yonkers would use urban renewal and condemnation to allow Otis to expand its plant in Yonkers and therefore remain in Yonkers. The parties' letter of intent provided in part that "[t]he purpose of this letter and of the commitments set forth herein is the realization of the following goal[ ]: the retention by Otis of its existing usable manufacturing facilities in Yonkers * * *." The letter of intent said nothing about how long Otis Elevator was committed to stay in Yonkers. The parties performed the agreement and Otis Elevator completed its expansion, but about six years later Otis Elevator determined to leave Yonkers because technological changes in elevator manufacturing meant that continued operation was economically unfeasible. Yonkers alleged that Otis Elevator had impliedly promised to continue its operations in Yonkers "for a reasonable time to be set by law * * * alleged to be at least sixty years." The court relied on deposition testimony of several witnesses that, according to the court, established "that Otis would not have agreed to a term requiring Otis to operate in Yonkers for a period of time or even for a reasonable time." The court, in affirming a grant of summary judgment to Otis stated in part:

[T]here is no contention that the parties specifically agreed that Otis would remain in onkers, much less remain for a fixed period of time. Both sides believed, however, that the size of Otis' reinvestment in its Yonkers facility would guarantee the long term presence of Otis in Yonkers. Mr. Weller [President of Otis Elevator] so testified, as did Alphons Yost, executive director of the Agency, and Alfred DelBello, then Mayor of Yonkers. Yost nonetheless testified that this was a "hope," and "that the length of time that Otis would operate in Yonkers could have been unilaterally determined by Otis.

The letter of intent, quoted above, similarly supports this view. That letter contains a clear distinction between 'goals' and 'commitments.' Otis' continuing presence was only a goal, not a commitment. Yonkers argues that this is mere semanticism, and if only one or the other term had appeared, that argument might have some merit. Both were employed, however, and there is a clear difference between them.

This distinction and its implications were noted by Brett Auerbahn, the project director of the Agency, who noted in a memorandum analyzing the letter of intent:

"Has Otis gone any further than stating that it is their goal to remain in Yonkers? There appear to be a great number of sanctions against the City should it fail to meet up to its part of the obligation but no similar sanctions against the Otis Elevator Company."

* * *

Whether one views the resulting situation as negating any limit on Otis' mobility or as creating an implied promise to stay only as long as the plant remained economically feasible, the result is the same. Yonkers does not dispute Otis' professed reason for closing the plant: technological changes in the product and a corresponding change in the manufacturing capability needed to produce that product.

* * *

We conclude that this is not an appropriate case for the imposition of the implied promise for which plaintiffs contend, and that no genuine issue of material fact concerning that question is presented by this record."

FARNSWORTH, DISPUTES OVER OMISSION IN CONTRACTS

68 Colum.L.Rev. 860, 891 (1968).

The traditional approach to disputes over omission in contracts has disguised the role played by the courts. It has referred to a fictional "intention" of the parties which is in turn supposed to take the form of fictional "terms" of the contract. The result has been to create an extensive framework of implied terms to deal with omissions. It has been suggested here that it is more realistic to assume that the parties form their expectations in connection with a limited number of significant situations, selected from a much larger number of foreseeable ones. As to those situations that are excluded by this process of selection, there is an absence of expectation. When they reduce their expectations to contract language, a second process of selection takes place, and they use their language only in connection with a limited number of the significant situations with respect to which they formed their expectations. As to the rest, there is an understatement of expectation.

A situation that does not survive these two processes of selection is a *casus omissus*. The process of determining whether there is a *casus omissus* is that of interpretation. The process of resolving the *casus omissus* is * * * based either on actual expectations or on general principles of fairness and justice. So where a dispute over omission concerns the qualification of a duty that has been expressed without qualification, a court must first determine by the process of interpretation whether the case at hand was one of the significant situations with respect to which the language was used. If it was not, then it is a *casus omissus* and the court should recognize that it is within its power to extend the duty by analogy to the case at hand, to refuse to extend it, or to reach an adjustment that lies between these extremes. In making these kinds of judgments it is sometimes helpful to view a dispute over omission in terms of the burden of expression.

HILLMAN, MORE CONTRACT LORE

94 Tulane L. Rev. 903, 908–909 (2020).

* * * [C]ourts curiously rely on the "intention of the parties" rubric even in cases involving stark contract gaps. Such gap cases are another illustration of the division between lore (contract law enforces the intentions of the parties) and law (contract law fills gaps in contracts from various sources having little to do with actual intentions).

A recent United States Supreme Court case, M & G Polymers USA, LLC v. Tackett best illustrates this division. The case considered whether certain retired union employees were entitled to lifetime healthcare benefits under their union's contract when the contract was silent on the duration of the benefits. In fact, trial testimony showed that drafting of the contract was "ill-informed and haphazard" and interviews with lawyers involved in such negotiations showed that for strategic reasons the parties purposely left a gap with respect to the duration of the benefits. Each side feared the other would prevail on the duration issue if it was raised and negotiated.

At oral argument, members of the Supreme Court certainly agreed that this was a gap case. "Justice Alito asked why the bargainers left the [collective bargaining agreement] silent on the duration of healthcare benefits." Justice Scalia then remarked, "I mean, this thing [the duration issue] is obviously an important feature. Both sides knew it was left unaddressed, so, you know, whoever loses deserves to lose for casting this upon us when it could have been said very clearly in the contract. Such an important feature."

The Court, in a unanimous decision written by Justice Thomas, faulted the United States Court of Appeals for the Sixth Circuit for applying to the case certain inferences and presumptions first enumerated in another Sixth Circuit case, which the Court believed failed to constitute "ordinary principles of contract law." These inferences and presumptions included that "retiree healthcare benefits can be a form of deferred compensation; healthcare benefits likely last while the former employee is a retiree; tying healthcare benefits to pension benefits [that vest] suggests that healthcare benefits vest." The Court therefore reversed and remanded the Sixth Circuit's decision that the employees were entitled to lifetime benefits for further proceedings that employed what the Court thought were authentic "ordinary contract principles."

The Supreme Court's opinion is full of language indicating that these "ordinary contract principles" were tools for finding the parties' intentions. For example, Justice Thomas wrote that the Court must apply "ordinary principles of contract law" and proceeded to invoke the "parties' intentions" and the "plainly expressed intent" of the agreement. The Court added that the Sixth Circuit's use of inferences "distort[ed] the attempt 'to ascertain the intention of the parties.' " And further, "[w]here the words of a contract in writing are clear and unambiguous, its meaning is to be ascertained in accordance with its plainly expressed intent."

The concurrence also fixated on the parties' intentions. Written by Justice Ginsburg, and joined by Justices Breyer, Sotomayor, and Kagan, the opinion directed the Sixth Circuit to search for the "intention of the parties." Further the concurrence noted that "clear and express language" is not necessary to prove that the parties intended lifetime benefits.

KEPPY v. LILIENTHAL, 524 N.W.2d 436 (Iowa App.1994). [Keppy and the Lilienthals orally agreed that Keppy would "revitalize [the Lilienthals'] pig herd which had been ravaged by pseudo-rabies." The Lilienthals agreed to lease sows and boars to Keppy, who would breed, feed, and otherwise care for them until their sale. Keppy agreed to lease the Turkle farm and farrowing facility to carry out the operation. The parties were to divide the proceeds from the sale of the offspring. After a disagreement over who should supply the feed, the Lilienthals terminated the agreement. Keppy sought an injunction barring the Lilienthals from removing the hogs. The Lilienthals counterclaimed, seeking the return of the hogs. They claimed the agreement was terminable at will, since it was silent as to duration.]

The law in Iowa is not well developed regarding the duration of contracts where the parties fail to specify a duration. A contract granting a sole distributorship for an indefinite period was found to continue for a reasonable time and could be terminated without cause only upon reasonable notice. Des Moines Blue Ribbon Distrib. v. Drewrys Ltd., 256 Iowa 899, 129 N.W.2d 731 (1964). When the duration of employment contracts is indefinite, the contract can be terminated at will by either party. Blackhawk Bldg. Sys. v. Law Firm, 428 N.W.2d 288 (Iowa 1988).

> If a period of duration can be fairly implied from the nature of the contract, its subject matter and relationship of the parties, the contract is not terminable at the pleasure of either party and the court will give effect to the manifest intent of the parties. It has also been held that a contract will be held terminable within a reasonable time or revocable at will, depending on the circumstances, where no termination date was within the contemplation of the parties, or where their intention in regard thereto could not be ascertained.
>
> 17A C.J.S. Contracts § 398, at 480 (1963).

Evidence was presented which fairly implied the duration of the contract given the nature of the contract and the surrounding circumstances. Lilienthals entered the agreement in order to revitalize their herd and earn money. There was also testimony that Keppy made it known to Lilienthals that she intended to have her own farrowing operation within three years. Keppy testified she told Lilienthals she leased Turkle's farm and farrowing facility for three years. Turkle's testimony supported Keppy's assertion that the duration of the contract with Lilienthals was to be about three years. We find there was substantial evidence to support the district court's conclusion the contract was not terminable at will.

HASLUND V. SIMON PROPERTY GROUP, INC.

United States Court of Appeals, Seventh Circuit, 2004.
378 F.3d 653.

POSNER, CIRCUIT JUDGE.

In a diversity suit for breach of contract governed by Illinois law, the district judge after a bench trial awarded Shannon Haslund $537,634.41 in damages, plus prejudgment interest, against Simon Property Group (SPG). 284 F.Supp.2d 1102 (N.D.Ill.2003). SPG's appeal argues that the provision of the contract that it was found to have violated was too indefinite to be enforceable, that no injury was proved, and that in any event no prejudgment interest should have been awarded.

During the dot-com boom of the late 1990s, SPG, a real estate company that operates hundreds of shopping malls, decided to form a subsidiary, "clixnmortar.com," to create Internet-related services ancillary to its mall business. It appointed its chief information officer, Melanie Alshab, to be the president of the new subsidiary. She approached Haslund, a management consultant who had done work for SPG in the past and was employed by Ernst & Young, to be clixnmortar's vice president for operations. Haslund was interested, but told Alshab that she wanted not only a substantial raise (from $125,000, her salary at Ernst & Young, to $175,000), but also equity in clixnmortar. She was taking a chance by leaving an established firm for a startup, and so she wanted upside potential. She made clear that unless she was given equity she wouldn't sign on with the new company. Alshab got authorization from her superiors to offer Haslund not only the salary increase that she requested but also one percent of clixnmortar's equity. The deal was confirmed in a letter to Haslund from SPG's director of human resources that under the caption "Annual Salary" recited "$175,000 plus 1% equity in clixnmortar.com, structure to be determined."

Haslund started her new job at the end of 1999 shortly after receiving this letter. No stock was issued to her, however, either then or later. She kept badgering SPG for the stock to no avail, and 10 months after starting work she was fired, having denounced SPG's boss in an email to a firm that was in the process of acquiring an interest in clixnmortar. The startup never turned a profit—in fact never had any significant income—and was soon moribund, though it wasn't dissolved until last year.

The fact that a contract is incomplete, presents interpretive questions, bristles with unresolved contingencies, and in short has as many holes as a Swiss cheese does not make it unenforceable for indefiniteness. Otherwise there would be few enforceable contracts. Complete contingent contracts are impossible. The future, over which contractual performance evolves, is too uncertain. We once decided a case in which the contract exceeded 2000 pages yet the dispute that gave rise to the suit had not been anticipated (or, if anticipated, provided for). *S.A. Healy Co. v. Milwaukee Metropolitan Sewerage District,* 50 F.3d 476 (7th Cir.1995). If contracting parties had to provide for every contingency that might arise, contract negotiations would be interminable. Contracts can be shorter and simpler and cheaper when courts stand ready to fill gaps and resolve ambiguities in the minority of contracts that get drawn into litigation.

But that is in general and not in every case. A contract is rightly deemed unenforceable for indefiniteness when it leaves out (1) a crucial term that (2) a court cannot reasonably be asked to supply in the name of interpretation * * *. An example is the contract price. * * * Not only is price central, so that if the choice of price could be delegated to a court it would be the court and not the parties that was the contract maker, but there is no interpretive path that leads from the terms the parties agreed on to the price they would have agreed on. In the division of functions between parties and the judiciary in the joint enterprise of fixing contractual meaning, the selection of the contract price falls clearly on the parties' side. What is more, the omission of crucial terms is powerful evidence that no contract was intended.

So if the employment agreement had said that Haslund would receive equity but hadn't indicated how much, a court could not supply the missing percentage. * * * No interpretive technique would enable the court to build a bridge between what the parties had agreed to and the percentage of the equity in the new firm that she would receive. But the contract did specify the percentage. What it omitted was a number of details, such as the form of the equity—would it be voting stock or nonvoting stock?—and whether there would be restrictions on vesting: could Haslund show up for work on December 27, 1999, and the next day announce she was quitting and demand her shares? Important details, to be sure; but their absence did not necessarily make the contract indefinite. A court might be able to fill them in without shouldering an inordinate burden of inquiry or creating an inordinate risk of error. There might for example be a custom in the industry with respect to whether stock in a startup issued to a new employee carries voting rights, whether the right to the stock vests immediately or only after the employee has been on the job for a reasonable period of time, whether the right is forfeited if the employee is fired for cause, and whether and when and to whom the employee can sell the stock once it is issued to him.

Evidence of trade usage is admissible to supply the answers to such questions. * * * Neither party presented such evidence, but Haslund presented evidence that, if not nearly as good, was nevertheless sufficient. This was Alshab's testimony that there were no restrictions on the equity interest that Haslund was to receive—that all that "structure to be determined" meant was that SPG had not yet decided on the form that equity in clixnmortar would take, for example the number of shares that would be issued and whether there would be classes of stock, such as voting and nonvoting. Alshab's testimony was implausible—it seems almost unthinkable that SPG would have agreed to give Haslund an unrestricted one percent interest in a company that SPG hoped not wholly without reason would be highly valuable; for if taken literally the absence of any restrictions would mean that she could quit and sell the stock the day she received it even if she'd been on the job for only five minutes. And Alshab had quit SPG before the trial and there was no love lost between her and her former employer; she may have been inclined to shade her testimony in favor of Haslund, whom after all she had recruited. Nevertheless, her testimony was not *so* implausible that the district judge's crediting it over the evasive and ambiguous denials of SPG's principal, David Simon, could be found to be reversible error.

SPG might have presented evidence, presumably in the form of expert testimony by management consultants knowledgeable about dot-com startups during the boom, that equity in a startup would *never* be given to a new employee without restrictions, specifically a restriction on vesting and sale. SPG presented no such evidence. It is common knowledge that such restrictions are the norm, but that doesn't mean that they are universal.

So the contract was enforceable, and was broken, and the next question is whether the district judge was right to award Haslund some half million dollars in damages (or, indeed, as we shall see, whether he was right to award her any amount of damages). The amount he awarded was one percent of his estimate that clixnmortar had a net worth when Haslund was fired of $54 million. The principal evidence on which he relied for this extravagant estimate—for remember that when Haslund was fired (indeed at all times) clixnmortar had not shown a profit, on the basis of which a capital value could be estimated by conventional methods, and apparently had no assets whose value could be appraised—consisted of two transactions. In the first a company named CPG Partners bought a 9.3 percent equity interest in clixnmortar from SPG for $5 million, which implies (arithmetically) a total value of clixnmortar of $54 million. [Discussion of the second transaction is omitted.]

These transactions—though the one with CPG, at least, was rich in the structure missing from Haslund's one percent interest, since the number of shares and the type of stock were specified, along with restrictions on transfer—constitute but poor evidence of clixnmortar's value. [The court explained, among other things, that no money actually changed hands in the CPG transaction because "at the same time that CPG paid $5 million for 50,000 shares in clixnmortar's common stock, SPG paid $5 million for 50,000 shares of the common stock of a subsidiary of CPG." The court surmised that the "aim of the transaction was to make each company seem to be worth $5 million more than it was." Thus, the "swap provided no information with regard to the value of either company." As a result, "[a]ll that Haslund has going for her on the proof-of-damages front is SPG's failure to propose an alternative damages figure other than zero."] * * * On this record, we have to say that it is more likely that zero is correct than that $537,000 is, and we are sufficiently confident about this conclusion to pronounce the district judge's contrary finding clearly erroneous and therefore not binding on us."

* * *

The judgment is reversed with instructions to enter judgment for the plaintiff for nominal damages only.

PROBLEM 6-7

On March 29, 2006, the New York Times reported that Britain's High Court was considering Apple Corps.' claim that Apple Computer was violating their 1991 trademark agreement. Despite Apple Computer's promise not to use its logo, an apple with a bite in it, in any sales of music, Apple Computer's iTunes digital music store nonetheless was transmitting digital music files to Internet customers. Apple Computer claimed that it served only as a conduit for the transfer of music owned by others, while Apple Corps. asserted that the parties' agreement kept Apple Computer out of the music business entirely.

A few excerpts from the agreement follow. The parties signed the agreement, as the Times put it, when the possibility of the transfer of digital files of music was at most "a glimmer in a programmer's eye." Does the agreement therefore contain a gap with respect to this dispute? If so, how should it be filled?

> Whereas, the context in which this Agreement arises is the parties' desire to reserve for Apple Corps' field of use for its trademarks, the record business, The Beatles, Apple Corps' catalog and artists and related material all as set forth in section 1.3 herein and to reserve for Apple Computer's field of use for its trademarks, the computer, data processing and telecommunications business as set forth in section 1.2 herein * * * ACCORDINGLY, THE PARTIES AGREE AS FOLLOWS:
>
> * * *
>
> 1.2 "Apple Computer Field of Use" means (i) electronic goods, including but not limited to computers, microprocessors * * * and computer software of any kind on any medium; (ii) data processing services * * *.
>
> 1.3 "Apple Corps. Field of Use" means * * * (ii) any current or future creative works whose principal content is music and/or musical performances; regardless of the means by which those works are recorded, or communicated, whether tangible or intangible * * *.
>
> * * *
>
> 4.1 Apple Computer shall have the exclusive worldwide right, as between the parties, to use and authorize others to use the Apple Computer Marks on or in connection with goods and services within the Apple Computer Field of Use.
>
> 4.2 Apple Corps. shall have the exclusive worldwide right, as between the parties, to use and authorize others to use the Apple Corps. Marks on or in connection with goods and services within the Apple Corps. Field of Use.

The parties settled the dispute in early 2007. The settlement allows Apple Computer to use its name and logos on iTunes, but the parties did not disclose the details.

NOTE:
GAP FILLERS UNDER THE UNIFORM COMMERCIAL CODE

The Uniform Commercial Code provides in section 2–204(3) that "[e]ven though one or more terms are left open a contract for sale does not fail for indefiniteness if the parties have intended to make a contract and there is a reasonably certain basis for giving an appropriate remedy." Under the Code, therefore, even if important terms, such as those dealing with duration, quantity, delivery, or price are omitted, the agreement can be enforced if the parties intended to contract and an appropriate remedy can be supplied.

How are gaps filled under the Code? The Code provides a series of sections to guide courts in filling such gaps. We now sample one court's approach to gap filling under the Code.

SOUTHWEST ENGINEERING CO. V. MARTIN TRACTOR CO.

Supreme Court of Kansas, 1970.
205 Kan. 684, 473 P.2d 18.

FONTRON, JUSTICE.

This is an action to recover damages for breach of contract. Trial was had to the court which entered judgment in favor of the plaintiff. The defendant has appealed.

Southwest Engineering Company, Inc., the plaintiff, is a Missouri corporation engaged in general contracting work, while the defendant, Martin Tractor Company, Inc., is a Kansas corporation. The two parties will be referred to hereafter either as plaintiff, or Southwest, on the one hand and defendant, or Martin, on the other.

We glean from the record that in April, 1966, the plaintiff was interested in submitting a bid to the United States Corps of Engineers for the construction of certain runway lighting facilities at McConnell Air Force Base at Wichita. However, before submitting a bid, and on April 11, 1966, the plaintiff's construction superintendent, Mr. R.E. Cloepfil, called the manager of Martin's engine department, Mr. Ken Hurt, who at the time was at Colby, asking for a price on a standby generator and accessory equipment. Mr. Hurt replied that he would phone him back from Topeka, which he did the next day, quoting a price of $18,500. This quotation was re-confirmed by Hurt over the phone on April 13.

Southwest submitted its bid on April 14, 1966, using Hurt's figure of $18,500 for the generator equipment, and its bid was accepted. On April 20, Southwest notified Martin that its bid had been accepted. Hurt and

Cloepfil thereafter agreed over the phone to meet in Springfield on April 28. On that date Hurt flew to Springfield, where the two men conferred at the airfield restaurant for about an hour. Hurt took to the meeting a copy of the job specifications which the government had supplied Martin prior to the letting.

At the Springfield meeting it developed that Martin had upped its price for the generator and accessory equipment from $18,500 to $21,500. Despite this change of position by Martin, concerning which Cloepfil was understandably amazed, the two men continued their conversation and, according to Cloepfil, they arrived at an agreement for the sale of a D353 generator and accessories for the sum of $21,500. In addition it was agreed that if the Corps of Engineers would accept a less expensive generator, a D343, the aggregate price to Southwest would be $15,000. The possibility of providing alternative equipment, the D343, was suggested by Mr. Hurt, apparently in an attempt to mollify Mr. Cloepfil when the latter learned that Martin had reneged on its price quotation of April 12. It later developed that the Corps of Engineers would not approve the cheaper generator and that Southwest eventually had to supply the more expensive D353 generator.

At the conference, Mr. Hurt separately listed the component parts of each of the two generators on the top half of a sheet of paper and set out the price after each item. The prices were then totaled. On the bottom half of the sheet Hurt set down the accessories common to both generators and their cost. This handwritten memorandum, as it was referred to during the trial, noted a 10 per cent discount on the aggregate cost of each generator, while the accessories were listed at Martin's cost. The price of the D353 was rounded off at $21,500 and D343 at $15,000. The memorandum was handed to Cloepfil while the two men were still at the airport. We will refer to this memorandum further during the course of this opinion.

On May 2, 1966, Cloepfil addressed a letter to the Martin Tractor Company, directing Martin to proceed with shop drawings and submittal documents for the McConnell lighting job and calling attention to the fact that applicable government regulations were required to be followed. Further reference to this communication will be made when necessary.

Some three weeks thereafter, on May 24, 1966, Hurt wrote Cloepfil the following letter:

"MARTIN TRACTOR
COMPANY, INC.

Topeka Chanute Concordia Colby

CATERPILLAR*

"P.O. Box 1698
Topeka, Kansas
May 24, 1966

Mr. R.E. Cloepfil
Southwest Engineering Co., Inc.
P.O. Box 3314, Glenstone Station
Springfield, Missouri 65804

Dear Sir:

Due to restrictions placed on Caterpillar products, accessory suppliers, and other stipulations by the district governing agency, we cannot accept your letter to proceed dated May 2, 1966, and hereby withdraw all verbal quotations.

REGRETFULLY,

/S/ KEN HURT
KEN HURT, MANAGER
ENGINE DIVISION"

On receipt of this unwelcome missive, Cloepfil telephoned Mr. Hurt who stated they had some work underway for the Corps of Engineers in both the Kansas City and Tulsa districts and did not want to take on any other work for the Corps at that time. Hurt assured Cloepfil he could buy the equipment from anybody at the price Martin could sell it for. Later investigation showed, however, that such was not the case.

In August of 1966, Mr. Cloepfil and Mr. Anderson, the president of Southwest, traveled to Topeka in an effort to persuade Martin to fulfill its contract. Hurt met them at the company office where harsh words were bandied about. Tempers eventually cooled off and at the conclusion of the verbal melee, hands were shaken all around and Hurt went so far as to say that if Southwest still wanted to buy the equipment from them to submit another order and he would get it handled. On this promising note the protagonists parted.

After returning to Springfield, Mr. Cloepfil, on September 6, wrote Mr. Hurt placing an order for a D353 generator (the expensive one) and asking that the order be given prompt attention, as their completion date was in early December. This communication was returned unopened.

A final effort to communicate with Martin was attempted by Mr. Anderson when the unopened letter was returned. A phone call was placed for Mr. Martin, himself, and Mr. Anderson was informed by the girl on the switchboard that Martin was in Colorado Springs on a vacation. Anderson then placed a call to the motel where he was told Mr. Martin could be reached. Martin refused to talk on the call, on learning the caller's name, and Anderson was told he would have to contact his office.

Mr. Anderson then replaced his call to Topeka and reached either the company comptroller or the company treasurer who responded by cussing him and saying "Who in the hell do you think you are? We don't have to sell you a damn thing."

Southwest eventually secured the generator equipment from Foley Tractor Co. of Wichita, a company which Mr. Hurt had one time suggested, at a price of $27,541. The present action was then filed, seeking damages of $6,041 for breach of the contract and $9,000 for loss resulting from the delay caused by the breach. The trial court awarded damages of $6,041 for the breach but rejected damages allegedly due to delay. The defendant, only, has appealed; there is no cross-appeal by plaintiff.

[The court first found that Hurt's handwritten memo satisfied U.C.C. § 2–201.]

Hurt * * * testified that in his opinion the thing which stood in the way of a firm deal was Martin's terms of payment—that had Southwest agreed with those terms of payment, so far as he was concerned, he would have considered a firm deal was made. Mr. Hurt acknowledged while on the stand that he penned the memorandum and that as disclosed therein a 10 per cent discount was given Southwest on the price of either of the generators listed (depending on which was approved by the Corps of Engineers), and that the accessories common to both generators were to be net—that is, sold without profit.

It is quite true, as the trial court found, that terms of payment were not agreed upon at the Springfield meeting. Hurt testified that as the memorandum was being made out, he said they wanted 10 per cent with the order, 50 per cent on delivery and the balance on acceptance, but he did not recall Cloepfil's response. Cloepfil's version was somewhat different. He stated that after the two had shaken hands in the lobby preparing to leave, Hurt said their terms usually were 20 per cent down and the balance on delivery; while he (Cloepfil) said the way they generally paid was 90 per cent on the tenth of the month following delivery and the balance on final acceptance. It is obvious the parties reached no agreement on this point.

However, a failure on the part of Messrs. Hurt and Cloepfil to agree on terms of payment would not, of itself, defeat an otherwise valid agreement reached by them. K.S.A. 84–2–204(3) reads:

> "Even though one or more terms are left open a contract for sale does not fail for indefiniteness if the parties have intended to make a contract and there is a reasonably certain basis for giving an appropriate remedy."

The official U.C.C. Comment is enlightening:

> "Subsection (3) states the principle as to 'open terms' underlying later sections of the Article. If the parties intend to enter into a binding agreement, this subsection recognizes that agreement as valid in law, despite missing terms, if there is any reasonably certain basis for granting a remedy. The test is not certainty as to what the parties were to do nor as to the exact amount of damages due the plaintiff. Nor is the fact that one or more terms are left to be agreed upon enough of itself to defeat an otherwise adequate agreement. Rather, commercial standards on the point of 'indefiniteness' are intended to be applied, this Act making provision elsewhere for missing terms needed for performance, open price, remedies and the like.
>
> "The more terms the parties leave open, the less likely it is that they have intended to conclude a binding agreement, but their actions may be frequently conclusive on the matter despite the omissions."

* * *

So far as the present case is concerned, K.S.A. 84–2–310 supplies the omitted term. This statute provides in pertinent part:

> "Unless otherwise agreed
>
> "(a) payment is due at the time and place at which the buyer is to receive the goods even though the place of shipment is the place of delivery;"

In our view, the language of the two Code provisions is clear and positive. Considered together, we take the two sections to mean that where parties have reached an enforceable agreement for the sale of goods, but omit therefrom the terms of payment, the law will imply, as part of the agreement, that payment is to be made at time of delivery. In this respect the law does not greatly differ from the rule this court laid down years ago.

* * *

We do not mean to infer that terms of payment are not of importance under many circumstances, or that parties may not condition an agreement on their being included. However, the facts before us hardly indicate that Hurt and Cloepfil considered the terms of payment to be significant, or of more than passing interest. Hurt testified that while he stated his terms he did not recall Cloepfil's response, while Cloepfil stated that as the two were on the point of leaving, each stated their usual terms and that was as far as it went. The trial court found that only a brief and casual conversation ensued as to payment, and we think that is a valid summation of what took place.

Moreover, it is worthy of note that Martin first mentioned the omission of the terms of payment, as justifying its breach, in a letter written by counsel on September 15, 1966, more than four months after the memorandum was prepared by Hurt. On prior occasions Martin attributed its cancellation of the Springfield understanding to other causes. In its May 24 letter, Martin ascribed its withdrawal of "all verbal quotations" to "restrictions placed on Caterpillar products, accessory suppliers, and other stipulations by the district governing agency." In explaining the meaning of the letter to Cloepfil, Hurt said that Martin was doing work for the Corps of Engineers in the Kansas City and Tulsa districts and did not want to take on additional work with them at this time.

The entire circumstances may well give rise to a suspicion that Martin's present insistence that future negotiations were contemplated concerning terms of payment, is primarily an afterthought, for use as an escape hatch. Doubtless the trial court so considered the excuse in arriving at its findings.

We are aware of Martin's argument that Southwest's letter of May 2, 1966, referring to the sale is evidence that no firm contract had been concluded. Granted that some of the language employed might be subject to that interpretation, the trial court found, on what we deem to be substantial, competent evidence, that an agreement of sale *was* concluded at Springfield. * * *

The defendant points particularly to the following portion of the May 2 letter, as interjecting a new and unacceptable term in the agreement made at Springfield.

> " * * * We are not prepared to make a partial payment at the time of placing of this order. However, we will be able to include 100% of the engine-generator price in our first payment estimate after it is delivered, and only 10% will have to be withheld pending acceptance. Ordinarily this means that suppliers can expect payment of 90% within about thirty days after delivery."

It must be conceded that the terms of payment proposed in Southwest's letter had not been agreed to by Martin. However, we view the proposal as irrelevant. Although terms of payment had not been mutually agreed upon, K.S.A. 84–2–310 supplied the missing terms, *i.e.*, payment on delivery, which thus became part of the agreement already concluded. In legal effect the proposal was no more than one to change the terms of payment implied by law. Since Martin did not accept the change, the proposal had no effect, either as altering or terminating the agreement reached at Springfield. * * *

* * *

We find no error in this case and the judgment of the trial court is affirmed.

SECTION FIVE: GOOD FAITH

We have already encountered the doctrine of good faith on several occasions. For example, we saw in Section Two of Chapter Two how it may impose an obligation on one party so that there is no want of mutuality of obligation; in Section Three of Chapter Three how it may serve as one factor influencing a court's choice between measures of damages; in Section Nine of Chapter Four how it helps define the scope of any legal obligation in an agreement to agree; and in Section One of Chapter Five how it can function as a policing doctrine. Moreover, we will see that good faith is relevant in the remaining chapters of this book. In this section, we see its special role in shaping the content of the duty to perform. We also take this occasion to identify the general authoritative sources of good faith doctrine, and to explore the nature of good faith concepts.

Many common law courts have held that in every contract "there exists an implied covenant of good faith and fair dealing." A leading example is Kirke La Shelle Co. v. Paul Armstrong Co., 263 N.Y. 79, 87, 188 N.E. 163, 167 (1933). A rapidly increasing number of judicial decisions recognizes the covenant of good faith and fair dealing in a wide variety of contexts. Section 1–304 of the Uniform Commercial Code also provides: "Every contract or duty within [the Uniform Commercial Code] imposes a duty of good faith in its performance or enforcement." A number of additional statutes also impose duties of good faith in various settings.

FORTUNE V. NATIONAL CASH REGISTER CO.

Supreme Judicial Court of Massachusetts, 1977.
373 Mass. 96, 364 N.E.2d 1251.

ABRAMS, JUSTICE.

Orville E. Fortune (Fortune), a former salesman of The National Cash Register Company (NCR), brought a suit to recover certain commissions allegedly due as a result of a sale of cash registers to First National Stores Inc. (First National) in 1968. Counts 1 and 2 of Fortune's amended declaration claimed bonus payments under the parties' written contract of employment. The third count sought recovery in quantum meruit for the reasonable value of Fortune's services relating to the same sales transaction. Judgment on a jury verdict for Fortune was reversed by the Appeals Court * * * and this court granted leave to obtain further appellate review. We affirm the judgment of the Superior Court. We hold, for the reasons stated herein, there was no error in submitting the issue of "bad faith" termination of an employment at will contract to the jury.

The issues before the court are raised by NCR's motion for directed verdicts. Accordingly, we summarize the evidence most favorable to the plaintiff. * * *

Fortune was employed by NCR under a written "salesman's contract" which was terminable at will, without cause, by either party on written notice. The contract provided that Fortune would receive a weekly salary in a fixed amount plus a bonus for sales made within the "territory" (i.e., customer accounts or stores) assigned to him for "coverage or supervision," whether the sale was made by him or someone else. The amount of the bonus was determined on the basis of "bonus credits," which were computed as a percentage of the price of products sold. Fortune would be paid a percentage of the applicable bonus credit as follows: (1) 75% if the territory was assigned to him at the date of the order, (2) 25% if the territory was assigned to him at the date of delivery and installation, or (3) 100% if the territory was assigned to him at both times. The contract further provided that the "bonus interest" would terminate if shipment of the order was not made within eighteen months from the date of the order unless (1) the territory was assigned to him for coverage at the date of delivery and installation, or (2) special engineering was required to fulfil the contract. In addition, NCR reserved the right to sell products in the salesman's territory without paying a bonus. However, this right could be exercised only on written notice.

In 1968, Fortune's territory included First National. This account had been part of his territory for the preceding six years; he had been successful in obtaining several orders from First National, including a million dollar order in 1963. Sometime in late 1967, or early 1968, NCR introduced a new model cash register, Class 5. Fortune corresponded with First National in an effort to sell the machine. He also helped to arrange for a demonstration of the Class 5 to executives of First National on October 4, 1968. NCR had a team of men also working on this sale.

On November 27, 1968, NCR's manager of chain and department stores, and the Boston branch manager, both part of NCR's team, wrote to First National regarding the Class 5. The letter covered a number of subjects, including price protection, trade-ins, and trade-in protection against obsolescence. While NCR normally offered price protection for only an eighteen-month term, apparently the size of the proposed order from First National caused NCR to extend its price protection terms for either a two-year or four-year period. On November 29, 1968, First National signed an order for 2,008 Class 5 machines to be delivered over a four-year period at a purchase price of approximately $5,000,000. Although Fortune did not participate in the negotiation of the terms of the order,[1] his name appeared on the order form in the space entitled "salesman credited." The amount of the bonus credit as shown on the order was $92,079.99.

On January 6, 1969, the first working day of the new year, Fortune found an envelope on his desk at work. It contained a termination notice addressed to his home dated December 2, 1968. Shortly after receiving the notice, Fortune spoke to the Boston branch manager with whom he was friendly. The manager told him, "You are through," but, after considering some of the details necessary for the smooth operation of the First National order, told him to "stay on," and to "[k]eep on doing what you are doing right now." Fortune remained with the company in a position entitled "sales support." In this capacity, he coordinated and expedited delivery of the machines to First National under the November 29 order as well as servicing other accounts.

Commencing in May or June, Fortune began to receive some bonus commissions on the First National order. Having received only 75% of the applicable bonus due on the machines which had been delivered and installed, Fortune spoke with his manager about receiving the full amount of the commission. Fortune was told "to forget about it." Sixty-one years old at that time, and with a son in college, Fortune concluded that it "was a good idea to forget it for the time being."

NCR did pay a systems and installations person the remaining 25% of the bonus commissions due from the First National order although contrary to its usual policy of paying *only* salesmen a bonus. NCR, by its letter of November 27, 1968, had promised the services of a systems and installations person; the letter had claimed that the services of this person, Bernie Martin (Martin), would have a forecasted cost to NCR of over $45,000. As promised, NCR did transfer Martin to the First National account shortly after the order was placed.

Approximately eighteen months after receiving the termination notice, Fortune, who had worked for NCR for almost twenty-five years, was asked to retire. When he refused, he was fired in June of 1970. Fortune did not receive any bonus payments on machines which were delivered to First National after this date.

At the close of the plaintiff's case, the defendant moved for a directed verdict, arguing that there was no evidence of any breach of contract, and adding that the existence of a contract barred recovery under the quantum meruit count. Ruling that Fortune could recover if the termination and firing were in bad faith, the trial judge, without specifying on which count,

[1] Fortune was not authorized to offer the price protection terms which appeared in the November 27 letter, as special covenant A, par. 3 of his contract prohibited him from varying the prices of items.

submitted this issue to the jury. NCR then rested and, by agreement of counsel, the case was sent to the jury for special verdicts on two questions:[2]

> "1. Did the Defendant act in bad faith * * * when it decided to terminate the Plaintiff's contract as a salesman by letter dated December 2, 1968, delivered on January 6, 1969?
>
> "2. Did the Defendant act in bad faith * * * when the Defendant let the Plaintiff go on June 5, 1970?"

The jury answered both questions affirmatively, and judgment entered in the sum of $45,649.62.[3]

The central issue on appeal is whether this "bad faith" termination constituted a breach of the employment at will contract. Traditionally, an employment contract which is "at will" may be terminated by either side without reason. * * * Although the employment at will rule has been almost uniformly criticised * * * it has been widely followed.

The contract at issue is a classic terminable at will employment contract. It is clear that the contract itself reserved to the parties an explicit power to terminate the contract without cause on written notice. It is also clear that under the express terms of the contract Fortune has received all the bonus commissions to which he is entitled. Thus, NCR claims that it did not breach the contract, and that it has no further liability to Fortune.[4] According to a literal reading of the contract, NCR is correct.

However, Fortune argues that, in spite of the literal wording of the contract, he is entitled to a jury determination on NCR's motives in terminating his services under the contract and in finally discharging him. We agree. We hold that NCR's written contract contains an implied covenant of good faith and fair dealing, and a termination not made in good faith constitutes a breach of the contract.

We do not question the general principles that an employer is entitled to be motivated by and to serve its own legitimate business interests; that an employer must have wide latitude in deciding whom it will employ in the face of the uncertainties of the business world; and that an employer needs flexibility in the face of changing circumstances. We recognize the

---

[2] The defendant reserved the right to argue on appeal that the judge should have directed verdicts, and that bad faith was not a proper issue in the case.

[3] The amount apparently represented 25% of the commission due during the eighteen months the machines were delivered to First National, and which was paid to Martin, and 100% of the commissions on the machines delivered after Fortune was fired.

[4] Damages were, by stipulation of the parties, set equal to the unpaid bonus amounts. Thus we need not consider whether other measures of damages might be justified in cases of bad faith termination. * * *

Although the order called for purchase of 2,008 Class 5 machines for a total sale of $5,040,080, at trial the parties stipulated that "1,503 machines were actually delivered and installed" under the First National order. The stipulated damages in the instant case were based on the number of registers actually delivered and installed.

employer's need for a large amount of control over its work force. However, we believe that where, as here, commissions are to be paid for work performed by the employee, the employer's decision to terminate its at will employee should be made in good faith. NCR's right to make decisions in its own interest is not, in our view, unduly hampered by a requirement of adherence to this standard.

On occasion some courts have avoided the rigidity of the "at will" rule by fashioning a remedy in tort.[5] We believe, however, that in this case there is remedy on the express contract.[6] In so holding we are merely recognizing the general requirement in this Commonwealth that parties to contracts and commercial transactions must act in good faith toward one another. Good faith and fair dealing between parties are pervasive requirements in our law; it can be said fairly, that parties to contracts or commercial transactions are bound by this standard. See G.L. c. 106, § 1–203 [current 1–304] (good faith in contracts under Uniform Commercial Code); G.L. c. 93B, § 4(3)(c) (good faith in motor vehicle franchise termination).

A requirement of good faith has been assumed or implied in a variety of contract cases. *Druker v. Roland Wm. Jutras Assocs.*, 348 N.E.2d 763 (1976). *Kerrigan v. Boston,* 361 Mass. 24, 33, 278 N.E.2d 387 (1972) (collective bargaining contract). *Murach v. Massachusetts Bonding & Ins. Co.,* 339 Mass. 184, 187, 158 N.E.2d 338 (1959) (insurance contract—insurer must exercise discretionary power to settle claims in good faith). *Krauss v. Kuechler,* 300 Mass. 346, 15 N.E.2d 207 (1938). *Clark v. State St. Trust Co.,* 270 Mass. 140, 153, 169 N.E. 897 (1930) (secondary agreement to a stock option agreement). *Elliott v. Kazajian,* 255 Mass. 459, 462, 152 N.E. 351 (1926) (broker's commission). *Chandler, Gardner & Williams, Inc. v. Reynolds,* 250 Mass. 309, 314, 145 N.E.476 (1924) (contracts to be performed to the satisfaction of the other party).

* * *

Recent decisions in other jurisdictions lend support to the proposition that good faith is implied in contracts terminable at will. In a recent employment at will case, *Monge v. Beebe Rubber Co.,* 114 N.H. 130, 133, 316 A.2d 549, 552 (1974), the plaintiff alleged that her oral contract of employment had been terminated because she refused to date her foreman.

---

[5] This theory has generally been utilized in order to protect public policy. See, e.g., *Montalvo v. Zamora,* 7 Cal.App.3d 69, 86 Cal.Rptr. 401 (1970) (employee terminated after hiring an attorney to negotiate a claim that the employer had violated the minimum wage law); *Petermann v. International Broth. of Teamsters, Local 396,* 174 Cal.App.2d 184, 344 P.2d 25 (1959) (employee discharged for refusing to commit perjury before government commission); *Frampton v. Central Ind. Gas Co.,* 260 Ind. 249, 297 N.E.2d 425 (1973) (employee fired for filing a workman's compensation claim); *Nees v. Hocks,* 272 Or. 210, 536 P.2d 512 (1975) (employee fired for performing jury duty in violation of company policy). Cf. *Geary v. United States Steel Corp.,* 456 Pa. 171, 319 A.2d 174 (1974) (tort remedy not available where employee fired for not following corporate hierarchy procedure in protesting company policy as to safety of a product).

[6] Thus, we do not reach the issues raised by count 3 for quantum meruit recovery.

The New Hampshire Supreme Court held that "[i]n all employment contracts, whether at will or for a definite term, the employer's interest in running his business as he sees fit must be balanced against the interest of the employee in maintaining his employment, and the public's interest in maintaining a proper balance between the two. * * * We hold that a termination by the employer of a contract of employment at will which is motivated by bad faith or malice * * * constitutes a breach of the employment contract. * * * Such a rule affords the employee a certain stability of employment and does not interfere with the employer's normal exercise of his right to discharge, which is necessary to permit him to operate his business efficiently and profitably."

We believe that the holding in the *Monge* case merely extends to employment contracts the rule that " 'in *every* contract there is an implied covenant that neither party shall do anything which will have the effect of destroying or injuring the right of the other party to receive the fruits of the contract, which means that in *every* contract there exists an implied covenant of good faith and fair dealing' [emphasis supplied]. *Uproar Co. v. National Broadcasting Co.,* 81 F.2d 373, 377 (1st Cir.), cert. denied, 298 U.S. 670, 56 S.Ct. 835, 80 L.Ed. 1393 (1936), quoting from *Kirke LaShelle Co. v. Paul Armstrong Co.,* 263 N.Y. 79, 87, 188 N.E. 163 (1933)." * * *

In the instant case, we need not pronounce our adherence to so broad a policy nor need we speculate as to whether the good faith requirement is implicit in every contract for employment at will. It is clear, however, that, on the facts before us, a finding is warranted that a breach of the contract occurred. Where the principal seeks to deprive the agent of all compensation by terminating the contractual relationship when the agent is on the brink of successfully completing the sale, the principal has acted in bad faith and the ensuing transaction between the principal and the buyer is to be regarded as having been accomplished by the agent. Restatement (Second) of Agency § 454, and Comment a (1958). The same result obtains where the principal attempts to deprive the agent of any portion of a commission due the agent. Courts have often applied this rule to prevent overreaching by employers and the forfeiture by employees of benefits almost earned by the rendering of substantial services. * * * In our view, the Appeals Court erroneously focused only on literal compliance with payment provisions of the contract and failed to consider the issue of bad faith termination. Restatement (Second) of Agency § 454, and Comment a (1958).

NCR argues that there was no evidence of bad faith in this case; therefore, the trial judge was required to direct a verdict in any event. We think that the evidence and the reasonable inferences to be drawn therefrom support a jury verdict that the termination of Fortune's twenty-five years of employment as a salesman with NCR the next business day after NCR obtained a $5,000,000 order from First National was motivated by a desire to pay Fortune as little of the bonus credit as it could. The fact that Fortune was willing to work under these circumstances does not constitute a waiver or estoppel; it only shows that NCR had him "at their mercy." *Commonwealth v. DeCotis,* 366 Mass. 234, 243, 316 N.E.2d 748 (1974).

NCR also contends that Fortune cannot complain of his firing in June, 1970, as his employment contract clearly indicated that bonus credits would be paid only for an eighteen-month period following the date of the order. As we have said, the jury could have found that Fortune was stripped of his "salesman" designation in order to disqualify him for the remaining 25% of the commissions due on cash registers delivered prior to the date of his first termination. Similarly, the jury could have found that Fortune was fired (or not assigned to the First National account) so that NCR could avoid paying him *any* commissions on cash registers delivered after June, 1970.

Conversely, the jury could have found that Fortune was assigned by NCR to the First National account; that all he did in this case was arrange for a demonstration of the product; that he neither participated in obtaining the order nor did he assist NCR in closing the order; and that nevertheless NCR credited him with the sale. This, however, did not obligate the trial judge to direct a verdict. Where evidence is conflicting, the rule is clear: "If upon any reasonable view of the evidence there is found any combination of circumstances from which a rational inference may be drawn in favor of the plaintiff, then there was no error in the denial of the motion, even if there may be other and different circumstances disclosed in the evidence which, if accepted as true by the jury, would support a conclusion adverse to the plaintiff." *Howes v. Kelman,* 326 Mass. 696, 696–697, 96 N.E.2d 394, 395 (1951).

We think that NCR's conduct in June, 1970 permitted the jury to find bad faith.

* * *

Judgment of the Superior Court affirmed.

HILLMAN, DRAFTING CHAPTER 2 OF THE ALI'S EMPLOYMENT LAW RESTATEMENT IN THE SHADOW OF CONTRACT LAW: AN ASSESSMENT OF THE CHALLENGES AND RESULTS

100 Cornell L. Rev. 1341 (2015).

[Under the employment Restatement] [e]mployees must * * * show that the employer's motivation was to deprive the employee of its just deserts. In a way, *Fortune* is an unfortunate precedent in this regard, at least from the perspective of those interested in employee rights. This is because the evidence appears almost a slam dunk for Fortune. As the court says, "[w]e think that the evidence and the reasonable inferences to be drawn therefrom support a jury verdict that the termination of Fortune's twenty-five years of employment as a salesman with NCR *the next business day after NCR obtained a $5,000,000 order* . . . was motivated by a desire to pay Fortune as little of the bonus credit as it could." Under the facts of *Fortune*, therefore, the court likely felt little contrition about interpreting the express terms of the contract to disapprove of such a termination. Employees likely will not have such striking evidence in the typical case.

TYMSHARE, INC. v. COVELL, 727 F.2d 1145 (D.C.Cir.1984). [Covell's employment contract with Tymshare granted Covell commissions on sales above a particular quota. The contract also expressly permitted Tymshare to increase the quota retroactively, which would have the effect of decreasing Covell's compensation: "(M)anagement reserves the right to change the quota plan and individual quota * * * payments at any time during the quota year within their sole discretion." Covell sued Tymshare, claiming that Tymshare exercised the clause in bad faith to deprive him of compensation. Tymshare appealed a grant of summary judgment in favor of Covell.]

SCALIA, CIRCUIT JUDGE.

* * *

Whether pursued under the rubric of "good faith" or the more traditional rubric (for most contracts) of "implied limitation," the object of our inquiry is whether it was reasonably understood by the parties to this contract that there were at least certain purposes for which the expressly conferred power to adjust quotas could not be employed. If not, then appellant is correct that no action in this regard could constitute "bad faith"—or, as we would put it, there is no implicit contractual restriction.

In conducting this inquiry we must reject at the outset the proposition which appellant seeks to extract from certain cases to the effect that "[a]s to acts and conduct authorized by the express provisions of the contract, no covenant of good faith and fair dealing can be implied which forbids such acts and conduct," *VTR, Inc. v. Goodyear Tire & Rubber Co.,* 303 F.Supp. 773, 778 (S.D.N.Y.1969). * * * We have no doubt that proposition is correct (assuming that the provisions of the contract are not void as unconscionable * * *) as an elaboration of the fundamental principle, set forth in another case cited by appellant, that "[w]hat the intent of the parties was in making the contract must control; it is possible to so draw a contract as to leave decisions absolutely to the uncontrolled discretion of one of the parties and in such a case the issue of good faith is irrelevant." *MacDougald Construction Co. v. State Highway Department,* 125 Ga.App. 591, 594, 188 S.E.2d 405, 407 (1972). But the trick is to tell *when* a contract has been so drawn—and surely the mere recitation of an express power is not always the test. Sometimes it may suffice, depending upon the nature of the expressed power. We cannot imagine, for example, entertaining a claim that a demand for payment of a demand note has been made "in bad faith." In the understood nature of human arrangements, a loan of money in exchange for a promise to repay on demand does not import an obligation to make the demand only if the money is really needed, or only without the purpose and effect of inconveniencing the obligor. But to say that every expressly conferred contractual power is of this nature is virtually to read the doctrine of good faith (or of implied contractual obligations and limitations) out of existence. Many cases, for example, place "good faith" limitations upon the reasons for which an express power to terminate a contract "at will" can be exercised, *see, e.g., Fortune v. National Cash Register Co.,* 373 Mass. 96, 364 N.E.2d 1251 (1977). (One application of this principle has been embodied in the RESTATEMENT (SECOND) OF AGENCY § 454 (1958).) And in much earlier times, before the "good faith" terminology was generally applied, the same principle was employed to find that an unqualified option to terminate if a specified event occurs "clearly implied" that the option had to be exercised within a reasonable time after the happening of the event. *Davidson Hardware Co. v. Delker Bros. Buggy Co.,* 170 N.C. 298, 300, 86 S.E. 958, 959 (1915); *see generally* Annot., 164 A.L.R. 1014, 1024–26 (1946).

Here, however, appellant does not rely solely upon the express conferral of a power to alter quotas, but also upon the expansive fashion in which that power is contractually described. The Compensation Plan states and reiterates that Tymshare may change the quota plan "within [its] sole discretion," Sections I A, V, *supra.* But as the administrative law concept of "abuse of discretion" suggests, *see* 5 U.S.C. § 706(2)(A) (1982), this phrase is not necessarily the equivalent of "for any reason whatsoever, no matter how arbitrary or unreasonable." As applied to some contractual powers, it may indeed connote the sort of unfettered authority appellant would wish. But just as, as discussed above, certain express powers, even without an expansive modifier, are implicitly absolute (the power to call a demand note) while others are not (the power to terminate certain continuing contractual arrangements); so also, the reasonably understood effect of an expansive modifier varies from case to case depending upon the nature of the power at issue. Where what is at issue is the retroactive reduction or elimination of a central compensatory element of the contract—a large part of the *quid pro quo* that induced one party's assent—it is simply not likely that the parties had in mind a power quite as absolute as appellant suggests. In the present case, agreeing to such a provision would require a degree of folly on the part of these sales representatives we are not inclined to posit where another plausible interpretation of the language is available. It seems to us that the "sole discretion" intended was discretion to determine the existence or nonexistence of the various factors that would reasonably justify alteration of the sales quota. Those factors would include (as the company's practice under the provisions bears out) an unanticipated volume of business from a particular customer unconnected with the extra sales efforts of the employee assigned to that account; and they may perhaps include other eventualities, such as a poor overall sales year for the company, leaving less gross income to be expended on commissions. The company's genuine determination that one or another of these factors exists can presumably not be questioned. But the language need not (and therefore can not reasonably) be read to confer discretion to reduce the quota for any reason whatever—including what Covell has alleged here, a simple desire to deprive an employee of the fairly agreed benefit of his labors.

[The court reversed the summary judgment in favor of Covell and remanded for a factual determination of Tymshare's motive.]

CITY OF MIDLAND v. O'BRYANT, 18 S.W.3d 209, 43 Tex. Sup. Ct. J. 884 (2000). [Plaintiffs were police officers who had previously brought claims against the city alleging violations of the Americans with Disabilities Act and the Texas Commission on Human Rights Act. After the plaintiffs voluntarily dismissed those lawsuits, the city reclassified their positions. Plaintiffs claimed in this lawsuit that the new positions were inferior and that the city reclassified them to retaliate for the previous lawsuits. One of the plaintiffs' theories was that the city's retaliation breached the duty of good faith and fair dealing.]

JUSTICE OWEN delivered the opinion of the court.

* * *

This Court has held that not every contractual relationship creates a duty of good faith and fair dealing. * * * We have "specifically rejected the implication of a general duty of good faith and fair dealing in all contracts." * * * But see Restatement (Second) of Contracts § 205 (1979) (providing that "[e]very contract imposes upon each party a duty of good faith and fair dealing in its performance and its enforcement"). * * *

As the plaintiffs recognize, this Court has imposed an actionable duty of good faith and fair dealing only when there is a special relationship, such as that between an insured and his or her insurance carrier. See Arnold v. National County Mut. Fire Ins. Co., 725 S.W.2d 165, 167 (Tex.1987). We have held that a special relationship exists in the insurance context because of "the parties' unequal bargaining power and the nature of insurance contracts which would allow unscrupulous insurers to take advantage of their insureds' misfortunes in bargaining for settlement or resolution of claims." Id. The Court concluded in Arnold that without a cause of action for breach of a duty of good faith and fair dealing, "insurers can arbitrarily deny coverage and delay payment of a claim" and that an insurer has "exclusive control over the evaluation, processing, and denial of claims." Id.

But the elements which make the relationship between an insurer and an insured a special one are absent in the relationship between an employer and its employees. First, in Texas, the employment relationship is generally at-will unless the parties enter into an express agreement that provides otherwise. Second, insurance contracts are typically much more restrictive than employment agreements. If an insured suffers a loss, he cannot simply contract with another insurance company to cover that loss. By contrast, an employee who has been demoted, transferred, or discharged may seek alternative employment. See, e.g., Foley v. Interactive Data Corp., 47 Cal.3d 654, 254 Cal.Rptr. 211, 765 P.2d 373, 390 (Cal.1988).

Moreover, this Court has thus far recognized only one limited common-law exception to the at-will employment doctrine. We held in Sabine Pilot Service, Inc. v. Hauck, 687 S.W.2d 733 (Tex.1985), that an employer may not discharge an employee for the sole reason that the employee refused to perform an illegal act that carried criminal penalties. Id. at 735. We have not, however, recognized other common-law exceptions to the employment at-will doctrine. We declined to recognize a common-law whistleblower cause of action * * *. We did so primarily on the basis that the Legislature has been active in crafting whistleblower statutes that often vary from one another in material respects.

The adoption of a general common-law whistleblower cause of action would have undercut the many distinctions drawn by the Legislature among the various statutory whistleblower causes of action. Similarly, we decline to impose a duty of good faith and fair dealing on employers in light of the variety of statutes that the Legislature has already enacted to regulate employment relationships. Recognizing a new common-law cause of action based on the duty plaintiffs advocate would tend to subvert those statutory schemes by allowing employees to make an end-run around the procedural requirements and specific remedies the existing statutes establish.

Here, for instance, plaintiffs have alleged claims for discrimination and retaliation under sections 21.051 and 21.055 of the Texas Labor Code. * * * But the court of appeals determined that plaintiffs had failed to exhaust their administrative remedies as required by the Labor Code, and that therefore the trial court did not have jurisdiction over those claims. * * * Plaintiffs do not contest this determination. Rather, they ask us to excuse them from the Labor Code's administrative requirements by creating a common-law cause of action for the same actions of the City on which they based their suit under the Labor Code. We decline to do so.

In holding that there is no duty of good faith and fair dealing in the employment context, we perceive no distinction between government and private employers, inasmuch as both types of employers are subject to applicable laws, regulations, and contractual agreements. Nor do we see any meaningful basis to distinguish between employment at-will and employment governed by an express agreement. A court-created duty of good faith and fair dealing would completely alter the nature of the at-will employment relationship, which generally can be terminated by either party for any reason or no reason at all, and we accordingly decline to change the at-will nature of employment in Texas. If, as plaintiffs argue, they could only be terminated or transferred for reasons of "merit," that fact militates against imposing a common-law duty of good faith and fair dealing because such a contractual limitation would afford more rights to the plaintiffs than at-will employees possess. Moreover, such a duty would be unnecessary when there are express contractual limits on an employer's right to terminate.

Accordingly, we hold that the City of Midland was entitled to summary judgment on the plaintiffs' claims that the defendants breached a duty of good faith and fair dealing. * * *

SUMMERS, "GOOD FAITH" IN GENERAL CONTRACT LAW AND THE SALES PROVISIONS OF THE UNIFORM COMMERCIAL CODE

54 Va.L.Rev. 195, 199–202 (1968).

What is the best way to determine a judge's meaning when he uses the phrase "good faith"? In the case law taken as a whole, does the term have a single general meaning of its own, or perhaps several such meanings? (The answers to these questions are closely linked.) Sometimes what a judge means by good faith will be instantly obvious, but frequently it will not be. When not, it may be that he is using the phrase loosely. But even if he is using it with care, there may still be unclarity. He might indicate only that, in a given context, parties are to act in good faith or that a party did or did not act in good faith, without elaborating at all. Or he might elaborate without communicating in any specific way—for example, by laying down some very general definition of good faith, such as acting "honestly" or "being faithful to one's duty or obligation." The analyst of such an opinion is likely to inquire: What is the meaning of good faith itself? He seems to assume that the phrase has some general meaning or meanings, one of which the judge presumably intends.

One of the principal theses of this Article is that in cases of doubt, a lawyer will determine more accurately what the judge means by using the phrase "good faith" if he does not ask what good faith itself means, but rather asks: What in the actual or hypothetical situation, does the judge intend to rule out by his use of this phrase? Once the relevant form of bad faith is thus identified, the lawyer can, if he wishes, assign a specific meaning to good faith by formulating an "opposite" for the species of bad faith being ruled out. For example, a judge may say: "A public authority must act in good faith in letting bids." And from the facts or the language of the opinion it may appear that the judge is, in effect, saying: "The defendant acted in bad faith because he let bids only as a pretense to conceal his purpose to award the contract to a favored bidder." It can then be said that "acting in good faith" here simply means: letting bids without a preconceived design to award the contract to a favored bidder.

If good faith had a general meaning or meanings of its own—that is, if it were either univocal or unambiguous—there would seldom be occasion to derive a meaning for it from an opposite; its specific uses would almost always be readily and immediately understood. But good faith is not that kind of doctrine. In contract law, taken as a whole, good faith is an "excluder." It is a phrase without general meaning (or meanings) of its own and serves to exclude a wide range of heterogeneous forms of bad faith. In a particular context the phrase takes on specific meaning, but usually this is only by way of contrast with the specific form of bad faith actually or hypothetically ruled out. Aristotle was one of the first to recognize that the function of some words and phrases is not to convey general, "extractable" meanings of their own, but rather is to exclude one or more of a variety of things. He thought "voluntary" was such a word. And the late Professor J.L. Austin of Oxford made much of "excluders."

RESTATEMENT (SECOND) OF CONTRACTS § 205.

Duty of Good Faith and Fair Dealing

Every contract imposes upon each party a duty of good faith and fair dealing in its performance and its enforcement.

Comment:

a. *Meanings of "Good Faith."* * * * The phrase "good faith" is used in a variety of contexts, and its meaning varies somewhat with the context. Good faith performance or enforcement of a contract emphasizes faithfulness to an agreed common purpose and consistency with the justified expectations of the other party; it excludes a variety of types of conduct characterized as involving "bad faith" because they violate community standards of decency, fairness or reasonableness. The appropriate remedy for a breach of the duty of good faith also varies with the circumstances.

* * *

d. *Good faith performance.* Subterfuges and evasions violate the obligation of good faith in performance even though the actor believes his conduct to be justified. But the obligation goes further: bad faith may be overt or may consist of inaction, and fair dealing may require more than honesty. A complete catalogue of types of bad faith is impossible, but the following types are among those which have been recognized in judicial decisions: evasion of the spirit of the bargain, lack of diligence and slacking off, willful rendering of imperfect performance, abuse of a power to specify terms, and interference with or failure to cooperate in the other party's performance.

1970 PROCEEDINGS OF THE AMERICAN LAW INSTITUTE

47 A.L.I.Proc. 489–91 (1970).

R. BRAUCHER[b] * * *

I should call attention to a limitation on this. The black letter is limited, as is the section of the Commercial Code, to good faith in performance and enforcement, and is not a requirement, as stated here, of good faith in bargaining, good faith in offer and acceptance.

Now, there are some obligations of good faith and fair dealing in the making of a contract, as distinguished from performance and enforcement. I don't think you can find a case in the whole history of the common law in which a court says that good faith is not required in the performance of a contract or in enforcement of a contract.

Now, the trouble with this section, of course, is that it's very general, very abstract, and it needs specification the worst way, and specification is not to be had. * * *

* * *

Anyway, the principle is to be found in judicial opinions. I haven't invented it. It's also to be found in the Commercial Code. I think there are more judicial opinions along this line in the New York Court of Appeals and the Supreme Court of California than there are in most of the other courts. * * *

Anyway, there it is. [There was no comment]

SUMMERS, THE GENERAL DUTY OF GOOD FAITH—ITS RECOGNITION AND CONCEPTUALIZATION

67 Cornell L.Rev. 810, 823–824 (1982).

In my view, a judge in a novel case posing an issue of good faith under section 205 with its excluder conceptualization is far from lacking meaningful guidance of the kind legitimately to be demanded in the name

[b] Robert Braucher was the Reporter of the Restatement (Second) of Contracts from 1960 to 1971. From 1946 to 1971, he was a member of the Harvard Law School faculty. In 1971, he was appointed Associate Justice of the Massachusetts Supreme Judicial Court, a position he held until his death in 1981.

of the rule of law. He should start with the language of the section. Second, he should turn to the purposes of section 205 as set forth mainly in Comment a. These purposive rationales will infuse the excluder analysis with meaning in all the ways that purposive interpretation is known generally to provide guidance to judges (as in the case of statutes). Third, after completing this, he should seek guidance by the time-honored common-law method of reasoning by analogy, not only from past cases, but from the various illustrations set forth in the Comments to section 205. Such reasoning, particularly that which is done with an eye to the *reasons* given by prior judges, can provide substantial insight into how novel cases should be decided. Fourth, also in light of the purposes of section 205 and any general analogies, he can analyze the relevant facts—alleged or proven—to see what specific reasons these facts, and the values they implicate, generate for and against characterizing the action or inaction in question as bad-faith behavior. Fifth, because of the very nature of the problem, the excluder analysis is not only faithful to the reality involved, but it is itself a distinctive source of illumination. It does not focus on some presumed positive and unitary element or cluster of elements called "good faith"; instead, it focuses on whether the alleged form of bad-faith behavior really is, in the context, ruled out by section 205, when considered in light of its purposes and in relation to the facts of the case. The foregoing factors do not exhaust all the forms of guidance that section 205 provides, but they are more than sufficient to rebut the charge that a section in which good faith is conceptualized as an excluder leaves the judges at sea and the "law" merely whatever the judges say it is.

FELD V. HENRY S. LEVY & SONS, INC.

Court of Appeals of New York, 1975.
37 N.Y.2d 466, 335 N.E.2d 320.

COOKE, JUDGE.

Plaintiff operates a business known as the Crushed Toast Company and defendant is engaged in the wholesale bread baking business. They entered into a written contract, as of June 19, 1968, in which defendant agreed to sell and plaintiff to purchase "all bread crumbs produced by the Seller in its factory at 115 Thames Street, Brooklyn, New York, during the period commencing June 19, 1968, and terminating June 18, 1969", the agreement to "be deemed automatically renewed thereafter for successive renewal periods of one year" with the right to either party to cancel by giving not less than six months notice to the other by certified mail. No notice of cancellation was served. Additionally, pursuant to a contract stipulation, a faithful performance bond was delivered by plaintiff at the inception of the contractual relationship, and a bond continuation certificate was later submitted for the yearly term commencing June 19, 1969.

Interestingly, the term "bread crumbs" does not refer to crumbs that may flake off bread; rather, they are a manufactured item, starting with stale or imperfectly appearing loaves and followed by removal of labels, processing through two grinders, the second of which effects a finer granulation, insertion into a drum in an oven for toasting and, finally, bagging of the finished product.

Subsequent to the making of the agreement, a substantial quantity of bread crumbs, said to be over 250 tons, were sold by defendant to plaintiff but defendant stopped crumb production on about May 15, 1969. There was proof by defendant's comptroller that the oven was too large to accommodate the drum, that it was stated that the operation was "very uneconomical", but after said date of cessation no steps were taken to obtain more economical equipment. The toasting oven was intentionally broken down, then partially rebuilt, then completely dismantled in the summer of 1969 and, thereafter, defendant used the space for a computer room. It appears, without dispute, that defendant indicated to plaintiff at different times that the former would resume bread crumb production if the contract price of 6 cents per pound be changed to 7 cents, and also that, after the crumb making machinery was dismantled, defendant sold the raw materials used in making crumbs to animal food manufacturers.

Special Term denied plaintiff's motion for summary judgment on the issue of liability and turned down defendant's counter-request for a summary judgment of dismissal. From the Appellate Division's order of affirmance, by a divided court, both parties appeal.

Defendant contends that the contract did not require defendant to manufacture bread crumbs, but merely to sell those it did, and, since none were produced after the demise of the oven, there was no duty to then deliver and, consequently from then on, no liability on its part. Agreements to sell all the goods or services a party may produce or perform to another party are commonly referred to as "output" contracts and they usually serve a useful commercial purpose in minimizing the burdens of product marketing (see 1 Williston, Contracts [3d ed.], § 104A). The Uniform Commercial Code rejects the ideas that an output contract is lacking in mutuality or that it is unenforceable because of indefiniteness in that a quantity for the term is not specified. * * * Official Comment 2 to section 2–306 * * * states in part: "Under this Article, a contract for output * * * is not too indefinite since it is held to mean the actual good faith output * * * of the particular party. Nor does such a contract lack mutuality of obligation since, under this section, the party who will determine quantity is required to operate his plant or conduct his business in good faith and according to commercial standards of fair dealing in the trade so that his output * * * will proximate a reasonably foreseeable figure." * * *

The real issue in this case is whether the agreement carries with it an implication that defendant was obligated to continue to manufacture bread crumbs for the full term. Section 2–306 of the Uniform Commercial Code, entitled "Output, Requirements and Exclusive Dealings" provides:

> "(1) A term which measures the quantity by the output of the seller or the requirements of the buyer means such actual output or requirements as may occur in good faith, except that no quantity unreasonably disproportionate to any stated estimate or in the absence of a stated estimate to any normal or otherwise comparable prior output or requirements may be tendered or demanded.
>
> "(2) *A lawful agreement* by either the seller or the buyer *for exclusive dealing* in the kind of goods concerned *imposes* unless otherwise agreed an obligation *by the seller to use best efforts to supply the goods* and by the buyer to use best efforts to promote their sale." (Emphasis supplied.)

The Official Comment thereunder reads in part: "Subsection (2), on exclusive dealing, makes explicit the commercial rule embodied in this Act under which the parties to such contracts are held to have impliedly, even when not expressly, bound themselves to use reasonable diligence as well as good faith in their performance of the contract. * * * An exclusive dealing agreement brings into play all of the good faith aspects of the output and requirement problems of subsection (1). It also raises questions of insecurity and right to adequate assurance under this Article."

Section 2–306 is consistent with prior New York case law. * * * Every contract of this type imposes an obligation of good faith in its performance. (Uniform Commercial Code, § 1–203 [current 1–304] * * *). Under the Uniform Commercial Code, the commercial background and intent must be read into the language of any agreement and good faith is demanded in the performance of that agreement * * * and, under the decisions relating to output contracts, it is clearly the general rule that good faith cessation of production terminates any further obligations thereunder and excuses further performance by the party discontinuing production. * * *

This is not a situation where defendant ceased its main operation of bread baking. * * * Rather, defendant contends in a conclusory fashion that it was "uneconomical" or "economically not feasible" for it to continue to make bread crumbs. Although plaintiff observed in his motion papers that defendant claimed it was not economically feasible to make the crumbs, plaintiff did not admit that as a fact. In any event, "economic feasibility", an expression subject to many interpretations, would not be a precise or reliable test.

There are present here intertwined questions of fact, whether defendant performed in good faith and whether it stopped its manufacture of bread crumbs in good faith, neither of which can be resolved properly on this record. The seller's duty to remain in crumb production is a matter calling for a close scrutiny of its motives (1 Hawkland, A Transactional Guide to the Uniform Commercial Code, p. 52, see, also, p. 48), confined here by the papers to financial reasons. It is undisputed that defendant leveled its crumb making machinery only after plaintiff refused to agree to a price higher than that specified in the agreement and that it then sold the raw materials to manufacturers of animal food. There are before us no componential figures indicating the actual cost of the finished bread crumbs to defendant, statements as to the profits derived or the losses sustained, or data specifying the net or gross return realized from the animal food transactions.

The parties by their contract gave the right of cancellation to either by providing for a six months' notice to the other. The apparent purpose of such a stipulation was to provide an opportunity to either the seller or buyer to conclude their dealings in the event that the transactions were not as profitable or advantageous as desired or expected, or for any other reason. Correspondingly, such a notice would also furnish the receiver of it a chance to secure another outlet or source of supply, as the case might be. Short of such a cancellation, defendant was expected to continue to perform in good faith and could cease production of the bread crumbs, a single facet of its operation, only in good faith. Obviously, a bankruptcy or genuine imperiling of the very existence of its entire business caused by the production of the crumbs would warrant cessation of production of that item; the yield of less profit from its sale than expected would not. Since bread crumbs were but a part of defendant's enterprise and since there was a contractual right of cancellation, good faith required continued production until cancellation, even if there be no profit. In circumstances such as these and without more, defendant would be justified, in good faith, in ceasing production of the single item prior to cancellation only if its losses from continuance would be more than trivial, which, overall, is a question of fact.

The order of the Appellate Division should be affirmed, without costs.

NOTE: *GOOD FAITH IN THE UNIFORM COMMERCIAL CODE*

As we have seen, Uniform Commercial Code section 1–304 provides that "[e]very contract or duty within [the Uniform Commercial Code] imposes an obligation of good faith in its performance or enforcement." In Feld v. Henry S. Levy & Sons, Inc., however, the New York Court of Appeals invoked section 2–306, one of several sections of Article 2 of the Code (on the sale of goods) that explicitly requires good faith. Numerous sections of Article 2 include comments which also use the phrase.

Article 1 of the U.C.C. ("General Provisions") defines good faith in section 1–201(b)(20) to mean (unless the context otherwise requires) "honesty in fact and the observance of reasonable commercial standards of fair dealing in the trade." Certain other articles of the Uniform Commercial Code also incorporate the term "good faith," usually with definitions. In cases in which the Code does not apply, courts often cite by analogy the Code's general provision on good faith, section 1–304.

CENTRONICS CORP. v. GENICOM CORP., 132 N.H. 133, 562 A.2d 187 (1989).

SOUTER, JUSTICE.

Despite the variety of their fact patterns, [good faith] cases illustrate a common rule: under an agreement that appears by word or silence to invest one party with a degree of discretion in performance sufficient to deprive another party of a substantial proportion of the agreement's value, the parties' intent to be bound by an enforceable contract raises an implied obligation of good faith to observe reasonable limits in exercising that discretion, consistent with the parties' purpose or purposes in contracting. A claim for relief from a violation of the implied covenant of good faith contractual performance therefore potentially raises four questions:

> 1. Does the agreement ostensibly allow to or confer upon the defendant a degree of discretion in performance tantamount to a power to deprive the plaintiff of a substantial proportion of the agreement's value? Contracts may be broken in a multitude of ways and theories of relief are correspondingly numerous, but the concept of good faith in performance addresses the particular problem raised by a promise subject to such a degree of discretion that its practical benefit could seemingly be withheld.
>
> 2. If the ostensible discretion is of that requisite scope, does competent evidence indicate that the parties intended by their agreement to make a legally enforceable contract?
>
> 3. Assuming an intent to be bound, has the defendant's exercise of discretion exceeded the limits of reasonableness? The answer to this question depends on identifying the common purpose or purposes of the contract, against which the reasonableness of the complaining party's expectations may be measured, and in furtherance of which community standards of honesty, decency and reasonableness can be applied.
>
> 4. Is the cause of the damage complained of the defendant's abuse of discretion, or does it result from events beyond the control of either party, against which the defendant has no obligation to protect the plaintiff? Although this question is cast

in the language of causation, it may be seen simply as the other face of question three. Suffice it to say here that its point is to emphasize that the good faith requirement is not a fail-safe device barring a defendant from the fruits of every plaintiff's bad bargain, or empowering courts to rewrite an agreement even when a defendant's discretion is consistent with the agreement's legally contractual character.

HOLMES, THE PATH OF THE LAW

10 Harv.L.Rev. 457, 459–60, 462 (1897).

The first thing for a business-like understanding of [a] matter is to understand its limits, and therefore I think it desirable at once to point out and dispel a confusion between morality and law, which sometimes rises to the height of conscious theory, and more often and indeed constantly is making trouble in detail without reaching the point of consciousness. * * *

* * *

* * * If you want to know the law and nothing else, you must look at it as a bad man, who cares only for the material consequences which such knowledge enables him to predict, not as a good one, who finds his reasons for conduct, whether inside the law or outside of it, in the vaguer sanctions of conscience. The theoretical importance of the distinction is no less, if you would reason on your subject aright. The law is full of phraseology drawn from morals, and by the mere force of language continually invites us to pass from one domain to the other without perceiving it, as we are sure to do unless we have the boundary constantly before our minds. * * *

* * *

Nowhere is the confusion between legal and moral ideas more manifest than in the law of contract. Among other things, here again the so called primary rights and duties are invested with a mystic significance beyond what can be assigned and explained. The duty to keep a contract at common law means a prediction that you must pay damages if you do not keep it,—and nothing else. If you commit a tort, you are liable to pay a compensatory sum. If you commit a contract, you are liable to pay a compensatory sum unless the promised event comes to pass, and that is all the difference. But such a mode of looking at the matter stinks in the nostrils of those who think it advantageous to get as much ethics into the law as they can.

L. FULLER, THE LAW IN QUEST OF ITSELF

93–95 (1940).

It is a very convincing figure which [Holmes] offers us, and it makes a working kind of positivism seem quite plausible. Yet it is apparent that this bad man of Holmes' is himself an abstraction, in two senses.

In the first place, it will be noted that it is a peculiar sort of bad man who is worried about judicial decrees and is indifferent to extra-legal penalties, who is concerned about a fine of two dollars but apparently not about the possible loss of friends and customers. To define the law in terms of the viewpoint of one with this attitude is to some extent a begging of the question, and amounts almost to saying that the law is that which concerns one who is concerned only with the law.

In the second place, Holmes assumes that his bad man has already reached a conclusion concerning the legal risks of a particular line of conduct, and he neglects to inquire into the process by which this man would actually arrive at such a conclusion. Let us see for ourselves how this bad man, faced with a specific problem of conduct, would have to reason. He wants to know what it is likely to cost him to attain a particular objective. Because of the peculiarly juristic orientation of his fears, he will be deterred only by judicial penalties. He must ask himself, then, "What are the chances that my conduct may lead to a detrimental interference in my affairs by the courts?" To answer that, he must ask, "How will my conduct be viewed by judges?" This question he cannot answer merely by consulting the letter of the law, for he will still not know in what direction the letter will be strained in cases of doubt. Nor will it be enough for him "to know his judge." Even if the judge who will decide his case has pronounced and recognizable biases, a bias is, after all, only one factor in a complex equation, and to calculate its effects one must analyze the ethical forces with which it will come in conflict. In the end, our bad man cannot escape having to decide a question of morality. He will have to ask, "How would I myself view my conduct if I were not interested in it? How would it be viewed by a disinterested third party? Would it seem to him to be good or evil?" Only when he has answered this question will he have rounded out the equation on the basis of which he can calculate accurately the chances of judicial intervention in his affairs.

In short, our bad man, if he is effectively to look after his own interests, will have to learn to look at the law through the eyes of a good man.

CHAPTER SEVEN

CONDITIONAL NATURE OF THE DUTY TO PERFORM, AND PERMISSIBLE RESPONSES TO FAILURE OF CONDITION AND BREACH OF DUTY

■ ■ ■

Since an express condition depends for its validity on the intentions of the parties, it has the same sanctity as the promise itself.

WILLISTON

The construction of conditions protects a party against impairment of expectation.

PATTERSON

SECTION ONE: CONDITIONS AND THE ROLE OF LAWYERS

Suppose Ben Builder and Oswald Owner negotiate for the construction of a new sidewalk for Owner at a price of about $4,500. A lawyer asked to draft an agreement between Builder and Owner will try to anticipate all important sources of dispute and deal with them in the agreement. Two major sources are the order of performance and the quality of performance. Who must perform first—Builder, by constructing the sidewalk, or Owner, by paying? And of what quality must Builder's completed performance be? Must it be perfect? By what standards? The lawyer should not leave gaps in the agreement with regard to such matters. To fill the first of these gaps, the lawyer can draft what is called an express condition precedent (pronounced pre*cee*dent) requiring Builder to perform the work before Owner's duty to pay matures: "Builder's constructing the sidewalk is a condition precedent to Owner's duty to pay." Why the language "condition precedent"? The duty of Owner to pay does not *mature* until the other party, Builder in our example, has first performed. Alternatively, the lawyer might expressly condition Builder's duty to perform on Owner first paying the $4,500. Of course, if a duty to perform does not mature because of the failure of an express condition, there can be no breach of that duty.

The lawyer can also specify the quality of performance required of Builder as part of an express condition precedent, and thus fill the second gap. Suppose the parties agree that Builder must perform first and that the job must be done in accord with specific standards, e.g., that the finished concrete has no cracks in it. The lawyer can then draft an express condition precedent requiring Builder to perform by constructing all sidewalk slabs without any cracking before Owner's duty to pay arises.

In preceding chapters, we saw that contracting parties frequently do not cover all matters in their express agreement (especially when they draft without the aid of lawyers), and we addressed how courts generally fill gaps.[a] In this chapter, we consider not only how the lawyer may plan and draft express conditions to deal with order of performance, quality of performance, and related problems, but also study how courts fill gaps in agreements that are silent on these matters.

Suppose, for example, that the drafter of the Builder-Owner contract fails to specify the order of performance and the quality of performance. Under principles of interpretation and gap-filling law, can Builder require that Oswald Owner pay him the $4,500 *before* Builder starts work? Or suppose that Builder builds the sidewalk, that it consists of 48 slabs, and that a crack emerges across one side of the eleventh slab. Despite this defect, is Builder entitled to the contract price—the $4,500—less any deduction for the cost to Owner of repairing the eleventh slab? Or would Builder have to perform perfectly to mature Owner's duty to pay the contract price?

When confronted with such gaps, courts turn to resources studied in the preceding chapter. Typically they first attempt to ascertain the intentions of the parties by examining contractual language and the overall circumstances. In some cases this evidence is sufficiently clear for a court to conclude that the parties intended a particular approach to a problem. For example, a course of dealing between the parties in which Builder always performed first may be enough to justify a finding that the parties actually intended Builder to perform first in this contract. In such a case, Owner's duty to pay is said to be *impliedly-in-fact* conditional on Builder's prior performance. In other cases, less substantial evidence, such as a general trade custom that builders perform before payment, may indicate the probable intentions of the parties as to the order of performance in their contract. Recognizing that such evidence is inconclusive, a court may present its findings simply as the reasonable expectations of the parties. In still other cases, there may be no evidence of the actual or probable

[a] See Chapter One, Sections Two and Three of Chapter Four, and Section Four of Chapter Six.

intentions of Builder and Owner with respect to the order of performance. In such cases, judges must fill the gap by devising a general *rule of law* such as: “in case of a gap in the contract as to the order of performance, builders must perform first.” Here, Owner’s duty to pay is said to be *impliedly-in-law* conditional on Builder’s performance, and the gap-filling rule invoked is justified not on the basis of the probable intentions of the parties but on general policies and principles. Courts have traditionally called the term supplied by such a gap-filler rule either an implied-in-law condition precedent, or a constructive condition precedent. Again, if such a condition does not occur, the duty to perform does not mature and there can be no breach.

Sometimes it will be difficult to tell whether a court’s decision is based on evidence of intentions, on some rule of law, or on a combination of both. In this chapter we will, with some refinement, use the terminology of “implied conditions” (and occasionally, “constructive conditions”) to refer to these forms of gap-filling. As we will see, the courts have developed a variety of gap-filler rules.

We now introduce some alternative terminology that was prominent in the older cases and still creeps into some modern opinions in which courts fill gaps with respect to the order of performance and the quality of performance. When a court holds that the performance of a promise is an implied condition precedent to the other party’s duty to perform—for example, suppose a court holds that Builder’s building of the sidewalk is a condition precedent to Owner’s duty to pay—the court might also refer to Owner’s duty as a “dependent covenant” and Builder’s duty as an “independent covenant.” The covenant to pay—Owner’s promise—is not to be performed in our example unless and until Builder performs. Hence Owner’s promise is “dependent” on Builder’s prior performance. On the other hand, the duty of Builder to build falls due prior to and thus “independently” of the owner’s duty to pay. Builder’s covenant is therefore an “independent” covenant. (As we will later see, however, circumstances may arise that excuse Builder from performing or tendering performance in light of the Owner’s circumstances, such as insolvency or a threat not to pay, so that Builder’s “prior” duty under his promise is not totally “independent” of the owner’s prospective performance or nonperformance.)

The leading common law case introducing the doctrine of implied conditions precedent (“dependency of covenants”) was the famous House of Lords decision in Kingston v. Preston, 2 Douglas 689 (1773). In that case, Lord Mansfield, confronted with a gap in an agreement as to the order of performance, chose to fill the gap in light of “the evident sense and meaning of the parties.” By this criterion, and if the agreement is otherwise silent, does it follow in our example that Builder is required to build before becoming entitled to payment from Owner? What further criteria are relevant here? Do the equities between the parties ever suggest an order of performance the court should adopt? Does custom? Does sound risk allocation? We return to these questions.

Let us consider further the second basic gap in our agreement between Builder and Owner, the "quality of performance" gap. Assume the agreement simply required the construction of a "48 slab sidewalk." What if Builder satisfactorily constructed 47 of 48 sidewalk slabs, but the eleventh one was cracked? By performing so substantially, would Builder have matured Owner's duty to pay the $4,500 contract price (less costs of repairing the cracked one), or would Builder have to perform *perfectly* in order to mature Owner's duty to pay the contract price? Again, a court will initially examine evidence of the actual or probable intentions of the parties and, if this evidence is sufficient, imply (in fact) the appropriate condition with respect to quality of performance. But here, too, the evidence may not be sufficient. In that event, the court must turn to gap-filler rules of law, i.e. implied-in-law conditions. These rules are not the same for all settings, however. In the construction setting, assuming a gap as to the quality of performance, a builder typically must "substantially perform" in order to satisfy an implied-in-law condition precedent to the owner's duty to pay. Would 47 good slabs and one cracked one constitute substantial performance? We treat this issue in detail later.

We have now introduced the problem of whether a contracting party's duty to perform has *matured* under an agreement. Suppose a duty to perform has not matured—e.g., suppose that Builder's constructing the sidewalk is a condition precedent to Owner's duty to pay and that Builder does not perform—at what point is Owner *discharged* from the agreement? Obviously Owner does not have to wait forever for Builder to perform. But can Owner bar Builder from performing and immediately hire someone else? Contract law's answer is that a party is discharged when it is "too late" for the condition to occur. This time may be stated expressly in the agreement or it may be implied from the circumstances. We consider this problem in detail in Section Nine of the present chapter.

SECTION TWO: SPECIFIC USES OF EXPRESS CONDITIONS AND THEIR OPERATION AND EFFECT

In Section One, we considered how parties, through their lawyers, might incorporate express conditions in their agreement as to order of performance and quality of performance, and thereby fill such gaps. The parties might use express conditions in further related ways, too. Compare the following examples:

(1) Ben Builder promises to construct a sidewalk during the month of October for Oswald Owner in accord with attached

plans. Oswald Owner promises to pay $4,500 for the sidewalk on condition that Builder construct the sidewalk.

(2) Ben Builder promises to construct a sidewalk during the month of October for Oswald Owner in accord with attached plans. Oswald Owner promises to pay $4,500 for the sidewalk on condition that Alice Taub, Architect, is satisfied that the sidewalk was built as agreed and has issued a certificate to Builder to that effect.

(3) Ben Builder promises to construct a sidewalk during the month of October for Oswald Owner in accord with attached plans on condition that weather conditions are satisfactory to Builder. Oswald Owner promises to pay $4,500 for the sidewalk.

(4) Oswald Owner promises to pay $4,500 to Builder on condition that Ben Builder constructs a sidewalk during the month of October in accord with attached plans.

In the first example, the subject matter of the express condition (the construction) is also the principal consideration moving to Owner. But in the second example, Owner is not bargaining principally for Builder's securing the certificate from the architect. Rather, Owner is bargaining principally for the construction of a sidewalk. (Of course, the subject matter of the express condition—the architect's approval and issuance of a certificate—is an event that signifies that the constructed sidewalk is of the quality Owner desires.) In the third example, the subject matter of the express condition (satisfactory weather) is again not the performance of a promise constituting one side of an agreed exchange. Rather, the subject matter is a qualification on the duty of one of the promisors to perform—if the weather is bad, Builder's duty to perform does not mature.

The fourth example *is* like the first because the subject matter of the condition—Builder's construction of the sidewalk—is the principal consideration that the other party, Owner, will receive. But there is this important difference. In the first example, the event of constructing the sidewalk is an express condition precedent to the duty of Owner to pay. In addition, Builder promises to construct the sidewalk. Builder makes no such promise in the fourth example. The subject matter of a condition precedent does not have to be a return promise. See also the third example, where the builder does not promise good weather. Such *non-promissory or pure conditions* are not uncommon. In the typical insurance contract, for example, the party who buys insurance coverage does not promise to pay the premium, but the contract makes the event of premium payment one of the conditions precedent to the insurer's duty to pay any insured loss that materializes.

Parties extract *promises* to bind the other party to a legal obligation. But why would a party want to make an event an *express condition* of that party's duty to perform a promise? The Restatement (Second) of Contracts' Introductory Note to Conditions and Similar Events, contains the following two possible explanations: "An obligor may make an event a condition of his duty in order to shift to the obligee the risk of its non-occurrence. * * * An obligor may also make an event a condition of his duty in order to induce the obligee to cause the event to occur." Which of these explanations accounts for the use of the express condition in our insurance example? Which accounts for the use of an express condition in each of the above four examples? Can you think of any other possible explanations for the use of express conditions?

Of course, as in example one, a contracting party such as Owner may choose *both* to make an event a condition of his own duty *and* to have the other party promise to bring the event about. The late Professor Corbin called an event that is both a condition and a promise a *promissory condition.*

It should be evident from what we have said so far that the lawyer must be able to differentiate between (1) an event that is merely promised by a party, (2) an event that is both promised by a party and designated as an express condition to the other party's duty—a promissory condition, and (3) an event that is merely an express condition to one party's duty—a non-promissory or pure condition. Thus, it is essential to understand the differences between a promise and an express condition. Professor Corbin once concisely summarized these differences:

CORBIN, CONDITIONS IN THE LAW OF CONTRACT

28 Yale L.J. 739, 743, 745–46 (1919).

The word "condition" is used in the law of property as well as in the law of contract and it is used with some variation in meaning. In the law of contract it is sometimes used in a very loose sense as synonymous with "term," "provision," or "clause." In such a sense it performs no useful service. * * * In its proper sense the word *"condition" means some operative fact subsequent to acceptance and prior to discharge,* a fact upon which the rights and duties of the parties depend. Such a fact may be an act of one of the two contracting parties, an act of a third party, or any other fact of our physical world. It may be a performance that has been promised or a fact as to which there is no promise.

* * *

A promise is always made by the act or acts of one of the parties, such acts being words or other conduct expressing intention; a fact can be made to operate as a condition only by the agreement of both parties or by the construction of the law. The purpose of a promise is the creation of a duty or a disability in the promisor; the purpose of constituting some fact as a condition is always the postponement of an instant duty (or other specified legal relation). The fulfilment of a promise discharges a duty; the occurrence of a condition creates a duty. The non-fulfilment of a promise is called a breach of contract, and creates in the other party a * * * right to damages; it is the failure to perform that which was required by a previous duty. The non-occurrence of a condition will prevent the existence of a duty in the other party; but it may not create any [right to recover damages] at all, and it *will* not unless someone has promised that it shall occur.

* * *

It may be observed that both a promise and a condition are means that are used to bring about certain desired action by another person. For example, an insurance company desires the payment of premiums. One means of securing this desired object would be to obtain a promise by the insured to pay premiums; on failure to pay them an action would lie. In fact, however, insurance policies seldom contain such a promise; the payment of the premiums is secured in a more effective way than that. The insurance company makes its own duty to pay the amount of the policy expressly conditional upon the payment of premiums. Here is no express promise of the insured creating a duty to pay premiums, but there is an express condition precedent to his right to recover on the policy. Payment by the insured is obtained not by holding a lawsuit over him *in terrorem* but by hanging before him a purse of money to be reached only by climbing the ladder of premiums. Before bilateral contracts became enforceable this was the only contractual way for a promisor to secure his desired object.

MERRITT HILL VINEYARDS INC. V. WINDY HEIGHTS VINEYARD, INC.

Court of Appeals of New York, 1984.
61 N.Y.2d 106, 460 N.E.2d 1077.

KAYE, JUDGE.

In a contract for the sale of a controlling stock interest in a vineyard, the seller's undertaking to produce a title insurance policy and mortgage confirmation at closing constituted a condition and not a promise, the breach of which excused the buyer's performance and entitled it to the return of its deposit, but not to consequential damages. On the buyer's motion for summary judgment seeking recovery of both the deposit and consequential damages, the Appellate Division 94 A.D.2d 947, 463 N.Y.S.2d 960, correctly awarded summary judgment to the buyer for its deposit and to the seller dismissing the cause of action for consequential damages, even though the seller had not sought this relief by cross appeal.

In September, 1981, plaintiff, Merritt Hill Vineyards, entered into a written agreement with defendants, Windy Heights Vineyard and its sole shareholder Leon Taylor, to purchase a majority stock interest in respondents' Yates County vineyard, and tendered a $15,000 deposit. The agreement provides that "[i]f the sale contemplated hereby does not close, Taylor shall retain the deposit as liquidated damages unless Taylor or Windy Heights failed to satisfy the conditions specified in Section 3 thereof." Section 3, in turn, lists several "conditions precedent" to which the obligation of purchaser to pay the purchase price and to complete the purchase is subject. Among the conditions are that, by the time of the closing, Windy Heights shall have obtained a title insurance policy in a form satisfactory to Merritt Hill, and Windy Heights and Merritt Hill shall have received confirmation from the Farmers Home Administration that certain mortgages on the vineyard are in effect and that the proposed sale does not constitute a default.

In April, 1982, at the closing, plaintiff discovered that neither the policy nor the confirmation had been issued. Plaintiff thereupon refused to close and demanded return of its deposit. When defendants did not return the deposit, plaintiff instituted this action, asserting two causes of action, one for return of the deposit, and one for approximately $26,000 in consequential damages allegedly suffered as a result of defendants' failure to perform.

Special Term denied plaintiff's motion for summary judgment on both causes of action. The Appellate Division unanimously reversed Special Term's order, granted plaintiff's motion for summary judgment as to the cause of action for return of the deposit, and upon searching the record pursuant to CPLR 3212 (subd. [b]), granted summary judgment in favor of defendants, dismissing plaintiff's second cause of action for consequential damages. Both plaintiff and defendants appealed from that decision. * * *

* * *

On the merits, plaintiff's right to return of its deposit or to consequential damages depends upon whether the undertaking to produce the policy and mortgage confirmation is a promise or a condition.

A promise is "a manifestation of intention to act or refrain from acting in a specified way, so made as to justify a promisee in understanding that a commitment has been made." (Restatement, Contracts 2d, § 2, subd. [1].) A *condition,* by comparison, is "an event, not certain to occur, which must occur, unless its non-occurrence is excused, before performance under a contract becomes due." (Restatement, Contracts 2d, § 224.) Here, the contract requirements of a title insurance policy and mortgage confirmation are expressed as conditions of plaintiff's performance rather than as promises by defendants. The requirements are contained in a section of the agreement entitled "Conditions Precedent to Purchaser's Obligation to Close," which provides that plaintiff's obligation to pay the purchase price and complete the purchase of the vineyard is "subject to" fulfillment of those requirements. No words of promise are employed.

Defendants' agreement to sell the stock of the vineyard, not those conditions, was the promise by defendants for which plaintiff's promise to pay the purchase price was exchanged.

Defendants' failure to fulfill the conditions of section 3 entitles plaintiff to a return of its deposit but not to consequential damages. While a contracting party's failure to fulfill a condition excuses performance by the other party whose performance is so conditioned, it is not, without an independent promise to perform the condition, a breach of contract subjecting the nonfulfilling party to liability for damages (Restatement, Contracts 2d, § 225, subds. [1], [3]; 3A Corbin, Contracts, § 663; 5 Williston, Contracts [Jaeger–3d ed.], § 665). This is in accord with the parties' expressed intent, for section 1 of their agreement provides that if defendants fail to satisfy the conditions of section 3 plaintiff's deposit will be returned. It does not provide for payment of damages.

On the merits of this case the Appellate Division thus correctly determined that plaintiff was entitled to the return of its deposit but not to consequential damages.

Accordingly, the order of the Appellate Division should be affirmed.

JACOB & YOUNGS, INC. V. KENT

Court of Appeals of New York, 1921.
230 N.Y. 239, 129 N.E. 889.

CARDOZO, J.

The plaintiff built a country residence for the defendant at a cost of upwards of $77,000, and now sues to recover a balance of $3,483.46, remaining unpaid. The work of construction ceased in June, 1914, and the defendant then began to occupy the dwelling. There was no complaint of defective performance until March, 1915. One of the specifications for the plumbing work provides that—

"All wrought-iron pipe must be well galvanized, lap welded pipe of the grade known as 'standard pipe' of Reading manufacture."

The defendant learned in March, 1915, that some of the pipe, instead of being made in Reading, was the product of other factories. The plaintiff was accordingly directed by the architect to do the work anew. The plumbing was then encased within the walls except in a few places where it had to be exposed. Obedience to the order meant more than the substitution of other pipe. It meant the demolition at great expense of substantial parts of the completed structure. The plaintiff left the work untouched, and asked for a certificate that the final payment was due. Refusal of the certificate was followed by this suit.

The evidence sustains a finding that the omission of the prescribed brand of pipe was neither fraudulent nor willful. It was the result of the oversight and inattention of the plaintiff's subcontractor. Reading pipe is distinguished from Cohoes pipe and other brands only by the name of the manufacturer stamped upon it at intervals of between six and seven feet. Even the defendant's architect, though he inspected the pipe upon arrival, failed to notice the discrepancy. The plaintiff tried to show that the brands installed, though made by other manufacturers, were the same in quality, in appearance, in market value, and in cost as the brand stated in the contract—that they were, indeed, the same thing, though manufactured in another place. The evidence was excluded, and a verdict directed for the defendant. The Appellate Division reversed, and granted a new trial.

We think the evidence, if admitted, would have supplied some basis for the inference that the defect was insignificant in its relation to the project. The courts never say that one who makes a contract fills the measure of his duty by less than full performance. They do say, however, that an omission, both trivial and innocent, will sometimes be atoned for by allowance of the resulting damage, and will not always be the breach of a condition to be followed by a forfeiture. * * * The distinction is akin to that between dependent and independent promises, or between promises and conditions. Anson on Contracts (Corbin's Ed.) § 367; 2 Williston on Contracts, § 842. Some promises are so plainly independent that they can never by fair construction be conditions of one another. Rosenthal Paper Co. v. Nat. Folding Box & Paper Co., 226 N.Y. 313, 123 N.E. 766; Bogardus v. N.Y. Life Ins. Co., 101 N.Y. 328, 4 N.E. 522. Others are so plainly dependent that they must always be conditions. Others, though dependent and thus conditions when there is departure in point of substance, will be viewed as independent and collateral when the departure is insignificant. * * * Considerations partly of justice and partly of presumable intention are to tell us whether this or that promise shall be placed in one class or in another. The simple and the uniform will call for different remedies from the multifarious and the intricate. The margin of departure within the range of normal expectation upon a sale of common chattels will vary from the margin to be expected upon a contract for the construction of a mansion or a "skyscraper." There will be harshness sometimes and oppression in the implication of a condition when the thing upon which labor has been expended is incapable of surrender because united to the land, and equity and reason in the implication of a like condition when the subject-matter, if defective, is in shape to be returned. From the conclusion that promises may not be treated as dependent to the extent of their uttermost minutiae without a sacrifice of justice, the progress is a short one to the conclusion that they may not be so treated without a perversion of intention. Intention not otherwise revealed may be presumed to hold in contemplation the reasonable and probable. If something else is in view, it must not be left to implication. There will be no assumption of a purpose to visit venial faults with oppressive retribution.

Those who think more of symmetry and logic in the development of legal rules than of practical adaptation to the attainment of a just result will be troubled by a classification where the lines of division are so wavering and blurred. Something, doubtless, may be said on the score of consistency and certainty in favor of a stricter standard. The courts have balanced such considerations against those of equity and fairness, and found the latter to be the weightier. The decisions in this state commit us to the liberal view, which is making its way, nowadays, in jurisdictions slow to welcome it. Dakin & Co. v. Lee, 1916, 1 K.B. 566, 579. Where the line is to be drawn between the important and the trivial cannot be settled by a formula. "In the nature of the case precise boundaries are impossible." 2 Williston on Contracts, § 841. The same omission may take on one aspect or another according to its setting. Substitution of equivalents may not have the same significance in fields of art on the one side and in those of mere utility on the other. Nowhere will change be tolerated, however, if it is so dominant or pervasive as in any real or substantial measure to frustrate the purpose of the contract. Crouch v. Gutmann, 134 N.Y. 45, 51, 31 N.E. 271, 30 Am.St.Rep. 608. There is no general license to install whatever, in the builder's judgment, may be regarded as "just as good." Easthampton L. & C. Co., Ltd. v. Worthington, 186 N.Y. 407, 412, 79 N.E. 323. The question is one of degree, to be answered, if there is doubt, by the triers of the facts (Crouch v. Gutmann; * * * supra), and, if the inferences are certain, by the judges of the law (Easthampton L. & C. Co., Ltd. v. Worthington, supra). We must weigh the purpose to be served, the desire to be gratified, the excuse for deviation from the letter, the cruelty of enforced adherence. Then only can we tell whether literal fulfillment is to be implied by law as a condition. This is not to say that the parties are not free by apt and certain words to effectuate a purpose that performance of every term shall be a condition of recovery. That question is not here. This is merely to say that the law will be slow to impute the purpose, in the silence of the parties, where the significance of the default is grievously out of proportion to the oppression of the forfeiture. The willful transgressor must accept the penalty of his transgression. Schultze v. Goodstein, 180 N.Y. 248, 251, 73 N.E. 21; Desmond-Dunne Co. v. Friedman-Doscher Co., 162 N.Y. 486, 490, 56 N.E. 995. For him there is no occasion to mitigate the rigor of implied conditions. The transgressor whose default is unintentional and trivial may hope for mercy if he will offer atonement for his wrong. * * *

In the circumstances of this case, we think the measure of the allowance is not the cost of replacement, which would be great, but the difference in value, which would be either nominal or nothing. Some of the exposed sections might perhaps have been replaced at moderate expense. The defendant did not limit his demand to them, but treated the plumbing as a unit to be corrected from cellar to roof. In point of fact, the plaintiff never reached the stage at which evidence of the extent of the allowance became necessary. The trial court had excluded evidence that the defect was unsubstantial, and in view of that ruling there was no occasion for the plaintiff to go farther with an offer of proof. We think, however, that the offer, if it had been made, would not of necessity have been defective because directed to difference in value. It is true that in most cases the cost of replacement is the measure. * * * The owner is entitled to the money which will permit him to complete, unless the cost of completion is grossly and unfairly out of proportion to the good to be attained. When that is true, the measure is the difference in value. Specifications call, let us say, for a foundation built of granite quarried in Vermont. On the completion of the building, the owner learns that through the blunder of a subcontractor part of the foundation has been built of granite of the same quality quarried in New Hampshire. The measure of allowance is not the cost of reconstruction. * * * The rule that gives a remedy in cases of substantial performance with compensation for defects of trivial or inappreciable importance has been developed by the courts as an instrument of justice. The measure of the allowance must be shaped to the same end.

The order should be affirmed, and judgment absolute directed in favor of the plaintiff upon the stipulation, with costs in all courts.

MCLAUGHLIN, J. I dissent. The plaintiff did not perform its contract. Its failure to do so was either intentional or due to gross neglect which, under the uncontradicted facts, amounted to the same thing, nor did it make any proof of the cost of compliance, where compliance was possible.

Under its contract it obligated itself to use in the plumbing only pipe (between 2,000 and 2,500 feet) made by the Reading Manufacturing Company. The first pipe delivered was about 1,000 feet and the plaintiff's superintendent then called the attention of the foreman of the subcontractor, who was doing the plumbing, to the fact that the specifications annexed to the contract required all pipe used in the plumbing to be of the Reading Manufacturing Company. They then examined it for the purpose of ascertaining whether this delivery was of that manufacture and found it was. Thereafter, as pipe was required in the progress of the work, the foreman of the subcontractor would leave word at its shop that he wanted a specified number of feet of pipe, without in any way indicating of what manufacture. Pipe would thereafter be delivered and installed in the building, without any examination whatever. Indeed, no examination, so far as appears, was made by the plaintiff, the subcontractor, defendant's architect, or any one else, of any of the pipe except the first delivery, until after the building had been completed. Plaintiff's architect then refused to give the certificate of completion, upon which the final payment depended, because all of the pipe used in the plumbing was not of the kind called for by the contract. After such refusal, the subcontractor removed the covering or insulation from about 900 feet of pipe which was exposed in the basement, cellar, and attic, and all but 70 feet was found to have been manufactured, not by the Reading Company, but by other manufacturers, some by the Cohoes Rolling Mill Company, some by the National Steel Works, some by the South Chester Tubing Company, and some which bore no manufacturer's mark at all. The balance of the pipe had been so installed in the building that an inspection of it could not be had without demolishing, in part at least, the building itself.

I am of the opinion the trial court was right in directing a verdict for the defendant. The plaintiff agreed that all the pipe used should be of the Reading Manufacturing Company. Only about two-fifths of it, so far as appears, was of that kind. If more were used, then the burden of proving that fact was upon the plaintiff, which it could easily have done, since it knew where the pipe was obtained. The question of substantial performance of a contract of the character of the one under consideration depends in no small degree upon the good faith of the contractor. If the plaintiff had intended to, and had, complied with the terms of the contract except as to minor omissions, due to inadvertence, then he might be allowed to recover the contract price, less the amount necessary to fully compensate the defendant for damages caused by such omissions. Woodward v. Fuller, 80 N.Y. 312; Nolan v. Whitney, 88 N.Y. 648. But that is not this case. It installed between 2,000 and 2,500 feet of pipe, of which only 1,000 feet at most complied with the contract. No explanation was given why pipe called for by the contract was not used, nor that any effort made to show what it would cost to remove the pipe of other manufacturers and install that of the Reading Manufacturing Company. The defendant had a right to contract for what he wanted. He had a right before making payment to get what the contract called for. It is no answer to this suggestion to say that the pipe put in was just as good as that made by the Reading Manufacturing Company, or that the difference in value between such pipe and the pipe made by the Reading Manufacturing Company would be either "nominal or nothing." Defendant contracted for pipe made by the Reading Manufacturing Company. What his reason was for requiring this kind of pipe is of no importance. He wanted that and was entitled to it. It may have been a mere whim on his part, but even so, he had a right to this kind of pipe, regardless of whether some other kind, according to the opinion of the contractor or experts, would have been "just as good, better, or done just as well." He agreed to pay only upon condition that the pipe installed were made by that company and he ought not to be compelled to pay unless that condition be performed. * * * The rule, therefore, of substantial performance, with damages for unsubstantial omissions, has no application. * * *

* * *

I am of the opinion the trial court did not err in ruling on the admission of evidence or in directing a verdict for the defendant.

For the foregoing reasons I think the judgment of the Appellate Division should be reversed and the judgment of the Trial Term affirmed.

HISCOCK, C.J., and HOGAN and CRANE, JJ., concur with CARDOZO, J.

POUND and ANDREWS, JJ., concur with MCLAUGHLIN, J.

Order affirmed, etc.

NOTE:
TWO COMMENTS ON JACOB & YOUNG

Jacob & Youngs, Inc. is a famous and important contracts case. According to J. Dawson, W. Harvey, and S. Henderson, Cases and Comment on Contracts 816–17 (4th ed. 1982), the record showed that the contract contained the following provision: "Any work furnished by the Contractor, the material or workmanship of which is defective or which is not fully in accordance with the drawings and specifications, in every respect, will be rejected and is to be immediately torn down, removed and remade or replaced in accordance with the drawings and specifications, whenever discovered." Further, Danzig and Watson report that another provision stated that "[w]here any particular brand of manufactured article is specified, it is to be considered as a standard." According to the provision, the plaintiff contractor had to obtain written approval of the architect before using a substitute. R. Danzig & G. Watson, The Capability Problem in Contract Law 99 (2004). Moreover, an original ad for Reading Pipe, unearthed by law professor John Newman, stated that "So that neither paint nor time will erase its identity we cut a band of spiral knurling upon every length of Reading Genuine Wrought Iron Pipe. It protects you against error or substitution and authenticates the installation forever after."

Two excerpts on the case follow. The first questions whether the owner should be required to pay for other than Reading pipe. The second focuses on the ambiguity in the idea of a willful breach. It compares Jacob & Youngs with the Peevyhouse case (see Chapter Three).

ATIYAH, BOOK REVIEW OF C. FRIED, CONTRACT AS PROMISE

95 Harv.L.Rev. 509, 522–23 (1981).

Consider the * * * case of *Jacob & Youngs v. Kent,* the Reading pipes case. Fried stigmatizes as "absurd" the owner's claim that he could keep the house without paying for it * * *. Even at the height of classical times, some might have agreed with Fried, though there is certainly evidence that others, including Baron Bramwell, would not. Faced with such a case, Bramwell might well have argued that he had no means of knowing whether the house as built was worth its price, or worth anything, to the owner. The defendant has decided what the house is worth with the Reading pipes. The court has no power to force him to pay for a house with different pipes. To do so would be to show disrespect for the defendant's autonomy, his free choice. I do not see anything illogical or absurd about such an argument. If it would seem unreasonable to most people today, that is surely because we no longer have quite the same respect for individual autonomy and free choice. We are prepared to overrule the owner's defense in such a case because we feel that the loss to the plaintiff would be too great, and we are prepared to judge for ourselves (through our courts) whether the change in pipes has in fact diminished the value of the house.

CRASWELL, WHEN IS A WILLFUL BREACH "WILLFUL"? THE LINK BETWEEN DEFINITIONS AND DAMAGES

107 Mich. L. Rev. 1501, 1502–03 (2009).

[C]onsider two staples of the contracts curriculum: Jacob & Youngs, Inc. v. Kent, and Peevyhouse v. Garland Coal & Mining Co. In Kent, a builder promised to use a particular brand of pipe to build a house; in Peevyhouse, a mining company promised to make certain repairs to the land after they finished mining the coal. The builder in Kent used the wrong brand of pipe, apparently by accident; but the mining company in Peevyhouse decided the promised repairs would cost too much, so it simply refused to make the repairs. Described in this way, Peevyhouse sounds deliberate or willful, while the breach in Kent sounds accidental.

However, Kent can be characterized as a willful breach if we focus on other events in the sequence. After all, as soon as the builder discovered his mistake, he could have torn the house down and started over, this time using the right brand of pipe. (Much of the pipe was in the interior walls and foundations, and so could not be replaced without demolishing the house.) The builder chose not to do this, for demolishing the house would have been extremely expensive, but there is no question that this choice—the choice not to demolish the house—was deliberate. Thus, if the intentionality of this part of the sequence is what matters, Kent must be classified with Peevyhouse as a deliberate or willful breach. Granted, we can avoid this characterization of Kent if we focus instead on the builder's earlier, unintentional mistake about what brand of pipe was being installed. But why should the intentionality of that event control our characterization of the breach, rather than the intentionality of the subsequent decision not to tear down the house and start over?

PROBLEM 7-1

You represent the defendant owner in Jacob & Youngs, Inc. v. Kent at the planning and drafting stage. Draft an express condition precedent that would have precluded the maturation of your client's duty to make the final payment on the contract price if the contractor failed to install Reading pipe.

BROWN-MARX ASSOCIATES, LTD. V. EMIGRANT SAVINGS BANK

United States Court of Appeals, Eleventh Circuit, 1983.
703 F.2d 1361.

GODBOLD, CHIEF JUDGE.

This diversity case concerns a dispute between a prospective borrower and a bank over a $1.1 million loan commitment for financing an office building. Emigrant Savings Bank refused to lend the money, maintaining among other things that Brown-Marx Associates, the would-be borrower, had failed to satisfy the minimum rental requirement of the commitment. Brown-Marx sued the bank alleging breach of contract and various tort theories of recovery. The matter was tried to a jury which found for Brown-Marx on its contract claim [and awarded $543,000 damages]. The district court granted the bank's motion for new trial, primarily on the ground it had erroneously instructed the jury on the applicable law. Later the court granted summary judgment for the bank on all claims. We affirm.

I. BACKGROUND

a. *The Initial Dealings*

Brown-Marx is an Alabama limited partnership with Gary Smith its sole general partner. Smith formed the partnership to purchase and renovate an office building in Birmingham. In May 1978 Brown-Marx obtained a loan commitment for permanent financing of the building from Emigrant Savings Bank of New York. Brown-Marx paid the bank $22,000 for the commitment, which was to expire May 1, 1979. Later Brown-Marx paid the bank $11,000 to extend the commitment to November 1, 1979.

Under the commitment the bank agreed to lend Brown-Marx $1.1 million, the "ceiling loan," if Brown-Marx provided satisfactory documentation of renovations, signed leases providing for at least $714,447 annual rentals, and a satisfactory appraisal that the building was worth at least $2.4 million. The commitment provided in the alternative for a "floor loan" of $750,000 if the major requirements for the ceiling loan were not met. The provisions for the alternative loans, floor or ceiling, are at the heart of the dispute:

> The Bank has agreed to lend the sum of $1,100,000 secured by a permanent mortgage on the * * * [building].
>
> * * *
>
> 2. Loan to close upon the following conditions being satisfactorily complied with:
>
> a. Exhibition of all required government certificates, permits, licenses, etc.

> b. [Details of renovation to be done "in a workmanlike manner satisfactory to the Bank."]
>
> c. Exhibition of signed leases for a term of not less than one year covering not more than 140,449 net rentable square feet at a rental of not less than $714,447 per annum and the space rented is rented on a basis so that if the building were 100% rented, the annual rentroll would be at least $840,526. Said rentals to be on an unfurnished basis without any concessions or offsets thereto. Leases to be approved by the Bank and assigned to the Bank.
>
> * * *
>
> It is also understood and agreed that in the event that condition 2.a. is met, but conditions 2.b. and c. are not, the loan shall be in the amount of $750,000 * * *.

The loan, whether ceiling or floor amount, was to be secured by a first mortgage on the building.

On the strength of this commitment Brown-Marx obtained from two Alabama banks $1.1 million interim financing to purchase and renovate the building, to be repaid from the proceeds of the permanent loan from Emigrant. Brown-Marx bought the building, renovated it, and proceeded to lease space in it.

* * *

II. THE CEILING LOAN: SUBSTANTIAL VS. PERFECT COMPLIANCE

The loan commitment imposed several conditions on the $1.1 million ceiling loan. Among these was the requirement in paragraph 2.c. for "[e]xhibition of signed leases for a term of not less than one year covering not more than 140,449 net rentable square feet at a rental of not less than $714,447 per annum * * * ". The main reason the bank gave for not making the ceiling loan was that Brown-Marx did not meet the $714,447 minimum annual rental requirement.

The trial judge submitted the breach of contract claim to the jury with an instruction that plaintiffs had the burden to prove by a preponderance of the evidence "that they had substantially performed all of the ultimately agreed upon conditions precedent to the ceiling loan." The court granted a new trial, concluding that this instruction was erroneous because substantial compliance was not applicable to the minimum annual rental clause in the commitment and Brown-Marx was, therefore, required to comply fully with the minimum annual rental requirement. Later the court granted the bank's motion for summary judgment with respect to the ceiling loan, finding there was no genuine issue of material fact as to whether Brown-Marx had failed to satisfy the minimum annual rental requirement.

There is no dispute in material facts concerning Brown-Marx's failure to comply fully with the minimum rental requirement, even when the leases brought to New York on closing day are considered. Five of the leases submitted were month-to-month leases rather than for a term of at least a year. Two leases covered space that was not in the building. Another had never been executed, and the supposed tenant had neither paid rent nor occupied the space. The rental amount on one lease was overstated. There was a shortfall in the dollar amount of annual rental. While there was considerable dispute about the size of the deficiency,[1] Brown-Marx does not contend that annual rentals were as much as $714,447, but rather that substantial compliance with the minimum rental provision was adequate. There is a paucity of Alabama case law on this subject. Alabama has applied the substantial performance doctrine in only one situation outside the field of construction contracts and then on facts that it found were analogous to a building contract situation. *See* discussion of *Bruner v. Hines,* 295 Ala. 111, 324 So.2d 265 (Ala.1975), below. We conclude that the Alabama courts would hold that substantial performance does not apply to the minimum required rental provision of the loan commitment.

Courts have usually treated the terms and conditions of a loan commitment as conditions precedent to the lender's obligation to perform. * * * The loan commitment fee is paid for the privilege of later borrowing the money if the conditions are met. The language of the loan commitment here expressly provides that compliance with the minimum annual rentals provisions is a "condition" to receiving the loan. Concerning such an express condition, 5 *Williston on Contracts* (Third Edition), Section 675, states:

> As a general rule, conditions which are either expressed or implied in fact must be exactly fulfilled or no liability can arise on the promise which such conditions qualify.

Id. at 184.

The substantial performance doctrine provides that where a contract is made for an agreed exchange of two performances, one of which is to be rendered first, substantial performance rather than exact, strict or literal performance by the first party of the terms of the contract is adequate to entitle the party to recover on it. The intent of the doctrine is equitable: to prevent unjust enrichment or the inequity of one party's getting the benefit of performance, albeit not strictly in accord with the contract's terms, with no obligation in return. The courts will allow recovery under the contract, less allowance for deviations, where a party in good faith has substantially performed its obligation. *See generally,* 3A *Corbin on Contracts,* Sections

[1] Brown-Marx, conceding that some leases were properly excludable from the tally, maintained below that annual rentals were $713,526. The bank calculated them as $700,826; the district court concluded that at most they were $706,176.

700–701; 6 *Williston on Contracts* (Third Edition), Section 842. The doctrine is widely applied to building contracts, though not always limited to them.

The doctrine is not primarily concerned with substantial performance of a "condition" but rather with substantial performance by one party of his obligations arising out of the agreed exchange under the contract. Its object is to prevent forfeiture of work, labor and materials supplied by the substantially performing party. Its application is illustrated in terms of construction contracts in 3A *Corbin on Contracts,* Section 701:

> [I]t is not with express conditions or interpretation that we are now primarily concerned. We are now dealing with a contract that consists of two exchanged promises requiring the rendition of two promised performances, without making either promise expressly conditional on anything. The builder promises to build and the owner promises to pay.
>
> * * *
>
> It is substantial performance of what the builder promised to do, of the construction work, of the equivalent for which the owner has promised to pay, that is the "condition" of the owner's duty to pay. It is not substantial performance of "a condition" that must be rendered; "substantial performance" *is* the condition—the fact that must exist before payment is due.

Id. at 314.

Under the Restatement of Contracts the loan commitment would be termed an "option contract" with Brown-Marx's performance being "acceptance" of the offer to lend money. Despite equity's dislike of forfeiture, the requirements of an option contract governing the manner of acceptance are strictly applied. *See* 1 *Restatement Second of Contracts* Section 2[5] and comment d.

* * *

Bruner v. Hines, 295 Ala. 111, 324 So.2d 265 (Ala.1975), is the only Alabama decision we have found that has applied substantial performance outside the field of construction contracts. In *Bruner* a sales contract included a "rough plat" drawn by the buyer describing the land to be sold, in which the road frontage of land was estimated at 366 feet based on a steel tape measurement, and the land was to contain 15 acres. The final survey showed 15.1 acres with 376.5 feet of road frontage. The buyer offered the seller $500 extra for the additional 0.1 acre, but the seller refused to convey, maintaining that the buyer's survey did not comply with the contract. The buyer sued claiming substantial performance. The Alabama Supreme Court held substantial performance applicable. The court reasoned that using a steel tape rather than survey equipment as the basis of the road frontage showed that the plat's acreage was only an estimate and that the seller's promise to convey should not be strictly conditioned on the buyer's furnishing a survey identical to the rough plat. The court emphasized the practical difficulty of surveying land to a numerically exact degree. It noted an analogy between building contracts and the facts before it. The court applied substantial performance but intimated that its application was limited:

> Because both the individual and societal interests are vital coordinates in a private enterprise system, the compromise of full performance should be kept minimal, and compensation should be paid whenever a party's bargained for exchange is not fulfilled.

Id. at 270.

Here the requirement for minimum annual rentals is expressed in paragraph 2.c. of the contract in a definite and precise manner. The contingency of less than perfect performance is specifically dealt with in the provision that if condition 2.a., but not conditions 2.b. and 2.c., is met, then the loan is to be made in the floor amount. In the face of these explicit contractual expressions there is no leeway for substantial performance without frustrating the intent of the parties. Nor is the requirement here inequitable. The minimum rental requirement is a matter of vital interest to the bank because it provides a major part of the loan's security. And, unlike *Bruner,* the requirement not met is possible to achieve as a practical matter.

* * *

We conclude that as a matter of Alabama law the bank was entitled to require total compliance with the minimum annual rental requirement. The district court correctly granted the motion for new trial and later the motion for summary judgment on the ceiling loan claim. * * *

[The court also held that Brown-Marx could not recover for breach of the agreement to make a loan in the floor amount because Brown-Marx did not establish that it wanted to "avail itself" of that loan and that it was ready to close a loan in that amount.]

AFFIRMED.

RESTATEMENT (SECOND) OF CONTRACTS § 237.

Comment d.

Substantial Performance. In an important category of disputes over failure of performance, one party asserts the right to payment on the ground that he has completed his performance, while the other party refuses to pay on the ground that there is an uncured material failure of performance. * * * A typical example is that of the building contractor who claims from the owner payment of the unpaid balance under a construction contract. In such cases it is common to state the issue, not in terms of whether there has been an uncured material failure by the contractor, but in terms of whether there has been substantial performance by him. This manner of stating the issue does not change its substance, however. * * * If there has been substantial although not full performance, the building contractor has a claim for the unpaid balance and the owner has a claim only for damages. If there has not been substantial performance, the building contractor has no claim for the unpaid balance, although he may have a claim in restitution. * * * If, however, the parties have made an event a condition of their agreement, there is no mitigating standard of materiality or substantiality applicable to the non-occurrence of that event. If, therefore, the agreement makes full performance a condition, substantial performance is not sufficient and if relief is to be had under the contract, it must be through excuse of the non-occurrence of the condition to avoid forfeiture.

NOTE:
SPECIAL RULES APPLICABLE TO EXPRESS CONDITIONS

As we have just seen in the Brown-Marx case, courts require strict compliance with express conditions precedent relating to quality of performance. (The same rule also applies to implied-in-fact conditions requiring perfect performance.) You should compare the rule of strict compliance with the very different gap-filling rule concerning quality of performance encountered in Jacob & Youngs v. Kent. When does the Jacob & Youngs rule apply? Why such a major difference? As a contract planner and drafter, you might want to insert an express condition precisely to avoid (or to try to avoid) the doctrine of substantial performance. Review once again Problem 7-1.

In subsequent sections of this chapter and in later chapters of this book, we encounter further special approaches and rules applicable only to express conditions. For example, courts approach the interpretation of claimed express conditions in distinctive ways, and apply special rules to excuse certain failures of express conditions.

SECTION THREE: INTERPRETATION OF CONTRACT LANGUAGE TO DETERMINE WHETHER IT CREATES AN EXPRESS CONDITION

Courts must often consider whether contract language means that (1) a party promises to bring an event about, or (2) the event is only an express condition precedent to a duty of the other party, or (3) the event is both a promise and a condition, or (4) the event is neither. From the cases that immediately follow, you should develop a list of factors that may influence a court's interpretation. In each case, you should also consider how a drafter of the language being interpreted could have made matters clearer.

GLAHOLM V. HAYS

The Court of Common Pleas, 1841.
133 Eng.Rep. 743.

TINDAL, C.J. * * *

The question raised upon this record is, whether the clause contained in the charter-party set out in the declaration, viz.: "the vessel to sail from England on or before the 4th day of February next," is a condition precedent on the part of the ship-owner, upon the non-compliance wherewith on his part, the defendants, the freighters, were at liberty to throw up the charter. The defendants, in their plea, have treated the clause as importing a condition; alleging in such plea that the vessel "did not sail from England on or before the said 4th day of February, but on the contrary remained and continued in England, without the leave and against the will of the defendants, for a long time after; whereupon the defendants refused to perform and fulfil the said charter-party, as they lawfully might;" and the plaintiff, having demurred to this plea, the question on the legal construction of the charter-party is thereby raised.

Whether a particular clause in a charter-party shall be held to be a condition, upon the non-performance of which by the one party, the other is at liberty to abandon the contract, and consider it at an end; or whether it amounts to an agreement only, the breach whereof is to be recompensed by an action for damages, must depend upon the intention of the parties to be collected, in each particular case, from the terms of the agreement itself, and from the subject matter to which it relates. "It cannot depend," as Lord Ellenborough observes, "on any formal arrangement of the words, but (must depend) on the reason and sense of the thing as it is to be collected from the whole contract:" see Ritchie v. Anderson (10 East 295). And looking, in the first place, at the terms of this agreement, we think some distinction must have been intended by the contracting parties, between this particular clause and those which precede and follow it, as to the nature of the obligations thereby respectively created. All the clauses of the charter-party, both prior and subsequent to the clause in dispute, are framed strictly and properly in the language of agreement only. The charter-party states, "it is mutually agreed between the parties that the ship being tight, & c., shall proceed to Trieste, and there load a complete cargo; that the said vessel being so loaded shall therewith proceed to a good and safe port in the United Kingdom; that the cargo shall be sent alongside; that the freight shall be paid in the manner therein stipulated; that forty running days shall be allowed the merchants." And then is interposed the clause now under discussion, viz.: "the vessel to sail from England on or before the 4th day of February next." After which, the charter-party continues in the same frame as before: That the vessel shall be addressed to the charterers' agents, & c. Referring, therefore, in the first place, to the variation between the language of the particular clause, and that of the clauses amongst which it is found, there is reasonable ground for surmising, that some distinction must have been intended between them; and no other distinction can exist, except that the one set of clauses sounds in agreement, and the other clause, in condition.

The very words themselves, "*to sail* on or before a given day," do, by common usage, import the same as the words "*conditioned* to sail," or "*warranted* to sail on or before such a day;" and, undoubtedly, if in the middle of a common bought and sold note, for a cargo of corn, or any other goods, were found the words, "to be delivered on or before such a day," they would be held to amount to a condition; and the purchaser would not be bound to accept the cargo, if not ready for delivery by the day appointed.

And looking at the subject matter of the contract, without regarding the precise words, we think that construing the words as a condition precedent, will carry into effect the intention of the parties, with more certainty, than holding them to be matter of contract only, and merely the ground of an action for damages.

Both parties were aware that the whole success of a mercantile adventure, does, in ordinary cases, depend upon the commencement of the voyage by a given time. The nature of the commodity to be imported, the state of the foreign and home market at the time the contract of charter-party is made, and the various other calculations which enter into commercial speculations, all combine to shew, that dispatch and certainty are of the very first importance to their success; and certainly nothing will so effectually insure both dispatch and certainty, as the knowledge that the obligation of the contract itself shall be made to depend upon the actual performance of the stipulation which relates to them.

The present case appears to us to be distinguishable from those cited on the part of the plaintiff, in both the particulars to which we have adverted; viz. that in this case the form of the stipulation is more nearly in the language of condition than in that of agreement, whilst in the cases cited the stipulation is in the language of covenant only; and again, that in this case the performance of the stipulation goes more to the very root and the whole consideration of the contract. And, indeed, in most or all of those cases, the objection has not been taken until after the voyage had been performed, nor, in many cases, until after the goods had been accepted; so that, it is manifest, the breach of the agreement of which the defendant complained, and which he sought to set up as the non-performance of a condition precedent, could not go *to the whole* of the consideration of the contract.

Such was the case of Constable v. Cloberie (Palmer 397, 81 Eng.Rep. 1141 (X.B. 1626),) where the shipowner covenanted, that his ship should sail with the first fair wind. * * *

Upon the whole, therefore, we think the intention of the parties to this contract sufficiently appears to have been, to insure the ship's sailing at latest by the 4th of February, and that the only mode of effecting this is by holding the clause in question to form a condition precedent; which we consider it to have been.

Judgment for the defendant.

RESTATEMENT (SECOND) OF CONTRACTS § 227(1).

In resolving doubts as to whether an event is made a condition of an obligor's duty, and as to the nature of such an event, an interpretation is preferred that will reduce the obligee's risk of forfeiture, unless the event is within the obligee's control or the circumstances indicate that he has assumed the risk.

HOWARD V. FEDERAL CROP INS. CORP.

United States Court of Appeals, Fourth Circuit, 1976.
540 F.2d 695.

WIDENER, CIRCUIT JUDGE.

Plaintiff-appellants sued to recover for losses to their 1973 tobacco crop due to alleged rain damage. The crops were insured by defendant-appellee, Federal Crop Insurance Corporation (FCIC). * * * The district court granted summary judgment for the defendant. * * * We remand for further proceedings. Since we find for the plaintiffs as to the construction of the policy, we express no opinion on the procedural questions.

Federal Crop Insurance Corporation, an agency of the United States, in 1973, issued three policies to the Howards, insuring their tobacco crops, to be grown on six farms, against weather damage and other hazards.

The Howards (plaintiffs) established production of tobacco on their acreage, and have alleged that their 1973 crop was extensively damaged by heavy rains, resulting in a gross loss to the three plaintiffs in excess of $35,000. The plaintiffs harvested and sold the depleted crop and timely filed notice and proof of loss with FCIC, but, prior to inspection by the adjuster for FCIC, the Howards had either plowed or disked under the tobacco fields in question to prepare the same for sowing a cover crop of rye to preserve the soil. When the FCIC adjuster later inspected the fields, he found the stalks had been largely obscured or obliterated by plowing or disking and denied the claims, apparently on the ground that the plaintiffs had violated a portion of the policy which provides that the stalks on any acreage with respect to which a loss is claimed shall not be destroyed until the corporation makes an inspection.

The holding of the district court is best capsuled in its own words:

> "The inquiry here is whether compliance by the insureds with this provision of the policy was a condition precedent to the recovery. The court concludes that it was and that the failure of the insureds to comply worked a forfeiture of benefits for the alleged loss."[1]

There is no question but that apparently after notice of loss was given to defendant, but before inspection by the adjuster, plaintiffs plowed under the tobacco stalks and sowed some of the land with a cover crop, rye. The question is whether, under paragraph 5(f) of the tobacco endorsement to the policy of insurance, the act of plowing under the tobacco stalks forfeits the coverage of the policy. Paragraph 5 of the tobacco endorsement is entitled *Claims*. Pertinent to this case are subparagraphs 5(b) and 5(f), which are as follows:

> "5(b) *It shall be a condition precedent* to the payment of any loss that the insured establish the production of the insured crop on a unit and that such loss has been directly caused by one or more of the hazards insured against during the insurance period for the crop year for which the loss is claimed, and furnish any other information regarding the manner and extent of loss as may be required by the Corporation. (Emphasis added)"

> "5(f) The tobacco stalks on any acreage of tobacco of types 11a, 11b, 12, 13, or 14 with respect to which a loss is claimed *shall not be destroyed until the Corporation makes an inspection.* (Emphasis added)"

The arguments of both parties are predicated upon the same two assumptions. First, if subparagraph 5(f) creates a condition precedent, its violation caused a forfeiture of plaintiffs' coverage. Second, if subparagraph 5(f) creates an obligation (variously called a promise or covenant) upon plaintiffs not to plow under the tobacco stalks, defendant may recover from plaintiffs (either in an original action, or, in this case, by a counterclaim, or as a matter of defense) for whatever damage it sustained because of the elimination of the stalks. However, a violation of subparagraph 5(f) would not, under the second premise, standing alone, cause a forfeiture of the policy.

---

[1] The district court also relied upon language in subparagraph 5(b), infra, which required as a condition precedent to payment that the insured, in addition to establishing his production and loss from an insured case, "furnish any other information regarding the manner and extent of loss as may be required by the Corporation." The court construed the preservation of the stalks as such "information." We see no language in the policy or connection in the record to indicate this is the case.

Generally accepted law provides us with guidelines here. There is a general legal policy opposed to forfeitures. *United States v. One Ford Coach,* 307 U.S. 219, 226, 59 S.Ct. 861, 83 L.Ed. 1249 (1939); *Baca v. Commissioner of Internal Revenue,* 326 F.2d 189, 191 (5th Cir.1964). Insurance policies are generally construed most strongly against the insurer. *Henderson v. Hartford Accident & Indemnity Co.,* 268 N.C. 129, 150 S.E.2d 17, 19 (1966). When it is doubtful whether words create a promise or a condition precedent, they will be construed as creating a promise. *Harris and Harris Const. Co. v. Crain and Denbo, Inc.,* 256 N.C. 110, 123 S.E.2d 590, 595 (1962). The provisions of a contract will not be construed as conditions precedent in the absence of language plainly requiring such construction. *Harris,* 123 S.E.2d at 596. * * *

Plaintiffs rely most strongly upon the fact that the term "condition precedent" is included in subparagraph 5(b) but not in subparagraph 5(f). It is true that whether a contract provision is construed as a condition or an obligation does not depend entirely upon whether the word "condition" is expressly used. Appleman, *Insurance Law and Practice* (1972), vol. 6A, § 4144. However, the persuasive force of plaintiffs' argument in this case is found in the use of the term "condition precedent" in subparagraph 5(b) but not in subparagraph 5(f). Thus, it is argued that the ancient maxim to be applied is that the expression of one thing is the exclusion of another.

The defendant places principal reliance upon the decision of this court in *Fidelity-Phenix Fire Insurance Company v. Pilot Freight Carriers,* 193 F.2d 812, 31 A.L.R.2d 839 (4th Cir.1952). Suit there was predicated upon a loss resulting from theft out of a truck covered by defendant's policy protecting plaintiff from such a loss. The insurance company defended upon the grounds that the plaintiff had left the truck unattended without the alarm system being on. The policy contained six paragraphs limiting coverage. Two of those imposed what was called a "condition precedent." They largely related to the installation of specified safety equipment. Several others, including paragraph 5, pertinent in that case, started with the phrase, "It is further warranted." In paragraph 5, the insured warranted that the alarm system would be on whenever the vehicle was left unattended. Paragraph 6 starts with the language: "The assured agrees, by acceptance of this policy, that the foregoing conditions precedent relate to matters material to the acceptance of the risk by the insurer." Plaintiff recovered in the district court, but judgment on its behalf was reversed because of a breach of warranty of paragraph 5, the truck had been left unattended with the alarm off. In that case, plaintiff relied upon the fact that the words "condition precedent" were used in some of the paragraphs but the word "warranted" was used in the paragraph in issue. In rejecting that contention, this court said that "warranty" and "condition precedent" are often used interchangeably to create a condition of the insured's promise, and "[m]anifestly the terms 'condition precedent' and 'warranty' were intended to have the same meaning and effect." 193 F.2d at 816.

Fidelity-Phenix thus does not support defendant's contention here. Although there is some resemblance between the two cases, analysis shows that the issues are actually entirely different. Unlike the case at bar, each paragraph in *Fidelity-Phenix* contained either the term "condition precedent" or the term "warranted." We held that, in that situation, the two terms had the same effect in that they both involved forfeiture. That is well established law. See Appleman, *Insurance Law and Practice* (1972), vol. 6A, § 4144. In the case at bar, the term "warranty" or "warranted" is in no way involved, either in terms or by way of like language, as it was in *Fidelity-Phenix*. The issue upon which this case turns, then, was not involved in *Fidelity-Phenix*.

The *Restatement of the Law of Contracts* states:

"§ 261. INTERPRETATION OF DOUBTFUL WORDS AS PROMISE OR CONDITION.

> Where it is doubtful whether words create a promise or an express condition, they are interpreted as creating a promise; but the same words may sometimes mean that one party promises a performance and that the other party's promise is conditional on that performance."

Two illustrations (one involving a promise, the other a condition) are used in the *Restatement*:

> "2. A, an insurance company, issues to B a policy of insurance containing promises by A that are in terms conditional on the happening of certain events. The policy contains this clause: 'provided, in case differences shall arise touching any loss, *the matter shall be submitted to impartial arbitrators,* whose award shall be binding on the parties.' This is a promise to arbitrate and does not make an award a condition precedent of the insurer's duty to pay.
>
> 3. A, an insurance company, issues to B an insurance policy in usual form containing this clause: 'In the event of disagreement as to the amount of loss it shall be ascertained by two appraisers and an umpire. The loss shall *not be payable until 60 days after the award of the appraisers when such an appraisal is required.*' This provision is not merely a promise to arbitrate differences but makes an award a condition of the insurer's duty to pay in case of disagreement." (Emphasis added)

We believe that subparagraph 5(f) in the policy here under consideration fits illustration 2 rather than illustration 3. Illustration 2 specifies something to be done, whereas subparagraph 5(f) specifies something not to be done. Unlike illustration 3, subparagraph 5(f) does not state any conditions under which the insurance shall "not be payable," or use any words of like import. We hold that the district court erroneously held, on the motion for summary judgment, that subparagraph 5(f) established a condition precedent to plaintiffs' recovery which forfeited the coverage.[2]

From our holding that defendant's motion for summary judgment was improperly allowed, it does not follow the plaintiffs' motion for summary judgment should have been granted, for if subparagraph 5(f) be not construed as a condition precedent, there are other questions of fact to be determined. At this point, we merely hold that the district court erred in holding, on the motion for summary judgment, that subparagraph 5(f) constituted a condition precedent with resulting forfeiture.

The explanation defendant makes for including subparagraph 5(f) in the tobacco endorsement is that it is necessary that the stalks remain standing in order for the Corporation to evaluate the extent of loss and to determine whether loss resulted from some cause not covered by the policy. However, was subparagraph 5(f) inserted because without it the Corporation's opportunities for proof would be more difficult, or because they would be impossible? Plaintiffs point out that the Tobacco Endorsement, with subparagraph 5(f), was adopted in 1970, and crop insurance goes back long before that date. Nothing is shown as to the Corporation's prior 1970 practice of evaluating losses. Such a showing might have a bearing upon establishing defendant's intention in including 5(f). Plaintiffs state, and defendant does not deny, that another division of the Department of Agriculture, or the North Carolina Department, urged that tobacco stalks be cut as soon as possible after harvesting as a means of pest control. Such an explanation might refute the idea that plaintiffs plowed under the stalks for any fraudulent purpose. Could these conflicting directives affect the reasonableness of plaintiffs' interpretation of defendant's prohibition upon plowing under the stalks prior to adjustment?

We express no opinion on these questions because they were not before the district court and are mentioned to us largely by way of argument rather than from the record. * * * Nothing we say here should preclude FCIC from asserting as a defense that the plowing or disking under of the stalks caused damage to FCIC if, for example, the amount of the loss was thereby made more difficult or impossible to ascertain whether the plowing or disking under was done with bad purpose or innocently. To repeat, our narrow holding is that merely plowing or disking under the stalks does not of itself operate to forfeit coverage under the policy.

The case is remanded for further proceedings not inconsistent with this opinion.

---

[2] The district court also referred to subparagraph 5(f) as a condition subsequent. The difference in terminology is of no consequence here.

Vacated and Remanded.

PROBLEM 7-2

A lawyer should not draft contract clauses without knowing how courts will interpret such clauses. Assume that an agreement being drafted in your office includes the following clause: "In return for Artist's promise to prepare and deliver holiday greeting card designs in accord with attached specifications by November 15, Manufacturer promises to pay $4,000 for those designs." Your senior partner has asked you to draft further alternative clauses for consideration which would make Artist's performance "by November 15": (1) only a duty of Artist; (2) only a condition of Manufacturer's duty; (3) both a duty of Artist and a condition of Manufacturer's duty. Draft the clauses.

PROBLEM 7-3

O & G Engineers rendered engineering services to Taleghani-Dabtary (T-D), a consultant to the Iranian government on the construction of water resource projects. Their letter agreement provided that "T-D agrees to make payments to O & G in the amount of $157,755.19 within fifteen days of the availability of funds." The parties agree that the purpose of the provision was to protect O & G by ensuring prompt payment, while simultaneously providing T-D a grace period in which to pay its obligation to O & G. After Iran failed to pay T-D, T-D claimed that such payment was a condition precedent to its obligation to O & G. Is it? Draft a provision that O & G should have insisted upon in its agreement with T-D, protecting O & G from such a defense.

SECTION FOUR: INTERPRETATION OF THE CONTENT OF EXPRESS CONDITIONS

In the cases in the preceding section, the court focused mainly on issues of interpretation with respect to the possible *existence* of an express condition precedent. Courts must also face important issues of interpretation with respect to the *content* of conditions. In the following cases, you should focus not only on techniques of interpretation but also on how the language in question could have been better drafted.

GIBSON V. CRANAGE

Supreme Court of Michigan, 1878.
39 Mich. 49.

MARSTON, J.

Plaintiff in error brought assumpsit to recover the contract price for the making and execution of a portrait of the deceased daughter of defendant. It appeared from the testimony of the plaintiff that he at a certain time called upon the defendant and solicited the privilege of making an enlarged picture of his deceased daughter. He says "I was to make an enlarged picture that he would like, a large one from a small one, and one that he would like and recognize as a good picture of his little girl, and he was to pay me."

The defendant testified that the plaintiff was to take the small photograph and send it away to be finished, "and when returned if it was not perfectly satisfactory to me in every particular, I need not take it or pay for it. I still objected and he urged me to do so. There was no risk about it; if it was not perfectly satisfactory to me I need not take it or pay for it."

There was little if any dispute as to what the agreement was. After the picture was finished it was shown to defendant who was dissatisfied with it and refused to accept it. Plaintiff endeavored to ascertain what the objections were, but says he was unable to ascertain clearly, and he then sent the picture away to the artist to have it changed.

On the next day he received a letter from defendant reciting the original agreement, stating that the picture shown him the previous day was not satisfactory and that he declined to take it or any other similar picture, and countermanded the order. A farther correspondence was had, but it was not very material and did not change the aspect of the case. When the picture was afterwards received by the plaintiff from the artist, he went to see defendant and to have him examine it. This defendant declined to do, or to look at it, and did not until during the trial, when he examined and found the same objections still existing.

We do not consider it necessary to examine the charge in detail, as we are satisfied it was as favorable to plaintiff as the agreement would warrant.

The contract (if it can be considered such) was an express one. The plaintiff agreed that the picture when finished should be satisfactory to the defendant, and his own evidence showed that the contract in this important particular had not been performed. It may be that the picture was an excellent one and that the defendant ought to have been satisfied with it and accepted it, but under the agreement the defendant was the only person who had the right to decide this question. Where parties thus deliberately enter into an agreement which violates no rule of public policy, and which is free from all taint of fraud or mistake, there is no hardship whatever in holding them bound by it.

Artists or third parties might consider a portrait an excellent one, and yet it prove very unsatisfactory to the person who had ordered it and who might be unable to point out with clearness or certainty the defects or objections. And if the person giving the order stipulates that the portrait when finished must be satisfactory to him or else he will not accept or pay for it, and this is agreed to, he may insist upon his right as given him by the contract. *McCarren v. McNulty,* 7 Gray 139; *Brown v. Foster,* 113 Mass. 136: 18 Amer., 465.

The judgment must be affirmed with costs.

FORMAN V. BENSON

Appellate Court of Illinois, Second District, 1983.
112 Ill.App.3d 1070, 68 Ill.Dec. 629, 446 N.E.2d 535.

HOPF, JUSTICE.

Defendant, Art Benson, appeals from an order of the circuit court of Lee County granting plaintiff Eric Forman specific performance of an installment contract to purchase commercial real estate owned by defendant. * * *

On March 23, 1981, the plaintiff, a chiropractor, executed an offer to purchase certain real estate in Dixon, Illinois, owned by the defendant, an electrician and a refrigeration and heating repairman. The offer was communicated the same day to the defendant at a conference attended by the defendant and three realtors. One of the realtors was Ken Burnell, with whom the defendant had listed the property. The other realtors attending the conference were Cheryl Blackorby and Bill Blackorby, spouses who are partners in another real estate firm. The plaintiff was a client of the Blackorbys, who had been assisting him for the previous several months in his search for a commercial building suitable for use as a chiropractic clinic.

The conference at which the offer was communicated took place in the office of the realtor, Ken Burnell. The terms of the offer were explained to defendant by Cheryl Blackorby. The offer proposed to purchase the property for $125,000, to be paid over a ten-year period. Payments were to be based upon a 30-year amortization rate at 9% interest. Plaintiff was to take possession of the property on September 1, 1981.

Before signing the agreement, defendant expressed concern over the plaintiff's credit worthiness, stating that he "didn't know him from a load of hay." Plaintiff's credit was of special significance to the defendant, since defendant was essentially "acting as a loan company" for plaintiff's benefit. As an assurance to the defendant, Mrs. Blackorby suggested that the contract be made subject to a favorable credit report. This suggestion eased defendant's feelings about the credit, and Ken Burnell thereafter added the following handwritten statement to the offer:

> "Subject to seller's approving buyer's credit report, oral on March 24, 1981, and written when ready."

The meaning of this statement was not explained in any detail at the time it was inserted by Mr. Burnell. However, it was uncontroverted that the clause was inserted for defendant's benefit. The contract was subsequently signed by defendant, and $1,000 was deposited by the plaintiff as earnest money.

Ken Burnell, defendant's realtor, testified on behalf of plaintiff Forman. Mr. Burnell stated that defendant indicated to him that he would approve the contract if plaintiff had a good credit report. Mrs. Blackorby also indicated that defendant said he would accept the contract if the credit report was favorable. However, it was defendant's understanding and belief that he would be given time to examine the credit documents, evaluate them and make a decision.

The day after the offer and acceptance was executed, Mrs. Blackorby telephoned the defendant and advised him that an excellent oral credit report had been received. She further told defendant that a written report would be ready in a few days. Defendant sounded agreeable to the oral report and stated he would pick up the written report when it arrived. On Friday, March 27, 1981, Mrs. Blackorby received the written credit report, as well as a personal financial statement prepared by the plaintiff and a letter from Dixon National Bank stating it would lend $35,000 to plaintiff. Mrs. Blackorby gave these documents to defendant that day, explaining the credit report in detail. Defendant stated the report "looks real good," and that he would have his attorney review it and begin the title work on the property.

Between Friday, March 27, 1981, and May 14, 1981, the plaintiff and defendant discussed the pending sale on three occasions. Those occasions took place in the latter part of April, at which time additional financial material, including copies of income tax returns, were furnished at the defendant's request. During those conversations the parties also discussed increases in the purchase price and the interest rate on the contract, as well as retention by the seller of certain personal property on the premises. Plaintiff testified that the seller wanted to raise the purchase price and interest rate, while the defendant testified that, prior to his rejection of the contract, he did mention a different price but not in terms of an ultimatum.

On May 14, 1981, the defendant, through the office of Ken Burnell, furnished a written statement rejecting plaintiff's credit and directing the realtor to refund the $1,000 deposit. Plaintiff attempted to discuss the matter further with the defendant, apparently making another offer as an inducement to complete the contract without litigation. Although defendant went to plaintiff's office to discuss another offer, no other offer was accepted by him. In July of 1981 the plaintiff brought this action seeking specific performance of the agreement. On September 1, 1981, plaintiff was ready and able to pay the balance of the down payment, complete the other obligations required by the installment agreement and take possession of the premises. The defendant denied the demand for possession under the terms of the agreement.

The defendant testified that he rejected the credit information because the plaintiff had liabilities of $80,000 and liquid assets of only $24,000.

When defendant sought additional information, he was furnished with a corporate tax return showing a $2,000 loss for the tax year. Based on this information, defendant believed the plaintiff was "just breaking even." He had asked for the additional information because he believed the information furnished in the credit bureau report was not very significant. Defendant has had no prior experience as a bank or loan officer.

Thomas Schmidt, loan officer with a local savings and loan association, testified on behalf of the plaintiff. His testimony was uncontroverted to the effect that the plaintiff had an excellent credit rating. Based upon the credit application and credit report of the plaintiff, the savings and loan association would not have hesitated to extend credit to the plaintiff, although not under the terms of this particular contract.

The trial court found that defendant was held to a standard of reasonableness in his rejection of the contract on the basis of plaintiff's credit report, and found that defendant's rejection here was unreasonable. The court also found that defendant attempted to renegotiate the contract prior to his rejection of plaintiff's offer and that this action waived any objection which defendant might reasonably have had to plaintiff's credit worthiness. Finally, waiver was also found in defendant's delay of over 30 days "before giving notice of his intention to rely upon the credit clause in question." The court found in favor of the plaintiff and entered a decree for specific performance. The instant appeal followed.

Defendant first argues that approval of the buyer's credit worthiness was intended to be a matter of personal satisfaction on the part of the seller and was not subject to a standard of reasonableness, as the plaintiff claims and the trial court held.

We have discovered no case dealing with the interpretation of the specific clause in question. However, there is some Illinois case law regarding the interpretation of "satisfaction" clauses in general. In *Reeves & Co. v. Chandler* (1904), 113 Ill.App. 167, 170, the court found that satisfaction clauses generally fall into one of two classes. In one class, the decision as to whether a party is satisfied is completely reserved to the party for whose benefit the clause is inserted, and the reasons for his decision may not be inquired into and overhauled by either the other party or the courts. Cases falling into this class generally involve matters which are dependent upon the feelings, taste, or judgment of the party making the decision. (*Reeves; The Union League Club v. The Blymyer Ice Machine Co.* (1903), 204 Ill. 117, 68 N.E. 409.) The second class of cases are those in which the party to be satisfied is to base his determination on grounds which are just and reasonable. (*Reeves.*) These cases generally involve matters which are capable of objective evaluation, or which involve considerations of operative fitness or mechanical utility. (*Reeves; The Union League Club.*) Matters of financial concern generally fall into this second category of cases. The adequacy of the grounds of a determination in this class are open to judicial scrutiny and are judged by a reasonable man standard. *Reeves; Wood Machine Co. v. Smith* (1883), 50 Mich. 565, 15 N.W. 906.

However, the *Reeves* case also made it clear that the parties may agree to a reservation in one party of the absolute and unqualified freedom of choice on a matter not involving fancy, taste, or whim. (113 Ill.App. 167, 170.) Quoting from *Wood Machine Co. v. Smith* (1883), 50 Mich. 565, 15 N.W. 906, the court stated:

> " 'It sometimes happens that the right is fully reserved where it is the chief ground, if not the only one, that the party is determined to reserve an unqualified option, and is not willing to leave his freedom of choice exposed to any contention or subject to any contingency. He will not enter into any bargain except upon the condition of reserving the power to do what others might regard as unreasonable.' " (113 Ill.App. 167, 170–71.)

Applying this reasoning, the court in *Reeves* found that a satisfaction clause regarding certain machinery—a matter which would normally be capable of objective evaluation—was intended to allow the purchaser of the machinery to exercise his judgment in accepting or rejecting the machinery:

> "It is apparent from the grammatical construction and arrangement of the clause in question that the words 'and satisfactory' were added thereto after the preceding portion was written and as a concession to defendant in error. It may be reasonably inferred that he was determined that no opportunity should be given plaintiff in error to force the outfit upon him if he finally concluded not to take it. The words referred to were undoubtedly added to the clause at his request or suggestion and for the purpose of inducing him to sign the order." (113 Ill.App. 167, 171.)

Thus, it is apparent that under *Reeves* the fact that the clause was added as a concession or inducement to one of the parties is significant in determining whether the reasonableness standard should be applied.

In *Quinn v. Daly* (1921), 300 Ill. 273, 133 N.E. 290, a provision similar to the one here in question was interpreted by the Illinois Supreme Court as providing for a decision based on personal judgment. In that case, the seller in a contract sale for realty stated that she would agree to the terms of the contract "if party is reliable and has other property clear * * *." (133 N.E. 290, 291.) The court held that this statement was intended to reserve in the seller the right to pass on the question of the buyer's reliability and trustworthiness. 133 N.E. 290, 291.

* * *

Although these * * * cases seem to stand for the proposition that personal judgment is involved when the evaluation of a credit rating is at issue, a different conclusion was reached in *Weisz Trucking Co., Inc. v. Emil R. Wohl Construction* (1970), 13 Cal.App.3d 256, 91 Cal.Rptr. 489. In that case a contract between a contractor and a subcontractor provided that "[t]he subcontractor shall furnish, if requested, a corporate surety contract bond * * * written * * * by a company acceptable to the contractor * * *." (13 Cal.App.3d 256, 258, 91 Cal.Rptr. 489, 490.) The subcontractor thereafter submitted a surety bond in the amount of $168,000 which was written by a company with a Treasury rating of only $61,000. The contractor rejected the bond, stating that it wanted a company with a Treasury rating of $500,000. The contractor cancelled the contract and the subcontractors sued for breach. The appellate court held that the sufficiency of the performance bond should be determined by the application of an objective test of reasonableness. In reaching this conclusion, the court relied upon numerous decisions dealing with satisfaction clauses in which it was generally found that "where the contract calls for satisfaction as to commercial value or quality or sufficiency which can be evaluated objectively, the standard of a reasonable person should be used in determining whether or not satisfaction has been received." 13 Cal.App.3d 256, 262, 91 Cal.Rptr. 489, 493.

It seems clear from the foregoing cases that a reasonableness standard is favored by the law when the contract concerns matters capable of objective evaluation. However, where the circumstances are such that it is clear the provision was added as a personal concession to one of the contracting parties, the subjective, rather than the objective standard, should be applied. *Reeves & Co. v. Chandler* (1904), 113 Ill.App. 167.

In the present case, it is uncontroverted that the clause in question was inserted as a concession to the defendant and as an inducement to him to sign the contract, which he subsequently did. Ken Burnell testified that the addition of the provision indeed eased defendant's mind about the plaintiff's credit worthiness. In light of the fact that the relationship between the parties was to endure over a ten-year period of time, we think it is a reasonable construction of the provision that it was intended to allow defendant the freedom of making a personal and subjective evaluation of plaintiff's credit worthiness. We, therefore, conclude that the trial court erred in applying a reasonableness standard to the instant case.

The personal judgment standard, however, does not allow the defendant to exercise unbridled discretion in rejecting plaintiff's credit, but rather is subject to the requirement of good faith. * * * In the instant case the trial court made no specific finding whether defendant Benson rejected plaintiff's credit in good faith. However, the trial court did find that between the time the contract was executed and the time the offer was rejected, defendant attempted to renegotiate the purchase price of the building as well as the interest rate. Defendant has challenged this finding on appeal, claiming it was against the manifest weight of the evidence. We disagree. Both plaintiff and defendant testified that an increased purchase price was discussed. Thus, the trial court's finding in this regard was supported by the record and was not against the manifest weight of the evidence. Further, we hold that while defendant may have had a basis in his personal judgment for rejecting plaintiff's credit (*i.e.,* outstanding debts and a $2,000 loss reflected in an income tax return), his attempted renegotiation demonstrates that his rejection was based on reasons other than plaintiff's credit rating and was, therefore, in bad faith.

* * *

For the foregoing reasons, the decree of the circuit court of Lee County granting specific performance to the plaintiff is affirmed.

Affirmed.

VAN DEUSEN, J., concurs.

LINDBERG, JUSTICE, dissenting.

I am compelled to disagree with the respected trial court and my colleagues in the majority. I believe the parties, the trial court and the majority have proceeded far deeper into the intricacies of contract law than the facts of this cause permit. I do not believe questions of reasonableness or good faith are involved where the issue is whether the seller accepted and assented to the contract.

* * *

The addendum to the contract "Subject to seller approving buyer's credit report, oral on March 24, 1981, written when ready" was indisputably a condition to the seller's acceptance of the buyer's offer. It is an elementary rule of contract law that a condition precedent must be performed before contractual liability arises. (*Godare v. Sterling Steel Casting Co.* (1981), 103 Ill.App.3d 46, 58 Ill.Dec. 588, 430 N.E.2d 620 (and the cases cited therein).) The seller's acceptance of the offer must be unequivocal. (*Milani v. Proesel* (1958), 15 Ill.2d 423, 155 N.E.2d 38.) The seller never approved the buyer's credit report and it is not suggested by the parties or the trial court that the seller performed this necessary act. Nor is it urged that his silence between March 23 and May 14 (except when he was solicited by the buyer two or three times in April and May) constituted an acceptance.

* * *

I conclude, * * * that neither the contract nor case law imposed upon the seller a standard of reasonableness in accepting or rejecting the contract. As to an implied agreement in every contract that the parties act in good faith I simply respond that there was no contract. But, also, the majority's conclusion that the seller lacked good faith by renegotiating other terms of the contract is not supported by the evidence. The buyer approached the seller and offered more documents regarding his "financial capabilities". During these meetings initiated by the buyer, seller indicated he might accept the contract at the original asking price of $135,000 and a half to one percent increase in the interest rate. Even if there was a contract, I would not hold that such discussions, where the seller has never indicated satisfaction with the buyer's credit, constitute bad faith.

I would reverse the judgment of the circuit court of Lee County.

NOTE: *FURTHER ASPECTS OF FORMAN V. BENSON*

Benson argued in his appellate brief that he had not (as the court ultimately found) acted in bad faith in seeking to renegotiate the price:

> The obvious innocent interpretation of any discussion of change in price or rates is that the Defendant saw a greater risk than anticipated and wished to have a greater return for that risk. There is no evidence of duplicity on the part of the Defendant, although the inference is attempted to be made by the Plaintiff. In any event it is clear from the facts that the seller sought additional financial information and examined it at length before rejecting the buyer's credit. Discussions regarding additional compensation, if any took place, would not necessarily suggest that the Defendant had approved the credit but wanted more money.

Should the appellate court have paid more attention to this argument? Could the argument have been drafted more persuasively?

The circuit court entered its decree of specific performance on January 5, 1982. On February 2, 1982, Benson's lawyer wrote a letter to him that stated in part:

> I received a call from Attorney Gehlbach. He advises me that his client is willing to make another offer in order to avoid the cost and delay of an appeal. He offers an additional $3,000 on the down payment. This would not increase the total amount of the contract, but would result in that additional amount paid "up front". As you know from my earlier conversations and correspondence I recommend that you work out some kind of accord with Dr. Forman. I believe it is in your best interests to avoid the expense of the appeal. Since your chances for success are not substantial, I urge you to either accept this proposal or make a counterproposal that is reasonable enough to induce Dr. Forman to accept. Perhaps a counterproposal for the additional $3,000 advance plus an increase of one-quarter of a per cent on the balance might be of interest to him.

Should Benson's lawyer have tried harder to bring about a settlement? What are the general constraints under which the lawyer operates?

LUTTINGER V. ROSEN

Supreme Court of Connecticut, 1972.
164 Conn. 45, 316 A.2d 757.

LOISELLE, ASSOCIATE JUSTICE.

The plaintiffs contracted to purchase for $85,000 premises in the city of Stamford owned by the defendants and paid a deposit of $8500. The contract was "subject to and conditional upon the buyers obtaining first mortgage financing on said premises from a bank or other lending institution in an amount of $45,000 for a term of not less than twenty (20) years and at an interest rate which does not exceed 8½ per cent per annum." The plaintiffs agreed to use due diligence in attempting to obtain such financing. The parties further agreed that if the plaintiffs were unsuccessful in obtaining financing as provided in the contract, and notified the seller within a specific time, all sums paid on the contract would be refunded and the contract terminated without further obligation of either party.

In applying for a mortgage which would satisfy the contingency clause in the contract, the plaintiffs relied on their attorney who applied at a New Haven lending institution for a $45,000 loan at 8¼ percent per annum interest over a period of twenty-five years. The plaintiffs' attorney knew that this lending institution was the only one which at that time would lend as much as $45,000 on a mortgage for a single-family dwelling. A mortgage commitment was obtained for $45,000 with "interest at the prevailing rate at the time of closing but not less than 8¾%." Since this commitment failed to meet the contract requirement, timely notice was given to the defendants and demand was made for the return of the down payment. The defendants' counsel thereafter offered to make up the difference between the interest rate offered by the bank and the 8½ percent rate provided in the contract for the entire twenty-five years by a funding arrangement, the exact terms of which were not defined. The plaintiffs did not accept this offer and on the defendants' refusal to return the deposit an action was brought. From a judgment rendered in favor of the plaintiffs the defendants have appealed.

The defendants claim that the plaintiffs did not use due diligence in seeking a mortgage within the terms specified in the contract. The unattacked findings by the court establish that the plaintiffs' attorney was fully informed as to the conditions and terms of mortgages being granted by various banks and lending institutions in and out of the area and that the application was made to the only bank which might satisfy the mortgage conditions of the contingency clause at that time. These findings adequately support the court's conclusion that due diligence was used in seeking mortgage financing in accordance with the contract provisions. Brauer v. Freccia, 159 Conn. 289, 293, 268 A.2d 645. The defendants assert that notwithstanding the plaintiffs' reliance on their counsel's knowledge of lending practices, applications should have been made to other lending institutions. This claim is not well taken. The law does not require the performance of a futile act. * * *

The remaining assignment of error briefed by the defendants is that the court erred in concluding that the mortgage contingency clause of the contract, a condition precedent, was not met and, therefore, the plaintiffs were entitled to recover their deposit. "A condition precedent is a fact or event which the parties intend must exist or take place before there is a right to performance." Lach v. Cahill, 138 Conn. 418, 421, 85 A.2d 481, 482. If the condition precedent is not fulfilled the contract is not enforceable. Lach v. Cahill, supra; Bialeck v. Hartford, 135 Conn. 551, 556, 66 A.2d 610. In this case the language of the contract is unambiguous and clearly indicates that the parties intended that the purchase of the defendants' premises be conditioned on the obtaining by the plaintiffs of a mortgage as specified in the contract. From the subordinate facts found the court could reasonably conclude that since the plaintiffs were unable to obtain a $45,000 mortgage at no more than 8½ percent per annum interest "from a bank or other lending institution" the condition precedent to performance of the contract was not met and the plaintiffs were entitled to the refund of their deposit. Any additional offer by the defendants to fund the difference in interest payments could be rejected by the plaintiffs. See Lach v. Cahill, supra, 138 Conn. 418, 85 A.2d 481. There was no error in the court's exclusion of testimony relating to the additional offer since the offer was obviously irrelevant.

There is no error.

SECTION FIVE: EXCUSE AND AVOIDANCE OF EXPRESS CONDITIONS

E.I. DU PONT DE NEMOURS POWDER CO. V. SCHLOTTMAN

United States Court of Appeals, Second Circuit, 1914.
218 Fed. 353.

WARD, CIRCUIT JUDGE. In July, 1908, one Grubb was negotiating with T.C. Du Pont, president of the Du Pont Powder Company, for the sale of the whole capital stock of the Pittsburgh Fuse Company to the Du Pont Company. July 20th Du Pont wrote to Grubb as follows:

> "Mr. Chas. G. Grubb, Building—Dear Sir: Should the deal now under discussion for the Pittsburgh Fuse Mfg. Co. go through, and after we have had the property a year, it is understood that if

in my judgment the property has for any reason been worth $175,000 to our company, and we manufactured double tape fuse at $2 per thousand with powder at $3.60 per keg, we are to pay you $25,000 in either bonds, preferred or common stock of our company as we may elect.

"Yours truly,

T.C. DU PONT, PRESIDENT."

On July 24th the deal referred to in the letter went through in a formal agreement whereby the Du Pont Company agreed to pay Grubb $75,000 of its preferred and $75,000 of its common stock for the whole capital stock of the Pittsburgh Fuse Company. Grubb delivered the Fuse Company's stock and the Du Pont Company transferred to it its own stock, but, after operating the plant for about six months, sold it to other parties, who dismantled it.

Grubb, the plaintiff's assignor, died before suit brought, and Mr. T.C. Du Pont did not testify to the circumstances attending the writing of the letter of July 20th. At the conclusion of the case each party asked Judge Ray to direct a verdict in his favor, and he did direct a verdict in favor of the plaintiff for $25,000.

The complaint treats the letter and the formal agreement as one contract, alleges that the defendant by selling the plant of the Fuse Company wrongfully prevented the test agreed upon, and claims damages for the difference between the fair and reasonable value of the Fuse Company's capital stock alleged to be $175,000 and the market value of the defendant's stock actually received, alleged to be $120,000.

The defendant contends that the letter of July 20th is a separate contract, and, as it is not to be performed within the year, is void under the statute of frauds, because it does not state any consideration. We think, however, that the two documents are to be considered together. The Du Pont Company was to pay $25,000 more in securities if in the judgment of T.C. Du Pont upon operating for one year, the plant was worth $175,000 to his company and was capable of making double tape fuse at $2 per thousand feet with powder at $3.60 a keg. This was to be additional compensation for additional value, so that the objection of the statute of frauds is unavailing.

The letter does not contain any express promise to operate the plant for one year, and the question is whether such a promise is to be implied. We think the court below rightly held that it was. The seller evidently thought the plant worth $175,000 in the defendant's securities, and the buyer was willing to pay the additional $25,000 if such value was demonstrated in the way provided. The letter implies a promise on the Du Pont Company's part to operate the plant for a year, and that promise must be taken as part of the consideration for which Grubb sold the capital stock. * * *

* * *

The question of damages is the only other question we think needing consideration. If the plaintiff could now perform or secure a performance of the agreed test, he might be obliged to do so as a condition of recovering the contract price. But the defendant has made performance impossible by selling the plant within the period of one year to a purchaser who has dismantled it. No similar test can be substituted. It was personal in its nature, viz., the operation for a year by a wealthy and expert corporation actuated by self-interest to make tape fuse at $2 a thousand feet. Because the defendant has made the performance of this test impossible, the plaintiff should not be remediless. We think he had the right to show, if he could, in other ways, that the value of the plant was greater by $25,000 than the sum paid for it. As Judge Bartlett said in Hopedale Co. v. Electric Storage Battery Co., 184 N.Y. 356, 364, 77 N.E. 394, 397:

> "In other words, the performance of a condition for valuation having been prevented by the act of the vendee, the price of the thing sold was to be fixed by the jury on a quantum valebant."

Though the contract contemplated that the defendant should pay the additional amount in its own securities, having refused to pay at all, the plaintiff has a right to recover money. New York Publishing Co. v. Steamship Co., 148 N.Y. 39, 42 N.E. 514. One witness stated that the plant was worth $175,000, and the Du Pont Company actually sold it for $150,000. The plaintiff's assignor received $122,000, the market value of the defendant's securities, aggregating $150,000. Therefore there was evidence to support the finding of the trial judge that the plant was worth $147,000, which may be implied from his direction of a verdict for $25,000.

Judgment affirmed.

HANNA V. COMMERCIAL TRAVELERS' MUTUAL ACCIDENT ASSOCIATION

Supreme Court of New York, Appellate Division, 1922.
204 App.Div. 258, 197 N.Y.S. 395, aff'd, 236 N.Y. 571, 142 N.E. 288 (1923).

Appeal from Supreme Court, New York County.

Action by William E. Hanna against the Commercial Travelers' Mutual Accident Association of America. From a judgment for plaintiff for $5,978.40, and from an order denying defendant's motion to set aside the verdict and for a new trial, defendant appeals. Judgment and order reversed, and complaint dismissed.

FINCH, J. The action is upon a policy of accident insurance. In 1913 the insured disappeared, and no trace of him was found until 1917, when his automobile was dredged up from the bottom of the Delaware river. When last seen he was driving this automobile upon a stormy, rainy morning in 1913. He had previously expressed an intention to go from Philadelphia to New York, and one of the usual routes existing at that time was down Dyott street, turning left for the ferry. Dyott street terminates in the Delaware river, and the only protection at the foot thereof was some posts extending across the street, two of which were found to be broken. It was the plaintiff's claim that the insured failed to turn off from Dyott street, and suffered death by accidentally driving his car from the street into the river. This claim, as well as a defense set up by the defendant that the alleged injury and death of the insured happened while he was under the influence of intoxicating drink, was determined in plaintiff's favor by the jury. Among other separate defenses pleaded, however, was failure to comply with the following provisions of the policy:

> "Notice of every accident for or on account of which a claim may be made shall be given immediately after it happens to the secretary at Utica, N.Y., in writing, with full particulars of the accident and injury, and failure to give such immediate notice shall invalidate all claims under this contract which may be made on account of such accident, and unless affirmative and positive proof of the death or injury and that the same resulted from causes covered by the contract shall be furnished within six months of the happening of such accident, then all claims based thereon shall be forfeited to the association. Notice of death for which a claim may be made shall be given in writing to the secretary of the association within ten days from the date of such death, and failure to give such notice within said ten days shall invalidate any claim for loss by death."

Concededly notice was not given within the time required by the terms of the policy, and, as was found by the trial court, no waiver of such provisions by the defendant was shown. It is the contention of the respondent that such noncompliance was excused by the impossibility of compliance before a discovery of the facts which gave rise to the claim. The weight of authority, however, appears to be that, while as a general rule, where the performance of a duty created by law is prevented by inevitable accident without the fault of a party, the default will be excused, yet when a person by express contract engages absolutely to do an act not impossible or unlawful at the time, neither inevitable accident nor other unforeseen contingency not within his control will excuse him, for the reason that he might have provided against them by his contract. Whiteside v. North American Accident Ins. Co., 200 N.Y. 320, 93 N.E. 948, 35 L.R.A. (N.S.)

696. In the case at bar by the express terms of the contract the provisions as to notice were made conditions precedent to any liability.

Defendant is only liable by reason of its promise and this promise cannot be enlarged by the court, so as to fasten a liability on the defendant, which the latter did not undertake. The insured was at liberty either to accept or reject the offer of the defendant. The defendant was within its rights in undertaking only to be responsible for those accidents which were reported to it in time to permit it to seek witnesses of the occurrence while it was still fresh and the witnesses were still living. As was said by Chief Judge Hiscock in the Whiteside Case:

> "All of these provisions and engagements enter into the substance of the contract which respondent is seeking to enforce, and under such circumstances the courts will not relieve either party under the conditions here presented from fulfillment of the engagement which he has voluntarily undertaken."

The plaintiff relies upon the case of Trippe v. Provident Fund Soc., 140 N.Y. 23, 35 N.E. 316, 22 L.R.A. 432, 37 Am.St.Rep. 529, as an authority for the contention that the time in which to give notice did not begin to run until discovery of the facts constituting the claim. It appears, however, that the decision arrived at in that case was in fact based upon a waiver by the defendant of the provisions of the contract, and therefore the statements of the court, upon which reliance is placed by the plaintiff, must be regarded as dicta, which have not been followed by the later decisions of the same court. Whiteside v. North American Accident Ins. Co., supra.

It follows that the judgment must be reversed, with costs, and the complaint dismissed, with costs.

MERRELL and GREENBAUM, JJ., concur.

CLARKE, P.J. (dissenting). With great respect to the opinion of the Court of Appeals, I do not believe that Whiteside v. North American Accident Insurance Co., 200 N.Y. 320, 93 N.E. 948, 35 L.R.A. (N.S.) 696, controls in the case at bar. In that case the facts were quite different. There the policy contained a provision:

> "That written notice from the insured or his representative, stating the time, place and nature of injury, or death, or commencement of sickness, must be mailed to the secretary of the company at its home office * * * within ten days after the date of such injury, * * * as conditions precedent to recovery."

And the complaint alleged that during the early part of said sickness he was delirious and unable to remember that he had said policy of insurance, and had wholly forgotten that fact until about the 10th day of December, 1904, when he caused notice to be sent to the defendant of such sickness, and the court said:

> "That [the plaintiff] must be held to the terms of the contract which he had voluntarily made, and that, having assented to a provision requiring notice of sickness within a certain time as a condition to recovery, he cannot be excused from fulfillment for the reasons alleged, and especially that this is true in view of the fact already mentioned that the notice called for by his contract might have been served by another person if he was disabled from personally so doing."

* * *

On April 28, 1913, insured disappeared. On May 24, 1913, the defendant wrote to Lyman, the insured, calling upon him to pay an assessment due under the policy on July 8, 1913. On July 10, 1913, Mrs. Lyman, the beneficiary, sent a check in payment of the assessment. This amount was never returned. On July 12, 1913, the defendant wrote inclosing a receipt and asking whether Lyman had changed his address. On July 17, 1913, a reply was sent stating that Lyman had disappeared on April 28, 1913, and had not been heard from since that date. On July 30th the defendant wrote saying, in view of Mr. Lyman's disappearance, the board of directors had terminated his membership in the association and canceled his certificate of insurance. On December 10, 1917, Mrs. Lyman's attorneys wrote the defendant, giving it notice that Lyman's automobile had been dredged from the Delaware river on December 5th, recalling to defendant the fact of his disappearance and the unsuccessful efforts to discover his whereabouts, and making a claim for the beneficiary for the full amount of the policy. On December 13, 1917, the defendant inclosed the usual proof of loss blanks, although not having been requested to do so by the beneficiary. On December 15, 1917, this letter was acknowledged with the statement, "We will prepare the proof of loss and forward same to you in due course," and on June 1, 1918, less than six months after Lyman's car was dredged from the river, Mrs. Lyman sent her proof of loss to the defendant, accompanied by a letter demanding a check for the amount of the insurance. This proof of loss was retained by the defendant, and after its receipt defendant communicated in no way with the plaintiff or her attorneys until the action was commenced.

The verdict of the jury upon the facts establishes that the insured met his death by accident on the 28th day of April, 1913, by reason of his car plunging from an unguarded street into the Delaware river. Of course it was impossible for him to give the notice required in case of accident by the policy. It was equally impossible for his widow to give such notice because the sole fact apparent at that time was that he had disappeared, and although investigations were immediately instituted, handbills printed, and every possible effort made to discover his whereabouts, it was not until three years later that in a dredging of the Delaware river his automobile was discovered and the cause of his disappearance established. It is obvious that the death occurred by accident and that it was within the terms of the policy. It is also obvious that the attempted cancellation of the policy above alluded to is without effect, because at that time the loss had occurred and the rights of the beneficiary to recover therefor were vested.

The sole question which survives the verdict of the jury is whether the failure under the facts and circumstances of this case to furnish the notice provided for in the policy, which it was impossible for any one to do by reason of the peculiar accident which caused the loss, is a complete defense to the action. * * *

* * *

In Ewing v. Commercial Travelers' Mutual Accident Association of America, 55 App.Div. 241, 66 N.Y.Supp. 1056, affirmed 170 N.Y. 590, 63 N.E. 1116, the insured died on June 23, 1897. The policy provided as a condition precedent to a recovery that immediate notice shall be given in writing of the accident or injury with full particulars. No one knew, until after the report of the chemist who had in charge the stomach and other organs of the deceased for chemical analysis upon an autopsy, the cause of death, which was from the effect of taking morphine accidentally. This report was made on the 8th or 9th of July following, and on July 9th the beneficiary notified the defendant. The court said:

> "The term 'immediate' should be interpreted reasonably. Trippe v. P.F. Society, 140 N.Y. 23. The context in which the word is here found implies that before notice is given the 'full particulars' must be first discovered by the person required to give the notice."

In Melcher v. Ocean Accident & Guarantee Corporation, Limited, 175 App.Div. 77, 161 N.Y.Supp. 586, this court reversed a judgment in favor of the plaintiff entered upon the verdict of a jury in an action on a policy whereby the defendant insured the plaintiff against accident upon and adjacent to his apartment house. One Didier was injured through the alleged negligence of the plaintiff on the premises on the 3d of November, 1913, from which injuries he died on the 22d day of March thereafter. By the terms of the policy it was provided that the assured upon the occurrence of an accident shall give immediate written notice thereof, with the fullest information obtainable at the time. Immediately after the accident, which occurred through the negligent operation of a freight elevator, which struck Didier when he was standing on an I-beam at work, he said he was not hurt and finished his job that afternoon, and the incident was not reported to the insurance company. On February 14, 1914, [more than three] months after the accident, the plaintiff received from an attorney employed by Didier a letter prior to Didier's death notifying him that Didier was seriously injured at the apartment on the 3d of November, 1913, while making certain repairs in an elevator shaft. The first notice that the defendant had of the accident was by the delivery of this letter to it by an insurance broker, employed by the plaintiff on the 17th day of February, 1914. This court reversed the judgment upon the ground of failure to give the notice required. The Court of Appeals reversed, quoting with approval Chapin v. Ocean Accident & Guarantee Corporation, 96 Neb. 213, 147 N.W. 465, 52 L.R.A.(N.S.) 227, which said:

> "If no apparent injury occurred from the mishap, and there was no reasonable ground for believing at the time that bodily injury would result from the accident, there was no duty upon the assured to notify the insurer."

While the majority of the court feel that they are constrained to reverse the judgment appealed from in the case at bar under the Whiteside Case, supra, it seems to me that the facts are so different from those presented in that case that the principle laid down in the cases cited by me ought to be applied, and therefore I vote to affirm the judgment appealed from.

DOWLING, J., concurs.

CONNECTICUT FIRE INSURANCE CO. V. FOX

United States Court of Appeals, Tenth Circuit, 1966.
361 F.2d 1.

[Plaintiffs, A.H. Fox and Edith Fox, sole proprietors of the Firebird Motor Hotel, Cheyenne, Wyoming, entered into a contract of fire insurance with Connecticut Fire Insurance Company. The contract was in force when, early in the morning of March 25, 1964, a substantial portion of the motel was either destroyed or damaged by fire. The contract provided that: "The insured shall give immediate notice to this company of any loss * * * and within sixty days after the loss, unless such time is extended in writing by this company, the insured shall render to this company a proof of loss. * * * " A Mr. Foster, an adjuster for General Adjustment Bureau, Inc. (G.A.B.), appeared on the scene the day after the fire and persuaded the Foxes to sign a "non-waiver" agreement (even though the Foxes' attorney apparently advised against it), which essentially provided that no action of the insurer in investigating the loss would waive any conditions of the policy and that no representative of the company had any authority to waive any conditions of the policy unless in writing. Mr. Foster explained to the Foxes the procedures to be followed to recover on the policy without mentioning the proof of loss requirement. On May 5, the parties met again, and according to Mr. Fox's testimony, he presented an inventory of losses.

On June 3, after the sixty day period for filing proof of loss had run, Foster met again with the Foxes and proposed a settlement, which was rejected. At this time, Foster also gave the Foxes a letter stating that although the sixty days had expired, if the proof of loss was filed before July 3, no objection would be made. According to Fox, he then told Foster he would fill out the proof of loss immediately and that he had not been aware that he had to do so because in the past an adjuster had always done such things. The Foxes filled out the proof of loss form and sent the inventories to the insurer on June 6. On June 8, two attorneys for the insurer met with the Foxes and assured them the whole thing would be settled soon. The Foxes heard nothing, and brought suit on July 7th. The insurer rejected the proof of loss thirty days later. The insurer defended on the ground that the Foxes caused the fire and on the ground that the Foxes failed to file a timely proof of loss. The jury found for the Foxes on both issues. On appeal the defendant insurer asserted, among other things, that the proof of loss was not timely as a matter of law.]

HILL, CIRCUIT JUDGE.

* * *

It is undisputed that the Foxes did not file their proofs of loss within sixty days after the fire as required by the policy. As a general rule, a proof of loss requirement is valid and may be considered as a condition precedent to recovery. However, this technical policy requirement may be waived by the insurer either directly or through the acts of its agents. The question to decide is whether under the facts and circumstances of this case, the insurer is deemed to have waived the proof of loss requirement.

Appellants' main contention is that the non-waiver agreement signed by the insured precludes a waiver by the insurer or its agents of a proof of loss requirement. Although we can find no Wyoming law directly in point, there can be no doubt of the validity of insurance non-waiver agreements, which, despite investigation into a claim by an insurer, nevertheless maintains the status quo of the policy and its conditions precedent to recovery. Had the insurer here through its adjusters done no more than investigate the fire loss, we would be loathe to say in light of the non-waiver agreement that this effectively waived the proof of loss requirement. But more was done than a mere investigation.

Non-waiver agreements are not so sacrosanct that they immunize an insurer from responsibility for any and all actions taken in adjusting a loss. The agreement being solely for the benefit of the insurer must be strictly construed against it under sound contract principles. In this case, the agreement merely allows the insurer to investigate to determine the cause and the amount of loss. The actions of the adjusters however went far beyond a mere investigation and to us cannot be considered protected under the non-waiver agreement. Nor can it be seriously doubted that the adjusters here, and particularly Foster, had the power to waive requirements of the policy like those under consideration.

At the first meeting, Agent Foster explained to the Foxes the conditions of the policy and their responsibility thereunder, but no mention was made of the proofs of loss. Foster did furnish inventory forms to be completed and submitted to the insurer and the accuracy and correctness of the forms thereafter seemed to be a main source of difficulty between the parties. No indication was ever made by Foster that proofs of loss were also required. On May 5th, when the Foxes had prepared these inventory forms, Foster rejected them as unsatisfactory. Fox submitted a bid to Foster at the May 5th meeting to completely rebuild the property but it was rejected for lack of detail. On May 12th, G.A.B. sent Mr. Wyatt of Underwriters Salvage Company to the motel to verify the inventory, which he did with Mr. Fox's assistance. Under the circumstances, Fox had a right to believe that once the inventory forms and bids were satisfactorily completed no further action on his part was necessary to perfect the claim. The cases are legion to the effect that once the insurer or its authorized agents indicate by a course of conduct that proofs of loss are unnecessary, such a requirement is waived. But Foster even went further. In taking complete charge of the loss, he instructed the Foxes to secure the property, to winterize the motel and to have the area cleaned and the remaining undamaged units made available for business, all of which was done. According to Mrs. Fox, Foster told them to keep a file on all these expenses and it would be included in settlement. Clearly by all these acts, Foster went beyond a mere investigation of the fire. It is no surprise in light of his apparent authority that the Foxes relied upon Foster to know what they must do to recover their loss.

One other factor certainly bears mentioning. The insurer actually paid a claim under the policy to a motel guest. Agent McMaster of G.A.B. in fact completed the proof of loss for the guest and the company paid $100. Having prepared a proof of loss and assumed liability for a guest in that instance under the policy, it seems rather astonishing that the insurer should now insist on proof of loss from the motel owner. As the final indication of the insurer's intention to waive the proof of loss requirement, appellee points to the letter of June 3rd, which waived the time for filing the proof of loss. The appellant insurer, while acknowledging this letter, contends that Foster had no authority to do so and, even if he did, the time for filing the proofs had already expired when the letter was given on June 3rd and that a waiver cannot be effectuated after the time for filing proofs of loss had expired. While there is some authority to that effect, we believe the other rule should prevail under the facts here and allow the insurer to waive or extend the requirement even though the original time requirement had expired. The contention that Foster lacked authority to make the waiver is not persuasive particularly in light of the company's reliance on the earlier non-waiver agreement which was also signed by Foster in behalf of the insurer. At any rate, had the insurer been dissatisfied with the waiver or extension for filing the proofs, the time for repudiating it would have been when the proofs were received on June 6th, not two months later after suit had been filed. In answer to an interrogatory, the jury expressly found that the agents of G.A.B., and specifically Foster, did have authority to extend the time for filing the proofs of loss. We are satisfied that finding is supported by substantial evidence and must therefore be affirmed.

8 CORBIN ON CONTRACTS

§ 33A.7 (Rev. ed. 2019).

Generally, the promisor's waiver of a condition is followed by the promisee's substantial change of position. At the very least, the promisee will be induced by the waiver not to perform the condition, if the condition consists of some act or forbearance of the promisee * * *

In many cases, however, the waiver takes place after the failure to perform the condition has already occurred, and the promisee makes no subsequent change of position on which to base an estoppel.

* * *

* * * A condition of a promisor's duty can be eliminated by a mere voluntary expression of his willingness to waive it, if its performance does not constitute a material part of the agreed equivalent of the promise and its non-performance does not materially affect the value the promisor received.

R. HILLMAN, PRINCIPLES OF CONTRACT LAW

321–22 (4th ed. 2019).

[W]aivers are, as Johnny Carson used to say, "some crazy stuff," and they represent a significant exception to the rule requiring that promises must be supported by consideration or be relied on to be legally enforceable. One significant limitation on all of this is that courts tend to restrict waivers without consideration or reliance to non-material relinquishments of a right, such as a waiver of an insured's duty to file proofs of loss within a particular time period. Parties generally cannot waive material terms without consideration or reliance. For example, suppose Champ's Sporting Goods promises to pay $2000 to Ron D. Jockefeller, a manufacturer of sports apparel, for 1000 athletic supporters. Contract law would not recognize Champ's waiver if, after paying, it released Jockefeller from its duty to deliver the goods.

PROBLEM 7-4

Your client, Betty Franklin, entered a retail installment contract with Essco Motors to purchase a used Ford Thunderbird. The price was $1,352, of which Franklin paid $300, leaving a balance of $1,052. With finance and insurance charges, Franklin's debt to Essco was $1,656. Her contract called for 24 monthly payments of $69 due on the 15th of each month. Franklin paid $69 on February 15, March 15, April 25, May 23, June 24, July 26, August 24, September 27 and October 27. On November 26, Essco repossessed the car for failure of Franklin to pay the November installment. Advise Franklin on her rights based on the following possible additional facts.

(A) Essco accepted the March through October payments without protest and had given no notice in November before repossessing the car.

(B) Essco accepted the March through October payments without protest, but had notified Franklin in writing on November 5 that payment for November and thereafter would have to be on time.

(C) Essco and Franklin had agreed in April that payment would be on the 27th of each month instead of the 15th and Essco had given no notice before repossessing in November.

(D) Essco and Franklin had agreed in April that payment would be made on the 27th of each month, but Essco had notified Franklin in writing on November 5 that payment for November and thereafter would have to be on time, *e.g.* on the 15th of each month.

Q. VANDENBERG & SONS v. SITER, 204 Pa.Super. 392, 204 A.2d 494 (1964). [Seller warranted that flower bulbs were capable of flowering properly. The contract provided, however, that "[a]ll claims hereunder shall be deemed waived unless presented within eight (8) days after receipt of the goods." The trial court struck buyer's evidence that defects in the bulbs, although existing at the time of delivery, were latent, and could not be discovered until long after the eight days. Held, error.] "A limitation which renders the warranties ineffective as regards latent defects, literally covered by the warranty but not discoverable within the limitation period of the contract, is manifestly unreasonable and therefore invalid under § 1–[205] of the code."

UNIFORM COMMERCIAL CODE § 1–205.

Reasonable Time; Seasonableness

(a) Whether a time for taking an action required by [the Uniform Commercial Code] is reasonable depends on the nature, purpose, and circumstances of the action.

(b) An action is taken seasonably if it is taken at or within the time agreed or, if no time is agreed, at or within a reasonable time.

SECTION SIX: THE OVERRIDING OF EXPRESS CONDITIONS TO PREVENT FORFEITURE

J.N.A. REALTY CORP. V. CROSS BAY CHELSEA, INC.

Court of Appeals of New York, 1977.
42 N.Y.2d 392, 366 N.E.2d 1313.

WACHTLER, JUDGE.

J.N.A. Realty Corp., the owner of a building in Howard Beach, commenced this proceeding to recover possession of the premises claiming that the lease has expired. The lease grants the tenant, Cross Bay Chelsea, Inc., an option to renew and although the notice was sent, through negligence or inadvertence, it was not sent within the time prescribed in the lease. The landlord seeks to enforce the letter of the agreement. The tenant asks for equity to relieve it from a forfeiture.

The Civil Court, after a trial, held that the tenant was entitled to equitable relief. The Appellate Term affirmed, without opinion, but the Appellate Division, after granting leave, reversed and granted the petition. The tenant has appealed to this court.

Two primary questions are raised on the appeal. First, will the tenant suffer a forfeiture if the landlord is permitted to enforce the letter of the agreement. Secondly, if there will be a forfeiture, may a court of equity grant the tenant relief when the forfeiture would result from the tenant's own neglect or inadvertence.

At the trial it was shown that J.N.A. Realty Corp. (hereafter JNA) originally leased the premises to Victor Palermo and Sylvester Vascellero for a 10-year term commencing on January 1, 1964. Paragraph 58 of the lease, which was attached as part of 12-page rider, granted the tenants an option to renew for a 10-year term provided "that Tenant shall notify the landlord in writing by registered or certified mail six (6) months prior to the last day of the term of the lease that tenant desires such renewal." The tenants opened a restaurant on the premises. In February, 1964 they formed the Foro Romano Corp. (Foro) and assigned the lease to the corporation.

By December of 1967 the restaurant was operating at a loss and Foro decided to close it down and offer it for sale or lease. In March, 1968 Foro entered into a contract with Cross Bay Chelsea, Inc. (hereafter Chelsea), to sell the restaurant and assign the lease. As a condition of the sale Foro was required to obtain a modification of the option to renew so that Chelsea would have the right to renew the lease for an additional term of 24 years.

The closing took place in June of 1968. First JNA modified the option and consented to the assignment. The modification, which consists of a separate document to be attached to the lease, states: "the Tenant shall have a right to renew this lease for a further period of Twenty-Four (24) years, instead of Ten (10) years, from the expiration of the original term of said lease * * *. All other provisions of Paragraph #58 in said lease, * * * shall remain in full force and effect, except as hereinabove modified." Foro then assigned the lease and sold its interest in the restaurant to Chelsea for $155,000. The bill of sale states that "the value of the fixtures and chattels included in this sale is the sum of $40,000 and that the remainder of the purchase price is the value of the leasehold and possession of the restaurant premises." At that point five and one-half years remained on the original term of the lease.

In the summer of 1968 Chelsea reopened the restaurant. JNA's president, Nicholas Arena, admitted on the stand that throughout the tenancy it regularly informed Chelsea in writing of its obligations under the lease, such as the need to pay taxes and insurance by certain dates. For instance on June 13, 1973 JNA sent a letter to Chelsea informing them that certain taxes were due to be paid. When that letter was sent the option to renew was due to expire in approximately two weeks but JNA made no mention of this. A similar letter was sent to Chelsea in September, 1973.

Arena also admitted that throughout the term of the tenancy he was "most assuredly" aware of the time limitation on the option. In fact there is some indication in the record that JNA had previously used this device in an attempt to evict another tenant. Nevertheless it was not until November 12, 1973 that JNA took any action to inform the tenant that the option had lapsed. Then it sent a letter noting that the date had passed and, the letter states, "not having heard from you as prescribed by paragraph #58 in our lease we must assume you will vacate the premises" at the expiration of the original term, January 1, 1974. By letter dated November 16, 1973 Chelsea, through its attorney, sent written notice of intention to renew the option which, of course, JNA refused to honor.

At the trial Chelsea's principals claimed that they were not aware of the time limitation because they had never received a copy of paragraph 58 of the rider. They had received a copy of the modification but they had assumed that it gave them an absolute right to retain the tenancy for 24 years after the expiration of the original term. However, at the trial and later at the Appellate Division, it was found that Chelsea had knowledge of, or at least was "chargeable with notice" of, the time limitation in the rider and thus was negligent in failing to renew within the time prescribed.

Chelsea's principals also testified that they had spent an additional $15,000 on improvements, at least part of which had been expended after the option had expired. Toward the end of the trial JNA's attorney asked the court whether it would "take evidence from" Arena that he had negotiated with another tenant after the option to renew had lapsed. However, the court held that this testimony would be immaterial.

It is a settled principle of law that a notice exercising an option is ineffective if it is not given within the time specified * * *. Thus the tenant had no legal right to exercise the option when it did, but to say that is simply to pose the issue; it does not resolve it. Of course the tenant would not be asking for equitable relief if it could establish its rights at law.

The major obstacle to obtaining equitable relief in these cases is that default on an option usually does not result in a forfeiture. The reason is that the option itself does not create any interest in the property, and no rights accrue until the condition precedent has been met by giving notice within the time specified. Thus equity will not intervene because the loss of the option does not ordinarily result in the forfeiture of any vested rights. * * *

But when a tenant in possession under an existing lease has neglected to exercise an option to renew, he might suffer a forfeiture if he has made valuable improvements on the property. This of course generally distinguishes the lease option, to renew or purchase, from the stock option or the option to buy goods. This was a distinction which some of the older cases failed to recognize. * * * More recently it has been noted that "although the tenant has no legal interest in the renewal period until the required notice is given, yet an equitable interest is recognized and protected against forfeiture in some cases where the tenant has in good faith made improvements of a substantial character, intending to renew the lease, if the landlord is not harmed by the delay in the giving of the notice and the lessee would sustain substantial loss in case the lease were not renewed" (2 Pomeroy, Equity Jurisprudence [5th ed.], § 453b, p. 296).

* * * In *Jones v. Gianferante,* 305 N.Y. 135, 138, 111 N.E.2d 419, 420, citing [F.B. Fountain Co. v. Stein, 97 Conn. 619, 118 A. 47], we held that the tenant was entitled to "the benefit of the rule or practice in equity which relieves against such forfeitures of valuable lease terms when default in notice has not prejudiced the landlord, and has resulted from an honest mistake, or similar excusable fault." The rule was extended in *Sy Jack Realty Co. v. Pergament Syosset Corp.,* 27 N.Y.2d 449, 453, 318 N.Y.S.2d 720, 722, 267 N.E.2d 462, 464, * * * to preserve the tenant's interest in a "long-standing location for a retail business" because this is "an important part of the good will of that enterprise, [and thus] the tenant stands to lose a substantial and valuable asset."

In neither of those cases were we asked to consider whether the tenant would be entitled to equitable relief from the consequences of his own neglect or "mere forgetfulness" as the court had held in the *Fountain* case, *supra.* In *Gianferante* the default was due to an ambiguous lease, and in *Sy Jack* the notice was mailed but never delivered (but see *Roy's of North Syracuse v. P & C Food Markets,* 51 A.D.2d 641, 377 N.Y.S.2d 1019, mot. for lv. to app. den. 38 N.Y.2d 711, 384 N.Y.S.2d 1026, 348 N.E.2d 927; and the dissenting opn. in *Sy Jack, supra,* 27 N.Y.2d p. 456, n. 1, 318 N.Y.S.2d p. 725, 267 N.E.2d p. 466, where it is noted that the three cases cited in Williston—the principle one being the *Fountain* case—"obviously warranted equitable relief. For not only in those cases was there 'excusable fault', but also in each one the tenant had made substantial improvements"). But the principle involved is well established in this State. A tenant or mortgagor should not be denied equitable relief from the consequences of his own neglect or inadvertence if a forfeiture would result (*Giles v. Austin,* 62 N.Y. 486; *Noyes v. Anderson,* 124 N.Y. 175, 26 N.E. 316; *Roy's of North Syracuse v. P & C Food Markets, supra;* see, also, 2 Pomeroy, Equity Jurisprudence [5th ed.], § 452, p. 287). The rule applies even though the tenant or mortgagor, by his inadvertence, has neglected to perform an affirmative duty and thus breached a covenant in the agreement (*Giles v. Austin, supra; Noyes v. Anderson, supra*).

On occasion the court has cautioned that equitable relief would be denied where there has been a willful or gross neglect (*Noyes v. Anderson, supra,* 124 N.Y. p. 179, 26 N.E. p. 317), but it has been reluctant to employ the sanction when a forfeiture would result. In *Giles v. Austin, supra,* p. 491, for instance, the landlord sought to recover possession of the premises after the tenant had neglected to pay the taxes as required by a covenant in the lease. We held that although the tenant had not paid the taxes since the inception of the lease in 1859, and had only paid them after suit was commenced in 1868, the tenant's default was not "so willful, or his neglect so inexcusable, that a court of equity should have denied him any relief."

There are several cases in which this court has denied a tenant or mortgagor equitable relief because of his own neglect to perform within the time fixed in the lease or mortgage, but only when it has found that there was "no penalty, no forfeiture". * * * Cardozo took a different view. He felt that even though there may be no penalty or forfeiture "in a strict or proper sense" equity should "relieve against it if default has been due to mere venial inattention and if relief can be granted without damage to the lender". Even in those cases he would apply the general equitable principle that "the gravity of the fault must be compared with the gravity of the hardship" (*Graf v. Hope Bldg. Corp.,* * * * 254 N.Y. pp. 9–10, 13, 171 N.E. p. 888 [Cardozo, Ch. J., dissenting]; see, also, 2 Pomeroy, Equity Jurisprudence [5th ed.], § 439, p. 220).

Here, as noted, the tenant has made a considerable investment in improvements on the premises—$40,000 at the time of purchase, and an additional $15,000 during the tenancy. In addition, if the location is lost, the restaurant would undoubtedly lose a considerable amount of its customer good will. The tenant was at fault, but not in a culpable sense. It was, as Cardozo says, "mere venial inattention." There would be a forfeiture and the gravity of the loss is certainly out of all proportion to the gravity of the fault. Thus, under the circumstances of this case, the tenant would be entitled to equitable relief if there is no prejudice to the landlord.

However, it is not clear from the record whether JNA would be prejudiced if the tenant is relieved of its default. Because of the trial court's ruling, JNA was unable to submit proof that it might be prejudiced if the terms of the agreement were not enforced literally. Its proof of other negotiations was considered immaterial. It may be that after the tenant's default the landlord, relying on the agreement, in good faith, made other commitments for the premises. But if JNA did not rely on the letter of the agreement then, it should not be permitted to rely on it now to exact a substantial forfeiture for the tenant's unwitting default. This, however, must be resolved at a new trial.

Finally we would note, as the dissenters do, that it is possible to imagine a situation in which a tenant holding an option to renew might intentionally delay beyond the time prescribed in order to exploit a fluctuating market. However, as the dissenters also note, there is no evidence to suggest that that is what occurred here. On the contrary there has been an affirmed finding of fact that the tenant's late notice was due to negligence. Of course a tenant who has intentionally delayed should not be relieved of a forfeiture simply because this tenant, who was merely inadvertent, may be granted equitable relief. But, on the other hand, we do not believe that this tenant, or any tenant, guilty only of negligence should be denied equitable relief because some other tenant, in some other case, may be found to have acted in bad faith. By its nature equitable relief must always depend on the facts of the particular case and not on hypotheticals.

Accordingly, the order of the Appellate Division should be reversed and a new trial granted.

BREITEL, CHIEF JUDGE (dissenting).

Relieving the tenant of its negligent failure to exercise its option to renew a lease within the prescribed time upsets established precedent, introduces instability in business transactions, and disregards commercial realities. I therefore dissent.

This case involves an option to renew a lease, not a mortgage foreclosure or an acceleration clause in a lease or mortgage. The categories and applicable precedents are not to be confused.

* * *

Had an honest mistake or similar "excusable fault", as opposed to what is undoubtedly mere carelessness, occasioned the tenant's tardiness, absent prejudice to the landlord, equitable relief would be available * * *. At issue, instead, is the availability of equitable relief where the only excuse for the commercial tenant's dilatory failure to exercise its option to renew is sheer carelessness.

Enough has been said to uncover a common situation. Experienced and even hardened businessmen at cross-purposes over the renewal of a valuable lease term seek on the one hand to stand by the written agreement, and on the other, to loosen the applicable rules to receive ad hoc adjustment of equities and relief from economic detriment. The landlord wants a higher return. The tenant wants to keep the old bargain. Which of the profit-seeking parties in this particular case should prevail as a matter of morals is not within the province of the courts. The well-settled doctrine is that with respect to options, whether they be lease renewal options, options to purchase real or personal property, or stock options, time is of the essence. The exceptions, namely, estoppel, fraud, mistake, accident, or overreaching, are few. Commercial stability and certainty are paramount, and always the dangers of unsolvable issues of fact and speculative manipulation (as with stock options) are to be avoided.

The landlord should be awarded possession of the premises in accordance with the undisputed language and manifested intention of the written lease, its 12-page rider, and modification. It does not suffice that the tenant may suffer an economic detriment in losing the renewal period. Nor does it suffice that the delay in giving notice may have caused the landlord no "prejudice", other than loss of the opportunity to relet the property or renegotiate the terms of a lease on a fresh basis. Once an option to renew a lease has been conditioned upon the tenant's giving timely notice, the commercial lessee should not be heard to complain that through carelessness a valued asset has been lost, anymore than one would allow the landlord to complain of the economic detriment to him in agreeing to an improvident option to renew.

* * *

In this State, as in others, relief has been afforded tenants threatened with loss of an expected renewal period (see, generally, Effect of Lessee's Failure or Delay in Giving Notice Within Specified Time, of Intention to Renew Lease, Ann., 44 A.L.R.2d 1359, esp. 1362–1369). But in New York, as elsewhere, the circumstances conditioning such relief have been carefully limited. It is only where the tenant can show, not mere negligence, but an excuse such as fraud, mistake, or accident, that is, one or more of the categories common and integral to invocation of equity, that courts have, despite the literal agreement and intention of the parties, stepped in to prevent a loss. * * *

* * *

The majority facilely disposes of the tenant's delinquency in exercising its option by relying on cases in which a party, notwithstanding its negligence, was relieved from a forfeiture * * *. But indiscriminate application of principles evolved to deal with mortgage foreclosures or a lessor's right to re-enter upon a tenant's failure to pay taxes and assessments when due does not withstand analysis. Since ever so long, enforcement of a mortgage has rested in equity * * *. It is also significant that as to foreclosure, time is not of the essence (see 10 N.Y.Jur., Contracts, § 270). Even where acceleration clauses are involved and a strong argument can be made for allowing relief, time has been of the essence and negligence has not been excused * * *. It is equally inappropriate to analogize to a lessee's failure to comply with a lease requirement that taxes and assessments be paid as they become due * * *. For the loss of an existing lease term subject to a condition subsequent distinguishes that situation from the loss of a possible option period subject to a condition precedent. An option is a right to purchase or acquire an interest in personal or real property in the future, and, if precise, it carries an invulnerable requirement to comply with all conditions, including that of time which is therefore of the essence in law and equity.

There are cases, not binding on this court, which express the principles discussed. For reasons that are not persuasive they would distinguish, however, between mere neglect or forgetfulness and gross or willful negligence, whatever that might be * * *. This is not a distinction generally accepted and is hardly a pragmatic one to apply in an area where the opportunities for distortion and manipulation are so great. The instability and uncertainty would be dangerous and would allow for ad hoc dispensations in particular cases without reliable rule so essential to commercial enterprise.

To begin with, under the guise of sheer inadvertence, a tenant could gamble with a fluctuating market, at the expense of his landlord, by delaying his decision beyond the time fixed in the agreement. The market having resolved in favor of exercising the option, the landlord, even though the day appointed in the agreement has passed, could be held to the return set out in the option, although if the market had resolved otherwise, the tenant could not be held to the renewal period.

None of this is to say that the tenant in this case was guilty of any manipulation. Hardly so. But what the court is concerned with is a rule for this case which perforce must cover other cases of like kind, where there will be no assurance that the "forgetfulness" is no more than that. The worst of the matter is that the kind of paltry record made in this case is hardly one on which a new rule with potential for mischief should be based. When the option, especially one requiring notice well in advance of the expiration of the lease, permits of economic manipulation, in commercial fairness the parties, especially if represented by counsel, should be held to their bargain, if plainly expressed.

Considering investments in the premises or the renewal term a "forfeiture" as alone warranting equitable relief would undermine if not dissolve the general rule upon which there is agreement. For, it is difficult to imagine a dilatory commercial tenant, particularly one in litigation over a renewal, who would not or could not point, scrupulously or unscrupulously, to some threatened investment in the premises, be it a physical improvement or the fact of good will. As a practical matter, it is not unreasonable to expect the commercial tenant, as compared with his residential counterpart, to protect his business interests with meticulousness, a meticulousness to which he would hold his landlord. All he, or his lawyer, need do is red-flag the date on which he has to act.

Having established no excuse, other than its own carelessness, Chelsea's claim is unfounded. Even if Chelsea honestly thought it enjoyed a 30-year lease, it does not change the result. Nor is it helpful to argue that Chelsea, always represented by a lawyer, was unable to procure a copy of the entire lease agreement. Indeed, it borders on the utterly incredible that experienced, sophisticated businessmen and their lawyers would not have assembled and scrutinized every relevant document affecting a long-term lease covering, with a renewal, a 30-year period.

That adherence to well-settled principles, like a Statute of Limitations or a Statute of Frauds works a hardship on some does not, alone, permit a court to depart from sound doctrine and principles. Even if precedent did not control the same doctrines and principles discussed should be applied.

Accordingly, I dissent and vote that the order of the Appellate Division should be affirmed, and the landlord awarded possession of the premises.

GABRIELLI, FUCHSBERG and COOKE, JJ., concur with WACHTLER, J.

BREITEL, C.J., dissents and votes to affirm in a separate opinion in which JASEN and JONES, JJ., concur.

Order reversed, with costs, and a new trial granted.

KNAPP, JUDGMENT CALL: THEORETICAL APPROACHES TO CONTRACT DECISION-MAKING

1988 Ann.Surv.Am.L. 307, 333, 336.

From the record, it appears that the tenant Chelsea had by 1973 established a profitable restaurant at the Howard Beach location, one which it wished to continue. You may assume that it would at that point have been possible for Chelsea to find comparable space in some other building close enough so that at least some of the "good will" attributable to location would be retained, but that the high costs of moving (including both the costs of physical removal and the loss of profits occasioned by an interruption of business) plus uncertainty about the transferability of its good will made Chelsea strongly prefer to stay at its present location on the JNA premises. This could have been the case even if rental levels in the area had not risen to levels higher than those provided for in its lease-renewal agreement with JNA; since apparently they had, Chelsea's decision to invest resources in an attempt to stay on at its present location is easily seen as the act of one motivated by rational self-interest.

For its part, the landlord JNA appears to have been motivated entirely by a desire to realize from the property a level of rental income higher than that provided by the lease extension agreement. To analyze more completely the economic factors at work, however, it appears relevant to note that landlords in similar cases (i.e., landlords resisting lease renewal) might well be motivated by a variety of concerns, and that these various possibilities should be taken into account in any economic analysis of the case. At least three distinguishable cases may be suggested: (1) The landlord may believe that the property could be sold for an advantageous price if it were unencumbered by this tenancy; (2) the landlord may be willing to continue to rent to a tenant of this type, perhaps even on comparable terms, but may wish to get rid of this particular tenant; (3) the landlord may be willing to continue to rent to this tenant, but only at a higher rental (as was apparently true in JNA's case). * * *

* * *

* * * So far as one can tell from the record or from discussions with the attorneys involved, JNA had no wish to sell the building or to convert it to another use; nor did it have any particular complaints about Chelsea as a tenant. It merely wanted to receive a higher rental than provided for in the lease extension agreement. This is the third situation imagined above. In this variation of the case, a decision in the landlord's favor serves neither to facilitate some fundamentally different utilization of the property in question nor to save the landlord (and society) the expense of effecting what might well be a deserved termination of the tenancy. Instead, [the] court's decision will merely affect the distribution of wealth as between the landlord and the tenant: the tenant either will be forced to agree to a rent increase, or it won't.

RESTATEMENT (SECOND) OF CONTRACTS § 229.

To the extent that the non-occurrence of a condition would cause disproportionate forfeiture, a court may excuse the non-occurrence of that condition unless its occurrence was a material part of the agreed exchange.

Illustrations:

3. A contracts to make repairs on B's house, in return for which B agrees to pay $10,000 "on condition that the repairs are completed by October 1." The repairs are not completed until October 2. A court may decide that there are two cumulative conditions, repair of the house and completion of the repairs by October 1, and that the non-occurrence of the second condition is excused to the extent of one day.

HOLIDAY INNS OF AMERICA, INC. V. KNIGHT

Supreme Court of California, 1969.
70 Cal.2d 327, 450 P.2d 42.

TRAYNOR, CHIEF JUSTICE.

Plaintiffs appeal from a judgment for defendants in an action seeking a declaration that a contract was still effective. The judgment was entered after plaintiffs' motion for summary judgment was denied and defendants' motion for summary judgment was granted.

The pleadings and affidavits of the parties establish the following undisputed facts.

Plaintiffs are the successors in interest to the optionee under a written option contract between the optionee and the owners of the option property, defendant D. Manley Knight and his mother, Mary Knight. Mary Knight is now deceased and D. Manley Knight is the sole owner of the property. Although his wife is also named a defendant herein, she has no interest in the contract or the option property. We will therefore refer to D. Manley Knight as defendant.

The contract, executed on September 30, 1963, granted an option to purchase real property in Orange County for $198,633, the price to be subject, however, to prescribed adjustments for changes in the cost of living. Unless cancelled as provided in the agreement, the option could be exercised by giving written notice thereof no later than April 1, 1968. The contract provided for an initial payment of $10,000 and for four additional payments of $10,000 to be made directly to the optionors on July 1 of each year, commencing in 1964, unless the option was exercised or cancelled before the next such payment became due. These payments were not to be applied to the purchase price. The cancellation provision provided that "it is mutually understood that failure to make payment on or before the prescribed date will automatically cancel this option without further notice." On December 9, 1963, the parties amended the contract by executing escrow instructions that provided that the annual payments were to be deposited in escrow with the Security Title Insurance Company, and that, in "the event you [Security Title] do not receive the $10,000 annual payments [by July 1] and upon receiving notice from Optionors to cancel the option, without further instructions from Optionee you are to terminate the escrow."

The initial payment of $10,000 and the annual installments for 1964 and 1965 were paid. After the execution of the contract, plaintiffs expended "great amounts of money" to develop a major residential and commercial center on the land adjacent to the option property. These expenditures have caused the option property to increase substantially in value since the contract was executed. Plaintiffs' purpose in entering into the contract was to put themselves in a position to secure the advantage of this increase in value resulting from their development efforts.

In 1966 plaintiffs mailed a check for $10,000 to defendant. It was made out to D. Manley Knight and his wife, Lavinia Knight, and dated June 30, 1966. Defendant received the check on July 2, 1966 and returned it to plaintiffs on July 8, stating that the option contract was cancelled. On July 8 plaintiffs tendered another check directly to defendant, and he again refused it. On July 15 plaintiffs deposited a $10,000 check with Security Title payable to defendant. Security Title tendered the check to defendant, but his attorney returned it to plaintiffs on July 27 and advised them that the agreement was terminated pursuant to the cancellation provision.

Plaintiffs contend that payment of the annual installment was timely on the ground that the check became the property of defendant when mailed; that even if the payment was late, the trial court should have relieved them from forfeiture and declared the option in force under section 3275 of the Civil Code; and that, in any event, the trial court erred in excluding extrinsic evidence offered to prove that the escrow instructions modified the contract to permit payment at any time before defendant notified the title company that the option was cancelled. Since the undisputed facts establish that plaintiffs are entitled to relief from forfeiture pursuant to section 3275, it is unnecessary to consider plaintiffs' other contentions.

Section 3275 provides: "Whenever, by the terms of an obligation, a party thereto incurs a forfeiture, or a loss in the nature of a forfeiture, by reason of his failure to comply with its provisions, he may be relieved therefrom, upon making full compensation to the other party, except in case of a grossly negligent, willful, or fraudulent breach of duty." The tumultuous history of this section has been recorded in a lengthy series of major decisions in the area of property and contract law.

Although most of the cases considering section 3275 have involved land sale contracts, its proscriptions against forfeiture apply in any case in which the party seeking relief from default has brought himself within the terms of the section by pleading and proving facts that justify its application. (Barkis v. Scott, 34 Cal.2d [16] at pp. 118, 120, 208 P.2d 367.) In determining whether a given case falls within section 3275, however, it is necessary to consider the nature of the contract and the specific clause in question. Although the contract in the instant case is an option contract, the question is not whether the exercise of the option was timely, but whether the right to exercise the option in the future was forfeited by a failure to pay the consideration for that right precisely on time. Defendant's reliance on Cummings v. Bullock (9th Cir.1966) 367 F.2d 182, and Wilson v. Ward (1957) 155 Cal.App.2d 390, 317 P.2d 1018, is therefore misplaced. Both those cases dealt with the time within which an option must be exercised and correctly held that such time cannot be extended beyond that provided in the contract. To hold otherwise would give the optionee, not the option he bargained for, but a longer and therefore more extensive option. In the present case, however, plaintiffs are not seeking to extend the period during which the option can be exercised but only to secure relief from the provision making time of the essence in tendering the annual payments. * * * In a proper case, relief will be granted under section 3275 from such a provision. (Barkis v. Scott, supra 34 Cal.2d at p. 122, 208 P.2d 367.)

The sole issue in this case is whether the plaintiffs have brought themselves within section 3275; whether there would be a loss in the nature of a forfeiture suffered by plaintiffs if the option contract were terminated. Essentially, the position of defendant is that there is no forfeiture since plaintiffs got precisely what they bargained for, namely, the exclusive right to buy the property for the three years during which they made payments. Cancellation because of the late 1966 payment amounts to nothing more than terminating a contract providing for that exclusive right during 1966. As viewed by defendant, this contract is in effect wholly executory and therefore its termination would not result in a forfeiture to either party. (Martin v. Morgan (1890) 87 Cal. 203, 25 P. 350.)

To sustain defendant's argument, the contract would have to be viewed as a series of independent contracts, each for a one-year option. Only if this were true, could it be said that plaintiffs received their bargained for equivalent of the $30,000 payments. (Sheveland v. Reed (1958) 159 Cal.App.2d 820, 822, 324 P.2d 633.) The economic realities of the transaction, however, do not support this analysis. First, the language of the agreement states that the "Optioners hereby grant to Optionee the exclusive right and option for a five year period * * *." The parties agreed to bind themselves to a period of five years with the price payable in five installments. On the basis of risk allocation, it is clear that each payment of the $10,000 installment was partially for an option to buy the land during that year and partially for a renewal of the option for another year up to a total of five years. With the passage of time, plaintiffs have paid more and more for the right to renew, and it is this right that would be forfeited by requiring payment strictly on time. At the time the forfeiture was declared, plaintiffs had paid a substantial part of the $30,000 for the right to exercise the option during the last two years. Thus, they have not received what they bargained for and they have lost more than the benefit of their bargain. In short, they will suffer a forfeiture of that part of the $30,000 attributable to the right to exercise the option during the last two years.[1]

Plaintiffs have at all times remained willing and able to continue with the performance of the contract and have acted in good faith to accomplish this end. Defendant has not suffered any injury justifying termination of the contract, and none of his reasonable expectations have been defeated. Moreover, he will receive the benefit of his bargain, namely, the full price of the option granted plaintiffs. As we stated in *Barkis,* "when the default has not been serious and the vendee is willing and able to continue with his performance of the contract, the vendor suffers no damage by allowing the vendee to do so." (Barkis v. Scott, supra, 34 Cal.2d at p. 122, 208 P.2d at p. 371.)

---

[1] Plaintiffs also allege forfeiture of "great amounts of money" expended for the development of surrounding land. Evidently none of the investment was made in the option property. Since there is nothing to indicate that the development was not highly profitable in its own right or that inclusion of defendant's property was necessary to make the development a success, it would not seem that any part of these expenditures can be considered forfeited by a termination of the contract. * * *

The judgment is reversed and the trial court is directed to enter a summary judgment for plaintiffs in accord with the views herein expressed.

PROBLEM 7-5

Compare once again Jacob & Youngs, Inc. v. Kent with Brown-Marx Assocs., Ltd. v. Emigrant Savings Bank. (See Section Two of this chapter.) We saw that the latter case affirms the general doctrine that a party must strictly comply with an express condition, while Jacob & Youngs holds that, in the absence of an express condition as to quality of performance, there is an implied condition of substantial performance. In light of the cases on excuse, avoidance, and overriding of express conditions, what remains of the initial sharpness of the foregoing distinction?

NOTE:
UNJUST ENRICHMENT AS A THEORY TO PREVENT FORFEITURE

As we have seen, courts avoid forfeiture resulting from the failure to satisfy a condition precedent under an "agreement with consideration." Courts also avoid forfeiture by invoking the unjust enrichment theory of obligation. In a particular case, of course, that theory may be unavailable because one or more of the requirements for an unjust enrichment recovery may not be met. See Chapter Two. Even when those requirements are met, the recovery may be less than a recovery on the contract. For example, suppose that an express condition precedent to Owner's duty to pay Builder $4500 for construction of a sidewalk is the completion of 48 slabs. Suppose further that Builder is only able to complete 36 slabs. The market value of 36 slabs is $2500 and Owner has not sustained any damages resulting from the breach. Builder may recover $2500 based on unjust enrichment, whereas a ratable portion of the contract price would be $3375.

SECTION SEVEN: EXPRESS CONDITIONS AND THE LAW OF PLEADING AND PROCEDURE

Sometimes a court allocates burdens of pleading and proof depending on whether a condition is cast in the form of a condition precedent or a condition subsequent. Suppose the buyer and the seller of a house agree that the buyer will pay $75,000 for the house on May 1 on condition that the buyer sells his own house by that date. Such a condition is usually denominated a condition precedent because the duty of the buyer to pay has not ripened—the buyer must sell his house first. In the seller's suit for the buyer's failure to pay, some courts allocate to the seller the burdens of pleading and proving that the buyer has sold his house and thus that the buyer's duty to perform has matured. Indeed, some court rules require such an allocation with respect to pleading. Rule 9(c) of the Federal Rules of Civil Procedure provides:

> In pleading the performance or occurrence of conditions precedent, it is sufficient to aver generally that all conditions precedent have been performed or have occurred. A denial of performance or occurrence shall be made specifically and with particularity.

Suppose, however, that the parties' agreement calls for the buyer to purchase the house on May 1, "but if the buyer is unable to sell his own house, the buyer is released from the duty to purchase." This condition is cast in the form of a condition subsequent. Here the buyer's duty to perform has already arisen, but is discharged if the buyer cannot sell the house. Some courts allocate to the buyer the burdens of pleading and proving that he has failed to sell his house and thus that his duty of performance has been discharged.

You can see that the drafters of a contract can draft most conditions in either precedent or subsequent *form* and thus have some control over the allocations of burdens of pleading and proof at a potential trial. But the law may also permit a court to take into account many additional factors in allocating burdens of proof, such as the probability of the truth of an allegation, and which party has better access to the available evidence.

Occasionally a court may view a condition subsequent as more than merely a matter of form. For example, a policy of fire insurance may require notice and proof of loss as conditions precedent to the insurer's duty to pay. The policy may also require that the insured bring any action within a certain time. Technically, the insured's duty to bring the action could be drafted as a condition precedent to the duty of the insurer to pay. But would this make sense? Instead, the insurance company drafts the duty to pay as subject to the condition subsequent that the insured bring the action. Therefore, once the insured files the notice and proof of loss, the insurer's duty to pay matures, but it is subsequently discharged if the insured does not sue within the specified time.

SECTION EIGHT: IMPLIED CONDITIONS FIXING THE ORDER OF PERFORMANCE

In Section One of this chapter, we introduced the problem that arises when the parties leave a gap in their agreement as to the order of performance. We now return to this problem. In subsection A, we consider gap-filler rules that apply when simultaneous exchange is possible. In subsection B, we consider gap-filler rules that apply when one party must perform before the other.

A. SIMULTANEOUS EXCHANGE

Assume that in a signed writing a vendor agrees to sell Blackacre to a vendee on July 2 for $215,000. Assume the agreement does not set forth whether one party is to perform first or whether the two are to perform simultaneously. Nor do the circumstances demonstrate that the parties intended any particular approach. Thus, there are no express or implied-in-fact conditions fixing the order of performance. In the absence of precedent, a court confronted with a dispute over the order of performance must fill the gap. One possibility would be to adopt a rule requiring the vendor to perform first by transferring a deed to the vendee and by allowing the vendee to enter possession before paying the $215,000 price. Another possibility would be to require the vendor to deliver the deed and the vendee to pay the $215,000 at the same time, with the vendee to take possession thereafter. Still another possibility would be to require the vendee to pay before the vendor transfers a deed. What policies are relevant to this choice of gap fillers? As we will see, one policy is facilitating the consummation of agreed exchanges. A related policy is eliminating, or at least minimizing, the risk that one party will perform without receiving due performance in return. Which of the alternative rules above would best serve these policies?

Suppose that the order of performance gap is filled by a rule of law requiring concurrent performances. Suppose also that the vendor does not perform at all, or does not substantially perform, but the agreement is silent on the consequences. Must the vendee nevertheless perform? A court might choose to fill this gap by adopting a rule that the non-performing party—here, the vendor—must pay any damages to the vendee for breach of contract, but that the vendee must still perform or be liable for breach as well. But such an approach would not make sense. As an alternative to the foregoing rule, a court might provide that the vendee can not only recover damages upon the vendor's breach but also can withhold his own promised performance. Put another way, contract law might make the vendor liable for breach and also regard the breach as a failure of an implied-in-law ("constructive") condition precedent to the vendee's duty to pay, with the result that the vendee's duty does not mature at all. Which of the foregoing basic alternatives would maximize the likelihood that agreed exchanges will take place? Which alternative would minimize the risk that one party will perform without receiving due performance in return?

An additional related problem is this. Let us suppose that the court adopts a rule requiring the parties to perform simultaneously and that the vendor does not show up on July 2 with the deed. What must the aggrieved vendee show in court to establish a right to damages for the vendor's nonperformance? One approach would be to require the vendee only to allege and prove the vendor's nonperformance of the contract. An alternative would be to require not only such allegations and proof, but *also* allegations and proof that the vendee duly tendered performance to the vendor (or that for some reason this tender was excused), that the vendee then demanded performance from the vendor, and that all this was unavailing. Which of these rules would reveal who was responsible for the failure of the exchange? Which of these rules would maximize the likelihood that agreed exchanges will occur without a default? One court set forth the law here as follows:

> In a contract with concurrent conditions, a party is not required to perform until the other party makes a valid offer to perform. Restatement (Second) of Contracts § 238 cmt. a. (1981). If no party performs, neither party is in default, nor liable for breach. *Id.* Thus, a claimant alleging breach of a contract that contains concurrent conditions must at least show that he or she offered to perform, and that the other party defaulted. *Id.* The Restatement further instructs that a valid offer to perform "must be made with the manifested present ability to make it good, but the offeror need not go so far as actually to hold out that which he is to deliver." *Id.* However, "[w]hen it is too late for either to make such an offer, both parties are discharged by the non-occurrence of a condition." *Id.*

Addie v. Kjaer, 737 F.3d 854 (3d Cir. 2013).

Observe that if the vendee were to sue for specific performance, the court could order a simultaneous exchange, with the vendor to deliver the deed upon the vendee's payment. According to this approach, the exchange would take place under court supervision without risk that one party would perform and the other not. But the court cannot so effectively facilitate the aims of the parties where it has no direct intervening role, such as in a damages action after the time for performance. The court can then only require that the vendee allege and prove that the vendee took those steps (in a timely fashion) that would have been likely, were the vendor willing, to lead to performance by both parties, or at least require that the vendee allege and prove that those steps would have been useless.

PASSEHL ESTATE V. PASSEHL

Supreme Court of Iowa, 2006.
712 N.W.2d 408.

STREIT, JUSTICE.

As the cynic Ambrose Bierce once said, "Death is not the end. There remains the litigation over the estate." Jerry and Volnetta Passehl claim the district court erred by enforcing a penalty provision in their settlement agreement with the Doris N. Passehl Estate (hereinafter "the Estate"). They now seek further review of the court of appeals' decision affirming the district court's ruling. Because we find the terms of the penalty provision were not met, we vacate the decision of the court of appeals and reverse and remand to the district court with instructions.

I. Facts and Prior Proceedings

Jerry, Karen, and David are the children of Doris N. Passehl. Doris died in 1997. At the time of her death, Doris owned approximately 160 acres of farmland in Franklin County. Jerry Passehl and his wife, Volnetta (hereinafter "Passehls"), have, for the past fifteen years, occupied a five-acre portion of this land and operated an auto salvage business thereon. The portion of land occupied by Passehls was covered with vehicles and, for the most part, surrounded by a fence. The fence was erected in 1990 after the Franklin County Zoning Board of Adjustment approved the use of the land as a dismantling and recycling center on the condition that a six-foot-high enclosure fence surround the premises. Two grain bins were also located within the fenced area. The other 155 tillable acres were, and still are, leased to a third party. The lease provides that the third party can use the two grain bins located on the land occupied by Passehls.

Karen and David serve as co-executors of the Estate. After Doris's death, family disputes over Passehls' operation of the salvage business resulted in two separate lawsuits. In one lawsuit, the Estate filed suit against Passehls for breach of contract, conversion, and nonpayment of rent. In another lawsuit, the Estate filed an ejectment action to remove Passehls from the land. In an effort to resolve their differences, the parties agreed to settle these lawsuits through a written settlement agreement. The settlement agreement, signed October 17, 2002, provides:

> 2. [Passehls] agree to return to Karen Zander and David Passehl the motorized Shriner's car and the cornsheller.
>
> . . . .
>
> 4. [The Estate] agrees to sell to [Passehls] and [Passehls] agree to buy from [the Estate] . . . [a]n approximate five acre tract . . . [t]he legal description [of such land] shall be established by survey which shall coincide with existing fence boundaries required by Franklin County Zoning Ordinances.
>
> [Passehls] agree to deposit into the Brian D. Miller Trust Account [Miller was the lawyer for the estate] Twenty Thousand Dollars ($20,000.00) on or before October 18, 2002. The purchase price for the above described real estate shall be Fifty Thousand Dollars ($50,000.00). Closing shall be held on or before March 1, 2003. The parties agree that the $20,000.00 deposited into the Brian D. Miller Trust Account shall be applied toward the purchase price at time of closing.
>
> In the event that [the Estate] provides marketable title to the *subject* real estate, *but closing does not occur* on or before March 1, 2003, *as a result of nonperformance* by [Passehls], then the

parties agree that the $20,000.00 deposited into the Brian D. Miller Trust Account shall be forfeited to [the Estate].

* * *

The district court approved the settlement agreement. Both lawsuits, along with an unrelated pending appeal by Passehls, were dismissed with prejudice. On the same day, the parties signed an Iowa State Bar Association real estate contract form for the land described in the settlement agreement. At the time the agreement and contract were drafted, neither party had a precise legal description of this land. In both the settlement agreement and the real estate contract, the land was described as the following:

> The acreage locally known as 513 160th St., Latimer, Iowa and described as: An approximate five acre tract located in the Northwest Quarter (NW1/4) of section 26, Township 92 North, Range 22 West of the 5th P.M., Franklin County, Iowa. The legal description shall be determined by survey, which shall coincede [sic] with existing fence boundaries required by Franklin County Zoning.

The real estate contract also stated the purchase price for the real estate:

> 1. PRICE. The total purchase price for the Real Estate is . . . ($50,000.00) of which . . . ($20,000) has been paid. Buyers shall pay the balance to Sellers at Hampton, Iowa or as directed by Sellers, as follows: Said down payment of $20,000.00 shall be deposited in the Brian D. Miller Trust account before October, 18, 2002. Closing shall be on or before March 1, 2003. In the event the [Estate] provide[s] marketable title to the subject real estate, but as a result of nonperformance by [Passehls], the sale does not close then the parties agree that the $20,000.00 deposited in the Brian D. Miller Trust Account shall be forfeited to the [Estate].

The real estate contract set March 1, 2003, as the closing date [which was later postponed].

A subsequent survey determined the fence did not "line-up" with the boundaries set forth by the zoning ordinance. The land zoned for the salvage business was approximately 22,457 square feet less than the land demarcated by the fence. The boundary line described in the zoning ordinance cut through an existing garage, horse barn, and driveway, while the fence boundary did not. After the survey, a disagreement developed between Passehls and the Estate as to whether the fence or the zoning ordinance boundary controlled the property to be conveyed.

On March 19, 2003, the Estate's attorney sent Passehls a letter with the following requirements for the real estate closing:

> 1. The motorized Shriner's car and corn sheller needs to be delivered by Jerry and Volnetta to Karen's residence, prior to the real estate closing.
>
> 2. Karen reports that the east bin cannot be accessed because of junk and junk vehicles stored around it. The junk and junk vehicles need to be cleared from the bins.
>
> * * *
>
> 4. The junk vehicles located outside the fence and on the tillable farm ground need to be removed. Karen and David would like to know if Jerry and Volnetta plan to move these junk vehicles and if so, the date by which they can expect them to be moved.
>
> 5. As we have already mentioned by letter, the junkyard fence is not properly located per the Franklin County Zoning Variance. Karen and David want to know if Jerry and Volnetta plan to move the fence to the legal description consistent with the County Zoning Variances and if so, when that work will be completed by.

On March 24, 2003, the parties met to close the sale. Passehls brought a check for $30,000, but the Shriner's car and cornsheller had not yet been delivered to Karen and David. The attorney for the Estate brought a deed, but the deed only conveyed the lesser amount of land defined by the zoning ordinance. An argument erupted between the parties. Karen, as co-executor of the Estate, stated Passehls had not performed because the Shriner's car and cornsheller had not been delivered, there were still vehicles surrounding one of the grain bins, and there were still vehicles outside of the fenced area. Jerry also objected because the property described in the deed did not match the property the parties had agreed upon. The discussions deteriorated, and the parties did not close the transaction.

On March 26, the Estate sent a letter to Passehls assigning April 1 as the new closing date. The letter declared "this will be the last time this real estate closing will be rescheduled . . . Karen and David are not willing to extend this matter further." The letter also reiterated the "five specific items that Jerry and Volnetta needed to take care of prior to the closing." The letter also stated the following:

> if the real estate closing cannot take place on April 1st, at the scheduled time, as a result of their non-compliance with the settlement agreement, my letter dated March 19, 2003, and this letter, the $20,000.00 currently being held in my Trust Account [will be] forfeited by Jerry and Volnetta.

On April 1, Passehls' attorney came to the closing with a check for $30,000. The Shriner's car and cornsheller had already been delivered to Karen and David; however, vehicles still surrounded one of the grain bins, and some junk vehicles still remained outside of the fenced-in area. The Estate came to the closing with a deed that did not conform to the existing fence boundaries. As before, Karen contended the terms of the contract were not fulfilled, and Jerry disputed the correct legal description of the property. Once again, the closing did not occur.

Days later, the Estate's attorney took the $20,000 out of his client trust account and paid it to Karen and David.

Passehls filed a motion to enforce the terms of the settlement agreement. The Estate filed a cross motion to enforce the settlement agreement.

* * *

After a bench trial, the trial court concluded the parties' intent was clear at the time the settlement agreement and real estate contract were signed-the fence was to remain, and the survey and conveyance would coincide with the fence. The court then concluded the $20,000 down payment was forfeited because Passehls "failed to perform by not only providing access to the grain bins but also by failing to remove junk cars from outside the fence boundary, an agreed upon contingency required prior to closing." The court then ordered the Estate to execute a deed and convey the property within the fenced boundary once Passehls: paid an additional $50,000 to the Estate, moved all junk vehicles away from the grain bins, removed an unrelated horse fence, and removed the junk vehicles that were still outside the fenced-in area. The court also enjoined Passehls from placing anything within twenty yards of the grain bins and from placing anything else outside the existing fence boundary. Passehls appealed.

The court of appeals affirmed the decision of the trial court, and we granted Passehls' application for further review.

* * *

III. Merits

Bad blood, demands outside the four corners of the settlement agreement and corresponding real estate contract, and real estate contract forfeiture law have unnecessarily clouded the facts of this case. The parties disagree on the size of the property; both parties claim the other failed to perform their obligations under the contract, and neither party can agree on the meaning of the penalty provision. Because this case can be resolved under basic contract principles, we will not obfuscate the matter with irrelevant Iowa Code provisions concerning real estate contract forfeitures.

A. Size of the Property

Both parties dispute the meaning of the terms describing the property to be conveyed.

* * *

The settlement agreement and the real estate contract both recite the following description of the property to be conveyed:

> The acreage locally known as 513 160th St., Latimer, Iowa and described as: An approximate five acre tract located in the Northwest Quarter (NW1/4) of section 26, Township 92 North, Range 22 West of the 5th P.M., Franklin County, Iowa. *The legal description shall be determined by survey, which shall coincede* [sic] *with existing fence boundaries required by Franklin County Zoning.*

(Emphasis added.) At trial, Passehls argued the parties wrote the contract so that Passehls could keep the junkyard as defined by the boundary fence. The Estate argued the fence was immaterial because the land to be conveyed was the land described by the zoning ordinance.

The record belies the Estate's argument. To conclude the intent of the parties was to convey only the property set forth in the zoning ordinance would require us to excise any reference to the fence in the property description * * * We value each word in a written contract, and we are not persuaded to eliminate the phrase "existing fence" when a more suitable explanation is apparent. *See id.* § 212 cmt. *b* ("the words of an integrated agreement remain the most important evidence of intention").

A more sensible interpretation of the contract is that the phrase "required by Franklin County Zoning Ordinances" described the "fence" that was to be the subject of the survey. * * * The boundary fence was erected in 1990 after the Franklin County Zoning Board of Adjustment approved the use of the site as a dismantling and recycling center on the condition that a six-foot-high enclosure fence surround the premises. The reference in the contract to the zoning ordinance was meant to describe the fence that controlled the size of the property; the zoning ordinance itself was not meant to control the size of the property.

The circumstances surrounding the signing of the contract also do not support the Estate's proposed description. Such a description would result in a property line that divided an existing garage, horse barn, and driveway. Such a description would also require that the existing fence be moved. * * *

We therefore agree with the finding of the trial court; the intent of the parties was clear at the time the agreements were signed-Passehls contracted to purchase the land contained within the fenced boundary.

Presenting a deed conveying property that is 22,457 square feet less than the property bargained for does not constitute substantial performance of the terms of the settlement agreement or the real estate contract. Therefore, the Estate effectively refused to perform its obligations under the contract.

B. Penalty Provision

The settlement agreement and contract contain a penalty provision which provides the following:

> In the event that [the Estate] provides marketable title to the subject real estate, but closing does not occur on or before March 1, 2003, as a result of nonperformance by [Passehls], then the parties agree that the $20,000.00 deposited into the Brian D. Miller [the Estate's attorney's] Trust Account shall be forfeited to [the Estate].

A plain reading of this provision indicates the Estate must provide a marketable title to the subject real estate *before* the penalty provision can be enforced. Because the penalty provision sets forth a specific order of performance, the Estate's obligation to provide title to the appropriate real estate is a precondition to the enforcement of the penalty provision. As mentioned above, the Estate never proffered a deed to the real estate described in the settlement agreement or the real estate contract. Therefore, the penalty provisions contained within the written settlement agreement and real estate contract were not triggered.

C. Breach

Despite the clear language of the penalty provision, the trial court still concluded the Estate was entitled to the $20,000 penalty because Passehls failed to perform "an agreed upon contingency prior to closing." The trial court found Passehls failed to perform this contingency by not providing access to the grain bins and not moving all junk vehicles into the fenced-in area. However, neither the settlement agreement nor the real estate contract expressly states this contingency. In order to find that this additional contingency existed, the trial court apparently accepted the Estate's argument that there was a subsequent oral modification to the contract.

The Estate contends a new oral agreement was formed on March 24 after Passehls "failed" to close. At that time Karen, the co-executor of the Estate, stated she would not enforce the $20,000 penalty so long as Passehls agreed to complete five specific items by April 1. These items included returning the Shriner's car and cornsheller, removing the junk vehicles from around the grain bins, removing the horse pasture fence, removing the junk vehicles from outside of the fenced areas, and moving the fence to comply with the zoning requirements. Although Passehls contends there was no such agreement, the Estate claims the agreement was memorialized through a letter prepared by the Estate's attorney and sent to Passehls on March 26.

[The court concluded that the Passehls did not agree to an oral modification in part because "the letter that purportedly contains the terms of the contract does not reference any new oral agreement; instead it threatens forfeiture." The court, influenced by the siblings five-year feud and three lawsuits, thought it "incredible" to believe that the parties would agree to a major modification of their agreement without reducing it to writing.]

D. Current Status of Contract

In a real estate transaction, the law contemplates that each party will only relinquish their tight grip on their money or deed once they have their other hand firmly planted on the other party's money or deed; therefore, the law generally requires simultaneous performance. *Braig v. Frye,* 199 Iowa 184, 189, 199 N.W. 977, 979 (1924); *see also* 13 Richard A. Lord, *Williston on Contracts* § 38:8, at 407 (4th ed. 2000) [hereinafter *Williston on Contracts*] (stating the obligation of each party in a real estate contract "is subject to the condition precedent that the other party either perform, or make an absolute or conditional tender of performance"). The penalty provision is the only language in either the settlement agreement or real estate contract which could possibly change the presumption of simultaneous performance. As discussed above, the penalty provision required the Estate to first tender a marketable title to the subject property before the penalty provision became applicable. At best, this means *the Estate* had to perform first by tendering marketable title to the subject property.

Even if we assume, arguendo, Passehls failed to tender proper performance on March 24 and April 1, we would still conclude *neither* party tendered proper performance on either date. If both parties fail to perform their mutual and simultaneous obligations under a contract, then neither is in default. *Braig,* 199 Iowa at 189, 199 N.W. at 979; *Wright v. Swigart,* 172 Iowa 743, 746, 154 N.W. 938, 939 (1915); *Waters v. Pearson,* 163 Iowa 391, 403, 144 N.W. 1026, 1031 (1914); *see also* 13 *Williston on Contracts* § 38:8, at 407 ("[b]efore either party can sue on a [real estate] contract, that party must first put the other party in default by tendering or offering to tender performance"). Without a default or breach by either party, the penalty provision becomes inapplicable and the contract continues as binding on both parties. *See Braig,* 199 Iowa at 189, 199 N.W. at 979.

IV. Disposition

Because the Estate never proffered a deed to the appropriate property, the trial court erred when it decided the Estate was entitled to the $20,000 "forfeiture." We therefore reverse the decision of the district court.

At present, all of the obligations explicitly set forth in the settlement agreement and real estate contract have been performed by Passehls. The pending appeal was dropped; the Estate received the $20,000 down payment; the remaining $30,000 rests in Passehls' attorney's trust account; the Shriner's car and cornsheller have been delivered; and Passehls acknowledged the easement for access to the grain bins.

Upon remand, the district court shall direct the Estate to tender performance by executing a court officer's deed to the property described herein. The remaining $30,000 shall be simultaneously transferred to the Estate.

DECISION OF COURT OF APPEALS VACATED; DISTRICT COURT JUDGMENT REVERSED AND REMANDED WITH INSTRUCTIONS.

WILLISTON ON CONTRACTS

§ 47:2 (4th ed. Lord 2020).

It is one of the consequences of concurrent conditions that a situation may arise where no right of action ever arises against either party. Since a conditional tender is necessary to put either party in default, so long as both parties remain inactive, neither is liable and neither has acquired a right of action. * * * The possibility of either party putting the other in default will also cease if the delay is too long. It may be supposed that, by the terms of the contract, the concurrent performances were to be rendered on a fixed day, or it may be supposed that no time was stated for the performance. Under the first supposition, if time was of the essence of the contract, both parties will be discharged unless one or the other takes the initiative and makes a conditional tender at or about the time stated in the contract. Even though time is not of the essence, or if no time is mentioned in the contract for its performance, the lapse of an unreasonable time must necessarily deprive the parties of the possibility of thereafter making an effective tender.

UNIFORM COMMERCIAL CODE § 2–507(1).

Tender of delivery is a condition to the buyer's duty to accept the goods and, unless otherwise agreed, to his duty to pay for them. Tender entitles the seller to acceptance of the goods and to payment according to the contract.

UNIFORM COMMERCIAL CODE § 2–511(1).

Unless otherwise agreed tender of payment is a condition to the seller's duty to tender and complete any delivery.

RESTATEMENT (SECOND) OF CONTRACTS § 234(1).

Where all or part of the performances to be exchanged under an exchange of promises can be rendered simultaneously, they are to that extent due simultaneously, unless the language or the circumstances indicate the contrary.

B. SEQUENTIAL PERFORMANCES

STEWART V. NEWBURY

Court of Appeals of New York, 1917.
220 N.Y. 379, 115 N.E. 984.

CRANE, J.

The defendants are partners in the pipe fitting business under the name of Newbury Manufacturing Company. The plaintiff is a contractor and builder residing at Tuxedo, N.Y.

The parties had the following correspondence about the erection for the defendants of a concrete mill building at Monroe, N.Y.:

"Alexander Stewart,
"Contractor and Builder,

"Tuxedo, N.Y., July 18, 1911.

"Newbury Mfg. Company, Monroe, N.Y.—Gentlemen: With reference to the proposed work on the new foundry building I had hoped to be able to get up and see you this afternoon, but find that impossible and am, in consequence, sending you these prices, which I trust you will find satisfactory.

"I will agree to do all excavation work required at sixty-five ($.65) cents per cubic yard.

"I will put in the concrete work, furnishing labor and forms only, at two and 05–100 ($2.05) dollars per cubic yard.

"I will furnish labor to put in reenforcing at four ($4.00) dollars per ton.

"I will furnish labor only to set all window and door frames, window sash and doors, including the setting of hardware for one hundred twelve ($112) dollars. As alternative I would be willing to do any or all of the above work for cost plus 10 per cent., furnishing you with first class mechanics and giving the work considerable of my personal time.

"Hoping to hear favorably from you in this regard, I am.

"RESPECTFULLY YOURS,
"[SIGNED] ALEXANDER STEWART."

"The Newbury Mfg. Co.,
"Steam Fittings, Grey Iron Castings,
"Skylight Opening Apparatus,
"Monroe, N.Y.

"Telephone Connection.

"Monroe, N.Y., July 22, 1911.

"Alexander Stewart, Tuxedo Park, N.Y.—Dear Sir: Confirming the telephone conversation of this morning we accept your bid of July the 18th to do the concrete work on our new building. We trust that you will be able to get at this the early part of next week.

"YOURS TRULY,
THE NEWBURY MFG. CO.,
"H.A. NEWBURY."

Nothing was said in writing about the time or manner of payment. The plaintiff, however, claims that after sending his letter, and before receiving that of the defendant, he had a telephone communication with Mr. Newbury and said: "I will expect my payments in the usual manner," and Newbury said, "All right, we have got the money to pay for the building." This conversation over the telephone was denied by the defendants. The custom, the plaintiff testified, was to pay 85 per cent. every 30 days or at the end of each month, 15 per cent. being retained till the work was completed.

In July the plaintiff commenced work and continued until September 29th, at which time he had progressed with the construction as far as the first floor. He then sent a bill for the work done up to that date for $896.35. The defendants refused to pay the bill and work was discontinued. The plaintiff claims that the defendants refused to permit him to perform the rest of his contract, they insisting that the work already done was not in accordance with the specifications. The defendants claimed upon the trial that the plaintiff voluntarily abandoned the work after their refusal to pay his bill.

On October 5, 1911, the defendants wrote the plaintiff a letter containing the following:

> "Notwithstanding you promised to let us know on Monday whether you would complete the job or throw up the contract, you have not up to this time advised us of your intention. * * * Under the circumstances, we are compelled to accept your action as being an abandonment of your contract and of every effort upon your part to complete your work on our building. As you know, the bill which you sent us and which we declined to pay is not correct, either in items or amount, nor is there anything due you under

our contract as we understand it until you have completed your work on our building."

To this letter the plaintiff replied the following day. In it he makes no reference to the telephone communication agreeing, as he testified, to make "the usual payments," but does say this:

> "There is nothing in our agreement which says that I shall wait until the job is completed before any payment is due, nor can this be reasonably implied. * * * As to having given you positive date as to when I should let you know what I proposed doing, I did not do so; on the contrary, I told you that I would not tell you positively what I would do until I had visited the job, and I promised that I would do this at my earliest convenience and up to the present time I have been unable to get up there."

The defendant Herbert Newbury testified that the plaintiff "ran away and left the whole thing." And the defendant F.A. Newbury testified that he was told by Mr. Stewart's man that Stewart was going to abandon the job; that he thereupon telephoned Mr. Stewart, who replied that he would let him know about it the next day, but did not.

In this action, which is brought to recover the amount of the bill presented, as the agreed price and $95.68 damages for breach of contract, the plaintiff had a verdict for the amount stated in the bill, but not for the other damages claimed, and the judgment entered thereon has been affirmed by the Appellate Division.

The appeal to us is upon exceptions to the judge's charge. The court charged the jury as follows:

> "Plaintiff says that he was excused from completely performing the contract by the defendants' unreasonable failure to pay him for the work he had done during the months of August and September. * * * Was it understood that the payments were to be made monthly? If it was not so understood, the defendants only obligation was to make payments at reasonable periods, in view of the character of the work, the amount of work being done, and the value of it. In other words, if there was no agreement between the parties respecting the payments, the defendants' obligation was to make payments at reasonable times. * * * But whether there was such an agreement or not, you may consider whether it was reasonable or unreasonable for him to exact a payment at that time and in that amount."

The court further said, in reply to a request to charge:

> "I will say in that connection, if there was no agreement respecting the time of payment, and if there was no custom that was understood by both parties, and with respect to which they

made the contract, then the plaintiff was entitled to payments at reasonable times."

The defendants' counsel thereupon made the following request, which was refused:

> "I ask your honor to instruct the jury that, if the circumstances existed as your honor stated in your last instruction, then the plaintiff was not entitled to any payment until the contract was completed."

The jury was plainly told that if there were no agreement as to payments, yet the plaintiff would be entitled to part payment at reasonable times as the work progressed, and if such payments were refused he could abandon the work and recover the amount due for the work performed.

This is not the law. Counsel for the plaintiff omits to call our attention to any authority sustaining such a proposition and our search reveals none. In fact, the law is very well settled to the contrary. This was an entire contract. * * * Where a contract is made to perform work and no agreement is made as to payment, the work must be substantially performed before payment can be demanded. * * *

This case was also submitted to the jury upon the ground that there may have been a breach of contract by the defendants in their refusal to permit the plaintiff to continue with his work, claiming that he had departed from the specifications, and there was some evidence justifying this view of the case; but it is impossible to say upon which of these two theories the jury arrived at its conclusion. The above errors, therefore, cannot be considered as harmless and immaterial. * * * As the verdict was for the amount of the bill presented and did not include the damages for a breach of contract, which would be the loss of profits, it may well be presumed that the jury adopted the first ground of recovery charged by the court as above quoted and decided that the plaintiff was justified in abandoning work for nonpayment of the installment.

The judgment should be reversed, and a new trial ordered; costs to abide the event.

PATTERSON, CONSTRUCTIVE CONDITIONS IN CONTRACTS

42 Colum.L.Rev. 903, 919–920 (1942).

[O]ne may ask, why should the party whose promised performance takes time be required to extend credit to the one whose performance does not? The typical case falling under this rule—of which it is a kind of extrapolation—is the contract to do work for money. The usual practice in the community to which the rule was applicable was to pay for the work after it was completed. This "belief as to the practice of a community or a class" is empirically verified, but it does not settle the questions of justice or policy with which the law is concerned. The practice may be ascribed to the influence of employers as a dominant class, and to judicial inertia which allows an outmoded rule to continue unchanged. The dominance of employers as a class is not what it used to be, yet no demand has appeared to require that employees generally be paid their wages or salaries in advance. There may be sufficient reasons for the survival of the rule. Professor Williston suggests two: 1. The normally greater responsibility of the employer; and 2., the fact that the employee cannot be compelled to perform specifically.

The policy of the law, here as in the tendency to construct concurrent conditions, is to minimize credit risks. If employers usually present less credit risks than employees, the rule of construction effectuates this end. That colleges and theatres ordinarily require payment in advance for the services which they furnish merely exemplifies the operation of the principle. A further justification may be found in the belief that a moderate postponement of reward stimulates productivity of social goods; such a belief is operative as a part of the mores of a particular culture. This justification, like the second reason given by Professor Williston, must be limited in scope of application, if it is not to conflict with the prohibition of involuntary servitude; that is, it may become a too-effective means of coercing the employee to work. The rule which makes performance by the employee a condition precedent of the duty of payment by the employer and which thus places the credit risk and the credit strain on the employee, has been mitigated in its severity by statutes requiring that wages be paid at short intervals (weekly or biweekly) to certain classes of employees (in the lower income brackets), by provisions making wage claims preferred in the case of bankruptcy of the employer and by a limited relief for unjust enrichment. The order-of-performance test of credit burdens is thus supplemented by custom and by policy.

PROBLEM 7-6

Buyer contracted with seller to buy five truckloads of chopped wood to be burned in fireplaces in buyer's motel. The price was $1100 for the five truckloads, delivery over a five week period. After seller delivered the first truckload, he demanded $220. Buyer refused to pay until seller delivered in full. Seller comes to your law office. How would this problem be resolved under the Uniform Commercial Code sections reproduced below?

§ 2–507. Effect of Seller's Tender; Delivery on Condition

(1) Tender of delivery is a condition to the buyer's duty to accept the goods and, unless otherwise agreed, to his duty to pay for them. Tender entitles the seller to acceptance of the goods and to payment according to the contract.

§ 2–511. Tender of Payment by Buyer; Payment by Check

(1) Unless otherwise agreed tender of payment is a condition to the seller's duty to tender and complete any delivery.

§ 2–307. Delivery in Single Lot or Several Lots

Unless otherwise agreed all goods called for by a contract for sale must be tendered in a single delivery and payment is due only on such tender but where the circumstances give either party the right to make or demand delivery in lots the price if it can be apportioned may be demanded for each lot.

SECTION NINE: IMPLIED CONDITIONS FIXING THE QUALITY OF PERFORMANCE

PLANTE V. JACOBS

Supreme Court of Wisconsin, 1960.
10 Wis.2d 567, 103 N.W.2d 296.

Suit to establish a lien to recover the unpaid balance of the contract price plus extras of building a house for the defendants, Frank M. and Carol H. Jacobs, who in their answer allege no substantial performance and breach of the contract by the plaintiff and counterclaim for damages due to faulty workmanship and incomplete construction. The defendants, Sterling Savings & Loan Association and Marguerite A. Hoenig, claim an interest in the property by virtue of a mortgage; and the defendant, City Bank and Trust Company, as a judgment lien creditor. After a trial to the court, judgment was entered for the plaintiff in the amount of $4,152.90 plus interest and costs, from which the defendants, Jacobs, appealed and the plaintiff petitioned for a review. The other defendants have not appealed.

The Jacobs, on or about January 6, 1956, entered into a written contract with the plaintiff to furnish the materials and construct a house upon their lot in Brookfield, Waukesha county, in accordance with plans and specifications, for the sum of $26,765. During the course of construction the plaintiff was paid $20,000. Disputes arose between the parties, the defendants refused to continue payment, and the plaintiff did not complete the house. On January 12, 1957, the plaintiff duly filed his lien.

The trial court found the contract was substantially performed and was modified in respect to lengthening the house two feet and the reasonable value of this extra was $960. The court disallowed extras amounting to $1,748.92 claimed by the plaintiff because they were not agreed upon in writing in accordance with the terms of the agreement. In respect to defective workmanship the court allowed the cost of repairing the following items: $1,550 for the patio wall; $100 for the patio floor; $300 for cracks in the ceiling of the living room and kitchen; and $20.15 credit balance for hardware. The court also found the defendants were not damaged by the misplacement of a wall between the kitchen and the living room, and the other items of defective workmanship and incompleteness were not proven. The amount of these credits allowed the defendants was deducted from the gross amount found owing the plaintiff, and the judgment was entered for the difference and made a lien on the premises subject to the mortgage of the Sterling Savings & Loan Association, but prior to the claims of the defendants, Marguerite A. Hoenig and The City Bank and Trust Company.

HALLOWS, JUSTICE.

The defendants argue the plaintiff cannot recover any amount because he has failed to substantially perform the contract. The plaintiff conceded he failed to furnish the kitchen cabinets, gutters and downspouts, sidewalk, closet clothes poles, and entrance seat amounting to $1,601.95. This amount was allowed to the defendants. The defendants claim some 20 other items of incomplete or faulty performance by the plaintiff and no substantial performance because the cost of completing the house in strict compliance with the plans and specifications would amount to 25 or 30 per cent of the contract price. The defendants especially stress the misplacing of the wall between the living room and the kitchen, which narrowed the living room in excess of one foot. The cost of tearing down this wall and rebuilding it would be approximately $4,000. The record is not clear why and when this wall was misplaced, but the wall is completely built and the house decorated and the defendants are living therein. Real estate experts testified that the smaller width of the living room would not affect the market price of the house.

The defendants rely on Manitowoc Steam Boiler Works v. Manitowoc Glue Co., 1903, 120 Wis. 1, 97 N.W. 515, for the proposition there can be no recovery on the contract as distinguished from *quantum meruit* unless there is substantial performance. This is undoubtedly the correct rule at common law. * * * The question here is whether there has been substantial performance. The test of what amounts to substantial performance seems to be whether the performance meets the essential purpose of the contract. In the Manitowoc case the contract called for a boiler having a capacity of 150 per cent of the existing boiler. The court held there was no substantial performance because the boiler furnished had a capacity of only 82 per cent of the old boiler and only approximately one-half of the boiler capacity contemplated by the contract. In Houlahan v. Clark, 1901, 110 Wis. 43, 85 N.W. 676, the contract provided the plaintiff was to drive pilings in the lake and place a boat house thereon parallel and in line with a neighbor's dock. This was not done and the contractor so positioned the boat house that it was practically useless to the owner. Manthey v. Stock, 1907, 133 Wis. 107, 113 N.W. 443, involved a contract to paint a house and to do a good job, including the removal of the old paint where necessary. The plaintiff did not remove the old paint, and blistering and roughness of the new paint resulted. The court held that the plaintiff failed to show substantial performance. The defendants also cite Manning v. School District No. 6, 1905, 124 Wis. 84, 102 N.W. 356. However, this case involved a contract to install a heating and ventilating plant in the school building which would meet certain tests which the heating apparatus failed to do. The heating plant was practically a total failure to accomplish the purposes of the contract. See also Nees v. Weaver, 1936, 222 Wis. 492, 269 N.W. 266, 107 A.L.R. 1405 (roof on a garage).

Substantial performance as applied to construction of a house does not mean that every detail must be in strict compliance with the specifications and the plans. Something less than perfection is the test of * * * performance unless all details are made the essence of the contract. This was not done here. There may be situations in which features or details of construction of special or of great personal importance, which if not performed, would prevent a finding of substantial performance of the contract. In this case the plan was a stock floor plan. No detailed construction of the house was shown on the plan. There were no blueprints. The specifications were standard printed forms with some modifications and additions written in by the parties. Many of the problems that arose during the construction had to be solved on the basis of practical experience. No mathematical rule relating to the percentage of the price, of cost of completion or of completeness can be laid down to determine substantial performance of a building contract. Although the defendants received a house with which they are dissatisfied in many respects, the trial court was not in error in finding the contract was substantially performed.

The next question is what is the amount of recovery when the plaintiff has substantially, but incompletely, performed. For substantial performance the plaintiff should recover the contract price less the damages caused the defendant by the incomplete performance. Both parties agree. Venzke v. Magdanz, 1943, 243 Wis. 155, 9 N.W.2d 604, states the correct rule for damages due to faulty construction amounting to such incomplete performance, which is the difference between the value of the house as it stands with faulty and incomplete construction and the value of the house if it had been constructed in strict accordance with the plans and specifications. This is the diminished-value rule. The cost of replacement or repair is not the measure of such damage, but is an element to take into consideration in arriving at value under some circumstances. The cost of replacement or the cost to make whole the omissions may equal or be less than the difference in value in some cases and, likewise, the cost to rectify a defect may greatly exceed the added value to the structure as corrected. The defendants argue that under the Venzke rule their damages are $10,000. The plaintiff on review argues the defendants' damages are only $650. Both parties agree the trial court applied the wrong rule to the facts.

The trial court applied the cost-of-repair or replacement rule as to several items, relying on Stern v. Schlafer, 1943, 244 Wis. 183, 11 N.W.2d 640, 12 N.W.2d 678, wherein it was stated that when there are a number of small items of defect or omission which can be remedied without the reconstruction of a substantial part of the building or a great sacrifice of work or material already wrought in the building, the reasonable cost of correcting the defect should be allowed. However, in Mohs v. Quarton, 1950, 257 Wis. 544, 44 N.W.2d 580, the court held when the separation of defects would lead to confusion, the rule of diminished value could apply to all defects.

In this case no such confusion arises in separating the defects. The trial court disallowed certain claimed defects because they were not proven. This finding was not against the great weight and clear preponderance of the evidence and will not be disturbed on appeal. Of the remaining defects claimed by the defendants, the court allowed the cost of replacement or repair except as to the misplacement of the living-room wall. Whether a defect should fall under the cost-of-replacement rule or be considered under the diminished-value rule depends upon the nature and magnitude of the defect. This court has not allowed items of such magnitude under the cost-of-repair rule as the trial court did. Viewing the construction of the house as a whole and its cost we cannot say, however, that the trial court was in error in allowing the cost of repairing the plaster cracks in the ceilings, the cost of mud jacking and repairing the patio floor, and the cost of reconstructing the non-weight-bearing and nonstructural patio wall. Such reconstruction did not involve an unreasonable economic waste.

The item of misplacing the living room wall under the facts of this case was clearly under the diminished-value rule. There is no evidence that defendants requested or demanded the replacement of the wall in the place called for by the specifications during the course of construction. To tear down the wall now and rebuild it in its proper place would involve a substantial destruction of the work, if not all of it, which was put into the wall and would cause additional damage to other parts of the house and require replastering and redecorating the walls and ceilings of at least two rooms. Such economic waste is unreasonable and unjustified. The rule of diminished value contemplates the wall is not going to be moved. Expert witnesses for both parties, testifying as to the value of the house, agreed that the misplacement of the wall had no effect on the market price. The trial court properly found that the defendants suffered no legal damage, although the defendants' particular desire for specified room size was not satisfied. For a discussion of these rules of damages for defective or unfinished construction and their application see Restatement, 1 Contracts, pp. 572–573, sec. 346(1)(a) and illustrations.

* * *

Judgment affirmed.

O.W. GRUN ROOFING AND CONSTRUCTION CO. v. COPE

Court of Civil Appeals of Texas, 1975.
529 S.W.2d 258.

[Defendant Grun installed a roof on Cope's home for $648, pursuant to a contract. When Cope refused to pay, claiming defects, Grun filed a mechanic's lien. Cope brought an action to set aside the lien and for damages. Grun filed a cross-claim for foreclosure on the mechanic's lien and for the money allegedly due. After a jury trial, the trial court entered judgment for Cope for $122.60 and set aside the mechanic's lien.]

* * * CADENA, JUSTICE.

The written contract required defendant to install a new roof on plaintiff's home for $648.00. The contract describes the color of the shingles to be used as "russet glow," which defendant defined as a "brown varied color." Defendant acknowledges that it was his obligation to install a roof of uniform color.

After defendant had installed the new roof, plaintiff noticed that it had streaks which she described as yellow, due to a difference in color or shade of some of the shingles. Defendant agreed to remedy the situation and he removed the nonconforming shingles. However, the replacement shingles do not match the remainder, and photographs introduced in evidence clearly show that the roof is not of a uniform color. Plaintiff testified that her roof has the appearance of having been patched, rather than having been completely replaced. According to plaintiff's testimony, the yellow streaks appeared on the northern, eastern and southern sides of the roof, and defendant only replaced the non-matching shingles on the northern and eastern sides, leaving the southern side with the yellow streaks still apparent. The result is that only the western portion of the roof is of uniform color.

When defendant originally installed the complete new roof, it used 24 "squares" of shingles. In an effort to achieve a roof of uniform color, five squares were ripped off and replaced. There is no testimony as to the number of squares which would have to be replaced on the southern, or rear, side of the house in order to eliminate the original yellow streaks. Although there is expert testimony to the effect that the disparity in color would not be noticeable after the shingles have been on the roof for about a year, there is testimony to the effect that, although some nine or ten months have elapsed since defendant attempted to achieve a uniform coloration, the roof is still "streaky" on three sides. One of defendant's experts testified that if the shingles are properly applied the result will be a "blended" roof rather than a streaked roof.

In view of the fact that the disparity in color has not disappeared in nine or ten months, and in view of the fact that there is testimony to the effect that it would be impossible to secure matching shingles to replace the nonconforming ones, it can reasonably be inferred that a roof or uniform coloration can be achieved only by installing a completely new roof.

The evidence is undisputed that the roof is a substantial roof and will give plaintiff protection against the elements.

The principle which allows recovery for part performance in cases involving dependent promises may be expressed by saying that a material breach or a breach which goes to the root of the matter or essence of the contract defeats the promisor's claim despite his part performance, or it may be expressed by saying that a promisor who has substantially performed is entitled to recover, although he has failed in some particular to comply with his agreement. The latter mode of expressing the rule is generally referred to as the doctrine of substantial performance and is especially common in cases involving building contracts, although its application is not restricted to such contracts.

It is difficult to formulate a definitive rule for determining whether the contractor's performance, less than complete, amounts to "substantial performance," since the question is one of fact and of degree, and the answer depends on the particular facts of each case. But, although the decisions furnish no rule of thumb, they are helpful in suggesting guidelines. One of the most obvious factors to be considered is the extent of the nonperformance. The deficiency will not be tolerated if it is so pervasive as to frustrate the purpose of the contract in any real or substantial sense. The doctrine does not bestow on a contractor a license to install whatever is, in his judgment, "just as good." The answer is arrived at by weighing the purpose to be served, the desire to be gratified, the excuse for deviating from the letter of the contract and the cruelty of enforcing strict adherence or of compelling the promisee to receive something less than for which he bargained. Also influential in many cases is the ratio of money value of the tendered performance and of the promised performance. In most cases the contract itself at least is an indication of the value of the promised performance, and courts should have little difficulty in determining the cost of curing the deficiency. But the rule cannot be expressed in terms of a fraction, since complete reliance on a mathematical formula would result in ignoring other important factors, such as the purpose which the promised performance was intended to serve and the extent to which the nonperformance would defeat such purpose, or would defeat it if not corrected. See, generally, 3A Corbin, Contracts Secs. 700–07 (1960).

* * *

* * * It should not come as a shock to anyone to adopt a rule to the effect that a person has, particularly with respect to his home, to choose for himself and to contract for something which exactly satisfies that choice, and not to be compelled to accept something else. In the matter of homes and their decoration, as much as, if not more than, in many other fields, mere taste or preference, almost approaching whimsy, may be controlling with the homeowner, so that variations which might, under other circumstances, be considered trifling, may be inconsistent with that "substantial performance" on which liability to pay must be predicated. Of mere incompleteness or deviations which may be easily supplied or remedied after the contractor has finished his work, and the cost of which to the owner is not excessive and readily ascertainable, present less cause for hesitation in concluding that the performance tendered constitutes substantial performance, since in such cases the owner can obtain complete satisfaction by merely spending some money and deducting the amount of such expenditure from the contract price.

In the case before us there is evidence to support the conclusion that plaintiff can secure a roof of uniform coloring only by installing a completely new roof. We cannot say, as a matter of law, that the evidence establishes that in this case that a roof which so lacks uniformity in color as to give the appearance of a patch job serves essentially the same purpose as a roof of uniform color which has the appearance of being a new roof. We are not prepared to hold that a contractor who tenders a performance so deficient that it can be remedied only by completely redoing the work for which the contract called has established, as a matter of law, that he has substantially performed his contractual obligation.

* * *

Finally, defendant argues that it was entitled to judgment at least on the theory of quantum meruit on its cross claim because the evidence establishes as a matter of law that defendant installed a good weatherproof roof which was guaranteed for 15 years, and that such roof was installed properly in accordance with factory specifications and was of use and benefit to plaintiff.

The evidence does not conclusively establish that the shingles were properly installed. There is evidence to the effect that if shingles of this type are properly installed the result will be a roof which "blends," rather than a roof with clearly discordant streaks. In any event, the evidence does not conclusively establish that plaintiff has received any benefit from defendant's defective performance. As already pointed out, there is evidence that plaintiff will have to install a completely new roof. Because of defendant's deficient performance, plaintiff is not in a position which requires that she pay for a new roof.

Nor does the evidence conclusively establish that plaintiff accepted the claimed benefit. She complained immediately and has expressed dissatisfaction at all times. We cannot infer an acceptance from the fact that plaintiff continued to live in the house. She was living in the house before defendant installed the new roof, and we know of no rule which would require that, in order to avoid a finding of implied acceptance, plaintiff was obligated to move out of her home.

The judgment of the trial court is affirmed.

NOTE: SUBSTANTIAL PERFORMANCE IN LAND SALE CONTRACTS

A land-sale agreement entitles the buyer to the seller's performance, but must the seller's tender be perfect? Or does substantial performance entitle the seller to the consideration? Some cases hold that substantial performance is enough in the absence of an express condition requiring perfect performance. Thus a mistake as to the quantity of land to be conveyed—seller promised ten acres when there were only nine—might not be so material as to permit the buyer to escape his or her obligations under the contract. For example, when the buyer is more interested in a particular plot of land than the precise amount of acreage, a small acreage deficiency may not permit the buyer to avoid the deal. The buyer, of course, would be entitled to damages for seller's breach of promise as to the number of acres. Conversely, even a very small deficiency in the number of acres promised might be material, thereby permitting the buyer to avoid the deal. Suppose, for example, the buyer wanted waterfront property and the acreage deficiency was land that bordered the water. A useful general treatment appears in D. Dobbs, Remedies 822–24 (2d ed. 1993).

WALKER & CO. V. HARRISON

Supreme Court of Michigan, 1957.
347 Mich. 630, 81 N.W.2d 352.

SMITH, JUSTICE.

This is a suit on a written contract. The defendants are in the dry-cleaning business. Walker & Company, plaintiff, sells, rents, and services advertising signs and billboards. These parties entered into an agreement pertaining to a sign. The agreement is in writing and is termed a "rental agreement." It specifies in part that:

> "The lessor agrees to construct and install, at its own cost, one [eighteen feet, nine inches high and eight feet, eight inches] wide pylon type d.f. neon sign with electric clock and flashing lamps * * *. The lessor agrees to and does hereby lease or rent unto the said lessee the said SIGN for the term, use and rental and under

the conditions, hereinafter set out, and the lessee agrees to pay said rental * * *.

"(a) The term of this lease shall be 36 months * * *.

"(b) The rental to be paid by lessee shall be $148.50 per month for each and every calendar month during the term of this lease; * * *.

"(d) Maintenance. Lessor at its expense agrees to maintain and service the sign together with such equipment as supplied and installed by the lessor to operate in conjunction with said sign under the terms of this lease; this service is to include cleaning and repainting of sign in original color scheme as often as deemed necessary by lessor to keep sign in first class advertising condition and make all necessary repairs to sign and equipment installed by lessor. * * *."

At the "expiration of this agreement," it was also provided, "title to this sign reverts to lessee." This clause is in addition to the printed form of agreement and was apparently added as a result of defendants' concern over title, they having expressed a desire "to buy for cash" and the salesman, at one time, having "quoted a cash price."

The sign was completed and installed in the latter part of July, 1953. The first billing of the monthly payment of $148.50 was made August 1, 1953, with payment thereof by defendants on September 3, 1953. This first payment was also the last. Shortly after the sign was installed, someone hit it with a tomato. Rust, also, was visible on the chrome, complained defendants, and in its corners were "little spider cobwebs." In addition, there were "some children's sayings written down in here." Defendant Herbert Harrison called Walker for the maintenance he believed himself entitled to under subparagraph (d) above. It was not forthcoming. He called again and again. "I was getting, you might say, sorer and sorer. * * * Occasionally, when I started calling up, I would walk around where the tomato was and get mad again. Then I would call up on the phone again." Finally, on October 8, 1953, plaintiff not having responded to his repeated calls, he telegraphed Walker that:

"You Have Continually Voided Our Rental Contract By Not Maintaining Signs As Agreed As We No Longer Have A Contract With You Do Not Expect Any Further Remuneration."

Walker's reply was in the form of a letter. After first pointing out that "your telegram does not make any specific allegations as to what the failure of maintenance comprises," and stating that "We certainly would appreciate your furnishing us with such information," the letter makes reference to a prior collateral controversy between the parties, "wondering if this refusal on our part prompted your attempt to void our rental contract," and concludes as follows:

> "We would like to call your attention to paragraph G in our rental contract, which covers procedures in the event of a Breach of Agreement. In the event that you carry out your threat to make no future monthly payments in accordance with the agreement, it is our intention to enforce the conditions outlined under paragraph G[1] through the proper legal channels. We call to your attention that your monthly rental payments are due in advance at our office not later than the 10th day of each current month. You are now approximately 30 days in arrears on your September payment. Unless we receive both the September and October payments by October 25th, this entire matter will be placed in the hands of our attorney for collection in accordance with paragraph G which stipulates that the entire amount is forthwith due and payable."

No additional payments were made and Walker sued in assumpsit for the entire balance due under the contract, $5,197.50, invoking paragraph (g) of the agreement. Defendants filed answer and claim of recoupment, asserting that plaintiff's failure to perform certain maintenance services constituted a prior material breach of the agreement, thus justifying their repudiation of the contract and grounding their claim for damages. The case was tried to the court without a jury and resulted in a judgment for the plaintiff. The case is before us on a general appeal.

Defendants urge upon us again and again, in various forms, the proposition that Walker's failure to service the sign, in response to repeated requests, constituted a material breach of the contract and justified

---

1 "(g) Breach of Agreement. Lessee shall be deemed to have breached this agreement by default in payment of any installment of the rental herein provided for; abandonment of the sign or vacating premises where the sign is located; termination or transfer of lessee's interest in the premises by insolvency, appointment of a receiver for lessee's business; filing of a voluntary or involuntary petition in bankruptcy with respect to lessee or the violation of any of the other terms or conditions hereof. In the event of such default, the lessor may, upon notice to the lessee, which notice shall conclusively be deemed sufficient if mailed or delivered to the premises where the sign was or is located, take possession of the sign and declare the balance of the rental herein provided for to be forthwith due and payable, and lessee hereby agrees to pay such balance upon any such contingencies. Lessor may terminate this lease and without notice, remove and repossess said sign and recover from the lessee such amounts as may be unpaid for the remaining unexpired term of this agreement. Time is of the essence of this lease with respect to the payment of rentals herein provided for. Should lessee after lessor has declared the balance of rentals due and payable, pay the full amount of rental herein provided, he shall then be entitled to the use of the sign, under all the terms and provisions hereof, for the balance of the term of this lease. No waiver by either party hereto of the nonperformance of any term, condition or obligation hereof shall be a waiver of any subsequent breach of, or failure to perform the same, or any other term, condition or obligation hereof. It is understood and agreed that the sign is especially constructed for the lessee and for use at the premises now occupied by the lessee for the term herein provided; that it is of no value unless so used and that it is a material consideration to the lessor in entering into this agreement that the lessee shall continue to use the sign for the period of time provided herein and for the payment of the full rental for such term."

repudiation by them. Their legal proposition is undoubtedly correct. Repudiation is one of the weapons available to an injured party in event the other contractor has committed a material breach. But the injured party's determination that there has been a material breach, justifying his own repudiation, is fraught with peril, for should such determination, as viewed by a later court in the calm of its contemplation, be unwarranted, the repudiator himself will have been guilty of material breach and himself have become the aggressor, not an innocent victim.

What is our criterion for determining whether or not a breach of contract is so fatal to the undertaking of the parties that it is to be classed as "material"? There is no single touchstone. Many factors are involved. They are well stated in section 275 of Restatement of the Law of Contracts in the following terms:

> "In determining the materiality of a failure fully to perform a promise the following circumstances are influential:
>
> "(a) The extent to which the injured party will obtain the substantial benefit which he could have reasonably anticipated:
>
> "(b) The extent to which the injured party may be adequately compensated in damages for lack of complete performance;
>
> "(c) The extent to which the party failing to perform has already partly performed or made preparations for performance;
>
> "(d) The greater or less hardship on the party failing to perform in terminating the contract;
>
> "(e) The wilful, negligent or innocent behavior of the party failing to perform;
>
> "(f) The greater or less uncertainty that the party failing to perform will perform the remainder of the contract."

We will not set forth in detail the testimony offered concerning the need for servicing. Granting that Walker's delay (about a week after defendant Herbert Harrison sent his telegram of repudiation Walker sent out a crew and took care of things) in rendering the service requested was irritating, we are constrained to agree with the trial court that it was not of such materiality as to justify repudiation of the contract, and we are particularly mindful of the lack of preponderant evidence contrary to his determination. Jones v. Eastern Michigan Motorbuses, 287 Mich. 619, 283 N.W. 710. The trial court, on this phase of the case, held as follows:

> "Now Mr. Harrison phoned in, so he testified, a number of times. He isn't sure of the dates but he sets the first call at about the 7th of August and he complained then of the tomato and of some rust and some cobwebs. The tomato, according to the testimony was up on the clock; that would be outside of his reach,

without a stepladder or something. The cobwebs are within easy reach of Mr. Harrison and so would the rust be. I think that Mr. Bueche's argument that these were not materially a breach would clearly be true as to the cobwebs and I really can't believe in the face of all the testimony that there was a great deal of rust seven days after the installation of this sign. And that really brings it down to the tomato. And, of course, when a tomato has been splashed all over your clock, you don't like it. But he says he kept calling their attention to it, although the rain probably washed some of the tomato off. But the stain remained, and they didn't come. I really can't find that that was such a material breach of the contract as to justify rescission. I really don't think so."

Nor, we conclude, do we. There was no valid ground for defendants' repudiation and their failure thereafter to comply with the terms of the contract was itself a material breach, entitling Walker, upon this record, to judgment.

* * * Judgment was, therefore, rendered for the cash price of the sign, for such services and maintenance as were extended and accepted, and interest upon the amount in default. There was no error.

Affirmed. Costs to appellee.

MACNEIL, A PRIMER OF CONTRACT PLANNING

48 S.Cal.L.Rev. 627, 680 & n. 151 (1975).

A constant risk of contractual relationships is the uncertain-duty-risk—the need to act or refrain from acting in the face of uncertainty concerning the duties of the parties. We associate this risk most often with disputes, but it also exists even in the absence of a present dispute. A party often has to act on his interpretation of performance obligations at the peril of being held wrong in the event of a subsequent dispute. Nevertheless, the uncertain-duty-risk is most likely to be serious where a dispute has arisen or seems likely to arise. In such circumstances parties often find themselves having to act or refrain from acting at considerable risk that their premises for action will subsequently be held erroneous.

It is impossible through planning of contractual relationships to avoid uncertain-duty-risks completely. Nevertheless, such risks can be drastically reduced in many ways through prior planning. * * *

At least one important technique, tender of performance, is available for reducing the uncertain-duty-risk after disputes arise. In many situations the best way to eliminate some or all of the uncertain-duty-risk is to make a tender of performance to the other party. "Tender is an offer to perform a condition or obligation coupled with the present ability of immediate performance, so that were it not for the refusal of cooperation by the party to whom tender is made, the condition or obligation would be immediately satisfied."

PROBLEM 7-7

Suppose Harrison had called you soon after the sign was installed and complained about the tomato and about Walker & Co.'s lack of maintenance. Would you have advised him that Walker & Co. had materially breached and that Harrison could cease paying rent? Suppose the delay in maintenance had been two weeks? Three weeks? Observe that the lawyer called on to advise a client after an allegedly defective performance by the other party must determine whether there has been a breach and, if so, whether the breach is sufficiently egregious to permit cessation of performance by the client. Do the criteria of the Restatement of Contracts § 275 offer sufficient guidance to the lawyer? What are the consequences if the lawyer mistakenly advises that the other party's breach is material?

Now suppose Harrison had called you before he entered the agreement with Walker & Co. What would you have advised him? Draft an express condition that would have protected him.

CONVENTION ON CONTRACTS FOR THE INTERNATIONAL SALE OF GOODS.

Article 25

A breach of contract committed by one of the parties is fundamental if it results in such detriment to the other party as substantially to deprive him of what he is entitled to expect under the contract, unless the party in breach did not foresee, and a reasonable person of the same kind in the same circumstances would not have foreseen, such a result.

Article 49(1)(a)

(1) The buyer may declare the contract avoided:

(a) If the failure by the seller to perform any of his obligations under the contract or this Convention amounts to a fundamental breach of contract * * *.

Article 64(1)(a)

(1) The seller may declare the contract avoided:

(a) If the failure by the buyer to perform any of his obligations under the contract or this Convention amounts to a fundamental breach of contract * * *.

NOTE: *DIVISIBLE CONTRACTS*

In the John v. United Advertising case that follows, we introduce the concept of divisibility. A nice definition is found in Coady v. Wellfleet Marine Corp., 816 N.E.2d 124 (App. Ct. Mass. 2004):

> [O]ne party's breach of a contract does not bar recovery for the other party's breach if the different parts of the contract can be considered separable or divisible. The law in Massachusetts is consistent with the flexible rule of the Restatement (Second) of Contracts § 240 (1981), which states that "[i]f the performances to be exchanged under an exchange of promises can be apportioned into corresponding pairs of part performances so that the parts of each pair are properly regarded as agreed equivalents, a party's performance of his part of such a pair has the same effect on the other's duties to render performance of the agreed equivalent as it would have if only that pair of performances had been promised." See Potter & McArthur, Inc. v. Boston, 15 Mass.App.Ct. 454, 455–456, 446 N.E.2d 718 (1983).
>
> Even where there is only one agreement covering all the terms of a contract, "it may be that the performance under the contract will be divided into different groups, each set embracing performances which are the agreed exchange for each other, the result being that the contract is entire but divisible." Bianchi Bros. v. Gendron, 292 Mass. 438, 445, 198 N.E. 767 (1935).

JOHN V. UNITED ADVERTISING INC.

Supreme Court of Colorado, 1968.
165 Colo. 193, 439 P.2d 53.

MCWILLIAMS, JUSTICE.

This is a contract case. The central issue is whether the contract in question is "entire" or "severable" in nature.

Dwight John, who will hereinafter be referred to as the plaintiff, as the owner and operator of two motels located on South Broadway Street in Englewood, Colorado entered into a written contract with United Advertising, Inc., a corporation which will hereinafter be referred to as the defendant. Under the terms and provisions of this contract the defendant agreed to construct, install and then maintain at its own expense for a period of three years seven outdoor display signs advertising the two motels owned and operated by the plaintiff, in return for which the plaintiff promised to pay the defendant the sum of $95 per month for three years.

In view of the trial court's ultimate disposition of this controversy, two other provisions of the contract between the parties should now be mentioned. The contract "broke down" the aggregate monthly rental of $95 and provided that the rental on one of the seven signs, which was to be 10

[by] 30 in size, would be $35 per month and that the rental on each of the remaining six signs, which were each to be 4 [by] 8 in size, would be $10 per month. As concerns possible termination or modification of the agreement, there was a provision that the termination or modification "of any item of this agreement constitutes that part of the agreement only and does not affect any other item or part of the agreement."

The present writ of error stems from the plaintiff's claim against the defendant for damages for an alleged breach of contract. In his complaint the plaintiff alleged that the defendant failed to erect and maintain the advertising signs as it had agreed to do and averred that as a result thereof plaintiff suffered damages in the total sum of $10,655. Of this amount, according to the plaintiff, $10,000 represented a so-called loss of business profits, and the remaining $655 represented monies paid the defendant under the contract.

By answer the defendant alleged that each of the seven signs had been properly erected and maintained, except for one small sign which will be referred to as sign No. 4. The defendant asserted no counterclaim for the reason that shortly before the institution of the present action, the defendant assigned its claim against the plaintiff for unpaid monthly rentals to a collection agency.

Trial of this matter was to the court, at the conclusion of which the trial court made very detailed findings of fact and conclusions of law. Specifically, the trial court found that five signs which were referred to as signs No. 1, 2, 3, 6 and 7 were erected in substantial compliance with the terms of the contract. However, the trial court found that sign No. 4 was never erected and that sign No. 5 though erected, was not erected in the particular location called for by the contract. In short, then, the trial court found that the defendant had in fact breached the contract in these two particulars.

It was in this particular setting, that the trial court then found that the contract in question was "divisible" and that the failure of the defendant to properly erect and maintain signs No. 4 and 5 constituted only a "severable breach." However, the trial court then went on to find that even though the plaintiff had established two so-called severable breaches, he nonetheless had failed to establish by "satisfactory evidence" that he sustained *any* damage by reason of the failure of the defendant to properly install signs No. 4 and 5. The trial court accordingly entered judgment dismissing the plaintiff's claim for relief, and by writ of error plaintiff now seeks reversal of the judgment thus entered.

As above indicated, probably the basic issue is whether the contract between the parties is entire or severable. In other words, whether the seven signs in question were, or were not, erected in substantial compliance with the terms and provisions of the contract is basically a question of fact.

Our review of the record convinces us that there is evidence to support the trial court's determination that signs No. 1, 2, 3, 6 and 7 were installed substantially in accord with the contract, but that on the contrary the defendant did in fact breach the contract as concerns signs No. 4 and 5. These findings then cannot be disturbed, as there is evidence to support them.

[The court sustained the trial court's determination that John had not proven that he had lost profit as a result of defendant's breach.]

* * * [T]here is one remaining item of damage which must be considered, and that is the money paid by plaintiff to defendant under the contract. The contract itself called for plaintiff to pay the defendant the *last* four months rent on *all* seven signs. This the plaintiff did, paying defendant the total sum of $380 upon the signing of the contract, or within a very short time thereafter. Then, while the defendant was in the process of erecting the various signs, plaintiff also paid defendant additional sums totaling $300. In other words, the evidence showed that the plaintiff paid defendant the *total* sum of $680 under the contract, and this was the eventual finding of the trial court. However, the trial court apparently did not consider this to be an item of damage, and in this particular it did err.

Of the total sum given defendant by the plaintiff, namely $680, our study of the findings made by the trial court indicates that $120 represented money paid for the two signs (signs No. 4 and 5) which defendant failed to properly install. So, if the contract be *severable* or *divisible,* then the plaintiff is *only* entitled to recover those monies paid defendant for signs No. 4 and 5, which sum is $120. But if the contract be deemed entire in nature, the plaintiff would be entitled to recover *all* of the monies paid by him to the defendant, which would be the sum of $680. It is in this setting that it then becomes necessary to determine the correctness of the trial court's determination that the contract is severable, and not entire.

Whether a contract is entire or severable is a matter which cannot be determined with mathematical precision, as it has been said that there is no set formula which furnishes a foolproof method for determining in a given case just which contracts are severable and which are entire. 12 Am.Jur. 870 and 17 C.J.S. Contracts § 98, p. 785. The primary objective is to ascertain the intent of the contracting parties, as such intent is manifested by not only the several terms and provisions of the contract itself, but also as such are viewed in the light of all the surrounding circumstances, including the conduct of the parties before any dispute has arisen. * * * And the singleness or apportionability of the consideration is said to be an important factor to be considered. * * *

It has also been stated that whether a number of promises constitute one contract, or more than one, is to be determined by inquiring "whether the parties assented to all the promises as a single whole, so that there would have been no bargain whatever, if any promise or set of promises were struck out." United States v. Bethlehem Steel Corp., 315 U.S. 289, 62 S.Ct. 581, 86 L.Ed. 855. * * *

Plaintiff's position on this point is that it was intended that this be a "package deal," that at least four of the signs were to be so situated as to "lead" tourists to the very doorstep of his motel, and that he received *no* benefit under the contract unless all seven signs were properly erected and in place. Therefore, it is argued, the contract is entire in nature.

The defendant, on the contrary, urges that it was the intent of the parties that the contract be severable. In support thereof defendant points to the fact that the money due it from the plaintiff was not a lump sum for the seven signs, but was apportioned as so much, per individual sign. Also, the defendant argues that the termination and modification clause, referred to at the outset of this opinion, certainly looks toward severability. Finally, defendant notes that the several billings were on a "so much per sign basis," and each sign is said to be complete within itself, with no one sign by any language printed thereon being "tied in" to any other sign.

The foregoing recital indicates that the testimony bearing on this particular matter is in at least a degree of conflict. Certainly reasonable persons could well differ as to the proper inferences to be drawn from the testimony and documentary evidence which was before the trial court. In such circumstances we are not at liberty to overturn the trial court's determination that the contract in the instant case was a severable one. There being evidence, then, to support this finding of the trial court, its determination must therefore be upheld. Briano, In Behalf of Rubio v. Rubio, 141 Colo. 264, 347 P.2d 497.

Accordingly, the judgment of the trial court dismissing plaintiff's claim is reversed and the cause remanded with direction that judgment be entered in favor of plaintiff and against defendant in the sum of $120, which is the rental paid on signs No. 4 and 5.

PATTERSON, CONSTRUCTIVE CONDITIONS IN CONTRACTS

42 Colum.L.Rev. 903, 927–28 (1942).

[U]njust enrichment is an influential factor in situations where the remedy is, or is conceived to be, contractual, not quasi contractual. * * * The rule that substantial performance of the promise is a sufficient compliance with the constructive condition to permit recovery "on the contract," is apparently limited to cases in which the defendant has received the benefit of the performance. * * * Another example is "severability," which divides and weakens the force of constructive conditions and which is influenced by the principle of avoiding unjust enrichment as well as by the terms of the contract. The doctrine of "waiver," which permits a partial failure of a constructive condition to be excused by loose and sometimes dubious manifestations of consent, is likewise influenced by the principle of unjust enrichment. Finally, the quasi contractual remedy for unjust enrichment has grown up alongside the contractual remedy, and even under the same procedural forms, to mitigate the hardships of constructive conditions.

CARRIG V. GILBERT-VARKER CORP.

Supreme Judicial Court of Massachusetts, 1943.
314 Mass. 351, 50 N.E.2d 59.

* * *

Action by James A. Carrig against Gilbert-Varker Corporation to recover for breach of construction contract, and cross-action by defendant to recover money due thereon. From adverse judgments, both parties appeal.

Judgment in original action affirmed, and judgment in cross-action reversed, and judgment entered for cross-complainant.

* * *

RONAN, JUSTICE.

Carrig, hereinafter referred to as the owner, entered into a contract with Gilbert-Varker Corporation, hereinafter called the contractor, for the construction of * * * thirty-five houses on a lot of land in Watertown. The declaration filed by the owner seeks * * * to recover damages on account of the refusal of the contractor to erect fifteen houses in Watertown, and damages for its failure to erect in accordance with the contract the twenty houses that it actually built. The action of the owner and the second action, brought by the contractor, were referred to an auditor, whose findings of fact were to be final. * * * [The auditor] found that the owner was not entitled to recover damages for breach of contract in the construction of the twenty houses in Watertown, and that the contractor had repudiated its contract in refusing to proceed with the construction of fifteen more houses. He found for the owner for $9,935 together with interest. The judge ordered judgment for this last mentioned amount with interest. The contractor appealed.

The second action is brought by the contractor to recover * * * a balance of $3,143.85 alleged to be due upon the Watertown contract. * * * The auditor found that the contractor had not been paid $2,816.35, after making certain adjustments and allowances for work performed and materials furnished in erecting the twenty Watertown houses, but he found and ruled that the contractor was not entitled to recover this amount, on the ground that he had refused to carry out the Watertown contract by not erecting the fifteen houses. * * * [The contractor appealed.]

The parties on May 2, 1941, entered into a written contract by which the contractor agreed to build thirty-five houses in Watertown in accordance with certain plans and specifications accompanying the contract. The contract set forth four types of construction together with the basic price to be paid for each type. A schedule was included in the contract showing the various prices that were to be allowed the contractor for such alterations or additions as the owner might desire to have made in the construction of any of these houses. The type of the house to be erected on each of the thirty-five lots was designated in the contract together with the basic price for the structure to be erected upon that particular lot. The total basic price for the erection of these thirty-five houses amounted to $132,928. The houses were to be built in groups of not less than ten. The owner agreed to place a temporary construction loan mortgage on each lot upon which a house was to be built and to assign the proceeds of these mortgages to the contractor, who was not required to commence work until such assignment was made. The contractor was to be paid on each house certain percentages of the contract prices when certain stages were reached in its construction, and the final payment was to be made forty days after its completion. After the work began the contractor agreed to release a certain amount from the proceeds of the mortgage on each lot to enable the owner to sell the house, and the latter agreed to reimburse the contractor from the first proceeds of the sale. The bank paid the amounts of the various mortgages to the contractor. The contractor made various releases of funds. As the work progressed it became necessary to keep full accounts so that the financial situation between the owner and the contractor could be determined from time to time.

[The court first affirmed the auditor's finding that the contractor repudiated the contract by failing to build the fifteen houses.] We think the proper measure of damages was the cost in excess of the contract price that would be incurred by the owner in having the houses built, and that there was no error * * * in ordering judgment for this amount, with interest.

The remaining question is the right of the contractor to recover the unpaid balance arising from the construction of the twenty Watertown houses. The auditor has found that this work was done in substantial compliance with the contract and has made allowances to the owner for minor defects and for a small amount of uncompleted work. It is a general rule that one who has breached an entire contract to be performed for an entire price cannot recover * * * on the contract * * * but that where the contract consists of several and distinct items to be furnished or performed by one party, the consideration to be apportioned to each item according to its value and as a separate unit rather than as a part of the whole, then the contract is severable or divisible. * * * Whether a contract is entire or divisible depends upon the intention of the parties as disclosed by the language of the contract, the manner in which it is to be performed, the method of payment, and the circumstances attending its execution and operation. * * * The contract covered the construction of thirty-five houses, the money for which was secured by a separate mortgage placed on each lot and from the sale of each house upon its completion. Payments to the contractor for each house were made in instalments as the construction of that house reached certain stages. Each house was treated as a unit. The sum of $132,928 named in the contract was nothing more than the sum total of the basic prices for the erection of thirty-five different houses according to the basic type of construction designated for each house. A portion of this sum equal to the basic price of each particular house was allocated to the construction of that house, and the final instalment payment became due and payable to the contractor forty days after its completion. The construction of each house and the payment therefor were mutual and dependent provisions of the contract. We think the contract was a divisible one, and that the refusal of the contractor to construct the fifteen houses included in the contract, which were in addition to the twenty houses erected by the contractor, did not bar the contractor from recovering the unpaid balance for work done and materials furnished in constructing the twenty houses. * * *

[Order reversed.]

K & G CONST. CO. V. HARRIS

Court of Appeals of Maryland, 1960.
223 Md. 305, 164 A.2d 451.

PRESCOTT, JUDGE.

Feeling aggrieved by the action of the trial judge of the Circuit Court for Prince George's County, sitting without a jury, in finding a judgment against it in favor of a subcontractor, the appellant, the general contractor on a construction project, appealed.

The principal question presented is: Does a contractor, damaged by a subcontractor's failure to perform a portion of his work in a workmanlike manner, have a right, under the circumstances of this case, to withhold, in partial satisfaction of said damages, an installment payment, which, under the terms of the contract, was due the subcontractor, unless the negligent performance of his work excused its payment?

* * *

The statement [of the case according to a Maryland rule] in relevant part, is as follows:

> "* * * K & G Construction Company, Inc. (hereinafter called Contractor), plaintiff and counter-defendant in the Circuit Court and appellant herein, was owner and general contractor of a housing subdivision project being constructed (herein called

Project). Harris and Brooks (hereinafter called Subcontractor), defendants and counter-plaintiffs in the Circuit Court and appellees herein, entered into a contract with Contractor to do excavating and earth-moving work on the Project. Pertinent parts of the contract are set forth below:

" 'Section 3. The Subcontractor agrees to complete the several portions and the whole of the work herein sublet by the time or times following:

" '(a) Without delay, as called for by the Contractor.

" '(b) It is expressly agreed that time is of the essence of this contract, and that the Contractor will have the right to terminate this contract and employ a substitute to perform the work in the event of delay on the part of Subcontractor, and Subcontractor agrees to indemnify the Contractor for any loss sustained thereby, provided, however, that nothing in this paragraph shall be construed to deprive Contractor of any rights or remedies it would otherwise have as to damage for delay.

" 'Section 4. (b) Progress payments will be made each month during the performance of the work. Subcontractor will submit to Contractor, by the 25th of each month, a requisition for work performed during the preceding month. Contractor will pay these requisitions, less a retainer equal to ten per cent (10%), by the 10th of the months in which such requisitions are received.[1]

" '(c) No payments will be made under this contract until the insurance requirements of Sec. 9 hereof have been complied with.

* * *

" 'Section 8. * * * All work shall be performed in a workmanlike manner, and in accordance with the best practices.

" 'Section 9. Subcontractor agrees to carry, during the progress of the work, * * * liability insurance against * * * property damage, in such amounts and with such companies as may be satisfactory to Contractor and shall provide Contractor with certificates showing the same to be in force.'

"While in the course of his employment by the Subcontractor on the Project, a bulldozer operator drove his machine too close to Contractor's house while grading the yard, causing the immediate collapse of a wall and other damage to the house. The resulting damage to contractor's house was $3,400.00. Subcontractor had complied with the insurance provision (Sec. 9) of the aforesaid contract. Subcontractor reported said damages to their liability

1 This section is not a model for clarity.

insurance carrier. The Subcontractor and its insurance carrier refused to repair damage or compensate Contractor for damage to the house, claiming that there was no liability on the part of the Subcontractor.

* * *

"Contractor was generally satisfied with Subcontractor's work and progress as required under Sections 3 and 8 of the contract until September 12, 1958, with the exception of the bulldozer accident of August 9, 1958.

"Subcontractor performed work under the contract during July, 1958, for which it submitted a requisition by the 25th of July, as required by the contract, for work done prior to the 25th of July, payable under the terms of the contract by Contractor on or before August 10, 1958. Contractor was current as to payments due under all preceding monthly requisitions from Subcontractor. The aforesaid bulldozer accident damaging Contractor's house occurred on August 9, 1958. Contractor refused to pay Subcontractor's requisition due on August 10, 1958, because the bulldozer damage to Contractor's house had not been repaired or paid for. Subcontractor continued to work on the project until the 12th of September, 1958, at which time they discontinued working on the project because of Contractor's refusal to pay the said work requisition and notified Contractor by registered letters of their position and willingness to return to the job, but only upon payment. At that time, September 12, 1958, the value of the work completed by Subcontractor on the project for which they had not been paid was $1,484.50.

"Contractor later requested Subcontractor to return and complete work on the Project which Subcontractor refused to do because of nonpayment of work requisitions of July 25 and thereafter. Contractor's house was not repaired by Subcontractor nor compensation paid for the damage.

"It was stipulated that Subcontractor had completed work on the Project under the contract for which they had not been paid in the amount of $1,484.50 and that if they had completed the remaining work to be done under the contract, they would have made a profit of $1,340.00 on the remaining uncompleted portion of the contract. It was further stipulated that it cost the Contractor $450.00 above the contract price to have another excavating contractor complete the remaining work required under the contract. It was the opinion of the Court that if judgment were in favor of the Subcontractor, it should be for the total amount of $2,824.50.

"* * * Contractor filed suit against the Subcontractor in two counts: (1), for the aforesaid bulldozer damage to Contractor's house, alleging negligence of the Subcontractor's bulldozer operator, and (2) for the $450.00 costs above the contract price in having another excavating subcontractor complete the uncompleted work in the contract. Subcontractor filed a counter-claim for recovery of work of the value of $1,484.50 for which they had not received payment and for loss of anticipated profits on uncompleted portion of work in the amount of $1,340.00. By agreement of the parties, the first count of Contractor's claim, i.e., for aforesaid bulldozer damage to Contractor's house, was submitted to jury who found in favor of Contractor in the amount of $3,400.00. Following the finding by the jury, the second count of the Contractor's claim and the counter-claims of the Subcontractor, by agreement of the parties, were submitted to the Court for determination, without jury. All of the facts recited herein above were stipulated to by the parties to the Court. Circuit Court Judge Fletcher found for counter-plaintiff Subcontractor in the amount of $2,824.50 from which Contractor has entered this appeal."

The $3,400 judgment has been paid.

It is immediately apparent that our decision turns upon the respective rights and liabilities of the parties under that portion of their contract whereby the subcontractor agreed to do the excavating and earth-moving work in "a workmanlike manner, and in accordance with the best practices," with time being of the essence of the contract, and the contractor agreed to make progress payments therefor on the 10th day of the months following the performance of the work by the subcontractor.[2] The subcontractor contends, of course, that when the contractor failed to make the payment due on August 10, 1958, he breached his contract and thereby released him (the subcontractor) from any further obligation to perform. The contractor, on the other hand, argues that the failure of the subcontractor to perform his work in a workmanlike manner constituted a material breach of the contract, which justified his refusal to make the August 10 payment; and, as there was no breach on his part, the subcontractor had no right to cease performance on September 12, and his refusal to continue work on the project constituted another breach, which rendered him liable to the contractor for damages. The vital question, more tersely stated, remains: Did the contractor have a right, under the

[2] The statement of the case does not show the exact terms concerning the remuneration to be paid the subcontractor. It does not disclose whether he was to be paid a total lump sum, by the cubic yard, by the day, or in some other manner. It does state that the excavation finally cost the contractor $450 more than the "contract price."

circumstances, to refuse to make the progress payment due on August 10, 1958?

The answer involves interesting and important principles of contract law. Promises and counter-promises made by the respective parties to a contract have certain relations to one another, which determine many of the rights and liabilities of the parties. Broadly speaking, they are (1) independent of each other, or (2) mutually dependent, one upon the other. They are independent of each other if the parties intend that *performance* by each of them is in no way conditioned upon *performance* by the other. 5 Page, The Law of Contracts, ¶ 2971. In other words, the parties exchange promises for promises, not the *performance* of promises for the *performance* of promises. 3 Williston, Contracts (Rev.Ed.), ¶ 813, n. 6. A failure to perform an independent promise does not excuse non-performance on the part of the adversary party, but each is required to perform his promise, and, if one does not perform, he is liable to the adversary party for such non-performance. (Of course, if litigation ensues questions of set-off or recoupment frequently arise.) Promises are mutually dependent if the parties intend *performance* by one to be conditioned upon *performance* by the other, and, if they be mutually dependent, they may be (a) precedent, i.e., a promise that is to be performed before a corresponding promise on the part of the adversary party is to be performed, (b) subsequent, i.e., a corresponding promise that is not to be performed until the other party to the contract has performed a precedent covenant, or (c) concurrent, i.e., promises that are to be performed at the same time by each of the parties, who are respectively bound to perform each. Page, op. cit., ¶¶ 2941, 2951, 2961.

Professor Page, op. cit., ¶ 2971, says there are three classes of independent promises left: (1) those in which the acts to be performed by the respective parties are, by the terms of the contract, to be performed at fixed times or on the happening of certain events which do not bear any relation to one another; (2) those in which the covenant in question is independent because it does not form the entire consideration for the covenants on the part of the adversary party, and ordinarily forms but a minor part of such consideration; and (3) those in which the contract shows that the parties intended performance of their respective promises without regard to performance on the part of the adversary, thus relying upon the promises and not the performances (Cf. Brown v. Fraley, 222 Md. 480, 161 A.2d 128).

In the early days, it was settled law that covenants and mutual promises in a contract were *prima facie* independent, and that they were to be so construed in the absence of language in the contract clearly showing that they were intended to be dependent. Williston, op. cit., ¶ 816; Page, op. cit., ¶¶ 2944, 2945. In the case of Kingston v. Preston, 2 Doug. 689, decided in 1774, Lord Mansfield, contrary to three centuries of opposing precedents, changed the rule, and decided that performance of one covenant might be dependent on prior performance of another, although the contract contained no express condition to that effect. Page, op. cit., ¶ 2946; Williston, op. cit., ¶ 817. The modern rule, which seems to be of almost universal application, is that there is a presumption that mutual promises in a contract are dependent and are to be so regarded, whenever possible. Page, op. cit., ¶ 2946; Restatement, Contracts, ¶ 266. Cf. Williston, op. cit., ¶ 812.

While the courts assume, in deciding the relation of one or more promises in a contract to one or more counter-promises, that the promises are dependent rather than independent, the intention of the parties, as shown by the entire contract as construed in the light of the circumstances of the case, the nature of the contract, the relation of the parties thereto, and the other evidence which is admissible to assist the court in determining the intention of the parties, is the controlling factor in deciding whether the promises and counter-promises are dependent or independent. * * *

Considering the presumption that promises and counter-promises are dependent and the statement of the case, we have no hesitation in holding that the promise and counter-promise under consideration here were mutually dependent, that is to say, the parties intended performance by one to be conditioned on performance by the other; and the subcontractor's promise was, by the explicit wording of the contract, precedent to the promise of payment, monthly, by the contractor. In Shapiro Engineering Corp. v. Francis O. Day Co., 215 Md. 373, 380, 137 A.2d 695, we stated that it is the general rule that where a total price for work is fixed by a contract, the work is not rendered divisible by progress payments. It would, indeed present an unusual situation if we were to hold that a building contractor, who has obtained someone to do work for him and has agreed to pay each month for the work performed in the previous month, has to continue the monthly payments, irrespective of the degree of skill and care displayed in the performance of work, and his only recourse is by way of suit for ill-performance. If this were the law, it is conceivable, in fact, probable, that many contractors would become insolvent before they were able to complete their contracts. As was stated by the Court in Measures Brothers Ltd. v. Measures, 2 Ch. 248: "Covenants are to be construed as dependent or independent according to the intention of the parties and the good sense of the case."

We hold that when the subcontractor's employee negligently damaged the contractor's wall, this constituted a breach of the subcontractor's promise to perform his work in a "workmanlike manner, and in accordance with the best practices." * * * And there can be little doubt that the breach was material: the damage to the wall amounted to more than double the payment due on August 10. Speed v. Bailey, 153 Md. 655, 661, 662, 139 A.

534. 3A Corbin, Contracts, § 708, says: "The failure of a contractor's [in our case, the subcontractor's] performance to constitute 'substantial' performance may justify the owner [in our case, the contractor] in refusing to make a progress payment * * *. * * * If the refusal to pay an installment is justified on the owner's [contractor's] part, the contractor [subcontractor] is not justified in abandoning work by reason of that refusal. His abandonment of the work will itself be a wrongful repudiation that goes to the essence, even if the defects in performance did not." * * * Professor Corbin, in § 954, states further: "The unexcused failure of a contractor to render a promised performance when it is due is always a breach of contract * * *. Such failure may be of such great importance as to constitute what has been called herein a 'total' breach. * * *. For a failure of performance constituting such a 'total' breach, an action for remedies that are appropriate thereto is at once maintainable. Yet the injured party is not required to bring such action. He has the option of treating the non-performance as a 'partial' breach only * * *."[b] In permitting the subcontractor to proceed with work on the project after August 9, the contractor, obviously, treated the breach by the subcontractor as a partial one. As the promises were mutually dependent and the subcontractor had made a material breach in his performance, this justified the contractor in refusing to make the August 10 payment; hence, as the contractor was not in default, the subcontractor again breached the contract when he, on September 12, discontinued work on the project, which rendered him liable (by the express terms of the contract) to the contractor for his increased cost in having the excavating done—a stipulated amount of $450. Cf. Keystone Engineering Corp. v. Sutter, 196 Md. 620, 628, 78 A.2d 191.

The appellees suggest two minor points that may be disposed of rather summarily. They argue that the contractor "gave no written notice to subcontractor for any services rendered or materials furnished by the contractor to the subcontractor," in accordance with the terms of the contract. It is apparent that the contractor's claim against the subcontractor for ill-performance did not involve, in any way, "services rendered or materials furnished" by the contractor; hence, the argument has no substance. They also contend that the contractor had no right to refuse the August 10 payment, because the subcontractor had furnished the insurance against property damage, as called for in the contract. There is little, or no, merit in this suggestion. The subcontractor and his insurance company denied liability. The furnishing of the insurance by him did not constitute a license to perform his work in a careless, negligent, or unworkmanlike manner; and its acceptance by the contractor did not

---

[b] The Restatement (Second) of Contracts in section 236(1) defines a claim for "total breach" as a claim for damages "based on all of the injured party's remaining rights to performance." A claim for "partial breach" is "a claim for damages based on only part of the injured party's remaining rights to performance."

preclude his assertion of a claim for unworkmanlike performance directly against the subcontractor.

Judgment against the appellant reversed; and judgment entered in favor of the appellant against the appellees for $450, the appellees to pay the costs.

UNIFORM COMMERCIAL CODE § 2–717.

Deduction of Damages From the Price

The buyer on notifying the seller of his intention to do so may deduct all or any part of the damages resulting from any breach of the contract from any part of the price still due under the same contract.

NOTE:
THE RIGHT UNDER THE SECOND RESTATEMENT NOT TO PERFORM AND TO CANCEL AFTER MATERIAL BREACH

The Restatement (Second) of Contracts sets forth a series of special rules dealing with the aggrieved party's rights in the face of a material breach. Under sections 237, 241 and 242, a material breach does not necessarily entitle the aggrieved party to cancel the deal. According to these sections, the aggrieved party may initially only suspend performance and must continue to stand by to accept cure. How long must this party wait? Until it is too late. How late is too late? Consider the rules below.

> § 237. Effect on Other Party's Duties of a Failure to Render Performance
>
> [I]t is a condition of each party's remaining duties to render performances to be exchanged under an exchange of promises that there be no uncured material failure by the other party to render any such performance due at an earlier time.
>
> § 241. Circumstances Significant in Determining Whether a Failure Is Material
>
> In determining whether a failure to render or to offer performance is material, the following circumstances are significant:
>
> (a) the extent to which the injured party will be deprived of the benefit which he reasonably expected;
>
> (b) the extent to which the injured party can be adequately compensated for the part of that benefit of which he will be deprived;
>
> (c) the extent to which the party failing to perform or to offer to perform will suffer forfeiture;
>
> (d) the likelihood that the party failing to perform or to offer to perform will cure his failure, taking account of all the circumstances including any reasonable assurances;

(e) the extent to which the behavior of the party failing to perform or to offer to perform comports with standards of good faith and fair dealing.

§ 242. Circumstances Significant in Determining When Remaining Duties are Discharged

In determining the time after which a party's uncured material failure to render or to offer performance discharges the other party's remaining duties to render performance under the rule[ ] stated in § 237 * * * the following circumstances are significant:

(a) those stated in § 241;

(b) the extent to which it reasonably appears to the injured party that delay may prevent or hinder him in making reasonable substitute arrangements;

(c) the extent to which the agreement provides for performance without delay, but a material failure to perform or to offer to perform on a stated day does not of itself discharge the other party's remaining duties unless the circumstances, including the language of the agreement, indicate that performance or an offer to perform by that day is important.

E. FARNSWORTH, CONTRACTS

561–62 (4th ed. 2004).

Suppose that in breach of a construction contract the owner has delayed making a required progress payment, and the builder, after first refusing to go forward with the work, has finally terminated the contract, leaving the building unfinished. * * * Under the concept of constructive conditions of exchange, the owner's payment of progress payments is an implied condition of the builder's duty to continue to work. Therefore, the owner's breach in failing to make a progress payment may have two effects on the builder's duty. First, further performance will not become due, so the builder will be justified in exercising a right to self-help by suspending performance. Second, after an appropriate period of time, the builder can choose to treat its remaining duties of performance under the contract as discharged and can exercise a right to self-help by terminating the contract. Two distinct issues are therefore raised. First, was the owner's breach in failing to make the progress payments significant enough to justify the builder's suspending performance? Second, did the owner's breach continue long enough to justify the builder's terminating the contract? If the answer to both questions is yes, the builder was entitled to terminate the contract and claim damages for total breach against the owner. But if the answer to either is no, the builder's action was precipitous and unjustified, itself amounting to a breach that gave the owner a right to terminate and claim damages for total breach against the builder.

This sensible two-step analysis is carefully articulated in the Restatement Second.

ROSETT, CONTRACT PERFORMANCE: PROMISES, CONDITIONS AND THE OBLIGATION TO COMMUNICATE

22 U.C.L.A. L.Rev. 1083, 1086–87, 1096–97, 1100–1101 (1975).

The parties have exchanged promises, committing themselves to future performance. But prior to or during performance one party finds its expectations are not being fulfilled: The promised building is not completed or does not conform to plans; the goods delivered may not be quite what was expected or they are late, etc. The disappointed party will ask two questions: (1) shall I continue to perform my half of the contract or will the deal be terminated, and (2) how will I be compensated for the loss associated with my disappointment?

In answering these questions, traditional theory makes four inquiries. First, it asks whether one or both parties breached a promise; if so, the breaching party is liable to the other for damages. Second, it asks whether one or more of these breaches was material, that is, whether the breach was so serious that it justified the other side in suspending and ultimately terminating his own performance. Since most ruptures involve an interrelated set of failures on both sides, the answer to the last question is likely to require analysis of a third inquiry: the relationship between the promises the parties have exchanged. If it is concluded that the promise of performance of one was given in exchange for the performance of the other, then the failure of one performance affects the obligation to render the return performance. On the other hand, if the promises are deemed independent, any disappointment with performance does not relieve the obligation of counter-performance. The answers to the last two inquiries are likely to provide the resolution of the fourth—the determination of who committed the first material breach. That party is liable, not only for losses associated with the partial breach, but for damages measured by the value of the entire contract.

* * *

Too little weight is given the likelihood that most failures of performance are curable when, or soon after they occur. Breaches and failures become material in part because they are treated that way rather than promptly adjusted. When a party is faced with present or threatened failure of performance, the Restatement II analyzes the issue in terms of whether his behavior is a breach and whether that breach is material. The party who is guilty of the first uncured material breach bears the loss. The Restatement emphasis is on characterizing the performance of the parties, not upon guiding them in determining whether to continue with the contract. Although the Restatement II recognizes the possibility of communication, assurance, and cure, little emphasis is placed on whether the parties have tried to communicate to adjust the difficulties. No duty to communicate candidly is imposed, nor are the parties bound by what they say if they do communicate. Not only are the parties not required to communicate, but there seems to be a real danger that candid communication advising the other side of the circumstances jeopardizing performance and requesting a modification to accommodate the changed circumstances, unless carefully phrased, will be interpreted as a repudiation—a material breach by the communicating party.

This traditional orientation is unrealistic, because most business transactions are part of an ongoing relationship between people who are or can easily be in direct communication. The first thing a contracting party in difficulty should do is contact the other party, explain the situation, and give assurances that the defect will be cured, or if that is not possible, seek to modify the agreement so that it can be performed, or else terminate it altogether. * * *

PROBLEM 7-8

Resolve the following problems under Restatement (Second) of Contracts sections 237, 241 and 242 set forth above.

1. Vendor promises to convey land to vendee on July 1, vendee to pay $100,000 on July 1 and the balance of $175,000 one year later. On July 1, vendee learns that vendor has sold the property to Edgar. When can vendee cancel?

2. Owner contracts with Builder for the construction of a warehouse to be built during the months of July, August, and September, Owner to make a $150,000 progress payment on the 15th of each month. Owner erroneously concludes that the work is being done contrary to specifications and withholds the first progress payment. On July 23, Builder suspends performance. He has fourteen employees on the project, who are paid weekly. Their pay is due July 23, and Builder has to borrow money to meet the payroll. On July 25, Owner tenders the $150,000 due on July 15. Builder wants to know if he can refuse the tender and cancel. He says he wants to turn to another job he has lined up "free of such difficulties." What would you advise?

HILLMAN, CONTRACT LORE

27 J. Corp. L. 505, 509–510 (2002).

Contracts people show no hesitancy in proclaiming that the reasons for a breach, whether willful, negligent, or unavoidable, have no bearing in determining the rights of the contracting parties. Contract liability is said to be "strict," meaning that the reasons for a breach are irrelevant. The goal is to make the injured party whole, not to punish contract breakers.

But a host of exceptions swallow up the rule, so much so that most theorists, if pressed, understand that the true "rule" is that the breacher's conduct matters a lot. For example, in construction contracts, the degree of willfulness of a contractor's breach helps courts determine whether to grant expectancy damages measured by the cost of repair or the diminution in value caused by the breach, the latter often a smaller measure. Deliberateness also constitutes an express factor in determining the materiality of a promisor's breach and whether the promisee is excused from the contract. Even after being excused from performance, a promisee may have to deal further with a contract breaker to minimize damages, depending on a promisor's motive for the breach. A promisor also may commit a bad-faith breach of contract and therefore trigger rights in favor of the promisee that are not expressly set forth in the contract. Finally, courts have created "independent torts" that arise in the contract setting, including when a party misrepresents facts during negotiations or recklessly performs a contract.

None of these rules should be surprising or even very controversial. Fairness principles such as the "rule of reciprocity" dictate that one should not try to increase one's gains at the expense of the other party. Moreover, on moral grounds, people should keep their promises, and unintentional breaches deserve less moral approbation than intentional ones. Considering the deliberateness of a breach makes sense on instrumental grounds too. Courts should deter a promisor from taking advantage of the promisee's reliance on an expected performance or of changed circumstances that back the promisee into a corner. By deterring such "opportunistic breaches," contract law encourages contracting and thwarts useless wealth transfers from an innocent party to a wrongdoer. Perhaps most obvious, judges and juries are human beings who cannot help but be influenced by the degree of nastiness and inconsiderateness of a breach.

PROBLEM 7-9

If a materially breaching party makes a new offer to perform, is the injured party under a duty to accept such an offer in order to mitigate damages? If so, is the "right" of an injured party to suspend performance after a material breach illusory? For example, suppose a seller, under contract to deliver lumber to a buyer on credit, refuses to perform except for cash (but at a price reduction equal to the amount of interest the buyer would lose by paying earlier). Assume the refusal constitutes a material breach. Must the buyer nevertheless take the lumber and pay cash in order to minimize damages? In Lawrence v. Porter, 63 F. 62, 66 (6th Cir.1894), the court answered affirmatively, stating: "[t]here seems to be no insurmountable objection in * * * permitting a delinquent contractor to minimize his loss." But see Parker v. Twentieth Century-Fox Film Corp., set forth in Chapter 3.

SECTION TEN: CONDITIONS AND ARTICLE 2 OF THE UNIFORM COMMERCIAL CODE

UNIFORM COMMERCIAL CODE § 2–601.

Buyer's Rights on Improper Delivery

Subject to the provisions of this Article on breach in installment contracts (Section 2–612) and unless otherwise agreed under the sections on contractual limitations of remedy (Sections 2–718 and 2–719), if the goods or the tender of delivery fail in any respect to conform to the contract, the buyer may

(a) reject the whole; or

(b) accept the whole; or

(c) accept any commercial unit or units and reject the rest.

UNIFORM COMMERCIAL CODE § 2–602(1).

Rejection of goods must be within a reasonable time after their delivery or tender. It is ineffective unless the buyer seasonably notifies the seller.

WILSON V. SCAMPOLI

District of Columbia Court of Appeals, 1967.
228 A.2d 848.

MYERS, ASSOCIATE JUDGE.

This is an appeal from an order of the trial court granting rescission of a sales contract for a color television set and directing the return of the purchase price plus interest and costs.

Appellee purchased the set in question on November 4, 1965, paying the total purchase price in cash. The transaction was evidenced by a sales ticket showing the price paid and guaranteeing ninety days' free service and replacement of any defective tube and parts for a period of one year. Two days after purchase the set was delivered and uncrated, the antennae adjusted and the set plugged into an electrical outlet to "cook out."[1] When the set was turned on however, it did not function properly, the picture having a reddish tinge. Appellant's delivery man advised the buyer's daughter, Mrs. Kolley, that it was not his duty to tune in or adjust the color but that a service representative would shortly call at her house for that

[1] Such a "cook out," usually over several days, allows the set to magnetize itself and to heat up the circuit in order to indicate faulty wiring.

purpose. After the departure of the delivery men, Mrs. Kolley unplugged the set and did not use it.[2]

On November 8, 1965, a service representative arrived, and after spending an hour in an effort to eliminate the red cast from the picture advised Mrs. Kolley that he would have to remove the chassis from the cabinet and take it to the shop as he could not determine the cause of the difficulty from his examination at the house. He also made a written memorandum of his service call, noting that the television "Needs Shop Work (Red Screen)." Mrs. Kolley refused to allow the chassis to be removed, asserting she did not want a "repaired" set but another "brand new" set. Later she demanded the return of the purchase price, although retaining the set. Appellant refused to refund the purchase price, but renewed his offer to adjust, repair, or, if the set could not be made to function properly, to replace it. Ultimately, appellee instituted this suit against appellant seeking a refund of the purchase price. After a trial, the court ruled that "under the facts and circumstances the complaint is justified. Under the equity powers of the Court I will order the parties put back in their original status, let the $675 be returned, and the set returned to the defendant."

Appellant does not contest the jurisdiction of the trial court to order rescission in a proper case, but contends the trial judge erred in holding that rescission here was appropriate. He argues that he was always willing to comply with the terms of the sale either by correcting the malfunction by minor repairs or, in the event the set could not be made thereby properly operative, by replacement; that as he was denied the opportunity to try to correct the difficulty, he did not breach the contract of sale or any warranty thereunder, expressed or implied.

D.C.Code § 28:2–508 (Supp. V, 1966) provides:

> (1) Where any tender or delivery by the seller is rejected because non-conforming and the time for performance has not yet expired, the seller may seasonably notify the buyer of his intention to cure and may then within the contract time make a conforming delivery.
>
> (2) Where the buyer rejects a non-conforming tender which the seller had reasonable grounds to believe would be acceptable with or without money allowance the seller may if he seasonably notifies the buyer have a further reasonable time to substitute a conforming tender.

A retail dealer would certainly expect and have reasonable grounds to believe that merchandise like color television sets, new and delivered as crated at the factory, would be acceptable as delivered and that, if defective

[2] Appellee, who made his home with Mrs. Kolley, had been hospitalized shortly before delivery of the set. The remaining negotiations were carried on by Mrs. Kolley, acting on behalf of her father.

in some way, he would have the right to substitute a conforming tender. The question then resolves itself to whether the dealer may conform his tender by adjustment or minor repair or whether he must conform by substituting brand new merchandise. The problem seems to be one of first impression in other jurisdictions adopting the Uniform Commercial Code as well as in the District of Columbia.

Although the Official Code Comments do not reach this precise issue, there are cases and comments under other provisions of the Code which indicate that under certain circumstances repairs and adjustments are contemplated as remedies under implied warranties. In L & N Sales Co. v. Little Brown Jug, Inc., 12 Pa.Dist. & Co.R.2d 469 (Phila.County Ct.1957), where the language of a disclaimer was found insufficient to defeat warranties under §§ 2–314 and 2–315, the court noted that the buyer had notified the seller of defects in the merchandise, and as the seller was unable to remedy them and later refused to accept return of the articles, it was held to be a breach of warranty. In Hall v. Everett Motors, Inc., 340 Mass. 430, 165 N.E.2d 107 (1960), decided shortly before the effective date of the Code in Massachusetts, the court reluctantly found that a disclaimer of warranties was sufficient to insulate the seller. Several references were made in the ruling to the seller's unsuccessful attempts at repairs, the court indicating the result would have been different under the Code.

While these cases provide no mandate to require the buyer to accept patchwork goods or substantially repaired articles in lieu of flawless merchandise, they do indicate that minor repairs or reasonable adjustments are frequently the means by which an imperfect tender may be cured. In discussing the analogous question of defective title, it has been stated that:

> The seller, then, should be able to cure [the defect] under subsection 2–508(2) in those cases in which he can do so without subjecting the buyer to any great inconvenience, risk or loss. Hawkland, Curing an Improper Tender of Title to Chattels: Past, Present and Commercial Code, 46 Minn.L.Rev. 697, 724 (1962).
> * * *

Removal of a television chassis for a short period of time in order to determine the cause of color malfunction and ascertain the extent of adjustment or correction needed to effect full operational efficiency presents no great inconvenience to the buyer. In the instant case, appellant's expert witness testified that this was not infrequently necessary with new televisions. Should the set be defective in workmanship or parts, the loss would be upon the manufacturer who warranted it free from mechanical defect. Here the adamant refusal of Mrs. Kolley, acting on behalf of appellee, to allow inspection essential to the determination of the cause of the excessive red tinge to the picture defeated any effort by the seller to provide timely repair or even replacement of the set if the difficulty could not be corrected. The cause of the defect might have been minor and easily adjusted or it may have been substantial and required replacement by another new set—but the seller was never given an adequate opportunity to make a determination.

We do not hold that appellant has no liability to appellee,[3] but as he was denied access and a reasonable opportunity to repair, appellee has not shown a breach of warranty entitling him either to a brand new set or to rescission. We therefore reverse the judgment of the trial court granting rescission and directing the return of the purchase price of the set.

Reversed.

UNIFORM COMMERCIAL CODE § 2–608.

Revocation of Acceptance in Whole or in Part

(1) The buyer may revoke his acceptance of a lot or commercial unit whose non-conformity substantially impairs its value to him if he has accepted it

(a) on the reasonable assumption that its non-conformity would be cured and it has not been seasonably cured; or

(b) without discovery of such non-conformity if his acceptance was reasonably induced either by the difficulty of discovery before acceptance or by the seller's assurances.

(2) Revocation of acceptance must occur within a reasonable time after the buyer discovers or should have discovered the ground for it and before any substantial change in condition of the goods which is not caused by their own defects. It is not effective until the buyer notifies the seller of it.

(3) A buyer who so revokes has the same rights and duties with regard to the goods involved as if he had rejected them.

ACCETTURA v. VACATIONLAND, INC., 100 U.C.C. Rep Serv 2d 154, 2019 WL 4509017 (Sup. Ct. Ill. 2019). [Purchaser sought to revoke acceptance of a defective recreational vehicle.] The plain language of the statute evinces the General Assembly's intention to allow a buyer to revoke acceptance of a substantially impaired commercial unit under two separate and distinct circumstances. The first circumstance is when the buyer

[3] Appellant on appeal has renewed his willingness to remedy any defect in the tender, and thus there is no problem of expiration of his warranties. He should be afforded the right to inspect and correct any malfunction. If appellee refuses to allow appellant an opportunity to do so, then no cause of action can lie for breach of warranty, express or implied, and the loss must be borne by appellee.

knows of the nonconformity, the buyer accepts the nonconforming unit with a reasonable assumption that the nonconformity will be cured, and the seller fails to seasonably cure it. 810 ILCS 5/2–608(1)(a) (West 2014). The second is when the buyer accepts the nonconforming unit without knowledge of the nonconformity and either the nonconformity was difficult to discover or the seller assured her that the unit conformed to the specifications. *Id.* § 2–608(1)(b). Both situations contemplate a nonconformity that substantially impairs the unit's value to the buyer. Where they diverge is in the buyer's expectation. The first contemplates a buyer who accepts a nonconforming unit and expects the seller to cure the nonconformity. When she does not get that cure seasonably, she can revoke her acceptance. The second contemplates a buyer who accepts what she believes to be a conforming unit. When she does not get that conforming unit, she can revoke her acceptance. Because we find this language plain and because subsection (1)(b) does not require that a buyer give the seller an opportunity to cure, we need not consider the requirements of other statutes that defendant argues are analogous.* * * We hold that the plain language of subsection 2–608(1)(b) of the Illinois Commercial Code does not require that the buyer give the seller an opportunity to cure a substantial nonconformity before revoking acceptance. We reverse and remand for further proceedings consistent with this opinion.

UNIFORM COMMERCIAL CODE § 2–612.

"Installment Contract"; Breach

(1) An "installment contract" is one which requires or authorizes the delivery of goods in separate lots to be separately accepted, even though the contract contains a clause "each delivery is a separate contract" or its equivalent.

(2) The buyer may reject any installment which is non-conforming if the non-conformity substantially impairs the value of that installment and cannot be cured or if the non-conformity is a defect in the required documents; but if the non-conformity does not fall within subsection (3) and the seller gives adequate assurance of its cure the buyer must accept that installment.

(3) Whenever non-conformity or default with respect to one or more installments substantially impairs the value of the whole contract there is a breach of the whole. But the aggrieved party reinstates the contract if he accepts a non-conforming installment without seasonably notifying of cancellation or if he brings an action with respect only to past installments or demands performance as to future installments.

HUBBARD V. UTZ QUALITY FOODS, INC.

United States District Court, W.D. New York, 1995.
903 F.Supp. 444.

Trial Decision and Order

LARIMER, DISTRICT JUDGE.

This is a breach-of-contract action brought by Daniel Hubbard ("Hubbard") against UTZ Quality Foods, Inc. ("UTZ"). Hubbard is a Bath, New York potato farmer and UTZ is a Pennsylvania corporation that purchases potatoes for processing into potato chips.

On April 20, 1992, Hubbard executed a written contract to supply UTZ with a quantity of potatoes. The contract, a two-page, form-contract prepared by UTZ, required that the potatoes comply with certain quality standards. Hubbard claims that he was ready and able to deliver the required shipments of potatoes but that UTZ wrongfully and without basis rejected his potatoes. Hubbard contends that the sample potatoes provided to UTZ complied with all the quality requirements and, therefore, he complied with all terms of the contract. Hubbard claims that UTZ breached the contract and claims damages for the full contract price, $68,750.

UTZ denies Hubbard's allegations. UTZ contends that the potatoes supplied by Hubbard did not meet the quality requirements of the contract and, therefore, they were properly rejected. UTZ filed a counterclaim against Hubbard contending that he breached the contract by failing to provide the potatoes required by contract.

The case was tried to the Court for 5 days. The Court took testimony from 13 witnesses and received numerous documents and deposition testimony in evidence. This decision constitutes my findings of fact and conclusions of law pursuant to Fed.R.Civ.P. 52.

Facts

April 20, 1992 Potato Contract.

On April 20, 1992, Hubbard signed the two-page contract prepared by UTZ for farmers who produced potatoes for UTZ. UTZ is a large food processor in Hanover, Pennsylvania whose principal products are potato chips and other snack foods. The contract required Hubbard, beginning "approximately September 5, 1992" to ship 11,000 hundred-weight of Norwis (657) new chipping potatoes. Hubbard was to ship 2,000 to 4,000 hundred-weight per week with schedules to be arranged with UTZ. The price was $6.25 per hundred-weight, F.O.B. New York.

The contract provided that the potatoes must meet certain quality standards. The buyer, UTZ, was entitled to reject the potatoes if they failed to do so. The potatoes had to meet United States Department of Agriculture ("USDA") standards for No. 1 white chipping potatoes. They had to have a minimum size and be free from bruising, rotting and odors which made them inappropriate for use in the processing of potato chips.

The principal standard at issue in this lawsuit is the color standard. UTZ did not want dark potato chips but white or light ones and, therefore, the potatoes had to be the whitest or lightest possible color. The specific paragraph in the contract relating to color reads as follows:

> "Color" shall be at least #1 or #2 on the 1978 Snack Food Association "Fry Color Chart."

The Fry Color Chart is a color chart prepared by the Potato Chip/Snack Food Association which has five color designations. Color designation No. 1 is the best or lightest and the chart contains a visual depiction of potato chips with that color. The last color designation, No. 5, is the darkest reading. The contract required that the chips produced from Hubbard's potatoes must at least meet the No. 2 color designation.

Claims of the Parties.

In a nutshell, this lawsuit revolves around the color of the potato chips processed from potatoes submitted by Hubbard to UTZ. UTZ rejected all of the submitted potatoes claiming that they did not meet the required "color" standard. UTZ claims that the samples were too dark and did not meet UTZ' standards for producing white or light chips. Hubbard, on the other hand, contends that UTZ was arbitrary in its refusal to accept his potatoes and that his potatoes substantially complied with the color requirement. Hubbard contends in his pleadings that UTZ' rejection was motivated by concerns about price, not by quality. Hubbard alleges that after rejecting his potatoes, UTZ obtained similar potatoes from other sources at prices below his contract price.

The ultimate factual issue in this case is whether the potato chips made from Hubbard's potatoes failed to meet the color specifications of the contract. In other words, was UTZ' rejection of the installments proper?

In large part, this case turns on matters of law relating to the rights of a buyer, such as UTZ, to reject a seller's goods that are deemed to be non-conforming. The facts and the rights and obligations of the parties must be analyzed pursuant to the New York Uniform Commercial Code ("UCC").

Before discussing the principal issue, whether UTZ wrongfully rejected Hubbard's potatoes, I will deal with several other issues raised by the parties at trial. Some are material, some are not. Based on the evidence and the reasonable inferences from that evidence, I find the following facts.

Rejection of Hubbard's Potatoes.

Hubbard contends that he sent several sample loads of potatoes to UTZ for inspection. On or about September 22, 1992, he sent 1,000 pounds of potatoes from one of his fields to UTZ for testing. These were rejected.

Hubbard thought that they looked good when he harvested them but UTZ reported that when they were processed the color was poor. Hubbard discussed this rejection with Richard P. Smith, UTZ' Potato Manager, who told Hubbard to keep sending samples.

Thereafter, on October 1, 1992, Hubbard sent an entire truck load of potatoes to UTZ for processing under the contract. This installment consisted of 425–450 one-hundred-pound bags. Hubbard did not accompany this shipment to Pennsylvania but he was advised by telephone that none of the potatoes would be accepted due to their poor color.

Hubbard requested that UTZ put the reasons for this rejection in writing and Smith did so in a letter dated October 1, 1992 (Ex. 404).

Smith stated in that letter that the load had been rejected because the color (a No. 3 color designation) was unacceptable under the contract. Smith attached a photograph of the potato chips which had been processed and he returned a sample bag of those processed chips.

Smith told Hubbard that he did not intend to cancel the entire contract but told [Hubbard] that more tests should be run on Hubbard's other fields to see if the contract could be filled with crops from those fields.

About a week later, on October 7, Hubbard and his brother prepared a 1,000 pound load of potatoes and drove it to UTZ' facility in Pennsylvania to see if the potatoes would pass muster. Hubbard watched the chips go through UTZ' lines, and he made a video tape of some of the process. On that tape, Hubbard is heard to say that when he saw the chips being processed, they looked "better" than he thought they would. Once again, the chips were rejected, this time by an UTZ employee Kim R. DeGroft. DeGroft had been employed by UTZ for 16 years and in 1991 he was a "lead" person or supervisor in the Potato Department. He recalled that when these chips were processed, Hubbard commented that they should have been sold to Wise, a company that routinely accepted darker chips for processing. DeGroft testified that he had been inspecting potatoes for 5–6 years, and he believed Hubbard's lot was in the No. 3 color range.

Hubbard testified that he became quite upset at this rejection, because he believed that the chips looked good enough to meet the No. 1 and No. 2 color designation. * * *

* * *

After October 7, Hubbard never delivered, or caused to be delivered, any other shipments of potatoes for UTZ pursuant to the contract.

After allegedly conversing with certain government officials, Hubbard advised UTZ by telegram that he intended to sell his potatoes on the open market and charge UTZ for the difference in price.

* * *

Inclement Weather.

I also find as a fact that the weather during the summer of 1992 was very bad for potato farming.

Virtually every witness at trial who was involved in farming or processing potatoes in 1992 testified that it was a cold, rainy growing season which had a negative impact on the potato crop. It appears that the rain produced an ample crop but the cool weather prevented the crop from maturing properly and, therefore, the entire crop that season was immature and very poor. To the extent that there was disagreement on this issue, I accept and find as fact that the poor weather adversely affected the potato crop in New York during the summer of 1992. I find as fact that the entire potato industry suffered that season because of the weather and that other farmers had their potatoes rejected by UTZ for the same reasons that Hubbard's potatoes were rejected.

Visual Inspection * * *.

* * *

Concerning testing, the primary issue is whether [UTZ's] rejection based on visual inspection was unreasonable. In other words, was it unreasonable for UTZ to visually inspect Hubbard's potatoes when more sophisticated machinery was allegedly available?

I find as a fact that under all the circumstances that existed in the fall of 1992, it was reasonable for UTZ to rely on visual inspection when it determined whether Hubbard's installments complied with the contract.

As mentioned, the contract did not require [use of machinery for inspection]. Therefore, the contract did not prevent UTZ from using visual inspections. Second, the testimony was uncontradicted that those in the industry consistently used visual inspections when grading potatoes under contracts of this nature. Even at the trial, almost three years after the events at issue, visual inspection is still the norm. Hubbard's expert, Wilbur Gould, testified that in his view the Agtron machine was the preferred method for testing, but he conceded that visual inspection is used in the industry. Some processors did not wish to incur the $20,000 cost of obtaining an Agtron machine and so visual inspections persist.

Furthermore, both Smith, UTZ' Potato Manager, and Jack Corriere, UTZ' General Manager, testified that the first Agtron machine obtained by UTZ was in October 1992, and that it was not properly calibrated and used until late October 1992, well after Hubbard's potatoes had been rejected. Both Smith and Corriere testified that visual inspection of chips was the standard in the industry at the time Hubbard presented his potatoes for inspection. Hubbard presented no evidence to contradict that testimony. Smith testified that he had been potato manager for UTZ for over 30 years and during that time he relied on visual inspection and his expertise to determine whether to accept or reject loads.

I credit the testimony, and I find as a fact, that in September and October 1992, visual inspection of potatoes was the standard used in the industry. I also find that plaintiff understood that his crop would be judged by the visual observations of UTZ' inspectors at the plant, since that was the standard procedure that had been used prior to 1992 when Hubbard and his father had sent potatoes to UTZ for processing.

Motivation of UTZ.

Hubbard has also failed to convince me, by a preponderance of the evidence, that UTZ benefited by its rejection of Hubbard's potatoes. Smith and Corriere testified that they had suffered significant losses in the past when their potatoes had turned bad in storage. In 1992, UTZ took steps to see that such a disaster did not reoccur and so they were careful in their decisions to accept or reject potatoes.

Furthermore, there is no compelling evidence that UTZ purchased potatoes at lower market prices after it rejected Hubbard's crop. On the contrary, the evidence (Ex. 39) suggests that the market price during late 1992 and early 1993 was equal to or higher than Hubbard's contract price. Hubbard has failed to convince me that UTZ' motivation for rejecting his potatoes was to obtain similar potatoes but at a reduced cost. Therefore, I find as a fact, that UTZ' reason and motivation for rejection was its belief that the potatoes failed to meet the quality standards in the contract.

Discussion

UTZ' Rejection of Hubbard's Potatoes.

The primary legal issue in this matter is whether UTZ' rejection of Hubbard's potatoes was proper or wrongful. It is clear that the transaction at issue is a sale of goods governed by the New York Uniform Commercial Code ("UCC") Article 2. Indeed, the parties have stipulated that both Hubbard and UTZ are "merchants" as defined by UCC § 2–104(3).

It is also clear that the contract between the parties is an "installment contract" as that term is defined in UCC § 2–612(1): it contemplates "delivery of goods in separate lots to be separately accepted." That the contract is an installment contract does not appear to have been disputed by the parties. However, it is also evident as a matter of law from terms found throughout the contract.

For instance, in paragraph 1, the contract calls for the sale of "11,000 hundred weight of new chipping potatoes * * * " to be shipped in quantities of "2,000 to 4,000 hundred weight per week" starting around September 5, 1992. This language clearly contemplates between 3 and 6 total shipments.

Additionally, paragraphs 3(a) and 3(b) specifically note that standards must be met by "all shipments," which suggests that more than one shipment is contemplated.

Finally, paragraph 4, concerning payment, states that "[b]uyer agrees to pay for all potatoes accepted within 30 days of acceptance. . . ." This language suggests paying per shipment, since each shipment is separately subject to inspection (and acceptance), as indicated by paragraph 3. Clearly this is an "installment" contract as defined in UCC § 2–612(1).

As an installment contract, the question of whether UTZ' rejection was wrongful or proper is governed by UCC § 2–612(2) and (3). UCC § 2–612(2) states that a "buyer may reject any installment which is non-conforming if the non-conformity substantially impairs the value of that installment and cannot be cured. * * * " UCC § 2–612(3) states that "whenever non-conformity or default with respect to one or more installments substantially impairs the value of the whole contract there is a breach of the whole."

The purpose of this "substantial impairment" requirement is "to preclude a party from canceling a contract for trivial defects." *Emanuel Law Outlines, Inc. v. Multi-State Legal Studies,* 1995 WL 559978, *7, No. 93 Civ. 7212 (S.D.N.Y.1995). In this case, UTZ rejected Hubbard's potatoes based upon their failure to satisfy the color standard set forth in paragraph 3(c) of the contract. Thus, the issue for me to decide is whether the failure of Hubbard's potatoes to meet the required #1 or #2 color minimum constitutes a "substantial impairment" of the installments.[1]

Whether goods conform to contract terms is a question of fact. * * * Moreover, in determining whether goods conform to contract terms, a buyer is bound by the "good faith" requirements set forth in N.Y.U.C.C. § 1–203—"Every * * * duty within this Act imposes an obligation of good faith in its enforcement or performance." Thus, UTZ' determination that Hubbard's potatoes failed to satisfy the contract terms must have been fairly reached.

The UTZ-Hubbard contract contains many specific requirements regarding the quality of the potatoes. In paragraph 1 the contract states that "only specified varieties as stated in contract will be accepted. * * * " Paragraph 3(a) states that

> All shipments shall meet the United States Standards For Grades of Potatoes for Chipping, USDA, January 1978 * * *, in addition to other provisions enumerated in this 'Section 3'. Loads that do not meet these standards may be subject to rejection. * * *

[1] There is no dispute that UTZ' rejection was timely and effective, as required by UCC § 2–602. I find as a fact that UTZ promptly notified Hubbard of its rejection.

Paragraph 3(b) sets forth specific size requirements (85% or better * * * graded to a 1 7/8 minimum size); paragraph 3(c) sets forth specific gravity requirements (at least 1.070 in a standard eight pound test); paragraph 3(d) contains the color requirements at issue in this case; and paragraph 3(f) sets forth a number of other defects or incidents of improper treatment or handling of the potatoes that provide UTZ with the right to reject the potatoes.

Clearly, the quality standards are of great importance to UTZ. They are the most detailed aspect of the contract—far more so than timing or even quantity specifications.

In a contract of this type, where the quality standards are set forth with great specificity, the failure to satisfy one of the specifically enumerated standards is a "substantial impairment." UTZ obviously cares the most about the specific quality specifications, as is evident from the numerous references throughout the contract.

Additionally, I find that UTZ' determination that the potatoes did not meet the required #2 color standard was made in good faith, as required by UCC § 1–203. As noted above, the manner of visual testing utilized by UTZ was reasonable and customary. Further, Smith and DeGroft, the UTZ testers who rejected Hubbard's potatoes, provided credible testimony about their respective experience (Smith—30 years, DeGroft—5–6 years) and method of making such determinations. Accordingly, I find that UTZ fairly and in good faith determined that Hubbard's potatoes were nonconforming.

Thus, I find that Hubbard's failure to meet the proper color standard amounted to a "substantial impairment" of the installments (§ 2–612(2)), substantially impairing the whole contract (§ 2–612(3)). Accordingly, I find that UTZ' rejection of Hubbard's potatoes was proper.[2]

* * *

Conclusion

I find that plaintiff has failed to establish the claims set forth in his complaint by a preponderance of the evidence and, therefore, I find in favor of defendant on plaintiff's claims. Plaintiff's complaint is dismissed and judgment shall be entered accordingly in favor of defendant.

Defendant has failed to prove its counterclaims against plaintiff, and they are all dismissed.

---

[2] This is not a case where UTZ has rejected the potatoes because they were a week (or a month) late or where the quantities were lower than anticipated. Such nonconformity would not constitute "substantial impairment" of this contract because timing and quantity are not its critical components. *See, e.g., Emanuel, supra,* (delay in installment shipment of bar review study aids not significant where shipment was still timely for the purposes of the contract); *Hudson Feather & Down Products, Inc. v. Lancer Clothing Corp.,* 128 A.D.2d 674, 513 N.Y.S.2d 173 (2d Dep't 1987) (delay in installment payment did not substantially impair value of whole contract).

IT IS SO ORDERED.

SECTION ELEVEN: ANTICIPATORY REPUDIATION AND PROSPECTIVE INABILITY TO PERFORM

HOCHSTER V. DE LA TOUR

Queens Bench, 1853.
2 Ellis & Bl. 678, 118 Eng.Rep. 922.

Action of Assumpsit.

On the trial, before Erle J., at the London sittings in last Easter Term, it appeared that plaintiff was a courier, who, in April, 1852, was engaged by defendant to accompany him on a tour, to commence on 1st June 1852, on the terms mentioned in the declaration. On 11th May 1852, defendant wrote to plaintiff that he had changed his mind, and declined his services. He refused to make him any compensation. The action was commenced on 22d May. The plaintiff, between the commencement of the action and the 1st June, obtained an engagement with Lord Ashburton, on equally good terms, but not commencing till 4th July. The defendant's counsel objected that there could be no breach of the contract before the 1st of June. The learned Judge was of a contrary opinion, but reserved leave to enter a nonsuit on this objection. The other questions were left to the jury, who found for plaintiff.

Hugh Hill, in the same Term, obtained a rule Nisi to enter a nonsuit, or arrest the judgment. * * *

* * *

LORD CAMPBELL C.J. * * *

On this motion in arrest of judgment, the question arises, Whether, if there be an agreement between A. and B., whereby B. engages to employ A. on and from a future day for a given period of time, to travel with him into a foreign country as a courier, and to start with him in that capacity on that day, A. being to receive a monthly salary during the continuance of such service, B. may, before the day, refuse to perform the agreement and break and renounce it, so as to entitle A. before the day to commence an action against B. to recover damages for breach of the agreement; A. having been ready and willing to perform it, till it was broken and renounced by B. The defendant's counsel very powerfully contended that, if the plaintiff was not contented to dissolve the contract, and to abandon all remedy upon it, he was bound to remain ready and willing to perform it till the day when the actual employment as courier in the service of the defendant was to begin; and that there could be no breach of the agreement, before that day, to give a right of action. But it cannot be laid down as a universal rule that, where by agreement an act is to be done on a future day, no action can be brought for a breach of the agreement till the day for doing the act has arrived. If a man promises to marry a woman on a future day, and before that day marries another woman, he is instantly liable to an action for breach of promise of marriage; *Short v. Stone* (8 Q.B. 358). If a man contracts to execute a lease on and from a future day for a certain term, and, before that day, executes a lease to another for the same term, he may be immediately sued for breaking the contract; *Ford v. Tiley* (6 B.C. 325). So, if a man contracts to sell and deliver specific goods on a future day, and before the day he sells and delivers them to another, he is immediately liable to an action at the suit of the person with whom he first contracted to sell and deliver them; *Bowdell v. Parsons* (10 East, 359). One reason alleged in support of such an action is, that the defendant has, before the day, rendered it impossible for him to perform the contract at the day: but this does not necessarily follow; for, prior to the day fixed for doing the act, the first wife may have died, a surrender of the lease executed might be obtained, and the defendant might have repurchased the goods so as to be in a situation to sell and deliver them to the plaintiff. Another reason may be, that, where there is a contract to do an act on a future day, there is a relation constituted between the parties in the meantime by the contract, and that they impliedly promise that in the meantime neither will do any thing to the prejudice of the other inconsistent with that relation. As an example, a man and woman engaged to marry are affianced to one another during the period between the time of the engagement and the celebration of the marriage. In this very case, of traveller and courier, from the day of the hiring till the day when the employment was to begin, they were engaged to each other; and it seems to be a breach of an implied contract if either of them renounces the engagement. * * *.

The declaration in the present case, in alleging a breach, states a great deal more than a passing intention on the part of the defendant which he may repent of, and could only be proved by evidence that he had utterly renounced the contract, or done some act which rendered it impossible for him to perform it. If the plaintiff has no remedy for breach of the contract unless he treats the contract as in force, and acts upon it down to the 1st June 1852, it follows that, till then, he must enter into no employment which will interfere with his promise "to start with the defendant on such travels on the day and year," and that he must then be properly equipped in all respects as a courier for a three months' tour on the continent of Europe. But it is surely much more rational, and more for the benefit of both parties, that, after the renunciation of the agreement by the defendant, the plaintiff should be at liberty to consider himself absolved from any future performance of it, retaining his right to sue for any damage he has suffered from the breach of it. Thus, instead of remaining idle and laying out money in preparations which must be useless, he is at liberty to seek service under another employer, which would go in mitigation of the damages to which he would otherwise be entitled for a breach of contract.

It seems strange that the defendant, after renouncing the contract, and absolutely declaring that he will never act under it, should be permitted to object that faith is given to his assertion, and that an opportunity is not left to him of changing his mind. If the plaintiff is barred of any remedy by entering into an engagement inconsistent with starting as a courier with the defendant on the 1st June, he is prejudiced by putting faith in the defendant's assertion: and it would be more consonant with principle, if the defendant were precluded from saying that he had not broken the contract when he declared that he entirely renounced it. Suppose that the defendant, at the time of his renunciation, had embarked on a voyage for Australia, so as to render it physically impossible for him to employ the plaintiff as a courier on the continent of Europe in the months of June, July and August 1852: according to decided cases, the action might have been brought before 1st June; but the renunciation may have been founded on other facts, to be given in evidence, which would equally have rendered the defendant's performance of the contract impossible. The man who wrongfully renounces a contract into which he has deliberately entered cannot justly complain if he is immediately sued for a compensation in damages by the man whom he has injured: and it seems reasonable to allow an option to the injured party, either to sue immediately, or to wait till the time when the act was to be done, still holding it as prospectively binding for the exercise of this option, which may be advantageous to the innocent party, and cannot be prejudicial to the wrongdoer. An argument against the action before the 1st of June is urged from the difficulty of calculating the damages: but this argument is equally strong against an action before the 1st of September, when the three months would expire. In either case, the jury in assessing the damages would be justified in looking to all that had happened, or was likely to happen, to increase or mitigate the loss of the plaintiff down to the day of trial. * * *

Upon the whole, we think that the declaration in this case is sufficient. It gives us great satisfaction to reflect that, the question being on the record, our opinion may be reviewed in a Court of Error. In the meantime we must give judgment for the plaintiff.

Judgment for plaintiff.

ROSETT, PARTIAL, QUALIFIED, AND EQUIVOCAL REPUDIATION OF CONTRACT

81 Colum.L.Rev. 93, 95 (1981).

Many repudiations in the real world are not total, absolute, and unequivocal. The repudiating party, without totally renouncing performance, indicates that his performance will be late; that he may not be able to deliver some items of performance; that unless problems are somehow resolved, he does not see how the contract payments can be made on time. He expresses doubt, temporizes, and equivocates. The repudiator may not intend to terminate the agreement; he may sincerely attempt to perform or may seek to induce an advantageous modification of the agreement by the vulnerable other party. The expression of doubt as to will or ability to perform shades subtly into a statement that the performance will not occur. Although for convenience I refer to these actions as repudiations or renunciations, it is not clear that those are appropriate characterizations for essentially uncertain signals.

RESTATEMENT (SECOND) OF CONTRACTS § 250.

When a Statement or an Act Is a Repudiation

A repudiation is

(a) a statement by the obligor to the obligee indicating that the obligor will commit a breach that would of itself give the obligee a claim for damages for total breach * * * or

(b) a voluntary affirmative act which renders the obligor unable or apparently unable to perform without such a breach.

Comment:

* * *

b. *Nature of statement.* In order to constitute a repudiation, a party's language must be sufficiently positive to be reasonably interpreted to mean that the party will not or cannot perform. Mere expression of a doubt as to his willingness or ability to perform is not enough to constitute a repudiation. * * * [L]anguage that under a fair reading "amounts to a statement of intention not to perform except on conditions which go beyond the contract" constitutes a repudiation. Comment 2 to Uniform Commercial Code § 2–610.

Illustrations:

1. On April 1, A contracts to sell and B to buy land, delivery of the deed and payment of the price to be on July 30. On May 1, A tells B that he will not perform. A's statement is a repudiation.

2. A contracts to build a house for B for $50,000, progress payments to be made monthly in an amount equal to 85% of the price of the work performed during the preceding month, the balance to be paid on the architect's certificate of satisfactory completion of the house. Without justification B fails to make a $5,000 progress payment and tells A that because of financial difficulties he will be unable to pay him anything for at least another month. If, after a month, it would be too late for B to cure his material failure of performance by making the delayed payment, B's statement is a repudiation. * * *

3. The facts being otherwise as stated in Illustration 1, A does not tell B that he will not perform but says, "I am not sure that I can perform, and I do not intend to do so unless I am legally bound to." A's statement is not a repudiation.

* * *

c. *Nature of Act.* In order to constitute a repudiation, a party's act must be both voluntary and affirmative, and must make it actually or apparently impossible for him to perform. * * *

Illustrations:

5. The facts being otherwise as stated in Illustration 1, A says nothing to B on May 1, but on that date he contracts to sell the land to C. A's making the contract with C is a repudiation.

6. The facts being otherwise as stated in Illustration 1, A says nothing to B on May 1, but on that date he mortgages the land to C as security for a $40,000 loan which is not payable until one year later. A's mortgaging the land is a repudiation. * * *

7. A contracts to employ B, and B to work for A, the employment to last a year beginning in ten days. Three days after making the contract B embarks on a ship for a voyage around the world. B's embarking for the voyage is a repudiation.

RESTATEMENT (SECOND) OF CONTRACTS § 256.

Nullification of Repudiation or Basis for Repudiation

(1) The effect of a statement as constituting a repudiation under § 250 or the basis for a repudiation under § 251 is nullified by a retraction of the statement if notification of the retraction comes to the attention of the injured party before he materially changes his position in reliance on the repudiation or indicates to the other party that he considers the repudiation to be final.

(2) The effect of events other than a statement as constituting a repudiation under § 250 or the basis for a repudiation under § 251 is nullified if, to the knowledge of the injured party, those events have ceased to exist before he materially changes his position in reliance on the repudiation or indicates to the other party that he considers the repudiation to be final.

UNIFORM COMMERCIAL CODE § 2–610.

Anticipatory Repudiation

When either party repudiates the contract with respect to a performance not yet due the loss of which will substantially impair the value of the contract to the other, the aggrieved party may

(a) for a commercially reasonable time await performance by the repudiating party; or

(b) resort to any remedy for breach (Section 2–703 or Section 2–711), even though he has notified the repudiating party that he would await the latter's performance and has urged retraction; and

(c) in either case suspend his own performance or proceed in accordance with the provisions of this Article on the seller's right to identify goods to the contract notwithstanding breach or to salvage unfinished goods (Section 2–704).

CONVENTION ON CONTRACTS FOR THE INTERNATIONAL SALE OF GOODS.

Article 72

(1) If prior to the date for performance of the contract it is clear that one of the parties will commit a fundamental breach of contract, the other party may declare the contract avoided.

(2) If time allows, the party intending to declare the contract avoided must give reasonable notice to the other party in order to permit him to provide adequate assurance of his performance.

(3) The requirements of the preceding paragraph do not apply if the other party has declared that he will not perform his obligations.

HATHAWAY V. SABIN

Supreme Court of Vermont, 1891.
63 Vt. 527, 22 A. 633.

MUNSON, J.

* * *

The contract required the defendant to furnish a hall for the concert, and to pay $75 after the entertainment. The plaintiff alleged readiness to perform on his part, and assigned as the breach the defendant's failure to furnish a hall. The court directed a verdict for the plaintiff for $75 and interest. The defendant insists that, inasmuch as the non-payment of the $75 was not assigned as the breach, and as there was no proof of any loss except in the non-payment of the $75, there was no proof of loss from any breach complained of, and that consequently there could be no recovery. We think it cannot be said that the proof of loss in the non-receipt of the $75 did not apply to the breach declared upon. The plaintiff was ready to give the concert, and on giving it would have been entitled to the $75, but he was prevented from giving it by the defendant's failure to furnish a hall. This failure was properly assigned as the breach from which the plaintiff suffered damage. The plaintiff does not sue for the compensation to which he would have been entitled if the contract had been carried out, but for the damages he has sustained in being compelled to leave the contract unperformed. The breach is not the non-payment of the unearned compensation, but the failure to perform the antecedent stipulation which would have enabled the plaintiff to earn it.

The defendant also contends that he was excused from opening and heating the hall by the apparent impossibility of the musicians' reaching the town. During the 36 hours preceding the evening appointed for the concert a snow-storm of unusual violence prevailed in Montpelier and vicinity, which early on the day of the concert rendered the streets of that village and the roads from the surrounding country practically impassable. The quartette by which the concert was to be given was in Barre, having gone there from Montpelier the evening before, and trains on the spur from Montpelier to Barre were suspended. Late in the afternoon, however, an irregular train went to Barre, and on this the musicians returned to Montpelier, arriving early in the evening, and going to the hall at the time appointed. It is claimed that the defendant's conduct must be tested by the situation as it was at the time when action on his part became necessary, and that he is saved from liability by the doctrine that, when one party ascertains that the other will not be able to perform what he has undertaken, the party ascertaining this is excused from performing the obligations resting upon him. It is doubtless true that, when one party has put it out of his power to perform, the other party can maintain an action without having tendered performance on his part. But a party who becomes involved in difficulties for which he is not responsible, if ultimately able to perform, is not to be deprived of the benefits of his contract because of an assumption by the other party that the difficulties would prove insurmountable. Here the defendant was mistaken in supposing that the plaintiff would not be able to perform, and we know of no rule which permits him to plead reasonable cause to believe so in excuse for the failure on his part. It is apparent, also, that the defendant's course was determined before the time when action on his part became necessary. It was not necessary to commence the heating of the hall until 4 o'clock in the afternoon, but about 10 o'clock in the forenoon the defendant telephoned the manager that, owing to the condition of the streets in Montpelier, it would be impossible to have the entertainment that evening. It is evident from this that the defendant based his action upon his belief that there would be no audience, rather than upon the supposition that the musicians could not reach the place of entertainment. He did not wait until it was necessary to take action about the hall before deciding that there could be no concert. But, at the time when action on his part became necessary, there was nothing in the situation which could relieve him from liability. The contract contains no provision for his protection from such a misfortune, and the loss must fall on him.

The defendant also insists that upon being held liable he was entitled to have the damages assessed by the jury. We think, however, that the plaintiff was entitled to have this verdict directed. Having incurred all the expense necessary to enable him to give the concert, the plaintiff's damages were necessarily the amount to which he would have been entitled for giving it. It is not for the defendant to say that the damages were less than the amount he had agreed to pay, when the plaintiff had done and incurred everything on his part, and was prevented from earning the compensation agreed upon solely by the defendant's failure. The message sent the manager in the forenoon, even if treated as a sufficient notice to stop performance, did not require any different action as regards the damages. It afforded no ground for an application of the doctrine which forbids the making of expense after receiving notice of the repudiation of a contract; for the expense afterwards incurred by the musicians was only such as was required by the situation in which the notice found them. Neither did the case permit an application of the rule which requires a party who is stopped in the performance of a contract for service to do what he can to lessen the damages by seeking like employment elsewhere. Judgment affirmed.

NOTE:
THE UNIFORM COMMERCIAL CODE, THE RESTATEMENT, AND THE RIGHT TO ADEQUATE ASSURANCES OF PERFORMANCE

U.C.C. section 2–609 provides in part:

> **Right to Adequate Assurance of Performance**
>
> (1) A contract for sale imposes an obligation on each party that the other's expectation of receiving due performance will not be impaired. When reasonable grounds for insecurity arise with respect to the performance of either party the other may in writing demand adequate assurance of due performance and until he receives such assurance may if commercially reasonable suspend any performance for which he has not already received the agreed return.
>
> * * *
>
> (4) After receipt of a justified demand failure to provide within a reasonable time not exceeding thirty days such assurance of due performance as is adequate under the circumstances of the particular case is a repudiation of the contract.

The approach of section 2–609, which entitles a promisee to demand assurance that the promisor will perform when the promisee has reasonable grounds to believe the promisor will not perform, has also been adopted by the Restatement (Second) of Contracts in section 251 and the Convention on Contracts for the International Sale of Goods in Article 71. Together the Code, Restatement (Second), and Convention offer contracting parties (and their lawyers who must render advice) a new tool designed to avoid contract breakdown. For example, suppose a seller of goods receives information that reasonably suggests that the buyer is in financial distress. Such facts might include that the buyer had defaulted on other loans and had misrepresented the size of its factory. A seller who has reasonable grounds for insecurity, may demand assurance before proceeding. But what are "reasonable grounds for insecurity" and when are assurances "adequate"? Both "standards" will engender more occasions for lawyers to give advice. Will the approach avoid contract breakdown?

PROBLEM 7-10

Review Illustration 1 to section 250 of the Second Restatement. Suppose A told B on May 1 that A was not sure that he could perform on July 30 and that he was looking for a better deal. You represent B. What course of action, if any, do you advise?

ADORE ME, INC. v. NPC GLOBAL CORP., 99 U.C.C. Rep Serv 2d 750, 2019 WL 3406545 (S.D.N.Y. 2019). NPC * * * argues that it was justified in suspending performance [of a contract to sell shipping boxes] or not performing. In support of its justification defense, it cites N.Y. U.C.C. §§ 2–609 and 2–610 and refers to "the instability of full payment explicitly threatened by AMI" and "instability with respect to the terms of delivery." * * * [T]hese arguments are misplaced. NPC never had reason to doubt that AMI was able and willing to pay the amount due under the contract if NPC performed its obligations. The threat of a chargeback for late delivery of goods does not constitute a contract repudiation or present a ground for insecurity. NPC had no right to expect complete and timely payment of the contract price if it failed to perform its obligations.

MAGNET RESOURCES, INC. V. SUMMIT MRI, INC.

Superior Court of New Jersey, Appellate Division, 1998.
318 N.J.Super. 275, 723 A.2d 976.

BROCHIN, J.

This appeal arises from a breach of contract action. The * * * legal issue[ ] of particular importance with which we deal [is]: the right of a contracting party that reasonably deems itself insecure because of the other contracting party's threatened material breach to demand concrete assurances of performance and to suspend its own performance pending their receipt * * *.

Plaintiff Magnet Resources, Inc. ("Magnet Resources") and defendant Summit MRI, Inc. ("Summit") each charged the other with a material breach of contract and sued for damages. * * * The parties' * * * breach of contract claims were tried to a jury. The jury found that both parties had breached, and it awarded $492,320 to Magnet Resources and $18,470 to Summit. Summit has appealed and Magnet Resources has cross-appealed.

Summit did not object to the trial court's jury instructions. However, it argues to us that the instructions were incomplete and misleading because the jury was not told that one party's material breach relieves the other party of its duty to perform. * * *

* * *

Magnetic resonance imagers ("MRIs") are devices used by physicians and hospitals for diagnostic purposes. Magnet Resources sells and services new and used MRIs. Summit operated MRI installations in Jersey City, Paterson and Irvington, New Jersey. Magnet Resources contracted with Summit to provide preventive maintenance and emergency repair services for the MRIs at Summit's Paterson and Irvington installations. Magnet Resources also supplied cryogens for all of Summit's installations, including its Jersey City installation.

The charge for the services to be provided for the Irvington installation was $120,000 for the first year and $150,000 annually for subsequent years of the contract. Payments were to be made monthly in advance beginning with the fourth month of the contract. The testimony of both parties implies that there was a separate service agreement for the Paterson installation with terms similar to those of the Irvington contract, but the Paterson contract was not offered into evidence. However, neither party attaches any significance to this omission. For purposes of the case, both parties treated the service agreements for the two sites as a single contract, and we will do the same.

Summit's monthly payments were habitually late. On May 10, 1994, Magnet Resources faxed a memorandum to Summit complaining that seven of its checks had been dishonored.[1] The memorandum declared that thereafter payments more than ten days late would have to be made by certified check, the provision of the service contracts imposing a surcharge for late payment would be enforced, and neither essential supplies nor emergency service would be provided except under special arrangements if an invoice was late by thirty days or more. On June 7, 1994, Magnet Resources faxed a memorandum to Summit complaining that it had still not received a $13,250 payment due for April.

On December 20, 1994, Summit requested repair service for its Jersey City installation. Magnet Resources had no contract for emergency service or preventive maintenance for that site. It declined to provide the service because Summit then owed it $35,000. Summit promised that if the necessary work was done, Magnet Resources would get "most of the money by the end of the week." In reliance on that promise, Magnet Resources

[1] The dishonored checks were paid within a few days after they were returned.

installed a necessary piece of equipment from its inventory for a total charge of $8,750.

Neither that charge nor the other unpaid bills had yet been paid when Summit called a Magnet Resources service person at his home on Saturday, December 24, requesting immediate emergency service for its Paterson installation. Under its service contract, however, Summit was entitled to service only from Monday through Friday. Magnet Resource did not make the emergency repair.

On Tuesday, December 27, Summit still had not paid its outstanding bills to Magnet Resources. That day, the person in charge of Summit's Paterson facility telephoned Magnet Resources and urgently requested service for that site. The caller was informed that Magnet Resources would not respond because of Summit's continuing failure to pay overdue bills.

The director of Summit's centers called Ronald Hynes, Magnet Resources' president. The amount due and unpaid was then more than $40,000. Summit offered $10,000 if the emergency service problem was taken care of. Hynes refused; he decided to suspend service until "things were improved, or somebody talked to us [Magnet Resources] and made some arrangements." He faxed a memorandum to Summit which referred to the previous week's payment promise and declared, "[W]e have suspended service to each site where payment is overdue." The suspension was effective December 27.

Some time after the suspension of service, Hynes spoke with Hanafy and complained that Summit had ordered cryogens from Magnet Resources' supplier on Magnet Resources' credit. Summit responded that it had made arrangements to have another company provide service for its sites. Summit changed the locks on its MRI installations to bar access by Magnet Resources' service personnel who previously had been able to enter to service the MRI's after regular business hours.

* * *

1. Failure to ask the jury whose breach was material

It is black letter contract law that a material breach by either party to a bilateral contract excuses the other party from rendering any further contractual performance. * * * Restatement (Second) of Contracts § 237 (1981). Neither Summit nor Magnet Resources asked the trial court to charge that proposition, and neither objected to the omission of that charge. Summit is therefore not entitled to a new trial because of this omission unless it constituted "plain error," * * * capable of producing an unjust result. * * *

"Material breach" has been described as follows:

> Where a contract calls for a series of acts over a long term, a material breach may arise upon a single occurrence or consistent recurrences which tend to "defeat the purpose of the contract." [citation omitted] In applying the test of materiality to such contracts a court should evaluate "the ratio quantitatively which the breach bears to the contract as a whole, and secondly the degree of probability or improbability that such a breach will be repeated." [citation omitted] [Medivox Productions, Inc. v. Hoffmann-LaRoche, Inc., 107 N.J.Super. 47, 59, 256 A.2d 803 (Law Div.1969).]

See Restatement (Second) of Contracts §§ 241 and 242. In the present case, there was evidence of three events or series of events which could arguably have constituted material breaches. In their order of occurrence, these were, first, Summit's continual late payments and, at the end, its failure to pay for either two or three months' service and for emergency service at Jersey City that was not covered by the contracts; second, Magnet Resources' failure and refusal to provide service for the Paterson installation beginning December 24, 1994; and third, Summit's cancellation of the service contracts the following week.

Whether conduct constitutes a breach of contract and, if it does, whether the breach is material are ordinarily jury questions. * * * However, the court's failure to pose those questions to the jury would have been prejudicial to Summit only if the jury could have found that Magnet Resources' refusal to provide service at the Paterson installation was a material breach which justified Summit's canceling the contract.

Magnet Resources has argued to us that its refusal to provide service was not a material breach because Summit's non-compliance with its payment obligations was itself a prior material breach that excused it from any further duty of performance. * * * Summit's non-compliance indisputably breached the contract. But Magnet Resources, by declaring a suspension and not a cancellation of its undertaking to service Summit's facilities, implied its willingness to resume service upon payment and, perhaps, upon adequate assurance of timely future payments. That statement of its implied readiness to continue the contract waived the materiality of the breach; that is, it precluded Magnet Resources from successfully relying on Summit's payment history to excuse its refusal to provide service. * * *

Nonetheless, Magnet Resources had the legal right to do what it said it was doing, suspend its performance pending Summit's cure of its defaults within a reasonable time. Magnet Resources was a relatively small company. It did not contract to extend credit. Just the opposite. Its contract called for payment in advance. After repeatedly failing to make payments when they were due, Summit promised to pay most of what it owed. When Summit failed to keep that promise, perhaps Magnet Resources would have been entitled to treat Summit's failure as a material breach. It did not do so. Instead, in order to avoid extending further credit which had not been bargained for, it withheld further performance of its contractual obligations until it had received either the payment that was due or reasonable assurances that payment would be promptly made. For the following reasons, we conclude that as a matter of law, this suspension of performance—refusing service at Paterson beginning December 24—did not materially breach Magnet Resources' contractual obligations.

Section 251 of the Restatement (Second) of Contracts has been accepted as part of New Jersey law. * * *

Section 251 states:

> (1) Where reasonable grounds arise to believe that the obligor will commit a breach by non-performance that would of itself give the obligee a claim for damages for total breach * * *, the obligee may demand adequate assurance of due performance and may, if reasonable, suspend any performance for which he has not already received the agreed exchange until he receives such assurance.
>
> (2) The obligee may treat as a repudiation the obligor's failure to provide within a reasonable time such assurance of due performance as is adequate in the circumstances of the particular case.

The Comment to this section explains that an obligee of an executory promise "who believes, for whatever reason, that the obligor will not or cannot perform without a breach, is always free to act on that belief" by withholding his own performance. But if he cannot prove that his belief was correct, his non-performance may itself be a material breach of the contract, making him liable for damages. The Comment continues:

> This Section affords him an opportunity, in appropriate cases, to demand assurance of due performance and thereby avoid the uncertainties that would otherwise inhere in acting on his belief. If it is then reasonable for the obligee to suspend his own performance while he awaits assurance by the obligor, he may do so under Subsection (1). * * * If the obligee does not, within a reasonable time, obtain adequate assurance of due performance, he may under Subsection (2) treat the obligor's failure to provide such an assurance as a repudiation.

Significantly for the present case, Summit's failure to pay in accordance with its contract or with the promise by which it induced the provision of emergency service for the Jersey City facility did not have to amount to a material breach in order to have entitled Magnet Resources to demand assurances that Summit would comply with its obligations and to suspend performance for a reasonable time until those assurances were forthcoming. * * *

Kunian v. Development Corp. of America, 165 Conn. 300, 334 A.2d 427 (Conn.1973), illustrates the application of § 251 to facts closely analogous to those of the present case. Although unian was decided on the basis of § 2–609 of the Uniform Commercial Code, it is an appropriate guide to the decision of the present case because, according to the Comment to Restatement (Second) of Contracts § 251, that section is "a generalization, applicable without regard to the subject matter of the contract, from [the rule stated in] Uniform Commercial Code § 2–609."

The contract in Kunian provided for A. Merowitz and Company, Inc. to sell and deliver plumbing and heating supplies for a total cost of $358,381 to DCA Builders, a general contractor building a low cost housing project. The deliveries were to be made to the job site when and as ordered by the contractor. Materials delivered before the fifteenth of the month were to be paid for on the twenty-fifth; materials delivered between the fifteenth and thirtieth were to be paid for on the tenth day of the following month. The contract also provided that DCA Builders could take a two percent discount if it complied with these payment terms. From approximately March 18, 1969 to October 31, 1969, DCA Builders paid all amounts invoiced for materials received except for $7,502.75. A. Merowitz continued to deliver materials despite the indebtedness and, by November 26, 1969, the contractor owed approximately $38,000. On December 12, 1969, A. Merowitz met with DCA Builders and insisted on full payment, but received only $5,000. However, DCA Builders promised to make payments during January 1970 to reduce its debt, provided that A. Merowitz continue to deliver materials as ordered. The seller complied, but the contractor did not make any further payments either to reduce its indebtedness or for the new deliveries. In early January 1970, DCA Builders began purchasing plumbing and heating supplies from another source; however, on January 14, 1970, it wrote A. Merowitz demanding delivery of the balance of the supplies due under its contract. DCA Builders had not performed its previous promise to make payments on what it already owed. In response to DCA Builder's January 14 letter, A. Merowitz stated that it would deliver the balance of the required materials but, in view of the large indebtedness outstanding, only if DCA Builders deposited sufficient cash in escrow to pay for the delivered materials. When DCA Builders refused to comply by January 27, 1970, A. Merowitz ceased making deliveries. DCA Builders then owed A. Merowitz approximately $51,000; materials previously delivered totaled approximately $200,000.

Rejecting DCA Builders' contention that A. Merowitz had breached the contract by refusing further deliveries without a guarantee of payment, the Court said:

> [DCA Builders] argues that [A. Merowitz] should have continued making deliveries and its failure to do so after January 27, 1970, was a breach of contract. It is undisputed, however, that at the December 12, 1969, meeting between the parties [A. Merowitz] demanded adequate assurance that [DCA Builders] would pay its outstanding indebtedness before [A. Merowitz] would continue making deliveries. Under the circumstances, this was equivalent to a written demand for adequate assurance. It is further undisputed that [DCA Builders] failed to abide by its promise made at the conference to pay its outstanding indebtedness or even to pay for the subsequent deliveries which it thus had induced [A. Merowitz] to make. [A. Merowitz] then had 'reasonable grounds for insecurity' and justifiably informed [DCA Builders] that it would deliver the balance of the material only if payment of the entire contract was guaranteed by [DCA Builders'] depositing sufficient cash in escrow to pay for the delivered materials. [DCA Builders'] failure, therefore, to provide adequate assurance of due performance within a reasonable time after the request and after the action had been brought was a repudiation of the contract and [A. Merowitz] was excused from further performance under the contract.

These legal principles reflected in Restatement (Second) of Contracts § 251 and illustrated by the cited cases lead us to the conclusion that Magnet Resources was entitled to condition service after December 24, 1994 on payment or an acceptable arrangement for payment of the amount which Summit owed in accordance with its contract. In our view, a properly instructed jury could not reasonably have found otherwise. Consequently, we hold that, as a matter of law, Magnet Resources' suspension of performance was not a breach and, therefore, not a material breach. Summit's repudiation of the contract by arranging to have another firm service its MRI installations was consequently the first material breach, making it liable to Magnet Resources for lost profits. Because, as a matter of law, Magnet Resources' withholding service beginning December 24 was not a material breach, Summit was not prejudiced by the trial court's failure to instruct the jury that one party's material breach avoids liability by the other party for subsequent non-performance. That omission therefore entitles Summit neither to reversal of the judgment and a new trial nor to a judgment notwithstanding the verdict.

We agree with Summit, however, that the jury's verdict awarding it $18,470 is inconsistent with the verdict awarding Magnet Resources $492,320. But we disagree with Summit about the consequence of this inconsistency. The only basis Summit offered for its claim of damages was Magnet Resources' refusal to provide emergency service for the Paterson installation on and after December 24, 1994. Since Magnet Resources was legally justified in withholding service, its doing so did not constitute a breach and does not make Magnet Resources liable for losses which Summit may have sustained as a consequence. There is therefore no legal basis for the verdict in favor of Summit on its counterclaim.

* * *

The judgment in favor of Magnet Resources is affirmed. The judgment in favor of Summit is vacated and the case is remanded to the Law Division for the entry of a judgment of no cause for action on Summit's counterclaim.

WHITE, EIGHT CASES AND SECTION 251

67 Cornell L.Rev. 841, 853–55 (1982).

Where there is a good-faith dispute between the parties and there are plausible arguments on both sides of the dispute, neither or both of the parties will have reasonable grounds for insecurity. In such cases sections 2–609 and 251 do little to advance one's analysis about which party should be held in default.

* * *

* * * If we assume that each party was sparring with the other in a wary but good-faith effort to get what it wanted out of the contract, we see that section 2–609 does little to resolve matters. If a party has reasonable grounds for insecurity, he may suspend his performance. If he does not have such grounds, his suspension will likely constitute an anticipatory repudiation. Presumably if each party is at all times willing and able to perform the contract, then there are no reasonable grounds for insecurity. * * * Conceivably each party could have asked for assurances from the other, each could have granted assurances, yet neither's position would have changed. The same is true where the parties have a legitimate disagreement about the meaning of the specifications or other terms in the contract. If each has a plausible and good-faith interpretation that favors his position, how does section 2–609 help to resolve that dispute? The section's impotence in good faith disputes is nicely illustrated by *Cherwell-Ralli, Inc. v. Rytman Grain Co.*[1] There a buyer of grain, Rytman, had become concerned that the seller, Cherwell-Ralli, might not complete performance because the market price of the grain had risen significantly above the contract price. In a telephone conversation, Cherwell-Ralli's president assured Rytman's president that deliveries would continue if Rytman would pay for the goods already delivered. Thereupon, Rytman sent Cherwell-Ralli a check for $9,824.60 to cover shipments already made.

---

1 180 Conn. 714, 433 A.2d 984 (1980).

Several days later, Rytman stopped payment when he was told by a truck driver not employed by Cherwell-Ralli that the shipment would be his last load. The trial court, affirmed by the Connecticut Supreme Court, concluded that Rytman, not Cherwell-Ralli, breached the contract. It found that Rytman had no reasonable grounds for insecurity and that Rytman had breached the contract by stopping payment and refusing to pay for goods already delivered.

If, as it seems, Rytman truly believed that Cherwell-Ralli was not going to perform yet Cherwell-Ralli was willing to perform but had an understandable wish to be paid, we have a classic case of capable parties involved in a good-faith dispute. Section 2–609 does nothing to eliminate Rytman's honest but misplaced anxiety. Having demanded assurances and stopped payment, he is left in exactly the same position as if he had merely stopped payment.

This is a body of repudiation cases with tangles that sections 2–609 and 251 will not unsnarl. In these cases the courts will continue to search unassisted to determine whether a given act was a repudiation. Each party will have to bear continued uncertainty about whether the other party's act is sufficiently egregious to allow him to suspend performance. With these cases we are back in the nineteenth-century common law of contract.

GREGUHN V. MUTUAL OF OMAHA INSURANCE CO.

Supreme Court of Utah, 1969.
23 Utah 2d 214, 461 P.2d 285.

[Plaintiff suffered a debilitating injury while working as a brick mason. After making some payments to plaintiff under a health and accident insurance policy, Mutual of Omaha and another defendant asserted that plaintiff's ailment was due to a preexisting illness and refused to make further payments. In plaintiff's action against the insurance company, the jury found that plaintiff was permanently disabled under the terms of the policy and that the disability resulted proximately from the accident. The trial court's judgment awarded not only the damages due plaintiff to the time of trial, but also awarded a lump sum for future benefits based on the plaintiff's life expectancy. Defendants appealed.]

TUCKETT, J.

* * *

This brings us to what we consider the most critical problem in the case. Did the court err in granting an award for future disability under the doctrine of anticipatory breach? This problem is one of first impression in this jurisdiction. * * * The decisions of a number of the states permit an insured to recover a money judgment for the present value of future payments based upon the insured's life expectancy. However, the great majority of decisions permit recovery under a disability policy only of installments accrued and unpaid. The doctrine of anticipatory breach has not ordinarily been extended to unilateral contracts. As stated in the Restatement of Contracts:[1] In a unilateral contract for the payment in installments after default of one or more, no repudiation can amount to an anticipatory breach of the rest of the installments not yet due. We are of the opinion that it was error for the trial court to enter judgment for future benefits to become due under the policies.

The verdict and the decision of the trial court amounts to a determination that the plaintiff is entitled to the monthly payments as specified in the insurance policies so long as he is totally and permanently disabled. Defendants are not relieved of the obligation of making the payments unless the plaintiff should recover or die. Should the defendants fail in the future to make payment in accordance with the terms of the policies without just cause or excuse and the plaintiff is compelled to file another action for delinquent installments, the court at that time should be able to fashion such relief as will compel performance.

This matter is remanded to the trial court with directions to modify its judgment so as to eliminate that part of the judgment pertaining to future benefits under the policies. Plaintiff (respondent) is entitled to costs.

CROCKETT, C.J., and CALLISTER and HENROID, JJ., concur.

ELLETT, JUSTICE (dissenting).

I dissent.

The plaintiff claimed that he was totally and permanently disabled under the terms of the policies written by the defendants. After making some periodic payments, the defendants denied any liability to make further payments on the grounds that if the plaintiff had any disability, it was not related to causes covered in the policies.

By rendering its verdict in favor of the plaintiff, the jury found that plaintiff was permanently and totally disabled under the terms of the policies. There was evidence to support the verdict and, therefore, the issue of the permanency and totality of the disability under the policies has been concluded, and the prevailing opinion accepts these facts.

While the majority of cases listed in the digests have held that recovery in actions involving health and accident policies is limited to accrued and past-due installments, there is respectable and, in my opinion, better reasoned authority to the contrary.

In those actions which have been brought to interpret, apply, or enforce the terms of a policy and where no repudiation of further liability

1 Restatement of Contracts, Vol. 1, Sec. 318 * * *.

is involved, then the recovery is properly limited to accrued and past-due installments. However, where there is a repudiation of all contractual obligations, I think it is the better policy to allow full recovery in one action, as was done in the case now before us.

Some of the cases which limit recovery to past-due installments do so because of a provision in the policy requiring the insured to furnish proof of continued disability as a condition of liability to pay. This should not be necessary where there has been a determination in court that the disability is *total* and *permanent.*

* * *

There can be no quarrel with the rule that where the contract has become wholly unilateral, as where nothing further is to be done by the plaintiff, the mere failure to pay one or more installments when due would not, in and of itself, be considered a repudiation of the contract as to future payments, since the breach does not go to the essence of the contract. However, where there is a failure to pay one installment, coupled with an announcement by the insurer that no future payments will be made, then damages for the partly anticipatory breach should be allowed. See Corbin on Contracts, Sec. 966.

Since the plaintiff in this case was determined to be totally and permanently disabled, the defendants cannot relitigate those matters. By assuming the defendants would pay according to the contract, the prevailing opinion ignores the fact that the plaintiff sued for damages, not specific performance, and would compel him to abide by terms of the contract when neither party requests such a ruling. The decision grants to the defendants an opportunity to refuse again to pay the installments to plaintiff and says that in such an event the trial court "should be able to fashion such relief as will compel performance." I am unable to know just what relief the decision has in mind. Under the pleadings as framed in this case, the relief to which plaintiff was entitled has already been given him.

If it appears, as in this case, that a party to a contract makes an outright refusal to comply with the terms thereof and so notifies the other party, then I can see no legal reason why the other party may not accept the anticipatory breach of the contract and sue for his damages. What reason is there in law or good conscience to give a locus penitentiae to the party whose wrongful conduct precipitates a lawsuit? Why should an appellate court set the stage for further litigation when the matters have already been fully determined?

By informing the plaintiff herein that no further payments would be made upon the policies, the defendants were guilty of an executory breach of the contracts which entitled the plaintiff to sue for his damages and to put an end to further litigation.

I would affirm the judgment of the trial court. * * *

PART FOUR

THE CESSATION PROCESS

■ ■ ■

Chapter Eight
GROUNDS OF RIGHTFUL CESSATION

CHAPTER EIGHT

GROUNDS OF RIGHTFUL CESSATION

■ ■ ■

In the ordinary course, contracts come to an end with performance.

RICHARDSON

The best laid schemes o' mice and men gang aft a-gley.

BURNS

SECTION ONE: CESSATION AND THE ROLE OF LAWYERS

We use the word "cessation" to refer to the termination of relations. Cessation may or may not be rightful. Our primary focus in this chapter is on the grounds of *rightful* cessation, including remedial issues.

The grounds of rightful cessation are numerous. Most often, the parties to a valid agreement with consideration terminate their relations simply because they have fully performed their duties under the agreement. For example, a builder may complete construction of a building and the owner may pay the builder in full. This type of cessation leaves little role for the lawyer. Yet it may represent the culmination of a well-planned and drafted agreement for which the lawyer's reward is the client's satisfaction and willingness to retain the lawyer in the future.

Although full performance is by far the most common ground of rightful cessation, a party may rightfully refuse to perform or may cease performing on a variety of other grounds. We have already studied some of these. For example, a party may claim lack of consideration or unconscionability, and rightfully refuse to go forward on these grounds. Or a party may show that the other party materially broke the agreement or that an express condition precedent failed to occur. At this point, you should review the various grounds of rightful cessation already studied: lack of consideration and non-compliance with the statute of frauds in Chapter Two, lack of a valid agreement in Chapter Four, unconscionability and the like in Chapter Five, and material breach and failure of condition in Chapter Seven. Here we concentrate on several new grounds of rightful cessation: mistake, impossibility of performance, impracticability of performance, and frustration of purpose. After studying these, you will be in a position to integrate them into an overall picture of the law of cessation.

The new grounds of cessation on which we now focus are based on either mistaken views of the facts at the time of contracting or on events that arise thereafter. For example, an oil supplier may seek an excuse from the duty to supply oil because of an unforeseeable oil boycott that causes huge price increases, even though the contract says nothing about such an excuse. Courts seldom allow such relief. After all, the oil supplier typically promises to supply the oil *without* condition. But did the supplier really agree to supply no matter what the circumstances?

One can see from this oil supply example that the law of conditions studied in Chapter Seven is also relevant here. If the lawyer for the oil supplier had included an *express* condition relieving the supplier from the duty to perform in the event of an oil boycott, the supplier's duty to perform would not mature. But if this is so, perhaps the supplier should be excused from performance on the basis of an *implied-in-fact* condition?

As we will see, courts do sometimes resolve disputes similar to our oil supply problem by invoking the concept of implied-in-fact conditions. But usually courts permit cessation only when the parties, without fault, were unaware of existing facts at the time of contracting or reasonably did not foresee the supervening circumstances. Generally, a court will find only in such situations that the parties "impliedly" conditioned their duties on the *absence* of such onerous facts or supervening circumstances. Of course, if the parties were unaware of the facts or failed to foresee the supervening circumstances, the court is not really enforcing the intentions of the parties when it "finds" an implied condition and excuses a party because the parties could not have had any intentions. In these instances, it is better to say that the agreement contains an unallocated risk that must be allocated by the court. Put another way, the agreement contains a gap calling for a condition *implied in law.*

As with the law governing duties of performance treated in Chapters Six and Seven, the parties, through their lawyers, can displace much of the cessation law that we study in this chapter. The lawyer must plan and draft not only with an eye to the grounds of rightful cessation that the client may wish to claim, but must also consider the various possible grounds on which the other party may wish to terminate. For example, the lawyer for the oil supplier in our example may seek both to assure that the supplier will be excused in the face of onerous events, and to bar escape hatches favoring the buyer. Of course, one cannot hope to foresee all events and even the best lawyer cannot always secure an excuse for the client or protect the client from the other party's claim of excuse.

When an unallocated risk materializes, the parties may want to renegotiate the agreement. Their lawyers will then assume many of the roles previously studied in this book, such as those of counselor, negotiator, and even planner and drafter. Some of these roles may be especially difficult to fulfill at this stage because the lawyers must evaluate the strength of the promisor's claim to cease performance. If, for example, the oil supplier has a strong case for relief, the buyer's lawyer must consider whether to counsel the buyer to agree to a price increase and the supplier's lawyer must consider whether to counsel the supplier to insist on one. The lawyers also must consider the effect on the reputation and good will of their clients of either insisting on performance when the other party is in a difficult position or of seeking an excuse from duties of performance.

When it is not possible to modify the agreement, the lawyer may be called upon, as litigator, to try to persuade the court that the contract expressly or impliedly in fact allocates the risk in favor of the client. Or, if the court believes that the case involves a true gap, the lawyer's task is to persuade the court to fill it favorably to the client. This may require the construction and evaluation of legal, business, and moral arguments.

Rightful cessation may occur immediately after the parties make their agreement. Thus a party may announce that he or she will not perform, claiming, for example, that the agreement is unenforceable because of indefiniteness or because the parties made a mutual mistake. Or a party may make such claims later, on the eve of performance. Or a party may begin performance, and then cease for the foregoing reasons or because of impossibility, impracticability, or frustration of purpose. A party may also cease performance because of failure of a condition or a material breach. In our treatment of cessation in this chapter, we will take up the various grounds of rightful cessation in the order that they most commonly arise during the life of an agreement.

SECTION TWO: INVALIDITY AND RELATED DEFENSES—A BRIEF RETROSPECT

In Chapters Two and Four, we studied the requirements of the leading theory of obligation in contract and related matters, agreement with consideration. An alleged agreement may fail for lack of consideration, for want of an offer and acceptance, for lack of definiteness, and so on. If an agreement is legally deficient in any one of these ways, either party may justifiably claim a right of cessation. As we have seen, however, usually a lawyer can, through careful planning and drafting, set up an arrangement that will not lack "formational" validity. At this point, you should review the central themes of the relevant sections of Chapters Two and Four.

You may also wish to review the related "policing" defenses studied in Chapter Five: duress, misrepresentation, unconscionability, conflict with public policy, and the like. With regard to each, we saw that the lawyer may have important planning, drafting, negotiating, counseling and litigating roles. To fulfill these well, the lawyer must understand the substantive requirements of each ground of invalidity as well as the various "policing" defenses.

SECTION THREE: MUTUAL MISTAKE

As with invalidity and related defenses, the mutual mistake ground of cessation, arises at the agreement stage. A party who learns that the circumstances at the time of contracting were materially different from what the parties had assumed at that time may claim relief on the ground of "mutual mistake."

SHERWOOD V. WALKER

Supreme Court of Michigan, 1887.
66 Mich. 568, 33 N.W. 919.

MORSE, J. Replevin for a cow. Suit commenced in justice's court; judgment for plaintiff; appealed to circuit court of Wayne county, and verdict and judgment for plaintiff in that court. The defendants bring error, and set out 25 assignments of the same.

The main controversy depends upon the construction of a contract for the sale of the cow. * * * The defendants reside at Detroit, but are in business at Walkerville, Ontario, and have a farm at Greenfield, in Wayne county, upon which were some blooded cattle supposed to be barren as breeders. The Walkers are importers and breeders of polled Angus cattle. The plaintiff is a banker living at Plymouth, in Wayne county. He called upon the defendants at Walkerville for the purchase of some of their stock, but found none there that suited him. Meeting one of the defendants afterwards, he was informed that they had a few head upon their Greenfield farm. He was asked to go out and look at them, with the statement at the time that they were probably barren, and would not breed. May 5, 1886, plaintiff went out to Greenfield, and saw the cattle. A few days thereafter, he called upon one of the defendants with the view of purchasing a cow, known as "Rose 2d of Aberlone." After considerable talk, it was agreed that defendants would telephone Sherwood at his home in Plymouth in reference to the price. The second morning after this talk he was called up by telephone, and the terms of the sale were finally agreed upon. He was to pay five and one-half cents per pound, live weight, fifty pounds shrinkage. He was asked how he intended to take the cow home, and replied that he might ship her from King's cattle-yard. He requested defendants to confirm the sale in writing, which they did by sending him the following letter:

"WALKERVILLE, MAY 15, 1886.

"*T.C. Sherwood, President, etc.*—DEAR SIR: We confirm sale to you of the cow Rose 2d of Aberlone, lot 56 of our catalogue, at five and a half cents per pound, less fifty pounds shrink. We inclose herewith order on Mr. Graham for the cow. You might leave check with him, or mail to us here, as you prefer.

"YOURS, TRULY,
HIRAM WALKER & SONS."

The order upon Graham inclosed in the letter read as follows:

"WALKERVILLE, May 15, 1886.

"*George Graham:* You will please deliver at King's cattle-yard to Mr. T.C. Sherwood, Plymouth, the cow Rose 2d of Aberlone, lot 56 of our catalogue. Send halter with the cow, and have her weighed.

"YOURS TRULY,
HIRAM WALKER & SONS."

On the twenty-first of the same month the plaintiff went to defendants' farm at Greenfield, and presented the order and letter to Graham, who informed him that the defendants had instructed him not to deliver the cow. Soon after, the plaintiff tendered to Hiram Walker, one of the defendants, $80, and demanded the cow. Walker refused to take the money or deliver the cow. The plaintiff then instituted this suit. After he had secured possession of the cow under the writ of replevin, the plaintiff caused her to be weighed by the constable who served the writ, at a place other than King's cattle-yard. She weighed 1,420 pounds.

When the plaintiff, upon the trial in the circuit court, had submitted his proofs showing the above transaction, defendants moved to strike out and exclude the testimony from the case, for the reason that it was irrelevant and did not tend to show that the title to the cow passed, and that it showed that the contract of sale was merely executory. The court refused the motion, and an exception was taken. The defendants then introduced evidence tending to show that at the time of the alleged sale it was believed by both the plaintiff and themselves that the cow was barren and would not breed; that she cost $850, and if not barren would be worth from $750 to $1,000; that after the date of the letter, and the order to Graham, the defendants were informed by said Graham that in his judgment the cow was with calf, and therefore they instructed him not to deliver her to plaintiff, and on the twentieth of May, 1886, telegraphed plaintiff what Graham thought about the cow being with calf, and that consequently they could not sell her. The cow had a calf in the month of October following. On the nineteenth of May, the plaintiff wrote Graham as follows:

"PLYMOUTH, MAY 19, 1886.

"*Mr. George Graham, Greenfield*—DEAR SIR: I have bought Rose or Lucy from Mr. Walker, and will be there for her Friday morning, nine or ten o'clock. Do not water her in the morning.

"YOURS, ETC.,
T.C. SHERWOOD."

Plaintiff explained the mention of the two cows in this letter by testifying that, when he wrote this letter, the order and letter of defendants was at his home, and, writing in a hurry, and being uncertain as to the name of the cow, and not wishing his cow watered, he thought it would do no harm to name them both, as his bill of sale would show which one he had purchased. Plaintiff also testified that he asked defendants to give him a price on the balance of their herd at Greenfield, as a friend thought of buying some, and received a letter dated May 17, 1886, in which they named the price of five cattle, including Lucy, at $90, and Rose 2d at $80. When he received the letter he called defendants up by telephone, and asked them why they put Rose 2d in the list, as he had already purchased her. They replied that they knew he had, but thought it would make no difference if plaintiff and his friend concluded to take the whole herd.

The foregoing is the substance of all the testimony in the case.

* * * The [circuit] court * * * charged the jury that it was immaterial whether the cow was with calf or not. * * *

* * *

It appears from the record that both parties supposed this cow was barren and would not breed, and she was sold by the pound for an insignificant sum as compared with her real value if a breeder. She was evidently sold and purchased on the relation of her value for beef, unless the plaintiff had learned of her true condition, and concealed such knowledge from the defendants. Before the plaintiff secured the possession of the animal, the defendants learned that she was with calf, and therefore of great value, and undertook to rescind the sale by refusing to deliver her. The question arises whether they had a right to do so. The circuit judge ruled that this fact did not avoid the sale and it made no difference whether she was barren or not. I am of the opinion that the court erred in this holding. I know that this is a close question, and the dividing line between the adjudicated cases is not easily discerned. But it must be considered as well settled that a party who has given an apparent consent to a contract of sale may refuse to execute it, or he may avoid it after it has been completed, if the assent was founded, or the contract made, upon the mistake of a material fact,—such as the subject-matter of the sale, the price, or some collateral fact materially inducing the agreement; and this can be done when the mistake is mutual. * * *

If there is a difference or misapprehension as to the substance of the thing bargained for; if the thing actually delivered or received is different in substance from the thing bargained for, and intended to be sold,—then there is no contract; but if it be only a difference in some quality or accident, even though the mistake may have been the actuating motive to the purchaser or seller, or both of them, yet the contract remains binding. "The difficulty in every case is to determine whether the mistake or misapprehension is as to the substance of the whole contract, going, as it were, to the root of the matter, or only to some point, even though a material point, an error as to which does not affect the substance of the whole consideration." *Kennedy v. Panama, etc., Mail Co.*, L.R. 2 Q.B. 580, 587. It has been held, in accordance with the principles above stated, that where a horse is bought under the belief that he is sound, and both vendor and vendee honestly believe him to be sound, the purchaser must stand by his bargain, and pay the full price, unless there was a warranty.

It seems to me, however, in the case made by this record, that the mistake or misapprehension of the parties went to the whole substance of the agreement. If the cow was a breeder, she was worth at least $750; if barren, she was worth not over $80. The parties would not have made the contract of sale except upon the understanding and belief that she was incapable of breeding, and of no use as a cow. It is true she is now the identical animal that they thought her to be when the contract was made; there is no mistake as to the identity of the creature. Yet the mistake was not of the mere quality of the animal, but went to the very nature of the thing. A barren cow is substantially a different creature than a breeding one. There is as much difference between them for all purposes of use as there is between an ox and a cow that is capable of breeding and giving milk. If the mutual mistake had simply related to the fact whether she was with calf or not for one season, then it might have been a good sale, but the mistake affected the character of the animal for all time, and for its present and ultimate use. She was not in fact the animal, or the kind of animal, the defendants intended to sell or the plaintiff to buy. She was not a barren cow, and, if this fact had been known, there would have been no contract. The mistake affected the substance of the whole consideration, and it must be considered that there was no contract to sell or sale of the cow as she actually was. The thing sold and bought had in fact no existence. She was sold as a beef creature would be sold; she is in fact a breeding cow, and a valuable one. The court should have instructed the jury that if they found that the cow was sold, or contracted to be sold, upon the understanding of both parties that she was barren, and useless for the purpose of breeding, and that in fact she was not barren, but capable of breeding, then the defendants had a right to rescind, and to refuse to deliver, and the verdict should be in their favor.

The judgment of the court below must be reversed, and a new trial granted, with costs of this court to defendants.

CAMPBELL, C.J., and CHAMPLIN, J., concurred.

SHERWOOD, J., (*dissenting.*) I do not concur in the opinion given by my brethren in this case. * * * I * * * agree with [my Brother Morse] that the plaintiff was entitled to a delivery of the property to him when the suit was brought, unless there was a mistake made which would invalidate the contract, and I can find no such mistake. * * *

As has already been stated by my brethren, the record shows that the plaintiff is a banker and farmer as well, carrying on a farm, and raising the best breeds of stock, and lived in Plymouth, in the county of Wayne, 23 miles from Detroit; that the defendants lived in Detroit, and were also dealers in stock of the higher grades; that they had a farm at Walkerville, in Canada, and also one in Greenfield in said county of Wayne, and upon these farms the defendants kept their stock. The Greenfield farm was about 15 miles from the plaintiff's. In the spring of 1886 the plaintiff, learning that the defendants had some "polled Angus cattle" for sale, was desirous of purchasing some of that breed, and meeting the defendants, or some of them, at Walkerville, inquired about them, and was informed that they had none at Walkerville, "but had a few head left on their farm in Greenfield, and asked the plaintiff to go and see them, stating that in all probability they were sterile and would not breed." In accordance with said request, the plaintiff, on the fifth day of May, went out and looked at the defendants' cattle at Greenfield, and found one called "Rose, Second," which he wished to purchase, and the terms were finally agreed upon at five and a half cents per pound, live weight, 50 pounds to be deducted for shrinkage. The sale was in writing, and the defendants gave an order to the plaintiff directing the man in charge of the Greenfield farm to deliver the cow to plaintiff. This was done on the fifteenth of May. On the twenty-first of May plaintiff went to get his cow, and the defendants refused to let him have her; claiming at the time that the man in charge at the farm thought the cow was with calf, and, if such was the case, they would not sell her for the price agreed upon. The record further shows that the defendants, when they sold the cow, believed the cow was not with calf, and barren; that from what the plaintiff had been told by defendants (for it does not appear he had any other knowledge or facts from which he could form an opinion) he believed the cow was farrow, but still thought she could be made to breed. The foregoing shows the entire interview and treaty between the parties as to the sterility and qualities of the cow sold to the plaintiff. The cow had a calf in the month of October.

There is no question but that the defendants sold the cow representing her of the breed and quality they believed the cow to be, and that the purchaser so understood it. And the buyer purchased her believing her to be of the breed represented by the sellers, and possessing all the qualities stated, and even more. He believed she would breed. There is no pretense that the plaintiff bought the cow for beef, and there is nothing in the record indicating that he would have bought her at all only that he thought she might be made to breed. Under the foregoing facts,—and these are all that are contained in the record material to the contract,—it is held that because it turned out that the plaintiff was more correct in his judgment as to one quality of the cow than the defendants, and a quality, too, which could not by any possibility be positively known at the time by either party to exist, the contract may be annulled by the defendants at their pleasure. I know of no law, and have not been referred to any, which will justify any such holding, and I think the circuit judge was right in his construction of the contract between the parties.

It is claimed that a mutual mistake of a material fact was made by the parties when the contract of sale was made. There was no warranty in the case of the quality of the animal. When a mistaken fact is relied upon as ground for rescinding, such fact must not only exist at the time the contract is made, but must have been known to one or both of the parties. Where there is no warranty, there can be no mistake of fact when no such fact exists, or, if in existence, neither party knew of it, or could know of it; and that is precisely this case. If the owner of a Hambletonian horse had speeded him, and was only able to make him go a mile in three minutes, and should sell him to another, believing that was his greatest speed, for $300, when the purchaser believed he could go much faster, and made the purchase for that sum, and a few days thereafter, under more favorable circumstances, the horse was driven a mile in 2 min. 16 sec., and was found to be worth $20,000, I hardly think it would be held, either at law or in equity, by any one, that the seller in such case could rescind the contract. The same legal principles apply in each case.

In this case neither party knew the actual quality and condition of this cow at the time of the sale. The defendants say, or rather said, to the plaintiff, "they had a few head left on their farm in Greenfield, and asked plaintiff to go and see them, stating to plaintiff that in all probability they were sterile and would not breed." Plaintiff did go as requested, and found there these cows, including the one purchased, with a bull. The cow had been exposed, but neither knew she was with calf or whether she would breed. The defendants thought she would not, but the plaintiff says that he thought she could be made to breed, but believed she was not with calf. The defendants sold the cow for what they believed her to be, and the plaintiff bought her as he believed she was, after the statements made by the defendants. No conditions whatever were attached to the terms of sale by either party. It was in fact as absolute as it could well be made, and I know of no precedent as authority by which this court can alter the contract thus made by these parties in writing,—interpolate in it a condition by which, if the defendants should be mistaken in their belief that the cow was barren, she could be returned to them and their contract should be annulled. It is not the duty of courts to destroy contracts when called upon to enforce them, after they have been legally made. There was no mistake of any material fact by either of the parties in the case as would license the vendors to rescind. There was no difference between the parties, nor misapprehension, as to the substance of the thing bargained for, which was a cow supposed to be barren by one party, and believed not to be by the other. As to the quality of the animal, subsequently developed, both parties were equally ignorant, and as to this each party took his chances. If this were not the law, there would be no safety in purchasing this kind of stock. * * *

I entirely agree with my brethren that the right to rescind occurs whenever "the thing actually delivered or received is different in substance from the thing bargained for, and intended to be sold; but if it be only a difference in some quality or accident, even though the misapprehension may have been the actuating motive" of the parties in making the contract, yet it will remain binding. In this case the cow sold was the one delivered. What might or might not happen to her after the sale formed no element in the contract. * * *

According to this record, whatever the mistake was, if any, in this case, it was upon the part of the defendants, and while acting upon their own judgment. It is, however, elementary law, and very elementary, too, "that the mistaken party, without any common understanding with the other party in the premises as to the quality of an animal, is remediless if he is injured through his own mistake." Leake, Cont. 338; *Torrance v. Bolton,* L.R. 8 Ch. 118; *Smith v. Hughes,* L.R. 6 Q.B. 597.

* * *

* * * In this case, if either party had superior knowledge as to the qualities of this animal to the other, certainly the defendants had such advantage. I understand the law to be well settled that "there is no breach of any implied confidence that one party will not profit by his superior knowledge as to facts and circumstances" actually within the knowledge of both, because neither party reposes in any such confidence unless it be specially tendered or required, and that a general sale does not imply warranty of any quality, or the absence of any; and if the seller represents to the purchaser what he himself believes as to the qualities of an animal, and the purchaser buys relying upon his own judgment as to such qualities, there is no warranty in the case, and neither has a cause of action against the other if he finds himself to have been mistaken in judgment.

* * * The judgment should be affirmed.

G. PALMER, MISTAKE AND UNJUST ENRICHMENT

95 (1962).

I find it most difficult to accept the statement of the majority of the court that the buyer, Sherwood, shared the mistake. Sherwood was a banker who also had a stock farm on which he raised purebred cattle. The whole sense of the matter suggested that he was not buying the purebred cow, known as Rose 2d of Aberlone, to fatten and sell for beef; rather, as a dissenting judge concluded, he thought there was a chance that Rose 2d would breed. This alone should have been enough to prevent Walker from insisting that Sherwood be held to Walker's mistaken assumption. In addition, if the dissenting judge was right on the facts, there probably was uncertainty as to a vital matter, since two men in the business had different opinions, with nothing in the circumstances to fairly prevent Sherwood from dealing on the basis of his own opinion.

Sherwood's state of mind does become important. If it were true that he shared Walker's erroneous belief, rescission of the sale would be proper. The gain would then be unanticipated, whereas, on the facts as found by the dissenting judge, it was within the range of the buyer's legitimate expectations.

WOOD v. BOYNTON, 64 Wis. 265, 25 N.W. 42 (1885). [Wood sold a small stone she had found, the value of which she did not know, for $1 to Boynton, the proprietor of a jewelry store. Later it was determined that the stone was a rough diamond worth about $700 and Wood sought return of the diamond. Boynton testified that at the time he bought the stone he had never seen an uncut diamond and had no idea the stone was a diamond.]

TAYLOR, J.

* * *

* * * The only question in the case is whether there was anything in the sale which entitled the vendor (the appellant) to rescind the sale and so revest the title in her. The only reasons we know of for rescinding a sale and revesting the title in the vendor so that he may maintain an action at law for the recovery of the possession against his vendee are (1) that the vendee was guilty of some fraud in procuring a sale to be made to him; (2) that there was a mistake made by the vendor in delivering an article which was not the article sold,—a mistake in fact as to the identity of the thing sold with the thing delivered upon the sale. This last is not in reality a rescission of the sale made, as the thing delivered was not the thing sold, and no title ever passed to the vendee by such delivery.

In this case, upon the plaintiff's own evidence, there can be no just ground for alleging that she was induced to make the sale she did by any fraud or unfair dealings on the part of Mr. Boynton. Both were entirely ignorant at the time of the character of the stone and of its intrinsic value. Mr. Boynton was not an expert in uncut diamonds, and had made no examination of the stone, except to take it in his hand and look at it before he made the offer of one dollar, which was refused at the time, and afterwards accepted without any comment or further examination made by Mr. Boynton. The appellant had the stone in her possession for a long time, and it appears from her own statement that she had made some inquiry as to its nature and qualities. If she chose to sell it without further investigation as to its intrinsic value to a person who was guilty of no fraud or unfairness which induced her to sell it for a small sum, she cannot repudiate the sale because it is afterwards ascertained that she made a bad bargain. *Kennedy v. Panama, etc., Mail Co.,* L.R. 2 Q.B. 580. There is no pretense of any mistake as to the identity of the thing sold. It was produced by the plaintiff and exhibited to the vendee before the sale was made, and the thing sold was delivered to the vendee when the purchase price was paid. * * * Suppose the appellant had produced the stone, and said she had been told it was a diamond, and she believed it was, but had no knowledge herself as to its character or value, and Mr. Boynton had given her $500 for it, could he have rescinded the sale if it had turned out to be a topaz or any other stone of very small value? Could Mr. Boynton have rescinded the sale on the ground of mistake? Clearly not, nor could he rescind it on the ground that there had been a breach of warranty, because there was no warranty, nor could he rescind it on the ground of fraud, unless he could show that she falsely declared that she had been told it was a diamond, or, if she had been so told, still she knew it was not a diamond.

* * *

The judgment of the circuit court is affirmed.

PROBLEM 8-1

1. Suppose Boynton had known that the stone was a diamond. Did Boynton have a duty to disclose that information? Reconsider the materials in Section Three of Chapter Five.

2. These facts are based on an actual episode at Cornell University. The Cornell Veterinary School sold a Holstein breeder cow, weighing 2300 pounds, for $1.2 million to a farm in upstate New York. Soon after the farm took delivery, the cow died of a genetic disorder. Neither Cornell nor the buyer had reason to know of the disease at the time of the sale. The buyer wants its money back. Please advise Cornell of the likely result under the doctrine of Sherwood v. Walker.

3. These facts are also true. A New York farmer hired Michael Stone for $65 to clean some pens and wash some cows at the State Fair. While performing the work, Stone became fond of a newborn calf and proposed to take the calf instead of receiving the $65. The farmer told Stone that the calf was not worth $65, but agreed to the proposition. Six years later, the calf, named Jacob, is a top breeder bull whose semen is marketed for $1.2 million per year. At the time of the original deal, no one realized that Jacob's father was himself a superior breeder. Does the farm have any legal rights against Stone?

LENAWEE COUNTY BOARD OF HEALTH V. MESSERLY

Supreme Court of Michigan, 1982.
417 Mich. 17, 331 N.W.2d 203.

RYAN, JUSTICE.

In March of 1977, Carl and Nancy Pickles, appellees, purchased from appellants, William and Martha Messerly, a 600-square-foot tract of land upon which is located a three-unit apartment building. Shortly after the transaction was closed, the Lenawee County Board of Health condemned the property and obtained a permanent injunction which prohibits human habitation on the premises until the defective sewage system is brought into conformance with the Lenawee County sanitation code.

We are required to determine whether appellees should prevail in their attempt to avoid this land contract on the basis of mutual mistake and failure of consideration. We conclude that the parties did entertain a mutual misapprehension of fact, but that the circumstances of this case do not warrant rescission.

I

The facts of the case are not seriously in dispute. In 1971, the Messerlys acquired approximately one acre plus 600 square feet of land. A three-unit apartment building was situated upon the 600-square-foot portion. The trial court found that, prior to this transfer, the Messerlys' predecessor in title, Mr. Bloom, had installed a septic tank on the property without a permit and in violation of the applicable health code. The Messerlys used the building as an income investment property until 1973 when they sold it, upon land contract, to James Barnes who likewise used it primarily as an income-producing investment.[1]

Mr. and Mrs. Barnes, with the permission of the Messerlys, sold approximately one acre of the property in 1976, and the remaining 600 square feet and building were offered for sale soon thereafter when Mr. and Mrs. Barnes defaulted on their land contract. Mr. and Mrs. Pickles evidenced an interest in the property, but were dissatisfied with the terms

[1] James Barnes was married shortly after he purchased the property. Mr. and Mrs. Barnes lived in one of the apartments on the property for three months and, after they moved, Mrs. Barnes continued to aid in the management of the property.

of the Barnes-Messerly land contract. Consequently, to accommodate the Pickleses' preference to enter into a land contract directly with the Messerlys, Mr. and Mrs. Barnes executed a quitclaim deed which conveyed their interest in the property back to the Messerlys. After inspecting the property, Mr. and Mrs. Pickles executed a new land contract with the Messerlys on March 21, 1977. It provided for a purchase price of $25,500. A clause was added to the end of the land contract form which provides:

> "17. Purchaser has examined this property and agrees to accept same in its present condition. There are no other or additional written or oral understandings."

Five or six days later, when the Pickleses went to introduce themselves to the tenants, they discovered raw sewage seeping out of the ground. Tests conducted by a sanitation expert indicated the inadequacy of the sewage system. The Lenawee County Board of Health subsequently condemned the property and initiated this lawsuit in the Lenawee Circuit Court against the Messerlys as land contract vendors, and the Pickleses, as vendees, to obtain a permanent injunction proscribing human habitation of the premises until the property was brought into conformance with the Lenawee County sanitation code. The injunction was granted, and the Lenawee County Board of Health was permitted to withdraw from the lawsuit by stipulation of the parties.

When no payments were made on the land contract, the Messerlys filed a cross-complaint against the Pickleses seeking foreclosure, sale of the property, and a deficiency judgment. Mr. and Mrs. Pickles then counterclaimed for rescission against the Messerlys, and filed a third-party complaint against the Barneses, which incorporated, by reference, the allegations of the counterclaim against the Messerlys. In count one, Mr. and Mrs. Pickles alleged failure of consideration. Count two charged Mr. and Mrs. Barnes with willful concealment and misrepresentation as a result of their failure to disclose the condition of the sanitation system. Additionally, Mr. and Mrs. Pickles sought to hold the Messerlys liable in equity for the Barneses' alleged misrepresentation. The Pickleses prayed that the land contract be rescinded.

After a bench trial, the court concluded that the Pickleses had no cause of action against either the Messerlys or the Barneses as there was no fraud or misrepresentation. This ruling was predicated on the trial judge's conclusion that none of the parties knew of Mr. Bloom's earlier transgression or of the resultant problem with the septic system until it was discovered by the Pickleses, and that the sanitation problem was not caused by any of the parties. The trial court held that the property was purchased "as is", after inspection and, accordingly, its "negative * * * value cannot be blamed upon an innocent seller". Foreclosure was ordered against the Pickleses, together with a judgment against them in the amount of $25,943.09.[2]

Mr. and Mrs. Pickles appealed from the adverse judgment. The Court of Appeals unanimously affirmed the trial court's ruling with respect to Mr. and Mrs. Barnes but, in a two-to-one decision, reversed the finding of no cause of action on the Pickleses' claims against the Messerlys. *Lenawee County Board of Health v. Messerly,* 98 Mich.App. 478, 295 N.W.2d 903 (1980). It concluded that the mutual mistake[3] between the Messerlys and the Pickleses went to a basic, as opposed to a collateral, element of the contract,[4] and that the parties intended to transfer income-producing rental property but, in actuality, the vendees paid $25,500 for an asset without value.[5]

We granted the Messerlys' application for leave to appeal. 411 Mich. 900 (1981).[6]

II

We must decide initially whether there was a mistaken belief entertained by one or both parties to the contract in dispute and, if so, the resultant legal significance.

A contractual mistake "is a belief that is not in accord with the facts". 1 Restatement Contracts, 2d, § 151, p. 383. The erroneous belief of one or both of the parties must relate to a fact in existence at the time the contract is executed. *Richardson Lumber Co. v. Hoey,* 219 Mich. 643, 189 N.W. 923 (1922); *Sherwood v. Walker,* 66 Mich. 568, 580, 33 N.W. 919 (1887) (Sherwood, J., dissenting). That is to say, the belief which is found to be in error may not be, in substance, a prediction as to a future occurrence or non-occurrence. *Henry v. Thomas,* 241 Ga. 360, 245 S.E.2d 646 (1978);

[2] The parties stipulated that this amount was due on the land contract, assuming that the contract was valid and enforceable.

[3] Mr. and Mrs. Pickles did not allege mutual mistake as a ground for rescission in their pleadings. However, the trial court characterized their failure of consideration argument as mutual mistake resulting in failure of consideration. Recognizing a potential difficulty in reversing the trial court on an issue not raised by the pleadings, the Court of Appeals devoted a footnote to an explanation of its decision to consider the mutual mistake argument. * * *

[4] Mr. and Mrs. Pickles did not appeal the trial court's finding that there was no fraud or misrepresentation by the Messerlys or Mr. and Mrs. Barnes. Likewise, the propriety of that ruling is not before this Court today.

[5] The trial court found that the only way that the property could be put to residential use would be to pump and haul the sewage, a method which is economically unfeasible, as the cost of such a disposal system amounts to double the income generated by the property. There was speculation by the trial court that the adjoining land might be utilized to make the property suitable for residential use, but, in the absence of testimony directed at that point, the court refused to draw any conclusions. The trial court and the Court of Appeals both found that the property was valueless, or had a negative value.

[6] The Court of Appeals decision to affirm the trial court's finding of no cause of action against Mr. and Mrs. Barnes has not been appealed to this Court and, accordingly, the propriety of that ruling is not before us today.

Hailpern v. Dryden, 154 Colo. 231, 389 P.2d 590 (1964). But see *Denton v. Utley,* 350 Mich. 332, 86 N.W.2d 537 (1957).

The Court of Appeals concluded, after a *de novo* review of the record, that the parties were mistaken as to the income-producing capacity of the property in question. 98 Mich.App. 487–488, 295 N.W.2d 903. We agree. The vendors and the vendees each believed that the property transferred could be utilized as income-generating rental property. All of the parties subsequently learned that, in fact, the property was unsuitable for any residential use.

Appellants assert that there was no mistake in the contractual sense because the defect in the sewage system did not arise until after the contract was executed. The appellees respond that the Messerlys are confusing the date of the inception of the defect with the date upon which the defect was discovered.

* * *

An examination of the record reveals that the septic system was defective prior to the date on which the land contract was executed. The Messerlys' grantor installed a nonconforming septic system without a permit prior to the transfer of the property to the Messerlys in 1971. Moreover, virtually undisputed testimony indicates that, assuming ideal soil conditions, 2,500 square feet of property is necessary to support a sewage system adequate to serve a three-family dwelling. Likewise, 750 square feet is mandated for a one-family home. Thus, the division of the parcel and sale of one acre of the property by Mr. and Mrs. Barnes in 1976 made it impossible to remedy the already illegal septic system within the confines of the 600-square-foot parcel.[7]

Appellants do not dispute these underlying facts which give rise to an inference contrary to their contentions.

Having determined that when these parties entered into the land contract they were laboring under a mutual mistake of fact, we now direct our attention to a determination of the legal significance of that finding.

A contract may be rescinded because of a mutual misapprehension of the parties, but this remedy is granted only in the sound discretion of the court. *Harris v. Axline,* 323 Mich. 585, 36 N.W.2d 154 (1949). Appellants argue that the parties' mistake relates only to the quality or value of the real estate transferred, and that such mistakes are collateral to the

---

7 It is crucial to distinguish between the date on which a belief relating to a particular fact or set of facts becomes erroneous due to a change in the fact, and the date on which the mistaken nature of the belief is discovered. By definition, a mistake cannot be discovered until after the contract is executed. If the parties were aware, prior to the execution of a contract, that they were in error concerning a particular fact, there would be no misapprehension in signing the contract. Thus stated, it becomes obvious that the date on which a mistaken fact manifests itself is irrelevant to the determination whether or not there was a mistake.

agreement and do not justify rescission, citing *A & M Land Development Co. v. Miller,* 354 Mich. 681, 94 N.W.2d 197 (1959).

In that case, the plaintiff was the purchaser of 91 lots of real property. It sought partial rescission of the land contract when it was frustrated in its attempts to develop 42 of the lots because it could not obtain permits from the county health department to install septic tanks on these lots. This Court refused to allow rescission because the mistake, whether mutual or unilateral, related only to the value of the property.

> "There was here no mistake as to the form or substance of the contract between the parties, or the description of the property constituting the subject matter. * * * In the case at bar plaintiff received the property for which it contracted. The fact that it may be of less value than the purchaser expected at the time of the transaction is not a sufficient basis for the granting of equitable relief, neither fraud nor reliance on misrepresentation of material facts having been established." 354 Mich. 693–694, 94 N.W.2d 197.

Appellees contend, on the other hand, that in this case the parties were mistaken as to the very nature of the character of the consideration and claim that the pervasive and essential quality of this mistake renders rescission appropriate. They cite in support of that view *Sherwood v. Walker,* 66 Mich. 568, 33 N.W. 919 (1887), the famous "barren cow" case. In that case, the parties agreed to the sale and purchase of a cow which was thought to be barren, but which was, in reality, with calf. When the seller discovered the fertile condition of his cow, he refused to deliver her. * * *

As the parties suggest, the foregoing precedent arguably distinguishes mistakes affecting the essence of the consideration from those which go to its quality or value, affording relief on a per se basis for the former but not the latter. See, *e.g., Lenawee County Board of Health v. Messerly,* 98 Mich.App. 478, 492, 295 N.W.2d 903 (1980) (Mackenzie, J., concurring in part).

However, the distinctions which may be drawn from *Sherwood* and *A & M Land Development Co.* do not provide a satisfactory analysis of the nature of a mistake sufficient to invalidate a contract. Often, a mistake relates to an underlying factual assumption which, when discovered, directly affects value, but simultaneously and materially affects the essence of the contractual consideration. It is disingenuous to label such a mistake collateral. *McKay v. Coleman,* 85 Mich. 60, 48 N.W. 203 (1891). Corbin, Contracts (One Vol. ed.), § 605, p. 551.

Appellant and appellee both mistakenly believed that the property which was the subject of their land contract would generate income as rental property. The fact that it could not be used for human habitation deprived the property of its income-earning potential and rendered it less valuable. However, this mistake, while directly and dramatically affecting the property's value, cannot accurately be characterized as collateral because it also affects the very essence of the consideration. "The thing sold and bought [income generating rental property] had in fact no existence". *Sherwood v. Walker,* 66 Mich. 578, 33 N.W. 919.

We find that the inexact and confusing distinction between contractual mistakes running to value and those touching the substance of the consideration serves only as an impediment to a clear and helpful analysis for the equitable resolution of cases in which mistake is alleged and proven. Accordingly, the holdings of *A & M Land Development Co.* and *Sherwood* with respect to the material or collateral nature of a mistake are limited to the facts of those cases.

Instead, we think the better-reasoned approach is a case-by-case analysis whereby rescission is indicated when the mistaken belief relates to a basic assumption of the parties upon which the contract is made, and which materially affects the agreed performances of the parties. *Denton v. Utley,* 350 Mich. 332, 86 N.W.2d 537 (1957); *Farhat v. Rassey,* 295 Mich. 349, 294 N.W. 707 (1940); *Richardson Lumber Co. v. Hoey,* 219 Mich. 643, 189 N.W. 923 (1922). 1 Restatement Contracts, 2d, § 152, p. 385–386. Rescission is not available, however, to relieve a party who has assumed the risk of loss in connection with the mistake. *Denton v. Utley,* 350 Mich. 344–345, 86 N.W.2d 537 * * *.

All of the parties to this contract erroneously assumed that the property transferred by the vendors to the vendees was suitable for human habitation and could be utilized to generate rental income. The fundamental nature of these assumptions is indicated by the fact that their invalidity changed the character of the property transferred, thereby frustrating, indeed precluding, Mr. and Mrs. Pickles' intended use of the real estate. Although the Pickleses are disadvantaged by enforcement of the contract, performance is advantageous to the Messerlys, as the property at issue is less valuable absent its income-earning potential. Nothing short of rescission can remedy the mistake. Thus, the parties' mistake as to a basic assumption materially affects the agreed performances of the parties.

Despite the significance of the mistake made by the parties, we reverse the Court of Appeals because we conclude that equity does not justify the remedy sought by Mr. and Mrs. Pickles.

Rescission is an equitable remedy which is granted only in the sound discretion of the court. *Harris v. Axline,* 323 Mich. 585, 36 N.W.2d 154 (1949); *Hathaway v. Hudson,* 256 Mich. 694, 239 N.W. 859 (1932). A court need not grant rescission in every case in which the mutual mistake relates to a basic assumption and materially affects the agreed performance of the parties.

In cases of mistake by two equally innocent parties, we are required, in the exercise of our equitable powers, to determine which blameless party should assume the loss resulting from the misapprehension they shared.[8] Normally that can only be done by drawing upon our "own notions of what is reasonable and just under all the surrounding circumstances".[9]

Equity suggests that, in this case, the risk should be allocated to the purchasers. We are guided to that conclusion, in part, by the standards announced in § 154 of the Restatement of Contracts 2d, for determining when a party bears the risk of mistake. * * * Section 154(a) suggests that the court should look first to whether the parties have agreed to the allocation of the risk between themselves. While there is no express assumption in the contract by either party of the risk of the property becoming uninhabitable, there was indeed some agreed allocation of the risk to the vendees by the incorporation of an "as is" clause into the contract which, we repeat, provided:

"Purchaser has examined this property and agrees to accept same in its present condition. There are no other or additional written or oral understandings."

That is a persuasive indication that the parties considered that, as between them, such risk as related to the "present condition" of the property should lie with the purchaser. If the "as is" clause is to have any meaning at all, it must be interpreted to refer to those defects which were unknown at the time that the contract was executed.[10] Thus, the parties themselves assigned the risk of loss to Mr. and Mrs. Pickles.

We conclude that Mr. and Mrs. Pickles are not entitled to the equitable remedy of rescission and, accordingly, reverse the decision the Court of Appeals.

---

[8] This risk-of-loss analysis is absent in both *A & M Land Development Co.* and *Sherwood,* and this omission helps to explain, in part, the disparate treatment in the two cases. Had such an inquiry been undertaken in *Sherwood,* we believe that the result might have been different. Moreover, a determination as to which party assumed the risk in *A & M Land Development Co.* would have alleviated the need to characterize the mistake as collateral so as to justify the result denying rescission. Despite the absence of any inquiry as to the assumption of risk in those two leading cases, we find that there exists sufficient precedent to warrant such an analysis in future cases of mistake.

[9] *Hathaway v. Hudson,* 256 Mich. 702, 239 N.W. 859, quoting 9 C.J., p. 1161.

[10] An "as is" clause waives those implied warranties which accompany the sale of a new home, *Tibbitts v. Openshaw,* 18 Utah 2d 442, 425 P.2d 160 (1967), or the sale of goods. M.C.L. § 440.2316(3)(a); M.S.A. § 19.2316(3)(a). Since implied warranties protect against latent defects, an "as is" clause will impose upon the purchaser the assumption of the risk of latent defects, such as an inadequate sanitation system, even when there are no implied warranties.

BRIEF OF DEFENDANT-APPELLANTS—PICKLES TO THE COURT OF APPEALS OF MICHIGAN

10–11, 24–27.

The property involved here had been utilized by Defendants Messerlys and Cross-Defendants Barnes as a three-unit apartment house, and prior to the sale to Pickles it was listed and advertised as such and was sold and purchased as an income property. Neither Messerlys, Barnes nor Pickles were aware at the time the land contract was executed that the property in question, the subject matter of the contract, was unfit and uninhabitable for humans.

Mr. and Mrs. Messerly and the Barnes, as evidenced by their listing of the property, thought they were selling a three-unit apartment house. The Pickles, by undisputed testimony, thought they were purchasing an income property. When the parties later learned that the property in question was absolutely devoid of any value, unfit for human habitation, it became apparent that both Buyer and Seller had been mistaken as to the nature and character of the subject matter of the contract.

Michigan courts have consistently held that mutual mistake constitutes a ground for rescission of a contract. * * *

* * *

Paragraph 17 of the Land Contract in question reads:

> "Purchaser has examined this property and agrees to accept same in its present condition. There are no other or additional written or oral understandings."

At trial, both the Messerlys and Barnes urged that such a provision appearing in the contract estopped the Pickles from relief in the form of rescission. The trial Judge noted in his opinion that the Pickles bought the subject property "as is".

Defendants-Appellants Pickles would respectfully disagree with the Court's conclusion that the sale was on an "as is" basis. A reasonable construction of the plain language utilized in Paragraph 17 reveals only that the Pickles agreed to accept the property in its present condition, premised upon their having inspected the parcel. Thus, it appears that the practical effect of Paragraph 17 is to charge the Purchaser merely with reasonable inspection of the premises.

* * *

The Court in the present case specifically found that the Pickles conducted a physical examination and inspection of the premises and interviewed tenants of the apartment house. It therefore appears that the Pickles satisfied that duty imposed upon them by Paragraph 17 of the contract and agreed to accept the property subject to conditions that would have been revealed by reasonable inspection. As to defects not discoverable through such inspection, there is no estoppel under the terms of Paragraph 17.

* * *

In summary, under the terms of the contract involved here, the Pickles are only estopped from complaining of conditions which would have been revealed by reasonable inspection. The record in this case is clear, the Pickles did conduct a reasonable examination and inspection and the condition complained of here could not have been discovered through such inspection. This is evidenced by the fact that the Barnes and Messerlys had owned and had contact with the tenants for a number of years. The Pickles, it is clear, could not have discovered in one or two inspections a condition which had not come to the attention of the Barnes or Messerlys over a period of years.

EISENBERG V. HALL

Supreme Court of New York, Appellate Division, 2017.
147 A.D.3d 602, 48 N.Y.S. 3d 71.

ACOSTA, J.P., MAZZARELLI, ANDRIAS, FEINMAN, WEBBER, JJ.

Jerome M. Eisenberg buys and sells antiquities. He is a principal of plaintiff Jerome M. Eisenberg, Inc. (Eisenberg, Inc.), and a Qualified Appraiser of the Appraisers Association of America. He is a self-proclaimed expert in classical antiquities with a doctorate in Roman, Egyptian, and Near Eastern Art.

Defendants Maurice E. Hall, Jr. (Hall), Michael Hall Collections, Inc., and Michael Hall Fine Arts, Inc. are art dealers that mainly deal in sixteenth to nineteenth century European art. Hall was a principal and sole shareholder of both Hall entities. Hall asserts that his expertise is in Renaissance art and that he is merely an "amateur collector" of classical antiquities. Eisenberg also stated that he did not believe Hall to be an expert in classical antiquities.

This appeal deals with plaintiff securing from defendants a bust and a statue that they believed to be ancient but were later revealed to be modern forgeries.

In February 2009, Eisenberg visited Hall's townhouse, out of which Hall operated his business, and secured a marble head or bust of Faustina II, purported to be ancient Roman, and a bronze warrior statue purported to be Etruscan or Roman era (the Etruscan Warrior). Some months later plaintiff sold the Faustina Bust to the Mougins Museum of Classical Art in France. In or about September 2011, the Mougins Museum informed plaintiff that the Faustina Bust was a fake in that it was modern and not ancient. The museum sent plaintiff a report by Professor R.R.R. Smith of

Oxford University and Susan Walker, a curator at the British Museum, who opined that the bust was likely modern.

In April 2011, plaintiff obtained from defendants the Etruscan Warrior and a bronze helmet. Plaintiff subsequently sent photographs of the statue to Dr. Michael Padgett at Princeton University, who opined that the piece had some stylistic inconsistencies. Plaintiff then submitted the statue to Oliver Bobin of the Centre d'Innovation et de Recherche pour l'Analyse et le Marquage for metallographic analysis. Bobin determined that the Etruscan Warrior was actually from the nineteenth or twentieth century and therefore was not ancient.

Plaintiff alleges that due to the "mutual mistake" of the parties regarding whether the items were ancient, it is entitled to summary judgment.

We agree with the motion court's decision that plaintiff is not entitled to summary judgment on its breach of contract claim pursuant to the doctrine of mutual mistake * * *. Although the record reflects that both plaintiff and defendants mistakenly assumed at the time of the transactions that the items at issue were ancient, issues of fact exist as to whether plaintiff bore the risk of that mistake due to its "[c]onscious ignorance" of the items' authenticity * * * Restatement [Second] of Contracts § 154 and Comment c.

"Generally, a contract entered into under a mutual mistake of fact is voidable and subject to rescission" because it "does not represent the 'meeting of the minds' of the parties" (Matter of Gould v. Board of Educ. of Sewanhaka Cent. High School Dist., 81 N.Y.2d 446, 453, 599 N.Y.S.2d 787, 616 N.E.2d 142 [1993]). In order to justify rescission, "[t]he mutual mistake must exist at the time the contract is entered into and must be substantial" (id.).

The doctrine of mutual mistake "may not be invoked by a party to avoid the consequences of its own negligence" (P.K. Dev. v. Elvem Dev. Corp., 226 A.D.2d at 201, 640 N.Y.S.2d 558). Where a party "in the exercise of ordinary care, should have known or could easily have ascertained" the relevant fact (id. at 202, 640 N.Y.S.2d 558)—here, whether the items were ancient-that party is deemed to have been "[c]onscious[ly] ignoran[t]" and barred from seeking rescission (id. at 201, 640 N.Y.S.2d 558 [second and third alterations added]) or other *605 damages. This is true "[e]ven where a party must go beyond its own efforts in order to ascertain relevant facts (such as obtaining experts' reports)" (id. at 202, 640 N.Y.S.2d 558).

The conscious ignorance exception applies only where a party is aware that his knowledge is limited but decides to contract anyway "in the hope that the facts accord with his wishes," thus assuming "[t]he risk of the existence of the doubtful fact . . . as one of the elements of the bargain" (Backus v. MacLaury, 278 App.Div. at 507, 106 N.Y.S.2d 401. * * *

We agree with the dissent that both plaintiff and defendants shared the mistaken belief that the Faustina Bust and the Etruscan Warrior were "ancient." Where we diverge is that we find that the record at this time does not support a finding that Eisenberg did not consciously ignore his uncertainty as to a crucial fact (see Feigen, 1992 N.Y. Misc. LEXIS 711, *12).

Questions exist as to whether Eisenberg genuinely believed the bust and statue to be ancient, or was aware that they might not be ancient but decided to assume this risk. Plaintiff presented evidence that Eisenberg is an expert on classical antiquities and a qualified appraiser who generally relies on his own expertise in evaluating works unless he is unsure of a piece's authenticity. He could thus have reasonably accepted that the items were ancient "based on [a] rational assessment of the source and style of work" (Feigen, 1992 N.Y. Misc. LEXIS 711, *15). Moreover, as to the Etruscan Warrior, Hall admittedly informed Eisenberg that he believed it to be from the private collection of renowned art collector J. Pierpont Morgan as signified by a painted red number. Eisenberg could have rationally relied on Morgan's reputation in addition to his own observations (id.).

However, plaintiff also admits in its complaint that several other items purchased from defendants later turned out to be inauthentic. This suggests that plaintiff should have been on notice that the items might not be ancient-at least by the time of the later Etruscan Warrior purchase.

The circumstances surrounding the transactions, including the visits to Hall's townhouse and bedroom, with little or no discussion of the provenance of the pieces, as well as plaintiff's admission that several other items purchased from defendants turned out to be inauthentic, cast plaintiff's professed certainty as to the authenticity of the items into doubt and could support a finding that plaintiff was on notice that the items might not be ancient.

All concur except ANDRIAS, J. who dissents in a memorandum as follows:

* * *

The majority finds that "[t]he circumstances surrounding the transactions, including the visits to Hall's townhouse and bedroom, with little or no discussion of the provenance of the pieces, as well as plaintiff's admission that several other items purchased from defendants turned out to be inauthentic, cast plaintiff's professed certainty as to the authenticity of the items into doubt and could support a finding that plaintiff was on notice that the items might not be ancient." I do not agree.

The record establishes that defendants presented the Faustina Bust and Etruscan Warrior to plaintiff as ancient items. As the majority concedes, Eisenberg could have reasonably accepted that the items were ancient based on his own expertise and a "rational assessment of the source and style of work". Moreover, as to the Etruscan Warrior, Hall admittedly informed Eisenberg that he believed it to be from the private collection of renowned art collector J. Pierpont Morgan. As the majority acknowledges, "Eisenberg could have rationally relied on Morgan's reputation in addition to his own observations." While Hall and Eisenberg disagreed whether that statue was Etruscan or Roman, the dispositive fact is that they both believed it to be ancient, and that there was a rational basis for that belief.

There is no evidence demonstrating that Eisenberg did not genuinely believe that the items were ancient or that he was "uncertain as to a crucial fact" regarding their authenticity following his inspections. That plaintiff purchased several items in the past that were later determined to be fakes does not establish conscious disregard of any facts pointing to the inauthenticity of the sculptures at issue. Plaintiff's money was refunded in each of those cases and the particular circumstances of those transactions and the discovery of the fakes is unclear. Moreover, given that those transactions were rescinded and did not result in a financial loss, they should not form the basis of imposing a heightened duty of inquiry on plaintiff.

PROBLEM 8-2

Turlway, president of Ajax Construction Co., comes to your law office with the following problem. Ajax was the successful bidder for the construction of New City's police headquarters. Ajax began the project on July 18, 2005 and the agreed completion date was August 6, 2007. Ajax actually completed the project on August 5, 2010, at a cost over twice the projected amount. Turlway explains that Ajax's excavation work was delayed because it encountered solid rock that required difficult and time-consuming blasting. The rock covered 45% of the excavation site. Turlway points out that the plans and specifications furnished to prospective bidders by New City contained information on test soil borings performed by the City. These test borings, concededly accurate, showed no rock under the planned construction area because only three such borings were taken and because the borings were not located over the rock area. Most plans and specifications of a project of this size contained at least ten test borings. Turlway believes that the plans and specifications were accurate as to all other points. Before submitting its bid, Ajax took seven additional test borings of its own, which also failed to discover the rock.

The contract between Ajax and New City contains the following pertinent term:

Article 4.16:

> The Bidder must ascertain for itself all of the facts concerning conditions to be found at the site of this project including all physical characteristics below the ground surface. The Bidder promises to

> make all necessary investigations relating to site conditions and the City assumes no responsibility whatsoever with respect to ascertaining for the Bidder such facts concerning physical characteristics at the site of the Project. The Contractor agrees that he will make no claim for additional payment or extension of time for completion of the work because of failure to fully acquaint itself with all conditions relating to the work.

Is Ajax entitled to any additional compensation resulting from the soil conditions?

KENDRICK V. BARKER

Supreme Court of Wyoming, 2001.
15 P.3d 734.

Opinion

GOLDEN, JUSTICE.

In this appeal, we consider whether the district court properly enforced an oral settlement agreement and ruled that, as a matter of law, Wyoming does not recognize unknown injury as grounds for finding that mutual mistake warrants setting aside an agreement to release all personal injury claims.

We affirm.

* * *

FACTS

Kendrick filed suit for injuries she received when her vehicle collided with a Barker tractor-trailer. * * *

A settlement conference was held on June 4, 1999. On June 7, 1999, the mediator wrote to both parties outlining the terms of the tentative settlement agreement that had been reached and stating that Kendrick had until close of business on June 8 to accept Barker's final offer. The letter noted that the offer was open to allow Kendrick to determine an issue about a vehicle damages payment. On June 8, 1999, Kendrick's attorney faxed to Barker's attorney and the mediator Kendrick's acceptance of "$40,000.00 in full settlement of all claims against the Defendant." The mediator responded with a letter that day instructing the parties to prepare the first drafts of closing and settlement documents within three weeks. Kendrick's attorney also notified the district court, and the trial setting was vacated. After Kendrick received the document drafts, she notified her attorney that she would not accept the settlement and hired a new attorney.

Barker filed a motion seeking enforcement of the settlement agreement and denial of the withdrawal of Kendrick's first attorney.

Kendrick opposed enforcement, contending [in part] that on July 19, 1999, after the settlement conference, she was diagnosed with a closed head injury, and she argued that mutual mistake precluded enforcement of the agreement.

* * *

Mutual Mistake

Kendrick contends that the basis for her mutual mistake claim is that the parties were unaware she had suffered a closed head injury at the time of the settlement. As she claims, many courts will set aside a release of all claims reached by settlement for an unknown injury usually after considering factors indicating that the settlement was unconscionable. *See* * * * *Wheeler v. White Rock Bottling Co. of Oregon,* 229 Or. 360, 366 P.2d 527, 530 (1961).

> The courts which have granted relief from premature releases in such cases have talked in terms of mutual mistake. The decisions recognize that ordinarily mistaken opinions, or bad guesses about future possibilities, do not constitute the kind of mutual mistake that will make a contract voidable at the option of either party. However, the courts following the policy of treating improvident releases as voidable apparently are guided by these factors: (a) the peculiar dignity the law accords the human person, as distinguished from articles of commerce; (b) the very real possibility of being mistaken about the long-range effects of damage to human tissue; and (c) the inequality of the bargaining positions of the contracting parties.

Wheeler, 366 P.2d at 530.

On the other hand, a competing set of policy reasons justify a decision that the mutual mistake of unknown injury is not grounds for setting aside an untainted agreement to release all claims:

> [T]his court has considered the settlement of claims prior to litigation to be in the public interest. . . . There is no reason in principle why an improvident settlement made before trial is any more to be set aside than a judgment rendered upon a verdict that hindsight later proves to have been obtained too soon and for too little.
>
> * * *
>
> [T]here are attractive policy reasons for adopting a rule that would permit perfectly honorable releases to be repudiated in the event of aggravation of an injury or the discovery of undiagnosed injuries. There are less compassionate but equally sound policy reasons for requiring persons of legal age and capacity to contract

> to stand by their covenants, including bargains containing an element of chance.

Wheeler, 366 P.2d at 530.

We have long held that the policy of the court is to encourage settling claims without litigation. Releases, or exculpatory agreements, are contractual in nature. * * * In Wyoming, we recognize that fraud, duress, mistake, or unconscionable bargain will vitiate a contract. Further, we recognize that there is a special relationship created by the unequal bargaining power that an insurer has over an insured. Absent these factors, however, when parties reduce a contract to writing, they must abide by its plainly stated terms. Courts are not free to rewrite contracts under the guise of interpretation where the contractual provisions are clear and unambiguous. * * *

A mutual mistake is one that is reciprocal and common to both parties, each alike laboring under the same misconception. A contract is voidable on grounds of mutual mistake when both parties independently make a mistake at the time the contract is made as to a basic assumption of the contract, unless the party seeking avoidance bears the risk of the mistake. Restatement (Second) of Contracts § 152 (1981). A party bears the risk of mistake when "he is aware, at the time the contract is made, that he has only limited knowledge with respect to the facts to which the mistake relates but treats his limited knowledge as sufficient." *Id.* at § 154(b). In such a situation, there is no mistake. Instead, there is an awareness of uncertainty or conscious ignorance of the future. *Id.* at § 154, cmt. c.

In this case, Kendrick entered into the release agreement years after the accident and with the advice of counsel. Kendrick knew there was uncertainty surrounding the extent or consequences of her injuries, as she was not yet cured. Therefore, by accepting Barker's settlement offer Kendrick accepted a known risk that the extent or consequences of her injuries could change in the future.

At the trial court hearing on September 16, 1999, Kendrick confirmed that she had understood the release was in full settlement of her claim against Barker. She did not contend that she had reserved certain claims. As stated by the Maryland Court of Appeals:

> If from the particular language of the release or from the circumstances of the negotiated settlement, there was a conscious and deliberate intention to discharge liability from all consequences of an accident, the release will be sustained and bar any future claims of previously unknown injuries.

Bernstein v. Kapneck, 290 Md. 452, 430 A.2d 602, 607 (1981).

* * *

* * * Kendrick bargained away all of her rights against Barker when she accepted the settlement offer. In light of these facts and available protections under the law, we do not find it necessary to adopt a rule providing for special treatment of releases for personal injuries.

* * *

The district court's order of judgment is affirmed.

PROBLEM 8-3

CNN's website reported on April 5, 2006, that Smith (a fictitious name), infected with AIDS and suffering from AIDS related cancer, entered a contract in 1994 with Life Partners. Life Partners bought Smith's $150,000 life insurance policy in return for $90,000 and a promise to pay her life and health insurance premiums if she lived more than two years. At Smith's death, Life Partners would recover the full $150,000 from the policy.

Some twelve years later, Smith is still alive, thanks to new medicines that fight the ravages of AIDS, but which were not yet discovered in 1994. Life Partners has already paid $100,000 in premiums (plus the initial $90,000 to Smith) and faces premiums of $29,000 per year. Life Partners wants to stop paying. Does it have any legal rights?

RESTATEMENT (SECOND) OF CONTRACTS § 152.

When Mistake of Both Parties Makes a Contract Voidable

(1) Where a mistake of both parties at the time a contract was made as to a basic assumption on which the contract was made has a material effect on the agreed exchange of performances, the contract is voidable by the adversely affected party unless he bears the risk of the mistake under the rule stated in § 154.

(2) In determining whether the mistake has a material effect on the agreed exchange of performances, account is taken of any relief by way of reformation, restitution, or otherwise.

RESTATEMENT (SECOND) OF CONTRACTS § 154.

When A Party Bears The Risk of A Mistake

A party bears the risk of a mistake when

(a) the risk is allocated to him by agreement of the parties, or

(b) he is aware, at the time the contract is made, that he has only limited knowledge with respect to the facts to which the mistake relates but treats his limited knowledge as sufficient, or

(c) the risk is allocated to him by the court on the ground that it is reasonable in the circumstances to do so.

G. PALMER, MISTAKE AND UNJUST ENRICHMENT

36, 37, 38–39 (1962).

When mistake in assumptions occurs, the context that shaped the making of the agreement is seen to be false, and if the discrepancy is radical the policies favoring enforcement of the contract lose much of their force. They may finally be overbalanced by hardship to one party or enrichment of the other. * * *

* * * In most cases permitting rescission for mistake, a serious lack of equivalence appears. The apparent equilibrium of the transaction is upset, and there is enrichment in its most obvious form if the one who is harmed is held to his promise or denied restitution. The mistake may either lessen the value he was to receive or enhance the value he was to give.

* * *

The recognition of unjust enrichment as a principal reason for giving relief for mistake in basic assumptions has come slowly in our law. Even today the problems are often discussed with little or no reference to this factor. This is not to say that unjust enrichment is always essential to relief, for later discussion will disclose occasional instances of rescission without regard to enrichment. Nonetheless, it is the idea that brings most of the cases together. I am using unjust enrichment to mean lack of economic equivalence, attributable to the mistake. * * *

The nature of the mistake interacts with the factor of enrichment in ways that cannot be charted. It is reasonably clear that the extent of enrichment required for relief may vary with the nature of the mistake, the type of transaction, the stage of performance reached, and many other factors.

PROBLEM 8-4

The following facts are true. They are taken from Siegel v. National Comics Publications, Supreme Court, Westchester County, 1099–1947 (unreported). In 1933, Jerome Siegel "conceived the idea of a cartoon strip, the feature character of which would be a man of superhuman strength and power who would perform feats of great magnitude for the public good." Together with Joseph Shuster, an artist, Siegel produced the first Superman comic strip.

In 1938, Detective Comics, Inc. sought material for a new publication, "Action Comics." It learned of the Superman strip, still unpublished after rejection by a major newspaper syndicate. Detective Comics had previously purchased other comics from Siegel and Shuster at the rate of $10 per page. Detective Comics and Siegel and Shuster agreed that the latter two would produce a "thirteen page production" of Superman for the first issue of Action Comics.

On March 1, 1938, Detective Comics sent a check to Siegel for $130 for the thirteen page Superman strip. Detective Comics also enclosed the following contract:

Detective Comics, Inc.
480 Lexington Avenue
New York, N.Y.

> I, the undersigned, am an artist or author and have performed work for strip entitled 'Superman'.
>
> In consideration of $130 agreed to be paid me by you, I hereby sell and transfer such work and strip, all good will attached thereto and exclusive right to the use of the characters and story, continuity and title of strip contained therein, to you and your assigns to have and hold forever and to be your exclusive property and I agree not to employ said characters or said story in any other strips or sell any like strip or story containing the same characters by their names contained therein or under any other names at any time hereafter to any other person, firm or corporation, or permit the use thereof by said other parties, without obtaining your written consent therefor.
>
> The intent hereof is to give you exclusive right to use and acknowledge that you own said characters or story and the use thereof exclusive. I have received the above sum of money.

Siegel and Shuster signed the contract.

In 1947, after a spectacular growth in popularity of the "man of steel," Siegel and Shuster sought to avoid the above and other contracts in which they had transferred all their rights in Superman. By that time, Detective Comics had substantially increased the rate per page paid to the authors, but insisted that the above contract was enforceable.

Assume you represent Siegel and Shuster. At stake are millions of dollars. What arguments will you make in their behalf? What are the strengths and weaknesses of your clients' case?

(Some post 1947 facts about the dispute: The court in Siegel v. National Periodical Publications, Inc., 364 F.Supp. 1032, 1032 (S.D.N.Y. 1973), held that the defendant's copyrights included all renewal rights. The court stated: "Although Clark Kent, generally known as Superman, is happily capable of solving all problems without going to court, his creators and exploiters, mere mortals like the rest of us, are not so fortunate." But in 2008, Siegel's widow and daughter won a declaratory judgment action that they had successfully terminated the original copyright grant. The court based its decision on the 1976 Copyright Act's authorization to grantors to terminate any grant executed before January 1, 1978, regardless of "any agreement to the contrary." According to the House Report No. 94–1476; Copyright Law Revision (1976) at 124, the authorization to terminate was "needed because of the unequal bargaining position of authors, resulting in part from the impossibility of determining a work's value until it has been exploited." The plaintiffs now own half of the copyright. See Siegel v. Warner Bros. Entertainment Inc., 542 F. Supp.2d 1098 (C.D. Cal. 2008)).

You may be interested to know that the actual check for $130 sent by Detective Comics to Siegel recently sold for $160,000.

SECTION FOUR: UNILATERAL MISTAKE

DEPRINCE V. STARBOARD CRUISE SERVICES

Court of Appeal of Florida, Third District 2015.
163 So.3d 586.

ROTHENBERG, J.

Thomas DePrince ("DePrince") appeals the trial court's order granting summary judgment in favor of Starboard Cruise Services, Inc. ("Starboard") on DePrince's claims against Starboard for breach of contract, specific performance, and conversion. Because we find that disputed issues of material fact remain to be resolved on all three counts of DePrince's complaint, we reverse and remand for further proceedings.

Historical Hollywood starlet Mae West once said, "I never worry about diets. The only carrots that interest me are the number of carats in a diamond." Thus, it appears quite likely that Ms. West would have been interested in the diamond in this case: a twenty carat diamond that Starboard offered to DePrince for a very low sum. As it turns out, the "too good to be true" price of the diamond was just that, and the price conveyed to DePrince was a mistake. Now DePrince wants his twenty carat diamond; Starboard wants out of its sales contract; and Starboard's supplier, who allegedly misquoted the price of the diamond upon which Starboard and DePrince relied, has not even been added as a party to the lawsuit. In short, this is truly a gem of a case.

Factual Background

DePrince embarked on a cruise from Miami in February 2013. During that cruise, DePrince visited an onboard jewelry shop that is wholly owned and operated by Starboard. When DePrince expressed some interest in a large loose diamond and specified to the sales manager of the store, Mihai Rusan ("Rusan"), that the stone should be between 15 and 20 carats, Rusan, who had never dealt with a diamond of such magnitude, sent an email inquiry to Starboard's corporate office in Miami ("the Miami Office").

Starboard maintains a consignment agreement with a supplier, Sophia Fiori ("Fiori"), that allows Starboard to obtain gemstones and jewelry for sale in its onboard stores. The consignment agreement between Starboard and Fiori specifies, in relevant part:

> **Title to the Consigned Merchandise shall at all times remain with Consignor until the time of its sale to**

> **customers of Consignee, whereupon the Consigned Merchandise shall be deemed to have been purchased from Consignor by Consignee.**

Upon receiving the email inquiry from Rusan, the Miami Office relayed the information to Fiori to determine whether Fiori could fill such an order should DePrince decide to purchase a diamond. Fiori responded to the Miami Office via email, informing Starboard that there were two diamonds of that size available. Fiori's email described the diamonds precisely as follows:

> **1. EMERALD CUT 20.64 carats D VVS2 GIA VG Price $235,000**
>
> **2. EMERALD CUT 20.73 carats E VVS2 GIA EX EX FNT Price $245,000**

The Miami Office relayed this information to Rusan via email exactly as Fiori had typed it. Rusan notified DePrince of the availability of the size of the diamond he was interested in purchasing and the pricing information contained in the email, telling him that the purchase prices for the diamonds were $235,000 and $245,000 respectively.

DePrince told Rusan that he was interested, but that he would like to take some time to think about the purchase. That night, DePrince spoke with his life partner, Vernon Crawford, a certified gemologist who was on the cruise with DePrince, and also DePrince's sister, Carolyn DePrince, who holds the highest available degree in gemology. Both advised DePrince against making the purchase, telling him that the sale price was too good to be true and that the price for a diamond that large should be at least $2 million.

DePrince, however, ignored their advice and opted to complete the transaction. DePrince returned to Starboard's onboard jewelry store and placed a special mail purchase order for the 20.64 carat diamond the next day. Rusan prepared and signed a one-page sales agreement that listed the total price for the diamond at $235,000 plus a $25 shipping charge. DePrince made an initial down payment of $125,000 on the spot and paid the balance ($110,025) the next day. The parties agreed to have the diamond shipped to the Gemological Institute of America laboratory in New York so that a neutral gemologist could verify that the diamond that was shipped was the same one specified in the sales agreement.

Soon after the sale was completed, Starboard learned that Fiori's $235,000 price quote in the email was the per carat price for the diamond rather than the total price for the diamond ($4,850,400), and thus, Starboard had inadvertently contracted to sell the diamond to DePrince for less than 1/20th of the diamond's actual value. Five days after the sales agreement was executed, Starboard contacted DePrince via telephone to explain the situation, stating that the price on the sales agreement was "seriously in error" due to the mix-up in the email. Starboard offered discounted future cruise rates to DePrince to compensate him for the inconvenience, but DePrince demanded that the sale be completed as specified in the sales agreement. Starboard unilaterally reversed the charges on DePrince's credit card to refund him all the money he had paid and then repudiated the sales agreement, informing DePrince that it would not be shipping the diamond as they had originally agreed. These communications were memorialized in an email Starboard sent to DePrince after the phone call. The record does not disclose how Starboard dealt with the cancellation of the sale with regard to Fiori.

Thereafter, DePrince filed a complaint against Starboard alleging counts for specific performance, breach of contract, and conversion. Starboard answered and pleaded the affirmative defense of unilateral mistake, among others, claiming that Rusan had misquoted DePrince the total price of the diamond rather than the per carat price and that DePrince had known about the error the whole time due to his extensive experience with jewelry. Starboard also counterclaimed for a declaratory judgment that the sales agreement was unenforceable and for rescission of the contract.

Starboard moved for summary judgment on the ground that there had clearly been a unilateral mistake in the pricing, and, after hearing argument on that issue, the trial court granted summary judgment against DePrince on all his claims. Specifically, the trial court ruled at the summary judgment hearing:

> "I don't find that the plaintiff has established that there were any actionable damages and I don't find that there was a valid and enforceable contract for either the breach of contract or the conversion count. Particularly as to conversion, I don't find that the plaintiff or the defendant ever—there's no record evidence that the plaintiff possessed the diamond, as opposed to remaining in the possession of the vendor. I find, quite frankly, that it may be unconscionable to enforce this particular contract."

This appeal followed.

Analysis

* * *

The trial court granted summary judgment against DePrince on his breach of contract action due to its finding that there had been a unilateral mistake of fact sufficient to rescind the otherwise-enforceable contract, [and because] enforcement of the contract would be "unconscionable" * * *. On DePrince's claim for specific performance, the trial court found that the diamond was not unique and was therefore not the proper subject of the remedy of specific performance. * * *

We do not agree with the trial court that there are no genuine issues of material fact such that Starboard is entitled to judgment as a matter of law on any of these claims. Thus, Starboard was not entitled to summary judgment.

I. Contract Formation and Enforcement

On appeal, Starboard has raised two defenses to the sales agreement's formation and enforcement. First and primarily, Starboard claims that a unilateral mistake of law prevents the contract from being formed. Second, Starboard summarily raised an unconscionability defense in its briefing and then pressed that point more extensively at oral argument. For the reasons that follow, neither of these arguments entitle Starboard to summary judgment on DePrince's breach of contract claim. Moreover, the trial court seemed to make a sua sponte finding that DePrince had not alleged any actionable damages to support his breach of contract claim. That ruling was also in error. We explain each of these theories at length because there appears to be a great deal of misunderstanding in each of these areas.

A. Unilateral Mistake

1. This Court's Four-Prong Test for Unilateral Mistakes of Fact

This Court has held that in order to rescind an otherwise-valid contract based on a unilateral mistake, the party seeking to avoid the contract must show:

(1) [T]he mistake was induced by the party seeking to benefit from the mistake,

(2) there is no negligence or want of due care on the part of the party seeking a return to the status quo,

(3) denial of release from the agreement would be inequitable, and

(4) the position of the opposing party has not so changed that granting the relief would be unjust. * * * Examining the facts as alleged and supported by DePrince, Starboard did not conclusively demonstrate either of the first two prongs of this analysis.[1]

First, Starboard presented no evidence that DePrince induced it into making the pricing mistake. The primary focus of Starboard's argument, both at the summary judgment hearing and in its brief, was that DePrince must have known of the mistake in pricing due to his background as a

[1] DePrince has not argued on appeal that the third or fourth prong has not been satisfied. He seems to agree that the transaction appears inequitable and that he has not changed his position in reliance on the purchase.

former antiques and jewelry dealer and the advice he received from his gemologist partner and his sister. DePrince, however, denied that he knew there had been a pricing mistake in his affidavit, which is sufficient at the summary judgment phase of the proceedings to create a genuine issue of material fact. More importantly, we note that even if DePrince had known that the price he was quoted to purchase the diamond was in error, knowledge of an error is markedly different than inducement of that error. * * * Because Starboard presented no evidence that the pricing mistake was induced by DePrince, the trial court clearly erred by granting summary judgment in Starboard's favor under the four-prong test.

Second, there is a factual dispute regarding the second prong of the unilateral mistake standard: that the party seeking to avoid the contract (Starboard) was not inexcusably negligent or failed to act with due care. DePrince avers in both his complaint and affidavit that Starboard did not act with due care when it sold him the diamond. Starboard claims it simply provided DePrince with the quote provided to it by Fiori, and that it did not act negligently. Thus, whether Starboard made a reasonable and understandable mistake or acted negligently in its handling of the sale is a disputed issue of fact, and, because questions involving reasonableness and negligence determinations are highly factual inquiries upon which reasonable people could disagree, they are rarely appropriately resolved on summary judgment. Spadafora v. Carlo, 569 So.2d 1329, 1331 (Fla. 2d DCA 1990). This case is no exception.

2. The Two-Prong Test for Unilateral Mistakes of Fact

Although we have determined that Starboard has not satisfied its burden of meeting the four-prong test adopted by this Court to set aside a contract for unilateral mistake for purposes of summary judgment, Starboard contends that the two-prong test for pleading and proving a unilateral mistake is the test that should be applied. Starboard's argument is not wholly without merit, and in fact, numerous Florida cases have relied on the two-prong standard. Most recently, in Garvin v. Tidwell, the Fourth District Court of Appeal stated "that a trial court may rescind an agreement based on unilateral mistake if '(1) the mistake did not result from an inexcusable lack of due care, and (2) defendant's position did not so change in reliance that it would be unconscionable to set aside the agreement.' " * * *

The two elements in the two-prong test are in substance nearly identical to two of the four prongs relied upon by this Court. Indeed, the four-prong test largely restates the two-prong test and adds the elements that "the mistake was induced by the party seeking to benefit from the mistake [and] . . . denial of release from the agreement would be inequitable." Rachid, 26 So.3d at 72 (quoting Lechuga, 533 So.2d at 857). * * *

Most importantly in this case, however, is the fact that both the two- and the four-prong tests require that the party seeking to invoke a unilateral mistake of fact as an affirmative defense establish that he was not unduly negligent in forming the contract. As explained above, a genuine question of fact remains regarding whether Starboard was negligent in this case, thereby precluding summary judgment under the two-prong standard as well.

* * *

B. Unconscionability as an element of Unilateral Mistake

Starboard also contends on appeal, and the trial court seemed to find, that the contract was unenforceable because the agreement was unconscionable. The independent affirmative defense of unconscionability requires that the party seeking to avoid enforcement of the contract prove both procedural and substantive unconscionability. * * *

* * *

To the extent that Starboard relies on unconscionability as an independent affirmative defense to the contract—not as part of the unilateral mistake analysis—that defense was not properly before the trial court on summary judgment, and the trial court did not and could not make the requisite findings to warrant rescission on that basis. Indeed, the word "unconscionable," or any variation thereof, only appears one time in the hearing transcript—when the trial court found that it would be unconscionable to enforce the contract. And to the extent that Starboard relies on "unconscionability" as a way to establish its unilateral mistake defense, the "unconscionability" it has demonstrated is merely a necessary component to the four-prong (or two-prong) test to establish a unilateral mistake of fact, not a sufficient basis for relief in and of itself. Thus, the trial court erred in granting relief based on "unconscionability."

* * *

II. Specific Performance

DePrince pled specific performance as a wholly separate cause of action from his breach of contract claim. Specific performance is an equitable remedy that may be invoked in a breach of contract action under certain circumstances. * * * "It is a well-established legal principle that a court of equity will grant specific performance of a contract involving personal property when the property is of a unique character and value, such as an antique, and there is no adequate remedy at law." Mangus v. Porter, 276 So.2d 250, 251 n. 1 (Fla. 3d DCA 1973) (citing Graham v. Herlong, 50 Fla. 521, 39 So. 111, 111 (1905)); see also § 672.716(1), Fla. Stat. (2013) ("Specific performance may be decreed where the goods are unique or in other proper circumstances.").

The trial court granted summary judgment in Starboard's favor on DePrince's claim for specific performance based on its determination that the diamond at issue is not unique. This ruling, however, is in conflict with the facts DePrince alleged and averred in his action. In fact, the only evidence submitted on this issue was an affidavit submitted by DePrince's expert gemologist averring that the gem was unique based on a variety of characteristics and a specific laser number assigned only to that gem. Thus, whether the diamond in this case is unique is a factual issue not properly resolved on summary judgment.

* * *

Reversed and remanded.

B2C2 LTD. V. QUOINE PTE LTD.

Singapore International Commercial Court Suit 7, 2017.

[Quoine operated a centralized currency exchange platform that primarily enabled trading of cryptocurrencies by users of Quoine's trading platform. Vastly simplifying a complex ecosystem, cryptocurrencies are new forms of money, secured through personalized encryption rather than money vaults. B2C2 was an "electronic market marker" that had developed a trading algorithm written by its president several years before the events of the case. In April 2017, Quoine, as it always did, had a program in place that received other trading platforms' market prices to ensure trades were consistent with those prices.

Unfortunately, the program that Quoine had written temporarily failed. The result was its prices were out of sync with the global market. Related to this failure, Quoine executed a program that required the sale of assets held by traders on its platform, who (it mistakenly) believed lacked sufficient collateral to satisfy their obligations.

B2C2, whose goal was to capture returns from market inefficiencies just like this, offered to fill seven particular orders made on behalf of these conscripted sellers at a price around 250 times that available on the broader market, making it a quick profit of several million dollars. Quoine would make an ordinary commission on each sale that it had, effectively, arranged and for which it had set the price.

The next day, Quoine reversed the trades in its order book. B2C2 sued, arguing that the reversal violated Quoine's terms and conditions, which provided that "once an order is filled, you are notified via the Platform and such an action is irreversible."

Quoine offered two principal defenses to its supposed obligation to complete the trades with B2C2.

First, it pointed out that its risk disclosure statement, uploaded prior to the trade but not expressly incorporated into the terms and conditions, permitted a reversal of trades if "market circumstances shift dramatically or something else happens." In a part of the opinion you will not read, the court held that because the statement was not expressly incorporated into the contract (that is, into the terms and conditions), it did not override the express language of the contract itself.

Second, the court considered whether the facts established a *mistake*, allegedly because the parties would not themselves have executed the trade in a hypothetical world where they talked about it in person in real time. That is, the parties' agents—the programs—had executed a deal which, though an accurate expression of the code's instructions, somehow failed to capture their "real intent." As Quoine argued, the platforms were "really complex platforms", in which "a lot of things [could] go wrong." The mistake in question was not a typographical error in the code, but rather an "oversight in the design of the system." Quoine asked the court to apply a "pragmatic and judicious stance" and void a "clearly erroneous trade."]

Opinion

SIMON THORLEY, IJ

[Quoine alleges] that Mr Boonen [B2C2's programmer and owner] included the [ability to exploit a lopsided trade] when writing the program with the knowledge not only that it would lead to orders being placed on the Platform at that level in cases of low liquidity but also with the knowledge that there were circumstances in which such orders might be met. Quoine amplified upon this in its written opening submissions. The suggestion that the placing of the deep prices was strictly the result of an innocuous defensive programming strategy was said to be highly artificial and strained. It was also suggested that the Plaintiff was being opportunistic in seeking to take advantage of forced and/or erroneous liquidations by programming its trading software to place orders at the deep prices which were not bona fide * * *.

In its Reply, the Plaintiff denied that it had any knowledge of the trades at the time they were made and asserted that it was speculative to assert that it had "any form of knowledge of any purported system failure, loss of order book, force-closure or otherwise of any alleged mistake" and denied that its trading software was programmed with the intentions and/or objectives alleged * * *.

In his written evidence, Mr Boonen said that he was not aware that the Platform was affected by any glitch, that the trading software was not programmed to detect such glitches and that the orders were placed because of the deep pricing strategy referred to * * * above. He accepted that there was always a possibility that such orders would be filled and that, if they were, B2C2 would be bound by them. It was for this reason that he pre-programmed the code so that the prices were sufficiently advantageous to cover the risk to B2C2 of uncertain liquidity and market conditions. He frankly stated that "the price levels had to be sufficiently advantageous so that B2C2 would not regret it if orders placed at or near those levels were filled."

* * *

> * * * "I could not even know that this situation would have occurred. If you had told me when I left my job at Goldman Sachs—and actually I remember I told my partner, my line manager, the guy I had to officially resign to, "I'm thinking that Bitcoin thing has some legs, I'm going to do it for maybe six months. Hopefully I can sell the company for $2 million". That's what I said, "$2 million", "then I'll come back". If you had told me at the time, "Max, your company is going to make tens of millions of dollars and you're going to be in a courtroom in Singapore in 2018", I would have thought that—I would have re-evaluated my life's choices. So, no. My objective here, in setting [the code to trade on lopsided deals up to an amount], was not that I was about to make obscene profit.
>
> * * *
>
> You're saying that my mind was set to try to do something nefarious for seven little orders that you agree were unlikely to ever trade anyway, it was unlikely that such a situation would ever occur. But if I had done that, I would have missed out on tens of millions of dollars of profit for my firm, because that's what I was focused on. You know, if I'm spending all my time trying to find some work-around to try to take advantage of Quoine, a tiny platform that I—I'm not sure in November 2014 they existed, maybe the company was created around that time, that makes absolutely no sense because it would have diverted so much focus away from all the other platforms, from all the other parts of the code. Frankly, that deep price stuff is minor.
>
> * * *
>
> And so I completely disagree. It makes no sense. It doesn't make any sense for me to have focused so much, with perfect foresight, on trying to take advantage of Quoine, when I did not need that at all. I did not need those trades. The reason I'm here is because I'm entitled to a profit. My profit has been illegally clawed back from me, and it simply is a big enough number that I have to be here.

What then was his mindset? At the time the original program was written, [cryptocurrencies] did not exist. In June 2016 [when Mr. Boonen wrote the computer code that seized the opportunity to make lopsided trades, the cryptocurrency being traded] was a fledgling currency and I accept Mr Boonen's evidence that he regarded it as representing the most risk. I also accept that his primary concern when writing the program was to protect the integrity of the B2C2 trading system so as to minimise the risk of any unwarranted exposure.

He was particularly careful because of the fact that the markets in virtual currencies were unregulated. He saw the need to protect B2C2 and anticipated that other traders and the platform operators would take similar steps. He appreciated that the way he had written the software, the deep prices could go on the Platform and that it was possible, although unlikely, that a trade would be executed at that level. It would only be, as he put it in the passage quoted above, when something very unusual happened or when the unfathomable actually crystallised. He frankly conceded that were this to happen he would hope to make a profit and that the price chosen was selected so as to maximise the possibility of not making a loss. His strategy was therefore not wholly defensive.

* * *

Defenses

Accordingly, in order to succeed in rendering a contract void under the common law doctrine of unilateral mistake, the Defendant must show, first, that there was a sufficiently important or fundamental mistake as to a term of the contract, in the sense that the offeror did not intend the terms of the offer to be that which on its face was offered and, secondly, that the Plaintiff who is seeking to enforce that contract must have actual knowledge of the mistake. Actual knowledge is to be determined by the court as a question of fact and it is sufficient if the court concludes that the person in question was probably aware of the mistake or that he or she was shutting her mind to the obvious.

* * *

That said, it is plain that applying the law to a case where algorithmic trading is involved does raise new questions. What mistakes have been made and to what extent are they fundamental? How does one assess knowledge or intention when the whole operation is carried out by computers acting as programmed? Whose knowledge is relevant? At what date is this knowledge to be assessed?

The researches of counsel and by the court have failed to identify any authority dealing directly with these questions.

Quoine submits that the Court should consider what the parties are likely to have known and intended if, hypothetically, they had met on the "floor of the exchange" for the purpose of reaching an agreement on the trades on 19 April 2017. On this basis, as I understand it, it is contended that mistakes can be identified by comparing theoretically what would have happened in face-to-face negotiations with what actually happened at the computer interface.

Quoine further submits that the law should treat the algorithms or computers used to enter contracts as the legal agents of their human principles and relied on two learned articles in support, namely L Scholz "Algorithmic Contracts" (2017) 20 Stanford Technology Law Review 128 and S Chopra & Laurence White "Artificial Agents and the Contracting Problems: A solution via an Agency Analysis" (2009) University of Illinois Journal of Law, Technology & Policy. On the basis of this, Quoine went on to contend that in answering the hypothetical question as to knowledge or intention on the part of the non-mistaken party, the Court should consider what the programmer of then software in question would have known and intended when writing the software at the time that software was written.

B2C2 contends that there must be a mistake as to a term of the contract and that the party placing the order, albeit by a computer, must be the person mistaken. It was not sufficient if there was a mistake as to facts surrounding that term. In this respect therefore B2C2's position was that the assessment of a relevant mistake was no different in the case of computer transactions than in face-to-face transactions.

Furthermore * * * B2C2 contends that the only relevant knowledge is knowledge at the time of contracting and suggests that it is wrong to assess knowledge or constructive knowledge at the time the deep price mechanism was programmed.

So far as concerns the nature of the mistake, I cannot accept Quoine's hypothetical meeting contention. The question is not what would have happened if the computer element was absent. The parties have chosen to use computers as the means of entering the Trading contracts. They have entered Platform contracts with Quoine so as to be able to enter Trading contracts and, in the case of margin traders, they have entered the Margin trading contracts to regulate their position vis-à-vis the lender, in this case Quoine. All parties were therefore aware that there was to be no human element in the trades and it is wholly artificial to work on the basis of what might have happened if a human element was involved. Equally whilst B2C2's position identifies what the nature of the mistake must be, it does not assist in determining how and when to identify it.

In the circumstances of this case, I have concluded that the relevant mistake must be a mistake by the person on whose behalf the computer placed the order in question as to the terms on which the computer was programmed to form a Trading contract in relation to that order. This mistake will have to be in existence at the date of the contract in question but may have been formed at an earlier date. The existence of a relevant mistake will be a question of fact in each case.

Turning to knowledge of the mistake, the law in relation to the way in which ascertainment of knowledge in cases where computers have replaced human actions is to be determined will, no doubt, develop as legal disputes arise as a result of such actions. This will particularly be the case where the computer in question is creating artificial intelligence and could therefore be said to have a mind of its own.

* * *

* * * Where the law is in a formative state it is, I think, appropriate for a court (of first instance at any rate) to develop the law only so far as necessitated by the facts of the case before it. With this in mind I do not intend to express any views on the precise legal relationship between computers and those who control or program them. The algorithmic programmes in the present case are deterministic, they do and only do what they have been programmed to do. They have no mind of their own. They operate when called upon to do so in the pre-ordained manner. They do not know why they are doing something or what the external events are that cause them to operate in the way that they do.

They are, in effect, mere machines carrying out actions which in another age would have been carried out by a suitably trained human. They are no different to a robot assembling a car rather than a worker on the factory floor or a kitchen blender relieving a cook of the manual act of mixing ingredients. All of these are machines operating as they have been programmed to operate once activated.

Where it is relevant to determine what the intention or knowledge was underlying the mode of operation of a particular machine, it is logical to have regard to the knowledge or intention of the operator or controller of the machine. In the case of the kitchen blender, this will be the person who put the ingredients in and caused it to work. His or her knowledge or intention will be contemporaneous with the operation of the machine. But in the case of robots or trading software in computers this will not be the case. The knowledge or intention cannot be that of the person who turns it on, it must be that of the person who was responsible for causing it to work in the way it did, in other words, the programmer. Necessarily this will have been done at a date earlier than the date on which the computer or robot carried out the acts in question. To this extent I reject B2C2's contention that that the only relevant knowledge is knowledge at the time of contracting.

Accordingly, in my judgment, in circumstances where it is necessary to assess the state of mind of a person in a case where acts of deterministic computer programs are in issue, regard should be had to the state of mind of the programmer of the software of that program at the time the relevant part of the program was written. In the present case that person is Mr Boonen.

* * *

* * * Can it be said that Mr Boonen knew that "it was never contemplated by [any trader] that any trades would be transacted on the Platform at prices which deviated so substantially from the actual market prices?" This amounts to a belief held by Mr Boonen at that date that the price was so abnormal that no trader would trade at that price otherwise by way of a mistake.

This is the aspect of this case that I have found to be most troubling but I have concluded on the basis of those findings of fact that Mr Boonen did not insert the deep prices with that belief. He foresaw that a number of factors might arise which would cause the deep prices to be inserted and the overriding reasons for them being inserted was to protect B2C2 in the event of the unexpected happening. He did not exclude the possibility of trades at those prices being executed. Whilst he was aware that one possible cause was that it could be the result, wholly or in part, of some error or omission on the part of someone, including himself, he did not turn his mind in any detail to the circumstances that might lead to such trades being executed. He knew that the Platform was an automated system and that therefore no opportunity would arise for any particular trade to be reviewed by the parties in advance. In the circumstances of this case, in order for him to have actual knowledge that other traders believed that in no circumstances would a trade be transacted on the Platform at prices which deviated so substantially from the actual market prices, I consider that it would be necessary for it to be demonstrated that he held that belief himself, which he did not. * * *

Accordingly, whilst I accept that the Counterparties held the second mistaken belief relied upon by Quoine, I do not accept that Mr Boonen had actual knowledge of that belief. The defence of unilateral mistake at common law therefore fails.

[The Court then concluded that Quoine was also not entitled to reverse the trades on the ground of mutual mistake: "Even if Quoine held the mistaken belief as to price, on the facts as they have been found, it is plain that Mr Boonen did not. Once therefore the hypothetical meeting on the floor of the exchange is rejected, it must follow that, if the defence of unilateral mistake fails, the defence of mutual mistake must fail also."]

* * *

NOTE:
FURTHER DEVELOPMENTS IN B2C2

In February, 2020, the Singapore Court of Appeals affirmed the decision you read in a 100-plus-page-opus, holding "We also agree with the Judge that it follows from this that in cases where contracts are made by way of deterministic algorithms, any analysis concerning knowledge of a mistake or unconscionably taking advantage of one must be done by reference to the state of mind of the programmers of the algorithms at the time of the programming (see Judgment at [211]) . . . the relevant inquiry might be framed thus: when programming the algorithm, was the programmer doing so with actual or constructive knowledge of the fact that the relevant offer would only ever be accepted by a party operating under a mistake and was the programmer acting to take advantage of such a mistake?"

This case, and the issue of "self-executing" contracts and their interaction with issues of interpretation, mistake, and party intent, is discussed in depth in Shaanan Cohney and David A. Hoffman, Transactional Scripts in Contract Stacks, Minn. L. Rev. (forthcoming 2021).

NOTE:
MORE UNILATERAL MISTAKES

1. The Ithaca Journal reported that the owner of Ball-Mart Baseball Cards and the thirteen-year-old buyer of a 1968 Nolan Ryan card settled their lawsuit over the ownership of the card. Ball-Mart sold the card, apparently worth $1200, to the buyer for $12. Ball-Mart claimed, however, that "an inexperienced clerk who didn't understand the '1200' marking" mistakenly sold the card to the buyer. Ball-Mart therefore sued for return of the card or money damages measured by the contract-market differential. The parties settled the dispute by agreeing to sell the card at an auction and to donate the proceeds to two charities. The junior-high-school student buyer observed that "people should settle their disputes themselves rather than let other people take them to court and settle them for them." Ithaca Journal, Apr. 24, 1991, § 1, at 6, Col. 3.

Question: Suppose the buyer were not so settlement-oriented. Would he have won the lawsuit?

2. In December, 2005, the Associated Press reported that a trader at one of Japan's largest brokerage firms sought to sell one share of a job-recruiting firm for 610,000 yen ($5,041) but, because of a typing error, actually sold 610,000 shares at 1 yen (less than one cent) per share. This cost the firm, according to the report, more than $225 million if the sale stands.

Question: What are the trader's rights, if any?

3. The electronic age may mean more clerical errors. In one actual episode, for example, a married couple sent a check to a zoo intending a donation of $130, but mistakenly made the check out for $93,447. How could this happen? The couple's computer placed their ZIP code where the dollar amount was supposed to go. The zoo returned about $30,000, but refused to return the rest, claiming it had already spent the money. Further, the zoo alleged that it received lots of large donations, so it was not tipped off that the check was a mistake. The parties settled the matter, but apparently neither side was satisfied with the settlement.

SECTION FIVE: IMPOSSIBILITY OF PERFORMANCE

In mutual mistake cases, the circumstances at the time of contracting are materially different from what the parties reasonably assumed. What if, instead, the circumstances materially change *after* the parties make their agreement? The effect of supervening events is the subject of Sections Five through Seven dealing with impossibility of performance, impracticability, and frustration of purpose. More than one writer has observed, however, that these doctrines are essentially concerned with "mistake as to the future" and are therefore "not basically different from * * * mistake with respect to an existing fact."[a]

We turn first to impossibility. Early contract cases excused performance on this ground only when performance was objectively impossible—when the promisor was literally incapable of performing due to circumstances "unforeseeable" at the time of contracting. But when is a promisor truly unable to perform?

TAYLOR V. CALDWELL

Queens Bench, 1863.
3 B. & S. 826, 122 Eng.Rep. 309.

BLACKBURN J. In this case the plaintiffs and defendants had, on the 27th May, 1861, entered into a contract by which the defendants agreed to let the plaintiffs have the use of The Surrey Gardens and Music Hall on four days then to come, viz., the 17th June, 15th July, 5th August and 19th August, for the purpose of giving a series of four grand concerts, and day and night fetes at the Gardens and Hall on those days respectively; and the plaintiffs agreed to take the Gardens and Hall on those days, and pay 100l. for each day.

The parties inaccurately call this a "letting," and the money to be paid a "rent"; but the whole agreement is such as to shew that the defendants were to retain the possession of the Hall and Gardens so that there was to be no demise of them, and that the contract was merely to give the plaintiffs the use of them on those days. Nothing however, in our opinion, depends on this. The agreement then proceeds to set out various stipulations between the parties as to what each was to supply for these concerts and entertainments, and as to the manner in which they should be carried on. The effect of the whole is to shew that the existence of the Music Hall in the Surrey Gardens in a state fit for a concert was essential for the fulfilment of the contract,—such entertainment as the parties contemplated in their agreement could not be given without it.

---

[a] H. Havighurst, The Nature of Private Contract 62 (1961). Of course, not all mistakes are mistakes as to the existing facts.

After the making of the agreement, and before the first day on which a concert was to be given, the Hall was destroyed by fire. This destruction, we must take it on the evidence, was without the fault of either party, and was so complete that in consequence the concerts could not be given as intended. And the question we have to decide is whether, under these circumstances, the loss which the plaintiffs have sustained [the costs of advertising and preparing for the concerts] is to fall upon the defendants. The parties when framing their agreement evidently had not present to their minds the possibility of such a disaster, and have made no express stipulation with reference to it, so that the answer to the question must depend upon the general rules of law applicable to such a contract.

There seems no doubt that where there is a positive contract to do a thing, not in itself unlawful, the contractor must perform it or pay damages for not doing it, although in consequence of unforeseen accidents, the performance of his contract has become unexpectedly burthensome or even impossible. The law is so laid down in 1 Roll.Abr. 450, Condition (G), and in the note (2) to *Walton v. Waterhouse* (2 Wms. Saund. 421 a. 6th ed.), and is recognised as the general rule by all the Judges in the much discussed case of *Hall v. Wright* (E.B. & E. 746). But this rule is only applicable when the contract is positive and absolute, and not subject to any condition either express or implied: and there are authorities which, as we think, establish the principle that where, from the nature of the contract, it appears that the parties must from the beginning have known that it could not be fulfilled unless when the time for the fulfilment of the contract arrived some particular specified thing continued to exist, so that, when entering into the contract, they must have contemplated such continuing existence as the foundation of what was to be done; there, in the absence of any express or implied warranty that the thing shall exist, the contract is not to be construed as a positive contract, but as subject to an implied condition that the parties shall be excused in case, before breach, performance becomes impossible from the perishing of the thing without default of the contractor.

There seems little doubt that this implication tends to further the great object of making the legal construction such as to fulfil the intention of those who entered into the contract. For in the course of affairs men in making such contracts in general would, if it were brought to their minds, say that there should be such a condition.

Accordingly, in the Civil law, such an exception is implied in every obligation of the class which they call obligatio de certo corpore. * * *

Although the Civil law is not of itself authority in an English Court, it affords great assistance in investigating the principles on which the law is grounded. And it seems to us that the common law authorities establish that in such a contract the same condition of the continued existence of the thing is implied by English law.

There is a class of contracts in which a person binds himself to do something which requires to be performed by him in person; and such promises, e.g. promises to marry, or promises to serve for a certain time, are never in practice qualified by an express exception of the death of the party; and therefore in such cases the contract is in terms broken if the promisor dies before fulfilment. Yet it was very early determined that, if the performance is personal, the executors are not liable; Hyde v. The Dean of Windsor (Cro.Eliz. 552, 553). See 2 Wms.Exors. 1560, 5th ed., where a very apt illustration is given. "Thus," says the learned author, "if an author undertakes to compose a work, and dies before completing it, his executors are discharged from this contract: for the undertaking is merely personal in its nature, and, by the intervention of the contractor's death, has become impossible to be performed." * * *

* * *

These are instances where the implied condition is of the life of a human being, but there are others in which the same implication is made as to the continued existence of a thing. For example, where a contract of sale is made amounting to a bargain and sale, transferring presently the property in specific chattels, which are to be delivered by the vendor at a future day; there, if the chattels, without the fault of the vendor, perish in the interval, the purchaser must pay the price and the vendor is excused from performing his contract to deliver, which has thus become impossible.

* * *

It may, we think, be safely asserted to be now English law, that in all contracts of loan of chattels or bailments if the performance of the promise of the borrower or bailee to return the things lent or bailed, becomes impossible because it has perished, this impossibility (if not arising from the fault of the borrower or bailee from some risk which he has taken upon himself) excuses the borrower or bailee from the performance of his promise to redeliver the chattel.

* * * The principle seems to us to be that, in contracts in which the performance depends on the continued existence of a given person or thing, a condition is implied that the impossibility of performance arising from the perishing of the person or thing shall excuse the performance.

In none of these cases is the promise in words other than positive, nor is there any express stipulation that the destruction of the person or thing shall excuse the performance; but that excuse is by law implied, because from the nature of the contract it is apparent that the parties contracted on the basis of the continued existence of the particular person or chattel. In the present case, looking at the whole contract, we find that the parties contracted on the basis of the continued existence of the Music Hall at the time when the concerts were to be given; that being essential to their performance.

We think, therefore, that the Music Hall having ceased to exist, without fault of either party, both parties are excused, the plaintiffs from taking the gardens and paying the money, the defendants from performing their promise to give the use of the Hall and Gardens and other things. Consequently the rule must be absolute to enter the verdict for the defendants.

Rule absolute.

THE OPERA COMPANY OF BOSTON, INC. v. THE WOLF TRAP FOUNDATION FOR THE PERFORMING ARTS, 817 F.2d 1094 (4th Cir. 1987). "The doctrine of impossibility of performance as an excuse or defense for a breach of contract was for long smothered under a declared commitment to the principle of sanctity of contracts. This rationale for constrained application of the doctrine was expressed by the United States Supreme Court in Dermott v. Jones (2 Wall.), 69 U.S. 1, 8, 17 L.Ed. 762 (1864):

> The principle which controlled the decision of the cases referred to rests upon a solid foundation of reason and justice. It regards the sanctity of contracts. It requires parties to do what they have agreed to do. If unexpected impediments lie in the way, and a loss must ensue, it leaves the loss where the contract places it. If the parties have made no provision for a dispensation, the rule of law gives none. It does not allow a contract fairly made to be annulled, and it does not permit to be interpolated what the parties themselves have not stipulated.

The growth of commercial activity in the nineteenth century, however, made this rigidity of the doctrine of impossibility both "economically and socially unworkable," *see Cook v. Deltona Corp.,* 753 F.2d 1552, 1558 (11th Cir.1985), and in *Taylor v. Caldwell,* 3 B. & S. 826, 122 Eng.Rep. 309, 324, 6 R.C. 603 (1863), the English courts recognized these changed conditions and, relying largely on civil law precedents, relaxed the constraints on the doctrine by the principle of sanctity of contracts as followed by the English courts since *Paradine v. Jayne,* Alleyn, 27, 23d Charles II (1670). It based such relaxation on the theory of an implied condition arising without express condition in the contract itself."

BELL v. CARVER, 245 Ark. 31, 431 S.W.2d 452 (1968). "In Williston and Thompson, Revised Edition on Contracts, Section 1975, at page 948, this statement appears:

> One who works upon a building or other property under an indivisible contract with the owner, requiring him to complete a certain task or accomplish a certain result, cannot perform his full undertaking if the building or property in question is destroyed. He is excused from liability for his failure, because the contract required the continued existence of the building. Equally clearly he cannot sue the owner for loss of profit. If the destruction of the building was without fault on the part of the latter, he, as well as the workman, is excused from liability on the contract. But most American decisions allow recovery on a quantum meruit for the value of the work which had been done prior to the destruction."

8 CORBIN ON CONTRACTS

§ 33A.7 (rev. ed. 2019).

In very numerous cases involving a contract for the sale of land, the question has arisen as to which party shall carry the risks of loss and destruction, of buildings or of the land itself, after the contract has been made but before the formal deed of conveyance has been delivered. The facts in these many cases vary in important respects. Again, variation and some conflict in the allocation of risks of loss occur across the jurisdictions. The question may be regarded as one of partial impossibility of performance by the vendor, or as one of partial frustration of the purposes and expectations of the purchaser.

UNIFORM COMMERCIAL CODE § 2–509.

Risk of Loss in the Absence of Breach

* * *

(3) In any case not [involving a carrier or a bailee] the risk of loss passes to the buyer on his receipt of the goods if the seller is a merchant; otherwise the risk passes to the buyer on tender of delivery.

(4) The provisions of this section are subject to contrary agreement of the parties * * *.

UNIFORM COMMERCIAL CODE § 2–104(1).

"Merchant" means a person who deals in goods of the kind or otherwise by his occupation holds himself out as having knowledge or skill peculiar to the practices or goods involved in the transaction or to whom such knowledge or skill may be attributed by his employment of an agent or broker or other intermediary who by his occupation holds himself out as having such knowledge or skill.

UNIFORM COMMERCIAL CODE § 2–613.

Casualty to Identified Goods

Where the contract requires for its performance goods identified when the contract is made, and the goods suffer casualty without fault of either party before the risk of loss passes to the buyer, * * * then

(a) if the loss is total the contract is avoided; and

(b) if the loss is partial or the goods have so deteriorated as no longer to conform to the contract the buyer may nevertheless demand inspection and at his option either treat the contract as avoided or accept the goods with due allowance from the contract price for the deterioration or the deficiency in quantity but without further right against the seller.

CANADIAN INDUSTRIAL ALCOHOL CO. v. DUNBAR MOLASSES CO.

Court of Appeals of New York, 1932.
258 N.Y. 194, 179 N.E. 383.

CARDOZO, C.J.

A buyer sues a seller for breach of an executory contract of purchase and sale.

The subject-matter of the contract was "approximately 1,500,000 wine gallons Refined Blackstrap [molasses] of the usual run from the National Sugar Refinery, Yonkers, N.Y., to test around 60% sugars."

The order was given and accepted December 27, 1927, but shipments of the molasses were to begin after April 1, 1928, and were to be spread out during the warm weather.

After April 1, 1928, the defendant made delivery from time to time of 344,083 gallons. Upon its failure to deliver more, the plaintiff brought this action for the recovery of damages. The defendant takes the ground that, by an implied term of the contract, the duty to deliver was conditioned upon the production by the National Sugar Refinery at Yonkers of molasses sufficient in quantity to fill the plaintiff's order. The fact is that the output of the refinery, while the contract was in force, was 485,848 gallons, much less than its capacity, of which amount 344,083 gallons were allotted to the defendant and shipped to the defendant's customer. The argument for the defendant is that its own duty to deliver was proportionate to the refinery's willingness to supply, and that the duty was discharged when the output was reduced.

The contract, read in the light of the circumstances existing at its making, or more accurately in the light of any such circumstances apparent from this record, does not keep the defendant's duty within boundaries so narrow. We may assume, in the defendant's favor, that there would have been a discharge of its duty to deliver if the refinery had been destroyed * * * or if the output had been curtailed by the failure of the sugar crop * * * or conceivably in some circumstances by unavoidable strikes * * *. We may even assume that a like result would have followed if the plaintiff had bargained not merely for a quantity of molasses to be supplied from a particular refinery, but for molasses to be supplied in accordance with a particular contract between the defendant and the refiner, and if thereafter such contract had been broken without fault on the defendant's part. Scialli v. Correale, 97 N.J. Law, 165, 117 A. 255; cf., however, Marsh v. Johnston, 125 App.Div. 597, 109 N.Y.S. 1106; Id., 196 N.Y. 511, 89 N.E. 1104. The inquiry is merely this, whether the continuance of a special group of circumstances appears from the terms of the contract, interpreted in the setting of the occasion, to have been a tacit or implied presupposition in the minds of the contracting parties, conditioning their belief in a continued obligation. * * *

Accepting that test, we ask ourselves the question: What special group of circumstances does the defendant lay before us as one of the presuppositions immanent in its bargain with the plaintiff? The defendant asks us to assume that a manufacturer, having made a contract with a middleman for a stock of molasses to be procured from a particular refinery, would expect the contract to lapse whenever the refiner chose to diminish his production, and this in the face of the middleman's omission to do anything to charge the refiner with a duty to continue. Business could not be transacted with security or smoothness if a presumption so unreasonable were at the root of its engagements. There is nothing to show that the defendant would have been unable by a timely contract with the refinery to have assured itself of a supply sufficient for its needs. There is nothing to show that the plaintiff, in giving the order for the molasses, was informed by the defendant that such a contract had not been made, or that performance would be contingent upon obtaining one thereafter. If the plaintiff had been so informed, it would very likely have preferred to deal with the refinery directly, instead of dealing with a middleman. The defendant does not even show that it tried to get a contract from the refinery during the months that intervened between the acceptance of the plaintiff's order and the time when shipments were begun. It has wholly failed to relieve itself of the imputation of contributory fault. 3 Williston on Contracts, § 1959. So far as the record shows, it put its faith in the mere chance that the output of the refinery would be the same from year to year, and finding its faith vain, it tells us that its customer must have expected to take a chance as great. We see no reason for importing into the bargain this aleatory element. The defendant is in no better position than a factor who undertakes in his own name to sell for future delivery a special grade of merchandise to be manufactured by a special mill. The duty will be discharged if the mill is destroyed before delivery is due. The duty will subsist if the output is reduced because times turn out to be hard and labor charges high. * * *

* * *

The judgment should be affirmed, with costs.

NOTE:
ADDITIONAL CASES FINDING IMPOSSIBILITY

The impossibility defense is often raised by a promisor, but is rarely successful. Courts typically find that the particular risk was allocated to the promisor or that performance was not impossible. See, e.g., Pillsbury Co. v. Wells Dairy, Inc., 752 N.W.2d 430 (Iowa 2008) (interpreting a force majeure clause, the court did not excuse an ice cream manufacturer even though its creamery exploded). The defense has succeeded, however, in some cases. For example, in UNCC Properties, Inc. v. Greene, 111 N.C.App. 391, 432 S.E.2d 699 (1993), the court excused a landowner from a contract to convey an easement when the county condemned the property for public use. In Oneal v. Colton Consol. School Dist. No. 306, 16 Wash.App. 488, 557 P.2d 11 (1976), the court excused a secondary school teacher on impossibility grounds because of deteriorating eyesight. In Net Realty Holding Trust v. Franconia Properties, Inc., 544 F.Supp. 759 (E.D.Va.1982), the court excused a real estate lessor from leasing space only to a department store under the trade name "Korvettes" when Korvettes went bankrupt.

SECTION SIX: IMPRACTICABILITY OF PERFORMANCE

Today, courts may permit cessation even when performance is not "objectively" impossible. Some courts recognize the lack of sense in compelling performance (or awarding damages for non-performance) in certain situations where performance has become extremely onerous due to an unanticipated event. Yet the line is fine between those cases where courts excuse performance on impracticability grounds and those where they refuse to do so, with refusal the rule and excuse the exception. Typically, the refusal is on the ground that the parties have expressly or impliedly allocated the risk to the promisor.

MARCOVICH LAND CO. V. J.J. NEWBERRY CO.

Court of Appeals of Indiana, 1980.
413 N.E.2d 935.

MILLER, JUDGE.

Paul March and Walter March (the latter being the executor of the estate of defendant Michael H. March, deceased), legal successors in interest to defendant-landlord Marcovich Land Corporation, appeal a judgment granting plaintiff-tenant, J.J. Newberry Company, a variety store chain, some $117,000, and denying the Marches the damages they requested in a counterclaim. Newberry, former tenant in a building owned by Marcovich located in East Chicago, Indiana, was awarded lost business profits for a period of three years[1] because Marcovich refused to rebuild the structure occupied by Newberry after it was destroyed by fire. The parties had a written lease which the trial court determined was enforceable and required such reconstruction by Marcovich. The court rejected the Marches' dual contentions in their counterclaim or set off that Newberry had not cooperated in efforts to rebuild and that in any event the covenant requiring rebuilding was impossible to perform. We affirm the trial court's judgment.

On appeal, the legal successors to Marcovich present several questions for our review, which issues may be summarized as follows:

> 1) that the lease does not anticipate or require rebuilding where there has been a total destruction as occurred under the circumstances of the instant case;
>
> 2) that it would be "unconscionable" as well as impossible (or, as the Marches contend, commercially impractical) to require such rebuilding in light of the amount of the insurance proceeds, the time remaining on the lease, the "blighted" condition of the area, and the alleged difficulty in obtaining financing;
>
> 3) that the trial court improperly ignored the prohibitive circumstances noted in 2) above, as evidenced by its findings and conclusions;

* * *

Newberry's complaint, filed January 4, 1973, generally alleged the parties entered into their 25-year written lease agreement on September 30, 1953 with respect to real estate and the improvements thereon located in the Indiana Harbor region of the City of East Chicago, and that thereafter, on July 14, 1958, Marcovich assigned its interest in the lease to Paul March and Michael H. March as trustees operating under the name

---

[1] Although the remaining term of its lease was 7 years, the land had been condemned, apparently as part of an urban renewal project, some 4 years after the building burned.

of March Realty. The parties do not dispute these general facts, nor the further assertion that a fire of unknown origin completely destroyed the building in question on December 30, 1971. * * *

Count II of the complaint presents the issue involved in the instant appeal, since specific performance was prevented by the condemnation of the property on June 16, 1976 by the City of East Chicago. Newberry contends it lost net profits as a result of the failure by Marcovich to reconstruct the demised premises, and accordingly, in its complaint requested damages of $210,000. As noted above, the trial court awarded Newberry approximately $117,000, consisting of lost profits of about $122,000 until June 16, 1976 minus $5,000 Newberry owed under the rental obligation imposed by the lease.

Because of its significance to the instant appeal, the so-called "fire clause" relied upon by both parties is quoted herein at the outset. That language in the lease provides as follows:

> "In the event the demised premises are damaged or destroyed by fire or other casualty, or damaged by the demolition of any portion of the building necessitated by the enforcement of any law or Ordinance, or declared unsafe by any public authority, the Landlord shall, at own cost [sic] and expense, immediately repair, reconstruct and replace the demised premises, including improvements, extensions, alterations and additions to building made by Landlord or Tenant, all such work to be done in compliance with State Laws and City Ordinances. If the extent or character of such damage, destruction or unsafe condition renders the demised premises unfit for the proper conduct of the business of the Tenant, all rent shall cease and abate during the cessation of business of the Tenant and until the complete restoration of the demised premises ready for occupancy. If, however, the Tenant is able to and does continue its business in said premises pending the restoration or reconstruction of the demised premises, then a fair and just proportion of the rent shall abate until the demised premises are restored and ready for occupancy. Any rent paid in advance beyond the happening of any of the contingencies above mentioned shall be returned by the Landlord to the Tenant."

Before applying such provision in its judgment and conclusions of law, the trial court, which decided this case without intervention of a jury, arrived at the following findings of fact significant to the rights of Newberry and the successors to Marcovich's interest:

> "6. That at the time the lease of September 30, 1953 was negotiated between the parties, the defendants, Paul March and Michael March, deceased, principals of the defendant, Marcovich

Land Corporation, were experienced and competent real estate brokers and landlords.

7. That the defendant, Paul March, had over 40 years of experience in the real estate field which included purchasing, selling and leasing of real estate including commercial properties.

8. That the defendant, Michael March, had over 60 years of experience in the real estate field which included purchasing, selling and leasing of real estate including commercial properties.

9. That at all times during the negotiation of the lease agreement of September 30, 1953, both the plaintiff and the defendants had equal bargaining power for the purposes of negotiating said lease.

10. That from September 30, 1953 until the time of the fire (December 30, 1971) both parties to the lease had completely performed pursuant to the terms of the lease and that neither of the parties to the lease had in any way breached the lease or its terms and conditions.

11. That on December 30, 1971, the building which was the subject-matter of the lease of September 30, 1953, was complete [sic] destroyed by fire. The building was a total loss and nothing was saved.

* * *

13. That on December 31, 1971 the defendants were advised by J.J. Newberry Company that the plaintiff wanted the building rebuilt pursuant to the lease agreement."

Significantly, the conclusions of law which accompanied the above findings determined that the lease agreement between the parties was in all respects valid, enforceable and conscionable, and that the parties to the lease had equal bargaining power when the agreement was made. Thus, since Marcovich did not rebuild, and according to the trial court was apparently not hindered in such efforts by Newberry, damages were awarded to Newberry under what the court thought to be a reasonable determination.

The ultimate award was based on the profits Newberry would have received from May of 1973 until June of 1976, (the latter being, as noted above, the date the property was condemned), apparently because it would take a year to construct a new building. Thus, the profit calculation did not include the 12 months following Michael March's abandonment of the lease in May of 1972. The findings listed specific predicted lost profits for the years (or parts thereof) 1973, 1974, 1975 and 1976.

We first address what amounts to a threshold question in this case, namely, whether the so-called "fire clause" in the parties' lease agreement applies on its face to a situation where, as here, the leased premises were not merely damaged by fire, but rather (as the trial court found) were completely destroyed with nothing saved. The Marches contend, relying principally on an early Kentucky case, *Davis v. Parker,* (1923) 200 Ky. 847, 255 S.W. 836, the language of the lease does not contemplate rebuilding where there has been such a total destruction.

We disagree. While it is true the Court in *Davis* found the lease there at issue anticipated only the restoration or reconstruction of premises which had merely been partially destroyed, as opposed to the complete rebuilding of a demised structure, it is significant that in the *Davis* case the relevant lease provision stated the landlord must "replace the buildings in the same condition as they now are" whenever they are "destroyed by fire or tempest *in such a manner as to render the same untenantable.*" *Id.* at 847, 255 S.W. at 836. (emphasis supplied by the Kentucky Court). The Court observed, "[i]f the word [destroyed] stood alone in the sentence there could be no discussion or question, * * *." *Id.* at 849, 255 S.W. at 836. This latter situation is now before this Court. Thus, even if we were to apply the general reasoning of that case in Indiana, it is evident the instant lease provision is distinguishable in light of the fact the modifying language found in *Davis* is omitted from the unambiguous promise in the case at bar to "repair, reconstruct and replace" the demised premises where they are "damaged *or* destroyed." (Emphasis added.)

Similarly, although the Marches contend in this context that "[p]arties to [a] contract are not always able to provide for all the possibilities of which they are aware," *quoting Transatlantic Financing Corp. v. United States,* (D.C.Cir.1966) 363 F.2d 312, 316 it is evident (in contrast to the position urged by the Marches) both sides in the instant litigation did anticipate and provide for what in fact occurred, namely, a fire which completely destroyed the building, consisting of the original premises plus "improvements, extensions, alterations and additions" made by Newberry. An unambiguous document such as the one at bar neither requires nor permits the extrinsic interpretative evidence offered by the Marches. *New Harmony Realty Corp. v. Superior Oil Co.* (1941) 108 Ind.App. 668, 31 N.E.2d 673. Although it is unnecessary to our interpretation of such lease provision we note, in this regard, that it was perhaps partly in anticipation of the landlord's clear duty to rebuild upon complete destruction of the premises that he was elsewhere in the lease required to insure the building and improvements against fire "to the extent of the reasonable insurable value thereof." We accordingly conclude the trial court did not err in its determination of the parties' intent based on the language of this lease agreement.

* * *

* * * With regard to [the Marches' impossibility] defense, both parties cite and discuss this Court's opinion in *Kruse, Kruse & Miklosko, Inc. v. Beedy,* (1976) 170 Ind.App. 373, 353 N.E.2d 514, where the theory is discussed at some length. By way of background—before considering the particular merits of the Marches' argument in the case at bar—we observe the following language in *Kruse* pertaining generally to the impossibility defense in this State:

> "The law in Indiana in regard to impossibility of performance as a defense to a contract action is well stated in *Krause v. Board, etc.* (1904), 162 Ind. 278, at 283–84, 70 N.E. 264, at 265:
>
> 'We regard it as thoroughly settled that the words of a mere general covenant will not be construed as an undertaking to answer for a subsequent event, happening without the fault of the covenantor, which renders performance of the covenant itself *not merely difficult or relatively impossible, but absolutely impossible,* owing to the act of God, the act of the law, or the loss or destruction of the subject-matter of the contract. Where performance is thus rendered impossible, the inquiry naturally arises as to whether there was a purpose to covenant against such an extraordinary and therefore presumably unapprehended event, the happening of which it was not within the power of the covenantor to prevent.' "

Id. 394, 353 N.E.2d at 528. (emphasis supplied in *Kruse.*)

Significantly (in light of this language in *Kruse*), it does not appear the Marches argue it was absolutely impossible to rebuild the structure rented by Newberry at the time of the fire, since they suggest in their brief "[p]erformance is possible, but the value (benefit) (investment) has been destroyed by an unforeseen event, a totally and completely destroyed building, * * *." Indeed, the only evidence presented at trial which was arguably intended to show such absolute impossibility of performance concerned the purported inability of the Marcovich representatives to obtain financing for a new building under the existing lease terms with Newberry. In this regard, however, we must note not only that there was no showing such financing was essential to permit rebuilding,[2] but also that the depositions of defendant-appellant Paul March and Michael March, deceased (for whom defendant-appellant Walter March acts as executor), suggest the family in fact never tried to obtain financing based on the remaining lease term. Paul March, for example, stated as follows:

> "Q. * * * Did you ever try to obtain financing from any bank or lending institution to rebuild the building?

[2] It is significant with respect to this question that the Marches acknowledge receiving $200,000 in insurance proceeds which could be applied toward rebuilding, along with whatever other assets the family may have had available.

A. I didn't, no.

Q. Did anyone that you know of try to do that?

A. It wasn't necessary yet. We hadn't gotten anywhere.

Q. As far as you know, nobody from March Realty ever tried to obtain financing or ever approached a bank concerning financing, is that correct?

A. Not as yet."

Similarly, Michael March asserted "I didn't have to try. I know [it was impossible]." These statements, which in essence amount to admissions by the parties they were unaware of any efforts to obtain such financing based on the original lease, were controverted (if at all) only by the unelaborated suggestion by Martin March, who was not a party either to the lease or this lawsuit, that the Marches were not able to get financing to rebuild under the remaining term of the lease. He did not explain the basis for such assertion. In this context, we also observe that the possible inability to obtain financing is not generally an unforeseeable circumstance which the parties do not consider in commercial leases or contracts. *See Kruse, Kruse & Miklosko v. Beedy, supra* at 394–95, 353 N.E.2d at 529, where the Court noted "the possibility that Small could not obtain financing not only should have been foreseen by the parties, but was provided for in their agreement."

The Marches maintain, however, that apart from any issue of "absolute" impossibility, the essential question raised by this appeal is whether in Indiana impossibility of performance should include the defense that performance is "impractical" where it involves "excessive and unreasonable cost." They concede such issue is unanswered in any Indiana precedent, but contend their position should be adopted in light of the practice in other jurisdictions, *citing Transatlantic Financing Corp. v. United States,* [363 F.2d 312 (D.C.Cir.1966)], a case in which Judge Wright acknowledged such a defense but concluded it was not "commercially impractical" under a contract to require a ship carrying wheat to travel 3,000 additional miles on an original 10,000-mile trip, at an alleged cost of almost $44,000, because of the closing of the Suez Canal. *See also Aluminum Co. of America v. Essex Group, Inc.,* 499 F.Supp. 53 (U.S.D.C., W.D.Pa.1980), a case purporting to apply Indiana law.

In response to such argument, we conclude, even assuming *arguendo* the affirmative defense in Indiana extends beyond "absolute" impossibility to encompass the doctrine urged by the Marches, that the trial court could properly have determined there was no evidence before it of the kind of commercially senseless expense contended by the Marches, but rather that the parties had *anticipated* and *allocated between them* the unextraordinary risk which in fact occurred.

* * *

Turning to the evidence relied on by the Marches in support of their theory we note the uncontroverted (though challenged by objection) testimony of the Marches' expert, Richard J. Kestle, that it would cost at least $452,000 in 1972 to construct a building on the site in accordance with certain rough plans prepared by Newberry. Additionally, the Marches presented evidence they received only $200,000 in insurance proceeds, such lesser figure presumably being attributable to the fact the Marches chose not to insure the structure for its replacement cost.[3] The Marches also presented evidence in this regard, however, in the form of testimony from a real estate appraiser using the $452,000 reconstruction figure and a six-year lease, that rebuilding would not be economically or commercially "feasible," a conclusion which he explained in an offer to prove took into account what return a prudent investor would want for his money invested in a new building in 1972, assuming such an investor "would want at least 8% on his money and we said that the recapture or depreciation rate would be 2½% or a total capitalization rate of 10½%." The same expert observed the property in question was in an "urban renewal" area in 1974 or 1975 (though not in 1972), and concluded, "I would advise my client that this is a very poor deal to get into."

In viewing such evidence we are cognizant that even under the standard advocated by the Marches, the test is not simply whether a particular performance would be a bad business risk or even a "very poor deal" for a prudent investor, but rather whether there was "*extreme* . . . difficulty, expense, injury, or loss" which goes well beyond the normal range of what might have been expected, Comment d to the proposed Restatement (Second) of Contracts, [§ 281] and whether the parties failed to allocate such risk. *Transatlantic Financing Corp. v. United States, supra.* We believe the trial court could properly have concluded the evidence in the instant case, involving regrettable but unextraordinary rebuilding considerations, did not rise to such a level, but that the risk was anticipated by the parties, and thus not [un]expected and that such risk was, moreover, intended to be allocated between them by the "fire clause" itself.

* * *

[Affirmed.]

---

[3] We are cognizant the trial court implicitly found the building had been insured for its "reasonable insurable value" when it concluded neither party had breached the lease, but we do not find such determination to be inconsistent with the Marches' right, if they chose, to protect themselves against their ultimate liability for rebuilding by insuring for the replacement cost.

MINERAL PARK LAND CO. V. HOWARD

Supreme Court of California, 1916.
172 Cal. 289, 156 P. 458.

SLOSS, J. The defendants appeal from a judgment in favor of plaintiff for $3,650. The appeal is on the judgment roll alone.

The plaintiff was the owner of certain land in the ravine or wash known as the Arroyo Seco, in South Pasadena, Los Angeles county. The defendants had made a contract with the public authorities for the construction of a concrete bridge across the Arroyo Seco. In August, 1911, the parties to this action entered into a written agreement whereby the plaintiff granted to the defendants the right to haul gravel and earth from plaintiff's land, the defendants agreeing to take therefrom all of the gravel and earth necessary in the construction of the fill and cement work on the proposed bridge, the required amount being estimated at approximately 114,000 cubic yards. Defendants agreed to pay 5 cents per cubic yard for the first 80,000 yards, the next 10,000 yards were to be given free of charge, and the balance was to be paid for at the rate of 5 cents per cubic yard.

The complaint was in two counts. The first alleged that the defendants had taken 50,131 cubic yards of earth and gravel, thereby becoming indebted to plaintiff in the sum of $2,506.55, of which only $900 had been paid, leaving a balance of $1,606.55 due. The findings support plaintiff's claim in this regard, and there is no question of the propriety of so much of the judgment as responds to the first count. The second count sought to recover damages for the defendants' failure to take from plaintiff's land any more than the 50,131 yards.

It alleged that the total amount of earth and gravel used by defendants was 101,000 cubic yards, of which they procured 50,869 cubic yards from some place other than plaintiff's premises. The amount due the plaintiff for this amount of earth and gravel would, under the terms of the contract, have been $2,043.45. The count charged that plaintiff's land contained enough earth and gravel to enable the defendants to take therefrom the entire amount required, and that the 50,869 yards not taken had no value to the plaintiff. Accordingly the plaintiff sought, under this head, to recover damages in the sum of $2,043.45.

The answer denied that the plaintiff's land contained any amount of earth and gravel in excess of the 50,131 cubic yards actually taken, and alleged that the defendants took from the said land all of the earth and gravel available for the work mentioned in the contract.

The court found that the plaintiff's land contained earth and gravel far in excess of 101,000 cubic yards of earth and gravel, but that only 50,131 cubic yards, the amount actually taken by the defendants, was above the water level. No greater quantity could have been taken "by ordinary means," or except by the use, at great expense, of a steam dredger, and the earth and gravel so taken could not have been used without first having been dried at great expense and delay. On the issue raised by the plea of defendants that they took all the earth and gravel that was available the court qualified its findings in this way: It found that the defendants did take all of the available earth and gravel from plaintiff's premises, in this, that they took and removed "all that could have been taken advantageously to defendants, or all that was practical to take and remove from a financial standpoint"; that any greater amount could have been taken only at a prohibitive cost, that is, at an expense of 10 or 12 times as much as the usual cost per yard. It is also declared that the word "available" is used in the findings to mean capable of being taken and used advantageously. It was not "advantageous or practical" to have taken more material from plaintiff's land, but it was not impossible. There is a finding that the parties were not under any mutual misunderstanding regarding the amount of available gravel, but that the contract was entered into without any calculation on the part of either of the parties with reference to the amount of available earth and gravel on the premises.

The single question is whether the facts thus found justified the defendants in their failure to take from the plaintiff's land all of the earth and gravel required. This question was answered in the negative by the court below. The case was apparently thought to be governed by the principle—established by a multitude of authorities—that where a party has agreed, without qualification, to perform an act which is not in its nature impossible of performance, he is not excused by difficulty of performance, or by the fact that he becomes unable to perform. * * *

It is, however, equally well settled that, where performance depends upon the existence of a given thing, and such existence was assumed as the basis of the agreement, performance is excused to the extent that the thing ceases to exist or turns out to be nonexistent. 1 Beach, Contr. § 217; 9 Cyc. 631. Thus, where the defendants had agreed to pasture not less than 3,000 cattle on plaintiff's land, paying therefor $1 for each and every head so pastured, and it developed that the land did not furnish feed for more than 717 head, the number actually put on the land by defendant, it was held that plaintiff could not recover the stipulated sum for the difference between the cattle pastured and the minimum of 3,000 agreed to be pastured. Williams v. Miller, 68 Cal. 291, 9 Pac. 166 * * *.

We think the findings of fact make a case falling within the rule of these decisions. The parties were contracting for the right to take earth and gravel to be used in the construction of the bridge. When they stipulated that all of the earth and gravel needed for this purpose should be taken from plaintiff's land, they contemplated and assumed that the land contained the requisite quantity, available for use. The defendants were not binding themselves to take what was not there. And, in determining whether the earth and gravel were "available," we must view the conditions in a practical and reasonable way. Although there was gravel on the land, it was so situated that the defendants could not take it by ordinary means, nor except at a prohibitive cost. To all fair intents then, it was impossible for defendants to take it.

"A thing is impossible in legal contemplation when it is not practicable; and a thing is impracticable when it can only be done at an excessive and unreasonable cost." 1 Beach on Contr. § 216. We do not mean to intimate that the defendants could excuse themselves by showing the existence of conditions which would make the performance of their obligation more expensive than they had anticipated, or which would entail a loss upon them. But, where the difference in cost is so great as here, and has the effect, as found, of making performance impracticable, the situation is not different from that of a total absence of earth and gravel.

On the facts found, there should have been no recovery on the second count.

The judgment is modified by deducting therefrom the sum of $2,043.45, and, as so modified, it stands affirmed.

TRANSATLANTIC FINANCING CORP. V. UNITED STATES

United States Court of Appeals, District of Columbia Circuit, 1966.
363 F.2d 312.

J. SKELLY WRIGHT, CIRCUIT JUDGE.

This appeal involves a voyage charter between Transatlantic Financing Corporation, operator of the SS CHRISTOS, and the United States covering carriage of a full cargo of wheat from a United States Gulf port to a safe port in Iran. The District Court dismissed a libel filed by Transatlantic against the United States for costs attributable to the ship's diversion from the normal sea route caused by the closing of the Suez Canal. We affirm.

On July 26, 1956, the Government of Egypt nationalized the Suez Canal Company and took over operation of the Canal. On October 2, 1956, during the international crisis which resulted from the seizure, the voyage charter in suit was executed between representatives of Transatlantic and the United States. The charter indicated the termini of the voyage but not the route. On October 27, 1956, the SS CHRISTOS sailed from Galveston for Bandar Shapur, Iran, on a course which would have taken her through Gibraltar and the Suez Canal. On October 29, 1956, Israel invaded Egypt. On October 31, 1956, Great Britain and France invaded the Suez Canal Zone. On November 2, 1956, the Egyptian Government obstructed the Suez Canal with sunken vessels and closed it to traffic.

On or about November 7, 1956, Beckmann, representing Transatlantic, contacted Potosky, an employee of the United States

Department of Agriculture, who appellant concedes was unauthorized to bind the Government, requesting instructions concerning disposition of the cargo and seeking an agreement for payment of additional compensation for a voyage around the Cape of Good Hope. Potosky advised Beckmann that Transatlantic was expected to perform the charter according to its terms, that he did not believe Transatlantic was entitled to additional compensation for a voyage around the Cape, but that Transatlantic was free to file such a claim. Following this discussion, the CHRISTOS changed course for the Cape of Good Hope and eventually arrived in Bandar Shapur on December 30, 1956.

Transatlantic's claim is based on the following train of argument. The charter was a contract for a voyage from a Gulf port to Iran. Admiralty principles and practices, especially stemming from the doctrine of deviation, require us to imply into the contract the term that the voyage was to be performed by the "usual and customary" route. The usual and customary route from Texas to Iran was, at the time of contract, via Suez, so the contract was for a voyage from Texas to Iran via Suez. When Suez was closed this contract became impossible to perform. Consequently, appellant's argument continues, when Transatlantic delivered the cargo by going around the Cape of Good Hope, in compliance with the Government's demand under claim of right, it conferred a benefit upon the United States for which it should be paid in *quantum meruit*.

The doctrine of impossibility of performance has gradually been freed from the earlier fictional and unrealistic strictures of such tests as the "implied term" and the parties' "contemplation." Page, *The Development of the Doctrine of Impossibility of Performance,* 18 MICH.L.REV. 589, 596 (1920). See generally 6 CORBIN, CONTRACTS §§ 1320–1372 (rev. ed. 1962); 6 WILLISTON, CONTRACTS §§ 1931–1979 (rev.ed.1938). It is now recognized that " 'A thing is impossible in legal contemplation when it is not practicable; and a thing is impracticable when it can only be done at an excessive and unreasonable cost.' " Mineral Park Land Co. v. Howard, 172 Cal. 289, 293, 156 P. 458, 460, L.R.A. 1916E, 1 (1916). *Accord,* Whelan v. Griffith Consumers Company, D.C.Mun.App., 170 A.2d 229 (1961); RESTATEMENT, CONTRACTS § 454 (1932); UNIFORM COMMERCIAL CODE (U.L.A.) § 2–615, comment 3. The doctrine ultimately represents the ever-shifting line, drawn by courts hopefully responsive to commercial practices and mores, at which the community's interest in having contracts enforced according to their terms is outweighed by the commercial senselessness of requiring performance.[1] When the issue is raised, the court is asked to

[1] While the impossibility issue rarely arises, as it has here, in a suit to recover the cost of an alternative method of performance, compare Annot. 84 A.L.R.2d 12, 19 (1962), there is nothing necessarily inconsistent in claiming commercial impracticability for the method of performance actually adopted; the concept of impracticability assumes performance was physically possible. Moreover, a rule making nonperformance a condition precedent to recovery would unjustifiably encourage disappointment of expectations.

construct a condition of performance[2] based on the changed circumstances, a process which involves at least three reasonably definable steps. First, a contingency—something unexpected—must have occurred. Second, the risk of the unexpected occurrence must not have been allocated either by agreement or by custom. Finally, occurrence of the contingency must have rendered performance commercially impracticable. Unless the court finds these three requirements satisfied, the plea of impossibility must fail.

The first requirement was met here. It seems reasonable, where no route is mentioned in a contract, to assume the parties expected performance by the usual and customary route at the time of contract. Since the usual and customary route from Texas to Iran at the time of contract was through Suez, closure of the Canal made impossible the expected method of performance. But this unexpected development raises rather than resolves the impossibility issue, which turns additionally on whether the risk of the contingency's occurrence had been allocated and, if not, whether performance by alternative routes was rendered impracticable.

Proof that the risk of a contingency's occurrence has been allocated may be expressed in or implied from the agreement. Such proof may also be found in the surrounding circumstances, including custom and usages of the trade. See 6 CORBIN, *supra,* § 1339, at 394–397; 6 WILLISTON, *supra,* § 1948, at 5457–5458. The contract in this case does not expressly condition performance upon availability of the Suez route. Nor does it specify "via Suez" or, on the other hand, "via Suez or Cape of Good Hope."[3] Nor are there provisions in the contract from which we may properly imply that the continued availability of Suez was a condition of performance.[4] Nor is there

---

2 Patterson, *Constructive Conditions in Contracts,* 42 COLUM.L.REV. 903, 943–954 (1942).

3 In Glidden Company v. Hellenic Lines, Limited, 2 Cir., 275 F.2d 253 (1960), the charter was for transportation of materials from India to America "via Suez Canal or Cape of Good Hope, or Panama Canal," and the court held performance was not "frustrated." In his discussion of this case, Professor Corbin states: "Except for the provision for an alternative route, the defendant would have been discharged, for the reason that the parties contemplated an open Suez Canal as a specific condition or means of performance." 6 CORBIN, *supra,* § 1339, at 399 n. 57. Appellant claims this supports its argument, since the Suez route was contemplated as usual and customary. But there is obviously a difference, in deciding whether a contract allocates the risk of a contingency's occurrence, between a contract specifying no route and a contract specifying Suez. We think that when Professor Corbin said, "Except for the provision for an alternative route," he was referring, not to the entire *provision*—"via Suez Canal or Cape of Good Hope" etc.—but to the fact that *an alternative route* had been provided for. Moreover, in determining what Corbin meant when he said "the parties contemplated an open Suez Canal as a specific condition or means of performance," consideration must be given to the fact, recited by Corbin, that in *Glidden* the parties were specifically aware when the contract was made the Canal might be closed, and the promisee had refused to include a clause excusing performance in the event of closure. Corbin's statement, therefore, is most accurately read as referring to cases in which a route is specified after negotiations reflecting the parties' awareness that the usual and customary route might become unavailable. Compare Held v. Goldsmith, 153 La. 598, 96 So. 272 (1919).

4 The charter provides that the vessel is "in every way fitted for *the voyage*" (emphasis added), and the "P. & I. Bunker Deviation Clause" refers to "the contract voyage" and the "direct and/or customary route." Appellant argues that these provisions require implication of a voyage by the direct and customary route. Actually they prove only what we are willing to accept—that

anything in custom or trade usage, or in the surrounding circumstances generally, which would support our constructing a condition of performance. The numerous cases requiring performance around the Cape when Suez was closed, see *e.g.,* Ocean Tramp Tankers Corp. v. V/O Sovfracht (The Eugenia), [1964] 2 Q.B. 226, and cases cited therein, indicate that the Cape route is generally regarded as an alternative means of performance. So the implied expectation that the route would be via Suez is hardly adequate proof of an allocation to the promisee of the risk of closure. In some cases, even an express expectation may not amount to a condition of performance.[5] The doctrine of deviation supports our assumption that parties normally expect performance by the usual and customary route, but it adds nothing beyond this that is probative of an allocation of the risk.[6]

---

the parties expected the usual and customary route would be used. The provisions in no way condition performance upon nonoccurrence of this contingency.

There are two clauses which allegedly demonstrate that time is of importance in this contract. One clause computes the remuneration "in steaming time" for diversions to other countries ordered by the charterer in emergencies. This proves only that the United States wished to reserve power to send the goods to another country. It does not imply in any way that there was a rush about the matter. The other clause concerns demurrage and despatch. The charterer agreed to pay Transatlantic demurrage of $1,200 per day for all time in excess of the period agreed upon for loading and unloading, and Transatlantic was to pay despatch of $600 per day for any saving in time. Of course this provision shows the parties were concerned about time, see GILMORE & BLACK, THE LAW OF ADMIRALTY § 4–8 (1957), but the fact that they arranged so minutely the consequences of any delay or speedup of loading and unloading operates against the argument that they were similarly allocating the risk of delay or speed-up of the voyage.

[5] UNIFORM COMMERCIAL CODE § 2–614(1) provides: "Where without fault of either party * * * the *agreed* manner of delivery * * * becomes commercially impracticable but a commercially reasonable substitute is available, such substitute performance must be tendered and accepted." (Emphasis added.) Compare Mr. Justice Holmes' observation: "You can give any conclusion a logical form. You always can imply a condition in a contract. But why do you imply it? It is because of some belief as to the practice of the community or of a class, or because of some opinion as to policy * * *." Holmes, *The Path of the Law,* 10 HARV.L.REV. 457, 466 (1897).

[6] The deviation doctrine, drawn principally from admiralty insurance practice, implies into all relevant commercial instruments naming the termini of voyages the usual and customary route between those points. 1 ARNOULD, MARINE INSURANCE AND AVERAGE § 376, at 522 (10th ed. 1921). Insurance is cancelled when a ship unreasonably "deviates" from this course, for example by extending a voyage or by putting in at an irregular port, and the shipowner forfeits the protection of clauses of exception which might otherwise have protected him from his common law insurer's liability to cargo. See GILMORE & BLACK, *supra* Note 8, § 2–6, at 59–60. This practice, properly qualified, see *id.* § 3–41, makes good sense, since insurance rates are computed on the basis of the implied course, and deviations in the course increasing the anticipated risk make the insurer's calculations meaningless. ARNOULD, *supra,* § 14, at 26. Thus the route, so far as insurance contracts are concerned, is crucial, whether express or implied. But even here, the implied term is not inflexible. Reasonable deviations do not result in loss of insurance, at least so long as established practice is followed. See Carriage of Goods by Sea Act § 4(4), 49 STAT. 1210, 46 U.S.C. § 1304(4); and discussion of "held covered" clauses in GILMORE & BLACK, *supra,* § 3–41, at 161. Some "deviations" are required. *E.g.,* Hirsch Lumber Co. v. Weyerhaeuser Steamship Co., 2 Cir., 233 F.2d 791, *cert. denied,* 352 U.S. 880, 77 S.Ct. 102, 1 L.Ed.2d 80 (1956). The doctrine's only relevance, therefore, is that it provides additional support for the assumption we willingly make that merchants agreeing to a voyage between two points expect that the usual and customary route between those points will be used. The doctrine provides no evidence of an allocation of the risk of the route's unavailability.

If anything, the circumstances surrounding this contract indicate that the risk of the Canal's closure may be deemed to have been allocated to Transatlantic. We know or may safely assume that the parties were aware, as were most commercial men with interests affected by the Suez situation, see The Eugenia, *supra,* that the Canal might become a dangerous area. No doubt the tension affected freight rates, and it is arguable that the risk of closure became part of the dickered terms. UNIFORM COMMERCIAL CODE § 2–615, comment 8. We do not deem the risk of closure so allocated, however. Foreseeability or even recognition of a risk does not necessarily prove its allocation.[7] Compare UNIFORM COMMERCIAL CODE § 2–615, Comment 1; RESTATEMENT, CONTRACTS § 457 (1932). Parties to a contract are not always able to provide for all the possibilities of which they are aware, sometimes because they cannot agree, often simply because they are too busy. Moreover, that some abnormal risk was contemplated is probative but does not necessarily establish an allocation of the risk of the contingency which actually occurs. In this case, for example, nationalization by Egypt of the Canal Corporation and formation of the Suez Users Group did not necessarily indicate that the Canal would be blocked even if a confrontation resulted.[8] The surrounding circumstances do indicate, however, a willingness by Transatlantic to assume abnormal risks, and this fact should legitimately cause us to judge the impracticability of performance by an alternative route in stricter terms than we would were the contingency unforeseen.

We turn then to the question whether occurrence of the contingency rendered performance commercially impracticable under the circumstances of this case. The goods shipped were not subject to harm from the longer, less temperate Southern route. The vessel and crew were fit to proceed around the Cape.[9] Transatlantic was no less able than the United States to purchase insurance to cover the contingency's occurrence. If anything, it is more reasonable to expect owner-operators of vessels to insure against the hazards of war. They are in the best position to calculate the cost of performance by alternative routes (and therefore to estimate the

---

[7] See Note, *The Fetish of Impossibility in the Law of Contracts,* 53 COLUM.L.REV. 94, 98 n. 23 (1953), suggesting that foreseeability is properly used "as a *factor* probative of assumption of the risk of impossibility." (Emphasis added.)

[8] Sources cited in the briefs indicate formation of the Suez Canal Users Association on October 1, 1956, was viewed in some quarters as an implied threat of force. See N.Y. Times, Oct. 2, 1956, p. 1, col. 1, noting, on the day the charter in this case was executed, that "Britain has declared her freedom to use force as a last resort if peaceful methods fail to achieve a satisfactory settlement." Secretary of State Dulles was able, however, to view the statement as evidence of the canal users' "dedication to a just and peaceful solution." THE SUEZ PROBLEM 369–370 (Department of State Pub. 1956).

[9] The issue of impracticability should no doubt be "an objective determination of whether the promise can reasonably be performed rather than a subjective inquiry into the promisor's capability of performing as agreed." Symposium, *The Uniform Commercial Code and Contract Law: Some Selected Problems,* 105 U.PA.L.REV. 836, 880, 887 (1957). Dealers should not be excused because of less than normal capabilities. But if both parties are aware of a dealer's limited capabilities, no objective determination would be complete without taking into account this fact.

amount of insurance required), and are undoubtedly sensitive to international troubles which uniquely affect the demand for and cost of their services. The only factor operating here in appellant's favor is the added expense, allegedly $43,972.00 above and beyond the contract price of $305,842.92, of extending a 10,000 mile voyage by approximately 3,000 miles. While it may be an overstatement to say that increased cost and difficulty of performance never constitute impracticability, to justify relief there must be more of a variation between expected cost and the cost of performing by an available alternative than is present in this case, where the promisor can legitimately be presumed to have accepted some degree of abnormal risk, and where impracticability is urged on the basis of added expense alone.

We conclude, therefore, as have most other courts considering related issues arising out of the Suez closure, that performance of this contract was not rendered legally impossible. Even if we agreed with appellant, its theory of relief seems untenable. When performance of a contract is deemed impossible it is a nullity. In the case of a charter party involving carriage of goods, the carrier may return to an appropriate port and unload its cargo, The Malcolm Baxter, Jr., 277 U.S. 323, 48 S.Ct. 516, 72 L.Ed. 901 (1928), subject of course to required steps to minimize damages. If the performance rendered has value, recovery in *quantum meruit* for the entire performance is proper. But here Transatlantic has collected its contract price, and now seeks *quantum meruit* relief for the additional expense of the trip around the Cape. If the contract is a nullity, Transatlantic's theory of relief should have been *quantum meruit* for the entire trip, rather than only for the extra expense. Transatlantic attempts to take its profit on the contract, and then force the Government to absorb the cost of the additional voyage.[10] When impracticability without fault occurs, the law seeks an equitable solution, see 6 CORBIN, *supra,* § 1321, and *quantum meruit* is one of its potent devices to achieve this end. There is no interest in casting the entire burden of commercial disaster on one party in order to preserve the other's profit. Apparently the contract price in this case was advantageous enough to deter appellant from taking a stance on damages consistent with its theory of liability. In any event, there is no basis for relief.

Affirmed.

---

[10] The argument that the UNIFORM COMMERCIAL CODE requires the buyer to pay the additional cost of performance by a commercially reasonable substitute was advanced and rejected in Symposium, *supra* Note, [11] 105 U.PA.L.REV. at 884 n. 205. In Dillon v. United States, 156 F.Supp. 719, 140 Ct.Cl. 508 (1957), relief was afforded for some of the cost of delivering hay from a commercially unreasonable distance, but the suit was one in which the plaintiff had suffered losses far in excess of the relief given.

THE OPERA COMPANY OF BOSTON, INC. v. THE WOLF TRAP FOUNDATION FOR THE PERFORMING ARTS, 817 F.2d 1094 (4th Cir. 1987). "The occurrence, as *Transatlantic* puts it, must be unexpected but it does not necessarily have to have been unforeseeable. A requirement of absolute non-foreseeability as a condition to the application of the doctrine would be so logically inconsistent that in effect it would nullify the doctrine. This was recognized by Judge Clark in *L.N. Jackson & Co. v. Royal Norwegian Government,* 177 F.2d 694, 699 (2d Cir.1949), where he said that to require an absolute absence of foreseeability would, if accepted,

> practically destroy the doctrine of supervening impossibility, notwithstanding its present wide and apparently growing popularity. Certainly the death of a promisor, the burning of a ship, the requisitioning of a merchant marine on the outbreak of a war could, and perhaps should, be foreseen. In fact, the more common expression of the rule appears to be in terms which tend to state the burden the other way, e.g., that "the duty of the promisor is discharged, unless a contrary intention has been manifested" or "in the absence of circumstances showing either a contrary intention or contributing fault on the part of the person subject to the duty.

Williston expressed the same objection to such an absolute rule. It said:

> It is frequently said that where an event which causes impossibility "might have been anticipated and guarded against in the contract," one who makes an absolute promise is bound by it unconditionally.
>
> Such a test, however, seems of little value. It has descended in the law from a time when it was more nearly true than it now is, because impossibility was more rarely an excuse. Any kind of impossibility is more or less capable of anticipation. The question is one of degree, and if anticipated, any circumstance whatever may be guarded against by the draftsman of the contract.

18 Williston on Contracts, § 1953, pp. 117–18."

POSNER AND ROSENFIELD, IMPOSSIBILITY AND RELATED DOCTRINES IN CONTRACT LAW: AN ECONOMIC ANALYSIS

6 J.Leg.Stud. 83, 89–91 (1977).

The typical case in which impossibility or some related doctrine is invoked is one where, by reason of an unforeseen or at least unprovided-for event, performance by one of the parties of his obligations under the contract has become so much more costly than he foresaw at the time the contract was made as to be uneconomical (that is, the costs of performance would be greater than the benefits). The performance promised may have been delivery of a particular cargo by a specified delivery date—but the ship is trapped in the Suez Canal because of a war between Israel and Egypt. Or it may have been a piano recital by Gina Bachauer—and she dies between the signing of the contract and the date of the recital. The law could in each case treat the failure to perform as a breach of contract, thereby in effect assigning to the promisor the risk that war, or death, would prevent performance (or render it uneconomical). Alternatively, invoking impossibility or some related notion, the law could treat the failure to perform as excusable and discharge the contract, thereby in effect assigning the risk to the promisee.

From the standpoint of economics—and disregarding, but only momentarily, administrative costs—discharge should be allowed where the promisee is the superior risk bearer; if the promisor is the superior risk bearer, nonperformance should be treated as a breach of contract. "Superior risk bearer" is to be understood here as the party that is the more efficient bearer of the particular risk in question, in the particular circumstances of the transaction. Of course, if the parties have expressly assigned the risk to one of them, there is no occasion to inquire which is the superior risk bearer. The inquiry is merely an aid to interpretation.

A party can be a superior risk bearer for one of two reasons. First, he may be in a better position to prevent the risk from materializing. This resembles the economic criterion for assigning liability in tort cases. * * * Discharge would be inefficient in any case where the promisor could prevent the risk from materializing at a lower cost than the expected cost of the risky event. In such a case efficiency would require that the promisor bear the loss resulting from the occurrence of the event, and hence that occurrence should be treated as precipitating a breach of contract.

But the converse is not necessarily true. It does not necessarily follow from the fact that the promisor could not at any reasonable cost have prevented the risk from materializing that he should be discharged from his contractual obligations. Prevention is only one way of dealing with risk; the other is insurance. The promisor may be the superior insurer. If so, his inability to prevent the risk from materializing should not operate to discharge him from the contract, any more than an insurance company's inability to prevent a fire on the premises of the insured should excuse it from its liability to make good the damage caused by the fire.

PROBLEM 8-5

Transatlantic has asked you to draft a clause protecting it in the future from the necessity of undertaking diversions from its "usual and customary" sea routes. Please draft the clause.

UNIFORM COMMERCIAL CODE § 2–615.

Excuse by Failure of Presupposed Conditions

Except so far as a seller may have assumed a greater obligation and subject to the preceding section on substituted performance:

(a) Delay in delivery or non-delivery in whole or in part by a seller who complies with paragraphs (b) and (c) is not a breach of his duty under a contract of sale if performance as agreed has been made impracticable by the occurrence of a contingency the non-occurrence of which was a basic assumption on which the contract was made or by compliance in good faith with any applicable foreign or domestic governmental regulation or order whether or not it later proves to be invalid.

(b) Where the causes mentioned in paragraph (a) affect only a part of the seller's capacity to perform, he must allocate production and deliveries among his customers but may at his option include regular customers not then under contract as well as his own requirements for further manufacture. He may so allocate in any manner which is fair and reasonable.

(c) The seller must notify the buyer seasonably that there will be delay or non-delivery and, when allocation is required under paragraph (b), of the estimated quota thus made available for the buyer.

CONVENTION ON CONTRACTS FOR THE INTERNATIONAL SALE OF GOODS.

Article 79(1)

(1) A party is not liable for a failure to perform any of his obligations if he proves that the failure was due to an impediment beyond his control and that he could not reasonably be expected to have taken the impediment into account at the time of the conclusion of the contract or to have avoided or overcome it or its consequences.

MISHARA CONSTRUCTION CO. V. TRANSIT-MIXED CONCRETE CORP.

Supreme Judicial Court of Massachusetts, 1974.
365 Mass. 122, 310 N.E.2d 363.

REARDON, JUSTICE.

In this action of contract a verdict was returned for the defendant. The case is here on the plaintiff's exceptions.

The plaintiff Mishara Construction Company, Inc. (Mishara) was the general contractor under contract with the Pittsfield Housing Authority for the construction of Rose Manor, a housing project for the elderly. In September, 1966, the plaintiff negotiated with the defendant Transit-Mixed Concrete Corp. (Transit) for the supplying of ready-mixed concrete to be used on the project. An agreement was reached that Transit would supply all the concrete needed on the project at a price of $13.25 a cubic yard, with deliveries to be made at the times and in the amounts as ordered by Mishara. This agreement was evidenced by a purchase order signed by the parties on September 21, 1966. That purchase order identified the Rose Manor project and indicated that delivery was to be made "[a]s required by Mishara Construction Company." Performance under this contract was satisfactory to both parties until April, 1967. In that month a labor dispute disrupted work on the job site. Although work resumed on June 15, 1967, a picket line was maintained on the site until the completion of the project in 1969. Throughout this period, with very few exceptions, no deliveries of concrete were made by Transit notwithstanding frequent requests by Mishara. After notifying Transit of its intention, Mishara purchased the balance of its concrete requirements elsewhere. Mishara sought in damages the additional cost of concrete incurred by virtue of the higher price of the replacement product, as well as the expenses of locating an alternate source.

The plaintiff's exceptions relate to the introduction of certain evidence and the failure of the trial judge to give certain requested instructions. * * *

* * *

[There was no] error in the refusal to give request 13, that on the evidence the jury "must find that [the] defendant breached its contract with [the] plaintiff by failing to deliver" Mishara's concrete requirements. The principal issue in the case was the defendant's claimed excuse of impossibility of performance. The determination of that issue depended on facts and circumstances which were for the jury to decide. While we suppose one could develop a nice technical argument that impossibility does not nullify a breach but rather provides an excuse for it, to give the instruction requested would surely have misled the jury on the ultimate question of liability. Moreover, the failure to give it was of no detriment to the plaintiff of which it can complain. See Howes v. Grush, 131 Mass. 207 (1881). * * *

The remainder of the plaintiff's exceptions relate to the proffered defense of the impossibility of performance. Objection was made to the introduction of all evidence regarding the existence of a picket line at the job site and the difficulty which Transit did encounter or might have encountered in attempting to make deliveries through that picket line. Furthermore, Mishara requested an instruction that Transit "was required to comply with the contract regardless of picket lines, strikes or labor difficulties."[1] As a result Mishara would have completely withdrawn the question of impossibility resulting from the picket line from the jury. We are asked to decide as matter of law and without reference to individual facts and circumstances that "picket lines, strikes or labor difficulties" provide no excuse for nonperformance by way of impossibility. This is too sweeping a statement of the law and we decline to adopt it.

The excuse of impossibility in contracts for the sale of goods is controlled by the appropriate section of the Uniform Commercial Code, G.L. c. 106, § 2–615. That section sets up two requirements before performance may be excused. First, the performance must have become "impracticable." Second, the impracticability must have been caused "by the occurrence of a contingency the non-occurrence of which was a basic assumption on which the contract was made." This section of the Uniform Commercial Code has not yet been interpreted by this court. Therefore it is appropriate to discuss briefly the significance of these two criteria.

With respect to the requirement that performance must have been impracticable, the official Code comment to the section stresses that the reference is to "commercial impracticability" as opposed to strict impossibility. G.L. c. 106, § 2–615, comments 3–4. This is not a radical departure from the common law of contracts as interpreted by this court. Although a strict rule was originally followed denying any excuse for accident or "inevitable necessity," e.g., Adams v. Nichols, 19 Pick. 275 (1837), it has long been assumed that circumstances drastically increasing the difficulty and expense of the contemplated performance may be within the compass of "impossibility." See Rowe v. Peabody, 207 Mass. 226, 233–234, 93 N.E. 604 (1911) (dictum); Fauci v. Denehy, 332 Mass. 691, 696–697, 127 N.E.2d 477 (1955). By adopting the term "impracticability" rather than "impossibility" the drafters of the Code appear to be in accord with Professor Williston who stated that "the essence of the modern defense of impossibility is that the promised performance was at the making of the contract, or thereafter became, impracticable owing to some extreme or unreasonable difficulty, expense, injury, or loss involved, rather than that it is scientifically or actually impossible." Williston, Contracts (Rev. ed.) § 1931 (1938). See Restatement: Contracts, § 454 (1932); Corbin, Contracts, § 1339 (1962).

The second criterion of the excuse, that the intervening circumstance be one which the parties assumed would not occur, is also familiar to the law of Massachusetts. Baetjer v. New England Alcohol Co., 319 Mass. 592, 600, 66 N.E.2d 798 (1946). Boston Plate & Window Glass Co. v. John

[1] Requests 16 and 17 essentially asked for instructions that in the absence of clauses in the contract to the contrary, the impossibility of performance provides no excuse. This, in effect, requires a charge that no set of circumstances will ever excuse a supplier from performing. Since we conclude in the text that request 15, to the effect that picket lines and labor disputes provide no excuse, is an incorrect statement of the law, it follows a fortiori that these requests were rightly refused.

Bowen Co., Inc., 335 Mass. 697, 699–700, 141 N.E.2d 715 (1957). The rule is essentially aimed at the distribution of certain kinds of risks in the contractual relationship. By directing the inquiry to the time when the contract was first made, we really seek to determine whether the risk of the intervening circumstance was one which the parties may be taken to have assigned between themselves. It is, of course, the very essence of contract that it is directed at the elimination of some risks for each party in exchange for others. Each receives the certainty of price, quantity, and time, and assumes the risk of changing market prices, superior opportunity, or added costs. It is implicit in the doctrine of impossibility (and the companion rule of "frustration of purpose") that certain risks are so unusual and have such severe consequences that they must have been beyond the scope of the assignment of risks inherent in the contract, that is, beyond the agreement made by the parties. To require performance in that case would be to grant the promisee an advantage for which he could not be said to have bargained in making the contract. "The important question is whether an unanticipated circumstance has made performance of the promise vitally different from what should reasonably have been within the contemplation of both parties when they entered into the contract. If so, the risk should not fairly be thrown upon the promisor." Williston, Contracts (Rev. ed.) § 1931 (1938). The emphasis in contracts governed by the Uniform Commercial Code is on the commercial context in which the agreement was made. The question is, given the commercial circumstances in which the parties dealt: Was the contingency which developed one which the parties could reasonably be thought to have foreseen as a real possibility which could affect performance? Was it one of that variety of risks which the parties were tacitly assigning to the promisor by their failure to provide for it explicitly? If it were, performance will be required. If it could not be so considered, performance is excused. The contract cannot be reasonably thought to govern in these circumstances, and the parties are both thrown upon the resources of the open market without the benefit of their contract. See Boston Plate & Window Glass Co. v. John Bowen Co., Inc., *supra,* at 699–700, 141 N.E.2d 715.

With this backdrop, we consider Mishara's contention that a labor dispute which makes performance more difficult never constitutes an excuse for nonperformance. We think it is evident that in some situations a labor dispute would not meet the requirements for impossibility discussed above. A picket line might constitute a mere inconvenience and hardly make performance "impracticable." Likewise, in certain industries with a long record of labor difficulties, the nonoccurrence of strikes and picket lines could not fairly be said to be a basic assumption of the agreement. Certainly, in general, labor disputes cannot be considered extraordinary in the course of modern commerce. See Restatement: Contracts, § 461, illustration 7 (1932). Admitting this, however, we are still far from the proposition implicit in the plaintiff's requests. Much must depend on the facts known to the parties at the time of contracting with respect to the history of and prospects for labor difficulties during the period of performance of the contract, as well as the likely severity of the effect of such disputes on the ability to perform. From these facts it is possible to draw an inference as to whether or not the parties intended performance to be carried out even in the face of the labor difficulty. Where the probability of a labor dispute appears to be practically nil, and where the occurrence of such a dispute provides unusual difficulty, the excuse of impracticability might well be applicable. Thus in discussing the defence of impossibility, then Chief Judge Cardozo noted an excuse would be provided "conceivably in some circumstances by unavoidable strikes." Canadian Industrial Alcohol Co., Ltd. v. Dunbar Molasses Co., 258 N.Y. 194, 198, 179 N.E. 383, 384 (1932). The many variables which may bear on the question in individual cases were canvassed by Professor Williston in Williston, Contracts (Rev. ed.) § 1951A (1938), and he concluded that the trend of the law is toward recognizing strikes as excuses for nonperformance. We agree with the statement of the judge in Badhwar v. Colorado Fuel & Iron Corp., 138 F.Supp. 595, 607 (S.D.N.Y.1955), affd. 245 F.2d 903 (2d Cir.1957), on the same question: "Rather than mechanically apply any fixed rule of law, where the parties themselves have not allocated responsibility, justice is better served by appraising all of the circumstances, the part the various parties played, and thereon determining liability." Since the instructions requested by the plaintiff and the exclusion of the evidence objected to would have precluded such a factual determination, the requests were more properly refused, and the evidence was properly admitted.

Exceptions overruled.

PROBLEM 8-6

Your client, Westinghouse Electric Corp., agreed to build and fuel two Florida Power and Light Company nuclear steam supply systems and to remove the spent fuel. Westinghouse agreed to a contract price fixed for ten years solely by reference to the amount of electricity generated by the systems and independent of its costs. The parties also contemplated that Westinghouse would reprocess the spent fuel, which would permit Westinghouse to recoup between $16 and $19 million over the life of the contract, although the contract expressly required only that Westinghouse remove the spent fuel and "dispose of it as Westinghouse sees fit." After the agreement was reached, a federal government order halted commercial reprocessing, but spent fuel could still be stored in storage racks. Is Westinghouse bound to its agreement with Florida Power?

Consider individually and collectively the import of the following additional facts: (1) At the time of the agreement no commercial reprocessing firm existed, but the government had been encouraging firms to engage in it. (2) If Westinghouse were excused, Florida Power would be forced to shut down its reactors and would incur potential future costs of $1 million per day for replacement power. (3) If forced to perform, Westinghouse would not lose money on the "package deal" of plant and fuel contracts with Florida Power. (4) Westinghouse had insufficient information in computing its costs for the fuel contract. (5) Florida had little knowledge of the nuclear power industry, whereas Westinghouse was knowledgeable. (6) From the outset, Florida sought a fixed-price contract and Westinghouse knew this. What additional information would you elicit?

SECTION SEVEN: FRUSTRATION OF PURPOSE

KRELL V. HENRY

King's Bench, 1903.
2 K.B. 740.

APPEAL from a decision of DARLING J.

The plaintiff, Paul Krell, sued the defendant, C.S. Henry, for 50*l.*, being the balance of a sum of 75*l.*, for which the defendant had agreed to hire a flat at 56A, Pall Mall on the days of June 26 and 27, for the purpose of viewing the processions to be held in connection with the coronation of His Majesty. The defendant denied his liability, and counterclaimed for the return of the sum of 25*l.*, which had been paid as a deposit, on the ground that, the processions not having taken place owing to the serious illness of the King, there had been a total failure of consideration for the contract entered into by him.

The facts, which were not disputed, were as follows. The plaintiff on leaving the country in March, 1902, left instructions with his solicitor to let his suite of chambers at 56A, Pall Mall on such terms and for such period (not exceeding six months) as he thought proper. On June 17, 1902, the defendant noticed an announcement in the windows of the plaintiff's flat to the effect that windows to view the coronation processions were to be let. The defendant interviewed the housekeeper on the subject, when it was pointed out to him what a good view of the processions could be obtained from the premises, and he eventually agreed with the housekeeper to take the suite for the two days in question for a sum of 75*l.*

On June 20 the defendant wrote the following letter to the plaintiff's solicitor:—

> "I am in receipt of yours of the 18th instant, inclosing form of agreement for the suite of chambers on the third floor at 56A, Pall Mall, which I have agreed to take for the two days, the 26th and 27th instant, for the sum of 75*l.* For reasons given you I cannot enter into the agreement, but as arranged over the telephone I

inclose herewith cheque for 25*l.* as deposit, and will thank you to confirm to me that I shall have the entire use of these rooms during the days (not the nights) of the 26th and 27th instant. You may rely that every care will be taken of the premises and their contents. On the 24th inst. I will pay the balance, viz., 50*l.*, to complete the 75*l.* agreed upon."

On the same day the defendant received the following reply from the plaintiff's solicitor:—

"I am in receipt of your letter of to-day's date inclosing cheque for 25*l.* deposit on your agreeing to take Mr. Krell's chambers on the third floor at 56A, Pall Mall for the two days, the 26th and 27th June, and I confirm the agreement that you are to have the entire use of these rooms during the days (but not the nights), the balance, 50*l.*, to be paid to me on Tuesday next the 24th instant."

The processions not having taken place on the days originally appointed, namely, June 26 and 27, the defendant declined to pay the balance of 50*l.* alleged to be due from him under the contract in writing of June 20 constituted by the above two letters. Hence the present action.

Darling J., on August 11, 1902, held, upon the authority of *Taylor v. Caldwell* and *The Moorcock,* that there was an implied condition in the contract that the procession should take place, and gave judgment for the defendant on the claim and counter-claim.

The plaintiff appealed.

* * *

Aug. 11. VAUGHAN WILLIAMS L.J. read the following written judgment. * * * The contract is contained in two letters of June 20 which passed between the defendant and the plaintiff's agent, Mr. Cecil Bisgood. These letters do not mention the coronation, but speak merely of the taking of Mr. Krell's chambers, or, rather, of the use of them, in the daytime of June 26 and 27, for the sum of 75*l.*, 25*l.* then paid, balance 50*l.* to be paid on the 24th. But the affidavits, which by agreement between the parties are to be taken as stating the facts of the case, shew that the plaintiff exhibited on his premises, third floor, 56A, Pall Mall, an announcement to the effect that windows to view the Royal coronation procession were to be let, and that the defendant was induced by that announcement to apply to the housekeeper on the premises, who said that the owner was willing to let the suite of rooms for the purpose of seeing the Royal procession for both days, but not nights, of June 26 and 27.

In my judgment the use of the rooms was let and taken for the purpose of seeing the Royal procession. It was not a demise of the rooms, or even an agreement to let and take the rooms. It is a licence to use rooms for a particular purpose and none other. And in my judgment the taking place of those processions on the days proclaimed along the proclaimed route, which passed 56A, Pall Mall, was regarded by both contracting parties as the foundation of the contract; and I think that it cannot reasonably be supposed to have been in the contemplation of the contracting parties, when the contract was made, that the coronation would not be held on the proclaimed days, or the processions not take place on those days along the proclaimed route; and I think that the words imposing on the defendant the obligation to accept and pay for the use of the rooms for the named days, although general and unconditional, were not used with reference to the possibility of the particular contingency which afterwards occurred.

It was suggested in the course of the argument that if the occurrence, on the proclaimed days, of the coronation and the procession in this case were the foundation of the contract, and if the general words are thereby limited or qualified, so that in the event of the non-occurrence of the coronation and procession along the proclaimed route they would discharge both parties from further performance of the contract, it would follow that if a cabman was engaged to take someone to Epsom on Derby Day at a suitable enhanced price for such a journey, say 10*l.*, both parties to the contract would be discharged in the contingency of the race at Epsom for some reason becoming impossible; but I do not think this follows, for I do not think that in the cab case the happening of the race would be the foundation of the contract. No doubt the purpose of the engager would be to go to see the Derby, and the price would be proportionately high; but the cab had no special qualifications for the purpose which led to the selection of the cab for this particular occasion. Any other cab would have done as well. Moreover, I think that, under the cab contract, the hirer, even if the race went off, could have said, "Drive me to Epsom; I will pay you the agreed sum; you have nothing to do with the purpose for which I hired the cab," and that if the cabman refused he would have been guilty of a breach of contract, there being nothing to qualify his promise to drive the hirer to Epsom on a particular day. Whereas in the case of the coronation, there is not merely the purpose of the hirer to see the coronation procession, but it is the coronation procession and the relative position of the rooms which is the basis of the contract as much for the lessor as the hirer; and I think that if the King, before the coronation day and after the contract, had died, the hirer could not have insisted on having the rooms on the days named. It could not in the cab case be reasonably said that seeing the Derby race was the foundation of the contract, as it was of the licence in this case. Whereas in the present case, where the rooms were offered and taken, by reason of their peculiar suitability from the position of the rooms for a view of the coronation procession, surely the view of the coronation procession was the foundation of the contract, which is a very different thing from the purpose of the man who engaged the cab—namely, to see the race—being held to be the foundation of the contract.

Each case must be judged by its own circumstances. In each case one must ask oneself, first, what, having regard to all the circumstances, was the foundation of the contract? Secondly, was the performance of the contract prevented? Thirdly, was the event which prevented the performance of the contract of such a character that it cannot reasonably be said to have been in the contemplation of the parties at the date of the contract? If all these questions are answered in the affirmative (as I think they should be in this case), I think both parties are discharged from further performance of the contract. I think that the coronation procession was the foundation of this contract, and that the non-happening of it prevented the performance of the contract; and, secondly, I think that the non-happening of the procession, to use the words of Sir James Hannen in *Baily v. De Crespigny,* was an event "of such a character that it cannot reasonably be supposed to have been in the contemplation of the contracting parties when the contract was made, and that they are not to be held bound by general words which, though large enough to include, were not used with reference to the possibility of the particular contingency which afterwards happened."

The test seems to be whether the event which causes the impossibility was or might have been anticipated and guarded against. It seems difficult to say, in a case where both parties anticipate the happening of an event, which anticipation is the foundation of the contract, that either party must be taken to have anticipated, and ought to have guarded against, the event which prevented the performance of the contract. * * * I myself am clearly of opinion that in this case, where we have to ask ourselves whether the object of the contract was frustrated by the non-happening of the coronation and its procession on the days proclaimed, parol evidence is admissible to shew that the subject of the contract was rooms to view the coronation procession, and was so to the knowledge of both parties. When once this is established, I see no difficulty whatever in the case. It is not essential to the application of the principle of *Taylor v. Caldwell* that the direct subject of the contract should perish or fail to be in existence at the date of performance of the contract. It is sufficient if a state of things or condition expressed in the contract and essential to its performance perishes or fails to be in existence at that time. In the present case the condition which fails and prevents the achievement of that which was, in the contemplation of both parties, the foundation of the contract, is not expressly mentioned either as a condition of the contract or the purpose of it; but I think for the reasons which I have given that the principle of *Taylor v. Caldwell* ought to be applied.

This disposes of the plaintiff's claim for 50*l.* unpaid balance of the price agreed to be paid for the use of the rooms. The defendant at one time set up a cross-claim for the return of the 25*l.* he paid at the date of the contract. As that claim is now withdrawn it is unnecessary to say anything about it.

I think this appeal ought to be dismissed.

ROMER L.J. With some doubt I have also come to the conclusion that this case is governed by the principle on which *Taylor v. Caldwell* was decided, and accordingly that the appeal must be dismissed. The doubt I have felt was whether the parties to the contract now before us could be said, under the circumstances, not to have had at all in their contemplation the risk that for some reason or other the coronation processions might not take place on the days fixed, or, if the processions took place, might not pass so as to be capable of being viewed from the rooms mentioned in the contract; and whether, under this contract, that risk was not undertaken by the defendant. But on the question of fact as to what was in the contemplation of the parties at the time, I do not think it right to differ from the conclusion arrived at by Vaughan Williams L.J., and (as I gather) also arrived at by my brother Stirling. This being so, I concur in the conclusions arrived at by Vaughan Williams L.J. in his judgment, and I do not desire to add anything to what he has said so fully and completely.

STIRLING L.J. said he had had an opportunity of reading the judgment delivered by Vaughan Williams L.J., with which he entirely agreed. Though the case was one of very great difficulty, he thought it came within the principle of *Taylor v. Caldwell.*

Appeal dismissed.

Krell? and Henry? in front of 56A Pall Mall.

NOTE: THE FRUSTRATION OF PURPOSE DEFENSE SOMETIMES WORKS!

From: Kate Young
Sent: May 7, 2015, at 5:41 PM
To: Robert Hillman
Subject: at long last, your Beatles concert story is being put to use

Dear Dean Hillman,

I just wanted to let you know that your story about attending a Beatles concert and not being able to hear "a note of music" over the screams of the enthralled girls came to mind as I was asked to request a refund from Ticketmaster for One Direction concert tickets purchased before Zayn Malik departed the band. I have just put to paper my best "frustration of purpose" argument, though I hold no greater hope than you did of getting a refund. Nonetheless, the memory made me smile and I wanted to let you know I'm putting my year in your contracts class and my summer as your research assistant to good use. Hope all is well with you.

From: Robert A. Hillman
Sent: Friday, May 08, 2015 4:32 AM
To: Kate Young
Subject: Re: at long last, your Beatles concert story is being put to use

Hi Kate. Very nice to hear from you. Good luck with your frustration of purpose argument, but I agree it's a longshot. Still, a great classroom hypothetical!

All is well here, and I hope you're enjoying your career.

From: Kate Young
Sent: On June 9, 2015, at 6:19 PM
To: Robert Hillman
Subject: at long last, your Beatles concert story is being put to use

I'm happy to report that I just heard back from TicketMaster, which is fully refunding my client's ticket purchase price. Trying to not be shocked. Feel free to share with your students. Might give you a chance to modernize your Beatles story, though that's hard to touch. What a classic that was!

PROBLEM 8-7

On March 15, 2006, Jenson entered a two-year lease of a tract of 700 acres in Fremont County, Iowa, with lessor Haynes. The parties agreed to semi-annual rent of $52,600. The first installment was paid on March 15, 2006, but in November, when the next installment was due, Jenson refused to pay. He claimed that farming of the land was "frustrated" by "unusual, sudden, violent and extraordinary floods of the East Nishnabotna River." Assume that the river had flooded the farm land for much of the summer of 2006, substantially impairing the prospect of cultivating crops on the leased land. Assume further that crop failures from causes such as excess moisture, drought and insect infestation are quite common in Iowa, but that the lease was silent on these problems. Evaluate Jenson's defense. What further facts do you need? If Jenson sought your advice before entering the lease, what would you have told him?

DOWNING v. STILES, 635 P.2d 808 (Wyo.1981). [Plaintiffs sold their half interest in the "Maverick Recreation Center," a restaurant, to their partner defendant, Stiles. Stiles gave plaintiffs a promissory note for $25,000 to pay for the interest in the restaurant. Much of Maverick's business resulted from patronage by customers of a bar in the same building. Six or seven months after the bar ceased doing business, Stiles stopped making installment payments to the plaintiffs on the purchase price of the restaurant. A month later, the building burned down. The trial court, in a non-jury trial, found in favor of Stiles based on commercial frustration in that Maverick "was dependent on the business with Rustler Bar." Held, reversed.]

ROONEY, JUSTICE.

In this case, Stiles did not contend that the supervening event was the fire. The discontinuance of the Rustler Bar business was the event designated as supervening. The contract was partly executory, the event occurred subsequent to the making of the contract, and appellants had not agreed, expressly or impliedly, to perform in spite of the occurrence of the event. Although subject to considerable dispute, it may even be said that the non-occurrence of the event was a basic assumption on which the contract was made. But the evidence does not establish the continuation of Rustler Bar's business as the principal purpose for which the contract was made, and, therefore, that the frustration was substantial. Certainly, the frustration was not "total or nearly total."

The principal purpose of the purchase was to carry on a restaurant business. The fact is that such restaurant business was continued to be carried on for six or seven months after the Rustler Bar ceased doing business. It was not until just prior to the fire that Stiles refused to make payment under the contract. This fact reflects the recognition that one of the risks assumed by Stiles under the contract was the decrease and discontinuance of Rustler Bar's business. Because of the lease, Stiles could not be evicted. But Stiles had not sought any provision in the agreement whereby Rustler Bar was bound to use Stiles for its food service. If such were the principal purpose of the purchase agreement between Stiles and appellants, assurance of such should have been secured along with the lease. And such assurance should designate the extent of such service. For otherwise, where is the line drawn? Can Stiles be discharged from performance of her contract with appellants when service to Rustler Bar's customers falls off 10%? or 25%? or 90%? In the language of Comment *a* to § 285, Restatement, Contracts 2d, supra:

> * * * It is not enough that the transaction has become less profitable for the affected party or even that he will sustain a loss. The frustration must be so severe that it is not fairly to be regarded as within the risks that he assumed under the contract. * * *

The circumstances of this case are similar to Illustration 7 to [Section 265] of the Restatement [Second]:

> 7. A leases a gasoline station to B. A change in traffic regulations so reduces B's business that he is unable to operate the station except at a substantial loss. B refuses to make further payments of rent. If B can still operate the station, even though at some loss, his principal purpose of operating a gasoline station is not substantially frustrated. B's duty to pay rent is not discharged, and B is liable to A for breach of contract. The result would be the same if the loss were caused by a governmental regulation rationing gasoline or a termination of the franchise under which B obtained gasoline.

* * *

Accordingly, it was error to apply the doctrine of commercial frustration to the circumstances of this case.

SMITH v. ROBERTS, 54 Ill.App.3d 910, 12 Ill.Dec. 648, 370 N.E.2d 271 (1977).

MILLS, JUSTICE.

We have here a lease.

And with it we have the doctrine of commercial frustration.

The trial judge held that the doctrine applied and that the lease was terminated thereby.

He was right. We affirm.

The Smiths and Roberts Brothers entered into a lease agreement for the rental of the first floor and basement of property located in Springfield at 111–113 North Sixth Street. Roberts Brothers was already operating a men's clothing store next to the leased premises and intended to make an opening through their east wall and Smith's west wall in order to establish a department which would be called the Gas Light Room. Thereafter, the main store building of Roberts Brothers was completely destroyed by fire. Questions concerning the rights and liabilities of the parties under the lease were raised as a result of that conflagration and those questions then ripened into litigation.

After Roberts Brothers failed to reoccupy the leased premises—which suffered only smoke damage—the Smiths filed suit for breach of the lease. * * * The trial court found that the lease had been terminated because the destruction of Roberts Brothers' main store excused performance on its part. * * *

We concur with the trial judge and affirm.

* * *

At issue is the doctrine of *commercial frustration.*

* * *

The doctrine of commercial frustration is not to be applied liberally. (*Greenlee Foundries v. Kussel* (1973), 13 Ill.App.3d 611, 301 N.E.2d 106.) However, the defense of commercial frustration is a viable doctrine in Illinois and will be applied when the defendant has satisfied two rigorous tests: (1) the frustrating event was not reasonably foreseeable; and (2) the value of counterperformance by the lessee had been totally or nearly totally destroyed by the frustrating cause. *Greenlee, citing Lloyd v. Murphy* (1944), 25 Cal.2d 48, 153 P.2d 47.

The factual circumstances here satisfy these stringent tests. First, although it might be foreseeable that the main Roberts Brothers' store would be destroyed and the leased premises would remain intact, it is a remote contingency to provide for in a lease. The parties were, in fact, diligent enough to put a catastrophe clause in the lease concerning destruction of the *leased* premises. We find that their failure to include such a clause as to Roberts Brothers' main store was not due to a lack of diligence since such a contingency was not reasonably foreseeable.

The second horn of the two-prong test is also satisfied—the value of the Smith counterperformance was totally—or nearly totally—destroyed. Although it would be physically possible to operate the leased premises as a separate entity, testimony revealed that operations would have to be changed drastically in order to make the premises self-sufficient. Furthermore, the record clearly demonstrates that the leased premises were never intended to be autonomous. Therefore, the trial court's finding that the existence of the main store was an implied condition of the contract between the parties and that its destruction frustrated the lease is an accurate interpretation of the lease. The court's finding results in the fairest disposition of the parties' respective interests.

* * *

Affirmed.

PROBLEM 8-8

You represent Alvin Parker, a 37 year-old bachelor, who believed his marriage prospects would improve if he took dancing lessons. He contracted for 2,734 hours of lessons for which he paid over $24,000 in advance. The contract signed by Parker contained the following clause:

> NON-CANCELLABLE * * * CONTRACT * * * I UNDERSTAND THAT NO REFUNDS WILL BE MADE UNDER THE TERMS OF THIS CONTRACT.

A few weeks after signing this agreement Parker was severely injured in an auto accident rendering him incapable of continuing his lessons. Can Parker get his money back? If Parker had asked you to review the agreement before signing, what would you have recommended?

SECTION EIGHT: FAILURE OF CONDITION, MATERIAL BREACH, AND THE LIKE— A BRIEF RETROSPECT

Grounds of rightful cessation include failure of a condition precedent to a party's duty to perform, material breach, anticipatory repudiation, and prospective inability to perform (all studied in Chapter Seven). You should review the specific requirements of each of these grounds of cessation and compare them with those studied in this chapter. The close kinship of these grounds of cessation and the excuse doctrines studied in this chapter should now be apparent.

In light of all the grounds of cessation studied earlier or for the first time in this chapter, some basic questions arise. Which ground or grounds seem most freely available? Which are least available? Which can a party effectively protect against at the planning stage?

SECTION NINE: REMEDIES AFTER A FINDING OF MISTAKE, IMPOSSIBILITY, IMPRACTICABILITY, OR FRUSTRATION

If a promisor is excused from performance based on mistake, impossibility, impracticability, or frustration, the promisee cannot assert a breach of contract and recover lost expectancy damages. Nevertheless, that party may have conferred a benefit on the excused promisor and thus may be entitled to recover for unjust enrichment. Or the promisee may have relied on the agreement before a court determined it was not enforceable and thus seek reliance damages. Although this chapter has already considered some remedial implications of cessation, we have reserved this section for a more unified look at the remedies question.

COMMENT, APPORTIONING LOSS AFTER DISCHARGE OF A BURDENSOME CONTRACT: A STATUTORY SOLUTION

69 Yale L.J. 1054, 1056–57 (1960).

A court which has discharged full performance of a contract can adopt five general approaches to the treatment of loss. (1) Conditions may be left as they are at the time of discharge, so that a party who has sustained any type of loss must bear it and a party who has gained any benefit may keep it. (2) A party may be required to disgorge benefit accruing to him from reliance expenditures made by the other. Under this "restitutionary" approach, non-recoverable reliance expenses not benefiting another party remain losses to the party incurring the expense. (3) A party may be allowed to set off some or all of the losses he has suffered against the value of any benefit received from the performance of the other party. Losses exceeding the value of any benefit received are sustained by the party who has suffered them. To the extent that losses are less than or equal to the value of benefit received, this approach allows the court equitably to divide losses between the parties. (4) All or some of the losses may be divided between the parties without regard to any benefit either or both may or may not have received. This approach allows the court equitably to apportion loss without the inhibition imposed by a requirement that loss be set off against correlative benefit. (5) The court may adjust contractual obligations of the parties in order to minimize the total loss of both; new obligations would be substituted for the original ones and enforced as if they were the terms of the contract. Loss remaining after performance of the modified obligations could then be apportioned.

Selection of the most appropriate method of treating losses suffered by parties to a discharged contract depends upon the decisionmaker's concepts of fairness and is intimately related to the fact of discharge and the circumstances which give rise to it.

SIEGEL v. EATON & PRINCE CO., 165 Ill. 550, 557–58, 46 N.E. 449, 451 (1896). "We think the law is, that where a contract is entered into with reference to the existence of a particular thing, and that thing is destroyed before the time for the performance of the contract, without the fault of either party, both parties are excused from performing the contract, but neither is entitled to recover anything for a part performance thereof."

FACTO V. PANTAGIS

Superior Court of New Jersey, 2007.
390 N.J.Super. 227, 915 A.2d 59.

The opinion of the court was delivered by SKILLMAN, P.J.A.D.

This is a breach of contract action arising out of the cancellation of a wedding reception due to a power failure.

Plaintiffs contracted with defendant Snuffy Pantagis Ent., Inc., t/a Pantagis Renaissance, a banquet hall in Scotch Plains, for a wedding reception for 150 people, to be held between 6 p.m. and 11 p.m. on Saturday, August 3, 2002. The total contract price was $10,578, all of which was to be paid in advance. The contract contained a *force majeure* clause, which stated: "Snuffy's will be excused from performance under this contract if it is prevented from doing so by an act of God (e.g., flood, power failure, etc.), or other unforeseen events or circumstances."

Less than forty-five minutes after the reception began, there was a power failure in the area where the Pantagis Renaissance is located. At the time, plaintiffs were in an upstairs room with the bridal party, and their guests were downstairs being served alcoholic beverages and hors d'oeuvres. The power failure caused all the lights, except emergency lights, to go out and the air conditioning system to shut off. In addition, the band plaintiffs had hired for the reception refused to play without lights or the electricity required to operate their instruments, and the lack of lighting impeded the wedding photographer and videographer from taking pictures.

On the day of the reception, the temperature was in the upper 80s or low 90s and the humidity was high. As a result, plaintiffs and their guests became extremely uncomfortable within a short time after the power failure. According to plaintiffs, some of the guests resorted to pouring water over their heads to keep cool.

When it became evident that electricity would not be restored quickly, the manager of the Pantagis Renaissance offered to reschedule the reception. However, many of plaintiffs' guests had traveled a substantial distance to attend the wedding and would not have been able to return on another date. Therefore, plaintiffs declined the offer.

There was some dispute regarding the services provided after the power failure. Plaintiffs testified that the Pantagis Renaissance stopped serving alcoholic beverages around 7:30 p.m. and that the only food it served in addition to hors d'oeuvres was salad. However, the banquet hall's general manager testified that the facility continued to serve alcoholic beverages until after 9 p.m. and that it served plaintiffs and their guests salad and pasta and started to serve them dinner.

Shortly after 9 p.m., there was some kind of altercation between one of plaintiffs' guests and an employee of the Pantagis Renaissance. As a result, the banquet hall called the police, who arrived around 9:30 p.m. By this time, the batteries operating the emergency lights had begun to run out of power, and the only illumination was provided by candelabras on the tables. Therefore, the manager of the Pantagis Renaissance asked the police to evacuate the facility, which was then occupied not only by plaintiffs and their guests but also the attendees at four other wedding receptions.

Plaintiffs subsequently brought this breach of contract action seeking recovery of the $10,578 they prepaid for the wedding reception plus the $6,000 paid to the band, $3,810 paid to the wedding photographer and $3,242.09 paid to the videographer. Plaintiffs' complaint also asserted a negligence claim.

The case was tried in a half-day bench trial. The trial court concluded in a brief oral opinion that plaintiffs' breach of contract claim was barred by the *force majeure* clause of the contract because the power failure was an "unusual extraordinary unexpected circumstance" that could not be avoided by "reasonable human foresight." The court dismissed plaintiffs' negligence claim on the ground there was no evidence the Pantagis Renaissance was responsible for the power failure or failed to take reasonable measures to respond to this unforeseen circumstance. Accordingly, the court entered judgment dismissing plaintiffs' complaint.

On appeal, plaintiffs challenge the dismissal of both their negligence and contract claims. Plaintiffs' arguments in support of their negligence claim are clearly without merit and do not warrant extended discussion. *R.* 2:11–3(e)(1)(E). Plaintiffs failed to present any evidence that could support a finding that defendants were negligent. Moreover, even if defendants had been negligent, their liability for failure to perform the contract would still be governed solely by the law of contracts. * * *

Plaintiffs' contract claim presents more difficult issues. We agree with the trial court's conclusion that the power failure relieved the banquet hall of the obligation to provide plaintiffs with a wedding reception. Therefore, the banquet hall's failure to perform the contract due to the absence of electricity did not constitute a breach. But even though there was no breach, the banquet hall's inability to perform the contract also relieved plaintiffs of their obligation to pay the contract price. Consequently, plaintiffs are entitled to recovery of the $10,578 they prepaid the banquet hall, less the value of the services they did receive.

Even if a contract does not expressly provide that a party will be relieved of the duty to perform if an unforeseen condition arises that makes performance impracticable, "a court may relieve him of that duty if performance has unexpectedly become impracticable as a result of a supervening event." Restatement (Second) of Contracts § 261 cmt. a (1981) * * *.

A *force majeure* clause, such as contained in the Pantagis Renaissance contract, provides a means by which the parties may anticipate in advance a condition that will make performance impracticable. *See* 8 *Corbin on Contracts* § 31.4 (Perillo rev. 1999). Such a clause conditions a party's duty to perform upon the non-occurrence of some event beyond its control and serious enough to interfere materially with performance. *Ibid.*

* * *

The *force majeure* clause in the Pantagis Renaissance contract provided: "Snuffy's will be excused from performance under this contract if it is prevented from doing so by an act of God (e.g., flood, power failure, etc.), or other unforeseen events or circumstances." Thus, the contract specifically identified a "power failure" as one of the circumstances that would excuse the Pantagis Renaissance's performance. We do not attribute any significance to the fact the *force majeure* clause refers to a power failure as an example of an "act of God." This term has been construed to refer not just to natural events such as storms but to "comprehend[ ] all misfortunes and accidents arising from inevitable necessity which human prudence could not foresee or prevent[.] *Meyer Bros. Hay & Grain Co. v. Nat'l Malting Co.*, 124 *N.J.L.* 321, 323, 11 A.2d 840 (Sup.Ct.1940); *see also* 14 *Corbin, supra,* § 74.4 (noting that "[t]he kinds of impossibility that [excuse performance under a contract] in many instances are caused by human beings, although the court might still refer to the event as an 'act of God.' "). Furthermore, the *force majeure* clause in the Pantagis Renaissance contract excuses performance not only for "acts of God" but also "other unforeseen events or circumstances." Consequently, even if a power failure caused by circumstances other than a natural event were not considered to be an "act of God," it still would constitute an unforeseen event or circumstance that would excuse performance.

The fact that a power failure is not absolutely unforeseeable during the hot summer months does not preclude relief from the obligation to perform. Indeed, even in the absence of a *force majeure* clause, absolute unforeseeability of a condition is not a prerequisite to the defense of impracticability. *See Opera Co. of Boston, supra,* 817 F.2d at 1100–01. The party seeking to be relieved of the duty to perform only needs to show that "the 'destruction, or * * * deterioration' of a 'specific thing necessary for the performance' of the contract 'makes performance impracticable.' " *Id.* at 1100 (quoting *Restatement (Second) of Contracts* § 263 (1981)). In this case, the Pantagis Renaissance sought to eliminate any possible doubt that the availability of electricity was a "specific thing necessary" for the wedding reception by specifically referring to a "power failure" as an example of an "act of God" that would excuse performance.

It is also clear that the Pantagis Renaissance was "prevented from" substantial performance of the contract. The power failure began less than forty-five minutes after the start of the reception and continued until after it was scheduled to end. The lack of electricity prevented the band from playing, impeded the taking of pictures by the photographer and videographer and made it difficult for guests to see inside the banquet hall. Most significantly, the shutdown of the air conditioning system made it unbearably hot shortly after the power failure began. It is also undisputed that the power failure was an area-wide event that was beyond the Pantagis Renaissance's control. These are precisely the kind of circumstances under which the parties agreed, by inclusion of the *force majeure* clause, that the Pantagis Renaissance would be excused from performance. Therefore, the trial court correctly concluded that defendants did not breach the contract.

However, the court erred in concluding that because defendants did not breach the contract, plaintiffs are not entitled to recover the money they prepaid for the wedding reception. Where one party to a contract is excused from performance as a result of an unforeseen event that makes performance impracticable, the other party is also generally excused from performance. *Restatement (Second) of Contracts* §§ 237, 239, 267 (1981). As explained in *Corbin:*

> A promisor should not be compelled to give something for nothing. The parties agreed upon an exchange of performances, and an exchange cannot now take place. Even if not stated in express terms, the promisor's duty is constructively conditional on the return performance by the promisee. Even though the nonperforming promissee is not in default because the impossibility doctrine discharges the duty, it cannot demand something for nothing from the other party.

[14 *Corbin, supra,* § 78.2.]

The same rule applies if a party to a contract is excused from performance by a *force majeure* clause that expressly sets forth certain categories of unforeseen events that will render performance impracticable. *See* 8 *Corbin, supra,* § 31.4 at 62. Therefore, the power failure that relieved the Pantagis Renaissance of the obligation to furnish plaintiffs with a wedding reception also relieved plaintiffs of the obligation to pay the contract price for the reception.

Nevertheless, since the Pantagis Renaissance partially performed the contract by starting the reception before the power failure, it is entitled, under principles of quantum meruit, to recover the value of the services it provided to plaintiffs. *See Shapiro v. Solomon,* 42 *N.J.Super.* 377, 383, 126 A.2d 654 (App.Div.1956) (noting that "where an express contract for work or services is abortive for * * * impossibility, or invalidity for other reasons, the plaintiff not being at fault * * * may have recovery for the value of his services[.]"); *see also Restatement (Second) of Contracts* § 272 (1981). The measure of damages is the benefit conferred upon the party against whom the quantum meruit claim is asserted. * * *

Accordingly, the final judgment dismissing plaintiffs' complaint is reversed and the case is remanded to the trial court for further proceedings in conformity with this opinion.

ALBRE MARBLE AND TILE CO. V. JOHN BOWEN CO.

Supreme Judicial Court of Massachusetts, 1959.
338 Mass. 394, 155 N.E.2d 437.

[Plaintiff agreed to supply labor and materials to defendant general contractor of a hospital building in Boston. The general contract with the state of Massachusetts was declared invalid because of irregularities in the contractor's bid and when, in counts 1 and 2 of its complaint, plaintiff brought an action for breach of two subcontracts, the court affirmed an "immediate entry of judgment" in favor of defendant on the grounds of impossibility. The plaintiff also sought in counts 3 and 4 of its complaint, on a quantum meruit theory, recovery for work and labor furnished the defendant. "Immediate judgment" was also in favor of defendant on this theory and plaintiff appealed.]

SPALDING, JUSTICE.

* * *

We turn now to counts 3 and 4 by which the plaintiff seeks a recovery for the fair value of work and labor furnished to the defendant prior to the termination of the general contract. The plaintiff seeks recovery in count 3 for "preparation of samples, shop drawings, tests and affidavits" in connection with the tile work; in count 4 recovery for similar work in connection with the marble contract is sought.

The defendant in its affidavit maintains that the tile and marble work to be furnished by the plaintiff could not have been done until late in the construction process; that no tile or marble was actually installed in the building; and that the expenses incurred by the plaintiff prior to the time the general contract was declared invalid consisted solely of expenditures in preparation for performance. Relying on the decision in Young v. Chicopee, 186 Mass. 518, 72 N.E. 63, the defendant maintains that where a building contract has been rendered impossible of performance a plaintiff may not recover for expenses incurred in preparation for performance, but may recover only for the labor and materials "wrought into" the structure. Therefore, the defendant says, the plaintiff should take nothing here.

The plaintiff places its reliance upon a clause appearing in both contracts which provides in part: "It is agreed you [the plaintiff] will furnish and submit all necessary or required samples, shop drawings, tests, affidavits, etc., for approval, all as ordered or specified * * *." The plaintiff in effect concedes that no labor or materials were actually [wrought] into the structure, but argues that the contract provision quoted above placed its preparatory efforts under the supervision of the defendant, and that this circumstance removes this case from the ambit of those decisions which apply the "wrought-in" principle.

* * *

The problem of allocating losses where a building contract has been rendered impossible of performance by a supervening act not chargeable to either party is a vexed one. In situations where the part performance of one party measurably exceeds that of the other the tendency has been to allow recovery for the fair value for work done in the actual performance of the contract and to deny recovery for expenditures made in reliance upon the contract or in preparing to perform. This principle has sometimes been expressed in terms of "benefit" or "lack of benefit." In other words, recovery may be had only for those expenditures which, but for the supervening act, would have enured to the benefit of the defendant as contemplated by the contract. See, e.g. Young v. Chicopee, 186 Mass. 518, 520, 72 N.E. 63. The "wrought-in" principle applied in building contract cases is merely a variant of this principle. It has long been recognized that this theory is unworkable if the concept of benefit is applied literally. In M. Ahern Co. v. John Bowen Co. Inc., 334 Mass. 36, 41, 133 N.E.2d 484, 487, we quoted with approval the statement of Professor Williston that "It is enough that the defendant has actually received in part performance of the contract something for which when completed he had agreed to pay a price." Williston on Contracts (Rev. ed.) § 1976.

Although the matter of denial of reliance expenditures in impossibility situations seems to have been discussed but little in judicial opinions, it has, however, been the subject of critical comment by scholars. See Fuller and Perdue, The Reliance Interest in Contract Damages, 46 Yale L.J. 52, 373, 379–383. Note, 46 Mich.L.Rev. 401. In England the recent frustrated contracts legislation provides that the court may grant recovery for expenditures in reliance on the contract or in preparation to perform it where it appears "*just to do so having regard to all the circumstances of the case*" (emphasis supplied). 6 & 7 George VI, c. 40.

We are of the opinion that the plaintiff here may recover for those expenditures made pursuant to the specific request of the defendant as set forth in the contract clause quoted above. A combination of factors peculiar to this case justifies such a holding without laying down the broader principle that in every case recovery may be had for payments made or obligations reasonably incurred in preparation for performance of a contract where further performance is rendered impossible without fault by either party. See Boston Plate & Window Glass Co. v. John Bowen Co. Inc., 335 Mass. 697, 702, 141 N.E.2d 715.

The factors which determine the holding here are these: First, this is not a case of mere impossibility by reason of a supervening act. The opinion of this court in M. Ahern Co. v. John Bowen Co. Inc., 334 Mass. 36, 133 N.E.2d 484, points out that the defendant's involvement in creating the impossibility [by submitting a bid that was unlawful] was greater than that of its subcontractors. The facts regarding the defendant's conduct are set forth in that opinion and need not be restated. Although the defendant's conduct was not so culpable as to render it liable for breach of contract (Boston Plate & Window Glass Co. v. John Bowen Co. Inc., 335 Mass. 697, 141 N.E.2d 715), nevertheless, it was a contributing factor to a loss sustained by the plaintiff which as between the plaintiff and the defendant the latter ought to bear to the extent herein permitted.

We attach significance to the clause in the contract, which was prepared by the defendant, specifically requesting the plaintiff to submit samples, shop drawings, tests, affidavits, etc., to the defendant. This is not a case in which all efforts in preparation for performance were solely within the discretion and control of the subcontractor. * * *

Moreover, the acts requested here by their very nature could not be "wrought into" the structure. * * *

* * *

We hold that the damages to be assessed are limited solely to the fair value of those acts done in conformity with the specific request of the defendant as contained in the contract. Expenses incurred prior to the execution of the contract, such as those arising out of preparing the plaintiff's bid, are not to be considered.

The plaintiff's exceptions as to counts 1 and 2 are overruled and are sustained as to counts 3 and 4; as to those counts the case is remanded to the Superior Court for further proceedings in conformity with this opinion. The appeal is dismissed.

So ordered.

RESTATEMENT (SECOND) OF CONTRACTS § 158.

Relief Including Restitution

(1) In any case governed by the rules stated in this Chapter [Mistake], either party may have a claim for relief including restitution * * *.

(2) In any case governed by the rules stated in this Chapter, if those rules together with the rules stated in Chapter 16 [Remedies] will not avoid injustice, the court may grant relief on such terms as justice requires including protection of the parties' reliance interests.

RESTATEMENT (SECOND) OF CONTRACTS § 272.

Relief Including Restitution

(1) In any case governed by the rules stated in this Chapter [Impracticability and Frustration], either party may have a claim for relief including restitution * * *.

(2) In any case governed by the rules stated in the Chapter, if those rules together with the rules stated in Chapter 16 [Remedies] will not avoid injustice, the court may grant relief on such terms as justice requires including protection of the parties' reliance interests.

PERILLO, RESTITUTION IN THE SECOND RESTATEMENT OF CONTRACTS

81 Colum.L.Rev. 37, 40 (1981).

Sections 158 and 272 of the *Restatement (Second)* were amended in 1979 to provide that where an obligation has been discharged or a contract avoided for impracticability, frustration, mistake, or the like, the court may grant, instead of or in addition to restitution, "relief on such terms as justice requires including protection of the parties' reliance interests."

Reliance has traditionally been linked to the doctrine of promissory estoppel, which renders binding a promise that induces foreseeable action or forebearance to the promisee's detriment, notwithstanding the absence of consideration or of other requirements for an enforceable promise. In each of the instances in which the *Restatement (Second)* engages promissory estoppel, the promisee's reliance interest is protected by enforcement of an otherwise defective contract against a party in breach. On the other hand, when a contract is discharged or avoided for impracticability, frustration, or mistake, there is no enforceable contract; no party is in breach. Heretofore, absent tortious conduct, the only common law action that was permitted in such circumstances was the quasi-contractual action of restitution—an action for reliance was unavailable. However, under the new formulation of sections 158 and 272, when a contract fails for impracticability, frustration, or mistake, an action for reliance is permitted. Although there is clearly some relationship between this action and the concept of promissory estoppel, the degree of kinship is unclear. If a new kind of action based solely on reliance is to be created, it should be given an analytic and procedural framework.

HUDEC, RESTATING THE "RELIANCE INTEREST"

67 Cornell L.Rev. 704, 715–16 (1982).

In what sense is the remedy of sections 158 and 272 different from contract liability and the more familiar forms of reliance liability (*e.g.*, section[ ] 90 * * *)? The distinction does not lie in the nature of the conduct that gives rise to liability. Sections 158 and 272 apply to parties who have made contracts, or other promises that are binding due to reliance. The conduct that gives rise to sections 158 and 272 liability is thus the same promise-making that triggers contract and other reliance liability.

The difference is that sections 158 and 272 have recognized additional obligations arising from the same conduct. Both contract liability and the more familiar reliance liability of [section] 90 * * * protect the promisee by imposing an obligation upon the promisor to perform. Breach of the duty of performance is the "wrong," and the harm to be compensated is the loss caused by that wrong. Sections 158 and 272 go beyond this and make promisors liable for some reliance losses that have not been caused by wrongful nonperformance, including some that occur because the promisee is unable to perform. It is difficult to be precise about the basis and the exact dimensions of this added liability. The justification is usually stated in terms of overall equities, and several different and even contradictory theories of justification may be involved.

The most distinctive theory of liability in this area would be a loss sharing theory which asserts that the parties to a contract are participants in a common venture, and so should bear common responsibility for losses caused by unforeseen disasters for which neither party is to blame. If one thinks about the basis of such a theory, it is evident that the *conduct* being relied upon to justify liability (for at least fifty percent, anyway), is no more than the ordinary promise-making behavior that began the contract venture. The liability does not depend on any further duty to do or not do anything. It is simply an insurance-type responsibility for disaster losses, resting on the reliance-inducing promise alone.

NOTE:
JUDICIAL REFORMATION

Judicial reformation of disrupted contracts is not uncommon. For example, a court may excuse only part of a promised performance and enforce the remainder. Professor Dawson set forth the following case: "A public accountant * * * sells for a lump sum ($30,000) his business assets, including accounts receivable, with an undertaking on his part to remain active for two years as an associate in that office. The seller dies not quite two months later. Since he is excused and the parties have 'separately agreed on' a contract price for the assets transferred ($4,682.20), this is the sum the seller's representative can recover."[b] To cite another example, courts also unhesitatingly reform agreements for the sale of land where the parties err as to the quantity of land sold. And in Chapter Five, we suggested that the judicial response to the Covid-

[b] Dawson, Judicial Revision of Frustrated Contracts: The United States, 64 B.U.L.Rev. 1, 7 (1984), citing Mullen v. Wafer, 252 Ark. 541, 480 S.W.2d 332 (1972).

19 pandemic of 2020 and the millions of disrupted contracts that resulted may be judicial reformation of the contracts on public policy grounds.

Some forms of court reformation are controversial. For example, in Aluminum Co. of America v. Essex Group, 499 F.Supp. 53 (W.D.Pa.1980), the parties adopted the Wholesale Price Index—Industrial Commodities (WPI) as a measure for adjusting certain production charges of Alcoa in processing aluminum pursuant to a long-term contract with Essex. The WPI did not reflect unexpected cost increases caused by inflation in oil prices and pollution controls and Alcoa stood to lose more than $75 million under the contract. The court agreed with Alcoa that "the shared objectives of the parties with respect to the use of the WPI have been completely and totally frustrated * * *." The court therefore reformed the contract according to a formula the court concocted to allow Alcoa a profit of "one cent per pound of Aluminum," subject to an already agreed contractual ceiling.

The excerpt that follows describes the Alcoa case's reception in some quarters.

HILLMAN, MAYBE DICK SPEIDEL WAS RIGHT ABOUT COURT ADJUSTMENT

46 San Diego L. Rev. 595, 595, 598–99, 602, 603 (2009).

A. Judicial Responses

Most courts have exhibited lots of skepticism about the ALCOA case. But much of the criticism has focused on the court's determination that ALCOA did not assume the risk of a rise in costs of the magnitude it had experienced, not on the court's decision to adjust the contract assuming some relief was in order. And even on the former issue, a few courts have cited the decision favorably, or have recognized that the risk of unanticipated events is not always allocated to the promisor—although these courts have not found the ALCOA court's line of reasoning applicable to their particular facts.

A few courts have singled out the ALCOA court's adjustment remedy for scorn primarily because of the perceived lack of certainty and finality in the approach: [One] court characterized judicial reformation as an improper role for courts: "It is not the responsibility or function of this court to rewrite the parties' contract to provide for [unforeseen] circumstances." * * *

B. Scholarly Discussions

1. Immediate Reactions

Jack Dawson led the charge against court adjustment, writing that the ALCOA court's adjustment remedy was thoroughly "bizarre." Two of Dawson's reasons stand out: courts lack the knowledge and resources to write a better contract than the parties, and courts do not have the power or authority to do so.

As for the court's expertise and resources, Dawson wrote: "Nothing in their prior training as lawyers or their experience in directing litigation and giving coherence to its results will qualify them to invent viable new designs for disrupted enterprises, now gone awry, that the persons most concerned had tried to construct but without success." Concerning the court's power, Dawson opined: "[F]rom what source does any court derive the power to impose on [the parties] a new contract without the free assent of both? * * *

2. More Recent Discussions

Scholarly discussion of court adjustment has not "faded away," at least not to the extent that the ALCOA case faded in the courts. In recent years, several writers have commented on the issue and it is fair to say that these comments are a bit more tempered than Dawson's. Some writers even seem willing, albeit grudgingly, to acknowledge that there may be a place for court adjustment.

Some writers emphasized that the parties in the ALCOA case thought their price formula would more reliably track ALCOA's costs. For example, George Geis asked: "Should the court reform the contract under the almost certainly correct assumption that the parties really meant to write a deal that tracked [ALCOA's] actual costs more closely?" For some, this assumption leads to the conclusion that Essex would have received an unfair windfall under the contract as written. In fact, Donald Smythe pointed out that Essex "took advantage . . . by reselling millions of pounds of aluminum for an enormous profit." Although these observations do not speak directly to court adjustment, the implication is that court adjustment should not automatically be ruled out. After all, if the court excused ALCOA, it would have received the windfall instead of Essex. If windfalls are the concern, the court's intermediate approach therefore may make some sense.

* * *

Those recent commentators most dissatisfied with the ALCOA decision are clearly motivated by ALCOA's failure to protect itself adequately in the contract. For example, Richard Posner pointed out that ALCOA was "highly sophisticated" with "long experience . . . in designing the price escalator clause" and noted that ALCOA consulted Alan Greenspan in formulating the term. Macaulay thought ALCOA's mistake occurred even though ALCOA was a "well-represented major corporation" attuned to "transaction plann[ing]." * * *

NOTE:
REMEDIES AND SUBSTANCE

The substantive grounds for granting relief to parties who confront unanticipated calamities are not likely to expand as long as courts are unwilling to be more flexible remedially: "Contract's all-or-nothing remedial tradition * * * disfavors an enthusiastic move to contract excuse. Excuse's balancing methodology too often underscores significant interests on both sides. Courts inclined to construct a remedy that reflects these interests would be forced to come to terms with their aversion to a solution based on sharing losses. A host of hurdles obstructs fabricating a sharing strategy: Consider the challenge of constructing standards for apportioning the loss and comprehending the contextual implications of complex deals. It is easier for courts to repress their urges to move to a sharing approach and simply find for the promisee on the basis of freedom of contract." Hillman, Contract Excuse and Bankruptcy Discharge, 43 Stan.L.Rev. 99, 109 (1990).

UNIFORM COMMERCIAL CODE § 2–615.

Official Comment

* * *

6. In situations in which neither sense nor justice is served by either answer when the issue is posed in flat terms of "excuse" or "no excuse," adjustment under the various provisions of this Article is necessary, especially the sections on good faith, on insecurity and assurance and on the reading of all provisions in the light of their purposes, and the general policy of this Act to use equitable principles in furtherance of commercial standards and good faith.

NATIONAL PRESTO INDUS., INC. v. UNITED STATES, 338 F.2d 99, 112 (Ct.Cl.1964). "[I]t is [sometimes] equitable to reform the contract so that each side bears a share of the unexpected costs, instead of permitting the whole loss to remain with the party on whom it chanced to light. In contract suits courts have generally seemed loath to divide damages, but in this class of case we see no objection other than tradition. Reformation, as the child of equity, can mold its relief to attain any fair result within the broadest perimeter of the charter the parties have established for themselves. Where that arrangement has allocated the risk to neither side, a judicial division is fair and equitable. The division can follow from the special circumstances if there are any; in their absence an equal split would fit the basic postulate that the contract has assigned the risk to neither party."

NOTE: ECONOMIC HARDSHIP CLAUSES

Contracting parties may desire to set forth their own remedial approach to problems of hardship caused by unanticipated circumstances. Especially in the long-term supply contract setting, drafters frequently include a "gross inequities adjustment provision" or an "economic hardship" clause. We set forth below a sample of the latter kind of clause actually found in some coal supply contracts. What problems do such clauses raise? Review the materials on Agreements to Agree in Section Nine of Chapter Four.

> (d) Ninety (90) days prior to the end of the fifth year of this agreement and ninety (90) days prior to the end of each subsequent fifth year, the parties shall jointly consider the effect of economic conditions and market prices in the coal industry to ascertain whether the Adjusted Price should be further adjusted in order to avoid economic hardship for SELLER or for BUYER. If it is thus ascertained that a substantial change has occurred in the economic conditions and/or market prices, then the Adjusted Price shall be further adjusted to compensate for such change and the amount of such adjustment and its effective date shall be mutually agreed upon by SELLER and BUYER.
>
> The intent of this Paragraph (d) is to avoid having SELLER experience a significant loss as a result of changed economic conditions and to insure that BUYER will not pay SELLER a price significantly higher than market prices for steam coal of similar quality, specifications, quantity, and long-term availability.
>
> If the parties are unable to agree with respect to a price adjustment, then either party may upon twelve (12) months written notice, terminate this contract.

PART FIVE

RIGHTS AND DUTIES OF THIRD PARTIES

■ ■ ■

CHAPTER NINE

THIRD PARTY BENEFICIARIES

■ ■ ■

In no department of the law has a more obstinate and persistent battle between theory and practice been waged. Nor is the strife ended.

WILLISTON

SECTION ONE: THIRD PARTY BENEFICIARIES AND THE ROLE OF LAWYERS

In previous chapters, we considered the rights and duties of immediate parties to agreements. Now we turn to the rights and duties of third parties—parties who are neither promisors nor promisees under an agreement, but who have some right (or owe some duty) under it.

When practicing law involving third parties, the lawyer must utilize virtually all of the skills heretofore explored in this book. For example, if Amy promises Helen to pay Esta $10,000 in return for Helen's promise to forgive Amy's $10,500 debt to Helen, Esta may seek to enforce Amy's promise if Amy reneges. The lawyer representing Esta, as a litigator, must show that contract law supports Esta's claim. The lawyer drafting the Amy-Helen deal must ascertain whether the parties desire to create a cause of action in Esta, and, if so, the lawyer must reflect that intent in the agreement. We will see that the law's approach to whether Esta can recover depends on whether the Amy-Helen agreement reflects such an intent.

SECTION TWO: INTENDED AND INCIDENTAL BENEFICIARIES

LAWRENCE V. FOX

Court of Appeals of New York, 1859.
20 N.Y. 268.

APPEAL from the Superior Court of the city of Buffalo. On the trial before MR. JUSTICE MASTEN, it appeared by the evidence of a bystander, that one Holly, in November, 1857, at the request of the defendant, loaned and advanced to him $300, stating at the time that he owed that sum to the plaintiff for money borrowed of him, and had agreed to pay it to him the then next day; that the defendant in consideration thereof, at the time of receiving the money, promised to pay it to the plaintiff the then next day. Upon this state of facts the defendant moved for a nonsuit, upon [the grounds that], viz.: * * * the agreement by the defendant with Holly to pay the plaintiff was void for want of consideration, and that there was no privity between the plaintiff and defendant. The court overruled the motion, and the counsel for the defendant excepted. The cause was then submitted to the jury, and they found a verdict for the plaintiff for the amount of the loan and interest, $344.66, upon which judgment was entered; from which the defendant appealed to the Superior Court, at general term, where the judgment was affirmed, and the defendant appealed to this court. The cause was submitted on printed arguments.

* * *

H. GRAY, J. * * * [I]t is claimed that notwithstanding [defendant's] promise was established by competent evidence, it was void for the want of consideration. It is now more than a quarter of a century since it was settled by the Supreme Court of this State—in an able and pains-taking opinion by the late Chief Justice SAVAGE, in which the authorities were fully examined and carefully analysed—that a promise in all material respects like the one under consideration was valid; and the judgment of that court was unanimously affirmed by the Court for the Correction of Errors. (*Farley v. Cleveland,* 4 *Cow.,* 432; *same case in error,* 9 *id.,* 639.) In that case one Moon owed Farley and sold to Cleaveland a quantity of hay, in consideration of which Cleaveland promised to pay Moon's debt to Farley; and the decision in favor of Farley's right to recover was placed upon the ground that the hay received by Cleaveland from Moon was a valid consideration for Cleaveland's promise to pay Farley, and that the subsisting liability of Moon to pay Farley was no objection to the recovery. The fact that the money advanced by Holly to the defendant was a loan to him for a day, and that it thereby became the property of the defendant, seemed to impress the defendant's counsel with the idea that because the defendant's promise was not a trust fund placed by the plaintiff in the defendant's hands, out of which he was to realize money as from the sale of a chattel or the collection of a debt, the promise although made for the benefit of the plaintiff could not enure to his benefit. The hay which Cleaveland [received from] Moon was not to be paid to Farley, but the debt incurred by Cleaveland for the purchase of the hay, like the debt incurred by the defendant for money borrowed, was what was to be paid. That case has been often referred to by the courts of this State, and has never been doubted as sound authority for the principle upheld by it. (*Barker v. Buklin,* 2 *Denio,* 45; *Hudson Canal Company v. The Westchester Bank,* 4 *id.,* 97) It puts to rest the objection that the defendant's promise was void for want of consideration.

The report of that case shows that the promise was not only made to Moon but to the plaintiff Farley. In this case the promise was made to Holly and not expressly to the plaintiff; and this difference between the two cases presents the question, raised by the defendant's objection, as to the want of privity between the plaintiff and defendant. As early as 1806 it was announced by the Supreme Court of this State, upon what was then regarded as the settled law of England, "That where one person makes a promise to another for the benefit of a third person, that third person may maintain an action upon it." *Schermerhorn v. Vanderheyden* (1 *John R.*, 140), has often been re-asserted by our courts and never departed from. * * * This question was subsequently, and in a case quite recent, again the subject of consideration by the Supreme Court, when it was held, that in declaring upon a promise, made to the debtor by a third party to pay the creditor of the debtor, founded upon a consideration advanced by the debtor, it was unnecessary to aver a promise to the creditor; for the reason that upon proof of a promise made to the debtor to pay the creditor, a promise to the creditor would be implied. * * * But it is urged that because the defendant was not in any sense a trustee of the property of Holly for the benefit of the plaintiff, the law will not imply a promise. I agree that many of the cases where a promise was implied were cases of trusts, created for the benefit of the promiser. The case of *Felton v. Dickinson* (10 *Mass.*, 189, 190), and others that might be cited are of that class; but concede them all to have been cases of trusts, and it proves nothing against the application of the rule to this case. The duty of the trustee to pay the *cestuis que trust,* according to the terms of the trust, implies his promise to the latter to do so. In this case the defendant, upon ample consideration received from Holly, promised Holly to pay his debt to the plaintiff; the consideration received and the promise to Holly made it as plainly his duty to pay the plaintiff as if the money had been remitted to him for that purpose, and as well implied a promise to do so as if he had been made a trustee of property to be converted into cash with which to pay. The fact that a breach of the duty imposed in the one case may be visited, and justly, with more serious consequences than in the other, by no means disproves the payment to be a duty in both. The principle illustrated by the example so frequently quoted (which concisely states the case in hand) "that a promise made to one for the benefit of another, he for whose benefit it is made may bring an action for its breach," has been applied to trust cases, not because it was exclusively applicable to those cases, but because it was a principle of law, and as such applicable to those cases.

It was also insisted that Holly could have discharged the defendant from his promise, though it was intended by both parties for the benefit of the plaintiff, and therefore the plaintiff was not entitled to maintain this suit for the recovery of a demand over which he had no control. It is enough that [Holly] did not release the defendant from his promise, and whether he could or not is a question not now necessarily involved; but if it was, I think it would be found difficult to maintain the right of Holly to discharge a judgment recovered by the plaintiff upon confession or otherwise, for the breach of the defendant's promise; and if he could not, how could he discharge the suit before judgment, or the promise before suit, made as it was for the plaintiff's benefit and in accordance with legal presumption accepted by him (*Berly v. Taylor,* 5 *Hill,* 577–584, *et seq.*), until his dissent was shown. The cases cited, and especially that of *Farley v. Cleveland,* establish the validity of a parol promise; it stands then upon the footing of a written one. Suppose the defendant had given his note in which, for value received of Holly, he had promised to pay the plaintiff and the plaintiff had accepted the promise, retaining Holly's liability. Very clearly Holly could not have discharged that promise, be the right to release the defendant as it may. No one can doubt that he owes the sum of money demanded of him, or that in accordance with his promise it was his duty to have paid it to the plaintiff; nor can it be doubted that whatever may be the diversity of opinion elsewhere, the adjudications in this State, from a very early period, approved by experience, have established the defendant's liability; if, therefore, it could be shown that a more strict and technically accurate application of the rules applied, would lead to a different result (which I by no means concede), the effort should not be made in the face of manifest justice.

The judgment should be affirmed.

JOHNSON, CH. J., DENIO, SELDEN, ALLEN and STRONG, JS., concurred. JOHNSON, CH. J., and DENIO, J., were of opinion that the promise was to be regarded as made to the plaintiff through the medium of his agent, whose action he could ratify when it came to his knowledge, though taken without his being privy thereto.

COMSTOCK, J. (Dissenting.) The plaintiff had nothing to do with the promise on which he brought this action. It was not made to him, nor did the consideration proceed from him. If he can maintain the suit, it is because an anomaly has found its way into the law on this subject. In general, there must be privity of contract. The party who sues upon a promise must be the promisee, or he must have some legal interest in the undertaking. In this case, it is plain that Holly, who loaned the money to the defendant, and to whom the promise in question was made, could at any time have claimed that it should be performed to himself personally. He had lent the money to the defendant, and at the same time directed the latter to pay the sum to the plaintiff. This direction he could countermand, and if he had done so, manifestly the defendant's promise to pay according to the direction would have ceased to exist. The plaintiff would receive a benefit by a complete execution of the arrangement, but the arrangement itself was between other parties, and was under their exclusive control. If the defendant had paid the money to Holly, his debt would have been discharged thereby. So Holly might have released the demand or assigned it to another person, or the parties might have annulled the promise now in question, and designated some other creditor of Holly as the party to whom the money should be paid. It has never been claimed, that in a case thus situated, the right of a third person to sue upon the promise rested on any sound principle of law. We are to inquire whether the rule has been so established by positive authority.

* * *

The cases in which some trust was involved are * * * frequently referred to as authority for the doctrine now in question, but they do not sustain it. If A delivers money or property to B, which the latter accepts upon a trust for the benefit of C, the latter can enforce the trust by an appropriate action for that purpose. (*Berly v. Taylor,* 5 *Hill,* 577.) If the trust be of money, I think the beneficiary may assent to it and bring the action for money had and received to his use. If it be of something else than money, the trustee must account for it according to the terms of the trust, and upon principles of equity. There is some authority even for saying that an express promise founded on the possession of a trust fund may be enforced by an action at law in the name of the beneficiary, although it was made to the creator of the trust. Thus, in *Comyn's Digest* (*Action on the case upon Assumpsit, B.* 15), it is laid down that if a man promise a pig of lead to A, and his executor give lead to make a pig to B, who assumes to deliver it to A, an assumpsit lies by A against him. The case of *The Delaware and Hudson Canal Company v. The Westchester County Bank* (4 *Denio,* 97), involved a trust because the defendants had received from a third party a bill of exchange under an agreement that they would endeavor to collect it, and would pay over the proceeds when collected to the plaintiffs. A fund received under such an agreement does not belong to the person who receives it. He must account for it specifically; and perhaps there is no gross violation of principle in permitting the equitable owner of it to sue upon an express promise to pay it over. Having a specific interest in the thing, the undertaking to account for it may be regarded as in some sense made with him through the author of the trust. But further than this we cannot go without violating plain rules of law. In the case before us there was nothing in the nature of a trust or agency. The defendant borrowed the money of Holly and received it as his own. The plaintiff had no right in the fund, legal or equitable. The promise to repay the money created an obligation in favor of the lender to whom it was made and not in favor of any one else.

* * *

GROVER, J., also dissented.

Judgment affirmed.

SEAVER V. RANSOM

Court of Appeals of New York, 1918.
224 N.Y. 233, 120 N.E. 639.

POUND, J. Judge Beman and his wife were advanced in years. Mrs. Beman was about to die. She had a small estate, consisting of a house and lot in Malone and little else. Judge Beman drew his wife's will according to her instructions. It gave $1,000 to plaintiff, $500 to one sister, plaintiff's mother, and $100 each to another sister and her son, the use of the house to her husband for life, and remainder to the American Society for the Prevention of Cruelty to Animals. She named her husband as residuary legatee and executor. Plaintiff was her niece, 34 years old in ill health sometimes a member of the Beman household. When the will was read to Mrs. Beman, she said that it was not as she wanted it. She wanted to leave the house to plaintiff. She had no other objection to the will, but her strength was waning, and, although the judge offered to write another will for her, she said she was afraid she would not hold out long enough to enable her to sign it. So the judge said, if she would sign the will, he would leave plaintiff enough in his will to make up the difference. He avouched the promise by his uplifted hand with all solemnity and his wife then executed the will. When he came to die, it was found that his will made no provision for the plaintiff.

This action was brought, and plaintiff recovered judgment in the trial court, on the theory that Beman had obtained property from his wife and induced her to execute the will in the form prepared by him by his promise to give plaintiff $6,000, the value of the house, and that thereby equity impressed his property with a trust in favor of plaintiff. Where a legatee promises the testator that he will use property given him by the will for a particular purpose, a trust arises. O'Hara v. Dudley, 95 N.Y. 403, 47 Am.Rep. 53; Trustees of Amherst College v. Ritch, 151 N.Y. 282, 45 N.E. 876, 37 L.R.A. 305; Ahrens v. Jones, 169 N.Y. 555, 62 N.E. 666, 88 Am.St.Rep. 620. Beman received nothing under his wife's will but the use of the house in Malone for life. Equity compels the application of property thus obtained to the purpose of the testator, but equity cannot so impress a trust, except on property obtained by the promise. Beman was bound by his promise, but no property was bound by it; no trust in plaintiff's favor can be spelled out.

An action on the contract for damages, or to make the executors trustees for performance, stands on different ground. Farmers' Loan & Trust Co. v. Mortimer, 219 N.Y. 290, 294, 295, 114 N.E. 389. The Appellate Division properly passed to the consideration of the question whether the judgment could stand upon the promise made to the wife, upon a valid consideration, for the sole benefit of plaintiff. The judgment of the trial court was affirmed by a return to the general doctrine laid down in the great case of Lawrence v. Fox, 20 N.Y. 268, which has since been limited as herein indicated.

Contracts for the benefit of third persons have been the prolific source of judicial and academic discussion. * * * The general rule, both in law and equity * * * was that privity between a plaintiff and a defendant is necessary to the maintenance of an action on the contract. The consideration must be furnished by the party to whom the promise was made. The contract cannot be enforced against the third party, and therefore it cannot be enforced by him. On the other hand, the right of the beneficiary to sue on a contract made expressly for his benefit has been fully recognized in many American jurisdictions, either by judicial decision or by legislation, and is said to be "the prevailing rule in this country." Hendrick v. Lindsay, 93 U.S. 143, 23 L.Ed. 855; Lehow v. Simonton, 3 Colo. 346. It has been said that "the establishment of this doctrine has been gradual, and is a victory of practical utility over theory, of equity over technical subtlety." Brantly on Contracts (2d Ed.) p. 253. The reasons for this view are that it is just and practical to permit the person for whose benefit the contract is made to enforce it against one whose duty it is to pay. Other jurisdictions still adhere to the present English rule (7 Halsbury's Laws of England, 342, 343; Jenks' Digest of English Civil Law, § 229) that a contract cannot be enforced by or against a person who is not a party (Exchange Bank v. Rice, 107 Mass. 37, 9 Am.Rep. 1). * * *

In New York the right of the beneficiary to sue on contracts made for his benefit is not clearly or simply defined. It is at present confined: First. To cases where there is a pecuniary obligation running from the promisee to the beneficiary, "a legal right founded upon some obligation of the promisee in the third party to adopt and claim the promise as made for his benefit." Farley v. Cleveland, 4 Cow. 432, 15 Am.Dec. 387; Lawrence v. Fox * * *. Secondly. To cases where the contract is made for the benefit of the wife (Buchanan v. Tilden, 158 N.Y. 109, 52 N.E. 724, 44 L.R.A. 170, 70 Am.St.Rep. 454 * * *), affianced wife, * * * or child * * * of a party to the contract. The close relationship cases go back to the early King's Bench case (1677), long since repudiated in England, of Dutton v. Poole, 2 Lev. 211 (s. c., 1 Ventris, 318, 332). See Schemerhorn v. Vanderheyden, 1 Johns. 139, 3 Am.Dec. 304. The natural and moral duty of the husband or parent to provide for the future of wife or child sustains the action on the contract made for their benefit. "This is the farthest the cases in this state have gone," says Cullen, J., in the marriage settlement case of Borland v. Welch, 162 N.Y. 104, 110, 56 N.E. 556.

The right of the third party is also upheld in, thirdly, the public contract cases * * * where the municipality seeks to protect its inhabitants by covenants for their benefit; and, fourthly, the cases where, at the request of a party to the contract, the promise runs directly to the beneficiary although he does not furnish the consideration. * * *

It may be safely said that a general rule sustaining recovery at the suit of the third party would include but few classes of cases not included in these groups, either categorically or in principle.

The desire of the childless aunt to make provision for a beloved and favorite niece differs imperceptibly in law or in equity from the moral duty of the parent to make testamentary provision for a child. The contract was made for the plaintiff's benefit. She alone is substantially damaged by its breach. The representatives of the wife's estate have no interest in enforcing it specifically. It is said in Buchanan v. Tilden that the common law imposes moral and legal obligations upon the husband and the parent not measured by the necessaries of life. It was, however, the love and affection or the moral sense of the husband and the parent that imposed such obligations in the cases cited, rather than any common-law duty of husband and parent to wife and child. If plaintiff had been a child of Mrs. Beman, legal obligation would have required no testamentary provision for her, yet the child could have enforced a covenant in her favor identical with the covenant of Judge Beman in this case. * * * The constraining power of conscience is not regulated by the degree of relationship alone. The dependent or faithful niece may have a stronger claim than the affluent or unworthy son. No sensible theory of moral obligation denies arbitrarily to the former what would be conceded to the latter. We might consistently either refuse or allow the claim of both, but I cannot reconcile a decision in favor of the wife in Buchanan v. Tilden, based on the moral obligations arising out of near relationship, with a decision against the niece here on the ground that the relationship is too remote for equity's ken. * * *

The court in [Lawrence v. Fox] attempted to adopt the general doctrine that any third person, for whose direct benefit a contract was intended, could sue on it. [The court here discusses cases interpreting Lawrence v. Fox in this way and cases limiting its holding to where " 'there has been a debt or duty owing by the promisee to the party claiming to sue upon the promise.' "]

* * *

But, on principle, a sound conclusion may be reached. If Mrs. Beman had left her husband the house on condition that he pay the plaintiff $6,000, and he had accepted the devise, he would have become personally liable to pay the legacy, and plaintiff could have recovered in an action at law against him, whatever the value of the house. * * * That would be because the testatrix had in substance bequeathed the promise to plaintiff, and not because close relationship or moral obligation sustained the contract. The distinction between an implied promise to a testator for the benefit of a third party to pay a legacy and an unqualified promise on a valuable consideration to make provision for the third party by will is discernible, but not obvious. The tendency of American authority is to sustain the gift in all such cases and to permit the donee beneficiary to recover on the contract. Matter of Edmundson's Estate (1918, Pa.) 103 Atl. 277, 259 Pa. 429. The equities are with the plaintiff, and they may be enforced in this action, whether it be regarded as an action for damages or an action for specific performance to convert the defendants into trustees for plaintiff's benefit under the agreement.

The judgment should be affirmed, with costs.

HOGAN, CARDOZO and CRANE, JJ., concur. HISCOCK, C.J., and COLLIN and ANDREWS, JJ., dissent.

Judgment affirmed.

RESTATEMENT (FIRST) OF CONTRACTS § 133.

Definition of Donee Beneficiary, Creditor Beneficiary, Incidental Beneficiary

(1) Where performance of a promise in a contract will benefit a person other than the promisee, that person is * * *

(a) a donee beneficiary if it appears from the terms of the promise in view of the accompanying circumstances that the purpose of the promisee in obtaining the promise of all or part of the performance thereof is to make a gift to the beneficiary or to confer upon him a right against the promisor to some performance neither due nor supposed or asserted to be due from the promisee to the beneficiary;

(b) a creditor beneficiary if no purpose to make a gift appears from the terms of the promise in view of the accompanying circumstances and performance of the promise will satisfy an actual or supposed or asserted duty of the promisee to the beneficiary, or a right of the beneficiary against the promisee which has been barred by the Statute of Limitations or by a discharge in bankruptcy, or which is unenforceable because of the Statute of Frauds;

(c) an incidental beneficiary if neither the facts stated in Clause (a) nor those stated in Clause (b) exist.

GRUNEWALD V. METROPOLITAN MUSEUM OF ART

New York Appellate Division, 2015.
125 A.D.3d 438, 3 N.Y.S.3d 23.

Orders, Supreme Court, New York County (SHIRLEY WERNER KORNREICH, J.), entered October 30, 2013, which, inter alia, granted defendants' motions to dismiss the causes of action seeking to enjoin defendant museum's admission fee policy as breach of a statute and breach of a lease between the City of New York and defendant museum, unanimously affirmed, without costs.

This appeal arises out of two separate actions in which members of the public seek to challenge a policy by the Metropolitan Museum of Art (MMA), in place since 1970, to have all visitors at all times pay an entrance fee. While the fee is currently "recommended" at $25, visitors may pay as little at 1¢, but they must pay something. Prior to 1970, MMA entry was free to all visitors, at least on certain days and times. Plaintiffs in each of these actions claim that they paid for tickets to enter the museum on days and at times that they allege admission was required to be free. In addition to other causes of action, each complaint alleges that MMA's policy of charging an entry fee, in any amount, separately violates both certain legislation and the lease by which MMA occupies its home in Central Park. In each action, plaintiffs seek a permanent injunction to enforce a free admissions requirement.

The narrow issue before this Court is not whether the legislation relied upon and/or the lease mandate free admissions to MMA, but simply whether plaintiffs have standing to raise the issue.

Plaintiffs lack standing to sue under the 1893 statute. The statute authorizes the Department of Public Parks in the City of New York to apply for up to an additional $70,000 of funds to keep, preserve and exhibit the collections in the MMA. As an express condition of the authorization, the MMA shall be free of charge for five days per week, including Sunday and two evenings per week. Clearly there is no express private right of action. Nor is there an implied right of action consistent with the legislative scheme (*see Sheehy v. Big Flats Community Day*, 73 NY2d 629, 633–635 [1989]). Regardless of whether the legislation is designated an appropriations bill or not, the plain language makes the two obligations of the bill interdependent. The Parks Department's authority to apply for the additional appropriations for MMA is expressly conditioned upon free admission. The plaintiffs in this case are not seeking to revoke the Parks Department's authorization to seek additional funds, but only to enforce the condition for that authority. No private remedy to enforce only the conditional portion of the statute is fairly implied. Nor would a private right of action to enforce only the condition be consistent with the mechanism of the statute (e.g. forfeiting the right to seek additional funds) (*see Rhodes v. Herz*, 84 AD3d 1, 10 [1st Dept 2011], *lv dismissed* 18 NY3d 838 [2011]). We decline to reach the issue of whether the 1893 statute was impliedly overruled by later legislation.

Plaintiffs also lack standing to sue under the MMA's lease with the City as third party beneficiaries because the benefit to them is incidental and not direct (*Burns Jackson Miller Summit & Spitzer v. Lindner*, 59 NY2d 314, 336 [1983]). Government contracts often confer benefits to the public at large. That is not, however, a sufficient basis in itself to infer the government's intention to make any particular member of the public a third party beneficiary, entitled to sue on such contract (*see Fourth Ocean*

Putnam Corp. v. Interstate Wrecking Co., 66 NY2d 38 [1985]; *Moch Co. v. Rensselaer Water Co.*, 247 NY 160 [1928]; Restatement [Second] of Contracts § 313). In order for the benefit to be direct, it must be primary and immediate in such a sense and to such a degree as to demonstrate the assumption of a duty to provide a direct remedy to the individual members of the public if the benefit is lost (*Moch Co.* at 164 [Cardozo, Ch. J.]). Neither the language of the lease nor any other circumstances indicate that the parties intended to give these plaintiffs individually enforceable rights thereunder (*see Oursler v. Women's Interart Ctr.*, 170 AD2d 407 [1st Dept 1991]; *Alicea v. City of New York*, 145 AD2d 315 [1st Dept 1988]).

Plaintiffs' other contentions address unappealable dicta (*see Edge Mgt. Consulting v. Irmas*, 306 AD2d 69 [1st Dept 2003]). Concur—MAZZARELLI, J.P., DEGRASSE, MANZANET-DANIELS AND GISCHE, JJ.

RESTATEMENT (SECOND) OF CONTRACTS § 302.

Intended and Incidental Beneficiaries

(1) Unless otherwise agreed between promisor and promisee, a beneficiary of a promise is an intended beneficiary if recognition of a right to performance in the beneficiary is appropriate to effectuate the intention of the parties and either

(a) the performance of the promise will satisfy an obligation of the promisee to pay money to the beneficiary; or

(b) the circumstances indicate that the promisee intends to give the beneficiary the benefit of the promised performance.

(2) An incidental beneficiary is a beneficiary who is not an intended beneficiary.

DRAKE v. DRAKE, 89 A.D.2d 207, 455 N.Y.S.2d 420 (1982). "[B]arring unusual circumstances, children have no standing to enforce the periodic support provisions of their parents' separation agreement, although they may enforce other specific provisions of the agreement clearly made exclusively for their benefit, such as a promise to pay college tuition or to make the child a beneficiary of a life insurance policy. The distinction drawn comports with the rules of law applicable to third party beneficiaries and further is rooted in considerations of public policy designed to promote familial harmony and foster the parent-child relationship. A parent's contractual promise to pay support is made with a view toward his statutory duty of support. * * *

"We have no doubt that circumstances may arise, such as death or disability, or outright refusal of a contracting parent to seek enforcement of periodic support provisions for a child, which would give a child the necessary standing to enforce the agreement."

PROBLEM 9-1

Alice Turlway, an intended beneficiary under the will of the deceased, Leon Faquar, tells you that Faquar's attorney, Walter Wemmick, poorly drafted the will and that she (Alice) would receive nothing. It seems that because of Wemmick's negligence, the bequest to Alice of an interest in a trust was invalid under applicable state law. Alice wants to know whether she can recover from Wemmick for breach of contract because Wemmick promised Faquar to prepare a will in which Alice would be a beneficiary. Please advise.

ALANIZ V. SCHAL ASSOCIATES

Appellate Court of Illinois, Second District, 1988.
175 Ill.App.3d 310, 529 N.E.2d 832.

JUSTICE DUNN delivered the opinion of the court.

Plaintiff, Horacio Alaniz, appeals from an order of the circuit court of Lake County which granted the motion of defendant, Thorne-McNulty Corporation, to dismiss count III of plaintiff's second amended complaint and which found no reason to delay appeal or enforcement thereof. Plaintiff contends that the trial court erred in dismissing that count because he was an intended third-party beneficiary of construction contracts entered into by Thorne-McNulty, defendant Schal Associates, and plaintiff's employer, Rite-On Roofing, Inc. We affirm.

Plaintiff's initial complaint alleged that on March 1, 1985, while he was working as a roofer at the construction site of the Bannockburn Green Shopping Center, he sustained personal injuries when an extension ladder he was using collapsed. He alleged that his injuries were caused by violations of the Structural Work Act (Ill.Rev.Stat.1985, ch. 48, par. 60 *et seq.*) by Schal Associates, the construction manager of the project. Thorne-McNulty was not named as a defendant in the original complaint.

On June 23, 1987, plaintiff filed his first amended complaint. Count II of that complaint named Thorne-McNulty as a defendant, alleging that Thorne-McNulty had also violated the Structural Work Act. Thorne-McNulty moved to dismiss that count as barred by the two-year statute of limitations pertaining to actions for damages for personal injury (Ill.Rev.Stat.1985, ch. 110, par. 13–202). The motion to dismiss count II was granted on August 21, 1987, and plaintiff does not challenge the dismissal of count II.

Prior to the dismissal of count II, plaintiff filed a second amended complaint adding count III against Thorne-McNulty. Count III alleged that plaintiff was an intended third-party beneficiary of contracts between Thorne-McNulty and Rite-On Roofing, and between Thorne-McNulty and

Schal Associates. The subcontract between Thorne-McNulty and Schal Associates called for Thorne-McNulty to perform certain construction work on the Bannockburn project, and article 12 of the general conditions of the subcontract contained the following provision:

"The subcontractor [Thorne-McNulty] has the responsibility for maintaining the safety and loss prevention programs covering all work performed by it, and its subcontractors."

The contract between Thorne-McNulty and Rite-On Roofing, entitled "Hold Harmless Agreement," provided that Thorne-McNulty consented to Rite-On Roofing's use of certain scaffolding under the conditions that Rite-On Roofing indemnify and hold harmless Thorne-McNulty for any claims arising out of the use by Rite-On or its agents of the scaffolding and that no guarantee or representation was made concerning the safety of the scaffolding. Plaintiff alleged that his injuries were a proximate result of Thorne-McNulty's breach of the aforementioned contracts. Thorne-McNulty moved to dismiss count III pursuant to section 2–615 of the Code of Civil Procedure (Ill.Rev.Stat.1985, ch. 110, par. 2–615), and, as noted above, the motion was granted.

On appeal, plaintiff argues that the contract between Thorne-McNulty and Schal Associates made plaintiff an intended third-party beneficiary due to the sentence which provided that Thorne-McNulty had the responsibility to maintain safety programs covering work by Thorne-McNulty and its subcontractor, Rite-On Roofing. Therefore, plaintiff contends, Thorne-McNulty had a contractual duty to him, as an employee of Rite-On Roofing, to have a safety program which provided safe work conditions, including safe equipment. He concludes that, due to Thorne-McNulty's contractual duty, he may maintain a cause of action against Thorne-McNulty for personal injuries resulting from unsafe work conditions and equipment used on the construction project.

Although apparently no case involving contractual language similar to that found here has been decided in Illinois, the law regarding third-party beneficiaries is well established. A third-party beneficiary may sue for breach of a contract made for his benefit. (*Carson Pirie Scott & Co. v. Parrett* (1931), 346 Ill. 252, 257, 178 N.E. 498.) A third-party may only sue for breach of contract, however, if the contract was entered into for the party's direct benefit; if the third-party's benefit is merely incidental, he has no right of recovery on the contract. * * * Whether a third-party is a direct beneficiary depends on the intention of the parties, which must "be gleaned from a consideration of all of the contract and the circumstances surrounding the parties at the time of its execution." *Parrett,* 346 Ill. at 258.

Our review of the contract here and the circumstances surrounding the parties at the time of its execution reveals that neither Thorne-

McNulty nor Schal Associates intended to confer a direct benefit to plaintiff by inclusion of the general language regarding safety and loss prevention programs. It appears, rather, that the contract was intended solely to benefit the contracting parties by setting forth their respective responsibilities during construction. As was stated by the court in *Kohlmeier v. Shelter Insurance Co.* (1988), 170 Ill.App.3d 643, 121 Ill.Dec. 288, 525 N.E.2d 94:

> " 'As people usually stipulate for themselves, and not for third persons, a strong presumption obtains in any given case that such was their intention, and that the implication to overcome that presumption must be so strong as to amount practically to an express declaration.' " * * *

Given the nature of the construction industry and the frequency with which construction injuries occur despite safety precautions, we do not believe the presumption set forth above has been overcome. Although plaintiff argues that the hold harmless agreement between Thorne-McNulty and Rite-On Roofing establishes that Thorne-McNulty was attempting to shift its responsibility towards plaintiff to plaintiff's employer, we construe the agreement as evidence that Thorne-McNulty never intended to directly benefit plaintiff or any other workers by guaranteeing their safety.

The cases cited by plaintiff do not alter our conclusion that the contracting parties did not intend to confer a direct benefit to plaintiff by inclusion of the general safety provision. * * *

In *Baker v. S.A. Healy Co.* (1939), 302 Ill.App. 634, 24 N.E.2d 228, the intent to directly benefit the third-party claimants was clear from the contract sued upon. There, property owners brought suit against a construction firm for damages they sustained as a result of blasting during construction of a sewer. In *Baker,* the contract between the contractor and the sanitary district of Chicago provided that the contractor would, at its own expense, repair any damage to property as well as to persons. (*Baker,* 302 Ill.App. at 655.) Because the language of the contract explicitly evidenced an intent to benefit the injured property owners, they were allowed to pursue their third-party claims. In contrast to *Baker,* the language of the contract in question here contains no promise directed specifically to third parties.

* * *

It is not enough that an incidental benefit will flow to third parties; only a direct beneficiary has a right under a contract. * * * We believe that more than the general safety provision found in the contract between Thorne-McNulty and Schal Associates is required to evidence an intent to directly benefit plaintiff. While plaintiff would most likely have received some benefit by implementation of safety programs, such benefit is incidental to the direct benefit intended for the contracting parties, and thus is not sufficient to allow him to maintain an action on the contract. Plaintiff's action is better characterized as a tort action. See *Pippin v. Chicago Housing Authority* (1979), 78 Ill.2d 204, 210, 35 Ill.Dec. 530, 399 N.E.2d 596.

The trial court's dismissal of count III of plaintiff's second amended complaint is affirmed.

AFFIRMED.

LINDBERG, P.J., and INGLIS, J., concur.

NOTE: FURTHER ASPECTS OF ALANIZ V. SCHAL ASSOCIATES

In a letter to the editors, Alaniz's lawyer explained his strategy:

> The case was satisfactorily settled against Schal which was the general contractor. It chose not to third-party any other defendant. As attorney for the plaintiff, I thought it would be helpful to have the subcontractor Thorne-McNulty as a defendant too. I argued the intended third-party beneficiary theory of contract law to make them a direct party defendant. But it was not accepted by either the trial or appellate courts. In any event, in retrospect, I'm not sure it was necessary to have Thorne-McNulty as a defendant. The reason being that Schal was clearly in charge of the work and thus liable to the plaintiff. I was thinking probably that I should have as many defendants as possible. But in the facts of this case, the general contractor required the subcontractors to purchase liability insurance so that there was the same insurance company for everyone or at least an understanding on liability among the insurers involved.

The oral argument of Thorne-McNulty's motion to dismiss count III in the Circuit Court contains the following interesting interchange involving the use of precedent:

THE COURT: Are there any personal injury cases?

MR. DANIAN: [Alaniz's lawyer]: The Baker case involved personal injury, Your Honor.

MR. POWER [Thorne-McNulty's lawyer]: Your Honor, the Baker case involved a sewer explosion. There is a specific contract in the case—There is a specific clause in the contract between two of the contracting parties, the sanitary district and one of the contractors, which says they shall at their own expense repair any damage to buildings or other property. That's one clause.

Then they say it requires replacement by the contractors of lawns, trees, shrubs and plants upon private property and then the clause goes on to say the contract in a case of injury by blasting to any portion of the sewer or other structure or to material supporting same to rebuild the sewer or other structure or to replace the material surrounding or supporting same without extra payment.

These are specific clauses that the party put in the contract which definitely expressed their intention to reimburse people for personal injuries and for property damage. The people are definitely referred to [as] intended beneficiaries. No such comparison can be made in this situation, Your Honor.

* * *

* * * There is no clause in the contract that says * * * that I, one of the contracting parties, promise that I am going to pay for this person if he gets injured. On the contrary, there [are] clauses in the contract which take steps, make plans just in case somebody is injured because they recognize the possibility, Your Honor. They are saying quite to the contrary. We hope that nobody gets injured, but if they do, here is what you are supposed to do. They are not saying we are promising that if you get injured we are going to pay for you, unlike what they did say in Baker.

* * *

MR. DANIAN: It is obvious that safety programs pertain to workers. Safe environment and safe equipment is to be provided for these individuals and obviously it can be reasonably inferred from that, although I think there is still language in the contract which these programs are designed for the safety and safety means personal injury. It doesn't mean anything else. And in that respect it's very analogous to the Baker case with respect to personal injury. So I would only cite that particular case at this time.

* * *

THE COURT: Okay. Thank you. The Court will grant the motion.

MR. POWER: To dismiss?

THE COURT: To dismiss.

MR. POWER: Thank you, Your Honor.

KAUFFMAN v. DREYFUS FUND, INC., 434 F.2d 727, 732 (3d Cir. 1970), *cert. denied,* 401 U.S. 974, 91 S.Ct. 1190, 28 L.Ed.2d 323 (1971). A stockholder of a corporation does not acquire standing to maintain an action in his own right, as a shareholder, when the alleged injury is inflicted upon the corporation and the only injury to the shareholder is the indirect harm which consists in the diminution in value of his corporate shares resulting from the impairment of corporate assets. In this situation, it has been consistently held that the primary wrong is to the corporate body and, accordingly, that the shareholder, experiencing no direct harm, possesses no primary right to sue.

MARCHMAN v. NCNB TEXAS NAT. BANK, 120 N.M. 74, 81–82, 898 P.2d 709 (1995). There are exceptions to the general rule that a shareholder cannot sue individually for injuries to his or her corporation. Those exceptions arise "where there is a special duty, such as a contractual duty, between the wrongdoer and the shareholder," and "where the shareholder suffered an injury separate and distinct from that suffered by other shareholders." [12B William M. Fletcher, *Fletcher Cyclopedia of the Law of Private Corporations]*, § 5911, at 484; *see also Bank of New Mexico v. Rice,* 78 N.M. 170, 176, 429 P.2d 368, 374 (1967) ("A stockholder may sue as an individual where the act complained of creates not only a cause of action in favor of the corporation but also creates a cause of action in favor of the stockholder as an individual, as where the act is in violation of duties arising from contract or otherwise, and owed to him directly. . . ." (quoting 12B Fletcher, *supra,* § 5921, at 519)). There must be a direct injury to the shareholder in his or her individual capacity, independent of any duty to the corporation, before the shareholder is entitled to sue.

NOTE:
IMAGINATIVE USE OF THIRD PARTY BENEFICIARY THEORY: SOME SUCCESSES AND FAILURES

We illustrate here how some imaginative lawyers have sought to utilize third party beneficiary theory:

(1) Plaintiff landlord was a third party beneficiary of an agreement between a tenant and her assignee that explicitly provided that the assignee "assumed all of the tenant's obligations" under the lease. Gateway Co. v. DiNoia, 232 Conn. 223, 654 A.2d 342 (1995).

(2) The personal representative of the estate of an inmate in a correctional facility who died while receiving treatment in the infirmary stated a good cause of action that the inmate was an intended third party beneficiary of a contract between the sheriff's department and a provider of "total health services for inmates." The contract expressly stated that it was made for the benefit of the inmates as well as for the parties themselves. Cherry v. Crow, 845 F.Supp. 1520 (M.D.Fla.1994).

(3) The owners of land with a creek stated a good cause of action as third party beneficiaries seeking damages resulting from defendant chicken processing and fertilizing plant's discharge of noxious wastes into the upstream sewer system of a municipality. According to the complaint, the contract between the municipality and the defendant provided that the latter would not oversaturate the municipality's sewer treatment facilities with certain refuse. Ratzlaff v. Franz Foods of Arkansas, 250 Ark. 1003, 468 S.W.2d 239 (1971).

(4) Plaintiffs were involved in an auto accident with defendant, who was uninsured. Plaintiffs were not intended beneficiaries of a contract between defendant and his employer, in which the employer provided funds to the defendant to purchase automobile liability insurance. Dudley v. Unisys Corp., 852 S.W.2d 435 (Tenn.App.1992).

(5) Purchaser of a yacht was not an intended beneficiary of a contract between the yacht manufacturer and a supplier of defective paint. Neither the contract nor the parties' course of dealing evidenced an intention to benefit the purchaser directly. Caretta Trucking, Inc. v. Cheoy Lee Shipyards, Ltd., 647 So.2d 1028 (Fla.App.1994).

(6) After a property owner ignored a court order to demolish a building that was a public nuisance, a municipality hired a wrecking company to do the work. When the wrecking company improperly demolished the building by failing to remove walls and foundations one foot below grade and to crush the slab, the property owner claimed to be a third-party beneficiary of the contract made by the wrecking company and the municipality. Held, the property owner was an incidental beneficiary rather than an intended beneficiary under the Restatement (Second) approach. Fourth Ocean Putnam Corp. v. Interstate Wrecking Co., Inc., 66 N.Y.2d 38, 495 N.Y.S.2d 1, 485 N.E.2d 208 (1985).

(7) Plaintiff's decedent was not an intended beneficiary of a contract between the New York State Thruway Authority and Chevron Oil Co., which gave Chevron the exclusive right to render service on the Thruway to disabled vehicles and which required Chevron to service the vehicles within 30 minutes from the time of a call for assistance. Plaintiff's decedent had a heart attack while changing a flat tire some 2½ hours after a call to the service station. Kornblut v. Chevron Oil Co., 48 N.Y.2d 853, 424 N.Y.S.2d 429, 400 N.E.2d 368 (1979).

(8) Plaintiff was not an intended beneficiary of a contract between plaintiff's father and defendant brokerage firm in which plaintiff's father used plaintiff's name and social security number to set up the account. The court stated, "The record is devoid of evidence that the plaintiff's father had sought a promise from the defendant to transfer possession of the funds to the plaintiff. Without evidence of such a promise by the defendant, there is no basis on which the finder of fact could conclude that the defendant, either expressly or implicitly, assumed a direct obligation to deliver those funds to the plaintiff." Wasniewski v. Quick & Reilly, Inc., 971 A.2d 8 (Conn. 2009).

UNIFORM COMMERCIAL CODE § 2–318.

Third Party Beneficiaries of Warranties Express or Implied

Alternative A

A seller's warranty whether express or implied extends to any natural person who is in the family or household of his buyer or who is a guest in his home if it is reasonable to expect that such person may use, consume or be affected by the goods and who is injured in person by breach of the warranty. A seller may not exclude or limit the operation of this section.

Alternative B

A seller's warranty whether express or implied extends to any natural person who may reasonably be expected to use, consume or be affected by the goods and who is injured in person by breach of the warranty. A seller may not exclude or limit the operation of this section.

Alternative C

A seller's warranty whether express or implied extends to any person who may reasonably be expected to use, consume or be affected by the goods and who is injured by breach of the warranty. A seller may not exclude or limit the operation of this section with respect to injury to the person of an individual to whom the warranty extends.

IN RE GENERAL MOTORS LLC CP4 FUEL PUMP LITIGATION, 99 U.C.C. Rep Serv 2d 500, 2019 WL 3315286 (N.D. Cal. 2019). [Plaintiffs brought a class action after purchasing diesel vehicles. They alleged the vehicles had defective fuel injection pumps incompatible with diesel fuel.] GM argues first, that a plaintiff cannot recover for breach of implied warranty under California law unless he directly purchased the product from the defendant. Thus, Plaintiffs who purchased vehicles from independent dealerships cannot make out this claim. Second, GM argues that plaintiffs do not qualify for the third-party beneficiary or advertising exceptions to this rule. * * * The Court disagrees that direct privity is strictly required to make out a breach of implied warranty claim. As this Court has held in an analogous context, under California law, "a third party beneficiary can enforce a contract made expressly for his benefit. . . . A contract made expressly for a third party's benefit does not need to specifically name the party as the beneficiary; the only requirement is that the party is more than incidentally benefitted by the contract." *Aberin*, 2018 WL 1473085, at *7 (citation omitted). As Plaintiffs assert, the third-party beneficiary exception applies to them as the intended beneficiaries of GM's contracts with its dealers.

SECTION THREE: DEFENSES

MORSTAIN V. KIRCHER

Supreme Court of Minnesota, 1933.
190 Minn. 78, 250 N.W. 727.

HILTON, JUSTICE.

Defendant appealed from a judgment of the municipal court of Minneapolis in the sum of $432.07.

Frances V. Brown and Thomas W. Brown, husband and wife, were the owners of certain real estate in Hennepin county. On May 4, 1928, they executed and delivered to plaintiff their promissory note for $400, payable in two years from date. The note was secured by a mortgage on the property. On June 12, 1928, the Browns conveyed the premises by warranty deed to defendant, subject to said mortgage, and, as part of the consideration, defendant assumed and agreed to pay the note and mortgage. Defendant, after the conveyance to him, paid two installments of interest to plaintiff. Later, and on November 1, 1928, defendant reconveyed the premises to the Browns by warranty deed for $15, subject to the mortgage.

Plaintiff commenced this action in April, 1931, to recover the amount due and unpaid on the note. At no time had any proceedings been instituted to foreclose the mortgage, nor any other action to collect on the note. The trial court made findings in which the salient facts were as above set forth. As a conclusion of law the judgment above referred to was ordered and was duly entered on February 24, 1933. The only question involved is as to the correctness of the conclusion of law. Defendant's contention is that because of his reconveyance of the land to the Browns his liability was extinguished.

It is settled law in this state that, where a purchaser of mortgaged property from the mortgagor assumes and agrees to pay the mortgage, he becomes personally liable therefor to the mortgagee, who may enforce it in an appropriate action. The right of the mortgagee is purely a personal one, and may be enforced without a foreclosure of the mortgage. 4 Dunnell, Minn.Dig. (2d Ed.) § 6294, and cases cited. The assumption of the mortgage debt by the grantee (defendant) was primarily for the protection of his grantors (the Browns). Nelson v. Rogers, 47 Minn. 103, 49 N.W. 526. It was also secondarily for the benefit of the mortgagee, and, had there been no reconveyance to the mortgagors, plaintiff could have recovered in this action.

By accepting a reconveyance of the property under the circumstances in this case, the Browns released defendant from any obligation to them. Manifestly they could not successfully maintain an action against defendant on his assumption agreement. Neither can their mortgagee. She paid no consideration for defendant's agreement to pay the mortgage debt, nor had she in reliance on the assumption contract placed herself in a position from which she could not retreat without loss. Plaintiff here was a creditor beneficiary. In American Law Institute, Restatement, Contracts, § 143, it is said: "A discharge of the promisor by the promisee in a contract or a variation thereof by them is effective against a creditor beneficiary if, (a) the creditor beneficiary does not bring suit upon the promise or otherwise materially change his position in reliance thereon before he knows of the discharge or variation. * * * "

This rule, as applied to the facts in this case, is a sound and just one, and is supported by many well-considered cases. See 21 A.L.R. page 462 et seq. See, also, Williston on Contracts, vol. 1, § 397.

Plaintiff now is in no worse position than she was when the note and mortgage were given. The property is again in the ownership of the Browns; the mortgage still remains a subsisting lien thereon; plaintiff may foreclose on the mortgage and also has the right to recover in a suit upon the note against the makers thereof.

Judgment reversed.

RESTATEMENT (SECOND) OF CONTRACTS § 311.

Variation of a Duty to a Beneficiary

(1) Discharge or modification of a duty to an intended beneficiary by conduct of the promisee or by a subsequent agreement between promisor and promisee is ineffective if a term of the promise creating the duty so provides.

(2) In the absence of such a term, the promisor and promisee retain power to discharge or modify the duty by subsequent agreement.

(3) Such a power terminates when the beneficiary, before he receives notification of the discharge or modification, materially changes his position in justifiable reliance on the promise or brings suit on it or manifests assent to it at the request of the promisor or promisee.

(4) If the promisee receives consideration for an attempted discharge or modification of the promisor's duty which is ineffective against the beneficiary, the beneficiary can assert a right to the consideration so received. The promisor's duty is discharged to the extent of the amount received by the beneficiary.

ROUSE V. UNITED STATES

United States Court of Appeals for the District of Columbia Circuit, 1954.
215 F.2d 872.

EDGERTON, CIRCUIT JUDGE.

Bessie Winston gave Associated Contractors, Inc., her promissory note for $1,008.37, payable in monthly installments of $28.01, for a heating plant in her house. The Federal Housing Administration guaranteed the note and the payee endorsed it for value to the lending bank, the Union Trust Company.

Winston sold the house to Rouse. In the contract of sale Rouse agreed to assume debts secured by deeds of trust and also "to assume payment of $850 for heating plant payable $28 per Mo." Nothing was said about the note.

Winston defaulted on her note. The United States paid the bank, took an assignment of the note, demanded payment from Rouse, and sued him for $850 and interest.

Rouse alleged as defenses (1) that Winston fraudulently misrepresented the condition of the heating plant and (2) that Associated Contractors did not install it satisfactorily. The District Court struck these defenses and granted summary judgment for the plaintiff. The defendant Rouse appeals.

Since Rouse did not sign the note he is not liable on it. D.C.Code 1951, § 28–119; N.I.L. Sec. 18. He is not liable to the United States at all unless his contract with Winston makes him so. The contract says the parties to it are not "bound by any terms, conditions, statements, warranties or representations, oral or written" not contained in it. But this means only that the written contract contains the entire agreement. It does not mean that fraud cannot be set up as a defense to a suit on the contract. Rouse's promise to "assume payment of $850 for heating plant" made him liable to Associated Contractors, Inc., only if and so far as it made him liable to Winston; one who promises to make a payment to the promisee's creditor can assert against the creditor any defense that the promisor could assert against the promisee. Accordingly Rouse, if he had been sued by the corporation, would have been entitled to show fraud on the part of Winston. He is equally entitled to do so in this suit by an assignee of the corporation's claim. It follows that the court erred in striking the first defense. We do not consider whether Winston's alleged fraud, if shown, would be a complete or only a partial defense to this suit, since that question has not arisen and may not arise.

We think the court was right in striking the second defense. "If the promisor's agreement is to be interpreted as a promise to discharge whatever liability the promisee is under, the promisor must certainly be allowed to show that the promisee was under no enforceable liability. * * * On the other hand, if the promise means that the promisor agrees to pay a sum of money to A, to whom the promisee says he is indebted, it is immaterial whether the promisee is actually indebted to that amount or at all. * * * Where the promise is to pay a specific debt * * * this interpretation will generally be the true one."

The judgment is reversed and the cause remanded with instructions to reinstate the first defense.

Reversed and remanded.

RESTATEMENT (SECOND) OF CONTRACTS § 309.

Defenses Against the Beneficiary

(1) A promise creates no duty to a beneficiary unless a contract is formed between the promisor and the promisee; and if a contract is voidable or unenforceable at the time of its formation the right of any beneficiary is subject to the infirmity.

(2) If a contract ceases to be binding in whole or in part because of impracticability, public policy, non-occurrence of a condition, or present or prospective failure of performance, the right of any beneficiary is to that extent discharged or modified.

(3) Except as stated in Subsections (1) and (2) and in § 311 or as provided by the contract, the right of any beneficiary against the promisor is not subject to the promisor's claims or defenses against the promisee or to the promisee's claims or defenses against the beneficiary.

(4) A beneficiary's right against the promisor is subject to any claim or defense arising from his own conduct or agreement.

PROBLEM 9-2

Felix and Edgar enter an agreement in which Felix promises to mow Edgar's lawn and Edgar promises Felix to pay David the $25 that Felix owes David. Felix mows only half of Edgar's lawn. What are David's rights? Suppose Felix breaks his leg and cannot mow any of the lawn. What are David's rights, if any?

SECTION FOUR: REVIEW OF THIRD-PARTY-BENEFICIARY THEORY

PROBLEM 9-3

The City of San Martin, California is considering entering an agreement with County Resource Recovery Inc. for the latter to build and operate a recycling plant for the city. It is clear such a plant will release pollutants into the environment and many concerned citizens oppose the project. These citizens can be mollified only if limits on emissions are established and they have a private right to enforce these limits against County Resource. (They believe that existing environmental laws are insufficient to protect them, that these laws might change, and that these laws are not self-executing.) County Resource is willing to agree to reasonable limits and to sign an agreement with the private group to that effect. Is such an agreement enforceable? What is the consideration? If it is not enforceable or if there is a question of enforceability, could the agreement between the city and County Resource establish a private right of action on behalf of the private group? Review: If the private group can sue, is it entitled to specific performance? (Damage from emissions would likely be in the form of incremental increases to long term irreversible effects of pollution.)

CHAPTER TEN

ASSIGNMENT AND DELEGATION

■ ■ ■

Who made the discovery which has most deeply affected the fortunes of the human race? We think—the person who first discovered that a debt is a saleable commodity.

MACLEOD

SECTION ONE: ASSIGNMENT, DELEGATION, AND THE ROLE OF LAWYERS

The law of assignment and delegation governs the transfer to third parties of rights and duties under existing contracts. For example, suppose Tex-Oil wishes to purchase the business of an oil supplier that has previously entered enforceable agreements to supply oil to various utilities. Must Tex-Oil assume existing duties of the supplier? What rights will Tex-Oil acquire under the supplier's existing contracts?

If the transaction between Tex-Oil and the oil supplier is itself an agreement with consideration, the lawyers representing the parties must utilize the planning and drafting skills previously studied in this book. The lawyer for Tex-Oil, for example, must determine the supplier's existing duties and whether Tex-Oil is willing to assume them. The lawyer must then plan, negotiate, and draft accordingly. A lawyer representing an oil purchaser under the original agreement with the oil supplier must also consider whether the oil supplier has the right to "assign" the supply contract to a party such as Tex-Oil.

The lawyer who works on an assignment or delegation problem frequently consults sources of law outside general contract law. For example, the Uniform Commercial Code incorporates a number of important provisions on assignment. See especially section 2–210 and various provisions of Article 9 governing secured transactions. We do not focus on the Article 9 provisions here. Also, state regulatory statutes deal, for example, with assignments of wages.

SECTION TWO: THE POWER TO ASSIGN RIGHTS—NATURE AND LIMITS

For centuries, the common law prohibited the assignment of rights. Various factors explain this, including the fear of an increase in litigation. Of course, one effect of the prohibition was to reduce the present value of a right to a future payment or other performance. With the rise of a market economy and of credit, the prohibition against assignment of rights could not be expected to survive, and by the 18th century most restrictions were gone. Professor Gilmore once described the indirect manner in which this was achieved by the common law:

> Although a person to whom a contract right was owed could not transfer it to one to whom the obligor was not bound in privity, he could appoint an agent or attorney to collect in his place or stead. In time the fictitious agency became irrevocable and the nominal owner, after notice of the assignment to the obligor, lost any power to interfere with the assignee's rights. Thus by the typically muddle-headed process of thinking known as the genius of the common law, assignments of intangibles were made effective in fact while basic theory still proclaimed them to be legal impossibilities.[a]

The general assignability of rights was hailed as a major advance of the law. The Farnsworth excerpt at the close of this section sets forth one of the major uses of assignments in today's world.

An assignment of a right is a legally valid present transfer of that right. Such a transfer manifests an intent on the part of the assignor to extinguish his or her own right to another's performance and to convey that right to the assignee. No special form of words is required. A valid assignment may be either gratuitous or for a consideration. According to section 332 of the second Restatement, a gratuitous assignment is irrevocable if it is (1) in writing signed by the assignor (or under seal) and delivered to the assignee, or (2) accompanied by delivery of a writing of a type customarily accepted as a symbol or as evidence of the right, such as a savings bank book. But the assignor can revoke an oral gratuitous assignment and the assignor's notification thereof or the assignor's death, incapacity, or subsequent assignment terminates the assignee's rights. A revocable gratuitous assignment becomes irrevocable if the assignee obtains payment or a judgment against the obligor, or enters a new contract with the obligor directly, or reasonably relies thereon. An assignment for consideration is irrevocable even though oral unless it falls within an applicable statute of frauds provision.

---

[a] 1 G. Gilmore, Security Interests In Personal Property, § 7.3 at 202 (1965).

The legal power to assign a right is not without limitations, however. We now consider several limitations.

CRANE ICE CREAM CO. V. TERMINAL FREEZING & HEATING CO.

Court of Appeals of Maryland, 1925.
147 Md. 588, 128 A. 280.

Action by the Crane Ice Cream Company against the Terminal Freezing & Heating Company. Demurrer to the declaration was sustained, and from the judgment entered thereon against plaintiff, it appeals. Judgment affirmed.

* * *

PARKE, J. The appellee and one W.C. Frederick entered into a contract for the delivery of ice by the appellee to Frederick, and, before the expiration of the contract, Frederick executed an assignment of the contract to the appellant; and on the refusal of the appellee to deliver ice to the assignee it brought an action on the contract against the appellee to recover damages for the alleged breach. * * *

The demurrer admitted the following material allegations: At the execution of the contract the Terminal Freezing & Heating Company, appellee, was a corporation engaged in the manufacture and sale of ice at wholesale within the state of Maryland, and William C. Frederick made and sold ice cream in Baltimore, where his plant was located. * * *

The contract imposed upon the appellee the liability to sell and deliver to Frederick such quantities of ice as he might use in his business as an ice cream manufacturer to the extent of 250 tons per week, at and for the price of $3.25 a ton of 2,000 pounds on the loading platform of Frederick. The contractual rights of the appellee were (a) to be paid on every Tuesday during the continuation of the contract, for all ice purchased by Frederick during the week ending at midnight upon the next preceding Saturday; (b) to require Frederick not to buy or accept any ice from any other source than the appellee, except in excess of the weekly maximum of 250 tons; (c) to annul the contract upon any violation of the agreement by Frederick; and (d) to sustain no liability for any breach of contract growing out of causes beyond its control. The converse of these rights and liabilities of the appellee were the correlative liabilities and rights of Frederick under the contract.

There was a further provision that the contract in its entirety should continue in force from term to term, unless either party thereto gave to the other party at least 60 days' notice in writing before the expiration of the term of the intention to end the contract. The contract did not expressly permit or inhibit an assignment, but neither did it contain any word, such as assigns, to indicate that the parties contemplated an assignment by either.

Before the first year of the second term of the contract had expired Frederick, without the consent or knowledge of the appellee, executed and delivered to the appellant, for a valuable consideration, a written assignment dated February 15, 1921, of the agreement between him and the appellee. The attempted transfer of the contract was a part of the transaction between Frederick and the appellant whereby the appellant acquired by purchase the plant, equipment, rights, and credits, choses in action, "good will, trade, custom, patronage, rights, contracts," and other assets of Frederick's ice cream business, which had been established and conducted by him in Baltimore. The purchaser took full possession and continued the former business carried on by Frederick. It was then and is now a corporation "engaged in the ice cream business upon a large and extensive scale in the city of Philadelphia, as well as in the city of Baltimore, and state of Maryland," and had a large capitalization, ample resources, and credit to meet any of its obligations "and all and singular the terms and provisions" of the contract; and it was prepared to pay cash for all ice deliverable under the contract.

As soon as the appellee learned of this purported assignment and the absorption of the business of Frederick by the appellant, it notified Frederick that the contract was at an end, and declined to deliver any ice to the appellant. Until the day of the assignment the obligations of both original parties had been fully performed and discharged.

* * *

The basic facts upon which the question for solution depends must be sought in the effect of the attempted assignment of this executory bilateral contract on both the rights and the liabilities of the contracting parties, as every bilateral contract includes both rights and duties on each side while both sides remain executory. I Williston on Contracts, § 407. If the assignment of rights and the assignment of duties by Frederick are separated, they fall into these two divisions: (1) The rights of the assignor were (a) to take no ice, if the assignor used none in his business, but, if he did (b) to require the appellee to deliver, on the loading platform of the assignor, all the ice he might need in his business to the extent of 250 tons a week, and (c) to buy any ice he might need in excess of the weekly 250 tons from any other person; and (2) the liabilities of the assignor were (a) to pay to the appellee on every Tuesday during the continuance of the contract the stipulated price for all ice purchased and weighed by the assignor during the week ending at midnight upon the next preceding Saturday, and (b) not directly or indirectly, during the existence of this agreement, to buy or accept any ice from any other person, firm, or corporation than the said the Terminal Freezing & Heating Company, except such amounts as might be in excess of the weekly limit of 250 tons.

Whether the attempted assignment of these rights, or the attempted delegation of these duties must fail because the rights or duties are of too personal a character, is a question of construction to be resolved from the nature of the contract and the express or presumed intention of the parties. Williston on Contracts, § 431.

The contract was made by a corporation with an individual, William C. Frederick, an ice cream manufacturer, with whom the corporation had dealt for 3 years, before it executed a renewal contract for a second like period. The character, credit, and resources of Frederick had been tried and tested by the appellee before it renewed the contract. Not only had his ability to pay as agreed been established, but his fidelity to his obligation not to buy or accept any ice from any other source up to 250 tons a week had been ascertained. In addition, the appellee had not asked in the beginning, nor on entering into the second period of the contract, for Frederick to undertake to buy a specific quantity of ice or even to take any. Frederick simply engaged himself during a definite term to accept and pay for such quantities of ice as he might use in his business to the extent of 250 tons a week. If he used no ice in his business, he was under no obligation to pay for a pound. In any week, the quantity could vary from zero to 250 tons, and its weekly fluctuation, throughout the life of the contract, could irregularly range between these limits. The weekly payment might be nothing or as much as $812.50; and for every week a credit was extended to the eighth day from the beginning of every week's delivery. From the time of the beginning of every weekly delivery of the ice to the date of the payment therefor the title to the ice was in the purchaser, and the seller had no security for its payment except in the integrity and solvency of Frederick. The performances, therefore, were not concurrent, but the performance of the nonassigning party to the contract was to precede the payments by the assignor.

When it is also considered that the ice was to be supplied and paid for, according to its weight on the loading platform of Frederick, at an unvarying price without any reference either to the quantity used, or to the fluctuations in the cost of production or to market changes in the selling price, throughout 3 years, the conclusion is inevitable that the inducement for the appellee to enter into the original contract and into the renewal lay outside the bare terms of the contract, but was implicit in them, and was the appellee's reliance upon its knowledge of an average quantity of ice consumed, and probably to be needed, in the usual course of Frederick's business, at all times throughout the year, and its confidence in the stability of his enterprise, in his competency in commercial affairs, in his probity, personal judgment, and in his continuing financial responsibility. The contract itself emphasized the personal equation by specifying that the ice was to be bought for "use in his business as an ice cream manufacturer," and was to be paid for according to its weight "on the loading platform of the said W.C. Frederick."

When Frederick went out of business as an ice cream manufacturer, and turned over his plant and everything constituting his business to the appellant, it was no longer his business, or his loading platform, or subject to his care, control, or maintenance, but it was the business of a stranger, whose skill, competency, and requirements of ice were altogether different from those of Frederick. The assignor had his simple plant in Baltimore. The assignee, in its purchase, simply added another unit to its ice cream business which it had been, and is now, carrying on "upon a large and extensive scale in the city of Philadelphia and state of Pennsylvania, as well as in the city of Baltimore and state of Maryland." The appellee knew that Frederick could not carry on his business without ice wherewith to manufacture ice cream at his plant for his trade. It also was familiar with the quantities of ice he would require, from time to time, in his business at his plant in Baltimore, and it consequently could make its other commitments for ice with this knowledge as a basis.

The appellant, on the other hand, might wholly supply its increased trade acquired in the purchase of Frederick's business with its ice cream produced upon a large and extensive scale by its manufactory in Philadelphia, which would result in no ice being bought by the assignee of the appellee, and so the appellee would be deprived of the benefit of its contract by the introduction of a different personal relation or element which was never contemplated by the original contracting parties. Again, should the price of ice be relatively high in Philadelphia in comparison with the stipulated price, the assignee could run its business in Baltimore and furnish its patrons, or a portion of them, in Philadelphia with its product from the weekly maximum consumption of 250 tons of ice throughout the year. There can be no denial that the uniform delivery of the maximum quantity of 250 tons a week would be a consequence not within the normal scope of the contract, and would impose a greater liability on the appellee than was anticipated. 7 Halsbury's Laws of England, § 1015, p. 501.

Moreover, the contract here to supply ice was undefined except as indicated from time to time by the personal requirements of Frederick in his specified business. The quantities of ice to be supplied to Frederick to answer his weekly requirements must be very different from, and would not be the measure of the quantities needed by his assignee, and, manifestly, to impose on the seller the obligation to obey the demands of the substituted assignee is to set up a new measure of ice to be supplied, and so a new term in the agreement that the appellee never bound itself to perform. Up to 250 tons of ice a week Frederick engaged not to buy or accept any ice from any other party than the appellee. After Frederick had sold away his business, this covenant could not bind the assignee of his business, and, even if it continued to bind Frederick, his refraining from not buying ice elsewhere was not a contemplated consideration for selling ice to any one except Frederick himself. Kemp v. Baerselman, [1906] 2 K.B. 604, 608, 609. It was argued that Frederick was entitled to the weekly maximum of 250 tons, and that he might have expanded his business so as to require this weekly limit of ice, and that therefore the burdens of the contract might have been as onerous to the appellee, if Frederick had continued in business, as they could become under the purporting assignment by reason of the increased requirements of the larger business of the assignee. The unsoundness of this argument is that the law accords to every man freedom of choice in the party with whom he deals and the terms of his dealing. He cannot be forced to do a thing which he did not agree to do because it is like and no more burdensome than something which he did contract to do.

Under all the circumstances of the case, it is clear that the rights and duties of the contract under consideration were of so personal a character that the rights of Frederick cannot be assigned nor his duties be delegated without defeating the intention of the parties to the original contract. When Frederick went out of the business of making ice cream, he made it impossible for him to complete his performance of the contract, and his personal action and qualifications upon which the appellee relied were eliminated from a contract which presupposed their continuance. Frederick not only attempted an assignment, but his course is a repudiation of the obligations of the contract. He is not even alleged to be ready to pay for any ice which might be delivered after the date of the purporting assignment, but the allegations of the declaration simply aver that the assignee alone had undertaken to perform the further contractual obligations of the assignor. Frederick, however, cannot be heard to say that he has not repudiated a contract, whose contemplated performance his own act has made it impossible for him to fulfill. Eastern Advertising Co. v. McGaw, 89 Md. 72, 88, 42 A. 923.

While a party to a contract may as a general rule assign all his beneficial rights, except where a personal relation is involved, his liability under the contract is not assignable inter vivos, because any one who is bound to any performance whatever or who owes money cannot by any act of his own, or by any act in agreement with any other person than his creditor or the one to whom his performance is due, cast off his own liability and substitute another's liability. If this were not true, obligors could free themselves of their obligations by the simple expedient of assigning them. A further ground for the rule is that, not only is a party entitled to know to whom he must look for the satisfaction of his rights under the contract, but in the familiar words of Lord Denman in Humble v. Hunter, 12 Q.B. 317, "you have a right to the benefit you contemplate from the character, credit, and substance of the person with whom you contract." For these reasons it has been uniformly held that a man cannot assign his liabilities under a contract, but one who is bound so as to bear an unescapable liability may delegate the performance of his obligation to another, if the liability be of such a nature that its performance by another will be substantially the same thing as performance by the promisor himself. In such circumstances the performance of the third party is the act of the promisor, who remains liable under the contract and answerable in damages if the performance be not in strict fulfillment of the contract. * * *

However, the analysis of the facts on this appeal leaves no room for doubt that the case at bar falls into the category of those assignments where an attempt is made both to transfer the rights and to delegate the duties of the assignor under an executory bilateral contract whose terms and the circumstances make plain that the personal qualification and action of the assignor, with respect to both his benefits and burdens under the contract, were essential inducements in the formation of the contract, and, further, that the assignment was a repudiation of any future liability of the assignor. The attempted assignment before us altered the conditions and obligations of the undertaking. The appellee would here be obliged not only to perform the subsequent stipulations of the contract for the benefit of a stranger and in conformity with his will, but also to accept the performance of the stranger in place of that of the assignor with whom it contracted, and upon whose personal integrity, capacity, and management in the course of a particular business he must be assumed to have relied by reason of the very nature of the provisions of the contract and of the circumstances of the contracting parties. The nature and stipulations of the contract prevent it being implied that the nonassigning party had assented to such an assignment of rights and delegation of liabilities. The authorities are clear, on the facts at bar, that the appellant could not enforce the contract against the appellee.

* * *

Judgment affirmed, with costs to the appellee.

RESTATEMENT (SECOND) OF CONTRACTS § 317.

Assignment of a Right

(1) An assignment of a right is a manifestation of the assignor's intention to transfer it by virtue of which the assignor's right to performance by the obligor is extinguished in whole or in part and the assignee acquires a right to such performance.

(2) A contractual right can be assigned unless

(a) the substitution of a right of the assignee for the right of the assignor would materially change the duty of the obligor, or materially increase the burden or risk imposed on him by his contract, or materially impair his chance of obtaining return performance, or materially reduce its value to him, or

(b) the assignment is forbidden by statute or is otherwise inoperative on grounds of public policy, or

(c) assignment is validly precluded by contract.

UNIFORM COMMERCIAL CODE § 2–210(2).

Unless otherwise agreed all rights of either seller or buyer can be assigned except where the assignment would materially change the duty of the other party, or increase materially the burden or risk imposed on him by his contract, or impair materially his chance of obtaining return performance. A right to damages for breach of the whole contract or a right arising out of the assignor's due performance of his entire obligation can be assigned despite agreement otherwise.

NOTE: *THE POWER TO ASSIGN RIGHTS UNDER GENERAL CONTRACT LAW AND ARTICLE 9 OF THE UNIFORM COMMERCIAL CODE*

In addition to limitations on the power to assign rights discussed in Crane Ice Cream Co., and set forth in section 317 of the second Restatement and in section 2–210(2) of the Uniform Commercial Code, a further limitation is that a right expected to arise under a contract not in existence is not a present assignment, but operates only as a promise to assign. Restatement (Second) of Contracts § 321. For example, A has not made an assignment if A, an unemployed gardener, promises to pay B money that A hopes to earn in the future from C, who is opening a new gardening store. As a result, even if C employs A, C does not have to pay A's salary to B. (C may have other defenses as well, such as a statutory prohibition of assignments of wages.)

Article 9 of the Uniform Commercial Code, dealing with secured transactions, permits the assignment of future accounts as collateral for present loans. You will encounter this subject in an upperclass commercial law course.

PROBLEM 10-1

To make an effective assignment, the assignor must manifest an intention to transfer his right to another person. The issue is one of intention—a court will examine any writing and the circumstances to determine intention in the manner we have studied in Chapter 6. This suggests that appropriate drafting can ensure the effectiveness of an assignment. The language should demonstrate that the assignor intends to extinguish its own right to another's performance and give the assignee the right to that performance. Consider whether any of the following constitutes appropriate language:

(1) A will pay B if A gets the money from C.

(2) B is entitled to the commission for the sale of C's home. (B is an employee of A, a real estate agent, with whom C has contracted.)

(3) I, A, for value received, hereby assign, transfer and set over to B my right, title and interest in the funds due me from C.

E. FARNSWORTH, CONTRACTS

680–81 (4th ed. 2004).

The * * * most complex situation is that of an owner of a business that furnishes goods or services to other businesses. If the owner (B) wants to transfer the business as a going concern to a buyer (C) by a sale of the assets of the business, the parties may also plan to transfer long-term contracts with, say, a supplier (A) and a customer (A′). With respect to both the supplier and the customer, such a transfer involves not only assignment but delegation. The seller wants both to assign to the buyer the seller's rights against the supplier and the customer, and also to delegate to the buyer the performances that the seller owes them. There are, therefore, two significant problems not present in the four earlier situations. The first is that, with respect to the supplier, the right that the seller wishes to assign is a right to a performance other than the payment of money. The second is that, with respect to both the supplier and the customer, the seller wishes not only to assign rights but also to delegate performance of duties—the duty of paying the supplier for what is supplied and the duty of furnishing the customer with goods or services. If the seller can overcome these problems and transfer these contracts, the buyer will have both a right to be supplied by the supplier in return for payment and a right to be paid by the customer in return for furnishing goods or services.

SECTION THREE: DEFENSES OF THE OBLIGOR AGAINST THE ASSIGNEE

Article 9 of the Uniform Commercial Code and other legislation figure heavily in this topic. You can investigate it fully in upperclass commercial law courses. Here we just scratch the surface by presenting two sections of the Restatement (Second) of Contracts and an excerpt from a very astute author.

RESTATEMENT (SECOND) OF CONTRACTS § 336.

Defenses Against an Assignee

(1) By an assignment the assignee acquires a right against the obligor only to the extent that the obligor is under a duty to the assignor; and if the right of the assignor would be voidable by the obligor or unenforceable against him if no assignment had been made, the right of the assignee is subject to the infirmity.

(2) The right of an assignee is subject to any defense or claim of the obligor which accrues before the obligor receives notification of the assignment, but not to defenses or claims which accrue thereafter except as stated in this Section or as provided by statute.

(3) Where the right of an assignor is subject to discharge or modification in whole or in part by impracticability, public policy, non-occurrence of a condition, or present or prospective failure of performance by an obligee, the right of the assignee is to that extent subject to discharge or modification even after the obligor receives notification of the assignment.

(4) An assignee's right against the obligor is subject to any defense or claim arising from his conduct or to which he was subject as a party or a prior assignee because he had notice.

RESTATEMENT (SECOND) OF CONTRACTS § 338.

Discharge of an Obligor After Assignment

(1) Except as stated in this Section, notwithstanding an assignment, the assignor retains his power to discharge or modify the duty of the obligor to the extent that the obligor performs or otherwise gives value until but not after the obligor receives notification that the right has been assigned and that performance is to be rendered to the assignee.

(2) So far as an assigned right is conditional on the performance of a return promise, and notwithstanding notification of the assignment, any modification of or substitution for the contract made by the assignor and obligor in good faith and in accordance with reasonable commercial standards is effective against the assignee. The assignee acquires corresponding rights under the modified or substituted contract.

(3) Notwithstanding a defect in the right of an assignee, he has the same power his assignor had to discharge or modify the duty of the obligor to the extent that the obligor gives value or otherwise changes his position in good faith and without knowledge or reason to know of the defect.

R. HILLMAN, PRINCIPLES OF CONTRACT LAW

392–94 (4th ed. 2019).

You assign to Taylor your right to the money Alice owes you for mowing her lawn. * * * Taylor, as an assignee, has a cause of action against Alice if she does not pay him. But does Alice have any defenses against Taylor's claim? Suppose, for example, that you have done a miserable job mowing Alice's lawn and your performance constitutes a material breach. (Suppose, you cut the lawn too low and Alice's lawn burned out.) If you had not assigned your right to payment, Alice could assert this defense against you. Because an assignee receives only what the assignor has to transfer,

Alice can also assert your material breach as a defense against Taylor. Similarly, if the contract between you and Alice is unenforceable because of impracticability (or another excuse doctrine), the failure of a condition, or public policy (or another policing doctrine), Alice can assert the defense against Taylor.

* * *

Suppose after you mow Alice's lawn and after your assignment of the $40 to Taylor, but before Alice pays anything to anyone, you accidentally hit Alice's car while backing out of your driveway. Alice's car sustains $40 of damage. (As you know, this is a highly unrealistic example. Car manufacturers make cars so that the slightest impact causes a minimum of $10,000 of damage.) Alice could have asserted your tort liability as a "set off" (a claim unrelated to the contract) if you had not already assigned your right to payment and you were suing her for your $40. But can she assert the set off against Taylor under the actual facts?

The answer depends on when Taylor notified Alice of the assignment and when her tort claim against you "accrued." If Taylor notified Alice before the tort claim accrued, Alice can not assert the set off against Taylor. Conversely if the tort claim accrued first, Alice can assert the set off against Taylor. You're probably wondering what "accrued" means. Basically, it is the time "when a cause of action comes into being." This can be technical, but here the cause of action accrued when you hit Alice's car. A breach of contract cause of action accrues, not when the parties make a contract, but when a party repudiates or breaches it. The moral of the story, of course, is that an assignee such as Taylor should notify the obligor of an assignment immediately to cut off potential set-off defenses.

There is another reason why an assignee should notify the obligor of the assignment immediately. Taylor's notification cuts off the right of you and Alice to modify your contract, for example, so that Alice must pay you instead of Taylor. Without such a notification, Alice would be discharged from her obligation to Taylor if she pays you the $40.

SECTION FOUR: DELEGATION OF DUTIES

MACKE CO. V. PIZZA OF GAITHERSBURG, INC.

Maryland Court of Appeals, 1970.
259 Md. 479, 270 A.2d 645.

SINGLEY, JUDGE.

The appellees and defendants below, Pizza of Gaithersburg, Inc.; Pizzeria, Inc.; The Pizza Pie Corp., Inc. and Pizza Oven, Inc., four corporations under the common ownership of Sidney Ansell, Thomas S. Sherwood and Eugene Early and the same individuals as partners or proprietors (the Pizza Shops) operated at six locations in Montgomery and Prince George's Counties. The appellees had arranged to have installed in each of their locations cold drink vending machines owned by Virginia Coffee Service, Inc., and on 30 December 1966, this arrangement was formalized at five of the locations, by contracts for terms of one year, automatically renewable for a like term in the absence of 30 days' written notice. A similar contract for the sixth location, operated by Pizza of Gaithersburg, Inc., was entered into on 25 July 1967.

On 30 December 1967, Virginia's assets were purchased by The Macke Company (Macke) and the six contracts were assigned to Macke by Virginia. In January, 1968, the Pizza Shops attempted to terminate the five contracts having the December anniversary date, and in February, the contract which had the July anniversary date.

Macke brought suit in the Circuit Court for Montgomery County against each of the Pizza Shops for damages for breach of contract. From judgments for the defendants, Macke has appealed.

The lower court based the result which it reached on two grounds: first, that the Pizza Shops, when they contracted with Virginia, relied on its skill, judgment and reputation, which made impossible a delegation of Virginia's duties to Macke; and second, that the damages claimed could not be shown with reasonable certainty. These conclusions are challenged by Macke.

In the absence of a contrary provision—and there was none here—rights and duties under an executory bilateral contract may be assigned and delegated, subject to the exception that duties under a contract to provide personal services may never be delegated, nor rights be assigned under a contract where *delectus personae* was an ingredient of the bargain. 4 Corbin on Contracts § 865 (1951) at 434. * * *

The six machines were placed on the appellees' premises under a printed "Agreement-Contract" which identified the "customer," gave its place of business, described the vending machine, and then provided:

> "TERMS
>
> "1. The Company will install on the Customer's premises the above listed equipment and will maintain the equipment in good operating order and stocked with merchandise.
>
> "2. The location of this equipment will be such as to permit accessibility to persons desiring use of same. This equipment shall remain the property of the Company and shall not be moved from the location at which installed, except by the Company.
>
> "3. For equipment requiring electricity and water, the Customer is responsible for electrical receptacle and water outlet

within ten (10) feet of the equipment location. The Customer is also responsible to supply the Electrical Power and Water needed.

"4. The Customer will exercise every effort to protect this equipment from abuse or damage.

"5. The Company will be responsible for all licenses and taxes on the equipment and sale of products.

"6. This Agreement-Contract is for a term of one (1) year from the date indicated herein and will be automatically renewed for a like period, unless thirty (30) day written notice is given by either party to terminate service.

"7. Commission on monthly sales will be paid by the Company to the Customer at the following rate: * * *."

The rate provided in each of the agreements was "30% of Gross Receipts to $300.00 monthly [,] 35% over [$]300.00," except for the agreement with Pizza of Gaithersburg, Inc., which called for "40% of Gross Receipts."

We cannot regard the agreements as contracts for personal services. They were either a license or concession granted Virginia by the appellees, or a lease of a portion of the appellees' premises, with Virginia agreeing to pay a percentage of gross sales as a license or concession fee or as rent * * * and were assignable by Virginia unless they imposed on Virginia duties of a personal or unique character which could not be delegated, S & L Vending Corp. v. 52 Thompkins Ave. Restaurant, Inc., 26 A.D.2d 935, 274 N.Y.S.2d 697 (1966).

The appellees earnestly argue that they had dealt with Macke before and had chosen Virginia because they preferred the way it conducted its business. Specifically, they say that service was more personalized, since the president of Virginia kept the machines in working order, that commissions were paid in cash, and that Virginia permitted them to keep keys to the machines so that minor adjustments could be made when needed. Even if we assume all this to be true, the agreements with Virginia were silent as to the details of the working arrangements and contained only a provision requiring Virginia to "install * * * the above listed equipment and * * * maintain the equipment in good operating order and stocked with merchandise." We think the Supreme Court of California put the problem of personal service in proper focus a century ago when it upheld the assignment of a contract to grade a San Francisco street:

> "All painters do not paint portraits like Sir Joshua Reynolds, nor landscapes like Claude Lorraine, nor do all writers write dramas like Shakespeare or fiction like Dickens. Rare genius and extraordinary skill are not transferable, and contracts for their employment are therefore personal, and cannot be assigned. But

> rare genius and extraordinary skill are not indispensable to the workmanlike digging down of a sand hill or the filling up of a depression to a given level, or the construction of brick sewers with manholes and covers, and contracts for such work are not personal, and may be assigned." Taylor v. Palmer, 31 Cal. 240 at 247–248 (1866).

* * * Moreover, the difference between the service the Pizza Shops happened to be getting from Virginia and what they expected to get from Macke did not mount up to such a material change in the performance of obligations under the agreements as would justify the appellees' refusal to recognize the assignment. * * *

* * *

Except for the fact that the result has been roundly criticized, see Corbin, *supra,* at 448–49, the Pizza Shops might have found some solace in the facts found in Boston Ice Co. v. Potter, 123 Mass. 28 (1877). There, Potter, who had dealt with the Boston Ice Company, and found its service unsatisfactory, transferred his business to Citizens' Ice Company. Later, Citizens' sold out to Boston, unbeknown to Potter, and Potter was served by Boston for a full year. When Boston attempted to collect its ice bill, the Massachusetts court sustained Potter's demurrer on the ground that there was no privity of contract, since Potter had a right to choose with whom he would deal and could not have another supplier thrust upon him. Modern authorities do not support this result, and hold that, absent provision to the contrary, a duty may be delegated, as distinguished from a right which can be assigned, and that the promisee cannot rescind, if the quality of the performance remains materially the same.

* * *

As we see it, the delegation of duty by Virginia to Macke was entirely permissible under the terms of the agreements. * * *

* * *

Judgment reversed as to liability. * * *

NEHF, WRITING CONTRACTS IN THE CLIENT'S INTEREST

51 S.C. L.Rev. 153, 179–80 (1999).

A deciding factor [in Macke] was that the contract did not mention these benefits which the non-assigning party now claimed were so important. The lesson for contract drafters is that all important expectations should be spelled out in the contract; otherwise, it may be difficult to contend later that they were material parts of the bargain that would be altered through an assignment.

NOTE:
"ASSIGNMENT OF CONTRACT" INCLUDES DELEGATION

If a contract between an assignor and assignee uses only general language such as "we assign the contract to," the Restatement (Second) of Contracts and the Uniform Commercial Code, which we set forth below, indicate that courts should treat the assignment as an assignment of rights *and* a delegation of duties. In addition, in such a situation, courts should construe the assignee-delegatee's implied promise to take on the duties of the assignor-delegator as creating in the original obligee a third-party beneficiary right. So if B "assigns its contract with A to C" courts should treat the contract as an assignment to C of B's rights against A and a delegation to C of B's duties to A. A is a third-party intended beneficiary of C's implied promise to take on B's duties to A. See, e.g., Brett Stone Painting and Maintenance v. New England Bank, 72 A.3d 1121 (Conn. 2015) (homeowner's obligation to contractor delegated to bank that was therefore liable to contractor).

RESTATEMENT (SECOND) OF CONTRACTS § 328.

(1) Unless the language or the circumstances indicate the contrary, as in an assignment for security, an assignment of "the contract" or of "all my rights under the contract" or an assignment in similar general terms is an assignment of the assignor's rights and a delegation of his unperformed duties under the contract.

(2) Unless the language or the circumstances indicate the contrary, the acceptance by an assignee of such an assignment operates as a promise to the assignor to perform the assignor's unperformed duties, and the obligor of the assigned rights is an intended beneficiary of the promise.

UNIFORM COMMERCIAL CODE § 2–210(3) and (4).

(3) Unless the circumstances indicate the contrary a prohibition of assignment of "the contract" is to be construed as barring only the delegation to the assignee of the assignor's performance.

(4) An assignment of "the contract" or of "all my rights under the contract" or an assignment in similar general terms is an assignment of rights and unless the language or the circumstances (as in an assignment for security) indicate the contrary, it is a delegation of performance of the duties of the assignor and its acceptance by the assignee constitutes a promise by him to perform those duties. This promise is enforceable by either the assignor or the other party to the original contract.

UNIFORM COMMERCIAL CODE § 2–210(1).

A party may perform his duty through a delegate unless otherwise agreed or unless the other party has a substantial interest in having his original promisor perform or control the acts required by the contract. No delegation of performance relieves the party delegating of any duty to perform or any liability for breach.

DEMOCRACY CAPITAL CORP. v. MARYLAND FINANCIAL BANK, 2020 WL 551095 (Ct. of Special App. Md. 2020). [T]he Court of Appeals differentiated between "the term 'assignment,' " meaning "the transfer of contractual rights[,]" and "the term 'delegation[,]' " meaning "the transfer of contractual duties." *Public Serv. Comm'n v. Panda-Brandywine, L.P.*, 375 Md. [185,] 197 [(2003)]. The Court explained that a contractual right may not be assigned if the assignment is validly precluded by contract, and that a contractual duty may not be delegated if the delegation is contrary to the terms of the obligor's promise. *Id.* at 198. Put differently, a "valid contractual provision prohibiting assignment or delegation" may limit "the extent to which rights may be assigned and duties of performance may be delegated[.]" *Id.* at 198–99.

SECTION FIVE: NOVATION

The general view is that a delegating party remains liable to the obligee even after a valid delegation of duties. Suppose, however, that the obligee agrees (expressly or impliedly) to release the delegating party in exchange for the new duty of the delegate. Contract law calls the new contract a novation. The delegate substitutes for the party delegating, who is discharged.

The Restatement (Second) of Contracts section 329 provides that a novation occurs if the obligee, without reservation of rights against the party delegating, accepts any performance from the delegate with knowledge that the party delegating has repudiated his or her obligation to the obligee.

UTICA MUTUAL INSURANCE COMPANY v. VIGO COAL COMPANY, INC.

United States Court of Appeals, Seventh Circuit, 2004.
393 F.3d 707.

POSNER, CIRCUIT JUDGE.

This diversity suit for breach of a suretyship contract, decided in favor of the defendants after a bench trial, presents questions primarily relating to the contract-law doctrine of "novation," but more broadly to principles of contract interpretation; all the questions are governed by the common law of Indiana.

In 1991 defendant Vigo purchased Buck Creek Coal, which operated a coal mine and was required by both federal and state law to post reclamation bonds as a condition of being permitted to operate the mine. 30 U.S.C. § 1259(a); 30 C.F.R. § 800.20; Ind.Code § 14–34–6–1. In connection with the purchase, Vigo, joined by defendant Atlas and by the owners of Vigo and Atlas (the Koesters and the Piepers, respectively, who are also defendants) and by Buck Creek Coal, signed a "General Indemnity Agreement." In it they agreed to indemnify Utica insurance company for any losses that Utica might incur from issuing reclamation bonds to the Indiana state government on behalf of Buck Creek. The following year (1992) another "General Indemnity Agreement" was signed, identical to the first, except that the only signers were defendant Schulties, who had not signed the previous agreement, and the Piepers (who, remember, are Atlas's owners). Mr. Pieper signed both individually and as president; and because of his having thus signed in his official capacity, as it were, as an agent apparently authorized to bind his principal, the district judge ruled that Atlas was bound by the second agreement. * * * Atlas has not challenged that ruling, even though it appears from the 1992 agreement that Pieper actually was signing in his capacity as president of Buck Creek, not of Atlas. So Atlas is bound; and to simplify our opinion we shall assume that Atlas and Schulties were the signers of the second agreement and Vigo and Atlas the signers of the first; in other words, we'll ignore not only the district court's unchallenged error but also the companies' owners. With this simplification, the case becomes Utica versus Vigo.

The surety bonds were later "forfeited"; that is, Buck Creek proving unable to fulfill its reclamation obligations, the state required the surety, Utica, to do the reclamation. Utica then brought this suit, against all the signers of either agreement, for reimbursement of the expense—some $400,000—of the reclamation.

The district court concluded that the signers of the 1991 indemnity agreement were off the hook (except Atlas, since it had signed the second agreement as well) because the second agreement was a "novation," that is, a replacement of the first agreement, which therefore released the obligors in that agreement. * * * But the judge also turned down these defendants' counterclaim, in which they sought to recover the attorneys' fees that they had incurred in defending against Utica's claim.

Unable to recover its entire loss from the signers of the 1992 agreement (Atlas and Schulties—the latter now bankrupt), and seeking therefore to enforce the 1991 agreement against Vigo, Utica challenges the finding that the 1992 agreement was a novation.

The agreement does not describe itself as a novation or a substitute, or purport to release the signers of the first agreement. The only clue in the agreements themselves that the second one might be a novation is that Atlas signed both, and if the only purpose of the second was to add an indemnitor, namely Schulties, why did Atlas sign it, having signed the identical first agreement, unless that wasn't the purpose, and the second agreement replaced rather than supplemented the first? Additional evidence, that is, evidence beyond the two agreements themselves, was presented at the trial, and that evidence, together with the anomaly we've just noted, persuaded the judge that the second agreement was indeed a novation.

That evidence revealed the following. In 1992, Vigo sold the coal mine to Atlas and Schulties and they agreed to use their best efforts to replace the existing reclamation bonds and obtain a release of Vigo's liability under those bonds. They failed to do so, but an insurance agent named Jones submitted a "reclamation bonding application" to Utica, proposing to "transfer these bonds over and have new Indemnity Agreements signed by Chuck Schulties." There was no mention of Vigo. The agent testified that the reason Vigo was left off the second agreement was that it and its owners, who had signed the 1991 agreement, "had no ownership, they had no control, they were not party to running the company." Asked at trial whether Vigo's omission from the agreement was "confirmatory of the conversations that you'd had with [Utica's Gerald Swarthout, who handled the negotiations leading up to the 1992 agreement] that they would not be indemnitors," the agent replied "of course, they were selling."

Swarthout gave contrary testimony, but the district judge disbelieved it, in part because Schulties had (at the time!) substantial assets. That fact, together with his substantial expertise in coal mining, suggested that an indemnity agreement signed by him as well as by Atlas would provide sufficient security to persuade Utica *or some other insurance company* to issue new reclamation bonds to replace those that Utica had issued. For although the General Indemnity Agreement (whether the 1991 or the 1992 version, since they were identical except for the signers) embraced replacement bonds, it was terminable by an indemnitor on 20 days' notice. And therefore as part of Vigo's sale of the coal mine to Atlas and Schulties, Atlas and Vigo could have withdrawn from the 1991 agreement and Atlas and Schulties, with a net worth between them of $7 million, could have persuaded Utica or some other insurance company to issue new surety bonds that Vigo, having withdrawn from the agreement, would not have been a guarantor of. Utica does not deny that its bonds could have been replaced in this fashion. Ind.Code § 14–34–6–14.6.

The consequence of replacing the bonds would have been to release Vigo. But given Schulties' financial wherewithal and mining expertise, and Vigo's natural reluctance to remain a guarantor of performance over which, as a result of the sale, it would no longer have any control, the judge was on solid ground in finding that Utica would have agreed to an express novation rather than lose to another insurance company a business relationship that yielded it significant premiums ($18,000 a year) in exchange for assuming what seemed at the time a modest risk. Modest because underground coal mines (Buck Creek's mine was an underground mine) tend to require less expense to restore the surface after the mine is exhausted than strip mines and because two substantial-seeming parties, Atlas and Schulties, had agreed to indemnify Utica for any loss.

The judge's reconstruction of the parties' deal—his conclusion that they intended the second agreement to substitute for rather than supplement the first—is not clearly erroneous. On the contrary, it makes commercial, economic, and common sense; and good sense, or such synonyms as commercial reasonableness, provides sound guidance for interpreting ambiguous contracts, in Indiana as elsewhere. * * * As Judge Boudin explained recently, "Agreements, especially commercial arrangements, are designed to make sense. If one reading produces a plausible result for which parties might be expected to bargain, that reading has a strong presumption in its favor as against another reading producing an unlikely result (*e.g.*, windfall gains, conditions that cannot be satisfied, dubious incentives)." *National Tax Institute, Inc. v. Topnotch at Stowe Resort & Spa,* 388 F.3d 15, 19 (1st Cir.2004).

The difficult question is whether the district judge was entitled to take evidence—to mine underground, as it were—rather than to stay on the semantic surface of the two agreements. A finding of novation is dynamite, as this case illustrates. Instead of supplementing a previous contract, it wipes it out. Parties that enter into multiple contracts with one another want protection against a trial that may convert a contract that says nothing about novation or release into a release of the obligors under a previous contract. Were it not for what we're calling the dynamite effect of a novation, there would be no reason to treat a novation any differently from any other contract modification.

One way to give obligees protection would be to have a rule that a novation or release must be explicit; that it can never be implied. Indiana rejects that approach, * * * no jurisdiction, to our knowledge, accepts it. So we can set it to one side. There are three alternatives. One, proposed by the Williston treatise, is to require that a novation be proved by clear and convincing evidence. 30 *Williston on Contracts, supra,* § 76:42. The cases do not support this alternative; *Johnston v. Holiday Inns, Inc.,* 565 F.2d 790, 797 (1st Cir.1977), rejects it outright. What the case law, including Indiana case law, does support is that proof of a novation must be "clear and definite" or "clear and satisfactory" or words to that effect. * * * We take this to be an appropriate reminder of the fell consequences of a finding of novation.

Another alternative, which would treat the determination of novation like other issues of contractual interpretation, is that a novation can be implied only if there is an ambiguity as to whether the agreement claimed to be a novation really is one, rather than merely a supplement to the earlier agreement. This approach also has support in Indiana, as in other states. * * *

Still another alternative * * * appears to allow extrinsic evidence to be introduced in *any* novation case, perhaps on the theory (not articulated in the cases, however) that the agreement claimed to be a novation cannot be interpreted without consideration of the meaning of the contract it is alleged to have replaced. This cannot be quite right; if the second agreement states "this is a novation" or "this is not a novation," that surely is the end of the case; extrinsic evidence will not be allowed.

Probably what we have described as alternative rules come to the same thing, in the following sense; the court can always peek at the earlier contract, and if in light of what that contract says it is uncertain whether the new contract is a novation, then the court can treat the interpretive issue as one of fact, that is, can take evidence on it, but always bearing in mind the need for the proof of a novation to be clear. The earlier contract is a bit of extrinsic evidence that is always already in the case, and if it shows that the new contract is ambiguous (as to whether it is a novation), the door is opened to the presentation of additional extrinsic evidence, which may make clear that the new contract really was intended to take the place of the old.

* * *

[E]xtrinsic ambiguity was adequately demonstrated here. There was no integration clause in the 1992 agreement (or in the prior one, for that matter, for remember that the terms, as distinct from their signatories, are identical). And so Judge Hamilton had to consider extrinsic evidence in order to decide whether the agreement was the complete agreement of the parties. It was not. From the sale of the mine and the other circumstances we've recounted it is apparent that the parties understood the 1992 agreement to replace rather than supplement the previous one.

* * *

So the judge's ruling that there was a novation stands. * * *

* * *

AFFIRMED.

APPENDIX A

JUDICIAL REASONS

▪ ▪ ▪

The reasons set forth by judges to support their decisions are of great importance. It is not possible to understand a court opinion without a firm grasp of these reasons.

It is useful to distinguish between three basic types of reasons: (1) authoritative reasons, (2) substantive reasons, and (3) institutional reasons. Authoritative reasons appeal to recognized authorities including case law, statutes, administrative regulations, and constitutions. These authorities are legally binding within the jurisdictions where they are applicable. They are also "persuasive" authority, or authority by analogy, in other jurisdictions. Other non-binding authorities that generate authoritative reasons are restatements, treatises, law review articles, and the like. The opinion in White v. Benkowski includes appeals both to binding and non-binding authorities.

The justificatory force of authoritative reasons that appeal to binding authorities derives from at least two sources: (1) the various values served when courts follow antecedent law, whatever its content: certainty, predictability, equality before the law, efficiency, etc. and (2) the various values that may inform the content of the case law, statutes, and other authorities involved. The first class of values might be called "formal rule of law values," the second class, simply "substantive values." The general rule denying punitive damages, invoked as an authoritative reason by the court in White v. Benkowski, reflects not only values of the first type but also substantive values, including the values associated with freedom of contract. That is, parties will contract more freely if they know that damages for breach generally do not include a sum for punishment.

Authoritative reasons do not necessarily incorporate values of both types. Thus a given authoritative reason might serve formal "rule of law" values, but not relevant substantive values. The rule invoked by the court might indeed by the relevant and authoritative rule, but the rule might be substantively unsound.

It is important to develop the ability to construct and evaluate authoritative reasons. One possible criticism of an authoritative reason is that it does not apply. For example, a rule may not apply because the case from which it derives is distinguishable—not "in point." Relatedly, a case-law rule may not apply because the reasons for the adoption of the rule are not applicable to the case at hand. Another possible criticism is that the substantive content of a rule is unsound in some way (e.g., perhaps punitive damages have no effect on a party's willingness to contract).

The terms of valid agreements may be viewed as a special class of authoritative reasons. Do you see why?

Substantive reasons do not involve appeals to authority. These reasons consist of moral, economic, political, and other social considerations. Those unfamiliar with the law may think that judges must decide cases according to antecedent law, and thus can give only authoritative reasons, preferably those of a binding nature. This view is reinforced by crude positivist philosophies of law which implicitly hold that truly legal reasons necessarily appeal to antecedent binding authority. In fact, judges frequently give substantive reasons to support their decisions. A judge may not only give an authoritative reason, but may also offer a substantive reason that supports the same result. Or a judge may be faced with an issue not previously decided in the jurisdiction. In such a case, the judge usually decides by comparing the justificatory force of the substantive reasons on each side of the issue. Or a judge may confront an issue on which the authorities are in conflict, or an issue of whether to overrule a prior case. Here, too, the judge usually decides in accord with the weight of the competing substantive reasons.

As with authoritative reasons, it is important to develop the ability to construct and critically evaluate substantive reasons. In this regard, it is useful to distinguish between two different types of substantive reasons. The first type of substantive reason is a "goal" reason. In Sullivan v. O'Connor (in Chapter 1), Justice Kaplan stated that: "If actions for breach of promise can be readily maintained, doctors, so it is said, will be frightened into practising 'defensive medicine.' " A goal reason, then, for not readily permitting such actions might be that this will promote effective health care. You can see that the justificatory force of a goal reason derives from the predicted salutary effects of the decision it supports. Two of the possible grounds for criticizing a goal reason are that the decision would not have effects that serve the goal, and that the goal is not a good one.

A second type of substantive reason may be called a "rightness" reason. In Sullivan v. O'Connor, Justice Kaplan offered a rightness reason when he stated: "We should recall that the fee paid by the patient to the doctor for the alleged promise would usually be quite disproportionate to the putative expectancy recovery." This is essentially a rightness argument that an expectancy recovery would be unfair. Unlike a good goal reason, the justificatory force of a good rightness reason does not depend on the predicted effects of the decision it supports. Rather, the justificatory force of a good rightness reason depends upon the soundness and applicability of the rightness norm in which the reason is grounded. Thus the force of the rightness reason set forth by Justice Kaplan depends on a norm that might in this context be articulated as follows: "In the absence of special circumstances, potential liability of a contracting party should be proportionate to that party's expected gain." A rightness reason is subject to criticism on various grounds, including the possible inapplicability of the norm to the facts, and the possible unsoundness of the norm.

Still another type of reason found in judicial opinions is "institutional" in character. In Sullivan v. O'Connor, Justice Kaplan set forth an institutional reason when he said: "But patients may transform such statements into firm promises in their own minds, especially when they have been disappointed in the event, and testify in that sense to sympathetic juries." Here are some further examples of institutional reasons:

—Because the plaintiff's claim calls for a change in the law that cannot justifiably be made without access to "general social facts" that only a legislature can adequately investigate or evaluate, the court ought not to make the change, but should leave it to the legislature.

—Because the court could not supervise the implementation of its decree without undue expenditure of resources, an order for specific performance of the contract will be denied.

—Because of difficulties of measurement, breach of contract damages should not include pain and suffering.

From these examples, it can be seen that an institutional reason is a special kind of goal reason or rightness reason. Such reasons are often influential, and it is important to develop the ability to construct and evaluate them. This requires, among other things, the acquisition of "institutional" knowledge about the processes, personnel, and roles involved.

We now return to the general question: why is it important to study closely the reasons judges give for their decisions? This is a very large subject which can only be introduced here. By close study of authoritative reasons, we can better understand the meaning and likely consequences of a judge's decision. For example, we can determine whether and to what extent a judge follows prior law. If the judge purports to follow applicable law but does not, then the decision rendered will be "lawless" in that respect. Moreover, it will have less precedential value.

The study of substantive reasons also has a special importance. First, substantive reasons may improve and shape the very content of law (and thus improve and shape future authoritative reasons).

Second, by focusing on the substantive reasons that support a rule (or other form of law), we may determine more reliably the true scope of the rule. This is largely because most judges, at least in regard to case law rules, follow Karl N. Llewellyn's maxim: "the rule follows where its reason leads, where reason stops, there stops the rule."

Third, as we have seen, substantive reasons are largely decisive in cases where there is no antecedent binding law, where case law is in conflict, or where a rule originally unsound or now outmoded should be overruled. And in all such cases, a judge may or may not formulate a general rule. When the judge does not formulate a rule, subsequent judges will very likely look upon the substantive reasons given by the first judge as the germ of a new rule. When a judge does formulate a general rule, later judges will consider accompanying substantive reasons in determining the contours of the announced rule.

Fourth, substantive reasons are necessary constituents of all forms of criticism of law and its operation. Those who are unable to construct and evaluate substantive reasons simply cannot engage in effective criticism. A legal system which lawyers and others do not subject to effective criticism almost certainly would not be of high quality.

It is sometimes said that the serious study of judicial reasons is pointless because judges seldom give their "real" reasons. We believe nearly all judges try to give their "real" reasons when writing opinions. But even if this were not so, the study of the reasons actually given would be far from pointless.

Authoritative reasons are analyzed and discussed further in H.L.A. Hart, Essays on Bentham 242–268 (1982), and also in Summers, Two Types of Substantive Reasons: The Core of a Theory of Common-Law Justification, 63 Cornell L.Rev. 707, 724–5 (1978). The latter article also extensively discusses substantive reasons. A related but somewhat different approach to substantive reasons appears in R. Dworkin, Taking Rights Seriously, ch. 4 (1977). An important critique of Dworkin's views on substantive reasons is Greenawalt, Policy, Rights, and Judicial Decision, 11 Ga.L.Rev. 991 (1977). Dworkin's reply appears in Dworkin, Seven Critics, 11 Ga.L.Rev. 1201, 1203–1241 (1977).

APPENDIX B

HISTORICAL BACKGROUND OF CONSIDERATION AND RELATED DOCTRINES[a]

■ ■ ■

From the mid 16th century to the late 19th century, courts and commentators often discussed "consideration" in connection with two separate problems. First, they wanted to ensure that the law went far enough in recognizing consensual liability. Early English law had dramatically under-recognized such liability. (In our terms, the courts failed to adopt sufficiently expansive theories of obligation.) The second problem was to see that such liability did not go too far—that due limits were imposed.

The English common law was, until the 19th century, encased in what were called "forms of action" administered primarily by the "common-law courts": Kings Bench, Common Pleas, and Exchequer. These courts were distinguished from the Court of Chancery that administered a body of law and a set of special remedies called "equity," until the merger of law and equity in the 19th century.

What then were these forms of action? We offer a general functional account. With few exceptions, a lawyer could start a legal proceeding in one of the common-law courts only by purchasing, from a clerk in the office of Chancery, a "writ" embodying the relevant form of action for the case at hand. The lawyer reviewed the Register of Writs (or a copy of it) to see if it included a writ embodying a form of action which covered the fact pattern his client related to him. The early writs (1) directed the sheriff of the shire where the episode occurred to have the defendant appear in court, and (2) authorized the common law court to take jurisdiction of the case. In general, there was no substantive right to a remedy if there was no available form of action. The form of action also usually prescribed certain procedural requirements, including modes of trial. Over hundreds of years, new writs were added to the Register of Writs, more or less haphazardly. As it grew, so the substantive law grew. Sir Henry Maine in his great work, Dissertations on Early Law and Custom, remarked in 1883 (at 389) that "[s]o great is the ascendency of the Law of Actions in the infancy of Courts of Justice, that substantive law has at first the look of being gradually

---

[a] The editors wish to thank Professor A.W.B. Simpson for reviewing this historical account.

secreted in the interstices of procedure; and the early lawyer can only see the law through the envelope of its technical forms."

In the field we now know as contract, the two most important early forms of action were called "covenant" and "debt." In medieval times, covenant was available only to recover for breach of promises under seal. The student should review the modern theories of obligation in Chapter Two and identify the one most analogous today to covenant. How, if at all, might Fuller justify the availability of this form of action? (See the extract, Consideration and Form, in Chapter 2.)

The form of action called debt had several uses. One use was to enforce a broken promise to pay a sum certain in money *in return* for a loan, or goods sold, or services received. The plaintiff (in our parlance) would have to prove (if denied) that the defendant had *actually received* the loan, the goods, the services, etc.—a *quid pro quo,* as it was called. The student should review the modern theories of obligation studied in Chapter Two and identify the one or ones most analogous today to debt (as we have here described it). Some scholars trace the emphasis on bargained-for exchange and on "benefit to the promisor" in 19th century consideration theory to the influence of the action of debt.

By about 1500, there were some extensions of debt beyond the above confines. For example, a seller could sue in debt for the agreed price (a "sum certain") of *undelivered* property.

The mode of trial in debt involved appeal to the supernatural. The defendant could "wage his law" and bring in so called "oath helpers" who would in effect swear that the defendant was not liable. Mode of trial aside, do you see how debt and covenant together were woefully deficient compared to the theories of obligation available today? The biggest gap in promissory liability, of course, was that a plaintiff could not, as a general matter, recover damages for the breach of a bilateral executory agreement not under seal. (Of course, the above noted extension of debt was a limited move in this direction.)

During the 1500s and 1600s major developments occurred in a further form of action called "assumpsit" (the Latin word for "undertook"). This form of action did not require a promise under seal, a sum certain, or trial by wager of law.

Assumpsit grew out of the tort form of action called "trespass on the case," and came very largely to supersede debt. Before 1500, assumpsit had become widely available where there was a consensual arrangement in which the defendant undertook to do something for the plaintiff and then did it poorly, i.e. "misfeasance." Here the loss occurred within a relationship defined by an agreement which shaped the contours of the duty later broken. For example, if D agreed to ferry P's horses, cart, goods, and family across the River Isis and D *negligently* dumped everything in the river, P could recover. The theoretical basis of this form of action at this time was not the failure to perform a promise, but rather the tortious wrong by the defendant, causing a loss to P. Some scholars trace the emphasis in 19th century consideration theory on "detriment" incurred by the promisee in reliance on the promisor to "misfeasance-assumpsit." You should again review the modern theories of obligation studied in Chapter Two and identify the one most analogous today to this use of assumpsit (as we have so far described it). Has Fuller failed to provide a "contractual" rationale for the recognition of this use of assumpsit as a form of action? Of course, this use of assumpsit did not satisfy the need for a general theory of relief for the broken bilateral *executory* agreement.

What, then, if the defendant in our example was guilty only of "nonfeasance?" For example, what if, after promising to ferry the agreed persons and things across the River Isis, the defendant simply refused to carry out the promise at all, thereby causing a loss? During the 1500s and 1600s, such a broken promise came to be redressable in assumpsit, at least if the plaintiff relied on the promise. A major early landmark case was Pickering v. Thoroughgood, decided in 1533. Spilman J. said in that case:

> And in some books a difference has been taken between nonfeasance and malfeasance; thus on the one an action of covenant lies, and on the other an action on the case lies. This is no distinction in reason, for if a carpenter for £100 covenants with me to make me a house, and does not make it before the day assigned, so that I am deprived of lodging, I shall have an action for this nonfeasance just as well as if he had made it badly.[b]

Even in the absence of reliance, a mere promise given in exchange for another's promise also came to be viewed as a "detriment," a "consideration," enabling courts to enforce purely executory exchanges. This was a major step in the growth of liability.[c] (For this use of "detriment" as consideration, see, for example, Hamer v. Sidway.) When these exchanges were enforced, the form of action was called "special assumpsit" because of the specificity required in the pleading form, which had to set forth how the obligation arose.

Assumpsit eventually also occupied most of the field formerly occupied by debt. In this use, assumpsit was called "indebitatus" or "general" assumpsit. The name general assumpsit arose because of the generality permitted in the pleading form. Unlike special assumpsit, it was not necessary to allege specifically how the obligation arose. It was necessary to allege only that the defendant, indebted to the plaintiff in a certain sum, promised or undertook to pay the debt. General assumpsit also grew to

---

[b] As found in A.W.B. Simpson's historical introduction to G. Cheshire & C. Fifoot, Law of Contract 5 (10th ed. M. Furmston, editor 1981).

[c] See, e.g., Strangeborough v. Warner, 4 Leon 3 (1589).

include certain very general stylized pleading forms called the "common counts." (The foregoing matters are treated more fully in A.W.B. Simpson, A History of the Common Law of Contract—The Rise of the Action of Assumpsit 303–07 (1975)).

By the 1600s, the presence of "consideration," even then sometimes sloganized as benefit to the promisor or detriment to the promisee,[d] enabled the plaintiff to maintain an action of assumpsit. Professor A.W.B. Simpson, the leading scholar of this branch of our subject, has said:

> The consideration, or considerations, for a promise meant the factors which the promisor considered when he promised, and which moved or motivated his promising. Although not a precise equivalent, "motive" is perhaps about as near as one can get by way of synonym. The essence of the doctrine of consideration, then, is the adoption by the common law of the idea that the legal effect of a promise should depend upon the factor or factors which motivated the promise. To decide whether a promise to do X is binding, you need to know why the promise was made. This basic idea can be elaborated in various ways—for example, one might or might not accept love of charity, or a future marriage, or a past payment, as sufficient in law to impose promissory liability. Whatever decisions are made about such matters as these can be fitted into the basic analysis.
>
> The recognition by the common law that a promise, to give rise to legal liability in assumpsit, must be "supported" by good, sufficient, or adequate consideration, entails the idea that a promise on its own, an unsupported promise, is not sufficient to impose liability. * * * In modern terms one can see the plausibility of the theory—a promise which lacks any adequate motive cannot have been serious, and therefore ought not to be taken seriously. (A.W.B. Simpson, A History of the Common Law of Contract—The Rise of the Action of Assumpsit 321–22 (1975).)

Thus the *presence* of consideration in the late middle ages helped to bring about full recognition of liability for the wholly unperformed promise as part of an executory exchange, and the *absence* of consideration imposed outer limits on the liability that came to be recognized. There is no inherent reason, however, why consideration must mean exactly the same thing in both of its manifestations. For example, if consideration is defined as requiring a bargain (and courts do not always so define it) the presence of a bargain might be held sufficient for prima facie liability, yet the absence of a bargain might not be held fatal. See Hamer v. Sidway. Yet it should be easy to see how *intellectual* pressure grew for a *unitary* conception of

[d] Stone v. Wythipol, Cro.Eliz. 126, 1 Leon 113, Owen 94 (1588).

consideration. Both Restatements of contract reflect this pressure, the second even more than the first.

APPENDIX C

THE RESTATEMENT IDEA

■ ■ ■

This book contains many sections of the contracts Restatements. They are a helpful learning tool. Some remarks about their usage follow.

CLARK, THE RESTATEMENT OF THE LAW OF CONTRACTS

42 Yale L.J. 643, 646, 652, 654–56 (1933).

[A] black letter sentence * * * can never * * * state pages of history and policy and honest deliberation * * *.

* * *

The * * * [Restatement] is apparently the final answer that the Word alone counts, and the long and tortuous way by which the Word was ascertained is to be forgotten.

* * *

Simplification as an end in itself is false. Simplification as a clarification and orderly statement of intellectual processes and conclusions is desirable. The idea that there is "the law"—the "common" *non-statutory* law—of our forty eight states, our territories and our federal system, which can be stated, is the former kind of simplification. Actually the resulting statement is the law nowhere and in its unreality only deludes and misleads. It is either a generality so obvious as immediately to be accepted, or so vague as not to offend, or of such antiquity as to be unchallenged as a statement of past history.

* * *

The process of statutory interpretation, though inevitable, is difficult and full of pitfalls. * * * [R]estatement interpretation is an unreality. And without interpretation, or *background* against which meaning can be discovered, the black letter statements are not understandable. The idea that words speak for themselves, without interpretation in the light of the circumstance under which they were composed or arranged, has been too often exploded with reference to wills, contracts and written instruments generally, to be believed again with respect to the restatements.

This fallacy, that words speak for themselves or convey a clear meaning of themselves, is * * * at the bottom of the Institute's insistence on the sanctity of the black letter.

* * *

* * * Moreover the black letter itself is, as must be expected, a compromise to cover various views. With one leg it steps forward; with the other it steps backward. It is caught between stating the law which should be and the law which is and often ends by stating only the law that was. * * * The necessity of agreement on black letter forces each participant to a choice of position which, when stated as a group result, must inevitably tend towards (a) the ancient historical rather than the modern rule or possible future trend, (b) the conventional safe and unoriginal point of view and (c) a compromise which goes only to the point whereon all are agreed.

PATTERSON, THE RESTATEMENT OF THE LAW OF CONTRACTS

33 Colum.L.Rev. 397, 399–400, 405 (1933).

Obviously some propositions of law must be rejected in favor of others with which they are inconsistent; the "weight of authority" test can be applied. The draftsmen of the Restatement were experts in applying this test. Other propositions of law, seemingly diverse, may be capable of translation into common terms. The translation formula is a product of expert opinion, to quote from the preface of the present work. The assertion (in the preface) that it is "the product of expert opinion" seems to imply that there are no divergent expert opinions. This is contrary to fact. The illusion that "the law" can be found in one and only one set of authoritative propositions is not wholly dispelled.

The meaning of Restatement becomes still more ambiguous when one looks at the diverse theories as to the interpretation of precedents. Can a judicial decision of an appellate court be taken to imply a proposition nowhere stated in the opinion? One knows that courts sometimes distinguish their prior decisions by this method; and there is expert opinion in favor of a more extensive use of this type of analysis. The opinion itself will frequently reveal statements of varying degrees of comprehensiveness or abstractness; add to this range of choice the possibility of others not mentioned in the opinion but seen by the divining eye of the expert, and one has a wide variety of choice as to the proposition for which a given precedent shall be taken to stand. A judicial precedent has, practically, a minimum and a maximum value, and a number of values in between these extremes. The expert has to choose between them.

What are the criteria of his choice? The "weight-of-authority" test furnishes some guidance. Yet this is no mere matter of counting cases; respect for the reasoning of an opinion or for the reputation of the court will be thrown into the scale. On many questions of law there either is no weight of authority, or none established beyond the peradventure of a doubt. In such a case one chooses the law that one thinks ought to be. The proposition thus chosen can be shown to be supported by cases; inconvenient facts become irrelevant detail, and incompatible portions of the opinion are disregarded. Listen to lawyers arguing a question of case-law, and then read the court's opinion. The Restatement Committee, no more than the judges, can avoid choices, value-judgments.

The re-assertion of this conclusion would be needless repetition were it not for the persistence of the belief that a unique and exclusively valid system of rules of law exists somehow and can be discovered by an inexorable process of deduction or of induction.

* * *

* * * As a rational system of norms the Restatement might be expected to reveal the basic ethical principles upon which it rests; but the ethical basis of the law of contract is scarcely mentioned.

HAVIGHURST, THE RESTATEMENT OF THE LAW OF CONTRACTS

27 Ill.L.Rev. 910, 914–15 (1933).

One of the objects of the Restatement as stated in the Introduction is to meet the difficulties occasioned by the ever growing mass of case material. The thought seems to be that the looking up of law will be greatly facilitated. This would suggest the danger of technological unemployment for young lawyers recently turned out. But it is doubtful if they have cause to worry. The Anglo-American lawyer is too thoroughly steeped in the tradition of using cases in building his arguments ever easily to relinquish his search for precedent before exhausting the field. No matter how perfect and authoritative his general principle, the better lawyer will feel on firmer ground if he has one supporting case with similar facts or furnishing an apt analogy.

* * *

Moreover, in some respects, apart from the expense of keeping up libraries, the increasing number of reports may well be a cause for satisfaction rather than alarm. In the preparation of a case, the study of prior cases dealing with a similar problem serves to call attention to elements and social implications which might otherwise be overlooked. In a sense lawyers and judges must educate themselves anew for each occurring problem. There is no method that is more efficient than the case method; and the more cases the better. This is true both for sound advocacy and for wise decision. The habit of using cases as authority rather than for their educational value is doubtless too firmly ingrained to be overcome. This habit, however, is wholesome in that lawyers who would otherwise be conscious of no need, are constantly re-educating themselves in spite of themselves. This, to my mind, is the great advantage of our Anglo-American system over the civil law system. A few cases sacrificed on the altar of blind precedent are a small price to pay for it. Moreover, it is doubtful if the idea that precedents are binding has an appreciable effect in producing stagnation in the law. There are so many possibilities of distinguishing facts. And courts have shown a disposition to feel free to overrule if the precedent seems outworn. We may thus in a sense eat our cake and have it too. The Restatement, if it should succeed in leading us away from the cases and back to first principles, will profit us something in flexibility, but such gain will be offset by the loss of the case method in legal self-education. We need case study; and the more complex becomes the organization of society, the more cases we need covering its manifold phases.

GORDLEY, EUROPEAN CODES AND AMERICAN RESTATEMENTS: SOME DIFFICULTIES

81 Colum.L.Rev. 140, 147–51, 153–54 (1981).

Now, as the *Restatement (Second) of Contracts* makes its official appearance, it may be a good time to ask again, what can a restatement or a code do to clarify the law?

* * * [T]here are benefits * * *. But there is no reason to believe that clarity is among them.

* * *

Although the problem of formulating rules is closely related to that of choosing the better rule, it will be helpful to consider each of these problems by itself. Suppose, then, that the main problem confronting judges and scholars is that they have been unable to formulate a plausible rule. They have in mind, in a general way, what they want this rule to do, the policy considerations to which it should respond, or the particular results that it should explain. But they still do not have a rule. They cannot clearly describe a class or category of cases and assign to it a definite legal result, or if they can, the result seems to be the wrong one for at least some of the cases falling within that class.

If that is the predicament of judges and scholars, it is likely to be the predicament of drafters as well, since they are in no better position to find a clear and plausible rule. They may even be in a worse position than scholars; while a scholar can concentrate on one problem and write a specialized article when he thinks he has it solved, drafters must produce a full set of rules. Consequently, the drafters may have only two alternatives. They may formulate a rule that is cloudy and does not clearly describe which cases should come out which way. Or they might formulate a rule that is clearer but is too broad or too narrow. It sweeps in some cases that call for the opposite result or leaves out some of that call for the same result.

* * *

When the drafters propose such a cloudy rule, it is hard to see how they have clarified prior law. The most they will have contributed is a hint about the direction in which to look for a solution. Their formulations, although vague, may be suggestive and so may give some guidance. But if so, it is guidance of a peculiarly dangerous kind. It is always perilous for anyone, a court, a scholar, or a draftsman, to tell others where to look for a solution that he himself has not found, even though it may sometimes be helpful, since he may have an insight into the problem without having a solution. But at least when a court formulates a rule, the formulation is regarded as tentative and subject to correction. At least when a scholar formulates a rule, the formulation has no more authority than his arguments or reputation may give it. When a drafter formulates a rule, there is the added danger that courts will look for a solution in the direction vaguely indicated by the rule even when, left to their own judgment, these courts would not regard that direction as particularly fruitful.

OBERER, ON LAW LAWYERING AND LAW PROFESSING: THE GOLDEN SAND

39 J.Legal Educ. 203, 211 (1989).

Why is reading law at large, in codes, a painful waste of time? Because codification entails the effort to capture in black-letter postulation the wisdom of the cases, of the ages. The reader is challenged to comprehend not only a "rule" but qualifications of that rule, and qualifications upon the qualifications. Words and phrases of "art" are of the essence of such distillation; they can be understood only against the backdrop of the cases, the decisions in factual situations that produce the "rule," and neighboring factual situations that qualify it. The factual situations that produce the rule and the qualifications upon the rule are subsumed. The foliage obscures the root, and, as an incident, defies comprehending retention.

Now, let us reverse the procedure; which is to say, let us examine the advantages of the "case method" for learning the law. The case method has been derided as repetitive and wasteful of time. What is its core justification? My answer is that it teaches the law *tentatively,* in a context that both justifies the resolution of the issue presented and confines that resolution to the factual context in which it occurs. Both the justification and the confinement are intimately related to the facts involved. The "rule of law" thus produced is inherently limited by the context of its creation and is understood by the student in a way that transcends, invades, black-letter treatment. The student so introduced to a legal "principle" goes to a code not passively but challengingly, as its master, not its minion.

In this regard, and as a culmination of my preachments, I seek to produce lawyers case-trained to an understanding of the "law" that emancipates them from feeling helpless when they represent clients whose cause they deem, after the caution and scrutiny induced by good-faith skepticism, to be meritorious. Their case has never before been decided; if they do the yin-yang job of relating relevant fact to relevant law and conclude, in that process, what the result *ought* to be, the chances are good that they can produce that result in their case.

INDEX

References are to Pages